The Palgrave Handbook of Ethnicity

Steven Ratuva
Editor

The Palgrave Handbook of Ethnicity

Volume 3

With 46 Figures and 57 Tables

Editor
Steven Ratuva
Department of Anthropology and Sociology
University of Canterbury
Christchurch, New Zealand

Macmillan Brown Centre for Pacific Studies
University of Canterbury
Christchurch, New Zealand

ISBN 978-981-13-2897-8   ISBN 978-981-13-2898-5 (eBook)
ISBN 978-981-13-2899-2 (print and electronic bundle)
https://doi.org/10.1007/978-981-13-2898-5

© Springer Nature Singapore Pte Ltd. 2019, corrected publication 2020
This work is subject to copyright. All rights are solely and exclusively licensed by the Publisher, whether the whole or part of the material is concerned, specifically the rights of translation, reprinting, reuse of illustrations, recitation, broadcasting, reproduction on microfilms or in any other physical way, and transmission or information storage and retrieval, electronic adaptation, computer software, or by similar or dissimilar methodology now known or hereafter developed.
The use of general descriptive names, registered names, trademarks, service marks, etc. in this publication does not imply, even in the absence of a specific statement, that such names are exempt from the relevant protective laws and regulations and therefore free for general use.
The publisher, the authors, and the editors are safe to assume that the advice and information in this book are believed to be true and accurate at the date of publication. Neither the publisher nor the authors or the editors give a warranty, express or implied, with respect to the material contained herein or for any errors or omissions that may have been made. The publisher remains neutral with regard to jurisdictional claims in published maps and institutional affiliations.

This Palgrave Macmillan imprint is published by the registered company Springer Nature Singapore Pte Ltd.
The registered company address is: 152 Beach Road, #21-01/04 Gateway East, Singapore 189721, Singapore

Preface

Since the end of the cold war, the world has seen an unprecedented multimodal transformation involving the complex interplay of various forces such as globalization and nationalism; the resurgence of extreme right and the unrelenting response from the left; the consolidation of neoliberal hegemony and creation of conditions for its own crisis; the rise of authoritarian leadership and the widespread democratic reactions; the popularization of the social media and the declaration of cyber wars; and the rise of China and how this poses a threat to US hegemony. A salient feature of many of these is the multiple expressions of ethnicity as a factor in shaping geopolitical, socioeconomic, and sociocultural relations. The explosion of ethno-nationalist conflicts and religious tension; the resurgence and electoral mainstreaming of ultra-right political groups with racial supremacist ideals; the widespread expressions of extremist Islamic groups; the anti-immigration policies of President Trump and various European states; the use of the cyberspace as an arena for racial vilification; the rise of extremist and terroristic violence; and the fluid nature of ethnic relations are just some of the manifestations of the new transformation. These have justifiably inspired a surge in interest in research and discourses around ethnicity.

Commissioned by Palgrave Macmillan, this comprehensive work on global ethnicity – which spans diverse national, political, cultural, and ideological boundaries, schools of thought, and methodological approaches – is a result of an exhaustive international search for the right experts, mobilization of a wide range of resources, writing, editing, reviewing, and production over 3 years. With 102 chapters (and more than 90 authors from around the world), this was a mammoth task, which involved the collective synergies of the editor-in-chief, section editors, chapter authors, the Palgrave editorial team, and the production team. It is a great example of transnational cooperation, innovative communication, systematic networking, and durable patience. At a time when academia is obsessed with the fetishization of individual output, as a result of the pervading audit and metric culture wrought by neoliberal reforms, a collaborative interdisciplinary and transnational effort of this scope and magnitude is a rarity. This is why all those involved in this mega project deserve whole-hearted congratulations.

The different parts and individual themes of the chapters are connected in a complex web of historical, intellectual, sociocultural, and political narratives and are meant to converse with each other using different contextual yet familiar discourses. Ostensibly, while they encapsulate different schools of thought and disciplinary traditions, they share a common thread of optimism and hope of expanding the horizons of knowledge of humanity and contributing to debates and discussions about creating a better world.

Ethnicity is not an easy subject to deal with because of its intersectional relationship with a host of factors including identity, inequality, conflict, religion, economic distribution, class, politics, and other aspects of everyday life. History is littered with the residues of ethnicity's connection with wars, mass killings, terrorism, poverty, and discrimination. History is also blessed with moments of interethnic embracement, multicultural engagements, and collective voices of humanity crying for justice and yearning for equality against the forces of discrimination, abuse, and oppression. These three volumes echo the multiple sentiments of history and capture some of the moments of human frailty and strength, human fiasco and fortitude, human retardation and progress, manifested in the different corners of the globe.

Some chapters are theoretical and some are based on empirical case studies and cover more than 70 countries around the world. Due to the massive size of the undertaking and the limited time available for its completion, the volumes are not able to cover all the countries in the world. Nevertheless, the existing chapters provide a wealth of discourses, experiences, reflections, and analysis, which would no doubt enrich our understanding of ethnicity as complex developments in our contemporary world unfold over time. The volumes are meant to inspire further debate and research and not meant to provide the panacea for global ethnic utopia. They are meant for a wide range of interests including scholars and researchers, policy makers, political leaders, corporate personnel, international agencies, peacebuilders, educators, security community, civil society organizations, and the public at large. This diversity reflects the underlying normative sentiments of inclusivity, accessibility, (in)formativeness, and enrichment.

Some chapters provide practical solutions to problems, while some provide abstract analyses of complex dynamics to unpack deeper and latent manifestations of social realities. While some are concerned with the global context, some revolve around geopolitical and geocultural regions, and some are focused on national and even local situation. These multiple layers of narratives are interconnected and provide intellectual enrichment for each other. The volumes do not pretend to provide definitive and conclusive analysis of ethnic issues that enshroud our times, but rather speak to them and raise important issues that need closer and serious scrutiny with the ambitious goal and sincere hope of making the world a better place for humanity.

Department of Anthropology and Sociology   Steven Ratuva
University of Canterbury   Editor
Christchurch, New Zealand

Macmillan Brown Centre for Pacific Studies
University of Canterbury
Christchurch, New Zealand

Contents

Volume 1

1   Exploring Global Ethnicity: A Broad Sociological Synopsis   1
Steven Ratuva

Part I   Nexus Between Ethnicity and Identity **27**

2   Ethno-cultural Symbolism and Group Identity   29
Elya Tzaneva

3   Cultural Socialization and Ethnic Consciousness   49
Sara N. Amin

4   Historical Memory and Ethnic Myths   65
Cindy Zeiher

5   Indian Identity in South Africa   77
Kathryn Pillay

6   The State and Minority Nationalities (Ethnic Groups) in
China   93
Roland Boer

7   Ethnic Blindness in Ethnically Divided Society: Implications
for Ethnic Relations in Fiji   109
Romitesh Kant

8   Post-Arab Spring: The Arab World Between the Dilemma of
the Nation-State and the Rise of Identity Conflicts   131
Hassanein Ali

Part II   The State, Society, and Ethnopolitics **147**

9   The Significance of Ethno-politics in Modern States
and Society   149
Joseph R. Rudolph

10	**Religion and Political Mobilization**	169
	Jóhanna K. Birnir and Henry D. Overos	
11	**Foreign Military Occupations and Ethnicity**	187
	Radomir Compel	
12	**Ethnic Politics and Global Justice**	209
	Geoff Pfeifer	
13	**Shared Citizenship and Sovereignty: The Case of the Cook Islands' and Niue's Relationship with New Zealand**	221
	Zbigniew Dumieński	
14	**State Hegemony and Ethnicity: Fiji's Problematic Colonial Past**	247
	Sanjay Ramesh	
15	**Ethnicity and Politics in Kenya**	265
	Jacob Mwathi Mati	
16	**Ethno-politics in the People's Republic of China**	283
	Matthew Hoddie	
17	**Ethnicity and Cultural Rights in Tibet**	301
	Jianxia Lin	
18	**Volga Tatars: Continuing Resilience in the Age of Uncertainty**	315
	Renat Shaykhutdinov	
19	**Identity and Conflict in Northern Ireland**	331
	Cathal McManus	
20	**Immigration Policy and Left-Right Politics in Western Europe**	347
	Trevor J. Allen and Misty Knight-Finley	
21	**Lost in Europe: Roma and the Search for Political Legitimacy**	363
	Neil Cruickshank	
Part III	**Stereotypes and Prejudices**	**381**
22	**Race and Racism: Some Salient Issues**	383
	Vijay Naidu	
23	**Media and Stereotypes**	397
	Tara Ross	
24	**Japanese Representation in Philippine Media**	415
	Karl Ian Uy Cheng Chua	

25	Racism in Colonial Zimbabwe Alois S. Mlambo	429
26	Ethnic Riots in United Kingdom in 2001 Paul Bagguley and Yasmin Hussain	447
27	Racialized Identity Under Apartheid in South Africa Suryakanthie Chetty	463
28	Racism and Stereotypes Paul Spoonley	483
29	Discussing Contemporary Racial Justice in Academic Spaces: Minimizing Epistemic Exploitation While Neutralizing White Fragility Adele Norris	499
30	Ethnicity, Race, and Black People in Europe Stephen Small	513

Volume 2

Part IV Ethno-nationalism and Power 535

31	Contemporary Ethnic Politics and Violence Adis Maksic	539
32	Ethnic Conflict and Militias Andrew Thomson	559
33	Evolution of Palestinian Civil Society and the Role of Nationalism, Occupation, and Religion Yaser Alashqar	577
34	Ethno-nationalism and Political Conflict in Bosnia (Europe) Aleksandra Zdeb	595
35	Ethnic Conflicts and Peace-Building Sergio Luiz Cruz Aguilar	613
36	Ethnicity and Violence in Sri Lanka: An Ethnohistorical Narrative Premakumara de Silva, Farzana Haniffa, and Rohan Bastin	633
37	Ethno-communal Conflict in Sudan and South Sudan Johan Brosché	655
38	Patterns and Drivers of Communal Conflict in Kenya Emma Elfversson	675

39	Elites in Between Ethnic Mongolians and the Han in China Chelegeer	695
40	Ethnicity and Cultural Wounding: Ethnic Conflict, Loss of Home, and the Drive to Return Amanda Kearney	715
41	Constitutional Features of Presidential Elections and the Failure of Cross-ethnic Coalitions to Institutionalize M. Bashir Mobasher	735
42	The Making of a Mobile Caliphate State in the African Sahel Hamdy Hassan	755
43	Consequences of Globalization for the Middle East Political Geography Mostafa Entezarulmahdy	773
44	National Imaginary, Ethnic Plurality, and State Formation in Indonesia Paul J. Carnegie	791
45	Ethno-nationalism and Ethnic Dynamics in Trinidad and Tobago: Toward Designing an Inclusivist Form of Governance Ralph Premdas	809
46	Islam in Trinidad Nasser Mustapha	825

Part V Indigeneity, Gender, and Sexuality **847**

47	Indigenous Rights and Neoliberalism in Latin America Jeffrey A. Gardner and Patricia Richards	849
48	Settler Colonialism and Biculturalism in Aotearoa/New Zealand Jessica Terruhn	867
49	Nuclear Testing and Racism in the Pacific Islands Nic Maclellan	885
50	Nagas Identity and Nationalism: Indigenous Movement of the Zeliangrong Nagas in the North East India Aphun Kamei	907
51	Reclaiming Hawaiian Sovereignty Keakaokawai Varner Hemi	927

52	**Perpetual Exclusion and Second-Order Minorities in Theaters of Civil Wars** .... Jovanie Camacho Espesor	967
53	**Indigenous Australian Identity in Colonial and Postcolonial Contexts** .... Michael Davis	993
54	**China: Modernization, Development, and Ethnic Unrest in Xinjiang** .... Kate Hannan	1011
55	**Ethnicity and Class Nexus: A Philosophical Approach** .... Rodrigo Luiz Cunha Gonsalves	1033
56	**Islamic Identity and Sexuality in Indonesia** .... Sharyn Graham Davies	1063
57	**LGBT and Ethnicity** .... Arjun Rajkhowa	1077
58	**Migration and Managing Manhood: Congolese Migrant Men in South Africa** .... Joseph Rudigi Rukema and Beatrice Umubyeyi	1111
59	**Race and Sexuality: Colonial Ghosts and Contemporary Orientalisms** .... Monique Mulholland	1129

Part VI Globalization and Diaspora **1147**

60	**Diaspora as Transnational Actors: Globalization and the Role of Ethnic Memory** .... Masaki Kataoka	1149
61	**Global Chinese Diaspora** .... Zhifang Song	1167
62	**Greek Identity in Australia** .... Rebecca Fanany and Maria-Irini Avgoulas	1185
63	**Italian Identity in the United States** .... Stefano Luconi	1203
64	**Faamatai: A Globalized Pacific Identity** .... Melani Anae	1223
65	**Migrant Illegalization and Minoritized Populations** .... Paloma E. Villegas and Francisco J. Villegas	1247

| 66 | Indian Diaspora in New Zealand | 1265 |

Todd Nachowitz

| 67 | Ethnic Migrants and Casinos in Singapore and Macau | 1313 |

Juan Zhang

| 68 | Ethnic Minorities and Criminalization of Immigration Policies in the United States | 1331 |

Felicia Arriaga

| 69 | Diaspora and Ethnic Contestation in Guyana | 1351 |

Ralph Premdas and Bishnu Ragoonath

Volume 3

Part VII Ethnic Relations and Policy Responses **1363**

| 70 | Role of Crown Health Policy in Entrenched Health Inequities in Aotearoa, New Zealand | 1365 |

Sarah Herbert, Heather Came, Tim McCreanor, and Emmanuel Badu

| 71 | Aboriginal and Torres Strait Islander Secondary Students' Experiences of Racism | 1383 |

Gawaian Bodkin-Andrews, Treena Clark, and Shannon Foster

| 72 | Stereotypes of Minorities and Education | 1407 |

Jean M. Allen and Melinda Webber

| 73 | Rural Farmer Empowerment Through Organic Food Exports: Lessons from Uganda and Ghana | 1427 |

Kristen Lyons

| 74 | Local Peacebuilding After Communal Violence | 1445 |

Birgit Bräuchler

| 75 | Cultural Identity and Textbooks in Japan: Japanese Ethnic and Cultural Nationalism in Middle-School History Textbooks | 1465 |

Ryota Nishino

| 76 | Asian Americans and the Affirmative Action Debate in the United States | 1483 |

Mitchell James Chang

| 77 | Affirmative Action: Its Nature and Dynamics | 1501 |

Ralph Premdas

| 78 | Negotiating Ethnic Conflict in Deeply Divided Societies: Political Bargaining and Power Sharing as Institutional Strategies | 1515 |

Madhushree Sekher, Mansi Awasthi, Allen Thomas, Rajesh Kumar, and Subhankar Nayak

Part VIII Ethnic Cleansing and Genocide 1537

79 The Threat of Genocide: Understanding and Preventing the "Crime of Crimes" 1539
Eyal Mayroz

80 Separation Versus Reunification: Institutional Stagnation and Conflict Between Iraq and Kurdistan Region 1555
Nyaz N. Noori

81 Ethnic Cleansing of the Rohingya People 1575
Nasir Uddin

82 Displaced Minorities: The Wayuu and Miskito People 1593
Christian Cwik

83 Ethnic Conflict and Genocide in Rwanda 1611
Wendy Lambourne

Part IX Ethnicity, Migration, and Labor 1643

84 Policing Ethnic Minorities: Disentangling a Landscape of Conceptual and Practice Tensions 1647
Isabelle Bartkowiak-Théron and Nicole L. Asquith

85 Romanian Identity and Immigration in Europe 1671
Remus Gabriel Anghel, Stefánia Toma, and László Fosztó

86 Refugee Protection and Settlement Policy in New Zealand 1689
Louise Humpage

87 Indian Indentured Laborers in the Caribbean 1711
Sherry-Ann Singh

88 New Middle-Class Labor Migrants 1729
Sam Scott

89 Slavery, Health, and Epidemics in Mauritius 1721–1860 1749
Sadasivam Jaganada Reddi and Sheetal Sheena Sookrajowa

90 The Legacy of Indentured Labor 1767
Kathleen Harrington-Watt

91 Global Capitalism and Cheap Labor: The Case of Indenture ... 1795
Brinsley Samaroo

92 United Nations Migrant Workers Convention 1813
Sheetal Sheena Sookrajowa and Antoine Pécoud

| 93 | The Rhetoric of Hungarian Premier Victor Orban: Inside X Outside in the Context of Immigration Crisis 1829
Bruno Mendelski

| 94 | Different Legacies, Common Pressures, and Converging Institutions: The Politics of Muslim Integration in Austria and Germany 1853
Ryosuke Amiya-Nakada

| 95 | Intended Illegal Infiltration or Compelled Migration: Debates on Settlements of Rohingya Muslims in India 1877
Sangit Kumar Ragi

| 96 | Indonesia and ASEAN Responses on Rohingya Refugees 1891
Badrus Sholeh

Part X Cultural Celebration and Resistance **1907**

| 97 | Rewriting the World: Pacific People, Media, and Cultural Resistance 1909
Sereana Naepi and Sam Manuela

| 98 | Kava and Ethno-cultural Identity in Oceania 1923
S. Apo Aporosa

| 99 | Museums and Identity: Celebrating Diversity in an Ethnically Diverse World 1939
Tarisi Vunidilo

| 100 | Artistic Expressions and Ethno-cultural Identity: A Case Study of Acehnese Body Percussion in Indonesia 1957
Murtala Murtala, Alfira O'Sullivan, and Paul H. Mason

| 101 | Ethnic Film in South Africa: History, Meaning, and Change ... 1977
Gairoonisa Paleker

| 102 | Multiculturalism and Citizenship in the Netherlands 1993
Igor Boog

Correction to: Diaspora and Ethnic Contestation in Guyana **C1**

Index **2015**

About the Editor

Steven Ratuva
Department of Anthropology and Sociology
University of Canterbury
Christchurch, New Zealand

Macmillan Brown Centre for Pacific Studies
University of Canterbury
Christchurch, New Zealand

Steven Ratuva is Director of the Macmillan Brown Center for Pacific Studies and Professor in the Department of Anthropology and Sociology at the University of Canterbury. He was Fulbright Professor at UCLA, Duke University, and Georgetown University and currently Chair of the International Political Science Association Research Committee on Security, Conflict, and Democratization. With a Ph.D. from the Institute of Development Studies at the University of Sussex, Ratuva is an interdisciplinary scholar who has written or edited a number of books and published numerous papers on a range of issues including ethnicity, security, affirmative action, indigenous intellectual property, geopolitical strategies, social protection, militarization, ethno-nationalism, development, peace, and neoliberalism. He has been a consultant and advisor for a number of international organizations such as the UNDP, International Labour Organization, International Institute for Democracy and Electoral Assistance, Commonwealth Secretariat, and the Asian Development Bank, and has worked in a number of universities around the world including in Australia, USA, New Zealand, Fiji, and UK.

About the Section Editors

Steven Ratuva
Department of Anthropology and Sociology
University of Canterbury
Christchurch, New Zealand

Macmillan Brown Centre for Pacific Studies
University of Canterbury
Christchurch, New Zealand

Steven Ratuva is Director of the Macmillan Brown Center for Pacific Studies and Professor in the Department of Anthropology and Sociology at the University of Canterbury. He was Fulbright Professor at UCLA, Duke University, and Georgetown University and currently Chair of the International Political Science Association Research Committee on Security, Conflict, and Democratization. With a Ph.D. from the Institute of Development Studies at the University of Sussex, Ratuva is an interdisciplinary scholar who has written or edited a number of books and published numerous papers on a range of issues including ethnicity, security, affirmative action, indigenous intellectual property, geo-political strategies, social protection, militarization, ethno-nationalism, development, peace, and neoliberalism. He has been a consultant and advisor for a number of international organizations such as the UNDP, International Labour Organization, International Institute for Democracy and Electoral Assistance, Commonwealth Secretariat, and the Asian Development Bank, and has worked in a number of universities around the world including in Australia, USA, New Zealand, Fiji, and UK.

Joseph R. Rudolph
Department of Political Science
Towson University
Baltimore, MA, USA

Joseph R. Rudolph, Jr. received his Ph.D. from the University of Virginia and is currently a Professor in the Department of Political Science at Towson University (Baltimore, Maryland, USA). He has served as a Fulbright appointee to Czechoslovakia (1991–1992) and Kosovo (2011–2012), and has published in the field of ethnic and nationalist politics for more than 30 years. Since 1997, he has also frequently been a part of the democratization operations of the Organization for Security and Cooperation in Europe (OSCE) in areas of the former Yugoslavia and former Soviet Union. His Palgrave publication *Politics and Ethnicity: A Comparative* Study (2006) is now in its second printing. More recent work includes compiling and contributing to *The Encyclopedia of Modern Ethnic Conflicts* (editor, 2nd edition, 2015), and *From Mediation to Nation Building: Third Parties and the Management of Communal Conflict* (coeditor, 2013).

Vijay Naidu
University of the South Pacific
Suva, Fiji

Vijay Naidu completed his undergraduate and M.A. studies at the University of the South Pacific in Fiji, and his doctoral degree at the University of Sussex in the UK. He has been Professor and Director of Development Studies in the School of Government, Development, and International Affairs at the University of the South Pacific (USP), and the School of Geography, Environment, and Earth Sciences at the Victoria University of Wellington. He is a Pacific development scholar and has written on aid, electoral politics, ethnicity, higher education, land tenure, migration, urbanization, social exclusion, the state, poverty and social protection, informal settlements, human security, and MDGs.

About the Section Editors

Paul J. Carnegie
Institute of Asian Studies
Universiti Brunei Darussalam
Bandar Seri Begawan, Brunei Darussalam

Paul J. Carnegie is Associate Professor of Politics and International Relations at the Institute of Asian Studies, Universiti Brunei Darussalam and the former Director of the Postgraduate Governance Program at the University of the South Pacific. He has research specializations in comparative democratization, human security, and localized responses to militant extremism in Southeast Asia, MENA, and the Asia Pacific with a particular focus on Indonesia. Paul has published widely in his fields including the monograph *The Road from Authoritarianism to Democratization in Indonesia* (Palgrave Macmillan) and the coedited volume *Human Insecurities in Southeast Asia* (Springer). He has been awarded multiple research grants with related output in leading international journals including *Pacific Affairs*, *Australian Journal of Politics and History*, the *Middle East Quarterly*, and the *Australian Journal of International Affairs*. Paul has extensive applied research experience and networks having lived and worked previously in Australia, Brunei Darussalam, Egypt, Fiji, and the United Arab Emirates.

Airini
Faculty of Education and Social Work
Thompson Rivers University
Kamloops, BC, Canada

Professor Airini is Dean of the Faculty of Education and Social Work at Thompson Rivers University, British Columbia, Canada (https://www.tru.ca/), and previously at the University of Auckland, Aotearoa New Zealand. Airini's research looks at how to build world-class education systems where success for all means all. Her current focus is on closing education achievement gaps experienced by Indigenous school and university students in Canada and internationally. Airini is the recipient of national research and teaching awards in New Zealand (*Success for All: What university teaching practices help/hinder Maori and Pasifika student success*) and Canada (*Knowledge Makers: Indigenous undergraduate and graduate student research mentoring*). To identify how we can influence better outcomes for all, Airini went to Washington DC as a Fulbright Scholar and investigated how to convert tertiary education policy into better results for underserved students (E-mail: airini@tru.ca; Twitter: @truAirini; LinkedIn: https://ca.linkedin.come/in/airini).

Melani Anae
Pacific Studies|School of Māori Studies
and Pacific Studies,
Te Wānanga o Waipapa
University of Auckland
Auckland, New Zealand

Lupematasila, Misatauveve Dr. Melani Anae, is Senior Lecturer in Pacific Studies, Te Wānanga o Waipapa, at the University of Auckland. Anae has been a former Director of the Centre for Pacific Studies (2002–2007), a recipient of the Fulbright New Zealand Senior Scholar Award (2007), and was awarded the Companion to the Queen's Service Order for services to Pacific communities in New Zealand (2008). In 2014, she was awarded the prestigious Marsden Grant from the Royal Society of New Zealand for her project "Samoan transnational matai (chiefs): ancestor god avatars or merely titleholders?" Focusing on her research interests of ethnic identity for first-/second-generation Pacific peoples born in the diaspora, social justice and Pacific activism, and the development of her teu le va paradigm in relational ethics, her transformational work has successfully developed strategies for policy formation, service delivery, and optimal research outcomes for Pacific peoples/families and communities across the sectors of education, health, and well-being for Pacific peoples, families, and communities in New Zealand. She has taught, researched, and published extensively in these specialty areas and is currently focused on transnational identity construction of Pacific peoples and communities in the diaspora. She carries two Samoan chiefly titles from the villages of Siumu and Falelatai in Samoa, is part of a large transnational Samoan aiga, and is a grandmother and mother of three children.

Radomir Compel
School of Global Humanities and Social Sciences
Nagasaki University
Nagasaki, Japan

Radomir Compel is Associate Professor of comparative politics at the Global School of Humanities and Social Sciences of Nagasaki University in Japan. He has edited or coauthored several books, including *Guns and Roses: Comparative Civil-Military Relations in the Changing Security Environment* (2019), *Hito to Kaiyo no Kyosei wo Mezashite VI* (2013), and *Ashida Hitoshi Nikki 1905–1945 V* (2012), and has published articles in Japanese and English on Okinawa, Japan, East Asia, Middle East, and maritime issues. He obtained a Ph.D. from Yokohama National University, and taught at Hosei University, Yokohama National University, Nihon University, University of Oulu, and other educational institutions in Japan and Europe.

Sergio Luiz Cruz Aguilar
Sao Paulo State University (UNESP)
Marilia, São Paulo, Brazil

Sergio Luiz Cruz Aguilar holds a Ph.D. in History (UNESP), and is Associate Professor at the Sao Paulo State University (UNESP), Brazil, where he coordinates the Group of Studies and Research of International Conflicts and the International Conflicts Observatory. He is also Professor of the postgraduation programs San Tiago Dantas Program on International Relations (UNESP/UNICAMP/PUC-SP) and Social Sciences (UNESP – Campus of Marilia/SP). He was visiting researcher at the Department of Politics and International Relations – University of Oxford, UK. He was military observer on the United Nations Peace Force (UNPF) and on United Nations Transitional Administration for Eastern Slavonia (UNTAES), during the civil war in the former Yugoslavia. Sergio was also Director of the Brazilian Defense Studies Association (ABED) and wrote four books, edited five books, and published many journal articles in Portuguese, English, and Spanish languages.

Lyndon Fraser
Department of Sociology and Anthropology
University of Canterbury
Christchurch, New Zealand

Historian **Lyndon Fraser** is currently the Head of Department (Sociology and Anthropology) at the University of Canterbury, Christchurch, New Zealand, and Research Fellow in Human History at the Canterbury Museum. He is coeditor (with Linda Bryder) of the *New Zealand Journal of History,* and his recent publications include *Rushing for Gold: Life and Commerce on the Goldfields of Australia and New Zealand* (Otago University Press, 2016, with Lloyd Carpenter) and *History Making a Difference: New Approaches from Aotearoa* (Cambridge Scholars Publishing, 2017, coedited with Katie Pickles, Marguerite Hill, Sarah Murray, and Greg Ryan).

Contributors

Sergio Luiz Cruz Aguilar Sao Paulo State University (UNESP), Marilia, São Paulo, Brazil

Yaser Alashqar Trinity College Dublin (the University of Dublin), Dublin, Ireland

Hassanein Ali Department of International Studies, College of Humanities and Social Sciences, Zayed University, Dubai, United Arab Emirates

Jean M. Allen Faculty of Education and Social Work, The University of Auckland, Auckland, New Zealand

Trevor J. Allen Department of Political Science, Central Connecticut State University, New Britain, CT, USA

Sara N. Amin School of Social Sciences, Faculty of Arts, Law and Education, The University of the South Pacific, Suva, Fiji Islands

Ryosuke Amiya-Nakada Tsuda University, Kodaira, Japan

Melani Anae Pacific Studies|School of Māori Studies and Pacific Studies, Te Wānanga o Waipapa, University of Auckland, Auckland, New Zealand

Remus Gabriel Anghel The Romanian Institute for Research on National Minorities, Cluj Napoca, Romania

S. Apo Aporosa Te Huataki Waiora: Faculty of Health, Sport and Human Performance, University of Waikato, Hamilton, Waikato, New Zealand

Felicia Arriaga Sociology Department, Appalachian State University, Boone, NC, USA

Nicole L. Asquith Western Sydney University, Kingswood, NSW, Australia

Maria-Irini Avgoulas School of Psychology and Public Health, College of Science, Health and Engineering, La Trobe University, Bundoora, VIC, Australia

Mansi Awasthi Tata Institute of Social Sciences (TISS), Mumbai, India

Emmanuel Badu Faculty of Health and Environmental Studies, Auckland University of Technology, Auckland, New Zealand

Paul Bagguley School of Sociology and Social Policy, University of Leeds, Leeds, UK

Isabelle Bartkowiak-Théron Tasmanian Institute of Law Enforcement Studies, University of Tasmania, Hobart, TAS, Australia

Rohan Bastin School of Humanities and Social Sciences, Deakin University, Geelong, VIC, Australia

Jóhanna K. Birnir Government and Politics, University of Maryland, College Park, MD, USA

Gawaian Bodkin-Andrews Centre for the Advancement of Indigenous Knowledges, University of Technology Sydney, Broadway, NSW, Australia

Roland Boer School of Liberal Arts, Renmin University of China, Beijing, People's Republic of China

Igor Boog Institute of Cultural Anthropology and Development Sociology, Leiden University, Leiden, The Netherlands

Birgit Bräuchler Monash University, Melbourne, VIC, Australia

Johan Brosché Department of Peace- and Conflict Research, Uppsala University, Uppsala, Sweden

Heather Came Faculty of Health and Environmental Studies, Auckland University of Technology, Auckland, New Zealand

Paul J. Carnegie Institute of Asian Studies, Universiti Brunei Darussalam, Bandar Seri Begawan, Brunei Darussalam

Mitchell James Chang University of California, Los Angeles, Los Angeles, CA, USA

Chelegeer University of Leeds, Leeds, UK

Karl Ian Uy Cheng Chua History Department, Ateneo de Manila University, Quezon City, Philippines

Suryakanthie Chetty University of South Africa, Pretoria, South Africa

Treena Clark Centre for the Advancement of Indigenous Knowledges, University of Technology Sydney, Broadway, NSW, Australia

Radomir Compel School of Global Humanities and Social Sciences, Nagasaki University, Nagasaki, Japan

Neil Cruickshank Political Scientist and Dean of the Faculty of Arts, Science, and Technology, North Island College, Courtenay, BC, Canada

Faculty Associate, Centre for European Studies, Carleton University, Ottawa, ON, Canada

Christian Cwik Department of History, The University of the West Indies, St Augustine, Trinidad and Tobago

Sharyn Graham Davies Auckland University of Technology, Aotearoa, New Zealand

Michael Davis Department of Sociology and Social Policy, The University of Sydney, Sydney, NSW, Australia

Premakumara de Silva Department of Sociology, University of Colombo, Colombo, Sri Lanka

Zbigniew Dumieński Auckland University of Technology, Auckland, New Zealand

Emma Elfversson Department of Peace and Conflict Research, Uppsala University, Uppsala, Sweden

Mostafa Entezarulmahdy Political Science Department, Robat Karim Branch, Islamic Azad University, Tehran, Iran

Jovanie Camacho Espesor Department of Political Science and International Relations, University of Canterbury, Christchurch, New Zealand

Department of Political Science, Mindanao State University, General Santos City, Philippines

Center for Middle East and Global Peace Studies, Universitas Islam Negeri Syarif Hidayatullah Jakarta, Tangerang, Indonesia

Rebecca Fanany School of Health, Medical and Applied Sciences, Central Queensland University, Melbourne, VIC, Australia

Shannon Foster Centre for the Advancement of Indigenous Knowledges, University of Technology Sydney, Broadway, NSW, Australia

László Fosztó The Romanian Institute for Research on National Minorities, Cluj Napoca, Romania

Jeffrey A. Gardner Department of Sociology, Sam Houston State University, Huntsville, TX, USA

Rodrigo Luiz Cunha Gonsalves European Graduate School (EGS), Saas fee, Switzerland

University of Sao Paulo (IPUSP), Sao Paulo, Brazil

Farzana Haniffa Department of Sociology, University of Colombo, Colombo, Sri Lanka

Kate Hannan Department of History and Politics, University of Wollongong, Wollongong, NSW, Australia

Kathleen Harrington-Watt Anthropology, Canterbury University, Christchurch, New Zealand

Hamdy Hassan College of Humanities and Social Sciences, Zayed University, Dubai, UAE

Keakaokawai Varner Hemi University of Waikato, Hamilton, New Zealand

Sarah Herbert Faculty of Health and Environmental Studies, Auckland University of Technology, Auckland, New Zealand

Matthew Hoddie Department of Political Science, Towson University, Towson, MD, USA

Louise Humpage Sociology, Faculty of Arts, University of Auckland, Auckland, New Zealand

Yasmin Hussain School of Sociology and Social Policy, University of Leeds, Leeds, UK

Aphun Kamei Department of Sociology, Delhi School of Economics, University of Delhi, Delhi, India

Romitesh Kant Institute for Human Security and Social Change (IHSSC), College of Arts and Social Sciences, La Trobe University, Melbourne, VIC, Australia

Masaki Kataoka University of Canterbury, Christchurch, New Zealand

Institute of Developing Economies, Japan External Trade Organization, Chiba, Japan

Amanda Kearney College of Humanities, Arts and Social Sciences, Flinders University, Bedford Park, SA, Australia

Misty Knight-Finley Department of Political Science and Economics, Rowan University, Glassboro, NJ, USA

Rajesh Kumar Tata Institute of Social Sciences (TISS), Mumbai, India

Wendy Lambourne Department of Peace and Conflict Studies, University of Sydney, Sydney, NSW, Australia

Jianxia Lin University of Leeds, Leeds, UK

Stefano Luconi Department of Education (DISFOR), University of Genoa, Genoa, Italy

Kristen Lyons School of Social Science, University of Queensland, Brisbane, QLD, Australia

Nic Maclellan Melbourne, Australia

Adis Maksic International Burch University, Sarajevo, Bosnia and Herzegovina

Sam Manuela University of Auckland, Auckland, New Zealand

Paul H. Mason School of Social Sciences, Monash University, Clayton, VIC, Australia

Department of Anthropology, Macquarie University, North Ryde, NSW, Australia

Jacob Mwathi Mati School of Social Sciences, Faculty of Arts, Law and Education (FALE), The University of the South Pacific, Suva, Fiji Islands

Society, Work and Politics (SWOP) Institute, The University of the Witwatersrand, Johannesburg, South Africa

Eyal Mayroz University of Sydney, Sydney, NSW, Australia

Tim McCreanor Te Rōpū Whāriki, Massey University, Auckland, New Zealand

Cathal McManus School of Social Sciences, Education and Social Work, Queen's University Belfast, Belfast, Northern Ireland

Bruno Mendelski Institute of International Relations (IREL), University of Brasilia, Brasilia, Brazil

International Relations at Department of Economics, University of Santa Cruz do Sul, Santa Cruz do Sul, Viamão, Brazil

Alois S. Mlambo University of Pretoria, Pretoria, South Africa

M. Bashir Mobasher Department of Political Science, American University of Afghanistan, Kabul, Afghanistan

Monique Mulholland College of Humanities, Arts and Social Sciences, The Flinders University of South Australia, Adelaide, Australia

Murtala Murtala Suara Indonesia Dance Troupe, Sydney, NSW, Australia

Nasser Mustapha Department of Behavioural Sciences, University of the West Indies, St Augustine, Trinidad and Tobago

Todd Nachowitz University of Waikato, Hamilton, New Zealand

Sereana Naepi Thompson Rivers University, Kamloops, Canada

Vijay Naidu University of the South Pacific, Suva, Fiji

Subhankar Nayak Tata Institute of Social Sciences (TISS), Mumbai, India

Ryota Nishino University of the South Pacific, Suva, Fiji

International Research Center for Japanese Studies (Nichibunken), Kyoto, Japan

Nyaz N. Noori Department of Economic History, Uppsala University, Uppsala, Sweden

Lecturer, Department of Economics, University of Sulaymaniyah, Sulaimaniyah, Kurdistan Region, Iraq

Adele Norris School of Social Sciences, Sociology and Sociology Program, The University of Waikato, Hamilton, New Zealand

Alfira O'Sullivan Suara Indonesia Dance Troupe, Sydney, NSW, Australia

Henry D. Overos Government and Politics, University of Maryland, College Park, MD, USA

Gairoonisa Paleker Department of Historical and Heritage Studies, University of Pretoria, Pretoria, South Africa

Antoine Pécoud University of Paris 13, Paris, France

Geoff Pfeifer Worcester Polytechnic Institute, Worcester, MA, USA

Kathryn Pillay University of KwaZulu-Natal, Durban, South Africa

Ralph Premdas University of the West Indies, St. Augustine, Trinidad and Tobago

Sangit Kumar Ragi Department of Political Science, Social Science Building, North Campus, University of Delhi, Delhi, India

Bishnu Ragoonath Department of Political Science, University of the West Indies Trinidad, St. Augustine, Trinidad and Tobago

Arjun Rajkhowa University of Melbourne, Melbourne, Australia

Sanjay Ramesh Department of Peace and Conflict Studies, University of Sydney, Camperdown, NSW, Australia

Steven Ratuva Department of Anthropology and Sociology, University of Canterbury, Christchurch, New Zealand

Macmillan Brown Centre for Pacific Studies, University of Canterbury, Christchurch, New Zealand

Sadasivam Jaganada Reddi Réduit, Mauritius

Patricia Richards Department of Sociology, University of Georgia, Athens, GA, USA

Tara Ross University of Canterbury, Christchurch, New Zealand

Joseph R. Rudolph Department of Political Science, Towson University, Baltimore, MA, USA

Joseph Rudigi Rukema School of Social Sciences, University of KwaZulu-Natal, Durban, South Africa

Brinsley Samaroo History Department, University of the West Indies, St. Augustine, Trinidad and Tobago

Sam Scott University of Gloucestershire, Cheltenham, UK

Madhushree Sekher Centre for Study of Social Exclusion and Inclusive Policies (CSSEIP), Tata Institute of Social Sciences (TISS), Mumbai, India

Renat Shaykhutdinov Florida Atlantic University, Boca Raton, FL, USA

Badrus Sholeh Department of International Relations, Faculty of Social and Political Sciences, Syarif Hidayatullah State Islamic University, Jakarta, Indonesia

Sherry-Ann Singh The University of the West Indies, St. Augustine, Trinidad and Tobago

Stephen Small Department of African American Studies, University of California, Berkeley, Berkeley, CA, USA

Zhifang Song University of Canterbury, Canterbury, New Zealand

Sheetal Sheena Sookrajowa Department of History and Political Science, Faculty of Social Sciences and Humanities, University of Mauritius, Réduit, Mauritius

Paul Spoonley College of Humanities and Social Sciences, Massey University, Auckland, New Zealand

Jessica Terruhn Massey University, Auckland, New Zealand

Allen Thomas Tata Institute of Social Sciences (TISS), Mumbai, India

Andrew Thomson Queens University of Belfast, Belfast, UK

Stefánia Toma The Romanian Institute for Research on National Minorities, Cluj Napoca, Romania

Elya Tzaneva Institute of Ethnology and Folklore Studies with Ethnographic Museum, Bulgarian Academy of sciences, Sofia, Bulgaria

Nasir Uddin Department of Anthropology, University of Chittagong, Chittagong, Bangladesh

Beatrice Umubyeyi School of Built and Environmental Studies, University of KwaZulu-Natal, Durban, South Africa

Francisco J. Villegas Department of Anthropology and Sociology, Kalamazoo College, Kalamazoo, MI, USA

Paloma E. Villegas Sociology, California State University, San Bernardino, CA, USA

Tarisi Vunidilo Department of Anthropology, University of Hawaii-Hilo, Hilo, HI, USA

Melinda Webber Faculty of Education and Social Work, The University of Auckland, Auckland, New Zealand

Aleksandra Zdeb Centre for Southeast European Studies of the University of Graz, University of Graz, Graz, Austria

Cindy Zeiher University of Canterbury, Christchurch, New Zealand

Juan Zhang Department of Anthropology and Archaeology, University of Bristol, Bristol, UK

Part VII
Ethnic Relations and Policy Responses

Part Introduction

There are many ways of conceptualizing relevance of ethnic relations to public policy. One of the key dimensions isthe historical relationship between the state and society, which was dramatically reframed with the rise of the welfare state and its reach into issues such as diversity and equitable development. In ethnicallydiverse societies, institutions and policies of statesare confronted with addressing the challenges of vertical inequalities (such asreduction of poverty and lack of opportunities) and horizontal injustices (such as leveling the playing field for historically discriminated ethnicities including indigenous populations, African Americans, Muslims, or ethnic minorities). Policies undertaken to address such injustices include affirmative action and other strategies related to diversity promotion.

Chapters in this part provide critical analyses of policies addressing problems associated with ethnic relations, such as healthcare, education, economic policy, political participation, and conflict resolution. Sarah Herbert, Heather Came, Tim McCreanor, and Emmanuel Badudiscuss New Zealand's health policies and the reasons fortheir failure to address the needs of Indigenous peoples, and the need to provide an inclusive "Tiriti-based" Maori transformational solution for more equitable healthcare. Gawaian Bodkin-Andrews, Tereena Clark, and Shannon Foster scrutinize the concept of racism in Australia, arguingthat academic discourses have insufficiently addressed personal, institutional, and collective racism experienced by aboriginal Australian and Torres Strait Islands peoples, especially among youth and children. Jean M. Allen and Melinda Webber reach similar conclusions in their sociopsychological study focusing on the negative impact of stereotyping of minorities in the educational context inAotearoa New Zealand. To cope with such negative stereotyping, they suggest educational methods such as limitation of competition, encouragement of trust, promotion of collaboration, ordevelopment of strong positive self-identification linked togrowth mindset (embedded achievement). Ryota Nishino discusses the persistence and change in Japanese national imagination through portrayals of linearity between ancient and modern Japanese in middle school textbooks, which over time have become less genealogy-based and more culturalas it increasingly accounts for multicultural and local influences.

Nevertheless, this hasforestalled any critical understanding of the present-day Japanese state. Finally, Mitchell James Chang evaluates US discriminatory policies towardAsian Americans in university entry examinations, pointing out their deficiencies and implicit defense of whiteness despite affirmative action projects adoptedto the contrary.

Kristen Lyons introduces an example of how trade and economic policy in Uganda and Ghanahas benefited local indigenous organic farmers producing for export. The two casessuggest that policy tools such as smallholder group certification and domestic organic inspection help empower local producers vis-à-vis their northern buyers. From a conflict resolution perspective and based on her fieldwork in Maluku of Eastern Indonesia, Brigit Bräucher argues that building on local culture and tradition may overcome violence induced by religious and cultural tensions accompanying colonialism or state consolidation. Madushree Sekher, Mansi Awasthi, Allen Thomas, Rajesh Kumar, and Subhankar Nayak investigate alternative channels of political representation in India, such as social movements and public protests, which help redress injustices. This is to take place within the framework of legally guaranteed but poorly implemented affirmative action policies to ensure the improvement of life conditions for the Dalit caste.

Finally, Ralph Premdas makes a critical review of affirmative action policies and challenges in India, US, Northern Ireland, Malaysia, South Africa, and Fiji, looking at their problems, achievements, and opportunities. In his view, a new order of affirmative action clearly requires a new frame of mind by both beneficiaries and the old guard. He argues that the success of such innovative policies will depend onhow far they win wide societal support. Premdas' comparative, empirical, and comprehensive study of multiethnic and deeply divided societiesoffers many thoughtful suggestions about framing and reframing ethnic relations and public policies addressed in this part.

Radomir Compel

Role of Crown Health Policy in Entrenched Health Inequities in Aotearoa, New Zealand

70

Sarah Herbert, Heather Came, Tim McCreanor, and Emmanuel Badu

Contents

Introduction	1366
Te Tiriti o Waitangi	1367
Te Pae Mahutonga	1368
New Zealand Health Policy	1369
Te Pae Māhutonga as a Framework for Health Policy in Aotearoa	1370
Ngā Manukura	1370
Te Mana Whakahaere	1371
Mauriora, Waiora, Toiora, Te Oranga	1373
Conclusion	1376
References	1378

Abstract

In Aotearoa (New Zealand), health disparities between Pākehā (non-Māori settler) and Māori (Indigenous person/s in Aotearoa) are deep, long-standing, and an indictment of decades of neglect, abuse, and racism despite the commitments of te *Tiriti o Waitangi* (te Tiriti) and ideological claims to a just and egalitarian social order. In this chapter we focus on the key health policy frameworks operated by the Crown and scrutinize the adequacy of their orientation to the provisions of te Tiriti and the effects they have in terms of health disparities. We undertake an analysis framed around the holistic Māori model of health promotion, *Te Pae Māhutonga* (Durie, Health Promot Forum Newsl 49:2–5, 1999), that supports the pursuit of the aspiration of health equity for the nation. We begin with an outline

---

S. Herbert (✉) · H. Came · E. Badu
Faculty of Health and Environmental Studies, Auckland University of Technology, Auckland, New Zealand
e-mail: Sarah.Herbert@aut.ac.nz; Heather.Came@aut.ac.nz; emmanuel.badu@aut.ac.nz

T. McCreanor
Te Rōpū Whāriki, Massey University, Auckland, New Zealand
e-mail: T.N.McCreanor@massey.ac.nz

© The Author(s), under exclusive license to Springer Nature Singapore Pte Ltd. 2019
S. Ratuva (ed.), *The Palgrave Handbook of Ethnicity*,
https://doi.org/10.1007/978-981-13-2898-5_104

of demography and health disparities, lay the foundation of critical analysis based on te Tiriti and *Te Pae Mahutonga*, introduce and critique three key health policies, and close with an argument for a transformational approach to health in Aotearoa.

Keywords

Māori · Health policy · Te Tiriti o Waitangi · New Zealand · Health equity · Health disparities · Health · Te Pae Mahutonga

Introduction

In 2013, the New Zealand population was 4,242,048, of whom 598,605 (14.9%) identified as Māori (Statistics New Zealand 2018). European people were 74%, while Pacific (7.4%), Asian (11.8%), Middle Eastern, Latin American, African (1.2%), and "other" (1.7%) peoples made up the balance. The population of Aotearoa is youthful with 20.4% aged under 15 years. The Māori population in particular has a youthful age structure with 33.8% aged under 15 years. However, Aotearoa is also experiencing population aging with 14.3% over 65 years, and by 2063 this segment is projected to reach 26.7%, while the proportion under 15 is expected to decrease to 15.5% by 2063.

Sociodemographic data allows important insights into the social determinants of heath. A total of 79.1% of people aged 15 years and over have a formal qualification, and 20% of these people hold a tertiary qualification. In contrast, only 66.7% Māori aged 15 years and over have a formal qualification, while only 10% are tertiary qualified. In the population as a whole, unemployment is at 7.1% among people aged 15 years and over, and the majority of those employed work in professional occupations. For Māori, the unemployment rate is more than double that figure, and those employed mostly occupy laboring occupations. Income differences are stark; 38.2% aged 15+ years earn less than $20,000 annually, while 26.7% earn over $50,000, but for Māori, the figures are 46.3% and 18.1%, respectively. Moreover, New Zealand European and others are more likely to attain higher-level educational qualifications, are more likely to be employed, feel safe at work, earn higher wages/salaries than Māori and Pacific people, and are the least likely to feel discriminated against or harassed (Statistics New Zealand 2017b).

Life expectancy provides a useful indication of how social, economic, behavioral, environmental, and health system factors interact to impact on a person's life from birth. Between 1996 and 2016 life expectancy from birth increased by 5 years for males and 3.6 years for females of all groups (Institute for Health Metrics and Evaluation 2016). Increases in life expectancy were largest among Māori males (6.4 years) and females (5.8 years). However, although the situation has improved steadily from a 15+ year deficit in 1951 when data were first collected, currently non-Māori males (80.3 years) and females (83.9 years) enjoy longer life – 7.3 and 6.8 years, respectively – than their matched Māori peers (Statistics New Zealand 2017a).

Better access to effective, quality healthcare means that New Zealand European and others are less likely to die prematurely (under age 75 years) from preventable diseases or injuries (Ministry of Health 2016a, 2018) than Māori or Pacific people. For instance, European and others are less likely to be diagnosed with, and die from, cancers than Māori and Pacific peoples (Ministry of Health 2017b). Similarly, New Zealand Europeans suffer stroke 15 years later than Māori and Pacific peoples and have seen a more accelerated decline in stroke incidence and mortality than Māori and Pacific (Feigin et al. 2015).

Beyond health system factors are individual behaviors that positively or negatively impact health. Engaging in health-promoting behaviors is not simply individual choices; they are the outcome of people responding to the systems and environments around them. The Global Disease Burden Study (Institute for Health Metrics and Evaluation 2016) identified obesity, diet, tobacco use, high blood pressure, and alcohol and other drug use as the leading modifiable risk factors for health loss in Aotearoa. Significant disparities exist such that New Zealand Europeans and others are about half as likely to be obese than Māori and Pacific and are less likely to smoke (Ministry of Health 2017b).

Te Tiriti o Waitangi

The founding document of the colonial state of New Zealand is te *Tiriti o Waitangi* (Māori text). It was negotiated and signed by Māori rangatira (chiefs or leaders) and the Crown at Waitangi and elsewhere beginning on 6th of February 1840. It outlines the intended strategic relationship between rangatira, representing hapū (sub-tribe), and the British Crown (Healy et al. 2012b) at a time of peace when Māori were the dominant population. Te Tiriti consists of a preamble and four articles. Within Article 1 Māori delegated limited kāwanatanga (governance responsibilities) to the British to oversee their often wayward citizens in Aotearoa. Article 2 reaffirmed the words of the 1835 *He Whakaputanga o Te Rangatiratanga o Nū Tīreni* (Declaration of Independence) guaranteeing Māori tino rangatiratanga (absolute sovereignty) over Māori lands and taonga (resources or treasured items). Article 3 relates to ōritetanga (equity) and promised Māori the same rights as British subjects. The fourth, oral article pertains to wairuatanga, protecting all faiths with a promise of religious freedom.

The Māori text is the document recognized under international law through the doctrine of contra proferentem. It was signed by more than 500 rangatira throughout Aotearoa and by Captain Hobson representing the Queen of England. Durie (1998) and others have argued that Māori remain committed to the Māori text, and the Waitangi Tribunal (2014) has ruled that in signing te Tiriti, rangatira did not cede sovereignty. The Crown has sought to limit the mana of the Māori text by developing a collection of "Treaty principles" (Hayward 1997) used by courts and government departments.

In the 170 plus years since the negotiation of te Tiriti, the many breaches have drawn resistance, protest, and legal action. Since the 1970s, the long-standing efforts of rangatira Māori and activists have achieved a substantial repositioning of te Tiriti in the social, cultural, and political life of Aotearoa (Walker 1990). The establishment of the Waitangi Tribunal was part of this re-engagement and reconciliation process that has seen the New Zealand government apologize for past misconduct and provide partial reparations through the transfer of whenua (land), money, and, in some instances, co-management arrangements. The Tribunal is a permanent Commission of Inquiry which has spent the first three decades of its existence dealing primarily with claims over land that have arisen from unjust confiscations, illicit purchase arrangements, and theft, all of which have impacted with terrible harm on the health, well-being, and sustainability of hapū Māori.

As the land issues have been slowly settled, attention has refocused on what are known as the kaupapa (theme or purpose) claims, the harms arising from breaches of te Tiriti that have damaged, limited, or undermined aspects of te ao Māori (the Māori world). There are currently 170 deeds of claim before the Tribunal relating to the actions and inactions of Crown Ministers and officials in the health sector. The longstanding existence of serious disparities between the health status of Māori and Pākehā is the sentinel issue.

Te Tiriti is of paramount importance to healthy relationships between Māori and the Crown and is therefore critical to the development, implementation, and effectiveness of any policy. This is never more obvious than in the context of health. For example, within te *Tiriti o Waitangi*, Māori sovereignty is guaranteed, Māori leadership is acknowledged, and there is provision that Māori models of health should be as visible and valued in policy. Te Tiriti affirms the right of Māori to see their taonga; in this instance health, theories, and aspirations advanced as part of their sovereign rights. In critique and analysis of established policy, te Tiriti is a foundational tool in understanding the Crown's shortcomings in their administration of the health system, and it underlies the standpoint of this chapter. It is also a vital underpinning of the Māori health promotion framework known as *Te Pae Mahutonga* (Durie 1999).

Te Pae Mahutonga

Te Pae Mahutonga identifies two te Tiriti-based (Article 2) prerequisites for healthy populations, ngā manukura (Māori leadership) and te mana whakahaere (autonomy), both of which can help us understand what health policy is doing in this context. It also points to four key tasks (relating to Articles 2 and 3 of te Tiriti) in relation to health, mauriora, facilitating access to te ao Māori and strengthening cultural identity; waiora, ensuring environmental protection; toiora, promoting healthy lifestyles; and te oranga, facilitating participation in society – that we argue policy should be able to fulfil if it aspires to health equity in Aotearoa.

Given entrenched systemic health inequities between Māori and Pākehā, we argue that existing health policy in Aotearoa has failed the nation by breaching te Tiriti and allowing preventable disparities to continue and in some circumstances worsen, harming the whole of society. Māori theory including *Te Pae Mahutonga* and other frameworks has been marginalized or regarded as of niche value only.

The six points of *Te Pae Mahutonga* provide an elegant framework, underpinned by te Tiriti, that can be used to understand why health policy has historically and particularly in the contemporary setting made no impression on health disparities and compounded the injustice of the ill-health of Māori introduced by colonization. We will use ngā manukura and te mana whakahaere as critical lenses to critique policy and the four tasks as markers of the degree to which policy reflects the aspiration of *Te Pae Mahutonga* for health equity – the elimination of health inequities.

New Zealand Health Policy

Despite pre-existing indigenous health systems in Aotearoa, in 1900 the New Zealand government established a Department of Health to oversee health policy development and the funding and delivery of health services. In the same period, it sought to destabilize the existing Māori health system by outlawing its practitioners via the introduction of the *Suppression of Tohunga* [expert Māori healer] *Act 1907* (Waitangi Tribunal 2011). Successive governments have reformed this system to reflect their ideological values (Dow 1995, 1999; Lange 1999) including the economic rationalism of recent neoliberal administrations, but none of these changes have eliminated health disparities, and some have made them worse (Ajwani et al. 2003).

Aotearoa has two core health policy documents: the *New Zealand Health Strategy* (Ministry of Health 2016b) and *He Korowai Oranga* (Ministry of Health 2014). These guide the health sector and inform funding decisions. The *Primary Health Care Strategy* (PHCS) (King 2001) is also of critical significance to Māori health, given its governance of first contact services. The NZHS and PHCS are minimalist in their engagement with te Tiriti. For example, the PHCS refers (once) to a "special relationship between Māori and the Crown" (King 2001, p. 2) but provides no detail of what this should mean in terms of policy implementation and outcomes. Māori are listed as a hard-to-reach group, the majority of whom will get their healthcare from generic services, to be approached with cultural "sensitivity" but essentially as just another minority rather than a partner under te Tiriti.

Broadly, the PHCS (King 2001) was published as part of a range of reforms within the New Zealand health sector to strengthen the population health focus, enable stronger community control and collaboration, introduce capitation funding, and shift from the medicalized emphasis of doctors to a more socioculturally oriented paradigm. These reforms were underscored by the need to reduce health inequalities and address causes of poor health status.

In the NZHS, which makes scant mention of te Tiriti, are the notions of lifestyle choice, the neoliberal requirement of people taking personal responsibility for their health, and the economic rationalization of services. The document is framed around five key themes – "people-powered," "closer to home," "value and high performance," "one team," and "smart system" (Ministry of Health 2016b, p. 15) – reflecting

Crown enthusiasm for disinvestment in health services and passing the responsibilities to markets, consumers, and communities (Came et al. 2016).

He Korowai Oranga (HKO) is a framework intended to assist DHBs and providers to achieve "the best" for Māori health. It has an overarching goal of pae ora (healthy future), which has three elements: (i) mauriora, healthy individuals; (ii) whānau ora, healthy families; and (iii) waiora, healthy environments. These elements are to be achieved through collaboration across the health sector to deliver high-quality and effective services as well as through embracing holistic definitions of health and well-being. HKO makes specific reference to rangatiratanga – the capacity to take control over one's destiny – as a core component of health and well-being. However, it also takes only the weakened principles of te Tiriti – partnership, protection, and participation – as its standpoint on Crown/Māori relationships.

Below NZHS, PHCS, and HKO are a series of lesser strategies pertaining to particular foci within the health sector. These include disease-based strategies such as cancer prevention, treatment strategies, and population-based strategies targeting groups such as older people. All are expected to align to directions set out in the NZHS, HKO, and PHCS.

Te Pae Māhutonga as a Framework for Health Policy in Aotearoa

Ngā Manukura

Ngā manukura concerns Māori concepts of leadership which, as Ratima and Ratima (2003) argued, are culturally constructed. Durie (1999, p. 5) promotes a relational approach to leadership which fosters alliances and brings together diverse contributions. Māori leadership must be present in all domains (community, tribal, academic, and political) which are collectively critical for health, since no single group is understood to hold all the necessary expertise to transform Māori health.

At present, most major health policy is drafted by Crown Officials from the Ministry of Health, often assisted by stakeholder or advisory groups. Despite the Treaty partnership, usually only one or two Māori experts are included. A study by Came et al. (Forthcoming) found Māori knowledge and experience is not consistently valued within such contexts with some participants reporting racism and tokenistic engagement with their contributions. Makowharemahihi et al. (2016) argued indigenous health advancement required structural mechanisms including expert advisory groups to optimize indigenous input into policy.

To enhance Māori leadership, it is necessary to invest, strengthen, and expand the Māori health workforce (Ratima et al. 2007; Sewell 2017). Recognizing the importance of Māori practitioners, Durie (1999) has consistently argued for 1 hauora kaimahi (health worker) for each active marae (traditional meeting place/s of Māori) or Māori community of 3000 people. Findings from a survey conducted by the New Zealand Medical Council (2016) showed only a marginal increase in the number of Māori doctors between 2005 and 2016 (2.6–3.3%). Ihimaera and Maxwell-Crawford (2012) found a twofold increase in the number of registered Māori nurses between 1991 and 2001, but Māori continue to be underrepresented in the clinical health workforce (Ihimaera and Maxwell-Crawford 2012; Sewell 2017) and occupy primarily support and administrative positions. These data suggest current government workforce development strategies (Ministry of Health 2006, 2007, 2008) are making limited progress in achieving the goal of an ethnic match between the health workforce and the communities in which they serve. Developing the Māori health workforce and addressing the systemic upstream challenges within the education system remains a necessity for Māori leadership within the health sector.

Ngā manukura constituted with a te Tiriti-based analysis suggests that Māori leadership needs to be embedded in the process of policy development. It is critical to Māori workforce development and central to the relationship between Māori and the Crown to ensure Māori have an equitable and sovereign voice in the development, application, and evolution of policy. Currently, NZHS, HKO, and PHCS make no substantive provision for Māori leadership. More broadly, this is not aligned to key international human rights instruments to which the Crown is a signatory, particularly the *Declaration on the Rights of Indigenous Peoples* (UN 2007) and the *Convention on the Elimination of All Forms of Racism and Discrimination* (UN 1966).

Te Mana Whakahaere

Te mana whakahaere implies Māori control over destiny, which is critical to the elimination of disparities. Durie (1999, p. 5) argued that little health gain can be achieved if health policy and programs are imposed without a sense of community ownership or control:

> Good health cannot be prescribed. Communities – whether they be based on hapū marae, iwi [tribe/s], whānau [family] or places of residence – must ultimately be able to demonstrate a level of autonomy and self-determination in promoting their own health.

This conceptualization relates to the concept of empowerment which is used extensively within the public health sector (Labonte 1990) and where researchers have highlighted the need for communities to determine their own priorities (Durie 1999, 2004; Hamerton et al. 2012; Laverack and Labonte 2000; Ropiha 1994; Simmons and Voyle 2003). This requires culturally tailored interventions, whose success is measured using indicators which are meaningful for Māori (Durie et al. 2002; Hamerton et al. 2012; Ropiha 1994; Simmons and Voyle 2003). Te mana whakahaere necessitates control of health to be held by Māori. This means prioritizing Māori aspirations within health policy and proceeding according to (diverse) Māori cultural preferences (Ratima et al. 2015).

Systemic inequities in social, educational, and health outcomes (Marriott and Sim 2014) are an indication of the presence of institutional racism and potentially breaches of te Tiriti. Institutional racism, inimical to te mana whakahaere, is a *pattern* of differential access to material resources, cultural capital, social legitimation, and political power that advantage one group over another (Came 2014). Lukes (2005) argued power can be exercised through the framing of policy, decision-making, agenda setting, prioritization, and imposing worldviews. In the context of Aotearoa, it manifests as:

> ... the outcomes of mono-cultural institutions which simply ignore and freeze out the cultures of those who do not belong to the majority. National structures are evolved which are rooted in the values, systems and viewpoints of one culture only. (Ministerial Advisory Committee on a Māori Perspective for the Department of Social Welfare 2018, p19)

Racism involves the structures, practices, and policies of a system that reflect and maintain cultural dominance (Paradies 2006). Racism becomes "naturalized" in the routine, mundane workings of established social orders (Adams and Balfour 2009). Detection requires vigilance in terms of examining organizational practices and reviewing action and inaction in the face of need (Human Rights Commission 2011).

Te mana whakahaere is largely absent or unrecognized within health policy partly due to the marginalization of te *Tiriti* within health policy. A study by Came et al. (2018) of te *Tiriti* and public health policy between 2006 and 2016 found only 12 out of 48 policy documents made any mention of the Māori text, the English version, or the Treaty principles. The marginalization of te *Tiriti o Waitangi* in health policy was a deliberate decision (Wall 2006) taken after a senior conservative politician made a speech about nationhood and Māori privilege, arguing that culturally tailored programs advantaged Māori, at the expense of other New Zealanders.

Data from the Ministry of Health and DHBs (2017a) shows in 2015/2016 total investment in Māori health providers was $270.3 million which equates to 1.86% of the total health budget. Māori health providers have proven themselves effective at delivering kaupapa Māori health interventions and services to diverse Māori (and non-Māori) communities (Cram and Pipi 2001; Pipi et al. 2001). Māori leaders have consistently maintained that such underfunding compromises efforts to achieve health equity and is a breach of te Tiriti.

Research by Came et al. (2017) revealed further complexity within health funding practices. Through a nationwide survey of public health providers, the authors showed statistically significant variations in length of contracts, intensity of monitoring, compliance costs, and frequency of auditing between Māori and non-Māori providers. This example of institutional racism reflects a failure of equitable practice which undermines the ability of Māori providers to enact te mana whakahaere within the health system.

In summary, te mana whakahaere, underpinned by te Tiriti, should be visible within contemporary health policy and health service provision. This would be illustrated by Māori having clear control over their health and well-being priorities and outcomes. However, institutional racism compromises the realization of te mana whakahaere, and, along with the marginalization of te Tiriti, this has flow-on effects to health investment decisions and health service provision which undercut Māori ability to exercise te mana whakahaere in the health sector.

Mauriora, Waiora, Toiora, Te Oranga

Health policies engage in passing with some of the four tasks of *Te Pae Mahutonga*. In the NZHS (Ministry of Health 2016b), mauriora is fleetingly implied within the theme of "people-powered" in the sense of recognizing the need for pathways to care "that meet individual needs... across all stages of their life" (p. 17). Specific recognition is given to waiora conceptualized as "the wider context of health." It is stated that "Waiora captures the idea that the environments in which we live have a significant impact on the health and wellbeing of individuals, whānau and communities" (p. 4). Toiora is incorporated in the NZHS through an emphasis on building health literacy as a pathway toward improved health outcomes, but health literacy is framed as a highly individualized set of health knowledges. The goal of te oranga is touched upon within the "investment approach" some agencies are using to ensure "best outcomes for all New Zealanders" (Ministry of Health 2016b, p. 5). Here investment in the health sector which supports increased participation in education and employment is acknowledged to have positive long-term financial impacts for the social sector (p. 6).

The PHCS (King 2001), while consistently referring to "tackling inequalities in health," nominally recognizes the importance of culturally appropriate healthcare (p. 1) which relates to the domain of mauriora. In outlining the new "vision" for the PHCS, attention is paid to education and prevention [of ill-health] as being important, thereby supporting notions of toiora. The need for community participation to improve health and well-being is also recognized which speaks to te oranga. However, there is little to no consideration of waiora.

Unsurprisingly, HKO has the most evolved consideration of the four key tasks, with explicit recognition and attention paid to both mauriora and waiora as key elements of Māori health (Ministry of Health 2014). Recognition of "living healthy lifestyles" – or toiora – is included within the notion of whānau ora (p. 5), and clear pathways toward "supporting Māori participation" (p. 3) are identified thereby supporting the notion of te oranga.

Mauriora is about facilitating access to te ao Māori in order to support the development of identity and sense of belonging. Implicit in this goal is the importance of Māori having access to economic, social, and cultural resources that support the development of Māori identity to achieve positive hauora (health and well-being). Cultural identity is recognized as a determinant of health (Auger 2016; Durie 2001), and 70% of Māori believe it to be important to them (Statistics New Zealand 2014). However, it has been compromised by long processes of colonization and forced assimilation. For instance, in 2013 only 21.3% of Māori reported they could hold a conversation in Māori about everyday things (Te Puni Kōkiri 2014). Deculturation has been linked to poor health (Reid and Robson 2007), and Durie (1999) notes few social institutions in contemporary Aotearoa are orientated to Māori values and worldviews, further impeding access to critical goods and services necessary for well-being. Mauriora should be highly visible in health policy in order to enhance its effectiveness as has been shown by examples such as Korikori a Iwi (Henwood 2007, p. 34) a successful Māori nutrition and physical activity program utilizing kapa haka (Māori performance or performing group), waka ama (Māori canoeing sport), and rongoā (medicine) activities.

Waiora refers to spiritual connections with the external world encompassing physical, temporal, and cosmic domains. Waiora thus reinforces the interconnectedness within te ao Māori and factors which promote, or detract from, hauora. As Durie (2017, p. 34) states "If the environment does not flourish, the people cannot flourish" meaning that environmental degradation is bad for human health, an idea central to "Ko Aotearoa Tenei" (Waitangi Tribunal 2011, p. 5). Health policy must prioritize the protection and nurturing of the environment in recognition of the healthy relationship between Indigenous and other humans and their environments as being central to hauora.

Toiora is about minimizing threats to health by supporting healthy lifestyles. Risks such as alcohol and tobacco use, poor-quality diets, unprotected sex, and sedentary habits have well-known and preventable health consequences. However, as Durie (1999, p. 4) has noted:

> ...it would be an over simplification to suggest that everyone had the same degree of choice regarding the avoidance of risks. Risks are highest where poverty is greatest.

The potential gains from reducing engagement in risk-laden lifestyles among Māori are significant (Marriott and Sim 2014). To effectively uphold the task of toiora, culturally appropriate interventions must stand alongside clear macro policy solutions that address poverty traps and deculturation. For instance, Glover et al. (2015) found that recruiting older Māori aunties to support pregnant women to quit smoking increased quit attempts and engagement with effective cessation methods.

New Zealand health policy is substantially cast in terms of the neoliberal notion of personal responsibility in relation to health outcomes. As mentioned, within the NZHS, this ideology manifests as strong emphasis on health literacy, that is, fostering people's ability to secure and understand health information and make informed decisions based on that information (Kickbusch and Abel 2013). Health literacy thus becomes a tool that transfers responsibility for health promotion and disease management from the powerful who administer the health system to the less powerful users of health services. The injustice of uneven access to the prerequisites of health, a key driver of health inequities, is minimized through this focus on health literacy and may contribute to limited fulfilment of toiora.

Moreover, health policy minimizes that lifestyle "choices" are shaped by the social and built environments in which citizens live. Healthy public policy initiatives are one way to support making healthy choices, easy choices (Warwick-Booth et al. 2012). New Zealand has had several successful legislative interventions from the introduction of seat belts (Garbacz 1991) to the decriminalization of prostitution (Healy et al. 2012a). However, Durie (1999) draws attention to the conflicting health goals of successive New Zealand governments. He notes a simultaneous investment in discouraging risky alcohol use among youth alongside legislation that allows for increasing the number of alcohol outlets, as well as a lowered drinking age. Similarly, Batty and Gee (2018) note the tension with promoting physical activity and the prevalence of sports clubs relying on funding from gambling, or the sale of soft drinks, fast food, and alcohol as fund-raisers. In order to fulfil the goal of toiora within health policy, the aims and objectives which support the attainment of toiora must be clearly outlined and remain consistent over time.

The notion of collective well-being is fundamental to preferred Māori lifestyles (Durie 1998). The whānau ora program (part of HKO) engages with the well-being of the collective, in this context the whānau unit. Whānau ora was established to provide resources for whānau to create and enact plans about health, housing, and employment. The Whānau Ora Taskforce (2010, p. 7) initially explained whānau ora:

> ... recognises the many variables that have the potential to bring benefits to whānau and is especially concerned with social, economic, cultural and collective benefits. To live comfortably today, and in the years ahead, whānau will be strengthened by a heritage based around whakapapa [genealogy], distinctive histories, marae and customary resources, as well as by access to societal institutions and opportunities at home and abroad.

A report from the Auditor General's Office (Provost 2015) gave considerable credit for achievements under this initiative, noting that the $137 m spent over 4 years was an efficient contribution to improving conditions of life for participating whānau.

Presently, whānau ora is an exception within health policy in its focus on collective/whānau well-being rather than individual health. However, research supports the effectiveness of a collective approach to improving health (Hamerton et al. 2012; Warbrick et al. 2016). The NZHS consistently includes rhetoric around whānau well-being, but this inclusion is not reflected in changes in relation to contracting for public, primary, secondary, and tertiary health services. We argue the need to emphasize a whānau-based approach as being central to all health policy in order to fulfil the aims of hauora. This would require a shift from individual capabilities such as health literacy which is emphasized in current health policy to considering the capabilities and potential within and across whānau in order to effect positive health change.

Te oranga is about participation and requires consideration of the broader sociostructural factors known to impact on health and well-being outcomes (Wilkinson and Marmot 2003). Such factors include political, historical, social, and cultural influences. Durie (1999, p. 4) argued:

> [Wellbeing] is also about the goods and services which people can count on, and the voice they have in deciding the way in which those goods and services are made available.

There is evidence that Māori participation is low across a number of areas such as electoral engagement (UMR Research 2006). The goal within health policy then would be to ensure equitable access to society's goods and services (Ratima et al. 2015), as well as ensuring Māori voice in the development of all social and economic policy.

The New Zealand health system is based on the premise of universally accessible services – the notion of equality – but in reality, there are innumerable barriers to equitable access. These include diverse aspects of social capital such as wealth, education, and inclusion as articulated in Wilkinson and Marmot's (2003) notion of the social gradient which accounts for variations in health outcomes at the population level because of the conditions in which people are born and raised and age within. Marmot (2010) argued that to reduce health inequities, interventions must be universal but at a scale and intensity that is proportional to the level of disadvantage. The absence of proportionate provision within New Zealand health policy means only a small part of the problem of inequalities is being addressed. In a colonial context such as Aotearoa, this requires acknowledging the intergenerational impacts of colonization as historic and contemporary determinants of health (Kiro 2000).

We argue the need for Māori voice to be present in the development and execution of all public policy, including social, economic, and health sectors in order to reduce the barriers to equitable access to the goods and services within society that support positive health outcomes.

Conclusion

The right to health is guaranteed for all within the Constitution of the World Health Organization (WHO 1948, p. 1) and specifically among Indigenous peoples in the *Declaration on the Rights of Indigenous Peoples* (UN 2007). In the context of Aotearoa, this is further promised/consolidated through te *Tiriti o Waitangi*. Prior to 1840 when te Tiriti was signed, hapū "had the right, capacity and authority to make politically binding decisions for the wellbeing of their people and their lands" (Matike Mai Aotearoa 2016, p. 8).

Enduring health disparities between Māori and Pākehā not only highlights the inadequacies of current key health policy frameworks in Aotearoa; they also illustrate a broader failure to uphold people's right to health and show clear breaches by the Crown of the provisions held within te *Tiriti o Waitangi*. In light of the identified failures of existing health policy, a transformational approach that is based on the framework of *Te Pae Mahutonga* offers pathways through which to support the pursuit of the aspiration of health equity for all who reside in Aotearoa. We believe that through adopting a framework based on *Te Pae Mahutonga*, this will allow for Māori to re-establish their decision-making capacity, thereby allowing for the realization of tino rangatiratanga and what is provided for within te *Tiriti o Waitangi*.

Through utilizing *Te Pae Mahutonga*, we suggest a transformational approach to health in Aotearoa. In the current health policy context, this requires emphasis and recognition of the need to build ngā manukura and te mana whakahaere; prerequisites for healthy populations. We argue these prerequisites are not currently upheld, effectively disabling the mana of Māori or warranting Māori powerless in determining their own health outcomes and thereby contributing in various ways to the ongoing disparities in health.

In the context of ngā manukura, this is illustrated through the lack of Māori leadership present in the policy development process, thereby marginalizing Māori agency in determining health priorities and approaches to advancing health in Aotearoa. It is further illustrated through the unmet need to develop the Māori health workforce in order to bolster Māori leadership in the health sector. Finally, the relationship between Māori and the Crown illustrates an unequal partnership, where Māori are not positioned as equal leaders alongside Crown equivalents. We have argued this relationship must be reconsidered in order to enable Māori leadership to contribute to improvements in health rather than Māori being constructed as high users of health services. These examples highlight a breach of the provision of kāwanatanga, as outlined by Article 1 of te Tiriti. To this end, we assert that, through building ngā manukura, Māori will be afforded an equitable and sovereign voice in the development and application of health policy.

Te mana whakahaere is also not upheld, as illustrated by the presence of institutional racism within the health sector and through the marginalization of te *Tiriti o Waitangi* which has led to an absence of recognition of te mana whakahaere within health policy. This compromises the realization of te mana whakahaere and further illustrates breaches of te Tiriti as Māori are not enabled to exercise their rights to tino rangatiratanga as guaranteed by Article 2 of te Tiriti. The flow-on effects are that te mana whakahaere is also not present in health investment decisions and health service provision, thereby diminishing Māori ability to be in control over their health and well-being outcomes.

The development of ngā manukura and te mana whakahaere must be prioritized and supported within the health sector. This needs to occur from the development of health policy through to health investment decisions and health service provision and within the health workforce, if we are to effectively transform health outcomes and achieve equitable health outcomes. We also argue the need for stronger recognition and clearer incorporation of the four key tasks of *Te Pae Mahutonga*, mauriora, waiora, toiora, and te oranga, which should be at the fore of health policy in order to fulfil health equity in Aotearoa.

In the context of mauriora, this requires health policy to prioritize Māori access to economic, social, and cultural resources that support the development of secure Māori identities and have positive health impact. Further, we argue the need for mauriora to be clearly visible in all health policy in order to enhance its effectiveness. Recognizing and incorporating waiora require prioritizing protection and nurturing of our environments in recognition of the positive role that healthy relationships between humans and their environments have on health and well-being outcomes. While toiora is focused upon in current health policy, we argue the need to provide clear, macro policy solutions that address poverty traps and deculturation as a way to fulfil the goals of toiora. The aims and objectives within health policy that support the attainment of toiora must also be clearly outlined and consistently held over time.

Further, the limitations and unequal access afforded to Māori when emphasizing health literacy as an appropriate vehicle toward toiora must be recognized as this is a present focus within health policy. We argue the need for whānau-based approaches, rather than individual approaches, as a culturally appropriate vehicle toward the attainment of toiora. This would require a shift from individual capabilities such as health literacy which is emphasized in current health policy to considering the capabilities and potential within and across whānau and hapū in order to effect positive health change. In order to fulfil the goal of te oranga, we argue the need for health policy to ensure equitable access to the goods and services available in society. This requires active Māori engagement in the development of all social and economic policy in recognition of the broader socio-structural factors which impact health outcomes.

Despite the rhetoric, policy development and expenditures entailed in adjustments to the health domain since 2000, outcomes measures show very little gain in terms of improved health equity between Maori and other New Zealanders. Given the long history of disparity, such approaches have little relevance to the aspiration for health equity, and it is time to respond to Tiriti-based Maori theorizing to drive transformational approaches that can address this deep-seated injustice.

References

Adams G, Balfour D (2009) Unmasking administrative evil: rethinking public administration, 3rd edn. M.E. Sharpe, Armonk

Ajwani S, Blakely T, Robson B, Tobias M, Bonne M (2003) Decades of disparity: ethnic mortality trends in New Zealand 1980–1999. Ministry of Health, Public Health Intelligence Group and University of Otago, Wellington

Auger M (2016) Cultural continuity as a determinant of indigenous peoples' health: a metasynthesis of qualitative research in Canada and the United States. Int Indigenous Policy J 7(4). https://doi.org/10.18584/iipj.2016.7.4.3

Batty RJ, Gee S (2018) Fast food, fizz, and funding: balancing the scales of regional sport organisation sponsorship. Sport Manag Rev. https://doi.org/10.1016/j.smr.2018.06.014

Came H (2014) Sites of institutional racism in public health policy making in New Zealand. Soc Sci Med 106(0):214–220. https://doi.org/10.1016/j.socscimed.2014.01.055

Came H, McCreanor T, Doole C, Rawson E (2016) The New Zealand health strategy: whither health equity? N Z Med J 129(1447):72–77

Came H, Doole C, McKenna B, McCreanor T (2017) Institutional racism in public health contracting: findings of a nationwide survey from New Zealand. Soc Sci Med. https://doi.org/10.1016/j.socscimed.2017.06.002

Came H, Cornes R, McCreanor T (2018) Treaty of Waitangi in New Zealand public health policy 2006–2016. N Z Med J 131(1469):32–27

Came H, McCreanor T, Haenga-Collins M (Forthcoming) Māori and Pacific experiences of New Zealand public health advisory group processes

Cram F, Pipi K (2001) Determinants of Maori provider success: provider interviews summary report (Report No.4). Te Puni Kokiri, Wellington

Dow D (1995) Safeguarding the public health: a history of the New Zealand Department of Public Health. Victoria University Press, Wellington

Dow D (1999) Maori health and government policy 1840–1940. Victoria University Press in association Department of Internal Affairs, Wellington

Durie M (1998) Whaiora: Māori health development, 2nd edn. Oxford University Press, Auckland

Durie M (1999) Te pae mahutonga: a model for Māori health promotion. Health Promot Forum Newsl 49:2–5

Durie M (2001) Mauri ora: the dynamics of Māori health. Oxford University Press, Auckland

Durie M (2004) An indigenous model of health promotion. In: Proceedings of 18th world conference on health promotion and health education, Melbourne, pp 1–21

Durie M (2017) Transforming mental health services in Aotearoa New Zealand. In: Kingi T, Durie M, Elder H, Tapsell R, Lawrence M, Bennett S (eds) Maea te Toi Ora: Māori health transformations. Huia Publishers, Wellington, pp 30–38

Durie M, Fitzgerald E, Kingi TK, McKinley S, Stevenson B (2002) Māori specific outcomes and indicators. Te Puni Kōkiri, Wellington

Feigin VL, Krishnamurthi RV, Jones A, Witt E, Brown P, Abbott M, . . . Anderson C (2015) 30-year trends in stroke rates and outcome in Auckland, New Zealand (1981–2012): a multi-ethnic population-based series of studies. PLoS One 10(8). https://doi.org/10.1371/journal.pone.0134609

Garbacz C (1991) Impact of the New Zealand seat belt law. Econ Inq 29(2):310–317

Glover M, Kira A, Smith C (2015) Enlisting "Aunties" to support indigenous pregnant women to stop smoking: feasibility study results. Nicotine Tob Res 146(1). https://doi.org/10.1093/ntr/ntv146

Hamerton H, Mercer C, Riini D, McPherson B, Morrison L (2012) Evaluating Maori community initiatives to promote Health Eating Healthy Action. Health Promot Int 29(1): 60–69. https://doi.org/10.1093/heapro/das048

Hayward J (1997) The principles of the Treaty of Waitangi. In: Ward A (ed) Rangahau whanui national overview report. Waitangi Tribunal, Wellington, pp 475–494

Healy, Bennachie C, Marshall R (2012a) Harm reduction and sex workers: a New Zealand response: taking the harm. In: Pates R, Riley D (eds) Harm reduction in substance use and high-risk behaviour: international policy and practice. Wiley-Blackwell, West Sussex, pp 252–262

Healy, Huygens I, Murphy T (2012b) Ngāpuhi speaks. Network Waitangi Whangarei, Te Kawariki, Whangarei

Henwood W (2007) Māori knowledge: a key ingredient in nutrition and physical exercise health promotion programmes for Māori. Soc Policy J N Z 32:155–164

Human Rights Commission (2011) A fair go for all? Structural discrimination and systemic barriers to ethnic equality. Human Rights Commission, Wellington

Ihimaera L, Maxwell-Crawford (2012) Whakapuāwaitia Ngāi Māori 2030: Māori health workforce priorities. Reanga New Zealand, Wellington

Institute for Health Metrics and Evaluation (2016) GBD compare. University of Washington, Seattle

Kickbusch I, Abel T (2013) Health literacy: the solid facts. World Health Organization Regional Office for Europe, Copenhagen

King A (2001) The primary health care strategy. Ministry of Health, Wellington

Kiro C (2000) Kimihia mo te hauora Maori: Maori health policy and practice. (Doctoral dissertation). Massey University, Auckland

Labonte R (1990) Empowerment: notes on professional and community dimensions. Can Rev Soc Policy 26:64–75

Lange R (1999) May the people live: a history of Maori health development 1900–1920. Auckland University Press, Auckland

Laverack G, Labonte R (2000) A planning framework for community empowerment goals within health promotion. Health Policy Plan 15(3):255–262

Lukes S (2005) Power: a radical view. Palgrave Macmillan, London

Makowharemahihi C, Wall J, Keay G, Britton C, McGibbon M, LeGeyt P, . . . Signal V (2016) Quality improvement: indigenous influence in oral health policy, process, and practice. J Health Care Poor Underserved 27:54. https://doi.org/10.1353/hpu.2016.0035

Marmot Review Team (2010) Fair society, healthy lives: the Marmot review: strategic review of health inequalities in England post-2010 (the Marmot review). Global Health Equity Group, Department of Epidemiology and Public Health, University College London, London

Marriott L, Sim D (2014) Indicators of inequality for Māori and Pacific people [Working paper 09/2014]. Victoria University, Wellington

Matike Mai Aotearoa (2016) He whakaaro here whakaumu mō Aotearoa. Matike Mai Aotearoa, New Zealand

Ministerial Advisory Committee on a Maori Perspective for the Departmetn of Social Welfare (2018) Puao te ata tu (Daybreak). Department of Social Welfare, Wellington, New Zealand

Ministry of Health (2006) Raranga tupuake: Māori health workforce development plan. Ministry of Health, Wellington

Ministry of Health (2007) Te uru kahikatea: the public health workforce development plan 2007–2016. Ministry of Health, Wellington

Ministry of Health (2008) He tipu harakeke: recruitment of Māori in the health and disability workforce. Ministry of Health, Wellington

Ministry of Health (2014) The guide to he korowai oranga: Māori health strategy. Ministry of Health, Wellington

Ministry of Health (2016a) Defining amenable mortality. Ministry of Health, Wellington

Ministry of Health (2016b) New Zealand health strategy: future directions. Ministry of Health, Wellington

Ministry of Health (2017a) Funding to Māori health providers by the ministry of health and district health boards, 2011/12 to 2015/16. Ministry of Health, Wellington

Ministry of Health (2017b) New Zealand health survey 2016/17. Ministry of Health, Wellington

Ministry of Health (2018) Health and independence report 2017. The Director-General of Health's annual report on the state of public health. Ministry of Health, Wellington

New Zealand Medical Council (2016) The New Zealand medical workforce in 2016. Wellington, New Zealand. New Zealand Medical Council, Wellington

Paradies Y (2006) Defining, conceptualizing and characterizing racism in health research. Crit Public Health 16(2):143–157. https://doi.org/10.1080/09581590600828881

Pipi K, Cram F, Hawke S, Huriwai T, Keefe V, Mataki T, ... Tuuta C (2001) Iwi and Māori provider success: a research report of interviews with successful iwi and Māori providers and government agencies. Te Puni Kōkiri, Wellington

Provost L (2015) Whanau Ora: the first four years. Office of the Auditor General, Wellington

Ratima M, Ratima K (2003) Māori public health action: a role for all public health professionals. National Health Committee, Wellington

Ratima M, Brown R, Garrett N, Wikaire E, Ngawati R, Aspin C, Potaka U (2007) Rauringa raupa: recruitment and retention of Maori in the health and disability workforce. Taupua Waiora Centre for Maori Health Research, Auckland University of Technology, Auckland

Ratima M, Durie M, Hond R (2015) Māori health promotion. In: Promoting health in Aotearoa New Zealand. Otago University Press, Dunedin, pp 42–63

Reid P, Robson B (2007) Understanding health inequities. In: Robson B HR (ed) Hauora Māori standards of health IV: a study of the years 2000–2005. Te Rōpū Rangahau Hauora a Eru Pōmare, Wellington, pp 3–11

Ropiha D (1994) Kia whai te māramatanga: the effectiveness of health messages for Māori. Ministry of Health, Wellington

Sewell J (2017) Profiling the Māori health workforce 2017. Te Kīwai Rangahau, Te Rau Matatini, Wellington

Simmons D, Voyle JA (2003) Reaching hard-to-reach, high-risk populations: piloting a health promotion and diabetes disease prevention programme on an urban marae in New Zealand. Health Promot Int 18(1):41–50

Statistics New Zealand (2014) Te Kupenga 2013. Retrieved from https://www.stats.govt.nz/information-releases/te-kupenga-2013-english

Statistics New Zealand (2017a) Life expectancy. Retrieved from http://archive.stats.govt.nz/browse_for_stats/snapshots-of-nz/nz-social-indicators/Home/Health/life-expectancy.aspx

Statistics New Zealand (2017b) Social indicators: He kete tatauranga. Retrieved from http://archive.stats.govt.nz/browse_for_stats/snapshots-of-nz/nz-social-indicators/Home.aspx

Statistics New Zealand (2018) 2013 census quickstats about a place: New Zealand. Retrieved from http://archive.stats.govt.nz/Census/2013-census/profile-and-summary-reports/quickstats-about-a-place.aspx?request_value=13067&tabname=

Te Puni Kōkiri (2014) Te rautaki reo Māori: Māori language strategy. Te Puni Kōkiri, Wellington

UMR Research (2006) Māori electoral engagement – a review of existing data. UMR Research, Wellington

UN (1966) International convention on the elimination of all forms of racial discrimination. UN, New York

UN (2007) Declaration on the rights of indigenous peoples. UN, New York

Waitangi Tribunal (2011) Ko Aotearoa tenei: a report into claims concerning New Zealand law and policy affecting Māori culture and identity (WAI 262). Waitangi Tribunal, Wellington

Waitangi Tribunal (2014) He Whakaputanga me te Tiriti – the declaration and the treaty [WAI 1040]. Waitangi Tribunal, Wellington

Walker R (1990) Ka whawhai tonu mātou: struggle without end. Penguin Books, Auckland

Wall T (2006) "The way forward": for Treaty statements in the health and disability sector. NGO report to the Committee on the Elimination of Racial Discrimination. Retrieved from http://www.converge.org.nz/pma/CERD71-PMA3.pdf

Warbrick I, Wilson D, Boulton A (2016) Provider, father, and bro – Sedentary Maori men and their thoughts on physical activity. Int J Equity Health 15(22):1–11. https://doi.org/10.1186/s12939-016-0313-0

Warwick-Booth L, Dixey R, South J (2012) Healthy public policy. In: Dixey R, Cross R, Foster S, Lowcock D, O'Neill I, South J, Warwick-Booth L, White J, Woodall J (eds) Health promotion: global principles and practice. Modular Texts, Oxfordshire, pp 54–77

Whānau Ora Taskforce (2010) Whānau ora: report of the taskforce on whānau -centred initiatives. Minister for the Community and Voluntary Sector, Wellington

WHO (1948) Constitution. WHO, New York

Wilkinson R, Marmot M (2003) Social determinants of health: the solid facts, 2nd edn. World Health Organization, Geneva

Aboriginal and Torres Strait Islander Secondary Students' Experiences of Racism

71

Gawaian Bodkin-Andrews, Treena Clark, and Shannon Foster

Contents

Introduction	1384
Positioning	1385
Indigenist Research	1386
Defining Racism	1387
Racism Matters	1389
This Study	1391
The Use of an Indigenous Ethno-methodology	1391
Overview	1391
Procedure	1392
Qualitative Yarning Method	1393
Qualitative Yarning Results	1393
Qualitative Yarning Summary	1397
Indigenous Quantitative Method	1397
Quantitative Inferential Analyses and Results	1399
Quantitative Methods Summary	1400
Discussion	1401
References	1403

Abstract

The issue of race and racism within varying Australian contexts is hotly contested politically and across a wide range of media narratives. These debates often center around questioning the very existence of racism, while simultaneously ignoring and denigrating the voices and lived experiences of minoritorized groups within Australia. This is particularly notable for Aboriginal and Torres Strait Islander peoples who have been continually forced to navigate the oppressive nature of

---

G. Bodkin-Andrews (✉) · T. Clark · S. Foster
Centre for the Advancement of Indigenous Knowledges, University of Technology Sydney, Broadway, NSW, Australia
e-mail: gawaian.bodkin-andrews@uts.edu.au

© The Author(s), under exclusive license to Springer Nature Singapore Pte Ltd. 2019
S. Ratuva (ed.), *The Palgrave Handbook of Ethnicity*,
https://doi.org/10.1007/978-981-13-2898-5_106

systemic racism throughout Australia's "colonial history." Drawing from the theoretical and methodological foundations of Indigenist research (Rigney, Wicazo Sa Rev 14(2):109–121, 1999; Martin, J Aust Stud 27(76):203–214, 2003) and Indigenous and First Nations standpoints on Historical Trauma (Brave Heart and DeBruyn, Am Indian Alsk Native Ment Health Res 8(2):56, 1998; Pihama et al. 2014), this chapter will commit to a parallel mixed-methods design to explore how Aboriginal and Torres Strait Islander secondary school students both understand and are impacted by racism today. These findings will be extended through an Indigenous quantitative methodology that will fully articulate the impact of racism over Aboriginal and Torres Strait Islander students' well-being. Themes emerging from the interviews ($n = 17$) suggested the Aboriginal and Torres Strait Islander students understood racism to be much more systematic and endemic (e.g., individual, teacher, community, politics, epistemic) than has been portrayed within previous literature. The quantitative analyses ($n = 49$) also revealed that a more complex understanding of racism is necessary to understand how racism, in its many guises, can negatively impact Aboriginal and Torres Strait Islander students today.

Keywords

Indigenous Australians · Indigenous peoples · Race · Racism · Historical Trauma

Introduction

Racism, in all of its manifestations, is intrinsically and inseparably tied to the ongoing forces of colonization. Although there may be some debate as to what preceded what, racism or colonization (Paradies 2016), it cannot be denied that racism is a powerful weapon through which colonization perpetually oppresses, denies, and erases the human and sovereign rights of Indigenous and First Nations peoples and communities around the world (Walter 2018). It may be argued that there is an abundance of academic literature highlighting strategies to either fight racism through anti-racism discourses (Brown 2011; Hollinsworth 2006; Pedersen et al. 2005) or resist the impact of racism through resiliency and strengths-based discourses (Bodkin-Andrews and Craven 2013; Dune et al. 2018); the ongoing pervasiveness and impact of racism on Indigenous and First Nations peoples cannot be ignored. Many Indigenous scholars though have noted that across contemporary nations forged through colonial invasion, not only are there dominant trends for an obsessive level of avoidance toward meaningfully discussing racism but also a pathological (and often hostile) denial of the very existence of racism itself (Bond 2017; Battiste 2013; Moreton-Robinson 2015; St Denis and Hampton 2002). This, in essence, is one of the key tactics for perpetuating racism, and we argue that while blatant racism and subsequent denial and avoidance of racism may be easily identified (for some), the depths through which racism has been ingrained into the very social fabric of colonial societies, and their agencies for knowledge production (e.g., universities, schools, media), need to be continually monitored and critiqued.

This is powerfully argued by Cree scholar Margaret Kovach (2009, p. 28) who identified that:

> While anti-racist efforts that attempt to decolonise human relationships within sites of research (e.g., the academy) move forward, albeit slowly, there has been little systemic shift in the ideology of knowledge production.... From an Indigenous perspective the reproduction of colonial relationships persists inside institutional centres.

So it is the purpose of this chapter to examine potential discrepancies in understanding racism itself within the secondary (high school) sector of an Australian education system. More specifically, this chapter will privilege the voices and lived experiences of Aboriginal and Torres Strait Islander secondary school students to understand how they may construe, and be impacted by, racism itself. These themes emerging from the student voices will then be utilized in a small sample of quantitative data, where the impact of racism on the well-being of Aboriginal and Torres Strait Islander students will be investigated.

Positioning

It is critical to note that the three authors of this chapter are not approaching the research from some allegedly benign position of neutrality – a neutrality, although often peddled as the pinnacle for scientific methods, is noted by many critical Indigenous scholars as a colonial illusion (Foley 2003; Kovach 2009; Smith 2012; Walter and Andersen 2013). Rather, each author has been racialized under the English-imposed homogenous label of Aboriginal Australian, and as a result, our diverse ancestral lineages since colonization, and our lived experiences, have continually been forced to navigate and survive the varying and ever-evolving manifestations of racism itself. So we come into this research with a drive, or "conscious bias," to uncover and combat the complexities of racism that our future generations will be forced to endure.

Gawaian Bodkin-Andrews identifies as Bidigal, an Aboriginal clan/family group connected to the bitter-waters (inland river systems influenced by the tides) of the D'harawal nation. He brings to this chapter his lived experiences as D'harawal, yet due to his mixed heritage, he also acknowledges his ability to pass as a non-Indigenous Australian. Regardless, he has always identified as D'harawal and has witnessed, experienced, and fought racism for much of his life. Salient to this chapter is one of his first clear memories of directly experiencing racism, where the legal overturning of *terra nullius* in 1992 (and subsequent media and political debates surrounding *Native Title*) reverberated within the very secondary school he was situated. Specifically, he remembers being targeted with taunts and threats by students (some of whom he thought were friends) who wanted no "abo" (a derogatory label for Aboriginal people) getting free land and living next to them. It is from experiences like this that he has developed a drive to understand how racism has long embedded itself within the wider Australian psyche and how this may impact many individuals' lives.

Treena Clark is a Kokatha and Wirangu woman born and raised in Adelaide, South Australia, who currently lives in Sydney. Treena is a PhD candidate at the University of Technology Sydney, where she is researching Aboriginal and Torres Strait Islander ways of conducting public relations, frameworks for decolonizing the western (Australian) practice of public relations, and privileging the voices of Indigenous women who have contributed and carved their path and name within it. Treena attended public high school in a low SES and multicultural area of Adelaide from the early to mid-2000s where she experienced casual racism among her peers outside of the classroom ("Abo" was the "friendly" word of choice) and systematic racism within the classroom (with the whitewashing of Australian history and classmates complaining about studying "Abos"). Treena had a relatively sheltered existence from racism in high school; she had many cousins and other Aboriginal students at school, which contributed to a support system. It wasn't until university that Treena experienced severe racism from people with a lack of understanding and prejudice mindset.

Shannon Foster is a Sydney D'harawal Saltwater Knowledge Keeper, educator, and artist who was raised and educated during the Integration Era of the 1970s, 1980s, and 1990s when there was no information regarding Indigenous cultures taught in her formal education whatsoever. During this time, Shannon experienced firsthand the devastating effects of colonization through the Western Eurocentric education system and what has been referred to as the "Great Australian Silence" (Stanner 1968) and the "silent apartheid" (Rose 2012). Shannon suffered significantly, not just from the silencing and erasure of her culture, but also in the views of the people in the predominantly white community surrounding her, who believed that she was not a "real Aborigine" because of her fair skin and green eyes – the product of government assimilation policies that impacted directly on her D'harawal father's life. It was these experiences of systemic and educational racism that has inspired Shannon to undertake a PhD in Education and document her family's Narinya stories (Living Dreaming) in an effort to decolonize and center the knowledges and lived experiences of her family for use in education and, importantly, to forge a connection to culture for future generations.

Together, the three Aboriginal authors have lived with racism for the majority of their lives and have seen the impact of racism on not only themselves but also their families and kin. Partly due to this positioning, the authors will also approach this chapter from an Indigenist research lens (Martin 2003; Rigney 1999).

Indigenist Research

Both nationally and internationally, many respected Indigenous scholars have stressed the importance of approaching research from the foundations of a diversity of Indigenous standpoint theories and research methodologies (Archibald 2008; Battiste 2013; Foley 2003; Kovach 2009; Martin 2008; Moreton-Robinson 2013; Nakata 2007; Smallwood 2015; Smith 2012; Walter and Andersen 2013). Indigenous standpoint theories critically engage with the historical and ongoing forces of colonization that perpetually seek to silence and erase Indigenous perspectives and knowledges

(Behrendt 2016; Moreton-Robinson 2015; Nakata 2007; Walter and Andersen 2013). While this critical engagement is an essential foundation for Indigenous standpoint theories, research must also seek to engage with constructive narratives that not only seek to break down dominant stereotypes associated with colonial-centered Indigenous research but also commit to the strengthening and centering of Indigenous realities (Martin 2003). A seminal work by Narungga scholar Lester-Irabinna Rigney (1999) labels this as the Indigenist research paradigms. Here, Indigenist research must first be an act of emancipation from the dominant colonial discourses ultimately oppressing Indigenous peoples and communities. Indigenist research must also commit to a political integrity where the research should be ultimately led by Indigenous peoples and communities. Finally, Indigenist research should privilege the voices of Indigenous peoples as the primary driver for knowledge production and understanding.

Quandamooka scholar, Karen Martin (2003), highlights the need for engaging with Rigney's (1999) Indigenist research paradigms not only as an act of resistance against colonization but as an act of centering the strengths deeply embedded within diverse Aboriginal heritages, epistemologies, and ontologies. As a result, Martin adds that Indigenist research must also recognize that Indigenous worldviews, knowledges, and realities are critical for our very survival (and thus should not be reduced to some exotic fringe within research and knowledge production). The social customs and protocols of Indigenous peoples and communities must also be deeply respected and engaged with (when permission is given), and it must be recognized that social, political, environmental, and historical contexts will continually influence these knowledge, customs, and protocols. As a result Martin (2003) stresses that the privileging of Indigenous voices is not just about listening (and hearing) but deeply engaging with holistic Indigenous worldviews that embed not only the voices of Indigenous peoples but Indigenous Country and all entities within it (e.g., spiritual animals, ancestral beings, medical plants, waterways, sacred lands – Martin 2008).

Rather than simply recognizing the principles of Indigenist research in some tokenistic gesture, this chapter will seek to engage with principles through the entirety of the chapter, particularly when it is necessary to engage with, and correct, non-Indigenous standpoints in Indigenous research. This is critical, for as Rigney (1999, p. 133) forcefully argued:

> This means that our struggle against racism is not solely the fight against racist lunatics on the fringe. The struggle against racism must also include the fight to deracialise micro- and macro-social formations left to us by colonization that continue to affect and shape the lives of my people.

Defining Racism

There is a popular trope within media and politics (and research) that race itself is not real, as it is not based on some "biological fact," but rather is a social construct. While identification of the "illusion" of race may be tied to resistance against (or failure of) biological and scientific racism (e.g., research espousing racial superiority), a number of critical scholars have noted that the denial of "race" has become linked to the denial of racism itself – for example, "I treat everybody equally" (Bond 2017; Bonilla-Silva 2013; Moreton-Robinson 2015; Walter and Butler 2013). Munanjahli and South Sea Islander scholar Chelsea Bond (2017, p. 6) powerfully rejects such assertions by arguing that although race may not be an immutable biological construct, it is certainly a powerful social construct that determines both the societal goods and barriers that particular racial groups may be chronically exposed to. Ongoing inequities and inequalities are thus a (colonially) imposed indicator for race itself and that "not talking about race does not render it less powerful or less real. Proclaiming that race is not real does not minimise racism as a lived experience; instead it trivialises the trauma of those who experience it..." (Bond 2017, p. 7).

The denial of race does not erase racism, but rather obfuscates any attempt to understand racism itself and to recognize the immense impact that racism has on the lives of Indigenous peoples around the world. Yin Paradies, a prolific Aboriginal Australian scholar whose work has done much to delineate the ongoing pervasiveness and complexities of racism targeting Aboriginal and Torres Strait Islander peoples today, defines racism as the "unfair and preventable disparities in resources, power, opportunities or capacities along ethnic, racial, religious, or cultural lines... racism may occur via cognitive beliefs (e.g., stereotypes), feelings (e.g., anxiety) or practices/behaviours that are discriminatory (e.g., disparate treatment)" (Paradies 2017, p. 170). Paradies extends on this definition to suggest that racism may manifest itself across internalized, interpersonal, and systemic (e.g., institutional/organizational racism) levels. What is critical about understanding the nature and impact of racism is that the methods and levels through which racism may be realized do not occur in isolated moments of time, place, or being, but are interconnected across the entirety of Indigenous people's historical and lived experiences with colonization itself.

In understanding the contemporary negative impacts of colonization beyond current (and arguably experientially individualistic) and rather fixed notions of inequality and blatant racisms, a number of Indigenous scholars have engaged with Historical Trauma through an Indigenous lens (Brave Heart and DeBruyn 1998; Brave Heart et al. 2011; Pihama et al. 2014). Lakota scholar Maria Yellow Horse Brave Heart et al. (2011) identified Historical Trauma as a collective and intergenerational source of emotional and psychological trauma and grief that has accumulated across the lifespans of Indigenous peoples. Historical Trauma for Indigenous peoples began with the first contact with colonizers, who over generations have threatened and destroyed Indigenous peoples' knowledges and heritages through the dispossession and rape of their lands. This is realized through the introduction of diseases, addictive substances, war and massacres, and the systemic epistemic violence where collective and sustainable epistemologies were replaced by economic and individualist greed. The enacting of racist ideologies of white supremacy resulted in child removal, abusive boarding schools, and oppressive poverties that became a systemically forced way of life (Duran and Duran 1995; Pihama et al. 2014). Brave Heart et al. (2011) notes that the impact of Historical Trauma is ongoing as the genocidal practices of colonization continue to exist through the perpetual colonial narratives that continue to silence and erase Indigenous peoples' existence (Behrendt 2016; Bodkin-Andrews et al. 2017a; Brave Heart et al. 2011; Moreton-Robinson 2015; Rigney 1999).

Within the Australian context, Aboriginal and Torres Strait Islander scholars have directly and indirectly engaged with Historical Trauma in theory and research (Atkinson and Atkinson 2017; Paradies 2016). The potential links between Historical Trauma and the experiences of Aboriginal and Torres Strait Islander peoples are numerous. They range from an Indigenous population that, after 230 years, has still yet to reach parity with estimates of their pre-colonial lives (Muller 2014), the role of disease and biological warfare waged against Aboriginal and Torres Strait Islander peoples, blatant massacres, and ongoing policies related to dispossession, poverty, starvation, and child removal (e.g., Stolen Generations) as colonial weapons used in the pursuit of the genocide of Aboriginal and Torres Strait Islander peoples and customs (Paradies 2016; Rose 2012; Smallwood 2015). As Paradies (2016) warns though, Historical Trauma is not just about the past, it is about the ongoing and transgenerational effects of colonization. It is about the ongoing practices of Indigenous child removal endorsed by successive governments and the mainstream media (McMillan and Rigney 2018); the essentialist and negative political and media narratives demonizing Aboriginal communities (Proudfoot and Habibis 2015; Stoneham et al. 2014; Williams et al. 2017), the assimilative and deficit discourses rampant within our educational, legal, and health institutions (Porter 2015); and, as is the emphasis within this chapter, the persistence of racism within individual attitudes, institutional practices, and the collective Australian psyche that seemingly attempts to minimize the existence of, and responsibility for, racism itself (Bodkin-Andrews and Carlson 2016; Walter and Butler 2013).

Racism Matters

In a landmark study just after the turn of the millennia, Mellor (2003) conducted a series of in-depth interviews with Aboriginal Australian adults in an attempt to understand their experiences of living with racism. What this study uncovered was that for Aboriginal peoples, racism could not be simplified into some blatant or subtle dichotomy, but rather racism was multidimensional and multileveled in nature. Racism was reported at the interpersonal level with verbal racism (e.g., name-calling, jokes, threats) and behavioral racism (e.g., avoidance, assault), as well as at the institutional (e.g., denial of services, overapplication of punishment) and at cultural/macro levels (e.g., media misinformation, selective views on history, lack of concern). In addition, Mellor (2003) found that regardless of the dimension or source of racism, the participants overwhelmingly reported that the racism was both an everyday occurrence and blatant in nature (see also Bodkin-Andrews and Craven 2013; Ziersch et al. 2011 for similar results).

A wealth of quantitative literature has emerged to not only highlight the prevalence of racism experienced by Aboriginal and Torres Strait Islander adults but also the negative impact of racism. Larson et al. (2007), in a study that included responses from 187 Aboriginal adults, found that over 40% had experienced interpersonal racism within the last 4 weeks (nearly four times more likely than non-Indigenous adults). Of Aboriginal adults who did experience racism, they were 3.6 times more likely to report lower levels of physical health and 9.2 times more likely to report lower levels of mental health. In a more recent study involving 755 Aboriginal adults, Ferdinand et al. (2013) found that after utilizing a multidimensional measure of interpersonal racism (eight items including name-calling, physical abuse, stereotypes, etc.), 97% of the respondents reported experiencing some form of racism in the last year. In addition, five of the eight types of racism measured were significantly associated with high or very high levels of psychological distress.

It is important to note that research on racism is not limited to Aboriginal and Torres Strait Islander adults. For example, two papers utilizing the data from the *Western Australian Aboriginal Child Health Survey* found that for Aboriginal youth who experienced racism, they were significantly more likely to partake in risky health behaviors such as alcohol, tobacco, and marijuana consumption (Zubrick et al. 2005) and for both children and youth, racism was linked to increased risks of developing clinically significant emotional, behavioral, and conduct problems (aged from 4 to 17 years – De Maio et al. 2005). A more recent study utilizing the *Longitudinal Study of Indigenous Children* database (see Martin and Walter 2017 for a detailed overview of this database) found that while only 14% of Aboriginal and Torres Strait Islander children (5–10 years of age) directly experienced racism (as reported by primary carers), those who did experience racism were significantly more likely to be at high risk of clinically significant emotional and behavioral difficulties, sleep difficulties, obesity, and asthma (Shepherd et al. 2017). Utilizing the same database, Bodkin-Andrews et al. (2017c) found that the impact of racism was not limited to the direct experiences of Aboriginal and Torres Strait Islander children. They found that not only were the parents' (primary carers) direct experiences of racism associated with significantly increased levels of worry, anger, and depression, but if their child experienced racism, then the carers showed significantly higher levels of worry and depression. The authors linked these findings to the previous work of Priest et al. (2010), who found that the worry or expectation of experiencing racism by Indigenous carers was enough to not only substantially increase the risk of carer drug taking but was associated with a significantly increased risk of physical illness (e.g., respiratory infections, diarrhea, vomiting, scabies) impacting upon their Indigenous children. These findings that emphasize that racism can impact the whole family both directly and indirectly led Bodkin-Andrews et al. (2017c) to conclude that researchers must more carefully consider not only the transgenerational impact of racism but also the shared and cyclical threat racism holds over not only individuals but their families and communities. In addition:

> ...racism must be understood more comprehensively, particularly with regards to its endemic and systemic nature and impact. Relying solely on non-Indigenous representations

of racism not only silences Aboriginal and Torres Strait Islander voices and scholarly research, but also dangerously underestimates the insidious and enduring ways in which racism manifests in society today and in the future. (Bodkin-Andrews et al. 2017c, p. 202)

This Study

While quantitative research has attested to the negative impact of racism on Aboriginal and Torres Strait Islander children, youth, and adults, such research, particularly within child and youth contexts, is often limited by simplistic measures of racism that may underestimate its prevalence and impact. This is highly problematic, as qualitative research has highlighted the complexity of ways in which racism may be experienced by Aboriginal and Torres Strait Islander adults. To what extent is our understanding of racism and its impact from Aboriginal and Torres Strait Islander children and youth standpoints limited by the very research methods utilized? Each one of the studies involving Aboriginal and Torres Strait Islander children and youth did not move beyond single-item measures. Is it possible that such research may be inevitably contributing to the minimization and even silencing of Indigenous perspectives on racism itself? For research to truly act as a tool for emancipation from colonial academic narratives, the voices of our Aboriginal and Torres Strait Islander children and youth must be heard. As a result, this study aims to:

1. Identify how Aboriginal youth within urban schooling environments may define, understand, and experience racism.
2. Assess the degree to which multiple levels of racism may impact upon the well-being of Aboriginal youth.

The Use of an Indigenous Ethno-methodology

Overview

This chapter has committed to a parallel mixed-methods design that will engage with both Indigenist research principles (Martin 2003; Rigney 1999) and an Indigenous quantitative research methodology (Walter and Andersen 2013). These approaches have been taken because Paradies (2006) has argued prior quantitative literature on racism may be inadequate to capture both the subtleties and true pervasiveness of racism targeting Aboriginal and Torres Strait Islander peoples. For example, in a report on the social and emotional well-being of Aboriginal and Torres Strait Islanders (Australian Institute of Health and Welfare [AIHW] 2009), "racial discrimination" was measured simply by asking if "you had been treated badly" because of your Indigenous background in the last 12 months. While the majority of participants responded "no" (84%), the Aboriginal steering committee noted this measure's inconsistently with other quantitative research (e.g., Paradies and Cunningham 2012) and argued against simplistic single-item measures of racism – "the workshop agreed that it is likely that the current definitions are too narrow. It was suggested that this concept should be expanded to capture oppression and racism" (p. 82).

Drawing from the foundations of Indigenist research (Martin 2003; Rigney 1999), it is critical to note that if research aims to understand and combat the racism that Aboriginal and Torres Strait Islander peoples and communities are forced to endure, such research must be built from Aboriginal and Torres Strait Islander standpoints. From this, qualitative research methods offer the unique opportunity to more precisely capture not only that which may not have been previously measured but also further substantiate important insights and results for the research topic (Sechrest and Sidani 1995). This chapter firstly utilized an Indigenous qualitative technique of yarning that incorporated semi-structured research yarns (Bessarab and Ng'andu 2010) with Aboriginal high school students to more fully understand their perceptions and experiences of racism within Australia.

It also should be recognized that while many Indigenous scholars note how often quantitative research has misrepresented Indigenous peoples (Nakata 2007), an increasing number of Indigenous scholars are committed to deeply engaging with Indigenous epistemologies as a primary driver for realizing Indigenous quantitative methodologies and methods that center measures (and discussion) on the standpoints of Indigenous peoples (Kukutai and Andersen 2016; Bodkin-Andrews et al. 2017c; Kukutai and Walter 2015; Lovett 2016; Rainie et al. 2017; Walter and Andersen 2013). As a result, Indigenous quantitative research methods can avoid prioritizing non-Indigenous standpoints, take part in the breaking down of systemic colonial dominance in knowledge production, and be continually mindful of the risk of perpetuating many (but not all) of the norms of colonization that statistics have too often reinforced (Walter and Andersen 2013). As a result, the second study in this chapter will adhere to an Indigenous quantitative research methodology by drawing from a multidimensional racism measure both written by an Indigenous scholar and constructed from Aboriginal standpoints (Bodkin-Andrews et al. 2010, 2013).

Procedure

After consultation (and ongoing negotiations) with NSW Aboriginal Educational Consultative Committee (AECG) representatives (both state and local), ethical approval was awarded from both the university Human Resources Ethics Committee and the NSW Department of Education and Committees (DEC) to conduct the research from 2013 to 2014. Schools were approached due to their high population of Aboriginal students from urban areas (around 10%) or being situated within a highly multicultural area. Both quantitative and qualitative data was gathered only from students and parents/primary carers who provided informed consent (a total of 563 secondary students gave full consent, with 49 students identifying as being of Aboriginal descent – see Bodkin-Andrews and Craven 2014 for more detail).

Qualitative Yarning Method

A total of 17 Aboriginal Australian secondary school students were interviewed for the project and came from five rural/urban public high schools in the Australian state of New South Wales. Due to necessary ethical considerations (both Indigenous and non-Indigenous), both timing of the interviews and selection of consenting students (with parental consent) were determined by the school representatives (either a nominated teacher representative for the project or an Aboriginal Education Officer) to minimize impact on their studies. While all identified as Aboriginal Australian, only six named their Aboriginal Nation and/or clan grouping. Nine of the students were female (eight male), and students ranged from 12 to 16 years of age (mean age of 13.94 years).

The qualitative data was collected through audio recordings (as agreed to by all participants) of the individual yarning sessions conducted by an Aboriginal researcher. These sessions were conducted in school rooms which had no other staff or students present (although the door was left open). The sessions began with what Bessarab and Ng'andu 2010 label as social yarning where the Aboriginal researcher and student shared information about their families and mob (i.e., nation and clan group) and/or the Aboriginal Country on which their school was located. As already noted, only a minority of students showed an awareness of their Aboriginal Nation and/or Clan/Tribal groups, so the Aboriginal researcher fluidly transitioned the discussion onto the Aboriginal Nation group in which the schools were located (to minimize feelings of cultural threat) and positive cultural activities within the school. This was followed by research yarning where the themes of the yarn were shared with the student (feelings about school in general, how students may or may not respect each other's cultural background, and overall levels of cultural respect and racism both within and outside the school). Once completed, students were offered a small gift for their time (usually a bag of lollies endorsed by the school representative) and thanked for their time. The yarning sessions generally took up to 30 min. All interviews were transcribed verbatim and then entered into the NVivo 11 (QSR International, 2012) for coding. Each transcript was dealt with on a sequential basis and was carefully read prior to entry into NVivo. All coding was done by the lead author of this chapter, and the coding processes for each participant went through a number of stages, beginning with basic descriptive coding for participant details and then the process of more detailed free coding where each interview generated its own set of analytical codes. Finally the coded data was revisited, and not only were shared themes identified, but inconsistencies between respondents were carefully noted (Richards 2009; Strauss and Corbin 1990).

Qualitative Yarning Results

For the Aboriginal students, a wide diversity of themes emerged surrounding not only the existence of racism within Australia but how the students themselves personally experienced these racisms. The emerging themes will be presented in order of how many Aboriginal students voiced their concerns about racism today.

Racism on the Outside

Fourteen of the seventeen students voiced concerns regarding the ongoing existence of racism within Australia (yet outside the direct schooling environment). This included repeated concerns about racism within their local communities, where, for example, a 13-year-old male student spoke of the racial tensions he was aware of:

> **Interview 5** – 13-year-old male student: *Because it's just a split community and I just want them to get together. That's what I figure, Australia has got to come together...*

Intrinsically linked to this theme was how Aboriginal and Torres Strait Islander peoples and communities were presented within the media, as students often spoke of how media and political representations seemed to fuel racial tensions. For example, one student spoke of a frustration toward ongoing debates about a national day commemorating the 2008 national apology for the *Stolen Generations*:

> **Interview 8** – Interviewer: *Why you think there was this resistance to Sorry Day?*
> 15-year-old female student: *Oh, because people in the past, when they got taken, and no-one had the guts to say sorry.*

Naturally, politics was also directly raised as an example of racism:

> **Interview 11** – Interviewer: *Can you think of any examples of what would constitute racism in Australia?*
> 12-year-old male: *Yes, in political reasons at the moment there are only two Aboriginals in political... parliament.*

That a majority of the students revealed an awareness that racism existed outside their own individual experiences is important to recognize. This ranged from references to community racial tensions, racism within the news media, and racism within the highest levels of governance. Although such "perceptions" may be reduced to notions of "vicarious racism," considering the possible links to Historical Trauma (Brave Heart and DeBruyn 1998), evidence for the effects of transgenerational racism (Bodkin-Andrews et al. 2017c), and evidence suggesting that macro racism is indeed detrimental to Aboriginal and Torres Strait Islander student school engagement and achievement (Bodkin-Andrews et al. 2010), one should not assume that these wider forms of racism may be meaningless occurrences that are unrelated to Aboriginal and Torres Strait Islander student well-being.

Racist Slurs

Ten of the 17 Aboriginal students spoke about racist slurs that frequently occurred within their schools. This was most frequently typified by direct name-calling:

> **Interview 1** – 15-year-old female: *Yeah. I got a scholarship once during school and this guy walked off stage and he said just because you're fucking Abo.*
> **Interview 12** – 14-year-old male: *Where they tease you about your culture and they put you down.*

Yet references to racist slurs were also typified by everyday "playground" dialogues that some of the students also revealed some discomfort over:

> **Interview 3** – 15-year-old male: *Like people might sort of say like the N word... it's like they won't sort of say it to a person of a different culture sort of offensively. Like they might say it sort of like – from what I've seen, it's like for emphasis sort of thing... I don't see why, but they like using it... It's just kind of a bit like – more like an insult, but not an insult directly...*

While name-calling and verbal abuse would easily fall into the more blatant types of racism, and identifiable by its intent to harm, some Aboriginal student concerns about nondirected dialogues (arguably normalized through popular culture) blurred attempts to separate intent and non-intent as a defining feature of racism itself.

Subtleties of Stereotyping

For 8 of the 17 Aboriginal students, the subtleties of racism were highlighted, yet they were voiced in a manner that suggested personal implications. Similar to nondirected racist slurs, although (possibly) not meant as direct insults, these subtle stereotypes were often seen to target their own lives or families. For example, one student spoke of his Aboriginal father and false stereotypes of Aboriginal people lacking intelligence:

> **Interview 11** – 12-year-old male: *Well my dad didn't pass through high school. He stopped at Year 11 and he's actually... Aboriginal so since he didn't pass, everyone thinks that he's not really smart but he knows quite a lot about maths.*

This is not to state that the use of stereotypes was due to lack of intent and naivety, for the following student spoke of a stereotype used as a direct attack through emphasizing derogatory false beliefs that Aboriginal communities and cultures are inherently violent:

> **Interview 9** – 14-year-old female: *They said oh, you don't belong here. You need to go and kill someone or whatever to fit in. It made no sense but it was just – like there was no need for it.*

Racism as Erasure

Six of the 17 Aboriginal students spoke of racism in a manner that either identified the erasure of Aboriginal people within varying forms of knowledge production or attempts to erase the individual students' right to identify as Aboriginal.

> **Interview 1** – 15-year-old female: *In history, we get told the minimum of what actually happened. Where if they get told to the full extent and what it does to people today, maybe, they actually would realise why we get scholarships and need a little bit more help.*

It should be noted that within the above quote, a direct link between Historical Trauma and the lived experiences of Aboriginal students can be observed, as the student notes the ongoing negative impact of colonization on Aboriginal and Torres Strait Islander peoples today. Extending on the implication of this quote, this student is suggesting that the erasure of Aboriginal standpoints in framing Australia's colonial history actually amplifies the impact of Historical Trauma, as the racism of erasure (also known as epistemological racism – Rigney 1999; Scheurich and Young 1997) seems to amplify the resistance to righting past wrongs. As suggested in the introduction to the erasure of racism though, this is not just limited to broad notions of understanding Aboriginal and Torres Strait Islander histories and knowledges but individual student connections to their very identity:

> **Interview 4** – 15-year-old female: *People always say stuff to me because they don't think I'm Aboriginal because I'm white. But I just tell them to shut up.*

No Racism

Somewhat encouragingly, six of the students initially spoke of not experiencing racism personally within the schooling environment yet had difficulty articulating why racial tensions may not exist.

> **Interview 8** – 15-year-old female: *Because everybody just – it's – no-one's really racist at this school so everybody gets on.*
> Interviewer: *Do you think there's any special ingredient that's helping people get along?*
> 15-year-old female: *Maybe... I don't know.*

It is important to note though that for three of the students who did not experience racism directly, they later highlighted examples of racism either impacting other student ethnic groups within the school (e.g., **Interview 14** – 12-year-old male: *Depends on what the background is like if they're Indian*) or, as already discussed, outside the schooling environment.

Physical Racism

Five of the 17 Aboriginal students spoke of racism manifesting in a physical manner within their schooling environment. While three of these reports were centered on witnessing fights due to racial tensions, two of the students directly experienced physical abuse. For example, when one student was asked about any racism they had witnessed in the school:

> **Interview 4** – 15-year-old female: *Some of the students have no respect. I've been spat on by some of them because they've got nothing better to do.... Just they think they're better than everyone else.*

Teacher Racism

Finally, the last substantial theme of racism to emerge centered on four of the students who were aware of teachers within their schools who held racist attitudes (although none of these examples were direct experiences of blatant racism). For example:

Interview 16 – 14-year-old female student: *One of the teachers. She does history. She doesn't teach me but she teaches my younger sister and my younger sister, she sits with all of her friends who are also Aboriginal, and the teacher never talks to them. She doesn't take any of their opinions or anything.*

It is important to note that each example of racism emanating from teachers, as listed by the Aboriginal students, was not centered on blatant forms of racism (e.g., name-calling, abuse), but rather aligned more closely to the themes of *racism as erasure* (epistemological racism). Another powerful example of this includes the following quote that alludes to a possible systematic denial of student experiences of racism:

Interview 4 – Interviewer: *Have the teachers supported you in any way in terms of these incidences?*
15-year-old female: *Not really, no.*
Interviewer: *No?...*
15-year-old female: *Yes – well, I reckon they should just find out who is targeting other people and deal with them, instead of just saying oh, they'll get over it or just ignore them – because just ignoring them doesn't help.*

Qualitative Yarning Summary

In answering the first aim, this chapter attempted to privilege the voices of a small number of Aboriginal secondary school students with regard to their lived experiences of racism both within and outside of the schooling environment. What can be noted is a diverse range of reoccurring themes centered on the existence of multiple dimensions of racism (both direct and indirect) that are significant to the lives of these students. By identifying the themes of *Racism on the outside*, *Racist slurs*, *Subtleties of stereotyping*, *Racism as erasure*, *Physical racism*, and *Teacher racism*, researchers must realize that simplistic measures of the "have you experienced racism" ilk are not enough to truly understand the nature and impact of racism itself, even for our younger generations. It is with this finding in mind that this chapter will now report on the quantitative component of this study.

Indigenous Quantitative Method

A total of 49 Aboriginal Australian students (25 male, 24 female, from years 7 to 11) participated in the quantitative survey from 4 separate schools. The schools were all classified as having a below-average socioeconomic status (as drawn from www.myschool.edu.au), with scores ranging from 844 to 967 (mean SES of 928.65, the national mean sitting at 1000).

As already stipulated within this chapter, an Indigenous quantitative research methodology (Walter and Andersen 2013) will guide the analyses within this chapter. This is not only done through the prioritizing of a previous measure created from Indigenous standpoints on racism (Bodkin-Andrews et al. 2010, 2013), but the specific engagement with this measure will center on the voices of the Aboriginal students within this study. Rather than utilizing the predefined generalized factor structure, the voices of the Aboriginal students were privileged to define specific item selection. As a result, the following items have been selected for analyses as per the themes raised in the qualitative yarning interviews (and they were scored on a six-point Likert scale ranging from 1 "False" to 6 "True" with regard to student experiences in the previous year) (Table 1):

In assessing the potential impact of racism, a variety of outcome variables were selected to capture both Aboriginal student well-being and engagement with school. For student well-being, single items were selected from the short version of the Depression Anxiety Stress Scale (Szabó 2010) and scored on a four-point Likert scale ranging from 1 "Did not apply to me at all" to 4 "Applied to me most of the time":

- Stress: I found it hard to wind down.
- Anxiety: I felt scared without any good reason.
- Depression: I felt downhearted and blue.

For engagement with school, single items were selected from a prior school enjoyment measure (Craven et al. 2005) and purposely written disengagement measure (Bodkin-Andrews and Craven 2014) and were scored on a six-point Likert scale ranging from 1 False to 6 True:

- School enjoyment: I enjoy being at school.
- School disengagement: I think school is a waste of my time.
- School helplessness: I don't know how to achieve at school.
- School truancy: I sometimes look for excuses to skip school.

Table 2 contains the descriptive statistics for each of the measures, including the percentage of students who agreed with each question (pending the Likert scale utilized). As can be noted from this table, the range of students agreeing to

Table 1 Quantitative measures of racism

Yarning theme	Quantitative measure
Racism on the outside	Most other Australians believe political parties who unfairly target people from my cultural background
Racist slurs	I have had people call me nasty names based on the culture I come from
Subtleties of stereotyping	I have had people rudely stare at me when they become aware of my culture
Racism as erasure	Most other Australians don't understand the history of my culture
Physical racism	I have been physically threatened because of my cultural background
Teacher racism	Some teachers don't seem to trust me or other people from my culture at school

Table 2 Descriptive statistics for the racism and student outcome measures

	Range	Mean	Standard deviation	% agree
Racism on the outside	1–6	3.50	1.77	51
Racist slurs	1–6	3.08	2.16	45
Subtle stereotype	1–6	2.80	1.89	39
Racism as erasure	1–6	3.29	1.88	47
Physical racism	1–6	2.27	1.69	29
Teacher racism	1–6	2.32	1.62	29
Stress	1–4	2.37	1.07	71
Depression	1–4	1.72	1.00	43
Anxiety	1–4	1.93	1.06	55
Enjoy	1–6	4.00	1.61	78
Disengage	1–6	1.93	1.93	45
Hopeless	1–6	1.69	1.69	41
Truancy	1–6	1.54	1.54	22

Note. Considering the small sample size and that individual variables contained no more than 8.2% of missing responses (namely, four or less participants), the expectation-maximization (EM) substitution technique was used to replace missing values (Hills 2010)

experiencing racism moved from 29% (teacher racism – lack of trust) to 51% (outside racism – people believing political parties). When these diverse experiences of racism are combined though, it is important to note that 38 (78%) students experienced at least one form of racism.

For the student outcome variables, with the well-being variables, scores of "2" or above on the Likert indicated that they had experienced some form of stress, depression, or anxiety in the last 2 weeks. Forty-three percent of students admitted to feeling depression, 55% admitted to feeling anxious, and 71% reported feeling stress. For the school engagement variables (responses were on the same Likert scale as the racism measures), 78% of the Aboriginal students enjoyed school, and a large minority of students felt disengaged (45%) and hopeless (41%) and showed a desire to be truant (22%) from school.

Quantitative Inferential Analyses and Results

The final analysis for this chapter consisted of an inferential statistical technique known as partial correlation (Hills 2010), which was used to ascertain if the varying racism measures were associated with the student well-being and school engagement outcomes after controlling for the effects of student year level, gender, and school socioeconomic status. Table 3 offers the results for the final set of analyses.

As can be noted from Table 3, a range of significant (or approaching significant) associations can be observed (and this is after controlling for the explained variance in student year level, gender, and school socioeconomic status). For student self-reports on stress in the last 2 weeks, the racial slur ($r = .32$) and physical racism ($r = .35$) variables were significantly associated with *higher levels of stress* (as

Table 3 Associations between racism and student outcomes after controlling for student year level, gender, and school socioeconomic status

	Outside racism	Racial slurs	Subtle racism	Erasure racism	Physical racism	Teacher racism
Stress	–	.32*		.26^	.35*	.28^
Depression	.33*	–	.28^	.31*	.32*	.37*
Anxiety		–	.26^	.27^	.42**	.34*
School enjoyment	−.30*	–	−.41**	–	–	−.35*
School disengage	–	–	–	–	–	.37*
School hopeless	–	–	–	–	.25^	.34*
School truancy	–	.43**	.33*	–	.36*	.40**

Note. ^ = $p < .10$, * = $p < .05$, ** = $p < .01$. – = nonsignificant

were erasure and teacher racism, but these only approached significance). Outside ($r = .33$), erasure ($r = .31$), physical ($r = .32$), and teacher ($r = .37$) racisms were all significantly associated with *higher levels of depression* for the Aboriginal students (subtle racism was approaching significance here). Finally physical racism ($r = .42$) and teacher racism ($r = .34$) were both associated with *increased levels of anxiety* (subtle and erasure racism were approaching significance).

For the school engagement outcomes, another wide range of significant associations were identified. With regard to school enjoyment, outside ($r = -.30$), subtle ($r = -.41$), and teacher ($r = -.35$) racisms were associated with *decreased levels of enjoyment at school*. For both school disengagement and school hopelessness, teacher racism ($r = .37$ and $r = .34$, respectively) was associated with *increased risk* of these outcomes. Finally for school truancy, racial slurs ($r = .43$), subtle racism ($r = .33$), physical racism ($r = .36$), and teacher racism ($r = .40$) were associated with increased risk of students looking for reasons to skip school.

Quantitative Methods Summary

In engaging with an Indigenous quantitative methodology (Walter and Andersen 2013) to prioritize the standpoints of the Aboriginal students within this study, two key findings emerged. Firstly, across the students the prevalence of lived experiences of racism varied according to the type of racism being measured, with students least likely to report teacher (29%) and physical (29%) racism but most likely to report outside (51%) and erasure (47%) racism. These figures may suggest that the majority of students don't experience most racisms over a year, yet, when tallied, the results revealed that 78% of the Aboriginal students experienced at least one form of racism in the last year. Disturbingly though, the inferential results suggest that every one of these experiences of racism was not superficial in nature, but rather has diverse negative effects. That is, varying forms of racism were associated with an increased risk of stress, anxiety, and depression for the Aboriginal students, in addition to negatively impacting how they may engage with school.

Discussion

Combined, the qualitative and quantitative results attest to not only the complexities of how racism may be experienced by Aboriginal students but also the potential negative impact of racism on the well-being and school engagement of Aboriginal students. Both sets of results speak together with regard to the complexity of racism that Aboriginal students in this research experienced and the negative effects of such racism. The results have built upon prior literature that revealed how racism may be a critical element toward the perpetuation of Historical Trauma for Aboriginal and Torres Strait Islander adults, youth, and children (De Maio et al. 2005; Ferdinand et al. 2013; Larson et al. 2007; Mellor 2003; Paradies 2016; Ziersch et al. 2011). This is particularly important as this study, in part, adds to the literature suggesting that understanding the experiences of racism should not be limited to direct interpersonal interactions but also vicarious, systematic, and transgenerational effects (Bodkin-Andrews et al. 2017c; Paradies 2016; Priest et al. 2010).

Returning to the theoretical and methodological foundations of this chapter, it has only partially met the conditions of Indigenist research paradigms though (Martin 2003; Rigney 1999). That is, in attempting to address potential misunderstandings and silences regarding Aboriginal and Torres Strait Islander youth and their experiences of racism, this chapter has contributed to an emancipatory narrative attempting to fight dominant colonial discourses about racism. It has also, in part, engaged with Aboriginal communities (e.g., AECG) and been led by Indigenous scholars and thus privileged the voices of Aboriginal and Torres Strait Islander peoples (both in the student participants and an emphasis on citing Indigenous scholars). This paper's engagement with Indigenist paradigms centered on a strengths-based approach (Martin 2003) though is lacking. One key feature of Indigenous research methodologies though is the emphasis on reflexivity, not only in the recognition of the positioning of the authors but through the entirety of the research practice itself (Archibald 2008; Bodkin-Andrews et al. 2016; Kovach 2009; Martin 2008; Smallwood 2015; Smith 2012; Walter and Andersen 2013). So the question remains, how can Martin's (2003) extensions of Indigenist research be met? At the very least, we can briefly engage with research that has explored this possibility.

Indigenous scholars who have recognized the existence and ongoing impact of Historical Trauma also stress that such recognition creates space for future narratives and processes that enable the development, and in some cases the strengthening, of Indigenous recovery and healing practices (England-Aytes 2013; Fast and Collin-Vézina 2010; Pihama et al. 2014). For example, in a chapter led by Métis scholar Fast (Fast and Collin-Vézina 2010), the overarching need for self-governance and self-determination is stressed (e.g., Indigenous Data Sovereignty – Kukutai and Taylor 2016), in addition to the advancement of cultural and spiritual renewal projects that strengthen the identities and cultural practices of Indigenous peoples (e.g., Archibald 2008; Linklater 2014). While the two overarching principles suggested by Fast and Collin-Vézina (2010) are indeed relevant to strengthening Indigenous communities, Cherokee scholar England-Aytes (2013) offers a more detailed set of principles that also warn against the dangers of homogenization and essentialism often plaguing Indigenous "intervention." That is, to meaningfully address Historical Trauma, there is also a need to:

- Recognize the diversities of histories and experiences of Indigenous peoples.
- Explore, share, and draw strength from the diversities of internal representations of Indigenous peoples, communities, and their knowledges.
- Respectfully engage with Indigenous community representatives and organizations to assist in the learning processes.
- Move beyond "authentic" colonial understandings of "Indigenous history" and engage with the lived experiences of Indigenous peoples.
- Be empathic and identify signs of distress that can be linked to both contemporary and historical contexts.
- Recognize the systemic nature of racism and discrimination across personal, institutional, and border governmental and societal contexts.

The need to recognize the ongoing impact of racism, in all its complexity, is of critical importance, for racism is not only a barrier to addressing Historical Trauma, but it is a perpetuator and enabler of Historical Trauma itself. This is powerfully evidenced by Pihama et al. (2014), who cited zealous reactions by New Zealand politicians and media representatives in response to an associate minister for Māori Affairs utilizing the term "holocaust" to describe (accurately) the impact of colonization on Māori peoples. Pihama et al. (2014) list not only repeated reprimands from the then New Zealand prime minister but highlight the resulting tensions within the wider non-Māori community and concluded that "these debates illustrated a limited acknowledgement or recognition of the history of colonization and the severity of the traumatic acts perpetuated against Māori" (p. 257).

Paradies (2017) offers five key principles for combatting systemic racism that too often targets Aboriginal and Torres Strait Islander peoples. While these key principles may also be seen as essential first steps in the reduction of risk factors associated with Historical Trauma itself (namely, persistent colonial attitudes and actions), any enthusiasm may need to be tempered with a degree of Indigenous cynicism. That is, the first, and arguably key principle, is the presenting of accurate information that may foster a greater level of awareness of the social and historical forces that work against Aboriginal and Torres Strait Islander peoples (yet see the Pihama et al. example 2014 above). It may be argued though that the remaining four principles (centered on promoting egalitarian beliefs, enhancing empathy, increasing positive inter-group contact, and promoting positive social norms) are intrinsically and deterministically tied to the original "accurate information" principle and non-Indigenous peoples' willingness to engage with this. Unfortunately, it can be argued that the media and political climate within Australia is not one that fosters accurate and positive knowledge production for or with Aboriginal and Torres Strait Islander peoples and communities (see also Parker et al. 2018). The very awareness of the complexities of racism within the ongoing Australian colonial context (and targeting Indigenous peoples around the world) will continue to be subdued, if not oppressed, by the very colonial systems that enable and perpetuate Historical Trauma and racism itself. That is perpetuated by the ongoing forces that deny racism and, knowingly and unknowingly, reinforce colonization – be it the schooling system, media, politics, or academia itself. And so racism lives on, and as per the findings of this chapter, and the many prior research findings cited within it, it is our children and youth who will continue to suffer.

References

Archibald JA (2008) Indigenous storywork: educating the heart, mind, body, and spirit. BC Press, Vancouver

Atkinson J, Atkinson C (2017) A healing foundation for Aboriginal community development. In: Kickett-Tucker C, Bessarab D, Wright M, Coffin J (eds) Mia Mia Aboriginal community development: fostering cultural security. Cambridge University Press, Cambridge, pp 110–127

Australian Institute of Health and Welfare (2009) Measuring the social and emotional wellbeing of Aboriginal and Torres Strait Islander peoples. Cat. no. IHW 24. AIHW, Canberra

Battiste M (2013) Decolonizing education: nourishing the learning spirit. UBC Press, Saskatoon

Behrendt L (2016) Finding Eliza: power and colonial storytelling. University of Queensland Press, St Lucia

Bessarab D, Ng'andu B (2010) Yarning about yarning as a legitimate method in Indigenous research. Int J Crit Indig Stud 3(1):37–50

Bodkin-Andrews G, Carlson B (2016) The legacy of racism and Indigenous Australian identity within education. Race Ethn Educ 19(4):784–807

Bodkin-Andrews G, Craven RG (2013) Negotiating racism: the voices of Aboriginal Australian post-graduate students. In: Seeding success in Indigenous Australian higher education. Emerald Group Publishing Limited, Bingley, pp 157–185

Bodkin-Andrews G, Craven R (2014) Bubalamai Bawa Gumada (Healing the wounds of the heart): the search for resiliency against racism for Aboriginal Australian students. In: Quality and equity: what does research tell us – conference proceedings. Australian Council for Educational Research, Camberwell, pp 49–58

Bodkin-Andrews G, O'Rourke V, Grant R, Denson N, Craven RG (2010) Validating racism and cultural respect: testing the psychometric properties and educational impact of perceived discrimination and multiculturation for Indigenous and non-Indigenous students. Educ Res Eval 16(6):471–493

Bodkin-Andrews GH, Denson N, Bansel P (2013) Teacher racism, academic self-concept, and multiculturation: investigating adaptive and maladaptive relations with academic disengagement and self-sabotage for Indigenous and non-Indigenous Australian students. Aust Psychol 48(3):226–237

Bodkin-Andrews G, Bodkin AF, Andrews UG, Whittaker A (2016) Mudjil'Dya'Djurali Dabuwa'Wurrata (How the white waratah became red): D'harawal storytelling and welcome to country "controversies". AlterNative Int J Indig Peoples 12(5):480–497

Bodkin-Andrews G, Bodkin F, Andrews G, Evans R (2017a) Aboriginal identity, worldviews, research, and the story of the Burra'gorang. In: Kickett-Tucker C, Bessarab D, Wright M, Coffin J (eds) Mia Mia Aboriginal community development: fostering cultural security. Cambridge University Press, Cambridge, pp 19–36

Bodkin-Andrews G, Whittaker A, Harrison N, Craven R, Parker P, Trudgett M, Page S (2017b) Exposing the patterns of statistical blindness: centring Indigenous standpoints on student identity, motivation, and future aspirations. Aust J Educ 61(3):225–249

Bodkin-Andrews G, Lovelock R, Paradies Y, Denson N, Franklin C, Priest N (2017c) Not my family: understanding the prevalence and impact of racism beyond individualistic experiences. In: Walter M, Martin KL, Bodkin-Andrews G (eds) Indigenous children growing up strong. Palgrave Macmillan, London, pp 179–208

Bond C (2017) Race and racism: keynote presentation: race is real and so is racism-making the case for teaching race in Indigenous health curriculum. LIME Good Pract Case Stud 4:5

Bonilla-Silva E (2013) Racism without racists: color-blind racism and the persistence of racial inequality in America. Rowman & Littlefield, New York

Brave Heart MYH, DeBruyn LM (1998) The American Indian holocaust: healing historical unresolved grief. Am Indian Alsk Native Ment Health Res 8(2):56

Brave Heart MYH, Chase J, Elkins J, Altschul DB (2011) Historical trauma among Indigenous peoples of the Americas: concepts, research, and clinical considerations. J Psychoactive Drugs 43(4):282–290

Brown R (2011) Prejudice: its social psychology. Wiley, New York

Craven RG, Tucker A, Munns G, Hinkley J, Marsh HW, Simpson K (2005) Indigenous students' aspirations: dreams, perceptions and realities. DEST. Commonwealth of Australia, Canberra

De Maio JA, Zubrick SR, Silburn SR, Lawrence DM, Mitrou FG, Dalby RB, Blair EM, Griffin J, Milroy H, Cox A (2005) The Western Australian Aboriginal Child Health Survey: measuring the social and emotional wellbeing of Aboriginal children and intergenerational effects of forced separation. Curtin University of Technology and Telethon Institute for Child Health Research, Perth

Dune T, Stewart J, Tronc W, Lee V, Mapedzahama V, Firdaus R, Mekonnen T (2018) Resilience in the face of adversity: narratives from ageing Indigenous women in Australia. Int J Soc Sci Stud 6:63

Duran E, Duran B (1995) Native American postcolonial psychology. State University of New York Press, Albany

England-Aytes K (2013) Historical trauma and its prevention in the classroom. In: Jacobs DT (ed) Teaching truly: a curriculum to Indigenise mainstream education. Peter Lang Publishing, New York, pp 31–50

Fast E, Collin-Vézina D (2010) Historical trauma, race-based trauma and resilience of Indigenous peoples: a literature review. First Peoples Child Fam Rev 5(1):126–136

Ferdinand A, Paradies Y, Kelaher M (2013) Mental health impacts of racial discrimination in Victorian Aboriginal communities. Lowitja Institute, Victoria, Australia

Foley D (2003) Indigenous epistemology and Indigenous standpoint theory. Soc Altern 22(1):44

Hills AM (2010) Foolproof guide to statistics using PASW: SPSS version 15 for Windows. Pearson Australia, Frenchs Forest

Hollinsworth D (2006) Race and racism in Australia, 3rd edn. Cengage Learning/Social Science Press. Victoria, Australia

Kovach M (2009) Indigenous methodologies. University of Toronto Press, Toronto

Kukutai T, Andersen C (2016) Reclaiming the statistical "native": quantitative historical research beyond the pale. In: Andersen C, O'Brien JM (eds) Sources and methods in indigenous studies. Routledge, New York, pp 55–62

Kukutai T, Taylor J (eds) (2016) Indigenous data sovereignty: toward an agenda. Anu Press, Acton

Kukutai T, Walter M (2015) Recognition and indigenizing official statistics: reflections from Aotearoa New Zealand and Australia. Stat J IAOS 31(2):317–326

Larson A, Gillies M, Howard PJ, Coffin J (2007) It's enough to make you sick: the impact of racism on the health of Aboriginal Australians. Aust N Z J Public Health 31(4):322–329

Linklater R (2014) Decolonizing trauma work: Indigenous stories and strategies. Fernwood, Winnipeg

Lovett R (2016) Aboriginal and Torres Strait Islander community wellbeing: identified needs for statistical capacity. In: Kukutai T, Taylor J (eds) Indigenous data sovereignty: toward an agenda. Australian National University Press, Acton, p 213

Martin K (2003) Ways of knowing, being and doing: a theoretical framework and methods for Indigenous and Indigenist research. J Aust Stud 27(76):203–214

Martin KL (2008) Please knock before you enter: Aboriginal regulation of outsiders and the implications for researchers. Post Pressed, Brisbane

Martin KL, Walter M (2017) The story of LSIC: it's all about trust and vision. In: Walter M, Martin K, Bodkin-Andrews G (eds) Indigenous children growing up strong. Palgrave Macmillan, London, pp 41–60

McMillan M, Rigney S (2018) Race, reconciliation, and justice in Australia: from denial to acknowledgment. Ethn Racial Stud 41(4):759–777

Mellor D (2003) Contemporary racism in Australia: the experiences of Aborigines. Pers Soc Psychol Bull 29(4):474–486

Moreton-Robinson A (2013) Towards an Australian Indigenous women's standpoint theory: a methodological tool. Aust Fem Stud 28(78):331–347

Moreton-Robinson A (2015) The white possessive: property, power, and Indigenous sovereignty. University of Minnesota Press, Minneapolis

Muller L (2014) A theory for Indigenous Australian health and human service work. Allen & Unwin, Sydney

Nakata MN (2007) Disciplining the savages, savaging the disciplines. Aboriginal Studies Press, Canberra

Paradies Y (2006) A systematic review of empirical research on self-reported racism and health. Int J Epidemiol 35(4):888–901

Paradies Y (2016) Colonisation, racism and Indigenous health. J Popul Res 33(1):83–96

Paradies Y (2017) Overcoming racism as a barrier to community development. In: Kickett-Tucker C, Bessarab D, Wright M, Coffin J (eds) Mia Mia Aboriginal community development: fostering cultural security. Cambridge University Press, Cambridge, pp 169–185

Paradies YC, Cunningham J (2012) The DRUID study: exploring mediating pathways between racism and depressive symptoms among Indigenous Australians. Soc Psychiatry Psychiatr Epidemiol 47(2):165–173

Parker PD, Bodkin-Andrews G, Parker RB, Biddle N (2018) Trends in Indigenous and non-Indigenous multidomain well-being: decomposing persistent, maturation, and period effects in emerging adulthood. Emerg Adulthood, published online. https://doi.org/10.1177/2167696818782018

Pedersen A, Walker I, Wise M (2005) "Talk does not cook rice": beyond anti-racism rhetoric to strategies for social action. Aust Psychol 40(1):20–31

Pihama L, Reynolds P, Smith C, Reid J, Smith LT, Nana RT (2014) Positioning historical trauma theory within Aotearoa New Zealand. AlterNative Int J Indig Peoples 10(3):248–262

Porter A (2015) Words can never hurt me? Sticks, stones and section 18C. Altern Law J 40(2):86–88

Priest N, Paradies Y, Stevens M, Bailie R (2010) Exploring relationships between racism, housing and child illness in remote Indigenous communities. J Epidemiol Community Health 66:440

Proudfoot F, Habibis D (2015) Separate worlds: a discourse analysis of mainstream and Aboriginal populist media accounts of the Northern Territory Emergency Response in 2007. J Sociol 51(2):170–188

Rainie SC, Schultz JL, Briggs E, Riggs P, Palmanteer-Holder NL (2017) Data as a strategic resource: self-determination, governance, and the data challenge for Indigenous nations in the United States. Int Indig Policy J 8(2):1–29

Richards L (2009) Handling qualitative data: a practical guide, 2nd edn. Sage, London

Rigney LI (1999) Internationalization of an Indigenous anticolonial cultural critique of research methodologies: a guide to Indigenist research methodology and its principles. Wicazo Sa Rev 14(2):109–121

Rose M (2012) The 'silent apartheid' as the practitioner's blindspot. In: Aboriginal and Torres Strait Islander education: an introduction for the teaching profession. pp 64–80. Cambridge University Press, Victoria, Australia

Scheurich JJ, Young MD (1997) Coloring epistemologies: are our research epistemologies racially biased? Educ Res 26(4):4–16

Sechrest L, Sidani S (1995) Quantitative and qualitative methods: is there an alternative? Eval Program Plann 18(1):77–87

Shepherd CC, Li J, Cooper MN, Hopkins KD, Farrant BM (2017) The impact of racial discrimination on the health of Australian Indigenous children aged 5–10 years: analysis of national longitudinal data. Int J Equity Health 16(1):116

Smallwood G (2015) Indigenist critical realism: human rights and first Australians' wellbeing. Routledge, London

Smith LT (2012) Decolonizing methodologies: research and Indigenous peoples. Zed Books, London

St Denis V, Hampton E (2002) Literature review on racism and the effects on Aboriginal education. Prepared for Minister's National Working Group on Education, Indian and Northern Affairs Canada, Ottawa

Stanner WE (1968) After the dreaming: Black and White Australians: an anthropologist's view. Australian Broadcasting Commission, Sydney

Stoneham M, Goodman J, Daube M (2014) The portrayal of Indigenous health in selected Australian media. Int Indig Policy J 5(1):1–13

Strauss A, Corbin J (1990) Basics of qualitative research. Grounded theory procedures and techniques. Sage, Thousand Oaks

Szabó M (2010) The short version of the Depression Anxiety Stress Scales (DASS-21): factor structure in a young adolescent sample. J Adolesc 33(1):1–8

Walter M (2018) The voice of Indigenous data: beyond the markers of disadvantage. Griffith Rev 60:256–263

Walter M, Andersen C (2013) Indigenous statistics: a quantitative research methodology. Left Coast Press, Walnut Creek

Walter M, Butler K (2013) Teaching race to teach Indigeneity. J Sociol 49(4):397–410

Williams M, Finlay SM, Sweet M, McInerney M (2017) # JustJustice: rewriting the roles of journalism in Indigenous health. Aust Journal Rev 39(2):107

Ziersch AM, Gallaher G, Baum F, Bentley M (2011) Responding to racism: insights on how racism can damage health from an urban study of Australian Aboriginal people. Soc Sci Med 73(7): 1045–1053

Zubrick SR, Silburn SR, Lawrence DM, Mitrou FG, Dalby RB, Blair EM, Griffin J et al (2005) The Western Australian Aboriginal Child Health Survey: forced separation from natural family, forced relocation from traditional country or homeland, and social and emotional wellbeing of Aboriginal children and young people. Curtin University of Technology and Telethon Institute for Child Health Research, Perth

Stereotypes of Minorities and Education

72

Jean M. Allen and Melinda Webber

Contents

Introduction	1408
Racism, Stereotype Threat, and Ethnicity	1409
Stereotype Threat in the Aotearoa New Zealand Context	1412
Impacts of Stereotype Threat	1413
Performance Burden	1413
Disidentification	1416
Combating Stereotype Threat	1419
Future Research and Conclusions	1421
Cross-References	1422
References	1423

Abstract

Stereotyping is a phenomenon that impacts a range of people from diverse racial groups, ethnicities, genders, sexualities, and socioeconomic statuses. While all people are subject to stereotyping, the development of the process of stereotype threat (Steele, Am Psychol 52(6):613–629, 1997) has provided insight into how people from ethnically diverse groups are negatively impacted by stereotype threat to a greater extent than those from dominant ethnic groups. Extensive social-psychological research on minority test performance demonstrates that ethnically diverse students suffer underperformance due to their response to stereotype threat in the academic domain. These threats, which are a result of stereotypical beliefs, impact ethnically diverse students in a plethora of ways. In the Aotearoa New Zealand educational context, impacts from stereotype threat hold especially damaging consequences for Māori and Pacific students. The persistent disparities in educational opportunities and achievement for Māori and Pacific students are created and sustained by negative academic stereotypes

J. M. Allen (✉) · M. Webber
Faculty of Education and Social Work, The University of Auckland, Auckland, New Zealand
e-mail: jean.allen@auckland.ac.nz; m.webber@auckland.ac.nz

© The Author(s), under exclusive license to Springer Nature Singapore Pte Ltd. 2019
S. Ratuva (ed.), *The Palgrave Handbook of Ethnicity*,
https://doi.org/10.1007/978-981-13-2898-5_107

that characterize these students as lacking in academic potential, motivation, and engagement with education. This chapter highlights how the stereotypes about Māori and Pacific student potential have a life of their own and can powerfully shape the educational opportunities and experiences of Māori and Pacific students. We end this chapter by suggesting concrete ways to mitigate stereotype threat, building upon the existing strengths of Māori and Pacific students.

Keywords
Pacific · Māori · Stereotype threat · Education · Ethnically diverse

Introduction

To increase the participation and achievement of ethnically diverse students in school, educators must actively work to counter the negative stereotypes that suppress their achievement. Long-standing cultural myths about the educational potential and abilities of ethnically diverse students have been shown to diminish the expectations of educators, resulting in differentiated learning opportunities. Through a process labeled stereotype threat, an awareness of negative perceptions and beliefs can affect ethnically diverse student test performance, their willingness to engage in challenging academic activities, and, as a result, their long-term academic development (Steele 1997, 1998; Steele and Aronson 1995). Stereotype threat has been defined as "the threat of being viewed through the lens of a negative stereotype, or the fear of doing something that would inadvertently confirm that stereotype" (Steele 2003, p. 109). It has also been described as "a disruptive apprehension about the possibility that one might inadvertently confirm a negative stereotype about one's group" (Taylor and Walton 2011, p. 1). Steele (1997) has postulated that there is a prior condition that must exist for stereotype threat to become an issue: the individual who is susceptible must be invested in the domain of interest. In essence, the domain must be a salient contributor to the individual's personal identity, having implications for his or her self-concept.

Everyone is vulnerable to stereotype threat, at least in some circumstances – because each of us possesses multiple social identities. In certain contexts, one or more of our social identities may be devalued. One needs not be in an extreme situation to feel the weight of a devalued social identity. More subtle situations may also place a burden upon individuals who are somehow stigmatized. In response to this devaluation, an individual's behavior or sense of self may change, disrupting their ability to perform to potential. Research has shown that stereotype threat can harm the academic performance of individual for whom the situation invokes a stereotype-based expectation of poor performance. Any salient social identity can affect performance on a task that offers the possibility that a stereotype might be confirmed. Stereotype threat effects have therefore been shown with a wide range of social groups and stereotypes including women in math (Spencer et al. 1999; Walsh et al. 1999); Whites with regard to appearing racist (Frantz et al. 2004); students from low socioeconomic backgrounds compared to students from high socioeconomic backgrounds on intellectual tasks (Croizet and Claire 1998; Harrison et al. 2006); Whites compared with Asian men in mathematics (Aronson et al. 1999); and Whites compared with Blacks and Hispanics on tasks assumed to reflect natural sports ability (Stone 2002). Consequently, stereotype threat is a robust phenomenon, well-replicated in different groups, on different tasks, and in different countries. Even groups that are not traditionally marginalized in society (e.g., White men) have been shown to exhibit stereotype threat effects if, for example, they are led to believe that their performance on a math test is being used to examine Asian superiority at math (Aronson et al. 1999). There are a number of factors which may play a role in one's "stereotype vulnerability" (Steele and Aronson 1995) including group membership, domain identification, group identification, internal locus of control/proactive personality, and stereotype knowledge and belief, among others.

School is an important context for identity development during adolescence, yet creating a positive academic identity may be more challenging for ethnically diverse students. Who must cope with negative academic stereotypes that undermine their engagement and attainment? Simply thinking about these stereotypes can lead to decreased attainment. When ethnically diverse students perform in a domain in which their personal identity is invested, and about which there exists a negative societal stereotype, stereotype threat can develop if the students believe that their performance is being judged by others who have the stereotype in mind. The result is an emotional reaction that interferes with their performance. In the long term, stereotype threat can lead to disidentification with the domain, as the ethnically diverse student who is afraid of constantly being judged decides that this domain in which they are judged stereotypically is no longer important, or too stressful, and they cease to invest energy in that domain. As such, stereotype threat often cause people to focus on negative stereotypes about their potential to perform, rather than their actual abilities, which can lead to decreased performance (Smith and Hung 2008). This "threat" of confirming the negative stereotype creates questions of self-perception and uncertainty about one's abilities.

Racism, Stereotype Threat, and Ethnicity

In almost all countries in the world, ethnically diverse students are confronted with unfavorable stereotypes about their ethnic group, stigmatization, and racism. Compared to ethnic-majority students, they have to deal with these racism more often and sometimes on a daily basis. Racism is highly consequential to societies, to intergroup contexts within societies, and to individual members of society. It is a complex phenomenon whose markers – stereotypes, prejudices, and discrimination – are distinct but interwoven. Negative beliefs (stereotypes) and attitudes (prejudices) toward other racial-ethnic groups can eventuate in discriminatory behavior, defined as "actions or practices carried out by members of dominant racial or ethnic groups that have a differential negative impact on members of subordinate racial or ethnic groups" (Feagin 1991, p. 102). Racism can include explicit, overt actions (e.g., verbal antagonism, physical aggression) and more subtle, covert actions (e.g., being ignored when queuing, being overlooked for a promotion). However, as Feagin's (1991) definition indicates, racism can transcend individual-level actions or personally mediated racism and encompass institutional practices that result in racial disparities in terms of access to goods, services, and opportunities.

As such, racism can be experienced by ethnically diverse students in multiple ways, including directly, from peers in the form of name-calling or social exclusion and/or from adults through stereotyping, hostility, rejection, or acts that reinforce negative expectations. However, an individual needs not be personally involved in racism to be negatively affected – ethnically diverse students may be affected by vicariously experiencing racism that is directed toward their peers, relatives, parents, and others. Hence, vicarious racism is another pathway of influence. In addition, ethnically diverse students need not be present in order for racism to be influential. For example, parents' experience of racism in schools when they were young may have an intergenerational effect, and/or the socialization strategies used by parents, in some cases, to promote mistrust against others may reflect the exposure to racism that parents experienced themselves (Hughes et al. 2006). And finally, racism is also a "system of advantage based on race" that includes institutional practices and policies, cultural messages, as well as the beliefs and actions of individuals (Tatum 1997, p. 7). Accounting for the persistence of racism requires consideration of its structural nature and the systematic advantages and disadvantages that it confers (Wellman 1977).

The negative impact of racism on children's development has been recognized in the psychological research since at least from the Clark and Clark (1950) doll study which focused on stereotypes and children's self-perception in relation to their race. The results of the above study were used to prove that school segregation in the United States was distorting the minds of young Black American children, causing them to internalize stereotypes and racism, to the point of making them hate themselves. Clark and Clark (1950) found that the Black children often chose to play with the white dolls more than the black ones. When the children were asked to fill in a human figure with the color of their own skin, they frequently chose a lighter shade than their actual skin color. The children also gave the color "white" positive attributes like "good" and "pretty." On the contrary, "black" was attributed to being "bad" and "ugly." The results of this study were interpreted as reliable evidence that Black children had internalized racism caused by being discriminated against and stigmatized by segregation.

Racism has also come under increased scrutiny as a force that shapes children's development and psychological functioning (Fisher et al. 1998; García Coll et al. 1996). It has been found that children as young as 6 years old have the ability to make attributions to racism and, by early adolescence, have a sophisticated understanding of both individual-level and institutional-level racism (Brown and Bigler 2005; McKown 2004). McKown and Weinstein (2003) found that the proportion of children that are aware of others' racism increases between ages 6 and 10, such that by age 10, 80% of African American children and 63% of White and Asian children manifest awareness of racism. Research also documents that older adolescents perceive more experiences with racism than children in early adolescence (Brown and Bigler 2005; Greene et al. 2006). Underlying these developmental changes are changes in children's social contexts and growth in abstract thought, cognitive processing skills, social perspective taking abilities, and the ability to integrate one's own experiences and the experiences of others (Steinberg and Silk 2002).

Although cognitive growth during adolescence may endow ethnically diverse students with more cognitive resources to deal with experiences of racism, it may also result in increased vulnerability to these experiences and circumstances. In particular, with the expansion in cognitive processing skills that occurs during this period, adolescents are not only more cognizant of the prevalence of racism but also have the ability to integrate individual- and group-level experiences with racism into their self-perceptions and world views (Tarrant et al. 2001), and the implications of this integration can be far reaching. These considerations, taken together, underscore the importance of better understanding how racism influences student engagement and achievement at school.

In addition to perceptions of racism, children's awareness of intellectual stereotypes about their social group appears to emerge during middle childhood (McKown and Strambler 2009; McKown and Weinstein 2003), and, by early adolescence, some children may personally endorse this stereotype (Rowley et al. 2007). Both awareness and endorsement of stereotypes about intellectual competence may have implications for motivation and achievement. Moreover, endorsement of negative racial stereotypes by significant others, including teachers, may indirectly influence academic outcomes for members of this group. As such, stereotype threat has been one of the most widely studied topics in social psychology research of the last decade.

Research on stereotype threat has provided important insights into the negative motivational consequences of racial stereotypes about intelligence. Although stereotype threat is considered to be a general psychological state applicable to any negative group stereotype, the construct originated in the achievement domain and has been applied to the study of ethnically diverse students' awareness of the cultural stereotypes associating their race with intellectual inferiority. That awareness can be quite debilitating, especially for those ethnically diverse students who are invested in doing well in school. Furthermore, it is not necessary that a student endorse the stereotype; mere awareness of its existence is sufficient to activate threat.

There appear to be both adaptive and maladaptive motivational consequences of the anxiety associated with thinking about race and intelligence in highly evaluative achievement contexts. On the adaptive side, like reactions to discrimination for particular students, stereotype threat might be a motivational enhancer. Webber et al.'s (2013) study showed that, in some circumstances, ethnically diverse students have higher educational achievement aspirations than their majority peers, despite stereotypes positing them as less likely to achieve academically. Moreover, the ethnically diverse students in Macfarlane et al.'s (2014) study indicated that they were "as good as anyone else if we really out our mind to it...I'm not restricted by those stereotypes out there" (p. 112). For many ethnically diverse students, succeeding in the face of threat can be "psychologically beneficial if the experience is used as a barometer of self-esteem" (Leitner et al. 2013, p. 18). It is evident that some ethnically diverse students may choose to work especially hard as a way of disconfirming the stereotype. Of course, high effort in the face of increasing academic challenge may be difficult to sustain and may even lead a student to question his or her abilities. One additional possibility is that situational threat does not directly decrease engagement. Instead, threat may increase sensitivity to all situational cues (Murphy et al. 2007).

Regarding maladaptive motivational consequences, it has been suggested that stereotype threat promotes performance-avoidant goals or concerns about public displays of low ability (Ryan and Ryan 2005; Smith 2004). Stereotype threat can also influence achievement values, causing students to minimize effort and downplay the importance of doing well in school. Steele (1997) coined the term "academic disidentification" to describe students who no longer view academic achievement as a domain that is important either to them or to their self-definition. Disidentification has been operationalized as the absence of a relationship between academic performance and self-esteem and has been associated with declining achievement between middle school and high school (Osborne 1997). A similar process, labeled "academic disengagement," occurs when students begin to discount the feedback they receive about their performance or to devalue achievement altogether (Major and Schmader 2001). Although there appears to be more empirical support for disidentification than disengagement among studies involving African American adolescents (Morgan and Mehta 2004), it is evident that each process is something of a double-edged sword. Both disidentification and disengagement may be self-protecting mechanisms for coping with negative racial stereotypes; however, in the long run, their detrimental effects on achievement motivation would probably outweigh any short-term self-enhancing effects.

Stereotype Threat in the Aotearoa New Zealand Context

Stereotypes about the abilities of many ethnically diverse students exist, and for Māori and Pacific students in the New Zealand school context, they are largely negative, depicting them as less intelligent and academically disengaged (Nakhid 2012; Turner et al. 2015; Webber 2011). Some Māori and Pacific students may feel challenged to work harder to disconfirm negative stereotypes but simultaneously worry that increased effort means they are not as smart as they thought, or as capable as others who appear to have to work less. Other Māori and Pacific students may choose to disengage completely and adopt the view that academic achievement is not important to their future or worse, not relevant to their ethnic self (Nakhid 2012; Webber 2011).

Research has suggested that culturally diverse students are more vulnerable to stereotype threat than other children (Ford et al. 2008). So too are students who care more about achieving in a particular subject or domain (Aronson and Juarez 2012). In essence, high-achieving culturally diverse students may feel they must make the choice between prioritizing academics (and playing down their ethnic identity) and prioritizing their ethnic identity (and playing down their academic identity) (Mila-Shaaf 2010; Webber 2008). In New Zealand, the underperformance of

Māori and Pacific Island students has been well documented (Hunter et al. 2016; Turner et al. 2015). It has been suggested that the deficit theorizing of teachers in relation to Māori students may result in lowered expectations for their achievement and a corresponding negative self-fulfilling prophecy for them (Ministry of Education 2003). Steele (1997) indicated that there was a 15-point IQ gap between Māori and New Zealand European students (and indeed between ethnic minorities and the dominant group across several other countries). He suggested that such groups like Māori and Pacific are vulnerable to stereotype threat and that the negative stereotyping of these students by teachers who are often White and middle class can lead to poorer school performance, higher dropout levels, and subsequent behavioral difficulties. St. George (1983) found that New Zealand teachers judged the Polynesian students in her study (most of whom were Māori) to come from less supportive home backgrounds than the New Zealand European students. St. George stated that, in most cases, teachers had not met the parents, let alone visited their homes, and hence such judgments were most likely made on the basis of ethnic stereotypes and staffroom conversations. Rubie-Davies et al. (2006) have further suggested that Maori students are aware of the stereotypes about them and become anxious about performing in line with such stereotypes, and the resulting anxiety actually causes declines in performance. Finally, research has suggested that the Māori and Pacific students most likely to succeed and, those most motivated to achieve academically, have the greatest risk of disengaging from school because of the many impacts of stereotype threat (Webber 2015).

Impacts of Stereotype Threat

The disengagement of ethnically diverse students from education is often due to the threat they feel within specific domains where their academic ability and ethnic identity are questioned and under scrutiny. Steele (2003) reiterates that though this threat may never be verbally communicated, it is still present, a threat that hangs in the air, rarely explicitly stated but there still the same (Bishop and Goodwin 2010). However, it is imperative to note that stereotype threat while having impacting ethnically diverse students is not an all-consuming or defeating process. Rather stereotype threat "becomes this extra thing you have to deal with, navigate, and figure out throughout your life" (Gates and Steele 2009, p. 256). Thus, stereotype threat in academic domains can affect students in various ways by adding pressure and requiring those impacted to multitask. In the following section, we review the impact of stereotype threat on performance burden and also highlight the long-term impact of disidentification.

Performance Burden

Performance burden is a short-term consequence of stereotype threat where Māori and Pacific students who feel the impact of particular stereotypes in testing situations underperform. The extra pressure to perform to an expected standard manifests due to the student concerns that to fail, or not reach a particular standard, reinforces the negative stereotype about their lack of intelligibility (Steele 1992, 1998). Feelings of anxiety, fear of confirming stereotypes, distraction, loss of motivation, and increased mental workload when trying to challenge stereotypes are commonly identified psychological reactions to stereotype threat. While the individual exploration of each of these reactions has been carried out here in this chapter, it is important to note that they do overlap and are not necessarily part of every student's experience of performance burden.

Anxiety

Experiencing performance burden can stem from feelings of anxiety. Individuals can experience additional levels of risk and pressure when participating in tests or evaluations (Aronson 2004). While some amount of anxiety is a typical reaction to high-pressure situations such as tests, anxiety due to performance burden is more intense and can often result in students becoming distracted (Osborne 2007). This distraction further influences the performance of minority students as "failure to perform up to expected standards is psychologically distressing because it implies that the stereotype may, in fact, be true" (Massey and Fischer 2005, p. 47). While some students try to challenge their feelings of anxiety by actively fighting the stereotype, Ewing (2015) states that this often causes further anxiety and leads to poor performance of students. Within the New Zealand context, research by Hill and Hawk (2000) found that Māori and Pacific students' school experiences were impacted when teachers did not believe in their student's ability to achieve academically. Similarly, Nakhid (2003) found that teachers felt that Pacific students were not "motivated enough to want to improve their level of achievement" (p. 308). In Allen (2015), young Pacific people from the predominantly Māori and Pacific community of South Auckland, New Zealand, spoke of how other students perceived Pacific people to be unmotivated. One of the young men shared his experiences of going to a predominantly White school where Pacific students were put down and comments were made about them not pushing themselves as much as their White counterparts (Allen 2015). While these studies did not necessarily identify anxiety as a consequence of others' expectations, they both reflect attitudes and situations in which Māori and Pacific students felt threatened. It is these stereotype threats that cause anxiety, because Māori and Pacific students can become preoccupied with the possibility of being marginalized because people around them believe negative stereotypes about them (Gates and Steele 2009).

Fear of Confirming the Stereotype

Fear of confirming negative stereotypes is another way anxiety manifests and impacts students who experience stereotype threat. While Māori and Pacific students may know that negative stereotypes are not true for all within their stereotyped groups, fear of failure and consequently confirming negative stereotypes can influence performance. Aronson (2004) found that some students embraced stereotype threat as extra motivation "to disprove the negative stereotype or, at least, to deflect it from being self-characteristic" (p. 16). However, extra motivation from stereotype threat can also manifest in increased anxiety, pressure, and underperformance (Massey and Fischer 2005; Steele 1997; Steele et al. 2002). The fear of confirming stereotypes can also cause extra anxiety and pressure due to ethnically diverse students believing that if they fail academically "it will reflect badly not only on themselves and their family, but on the entire race" (Massey and Fischer 2005, p. 49). Similarly, New Zealand studies by Allen (2015), Warren (2017), and Webber (2012) alluded to Māori and Pacific students' tension regarding fear of confirming negative stereotypes and expectations that others had of them based on their ethnic identification. Collective ethnic stereotypes cause anxiety for students where "any discipline enforced for *one* of the group was perceived as confirming a negative stereotype for *all* in the group" (Warren 2017, p. 58 *emphasis added*). However, like Aronson (2004), students in Allen's (2015) project reiterated that stereotypes that linked their ethnicity and academic ability made them want to work harder and do better to prove people wrong. Though the fear of confirming negative stereotypes about ethnic group intelligence can have both a positive and negative impact on performance, it is an impact that can take over ones thought process and resulting in underperformance. Gates and Steele (2009) reiterate:

> the detriment in performance comes from the attempt to disprove the stereotype. It doesn't come from giving up. It comes from the person saying 'I'm going to beat this thing,' because the person cares about it. They don't want to be seen that way. And it's that extra over-effort that causes all the physiological reactivity. (p. 255)

This over-effort causes further anxiety. Therefore, the pressure placed on ethnically diverse students to perform for fear of confirming stereotypes about their ethnic groups inevitably results in them becoming distracted and unmotivated.

Distraction and Loss of Motivation

Performance burden and anxiety can also impact student efforts by distracting them from their academic work and causing them to lose motivation in academic settings. For some ethnically diverse students, the threat of reinforcing negative stereotypes causes a lack of effort on their part. Student lack of effort can manifest in avoidance of challenging work and selecting easier options where students have less chance of failure. These choices work as a defense mechanism that does not necessarily challenge the negative stereotype but attempts to protect the minority students from the initial threat. However, an outcome of these "easier" choices is that ethnically diverse students "rob themselves of opportunities to expand their skills and intelligence" (Aronson 2004, p. 17). By not extending their skills and intelligence, by being off task and not participating, Māori and Pacific students are understood to be conforming to negative stereotypes (Warren 2017). Siope (2011) found that Pacific students often kept quiet and did not participate as often as their peers in educational settings as a way of "not being so visible or noticeable as to bring negative attention from school peers and, dare I say it, teacher's in general" (p. 12). Perhaps wanting to remain unnoticed is also a defense mechanism as

Aronson (2004) reiterated that some students "report feeling a sense of unfairness, that there will be less patience for their mistakes than for white students' mistakes, and that their failure will be seen as evidence of an unalterable limitation rather than as the result of a bad day" (p. 16). While some ethnically diverse student experiences of stereotype threat cause them to lose motivation and become distracted, for others the same threat causes them to increase their mental workload and attempt to challenge the stereotype that is threatening them.

Increased Mental Workload due to Challenging Stereotypes

For some students, the fear of confirming negative ethnic stereotypes about academic ability resulted in ethnically diverse students increasing their workload as a way of proving the negative stereotype wrong. Stereotype threat has caused students to respond by trying harder on assessments and increasing their academic efforts to challenge or disprove negative stereotypes about the academic ability of minority students (Aronson 2004). Māori and Pacific students in New Zealand schools have also exhibited attitudes and practices that attempted to challenge negative stereotypes about their academic ability. Pacific and Māori students in Allen's (2015) study spoke of the way they use negative stereotypes as motivation to try harder and to do better. Similarly, Pacific students in Warren's (2017) project reiterated the same sentiment, in that they reworked negative stereotypes to their advantage by using them to push harder for academic success. In Webber's (2012) study, Māori students felt it was imperative to challenge and dispel negative stereotypes about intellectual inferiority attached to their ethnic identity. Though challenging negative stereotypes of academic inferiority is essential for many ethnically diverse students, Aronson (2004) and Steele (1997) question whether individual effort can impact the stability of stereotypes. Aronson (2004) suggests that "such a reflex can be advantageous in situations requiring brute effort" (p. 16). Therefore, questions need to be asked as to whether the increased workload that some ethnically diverse students take on to challenge negative stereotypes is not only causing underperformance but is also pointless.

Disidentification

Disidentification is a form of disengagement that is a result of a long-term reaction to stereotype threat. It occurs when the stereotype threat pressures result in not only underperformance within a specific domain but also a lack of care for their underperformance and no desire to try and improve their ability within the domain. Thus, disidentification disrupts a person's identification with schooling and/or specific academic subjects (Steele 1997). Students may try to justify underperformance by expressing a lack of concern or interest in the subject (Good et al. 2007), and if they are disidentified with the domain, "they no longer incorporate the domain into their identities" (Good et al. 2007, p. 124). While disidentification may seem like a choice students make, it has far-reaching consequences for their futures as they distance themselves from educational spaces. A secondary consequence of disidentification is the distancing of themselves from the domain where the stereotype has been most salient. The distancing of individuals from specific educational domains has significant impacts for ethnically diverse people, and their career trajectories as limited specific domain involvement can limit career opportunities (Good et al. 2007; Steele and Aronson 1995; Pronin et al. 2004). While disidentification is a long-term impact of stereotype threat, there are a number of practices that contribute to de-identification, such as students feeling a lack of belonging within educational domains. Part of this lack of belonging is a result of teachers having low expectations of minority student's academic ability. Dealing with the stereotype threat of low expectations can be troublesome, and for Māori and Pacific students who place such importance on the development of relationships, it can be detrimental to their continuation in education.

Lack of Belonging and Low Teacher Expectations

Extensive educational research reiterates the importance to ethnically diverse students feeling like they belong in educational settings. One of the most significant contributors to this sense of belonging is teachers' expectations and belief in their student's ability to achieve. However, if teachers have low expectations or reflect negative stereotypical perceptions about specific ethnic groups of students, then this can affect their sense of belonging and result in a threat "by creating a belief that the school views certain students as weak links in the chain" (Aronson 2004, p. 18). This threat to ethnically diverse students belonging can become discouraging, and thus students feel that not only do teachers but others within their school environments doubt their academic ability (Steele 1997). Māori and Pacific students value relationships and see teacher-student relationships specifically as an important part of their learning success (Hill and Hawk 2000). However, New Zealand research by Rubie-Davies et al. (2006) and Webber et al. (2013) found that teacher expectations were often founded on ethnic stereotypes and that this was particularly damaging to Māori and Pacific students' academic success. Similarly, Warren (2017) found that teachers in her study consciously and subconsciously had lower expectations for Pacific student while "implicitly or explicitly ascribing expectations of success to other ethnic groups" (p. 58). For indigenous Māori students, a comparable pattern arises where "teachers expected Māori achievement gains to be less than for any other ethnic group" (Turner et al. 2015). Teachers' negative perceptions of Māori and Pacific students have been shown to have considerable effects on students' sense of belonging, to the point where it can undermine their feelings of membership within academic communities and thus affect their intent to stay in school (Good et al. 2007).

Rejection of Ethnic and Academic Identification

Another consequence of stereotype threat that contributes to disidentification is when ethnically diverse students distance themselves from the group identity that is being threatened. For many ethnically diverse students, stereotype threat is a daily issue that they must cope with. Many ethnic stereotypes are negative and thus have an extensive effect on students' academic efficacy. Therefore, a result of this stereotype threat is that negative stereotypes can become internalized and can "cause rejection of one's own group, even of oneself" (Steele 1997, p. 621). As a result of this added pressure, some ethnically diverse students attempt to distance themselves from the identity which carries the threat. The process of rejection of ethnic and academic identity is understood to be part of a defense mechanism where as a way of protecting one's self from the stereotype, threat individuals distance themselves from specific identities (Good et al. 2007). For Māori and Pacific students, stereotype threat is often attached to ethnic identity and promotes the belief of academic inferiority. This threat often results in minority students either distancing themselves from their ethnic identity or from an academic identity. International research such as Pronin et al. (2004), who focused on female participation in mathematics courses, purports that this abandonment may be a result of the need for those experiencing stereotype threat to assimilate into another group and "abandon previously valued aspects of identity and sources of self-esteem" (p. 153). Some Pacific students in Warren's (2017) project rejected their ethnic identity by taking on "'plastic' traits" (p. 58). These "plastic" traits included socializing with students outside of their ethnic group. Socializing with other ethnic groups, rather than their own, was done as a way for Pacific students to remove or make the threat of negative stereotypes associated with their ethnic identity as Pacific Islanders less salient. However, the rejection of ethnic and academic identities is detrimental to minority Māori and Pacific students as when they reject their academic identity they are also affecting their ability to succeed later in life.

Distancing of Self from Educational Spaces

Long-term impacts from stereotype threat can also result in students distancing or completely disengaging from educational spaces. Students who feel the effect of stereotype threat over a sustained period of time may decide to protect themselves by distancing themselves from classes where they feel threatened or may leave educational institutions entirely (Steele 1997). One of the reasons for this distance is due to academic spaces not feeling welcoming or safe for minority students. As Good et al. (2007) state, "An extremely serious consequence of stereotypes for social identity is that they can make an academic community an uncomfortable place to be" (p. 123). For Pacific students in Allen's (2015) project, discomfort was felt in various educational settings, where students who attended open days at tertiary institutions and career expos were made to feel unwelcome due to the fact that they came from low-income communities, as well as the fact they were Pacific students. While it has been established that individuals react differently to stereotype threats, one of the serious consequences of distancing oneself from educational institutions is that it can greatly alter "stereotyped students' professional identities by redirecting the career paths that they pursue" (Good et al. 2007, p. 123). For Māori and Pacific peoples in Aotearoa New Zealand – who are already underrepresented in tertiary institutions and high paid employment – distancing themselves from educational sights has severe consequences for diversity in our workforce, though there are steps that educators can take to minimize stereotype threat within their classrooms and educational institutions.

Combating Stereotype Threat

Though stereotype threat is a concerning phenomenon with far-reaching consequences for ethnically diverse students, there are steps that educators can take to reduce the impact of stereotype threat within their classrooms and educational institutions. Within the classroom setting, Aronson (2004) suggests teachers develop environments that reduce competition, encourage trust, and limit stereotyping. Learning environments can be changed to nurture students and limit competition in multiple ways, through creating a collaborative environment where students work together (Aronson 2004) and also through changing the way tests and assessments are carried out to encourage more positive attitudes toward groups who experience stereotype threat (Ewing 2015). By taking steps toward reducing stereotype threat within the classroom, Aronson believes that minority student's engagement and grades can improve.

Another way of combating stereotype threat is through teaching students that intellectual ability is expandable and not fixed. Teaching expandability of intellectual ability can help students realize that stereotypes that link ethnicity and academic ability are flawed, and therefore the threat can be reduced. Aronson (2004), Good et al. (2007), and Steele (1997) suggest educators can do this by providing students with challenging work and providing the appropriate supports for achieving their academic goals. Providing students with challenging work demonstrates to students that teachers have respect for their academic potential and that they do not believe stereotypical deficit views regarding links to ethnicity and academic ability. Osborne (2001) recommends reminding students of how far they have come and how much they have learnt as a way of diminishing stereotype threat and removing feelings of anxiety.

The development of optimistic teacher and student relationships is highlighted by Steele (1997) and Webber (2015) as a critical strategy that may work for all students who suffer from stereotype threat. In the New Zealand context, extensive research into Māori and Pacific student-teacher relationships all highlight the link between teacher expectations and student achievement (e.g., Iosefo 2014; Fasavalu 2015). Pacific students in Hill and Hawk's (2000) project talked extensively about the need for the teacher to develop relationships and understand the worlds that their Pacific students live in. Webber et al. (2013) also reiterate the importance of students feeling like they belong. Teachers who take the time to develop relationships and get to know their students show their class that they care, that they want to know more about them, and that they are attempting to understand the worlds that they live in (Siope 2011; Wendt Samu et al. 2008). For Māori and Pacific students to be successful, they need to know that they belong and are valued and that teachers believe in their ability to succeed in education. If students feel this way, then stereotype threat may be diluted in situations in the classroom.

Students who experience stereotype threat should be encouraged to develop a strong sense of ethnic identity and ethnic group connectedness. Research by Webber (2012) and Webber et al. (2013) reiterate the importance of students processing and developing ethnic identities and how strong identities can ameliorate negative stereotypes. As Webber (2012) states:

> Positive racial-ethnic identity is important for Māori adolescents attending multi-ethnic schools because when they develop healthy, positive and strong racial-ethnic identities they are able to repel negative stereotypes and accommodate other positive attributes, such as academic achievement into their Māori identity. (p. 26)

Developing a strong sense of Māori identity "has been defined in terms of positive self-identification as Māori" (Webber 2012, p. 22). Positive self-identification includes understandings of language, culture, involvement with social activities, and close attachments to family groups. Like Māori, Pacific student opportunities to self-identify and build cultural strength are important, but Siteine (2010) and Warren (2017) found that teachers often unconsciously allocated static forms of identity to students rather than allowing them to develop for themselves. Rather than teacher's assigning static forms of identity and what it means to be Māori or a Pacific Islander, teachers can "create contexts where students can seek answers to the questions 'Who am I?' and 'How do I belong?'" (Webber 2012, p. 21). Developing this deep sense of ethnic identity could benefit those students who experience stereotype threat within educational settings and potentially work as a defense mechanism against threats of underperformance. Other researchers have proposed that there are two key questions affecting the academic choices that students make – "can I do it" and "do I want to do it?" (Eccles 2006). If Māori and Pacific students believe that doing well in school is important to their future success and will reap the same rewards for them as for other cultural groups in society, they are more likely to work hard to get good grades despite stereotype threat. Similarly, if Māori and Pacific students believe that they can succeed in challenging classes, despite negative ethnic stereotypes, they are more likely to have a strong sense of embedded achievement (Altshul et al. 2006) and put forth the effort needed to qualify for those classes.

Embedded achievement refers to believing that group membership involves valuing and achieving in academics (Oyserman and Lewis 2017). Embedded achievement is related to an ethnically diverse student's belief that academic achievement is an in-group identifier, that is, a key part of being a member of their ethnic group and a way to enact their ethnic identity. It also includes the related sense that achievement of some in-group members helps other in-group members succeed. Because negative stereotypes about Māori and Pacific students include low academic achievement, disengagement from school, and lack of academic ability (Webber 2011, 2012), some students may be less able to recruit sufficient motivational attention to override these messages and stay focused on school success. By viewing achievement as part of being a member of one's ethnic group, identification with this goal may be more easily facilitated. If Māori and Pacific students have a sense of embedded achievement and believe that their teachers expect them to do well, they are more likely to persist in challenging learning tasks with increased effort and persistence. When Māori and Pacific students experience success, they simultaneously develop and enhance their self-confidence, self-efficacy, and growth mind-set and increase the perceived value of academic tasks and opportunities. In this way, the social-psychological characteristics supportive of embedded achievement can be cultivated.

However, the extant research has shown that Māori and Pacific students who believe that their ability is flexible rather than fixed are more likely to be focused on learning, growth, and improvement and embrace challenge because of the opportunity to grow intellectually and gain competence. They more likely persist in the face of stereotype threat and believe persistent effort and study can positively impact their academic performance (Good 2012). Aronson and Juarez (2012) and Tarbetsky et al. (2016) have postulated that vulnerability to stereotype threat would be lessened if students hold a growth mind-set about intelligence. Schools that place more emphasis on a growth mind-set, and stress effort rather than innate intelligence, are more likely to create a sense of persistence in Māori and Pacific students, which is critical to retaining them in education.

Future Research and Conclusions

Research about stereotyping of ethnically diverse students and stereotype threat is extensive, but there is still work that needs to be done in the area to further unravel the complexity of this phenomenon. Projects have highlighted how various groups have been affected by stereotype threat including women in mathematics (Spencer et al. 1999; Walsh et al. 1999); White people who have been viewed as being racist (Frantz et al. 2004); students belonging to various socioeconomic groups (Croizet and Clair 1998; Harrison et al. 2006); White men compared with Asian men in mathematics (Aronson et al. 1999); and White and Asian people whose natural athletic abilities are compared with Black and Hispanics. These projects identify a range of factors that contribute to stereotype threat, but there are a few where our understandings of stereotype threat could be extended.

Aronson (2004) has encouraged researchers to think more broadly about what contributes to the underperformance of ethnically diverse students in education. Though stereotype threat provides significant insight into how ethnically diverse students' performance is impacted social-psychologically, it provides only one avenue of insight. Instead, moving forward, research in the area of stereotype threat and education needs to look more broadly at what other factors contribute to the underperformance of minority students in educational domains. Firstly, as stereotype threat is understood to be situational and context specific, it is recommended that further research pay particular attention to the various contexts that stereotype threat is present in. Focusing on contexts may provide extra evidence of the correlation between stereotype threat and specific situations or environments as we know that stereotype threat does not necessarily impact or affect people possessing the same social identity in the same ways (Good et al. 2007). Secondly, while attention to context is essential, focus needs to be paid to the minute details within specific contexts. A critique of stereotype threat theory is that researchers who embrace these projects run the risk of treating ethnic and racial groups as similar and homogeneous. However, extensive research reiterates that this is not the case (Ferguson et al. 2008). Therefore, stereotype research needs to further explore these differences and the diversity within ethnic and racial groups such as Blacks and Hispanics on an international level and Māori and Pacific groups within Aotearoa New Zealand.

There also appears to be a dearth of literature that examines stereotype threat and its impacts over an extended period. Examination of the increase, decrease, or static nature of stereotype threat on groups and individuals may provide added value to this field and provide greater insight into the nuances of stereotype threat on various groups of people. Stereotype threat literature appears to focus heavily on the causes and impacts, but there needs to be more research which focuses on strategies that reduce stereotype threat and more specifically what makes these strategies successful (or not) within various contexts and with various groups of people. Nguyen and Ryan (2008) believe there is an assumption that strategies that reduce stereotype threat result in positive outcome for those who are affected, but there is a lack of literature that supports this assumption. Finally, within the local context of New Zealand, Aotearoa, stereotype research needs to be extended to not only examine stereotype threat but also to contribute toward purposeful culturally responsive pedagogies and practices for educational sites. Providing guidelines for teachers is not necessarily helping them address stereotypes, limit stereotype threat, or help students develop protective factors like strong racial and ethnic identities. Instead, teachers need to receive professional development in how to incorporate the teaching of strong ethnic and racial identities within their classrooms without losing teaching time from other subjects (Siteine 2017). Therefore, more development for teacher training based on stereotype threat research needs to be done in this area. By extending research in these ways identified above, the complex nature of stereotype threat, its impacts and strategies to challenge it may be further examined and explained.

Discussing stereotype threat its impacts and consequences can be uncomfortable work, especially when questions about individual and group bias are challenged. However, research into the phenomenon of stereotype threat demonstrates the seriousness of these experiences and the far-reaching consequences for their lives. Perhaps one of the most disturbing aspects of stereotype threat is that it most strongly affects academically motivated students. Steele (2010) has argued that:

> No special susceptibility is required to experience this pressure. Research has found but one prerequisite: the person must care about the performance in question. That's what makes the prospect of confirming the negative stereotype upsetting enough to interfere with that performance. (p. 98)

This chapter has presented a review of the field of stereotype threat and its impact on ethnically diverse students internationally as well as focusing on Māori and Pacific people in Aotearoa New Zealand. It has suggested that Māori and Pacific students need to develop and maintain particular affective and social-psychological strengths in order to reconcile their academic selves with their ethnic selves.

Cross-References

▶ Ethnicity and Class Nexus: A Philosophical Approach
▶ Settler Colonialism and Biculturalism in Aotearoa/New Zealand
▶ Media and Stereotypes

▶ Racism and Stereotypes
▶ State Hegemony and Ethnicity: Fiji's Problematic Colonial Past

References

Allen JM (2015) Who represents the Southside? Youth perspectives and news media representations of South Auckland. Unpublished master's thesis, The University of Auckland

Altschul I, Oyserman D, Bybee D (2006) Racial-ethnic identity in mid- adolescence: content and change as predictors of academic achievement. Child Dev 77(5):1155–1169

Aronson J (2004) The threat of stereotype. Educ Leadersh 62(3):14–19. Retrieved from http://www.ascd.org/publications/educational-leadership.aspx

Aronson J, Juarez L (2012) Growth mindsets in the laboratory and the real world. In: Subotnik RF, Miller L (eds) Malleable minds: translating insights from psychology and neuroscience to gifted education. Department of Education, Washington, DC, pp 19–36

Aronson J, Lustina MJ, Good C, Keough K, Steele CM, Brown J (1999) When white men can't do math: necessary and sufficient factors in stereotype threat. J Exp Soc Psychol 35:29–46. https://doi.org/10.1006/jesp.1998.1371

Bishop L, Goodwin S (2010) 'Whistling Vivaldi' and beating stereotypes [audio file]. In: Conan N (ed) Talk of the nation. National Public Radio, Washington, DC

Brown C, Bigler R (2005) Children's perceptions of gender discrimination: a developmental model. Child Dev 76(3):533–553. https://doi.org/10.1111/j.1467-8624.2005.00862.x

Clark K, Clark M (1950) Emotional factors in racial identification and preference in Negro children. J Negro Educ 19(3):341–350. https://doi.org/10.2307/2966491

Croizet JC, Claire T (1998) Extending the concept of stereotype threat to social class: the intellectual underperformance of students from low socioeconomic backgrounds. Personal Soc Psychol Bull 24(6):588–594. https://doi.org/10.1177/0146167298246003

Eccles JS (2006) A motivational perspective on school achievement: taking responsibility for learning, teaching, and supporting. In: Sternberg RJ, Subotnik RF (eds) Optimizing student success with the other three Rs: reasoning, resilience and responsibility. Information Age, Greenwich, pp 199–224

Ewing H (2015) Stereotype threat and assessment in schools. J Init Teach Inq 1:7–9. Retrieved from https://ir.canterbury.ac.nz/handle/10092/11471

Fasavalu M (2015) Tales from above 'the tail': Samoan students' experiences of teacher actions as culturally responsive pedagogy. Unpublished master's thesis, The University of Auckland

Feagin J (1991) The continuing significance of race: anti-black discrimination in public places. Am Sociol Rev 56(2):101–116. Retrieved from http://journals.sagepub.com/home/asr

Ferguson PB, Gorinski R, Wendt Samu T, Mara D (2008) Literature review on the experiences of Pasifika learners in the classroom. Ministry of Education, Wellington

Fisher C, Jackson J, Villaruel F (1998) The study of African American and Latin American children and youth. In: Damon W, Lerner R (eds) Handbook of child psychology: theoretical models of human development. Wiley, New York, pp 1145–1207

Ford DY, Grantham TC, Whiting GW (2008) Culturally and linguistically diverse students in gifted education: recruitment and retention issues. Except Child 74(3):289–306. https://doi.org/10.1177/001440290807400302

Frantz CM, Cuddy AJC, Burnett M, Ray H, Hart A (2004) A threat in the computer: the race implicit association test as a stereotype threat experience. Personal Soc Psychol Bull 30:1611–1624. https://doi.org/10.1177/0146167204266650

García Coll C, Lamberty G, Jenkins R, McAdoo H, Crnic K, Wasik B et al (1996) An integrative model for the study of developmental competencies in minority children. Child Dev 67(5):1891–1914. https://doi.org/10.1111/j.1467-8624.1996.tb01834.x

Gates HL Jr, Steele CM (2009) A conversation with Claude M. Steele. Stereotype threat and black achievement. Du Bois Rev 6(2):251–271. https://doi.org/10.1017/s1742058X09990233

Good C (2012) Reformulation the talent equation: implications for gifted students' sense of belonging and achievement. In: Subotnik RF, Robinson A, Callahan CM, Gubbins EJ (eds) Malleable minds: translating insights from psychology and neuroscience to gifted education. University of Connecticut National Research Center on the Gifted and Talented, Storrs, pp 37–54

Good C, Dweck CS, Aronson J (2007) Social identity, stereotype threat, and self-theories. In: Fuligni AJ (ed) Contesting stereotypes and creating identities. Russell Sage Foundation, New York, pp 115–134

Greene M, Way N, Pahl K (2006) Trajectories of perceived adult and peer discrimination among Black, Latino, and Asian American adolescents: patterns and psychological correlates. Dev Psychol 42(2):218–238. https://doi.org/10.1037/0012-1649.42.2.218

Harrison LA, Stevens CM, Monty AN, Coakley CA (2006) The consequences of stereotype threat on the academic performance of white and non-white lower income college students. Soc Psychol Educ 9:341–357. https://doi.org/10.1007/s11218-005-5456-6

Hill J, Hawk K (2000) Making a difference in the classroom: effective teaching practice in low decile, multicultural schools. Massey University, Albany

Hughes D, Rodriguez J, Smith EP, Johnson DJ, Stevenson HC, Spicer P (2006) Parents' ethnic-racial socialization practices: a review of research and directions for future study. Dev Psychol 42(5):747–770. Retrieved from http://www.apa.org/pubs/journals/dev/index.aspx

Hunter J, Hunter R, Bills T, Cheung I, Hannant B, Kritesh K, Lachaiya R (2016) Developing equity for Pāsifika learners within a New Zealand context: attending to culture and values. N Z J Educ Stud 51(2):197–209

Iosefo J (2014) Moonwalking with the Pasifika Girl in the Mirror: an autoethnography on spaces in higher education. Unpublished master's dissertation, The University of Auckland

Leitner JB, Jones JM, Hehman E (2013) Succeeding in the face of stereotype threat: the adaptive role of engagement regulation. Personal Soc Psychol Bull 39(1):17–27

Macfarlane A, Webber M, Cookson-Cox C, McRae H (2014) Ka Awatea: An iwi case study of Maori students' success. [Manuscript]. University of Auckland, Auckland. Retrieved from http:www.maramatanga.co.nz/projects_publications

Major B, Schmader T (2001) Legitimacy and social construal of disadvantage. In: Jost J, Major B (eds) The psychology of legitimacy: emerging perspectives on ideology, power, and intergroup relations. Cambridge University Press, New York, pp 176–204

Massey DS, Fischer MJ (2005) Stereotype threat and academic performance: new findings from a racially diverse sample of college freshmen. Du Bois Rev 2(1):45–67. https://doi.org/10.1017/S1742058X05050058

McKown C (2004) Age and ethnic variation in children's thinking about the nature of racism. J Appl Dev Psychol 25(5):597–617. https://doi.org/10.1016/j.appdev.2004.08.001

McKown C, Strambler M (2009) Developmental antecedents and social and academic consequences of stereotype consciousness in middle childhood. Child Dev 80(6):1643–1659. Retrieved from https://onlinelibrary.wiley.com/journal/14678624

McKown C, Weinstein R (2003) The development and consequences of stereotypes consciousness in middle school. Child Dev 74(2):498–515. Retrieved from https://onlinelibrary.wiley.com/journal/14678624

Mila-Schaaf K (2010) Polycultural capital and the Pasifika second generation: negotiating identities in diasporic spaces. Unpublished doctoral thesis, Massey University, Albany

Ministry of Education (2003) Te Kotahitanga. Learning Media, Wellington

Morgan S, Mehta J (2004) Beyond the laboratory: evaluating the survey evidence for the disidentification explanation of black–white differences in achievement. Sociol Educ 77(1):82–101. https://doi.org/10.1177/003804070407700104

Murphy MC, Steele CM, Gross JJ (2007) Signaling threat: how situational cues affect women in math, science, and engineering settings. Psychol Sci 18(10):879–885

Nakhid C (2003) "Intercultural" perceptions. Academic achievement and the identifying process of Pacific Islands students in New Zealand schools. J Negro Educ 72(3):297–317. Retrieved from http://www.jstor.org/stable/3211249

Nakhid C (2012) 'Which side of the bridge to safety?' How young Pacific Islanders in New Zealand view their South Auckland community. Kotuitui: NZ J Soc Sci Online 7(1):14–25. https://doi.org/10.1080/1177083X.2012.670652

Nguyen HHD, Ryan AM (2008) Does stereotype threat affect test performance of minorities and women? A meta-analysis of experimental evidence. J Appl Psychol 93(6):1314–1334. https://doi.org/10.1037/a0012702

Osborne J (1997) Race and academic disidentification. J Educ Psychol 89(4):728–735. https://doi.org/10.1037/0022-0663.89.4.728

Osborne J (2001) Testing stereotype threat: does anxiety explain race and sex difference in achievement? Contemp Educ Psychol 26(3):291–310. https://doi.org/10.1006/ceps.2000.1052

Osborne J (2007) Linking stereotype threat and anxiety. Educ Psychol 27(1):135–154. https://doi.org/10.1080/01443410601069929

Oyserman D, Lewis NA (2017) Seeing the destination and the path: using identity-based motivation to understand and reduce racial disparities in academic achievement. Soc Issues Policy Rev 11(1):159–194

Pronin E, Steele CM, Ross L (2004) Identity bifurcation in response to stereotype threat: women and mathematics. J Exp Soc Psychol 40(2):152–168. https://doi.org/10.1016/S0022-1031(03)00088-X

Rowley S, Kurtz Costes B, Mistry R, Feagans L (2007) Social status as a predictor of race and gender stereotypes in late childhood and early adolescence. Soc Dev 16(1):150–168. https://doi.org/10.1111/j.1467-9507.2007.00376.x

Rubie-Davies C, Hattie J, Hamilton R (2006) Expecting the best for students: teacher expectations and academic outcomes. Br J Educ Psychol 76(3):429–444. https://doi.org/10.1348/000709905X53589

Ryan K, Ryan A (2005) Psychological processes underlying stereotype threat and standardized math test performance. Educ Psychol 40(1):53–63. https://doi.org/10.1207/s15326985ep4001_4

Siope A (2011) The schooling experiences of Pasifika students. SET 3:10–16. Retrieved from http://www.nzcer.org.nz/nzcerpress/set

Siteine A (2010) The allocation of Pasifika identity in New Zealand classrooms MAI Review 2010(1):1–12. Retrieved from http://www.journal.mai.ac.nz

Siteine A (2017) Recognising ethnic identity in the classroom: a New Zealand study. Int Stud Sociol Educ 26(4):393–407. https://doi.org/10.1080/09620214.2016.1264869

Smith J (2004) Understanding the process of stereotype threat: a review of mediational variables and new performance goal directions. Educ Psychol Rev 16(3):177–206. https://doi.org/10.1023/B:EDPR.0000034020.20317.89

Smith S, Hung L (2008) Stereotype threat: effects on education. Soc Psychol Educ 11:243–257. https://doi.org/10.1007/s11218-008-9053-3

Spencer S, Steele C, Quinn D (1999) Stereotype threat and women's math performance. J Exp Soc Psychol 35:4–28. https://doi.org/10.1006/jesp.1998.1373

St. George A (1983) Teacher expectations and perceptions of Polynesian and Pākehā pupils and the relationship to classroom behaviour and school achievement. Br J Educ Psychol 53(1):48–59

Steele C (1992) Race and the schooling of Black Americans. The Atlantic Monthly 269(4): 68–78

Steele CM (1997) A threat in the air. How stereotypes shape intellectual identity and performance. Am Psychol 52(6):613–629. Retrieved from http://www.apa.org/pubs/journals/amp/

Steele C (1998) Stereotyping and its threat are real. Am Psychol 53:680–681. Retrieved from http://www.apa.org/pubs/journals/amp/

Steele C (2003) Stereotype threat and African-American student achievement. In: Perry T, Steele C, Hilliard A (eds) Young, gifted, and black: promoting high achievement among African-American students. Beacon Press, Boston, pp 109–130

Steele C (2010) Whistling Vivaldi. W.W. Norton & Company, New York

Steele C, Aronson J (1995) Stereotype threat and the intellectual test performance of African-Americans. J Pers Soc Psychol 69(5):797–811. https://doi.org/10.1037/0022-3514.69.5.797

Steele CM, Spencer SJ, Aronson J (2002) Contending with group image: the psychology of stereotype and social identity threat. In: Zana MP (ed) Advances in experimental social psychology. Academic, San Diego, pp 379–440

Steinberg L, Silk J (2002) Parenting adolescents. In: Bornstein M (ed) Handbook of parenting: children and parenting. Erlbaum, Mahwah, pp 103–133

Stone J (2002) Battling doubt by avoiding practice: the effect of stereotype threat on self-handicapping in white athletes. Personal Soc Psychol Bull 28:1667–1678. https://doi.org/10.1177/014616702237648

Tarbetsky AL, Collie RJ, Martin AJ (2016) The role of implicit theories of intelligence and ability in predicting achievement for Indigenous (Aboriginal) Australian students. Contemp Educ Psychol 47:61–71

Tarrant M, North A, Edridge M, Kirk L, Smith E, Turner R (2001) Social identity in adolescence. J Adolesc 24(5):597–609. https://doi.org/10.1006/jado.2000.0392

Tatum B (1997) "Why are all the black kids sitting together in the cafeteria?" And other conversations about race. Basic Books, New York

Taylor VJ, Walton GM (2011) Stereotype threat undermines academic learning. Personal Soc Psychol Bull 37(8):1055–1067. Retrieved from http://journals.sagepub.com/home/psp

Turner H, Rubie-Davies CM, Webber M (2015) Teacher expectations, ethnicity and the achievement gap. N Z J Educ Stud 50(1):55–69. https://doi.org/10.1007/s40841-015-0004-1

Walsh M, Hickey C, Duffy J (1999) Influence of item content and stereotype situation on gender differences in mathematical problem solving. Sex Roles 41:219–240. https://doi.org/10.1023/A:1018854212358

Warren P (2017) A teacher like me: ethnic congruence and Pasifika student-teacher relationship. Unpublished master's thesis, The University of Auckland

Webber M (2008) Walking the space between: identity and Maori/Pakeha. New Zealand Council for Educational Research Press, Wellington

Webber M (2011) Gifted and proud: on being academically exceptional and Maori. In: Whitinui P (ed) Ka tangi te titi – permission to speak: successful schooling for Maori students in the 21st century. New Zealand Council for Educational Research, Wellington, pp 227–241

Webber M (2012) Identity matters: racial-ethnic identity and Māori students. SET 2:20–27. Retrieved from http://www.nzcer.org.nz/nzcerpress/set

Webber M (2015) Optimizing Maori student success with the other three Rs: racial-ethnic identity, resilience and responsiveness. In: Rubie-Davies C, Watson P, Stephens J (eds) The social psychology of the classroom international handbook. Routledge, New York, pp 102–111

Webber M, McKinley E, Hattie J (2013) The importance of race and ethnicity: an exploration of New Zealand Pākeha, Māori, Samoan and Chinese adolescent identity. N Z J Psychol 42(2):17–28. Retrieved from http://www.psychology.org.nz/publications-media/new-zealand-journal-of-psychology/?#.WzIpkacza00

Wellman D (1977) Portraits of Māori racism. Cambridge University Press, New York

Wendt Samu T, Mara D, Siteine A (2008) Education for Pacific peoples for the 21st century. In: Carpenter VM, Jesson J, Roberts P, Stephenson M (eds) Ngā Kaupapa here: connections and contradictions in education. Cengage Learning, Victoria, pp 145–167

Rural Farmer Empowerment Through Organic Food Exports: Lessons from Uganda and Ghana

73

Kristen Lyons

Contents

Introduction	1428
Global Development and Agri-Food Governance	1430
Governing Organic Agriculture	1432
Research Methods	1433
Organic Standard Setting and Deliberative Capacity	1435
Group Certification and Democratic Legitimacy	1437
Conclusions: Organic Governance and Southern Actor Empowerment?	1440
References	1441

Abstract

Export of certified organic agricultural products provides a market-based development strategy to deliver socioeconomic and ecological benefits to smallholder farmers in the global South. Yet the outcomes of participation in organic export-led initiatives are mixed. The extent to which organic export agriculture can deliver benefits to smallholders is, at least in part, tied to the capacity of organic governance to include smallholder farmers as active participants in shaping the outcomes of inclusion in export markets. This chapter contributes to understandings of local-level impacts of organic exporting by evaluating smallholder empowerment as part of two central components of organic governance: organic standard setting and group certification. Drawing from fieldwork in Uganda and Ghana, results demonstrate that organic governance arrangements that developed alongside the initial emergence of global South-North organic exporting provided limited opportunities for Southern actor empowerment; standard setting processes mostly excluded smallholder and other Southern interests, and created new forms of dependency upon exporters. However, the introduction of group

---

K. Lyons (✉)
School of Social Science, University of Queensland, Brisbane, QLD, Australia
e-mail: kristen.lyons@uq.edu.au

© The Author(s), under exclusive license to Springer Nature Singapore Pte Ltd. 2019
S. Ratuva (ed.), *The Palgrave Handbook of Ethnicity*,
https://doi.org/10.1007/978-981-13-2898-5_109

certification has provided smallholders' deliberative capacity, bringing with it opportunities for democratic legitimacy as part of global organic governance. As South-North organic exporting has continued to expand, the industry has grappled with the ongoing challenge of greater smallholder inclusion, with outcomes that have continued to establish the basis for legitimate deliberative capacity. The chapter concludes by pointing to the possibilities for smallholder empowerment alongside ongoing organic industry maturation.

Keywords

Empowerment · Export agriculture · Ghana · Organic food and agriculture · Uganda

Introduction

Pathways for global South development frequently situate the globalization and modernization of rural land and labor as central to economic growth. This "global development" agenda extends colonial legacies of land expulsion and enclosure, alongside disruption of traditional and Indigenous food ways, with outcomes that often exacerbate domestic food insecurity and food import dependence in many countries and regions (Campbell 2013; McMichael 2014). Despite its failings, especially in terms of its capacity to deliver national- and local-level food security, this global development agenda is institutionalized via neoliberal policy frameworks, and enabled via private sector and philanthro-capital (McMichael 2005; Cotula 2012; Holt-Gimenez and Altieri 2013).

On the ground, there is a diversity of responses to this development model. On the one hand, civil society, smallholder farmers, consumers/citizens, and researchers have coalesced as part of a global food sovereignty movement, and among these includes seed saving, women's cooperatives, the formation of local food and farming networks, as well as opposition to genetic engineering and inappropriate forms of food aid (Holt-Gimenez et al. 2009). Many of these movements aim to localize markets, shorten agri-food supply chains, provide localized responses to the global challenge of climate change, including centring local and Indigenous knowledges, and supporting peasant and subsistence agriculture (Whittman et al. 2010; McMichael 2014). Central to many of these responses is the right to food, land, livelihoods, and cultural expression as the basis for ensuring fair and equitable food systems. In contrast to food sovereignty movements that actively resist the globalization and commodification of land and labor, others have sought to reform global agri-food systems, including embedding socially and environmentally sustainable agricultural and food standards, such as Fair Trade, organic agriculture, and ethical trade initiatives. It is these latter initiatives that form the focus of this chapter.

In recent years, the certified organic food and agriculture sector has experienced significant growth in the global South, with sustained expansion in South/North organic trade occurring at a rate of 20% each year (FAO 1999; Willer and Lernoud 2017). On the basis of this growth, around 80% of the world's organic producers are now located in developing countries, or in emerging markets (Bouagnimbeck 2008; Willer and Lernoud 2017). Turning to the African continent – the focus of this chapter – organic agriculture has expanded significantly – growing by 33.5%, or 0.4 million hectares – between 2014 and 2015 alone, including significant expansion in Kenya, Madagascar, Zimbabwe, and Côte d'Ivoire. As a result, certified organic farming now covers 1.7 million hectares on the African continent, and comprises 3% of the global organic farming community (Willer and Lernoud 2017). The African organic industries' coming of age is reflected in the institutionalization of the African Organic Network in 2016 – acting as an umbrella organization for the sector. The majority of Africa's certified organic produce is destined for export markets, demonstrating the emphasis on certified organic agriculture as a "trade not aid" approach to development, as well as the limited domestic organic market and local alternative food trading networks (see Freidberg and Goldstein 2011; Willer and Lernoud 2017).

The expansion of African organic exporting – including significant growth over the last two decades alongside sustained global consumer demand for organic produce – raises a number of questions and concerns for those interested in empowerment and democracy for smallholder farmers in the global South. For example, food justice and sovereignty activists argue export-led agriculture reduces the land and labor available for local and/or national food security, as well as tying smallholders' livelihoods to the whims of northern consumer preferences, corporate actors, and organic certification requirements (see Freidberg 2004; Smith and Lyons 2012; Lyons et al. 2012). Some also oppose African organic exporting based upon concerns that airfreight of organic food – the "food miles" or "carbon footprint" – and the associated carbon emissions are antithetical with core environmental principles of the organic movement.

It is in the contested terrain of South/North organic exporting, and the nexus of empowerment and agri-food governance, this chapter is located. Specifically, it aims to examine the expansion of export-led certified organic agriculture, including the possibilities for empowerment of local communities within this context. To do this, the chapter examines the extent to which smallholder farmers, and other Southern actors, are empowered to shape their socioeconomic and ecological realities, including the terms – and outcomes – of their participation in organic export markets. The empirical data presented in this chapter is drawn from Uganda and Ghana, countries that have undergone varying degrees of expansion in organic exporting across commodities and sectors, thereby providing valuable comparative analysis. While Uganda comprises one of the largest sectors on the African continent – with over 190,000 organic producers – Ghana has just 2,600 farmers, but with well-developed in-country organic processing and exporters (Willer and Lernoud 2017).

The results presented here demonstrate mixed outcomes in terms of smallholders' and other Southern actors' empowerment in the context of governance of the global organic industry. On the one hand, the analysis presented demonstrates emergence of the certified organic sectors in Uganda and Ghana has occurred alongside the exclusion of Southern actors – including national organic peak bodies, civil society, and farmer groups – from the governance of organic agriculture. This is demonstrated in the dominance of Northern actors in defining both organic governance arrangements and the content of organic standards. It is also demonstrated via the limited extent to which Ugandan and Ghanaian organic farm and civil society organizations and smallholders have succeeded in shaping organic agri-food export networks to reflect their socioeconomic and ecological interests. However, some organic farmer and civil society organizations, alongside smallholder farmers, have also been effective in negotiating the terms for their participation in export markets, including their relationships with export buyers. The formation of a smallholder group certification scheme has been central to this. On this basis, Southern actors can be seen as shaping aspects of organic agri-food governance. The global organic industry continues to experiment in developing governance pathways that might expand deliberative capacity to center the voices and interests of global South actors. Grappling with this ongoing global organic agri-food governance challenge will be vital to build democratic legitimacy for the organic industry, which is now comprised of over 80% of global south producers.

Global Development and Agri-Food Governance

Agriculture and food systems have been significantly transformed and restructured via processes and policies of neoliberalization, alongside structural adjustment, modernization and industrialization (see McMichael 2009; Wiegratz et al. 2018). McMichael (2009) describes the emerging corporate food regime as shaped by corporate markets and global value chains, and mediated via global private standards and regulations (McMichael 2009; Oya 2012). In the global South, this agricultural transformation reflects the extension of patterns that established during political, economic, and cultural colonization, including the enclosure of land, and privatization and commodification of natural resources (Campbell 2013). Export agriculture has continued to expand since the early colonial period, including via the production of tropical commodities destined for the so-called developed world (Austin 2010; Campbell 2013). The expansion of commercial export agriculture during the colonial period provided a conducive environment for wealth accumulation (often to colonial elites and off-shore interests) via often violent exploitation of land and labor, and established the foundations for new forms of industrial commodity production in postcolonial contexts.

The policies and practices underpinning the colonial corporate food regime have integrated smallholder and peasant farmers into cash cropping and export markets (Freidberg 2004; Dolan 2008; Holt-Gimenez et al. 2009). This transformation from traditional and/or domestic production to production for export markets – alongside the imposition of western scientific knowledge and devaluing of Indigenous and local agricultural knowledges – has occurred unevenly across temporal, geographic, and social locations (Borras et al. 2008). Despite this, general trends demonstrate growing import dependence and food deficits for countries in the South, the results of which have greatly reduced Southern farmers' capacity to control their food systems (Holt-Gimenez et al. 2009). Demonstrating this, while the African continent was self-sufficient in food through the 1960s – and between 1966 and 1970 was a net exporter – by 2008 the continent was importing 25% of its food (Holt-Gimenez et al. 2009). The expansion of the colonial corporate food regime has also reduced the viability of agro-ecological and low carbon farming systems (Patel and McMichael 2009).

In this context, what might be the opportunity for export-led organic agriculture to address some of the challenges associated with this global agricultural development agenda, including specifically related to smallholder farmers' empowerment? While there are a range of ways this question might be approached, this chapter focuses on the role of organic governance arrangements – including scrutiny of deliberative capacity and democratic legitimacy – and their opportunities for empowering local communities.

To do this, the chapter draws from deliberative democratic political theory. Dryzek (2009) and others argue that deliberation and participation are widely recognized norms for democratic decision-making (see also Sarkissian et al. 2009; Pretty 2012). Proponents of deliberative democracy assert those affected by decision-making should be engaged in dialogue related to these decisions, and in so doing, to shape outcomes in ways that reflect their locally specific social, economic, ecological, and other aspirations and needs (see for example Dryzek 2009).

Within this literature, "inclusive" and "empowering" discourses are widely scrutinized, including for their capacity to mask the exclusion of certain groups – including minority groups – with outcomes that reinforce the interests of the most powerful (see Cooke and Kothari 2001). Similarly, inclusion in deliberative dialogue is critiqued when it fails to influence decision-making so as to deliver positive social and environmental changes (Schlosberg and Dryzek 2002).

In the context of these critiques, Dryzek (2009) has articulated some of the terms and conditions that might be required for effective democratic dialogue and decision-making – or what he names "deliberative capacity." Firstly, he argues deliberation must be authentic, enabling participants to freely reflect on their values and beliefs, including the freedom to change one's mind, as well as to reciprocate with others engaged in deliberative processes. Secondly, deliberative processes should be inclusive of a diverse range of actors, representing a broad range of interests and discourses. Thirdly, deliberative processes should result in outcomes that have consequences for decision-making.

Turning to the question of deliberative democracy in the context of agriculture and food systems, Fuchs et al. (2011) describe the rise of private sector actors across this governance space as demanding increased evaluation of its capacity to deliver legitimate democratic outcomes. They identify participation, transparency, and legitimacy as central factors in securing democratic legitimacy (Fuchs et al. 2011).

To critically evaluate the extent to which organic governance arrangements might engender legitimate democratic dialogue and decision-making – and with outcomes that may empower local actors – this chapter examines decision-making processes related to organic standards, alongside the emergence of group certification. Specifically, it critically evaluates the extent to which the socioeconomic and ecological realities and priorities of smallholders, and other Southern actors, are brought to bare as part of organic standard setting and organic certification.

This chapter now turns to an overview of organic agriculture governance. This provides the context to examine possibilities for smallholder empowerment in two selected countries, Uganda and Ghana.

Governing Organic Agriculture

The colonial corporate food regime has driven the production of high volume and low cost food. Yet recent spikes in food prices (in 2007/08, and again in 2011) – an outcome of a combination of factors, including speculative investment by finance capital, the burgeoning agro-fuels industry, and climate change – signify what some posit as the end of cheap food (see Moore 2012). Increasingly costly – in economic, social, and ecological terms – bulk and largely undifferentiated food is also incompatible with the values of a growing number of producers, consumers, retailers, and others, who value "quality" foods, including those differentiated on the basis of their social, environmental, and animal welfare attributes. Reflecting this, in recent years, there has been significant expansion of market and nonmarket arrangements for the provision of quality produce – including via farmers' markets, community supported agriculture (CSA), and box schemes (Donati et al. 2010) – as well as the proliferation of private sector-led quality agri-food production standards (including Fair Trade, Rainforest Alliance and organic standards) (Jaffee and Howard 2010; Fuchs et al. 2011; Oya 2012). These standards, and the alternative agri-food governance upon which they rely, provide traceability across complex agri-food chains, including South/North organic export trade relationships (Campbell 2009; Chkanikova and Lehner 2015).

This chapter is focused on governance arrangements for one selected quality agri-food initiative, the expanding global organic agriculture sector. Since the introduction of the first organic standard in 1973, Willer et al. (2008) estimate there are at least 468 government and nongovernment agencies that offer organic certification services. Organic certification is obtained via compliance with a set of standards, and often with verification via third-party certification. Organic standards stipulate allowable inputs (e.g., animal manures and some natural herbicides), allowable practices (e.g., crop rotations, companion planting, and animal husbandry practices), as well as prohibited substances (including synthetically derived agricultural chemicals, genetically modified organisms, and antibiotics). In addition, organic standards stipulate a range of social criteria (including reference to labor relations, gender equity, and child labor), as well as a range of environmental management criteria (biodiversity, soil fertility, and water conservation), and detailed record keeping requirements.

The expansion of certified organic agriculture – including the integration of Southern farmers and smallholders into global organic export markets – is the focus of a growing body of scholarship. Prior research has examined the extent to which organic governance (alongside other factors, including the entry of corporate firms, upscaling, and retailer home branding) signifies the "conventionalization" and "institutionalization" of organic agriculture (see Burch et al. 2001; Guthman 2004; Lockie et al. 2006; Campbell et al. 2010). Research in this area has also identified the co-option of organic movement interests by powerful northern actors, including corporate interests, and the subsequent weakening of organic standards. The complex bureaucratic requirements and costs associated with compliance processes are also tied to adverse impacts for farmers (see Buck et al. 1997; Guthman 2004; Gomez Tovar et al. 2005; Jaffee and Howard 2010).

Other research has examined the gendered – and including intersection with other categories (including race, ethnicity, and class) – livelihood impacts associated with entry into certified organic agriculture. Among this literature, Qiao et al. (2016) have documented the economic livelihood benefits of conversion to organics (see also Lyons and Burch 2007). Meanwhile, Gomez Tovar et al. (2005) describe expansion of the organic sector as privileging larger farms, structural conditions that are associated with land and water grabbing (Dell'Angelo et al. 2017). More broadly, Raynolds (2004) identified the dominance of northern actors in defining the content of organic standards.

There is also a nascent literature that analyses southern actors' engagement in organic governance processes (including standard setting, audit processes, etc.), and the extent to which such engagement might empower local actors, in other words, enabling what Dryzek (2009) refers to as "deliberative capacity." In their analysis of organic cocoa in Ghana, for example, Glin et al. (2014) describe a hybrid organic governance arrangement whereby the state, and alongside national and transnational NGOs and businesses, emerge as key players in organic standards formation. Similarly, describes organic standards as sociotechnical devices that are influenced by a diversity of actors. In this way, organic standards can be understood as part of the enactment of values and performance of agri-food governance. Raynolds et al. (2007) also identifies the role of civil society organizations, in particular, in shaping new organic governance arrangements.

In this context, what role might Ugandan and Ghanaian local actors play in shaping organic governance, and what might this mean for empowerment of southern actors? This chapter aims to answer these questions, and in so doing, contribute to the nascent literature on smallholders, governance, and organic agriculture in the global South.

Research Methods

The results presented in this chapter draw from fieldwork undertaken over 4 months in Uganda and 1 month in Ghana between 2005 and 2006, a period when the organic industry began to expand rapidly on the African continent. Given the time lapse between data collection and the writing of this chapter, this data is supplemented by contemporary organic industry data and sector reporting, alongside analysis of contemporary literature. These countries were selected to examine Southern actors' participation in, and experiences of, organic governance for a number of reasons. In

2005, when this research began, Uganda was experiencing rapid industry growth, and had quickly emerged as home to the largest area under certified organic production in Africa. Uganda remains one of the largest producers of organic crops – in terms of certified organic land – in Africa, with 226,954 hectares of certified organic or around 1.74% of Uganda's total agricultural land (Willer and Kilcher 2017). There has been significant investment in Uganda's organic sector from development agencies, including the Swedish International Development Corporation Agency's (SIDA) support for the Export Promotion of Organic Products from Africa (EPOPA) to facilitate organic exports (Bolwig and Odeke 2007). The EPOPA program ran between 1995 and 2008 (operating in three east African countries; Uganda, Tanzania, and Zambia), and provided financial support to 30 organic export companies (Parrott et al. 2006). According to Agro Eco and Grolink (Agro-Eco-Louis Bolk Institute n.d.), EPOPA supported the conversion of an estimated 30,000 smallholder farmers to organic farming practices in Uganda. In 2005, when fieldwork in Uganda was conducted, EPOPA was providing financial support to at least 11 companies engaged in export of tropical fruits, cotton, vanilla, coffee, Nile perch, tilapia, sesame, and spices, with a number of additional companies in the process of obtaining organic certification (including for shea butter, essential oils, and honey).

In contrast, organic agriculture in Ghana represents just 22,276 hectares, or 0.15%, of total agricultural land (Willer and Kilcher 2017). The Ghanaian organic agriculture sector has received limited international financial support, but with some funding from the UK Department for International Development (DFID) to establish a national peak body, the Ghana Organic Agriculture Network (GOAN). A number of large commodity traders – including the Ghana Oil Palm Development Company and the Ghana Cocoa Board – are also engaged in the production of small quantities of organic produce, alongside their much larger conventional production. An estimated 2600 farmers were certified organic in 2015, producing essential oils, herbs, horticultural crops, palm oil, and cocoa (Willer and Kilcher 2017). Interviews were undertaken with smallholder vegetable producers, cocoa, and oil palm producers.

Fieldwork included in-depth interviews with over 60 women and men organic smallholders, including 40 pineapple and coffee growers in Uganda; and 20 cocoa, oil palm, and mixed vegetable growers (including cabbage and tomatoes) in Ghana. Interviews were also undertaken with representatives from export companies: Amfri Farms, a domestically owned tropical fruit export company; and the international coffee trading company, Kawacom International in Uganda; and the Ghana Oil Palm Development Company. In addition, interviews were conducted with representatives from the national peak organic organizations (National Organic Agricultural Movement of Uganda – NOGAMU, and Ghana Organic Agriculture Network – GOAN), as well as from national and international organic certification organizations and development agencies. It also included participant observation at a number of events, including meetings, training days, and workshops, as well as textual analysis of a range of government and industry documents, including research papers, advertising and promotional print and web-based material. This data have been complemented with contemporary industry data.

The data collected as part of this research have been analyzed with a focus on smallholders' and other Southern actors' lived experiences in the context of South/North organic governance arrangements, with a specific focus on evidence of empowerment, including via deliberative capacity and democratic legitimacy related to organic standards setting processes, and group certification. Data presented reflect a particular historical moment – the rapid expansion of Africa's organic industry – thereby providing insights at a period of unprecedented social and agricultural change.

Organic Standard Setting and Deliberative Capacity

As detailed above, entry into organic export markets relies on organic certification, which is granted on the basis of compliance with a set of organic standards. The codification of organic principles, beliefs, and practices into systematic production, auditing and certification standards, and requirements is neither straightforward nor normative. Rather, standards are negotiated by movement and market actors, including farmers, farmer organizations, development agencies, processors, retailers, traders, consumer groups, and others (Guthman 2004; Lockie et al. 2006; DuPuis and Gillon 2009). Friedmann and McNair (2008, 409) have described these messy negotiations related to organic standard setting as "arena(s) for contestation, multiplication, (and) confusion." On this basis, dialogue and negotiations related to the content of standards and compliance provide opportunities for actors to (re)-shape the technologies of organic governance. The extent to which Southern actors have been effective in shaping organic governance processes, thereby signifying the deliberative capacity of these processes, appears mixed. To assess both the deliberative capacity and democratic legitimacy of South/North organic governance arrangements, and the impacts for empowerment of local actors, this chapter starts by examining the place of African smallholders, farm organizations and civil society in shaping processes related to the content of organic standards.

There is a little doubt that some local actors have succeeded in ensuring the inclusion of their interests in dialogic processes with international actors regarding setting organic standards. Demonstrating this, since at least the early 2000s, a number of representatives from Uganda have attended events organized by the international organic agriculture peak body, the International Federation of Organic Agriculture Movements (IFOAM), including conferences and trade fairs (e.g., BioFach). These events are increasingly attended by Southern stakeholders, given 75–80% of IFOAM's current membership base is located in the Global South (Raynolds 2004; Willer and Lernoud 2017). Yet these forms of inclusion appear at the lower end of the participatory spectrum (see Sarkissian et al. 2009), with Ugandan actors included in this research often describing their "observer" roles, and African organic produce often positioned as part of an exotic "display." While Ugandan actors (both people and products) were present during the period of rapid growth in global South organic exporting, they were frequently positioned as passive recipients of information and standards, rather than engaged as part of authentic deliberation that might impact governance outcomes.

Signifying a shift from this passive status, a Ugandan representative was elected to the IFOAM World Board in 2008 (and following this, a Kenyan representative was elected 2017–2020). There are also currently an additional 4 global south representatives (South Korea, India, Argentina, Fiji), out of a total of 10 IFOAM board members (2017–2020). While the inclusion of a Ugandan representative could be understood as widening of scope – in terms of both the actors and interests included as part of dialogic processes – local actors described significant limits in the extent to which this is translated into outcomes representative of their local interests and concerns. Despite inclusion in dialogue related to international standards setting, for example, representatives from national organic organizations in both Uganda and Ghana lamented they had been unsuccessful in delivering outcomes that shaped the content of organic standards. As a result, organic standards fell short in terms of reflecting the interests and realities of African smallholders, and other Southern actors. The failure to recognize equivalence between Ugandan and IFOAM standards related to livestock handling was demonstrative of this.

Organic standards for livestock handling require animals to be reared on land that is certified organic. In north-east Uganda, the Karamojong – an ethnic group of pastoral herders that have resided in the region since at least the 1600s – frequently move cattle across large areas of land, not all of which is certified organic. Representatives from Ugo-Cert and NOGAMU concurred it was highly unlikely activities that could exclude land from compliance with organic standards occurring in this region. As such, Ugo-Cert requested principles of equivalence (see Barrett et al. 2002) to support Karamojong to achieve compliance with organic certification. A representative from Ugo-Cert explained land that cattle were grazed upon, while not certified organic, was equivalent to certified organic land. Despite years of negotiation on this issue, IFOAM rejected this proposal, a decision that, at the time, excluded some herders from obtaining organic certification. A representative from Ugo-Cert reflected on this: "We have no bargaining power; we have absolutely no say."

The challenges related to organic standards equivalence were demonstrative of a broader concern raised by many Ugandan and Ghanaian organic advocates that inequitable power relations enable Northern interests to "speak for" southern stakeholders. While the deliberative turn in organic governance has encouraged Northern organic inspectors and certifiers to "speak with" Southern farmers, farm organizations and organic organizations, at the time of this research, there was little evidence this dialogue translated into significant shifts in the actual content of organic standards. As an outcome, smallholder farmers and representatives from organic organizations frequently described organic standards as disconnected from their lives.

The disconnect between the content of standards and smallholders' lived realities was also raised in regard to other quality standards. For example, a number of smallholder producers were certified with Fair Trade and Utz Kapeh. Like organic standards, these quality standards imposed requirements of some smallholders described as "inappropriate." For example, at a Fair Trade standards training day for organic smallholder pineapple producers in southwest Uganda, extension officers explained smallholders were required to wear gumboots as protective footwear. This engendered strong opposition from smallholders who were otherwise supportive of Fair Trade principles, and enthusiastic at the prospects of a price premium derived from Fair Trade certification. Yet one smallholder exclaimed: "why would we buy gumboots when we can't always afford food." It was not simply the cost of purchasing gumboots that elicited a strong response from smallholders, but also the widely shared view that protective footwear was not an urgent and important health and safety concern, particularly compared to other health challenges in the community.

Overall, the evidence presented points to limited southern actor inclusion in standards setting processes. This included Southern actor representation on international standard setting committees, such as IFOAM, thereby providing a site for inclusion in negotiations related to the content of organic standards. However, this was not matched – at least at the time of research – by substantial changes in the actual content of organic standards. Indeed, the results presented in this chapter demonstrate that while some Southern actors were included in standard setting negotiations, their interests were excluded from decisions arising from such dialogue. In short, organic standards setting processes – during the early stages of south/north exporting – fell short in terms of their deliberative capacity, leaving little room for southern actors' empowerment as part of organic standards formation.

However, over at least the last decade, the global organic industry has continued to grapple with this issue. The expansion of standards equivalence arrangements – whereby locally specific practices are recognized as "equivalent" to organic standards – alongside the emergence of alternative certification systems – including the Participatory Guarantee System (PGS) – each signify strategies to establish authentic and inclusive governance structures.

Group Certification and Democratic Legitimacy

While the experiences of smallholders and farm organizations in Uganda and Ghana related to standard setting processes pointed to limited deliberative capacity, other activities pointed to openings for democratic legitimacy of organic governance. Foremost among these activities included the formation of smallholder group organic certification schemes.

To obtain organic certification, farmers are required to verify compliance with organic standards through detailed record keeping of farm activities. The imposition of this individualized audit model has been widely critiqued, especially for global South (mostly smallholder) farmers (see Mutersbaugh 2002; Raynolds 2004; Dolan 2010). One agricultural consultant expressed frustration at what he, and others, described as an inappropraite "European model" for organic certification. Based on this critique, he was advocating for significant changes in organic compliance:

... Early on, they were trying to use audit systems developed for EU large farmers rather than smallholders, so we ended up trying to develop something that was a bit more appropriate (Agricultural consultant, Kampala, Uganda).

In East Africa (and elsewhere), there have been strong calls to restructure organic audit arrangements in ways that can more appropriately reflect the diverse and locally specific circumstances of smallholders. It is in this context the impetus to develop smallholder group certification schemes arose. Group certification is based on the organization of smallholders into groups, and with an organic certificate awarded to the group – and generally held by the export company – rather than individual smallholders. Management of the group occurs via an Internal Control System (ICS). The ICS employs an internal quality control document that stipulates requirements related to growing methods, post-harvest handling, record keeping, and other activities.

This audit model has reduced the cost associated with organic certification. Yet while this new smallholder-specific audit model enables the inclusion of smallholders in certified organic export trade, many farmers described being unable to join organic groups. Some organic pineapple and coffee smallholders in Uganda, and cocoa producers in Ghana, for example, recounted stories of neighbors they knew who were unable to join their organic smallholder group, due to the limited quantity of certified organic produce their export buyer was able to take. They described the export buyer as responsible for deciding which smallholders would be included in the group; circumstances that positioned exporters as arbiters of the so-called democratic governance.

Some smallholders also described familial ties determining purchasing arrangements. Some pineapple producers in Uganda, for example, expressed frustration that certain group members were able to sell greater quantities of pineapples to the export buyer. While a representative from Amfri Farms explained that decision making related to the distribution and quantity of purchases across group members was determined by smallholders' capacity to comply with "quality" indicators, including size and color, some smallholders were not convinced. Organic coffee producers that sold to Kawacom International raised similar concerns, citing favoritism as a frequent factor in shaping organic coffee buying arrangements.

These concerns indicated that while group certification enabled the entry of increasing numbers of smallholders into organic export markets, inequalities persisted; manifest in a disproportionate distribution of benefits across group members. Export companies played a determining role in the distribution of these benefits, given their opportunity for granting preference to some growers. Despite attempts by export companies to make decisions related to buying arrangements transparent, perceptions of these processes as opaque and biased limit the capacity for deliberative legitimacy.

There are other aspects of group certification that, while opening spaces for smallholder entry into organic export trading, have also constrained smallholders', and other Southern actors', capacities to negotiate the terms of their involvement. For example, the export company holds the organic certificate, leaving smallholders' dependent upon the company they supply. On the one hand, smallholders identified a number of benefits associated with this arrangement, including a reliable market for the sale of their organic crops, the provision of extension services, training, equipment, and other materials for use on the farm (see Lyons and Burch 2007). Some organic coffee smallholders also spoke of the difficulties in finding a market for their coffee beans prior to the arrival of Kawacom. The arrival of Kawacom had, for many growers, simplified market access arrangements.

On the other hand, smallholders also argued that tying recognition of their organic status to an export company created unequal power relations, including enabling export companies to "call all the shots." Such findings are not unique to organic trade, with similar findings in research of the impacts of contract farming for African smallholder farmers (see Oya 2012). For example, some organic coffee and cocoa smallholders reported that their buyers did not always make payment on time, as well as describing frequent delays in payment for their crops. Similarly, coffee smallholders at Sipi Falls in Uganda expressed frustrations with unfulfilled promises from Kawacom International. Many coffee smallholders, for example, described Kawacom International committing to supply tarpaulins for utilization during coffee drying, and lamented that only a few households in the community had ever received these.

The arrangement upon which group certification is based – with certification held with the export buyer rather than individual growers – was understood as imposing constraints upon smallholders, and with mixed impacts in terms of empowerment. On the one hand, the rights of smallholders to negotiate were sidelined; they occupied the role of price takers, and were passive recipients of export companies' corporate social responsibility provisions, with little capacity to negotiate the terms of their relationship with their buyer.

Yet this was not the only story. In one instance, for example, the Katuulo organic smallholder group was effective in shaping South/North negotiations, with outcomes of social and economic benefits. Through the Katuulo Organic Pineapple Cooperative, members negotiated with their buyer – Amfri Farms – to transport produce to local markets. Prior to negotiating this arrangement, smallholders travelled by foot, or in a few cases, bicycle, to sell produce on the local markets. According to some smallholders from the Cooperative, the provision of transport by Amfri Farms reduced this time-consuming and physically demanding task. Also in response to Cooperative requests, Amfri Farms provided resources and other supports required for construction of a community health clinic.

The Katuulo Cooperatives' capacity to negotiate in their interests with Amfri Farms was assisted by their long-standing credibility as a local organization, and their formalized structure of governance with elected representatives, regular meetings, and a cooperative bank account and communal savings plan. A representative from Amfri Farms explained the cooperative structure, as well as other attributes of the group, readied them for compliance with group certification processes. He also emphasized the simplicity of working with an already formed cooperative, especially in terms of ensuring compliance with the Internal Control System. He described the Katuulo Cooperative as "effective and coordinated," and one of their "best groups" of organic smallholders. He also stated the company "depended" upon "good farmers," including members of the Katuulo Organic Pineapple Cooperative, to ensure the regular supply of quality fresh fruit to their international buyers. While Katuulo was one of their most remote suppliers (over 200 km from Kampala, where Amfri Farms dries and packages fruit prior to export), representatives from Amfri Farms explained that the cost associated with extra travel was more than compensated by the benefits of working with this cooperative.

Conclusions: Organic Governance and Southern Actor Empowerment?

Global rural development and the colonial corporate food regime have driven an export agriculture agenda that delivers food insecurity, alongside social and ecological problems, for the global South. The expansion of export-led organic markets in the global South raises tensions among supporters of alternative agri-food initiatives related to the extent to which this pathway for rural development – often driven by development agencies, corporate actors, and Northern consumers – might perpetuate similar inequity and injustice. Among these includes concerns organic exporting will simply replicate unfair and ecologically destructive South/North relations that have come to underpin conventional trade, while at the same time rendering organic smallholder's dependent upon organic governance regimes and Northern stakeholder interests.

This chapter has contributed to this debate through an analysis of some of the relationships emerging as part of the politics of organic governance. In particular, this chapter has contributed to debates about the extent to which organic governance – upon which South/North organic export markets rely – might provide opportunities to empower smallholder farmers. To do this, this chapter has focused on Uganda and Ghana, and drawn from data collected during a period of rapid expansion in the African organic sector (2005–2006).

The results presented paint a mixed picture. On the one hand, Ugandan and Ghanaian smallholders, and other local Southern actors, have been limited in the extent to which they have been able to shape organic governance arrangements. This was particularly the case during the period of rapid global South organic industry expansion, the time when data presented included in this chapter were collected. Demonstrating this, while some Ugandan actors participated in standard setting processes, they gained little ground in actually shaping the content of organic standards. Rather, research findings demonstrate processes to define the socioeconomic and ecological conditions of certified organic agriculture were – at least during the period of rapid expansion of organics on the African continent – largely captured by Northern stakeholder interests, with little deliberative capacity for Southern actors to meaningfully shape the outcomes of dialogic processes (see Dryzek 2009). Group certification too created new forms of dependency between smallholders and export buyers, circumstances maintained by the opacity of aspects of organic governance arrangements. Such findings stand counter to Fuchs' et al. (2011) call for transparency as a precursor for building democratic legitimacy in agri-food governance.

At the same time, Ugandan and Ghanaian smallholders, alongside local farm and civil society organizations, were successful in shaping some aspects of organic governance arrangements, including aspects of the smallholder group certification scheme. There was also evidence of smallholder groups negotiating with their buyers in ways that delivered outcomes reflecting smallholders' needs and interests. Such activities represent openings for democratic legitimacy, and possibilities that South/North organic exporting can rupture inequalities bound to the colonial corporate food regime.

Over at least the last decade – since primary data presented in this chapter were collected – the global organic industry has continued to expand governance approaches that further support deliberative capacity, especially for Southern actors. This includes ongoing developments in processes related to smallholder group certification, alongside significant expansion of standards equivalence arrangements, thereby enabling recognition of farming practices in the global South as commensurate with those stipulated in organic standards. The global organic industry has also made significant investment and support to expand the Participatory Guarantee System (PGS); a low cost and oft described culturally appropriate certification system. These, and other initiatives, reflect the transformation that has occurred within the certified organic industry over at least the last decade; from its origins in the global North, to the current situation whereby the majority of IFOAM members and certified organic farmers now reside in the global South. With this as context, inclusivity, transparency, and meaningful engagement with global South actors has become increasingly normalized as part of organic agri-food governance. Further research is needed in the field of organic agriculture, smallholders, and agri-food governance, to better understand the contributions of these shifts in empowering Southern actors to shape agri-food futures. In the current era of climate constraint and its intersection with food precarity, centring the rights and interests of global South smallholders will be vital to ensure globalized organic agri-food systems can empower local communities, and thereby be part of building a democratic food future.

References

Agro-Eco-Louis Bolk Institute (n.d.) The natural source of knowledge. Advice, research and development in the field of organic and sustainable agriculture, nutrition and health care. Agro-Eco-Louis Bolk Institute, The Netherlands

Austin G (2010) African economic development and colonial legacies. International Development Policy Revue internationale de politique de dévelopement. http://poldev.revues.org/78. Accessed 20 Nov 2017

Barrett H, Browne A, Harris P, Cadoret K (2002) Organic certification and the UK market: organic imports from developing countries. Food Policy 27(4):183–199

Bolwig S, Odeke M (2007) Household food security effects of certified organic export production in tropical Africa. A gendered analysis. Export promotion of organic products from Africa (EPOPA)

Borras S, Edelman M, Kay C (2008) Transnational agrarian movements: origins and politics, campaigns and impacts. J Agrar Chang 8(2):169–204

Bouagnimbeck H (2008) Organic farming in Africa. In: Willer H, Yussefi M (eds) The world of organic agriculture: statistics and emerging trends. International Federation of Organic Agriculture Movements, Bonn, pp 90–102

Buck D, Getz C, Guthman J (1997) From farm to table: the organic vegetable commodity chain of northern California. Sociol Rural 37(1):3–20

Burch D, Lyons K, Lawrence G (2001) What do we mean by green? Consumers, agriculture and the food industry. In: Lockie S, Pritchard W (eds) Consuming foods, sustaining environments. Australian Academic Press, Brisbane

Campbell H (2009) Breaking new ground in food regime theory: corporate environmentalism, ecological feedbacks and the 'food from somewhere' regime? Agric Hum Values 26:309–319

Campbell OM (2013) The political ecology of agricultural history in Ghana. Nova Science Pub Inc, Ghana

Campbell H, Rosin C, Norton S, Carey P, Benye J, Moller H (2010) Examining the mythologies of organics: moving beyond the organic/conventional binary? In: Lawrence G, Lyons K, Wallington T (eds) Food security, nutrition and sustainability. Earthscan, London, pp 238–251

Chkanikova O, Lehner M (2015) Private eco-brands and green market development: towards new forms of sustainability governance in the food retailing. J Clean Prod 107:74–84

Cooke B, Kothari U (2001) Participation. The new tyranny. Zed Books, London

Cotula L (2012) The international political economy of the global land rush: a critical appraisal of trends, scale, geography and drivers. J Peasant Stud 39(3–4):649–680

Dell'Angelo J, D'Odorico P, Rulli M (2017) Threats to sustainable development posed by land and water grabbing. Curr Opin Environ Sustain 26–27:120–128

Dolan C (2008) Arbitrating risk through moral values: the case of kenyan fair trade. Res Econ Anthropol 28:271–296

Dolan C (2010) Virtual modalities: the mainstreaming of Fairtrade in Kenyan tea fields. Geoforum 41(1):33–43

Donati K, Cleary S, Pike L (2010) Bodies, bugs and dirt. Sustainability re-imagined in community gardens. In: Lawrence G, Lyons K, Wallington T (eds) Food security, nutrition and sustainability. Earthscan, London, pp 207–222

Dryzek J (2009) Democratization as deliberative capacity building. Comp Pol Stud 42 (11):1379–1402

DuPuis M, Gillon S (2009) Alternative modes of governance: organic as civic engagement. Agric Hum Values 26:43–56

Food and Agriculture Organisation (FAO) (1999) Organic agriculture. (COAG/99/9). FAO, Rome

Freidberg S (2004) French beans and food scares. Culture and commerce in an anxious age. Oxford University Press, Oxford

Freidberg S, Goldstein L (2011) Alternative food in the global south: reflections on a direct marketing initiative in Kenya. J Rural Stud 27:24–34

Friedmann H, McNair A (2008) Whose rules rule? Contested projects to certify local production for distant consumers. J Agrar Chang 8(2):408–434

Fuchs D, Kalfagianni A, Havinga T (2011) Actors in private food governance: the legitimacy of retail standards and multistakeholder initiatives with civil society participation. Agric Hum Values 28(3):353–367

Glin L, Oosterveer P, Mol A (2014) Governing the organic cocoa network from Ghana: towards hybrid governance arrangements? J Agrar Chang. https://doi.org/10.1111/joac.12059

Gomez Tovar L, Martin L, Angel Comez Cruz M, Mutersbaugh T (2005) Certified organic agriculture in Mexico: market connections and certification practices in large and small producers. J Rural Stud 21:461–474

Guthman J (2004) Agrarian dreams? The paradox of organic farming in California. University of California Press, Berkeley

Holt-Gimenez E, Altieri M (2013) Agroecology, Food Sovereingty and the New Green Revolution. Journal of Sustainable Agriculture 37(1):90–102

Holt-Gimenez E, Patel R, Shattuck A (2009) Food rebellions: crisis and the hunger for justice. Food First Books/Fahamu Books/Grassroots International, Oxford, UK/Oakland

Jaffee D, Howard P (2010) Corporate cooptation of organic and fair trade standards. Agric Hum Values 27(4):387–399

Lockie S, Lyons K, Lawrence G, Halpin D (2006) Going organic. Mobilising networks for environmentally responsible production. CABI, Cambridge

Lyons K, Burch D (2007) Socio-economic effects of organic agriculture in Africa. International Federation of Organic Agriculture Movements (IFOAM), Bonn

Lyons K, Palanippan G, Lockie S (2012) Organic agriculture and empowerment, human and social capital building. In: Halberg N, Muller A (eds) Organic agriculture for sustainable livelihoods. Earthscan, London

McMichael P (2005) Global development and the corporate food regime. In: Buttel F, McMichael P (eds) New directions in the sociology of global development. Research in rural sociology and development, vol 11. Emerald Group Publishing, Cambridge. pp 265–299

McMichael P (2009) Banking on agriculture: a review of the 'world development report 2008'. J Agrar Chang 9(2):235–246

McMichael P (2014) Historicizing food sovereignty. J Peasant Stud 41(6):933–957

Moore J (2012) Cheap food and bad money. Food, frontiers and financialization in the rise and demise of neoliberalism. Review 33(2–3)

Mutersbaugh T (2002) The number is the beast. A political economy of organic-coffee certification and producer unionism. Environ Plan A 34(7):1165–1184

Oya C (2012) Contract farming in sub-Saharan Africa: a survey of approaches, debates and issues. J Agrar Chang 12(1):1–33

Parrott N, Olesen J, Hogh-Jensen H (2006) Certified and non-certified organic farming in the developing world. In: Halberg N, Alroe H, Knudsen M, Kristensen E (eds) Global development of organic agriculture: challenges and prospects. CABI Publishing, Cambridge

Patel R, McMichael P (2009) A political economy of the food riot. Review xxxii(1):9–35

Pretty J (2012) Agriculture and food systems: our current challenge. In: Rosin C, Stock P, Campbell H (eds) Food systems failure. The global food crisis and the future of agriculture. Earthscan, London

Raynolds L (2004) The globalisation of organic agro-food networks. World Dev 32(5):725–743

Raynolds L, Murray D, Heller A (2007) Regulating sustainability in the coffee sector: a comparative analysis of third-party environmental and social certification initiatives. Agric Hum Values 24:147–163

Sarkissian W, Hofer N, Shore Y, Vajda S, Wilkinson C (2009) Kitchen table sustainability. Practical recipes for community engagement with sustainability. Earthscan, London

Schlosberg D, Dryzek J (2002) Political strategies of American environmentalism: inclusion and beyond. Soc Nat Resour 15(9):787–804

Smith K, Lyons K (2012) Negotiating organic, fair and ethical trade: lessons from smallholders in Uganda and Kenya. In: Rosin C, Stock P, Campbell H (eds) Food systems failure. The global food crisis and the future of agriculture. Earthscan, London

Qiao Y, Halberg N, Vaheesan S, Scott S (2016) Assessing the Social and Economic Benefits of Organic and Fair Trade Tea Production for Small-Scale Farmers in Asia: a Comparative Case Study of China and Sri Lanka. Renewable Agriculture and Food Systems 1:1–12

Whittman H, Desmararais A, Wiebe N (2010) Food sovereignty. Reconnecting food, nature and community. Fernwood Publishing/Food First Books/Pambazuka Press, Halifax/Winnipeg/Oakland/Cape Town

Wiegratz J, Martiniello G, Greco E (2018) Uganda: the dynamics of neoliberal transformation. Zed Books, London

Willer H, Kilcher L (eds) (2017) The world of organic agriculture – statistics and emerging trends 2017. IFOAM/FiBL, Bonn

Willer H, Lernoud J (2017) The World of Organic Agriculture: Statistics and Emerging Trends 2017. FIBL and IFOAM - Organics International

Willer H, Yussefi-Menzler M, Sorensen N (2008) The world of organic agriculture. Statistics and emerging trends 2008. International Federation of Organic Agriculture Movements (IFOAM), Bonn

Local Peacebuilding After Communal Violence

74

Birgit Bräuchler

Contents

Introduction	1446
Culture, Ethnicity, and Community	1447
Local Turn and Traditional Justice	1449
Communal Violence and Its Aftermath in Maluku	1452
Adapting Local Tradition	1454
Raja	1455
Pela	1456
Hatuhaha	1457
Conclusion	1459
References	1461

Abstract

This chapter aims to take an anthropologically informed look into local conflict dynamics and local negotiation processes aimed at the restoration of social relations and the reintegration of society after mass violence. It analyzes local processes of peacebuilding taking place independent of international interventions and how local actors inventively adapt local traditions to the requirements of a post-conflict society, thus challenging predominant notions of liberal peace. The chapter builds on current anthropological notions of culture, ethnicity, and tradition and argues that ethnographic research of contemporary local approaches to peace needs to be contextualized in broader history and power politics. The argument derives from multi-sited and multi-temporal ethnographic fieldwork

---

In this chapter I am drawing on my long-term research on conflict and peace in Eastern Indonesia and related publications, in particular (Bräuchler 2009a, d, 2010, 2014a, c, 2015, 2017b, 2018a, b)

B. Bräuchler (✉)
Monash University, Melbourne, VIC, Australia
e-mail: birgit.braeuchler@monash.edu

© The Author(s), under exclusive license to Springer Nature Singapore Pte Ltd. 2019
S. Ratuva (ed.), *The Palgrave Handbook of Ethnicity*,
https://doi.org/10.1007/978-981-13-2898-5_110

conducted in Maluku, an archipelago in Eastern Indonesia, for more than a decade and highlights the importance of culture and tradition for the restoration of sustainable peace in a society that has been torn apart by an alleged religious war. The response to the long-lasting violence was to activate an overarching ethnic identity to rebuild bridges and restore peace. These efforts are analyzed against the backdrop of changing sociopolitical developments in which group boundaries shift and ethnic and religious identity markers change meanings or merge. The chapter thus also argues against the stereotypification of violent religion and harmonious tradition as both religion and ethnicity are aspects of the same social dynamics.

Keywords

Traditional justice · Revival of tradition · Local turn · Religion · Communal violence · Indonesia · Maluku

Introduction

Ethnic conflict remains one of the prevailing challenges to international security in our time. Left unchecked, or managed poorly, it threatens the very fabric of the societies in which it occurs, endangers the territorial integrity of existing states, wreaks havoc on their economic development, destabilises entire regions as conflict spills over from one country into another, creates the conditions in which transnational organised crime can flourish, and offers safe havens to terrorist organisations. (Cordell and Wolff 2011: 1).

Despite such doomsday scenario, there is still little understanding of the dynamics and complexities of ethnic conflicts, let alone how to sustainably solve them. The international peace industry usually tries to fix problems through a top-down interventionist approach. The basic assumption is that the building of a democratic state plus market economy will produce peace, which is a rather hegemonial and evolutionist supposition. These interventions are normative, mechanistic, and solutionist – presuming a hierarchy of knowledge "between capable interveners and incapable intervened" (Finkenbusch 2016: 2). As such "reconciliation toolkits" (Bräuchler 2009b: 3) often fail, peace workers increasingly promoted the inclusion of local elements that are part of the conflict-affected environment, into the toolkit. However, rather than taking local agency seriously, such interventions often simply co-opt the local and are highly selective and essentializing, mostly ignorant of broader historical, political, and sociocultural contexts (see, e.g., Bräuchler 2018a; Bräuchler and Naucke 2017). One of the reasons is that ethnic and cultural identities are simply too complex to deal with, in a world, in which issues of concern are largely framed from the standpoint of economic, political, and strategic interests of the dominant powers. Local initiatives and actors are usually seen as part of larger international intervention and aid programs, with peace and conflict scholars focusing on the interplay of the international and the local (see, e.g., Donais and Knorr 2013; Wanis-St John 2013). Local people affected by mass violence thus continue to be reduced to victims or troublemakers, rather than active peacemakers with their own resources and cultural competence to draw on.

This chapter aims to take an anthropologically informed look into local dynamics and local negotiation processes aimed at the restoration of social relations and the reintegration of society after mass violence in Eastern Indonesia. It analyzes local processes of peacebuilding taking place independent of international interventions and how local actors inventively adapt local traditions to the requirements of a post-conflict society – with all its challenges. The chapter builds on current anthropological notions of culture, ethnicity, and tradition and argues that ethnographic research of contemporary local approaches to peace needs to be contextualized in broader history and power politics. My argument derives from multi-sited and multi-temporal ethnographic fieldwork conducted in Maluku, an archipelago in Eastern Indonesia, for more than a decade and highlights the importance of culture and tradition for the restoration of sustainable peace in a society that has been torn apart by an alleged religious war. The response to the long-lasting violence was to activate an overarching ethnic identity to rebuild bridges and restore peace. These efforts are analyzed against the backdrop of changing sociopolitical developments in which group boundaries shift and ethnic and religious identity markers change meanings or merge. The chapter thus also argues against the stereotypification of violent religion and harmonious tradition as both religion and ethnicity are aspects of the same social dynamics.

The first part of this chapter provides the conceptual framework with which I will work in the second part of the chapter that is dedicated to the case study. The first part deals with changing conceptualizations of ethnicity, the local, culture, and community that are important to better understand dynamics of local peacebuilding after communal violence. It then provides a brief overview of the local and cultural turn in peace studies and the rise of traditional justice as a means to cope with mass violence. The second part first offers insights into the Moluccan conflict and peace dynamics and then explores the particularities of Moluccan efforts to revive, restrengthen, and reconstruct local traditions as means to restore interreligious relations, with all its challenges. The chapter concludes with some lessons learned.

Culture, Ethnicity, and Community

Barth's *Ethnic Groups and Boundaries* (1969) was an important milestone to move away from an essentialist notion of ethnicity and focus on the relational aspect of collective identities. Sociopolitical and historical contexts influence and shape the making of boundaries, which suggests continuous change. Contemporary anthropological theory depicts culture no longer as an isolated whole with a fixed set of characteristics, but as something processual and dynamic, something that is continuously contested from within and outside and renegotiated, influenced by local and global factors, and continuously in the making (Bräuchler 2014b: 38). Construction must not be confused with invention though and needs to resort to a repertoire of materials, symbols, rituals, and geographical references that depend strongly on a specific cultural and historical context if they are to create effective identity projects. For Weber (1976: 234, 239), ethnicity implied a subjective feeling of community and of integrative, shared action versus the exclusion and despising of others who are different, thus implying both similarity and difference (Cohen 1985: 12), which renders both the relational aspect and symbolic content important. The materials used are, however, filtered and constructed by the memory, imagination, narratives, and myths of the respective actors (Hall 1994: 395). Simply outlining the construction of groups and boundaries is therefore inadequate, as this does give no explanation as to why people continue to refer to essentialist identities and why these often trigger profound emotions (Calhoun 1995: 198–199).

Focusing on shifting borders and the relational aspect of ethnicity or community only would imply dismissing the lived reality of community through sociality and the vitality of a culture in the community members' social lives (Amit 2002). This is important in the Moluccan context, where peace activists and local leaders are trying to develop a pan-Moluccan identity. Given the vastness of the archipelago, such an identity needs to be imagined (cf. Anderson 1983). However, it stays futile, if it is not embodied and lived, at least to a certain extent so that Moluccans can relate to it. A one-sided focus on fluidity, construction, and manipulation would also ignore the relevance of "socialisation, the transmission of knowledge and skills from one generation to the next, the power of norms, the unconscious importance of religion and language for identity and a sense of community" and culture "as a shared system of communication" (Eriksen 2010: 68). It would neglect a community's self-identity, which is "likely, in part, to be non-relativistic and non-contingent" (Cohen 2002: 166–167). It is actually in conversation with changing sociopolitical settings and selected "content" that ethnicity and group boundaries are constantly (re)negotiated, through daily interaction, conflict, and the search for peace and that engender frameworks in which collective actions can occur (Melucci 1995: 44).

What is particularly relevant for the study of reconciliation processes is that the focus is no longer on outlining and describing difference, but the analysis of processes of differentiation (Gupta and Ferguson 1992: 16) and contextualization – in power relations, global processes and political histories, and conflict and peace dynamics – and of agency as prominently signaled by the practice turn in anthropology. Such reformulation enables a focus on negotiation processes between formerly warring parties but also between those affected by the conflict and outside interventionists. In such context, the question is not primarily whether certain cultural elements have actually been invented or introduced from the outside in the (colonial) past (e.g., Brigg 2008: 35–39), but whether and for what reason they are important to current negotiation processes. Today, a dynamic and relational concept of culture is acknowledged and promoted by those peace scholars who attribute culture a role in peacebuilding processes (e.g., Avruch 1998; Brigg 2010). However, as Brigg (2008: 48) proposes, it is exactly this moving away from fixed categories and separateness toward culture in a relational sense that poses "challenges to mainstream quantitative social science practice" and makes peace scholars even more hesitant to engage with it.

Local Turn and Traditional Justice

Whereas the de-essentialization of culture and the local in the wake of globalization almost led to its disappearance as an anthropological category (Bräuchler and Naucke 2017), peace and conflict studies have only recently discovered the local and the everyday. Through comparative studies, peace researchers and workers worldwide became aware that an internationally established toolkit consisting of instruments such as truth commissions and law enforcement often failed and that they increasingly needed to draw on local resources and local cultural capital to provide legitimacy to international peace interventions. This triggered a local turn (Mac Ginty and Richmond 2013) in peace research and work that aims to move "the local" and, much less explicitly, "culture" (Bräuchler 2018b) into the center of attention and action – with mixed outcomes. "Local ownership," "participation," and "traditional justice" have become keywords. Ideally, conflict analysis and resolution as well as peace and reconciliation initiatives shall be conducted by locals themselves, nonlocal actors only acting as facilitators, if at all. "No one can make anyone else's peace" (Anderson and Olson 2003: 32). Lederach and Avruch were early promoters of that paradigm shift. As Lederach (1997: 94) put it, "the greatest resource for sustaining peace in the long term is always rooted in the local people and their culture." Scholars like Lederach are targeting a positive peace that goes beyond statist diplomacy and the mere absence of violence toward profound reconciliation through relationship rebuilding and addressing the root causes of enmity, which requires a very different timeframe from the one that peace interventions usually allow for.

However, the disciplines dominating peace and conflict studies have difficulties grasping the meaning of culture, the local, or "local ownership" that are often mere strategic proposal rhetoric or seen as nice accessory to top-down interventionist models, with some notable exceptions such as Autesserre's work (2010) on conflict and the international peace industry in the Democratic Republic of the Congo (Bräuchler and Naucke 2017). Culture and the local in mainstream peace research are often reified and denied its flexibility and heterogeneity in order to being able to deal with them better. Often the local is reduced to eloquent representatives of local communities or decontextualized rituals; it is stereotypically depicted as inherently bad or good, disorderly or harmonious, with values and needs that are not in line with liberal standards or ethnographic complexities simply not fitting the abstract categories or normative dimensions of international peace paradigms (Bräuchler 2018b: 20–21). Western-oriented interveners or aid workers "perform to localize, but the rhetoric is not matched by their everyday practices" (Anderl 2016: 197) and has not been able yet to seriously undermine the predominant liberal peace paradigm.

A few critical peace scholars recently started promoting anthropology as an important partner in peace research (e.g., Mac Ginty 2015; Millar 2018; Richmond 2018a, b). Generally, they do not go far enough yet in their approach, either taking anthropology as an auxiliary science (Finlay 2015), reducing it to the ethnographic method (as yet another tool for the peace industry), or dealing with the local only as part of larger international efforts and thus bracketing out local peace making initiatives and local social engineering processes as they are discussed in this chapter (Bräuchler 2018a: 23). In a recent article, Richmond thus asked for the involvement of anthropology as the discipline "rescuing peacebuilding from neoliberal epistemological frameworks" and preventing mainstream IR's projects "from verging into hegemonic illegitimacy" (2018b: 221, 230). As proposed by Galtung (1969) five decades ago, it is important to choose a broader perspective toward peacebuilding, which not only includes the ending of violence and dealing with its immediate aftermaths but also looking into less visible forms of violence that continue those structures and power relations that were, at least partly, responsible for the outbreak of violence. Universalist and interventionist approaches, however, rather reproduce power hierarchies and do little, if nothing, to counter structural violence (Richmond 2018a: 11, b: 227), and they essentially fail in locally anchoring a peace they aim to introduce from the outside.

One concomitant of the turn toward the local and an increasing number of so-called religious and ethnic conflicts in the post-Cold War era was the increasing involvement of non-state traditional justice mechanisms (TJM) into transition processes. In particular, in situations where retributive justice and truth commissions are out of reach, national justice systems are not in place and weak or refuse to take responsibility, local (restorative) justice mechanisms are increasingly used to cope with the aftermath of large-scale conflicts. Main features of TJM are their focus on the restoration of social relations, including the restoration of the victim and the communities affected and the reintegration of the offenders into the communities – in case such categorization does make sense at all, which is difficult in communal violence as in Maluku. TJM thus pursue the transformation toward (or back to) a more inclusive collective identity. Important for their success is that both sides actively participate in the process, in which cultural values and local decision-making mechanisms figure prominently. Traditional leaders or arbitrators, who know the sociocultural context and the conflict parties, play important roles. TJM are thus highly contextual, mostly communal and participatory, which makes them accessible for most, with regard to geographical, cultural, and linguistic closeness (Boege 2006). Just like community or culture, reconciliation fails when limited to the symbolic realm; instead it needs to be "embodied and lived out in new relationships between people at all levels of society" (Rigby 2001: 189). Enacting justice here often implies the restoration of social order according to local worldviews, in which the isolation of perpetrators (e.g., through imprisonment) is rather counterproductive. Such reconciliation processes can take a long time, involve several rounds of negotiation, and are often publicly sealed by rituals (Bräuchler 2015: 15–16).

Symbols and rituals give expression to how an ethnic or cultural community sees the world and "the other." Often, they are emotionally charged and can thus easily be instrumentalized. They are important elements in conflict and peace, for the creation of conflict lines and for closing the gaps. As Turner (1967) has argued, symbols are usually polysemic or multivocal. They can invoke diverse associations and stand for a variety of ideas and phenomena, depending on context and persons involved. Rituals and symbols can thus become means to (re)integrate and unify people, without taking away the possibility of difference. Turner (1967) emphasizes the liminality of rituals as creative phases of anti-structure that open up in-between spaces where rules for acting and interpreting can be negotiated anew. In post-conflict societies, there is a clear need for such spaces that acknowledge the past and image a different (shared) future (Ross 2004: 216–217). Cultural performances are an ideal space for the embodiment and lived experience of ethnic or collective identity that cannot be reduced to mechanisms of border management. As the case study will show, it is the flexibility of culture and symbols that allow for identity transformation and the active involvement of people affected by conflict to "take up locally rooted cultural symbols and rituals, and adapt, (re)construct, or (re)invent them according to the needs of a society in search of peace" (Bräuchler 2015: 35).

The turn to tradition and culture presents many new challenges for local and international communities involved in peacebuilding – challenges that arise from the intrinsic nature of TJM, from selection, adaptation, and social engineering processes involved, and the instrumentalization and misinterpretation of "tradition" by insiders and outsiders. As customary law is usually transmitted orally, TJM are more flexible than formal justice and can be adapted to changing circumstances such as political upheavals and efforts to reclaim political and economic rights, instigate conflict, or search for conflict solutions (Bräuchler and Widlok 2007). Moore (1986: xv, 39, 317) describes customary law as a "cultural construct with political implications" and "a set of ideas embedded in relationships that are historically shifting" and undergoing constant negotiations and modifications. However, the instrumentalization of tradition often strips it of such flexibility. Seeking (or pretending to seek) local legitimization, selected traditions have often been decontextualized, instrumentalized, romanticized, or mutilated. A prominent example is the restoration and adaptation of the "traditional" *gacaca* courts in post-genocide Rwanda in order to help the state process the hundreds of thousands of court cases and uncover the truth in a culturally apt way. Through their multiplication, the change of their field from property and marriage issues to crimes such as murder, and the use of newly elected judges, the *gacaca* tribunals were manipulated up to a point where there was not much resemblance left with the traditional communal gatherings they were, meant to negotiate, settle disputes, and bring about reconciliation (Waldorf 2010).

Adaptability and transferability of TJM clearly have their limits, especially when they are transferred to settings outside the sociocultural context in which they are usually rooted, in cases where "outsiders" are involved who don't share the same cultural values and laws, when applied to large-scale conflicts such as mass killings and genocide or when mistaken to be or instrumentalized by outsiders as one-off events. The latter, for instance, happening in Aceh with the military using a traditional *peusijuek* ceremony as an easy way out of accountability (Avonius 2009) or the Acholi ritual *mato oput* in Northern Uganda as a popular means to seemingly localize elitist or outside peace initiatives (Meier 2011) – both of them traditionally being the end of a long process of negotiations and peacebuilding, in order to finalize, legitimize, and socialize it. In Maluku, the revival of local traditions did bring to the fore old power hierarchies and the exclusionary power of culture, but it also provided means to develop a more inclusive Moluccan identity. Another extreme is peace workers and interveners explicitly excluding customary laws from peacebuilding as they may (re)enforce traditional hierarchies (based on inheritance, ethnicity, age, gender) and may not comply with international human rights standards (Bräuchler 2015: 14–23). These approaches refrain from a deeper engagement with local mechanisms in order to fully understand their implications and underlying local power structures; the impact of colonialism, independence, and modernization; or the politicization through the state or mass violence, genocide, and civil war, during which traditional leaders or arbitrators might also have lost legitimacy and influence.

Communal Violence and Its Aftermath in Maluku

My work on peacebuilding in Indonesia is an attempt to start closing those gaps through ethnographic research, anthropological conceptualizations, and, as Richmond (2010: 33) acknowledges, a "detailed understanding (rather than co-option or 'tolerance') of local culture, traditions, and ontology." The Moluccan archipelago in Eastern Indonesia covers several hundred islands and became famous as the "Spice Islands," the source of nutmeg and clove that attracted early traders and colonial powers, who also brought Islam and Christianity. This chapter looks at one of two Moluccan provinces, called Maluku. Maluku provided the scene for one of the most protracted conflicts that broke out shortly after the step-down of Indonesia's authoritarian president Suharto (1966–1998). This conflict tore apart villages, families, and other kin groups and resulted in an ideational and geographical divide of Moluccan society. The scale of violence that erupted in January 1999 in Maluku's capital Ambon and went on for almost 4 years took most observers by surprise, as Maluku and its roughly half Christian, half Muslim population used to be praised for interreligious harmony in a majority Muslim country. Thousands died on both sides and almost a third of the Moluccan population was displaced. Whereas initially it looked as if Christian Ambonese mainly targeted migrant Muslims, religion soon became the principal identity marker in the conflict. Rumors that central mosques and churches had been set alight and the fact that Ambon City is home to people from all over Maluku put the conflict on a higher (transcendental) scale and made it spread rapidly throughout Maluku.

The conflict's depiction as religious war is in line with predominant discourses on the rise of religious fundamentalisms worldwide and a national scenario, where interreligious violence erupted in many places. It is, however, a rather simplifying interpretation of a much more complex setting that requires a look into historical developments, the corresponding shifts in group and identity formations, and the structural problems and inequalities underlying the violence. Ever since the arrival of the colonial powers in Maluku, religion has become a politicized subject. Although Moluccans had developed means to maintain harmony and keep their society integrated, developments such as the Islamization of politics from Indonesia's center from the late 1980s and 1990s challenged this. A demographic shift in Maluku through spontaneous (mainly Muslim) immigration but also governmental transmigration programs from the 1970s onward further increased hidden tensions and competition in a precarious job market. The Indonesian security forces took sides in the violence, as a means to uphold their power that was supposed to be curtailed in the post-Suharto reformation era, but also giving expression to the central government's failure to control its security forces. The involvement of a militant Muslim group from Java called Laskar Jihad that government and military did not prevent from setting off to Maluku in 2000 led to new scales of destruction and violence. Colonial powers and neocolonial unification policies had also substantially manipulated and weakened TJM and imposed hierarchies that grant very unequal access to power and decision-making, resulting in land and resource grabbing through outside forces. The central government, however, mainly blamed Moluccans themselves for the recent violence and refused to set up formal transitional justice mechanisms. They mainly set on military power. The report of an independent national fact finding commission that was sent to Maluku after the Malino peace agreement in 2002 was never published, and masterminds behind the conflict were never named, let alone called to court. Moluccans thus had to themselves find means to reconcile and restore peace, without formal justice and "truth" (Bräuchler 2013, 2015).

A historical perspective and the analysis of evolving conflict dynamics and peace narratives substantiate or better provide the material to develop the theoretical and conceptual assumptions about the dynamics of culture, ethnicity, and community outlined in the chapter's first part. Changing identity and group patterns during conflict and peacemaking are the continuation of shifting relationships between Islam, Christianity, and adat in Maluku (Bräuchler 2014a, c). Whereas Islam came as a peaceful concomitant to trade, Christianity was forcefully imposed on the Moluccan people by colonial powers, starting with the Portuguese in 1512. The Dutch followed in the early seventeenth century and, together with indigenous preachers, promoted a purified Christianity and took action against adat that was not in line with it (e.g., Müller-Krüger 1968). Whereas Islam and adat merged on the village level (at least until an increasing influx of reformatory ideas from the Middle East from the nineteenth century onward), adat and church constituted two different and often competing institutional hierarchies (von Benda-Beckmann and Benda-Beckmann 1988). From the outset, religion had thus become politicized. In their effort to push through the spice monopoly, the colonial powers made massive use of existing local power struggles and traditional rivalries, thus sharpening existing group boundaries. Under Dutch colonial rule, Christians were given preferential treatment in education and the bureaucracy. In the struggle for independence, hundreds of Christians in the colonial army fought side by side with the Dutch against their brothers and sisters who favored an independent country. After independence, many Christian Moluccans were worried about an overpowering Muslim majority, and a group of western-educated and politically active Moluccan figures proclaimed the independence of a South Moluccan Republic (RMS) on 25 April 1950 that was crushed by the military a short while after. This was a major issue in the recent conflict, when Moluccan Christians were reproached for their closeness to the former colonial government, their (previous) claim for superiority and separatism. Indonesian government policies of the last decades (see above) further amplified the role of Islam and Christianity as identity markers.

A typical quarrel between a Christian bus driver and a Muslim passenger on 19 January 1999 thus fell on fertile ground and quickly turned into a bushfire that was difficult to control. Old grievances and resulting social inequalities came to the fore, and religion provided a welcome means to elevate this onto a higher level and bring together very heterogeneous communities under the seemingly unifying umbrella of religion as, to speak in Cohen's words, a symbolically simple public face that glossed over a symbolically complex private face (Cohen 1985: 74, 107, 116). The idleness and incapacity of the central government of Indonesia to put an end to the violence and the disastrous effects of the instrumentalization of religion drove people in Maluku to restrengthen, revive, and reconstruct culture and tradition that goes beyond religion and is meant to become the common ground for peace. That trend was supported by new autonomy laws in post-Suharto Indonesia that enabled the restoration of traditional sociopolitical structures in the villages. Community peacebuilding in Maluku is a continuation of the shifting and merging of group boundaries, in which religion (Christians vs Muslims), indigeneity (locals vs migrants), and adat (Moluccans vs outside intrusion) play determinant but changing roles.

Adapting Local Tradition

Countless peace initiatives took place in Maluku by local, national, and international actors (for an overview see Bräuchler 2015: Chap. 3). Religious and adat figures as well as students appealed to the Moluccan people from the very beginning of the conflict to honor their common roots and shared adat and stop the violence. Whereas those pleas were not very successful first, after several years of violent conflict, people from all levels of society put their hopes in adat as bridge builder. In the center of attention are traditional alliances binding villages together irrespective of their religious affiliation and traditional leaders. Moluccans were out to develop a narrative that would allow for the reintegration of society and the restoration of social relationships with their neighbors. As most of them were involved in the violence, one way or the other, it made no sense to look for culprits in their own ranks. They knew they were all guilty, but they also knew that they had been living in harmony before. The unifying narrative that most Moluccans could identify with was that outside provocateurs triggered the unrests and used religion to turn Moluccans against each other. The many Moluccans I spoke to over the years were convinced that reconciliation and restoration of social relations were not triggered by outside initiatives, but occurred naturally, from the bottom-up, by drawing on local resources and institutions, cultural capital, and social ties.

The rest of this section engages with three examples, where Moluccans have taken great efforts to revive, restrengthen, and at the same time reconstruct local traditions to make them fit post-conflict requirements. They are good examples of how identity patterns change over time due to changing sociopolitical settings.

(I can here only provide brief overviews of cases, for which I have provided more detail in previous publications, in particular Bräuchler 2009a, c, 2011, 2015). I will start with outlining the changing role of traditional village heads in Maluku, the raja, from the colonial past to the current peace process, and then turn to a Moluccan alliance system called pela that was influential in bringing about Maluku's image as a place of interreligious harmony. The last example deals with a specific village association that progressed from being a key warmonger to be a symbol for peace.

Raja

Maluku's traditional leaders look back on a tumultuous history, and the increasing attention they attract in contemporary Maluku is not without its challenges (Bräuchler 2011). In pre-colonial times, the raja were primus inter pares and had no authoritative power. In the colonial period, they were turned into intermediaries between the local population and the Dutch East India Company and were crucial for pushing through the spice monopoly. They were in charge of security and order in the villages and had to make sure that the villagers delivered sufficient quantities of spices and labor to the colonial rulers. In return, the raja were equipped with certain status symbols. Their power was backed by their ancestors, as well as the colonial government (Cooley 1969: 145), always torn between diverging loyalties. Through the abolition of the spice monopoly in 1863, "the raja had lost their economic utility" (Chauvel 1990: 97) and thus their special status. Conservative raja became outspoken opponents of the new nationalist movement in the Indonesian archipelago, which further threatened their position, and joined hands with RMS activists and Moluccan nationalism that builds on local tradition and leadership (Chauvel 1990: 224). In independent Indonesia, all village heads officially were to be elected by the village population (as opposed to hereditary succession that survived in many villages until today). Suharto's unification efforts resulted in the standardization of governmental structures down to the village level, which turned the raja into insignificant cogs in the Indonesian bureaucracy. Such changing policies left many villages in a rather chaotic state, resulting in power struggles that continue to the present between lineages that were in charge in pre-colonial times versus those in power during the colonial period or thereafter. Post-Suharto decentralization laws give villagers the opportunity to return to their "traditional" political structures and put the raja back on stage, which is challenging given their tumultuous history. This turned the raja into crucial figures in the translation process of state law, the management of higher government funds, and the revival of traditional justice systems, which triggered extensive debates and negotiations in most of the villages I have been to in Maluku about hereditary raja succession, democracy, and the revival of tradition for peace.

In the recent violence, some raja had fuelled the fighting by leading their people to go to war. During and after the violence, many became central peace actors in the reconciliation process due to their knowledge of traditional structures, their still major influence on local communities, and their interface function between local and regional politics. As they are thus ideally able to facilitate the restoration of peaceful relations toward the inside and the outside, actors from all levels wanted to make the raja multipliers of their peace initiatives, from local and international NGOs to the government. Raja installation ceremonies became important peace events, bringing hundreds and thousands of Christians and Muslims together. In 2008, some peace activists and raja set up a Moluccan-wide raja forum called Majelis Latupati Maluku (MLM) in an effort to bring all Moluccan raja together in a body that helps to reintegrate society, improve and facilitate communication between villages and government, and anticipate and prevent any future conflict. The MLM took years of preparation in a still very volatile setting. It was an important step toward developing a pan-Moluccan identity, as the colonialists of the past had taken great effort to destroy any overarching organization beyond the village level. Given the vastness of the Moluccan archipelago and the multitude of islands and cultures, it is a highly ambitious project and necessarily raises issues of representativeness. So far, the MLM got active as a representative board or to solve border issues between newly established districts; district level MLMs get active to anticipate and resolve conflicts between individual villages. Critics dismiss the MLM as a political instrument for regional power politics or as a means by the central government to co-opt traditional Moluccan leadership.

Pela

Pela is a traditional alliance system known throughout Maluku, although named differently in the various regions (Bräuchler 2009a). It ties two or more villages together, irrespective of their religious affiliation. Historical events such as war, headhunting, accidents, or financial difficulties, in which the parties involved helped each other or formed an alliance in order to consolidate peace, form the background for pela. Pela partners shall help each other in times of crisis or for the conduct of big projects such as building a church or mosque, and are not supposed to marry each other. As pela has positive connotations for most people and overcomes religious difference, it quickly advanced to be the symbol for Moluccan culture, local ownership, security, and peace. In the end, as an adat elder in Western Seram emphasized, it was their pela gandong culture that brought them back to their senses and stop the carnage. Pela pacts were, and still are, used as important mediating forces in the reconciliation process, and pela renewal ceremonies are crucial in reuniting Muslims and Christians, often merging with raja inauguration ceremonies. Such events are much closer to the lived reality of most villagers than the abstract MLM. The raja of Muslim Tulehu, for example, claimed that his installation ceremony attracted more than 4000 visitors in February 2003, among them Christian pela and gandong partners who were treated as special guests (gandong derives from the Indonesian word kandungan = womb to symbolize the strongest form of pela). Although one pela only connects up to a handful of villages, through their combination it has the potential to integrate Moluccan society (for a sketch see Bartels 1977).

One problem is that pela pacts were often concluded against a third party (Moluccan or not), thus questioning its praised integrative character (Hohe and Remijsen 2003). This became the cruel truth in the conflict, where only pela partners were spared among the religious "other." Immigrants can traditionally neither participate in the pela system nor become raja or other traditional functionaries, although some of them have been living in Maluku for generations. Formerly, Maluku had mechanisms in place to accommodate outsiders in local traditional structures. These mechanisms were gradually undermined or destroyed, most prominently through central government's transmigration programs that brought substantive amounts of outsiders, which the traditional systems could simply not deal with and that led to rising economic competition and land scarcity (Bräuchler 2010, 2017a; Platenkamp 2001). In the early days of the conflict, violence was primarily directed toward immigrants.

To address such shortcomings, some Ambonese scholars and peace activists want to take pela's integrative potential to new grounds. They want it to accommodate not only a couple of villages, but, ideally, Moluccan society at large, including both locals and permanent migrant settlers (e.g., Ohorella 1999). The idea is not to exclude any group residing in Maluku, but to strengthen Maluku and its culture against destructive outside forces. Given the fact that the past has seen the emergence of new kinds of pela, the Moluccan conflict could become an excuse to establish new pacts between former conflict parties. The challenging task is to develop rules and mechanisms for upscaling, beyond the village level, and set up, for example, pela between sub-districts or interethnic pela. Although the post-conflict phase saw an enormous strengthening of pela, none of these ideas have been realized yet. Pela ceremonies are also popular among politicians and international organizations. In an effort to support those events, mobilize their constituencies, or locally root their peace initiatives, regional politicians, for example, show up at well-attended pela ceremonies, sometimes contributing to the high costs, or international actors use pela as a catchy program title (e.g., UNIDO and ILO 2011). In 2016, the Christian University and the State Islamic Institute in Ambon even labelled their relationship as pela. Although this is meant to promote the peacebuilding potential of pela, it risks its instrumentalization and its reduction to a one-time event that ignores underlying long-term reciprocity and mutual trust.

Hatuhaha

My third example is Hatuhaha, a traditional village union in the northern half of Haruku Island, Central Maluku, that is known for its strong anti-colonial resistance and political stance after independence, for fighting at the front line of the recent violence, and for being a symbol of peace. Hatuhaha consists of four Muslim villages and one Christian village. This case shows particularly well how social and cultural memories played into the conflict pattern and complicated the simplifying "grand narrative" of a religious war (Bräuchler 2009c). Changing circumstances on an international, national, and local level changed the prioritization of certain identity aspects over time which prevents an easy patterning of the interrelationship of religion and adat in the Moluccan conflict and beyond. The village union goes back to five brothers who came to Haruku from Seram and jointly converted to Islam. Despite various challenges, it was one of the few that the

Dutch were not able to crush. To save its brothers from the colonialists' constant pestering, one Hatuhaha member, Hulaliu village, gave in and converted to Christianity. The Hatuhaha union was tested again, when its very localized version of Islam (so-called Islam adat) was confronted with the rise of orthodox Islam in Indonesia. To this day, that divide is an extremely sensitive topic. Involved in all this are struggles between village clans over who has the power to define what adat is, what needs to be continued, and what can be replaced or adapted to the wider cultural and religious context. Increasingly involved also get power struggles related to high-level politics, that is, the competition among (Muslim) Hatuhaha clans whose turn it is to get an influential position in the district or provincial government (Bräuchler 2014a).

The Moluccan conflict, at least momentarily, had reunited Hatuhaha Muslims. It brought back memories of past repression and made them fight on the front lines against Christians. Kariu, the neighboring Christian village of Hatuhaha Pelauw (Muslim), is not part of the Hatuhaha union and was completely destroyed in February 1999; its population forced to flee. Hulaliu, the Christian Hatuhaha village, tried to help its coreligionist Kariu, but in vain. While it was good neighborliness and economic interdependencies that shaped the relationship between Pelauw and Kariu before the conflict, it was their religious backgrounds and the missing adat link that were in focus during the conflict. Both Kariu and Pelauw claim to be the original inhabitants of Kariu's village territory. Kariu people fled to Hualoi (Muslim) in Seram and Aboru (Christian) in South Haruku, both long-standing gandong partners. In December 1999, Pelauw and its Muslim allies attacked Hulaliu but broke off after a short while as the ancestors were calling them back. Hatuhaha union stumbled and people were killed on both sides during the attack but ultimately withstood the religious challenge – and this is how the Hatuhaha people themselves see it. They thus consciously fade out Hatuhaha internal problems and its general weakening through Indonesia's unification policies and its immersion in broader regional power politics. They organized a Hatuhaha internal reconciliation ceremony, a peace march to Ambon City in 2002, and a 2-week-long ceremony to celebrate the restoration of the Hatuhaha mosque in Rohomoni in 2006 to promote Hatuhaha as a symbol of internal unity and peace between Christians and Muslims.

Hatuhaha's claim to be the key to peace in Maluku is highly contested by non-Hatuhaha people. It was only in 2005, after long negotiations, that Kariu people could finally return to their ancestral lands, and they did so in a big neo-traditional ceremony, in which people from both sides actively participated. Given the perceived nature of the Moluccan conflict, it was important to emphasize that Kariu people did not explicitly return as Christians, but as adat people. A recategorization of the former enemy had to take place, and it took place in a carefully planned repatriation ceremony that included adat elements well-known to all parties to create commonality, but in a way that each individual group could also preserve its specific identity and its specific interpretation of history and conflict. The joint adat ceremonies did not only build up bonds and create a new and shared repatriation history, but at the same time imposed responsibilities on those involved: the responsibility to maintain their shared reality, good relationships, and peace. A rash identification of religion as a dividing and adat as a unifying force, however, is misguided. Adat rituals not only unified people after conflict; local traditions also formed the basis for the development of divided memories that were invoked to legitimize the use of violence. A short while after Kariu's return, the head of the Moluccan Refugee Coalition, himself a Kariu descendant, suggested to establish a new pela between Kariu and Pelauw. The proposal did not find much favor with the villagers, who were still traumatized by the conflict or thought that the time was not ripe yet. Reconciliation is not just a matter of having the right peacebuilding mechanisms in place, but also a matter of time (Bräuchler 2009c, 2014a).

Conclusion

There are a couple of lessons to be learned from our case studies for the broader debate on community peacebuilding after violent conflict. What they clearly showed is that the relationships between adat and world religion, if detachable at all, are constantly renegotiated depending on changing sociopolitical circumstances, thus resulting in the continuous renegotiation of culture and ethnicity. What is "traditional" is relative, fluid, and constantly challenged, but not random. Customary law in post-colonial societies, which people refer to or want to revitalize nowadays, is not an unchanging heritage to be rediscovered from the pre-colonial past, but something that is constantly reconstructed in changing settings, which allows for its survival. Many conversations I had in Maluku show that local peace activists and academics as well as some raja and villagers are aware of the evolving character of adat. The Ambonese sociologist Pariela argues for "social engineering" as a comprehensive and integrative tool to manage diversity and create a shared reality for the whole (increasingly heterogeneous) Moluccan population (e.g., Pariela and Soumokil 2003). A juridical research team of Ambon's state university considers social engineering (*rekayasa sosial*) to be a necessary means to empower the local population and even out drawbacks of customary law, such as the domination of the revival process by a certain adat elite (Tim Peneliti Pusat Kajian Konstitusi 2005–2010). Similarly, Kaartinen (2014: 323), looking at neo-traditional conflict resolution practices in Kei in Southeastern Maluku, emphasizes that people are pragmatic about how and in what combinations they make use of their traditional law.

As our three case studies show, Maluku faces most of the challenges involved in using TJM in the aftermath of large-scale violence, including issues of democracy and representation, idealization and manipulation, integration and exclusion, and transferability and adaptation. On the positive side, it allows for easy access, connects to people's culture and lived realities, resonates with what constitutes a human being in an adat community, and implies ownership of the affected people and their empowerment with regard to outside forces that brought disaster to the area. It locally roots peace, with many of the ideas born from within. However, in my broader research on peacebuilding in Maluku, I have identified three kinds of limitations of *adat* that need to be dealt with by villagers, revival activists, academics, and the government: (1) where *adat* fails due to the kind and scale of conflict it is applied to, (2) where we face long-standing problems with *adat* such as land issues or *raja* succession regulations, and (3) when *adat* is supposed to integrate an increasingly heterogeneous society. It needs to be discussed, for instance, what space migrants are given in these processes and how they can be accommodated within local cultural structures and the other way around. Given the vastness and cultural diversity of the Moluccan archipelago, this implies a reflected revival within a long timeframe, where adaptation and (re)invention are supposed to overcome and transform limitations of current adat.

One way to overcome adat limitations with regard to scale was to take cultural concepts of mutual complementarity and reciprocity such as pela or traditional leadership concepts such as the raja, elevate them to a higher level, and make them cultural symbols of reconciliation and peace for all Moluccan people, with not only philosophical but also practical implications – with all the challenges as outlined above. Migrant communities, such as the Butonese, seem to think highly of cultural systems like pela that resonate with their own cultural values. Now they need to work together with Moluccans to reconstruct and develop further mechanisms for outsider integration that have been challenged through national political developments in Indonesia. They have also been challenged by current decentralization efforts that some local elites misuse to reclaim access to land that is occupied by migrant communities, some of them having resided in the area for generations (e.g., Adam 2009). As Ratuva (2003: 150) emphasized for Fiji, traditional models must not be imposed, but need to be negotiated between the different ethnic groups in order to work in such contexts. It also needs to be discussed in how far both local and migrants should have the right to exit (Chua 2004), that is, the "right to resist and opt out of the norms and expectations of particular social and cultural groupings" (Rapport 2002: 158), and how this would affect the setup and functioning of TJM.

Some outside peace workers (but also scholars) take such seeming misfits as an excuse to either ignore and exclude those traditions from any peace discourse or to only cursorily accommodate culture in the form of popular rituals, ceremonies, or some spokespersons. I want to argue that acknowledging difficulties and challenges involved in bottom-up peacebuilding (McEvoy and McGregor 2008: 9–10) and critically engaging with them – as part of local negotiation processes – is a first step in acknowledging that local agency is crucial for reconciliation and sustainable peace. As scholars and activists in Maluku stress, the shortcomings of existing adat law should not become an excuse to not foster its revitalization and refunctionalization (Tim Peneliti Pusat Kajian Konstitusi 2005–2010; Titahelu 2005). The involvement of outside actors as facilitators is sometimes necessary, e.g., when setting up the MLM or supporting the Hatuhaha repatriation ceremony, but one carefully needs to deal with issues of representation and legitimacy.

Pela or the raja forum as culturally legitimized and extended structures constitute shared institutions that are meant to reintegrate society to an unprecedented extent and to prevent future violence. They thus pursue the transformation toward (or back to) a more inclusive collective identity within Moluccan society. We can here learn from Popper's piecemeal approach to social engineering (Bräuchler 2017b), which does not believe in an "absolute and unchanging ideal," but operates at various smaller "building sites," learning "by trial and error, by making mistakes and improvements" (Popper 1971: 279). As Popper emphasizes, "piecemeal social experiments can be carried out under realistic conditions, in the midst of society" and allow for continuous readjustments (280). The Moluccan case certainly requires multilevel agency, involving members of all societal groups concerned in the negotiation process as well as government representatives, thus jointly becoming the owners of the peace process. Traditional justice is no panacea and it is no solution to delegate all responsibility to local communities. National political frameworks and regional politics also need to be adapted to challenges at the local level. The government needs to support physical and moral reconstruction but also the economic empowerment of people. As the coordinator of the repatriation ceremony of the Kariu refugees warned, adat is important and necessary to enable collective reconciliation, but it cannot prevent individual feelings of revenge or injustice coming to the surface again (e.g., due to unequal compensation after the conflict, unsolved land issues, or continuing economic and political injustices).

An essentialized notion of culture or ethnicity – as it still prevails in mainstream peace and conflict studies – would rather miss the point. Tradition in Maluku does not imply a step-back into the past, but, as Akin argues for the Solomon Islands, future-oriented (often political) acts that are "rooted ... in shared historical experiences and ongoing political realities" (Akin 2013: 343); acts that forward custom (or culture or adat) as a symbol of unity that helps to restore sociality and make diverse local societies join hands to fight colonial intruders, central governments, or other outside forces that triggered conflict and split local societies. Anthropology's role is to promote an open and reflected notion and understanding of the local, ethnicity, tradition, and culture; raise awareness of their historicity, ambiguity, contestedness, flexibility, and their embeddedness in relational webs that go far beyond the specific conflict; and try to track the intricacies and dynamics of identity transformations and peacebuilding through ethnographic fieldwork (Bräuchler 2015: 182).

The most important thing is the realization that peace and reconciliation are no fixed-term endeavors, but continuing processes. The ideational divide in Moluccan society only gradually dissolves, and tensions continue to run high until today, which requires continuous investment in relationship-building. Incidents that involve members from both religions quickly trigger fears that large-scale violence might flare up again, which is, unfortunately, often supported through sensational headlines in national mainstream media. This has prompted experienced peace activists in Maluku to set up a network of peace provocateurs in 2011, who make efficient use of traditional networks and social media to anticipate this from happening and to refute rumors immediately. They endeavor to open up spaces for a creative engagement with tradition, the violent past and a shared future.

References

Adam J (2009) The problem of going home: land management, displacement, and reconciliation in Ambon. In: Bräuchler B (ed) Reconciling Indonesia: grassroots agency for peace. Routledge, London/New York, pp 138–154

Akin DK (2013) Colonialism, Maasina rule and the origins of Malaitan Kastom. University of Hawai'i Press, Honolulu

Amit V (2002) Reconceptualizing community. In: Amit V (ed) Realizing community. Concepts, social relationships and sentiments. Routledge, London/New York, pp 1–20

Anderl F (2016) The myth of the local. How international organizations localize norms rhetorically. Rev Int Organ 11(2):197–218

Anderson B (1983) Imagined communities: reflections on the origin and spread of nationalism. Verso, London

Anderson MB, Olson L (2003) Confronting war: critical lessons for peace practitioners. The Collaborative for Development Action, Cambridge, MA

Autesserre S (2010) The trouble with the congo. Local violence and the failure of international peacebuilding. Cambridge University Press, New York

Avonius L (2009) Reconciliation and human rights in post-conflict Aceh. In: Bräuchler B (ed) Reconciling Indonesia: grassroots agency for peace. Routledge, London/New York, pp 121–137

Avruch K (1998) Culture and conflict resolution. United States Institute of Peace Press, Washington, DC

Bartels D (1977) Guarding the invisible mountain: intervillage alliances, religious syncretism and ethnic identity among Ambonese Christians and Moslems in the Moluccas. Cornell University, Ithaca

Barth F (ed) (1969) Ethnic groups and boundaries. The social organization of culture difference. Universitetsforlaget, Bergen-Oslo

Boege V (2006) Traditional approaches to conflict transformation – potentials and limits. Berghof Research Center for Constructive Conflict Management, Berlin. www.berghof-foundation.org/fileadmin/redaktion/Publications/Handbook/Articles/boege_handbook.pdf

Bräuchler B (2009a) Cultural solutions to religious conflicts? The revival of tradition in the Moluccas, Eastern Indonesia. Asian Soc Sci 37(6):872–891

Bräuchler B (2009b) Introduction: reconciling Indonesia. In: Bräuchler B (ed) Reconciling Indonesia: grassroots agency for peace. Routledge, London/New York, pp 3–33

Bräuchler B (2009c) Mobilising culture and tradition for peace: reconciliation in the Moluccas. In: Bräuchler B (ed) Reconciling Indonesia: grassroots agency for peace. London. Routledge, London/New York, pp 97–118

Bräuchler B (ed) (2009d) Reconciling Indonesia: grassroots agency for peace. Routledge, London/New York

Bräuchler B (2010) The revival dilemma: reflections on human rights, self-determination and legal pluralism in eastern Indonesia. J Legal Pluralism Unofficial Law 42(62):1–42

Bräuchler B (2011) Kings on stage: local leadership in the post-Suharto Moluccas. Asian J So Sci 39(2):196–218

Bräuchler B (2013) Cyberidentities at war: the Moluccan conflict on the internet. Berghahn Books, New York

Bräuchler B (2014a) Christian-Muslim relations in post-conflict Ambon, Moluccas: adat, religion and beyond. In: Platzdasch B, Saravanamuttu J (eds) Religious diversity in Muslim-majority Southeast Asia: areas of toleration and conflict. ISEAS, Singapore, pp 154–172

Bräuchler B (2014b) Modes of belonging in West Papua: local symbolism, national politics and international cultural concepts. Rev Indones Malaysian Aff 48(1):35–66

Bräuchler B (2014c) Modes of interreligious coexistence and civility in Maluku. In: Gottowik V (ed) Dynamics of religion in Southeast Asia. Amsterdam University Press, Amsterdam, pp 193–215

Bräuchler B (2015) The cultural dimension of peace. Decentralization and reconciliation in Indonesia. Palgrave Macmillan, London

Bräuchler B (2017a) Changing patterns of mobility, citizenship and belonging in Indonesia. Soc Identities 23(4):446–461

Bräuchler B (2017b) Social engineering the local for peace. Soc Anthropol 25(4):437–453

Bräuchler B (2018a) Contextualizing ethnographic peace research. In: Millar G (ed) Ethnographic peace research: approaches and tensions. Palgrave Macmillan, London, pp 21–42

Bräuchler B (2018b) The cultural turn in peace research: prospects and challenges. Peacebuilding 6(1):17–33

Bräuchler B, Naucke P (2017) Peacebuilding and conceptualisations of the local. Soc Anthropol 25 (4):422–436
Bräuchler B, Widlok T (2007) Die Revitalisierung von Tradition/The Revitalisation of Tradition (Special issue of the Zeitschrift für Ethnologie 132)
Brigg M (2008) The new politics of conflict resolution. Responding to difference. Palgrave Macmillan, Hampshire/New York
Brigg M (2010) Culture: challenges and possibilities. In: Richmond OP (ed) Palgrave advances in peacebuilding. Critical developments and approaches. Palgrave Macmillan, Hampshire/New York, pp 329–346
Calhoun C (1995) Critical social theory: culture, history, and the challenge of difference. Blackwell, Oxford UK/Cambridge, MA
Chauvel R (1990) Nationalists, soldiers and separatists. The Ambonese Islands from colonialism to revolt, 1880–1950. Verhandelingen van het Koninklijk Instituut voor Taal-, Land- en Volkenkunde. KITLV Press, Leiden, p 143
Chua BH (2004) Communitarian politics in Asia. In: Chua BH (ed) Communitarian politics in Asia. Routledge, London/New York, pp 1–24
Cohen AP (1985) The symbolic construction of community. Ellis Horwood, Chichester
Cohen AP (2002) Epilogue. In: Amit V (ed) Realizing community. Concepts, social relationships and sentiments. Routledge, London/New York, pp 165–170
Cooley FL (1969) Village government in the Central Moluccas. Indonesia 7:138–163
Cordell K, Wolff S (2011) The study of ethnic conflict. An introduction. In: Cordell K, Wolff S (eds) Routledge handbook of ethnic conflict. Routledge, New York, pp 1–12
Donais T, Knorr AC (2013) Peacebuilding from below vs. the liberal peace: the case of Haiti. Can J Dev Stud/Revue canadienne d'études du développement 34(1):54–69
Eriksen TH (2010) Ethnicity and nationalism: anthropological perspectives, 3rd edn. Pluto Press, London/East Haven
Finkenbusch P (2016) 'Post-liberal' peacebuilding and the crisis of international authority. Peacebuilding 1–15
Finlay A (2015) Liberal intervention, anthropology and the ethnicity machine. Peacebuilding 3(3):224–237
Galtung J (1969) Violence, peace, and peace research. J Peace Res 6(1):167–191
Gupta A, Ferguson J (1992) Beyond "Culture": space, identity, and the politics of difference. Cult Anthropol 7(1):6–23
Hall S (1994) Cultural identity and diaspora. In: Williams P, Chrisman L (eds) Colonial discourse and post-colonial theory. Columbia University Press, New York, pp 392–403
Hohe T, Remijsen B (2003) Peacemaker for religious conflicts? The value of pela relationships in Ambon. In: Ramstedt M (ed) Hinduism in modern Indonesia: Hindu Dharma Indonesia between local, national, and global interests. Routledge, London, pp 126–143
Kaartinen T (2014) Perceptions of justice in the making: rescaling of customary law in post-Suharto Maluku, Indonesia. Asia Pac J Anthropol 15(4):319–338
Lederach JP (1997) Building peace: sustainable reconciliation in divided societies. United States Institute of Peace Press, Washington, DC
Mac Ginty R (2015) Where is the local? Critical localism and peacebuilding. Third World Q 36(5):840–856
Mac Ginty R, Richmond OP (2013) The local turn in peace building: a critical agenda for peace. Third World Q 43(5):763–783
McEvoy K, McGregor L (2008) Transitional justice from below: an agenda for research, policy and praxis. In: McEvoy K, McGregor L (eds) Transitional justice from below: grassroots activism and the struggle for change. Hart, Oxford/Portland, pp 1–13
Meier B (2011) *Mato oput* – Karriere eines Rituals zur sozialen Rekonstruktion in Norduganda. In: Buckley-Zistel S, Kater T (eds) Nach Krieg, Gewalt und Repression: Vom schwierigen Umgang mit der Vergangenheit. NOMOS, Baden-Baden, pp 185–203
Melucci A (1995) The process of collective identity. In: Johnston H, Klandermans B (eds) Social movements and culture. Social movements, protest, and contention 4. University of Minnesota Press, Minneapolis, pp 41–63

Millar G (ed) (2018) Ethnographic peace research: approaches and tensions. Palgrave Macmillan, London

Moore SF (1986) Social facts & fabrications: customary law on Kilimanjaro, 1880–1980. Cambridge University Press, Cambridge, UK

Müller-Krüger T (1968) Der Protestantismus in Indonesien. Geschichte und Gestalt. Evangelische Verlagswerk GmbH, Stuttgart

Ohorella MG (1999) Part 1: Budaya Pela dan Gandong: Suatu Sistem Nilai untuk Hidup Berkasihkasihan. Part 2: Modifikasi Bentuk – Isi – Fungsi Lembaga Pela dan Gandong Menuju Abad Modern. Tulehu, Ambon. YP2 MARHAN MALTENG

Pariela TD, Soumokil T (2003) Konflik dan Dampaknya Serta Upaya-upaya Rekonsiliasi. [Penelitian Kerusuhan, Laporan Akhir, Universitas Pattimura, Ambon]

Platenkamp JDM (2001). Intercultural conflicts in Indonesia. Paper presented at the Symposium on "Integrating Others: The Appropriation of Modernity". Institut für Ethnologie, Westfälische Wilhelms-Universität Münster, 21–23 November 2001

Popper K (1971) The open society and its enemies (originally published in 1943). Princeton University Press, Princeton

Rapport N (2002) Post-cultural anthropology. The ironization of values in a world of movement. In: Amit V (ed) Realizing community. Concepts, social relationships and sentiments. Routledge, London/New York, pp 146–164

Ratuva S (2003) Re-inventing the cultural wheel: Re-conceptualizing restorative justice and peace building in ethnically divided Fiji. In: Dinnen S (ed) A kind of mending: restorative justice in the Pacific Islands. Pandanus Books, Canberra, pp 149–163

Richmond OP (2010) A genealogy of peace and conflict theory. In: Richmond OP (ed) Palgrave advances in peacebuilding. Critical developments and approaches. Palgrave Macmillan, Hampshire/New York, pp 14–38

Richmond OP (2018a) Peace and the formation of political order. Int Peacekeeping 1–26. https://doi.org/10.1080/13533312.2018.1511374

Richmond OP (2018b) Rescuing peacebuilding? Anthropology and peace formation. Glob Soc 32(2):221–239

Rigby A (2001) Justice and reconciliation: after the violence. Lynne Rienner Publishers, Boulder

Ross MH (2004) Ritual and the politics of reconciliation. In: Bar-Siman-Tov Y (ed) From conflict resolution to reconciliation. Oxford University Press, Oxford, pp 197–223

Tim Peneliti Pusat Kajian Konstitusi (2005–2010) Laporan Penelitian Sistem Pemerintahan Adat di Kabupaten Maluku Tenggara. Ambon. Fakultas Hukum Universitas Pattimura

Titahelu RZ (2005) Hukum Adat Maluku Dalam Konteks Pluralisme Hukum: Implikasi Terhadap Manajemen Sumber Daya Alam Maluku (Pidato Pengukuhan, 13 Agustus 2005). Fakultas Hukum Universitas Pattimura, Ambon

Turner V (1967) The forest of symbols: aspects of Ndembu ritual. Cornell University Press, Ithaca

UNIDO & ILO (2011) Maluku Pelagandong Project. http://www.ilo.org/jakarta/whatwedo/publications/WCMS_318403/lang%2D%2Den/index.htm. 28.11.2016

von Benda-Beckmann F, von Benda-Beckmann K (1988) Adat and religion in Minangkabau and Ambon. In: Claessen HJM, Moyer DS (eds) Time past, time present, time future. Perspectives on Indonesian culture. Verhandelingen van het Koninklijk Instituut voor Taal-, Land- en Volkenkunde, vol 131. KITLV Press, Leiden, pp 195–212

Waldorf L (2010) "Like Jews waiting for Jesus": posthumous justice in post-genocide Rwanda. In: Shaw R, Waldorf L (eds) Localizing transitional justice: interventions and priorities after mass violence. Stanford University Press, Stanford, pp 183–202

Wanis-St. John A (2013) Indigenous peacebuilding. In: Mac Ginty R (ed) Routledge handbook of peacebuilding. Routledge, London/New York, pp 360–374

Weber M (1976) Wirtschaft und Gesellschaft: Grundriß der verstehenden Soziologie. Mohr, Tübingen. Originally published in 1921, 5., rev. edn

Cultural Identity and Textbooks in Japan: Japanese Ethnic and Cultural Nationalism in Middle-School History Textbooks

75

Ryota Nishino

Contents

Introduction	1466
The Hegemony of Monotony: The Power of Curricula and Headings in Textbooks	1468
How "Japanese" Were the Jōmon People? Group 1 Textbooks	1470
Group 2 Textbooks	1473
Conclusion	1478
References	1479

Abstract

This chapter analyzes the descriptions of antiquity in middle-school (*Chūgakkō*) Japanese History textbooks to probe the nature of popular perceptions amongst the Japanese: the Japanese are biologically and culturally homogenous. This perception persists despite the empirical and logical flaws of the claim of homogeneity. A total of 20 textbooks, approved and published in two periods, between 1951 and 1993, and 2015–16, presume the Jōmon era (ca. 10,000–2400 BP) to be the foundational period of the Japanese race, culture, and state under the unquestioned premise of Japan as the overarching framework. The textbooks repeat the idea that racial and cultural hybridization during the Jōmon era led to a homogenous Japanese people. What varied was the intensity of the language that lauded the Jōmon era as the source of Japanese uniqueness and superiority. The celebration of Japanese homogeneity and uniqueness is a salient feature of *Nihonjin-ron*: the popular discourse on Japanese cultural identity. This chapter considers the textbook as a medium conveying *Nihonjin-ron* through the bureaucratic processes it has to fulfil before approval and the potential influence

---

R. Nishino (✉)
University of the South Pacific, Suva, Fiji

International Research Center for Japanese Studies (Nichibunken), Kyoto, Japan
e-mail: look4ryota@gmail.com; Nishino_r@usp.ac.fj

that the textbook version of history can have on students. The analysis here places textbooks on the spectrum of hard and soft *Nihonjin-ron*. While hard *Nihonjin-ron* openly celebrates Japanese uniqueness, soft *Nihonjin-ron* is subtle. This chapter demonstrates the most recent textbooks are polarized between soft and hard *Nihonjin-ron*. What remains in common, however, is that the textbooks discuss the Jōmon era without posing questions of what being Japanese means.

Keywords

History textbooks · Japan · *Nihonjin-ron* · The Jōmon period · Cultural nationalism

Introduction

Japanese History textbooks have generated a great deal of heated debate over their descriptions of the Asia-Pacific War, or lack thereof, as a manifestation of Japan's nationalism. The controversy overshadows another significant theme that can arouse nationalistic sentiments amongst the Japanese. This chapter focuses on the Jōmon period (ca. 10,000–2400 BP), the period that both primary and middle-school History textbooks feature early in the volumes and presents as the beginning of Japanese history. The Japanese cultural nationalists even claim the period as the cradle of the Japanese people, culture, tradition, and state that accord Japan its unique characteristics in the world. This chapter analyzes the descriptions of the Jōmon period in a total of 20 middle-school History textbooks approved for use after 1951 against the popular discourse of *Nihonjin-ron* (also known as *Nihon shakairon, Nihon bunkaron*, and *Nihonron*). The proponents of *Nihonjin-ron* claim that Japan's inherent uniqueness in the world rests on its cultural and racial homogeneity. This essentialist claim overlooks the ethnic minorities, who make up approximately 5% of the population today (ca. 126 million) and Japan's interactions with the outside world (Befu 2009: 25–27; Sugimoto 2003: 4).

This chapter radically revises the author's previously published article as a result of incorporating an analysis of eight textbooks in current use (Nishino 2010). It argues that the textbooks articulate a mixture of hard and soft *Nihonjin-ron* with constant and varying features and messages that inform their implications. Under scrutiny are the subject headings and the descriptions of the Jōmon-era people and their culture. While the textbooks present empirical historical and archaeological information, they show more significant variation in the use of emotive language to stress the exceptional quality of the Jōmon era. This analysis plots the textbooks on a spectrum of hard and soft *Nihonjin-ron*. On the hard side are the explicit claims of Japan's uniqueness and superiority, purporting to persuade students to identify antiquity as the root of Japanese identity. By contrast, soft *Nihonjin-ron* articulates the primordial sentiment that identifies the Jōmon era as the bedrock of Japanese culture without excessive emotive language.

One of many claims that *Nihonjin-ron* makes is that the Jōmon era was the cradle of Japanese culture and the *minzoku* (the people or *volk*). This claim stands on several weak empirical and logical bases. Archaeologists agree that the biological makeup of the Japanese people derives mostly from the Korean and Chinese migrants of the Yayoi era (BC fifth to AD third centuries) who outnumbered the Jōmon-era inhabitants (Hudson 1999: 60–61). Befu reminds us that even the critics of *Nihonjin-ron* fail to mention the significance of Chinese culture, which came to Japan through China and Korea from fourth century AD. The Chinese culture shaped many aspects of Japanese culture and customs such as political structure, spirituality, and the writing system. Moreover, *Nihonjin-ron* proponents fail to note the impact of the Meiji Restoration (1868), which turned Japan into a nation-state under a Western-modelled centralized government. The unification of "the Japanese territory" accompanied the standardization of various regional variations in architecture, diet, weddings, funerals, clothing, and language (Befu 2009: 26–72). The historian Amino Yoshihiko maintains that the ignorance of diversity, and of the processes toward unification can mislead many into believing in the "in the beginning we the Japanese" primordial claims: the Japanese have always been a singular ethnic group and the Japanese state began from time immemorial (1992: 3).

Determining when the Japanese polity was formed is a matter of conjecture and ideology. The mythological explanation propagates the mythological, not archaeological or biological, origins of the Japanese people, culture, land, and state. It holds that the Japanese territory and the state are the products of divine provenance; the reigning Emperor is the direct descendant of the Sun Goddess Amaterasu. This mythological explanation became the fodder of wartime ultranationalism and nationalist education, particularly in History. Only in the postwar era could school children learn the evolutionist origins. A secular yet ancient persuasion claims that the seventh century CE was when the first centralized state began calling itself *Nihon*, although the territory was far smaller than today's. The modernists would argue for the Meiji Restoration of 1868. Nonetheless, part of the longevity of *Nihonjin-ron* might lie in the flexibility of the word *Nihon*. As John Lie notes (1998: 115–116), *Nihon* can mean the Japanese people, territory, state, or all at once; it comes with an implicit expectation that the receiver of the information understands and accepts the context and the meaning of the referent. Investigating the descriptions of the Jōmon era in the History textbooks can illuminate the commonality with the logic of *Nihonjin-ron*. It helps us to understand how the textbooks can prepare students to be receptive to ethnocentric claims of Japanese uniqueness, both inside and outside the classroom.

This analysis divides the 20 textbooks into two groups. Group 1 comprises 11 textbooks approved for use between 1951 and 1993. This period roughly coincides with the mostly single-party rule under the Liberal Democratic Party (the LDP) that spanned from 1955 to 1993. Group 2 comprises eight textbooks approved in 2015 and published in 2016 for current use. By 2015, Prime Minister Abe Shinzō of the LDP (2006–2007 and 2012 to date) had introduced educational reforms that emphasized the cultivation of patriotism from the teaching of cultural heritage and tradition. Two Group 2 textbooks by Jiyūsha and Ikuhōsha grew out of an internal schism in Atarashii Rekishi o Tsukurukai (hereafter Tsukurukai). Hence, the analysis uses the Tsukurukai textbook, approved in 2001, to compare how much the Jiyūsha and the

Ikuhōsha textbooks carry the ethos of the 2001 Tsukurukai textbook. The year 2015 saw the publication of a dissenting textbook by the publisher Manabisha. This textbook rejects the teleological narrative of the Japanese nation.

An awareness of the textbook certification and adoption processes should provide an indication of the authority that the textbook has in the classroom, even though the students might not enjoy History classes and could forget the content. In Japan, middle-school History compulsory. The textbook might still occupy a prominent position in the mind-sets of students' understanding of history. In Japan, private publishers commission teams of authors, whose numbers vary from 8 to 50, and submit manuscripts to the Ministry of Education (Monbushō, hereafter MoE, now known as Mombu kagakushō; in English, the Ministry of Education, Culture, Sports, Science and Technology, MEXT). The MoE evaluates the manuscripts against the curriculum and the ministerial regulations concerning the content, interpretation, organization, pedagogy, and formatting of the textbook. These regulations affect, among other things, the number of pages that an average textbook spends on each topic. After approval, regional boards of education across Japan adopt a single textbook per subject for classroom use out of several approved textbooks. These bureaucratic layers make the textbooks a highly contested and political medium. The numbers of pages average around 300 for the Group 1 textbooks and 200 for the larger-sized Group 2 textbooks. The section on the Jōmon era is about two pages long in the Group 1 and Group 2 textbooks. The length is no different from other eras and themes, including the much-debated Second World War in Europe and the Asia-Pacific region. The limited space increases the contestation over every word, sentence, and visual aid on the pages (Dierkes 2010; Nishino 2011).

The Hegemony of Monotony: The Power of Curricula and Headings in Textbooks

The headings of the sections on antiquity can give us an indication of the hard and soft *Nihonjin-ron* in the textbooks. Both Group 1 and Group 2 textbooks associate the Jōmon era with the dawn of the Japanese people, state, and culture. The headings in both groups repeat the word Japan in such examples as "Ancient Japan" (Inoue 1965: 14; Aoki 1984: 22. All translation from Japanese to English is by the author), "The Beginning of Japan" (Takeuchi 1975: 16), and "Daybreak for Japan" (Kasahara 1975: 22). Subheadings such as "The Land and the *Volk* of Japan" (Kawata 1990: 13; Kawata 1993: 14) and "When Elephants Lived in Japan" (Inoue 1965: 14; Aoki 1984: 22) validate the "in the beginning we the Japanese" linear and teleological narrative as Amino lamented (1992: 3). The Group 2 textbooks continue the trend. Two textbooks feature an identical heading, namely, "Japan until antiquity" (Sakagami 2016: 20; Fujii 2016: 26). Other Group 2 textbooks situate the content in the regional context. The textbooks use headings such as "The birth of the Japanese archipelago and the exchange with the content" (Sakagami 2016: 32), "The Dawn of the Japanese archipelago" (Fukuya 2016: 24), "Japan until the antiquity," and "The Roots of the Japanese: Where did the ancestors of us Japanese come from? How did they live?" (Mitani 2016: 26). These headings in both the Group 1 and Group 2 textbooks do not carry the emotive language of hard *Nihonjin-ron* but, rather, verge on soft *Nihonjin-ron*. This serves the function of packaging the Jōmon era within the singular framework of Japan (Table 1).

Near uniformity in headings are not coincidental; they reveal the extent of bureaucratic control that binds the textbooks to the curriculum (Dierkes 2010: 135–144; Nishino 2008). Successive curricula, to which the textbooks have to comply, name the prehistory section as follows:

Given the tight alignment between the headings in the curricula and the textbooks, the presentation of Japan as the primary category seems to be nonnegotiable. However, the headings in the current textbooks could suggest a level of tension between hard *Nihonjin-ron* and an attempt to disengage from *Nihonjin-ron*. Hard *Nihonjin-ron* manifests when one compares textbooks by two publishers, Jiyūsha and Ikuhōsha (both offshoots of Tsukurukai), against one from another publisher,

Table 1 Curricula content unit headings and subheadings

Year curriculum	1947	1951	1955	1958	1969
Headings and subheadings in the curriculum. Explanations in italics.	*No specific mention of ancient history. History was part of integrated social studies.*	*Curriculum emphasizes that these are merely suggestions to teach as "units"* Unit 1: How did the people who left stone implements and middens sustain their livelihood? Unit 2: Under what societal circumstances were cities such as Nara and Kyoto constructed? 第1単元 石器や貝塚を残した人々は，どのようにして，生活を切り開いていったか 第2単元 奈良や京都のような都は，どのような世の中で作られたか	Human culture and prehistory 人類文化の始原時代	*From this year onward, the curriculum documents were no longer "suggested plans." The curricula became legally binding.* The origin of civilization The beginning of the human race The dawn of world civilization The primitive Japanese society 文明のおこり 人類のはじめ 世界の文明のあけぼの 日本の原始社会	The forming of prehistoric Japan and Asia The land and *Minzoku* of Japan 古代日本の形成とアジア 日本の国土と民族

(*continued*)

Table 1 (continued)

Year curriculum	1977	1989	1998	2005	2008
Headings and subheadings in the curriculum	The forming of prehistoric Japan and Asia The land and *Minzoku* of Japan 古代日本の形成とアジア 日本の国土と民族	The origin of civilization and Japan The beginning of life for the Japanese 文明の起こりと日本 日本人の生活の始まり	The course of history and regional history Japan until ancient times 歴史の流れと地域の歴史 古代までの日本	The course of history and regional history Japan until ancient times 歴史の流れと地域の歴史 古代までの日本	How to approach history Japan until ancient times 歴史のとらえ方 古代までの日本

Sources: MoE, *Gakushū shidō yōryō*. A list of curriculum documents from 1947 to 2008 is available on the website of the National Institute of Educational Research, Tokyo. http://www.nier.go.jp/guideline/, translation by the author.

namely, Manabisha. The Jiyūsha textbook uses the subheadings "Where did the Japanese come from?" and "The bounty of nature and the Jōmon culture" (Sugihara 2016: 26, 30). Ikuhōsha follows suit: "The Dawn of Japan and world civilization" and "The Jōmon culture and the abundant nature" (Itō 2016: 18, 20). Manabisha frames antiquity as "The beginning of civilization and the Japanese archipelago" and "Living with animals: chasing elephants at lakes" (Yasui 2016: 10, 24). While Japan is a prominent category in the Jiyūsha and Ikuhōsha textbooks, Manabisha foreshadows the global and regional contexts and avoids conflating prehistory as Japanese history.

It is worth noting that the MoE refused to approve the draft copies of the Jiyūsha and Manabisha textbooks. The MoE judged the Jiyūsha textbook to contain sentences with inaccurate details and declarative tones that could cause misunderstandings to occur for students (MoE 2015, no. 26–68). The MoE failed the Manabisha textbook, among other things, for placing less emphasis on Japan and for giving undue emphasis to world history when presenting Japanese history (MoE 2015). From these judgements, the MoE seems to prefer the textbooks to strike a balance between hard and soft *Nihonjin-ron*. Further analysis of the contents might show the fluctuations of hard and soft *Nihonjin-ron* that occur as a result of the certification process.

How "Japanese" Were the Jōmon People? Group 1 Textbooks

Within Group 1, the textbooks published between 1951 and 1957 typically identify the proto-Japanese as the original inhabitants who lived on the Japanese archipelago 5000–6000 years ago. A 1951 textbook by Gakkō Tosho explains that the continental migration formed the basis of the ethnic Japanese people: "They arrived over many months and years, and many times. While they lived on this archipelago, they mixed blood and created the common language and customs. This [mixing] marked the birth of the Japanese *volk"* (Sakamoto and Ienaga 1951: 10). Later, the textbook discusses the origins of the continental migrants: "Although it is uncertain where overseas people came from, it is thought that they were both northern and southern Asian people" (ibid.: 10). The narrative breaks away from the mythological explanation of wartime and endorses the hybridization theory: the contemporaneous academic consensus on the origins of the Japanese. It states that the original inhabitants, "the proto-Japanese," absorbed the subsequent migrants from the north and the south and gradually evolved into the modern Japanese people (Hudson 1999: 45–46).

Despite introducing the hybridization theory, the text is not immune to the ideological implications of conveying soft *Nihonjin-ron* on three accounts. Firstly, the textbook uses Japan without elucidating what this means. A mere mention of "this archipelago" rests on the common assumption of it being Japanese (Sakamoto and Ienaga 1951: 10). Secondly, the textbook fails to distinguish the mythological origins and history. This flaw might hark back to the mythological history of the prewar and wartime textbooks. Thirdly, insufficient causes of migration make Japan seem to be a natural destination for the migrant, thus making Japan look like a desirable center. These oversights implicitly position Japan in the center of history and the textbook in the soft *Nihonjin-ron* spectrum (ibid.: 10).

Another textbook published in 1951 by Nihon Shoseki provides a blatant example of the biological explanation not found in other textbooks: "Today there is a race in the hinterland of Siberia who has downward-slanting eyes and exudes much body odor. The constitution of those people had many similarities to those of the ancient Japanese" (Kodama 1951: 4). This textbook employs the idioms of geographical positioning and pseudo-biology to attenuate the hard *Nihonjin-ron* of open ethnocentrism and racism. Placing Siberia as the hinterland brings Japan to the center and marginalizes the Siberians. The authors note the shape of the eye and the body odor as the physical features that the Siberians and the ancient Japanese shared, thus distinguishing contemporary Japanese people as being more evolved. This textual representation exemplifies what anthropologist Johannes Fabian calls the denial of coevalness, which consigns the other to another temporal realm (Fabian 1986: 31, 153–154). The last quoted sentence intimates the gradual evolution of the Japanese and distinguishes ancient Japanese people from the contemporary Japanese people. The reference to body odor is a pseudoscientific cloak that not only denigrates the Siberians but also places them behind the Japanese on a queue of perceived evolutionary progress.

Subsequent Group 1 textbooks convey the hybridization theory with a mixture of soft and hard *Nihonjin-ron*. Ōsaka Shoseki's 1965 textbook represents this ambiguous mix. It repeats the hybridization thesis of migrants from Asia and the southern seas and states:

> It is thought that the Japanese masses with the common language and culture came into being. ... Therefore, it seems that the Japanese have lived on this national territory since about 10,000 years ago, and improved the standards of living gradually. (Inoue 1965: 28)

On the one hand, the author's use of "it seems" and "it is thought" indicates caution against making definitive judgements about the origins of the Japanese people, languages, and customs. This hedging undermines the populist appeal of *Nihonjin-ron*, which presents scientific and empirical evidence in scholarly terms. Nevertheless, the phrase "on this national territory" presents a teleological history and bolsters the primordial "in the beginning us Japanese" mind-set that conflates two notions of Japan: the Japanese archipelago and the Japanese state. This use flattens the biological, political, and cultural diversity across Japan and credits the singularity of people for the attainment of improved standards of living.

The 1969 edition of Nihon Shoseki's textbook narrates: "Just like other peoples around the world, our Japanese ancestors progressed from prehistoric to civilized living. But the way to progress had Japanese characteristics" (Abe 1969: 29). The text combines the elements of hard and soft *Nihonjin-ron*. It celebrates the Japanese progress toward "civilized living," which is in sync with the universal path that "other peoples" have trodden. Nevertheless, the text credits "the Japanese characteristics." This ambiguous message seems to resonate with the *zeitgeist* of the 1960s. As the historical sociologist Oguma Eiji (2002) demonstrates, the postwar intelligentsia asserted a new vision of the Japanese people as they gained confidence through the economic recovery. They maintained that the Japanese were a homogeneous *volk* (*tan'itsu minzoku*) who lived within an island nation (*shimaguni*) with distinct ethnic and cultural characteristics from East Asia and beyond. This vision contrasts with the prewar vision of Japanese imperialism, which states that the Japanese people share blood ties with Asian peoples and that Japan accommodates multiple races (Oguma 2002). The textbooks of the 1960s appear to echo the desire to place Japan in the world while reminding the reader to take pride in Japanese identity.

Textbooks from the mid-1980s show a new trend. The reference to biological hybridization disappeared, while the language and culture remained. Shimizu Shoin's textbook of 1987 states that:

> The connection between the people [of the Palaeolithic era, preceding the Jōmon era] and today's Japanese is not certain. It is thought that today's Japanese were created through the common language and customs with immigrants from the continent and the southern regions. (Mori 1987: 21)

Of all the textbooks surveyed, this textbook makes a rare admission: the similarity between the ancient and the contemporary Japanese people might not be as convincing as once believed. This admission undermines the biological connection, but the text still preserves the cultural and linguistic connection. Another textbook published in 1993 follows suit:

There are things amongst the Japanese myths and Japanese words that seem to have come from the Eurasian continent and the Pacific islands such as the Polynesian islands. These help us understand that the Japanese culture was created through interaction with the world at large. (Sasayama 1993: 25)

Unlike its contemporary counterparts, this textbook signals a new variant of *Nihonjin-ron* that places Japan on the world map. The mention of Eurasia and Polynesia might be stretching the historical license too far. Nonetheless, the authors extend the cultural gene pool of the Japanese people to reposition Japan in the international context. In the mid-1980s and the early 1990s, the "bubble economy" enabled many Japanese people to reap the cultural and material benefits of internationalization (Lie 1998: 23 and 30–31). These textbooks seem to laud the ability to indigenize languages and culture into "our own." This expression is a subtle celebration of Japanese ingenuity and calls to mind a more blatant statement made by Prime Minister Nakasone Yasuhiro. In 1986, he made a speech that drew international criticism. He stated that the Japanese had higher educational attainment than the multiethnic Americans, because the blacks and the Hispanics performed poorly than the others (Lie 1998: 173). Although not as blatant as Nakasone's hard *Nihonjin-ron*, the textbook shares the kernel of the message: ethnic and cultural homogeneity endows the Japanese people with a unique and superior quality. However, not all the textbooks agreed. A contemporary textbook by Tokyo Shoseki, published in 1990, continues to represent the *Nihonjin-ron* of the previous decades:

The Jōmon culture had a unique characteristic compared to the cultures in various parts of the world. Also, it is believed that the people of this era were the prototype of the Japanese. Later, they mixed with the people who emigrated from the continent. It is thought that the Japanese, possessing the common language and culture, were formed over an extended period. (Kawata 1990: 15)

While using the keyword of hard *Nihonjin-ron*, namely, "unique," the rest of the text conveys the bare facts of the hybridization without an obviously celebratory tone. Phrases such as "it is believed" and "it is thought" hedge against making a hasty pseudoscientific claim; they balance the claim of uniqueness. This textbook seems to aim to expose the reader to the fundamentals of the *Nihonjin-ron* discourse without forcing them onto the reader. The changing contours in Group 1 textbooks show the Jōmon period as the foundational era of Japanese race and culture. By the 1990s, however, declarative statements on racial origins and hybridization receded, which brought the cultural argument concerning hybridization toward homogeneity to the fore.

Group 2 Textbooks

The most striking features about the Group 2 textbooks, albeit superficial, are the changes to the page size (larger), the page numbers (fewer), and the visual aids (more picures and photosgraphs in color). The Group 2 textbooks feature more colorful illustrations and photographs than those in Group 1. Another change is the increase in additional readings on Japanese ancient culture and tradition. The Group 1 textbooks featured these additional features, but the Group 2 counterparts deliver a direct and graphic celebration of Japanese culture and tradition. The best-selling textbook by Tokyo Shoseki (Table 2) features a two-page spread on the inside front and back covers, entitled "National Treasure" and "Important Items of Cultural Heritage" from the Jōmon period to the Meiji period. These illustrative materials present Japanese culture as the result of a linear progression from antiquity to the present and cultivate the reductive primordial approach to the Jōmon era which Amino found problematic (1992: 3).

Another significant development in the Group 2 textbooks is the higher concentration of the market share by three publishers and the emergence of the neo-nationalist voice. The combined share of the "big three" increased to 83% in 2016, from 81.5% in 2015, and the textbook by Ikuhōsha, a successor of the Tsukurukai, jumped from 3.9% to 6.3% in the same period: a significant growth considering that the market share of the first Tsukurukai History textbook of 2001 was merely 0.039%. New in 2016 was the textbook by Manabisha, which aims to provide a

Table 2 The adoption of middle-school History textbooks, 2016

Rank in 2016	Publisher	Copies adopted, 2016	Market share %, 2016	Copies adopted, 2015	Rank in 2015	Market share %, 2015	Fluctuation
1	東京書籍 Tokyo Shoseki	607,856	51.0	630,460	1	52.9	−22,604
2	帝国書院 Teikoku Shoin	213,077	17.9	168,096	3	14.1	+44,981
3	教育出版 Kyōiku Shuppan	168,178	14.1	172,776	2	14.5	−4598
4	日本文教 Nihon Bunkyō Shuppan	111,513	9.4	149,364	4	12.5	−37,851
5	育鵬社 Ikuhōsha	75,238	6.3	46,778	5	3.9	−28,460
6	清水書院 Shimizu Shoin	9267	0.8	23,824	6	2.0	−14,557
7	学び舎 Manabisha	5704	0.5	0	–	0	+5704
8	自由社 Jiyūsha	567	0.0	879	7	0.1	−312
	Totals	1,191,400	100	1,192,177		100	−777

Source: Anon. *Naigai Kyōiku*, no. 6463, 8 Dec. 2015, p. 6. (Data from MoE)

student-centered and critical pedagogy. Its market share reached a modest 0.5% (Table 2).

Along with Tokyo Shoseki, the fourth best-selling textbook by Nihon Bunkyō Shuppan has an additional two-page feature: "Searching the roots of the Japanese cuisine: the beginning of *washoku* [Japanese cuisine]" (Fujii 2016: 30). It heralds the UNESCO registering the Japanese cuisine as a world intangible heritage in 2013, and introduces the reader to the cuisines of the Jōmon and the Yayoi eras. The text lists the four features of Japanese cuisine:

1. A variety of fresh food items;
2. The rice as the staple. Has an excellent balance of nutrition;
3. Express the beauty of nature and the change of season; and
4. A close association between feasts and annual events (ibid.: 30).

The subsequent text then explains the change of diet in antiquity, and magnifies the role that rice cultivation has played on the diet, while marginalizing the contributions of other influences from East Asia and the West, and other ingredients such as soybeans (ibid.: 31). The reading invokes a well-known *Nihonjin-ron* celebration of rice as the essential staple in the Japanese people's diet and, indeed, in an identity whose origin goes back to antiquity. This view can endorse the supporting of the state-centric historiography as the state finances depended on rice for much of the pre-modern period in Japan. It contradicts the notion that many regions had alternative grains as the staple and the view that the nation-wide acceptance of rice only began in the nineteenth century (Lie 1998: 75).

The recent reforms in textbook regulations can, to some extent, explain the renewed emphasis on culture and tradition. Group 2 is the first cohort of textbooks that the MoE evaluated and approved under the newly revised regulations on textbook certification. In 2006, the government overhauled the Fundamental Law of Education (initially promulgated in 1947) that serves as the guiding principle of education. The revision curtailed academic freedom and introduced the concepts of "respect for tradition and culture" and "love for our nation and homeland" (MoE 2006). The History curriculum of 2008 states that the first aim of a History education is to "deepen the affection for our country's history and to nurture self-awareness as the nationals (*kokumin*)" (MoE 2008). A further reform on textbook screening by the MoE, introduced in 2014, mandates that textbooks impart a patriotic ethos and respect for tradition, alongside accurate historical information (MoE 2011). The postwar curricula have always regarded Japan as the central paradigm of the History curriculum, and have stated History should cultivate patriotism and respect for tradition. The recent reforms further pushed patriotism to the fore and tightened the alignment between the textbooks and the ministerial reforms.

In the main text, however, the Group 2 textbooks differ in the portrayal of the cultural homogeneity of the ancient era. The best-selling Tokyo Shoseki follows the orthodox narrative of the hybridization theory, starting with the formation of the

Japanese archipelago to the Jōmon-era's hunter-gatherers: "... The people of the Jōmon era and the people who moved from the continent mixed. Over many years, the people with common language and culture began to spread across the Japanese archipelago" (Sakagami 2016: 33). Compared with the publisher's 1990 edition, this edition stripped off its hard *Nihonjin-ron* tone. Its removal of the claims of uniqueness makes the narrative dry. The text refers to the people of the Japanese archipelago and the Jōmon era simply as "human beings" (ibid.: 32–33). However, the new emphasis on culture and tradition in the illustrations and additional readings supplement the dryness of the main text.

The second best seller, Teikoku Shoin follows suit. It tells us that the introduction of rice cultivation spread across Japan as the continental migrants and the Jōmon people "mixed gradually," which "shaped the subsequent Japanese culture" (Kuroda et al. 2016: 23). The third, fourth, and sixth best-selling textbooks by Kyōiku Shuppan, Nihon Bunkyō Shuppan, and Shimizu Shoin, respectively, lean toward soft *Nihonjin-ron*. The main texts of these three textbooks deliver plain descriptions without stressing the ancient people as the original source of present-day Japanese culture or customs. Instead, Kyōiku Shuppan and Shimizu Shoin acknowledge the parallel existence of the agriculturalists and the hunter-gatherers across the archipelago and challenge the assumption of uniformity of livelihood (Fukaya 2016: 24–25; Mitani 2016: 10–11). These Group 2 textbooks represent soft *Nihonjin-ron*, presenting the bare facts in a linear national narrative, without the emotive language of hard *Nihonjin-ron*.

What gives greater variation to the intensity of *Nihonjin-ron* in Group 2, both in the main text and in the additional features, is the emergence of hard *Nihonjin-ron*. Two publishers, Jiyūsha and Ikuhōsha, who originate from Tsukurukai, represent hard *Nihonjin-ron* in both the formal text and the additional features. The headings celebrate the inherent uniqueness and singularity of Japan. Both textbooks open a chapter with the identical heading "The bounty of nature and the Jōmon period" (Itō 2016: 20; Sugihara 2016: 30). The Ikuhōsha textbook heralds the earthenware of the Jōmon era as "one of the oldest in the world" (Itō 2016: 20). We also learn that the people, although not described as "the Japanese people," have lived in nature. In this abundance, the people did not start mass-scale agricultural processes or herding:

> During the Jōmon era that spanned over 10,000 years, the people lived in harmony with abundant nature. This period made the foundation for the subsequent Japanese culture. Also, the Jōmon-era people and the people from the continent mixed, who shaped the Japanese sharing a common language and culture. (ibid.: 21)

The presentation of a "bountiful Japan" disregards the regional varieties and presents the whole of Japan as equally enjoying the riches of the land. The praise for Japan's natural abundance can distort the student vision, as there were other parts of the world around the same era that sustained people due to their abundant nature. The other "neo-nationalist" textbook from Jiyūsha concludes that in the Jōmon period:

People thanked the bounty of nature and prayed for the upbringing of children and grandchildren by dedicating clay dolls in the shape of women and lacquer-painted accessories. It is said that peace and stability prevailed in society, and the bases for the modest character of the Japanese and Japanese culture were nurtured in this period. (ibid.: 31)

Immediately following this conclusion is a two-page additional reading entitled "The Culture of Harmony: Jōmon" (ibid.: 32–33), which details the Sannaimaru ruin in Aomori as a case study of the "prosperous Jōmon lifestyle" (ibid.: 33). Archaeological findings attest to a plentiful food supply and regular spiritual worship. The absence of weapons leads the authors to assert that the people maintained "a harmonious society in which people helped each other. . . . The Jōmon people, our ancestors, built a society of moderation which we can call 'a civilization of harmony'" (ibid.: 33). Ikuhōsha and Jiyūsha turn the Jōmon era and its *zeitgeist* into a morality lesson. What remains equally problematic is the implicit prejudice toward subsequent continental migrants from China and Korea that lies behind this hard articulation of *Nihonjin-ron*. Readers might interpret this text as foregrounding the subsequent continental migrants as unwelcome intruders. Such a presentation accentuates ethnocentrism and downplays the regional context (Kawase 2006: 26).

Similar to other textbooks, the Tsukurukai textbook of 2001 describes the geographical setting as "Japan" and "the Japanese archipelago" without a clear definition. To its credit, it refers to the ancient population not as "the Japanese" but in more neutral terms such as "people" (*hitobito*) and "the inhabitants of the Japanese archipelago" (*Nihon rettō no jūmin*) (Nishio 2002: 23–24). Nonetheless, its hard *Nihonjin-ron* emerges from opinions on the natural environment of Japan:

Especially East Japan was blessed with plentiful nuts, berries and yams, and, in addition, river fish such as salmon and trout; the bounty of the sea included tuna, red sea bream, sea bass, and various shellfish; and the bounty of the mountain had the game like boars, deer, and pheasants. The inhabitants of the Japanese archipelago were comparatively blessed with food. Therefore, there was no need to begin mass-scale agriculture urgently. (ibid.: 23)

It continues to say:

Four great [world] civilizations were sustained by agriculture and stock-farming. Each developed in areas surrounded by desert and large rivers. On the other hand, on the Japanese archipelago, a way of living surrounded by forests and clean water continued for over 10,000 years. (ibid.: 24)

Where the above extract becomes problematic is the latent ethnocentrism and geographical isolationism in support of hard *Nihonjin-ron*. In his critique of the textbook, Kawase Kenichi accepts its empirical validity, but finds that the textbook presents the Japanese archipelago as the only place in the region with exceptional bounty. Kawase continues to explain that, during the late Ice Age, much of Europe and North America was still under ice and tundra; other parts of the world such as Africa also had a bounty of nature like Japan (Kawase 2006: 25). While this caveat applies to other textbooks, the Tsukurukai textbook amplifies the underhand claims of Japan's exceptionalism. The unqualified assessment of the Jōmon era, as the final sentence tells, resembles the pseudoscientific character of *Nihonjin-ron* for an impassioned presentation without adequate consideration of competing hypotheses.

Manabisha's textbook takes an original approach. The title of the first section, in which a chapter on the Jōmon era appears, is "The Beginning of Civilization and the Japanese Archipelago." Although the textbook uses the word "Japanese" possibly to obtain the MoE approval, it still pays greater attention to world civilizations, and places Japan as but one area (Yasui 2016: 10–31). In the chapter on the Jōmon era, the text relates the not-so-glorious facts of the rise and fall of the era:

> A scholar has calculated the total population across the Japanese archipelago exceeded 300,000. Later on, however, many villages perished due to excessive hunting and change in the climate. Population decreased drastically. Many died in their infancy. Very few bones of people over the age of 40 years can be excavated. Also found were bones hinting death by starvation and bones showing marks of prodigious fractures. (Yasui 2016: 27)

This textbook attests to the axiom of the "short, nasty, and brutish" lives of the ancient people. Japan was no exception. High infant mortality and short lifespans remind us that the standards of living were far from paradisiacal. Instead, this textbook relates the facts of people who perished from overhunting and from a change in climate. The absence of "Japan" in the text can potentially obscure the link between the ancient people and the contemporary Japanese; this undermines the hard *Nihonjin-ron* claim that the contemporary Japanese identity originates from the Jōmon era. The Group 1 and Group 2 textbooks generally replicate the linear narrative of Japan and the Japanese people, whose identity rests on the formula of "land = people = culture = polity" rooted in antiquity (Befu 2009: 21). The Manabisha textbook distances itself from the "us Japanese" *Nihonjin-ron* paradigm.

Conclusion

This chapter has analyzed the descriptions of the foundational era in 20 middle-school Japanese History textbooks approved for use in postwar Japan and has demonstrated the changing and stable features of *Nihonjin-ron*. A constant feature in both Groups is the durability of the teleological paradigms of the homogenous Japan and the Japanese people. The stability underlines the power of the curriculum and the certification processes. The variations in hard and soft *Nihonjin-ron* depend on both the confidence and anxiety surrounding the time of publication, as well as the scholarly consensus and the opinions of the intelligentsia.

The Group 1 textbooks show more uniformity than variations; they present the Jōmon era as the foundational period of the teleological narrative of the Japanese people. The textbooks agree that the hybridization of people during antiquity led to the subsequent homogeneity. The earlier textbooks state that the Jōmon people were the prototypes of the Japanese people, in the biological and cultural sense. The textbooks approved after the mid-1980s stress the cultural over the biological hybridization and homogeneity.

The Group 2 textbooks show more variations in hard and soft *Nihonjin-ron* even though they were published in the same year. These textbooks underscore the influence of the education reforms that worked their way into not only the descriptions but also the additional features outside the main text. Two neo-nationalist textbooks that grew out of the original Tsukurukai textbook of 2001 have continued to promote hard *Nihonjin-ron*. While the others amplify soft *Nihonjin-ron* in the main text, the additional features supplement the hard elements that the formal text lacks. The significant exception is the textbook by Manabisha, which distances itself from both hard and soft *Nihonjin-ron*.

The comparison between the textbooks published over the decades tells us that questions of Japanese identity, be they racial, cultural, political, or otherwise, are far from settled. It would seem that, depending on the textbook, the teacher and the students can come away with a firm and at times impassioned understanding of the Jōmon era as the foundation of present-day Japan. The less explicit or the more nuanced is the soft *Nihonjin-ron* that presents Japan as the overarching paradigm of history without distinguishing its meanings as a territory, a state, or a people. Such a presentation is problematic as it forestalls any meaningful and critical understanding of when and how the present-day Japanese state and territory were formed and to what extent we can claim the contemporary Japanese people have their biological and cultural roots in the Jōmon people. How far the ideology of *Nihonjin-ron* in those textbooks permeates to the individual mind-set of the students and teachers remains to be seen. Nonetheless, the linear history that the textbooks have presented over the decades is likely to make the students receptive to *Nihonjin-ron*.

References

Notes

All Japanese publishers are in Tokyo, unless otherwise stated.

The Ministry of Education Documents

Mombu kagakushō (2006) "Kyōiku kihon hō" [Fundamental law of education], Article 5. http://www.mext.go.jp/b_menu/houan/an/06042712/003.htm. Accessed 17 June 2018

Mombu kagakushō (2008) *Chūgakkō gakushūō yōryō* (Course of Studies: middle school), partially revised in 2010. https://www.nier.go.jp/guideline/h19j/index.htm. Accessed 16 Feb 2018

Mombu kagakushō (2011) "Gimu kyōiku shogakkō kyōkayō tosho kentei kijun" [Textbook screening standards for compulsory education sector], Ministerial notice, no. 33, 4 March 2011. Ratified on 17 Jan 2014. http://www.mext.go.jp/a_menu/shotou/kyoukasho/1260042.htm. Accessed 8 Mar 2018

Mombu kagakushō (2015) "Kentei shinsa fugōkaku to narubeki riyūsho", no 26–68, Heisei 26 nendo, kentei ikensho, April, 2015. http://www.mext.go.jp/a_menu/shotou/kyoukasho/kentei/1356423.htm. Accessed 8 Mar 2018

Group 1 Textbooks, 1951–1995

Under Group 1 are five periods, which coincide with the curricula in effect. The bibliography features the first authors for textbooks with more than three authors. The space permits listing only the textbooks quoted in the chapter. For a full list, see Nishino (2010 and 2011). The bibliography features the first authors.

Period 1: 1951–1957

Kodama K (1951) Chūgakusei no rekishi [History for middle-school students]. Nihon Shoseki
Sakamoto T, Ienaga S (1951) Chūgaku Nihon-shi [Middle-school Japanese History]. Gakkō Tosho

Period 2: 1958–1971

Abe Y (1969) Chūgaku shakai 2: rekishiteki bunya [Middle-school social studies 2: History]. Nihon Shoseki
Inoue C (1965) Chūgaku shakai: rekishiteki bunya [Middle-school social studies: History]. Osaka Shoseki, Osaka

Period 3: 1972–1980

Kasahara K (1975) Chūgakusei shakaika rekishiteki bunya [Middle-school social studies: History]. Gakkō Tosho
Takeuchi R (1975) Chūgaku shakai rekishi [Middle-school social studies: History]. Teikoku Shoin

Period 4: 1981–1989

Aoki K (1984) Nihon no ayumi to sekai (rekishi) [The footsteps of Japan and the world (History)]. Chūkyō Shuppan
Mori M (1987) Nihon no rekishi to sekai [History of Japan and the world]. Shimizu Shoin

Period 5: 1990–1993

Kawata T (1990) Atarashii shakai: Rekishiteki bunya [New social studies: History]. Tokyo Shoseki
Kawata T (1993) Atarashii shakai: Rekishiteki bunya [New social studies: History]. Tokyo Shoseki
Sasayama H (1993) Chūgakusei shakai rekishi [Middle-school social studies: History]. Kyōiku Shuppan

Group 2: Tsukurukai Textbook and Current History Textbooks

Fujii J (2016) Chūgaku shakai rekishi teki bunya [Middle-school social studies: History]. Nihon Bunkyō Shuppan, Osaka

Fukaya K (2016) Chuūgaku shakai rekishi: mirai o hiraku [Middle-school History: Pioneering the future]. Kyōiku Shuppan

Itō T (2016) Shinpan atarashii rekishi [A new History]. Ikuhōsha

Kuroda H (2016) Shakaika chūgakusei no rekishi: Nihon no ayumi to sekai no ugoki [Middle-school History: The footsteps of Japan and the movements in the world]. Teikoku Shoin

Mitani H (2016) Chūgaku rekishi: Nihon no rekishi to sekai [Middle school History: Japanese and world history]. Shimizu Shoin

Nishio K (2002) Shihanban atarashii rekishi kyōkasho [A new History textbook: A retail edition]. Fusōsha

Sakagami Y (2016) Shinpan atarashii shakai rekishi [New Social Studies: History]. Tokyo Shoseki

Sugihara S (2016) Shinpan atarashii rekishi kyōkasho [A revised new History textbook]. Jiyūsha

Yasui T (2016) Tomoni manabu ningen no rekishi [We study human History together]. Manabisha, Tachikawa

Secondary Sources

Amino Y (1992) Deconstructing Japan (trans: Gavan McCormack). East Asian Hist 3:121–142

Anon. '91 man satsu zō no 3455 man satsu' [A total of 34.55 million copies of textbooks, an increase of 910,000 copies], Naigai Kyōiku. no. 6463, 8 Dec 2015

Befu H (2009) Concepts of Japan, Japanese culture and the Japanese. In: Sugimoto Y (ed) The Cambridge companion to modern Japanese culture. Cambridge University Press, Cambridge, MA, pp 21–37

Dierkes J (2010) Postwar history education in Japan and the Germanys: guilty lessons. Routledge, Abingdon

Fabian J (1986) Time and the other: how anthropology makes its object. Columbia University Press, New York

Hudson M (1999) Ruins of identity: ethnogenesis in the Japanese islands. University of Hawai'i Press, Honolulu

Kawase K (2006) Tettei kenshō "Atarashii rekishi kyōkasho" dai ikkan kodai hen: Higashi ajia, kyōkai Iki, tennōsei, jyoseishi, shakaishi no shitenkara [A comprehensive survey of "Atarashii rekishi kyōkasho", vol. 1 ancient history: from prisms of East Asia, borders, the emperor system, women's history and social history]. Dōjidaisha, Tokyo

Lie J (1998) Multiethnic Japan. Harvard University Press, Cambridge, MA

Nishino R (2008) The political economy of the textbook in Japan: with particular focus on middle-school history textbooks, ca. 1945–1995. Int Schulbuchforschung (Int Textb Res) 30:487–514

Nishino R (2010) Narrative strategies regarding Japanese ethnic origins and cultural identities in Japanese middle-school history textbooks. J Educ Media, Mem Soc 2:97–112

Nishino R (2011) Changing histories: Japanese and South African textbooks in comparison (1945–1995). V&R Unipress, Göttingen

Oguma E (2002) A genealogy of 'Japanese' self-images (trans: Askew D). Trans Pacific Press, Melbourne

Sugimoto Y (2003) An introduction to Japanese society, 2nd edn. Cambridge University Press, Cambridge, MA

Asian Americans and the Affirmative Action Debate in the United States

76

Mitchell James Chang

Contents

Introduction	1484
Admissions Discrimination Charges	1485
Guarding White Privilege	1488
The Persistent Bond Between Whiteness and Privilege	1490
Pursuing Whiteness	1493
Discussion	1496
Conclusion	1497
References	1499

Abstract

The controversy over the discrimination of Asian American applicants in college admissions in the United States has returned with even higher stakes. Unlike the complaints filed in the 1980s, the current set also targets the elimination of race-conscious admissions practices that were implemented to increase enrollment of underrepresented students at elite institutions, including those from African American and Latino populations. The purpose of this chapter is to make sense of this recurring admissions controversy by applying a critical race analysis toward interpreting the sociohistorical roots that animate this controversy. The results of this analysis undermine the characterization of those institutions as color-blind engines of upward mobility and instead portray them as guardians of dispensing and protecting the privileges accompanying whiteness. Broader implications of those findings for achieving greater racial equity and justice are discussed.

M. J. Chang (✉)
University of California, Los Angeles, Los Angeles, CA, USA
e-mail: mjchang@gseis.ucla.edu

Keywords

Asian American · Race conscious admissions · Affirmative action · White privilege · Critical race · Selective admissions · White supremacy · Elitism · U.S. Office of Civil Rights

Introduction

In the United States, Asian Americans have "become the immigrant group that most embodies the American promise of success driven by will and resolve," declared cultural critic Lee Siegel (2012) writing for *The Wall Street Journal*. (I intentionally use the label *Asian Americans* as opposed to other racial or ethnic labels because I believe that this one is still meaningful. It emerged in the late 1960s to signal a pan-Asian solidarity that rejected old labels and made assertive claims to American belonging. The goal to achieve a new humanity and new humanism through empowered identities in the 1960s is still incomplete, however, and this struggle remains relevant today.) He noted that Asian Americans are now the country's best-educated, highest-earning, and fastest-growing racial group. With such "breathtaking success," he considered it peculiar that "Americans" don't share the fears once expressed by Tom Buchanan, the racist bully character in F. Scott Fitzgerald's *The Great Gatsby*, who worried that "the white race will be utterly submerged" if "we don't look out." Siegel speculated that perhaps "physiognomies" and "a deeply ingrained modesty" have "kept most Asian-American groups away from the public glare and thus out of the cross hairs of American bias and hatred." He questioned, however, how long "they will be able to resist attracting the furies of fear and envy."

If Siegel were a more astute observer of what he termed the "Rise of the Tiger Nation," he would have noticed that Asian Americans have indeed been recurrent targets of racial panic and their pursuit of the "American Dream" has not been a magic carpet ride. Curiously, Siegel pointed to one example of this racial panic, noting that "threatened elites at Ivy League schools like Harvard and Yale ... stand accused of discrimination against Asian-American students who, according to recent studies, must score higher than whites on standardized tests to win a golden ticket of admission." However, Siegel brushed this issue aside as merely a minor impediment that has not stood in the way of what he described as Asian Americans' "astounding success."

If this admissions problem for Asian Americans were merely a trivial issue that is nothing more than an insignificant footnote in an otherwise compelling model minority success narrative, this admissions problem would have been settled in the 1980s. During the early part of that decade, Asian American activists initiated and advanced claims of discrimination in undergraduate admissions against U.C., Berkeley, Brown, Harvard, Princeton, Stanford, and UCLA (Takagi 1992). Thirty years later, a similar set of complaints has been filed in a lawsuit but, this time, by a different set of even better organized coalitions who have added the elimination of race-conscious admissions to their agenda.

The purpose of this manuscript is to make sense of this persistent admissions controversy in the United States, which has pressed Asian Americans into the service of particular political agendas. To do this, I examine the link between race and political, economic, and social issues in contemporary United States to uncover deeper meaning underlying this admissions controversy. I first provide a brief backdrop of this controversy then draw from sociohistorical patterns of admissions and critical race theory to reinterpret the complex set of issues surrounding it, which serves to redefine the fundamental issues that contextualize this recurrent social problem.

Admissions Discrimination Charges

Asian American enrollment into those few select institutions of higher education that consistently rank on the very top of popular national rankings, or what I will generally refer to in this chapter as elite institutions (i.e., Harvard, Stanford, UCLA, Michigan, etc.), grew at an extraordinary pace, nearly tripling their proportion of the undergraduate enrollment between 1976 and 1985 (Karabel 2005). By the early 1980s, however, another peculiar trend was spotted. Although the number of Asian Americans applying to elite institutions had been rising every year, their admission rate at those campuses was actually dropping. Accordingly, complaints were filed, which resulted in formal investigations conducted by the Office of Civil Rights of the Department of Education (OCR) beginning in 1988. Dana Takagi (1992), whose book *The Retreat from Race* examined this controversy, pointed to three basic complaints filed during the 1980s. One was that Asian American applicants had lower admission rates than their white counterparts. Another was that enrollments of Asian Americans at those elite institutions had not risen in proportion to increases in the number of Asian American applicants. Third, university officials used illegal quotas and ceilings to limit Asian American enrollment.

In the Fall of 1990, OCR cleared Harvard of discrimination. Although OCR noted that Asian American applicants had been admitted at a significantly lower rate between the years of 1979 and 1988 than similarly qualified white applicants, Takagi (1992) noted they did not attribute this disparity to discriminatory policies or procedures. Instead, OCR concluded that the lower admission rate for Asian applicants was due to plus factors (legacy and athletics) that tipped in favor of whites. According to Karabel (2005), OCR considered the preferences for children of alumni and recruited athletes to be "legitimate institutional goals" and, subsequently, protected university officials' wide discretion with respect to the manner of selecting students. While OCR concluded that Harvard could justify those disparities, UCLA could not. According to Takagi, OCR ordered UCLA to make belated admissions offers to five Asian applicants who were rejected although their academic records were comparable to white students who had been admitted. The outcome of those investigations hardly settled the controversy, which has returned more recently with even higher stakes.

On May 23, 2016, the Asian American Coalition for Education (AACE) filed a complaint (AACE 2016) charging that Yale University, Brown University, and Dartmouth College engaged in unlawful discrimination against Asian American applicants in their undergraduate admissions process. The AACE, a coalition that was formed in 2015 to "achieve equal education rights for Asian Americans" (http://asianamericanforeducation.org/en/about/mission/), noted that their complaint was joined by 130 other concerned Asian American organizations and "Asian Americans students who, because of their race, were unfairly rejected by these Institutions because of such unlawful use of race in the admissions process and/or who seek the opportunity to apply for admission to these Institutions without being discriminated against because of their race" (p. 2). They charged that:

> The evidence is overwhelming that the Ivy League Colleges discriminate severely against Asian-American applicants, placing them at a disadvantage vis-a-vis individuals of all other races. The holistic approach to evaluating applicants utilized by these Institutions is implicated in the discrimination. There therefore must be an objective investigation into how the Ivy League Colleges use their holistic admissions procedures to discriminate, and into what safeguards should be put into place to ensure that this unlawful discrimination ends. (p. 19)

Those unfamiliar with this controversy might find it odd that two of the most selective Ivy League colleges, Harvard and Princeton, were not listed in the AACE complaint. Those two institutions, however, were among the first to receive formal complaints against them. Regarding complaints that Princeton discriminates against Asian American applicants, the US Department of Education Office of Civil Rights (OCR) in a letter (September 9, 2015) addressed to the institution's President, Christopher Eisgruber, noted that after conducting a compliance review of the university's consideration of race and national origin, which began in January 2008, "OCR determined that there was insufficient evidence to substantiate that the University violated Title VI or its implementing regulation with regard to the issue investigated" (p. 1). Earlier that year in July 2015, OCR dismissed parallel complaints that were filed in May 2015 against Harvard because a similar case is pending in federal courts (Lorin 2015).

That lawsuit, filed by Students for Fair Admissions (SFFA), seeks to more broadly prohibit Harvard from engaging in intentional discrimination on the basis of race and ethnicity (SFFA 2015). According to their website (https://studentsforfairadmissions.org/about/), SFFA is a "membership group of more than 20,000 students, parents, and others who believe that racial classifications and preferences in college admissions are unfair, unnecessary, and unconstitutional." Among their members is an Asian American student with a demonstrated extraordinary academic record and high school extracurricular activities but was denied admissions to Harvard in 2014. Apparently representing such members, SFFA charged in its brief that:

> Harvard intentionally discriminates against Asian-American applicants. This discrimination is shown through both direct and circumstantial evidence, including statistical studies of Harvard's admissions decisions. These studies confirm what Asian-American applicants and

their parents already know: Harvard intentionally and artificially limits the number of Asian Americans to whom it will offer admission. (at 200)

While the recent complaints are basically the same as those filed decades earlier, one major difference stands out. Unlike previous complaints, the current set points more directly to race-conscious admissions practices and the interest in "racial balancing" as the main source of the problem and, subsequently, seeks to eliminate such practices. For example, SFFA (2014) claimed that Harvard's violation of Title VI of the Civil Rights Act of 1964 entitles the plaintiff to a permanent injunction prohibiting Harvard from using race as a factor in future undergraduate admissions decisions. Likewise, AACE (2016) maintained in its complaint that Asian Americans have:

> been adversely and unlawfully affected by race-based affirmative action in college admissions, we do not support its continuation or application beyond the strict limits set by the United States Supreme Court. We believe economic-condition-based affirmative action in college admissions is a better alternative to the current race-based approach because it would be fair and would target individuals who are actually disadvantaged (rather than just members of a particular race). (p. 26)

The targeting of race-conscious admissions as the primary source of discrimination against Asian Americans is a continuation of an established political agenda. Takagi (1992) maintained that:

> Between 1989 and 1990, various conservatives and neoconservatives argued that discrimination against Asians was the direct and inevitable result of racial preferences for blacks. In essence, neoconservatives forced Asian Americans and university officials into a reconstructed debate over affirmative action. (p. 139)

Takagi chronicled this deliberative apportionment of Asian American students as the new victims of affirmative action, which re-casted the admissions complaints as a continuation of reverse discrimination toward whites. Accordingly, Takagi maintained, "Asian Americans were pressed into the service of a broader critique of diversity" (p. 117). She added:

> The emergence of a "good"—Asian—suffering discrimination as a result of preferences for "underrepresented minorities"—that is, blacks and Hispanics—offered liberals a difficult choice; scrap affirmative action or change it. (p. 176)

As Takagi warned, the controversy over Asian American admissions confronts liberalism with the difficult task of "reconciling equality of individual opportunity with equality of group opportunity in the zero-sum game of admissions" (p. 169). The inability to reconcile those principles has worked in favor of those calling to eliminate affirmative action. Yet, as this controversy evolved over time, it has also concealed more deeply rooted interests that serve to undermine racial progress for Asian Americans in the long run.

In the next sections, I examine past admissions practices at elite colleges and universities to uncover the sociohistorical roots that animate this controversy concerning Asian American admissions. I then apply a critical race framework to make sense of those sociohistorical patterns. Lastly, I discuss the implications from this analysis to illuminate the efforts that seek to press Asian Americans into the service of eliminating race-conscious admissions practices.

Guarding White Privilege

Elite institutions of higher education are widely regarded as occupying an extraordinarily special place in US society. In his study of privilege, Khan (2011) noted, "One of the best predictors of your earnings is your level of education; attending an elite educational institution increases your wages even further... elite schooling is central to becoming an elite ..." (p. 7). To understand better the meaning of their elite status and contribution to elitism in US society, it is instructive to point to Jerome Karabel's findings in his book *The Chosen* (2005). His study is perhaps the most rigorous sociohistorical examination of admissions ever undertaken of Harvard, Yale, and Princeton. While the study is limited to the "Big Three" because they graduate a disproportionately high number of the "American elite" (p. 3), the findings are especially relevant given the recent lawsuit and complaints filed against Ivy League institutions.

While it is well known that the Big Three have a repugnant history of discrimination, Karabel's account of their exclusionary practices is especially discerning because it connects those practices directly to each institution's interest in guarding admissions for whites only. For example, he pointed to modifications in the admissions criteria made in the 1920s among the Big Three, which shifted away from admitting students entirely on the basis of scholastic performance. This shift was implemented to address stark increases in the enrollment of Jews or what was referred to as the "Jewish problem" and intended to restore the Big Three's protection of privilege for White Anglo-Saxon Protestants (WASPs), which defined whiteness. As expressed by W. F. Williams, a Harvard alumnus, in a letter he sent on December 17, 1925, to then President of Harvard, Lawrence Lowell, which Karabel quoted at length and is worth doing so as well here:

> There were Jews to the right of me, Jews to the left of me, in fact they were so obviously everywhere that ... left (me) with a feeling of utter disgust of the present and grave doubts about the future of my Alma Mater... I cannot but feel that your New England blood must run cold when you contemplate their ever-increasing numbers at Harvard but what I cannot fathom is why you and the other Overseers don't have the backbone to put you (sic) foot down on this menace to the University. It is self-evident, therefore, that by raising the standard of marks he (Jews) can't be eliminated from Harvard, whereas by the same process of raising the standard "White" boys ARE eliminated... Are the Overseers so lacking in genius that they can't devise a way to bring Harvard back to the position it always held as a "white man's" college? (p. 105)

Rather than be appalled by such a letter that unapologetically guards admissions for whites, Karabel wrote that Lowell told Williams that he was "glad to see from your letter, as I have from many other signs, that the alumni are beginning to appreciate that I was not wholly wrong three years ago in trying to limit the proportion of Jews" (p. 109).

By the Fall of 1926, a new admissions regime was set in place at Harvard, one that, according to Karabel, would emphasize "character" – "a quality thought to be in short supply among Jews but present in abundance among high-status Protestants" (p. 2) and was thought to be "in accordance with the probable value of a college education ... to the university, and the community" (p. 108). Similar admissions practices that considered nonacademic factors were also adopted at Princeton and Yale. Remarkably, such "plus factors" are still being applied to admit students at all three institutions.

Karabel's sociohistorical account shows that the three most elite institutions of higher education in the United States and arguably in the world have, at least in the past, excluded certain groups by approaching admissions in two distinct ways that bitterly guarded the privileges bestowed by those institutions to their graduates. First, those institutions intentionally altered their admissions practices to favor white applicants. In other words, they altered the rules to determine who was or was not "white enough" to enjoy those privileges accompanying whiteness. Second, they grudgingly guarded those privileges by applying nonacademic factors in judging applicants, which on the surface appeared to be race blind but was coded in whiteness. In other words, they employed plus factors that appeared on the surface to be race blind but actually tipped in favor of white applicants, concealing their interests in reproducing white privilege.

The practice of un-leveling the playing field in deceptive ways that further advantage and privilege whites is a well-documented and long-standing pattern in the United States. In Cheryl Harris' groundbreaking article titled *Whiteness as Property* (1993), she argued that American law protects settled expectations based on white privilege, which forms the background against which legal disputes are framed, argued, and adjudicated. Through a rigorous historical and legal analysis, she traced, for example, how "slavery as a system of property facilitated the merger of white identity and property" (p. 1721). Those and similar laws set in place a legal recognition of property interest coded in whiteness, which subsequently reinforced white privilege and reproduced black subordination. According to Harris, the:

> ... relative economic, political, and social advantages dispensed to whites under systematic white supremacy in the United States were reinforced through patterns of oppression of Blacks and Native Americans. Materially, these advantages became institutionalized privileges, and ideologically, they became part of the settled expectations of whites .... (p. 1777)

Even today, Harris maintained, the courts regularly fail to "... expose the problem of substantive inequality in material terms produced by white domination and race segregation" (p. 1753).

Although Harris did not directly implicate elite colleges and universities, Karabel's sociohistorical account clearly shows that those institutions have advanced what Harris called "the institutional protection of benefits for whites that have been based on white supremacy" (p. 1767). Institutions with the capacity to do this, Harris argued, are "bound up by those essential features that afford them great power (p. 1761)," which include the exclusive rights to exclude and determine rules in ways that reproduce white privilege. Harris explained that:

> The possessors of whiteness were granted the legal right to exclude others from the privileges inhering in whiteness; whiteness became an exclusive club whose membership was closely and grudgingly guarded—determining who was or was not white enough to enjoy the privileges accompanying whiteness. (p. 1736)

Because elite colleges and universities operate within a system that is historically rooted in reproducing white privilege and are also highly selective and, by definition, exclusive, Harris' critique ostensibly applies to those institutions as well. Thus, Harris' framework challenges us to make new meaning of those elite institutions. They are more than simply engines for promoting upward social mobility, which is how they are often characterized, but also play a determining role in dispensing and protecting material advantages for whites. Since the latter characterization of elite institutions is quite provocative and those institutions have been transformed over the past century, the next section considers the extent to which they have abandoned their role in dispensing and protecting the privileges accompanying whiteness.

The Persistent Bond Between Whiteness and Privilege

Indeed, the Big Three have been transformed over the last century from what Karabel called "the enclaves of the Protestant upper class into institutions with a striking degree of racial, ethnic, and religious diversity" (p. 536). For example, Asian Americans are now overrepresented in the student body at those elite institutions relative to their proportion in the US population. Even Karabel acknowledged that in "virtually all the major institutions of American life, WASP men were now a small and beleaguered minority ..." (p. 536).

Karabel claimed that the Big Three are "well aware that it is possible to overinvest in traditional elites, especially when they show signs of decline" (p. 545). Unless the Big Three can appear to make real the American Dream of upward mobility through education, Karabel maintained it would bring into question the legitimacy of those institutions:

> ... the legitimacy of the American social order depended in good part on the public's confidence that the pathways to success provided by the nation's leading universities were open to individuals from all walks of life. (p 543)

Thus, diversifying their student body enabled elite universities not only to remain legitimate but also to benefit from enrolling "rising social groups" such as Asian Americans who can add to the prominence of those institutions especially in emerging fields of science and technology (p. 545).

Although the Big Three provided the "appearance" of equal opportunity by making available scholarships and widely publicizing efforts to recruit a racial and ethnically diverse student body, Karabel argued that in truth, enrollment is "a realistic possibility only for those young men and women whose families endow them with the type of cultural capital implicitly required for admission," which "is heavily concentrated among the scions of the privileged" (p. 549). Thus, he claimed that beneath this dramatic and highly visible change in the physiognomy of the student body was a surprising degree of stability in one crucial regard – the privileged class origins of students at the Big Three.

As Karabel argued, diversifying the student body does not necessarily mean that elite universities have forsaken their deeply rooted interest in protecting white privilege. To be sure, Karabel showed that even though the Big Three slowly transformed their admissions practices from emphasizing hereditary privilege into merit, "the qualities that came to define 'merit' tend to be attributes most abundantly possessed by dominant social groups" (p. 549). Not only was the standard for merit broadened to consider individual talent and accomplishments beyond scholastic achievements, including athletic talent in such sports as rowing, field hockey, sailing, golf, squash, fencing, and others that systematically favor the privileged, but also considered meritorious were connections to powerful external constituencies, including alumni. Karabel reported that "While the percentage of legacies in the entering class has gone down over the past decade, the relative admissions advantage for legacy applicants has actually increased" (p. 550). Given the history of systematic exclusion in the Big Three that shaped the composition of the alumni, this is a clear added advantage for a group that is predominantly wealthy and white. Thus, although those institutions may no longer be racially exclusive, they still excluded in ways that favor whiteness and thereby continued to guard the privileges accompanying whiteness.

This unchecked preference for white students is not simply a matter of past history. As part of the recent lawsuit discussed earlier filed against Harvard, Students for Fair Admissions (SFFA 2015) pointed to "decisive statistical evidence that Harvard discriminates against Asian American applicants":

> ... Asian Americans needed SAT scores that were about 140 points higher than white students, all other quantifiable variables being equal, to get into elite schools. Thus, if a white student needed a 1320 SAT score to be admitted to one of these schools, an Asian American needed a 1460 SAT score to be admitted. That is a massive penalty .... (at 208)

Moreover, SFFA allege that Asians would be 43% of the admitted class if Harvard considered academics alone, but instead, Harvard's holistic approach using plus factors for nonacademic characteristic drops Asians all the way down to 19% (Richwine 2018). Similarly, the complaint filed by the Asian American Coalition for

Education (AACE) in 2016 also pointed out that "Asian applicants have 67% lower odds of admission than white applicants with comparable test scores" (p. 13). Such charges about tipping admissions in favor of white applicants over Asian ones were also at the core of the OCR investigations conducted in the 1980s.

Those complaints pointing to white advantage are remarkably consistent with the admissions pattern documented by Karabel. According to him, the Big Three have always tilted in favor of the privileged. While they might slightly alter their admissions practices to remain socially relevant, they have a vested interest in maintaining the social order and their position in it, so there is little reason to believe that this preference will change anytime soon. Similarly, Harris also argued that US laws historically have cemented advantages for whites and those privileges were reproduced through institutional power to exercise exclusionary practices that limited access to those key institutions. Therefore, as long as the exclusionary practices of elite colleges and universities continue to be coded in favor of whiteness and those institutions retain exclusive rights to determine who is or is not white enough to enjoy the privileges accompanying whiteness, they will invariably reproduce the position of whites at the very top of the social order.

Indeed, a common practice that has largely defined the identity of institutions that are well positioned to dispense the privileges accompanying whiteness, according to Harris, is that they all grudgingly guard their exclusive rights both to exclude and establish rules to determine who was or was not white enough to enjoy those privileges (p. 1761). Fittingly, the Big Three have actively guarded those rights, especially when it comes to protecting the autonomy to set their own admissions standards. As an example of how they fiercely guard their rights so that they can continue to set the standards for exclusion, Karabel pointed to their defense of race-conscious admissions. According to him, their defense of race-conscious admissions "went well beyond the issues of blacks and other minorities; it raised the specter of an encroachment on the institutional discretion that Harvard believed indispensable to the protection of vital institutional interests" (p. 489). Harvard was involved in every single challenge to race-conscious admissions to reach the US Supreme Court, and at the heart of their defense of such practices, according to Karabel, was that to flourish, colleges and universities should be accorded freedom from external influence and intrusion (p. 492). The US Supreme Court agreed and allowed universities to retain their historic discretion and independence, upholding Harvard's admission policy as a "model of how to consider race within the bounds of the law and the Constitution" (p 498).

That the racial representation of the student body and to a much lesser extent the faculty on elite institutions have changed, according to Harris, only indicates that not "all whites will win, but simply that they will not lose ..." (p.1759). "Of course, there's still diversity," one Ivy alumnus was quoted as saying in a *New York Times* article (Yazigi 1999) concerning eating clubs at Princeton, "About 20 percent. They are there to make the other 80% show they are democratic and feel more superior." Unless the rights of those elite institutions to practice exclusion with impunity is challenged, Harris maintained, they will continue to dispense privileges in ways that are coded in favor of whiteness, reproducing the social order.

Pursuing Whiteness

Harris and Karabel's insights shed a new light on the discrimination complaints concerning Asian American admissions. By making clear the role of elite higher education in cementing the durable bond between whiteness and privilege, their insights raise serious questions about the meaning Asian Americans have generally attributed to those elite colleges and universities. Clearly, Asian Americans recognize the distinctive role of those institutions as a training ground for achieving the American Dream of upward mobility, as evidenced by their increasing application to and enrollment in elite colleges and universities. Their faith in and love affair with a very select group of institutions is illustrated well by Jeff Yang (2014), who confessed that:

> ... to my parents, it wasn't enough for me to just go to college. There was only one school they saw as a fitting goal, and it was the reason they came to America, my mother said, hoping that one day they would have kids who would grow up to attend it. That was Harvard University, the only school whose brand name shone brightly enough to reach across the waters to Taiwan. Other schools might offer a more dynamic curriculum, better access to senior faculty, a greater amount of financial aid. None of that mattered. To them, it was *Hafu Daxue* or bust.

Likewise, Amy Chua (2011) quipped that the US-born children of Chinese immigrants followed a remarkably common pattern as they:

> ... will typically be high-achieving. They will usually play the piano and/or violin. They will attend an Ivy League or Top Ten university. They will tend to be professionals—lawyers, doctors, bankers, television anchors—and surpass their parents in income ... If they are female, they will often marry a white person. (p. 29)

While both Yang and Chua's remarks suggest that the pursuit of elite college admissions among Asian Americans as a pathway to success is racially coded, Harris' framework adds even more meaning to this racial coding. She reminds us that success is primarily coded in whiteness because material privileges such as owning property and gaining membership into elite institutions have historically been reserved for only whites, and subsequently, "Becoming white meant gaining access to a whole set of public and private privileges that materially and permanently guaranteed basic subsistence needs and, therefore, survival" (p. 1713). Because elite institutions play a key role in dispensing the privileges accompanying whiteness and lean in favor of admitting those who are "white enough" as discussed earlier, this dogged pursuit of admissions among Asian Americans into elite institutions can be understood generally as a keen interest in obtaining the set of assumptions, privileges, and benefits that accompany the status of being white. In other words, obtaining credentials from those institutions can eventually provide one with a "pass" to enjoy the privileges accompanying whiteness. If so, Harris' framework suggests that the zeal for attending elite educational institutions as a pathway for success among a disproportionally high number of Asian Americans is in many respects a pursuit of a pathway toward becoming white.

On the surface, pursuing this pathway to obtain the privileges accompanying whiteness seems completely sensible. After all, gaining membership into those elite institutions still pays high material dividends and enhances one's social and economic status, which enables one to exercise more control over critical aspects of one's life rather than remain the object of white domination. According to Khan (2011), modern-day elite education provides students with "carefully cultivated lives" that "solidify their position as masters of our economy and government" and "credentials, relationships, and culture, all of which ensured their future success" (p. 13). Those elite institutions accomplish this not so much by deeply engaging students with ideas and text, Khan argued, but by "... develop(ing) privilege: a sense of self and a mode of interaction that advantage them" (p. 14), which ensures the future protection of their position. In short, those who obtain membership into those elite institutions come to enjoy essential privileges accompanying whiteness. Although Harris also acknowledged that there is a certain economic logic to becoming white and accumulating the material privileges inhering in whiteness, she also warned that a blind pursuit of those advantages may strengthen rather than weaken the bond between whiteness and privilege, reinforcing racial inequality. I will point to two major issues associated with the blind pursuit of whiteness particularly for Asian Americans.

Firstly, educational success has not always translated into expected career success for Asian Americans. Wesley Yang (2011) discussed this paradox in his featured article in *The New York Times Magazine*. He pointed to the bamboo ceiling "an invisible barrier that maintains a pyramidal racial structure throughout corporate America, with lots of Asians at junior levels, quite a few in middle management, and virtually none in the higher reaches of leadership." Yang argued that "... it is a part of the bitter undercurrent of Asian-American life that so many Asian graduates of elite universities find that meritocracy as they have understood it comes to an abrupt end after graduation."

That even those who have gained membership into elite institutions still face racial discrimination suggests that the context of contemporary discrimination is in constant flux. According to Carbado et al. (2008), "Although access is important, the story of discrimination does not end at the moment of access. *Inclusion in* does not mean the absence of *discrimination from*" (p. 85). They maintained that exclusion does not exhaust how discrimination operates but in fact access often facilitates certain conditions of discrimination. These forms of discrimination by inclusion contain a range of evolving subtle institutional practices and interpersonal dynamics, which in turn transforms "the role of race in society and the nature and sources of racial inequality" (p. 98).

Thus, one's vulnerability to discrimination cannot be eradicated merely by earning credentials from elite institutions. Just because one obtains a "pass" to access one setting does not necessarily mean that the pass will provide unrestricted access free of discrimination. A Chinese American scientist with multiple degrees from Harvard, for example, is still less likely than her white male colleague with a comparable set of degrees from elite institutions to be promoted into higher reaches of leadership. Similarly, the same Asian scientist is much more vulnerable of being persecuted for international espionage than her white colleague who works in the same high-tech company but attended an "insufficiently elite" college.

Secondly, Carbado and Gulati (2013) considered in another study whether African American employees at the bottom of the corporation would yield "trickle down" benefits from African Americans at the top. After closely examining this proposition, they remained "cynical that having more minorities at the top of the hierarchy will necessarily improve the conditions for those on the bottom" (p. 166). They reasoned that those who possess the skill set to race to the top of the hierarchy are also incentivized to "pull the ladder up behind them when they get there" (p. 165). Likewise, there is little reason to believe that those Asian Americans who over-attribute hard work and "individual merit" in gaining admissions to an elite college or university will necessarily "lift as they climb," unless, perhaps, they have seriously considered the underlying sources that both shape and derail the pursuit of the American Dream.

Although arguably limited, the discussion above at least raises doubts that gaining membership into elite institutions that provide access to white privilege necessarily translates into transformative racial progress for a majority of Asian Americans. While those individuals who gain membership to elite institutions certainly benefit by improving their capacity to accumulate privileges accompanying whiteness, there is reason to suspect that the unbridled pursuit of this pathway to success would necessarily curb other forms of discrimination against Asian Americans or significantly lift a majority of them, especially those with limited access to opportunities. Thus, it is not altogether clear how efforts to increase only slightly the chances of admissions for a very select group of Asian Americans into a few elite colleges and universities that have only a very limited number of available spots would meaningfully weaken the durable bond between whiteness and privilege. (Let's just look at Harvard admissions from a numerical standpoint, putting aside a more complex educational or social analysis for now. According to Jon Marcus, Asian Americans represent 17.8% or 383 of the students admitted to begin studies at Harvard in Fall 2011. Now imagine that activists wage an expensive legal battle and successfully double the representation of Asian Americans to a remarkable 40% for next year's class. Let's also assume in this scenario that Harvard receives 34,000 applications and that Asian Americans make up 20% of that pool (34,000 × 0.2 = 6800). If the overall admit rate remains at 6%, there would still only be 2040 total admitted (34,000 × 0.06). If 40% of the admitted students are Asian Americans under this scenario, 816 (2040 × 0.4) would be admitted. This still leaves 5984 Asian American applicants (6800–816) without a spot at Harvard. Try telling the rejected Asian American families that the Harvard admissions process is now fairer than before. By hypothetically doubling the proportion of Asian Americans in the admitted class from 20% (2040 × 0.2 = 408) to a ridiculous 40% (816), we have effectively only lowered the proportion of rejected Asian American applicants from 94% ([6800–408]/6800) to 88% (5984/6800), or a 6 percentage point change in the likelihood of being rejected. Unless Harvard doubles or triples the number of students admitted, the actual number of Asian American applicants who would gain admissions even under farfetched proportional increases is relatively small.)

Discussion

The complaints filed by Students for Fair Admissions that Asian Americans are discriminated against in admissions by Harvard will eventually be decided in US courts. Those and other related complaints ostensibly extend a familiar historical pattern that has been well documented by Karabel's exhaustive research into the history of admission at Harvard, Yale, and Princeton. Those complaints, however, fail to point to the fundamental source of racial discrimination and the role of affirmative action in addressing that source. As such, I applied Harris' critical race framework to make meaning of this shameful pattern in college admissions. Her framework, based on a deep analysis of the historical and continuing pattern of white racial domination and economic exploitation in the United States, illuminated the underlying racial implications of this pattern of exclusion and the role of elite colleges and universities in reinforcing racial inequality. Although elite institutions regularly alter their admissions to remain socially relevant, they also continue to exclude in ways that favor attributes that are coded in whiteness. This critique undermines the characterization of those institutions as color-blind engines of upward mobility and instead portrays them as guardians of dispensing and protecting the privileges accompanying whiteness.

Overall, this provocative interpretation of elite colleges and universities raises serious questions about the current set of complaints regarding competitive college admission, which casts Asian Americans as victims of affirmative action unlike the original ones filed in the early 1980s. As expressed by Swann Lee who helped to organize the filing of the 2015 complaint against Harvard, "Asian-American applicants shouldn't be racially profiled in college admissions ... " and "... should have the playing field leveled" (Carapezza 2015). While those complaints condemn racism, they fail to meaningfully critique the underlying conditions that contribute to discrimination and reproduce racial inequality.

By contrast, applying Harris' framework to account for white supremacy and privilege makes more explicit the underlying interests and assumptions that animate admissions discrimination, which compels us to reconsider the conditions that contextualize that controversy. For Harris, the fundamental problem regarding the admissions controversy is not simply what is observed on the surface – racial profiling – but what animates that problem in the first place, the tyranny of whiteness. Thus, the overarching goal for Harris is to "dismantle the institutional protection of benefits for whites that have been based on white supremacy and maintained at the expense of Blacks" (p. 1767). Race-conscious policies such as affirmative action, according to Harris, advance that goal by exposing "... the illusion that the original or current distribution of power, property, and resources is the result of 'right' and 'merit' ... It unmasks the limited character of rights granted by those who dominate. In a word, it is destabilizing" (p. 1778). By contrast, color-blind approaches tend to conceal the privileges accompanying whiteness, as documented, for example, by Karabel regarding certain "plus factors" that tipped admissions in favor of wealthy white applicants.

Applying an analysis that offers a serious critique of whiteness, either its role in discrimination or how it structures opportunity, redefines the problem and the target of the discrimination complaints in question. By placing the spotlight more squarely on the advantages that white applicants have over Asian ones, it serves to divorce race-conscious admissions practices from those complaints. These practices after all are applied to dismantle the institutional protection of benefits for whites by specifically increasing enrollment of those who have been historically excluded for not being white enough. At the very least, applying a critique of whiteness to those complaints raises serious doubts that removing an admissions practice that seeks to eradicate the settled advantages afforded to whites would actually curb the persistent advantages whites have over Asian Americans.

Moreover, focusing on eradicating white privilege problematizes efforts to place even more Asian Americans into elite institutions, raising issues about how such outcomes would actually serve the long-term collective interests of Asian Americans. Harris' framework suggests that while those Asian Americans who "pass" into such institutions obtain advantages associated with institutionalized privileges, their race to the top of the economic and social food chain will not necessarily lift all Asian Americans nor enable them to escape other forms of discrimination. In short, there is little reason to believe that placing even more Asian Americans into elite institutions that have become part of the "settled expectations of whites" will necessarily lead to achieving the broader goal of dismantling a deeply rooted system that continues to structure opportunities in favor of whiteness. While there may well be individual gains accrued for those who get a "pass," in the long run, protecting those policies that unmask white domination and dismantle a system that privileges whiteness would yield greater collective benefits for Asian Americans.

Conclusion

If the concerns raised about the discrimination of Asian Americans in college admissions are supposed to advance the collective interests of this population, then Asian Americans should rethink the meaning they attribute to those elite colleges and universities and better appreciate the role of those institutions in reinforcing white domination. As it stands, the current set of complaints tend to conceal the context of racial discrimination, failing to make clear the fundamental source of that problem. Without a better understanding about the fundamental problems that animate racial inequality, Asian Americans can be pressed into service of an agenda that stands to hurt more than help them in the long run. According to Park and Liu (2014), Asian Americans are regularly boxed into political discourses that constrain their actions such as in the case regarding race-conscious admissions whereby opponents of those practices frame the context for them as "having to relinquish their own self-interest in favor of 'less qualified' URMs [underrepresented racial minorities]" (p. 57). Park and Liu argue that the deployment of such misleading discourses conceals how Asian American interests diverge from the anti-affirmative action movement and distorts this population's commitment to access and equity in higher education. Even if there were genuine discrimination claims against elite colleges and universities, my analysis suggests that those complaints should be decoupled from affirmative action and should not target race-conscious admissions practices.

Additionally, Asian Americans need to consider the bigger picture when it comes to eliminating racial discrimination and achieving full participation. To achieve those goals, Wesley Yang (2011) argued that it will probably have less to do with any form of behavior assimilation that reproduces white domination than with the emergence of risk-takers whose success obviates the need for Asians to meet someone else's behavioral standard. According to him, Asian Americans will need more people to exercise proud defiance and "... to stop doggedly pursuing official paper emblems attesting to their worthiness, to stop thinking those scraps of paper will secure anyone's happiness, and to dare to be interesting." Likewise, Stephen Colbert host of *The Late Show* paid tribute to Muhammad Ali (aired on June 6 on *CBS*) who passed away on June 4, 2016, and quoted him as having said in 1970, "I am America. I am the part you won't recognize. But get used to me. Black, confident, cocky; my name, not yours; my religion, not yours; my goals, my own; get used to me." Colbert praised Ali for having helped "...create the America we live in today."

Perhaps it takes the kind of audacious defiance as demonstrated by Ali's statement and suggested by Yang to make a transformative and lasting imprint on American society. After all, blind faith and over-investment in pursuing those well-worn paths of achieving success, including what Yang called the dogged pursuit of "official paper emblems," are more likely to steer Asian Americans toward accepting rather than challenging white privilege and domination as being the natural order of things that cannot be disturbed. Moreover, there is little reason to believe that the few who get a "pass" to enjoy privileges accompanying whiteness by gaining membership into elite institutions would necessarily "lift as they climb" to the top of the social and economic hierarchy. As it stands, Asian American enrollments at those institutions already far exceed their representation in the national population. (For example, according to Harvard's *Admissions and Financial Aid* website (https://college.harvard.edu/admissions/admissions-statistics), Asians who presumably entered college in Fall 2017 make up 22.2% of their class of 2021. This compares to 5.6% Asians of the total US population in 2010, according to the US Census Bureau.)

By contrast, an audacious defiance that emphasizes active engagement in delegitimizing racial assumptions while simultaneously challenging over-investment in pursuing the privileges accompanying whiteness would ostensibly press Asian Americans toward the service of an alternative agenda. Pivoting more intentionally toward such an agenda that addresses the fundamental issues that animate those recurring admissions complaints can empower Asian Americans in ways that will actually resolve that problem for good. According to Takagi (1992), such pivots, even if only discursive, can facilitate "... a subtle but decisive shift in public and intellectual discourse about and at some universities, in practices of, affirmative action" (p. 10). Takagi argues that in the end, "... facts and statistics were less important than what people made of them ... the core of the debate over admissions pivoted not on the facts per se but on interpretation of the facts ..." (p. 11).

Whatever approach taken to interpret and address the facts, Asian Americans are at a crucial juncture when it comes to US racial politics. The admissions controversy returned with even higher stakes to include the elimination of practices that were designed to delegitimate structural advantages afforded to whites and address the illusion that there is a level playing field. Given the increasingly higher stakes, Asian Americans should ask tougher questions of those who are trying to press them into service of a particular racial or political agenda. The position that they stake out is indeed pivotal and can well determine whether Asian Americans remain the poster child for the mythical American Dream or participate more boldly in dismantling institutional structures that reproduce privileges accompanying whiteness.

References

Carapezza K (2015) Is Harvard showing bias against Asian-Americans [Electronic Version]? National Public Radio. Retrieved from http://www.npr.org/sections/ed/2015/05/20/408240998/is-harvard-showing-bias-against-asian-americans

Carbado D, Gulati M (2013) Acting white: rethinking race in "post-racial" America. Oxford University Press, New York

Carbado D, Fisk C, Gulati M (2008) After inclusion. Ann Rev Law Soc Sci 4:83–102

Chua A (2011) Battle hymn of the tiger mother. Penguin Press, New York

Complaint of the Asian American Coalition for Education v. Yale University, Brown University, and Dartmouth College. For unlawful discrimination against Asian-American applicants in the college admissions process. Submitted to Office for Civil Rights U.S. Department of Education on May 23, 2016. Retrieved from http://asianamericanforeducation.org/wp-content/uploads/2016/05/Complaint_Yale_Brown_Dartmouth_Full.pdf.

Harris C (1993) Whiteness as property. Harv Law Rev 106(8):1707–1791

Karabel J (2005) The chosen: the hidden history of admission and exclusion at Harvard, Yale, and Princeton. Houghton Mifflin, Boston

Khan SR (2011) Privilege: the making of an adolescent elite at St. Paul's school. Princeton University Press, Princeton

Lorin J (2015) Education department dismisses Harvard Asian-American discrimination complaint [Electronic Version]. Bloomberg News. Retrieved from http://www.bloomberg.com/news/articles/2015-07-07/harvard-bias-complaint-dismissed-by-education-department

Park JJ, Liu A (2014) Interest convergence or divergence?: A critical race analysis of Asian Americans, meritocracy, and critical mass in the affirmative action debate. J High Educ 85(1):36–64

Richwine J (2018) Who benefits from Harvard's Asian Quota? [Electronic Version]. National Review. Retrieved from https://www.nationalreview.com/corner/harvard-asian-quota-who-benefits/

Siegel L (2012) Rise of the tiger nation [Electronic Version]. Wall Street Journal. Retrieved from http://www.wsj.com/articles/SB10001424052970204076204578076613986930932

Students for Fair Admissions, Inc. v. President & Fellows of Harvard Coll., 308 F.R.D. 39, 52–53 (D. Mass. 2015)

Takagi DY (1992) The retreat from race: Asian-American admissions and racial politics. Rutgers University Press, New Brunswick
Yang W (2011) Paper tigers [Electronic Version]. New York Magazine. Retrieved from http://nymag.com/news/features/asian-americans-2011-5/
Yang J (2014) Harvard lawsuit is not what it seems [Electronic Version]. CNN. Retrieved from http://www.cnn.com/2014/11/24/opinion/yang-harvard-lawsuit/
Yazigi M (1999) At Ivy club, a trip back to elitism [Electronic Version]. New York Times. Retrieved from http://www.nytimes.com/1999/05/16/style/at-ivy-club-a-trip-back-to-elitism.html?pagewanted=all

Affirmative Action: Its Nature and Dynamics 77

Ralph Premdas

Contents

Introduction 1502
Distributive Sites of Contest: Material and Symbolic Goods 1507
Entitlement and the Eligibility of Groups 1508
Legal Mandates and Legitimating Sources 1510
Conclusion 1511
Cross-References 1512
References 1512

Abstract

The incidence of affirmative action policies has occurred most frequently in internally heterogeneous states marked by deep ethno-cultural divisions and in which one of the ethno-cultural communities tended to dominate the rest. The response has led to the adoption of affirmative action programs to rectify old wrongs and eradicate injustices and extend benefits and provide special preferences toward establishing a new, just, and equal society. Alternative views of equality and justice undergird much of the controversy over affirmative action. Justice and equality are commonly shared calls evoked by both proponents and opponents of affirmative action. However, there are no universal and generally accepted set of values which define justice and equality. Lacking commensurability, rival meanings are almost always caught up in contentious struggles over power and resources in affirmative action programs.

Keywords

Affirmative action · Injustice · Inequality · Merit · Preference · Ethno-cultural division · Domination · Redistribution

R. Premdas (✉)
University of the West Indies, St. Augustine, Trinidad and Tobago
e-mail: ralphpremdas@hotmail.com

Introduction

Alternative views of equality and justice undergird much of the controversy over affirmative action (Rosenfeld 1991; Premdas 2016). Justice and equality are commonly shared calls evoked by both proponents and opponents of affirmative action. However, there are no universal and generally accepted set of values which define justice and equality (Ryan 1993; Campbell 2000; Rawls 1971). In practical terms, equality and justice are concepts that are culturally and contextually defined, may opportunistically shift their meanings, but almost always they are a creature of struggles over power and resources. The lack of commensurability of cultures and values renders all preferences for a system of justice and equality, especially in multicultural states, contentious.

Affirmative action addresses issues of official state policy pertaining to justice and equality on behalf of certain groups that have been historically disadvantaged and discriminated against (Goldman 1976; Kellough 2006; Anderson 2004; Sterba 2003). Basically, affirmative action may be regarded as a variant of rectificatory or compensatory justice that seeks to establish equality through special policy preferences and programs for a short time. In effect affirmative action seeks to reorganize the distribution of the benefits and burdens of society for the inclusion of the previously disadvantaged who have been the victims of past injustices and discrimination. In part because the historically disadvantaged have tended to be ill prepared immediately for equal competition with others in the open marketplace for benefits in jobs, education, and business opportunities, affirmative action policies have rescinded the merit-based principles of equality by offering special preferences to temporarily compensate for and empower the disadvantaged toward eventual equal participation in society (Young 1990). Generally then, affirmative action policies create arbitrary preferences in abridging principles of equality based on individual merit suggesting reverse discrimination (Fullinwider 1980; Goldman 1979; Pojman 1998; Sher 1979; Nagel 1973). Depending on who the beneficiaries targeted, it can serve toward promoting the well-being of any community, both blacks and whites (Katznelson 2005). Further, as against the embedded societal value of rewarding work and effort based on individual merit, affirmative action policies may assign benefits on a group basis, and even when the better off in these groups have tended to be the main beneficiaries, these programs have been defended and maintained (Young 1990; Fullinwider 1975). Wherever it is practiced, it seeks to promote unity by a policy of wider inclusion by compensating for discrimination against entire classes, castes, and groups of persons in the past (Gomez and Premdas 2012).

Alternative views of equality and justice undergird much of the controversy over affirmative action (Rosenfeld 1991; Premdas 2016). Justice and equality are commonly shared calls evoked by both proponents and opponents of affirmative action. However, there are no universal and generally accepted set of values which define justice and equality (Ryan 1993; Campbell 2000; Rawls 1971). In practical terms, equality and justice are concepts that are culturally and contextually defined, may opportunistically shift their meanings, but almost always they are a creature of struggles over power and resources. The lack of commensurability of cultures and values renders all preferences for a system of justice and equality, especially in multicultural states, contentious (Sen 1992; Loury 1987; Glazer 1975; Phillips 1996; Nagel 1973; Westen 1985). In particular, equality, which is nearly always invoked to justify the claims for justice in affirmative action policies, is not a neutral principle that is crystal clear. Waltzer referred to it as a "procrustean bed" (Waltzer 1983). It invariably raises controversies on the appropriate formula to be applied over what goods and resources to be distributed and about who are the rightful and eligible recipients (Guinier and Sturm 2001; Sheth 1997; Nozick 1972). The arguments come from philosophers, publicists, artists, religious leaders, and opinion makers resulting in a massive outpouring of literature and pamphlets. They often combine philosophical positions on justice and equality with practical political and sectional interests particular to a community (Premdas 2010).

The incidence of affirmative action policies has occurred most frequently in internally heterogeneous states marked by deep ethno-cultural divisions and in which one of the ethno-cultural communities tended to dominate the rest. In the evolution of these plural societies most of which were created by colonialism, a coercively institutionalized order was established so that the distribution of economic, social, and political advantages was concentrated unevenly in favor of and against certain communities. Regardless of how this skewed distribution of power, benefits, and burdens eventuated, in the contemporary international order of universal human rights, they have triggered anger, frustrations, and violent protests to secure equality and justice. The response has led to the adoption of affirmative action programs to rectify old wrongs and eradicate injustices and extend benefits and provide special preferences toward establishing a new, just, and equal society. Thus, affirmative action policies can be conceived at once to be a form of conflict management as well as a longer-term project to remedy inequality and restore justice (Ratuva 2013).

Affirmative action policies are often proposed as a temporary preparatory measure necessary to establish a level playing field for the enactment of fair competition in the long term. In practice, these temporal limits are often breached as programs expand and beneficiaries increase. As one scholar remarked in relation to the Indian case:

> Reservations were supposed to be temporary measures devised primarily to ensure equality of opportunity. However, over the years, they have assumed the form of permanent and non-retractable concessions. Indeed, policies of positive discrimination have been used and abused by parties to augment their political support. (Gupta 1998:509)

Aimed in part at eliminating divisive communal politics and sectional alienation, affirmative action policies seek in part to promote societal unity by rectifying historical discriminatory wrongs and lessening inequality. Despite many valid criticisms against these preferential programs, they have in most cases substantially succeeded in creating a new middle class among the erstwhile oppressed and disadvantaged and in bestowing on them symbolic gratification, recognition, and dignity. Orlando Patterson, in evaluating the impact of affirmative action in the USA, concluded:

> For all its Imperfections, affirmative action has made a major difference helping to realize, as no other policy has done, the nation's constitutional commitment to the ideals of equality, fairness and integration...it is hard to find a program that has brought so much gain to so many at so little cost. It has been the single most important factor accounting for the rise of a significant Afro-American middle class. (Patterson 1998:147)

Overall, as an experiment in institutional reform, affirmative action policies and programs have left in their wake among the states that have adopted them a mixed record pointing to setbacks and achievements, successful changes in institutions and practices toward promoting equality, winners and losers, contested economic gains and losses, as well as unanticipated problems and solutions (Sowell 2004; Gomez and Premdas 2012).

In many ways, affirmative action signaled a new dawn for the disadvantaged and entailed institutional changes that went to the root of the society's traditional ways of life. However, affirmative action was not new with various forms having long existed with preferences extended to veterans of wars, to the elderly, to the disabled, to students, and to the handicapped. That apart, proto-affirmative action policies have existed in many legal programs for minorities and the disadvantaged in nearly all states. These however were small scale, generally incremental if not sporadic reformist programs, nothing like what would subsequently be launched from anti-colonial and revolutionary movements in the post-WWII era, engaging broad swaths of racial and gender disadvantaged groups and persons.

What would transform these small programs into full-blown comprehensive affirmative action structures stemmed in many cases from the failure of voluntary compliance of basic reform by power holders and the privileged in frequently drawn out and delayed actions if not outright sabotage so that the urgency of the need for compensatory justice was effectively denied. It was in the soil of this lack of meaningful progress and hypocritical delays leading to explosive violent crises that affirmative action policies germinated and emerged as full-blown affirmative action regimes as occurred in the American and South African cases (Skrentny 1996), In Malaysia, riots occurred in 1969; in the USA, sustained riots and demonstrations in the mid-1960s onwards; in South Africa a radical change of government and constitution; in Fiji a military coup; in Northern Ireland; violent activities by the Provisional IRA; etc. Even, in the case of India where affirmative action policies on behalf of the untouchables were not prompted by any immediate violence, the potential threat of such a crisis lingered in the background (Parikh 2012). In its demand for remedy and for decisive change, affirmative action pushed by years of frustrations and ignited by great expectations demanded specific timetables, quotas, and monitoring with penalties to sustain momentum and prevent delays and foot dragging (Skrentny 1996).

As a distributive policy over limited and scarce resources in society then, affirmative action policies tend to engage zero-sum contests and struggles between the privileged and underprivileged creating winners and losers for both individuals and groups. Typically, the competition is manifested in such material areas as employment (public and private) and access to educational and business opportunities including government procurement, contracts, and licenses. Also in symbolic areas like political representation, recognition of cultural symbols of identity, e.g., religion and language, titles, and statuses (Taylor 1994). Additionally, in relation to access to important services such as medical; water; transportation. Where the contest and competition become group-based and communalized, as it often does, it tends to evoke strong irrational passions that are difficult to reconcile and easy to manipulate by political entrepreneurs for political gain. While affirmative action policies may empower and promote full participant citizenship, with numerous tangible instances of meritorious achievements, they may simultaneously so shield and overly protect groups that, instead of their getting stronger, they become habitually dependent, inviting unfair collective stigmatization as genetically inferior, and thus in the long term, these groups may become disabled and unprepared for market competition (Sowell 2004). These policies may thus ghettoize the entire disadvantaged communities into self-perpetuating inferiorized groups maimed and consigned to the periphery of the society.

Affirmative action may be formally embodied and legalized in a variety of documents and practices including constitutions, laws/legislation, executive and administrative directives, court decisions, and popular referendums. The term "affirmative action" itself was first embodied as part of an executive order (number 10925) issued by an American President (Anderson 2004:60; Katznelson 2005:216). Affirmative action policies tend to involve a variety of programs and strategies of implementation in different targeted areas of remedy such as employment and education with different consequences in each sector of activity. Implementation is not a quick fix that is undertaken and completed overnight. In practice, in many cases including affirmative action policies, it is a long-drawn-out experimental process that is marked by successes and failures, with constant revisions and redesigns, unending challenges and conflicts, changing friends and enemies, new unanticipated problems, and threats of abandonment and exhaustion. Just as problematic is the loss of focus and changing aims in a meandering stream in the life of a policy during the implementation phase. Having started off as one thing, in a checkered career, it may metamorphose into a different creature with new accumulated interests, beneficiaries, and programs and become, instead of a short term temporary measure, almost rooted permanently into an ineradicable governmental patronage structure with strong political constituencies (Gomez and Premdas 2012).

Despite its noble aims and justifiable remedies, the introduction of affirmative action policies confronted resistance from the outset. This came typically from advocates who vehemently opposed the assignment of benefits and rewards collectively to groups as is espoused by all affirmative action policies and the corresponding abridgement of the principles of individualism and merit (Cohen 1998:14–22; Cohen and Sterba 2003). In particular, they argue that affirmative action is detrimental to equal citizenship for it destroys the relationship between equal work for equal reward, between work and desert (Pojman 1992). This is wrong from this point of view for it destroys incentives for individual effort and similarly discourages responsibility for the individual's own choices and self-determination. (Cohen 1998). Merit and individual identity are regarded as sacred values in the architecture in the Western democratic system of justice and governance. Hence, affirmative action bears the mark of an alien strain, a deviant and subversive intervention that threatens a just equal democratic order at its very core. To invoke merit in an argument therefore, even in all of its contradictions, is to assert an article of faith that seems to be beyond reasonable counter claims. It reverses discrimination which cannot remedy a wrong by committing another wrong, it is argued (Cohen and Sterba 2003).

The iconic status of the merit principle however has been challenged by many including Professor Iris Marion Young who has argued that "impartial, value neutral, scientific measures of merit do not exist" (Young 1990:193). She goes on to say:

> For the merit principle to apply, it must be possible to identify, measure, compare, and rank individual performance of job-related tasks using criteria that are normatively and culturally neutral. For most jobs, however, this is not possible, and most criteria of evaluation used in our society, including educational credentials and standardized testing, have normative and cultural content. (Ibid.)

What is also ironic, it has been pointed out, is that the resistance against affirmative action eventuated in those very merit-based societies had already extended group benefits to the handicapped, senior citizens, veterans of wars, special title holders, etc. Hence, affirmative action programs were generally not new in modifying the merit principle or in granting group benefits. What would however define their uniqueness in the era of widespread affirmative action regimes around the world were two salient facts: (1) the scope of entitlement which was exponentially extended more widely to entire ethnic and racial communities as well as women, signaling an upheaval of revolutionary proportions, and (2) the promulgation of mandatory performances in timetables, quotas, and reviews in the implementation of affirmative action policies. This latter feature became necessary when voluntary compliance by privileged incumbents in both the public and private sectors in offering positive discriminatory opportunities to the historically disadvantaged and discriminated against was deliberately ignored or cynically manipulated so as to fail. These changes evoked passionate resistance from communities which felt that they faced reverse discrimination and a radical reversal of fortunes, status, and privileges. Many openly engaged in acts of noncooperation and even sabotage. In a number of cases, the new order of affirmative action justice was carried out by and on behalf of groups that were a majority in the population and which had either seized power or wrested it by majoritarian democratic means. In these cases, the swift and massive application of the compensatory features in the special preferences that were allocated to the historically disadvantaged caused trauma, withdrawal, and emigration among the previously privileged. Cases include South Africa after the dissolution of apartheid, Malaysia after the riots and widespread violence in 1969, after the military coup of 1989 in Fiji, and after general elections in Sri Lanka in 1956. Affirmative action programs also were initiated by majorities on behalf of disadvantaged minorities as occurred in India, Brazil, and the USA even though in the latter, it truly got under way following sustained street demonstrations and demonstrations in the 1960s (Skrentny 2001).

Distributive Sites of Contest: Material and Symbolic Goods

Society can be conceived as a distributive community, argues Waltzer: "We come together to share, divide and exchange" (Waltzer 1983:3). Distribution includes both material and nonmaterial symbolic values and goods. Societies differ in how much they emphasize the relative worth of these scarce goods and constructs and confers on them their cultural meanings. Distribution is thus culturally constructed. Distribution sits on shifting sands and can best be understood as a political contest and power struggles.

Affirmative action is a particular variant of a just distributive principle. It is about scarce goods and values; it is about one principle of equity against another with zero sum consequences; and it is a moral claim seeking to displace another. It stirs passions and compels conviction evoking insecurities and fears for possible losers and winners alike. In affirmative action resides an accusation. It lays charges of oppression, exploitation, and marginalization onto another group. It argues that that the misfortune of one group in acquiring well-being and power has not been legitimate or right. It seeks in a new distributive order to right old wrongs, to obtain compensation, and to gain unequal advantages for a more just equal order. Those who have will not readily give up their shares until faced with greater loss by their resistance. Affirmative action challenges the holders of power and influence and can result in a radically reconfigured rearrangement of wealth, status, and power.

Affirmative action seeks both procedural and substantive rectification in the distribution of scarce goods and values. Procedural rectification refers to equal access via removal of artificial and legal barriers against a group seeking to compete for opportunities so as to obtain substantive benefits. However, these procedures themselves are only fair when applied to equally endowed and positioned participants in competition for benefits and opportunities. Hence, to offset the handicap in the lack of preparedness among the historically disadvantaged, it is necessary to offer special substantive compensating programs in the short run with the view of preparing them for full equal competition later. This in part what affirmative action is about focused programmatically on preferences which in a limited temporal frame seeks to restore an equal playing field in the competition for the values and opportunities in the state.

In affirmative action and other similar movements for remedy and rectification for past wrongs, certain values and goods have emerged as the sites of contest, competition, and struggle. Jobs and employment, both in the public and private sectors, are at the very foundation of solving poverty and inequality, and in practically all cases of affirmative action, it has been the critical arena of contest and accommodation. Education is another site of contested distribution. Access to it at all levels may determine other values such as employment opportunity and standard of living. Much struggle over educational opportunity has focused on tertiary training and university admissions. The symbolic category of goods and values includes both political and cultural items. The political aspect refers to participation in the polity by way of equal enfranchisement and more particularly in representation in the councils of decision-making. In a program of affirmative action, the demand for representation may be incorporated in a grand constitutional and political design such as in consociational democracy. In South Africa and Northern Ireland, this took the form in power sharing and institutional guarantees for legislative representation. In other cases, such as India, a dominant group without threat to its hold on power may accede to a fixed proportion of parliamentary seats for minority and disadvantaged groups. In regard to other symbolic goods, recognition of all cultural groups, their language or religion as well as certain holidays, is critical. An associated symbolic category refers to citizenship which stands for equal membership in a society and an end to inequality and discrimination. Granting of citizenship clearly has dire power implications in a democratic system by creating a new block of voters, and it becomes very potent where affirmative action encompasses a majority community that has been historically excluded. The claims for equality in the grant of citizenship are usually part and parcel of a claim to a historical identity in the national narratives of the state. Obtaining jobs and educational training in special programs of affirmative action is linked to the larger project of meaningful citizenship.

Entitlement and the Eligibility of Groups

Eligibility criteria for affirmative action beneficiaries have become mired in controversy mainly around issues of defining who is entitled, over the tendency for the size of affirmative action groups to expand, over undeserving individuals within these groups, and over the growth of entrenched dependency of affirmative action groups without an end in sight to the affirmative action program. Issues also arise regarding the stigmatization and ghettoization of these groups who remain permanently dependent and uncured of external support and forever require affirmative action for remedy. Despite all of these critical evaluations of affirmative action gathered from all societies where the policy has been adopted, affirmative action seems to be perfectly justified for those who have suffered historical discrimination and have emerged as marginalized and poverty stricken citizens. Affirmative action has been designed as an act of justice to rectify systemic inequality and not simply as optional humanitarian program.

This has not always been the case. At least in two major cases, affirmative action was designed to benefit a white group with deliberate intent to further marginalize a black community. In his major work on how affirmative action benefitted whites at the expense of blacks, Ira Katznelson referring to bias against blacks from the 1930s to 1940s under Social Security and the GI Bill that excluded African-Americans summarized the impact of such policies thus:

> But most blacks were left out. The damage to racial equality caused by each program was immense.Taken together, the effects of these public laws were devastating. Social Security, from which the majority of blacks were excluded until well into the 1950s, quickly became the country's most important social legislation. The labor laws of the New Deal and Fair Deal created a framework of protection for tens of millions of workers who secured

minimum wages, maximum hours, and the right to join industrial as well as craft unions. African Americans who worked on the land or as domestics, the great majority lacked these protections. Perhaps most surprising and most important, the treatment of veterans after the war, despite the universal eligibility for the benefits offered by the GI Bill, perpetuated the blatant racism that had marked military affairs during the war itself. (Katznelson 2005:141–142)

Something similar occurred under South Africa's apartheid laws and practices involving black exclusion. In the contemporary era after the fall of the apartheid South African regime and the emergence of more equitable racial practices in the USA, the issue of eligibility has turned in favor of nonwhite communities. In most cases, it seems rather obvious which groups are eligible as beneficiaries of affirmative action programs. In case after case, these groups are conspicuous publicly marked off by some diacritica such as color, phenotype, abject condition, lowly occupations, resident in marginal neighborhoods, etc. such as found among African-Americans in the USA, Africans in South Africa, indigenous Fijians in Fiji, untouchables in India, etc. Because affirmative action entails the potential availability of new job opportunities and/or access to scarce and prized goods and values, it tends to draw new claimants. Over time, the eligible groups become enlarged, and often their composition bears little resemblance from the original set of so conspicuous beneficiaries. Hence, as an example, added to the list of eligible groups in the USA are nonwhite recent immigrants of all hues and complexions bearing no history of discrimination and disadvantage in American history. Quickly, competition among the old and new claimants turn bitter as the struggle degenerates into complex and finer distinctions of who are truly eligible for affirmative action benefits. Who is indigenous? How long does it require to become indigenous if ever? What about mixed marriages and their progenies? Who is really Black? Does brown mixed race count? It has been estimated that some 90% of African-Americans are mixed. Who is a low caste? Can caste be acquired for the purpose of getting access to affirmative action benefits? Should recent arrivals be eligible or should they be descended from old native born citizens? In this regard, the debate and disputes turn their focus on the deserving candidates for remedial benefits. Should groups regardless of the internal differences in terms of economic need and endowment all be equally eligible? This issue evokes the old arguments mounted by opponents of affirmative action who hold that affirmative action and compensatory justice should not be allocated to groups but to individuals (Glazer 1983). Similarly, it evokes arguments about the merit of class- and needs- based eligibility rules as against broad group-assigned benefits. When women are thrown into the mix and they have been among the conspicuous disadvantaged, the same issues arise regarding eligibility based on need versus group membership. Women add an entirely new dimension to eligibility questions mainly because they are at least half of the population, and they display a wider array of internal differences in the distribution of wealth and well-being. Should only Black or indigenous or lower caste women be made beneficiaries regardless whether they are relatively well of or not? Should affirmative action be genderized so that there is a separate category for men and women?

Among the more prominent markers of eligibility, especially in the USA, is diversity. In the Bakke v. Regents of University of California case, Justice Powell writing for the majority rejected race as a legitimate criterion for affirmative action. However, he felt that "diversity" was a legitimate claim and constituted an important state interest for preferential treatment in university admissions. This was reaffirmed by Justice Sandra day Conner in 2003 in Grutter v. Bollinger. However, diversity was not taken as an automatic group criterion for preferential treatment but had to be evaluated on an individual basis along with other criteria. Diversity however has emerged as a surrogate for African-Americans, Hispanics, and indigenous peoples in the American context. Outside the USA, the diversity argument has failed to gain traction as an eligibility criterion.

Thus, finding objective and generally acceptable criteria of eligibility for affirmative action is practically impossible. As a result, eligibility has become a creature of political calculation and opportunism. Affirmative action groups are voters in a democracy, and political support for them may be fashioned with a view to cultivate and capture a community for the political gain of a party. Eligibility rules become a patronage football, and all sorts of new and invented groups are made candidates for inclusion regardless of a background in historical discrimination. Some of the main issues regarding eligibility focus on the fact that in many cases, the beneficiaries are not those who are the truly deserving. Rather, it has been argued that a small group within a broadly defined disadvantaged community has seized affirmative action benefits for its own aggrandizement.

Legal Mandates and Legitimating Sources

In most affirmative action regimes, some sort of formal instrument legalizes and legitimates preferential allocation of opportunities and goods usually also defining the identities of beneficiaries. These instruments include constitutions, legislation, court decisions, executive directives, and administrative rules. In the USA, it is found in the Civil Rights Act of 1964 as well as in the 5th and 14th Amendment of the US constitution; in South Africa in the Employment Equity Act No.55, of 1998a; in India in Section 335 of the Constitution; in Malaysia in Article 153 of the constitution; and in Northern Ireland in the Good Friday Agreement of 1998 and the Fair Employment and Treatment Order of 1998. Along with these instruments are court decisions which seek to adjudicate conflicts and challenges to the constitutional and legal instruments becoming themselves hallmark events in the life of affirmative action programs. Another source of legitimizing affirmative action preferences is found in executive directives and administrative rules and discretion. President Kennedy's Executive Order 10925 and President Johnson's Executive Order 11246 in the US experience have obtained legendary status in the life of affirmative action.

Laws and executive directives can be transformative in incremental as well revolutionary ways. Their impact may depend on how the recipients react to or manipulate the laws governing affirmative action. In Malaysia, "Ali baba" practices have become common in which indigenous Malays illegally transfer their contracts and licenses to non-indigenous individuals who are not eligible for affirmative action benefits (Gomez 2012). This assumes the form of "fronting" in South Africa. Another very significant way in which recipients may influence the implementation of affirmative action programs refers to what can be called their absorptive capacity. This points to the fact that in many instances, affirmative action opportunities and awards could simply not find qualified recipients for a variety of reasons. In South Africa and India, because of late availability of educational facilities against a history of illiteracy, many opportunities went either unfilled or were claimed by the same small group of qualified eligible persons. This inevitably in turn facilitated the emergence of a self-perpetuating well-off group, many very wealthy within the disadvantaged community. In some cases as in India, deliberate implementation hurdles such as special examinations to determine qualified beneficiaries have been created by privileged bureaucrats opposed to affirmative action.

Bridging the gap between formal legal instruments and their implementation for justice and equality therefore has been buffeted by an assortment of anticipated and unanticipated obstacles making doubly difficult to achieve the aims of affirmative action, some stemming from ongoing strife and litigation regarding defining who are eligible for benefits, some from the expansion of the eligible list of beneficiaries, some from resistance by employers engaged in superfluous schemes of avoidance from recipients undermining the intent of the law by engaging in "Ali Baba" practices, some from limited absorptive capability of the recipient communities, some from rear guard opposition from entrenched bureaucrats and administrators opposed to affirmative action, and some from violence against recipients as in India where untouchables have been habitually assaulted (Seth 1998:503).

Conclusion

The number of states which have now embarked on affirmative action policies has been growing, and the results have been diverse and require tracking. The experiences have differed even as these affirmative action states have tended to utilize a common vocabulary to describe their policies and programs. These policies and programs have left in the experiences of the societies that have adopted them setbacks and unanticipated problems as well as achievements and opportunities. They have often witnessed major societal changes in institutions and practices and to significant departures from the original aims and intentions. Overall, a critical and comparative examination of affirmative action policies has bequeathed in their wake a number of outstanding issues and questions. Does prolonged affirmative action tend to sustain and encourage ethno-cultural divisions in the society, that is, establish identity politics as a norm of political life so that divisions and mutual antipathy and systemic interethnic malaise and even hate and bigotry become routinized and normalized in daily citizen life? Is it culture war in which incommensurable cultural values of justice of one community confronts another in ongoing warfare? Is it covert class warfare in which cross-communal elites cultivate, mobilize, and manipulate ethnic group divisions and communal segmentation for their own benefit? Is there a problem of incommensurability that argues that each affirmative action policy is culture specific? If so, then no comparisons can be validly made and policy lessons across borders futile? Or on the contrary, these experiments in social engineering do share much in common and from them much can be leant and shared? Overall, it raises the fundamental issue of whether justice been served on behalf of the original victims. What lessons have been learnt for the benefit of reframing public policy on affirmative action? Are there universal principles of affirmative action as a mode of distributive justice that can create a new society based on shared beliefs?

A new order in affirmative action clearly requires a new frame of mind for both beneficiaries and the old guard. Clearly, affirmative action is an experiment in social engineering with no guarantees and clearly would require a new set of habits for compliant transformation in instituting more just and equal order. Its programs tend to be very sensitive and easily liable to sabotage and acts of noncooperation and therefore depend in wide societal support for successful implementation.

Cross-References

▶ Diaspora and Ethnic Contestation in Guyana

References

Anderson TH (2004) The pursuit of fairness: a history of affirmative action. Oxford University Press, New York
Campbell T (2000) Justice. Macmillan, London
Cohen C (1998) The corruption that is group preference. Acad Quest 11(summer):14–22
Cohen C, Sterba J (2003) Affirmative action and racial preferences: a debate. Oxford University Press, New York
Fullinwider RK (1975) Preferential hiring and compensation. Soc Theory Pract 3(spring):307–320
Fullinwider RK (1980) The reverse discrimination controversy: a moral and legal analysis. Rowman and Littlefield, Totowa
Glazer N (1975) Affirmative discrimination: ethnic inequality and public policy. Basic Books, New York
Glazer N (1983) Individual rights and group rights. In: Glazer N (ed) Ethnic dilemmas. Harvard University Press, Cambridge
Goldman A (1976) Affirmative action. Philos Public Aff 5(winter):178–195
Goldman A (1979) Justice and reverse discrimination. Princeton University Press, Princeton
Gomez T (2012) In: Premdas R (ed) Affirmative action, ethnicity, and conflict. Routledge, London
Gomez T, Premdas R (eds) (2012) Introduction: affirmative action, horizontal inequality and equitable development, in Gomez and Premdas, op.cit.
Guinier L, Sturm S (2001) Who's qualified? Beacon Press, Boston
Gupta D (1998) Recasting reservations in the language of rights. In: Mahajan G (ed) Democracy, difference, and social justice. Oxford, Mumbai,Ibid.p.509
Katznelson I (2005) When affirmative action was white: an untold history of racial inequality in the twentieth century America. W.W. Norton, New York
Kellough JE (2006) Understanding affirmative action: politics, discrimination, and the search for justice. Georgetown University Press, Washington, DC

Loury G (1987) Why should we care about group inequality. In: Miller P, Ahrens J (eds) Equal opportunity. Basil Blackwell, Oxford
Nagel T (1973) Equal treatment and compensatory discrimination. Philos Public Aff 2 (summer):348–363
Nozick R (1972) Anarchy, state, and utopia. Blackwell Publishers, London
Parikh S (2012) Poverty, equality, and affirmative action in India, in Gomez and Premdas, op.cit.
Patterson O (1998) The ordeal of integration: progress and resentment in America. Basic Civitas books, Washington DC
Phillips A (1996) Which equalities matter? Polity Press, London
Pojman L (1992) The moral status of affirmative action. Public Aff Q 6(April):181–206
Pojman L (1998) The case against affirmative action. Int J Appl Philos 12(spring):97–115
Premdas R (2010) Ethnic conflict. In: Collins PH, Solomos J (eds) The Sage handbook of race and ethnic studies. Sage, London
Premdas R (2016) Social justice and affirmative action, review. Ethn Racial Stud 39(3):449–462
Ratuva S (2013) Politics of preferential development: trans-global study of affirmative action and ethnic conflict in Fiji, Malaysia and South Africa. Australian University Press, Canberra
Rawls J (1971) A theory of justice. Harvard University Press, Cambridge
Rosenfeld M (1991) Affirmative action and justice: a philosophical and constitutional inquiry. Yale University Press, New Haven
Ryan A (1993) Justice. Oxford University Press, London
Sen A (1992) Inequality examined. Sage, London
Sher G (1979) Reverse discrimination, the future, and the past. Ethics 90(October):81–87
Sheth DL (1997) Reservations Policy Revisited in Democracy, Difference and Social Justice edited by Gurpreet Manhajan. New Delhi: Oxford University Press, pp. 489–508
Skrentny JD (1996) The ironies of affirmative action: politics, culture, and justice in America. University of Chicago Press, Chicago
Skrentny JD (ed) (2001) Color lines: affirmative action, immigration, and civil rights options for America. university of Chicago Press, Chicago
Sowell T (2004) Affirmative action around the world. Yale University Press, New Haven
Sterba JP (2003) Defending affirmative action, defending preferences. J Soc Philos 34 (June):285–300
Taylor C (1994) The politics of recognition. In: Guttman A (ed) Multiculturalism. Princeton University Press, Princeton
Waltzer M (1983) Spheres of justice: a defense of pluralism and equality. Basic Books, New York
Westen P (1985) The concept of equality. Ethics 95:830–850
Young IM (1990) Justice and the politics of difference. Princeton University Press, Princeton

Negotiating Ethnic Conflict in Deeply Divided Societies: Political Bargaining and Power Sharing as Institutional Strategies

78

Madhushree Sekher, Mansi Awasthi, Allen Thomas, Rajesh Kumar, and Subhankar Nayak

Contents

Introduction: Contextualizing India's Democracy	1516
Methodological Issues	1517
Democracy and Representation: A Brief Review	1518
Representation and Conflict Literature	1520
Reflections on Indian Electoral Democracy and Representation	1521
Representation: A Situational Analysis	1522
EPR: The Ethnic Power Relations Dataset	1523
Understanding and Analyzing "Ethnicity" in India	1525
Findings from the Field	1526
Emerging Debates	1534
Concluding Remarks	1535
Appendix	1535
References	1536

Abstract

With interest in social institutions expanding, and the centering of attention on state as an institution that is essentially cultural, a major interest in recent literature on ethnicity studies is on people, communities, and societies – (i) as collective actors in relation with the state as the sovereign authority and (ii) the process of interface between the state and the ethnic groups that constitute the ethno-demographic profile of the state. This, on one hand, has brought a shift in the focus on state and the modern state-system in studies on ethnic conflict, from the conventional perspective that viewed ethnic conflicts as a condition under

---

M. Sekher (✉)
Centre for Study of Social Exclusion and Inclusive Policies (CSSEIP), Tata Institute of Social Sciences (TISS), Mumbai, India
e-mail: madhusekher@gmail.com; madhusekher@tiss.edu

M. Awasthi · A. Thomas · R. Kumar · S. Nayak
Tata Institute of Social Sciences (TISS), Mumbai, India

© The Author(s), under exclusive license to Springer Nature Singapore Pte Ltd. 2019
S. Ratuva (ed.), *The Palgrave Handbook of Ethnicity*,
https://doi.org/10.1007/978-981-13-2898-5_152

state failure. On the other hand, the emphasis on the cultural base of the state has brought the state-system into the core of the state-society causal argument, driving interactive processes. An important condition that underlies the state-ethnic group(s) causal interface is the perceived inequalities of communities. It is this that can become a condition for likelihood of ethnic conflict. Political representation, beyond the domain of electoral politics, is an important non-military institutional strategy for expressing perceived inequalities and for negotiating conflict in ethnically divided societies. With movements and protests becoming central to state-society interactive processes, this chapter looks at power sharing and political bargaining as an institutional strategy that ethnic groups employ for addressing their grievances, particularly in diverse societies. The chapter is based on a study carried out in India. It redraws the focus away from formal structures to various methods of power sharing that run through all levels of society and the role played by civil society organizations, interest groups, and ethno-political organizations.

Keywords

Ethnic conflict · Perceived inequalities · Political representation · Power sharing · India's democracy

Introduction: Contextualizing India's Democracy

For the volumes written on the state of India's democracy, it is intriguing to find that most scholars approach the subject with a tone of surprise, starting typically by questioning how a society with such complex matrix of heterogeneous identities has managed to maintain order in the face of frequent violent social conflict (Weiner 1989). Pedagogically, this line of enquiry resembles the structural-functionalist approach to some extent, since it occupies itself with determining factors behind the sustenance of the whole along with the internal dysfunctions. Scholars have chosen to engage with different elements of the Indian democratic structure ranging from the structure and functioning of a parliamentary democracy (Kholi 1998; Singh and Verney 2003; Kashyap 2004; Beteille 2011; Mehta 2012); role and relationship of the legislature, judiciary, and executive (Rao 2005; Mehta 2007); nature of the Indian federalism (Bagchi 2000; Srikrishna 2011; Tillin 2018); and working of electoral politics and voting patterns. The process of electoral representation can be conceived of as a zero-sum game wherein one gets elected and becomes a representative or not. This conceptualization has an institutionally locked-in perspective where elections are seen as the mechanism that confers representative while being both structurally deterministic and politically conservative. It is imperative to go beyond this classical understanding of representation in democracy, as politics is an open arena of contestable opinions where elections are not the only mechanism through which representatives are made.

Essentially the classical understanding of representation in democracy implies that a group be organized collectively around an issue of shared interest and participate in the election process. This provides the group a better platform to negotiate their claims. Even though this procedure seems fairly self-evident, the structure of the Indian democracy is rather complex to lend itself to such a straightforward reasoning. Intense competition among groups/collective actors vying for state power results in the groups to mobilize considerable support for their mandate, notwithstanding the "rule of numbers" and the complications that arise by the virtue of coalition formation/power sharing.

When most of the data and literature on ethnic conflict is concentrated around the objective of social inequalities, this chapter offers an insight to the processes by which perceived inequalities and grievances of ethnic groups structure their institutional strategy and define the process that shapes their political representation. This process in the causal interaction defining state-society relations often goes unaddressed and can be a significant indicator of conflict likelihood. The chapter argues that one of the most underrated issues in understanding ethnicity and ethnic conflicts has been how communities connect with the state and the state-system characterized by its various agencies. The chapter, thus, makes an attempt to add to the growing body of knowledge that seeks to understand political representation, beyond the domain of electoral politics and elections. It finds resonance in the claim that people rely least on the state for the redressal of their grievances. In that regard, the chapter makes an empirical contribution to substantiate these claims and provide insight on the nature of institutions citizens associate with for redressing their grievances.

Methodological Issues

An obverse line of enquiry has been made here to assess what elements of democracy have been largely associated with social conflicts. A vast amount of conflict literature (Collier and Hoeffler 2004; Fearon and Laitin 2003; Cederman et al. 2010; Christin and Hug 2012) has adopted the method of identifying "independent" variables such as scale of public funding, measures of poverty, federal structure, etc., which contribute to the "dependent" variable, being the likelihood of conflict occurrence. These studies are largely statistical in their orientation and can be restricted to a certain time and space, given their preoccupation with highlighting correlations between variables and a dependence on datasets/databases, such as the $GROW^{up}$ and the Ethnic Power Relations-EPR data (ETH-International Conflict Research Data. URL- https://icr.ethz.ch/data/). In contrast, this chapter looks at how marginalized and excluded voices find avenues to express their grievances beyond the formal electoral process of gaining representation. Drawing on a combination of desk reviews and qualitative data collected from fieldwork carried out across sites in India (for details, see section "Appendix"), this chapter first familiarizes on how grievances regarding political representation emerge at the first place. Secondly, it assesses the formal structures such as the electoral machinery to assess how grievances may or may not be institutionally accommodated. The chapter, then, makes an attempt to analytically explore avenues other than the formal political space provided by electoral system, through which such grievances find expression. Consequently, the chapter highlights the various institutional strategies and mechanisms surrounding ethnic mobilization toward collective action and interest representation.

While empirical studies have convincingly shown that political and economic inequalities along ethnic lines increase the risk of violence (Cederman et al. 2011; Kuhn and Weidmann 2015; Vogt 2011), we know much less about the mechanism by which ethnic grievances are translated into political action. In this sense, the chapter aims to redraw the focus away from formal structures to methods of power sharing that run through all levels of society and the role played by civil society organizations, interest groups such as student union bodies, and other ethno-political organizations that translate perceived inequalities and grievances to political action. Through this trajectory, the chapter discusses issues regarding why voices feel excluded or disenchanted with formal structures of power sharing and representation.

Democracy and Representation: A Brief Review

Representation has been an integral part of democracy. While there has been significant debate over the meanings and applications of representation and democracy, the concern here is not with determining the complementary or antagonistic epistemologies and etymologies of these concepts. Rather, the attempt in this chapter is to explain the functioning of "political representation" in a postcolonial democratic India, through a discussion around its forms, manifestations, structures, and actors. Most of the scholarship on representation and democracy has been concerned with the formal aspect of democracy, engaging mainly with structures of representation and the institutional design of a democracy. However, contemporary scholarship has questioned and critiqued this over reliance on the formalistic element and proposed new ways of understanding representation beyond the electoral domain. This section provides a review of the approaches to understanding political representation in a democracy.

The institutionalization of representation in a democracy is most clearly manifested through elections wherein citizens elect representatives, giving them legitimacy as legal constitutional functionaries in the democratic process. It is not surprising thus that most of the literature on democracy – its assessment and forms, as well as academic debates around the concept of representation – have coalesced around the phenomenon of elections. In fact "election studies" as a discipline is concerned with precisely this aspect of a democracy, i.e., studying the various aspects of the elector and the elected, alongside the nature of the democratic process, such as nature of campaigning and political participation (Lama-Rewal 2009). This approach typically employs surveys in order to gauge general voting patterns, behavior, and attitude of the polity in order to arrive at some generalizations regarding people's choice of representatives. In essence, such studies provide insight on, and are thus limited by, their engagement with how people vote or who they vote for.

In India, this nature of enquiry was spearheaded by the *Lokniti* Network at the Centre for Study of Developing Societies (CSDS – http://www.lokniti.org), conducting large-scale survey research on *pre* and *post* polls, both at national (general elections) and the state level (assembly elections). The database hosted by CSDS revolutionized the study of the Indian polity, such that almost every publication has made a reference to the data derived thereof. However, given the inherent nature of the discipline alongside the limitations presented by the survey method, the analysis remains limited on several accounts. Thus, while this approach helps us in understanding how people vote and draw subsequent analysis from it, it does not provide adequate answers to "why people vote" (Banerjee 2017). Secondly, it remains limited to national- and state-level electoral politics, without providing any information about local-level political activity and participation, candidates/ representatives, or governance structures. While anthropological excursions such as Banerjee (2017) attempt to remedy the first by engaging in depth with why people vote, there seems to be systemic lack of data available, for use by scholars and researchers, on local-level electoral politics such that even the official election commission website of the country does not host this information (barring a few state government websites that are updated regularly).

The academic engagement on the question of political representation has now far surpassed its traditional understanding, which was largely restricted to studying representation through the paradigm of *the general will of the sovereign body*. Contemporary political theory has questioned the limitations of perspectives focused solely around the nature of the elector and the elected, proposing new ways to understand representation beyond the domain of elections and elected representatives. Historically speaking, the theoretical literature around the concept of political representation was largely focused on whether representatives should act as delegates or as trustees (Dovi 2006). Each of these posits own interpretation of how a representative ought to act, placing opposing emphasis on representative as a delegate enacting the will of those being represented or as trustee who must follow his own course of action based on his/her own judgment. Pitkin (1967) suggests maintaining this paradox as inherent to the concept of "representation," outlining four different approaches to understand representation, namely, formal, descriptive, symbolic, and substantive representation. This typology aims to provide a direction to discussions around what representatives ought to do by underlining the different expectations associated with each. In essence, disagreement over the role of the representative is judged based on which element of the schema is being applied, and tensions are levied onto the misapplication of standards laid out (Dovi 2006).

Formal representation is concerned with institutional design of a democratic regime, laying out the methods by which representatives come to power and acquire legitimacy, alongside sanctioning mechanisms to "punish" them, if they fail to perform. Pitkin (1967) refers to these two dimensions as authorization and accountability. Most scholarship on the nature of a democracy has been dominated by an engagement with the formal aspect of representation, i.e., the structures of representation, the institutional arrangements, the mechanism through which representatives are chosen, and the functions associated with the status of an elected representative. As a result, most discussions around the state of a democracy ultimately collapse into an engagement with electoral politics. This idea of representation as a principal agent relationship alongside the emphasis on institutional design and electoral politics implied that studies on state of democracies were devoted to determining the disjuncture between what elected representatives ought to do and the activities they undertook while in office (Yadav 2010). In fact, this tension between representation and responsiveness is the foundational paradox of the Indian democracy (Mehta 2012).

Recent works in contemporary democratic theory, however, have paved the way to take the discussion around representation beyond the domain of formal structures and processes (Dovi 2006). There is a recognition of the need to approach the process of political representation in the plural and to consider representational practices as they unfolded within, but also outside of the electoral process and in different modes (Lama-Rewal 2009). It is obvious that as political realities acquire greater complexity, the focus of representation must expand beyond its institutional embodiment.

One such formulation is Michael Saward's idea of *representative claim* wherein representation is seen as what it does rather than what it is (Saward 2010). Describing representation as a dynamic practice, he argues that it can be seen all around us and is across societies rather than simply a fixed feature of government (Saward 2010). The emergence of this literature has led scholars to argue that the study of representation has experienced a constructivist turn in the wake of a crisis of representation (Lama-Rewal 2009; Mehta 2012). This thesis of a crisis of representation follows from a set of changes that democracies worldwide are currently experiencing, such as a decline in electoral voting rates and electoral participation, an increasing distrust of politicians, and a decline in the popularity of political parties. The primary feature of this thesis is the rising importance of non-state or para-statal actors such as NGOs, interest groups, and social movements in the civil society domain, implying a shift from older and traditional forms of representation such as political parties and trade unions to newer models such as social movements, informal citizen groups, and NGOs (Chandhoke 2005).

However, there is a genuine lack of scholarly attention paid to "non-electoral forms of representation" in the Indian scenario. The accusation leveled against non-electoral forms of representation is that they are non-democratic since there is no generally agreed-upon mechanism, such as elections that accrue to them legitimacy of people. Building on the scholarship on representation, as cited above, this chapter makes an attempt to delineate how people view representation and representatives, as citizens of a democracy. Thus, questions asked in the field centered around whether or not people of community felt represented at the national, state, and local level, if they knew their elected representatives and if they voted regularly, who they approached for their grievances ranging from state actors to non-state ones, and whether they participated in any form of political activity such as protests, rallies, etc. The idea is to highlight how citizens relate to the state and elected representatives.

Representation and Conflict Literature

A new wave of conflict studies, especially international conflict literature, has been geared to exploring how lack of sufficient representation of ethnic groups relates with the likelihood of civil conflict. There is a general understanding that conflicts are the result of inequality, but not all inequalities acquire salience. Conflicts do not arise out of the mere existence of different ethnic groups, but when there is differential access and distribution of things commonly valued by groups comprising a polity. These include not only materialistic resources but also political power and opportunities which result in perceived inequalities. Studies on ethnic conflict have shown that the likelihood of conflict is higher in situations/areas wherein ethnic groups do not have/or have limited access to political power or state power (Cederman et al. 2013). Particularly, when political and economic power is unevenly distributed across ethnic lines, it gives rise to inequalities which manifests itself through grievances that have the potential to turn into issues of violent collective action (Cederman et al. 2010). Taking the case of India's linguistic reorganization of provinces as a case in point, it is also argued that asymmetrical access to state power or disproportionate representation of ethnic groups can increase the likelihood of violent conflict (Lacina 2014).

However, it is imperative that representation be seen beyond the national level given the nature of Indian politics in the post-Congress dominance era, which is marked by a shift in the arena of contestation from national level to the state level, as regional parties have gained importance with the rise of coalition politics. Moreover, by judging relevance as representation in the parliament, it is limited to institutional validation of relevance, as being measured by electoral legitimacy. It is our contention that in areas of conflict, non-electoral forms of representation may acquire greater salience, especially in cases where there is an abject distrust for the state-system, as seen in the case of Kashmir.

Reflections on Indian Electoral Democracy and Representation

As a result, while on the voter side the universal adult franchise in India recognizes that one vote accords one and equal value, there are also constituencies and seats reserved for the minority community. Moreover, with the demise of the Congress as the only national party in the 1970s, India saw the great rise of regional parties and was catapulted into an era of coalition politics. These factors mark particular turning point in India's democratic history since it also made actors at local level significant in the entire electoral mechanism. This is precisely why any analysis limited to the national level proves not only incomprehensible but also incorrect due to circumstantial and contextual diversities. While linguistic ethnic groups and the indigenous (Scheduled Tribe) population are relatively concentrated, the persistence of caste and gender hierarchy is a feature of nearly every state/district/region. Being mindful of these differentials and their variations over time, alongside the predominantly rural character of the Indian polity, measure for decentralized local governance was instituted in India through a Constitutional Amendment in 1992, with a vision to diffuse power down to the last mile, with the last tier of democratically elected governance structure being the Village – the Village *Panchayat/Gram Panchayat*. Thus, the rural local government system in India, through the Panchayati Raj Institutions (PRIs), makes provision for this involving devolution of functions, finances, and functionaries to the local government institutions. It was introduced, recognizing the ability of the local people to better manage their issues and to act as a buffer to prevent local tensions from escalating.

The PRIs and its conception must be assessed against the backdrop of conflict literature which has focused on the nature of relationship between the center/national government and the provinces, as a source of tension. A vast amount of literature is organized around the distribution of resources and power between the center and the provinces and how these might propel likelihood of conflict. Lacina (2014) in her essay has critiqued this line of enquiry preoccupied with distributional resource patterns as a source of conflict by making an appeal to bring the government back into the study of civil conflict.

Taking cues from these two approaches, this chapter redirects attention to the distribution of not just resources but also political power, by looking at how groups engage with the state/democratic structures at the local level. This is imperative since one of most ardent arguments behind advocating the decentralized governance was that it would act as a pacifier to situations of conflict, since it would give smaller groups the ability to gain power and representation at the local level, hence having a significant say in decision-making matters of governance that directly affect them. This is precisely where attention needs to be redirected from the national level and be redrawn to assess the nature of local-level politics – that is, the institutional strategies and processes underlying political bargaining and power sharing – how groups acquire positions of power; how they articulate their grievances; how they mobilize to achieve their demands; or how they strike alliances with other ethnic groups and also the state.

Representation: A Situational Analysis

It is the contention in this chapter that when voices feel marginalized and/or underrepresented by being excluded from the larger democratic process, they may react in or more of the following ways:

(I) The first occurs within the institutionally organized electoral process, as people exercise their dissent by choosing not to enact their vote and abstain from participating in elections. Hence a boycott of the elections becomes a manifestation of their grievances against the state, as an expression for their discontent against the political system. This situation is exemplified by the case of Kashmir, in its ideal-typical manifestation. In Kashmir, often there is a call for boycott by groups demanding secession from India, or sometimes the call for boycott may be made by mainstream political parties to show opposition toward certain government policies, as is being witnessed in recent months Kashmir where regional political parties like National Conference and People's Democratic Party have threatened to boycott the upcoming *Panchayat* (rural) and urban local body elections scheduled later this year, as a protest against certain decisions of the national government (for details, see https://www.indiatoday.in/india/story/jammu-and-kashmir-why-centre-backs-panchayat-polls-despite-boycott-by-national-conference-pdp-1338065-2018-09-11).

(II) Grievances relating to representation may range from demands for greater territorial autonomy to reservation quotas. Hence, unlike the scenario in Kashmir, ethnic groups to showcase their discontent, also, express grievances through collective mobilization and protests. Collective action could be violent or nonviolent. Since the aim here is not necessarily secession from the mainland, mobilization may not be against the electoral process but for a greater accommodation within that system as exemplified by demands for greater autonomy or reservation, etc. Mobilization of groups finds expression in several interest groups and beyond the domain of the state and the state-system, such as through student union groups and other organizations. However, there has been no clear way of establishing a relationship between a single factor and protest mobilization.

This section aims to provide a picture of the process of political bargaining and claims for power sharing (representational politics), in India, based on data from secondary sources and primary findings from two field sites where the study was carried out – in the provinces of Jammu and Kashmir and in Assam. First, the section provides an insight into how large-scale databases such as the Ethnic Power Relations (EPR) dataset, referred to in the foregoing section on methodological issues, have analyzed and assessed political representation in ethnic terms at the group level in the subcontinent and their political relevance. The intention here is to provide an all India picture of politically dominant/powerless ethnic groups. Second, since the dataset is based purely on figures accruing from the number of formal elected representatives per community grouping, the section also outlines people's perceptions around the question of representation extrapolating from the primary findings of the field study.

EPR: The Ethnic Power Relations Dataset

The Ethnic Power Relations dataset, as outlined before, is one of the few large-scale datasets that hosts information on political representation across countries at the group level. It codes the political relevance of various ethnic groups as senior partner, junior partner, or powerless based on a group's representatives in the national parliament, relative to their demographic size. The EPR India dataset shows the association between the demographic size of "politically" relevant ethnic groups in the country and their representation in the ethno-political system of India. EPR dataset is an attempt to unravel the pathway of inequality in political representation between different ethnic groups both at national and state level over time. As a result, one can assess over time periods, how an ethnic group's political relevance and representation changes over time. When data for the Indian subcontinent alone is extracted from the dataset, across all time periods, the following scenario emerges, as shown in Table 1.

Table 1 unveils that the Hindu forward category from Hindi heartland and from the provinces of Maharashtra, Gujarat, Karnataka, Kerala, Tamil Nadu, and West

Table 1 Status of political representation of ethnic groups (PREGs) in the national executive

Time periods	Status	Representation of PREGs in executive power		
1947–2015	Senior partner	Hinduism	Others	Hindi heartland (Uttar Pradesh, Madhya Pradesh, Bihar, Rajasthan, Haryana), Maharashtra, Tamil Nadu, Punjab, West Bengal, Karnataka, Gujarat, Orissa, Andhra Pradesh, Assam
		Sikhism	Others	Punjab[#]
	Junior partner	Hinduism	SC, ST, OBC	All states and Assam except northeastern states
		Islam, Christian, Sikhism	All*	States where these religions are present
	Powerless	Islam, Christian, Sikhism, Others	SC, ST, OBC, Others	**Northeastern states,** except Assam

Note: (1) *All and SC, ST, OBC, and Others have been merged in Islam, Christian, and Sikhism because this doesn't make a difference on their status unlike Others in Hinduism (in almost every state) which has absolute influence and labeled as senior partner. The consolidation of social categories in Islam, Christian, and Sikhism doesn't affect the absolute influence in the executive and hence their status, which is measured by the number and importance of the positions controlled by them. They have been categorized as junior partners because adding social categories up doesn't make them senior partners by numbers and they have their presence in the executive in almost all periods. (2) #Occasional representation. (3) *Senior Partner*: Representatives of the group participate as senior partners in a formal or informal power-sharing arrangement. Power sharing is defined as any arrangement that divides executive power among leaders who claim to represent particular ethnic groups and who have real influence on political decision-making. *Junior Partner*: Representatives participate as junior partners in government. The choice between senior and junior partner depends on the group's absolute influence in the executive – that is, irrespective of group size – measured by the number and importance of the positions controlled by group members. *Powerless*: Elite representatives hold no political power (or do not have influence on decision-making) at the national level of executive power – although without being explicitly discriminated against. (4) Coders were asked to focus on groups' absolute access to power, rather than on the groups' under or overrepresentation relative to their demographic size

Bengal enjoys the status of senior partner implying, thus, that this category holds much greater political relevance compared to the rest of the groups and enjoys significant representation. In fact, even India's Presidents, Prime Ministers, and Union Cabinet Ministers over the 1947–2014 predominantly belong to this category, which shows that this ethnic group has sustained its power and relevance throughout all elected terms of *Lok Sabha* – the Lower House/House of People's Representatives in India's Parliament. The EPR's time variant coding of politically relevant ethnic groups coded this group as "Senior Partner" in the formation of government. It is quite shocking that there is zero representation from the states of Tripura, Manipur, Mizoram, Arunachal Pradesh, and Nagaland at the central level of executive power, despite their *full provincial state* status within the Indian federal system.

This reflects the failure of proportional representation system in India – representation from minorities and smaller linguistic regions has been either disproportionate or completely absent in the legislative bodies.

Since independence, the Scheduled Castes and Scheduled Tribes were given reservation status, guaranteeing political representation. Owing to the recommendation of the Mandal Commission, affirmative action was extended to the Other Backward Class (OBC) group, resulting in a total of 49.5% reservation quota. Consequently, there was a rise of OBCs representation in the Lok Sabha. This phenomenon coincided with the rise of regional parties, which are largely dominated by non-upper caste groups. While the EPR dataset allows us to draw conclusions on nature of representation at the national level, by highlighting groups that hold power in state's executive body, it is not able to capture the representation matrix at the provincial government assembly level:

(i) Given the nature of Indian politics, as argued, with the rise of coalition politics and regional parties, the competition at the provincial level has acquired greater relevance. The decentralized system along with the federal structure has also meant that local-level governance and politics have become a site unto itself. The data on this third tier of democracy – the local government system – is conspicuously absent for analysis by researchers in such large-scale datasets. In fact, even the official Election Commission website of the country does not have systematic account of elected representatives at the local level for each region/administrative unit.

(ii) Moreover, it is noted that citizens are often more concerned about and in sync with local- and provincial-level politics, compared to the national level. In fact, one of the narratives which emerged in the media at the time of last General/Lok Sabha elections in 2014 was that people did not really scrutinize their choice when it came to voting for the Prime Minister in terms of party affiliation, social background, etc., since they felt too distanced from the consequences of that choice. This was in contrast to the scenario at the local government level, where people felt they knew the candidate and that they had more power to directly persecute the local government representative for unsatisfactory performance. Such nuanced perceptions underlying electorate choices are also not captured in the larger datasets.

Understanding and Analyzing "Ethnicity" in India

EPR dataset has offered a global picture of ethnic groups both which are in majority and at risk. Though this data is important, it fails to capture ethnicity and its influence on ethnic politics within the country. India is an unparalleled heterogeneous and complex society. Wide array of identities are attached to the people, and these include caste identities, religious identities, and identifications with clans and lineages as well as linguistic, regional, subregional, and local identities and often varying types of "tribal" identities. Most of these often cut across one another. The formation of an ethnic identity or transformation of that identity into ethnic nationalism is either the result of the actions taken by elites within the group to promote the change(s) or favorable conditions which arise from the broader political and economic environments rather than from the cultural values of the ethnic groups in question (Manor 1996). Individuals have multiple dimensions of identity – "identity complex" – at the same time. If power sharing and political bargaining, as institutional strategies, are to be understood, it is important to comprehend the identity complexities that ethnic groups employ for negotiating their grievances. Equally crucial is to understand how a group of people with similar identity get mobilized and at what point of time. With regard to identity politics, in India group identities are linked to religion, linguistic, tribe, and caste affiliations – all are prominent in national politics. Language and tribe tend to be geographically concentrated, whereas religion and caste are more evenly spread throughout the country. The foremost thing is to understand India's multicultural identities and how they play a role in defining group identities and their political bargaining and power sharing strategies to negotiate the ethnic politics. It is this that the following section attempts to make, drawing from the case studies carried out in Jammu and Kashmir and Assam.

Findings from the Field

This section provides a state-wise analysis of the findings based on the data collected from the two field sites of Jammu and Kashmir and Assam, respectively. Instead of looking at inequality in representation purely objectively, an attempt is made here to assess perceived inequalities by asking people if and how adequately they feel represented at the national, state, and local level and if not, why.

- Firstly, the questionnaire asked people whether or not they had exercised their voting rights in the past 10 years (and, at which level of electoral competition – national, provincial, local). These findings provide an insight on how people view formal structures and processes of representation, specifically elections and electoral politics.
- Another set of questions enquired people about their representatives at local, provincial, and national level. The answers to this, second set of questions, did not always match actual representatives in power-holding elected office, thus showing how perceived notions of representation may vary.
- Further, respondents were also asked about whom they approached to redress their grievances pertaining to common/local matters such as access to public services and who among them was most easily approachable and most responsive, looking at both state and non-state actors.
- Subsequently, respondents were asked as to who they most relied on in times of unrest and, more specifically, with respect to getting access to essential services such as food, healthcare, education, etc.

In order to have a clear picture of people's perceptions regarding the above outlined factors, the analysis is discussed in the following section, thematically, covering the issues separately for each study site.

Elections and Voting

One of the primary questions of the study sought to determine people's participation in electoral politics by asking them if they had exercised their voting right in the past 10 years (2005–2015) and at what level of electoral enterprise (local, provincial, national) and if not, why. The universal adult franchise is often cited as the basic criteria common to all existing democracies. Thus, the intention was to gauge whether people of the state participated in the enterprise or how they perceived it, by asking the question in a qualitative formulation.

Jammu and Kashmir

In the last 10 years, an overwhelming majority of the households in the region under study did not exercise their voting rights. Those who abstained from voting said they did not identify with the political establishment, arguing that the electoral system was an imposed order to which the people did not subscribe. Many of respondents supported their abstention of the electoral process by stating their ideological belief, which views Kashmir as being illegally and unjustly occupied by India. They neither believe in the Indian democracy, nor do they identify with the Indian rule. Even the households that voted in the last 10 years regretted having exercised their franchise. The promises and the assurance from the politicians and the political parties about initiating development and growth along with other basic facilities did manage to pull people out to vote, but could not garner their confidence for long as they failed to keep their promises, even the basic ones. The respondents felt that most elected representatives were corrupt and inefficient, which further amplified their alienation from and for the structural establishment. People voted not to live the spirit of democracy but just to fix their basic grievances. But when they realized that none of their grievances are addressed, they lost faith in the democracy and rather developed a negative perception toward the state and its administrative machinery.

However, does the erosion of faith in the electoral enterprise of a democracy imply that there is no case to be made for capturing political representation in the region? If research were to rely on data limited to elected representatives at various levels of governance based on their political party and ethnic group affiliations, drawn from the EPR dataset, it would show that "Kashmiri Muslims" hold at least some relevance. However, such datasets often decontextualize representation, as a result of which they fail to capture the perceived notions around representation as outlined above. Thus, in the case of a region where there is a strong movement for self-rule and secession, an analysis of representation limited to elected representatives and election process, serves no analytical purpose. Firstly, even if such an analysis is attempted, it must make some reference to the actual voter turnout rates and polling percentage, given area-wise, to be able to provide some sense of how many people's choices it represents. Secondly, by focusing on representation on national level alone, the EPR dataset fails to capture nature of representation at the provincial government level which, as shown in the case of Kashmir, resonates more with people's perceptions about and their own political life, compared to national-level politics (as discussed in the following section). Moreover, the decontextualization glosses over the fact that Jammu and Kashmir enjoys a constitutionally special autonomous position within the federal structure of India, given to it under Article 370 of the Indian Constitution.

Assam

Contrarily in Assam, with an average voter turnout around 60 percent of the total electorate, households permanently residing in the region exercised their voting rights at least once in the last 10 years – that is, voted in the national general election, in the provincial legislative assembly elections, and in the elections to the Bodoland Territorial Council (BTC), a special category local government institution constituted in 2003 to fulfill economic, educational, and linguistic aspiration and ethnic identity of the Bodos (for details on BTC, see https://wptbc.assam.gov.in/portlets/bodoland-territorial-council).

But, at the same time, it is difficult to make conclusive statements regarding the voters' awareness about the different elections conducted in the province, even if they exercised their franchise. For instance, few responded, stating that they had voted in *Rajya Sabha*/Council of States elections, not aware the *Rajya Sabha* is upper house of the Parliament of India which comprises of members indirectly elected by the provincial legislative assembly. This response of the people puts their general comprehension about the whole exercise of elections into question. However, the general attitude about elections was largely positive, with people recognizing and emphasizing the importance of the adult franchise. On the whole thus, the responses are suggestive of absence of any barriers in exercising voting rights in this region at any level.

Community's Representation at Local-, State-, and National-Level Legislatures

As part of the field study, a series of questions were asked to the respondents to understand whether they felt sufficiently represented in the three levels of governance within the country's federal structure in the national, provincial, and local government. Table 2 shows the number of households who answered in the positive to the question on whether their community had representatives at each of the three levels. However, these figures must be read alongside the qualitative responses of the people as highlighted below, as well as ethnic composition of the respondents' profile (see "Appendix").

Jammu and Kashmir

When we compare the representation of the community or the ethnic group at the local, the state, and the national level, we find that majority of the households in the region are feel represented (Table 2). It also shows that people may perceive representation in different terms and not necessarily in the electoral sense. An

Table 2 Community's political representation at different levels

Field site	Local government institutions	State legislative assembly (provincial government)	National parliament
Jammu and Kashmir	18 (36)	20 (37.1)	15 (29.4)
Assam	23 (39.0)	17 (28.3)	0
N	107	114	111

Note: Valid N for Assam: local (59), state, and national (60). Valid N for JandK: local (50), state (54), and national (51). Figures in parenthesis indicate percentages

overwhelming majority of households though (32 out of the 50 who attempted to answer) said they did not feel represented at the local level. At the state level, 20 of the 54 households believed they knew their representative at state level, out of which most responses corroborated with the actual representatives. However, a comparison with the figure for the national level is revealing, with only 15 of the 51 households knowing their representative and feeling represented in the national parliament. It must be kept in mind, however, that the reason for feeling inadequately represented is to be seen relative to the number of people who abstained from voting. These two factors seem to run a vicious cycle; people don't vote because they feel that none of the mainstream parties represent their ideological beliefs, and since they don't vote, they do not feel represented.

In terms of feeling sufficiently represented at all three levels, the satisfaction level with regard to their representation in the governing bodies is abysmally low with only few households being satisfied in this regard. Majority of the households in this region show lukewarm response to any political processes and generally do not participate in it. Their opinion of being non-represented is because of the two major reasons – first, their perception of the political system as imposed on them and second, the perceived disconnect of the elected representatives from the populace. There was a general perception that their or their community's interests were not sufficiently represented at each of the levels.

Assam

In the BTC region of Assam where the field study was carried out, response to the question regarding representation varied. While *Bodo* community dominated in maintaining the highest number of representations of their community members in local government in comparison to other communities, others like *Bengalis*, Scheduled Caste, and Other Backward Classes like *Santhalis* and *Koch Rajbongshi* felt they had no representation in the local government institutions. *Garos*, *Nepalis*, and *Rabhas* had at least one representatives of their community in the local government institution (the *Bodo* Territorail Council- BTC). But, despite the variation in ethnic profile, most households felt better represented at the local-level government, compared to the state and national level (Table 2).

At the state level, only households belonging to *Bodo* community responded that they felt represented in state legislature. Even this does not mean that all of the households belonging to the community are aware of their representatives. But their responses also reflect their ambiguity regarding their understanding about the legislative and political institutions. Mr. Chandan Brahma and Mrs. Pramila Rani Brahma are the representatives of the *Bodo* community from Kokrajhar region in the State Legislature. Though majority of households in the Kokrajhar region belonged to Bodo community, and the representatives from the region in the State Legislature were from the Bodo community, the people from the region did not know who were their elected representatives, and also named other local prominent leaders as members of the State Legislative Assembly, who were actually not the elected representatives. Few households even had the misconception that members of Bodo Territorial Council (BTC) are members in State Legislature. This also indicates the link between the representatives and the citizens.

Most of the households belonging to *Bodo* community in the Assam are positive about their representation in the political institutions of different levels. This is also because of the fulfillment of their demand for a territorial council – the BTC which was constituted on 2003. The people believe that it has led to increased development activities including infrastructure like road and electricity, which in turn steered more opportunities for people. People acknowledge that there have been better educational facilities with the setting up of territorial council, which they believe is due the better representation of the community by their political leaders at institutions and organizations. But interestingly, this representation is limited to local level, mostly leaders from their own locality.

The *Garo* community, an ethnic group of the Kokarajhar region feels they are not sufficiently represented even at local institutions. Except for the village headman, they are not convinced about the responsibilities carried out by their representatives. They held that their needs and demands are not met by the government due to the lack of adequate representation of their community. The communities under the Other Backward Class (OBC) category (mainly *Nepali*, *Santhal*, and *Koch Rajbongshi*) do not have ample political representation at any level. This deprives them of proper facilities and infrastructure, which affects the overall development in their village. Households belonging to *Rabha* and *Bengali* community also have similar concerns. Only few households agree that politicians have worked toward expanding their livelihood opportunities for the community.

Choice of Institution for Grievance Redressal

To evaluate whom respondents approached to redress their grievances, the questionnaire asked which institution or actor/agency the people approached and who among them was most responsive (Table 3).

Jammu and Kashmir

As seen in Tables 3 and 4, an overwhelming majority of the households in this region have faith in their community leader compared to any other institutions or personnel of the state, when it comes to settling their basic lawful grievances. Only 8 of the 60 households felt they could approach the local administration for addressing grievances over common matters, compared to mere 3 who said they had some level of faith in the judiciary, while virtually none of the elected political leaders were even considered an option.

Table 3 Grievance redressal over common matters

State	Judiciary	Local administration	Elected political leaders	Local community leader
Jammu and Kashmir	3 (5)	8 (13.3)	0	53 (88.3)
Assam	1(1.8)	5 (8.8)	5 (8.8)	46 (80.7)
N	117	117	117	117

Note: Valid N for Assam, 57; valid N for Jammu and Kashmir, 60. Figures in parenthesis indicate percentages

Easy availability, quick response, honesty, and sincerity of the community leaders make them the people's first choice for majority of the households. These features are completely missing either in the political leaders or in the administrative officials. The community leaders are more approachable, and there is a greater bond between them than the administration or the political leaders, and people relied on their community as the choice of first approach.

Besides, majority of the households relied on the *Awqaf*, a charitable endowment under Islamic personal law, rather than the statutory PRIs to redress their grievances. Such community organizations are trusted because of their easy availability and immediate as well as effective responses. These institutions are like their own family with whom they share a very strong bonding. In fact, some households even make voluntary financial deposits to these organizations in recognition of the services render and the role they play in the community. The district administration, which exists primarily to provide public services to the locals and with whom citizens have to interact, is perceived to be corrupt and inefficient – primarily seen in terms of weaknesses of the bureaucracy, growing complexities of administration, and absence of commitment and responsiveness of this frontline administrative wing of India's public administration (Sekher et al. 2018). In a region that is witnessing ethnic tensions like Jammu and Kashmir, it was not surprising that distrust of the district administration was more evident. Nevertheless, as reported by some respondents, people interacted with this institution to access public services.

Assam

Even in the case of Assam, it is the village headman who is the most preferred authority to settle grievances and is their point of contact to connect the local with the government institutions like local administration and police (Tables 3 and 4). Mostly households, who belong to Bodo community, approach community leaders. This distinction that respondents make between village headman and community leaders further complicates matters. While non-Bodo communities like Garos, Santhals, Bengalis, and other social categories, SC, and OBCs did not prefer to approach authorities other than village headman and community leaders for settling common disputes, the Bodo community seems to prefer the administrative authorities including local administration, and local elected leaders, for resolving their grievances in varying degrees. However, this point requires further interrogation in order to establish it as a trend.

Table 4 Reliance in times of social unrest/tensions

	Neighbors		Administration		Police/security forces		Political leaders		Civil society/community	
	Jammu and Kashmir	Assam	Jammu and Kashmir	Assam	Jammu and Kashmir	Assam	Jammu and Kashmir	Assam	Jammu and Kashmir	Assam
Most	51 (87.9)	54 (96.4)	0	10 (17.9)	1 (1.7)	13 (23.2)	0	12 (21.4)	15 (25.9)	18 (32.1)
Sometimes	5 (8.6)	1 (1.8)	19 (32.8)	17 (30.4)	0	6 (10.7)	2 (3.3)	13 (23.2)	11 (19.0)	13 (23.2)
Least	2 (3.4)	1 (1.8)	37 (63.8)	26 (46.4)	50 (86.2)	34 (60.7)	49 (84.5)	24 (42.9)	29 (50.0)	24 (42.9)
Never	0	0	2 (3.4)	3 (5.4)	7 (12.1)	3 (5.4)	7 (12.1)	7 (12.5)	3 (5.2)	1 (1.8)
Pearson correlation	−0.133		−0.220[a]		−0.3944[b]		−0.393[b]		−0.111	
N	114		114		114		114		114	

Note: Valid N for Assam: 56; valid N for JandK: 58. Figures in parenthesis indicate percentages
[a] Correlation is significant at 0.05 level (two tailed)
[b] Correlation is significant at 0.01 level (two tailed)

On the whole, the local administration, village headman, and community leaders were identified as the most responsive local agency. Highest number of households stated that the local government, including Village Council Development Committees (VCDC), and the district administration were responsive to people's requirements. Nongovernmental agencies, including different students' union, also featured among those entities that are sensitive about concerns of people. The nature of grievances raised is also relevant in determining which entity is more responsive to people. For instance, issues like incidents of missing persons or kidnapping are directly referred to and addressed by the government administration. If the complaints are related to village development or are pertaining to local community concerns, political and community leaders are most likely to be involved. People consult with different entities based on the assessment of their needs and requirements in terms of sensitivity, urgency, and significance. This is an important insight and holds much relevance for the grievance approach to understand representation and conflict. It implies that the nature of grievance is important to understand its link with collective action and choice of institution for redressal.

While the village headman is often the initial point of contact of locals to connect with political leaders or students' unions in the region, among Bengalis in the region, it is seen that community leaders and nongovernmental organizations are mostly contacted. Most households belonging to *Santhali* and *Rabha* community preferred going to government institutions, while the Nepali community did not show any specific preference in their choice of institutions to redress grievances, as all the institutions featured in their response except political leaders.

Though households belonging to *Bodo* community tend to prefer political leaders, and community and civil society organizations representatives, than other communities in the region, none of this observation can be generalized as there are households even among *Bodo* community who least preferred administration and political leaders due to their feeble receptiveness to crisis situations. For instance, when the Bodo-Garo community conflict happened in one of their regions, the Garos had to move out of their village to relief camps for security purposes. A Bodo leader visited the camp and ensured that they were provided with basic necessities. These kinds of community dynamics emerge at the time of crisis between communities, which can actually reverse the effects caused by conflict situations. To sum up, it implies that while neighbors are overwhelmingly the first option for households as most relied upon support systems during unrest, the variation in choice of other actors and agencies is not clearly attributable to any single factor.

While personal networks inevitably scored the highest trust of people, these arrangements with neighborhood need not be feasible if strikes or curfews continued for longer periods. In such situations there is a need for much institutionalized form of support system, which can be better provided by administration, political leaders, and civil society. There have been instances in recent past when conflict situations forced many households to leave their village and take shelter in relief camps, which are mostly set up as a part of such institutional mechanisms. Moreover, as outlined before, it must be underscored that responses be seen alongside the social profile of the respondents.

Emerging Debates

The nature of political representation, beyond the domain of electoral politics, an important nonmilitary institutional strategy for expressing perceived inequalities, and for negotiating conflict in ethnically divided societies, is gaining more credence with movements and protests becoming central to interactive processes between ethnic groups and the state-system (Carciumaru 2015). An emerging trend in this regard is the sudden upsurge among many economically upper class and upper castes, constituting important collective actors within India's ethnic landscape, who are now demanding affirmative quota benefits in education and employment, under Other Backward Class (OBC) category. This rise of dissent among dominant groups can be seen, for instance, in the agitations of *Jats* and the *Gujjars* spread across several provinces in North India and the *Patidars* in Gujarat, who are protesting to interact changes in public politics to address perceived inequalities.

On the other hand, the Dalit resistance movements seen in the country are the result of their decades of suppression and oppression by several agencies. With the rise of low castes and emerging new (often caste-based) political organization, there has been huge transformation, which has benefitted the Dalit community politically and symbolically, in terms of not only securing to them the advantages through affirmative policies guaranteed under the Indian Constitution in education and government employment but also at the same time creating a better social positioning for Dalits in the class hierarchy through the accrued opportunities. The Dalit resistance movements are for asserting their rights for land, minimum wages, control in the local government institutions, and for a dignified life. The flogging of Dalit youths, for instance, in Una administrative block of Gir Somnath district in the province of Gujarat by the village cow vigilantes (*gaur raksha*) in July 2016, and the subsequent denial by the Dalits to remove carcasses of animals from public places as a token resentment to the brutal incident, is a testimonial to the discrimination and atrocities that continue unabated. But, what is relevant in the discussion here is the Dalit mobilization that took place as a protest, wherein group representation became the strategy used to advance the interests of the ethnic group through political positioning and non-electoral processes against the exploitation. The massive 10 days rally (*Azadi Kooch* or March for Freedom) from Ahmedabad to Una in protest against the Una incident, with demands like alternative livelihood options, reservation for Dalits, land for Dalit families and a strong legal framework to fight the atrocities against Dalits, and above all the total end to manual scavenging marked a new era in the Dalit struggle for their rights and dignity. The organized social base, motivating leaders and the clear cut agenda a massive protest movement, not only forced the government to weigh their might carefully but also aroused the homogeneous consciousness among the community to fight for their cause more vociferously.

In contrary to Dalit mobilization, an upper class can also be seen for claiming affirmative benefits. The *Jats* and the *Patidars* who belong to agricultural landholding class are generally regarded as economically sound communities. However, both the communities have recently resorted to mass protest rallies and demonstrations seeking their inclusion into the OBC category for reservations in higher educational institute and government jobs. The *Jats* in Haryana, followed the footsteps of the Gujjars, who through violent movements, successfully secured reservations for their community by getting included in the scheduled tribe (ST) category much ahead of these recent caste consciousness-based movements led by *Jats* or *Patidars*.

Concluding Remarks

This chapter looks at political representation, beyond the domain of electoral politics and elections that people rely on for the redressal of their grievances. Looking at the case of India, the chapter argues that if diversities are not recognized within the political imagination of the modern state, it can lead to ethnic tensions where political bargaining and power sharing become instrumentalities for negotiating ethnic grievances. In the Indian case, linguistic groups, social category, and religion need to be grouped, as a triad to capture the nature of ethnicity and contestations seen in the micropolitics characterizing representation.

Acknowledgments Research for this chapter was carried out as part of the R4D project on "Ethnic Power Relations" (see http://www.r4d.ch). The financial support from the Swiss National Science Foundation and the Swiss Development Agency through Grant No. 400240-147210 is gratefully acknowledged. We also acknowledge the support and expert advice of Lars-Erik Cederman, Simon Hug, and Radu Carciumaru and the comments from participants at the International Political Science Association (IPSA) conference at Brisbane, 2018.

Appendix

Ethnic profile of the respondents ethnic community/state respondents Jammu and Kashmir

State	Ethnic community	Respondents
1. Jammu and Kashmir	Kashmiri Muslim Others	58
	Kashmiri Muslims OBC	2
2. Assam	Christian OBC (Santhali)	5
	Christian SC (Sadri)	1
	Christian ST (Garo)	8
	Hindu OBC (Nepali)	3
	Hindu OBC(Rajbongshi)	3
	Hindu Others	2
	Hindu Others(Assamese)	1
	Hindu ST (Bodo-Kachari[a])	31
	Hindu ST (Nepali)	1
	Muslim others (Assamese)	2
	Muslim Other (Bengali)	3

Note: Sample size for both field sites is 60 each
[a]Hindu ST (Bodo-Kachari) includes both Bodo and Rabha tribes

References

Bagchi A (2000) 'Rethinking Federalism': overview of current debates with some reflections in Indian context. Econ Polit Wkly 35(34):3025–3036
Banerjee M (2017) Why India votes? Routledge, New Delhi
Beteille A (2011) The institutions of democracy. Econ Polit Wkly 46(29):75–84
Carciumaru R (ed) (2015) Negotiating conflict and accommodating identity in South Asia. Samskriti, New Delhi
Cederman L-E, Wimmer A, Min B (2010) Why do ethnic-nationalist groups Rebel: New data and analysis. World Polit 62(1):87–119
Cederman LE, Weidmann NB, Gleditsch KS (2011) Horizontal inequalities and ethnonationalist civil war: a global comparison. Am Polit Sci Rev 105(3):478–495
Cederman LE, Gleditsch KS, Buhaug H (2013) Inequality, grievances, and civil war. Cambridge University Press, Cambridge
Chandhoke N (2005) Revisiting the crisis of representation thesis: the Indian context. Democratization 12(3):308–330
Christin T, Hug S (2012) Federalism, the geographic location of groups, and conflict. Conflict Manag Peace Sci 29(1):93–122
Collier P, Hoeffler A (2004) Greed and grievance in civil war. Oxf Econ Pap 56(4):563–595
Dovi S (2006) Political representation. Retrieved from Stanford Encyclopedia of Philosophy: https://plato.stanford.edu/entries/political-representation/
Fearon JD, Laitin DD (2003) Ethnicity, insurgency, and civil war. Am Polit Sci Rev 97(1):75–90
Kashyap SC (2004) Executive–legislature interface in the Indian polity. J Legis Stud 10(2–3):278–294
Kholi A (ed) (1998) India's democracy: an analysis of changing state-society relations. Princeton University Press, Princeton
Kuhn PM, Weidmann NB (2015) Unequal we fight: between- and within-group inequality and ethnic civil war. Polit Sci Res Methods 3(3):543–568
Lacina B (2014) How governments shape the risk of civil violence: India's federal reorganization, 1950–56. Am J Polit Sci 58(3):720–738
Lama-Rewal ST (2009) Studying elections in India: scientific and political debates. Retrieved from South Asia Multidiscip Acad J. http://samaj.revues.org/2784
Manor J (1996) 'Ethnicity' and politics in India'. Int Aff 72(3):459–475
Mehta PB (2007) The rise of judicial sovereignty. J Democr 18(2):70–83
Mehta PB (2012) State and democracy in India. Polish Sociol Rev. Polish Sociological Association 178:203–225
Pitkin HF (1967) The concept of representation. University of California, Berkeley
Rao PP (2005) Separation of powers in a democracy: the Indian experience. Peace Res 37(1):113–122
Saward M (2010) The representative claim. Oxford University Press, New York
Sekher M, Parasuraman S, Kattumuri R (eds) (2018) Governance and governed: multi-country perspectives on state, society and development. Springer, Singapore
Singh MP, Verney DV (2003) Challenges to India's centralized parliamentary federalism. Publius: J Fed 33(4):1–20
Srikrishna BN (2011) Beyond federalism. India Int Centre Q 38(3/4):386–407
Tillin L (2018) Federalism and democracy in today's India. Econ Polit Wkly 53(33):49–53
Vogt M (2011) A new dawn? Indigenous movements and ethnic inclusion in Latin America. Int Stud Q 60(4):790–801
Weiner M (1989) The Indian paradox: essays in Indian politics. Sage, New Delhi
Yadav Y (2010) Representation. In: Jayal NG, Mehta PB (eds) The Oxford companion to politics in India. Oxford University Press, New Delhi, pp 347–360

Part VIII
Ethnic Cleansing and Genocide

Part Introduction

The presence of diverse ethnic groups in a specific country or region is a secular characteristic in many parts of the world. In some cases, ethnicity can be linked to social divisions and tensions and become the center of armed conflicts. Although large-scale violence against ethnic minorities has been part of the history, the terms genocide and ethnic cleansing themselves are relatively new.

The term genocide was devised by Ralph Lemkin, a Polish Jew and academic lawyer, in his book *Axis rule in occupied Europe*, first published in 1944. Later, the United Nations Convention on the Prevention and Punishment of the Crime of Genocidedefined the term encompassing acts committed with intent to destroy (in whole or in part) a national, ethnical, racial, or religious group through killings; serious bodily or mental harm; physical destruction by inflicting on the group conditions of life; prevention of births within the group; and forcibly transferring children of the group to another group. When the Convention entered into force, the term genocide acquired a legal status.

The crime of genocide was legally framed almost 60 years ago and states have the obligation to adopt measures to prevent and punish both individuals and states if certain acts are deemed to fall within the legal definition of genocide. Treaties do not specify number of deaths that must occur to constitute genocide. Occurrence of deaths is only one of the few characteristics of the definition of genocide in the Genocide Convention. A major aspect is that there has to be a "specific intent," i.e., it has to be proved that the perpetrator clearly seeks to destroy, in whole or in part, a national, ethnical, racial, or religious group. This necessity limits the possibility of charging individuals or states due to the difficultyin providing proof of intention.

Ethnic cleansing is an even newer term, which arose from atrocities in the former Yugoslavia in the 1990s as a literal translation of the Serbo-Croatian term *etnicko cis cenje*. The United Nation Commission of Experts defined ethnic cleansing in relation to forced removal of an ethnic or religious group from a particular area through the use of force, violence, terror, or intimidation.

The ultimate consequence of both genocide and ethnic cleansing is to "clean" certain areas of certain groups deemed "unwanted." Nevertheless, unlike genocide, there is no legal definition of ethnic cleansing.

Eyal Mayroz outlines key underlying causes for the outbreak of genocide and presents insights about its distinctiveness from other mass atrocity crimes. Nyaz Noori explores the Kurdistan Region in Iraq, outlining the interdependencies between the institutional stagnation, partnership failure, and conflict between the federal government of Iraq and the Kurdistan Regional government. Nasir Uddin addresses the ethnic cleansing of the Rohingya people in Myanmar, from the ethnic, regional, and political history of Arakan/Rakhine and of Burman/Myanmar across time to the current challenges faced by the Rohingyas. Christian Cwik examines thesituation of the displaced Wayuu Indigenous minorities of the northern part of South America and the Miskito of Eastern Central America. The chapter examines the displacement triggered by the Conquista and the Trans-Atlantic-Slave-Trade andhow these two ethnic groups were able to maintain autonomous structures despite themass murder and displacement they suffered from the 1960s to the present. Wendy Lambourne explores the Rwandan case in the context of the precolonial relations between three identity groups,the construction of ethnic identity by the colonial powers, and how this was reinforced by the postindependence governments and became a factor in theviolent conflict and the genocide in the 1990s.

Although there are many other cases of genocide and ethnic cleansing, the ones presented in this part offer some critical lessons for the future. Despite being morally and legally opposed by the international community, genocide and ethnic cleansing continues to be practiced in different forms and guises in some parts of the world.

Sergio Luiz Cruz Aguilar

The Threat of Genocide: Understanding and Preventing the "Crime of Crimes"

79

Eyal Mayroz

Contents

Introduction	1540
Efforts and Failures to Prevent or Halt Genocide	1540
The Characteristics of Genocide	1541
Legal Foundations	1541
Genocide Debates	1542
The Crime of Crimes	1544
The Duty to Prevent	1546
The Underlying Causes of Genocide	1547
The Distinctiveness of Genocide	1549
Conclusion	1550
Cross-References	1551
References	1552

Abstract

This chapter provides a brief introduction to the concept of genocide. From its genesis in the 1940s amid the horrors of World War II, to recent "genocide debates" over the applicability of the word to the plight of the Rohingya people in Myanmar, few legal terms have received as much exposure and notoriety as the "G word" has. A central motivation behind the term's creation was to sow fear in the hearts of would-be perpetrators of mass atrocities and thus help to prevent future attempts at annihilation of human groups. Seven decades later it may be said that while the power and intensity acquired by the term have exceeded most expectations, the goal of preventing the "crime of crime" from reoccurring remains a vision yet to be fulfilled. The chapter outlines key underlying causes for the perpetration of genocide, presents new insights about its distinctiveness from

E. Mayroz (✉)
University of Sydney, Sydney, NSW, Australia
e-mail: Eyal.mayroz@sydney.edu.au

© The Author(s), under exclusive license to Springer Nature Singapore Pte Ltd. 2019
S. Ratuva (ed.), *The Palgrave Handbook of Ethnicity*,
https://doi.org/10.1007/978-981-13-2898-5_112

other mass atrocity crimes, and offers points for continued discussion, as part of the ongoing struggle for transforming the "never again" promise from a cliché to a reality.

> **Keywords**
> Genocide · Ethnicity · Prevention · Genocide Convention · Intervention · Crime of crimes

Introduction

In the few decades since it was coined, the word genocide has acquired a capacity to provoke powerful emotional reactions in millions of people around the world. It is said that no other term attained greater normative notoriety in so short a time as "genocide." What then are the characteristics which have made the "G" word so unique: a menace to perpetrators and at the same time a sought-after descriptor for their victims? And how have these characteristics varied from or paralleled those of other internationally recognized atrocity crimes? These questions carry special significance for scholars and activists working on advancing agendas of atrocity prevention. To many of them, detailed understanding of the past and its lessons is seen to be crucial for constructing better strategies and policies for the future.

The brutal acts of violence that accompanied our evolution have not been inimitable to what we call genocide. Indeed, incidents of cruelty inflicted by, between, and within human groups can be traced thousands of years back to a range of instances involving different forms of violence and divergent motivations. Consequently, a broad vocabulary was developed to capture these divergences. But when Raphael Lemkin, a Polish Jewish Jurist soon to be fleeing the horrors of the Holocaust in Europe, sought a terminology with which to describe "the destruction of a nation or of an ethnic group" (Lemkin 1944), no existing word or phrase met his purpose.

How and why has genocide evolved to epitomize definitive evil in the minds of so many? Based on what factors and, more importantly, to what effects? This chapter addresses these questions, tracing the development of the term in the lead up to, during, and after World War II. Integrating political, social, ethical, legal, economic, cultural, historical, and linguistic perspectives, it reviews key milestones in the story of genocide: its birth; makeup; acceptance as a crime under international law; the efforts to codify its prevention and punishment; and the failures ever since to fulfill the vision of its creator of establishing a powerful term, which by sheer association would help to prevent or halt the annihilation of human groups.

Efforts and Failures to Prevent or Halt Genocide

On 9 December 1948, a special meeting of the United Nations (UN) General Assembly adopted unanimously the Convention on the Prevention and Punishment of the Crime of Genocide, known as the Genocide Convention (United Nations

1948). Highlighting prevention and punishment, the treaty intended to challenge the protection offered to perpetrators of genocide by the nonintervention principle in the UN Charter (UN 1945). After a 2-year drafting process, all 55 member states of the newly founded United Nations voted in favor of the final text. Yet, in the following decades, the international community failed time and again to uphold the hope and promise embedded in the words of the Convention.

During the Cold War, international responses to the threats and realities of genocide were characterized by neglect (Whitaker 1985). No serious attempts were made to prevent or halt genocide, to rescue the millions who were dying in genocidal outbreaks, or to address the legal ambiguities that crippled the implementation of the Genocide Convention. An emerging bipolar divide was affecting the ability and willingness of states to act in the "common good" (Alvarez 2007). Additionally, the sanctity of state sovereignty, which for a long time had been offering cover to perpetrators, was merely dented at the Nuremberg trials, and so short a time after the end of World War II, the focus was on the risks posed by interstate conflicts. The link between domestic violations of human rights and the maintenance of international peace and security was much less clear than it is today, and systematic early prevention was an underdeveloped concept at the time.

The end of the Cold War saw certain increase in the deference exhibited by states to the moral and legal injunctions against the commission of genocide. During the 1990s, a small number of coercive multilateral interventions were carried out; often belatedly, based mostly on the self-interest of interveners, with some humanitarian imperatives and to varying degrees of success. These operations were generally referred to as humanitarian interventions, a modern term for a centuries-old concept. From the beginning of the twenty-first century, amid growing criticisms of this contested norm, discussions of responses to mass atrocities took up a new language and arguably a new substance in the form of the Responsibility to Protect (R2P) doctrine. Still, notwithstanding the modest increase in atrocity prevention efforts, responses to genocidal situations – threatened, impending, or ongoing – have remained ineffective to this day. The great powers continue to default on their self-proclaimed stewardship of international peace and security, and in some cases exacerbate or contribute to violent conflicts. Remarkably, these behaviors have not led to meaningful domestic political repercussions for the offending governments, even in the most democratic states.

The Characteristics of Genocide

Legal Foundations

Genocide was created as, and is still predominately, a legal concept. Raphael Lemkin had coined the term in 1943 by merging together the Greek word *genos* (race, tribe) and the Latin word *cide* (killing). In his seminal work, *Axis Rule in Occupied Europe*, he described it as "an old practice in its modern development" and argued that new conceptions required new terms (Lemkin 1944). As an amateur historian, Lemkin had studied the story and history of mass murder, and his conception of his "linguistic brainchild" extended beyond the events unfolding at that time in Europe (Moses 2010). His broader definition of the term described:

> a coordinated plan of different actions aiming at the destruction of essential foundations of the life of national groups, with the aim of annihilating the groups themselves. The objectives of such a plan would be disintegration of the political and social institutions, of culture, language, national feelings, religion, and the economic existence of national groups, and the destruction of the personal security, liberty, health, dignity, and even the lives of individuals belonging to such groups. (Lemkin 1944)

A few years later, in 1948, the UN General Assembly adopted a legal definition of genocide, as part of the new Genocide Convention. Article II of the Convention defined "genocide" to mean:

[A]ny of the following acts committed with intent to destroy, in whole or in part, a national, ethnical, racial or religious group, as such:

(a) Killing members of the group;
(b) Causing serious bodily or mental harm to members of the group;
(c) Deliberately inflicting on the group conditions of life calculated to bring about its physical destruction in whole or in part;
(d) Imposing measures intended to prevent births within the group;
(e) Forcibly transferring children of the group to another group.

Article III enumerated a list of five punishable acts:

(a) Genocide
(b) Conspiracy to commit genocide
(c) Direct and public incitement to commit genocide
(d) Attempt to commit genocide
(e) Complicity in genocide

The definition of genocide in Article II fell short of Lemkin's original conception in at least two ways (Mayroz 2018a). First, political calculations and interests of key states led to a narrower definition of the targeted groups and to the omission of some other, most importantly, social, economic, and political, groups (Schabas 2009a; Jones 2010). Second, the emphasis in the definition had come to rest mainly on physical manifestations of the crime, reducing the cultural aspects which were central to Lemkin's conception (Moses 2010). As a lawyer Lemkin understood the importance of a compromise for the benefit of a consensus. Whether or not he understood the implications of some of the compromises made is a different matter.

Genocide Debates

Over the years, a number of controversies have arisen in relation to words or phrases in the 1948 definition of genocide. The most perceptible among them debated questions around the meaning and the scope of the "intent to destroy," protected groups, and "in whole or in part."

The intent to destroy – charging individuals with acts of genocide or a state with a failure to prevent or punish genocide requires proof that "genocide" has actually taken place, is taking place, or (arguably) was intended to take place. Such a legal genocide determination requires first and foremost a proof of intent (Schabas 2009a). The difficulty to prove intent at an early enough stage to prevent the perpetration of genocide was perhaps the greatest letdown of the Genocide Convention. Given the critical significance of intent to the international community's response to genocide, much of the debate revolved around the level of proof required to satisfy its existence or absence. Whereas the benchmark used commonly in relation to the Genocide Convention has been the restrictive test of "specific intent" or *dolus specialis*, many over the years have been calling for a less restraining and knowledge-based approach. A common claim was that the focus of the Convention's drafters had been on protecting human groups, not on the exact nature of the perpetrators' motives (Goldsmith 2010). Hence, failures to provide the level of proof required for *specific intent* would go against the purposes of the Convention – so it was argued.

Protected groups – the decision by the Convention's drafters to restrict the list of protected groups in Article II to four categories (national, ethnical, racial, or religious) ended up excluding from the definition cases of otherwise clear attempts at genocidal annihilation of human groups. One example was that of Cambodia between 1975 and 1979, where an estimated two million people, most of them from the Khmer majority ethnic group, were murdered or starved to death by Pol Pot's brutal regime (Fawthrop and Jarvis 2004). As most of those targeted were members of particular social classes and political groups, the legal determination of "genocide" was confined in Cambodia to the Vietnamese and to other ethnic minority groups (Lemarchand 2003). Genocidal campaigns against political, social, or economic groups are categorized nowadays by some as "politicides," a term coined by Barbara Harff. In politicides the victim groups are not defined by their communal characteristics as in genocide (e.g., ethnicity, religion, nationality) but primarily in terms of their hierarchical position or political opposition to the regime and dominant groups (Harff and Gurr 1988).

In whole or in part – considerable debate has focused on the meaning of "in part" in Article II. Since the Genocide Convention did not elaborate further, it has been left for the courts to interpret the term. Schabas distinguished two basic approaches among jurists: "substantial part" and, a "significant part" (Schabas 2009a). The word "substantial" was interpreted by the Appeals Chamber of the International Criminal Tribunal for the former Yugoslavia (ICTY) as primarily numeric, i.e., the size of the targeted part in relation to the overall size of the group. However, the Chamber specified also a second consideration of prominence or significance, i.e., how emblematic was the targeted part of the group and how essential it was to the survival of the entire group (Schabas 2008b). Despite concerted efforts, mainly by the ICTY (Scheffer 2006), no court ruling has conclusively resolved the definition, and disagreements remain.

In summary, a genocide finding by a court is conditioned upon the court being satisfied that special intent existed; that the group targeted was one of the four specified in the definition; and that the intent to destroy extended to a substantial and/or significant part of the group. In addition, one or more of the acts carried out, attempted, or incited by the perpetrators have to match one of those enumerated in Article II of the Convention, i.e., killing, causing serious physical or mental harm, inflicting on the group conditions calculated to bring its destruction, preventing births, or transferring of children (Genocide Convention 1948).

Together, the four elements comprise the essence of what many call "the genocide debate," i.e., legal or political discussions over the applicability of the genocide label to a specific crisis. If a state were to ever again consider invoking the Genocide Convention in relation to a crisis, the difficulty of satisfying all four criteria, and especially that of "intent," would be a discouraging factor. Yet, in spite of these definitional controversies, which impeded the implementation of the vision at the heart of the Genocide Convention, half a century later, the drafters of the Statute of the International Criminal Court (ICC) ended up incorporating the exact same definition into Article VI of the treaty (Schabas 2008b).

The Crime of Crimes

Discussing the effects of the genocide label in relation to the crisis in Darfur, French historian Gerard Prunier wrote in 2005:

> At the immediate existential level this [determining whether or not genocide has occurred in Darfur] makes no difference; the horror experienced by the targeted group remains the same, no matter which word we use. But this does not absolve us from trying to understand the nature of what is happening. Unfortunately, whether the "big G-word" is used or not *seems to make such a difference*. It is in fact a measure of the jaded cynicism of our times that we seem to think that the killing of 250,000 people in a genocide is more serious, a greater tragedy and more deserving of our attention than that of 250,000 people in non-genocidal massacres. (Prunier 2005)

To be sure, the "genocide debate" on Darfur was said to have shifted public attention away from the urgency to act and to have provided politicians with alternative focus and a pretext for justifying inaction (Power 2004; Evans 2005; Prunier 2005; Straus 2006; Mendez 2006; Mennecke 2007).

While genocide debates had been triggered mostly by ambiguities in the Genocide Convention or insufficient information on a crisis, they were exploited also by states reluctant to act, to justify bystander behaviors (Mayroz 2018b). The calculated rationale would have been twofold: first, that a diminished consensus over the genocidal nature of a violent conflict could tamper with public understandings of the moral and legal obligation to act and, second, that preoccupation with a "genocide debate" would distract publics and politicians away from the need to take real action. A genocide debate could persist many decades after the events and end up transforming into "genocide denial." The most well-known example is that of the long-standing efforts by successive Turkish governments to prevent the use of the genocide label in relation to the extermination campaign conducted during World War I by the Young Turks against the Empire's Armenian minority. Other cases to mention include Serbs' retrospective portrayals of the 1995 Srebrenica massacres, Pakistani representations of the 1971 atrocities in Bangladesh, and the rejection of the 1966 Igbo genocide by Nigeria (Mayroz 2018b).

In parallel to the legal controversies, and despite efforts to develop an agreed upon typology of genocide (Dadrian 1975; Kuper 1985; Fein 1990; Chalk and Jonassohn 1990; Smith 2000), the conceptualisation of the term remains contentious. What attributes single out genocide as the "crime of crimes"? It has been noted that in situations of genocide, victims were targeted simply because they existed. However, this characteristic has proven typical also in some cases to other instances of crimes against humanity (Destexhe 1998). In these instances, the perpetrators were said to offend against humanity as a whole.

One unique attribute of genocide is the perpetrator's intent to destroy not only individuals as human beings, or as members of a particular group, but the *group* itself in whole or in part (Destexhe 1998). Early on, Lemkin had placed particular emphasis on the diversity of the human race and the cultural loss to the world if human groups were to be annihilated (Lemkin 1945). As described also by genocide scholar Roger Smith, genocide had the inherent potential to:

> distort and alter the very meaning for 'humankind', erasing for all time particular biological and cultural possibilities...For a particular group to claim for itself a right to determine what groups are, in effect, human, possessing the right to life, is a threat to the existence of all other humans. (Smith 2002)

Another reprehensible characteristic of genocide is the indelibility of victims' membership in the targeted group. In many cases these individuals were not allowed to discontinue their membership to escape persecution or extermination (Roth 2002). Furthermore, in Nazi Germany, as in 1994 Rwanda, the right to classify a person as a Jew, a Roma, or a Tutsi was one-sidedly appropriated by the perpetrators (Mayroz 2008a).

While the destruction of a human group may be regarded as more serious than the murdering of as many group members without destroying the group as such, this position was challenged by views which prioritized the value of the group members' lives over the survival of the group. Arguably, genocide does not necessarily affect more individuals in terms of magnitude, death toll, or level of suffering than other mass atrocity crimes (Lee 2009). The US bombings of Hiroshima and Nagasaki in 1945 – allegedly war crimes as well as crimes against humanity – could be said to have resulted in more casualties and no less grief than many genocidal campaigns. The same applied to the non-genocidal killings of millions of Russians and Chinese citizens by their own governments during the twentieth century (Rummel 1994). It is therefore not statistics nor levels of suffering which have made genocide stand out but perhaps the cruelty of the perpetrators (Mayroz 2018a).

The ethical debates are ongoing, but in international politics the tendency has been to pay more attention to the legal implications of genocide than to its moral distinctiveness. Central to this question is the nature and significance of the duty to prevent genocide in the Genocide Convention.

The Duty to Prevent

As implied in its formal title: "The Convention on the Prevention and Punishment of the Crime of Genocide," the 1948 Convention was envisaged by its architects as an instrument of "prevention." Instructions to that effect were conveyed by the General Assembly to the Committees that were to draft the treaty (UNGA 1946). Despite these intentions, the final text of the treaty ended up focusing mainly on the punishment of the crime. It has been noted though that this focus had reflected also the prevailing view of prosecution as a strong deterring factor, and as such, as an influential preventative element. The motivation had not been to allow genocide to occur and then punish the perpetrators but rather, to use the threat of prosecution to prevent the crime from ever taking place. In any event, the final version included only two references to prevention: in Articles I and VIII. Article I read:

> The Contracting Parties confirm that genocide, whether committed in time of peace or in time of war, is a crime under international law which they *undertake to prevent* and to punish. (Genocide Convention 1948)

The text established the legal basis for states parties' obligations to prevent genocide. Unfortunately, the Convention's drafters did very little to clarify what events would trigger the duty and what preventative measures had to be taken by states once it was activated. The second and only other occurrence of the word "prevention" was included in Article VIII, which stated:

> Any Contracting Party may call upon the competent organs of the United Nations to take such action under the Charter of the United Nations as they consider appropriate for the prevention and suppression of acts of genocide or any of the other acts enumerated in article III. (Genocide Convention 1948)

Most legal scholars have supported the view that the directive in the Article did not extend in significant ways beyond *allowing* states parties to refer a situation – deemed by them genocidal (or, arguably, likely to become genocidal) – to the "competent organs" of the UN (Luban 2006; Flint and De Waal 2006; Straus 2006). Once again however, the drafters did not specify what actions would have to be taken, if at all, by these organs (Toufayan 2002).

As noted earlier, the Cold War had come and gone without meaningful attempts being made to put the Genocide Convention into effect. The first significant development took place in March 1993. Eleven months into the civil war in Bosnia, the government of Bosnia-Herzegovina took the Federal Republic of Yugoslavia (Serbia and Montenegro, hereafter FRY) to the ICJ on charges of violations of the Genocide

Convention and requested the court to issue provisional measures that would help protect Bosnia's citizens (ICJ 1993). In addition to charges of genocide, Bosnia-Herzegovina accused also the FRY of failing to prevent genocide under Article I of the Convention (Mayroz 2012). Fourteen years later, in February 2007, the ICJ issued its final judgment on the Application of the Genocide Convention Case. In it, the court described the Convention's provision of "undertaking to prevent genocide" as normative and compelling, unqualified, and bearing direct obligations on states parties (ICJ 2007). A referral to the Security Council did not relieve states parties of the general obligation of prevention, the court noted. It further concluded that the obligation to prevent was one of conduct rather than of result, in the sense that compliance was to be measured by action and not by outcome. States had to manifestly take all measures within their power which would contribute to the prevention of genocide, with the obligation not to succeed but to exercise "due diligence" by employing all means reasonably available to them to prevent genocide, so far as possible (ICJ 2007). These obligations varied according to their capacity "to influence effectively the action of persons likely to commit, or already committing, genocide."

The judgment addressed also the politically thorny question of when a state's obligation to prevent genocide begins. Discounting the widespread notion that activation of the Convention required a legal determination of genocide, the ICJ argued: "[To suggest] that the obligation to prevent genocide only comes into being when perpetration of genocide commences...would be absurd *since the whole point of the obligation is to prevent, or attempt to prevent, the occurrence of the act*" (ICJ 2007). It therefore determined that "[a] State's obligation to prevent, and the corresponding duty to act, arise at the instant that the State learns of, or should normally have learned of, the existence of a *serious risk* that genocide will be committed." From that moment, a state with means at its disposal that are likely to have a deterrent effect on would-be perpetrators would be duty bound to make use of them "as the circumstances permit" (ICJ 2007). Crucially, the definition of what a "serious risk" is was left open to case-by-case interpretations by states or courts (Mayroz 2012).

The Underlying Causes of Genocide

The correlations between the segmentation of societies and the occurrence of genocide are well established. As James Hughes proposes, communally fragmented societies, multiethnic societies, composite societies, and internally colonized societies are all at a considerably higher risk of facing a domestic genocide. Analogous conditions are fostered by "diversity of racial, ethnic and/or religious groups that are politically, economically, socially and/or culturally distinct, organized and competing" (Hughes 2010). However, as Hughes noted, the majority of today's states are structured pluralistically, and so, these insights offered but a starting point for a more nuanced analysis of the causes for genocide.

In their pioneering studies of the threats posed by genocidal violence, Barbara Harff and Ted Gurr identified key indicators for early warning against the risks of genocide and politicide. Testing multitudes of causal factors over the years, by 2015

Harff and Gur had narrowed down their list to five predictive indicators, said to offer up to 90 percent accuracy in their model when temporal inconsistencies in the data were taken into account (Harff and Gurr 1988, 2015; Harff 2003). The five indicators are the existence of state-led discrimination against ethnic or religious minorities; exclusionary ideology held by ruling elites; the existence of minority elite or contention over elite ethnicity; the type of polity, i.e., autocracy versus democracy; and past employments of genocidal policies (Harff and Gurr 2015).

In a complementary effort to Harff and Gurr's, Gregory Stanton developed a predictive model consisting at present of ten conceptual stages in the evolution of genocide. The model helps to identify the existence or emergence of political and societal conditions for the onset of the crime – findings that could support subsequent efforts at prevention. The ten stages include processes of classification, symbolization, discrimination, dehumanization, organization, polarization, preparation, persecution, extermination, and denial. As Stanton notes, these stages are not necessarily linear, as they could evolve simultaneously and not inevitably in a set order (Stanton 2013). Linking his model to Harff and Gur's early warning indicators, he writes:

> Targeted groups of state-led discrimination are victims of Discrimination. An exclusionary ideology is central to Dehumanization. Autocratic regimes foster the Organization of hate groups. An ethnically polarized elite is characteristic of Polarization...Massive violations of human rights is evidence of Persecution. Impunity after previous genocides or politicides is evidence of Denial. (Stanton 2013)

The two models and other concerted emphases on country risks and on the modern state as the core unit of analysis of genocide (see also Fein 2001; Mann 2005) have been expanded to account for later developments, such as the emergence of Islamist extremism. Historic, ideological, ethnic, and religious enmities were thus found to manifest at national but also transnational settings (Hughes 2010).

The instigation of a genocidal campaign involves by definition a premeditated decision, usually by the leadership of the state or of a dominant (majority or minority) group. These decisions are anchored in, or at least invoke and manipulate, perceptions of existential threats from victim groups, perceptions which are strong enough to warrant their physical extermination. Hughes is right to warn though against clustering the analytical focus of research around threat perceptions and security dilemmas. Political ambitions of ruling elites, material interests such as the seizing of land or other resources (during colonization and even today), racist ideologies, deteriorating economic situations, rising social inequalities, and subsequent intensification of group competition - all these have accounted for or contributed to some of the most horrific genocides of the past hundred years and more (Jones 2004; Moses and Stone 2006; Moses 2008; Kiernan 2009). From among these factors, fear and greed have played particularly significant roles in legitimating and mobilizing the apparatuses that ended up perpetrating the genocide on the ground. Manufacturing an "enemy," dehumanizing the "other," and framing scapegoats were as essential to the process as the foot soldiers without which the genocidal campaign could not have been carried out. Studies of the Armenian genocide, the

Holocaust, the 1994 genocide in Rwanda, the genocide of the Australian aboriginals by the European colonizers, and the genocide of Muslims by ethnic Serbs in Bosnia have demonstrated how likening the victims to animals by the perpetrators could alter psychological mind-sets and prepare societies to partake or acquiesce in extermination projects. As discussed by Savage, depicting the victims as menacing animals had transformed them into a threat to society, enough to place them outside a common universe of mutual human moral obligation. The victim group would then become a problem requiring an immediate action, to which extermination would come to be seen a legitimate solution (Savage 2006; Stanton 2013).

The Distinctiveness of Genocide

Studies have attributed the failures to prevent or stop genocide to a wide variety of factors in the policymaking of key states, most notably to interplays of opposing interests and concerns – material and ideational, recurring, and case specific (Mayroz 2019). Moral and legal imperatives which may have existed for strong action had failed time and again to override cost-benefit calculations dominated by concerns over risks of military action, lack of national interests, or the continuing influence of state sovereignty. Structural weaknesses in the procedures of the UN Security Council erected additional obstacles to international action, since any one of the five permanent members of the Council (the P-5) could block such action based on self-interest and with little or no legal checks to prevent it from doing this. These conditions had left millions of vulnerable people around the world at the mercy of cold foreign policy calculations and power struggles between, and sometimes within, dominant states.

In a forum on genocide prevention held in Stockholm in 2004, UN Secretary-General at the time Kofi Annan spoke of the need for "clear ground rules to distinguish between genuine threats of genocide, which require a military solution, and other situations where force would not be legitimate" (Inter Press 2004). In contrast to this (later disavowed) distinction, the evidence points to more similarities than divergences between responses to genocide and to non-genocidal atrocity crimes, including other instances of crimes against humanity, war crimes, and ethnic cleansing. First, conferring the label on conflict situations had not resulted necessarily in the past in stronger action. In fact, given the inverse ratio between interventions in non-genocides and noninterventions in genocide, it may have been the opposite. The significance and normative preeminence of the label are thus put in question, since, if the "seriousness" of events would have correlated positively with the strength of responses, we might have seen more interventions to stop genocide (Mayroz 2019).

Second, similarities between genocide and other atrocity crimes have extended also to the constraints to action. Out *of 18* recurring obstacles examined by this author to the international community's ability to prevent or stop mass atrocities, only two were linked specifically to situations of genocide. All other constraints applied to non-genocidal events as well. The first of the two constraints were the effects of the "genocide debate." As noted earlier, various commentators pointed to these debates as distractions from, or excuses by, states to avoid taking meaningful steps. The second constraint applied to alleged reluctance by policymakers to commit to action on genocide, of fear of having to bear the legal and moral obligations purportedly generated by the label (Reeves 2004a; Scheffer 2006; Mayroz 2019). Notably, during the 1990s the Bush and Clinton administrations opted both overwhelmingly for the deceivingly sterile "baggage-free" and legally harmless phrase "ethnic cleansing" in references to the violence in Bosnia and later in Kosovo, arguably, to avoid using the "G word" (Blum et al. 2007; Mayroz 2008).

As a final point, rhetorical justifications of action, employed in the past during anti-genocide advocacy campaigns, did not seem to differ significantly to those raised in relation to non-genocidal situations.

In contrast to the abovementioned similarities, adoptions or circumventions by US officials of genocide rhetoric in relation to various crises were found to have led to different results, particularly in the case of media coverage, public attention, and the robustness of civil society's efforts in promoting action (Mayroz 2019). A key example was the relative visibility of Darfur during 2004, compared to the deadlier yet non-genocidal violence in the Democratic Republic of Congo (DRC) (Haeri 2008; Hamilton 2011; Mills 2015; Mennecke 2007). However, years later both conflicts continue to fester, and Darfur has long been absent from attention of the world's media, or of a no longer concerned international community.

William Schabas has made the argument that the prosecutorial utility of genocide had declined in favor of crimes against humanity. Taking perpetrators to court on charges of genocide is more difficult than on charges of crimes against humanity, he says, as the latter does not require proof of special intent (Schabas 2006). Furthermore, once the scope of crimes against humanity had been extended to cover times of peace by the Rome Statute of the ICC – earlier a unique characteristic of genocide – prosecuting under the former has become much easier. It was the nexus to armed conflict, imposed on "crimes against humanity" by the great powers in Nuremberg, which led to the internationalization of the term genocide in 1946. While the powers feared being targeted for repressive acts by a peacetime crime, emerging states, specifically India, Cuba, Panama, and Saudi Arabia, were pushing for an instrument that could protect them, and settled on genocide (Schabas 2008a).

On the other side of the scales was the normative force embedded in the popular, political and legal conceptions of the term genocide. Defendants coming before international criminal tribunals have been said to favor being indicted and convicted for war crimes, or crimes against humanity, over the prospect of being labelled *génocidaires*. Schabas wrote: "Plea agreements systematically involve[d] withdrawing charges of genocide in favour of convictions for crimes against humanity" (Schabas 2009). It is far from certain, however, that these concerns would deter perpetrators in the preparatory stages of genocide from launching their campaign.

Conclusion

Adam Jones has pointed to two key concerns for genocide scholars: the wish to define and conceptualize genocide, and the desire to learn how to prevent it (Jones 2010). Had the legal definition of the crime in the Genocide Convention, or the jurisprudence around it thereafter, been true to Lemkin's dream, the modern history of genocide would not have been as tragic as it has. The vision of a world joining hands to prevent the destruction of human groups had gone estray. What genocide *is* may be construed as too narrow or too broad. The stringent criteria in the 1948 definition have made it a very specific and difficult to substantiate crime. At the same time, the attempts to pigeonhole reality into a distinct criminal activity called "genocide" may have undermined the value of the term for saving lives. To raise the stakes higher, wide perceptions of genocide as "the crime of crimes" continue to lead survivors of legally recognized, contested, or even mistaken instances of genocide to believe that nothing short of the "G" label would capture and bestow public recognition on their personal tragedies. These attempts to effectively broaden the scope of what genocide is have been criticized for diminishing or diluting the potency of the term (Mayroz 2019).

Two decades into a new millennium, the world has not become perceptively safer for vulnerable human groups. The massacres of the twentieth century were followed by fresh cycles of mass violence in Darfur, Syria, Yemen, South Sudan, and other places. The targeting of ethnic and religious minorities in Iraq and Syria (Kerry 2016; US House of Representatives 2016) and more recently of the Rohingyas in Myanmar continues to shape the reality of the threat of genocide. Although we did witness in recent years quicker and at times more vocal responses from the UN, civil society, or even some states, these did not always lead to more effective outcomes. The proxy wars waged on the backs (and graves) of innocent Syrians have invoked echoes from Vietnam and other killing fields of the Cold War. Furthermore, the failures to stop the violence in Syria underscore the potentially disastrous consequences of power struggles among global and regional actors and interests. They reiterate also the question raised earlier by Prunier about the difference between genocidal and non-genocidal mass atrocities and the rationale for prioritizing one over the other.

How to enlist the support of the major powers for stronger international responses to genocide and other mass atrocities? How to challenge the cost-benefit calculations of key states against meaningful action? One strategy is to try to increase the political costs of failures to act, both domestically and internationally. In this scenario, a higher price for bystander practices could help transform routines of moralizing rhetoric and moral outrage – real or fake – into more effective meaningful measures. Beginning in the 1990s, the "genocide" label has served to encourage the former but created also significant hindrances for the latter. Overcoming governments' reluctance to commit to strong responses to "genocide" without surrendering the normative capital encapsulated in the label is a challenge waiting for creative solutions. In an increasingly populist global environment, where peoples' power is alleged to matter more than it did so far, the potential for change may well be greater. Arguably though, so could the difficulties.

Cross-References

▶ Ethnic Cleansing of the Rohingya People
▶ Ethnic Conflict and Genocide in Rwanda

References

Alvarez A (2007) The prevention and intervention of genocide during the Cold War Years. In: Totten S (ed) The prevention and intervention of genocide. New Brunswick, N.J.: Transaction Publishers, pp 7–30

Blum R, Stanton GH, Sagi S, Richter ED (2007) "Ethnic cleansing" bleaches the atrocities of genocide. Eur J Pub Health 18(2):204–209

Chalk F, Jonassohn K (eds) (1990) The history and sociology of genocide: analyses and case studies. Yale University Press, New Haven

Dadrian V (1975) A typology of genocide. Int Rev Sociol 5(12):201–212

Destexhe A (1998) The crime of genocide. In: Destexhe A (ed) Rwanda and genocide in the twentieth century. New York University Press, New York

Evans G (2005) Genocide or crime? Actions speak louder than words in Darfur. Politico 16 February

Fawthrop T, Jarvis H (2004) Getting away with genocide: elusive justice and the Khmer Rouge Tribunal. Pluto Press, London

Fein H (1990) Genocide: a sociological perspective. Sage Publications, London

Fein H (2001) Denying genocide. From Armenia to Bosnia. Series: Occasional papers in comparative and international politics 1. London School of Economics and Political Science, Department of Government, London

Flint J, De Waal A (2006) Darfur: a short history of a long war. Zed Books, New York

Goldsmith K (2010) The issue of intent in the genocide convention and its effect on the prevention and punishment of the crime of genocide: toward a knowledge-based approach. Genocide Stud Prev 5(3):238–257

Haeri M (2008) Saving Darfur: does advocacy help or hinder conflict resolution? Praxis: the fletcher. Journal of Human Security 23:33–46

Hamilton R (2011) Fighting for Darfur: public action and the struggle to stop genocide. MacMillan, New York

Harff B (2003) No lessons learned from the Holocaust? Assessing risks of genocide and political mass murder since 1955. Am Polit Sci Rev 97:57–73

Harff B, Gurr TR (1988) Toward empirical theory of genocides and politicides: identification and measurement of cases since 1945. Int Stud Q 32:359–371

Harff B, Gurr TR (2015) Hazard of onsets of genocide/politicide in 2015: risk assessments 2015: potential state perpetrators of genocide and politicide. Genocide Prevention Advisory Network. Available: http://gpanet.org/content/hazard-onsets-genocidepoliticide-2015. Accessed 2 Oct 2018

Hughes J (2010) Genocide and ethnic conflict. In: Cordell K, Wolff S (eds) Routledge handbook of ethnic conflict. Routledge, Abingdon, pp 1–22

ICJ (1993) Application of the genocide convention, 1993 ICJ 3. (Request for the Indications of Provisional Measures, Order of 8 April)

ICJ (2007) Case concerning the application of the convention on the prevention and punishment of the crime of genocide. (Bosnia and Herzegovina vs. Serbia and Montenegro), 26 February

Inter Press Service (2004) (Stockholm), 30 January 2004

Jones A (ed) (2004) Genocide, war crimes and the west: history and complicity. Zed books, London

Jones A (2010) Genocide: a comprehensive introduction, 2nd edn. Taylor & Francis, Hoboken

Kerry J (2016) Remarks on Daesh and genocide. US Department of State, 17 March. Available: https://2009-2017.state.gov/secretary/remarks/2016/03/254782.htm. Accessed 2 Oct 2018

Kiernan B (2009) Blood and soil: a world history of genocide and extermination, from Sparta to Darfur. Yale University Press, New Haven

Kuper L (1985) The prevention of genocide. Yale University Press, New Haven

Lee SP (2009) The moral distinctiveness of genocide. J Polit Philos 18(3):335–356

Lemarchand R (2003) Comparing the killing fields: Rwanda, Cambodia and Bosnia. In: Jensen SLB (ed) Genocide: cases, comparisons and contemporary debates. Copenhagen: The Danish Center for Holocaust and Genocide Studies, pp 141–174

Lemkin R (1944) Axis rule in occupied Europe. Laws of occupation. Analysis of government. Proposals for redress. Carnegie Endowment for International Peace, Division of International Law, Washington, DC

Lemkin R (1945) Genocide: a modern crime. 4 Free World 39:39–43. Available: http://www.preventgenocide.org/lemkin/freeworld1945.htm. Accessed 2 Oct 2018

Luban D (2006) Calling genocide by its rightful name: Lemkin's word, Darfur and the UN report. Chic J Int Law 7(1):303–320

Mann M (2005) The dark side of democracy: explaining ethnic cleansing. Cambridge University Press, Cambridge, UK

Mayroz E (2008) Ever again? The United States, genocide suppression, and the crisis in Darfur. J Genocide Res 10(3):359–388

Mayroz E (2012) The legal duty to prevent: after the onset of genocide. J Genocide Res 14(1):79–98

Mayroz E (2018a) Genocide: to prevent and punish "Radical Evil". In: Kastner P (ed) International criminal law in context. Routledge, Oxon, pp 71–90

Mayroz E (2018b) The distinctiveness of genocide and implications for prevention: destroying groups versus mass killing of people. In: Totten S (ed) Teaching about genocide. Rowman & Littlefield Publishers, Lanham

Mayroz E (2019) Reluctant intervenes: America's failed responses to genocide, from Bosnia to Darfur. Rutgers University Press, New Brunswick

Mendez JE (2006) United Nations Report from the Special Advisor on genocide prevention. Voices on Genocide Prevention (Interview), 16 February

Mennecke M (2007) What's in a name? Reflections on using, not using, and overusing the "G-Word". Genocide Stud Prev 2(1):57–71

Mills K (2015) International responses to mass atrocities in Africa: responsibility to protect, prosecute, and palliate. University of Pennsylvania Press, Philadelphia

Moses D (ed) (2008) Empire, colony, genocide: conquest, occupation, and subaltern resistance in world history. Studies on War and Genocide 12. Berghahn Books, New York

Moses D (2010) Raphael Lemkin, culture, and the concept of genocide. In: Bloxham D, Moses D (eds) The Oxford handbook on genocide studies. Oxford University Press, Oxford

Moses D, Stone D (eds) (2006) Colonialism and genocide. Routledge, London

Power S (2004) Dying in Darfur: can the ethnic cleansing in Sudan be stopped? The New Yorker, 23 August

Prunier G (2006) Darfur: the ambiguous genocide. Cornell University Press, Ithaca

Reeves E (2004a) New attacks on civilians far to the North in Darfur; more than 1,000 human beings now dying weekly in Darfur: what is the threshold for an emergency humanitarian intervention? sudanreeves.org, 8 February

Reeves E (2004b) No further evasion of the essential question: what will we do in Darfur? sudanreeves.org, 4 April

Roth JK (2002) The politics of definition. In: Rittner C, Roth JK, Smith JM (eds) Will genocide ever end? Paragon House, St. Paul

Rummel RJ (1994) Death by government. Transaction Publishers, New Brunswick

Savage R (2006) 'Vermin to be cleared off the face of the earth': perpetrator representations of genocide victims as animals. In: Tatz C et al (eds) Genocide perspectives III. Brandl & Schlesinger, Sydney, pp 17–45

Schabas WA (2006) Genocide, crimes against humanity, and Darfur: the commission of inquiry's findings on genocide. Cardozo Law Rev 27(2):1703–1721

Schabas WA (2008a) Origins of the genocide convention: from Nuremberg to Paris. Case W Res J Int'l L 40:35–55

Schabas WA (2008b) Article 6 genocide. In: Triffterer O (ed) Commentary on the Rome statute of the international criminal court, 2nd edn. Hart Publishing & Verlag C.H. Beck, Oxford

Schabas WA (2009a) What is genocide? What are the gaps in the convention? How to prevent genocide? Politorbis 47(2):33–46

Schabas WA (2009b) Genocide in international law: the crime of crimes, 2nd edn. Cambridge University Press, Cambridge, UK

Scheffer D (2006) Genocide and atrocity crimes. Genocide Stud Prev 1(3):229–250
Smith RW (2000) Human destructiveness and politics: the twentieth century as an age of genocide. In: Wallimann I, Dobkowski M (eds) Genocide and the modern age: etiology and case studies of mass death. Syracuse University Press, Syracuse
Smith RW (2002) As old as history. In: Rittner C, Roth JK, Smith JM (eds) Will genocide ever end? Paragon House, St. Paul
Stanton G (2013) Ten stages of genocide. Genocide Watch. Available: http://www.genocidewatch.org/genocide/tenstagesofgenocide.html. Accessed 2 Oct 2018
Straus S (2006) Rwanda and Darfur: a comparative analysis. Genocide Stud Prev 1(1):41–56
Toufayan M (2002) Deployment of troops to prevent impending genocide: a contemporary assessment of the UN Security Council's Powers. Can Yearb Int Law 40:195–249
UN General Assembly 179th Plenary meeting (UN document a/pv.179) (1945)
United Nations (1946) UNGA Resolution 96(I), 11 November
United Nations (1948) Convention on the prevention and punishment of the crime of genocide
United States House of Representatives (2016) H.Con.Res.75, 'Expressing the Sense of Congress that the Atrocities Perpetrated by ISIL Against Religious and Ethnic Minorities in Iraq and Syria Include War Crimes, Crimes Against Humanity, and Genocide, 14 March 2016'. Available: https://www.congress.gov/bill/114th-congress/house-concurrent-resolution/75. Accessed 2 Oct 2018
Whitaker (1985) Revised and updated report on the question of the prevention and punishment of the crime of genocide (the 'Whitaker Report'). United Nations, ECOSOC, UN Doc E/CN.4/Sub.2/1985/6, 2 July

Separation Versus Reunification: Institutional Stagnation and Conflict Between Iraq and Kurdistan Region

80

Nyaz N. Noori

Contents

Introduction	1556
Institutional Stagnation and Partnership Failure	1557
Economic and Political Aspects of Partnership Failure and Conflict	1560
Factors of Institutional Stagnation and Conflict	1562
Path Dependence	1562
The Neighbors' Effects	1564
Collective Action and Opportunity Costs	1566
Exit–Enter Costs	1567
Separation or Reunification: What to Do?	1568
Conclusions	1571
References	1571

Abstract

This chapter outlines the interdependencies between the institutional stagnation, partnership failure, and conflict between Iraq and the Kurdistan region. It identifies the pathways through which the institutions have emerged and stagnated since the mid-1960s. It explores why these two partners, the federal government of Iraq and the Kurdistan regional government, are unable to live together or separate peacefully.

Keywords

Kurdistan · Iraq · Institutional stagnation · Conflict resolution

---

N. N. Noori (✉)
Department of Economic History, Uppsala University, Uppsala, Sweden

Lecturer, Department of Economics, University of Sulaymaniyah, Sulaimaniyah, Kurdistan Region, Iraq
e-mail: niaz_najm@yahoo.com

© The Author(s), under exclusive license to Springer Nature Singapore Pte Ltd. 2019
S. Ratuva (ed.), *The Palgrave Handbook of Ethnicity*,
https://doi.org/10.1007/978-981-13-2898-5_115

Introduction

Baxtyar Ali, a well-known Kurdish novelist, in one of his poems describes the structure of partnership, or social contract, in the Kurdistan Region of Iraq (KRI) as follows: "Oh darling...come and loot me, because I am here to loot you." This is the rule between spouses and individuals as well as the center and the KRI.

The history of the last 50 years or so has shown that Iraq and the KRI, established in 1992 with recognition in 2005 Constitution of Federal government of Iraq, have continuously confronted internal volatility, political conflict, and macroeconomic fluctuation – whether they are rich or bankrupt and whether they are independent or a colony.

Hence, two questions can touch the core objectives of this chapter

- Why are these two parts of the same country neither able to live or separate peacefully? How has institutional stagnation left consequences on the partnership failure and conflict within and between Iraq and the KRI?

The author attempts to find the answers of these questions by illustrating and contributing to two related yet very different literatures: institutions and economic crisis and institutions and conflict.

The major argument of this chapter can be summarized as follows. First, uncivic, or bad, institutions have altered the behavior of the individuals, social groups, and political elites in Iraq, including the KRI, encouraging and enforcing them to engage in cheating and shirking and thrusting them into prolonged bloody conflict. Second, both "internal" enforcement party, the governments, and informal rules are the major obstacles for the institutional development and promoting peace between the center in Baghdad and the KRI, which confirms that designing institutions may not help in breaking vicious circles of institutional stagnation at once, it is a process. Still, the way institutions destine and the "external" enforcement party, the international community, interfere to reduce levels of conflict between these two parts of the same country actively contributes to determine the path of development. Third, an "angel versus evil" analysis does not help understanding what has been happening between these two parties, or partners, and why they do not interact or separate peacefully. A challenger, the Kurds in this case, and a target, the Arabs of Iraq in this case, have built trustless economic and political relations.

In showing aspects of conflict and supporting these arguments and hoping to fill the literature gap on the partnership failure and conflict between the Iraqi state and the KRI, the chapter follows a historical approach to explain the impact of path dependency on the performance of current institutions. It turns to look at economic policies used against each other before and after removing Saddam Hussein in 2003. A particular attention to spouses' and the political parties' relations will be part of the story in order to further investigate the roots and levels of disintegration. Finally, the study brings evidence from the formal rules, especially new constitution of Federal Republic of Iraq, too.

The rest of the chapter is organized as follows: section "Institutional Stagnation and Partnership Failure" explores the roles and causes of institutional stagnation. Section "Aspects of Partnership Failure and Conflict" provides a historical review on the aspects of political and economic conflict since the mid-1950s. Section "Factors of Institutional Stagnation and Conflict" explores sources of disintegration and conflict. Section "Separation or Reunification: What to Do?" explains the return of Kurdish nationalism euphoria, the internal weaknesses and characteristics of institutions in the KRI, and recommendations for conflict resolution. The final section devotes to conclusions.

Institutional Stagnation and Partnership Failure

Interactions between individuals in a society are not a simple process. Individuals need to be guided in order to develop their social capacity, live the life they value, and begin to be positive creatures toward themselves. They may not cooperate due to free riding and coordination costs, or other factors.

Generally speaking, better law and order situation promotes businesses through enhancing the confidence of investors by minimizing uncertainties and risks. With weak democratic institutions, politicians and public officials have fewer checks on their power, making it easier for them to engage in rent seeking, thereby causing a lower economic growth (Nawaz 2014). Francesca Gagliardi (2008) argues that "(T)he evolution of institutions can produce a favorable environment for the adoption of cooperative solutions that will foster economic change, hence growth." Otherwise, opportunism harms cooperation, exchange, and growth, and brings crisis.

Institutions, as North states, consist of three elements. The first element is a set of formal rules. These are codified laws that can be written in a democratic process or imposed by political elites otherwise. Constitutions, common laws, and contracts are examples of formal rules. The second element, norms of behavior or informal rules, is informal constraints on behavior that structure repeated human interaction. These rules tend to be inherited from the past and traditional culture of that society and/or through interactions with the world, especially the society's regional neighbors. Meanwhile, they are determined by individuals' expectations toward "others" behavior and policies. Accordingly, they influence the individuals' choices, motives, decisions, options, and shape their present and future.

Although formal rules are important, they require a third element, the government, to enforce them, or will not be followed. However, government's plans and strategies may be influenced by informal rules that can affect policies of enforcement. As North states, a Mafia-like character of the government can always standstill the process of development as the standard problems of agency may arise; thus, "embodying modem legal institutions and instruments is a major part of the history of freedom"(North 1989). As we shall see, the rise of a predatory state/government was part of the history of Iraq since its birth.

This three-pronged framework, elements of institutions, draws a clear line between the institutional approach and rational choice theory. Rational choice underlies theories of economic development through linearization and free trade. The specialization and division of labor results in increasing productivity of the factors of production, particularly the labor force, leading to arise of production, income, etc. Finally, the nation can accumulate wealth and will rise above poverty. Accordingly, nations shall move from personal to impersonal exchange models at a wide space.

North argues the latter change often accompanies with another path: poisoning the social relations, which limit further expansion of the economy. Once engaged in trade, a nation's economies experience short-lived prosperity. Meanwhile, these changes may change the behavior of individuals and social groups to incentivize shirking and cheating, thus resulting in recession, financial mismanagement, and other types of crisis. In personal model of exchange, the cost of gathering information on each party was low due to small numbers, and contract dealings were repeated among them. With impersonal exchange model and in the absence of good institutions, cheating, stealing, and thrive will be tolerated (North 1989).

At one point of time, when a relationship stagnates, or goes in favor of one party more than the other party, one of the parties may plan to exit. Although Mark Crescenzi's study focuses on trade agreement, it can still help in understanding decisions of exit in similar situations. This decision depends on its opportunity cost, of switching from this option to the next alternative. Assume that the game is between two states, a *challenger* and a *target*. The challenger attaches a threat of economic exit to its demand in an attempt to compel the target to concede. The "exit costs" define the likelihood of success of each party. Three factors cause current relationships between two partners more costly to break:

- *Trade routes:* Geographical and political boundaries that limit transport of goods and services increases costs of exit.
- *Asset specificity:* Rigid, immobile resources make states vulnerable to trading partners.
- *Market structure*: A partner may stay in an agreement if s/he has no other potential partners with which to establish new ties.

In this case, a type of *"constraint equilibrium"* emerges, which reduces conflict. However, this study does not explain why the challenger may choose "a crisis equilibrium, in which the use of economic tools of persuasion fails and militarized conflict ensues," as the partnership between Iraq and the KRI shows, though the latter may be called a quasi-state; or why "a *bargaining power equilibrium*, in which the costs of exit for the target allow the challenger to induce the target to agree to its demands" may not occur (Crescenzi 2003). In any case, with institutional stagnation, both enter and exit costs of a relationship increase.

There are combined factors that make institutions stagnate, or preferences for institutional change to prefer an efficient set of property rights not to occur, and partners fail to stay together or leave an agreement with minimizing its costs on both. The factors focused in this study, with a partial attention to the fifth point, can be listed as follows:

- **Path dependence:** accumulative events, organizations, and beliefs inherited from the past. A centralized distributional system supported by a political culture and rent seeking were the children of path dependency.
- **Collective action and high opportunity costs** of challenging the ruling class.
- **The neighbor effect:** Institutional weaknesses of the states/families surround the country/family (the KR's neighbors and Kurdish families in this example).
- **Exit–enter costs:** partially represented itself in Sectarian-Nationalism project in Iraq (among Sunnis and Shi'a Muslims in Iraq and between the Arab and the Kurds of Iraq).
- **International competition:** powerful states and counterproductive forms of international intervention (military intervention, developmental aid, sanctions, etc.).

Let's keep in mind that the institutional development can be achieved by accumulation, not designing. By bringing evidence from the Bill of Rights in 1689 and the Act of Settlement in 1701 in the United Kingdom, Peter Murrell's argument supports Fredrik Hayek's view (1960) on the evolution side of informal rules as well as legal structure. As Hayek, he stresses that institutions accumulate "as a result of trial and error and survival of the successful, with design secondary.... The institutions of government and the rights of the English arose in a very long process, which reached culmination in the mid-seventeenth century and thereafter bore fruit." Accordingly, a common set of ideas on rights and on the nature of government, plus many lesser instruments and habits of governance, hand in hand with law, supported social change in the United Kingdom (Murrell 2017).

However, designing the right institutions does help in getting rid of the problem of institutional stagnation. To challenge the problem of free riding and conflict, and perhaps to reduce exit or unification costs, Chatagnier and Kavakl point out that economic interdependency may not impose a low-level of conflict, particularly when they export similar goods (e.g., oil). Enforcement party plays a significant role. In this respect, the enforcement school states that "a punishment strategy is sufficient to enforce an agreement" and avoid cheatings, because "the net benefit will not be positive." In contrast, the managerial school argues that improving dispute resolution procedure, supplying technical and financial assistance, and increasing transparency address noncompliance problem (Chatagnier and Kavakl 2017). Still, it is not clear what type of facilities shall be provided and who shall be punished and how.

In one of their experiments for three different treatments, Stine Aakre et al. find that average participation rises sharply when "insiders" can punish other insiders. Interestingly, "when would-be free riders do not have an escape option, enforcement enhances the average total contribution substantially" (Aakre et al. 2016). Moreover, insiders may not be able to punish outsiders; therefore, an insider with another insider might be in conflict due to the hegemony of the outsiders. Hence, both compliance and participation are necessary condition to share power among insiders and resist the hegemony of outsiders (Iran and Turkey in this case).

Briefly, history has shown that the transformation from a less institutionally advanced society to a more institutionally advanced society was not possible unless the three major elements of institutions (norms of behavior, the formal rules, and enforcement) did not develop in a way that promotes the growth of social capital. However, due to several reasons, these elements may change very slowly, imposing "crisis equilibrium."

Economic and Political Aspects of Partnership Failure and Conflict

The problem of partnership failure and conflict between the governments and political leaders mentioned above has become a norm over time. It was more deteriorated by enforcing people to move from rural to urban areas within Anfal campaigns in late 1980s.

Understanding conflict at microlevel helps in tackling puzzles of partnership failure at macrolevel, too. Briefly, partners are suffering from finding a way to live together or leave their relationship peacefully. In the last few years, the divorce rate has sharply increased. Social media, economic hardship, and infidelity are the major motivations for these broken up relationships. The divorce rate could have even been higher if breaking up were socially and economically possible for many families while exhausted in daily fighting.

Similarly, from the birth of Iraq to the birth of the KRI, the center and the region were at war for almost 41 years. Prior to 1991, the center tried to marginalize the Kurds except for those groups who supported the regime. The economic reforms have not become a real alternative; they also had a catastrophic end. For example, 3 months after the 11 March 1970 agreement, which was supposed to grant autonomy to the Kurds, the Sulaimaniyah Sugar Factory contract was put into force with a 6,651,811 IQD investment, though it was not fully functional until 1976, when the factory employed 869 people. When a centralized system strengthened, another choice appeared for the Ba'ath party: in the 1975 Algiers Agreement, Iran and Iraq tackled the issue of the Persian Gulf; thus, Iran withdrew its support for the Kurds. From then on, the Ba'ath party did not need the Kurds any more. The Kurdish revolt ended, following a bloody conflict, with a total collapse of the autonomy project. During this period, the center's remedies were a cure to relieve the pain, rather than to develop the region.

As they created a headache for the regime, the countryside was severely attacked by subsequent governments, in the 1930s, 1950s, 1960s, 1970s, and most notably within the *Anfal* campaign's operational phases in 1988–1989 when nearly 4000 villages were razed by the central government. All these caused the decline of production, particularly wheat and barley, the two most important yields in the KRI to this day (Noori 2018).

Since then, except for a period of cooperation between removing the Saddam's regime up to 2012, lack of cooperation has been becoming a norm and conflict extended to the present time. As between couples within a family or political parties, the KRI and the central government often have learnt to use economic policies against the other. Controlling the monetary policy by the center is of vital to focus on. After removing the Ba'ath regime, private banks have opened their branches in the KRI, but mostly under the control of the central bank in Baghdad. Recently, when the Kurdistan Regional government (KRG) has taken people deposits in both public and private banks in the name of paying public wages, the central bank in

Baghdad could not interfere, and did not care if bankruptcy occurs in the KRI. In general, as the governments of Iraq and the KRI are less trusted, almost IQD 40 trillion, over USD 35 billion, is hoarded by Iraqi people (Fadiya Al-Jauary). The KRI has had less impact on the economic policies and punished decision makers of Iraq, though they have over 50 seats in Iraqi Parliament.

Irresponsibility toward the KRG employees after cutting its budget (17% minus sovereignty budget) since 2014; sanctioning the KRI on many occasions, even under the Federal system following the independence referendum in 2017; and neglecting the huge budget deficit of the KRG are only some examples that show disintegration of national economy as well as lack of national vision. On the other side, the KRI is not transparent in providing a clear budget statement to the center, one of the reasons for the delay of spending the latter's budget by the central government from 2014 onwards. In building the Ceyhan oil pipeline, exporting oil unilaterally, and moving Kurdish security forces into disputed areas between the Iraqi and KR governments, the Kurdish political leaders did not have sufficient justifications, though lack of clarity in the language of the 2005 constitution was contributed to create this problem.

In designing Federal Constitution in 2005, Dawoody states that the Kurdish as well as the Shiites leaders, more or less, used their experience for their own empowerment. In reality, the 2005 Constitution was boycotted by most Sunni organization. Whether the Federal government, the KRI, or both have the authority to extract and market Iraq's oil is unclear in the constitution. In 2005 Constitution, Article 111 states that "oil and gas are owned by all the people of Iraq," but Article 112 states "the federal government, with the producing governorates and regional governments, shall undertake the management of oil and gas extracted from *present* fields" (Dawoody 2006). The Constitution also identifies the unity of Iraq as a "free" act of its people. This indirectly acknowledges that the Iraqi union is a form of "union at will." Accordingly, the Kurds can use it as an entitlement for separation, though the Iraqi courts have decided that it is not a separation clause. Article 140, which finds a way to determine the fate of disputed area, including Kerkuk, has not yet been implemented. Ironically, Article 9 (sec B) bans militias from being formed outside of the framework of armed forces. However, many Shiite, Sunnis, and Kurdish units take their orders from the Shiites, Sunnis, and the Kurdish political parties (Arsalan Haji Issa Al-Mizory, October 2014). Paradoxically, Dawoody mentions, "Article 129 identifies additional powers for the regions by stating that: The region's government is responsible for all that is required to manage the region, in particular establishing and organizing internal security forces for the region such as police, security and regional guards." It also confirms that these two partners are not responsible for the possible mistakes that happen by one side. Violating the federal constitution is demonstrating that the problem lies with the enforcement party and norms of behavior more than the rules of law. Designing institutions has not encouraged cooperation between them too.

Putting the analysis above altogether, in Iraq and the KRI, partners are stuck in their relations, neither able to separate nor capable of living peacefully together. To analyze the influence of economic, socail, and political factors producing institutional stagnation, I would turn.

Factors of Institutional Stagnation and Conflict

Establishing the Iraqi state in early 1920s was the beginning of a new round of social relations among different social groups within Iraq and between the two major ethnic groups, Arabs and Kurds. However, the Iraqi national project was flawed from the start for several reasons that shall be discussed below.

Elsewhere, I have argued that the major factors that blockaded the process of long-term economic growth in the KRI are uncivic traditions, resource curse, and centralization. These factors are complementary in a sense that each produces the other (Noori 2018). Hence, a deep explanation for the causes of uncivic traditions alongside other factors leading to lack of cooperation and raise of conflict shall be paid attention to.

Path Dependence

The present time has been largely shaped by its past. Path dependence has represented itself in both a centralized planning system that made individuals a "means," not "ends" and a political culture supported by rent seeking produced disintegration in the society.

Briefly, as elsewhere, economic recession and political chaos provided the state with a pretext to institute centralized planning policy. Matin properly analyzes that from the fall of Ottoman Empire, to British Mandate, up to the fall of Ba'athiest regime and establishing the Federal government, in each period, a new regime substitutes its precedent but never national project successes. The combined factors in each round let the domestic landlords, tribe leaders, and the political leaders a chance to survive, recover their position, and rise to power. People were largely concentrated on what was removed, not its substitute (Matin 2018).

Due to lack of space, the focus here is on the second half of the twentieth century. In fact, institutions in their primary forms were an extension of primordial power relations. During the period of Iraq's monarchy (1921–1958), parliament candidates were treated as representatives of sects, ethnics, and tribal associations. Their power was largely relied on these associations' power. Up to date, parliament as a political institution is seen the same way both in Iraq and the KRI as it is clear from closing it by the KDP in recent year after the Gorran parliament members insisted on not extending the terms of president of the region for another 2 years.

After the fall of monarchy in Iraq in 1958, the legislative, executive, and judicial powers were powerless in reality, replaced by an unaccountable single-ruler and his party that had entitled to sensor every space. Especially after 1968, the Ba'ath leaders used every single means to strengthening their power. Distributing society into two camps, the counterrevolutionaries and revolutionaries, with the latter being regarded as traitors, was an effective one. The priority, as they claimed, aimed at building a more egalitarian society; thus, the individuals should support the party's strategy during transition period if they would reach the coasts of prosperity (al-Khafaji 2000). The Ba'ath regime, which was ruled by Saddam Hussein since 1979, deployed resources for military expansion under the party's control. In the first year of Iran–Iraq war, military expenditure constituted some 70% of Iraq's GDP. Preparing and making war, for example, with Iran's Shi'a regime, were followed to complete their hegemony over society.

Expelling the Jews from the country during 1940s, who were dominating the private sector and trade, eroding monarchy regime, and a breakdown of semifeudal system in agriculture marked an economic transformation into a fully rentier state, which pushed the rural people to move into the urban areas and changed terms of trade as oil dominated over the economy (al-Khafaji 2000). The social groups had now to follow the *Ba'ath leaders,* instead of becoming *free traders.* Restricting integration between domestic and the international markets, including the capital market, limited developing new ideas and left the domestic markets under the control of the government and/or recruited in the free officers' organizations: political party, military organizations, etc. Step by step, the Ba'ath party, through the state, specialized in everything and enforced an inefficient set of property rights while the rest (the ordinary people) were encouraged or enforced to specialize in protecting the state's/ elite's property rights and their robust political regime. By borrowing from Trotsky, with some modifications, Matin describes the political model of the Ba'athiest party as follows: "the army was substituted for the nation, the party for the army, the security apparatus for the party, and eventually the person of Saddam Hussein for the security apparatus" (Matin 2018).

Throughout the process of war preparation, war making, centralization, and bureaucratization, the "actual conflict reinforced and legitimated the efforts of successive ruling elites to centralize political authority and control the accumulation and distribution of national income"(al-Khafaji 2000). Due to these all, the political culture has been changed in favor of the different political elites in Arab and Kurdish regions in a sense that reproduced the same circles of institutional stagnation when Saddam removed.

As in 1970s, the oil sector is still the main source of economic growth in Iraq. The Kurdish political elites in the KRI have followed the same paths, particularly following the creation of the KRI-*Cihan* oil pipeline, which brings almost 75% of the monthly revenue needed to pay the KRG's soldiers and civil servants' salaries alone, which is about $850 million. There were 47 international oil companies from 17 countries operating in KRI. After all, the international relations with the governments as well as foreign companies have altered incentives of the political Kurdish and Arab elites to cooperate with each other. Instead, each group has tried to consolidate its power within it.

Elements of the political model of the Ba'ath party have been inherited by the Kurdish political parties. Again with some modifications of Matin's description, the Kurdish political parties model can be put into this context: The individuals' dreams and needs were shortening in serving his or her homeland, the latter was substituted for "the Kurdish nation," the Kurdish nation for "my own party," the latter for "my own tribe," reaching to the leader of the that tribe/party (Noori and Chomani 2018). Therefore, once the head of the institutions leaves his or her position, the whole organization confronts the risk of a total collapse. Tensions intensify and, after a period, another group may control it for another purpose. Thus, one may correctly claim that establishing an organization is part of the leaders' wants and wills.

The political elite's power extends to every single space in the labor market. At least four of the universities, the American University of Iraq-Sulaimaniayh, the University of Kurdistan Hawler, the University of Human Development, and the American University of Kurdistan in Duhok, were established by four famous politicians, mostly the politburo members of the parties, though their programs of study are generally much better in comparison to the rest of the universities available in the KRI. The same goes for the Kurdish news press and broadcasts. Without an exception, each belongs to a party or a group within that party and supports its political agenda.

Then education shall contribute to enrich human capital through producing talents and skills that match the contemporary business as well as make employees free from domestic political organizations. In essence, during the Saddam's ascend to power, the education sector gained a short-lived attention, then damaged, but became places for controlling subjects. The major two universities of Salahaddin in Erbil and Sulaimani in Sulaimaniyah city were the only available public universities in the KRI. In the last few years, their numbers, along with the private universities, have been increased. The public universities, and some of the private universities, however, are not qualified for dedicating a high-quality labor force, even totally damaged after cutting the KRG's budget in 2014. The focus here is the quality of public education. For instance, graduation research project (GRP) is a main course at any University that must be taken in year 4. The GRP is often conducted by a group of two to five students. In most of the cases, the students write their GRP in Arabic, but their level of Arabic is not proficient, even though they have studied it for years before reaching university. A large fraction of the students in these departments did not even understand the content of their GRP, and plagiarize by submitting a paper that had been submitted in another department (Noori 2015). Students expect that their fortune in the labor market does rely on patronage, tribal chiefs, and the like, rather than on their skills and talents. Above all, within these institutions, decisions are made centrally (Noori 2018).

Here lies the biggest problem: human beings can be converted from a cooperative one to a looting one who steals not just public resources but life itself from others; thus, the path of social development can be devastated. Ideologically, that conversion has been supported by a kind of "authoritarian education" in which subjects of a society are taught based on two principles. On the one hand, the individual sanctifies ideas as well as leaders (of a tribe, a party, mosques, etc.). On the other hand, authoritarian rulers (from family to state) teach individuals to reduce their opposition to an enemy who shall be eliminated. This has become part of sectarianism–nationalism identity in Iraq, including the KRI, and has been embodied by the organizations, which made a type of human beings that could not build a peaceful relation or separation.

The Neighbors' Effects

No doubt, the analysis above is not sufficient to convince that the path of social change had no chance to switch onto the railway of development but trapped in conflict.

Mostly due to the rise of the USA as the world leader, who put pressure on colonies to open up to free trade by announcing the Wilsonian maxim of "self-determination," and by seeing oil as a strategic commodity for new political era, the KRI was arbitrarily annexed to Iraq by Britain and France after the collapse of Ottoman Empire (Matin 2018).

Iraq is surrounded by authoritarian regimes. The "Neighbors doing the same" justification for authoritarianism motivated the rise of such regimes, particularly in Iraq, Syria, Iran, and Turkey. In Syria, there were some 13 members of the armed forces for every 1000 Syrians in 1970, growing to more than 35 in every 1000 persons by the second half of the 1980s (Perthes 2000). The rise of Ayatollah Khomeini to power in Iran by late 1979 and his success in consolidating an Islamic Shi'a regime was partially an outcome of his neighbors' political economic strategies and their expenditure on so-called national security, including Israel, which gave a pretext to replace the tyranny of Pahlavi dynasty with the Islamic Republican one. Thus, each country has copied its neighbors' political and economic model, which all was based on militarization, authoritarian, and centralization, no matter whether they were secular or religious. Therefore, it was difficult for the political elite in Iraq and the Kurdistan of Iraq to follow a different way that may have ended with a more egalitarian and democratic society. It even gave a justification to orient people through the tunnels of authoritarian regimes.

As between the Kurdish and perhaps Arab spouses in a traditional communities in which their tribe members advise them not to rely on court for separation even if one of the partners, often the husband, is unfaithful, Iraq and the KRI are surrounded by tribal-like regimes that do not support any sort of separation. When the partners fight, laws are rarely in between; their tensions are mostly tackled by tribesmen. Each neighbor interferes from its own interest or point of view. The outcome is that the major political parties inside Iraq, in addition to building or controlling several private and public organizations, protect themselves by coalition with one of the external powers, particularly due to incapability to punish outsiders, their neighbors. Matin's evidence in this regard is evidence. Since establishing federal system in Iraq, Iran has interfered for impeding Sunni insurgency. In response, the Sunni sect has been backed by Saudi Arabia and some other countries (Matin 2018).

Just as being single or being widow is not socially accepted for the individuals in the present KRI and Iraq, separation may encourage others to do the same – therefore, shall not be tolerated. One of the fears is still that it will raise the demands of the Kurds in Turkey, Syria, and Iran. Despite of these, the KRI leaders have unilaterally announced referendum for independence, a relative point to be returned to in the coming section.

Although it is out of the scope of this chapter to get into details, during Cold War, the superpowers, particularly, the USA and Russia, have supported Iraq against the Islamic regime in Iran. They have weakened these two countries' power through wars. The economic sanctions imposed on Iraq further activated sectarian and tribal relations as means of access to the state's scarce resources (Matin 2018).

Collective Action and Opportunity Costs

Did the hegemony of the political elite over public and private institutions have simply gone without resistance? The answer is NO. The recent strikes in August 2018 in Baghdad and other cities are demonstrating this resistance. The focus here is on the KRI's experience.

Despite many attempts and campaigns against corruption and authoritarian agents, individuals have accepted elite domination over the KRG economy because collective action against the system and its agents was likely fruitless. The benefit of participation in a strike, experiences have shown, is not clear as they do not trust each other and the outcome might be going to someone else's pocket or another political elite's. And it is not clear who runs the demonstrations in behind.

External threats contributed to the remaining existing set of institutions. During the 1990s, the threat was Saddam Hussein and his regime: you either choose the ruling parties or Saddam would be back. Recently, external threat has come majorly from two sources: ISIS's capture of Mosul and parts of Syria which deteriorating political tensions in Syria and motivated people to keep the status quo as the likelihood of having 'another Syria in Iraq and the KRI' was expected.

Both in Iraq and the KRI, one way that the political parties and elite were able to limit the growth of political opposition or civil society was by, as previously mentioned, sharing rents with the subjects. A form of this has been by controlling the public labor market. By 2012, about 50% of the labor force was recruited in the public sector in the KRI. The government budget consists of 66% of GDP. By and large, these numbers are scary as the KRG have not had its own stable sources of income. Moreover, in the KRI, "Fraud and abuse have become commonplace. In many cases people get paid without ever showing up for work or receive multiple fraudulent payments from different departments." According to the results of "biometric system" recently implemented for refining payments of the KRG employees, out of 1.4 million employed, including pension payments, about 150,514 were ghost employees. Some of them could earn up to five salaries from the KRG at the same time (Fadiya Al-Jauary 2017). Having over 150 thousand ghost employees emphasize that the major problem is with the norms of behavior and the enforcement party. Enforcement of the rules is usually reserved for non-elites. Recently, a man was sentenced 11 years in prison for stealing milk from a corner minisupermarket. Not surprisingly, to protect themselves or gain an economic opportunity, individuals may believe that reliance on "guns" and connections to the politicians and military officers are the only options.

Challenging the political regime is costly, because the political parties are controlling security forces and willing to resist any change even if it costs lives of their subjects, along with having hegemony over the labor market. As already examples given in the previous section, the political parties' sector in more powerful than the public and private sectors. Each party has tens of organizations (private, public, or political) in which their employees are not allowed to speak freely. Worth to note that the ruling parties have successfully used sectarian–nationalistic strategy against each other, claiming that any movement against, for example, the Sunni or the Kurds will be in favor of Shi'a sects or Arabs. The opposite is just true.

Alternatively, as the society was deeply divided over different political groups, the individuals have tried to protect themselves by finding a position among one of the lines of the ruling class' network (tribes, landlords, businesspeople, the political party companies and organizations, etc.) or migrate to a more safer part of the world to have a lesser gloomy stories of war and conflict.

Coalition with sheikhs, tribesmen, and landlords is not indispensable from the history of the ruling class since the Ottoman dynasty. By the time of abolition of the Ottoman in 1916 and due to war, economic decline, and the victory of the Russian revolution, the tribal sheikhs', who controlled the rural area where 80% of the Iraqi population settled, status valorized by incorporating the Tribal Civil and Criminal Disputes Regulation (TCCDR) into the 1925 Constitution, which "gave certain selected sheikhs the authority to settle all disputes within their tribes and to collect taxes for the government." During Faisal's kingship, the government possessed 1500 rifles, while the tribes had 100,000. Since late 1940, the oil revenues were spent largely to promote the interests of the tribal oligarchy and to reproduce noncapitalist agriculture. The combined sociological effect of these circumstances was that most Iraqis' membership of the purportedly emerging Iraqi nation was mediated through their more basic and determinative membership of a particular sect, tribe, or village community, instead of joining a national umbrella or a movement to impose democratic rules (Matin 2018). Thus cooperation or collective action among individuals is the most difficult task.

Exit–Enter Costs

At the time being, a 'velvet divorce' between Iraq and the KRI can be a myth, though exhausted in their relationship. When partners live together for ages, each invests on his or her relation. At a point of time, one of them may bear a larger cost than the other if his partner chooses to split up; therefore, secession would not be accepted. The disputed area rich in oil, from Khanaqin to Kirkuk and up to Mosel border, is another issue. None of the players would give it up, just like children become an obstacle between husband and wife when they would like to separate.

Up to date, a peaceful reunification is also not possible. One possible strategy is that each partner is saying that "I have sacrificed more; thus, I am entitled to have the lion's share of the opportunities, recourses, etc." By borrowing words from Fanar Haddad, the Sunni-Shiite relation and the relation between them and the Kurds are established on victimhood politics(Haddad 2014). It reaches to the coasts of de facto politics. Each tries to impose her/his preferences upon the other by threatening her/his partner through military intervention, war, sanctions, economic exit, and the like.

Fearing from expanding each other's power through economic growth encourages them to try to restrict other's progress. At micro and macro levels (e.g., family and governments), these strategies are followed as they live in uncertainty toward the other, though they might be exhausted. More importantly, one of the "insiders," the Iraqi state, is able to punish the other insider, the KRI. Consequently, the latter tend to violate the rules, either cheat or rely on rebellion in many ways.

Separation has its cots on third party too. From the perspective of the international community, the major question is that what will be the impact of moving a new star, a state, to our (political) solar system? There are many justifications for impeding this move. Previously, the fear of jeopardizing the security of neighboring states was discussed. A domino effect, as stated by Nye, is another reason: an internationally sanctioned secession anywhere could encourage secessionists everywhere. Richard Haass argues that the new stars will have their own lights, or voices, and may lead to produce difficulty in decision-making, as in EU. He also points out that the world already has enough failed states. An example is South Sudan where 3 years after its creation in 2011 "embroiled in military confrontation with its northern neighbor over disputed border territories and oil fields," in addition to "violent confrontation between some of its tribes." Ferguson argues that international interactions, due to new comers, can lead to conflict, causing an increase in the cost of defense per capita at international level. Thus, it is hard for today's capitalist relations to support establishing a state for the Kurds in Iraq.

Separation or Reunification: What to Do?

The state in Iraq failed to impose a shared identity from the above, or set an efficient property rights that could support economic national integration. However, the Kurds political elites have been contributing to this failure.

The quest for Kurdish autonomy and statehood is a long story (Dawoody 2006). Its historical perspective is out of the scope of this study. The recent referendum for independence on September 25th 2017, with over 93% of "Yes for Independence," though over a million people boycotted voting, demonstrates that the Kurds of Iraq are pessimistic in their partnership with Iraq and believe that the only solution to tackle conflict and develop good institutions is to enjoy their own state. It was an attempt that also increased uncertainty between them.

Whether the aim was really to outright independence or not, the major political parties in the KRI announced a unilateral referendum for the second time in 12 years. Some believe that separation supports democratization process, at least in some geographic areas and for some ethnic groups. A French philosopher Bernard-Henri argues that a "Kurdish nation-state will be a 'shining city on a hill,' and can tackle the complicated predicaments of part of the Middle East" (Levy 2017). Others argue that arriving "new stars" at this planet will provide the global system more choices of integration through cartels and free trade zones (e.g., the European Union and the North American Free Trade Area), meaning that more small countries are economically viable than was the case in the era of protectionist national trade policies. One can add that new comers will foster competition across the world and limit the power of large, hegemonic states too.

In addition to the analysis presented in the previous section, history has shown that there is a weak correlation between "my own state," or "self-state," democracy and well-being. After all, how many states are democratic? Not so many. Experiences of other nations and institutional weaknesses of their own give an outlook to make a proper political decision and pave the way to avoid building unviable state when the opportunity arrives.

The first wave of separation started in Africa where about 25 new states were formed between 1957 and 1964, with an over-optimistic view that future would be brighter. Nevertheless, "the honeymoon of Africa independence," writes Martin Meredith, "was brief but memorable." Just as in the KRI today, the priority was first to get rid of colonialists and only then to build institutions. "Seek first the political kingdom," KwameNkrumah, Ghana's first president had told his followers, "and all else shall be added onto you." Euphoria of nationalism captured the mind of poor, illiterate, and isolated Africans. While the people celebrated the end of colonial rule, the first generation of nationalists worked hard to consolidate power through a command economy and overspending policies, mostly on patronage. Combined with an ugly competition mainly between the United States and the former Soviet Union over Africa, the outcome was often the establishment of volatile institutions that succumbed to civil war, brutal coup, mountains of debt, dreams of development shattered, and national hangover.

Almost 30 new states, mostly in Eastern Europe, were established between 1981 and 1997 (Campanella 2017). Some of them were due to the collapse of Soviet Union and have not yet been recognized. An unrecognized state, such as Transnistria (TMR), by the international community is similar to a state under a prolonged sanction: they suffer from lack of a formal document to travel; immigration rate is high; they are controlled by a powerful state, Russia in this case; and they are facing huge debt, corruption, inflation, etc. (Isachenko 2010). South Ossetia and Abkhazia were two of the four so-called frozen conflicts after the breakup of the Soviet Union (Chamberlain-Creanga and Allin 2010). The political lesson here is that stateless nations/ethnics shall not take the risk of independence if they are not sure of its recognition by the international community.

Turning to the third wave of independence, it shall be observed that only five states have emerged since 2000. It seems that some nations have learnt from the previous waves so far, perhaps Ache in Indonesia, Flanders in Belgium, Biafra in Nigeria, and even Scotland are among the list. However, English-speaking ethnicity in Cameron has already announced their independence.

The outcomes of "referendum for independence" in the KRI were catastrophic. Three weeks after the referendum, the KRG has lost almost half of oil field capacities in Kirkuk, and nearly 30% of its revenue. The Kurdish forces lost over 100 Peshmerga in the few days clash with the central government forces as well as Iraqi militias, especially the Popular Mobilization Units (PMUs), known as al-Hashad al-Sha'bi. Had people and decision makers have observed the impacts of path dependence, institutional weaknesses of the KRI, and the factors affecting "exit costs" discussed in the "literature review" section(*trade routes, asset specificity, and Market structure*), the planners could not design the plan or the Kurdish forces' escape after referendum could have been expected as it happened on many occasions: 1975's total Kurdish rebellion collapse, 1988 and 1989's Anfal Campaigns, 1991's uprising, and not to mention Sinjar's recent flee in front the ISIS forces.

Likewise, it is shown that the institutional structure in the KRI has still several weaknesses that restrict social change and democratization even if this Region outrights her own state. Due to all these, the simplest solution is to claim that separation tackles the chronic predicaments of Iraq. Instead, the institutional change, and unification at this stage, is the key (Maruf and Noori 2016). But how agents of change motivate to do this?

According to Crescenzi's study, "a challenger whose actual exit costs exceed its exit cost threshold, the level of exit costs beyond which a player cannot endure exit, will not move to initiate economic exit in the game." Similarly, a target state with exit costs that exceed its threshold will accept a demand before the challenger exits. The idea suggests that the calculations of costs alongside increasing/decreasing these costs are vital for conflict resolution between partners.

Although reality goes according to the interest of several social/political groups, therefore hard to change through planning and policies; one cannot still stand by and watch conflict between Iraq and the KRI. Putting into the right nerve, some cure can encourage them to interact.

Financial support to the KRI can be one of the policies. More importantly, although the Kurds have been given some seats in parliament, government, and the Republic presidency, compliance and participation do mean that people and leaders in the KRI should have more space in designing the economic policies of Iraqi state with the ability to rely on Federal Court of Iraq when tensions occurs. The Kurds then do not need to rely on any type of rebellion against the center. Unlike Article 129 in the constitution mentioned above, each party should be responsible toward the other. Otherwise, one of the parties pays for the mistakes of the other.

Moreover, building trust between them will have profound impact on getting rid of crisis and investing in their relationship. This is the most difficult task. In order to achieve it, one shall not forget that the internal third party, the central government and the KRG, has no capacity or willingness to do so. Also, the last referendum has further deteriorated their relationship. Therefore, the third "international" party shall intervene into this relationship.

One possible effective remedy is that the international community alters the international law for independence or separation, announcing that no more states will be welcomed in the next two decades and during these two decades those nations who would separate must change their institutional structure. In other words, as no more direct invaders are around, states will not be given unless two parties are agreed and some levels of institutional development are observed (e.g., regular and fair election, autonomous courts, civil society's participation in decision-making, achieving an accountable government, and a continuous economic growth).

On the one hand, this credit screening blocks a tendency for separation, either by the Kurds, Sunnis, Shi'a, or even other ethnic groups around the world. It also encourages them to get rid of institutional stagnation; thus, the outcome can be an institutional change. On the other hand, this policy motivates the "mother-state," or the target, Iraq in this example, to spend more on her partner, the challenger, the KRI in this case, as certainty between them increases.

One can argue that the mother-state could also have less incentive to invest as it is clear that her partner will have no choice but to stay. However, as her partner has the right to separate under some conditions, the target state will be willing to invest in a right way. Eventually, progress may reach a point that both partners prefer to stay rather than to separate, or simply a velvet divorce takes place. The same policy can be applied on similar relationships around the world.

These two parts of the same country shall do their best to integrate their economy as well as society, which is much better than fall under the control of Iran or Turkey (Noori and Chomani 2018). However, a right intervention by the international community may push them to do good, instead of punishing them, hence, is supportive.

Conclusions

History has shown that the abolishment of institutional stagnation is precondition for a more stable society, avoids severe crisis, decreases rate of divorce or provides a peaceful unification, and achieves development. Institutions in Iraq and the KRI are stagnant for several reasons.

Path dependence has shaped the present and future. Challenging the path was failed due to the high opportunity cost of change, neighborhood interference, and sharing rents with the subjects. Institutional structure is not strong to restrict opportunistic behavior. The formal and informal rules are mostly supporting rent-seeking behavior and favor elitism. However, norms of behavior reflect on the enforcement party more than the rules of the game. Both formal and informal rules contribute to impede juncture points, the time a society breaking with its past, not to occur, and resulting in a short-economic growth and a severe predicament that exceeds economic crisis, reaches bloody conflict and catastrophe. The Kurds tried to break from the past through building their own autonomy. They also had an official attempt to separate and build their own. However, history, or path dependence, has no good news for arriving new stars, something that both the stateless ethnicities and the international community shall carefully prepare for in order to prevent further disorder in the system.

References

Aakre S, Helland L, Hovi J (2016) When does informal enforcement work? J Conf Resol 60(7):1312–1340 [a] The Author(s) 2014, pp. 1319–1324

al-Khafaji I (2000) War as a vehicle for the rise and demise of a state-controlled society: the case of Ba'thist Iraq. In: Heydemann S (ed) War, institutions, and social change in the Middle East. University of California Press, Berkely, p 262

Arsalan Haji Issa Al-Mizory (October/2014) Towards a New Understanding of the Right of Self-Determination in the Post-Colonial Context: The case of the Iraqi Kurdistan Region, a thesis submitted to the Department of Law/Bangor University in partial fulfilment of the requirements for the degree of Doctor of Philosophy, Bangor University

Campanella E (2017) Understanding the Secessionist Surge. https://www.project-syndicate.org/onpoint/understanding-the-secessionist-surge-by-ps-editors-2017-10?barrier=accesspaylog

Chamberlain-Creanga R, Allin LK (Fall 2010) Acquiring assets, debts and citizens: Russia and the micro-foundations of Transnistria's stalemated conflict. Demokratizatsiya 18(4):329–356. Washington

Chatagnier JT, Kavakl KC (2017) From economic competition to military combat: export similarity and international conflict. J Confl Resolut 61(7):1510–1536. (p 1511)

Crescenzi MJC (2003) Economic exit, interdependence, and conflict. J Polit 65(3):811–816. The University of Chicago Press, the Southern Political Science Association

Dawoody A (2006) The Kurdish quest for autonomy and Iraq's statehood. J Asian Afr Stud 41(5/6): 483–505. SAGE, London, Thousand Oaks/New Delhi. Accessed through Uppsala University, ibid, p. 494

DeWeaver MA (2017) Making ends meet: economic reforms in the Kurdistan region, AUIS, IRIS Iraq Report, p 4. http://www.auis.edu.krd/iris/sites/default/files/IIR_Making%20Ends%20Meet_DeWeaver%202017.pdf

Dewhurst, in Arsalan Haji Issa Al-Mizory. Assessing the Kurdish question: what is the future of Kurdistan, p 270

Fadiya Al-Jauary, the hoarding cash mass is estimated at IQA 40 trillion. ALMADA Newspaper, 28 May 2017., available at: http://almadapaper.net/ar/printnews.aspx?NewsID=530569

Ferguson N (2001) The cash nexus: money and power in the modern world, 1700–2000. Basic Books, New York, p 384

Gagliardi F (2008) Institutions and economic change: a critical survey of the new institutional approaches and empirical evidence. J Socio-Econ 37:416–443

Haddad F (2014) A sectarian awakening: reinventing Sunni identity in Iraq after 2003. Curr Trends Islam Ideol 17:75

Isachenko D (2010) On the political economy of unrecognised state-building projects. Ital J Int Aff 44(4):62–65. 13 Jan 2010, Download by: [Lund University Libraries], Date: 09 October 2015

Levy BH (2017) Address to the Kurdish nation. https://www.project-syndicate.org/commentary/address-to-the-kurdish-nation-by-bernard-henri-levy-2017-03?barrier=accesspaylog

Maruf H, Noori NN (2016) Macroeconomics: theory and policy. In: Kurdish 'Macroaburi: theory w siyaset. Haval Bookshop, Erbil, p 184

Matin K (2018) Lineages of the Islamic state: an international historical sociology of State (de-) formation in Iraq. J Hist Sociol, Special Issue, 018;31: 6–24, pp. 11–15

Murrell P (2017) Design and evolution in institutional development: the insignificance of the English Bill of Rights. J Comp Econ 45:36–55, access through Uppsala University library, p. 37

Nawaz S (2014) Growth effects of institutions: a disaggregated analysis. Econ Model 45:118–126

Noori NN (2015) The impact of the public expenditure on the government universities (2005–2014): The Universities of Sulaimani and polytechnic as evidence. Acad J Sulaimani University. In Kurdish, KarigeriXerjGishtileserzankokaniHkumet (2005–2014): ZankokaniSlemani w Polytechnic weknmune. Sci J 46:137–162, p 149

Noori NN (2018) The failure of economic reform in the Kurdistan region of Iraq (1921–2015): the vicious circle of uncivic traditions, resource curse, and centralization. Bri J Mid East Stud 45(2):7

Noori NN, Chomani K (2018) Economic and political reform in the Kurdistan region", in Kurdish, "ChaksazeeAburee w Siasee le HermiKurdistaniIraqda", 19/06/2018, published online: http://diplomaticmagazine.net/politics/704

North DC (1989) Institutions and economic growth: an historical introduction. World Dev 17:1321–1323, No. 9, Printed in Great Britain, Pergamon Press plc

Perthes V (2000) Si Vis Stabilitatem, Para Bellum: state building, national security, and war preparation in Syria. In: Heydemann S (ed) war, institutions, and social change in the Middle East. University of California Press, Berkeley, p 152

Online Reports and Articles

Kurdistan Region, Facts & Figures, http://investingroup.org/country/kurdistan/facts-figures/

Kurdish man sentenced to 11 years in prison for stealing milk, diaper, May 01–2017, http://www.kurdistan24.net/en/news/c3d68eb5-63ca-4188-a9d0-45e48dfd6f88/Kurdish-man-sentenced-to-11-years-in-prison-for-stealing-milk%2D%2Ddiaper

Gov't biometric payroll system unveils widespread fraud in Kurdistan Region By Rudaw 1/2/2017. Available athttp://www.rudaw.net/english/kurdistan/01022017

Iraq after the May 2018 Elections: Building Democracy or Becoming an Iranian Satellite?, Wednesday, January 31, 2018, http://new-middle-east.blogspot.se/2018/01/iraq-after-may-2018-elections-building.html

The labour force survey in Kurdistan Region (2010), a report (in Arabic), the KRG, Ministry of Planning, Board of Statistics, Rand Organization, pp. 12–14

Barham A.. Salih is the founder of the American University of Iraq. He is the former deputy of PUK leader as well as deputy of Prime Minster of the central government. See this link; http://auis.edu.krd/board/barham-salih

The chancellor of. the University is NechirvanBarzani, prime minster of the KRG and nephew of, and deputy of KDP president, MasoudBarzani, and, too

The president's letter Ali Qaradaghi, who is the founder and president of the Islamic Kurdish League founded in 1988, can be found on: http://uhd.edu.iq/pages.php?nid=3

The chairman's letter, Mansur Barzani, who is the son of former president of Kurdistan MasudBarzani, can be found on: http://auk.edu.krd/about/letter-from-chairman/

World Bank group, The Kurdistan Region of Iraq: Assessing the economic and Social Impact of the Syrian Conflict and ISIS, 2015 International Bank for Reconstruction and Development / The World Bank, http://documents.worldbank.org/curated/en/579451468305943474/pdf/958080PUB0Apri0PUBLIC09781464805486.pdf

Not so happily ever after – as Kurdish divorce rate grows, 13/9/2016,http://www.rudaw.net/english/kurdistan/13092016. See also: Rate of Divorce in Sulaymaniyah Doubled Since 2012:https://www.google.se/search?dcr=0&source=hp&ei=LMeRWqmZGoi00gWjxIXwDw&q=rate+of+divorce+in+kurdistan&oq=rate+of+divorce+in+kur&gs_l=psy-ab.3.0.33i22i29i30k1.79977.89392.0.91190.25.16.1.3.4.0.819.3110.1j3j0j2j1j1j1.9.0....0...1c.1.64.psy-ab..12.13.3135.0..0j35i39k1j0i67k1j0i22i30k1.0.E8C9VzjM5Ik

Ethnic Cleansing of the Rohingya People

81

Nasir Uddin

Contents

Introduction	1576
What Are the Rohingyas?	1576
"Seek and Hide" of History: The Politics of Rohingya Existence	1580
Citizenship, Statelessness, and Refugeehood	1583
Evidence of Ethnic Cleansing	1585
Conclusion	1588
References	1588

Abstract

The world has recently witnessed a massive influx of the Rohingyas, known as the most persecuted ethnic minority in the world, to Bangladesh as they fled unprecedented atrocities perpetrated by the Myanmar security forces in 2017. The denial of citizenship through adaptation of the Myanmar Citizenship Law in 1982 rendered the Rohingya people stateless which became instrumental behind merciless killing, ruthless violence against Rohingya women including random raping, reckless burning house and properties, and an unexplainable persecution in Rakhine state. Though it has recently taken an extreme form and drew a wider global attention, the Rohingya people had been undergoing various forms of discrimination, forced displacement, arbitrary detention, and an acute vulnerability in their everyday lives since 1962 when for the first time the military took over the power of then Burma. Since then state-sponsored violence, systemic persecution under state policy, massive human rights violations, and forcibly pushing them to cross the border became everyday experiences of Rohingya people. The latest one that started from August 25, 2017, superseded all previous records, and the intensity of brutality was so extreme that the United Nations Human Rights

---

N. Uddin (✉)
Department of Anthropology, University of Chittagong, Chittagong, Bangladesh
e-mail: nasir.anthro@cu.ac.bd

© The Author(s), under exclusive license to Springer Nature Singapore Pte Ltd. 2019
S. Ratuva (ed.), *The Palgrave Handbook of Ethnicity*,
https://doi.org/10.1007/978-981-13-2898-5_116

Council termed it as "the text book example of ethnic cleansing." This chapter presents the scenario and evidence of ethnic cleansing of Rohingya people with a vivid picture of their present conditions along with their struggling past in the borderland of Bangladesh and Myanmar.

Keywords
Rohingyas · Ethnic-cleansing · Genocide · Refugees · Bangladesh · Myanmar

Introduction

The Rohingya, an ethnolinguistic and religious minority, have been living in Arakan (Rakhine since 1989) state of Burma, now Myanmar, for centuries (see Buchanan 1799; Charney 1999; Karim 2016; Ibrahim 2016; Uddin 2017). In August 2017, worldwide attention was drawn to this region when the Myanmar Military began unprecedented campaign that forced more than 750,000 Rohingya people to cross the border in Bangladesh. Combined with the previous 550,000, now Bangladesh is hosting about 1.3 million Rohingyas in its Southeastern part (WHO Report 2018). The Rohingya people became stateless when Myanmar enacted the *Citizenship Law* in 1982 conferring citizenships to 135 nationals excluding the Rohingya people. In Myanmar, the Rohingya people are often identified as "illegal Bengali migrants," and in Bangladesh they are called "illegal Burmese migrants." The Government of Bangladesh has recently prepared their biometric database terming them as "Forcibly Displaced Myanmar Nationals." Apparently the Rohingya people exist nowhere as Myanmar does not recognize them as citizens, and Bangladesh denies recognizing them even as refugees. Factually, the denial of citizenship and subsequent statelessness turned into an instrument what Myanmar has been exploiting to drive them out of the country creating an "unlivable and atrocious conditions" (see Uddin 2019, forthcoming) in Rakhine state. However, it started from 1962 when the military first took over the state power, but the large-scale influx of Rohingyas to Bangladesh began from 1978 following the "Operation Nagamin" executed by then Burmese armies (Uddin 2012). The recent phenomenon is the prolongation of previously continued atrocious and exclusionary policy of the state of Myanmar. The chapter addresses the current situation of Rohingyas what has reached here through different political upheavals in Burma/Myanmar that has gradually pushed them to the struggle for existence. The chapter presents the ethnic, regional, and political history of Arakan/Rakhine and of Burman/Myanmar across time and space in an attempt to find the position of Rohingyas and the reasoning behind ethnic cleansing of Rohingya people.

What Are the Rohingyas?

The Rohingya people are widely known as the inhabitants of Rohang (or Rowsang or Rossan) which was the earlier name of Arakan, but now known as Rakhine state (Alam 1999). In the medieval works of the poets of Arakan and Chittagong, like

Quazi Daulat, Mir Mardan, Shamser Ali, Quraishi Magan Thakur, Alaol, Abdul Ghani, and others, they frequently referred to Arakan as "*Roshang*," "*Roshanga*," "*Roshango Shar*," and "*Roshango Des*" (see Karim 2016 [1997]). It is admitted here that literary works should not be used as a source of history, but the names of places could be found in the contemporary literature which could be academically authenticated. Besides, characters of fiction/literature are made of imagination, but the names of places are often used in the real forms. Therefore, it is widely accepted that Arakan's earlier name was Rohang (or Rowsang or Rossan). Besides, many historians (Phayre 1883; Harvey 2000 [1925]; Chowdhury 2004; Siddiquee 2012; Karim 2016; Iqbal 2017) supplemented to this paradigm of naming. Mrohong was the original Arakanese word of Rohang, and the Rohingya people were believed to be the inhabitants of Mrohong [Rohang] (Chowdhury 2004). Arakan is an old coastal country in Southeast Asian region. Historian Siddiquee wrote, "The word Arakan is the corruption of the word *Al-Rukun*....In Ptolemy's *Geografia* (150 AD) it was named '*Argyre*'. Early Buddhist missionaries called Arakan as '*Rekkha Pura*'. In the Ananda Chandra stone pillar of Chandra dynasty (8th Century) at Shitthaung Pagoda in Mrauk-U the name of Arakan was engraved as '*Arakades's*'. In a Latin Geography (1597 AD) by Peta Vino, the country was referred to as '*Aracan*'. Friar Manrique (1628–43 AD) mentions the country as *Aracan*" (Siddiquee, 2012: 15).

Historian Alam wrote, "Arab geographer Rashiduddin (1310 AD) termed it '*Rahan* or *Raham*', the British traveler Relph Fitch (1586 AD) called it *Rocon*, Rennell's map (1771 AD) indicated it '*Rassawn*', legendry Tripura Chronicle *Rajmala* named it *Roshang* and Francis Hamilton Buchanan mentioned it *Roung*, or *Rossawn*" (Alam 1999). We also find in Siddiquee's writing, "By the Bengal Hindus, at least by such of them as have been settled in Arakan, the country is called '*Rossawn*'. The Mahammedans who have long settled at Arakan call the country '*Rohingaw*' and called themselves *Rohinga* or the native of Arakan. The Persians called it *Rkon*" (Siddiquee 2012: 16). "Today the Muslims of Arakan call the country '*Rohang*' or '*Arakan*' and call themselves '*Rohingya*' or native of Rohang" (Amanullah 1997). Arguably, the inhabitants of Rohang were easily identified what is now known as the Rohingyas people.

Many renowned historians (Charney 1999; Karim 2016; Iqbal 2017) and scholars (Ahmed 2014; Ibrahim 2016; Fahmida 2017; Akhanda 2018; Uddin 2019, forthcoming) are of opinions that the Rohingya people are not a unique ethnic group but a group developed from different stocks of people during different turns of the history of this region. However, the Rohingya people are predominantly Muslim by religion with distinct culture, social-cultural organizations, and ethnic markers of their own (see Uddin 2019, forthcoming). Siddiquee wrote, "they trace their ancestry to Arabs, Moors, Pathans, Moghuls, Central Asians, Bengalis and some Indo-Mongoloid people. Since Rohingyas are mixture of many kinds of people, their cheekbone is not so prominent and eyes are not so narrow like Rakhine Maghs and Burmans. Their noses are not flat and they are a bit taller in stature than the Rakhine Maghs, but darker in complexion. They are of some bronzing colored and not yellowish. The Rohingyas of Arakan still carried the Arab names, faith, dress, music and customs" (Siddiquee 2012: 16. Also see, Ahmed 2014). So, "the Rohingyas are nationals as well as an indigenous ethnic group of Burma. They are not new born racial group of

Arakan; rather they are as old an indigenous race of the country as any others" (Alam 1999: 26). The historical records and the earlier history of their settlement in Arakan region, then known as Rohang, Rowshang or Rohaing, altogether confirm that the Rohingya people are one of the oldest residents of Arakan which discards the state discourse of Myanmar that "Rohingyas are illegal Bangladeshi migrants in Myanmar."

In order to justify the ongoing ethnic cleansing in Rakhine state, Myanmar has produced a state narrative about the demographic appearance of the Rohingya people in Arakan. According to Myanmar's narratives that I have summarized based on the available information (Radio Free Asia 2017) circulated by the Myanmar state authority and the remarks of military and political establishment: "the Rohingyas are not the inhabitants of the Myanmar and they have never been the permanent residents of Burma. The Rohingyas people are illegal Bengali migrants who migrated to the Rakhine, formerly Arakan, state during the British colonial period. The British brought a large number of Bengalis from then Bengal to the British Burma for various reasons including agriculture, fishing, and day labour. The Rohingyas are not Burmese people at any level in the history of Burma. Their religion, their culture, their language, and their physical appearance are unlike Burmese people. Rather, they are very similar to the South Asian people." This is sort of state narratives that have been supported by some pro-Myanmar (e.g., Chan 2005; Tonkin 2014; Ware and Laoutides 2018) and the military-backed historian (e.g., Leider 2013, 2015; Leiden 2018) and some extremist Burmese writers (e.g., Saw 2001). However, the emergence of Islam in the Arakan state, the history of colonization and decolonization, and earlier records of people's settlement in this region do not support the state narratives of Myanmar.

As per historically authenticated fact, the first group of Muslims people arrived in Arakan in the eighth century when Arab traders got shelter after their ship wrecked on the bank of Rumbee River (see Phayre 1883; Harvey 2000 [1925]; Chowdhury 2004; Akhanda 2013). It was the tenure of Mohathaing Sandia (788–810) when this incident took place in Arakan. According to the history of the Muslims in Arakan, some traders and soldiers were said to have died, while the remaining ones took shelter with the kind and generous consideration of the King Sandia. Those traders and soldiers are known as Kular or foreigners in the history of Arakan (Chowdhury 2004). They started living in Arakan and gave birth to new generations and continued lineages, which are considered, by some scholars and historians (see, for details, Chowdhury 2004; Siddiquee 2012; Akhanda 2013; Karim 2016), the earlier ancestors of today's Rohingya population. Then in 1430, the second phase of Muslims in Arakan came when ousted Arakanese King Mun Shaw Moon alias Normikhla regained his thorn defeating Burmese king with the help of 30,000 Mughal soldiers who were predominantly Muslims. A noted historian of Arakan, A P Phayre, "...apprehending trouble [from Burmese King], the king of Arakan made communication with the king of Bengal, established friendly relations with him and both King exchanged parents" (cited in Chowdhury 2004: 26). I wrote in elsewhere that "Normikhla stayed in Gorh for about 26 years and re-captured his lost thorn and kingdom in 1430 with the help of 30,000 soldiers provided by then Bengal King

Sultan Jalal Uddin Mohammad Shah. After regaining his throne, Normikhla wanted the Muslim soldiers to stay in Arakan state to protect the region and frontier areas from any further attack by then Burmese king" (see Uddin 2019, forthcoming). During this time, Rohang was made the capital of Arakan state. Normikhla provided land and space to the 30,000 soldiers from Bengal who then settled in Arakan. Most of them got married in Arakan and settled down there. According to many historians (e.g., Chowdhury 2004; Siddiquee 2012; Akhanda 2013; Karim 2016; Akhanda 2018 etc.), Normikhla took a Muslim name known as Sulaiman Shah and introduced an official coin in Arabic fonts as an acknowledgment of the supports by the Sultan of Gorh. In the history of Arakan, this branch of settlement is recorded as the second phase of Muslim settlement in this region (for details, see Phayre 1883: 78; Chowdhury 2004: 53–55; Forster 2011: 64; Siddiquee 2012: 21; Akhanda 2013: 38–39; Hossain 2014:14; Karim 2016:24–25; Iqbal 2017: 04; Uddin 2019, forthcoming). The next phase of Muslim settled in Arakan when Shah Suja arrived in 1660. Shah Suja was defeated by Mir Jumla, the Commander in Chief of Mughal Battalion, during the dynasty of Emperor Awrongajeb. According to many historians, in response to the assurance of the then Arakanese King for ensuring their safety, Shah Suja with his family, relatives, bodyguards, security soldiers, caretakers, cooks, followers, advisors, carriers, domestic servants, and trusted soldiers took shelter in Arakan (Uddin 2017: 31–32). But, later on, Shah Suja was killed with his family and trusted bodyguards in conspiracy executed by the then Arakanese King. After the killing of Shah Suja, the remaining soldiers were allowed to stay in Arakan who got married with the locals and settled down there. These group of people were Muslims, and their offsprings formed a large group of Muslim community in Arakan state who were later known as Kamanchi (see, for details, Phayre 1883: 78; Harvey 2000 [1925]: 95; Chowdhury 2004: 128–132; Siddiquee 2012: 26–27; Akhanda 2013: 43; Hossain 2014:14; Karim 2016:41–44; Uddin 2019, forthcoming). The last phase of Muslims' arrival in Arakan was recorded in 1824 when the British occupied Arakan. From 1430 to 1784, Arakan was an independent state until the Burmese King Budapaya captured it once again and controlled until 1824. Soon after Budapaya occupied the Arakan state, hundreds of thousands of Rakhine Buddhists and Arakanese Muslims took shelter in then Bengal as a frontier territory. After 40 years of Burmese occupation (1784–1824), when the British captured the Arakan state, a large number of Muslims and Hindus returned to Arakan. This migration is historically considered as the fourth phase of Muslim, along with some Hindus, settlements in Arakan (for details, see Phayre 1883; Harvey 2000 [1925]; Chowdhury 2004; Siddiquee 2012; Akhanda 2013; Hossain 2014; Karim 2016; Uddin 2017; Uddin 2019, forthcoming).

Given the aforementioned historical contexts of Muslim arrival and settlement in Arakan state, it is clear that Islam and Muslim have been the part of Arakan history for more than thousand years. But, the emergence of Islam and demographic appearance of Muslim do not essentially confirm that the history of Muslim and Islam is the history of Rohingya people in Arakan state. Because the arrival of Arab traders in the eighth century, Gorh's soldiers in 1430, Kamanchi in 1660, and the return of Muslims during the British period were not the Rohingya people by ethnicity. There is no space for controversy that the emergence of Islam and the appearance of Muslim in the demographic composition of Arakan took place more than thousands of years ago as many authentic historical records justify it (see Eaton 1993; Ezzati 2002; Akhanda 2013; Leitich 2014; Karim 2016). Besides, many renowned historians on Arakan also endorsed the thousand years of history of Islam and Muslim in Arakan (see Phayre 1883; Buchanan 1799; Harvey 2000 [1925]; Charney 1999), but no record has endorsed that the history of Muslim is the history of Rohingya people in Arakan (see Uddin 2017: 32). Many researchers and historians (Siddiqqui 2000; Chowdhury 2004; Siddiquee 2012; Akhanda 2013; Karim 2016; Iqbal 2017), many Rohingya activist-historians (Siddiquee 2012; Bahar 2012; Yunus 1994), and many scholars compassionate to Rohingyas (Elahi 1987; Ezzati 2002; Zarni and Cowley 2014; Ibrahim 2016; Farzana 2015, 2016) have been struggling and trying to establish the theory that the arrival of Muslims in Arakan is "the origin of Rohingyas" in Burma, but it does not stand because Arab traders, if we take as the first arrivals of Muslims, were not Rohingyas under any circumstances. But it is easily understandable and more sensible to assume that with the combination of many trends of people, their lifestyles, languages, and their culture like Arabs, Moors, Pathan, Mughal, and Bengals, the Rohingyas have been emerged as distinctive ethnic community in Arakan state over the long period of time. So, in that consideration, the Rohingyas are a "mixed race" (Uddin 2017: 37), since there is no "pure race" in this world as "pure race in an unscientific idea" (Sussman 2014) particularly in today's world when the entire idea of "indigeneity is on the move" (see Gerhrz et al. 2018) and the notion of "identity is deterritorialised" (Uddin 2018). It altogether confirms two theses: Firstly, Myanmar's state narrative about the Rohingya people that they are not the inhabitants of the Burma and they had never been in Burma but are illegal Bengali migrations who migrated during the British colonial period is a "manufactured history" and "distorted truth" invented to support the execution of Myanmar's state policy to drive the Rohingya people out of the country. Secondly, the Rohingyas, particularly their ancestors, have been the inhabitants of Arakan for more than 1000 years since the emergence of Islam and arrivals of Muslim in this region. However, the Rohingyas are a mixed "race" formed over centuries based on the combination of many trends of people, and now the Rohingyas constitute a particular ethnic category with their distinctive language, culture, and social organizations with large adaptation of Islamic culture.

"Seek and Hide" of History: The Politics of Rohingya Existence

Myanmar is deliberately utilizing this academic and historical vacuum to justly various forms of discrimination and atrocities against the Rohingya people what the UN Human Rights Council terms as "ethnic cleansing." Myanmar claims that Rohingyas were never the residents of Burma and they were migrated to Arakan from Bengal during the British colonial period started from 1824. Before that, there were no Rohingyas in the land of Burma. Myanmar has constructed this state narrative and used it in the formulation of its citizenship law enacted in 1982 where eligibility criteria were set that those who are entitled to the citizenship of Myanmar are those who were living in Burma before the British colonized this territory. Under the pretext of this clause, the citizenships of the Rohingya people were taken away as, according to state narratives, Rohingyas came in Burma during the British colonial period and there were no Rohingyas before 1824. This is a fair politics of exclusion and deliberately "manufactured historical narrative" (Uddin 2017) because there are some very authentic evidences and records which confirmed the presence of Rohingya people in Burma even long before the British colonized Burma. In order to dismantle the myth of this Myanmar's state narrative, I will cite some authentic historical records which are good enough to locate the Rohingya people in the historical-demographic canvas of Arakan long before the British colonized Burma.

Francis Hamilton Buchanan's travel notes have been recognized as a globally accepted authentic historical document. He published an article in 1799 titled "A Comparative Vocabulary of Some of the Languages Spoken in the Burma Empire" in the journal *Asiatic Researcher*. Buchanan categorically mentioned that he talked to a group of people living in the Arakan region who speak in a particular language and identified themselves as Rooinga (Buchanan 1799: 55). It is considered the first record of Rooinga in the history of Burma which later transformed and took shape into the Rohingya. Before this record, there were many indications, authentic notations, and historical evidences of the presence of Muslims in Arakan, but were recorded in different names. Buchanan for the first time recorded the presence of Rohingyas by using their self-identification as "Rooinga." It clearly manifests the Rohingya people as a distinctive group of people living in the Arakan even before 1799, 25 years before the British occupied Arakan. It is to be mentioned here that Rohingya people still identify themselves as "Rooinga" (see Uddin 2017).

The *Classic Journal* has often been considered as the historical baseline of the people of the Southeast Asian region. In the *Classic Journal* published in 1811, there was a clear indication that a group of people were living in the Arakan region and speaking "Rooinga language," and they used to call themselves as Rooingas (the *Classical Journal* 1811). It is also mentionable here that the *Classic Journal* of 1811 has been used as one of the authentic historical records for the early history of Burma (Uddin 2017:33). Many internationally acclaimed scholars (e.g., Tarling 2001; Gutman 2001; Singer 2008; Cotterell 2015) have used the *Classical Journal* as a historical source to write the history of Arakan. So, according to the information recorded in the *Classical Journal* of 1811, it is clearly evident that a group of people who identified themselves as Rooingas were living in the Arakan region in and before 1811.

Another record was found in an edited book titled *Examples of German vernaculars: Dr. Seetzen's linguistic legacy and other linguistic research and collections, in particular on East India* edited by Dr. Johann Severin Vater published in 1816 before the British colonized Burma. A German ethnologist Johann Severin Vater mentioned a name of ethnic group, with the reference to Francis Buchanan, who identified themselves as "Ruinga" what is now known as Rohingyas (Vater 1816). According to Vater these Ruinga people were speaking in a particular language what they called

"Ruinga language" (cited in Ibrahim 2016: 25). Vater's notation about a "Ruinga language"-speaking ethnic group then living in Arakan also clearly demonstrates that the Rohingya people were the residents and inhabitants of Arakan state in and before 1816.

Walter Hamilton (1820) wrote a book titled *A Geographical, Statistical, and Historical Description of Hindostan and the Adjacent Countries* published in 1820 where he clearly stated that "the Moguls know this country by the name of Rakhang, and the Mahomeddans, who have been long settled in this country call themselves Rooinga or the natives of Arracan" (1820: 802). Hamilton statement historically authenticates three important facts:

1. A group of people identified themselves in the name of Rooinga. It means that Rohingya people were living in Arracan (Arakan) before 1824 when the British colonized Burma.
2. "Rooinga people have been long settled there" indicates the Rohingya people had been living in Arakan long centuries before 1824.
3. The Rooinga were the natives of Arracan even in 1820 when the book was published and 4 years before the British colonized Burman. It clearly indicates the Rohingya people have been the natives of Arakan (now Rakhine) for centuries.

There are more historical records of Rohingya presence before 1824 in Arakan that I have presented and explained in elsewhere (Uddin 2019, forthcoming), but I am not going to further detail it here because this chapter is not about the identity and ethnicity of the Rohingya people. However, it is an important point to be noted here that the four historical records that I have used here were documented during the period (1784–1824) when Burmese king ruled the Arakan region and definitely before the British colonized the Arakan territory. "Thus, there is a plentiful evidence of the existence of the Rohingyas in Arakan by the early nineteenth century in a sequence of works published at the time. None of these sources had any partial political interest in the ethnic make of this regions; none of them has any reason to invent such a new group like Rohingyas any more than they had an interest in suppressing such groups, and all clearly point to the fact that there was a major ethnic group in the region with a distinct language at the time clearly identifiable as Rohingyas" (Ibrahim 2016: 25). So, it fairly delegitimizes the fabricated claims and manufactured narrative by the Myanmar state that Rohingya people were not the residents of Burma before the British colonized the region. The real fact is that the Rohingya people were the residents and inhabitants of the Arakan region long even before the British colonized it. It is also to be mentioned here that factually Burma occupied and ruled the Arakan state only for 66 years (26 years from 1406 to 1430 and 40 years from 1784 to 1824) during more than 2000 years of history of independent Arakan. Therefore, what Myanmar claims today regarding the ownership of Arakan state could be outright discarded by the historical facts. Rather it could be a valid question to raise whether Rohingyas or Burmese are the earlier migrants and residents of Arakan now known as the Rakhine state. Noted historian

Michael Charney wrote, "both Rohingyas Muslims and Rakhine Buddhists migrated and got settled down in Rakhine state 1000 year ago and factually the Rohingya people, perhaps not its present form, came to Arakan state before the Bamar came" (see, for detail, Charney 1999). If it is the fact, the Rohingya people could claim themselves as the natives of Arakan.

Citizenship, Statelessness, and Refugeehood

Arakan was an independent kingdom until 1784, when it encompassed the Chittagong region in the southern part of today's Bangladesh. I have already discussed that "The Rohingyas are [claimed to be] the descendants of [this first group of Muslims] Moorish, Arab and Persian Traders, including Mughal, Turk, Pathan and Bengali soldiers cum migrants, who arrived between the 9th and 15th centuries, married local women, and settled in the region" (Ahmed 2002–2003: 03). The Burmese king Bodawpaya conquered and annexed Arakan in 1784, triggering a long guerrilla war in which the Burmese allegedly killed more than 200,000 Arakanese. A failed attempt was made in 1796 to overthrow Burmese rule, resulting in the exodus of two-thirds of the Muslim Arakanese into the neighboring Chittagong area (see, for details, Harvey 2000 [1925]; Karim 2016; Médecins Sans Frontiers Report 2002; 2017; Uddin 2012). This marked the start of an influx of Arakanese Muslim refugees into Bengal. When the British incorporated Arakan into its empire in 1885, many refugees returned. For centuries, the Buddhist Rakhine (see Uddin 2019, forthcoming) and Arakanese Muslims lived together in the territory until the World War II. However, the advance of the Japanese army in 1942 sparked both the exodus of thousands of Muslims and the evacuation of the British from Arakan. Karim wrote, "Communal riots between the Rakhine Buddhists and Rohingyas erupted, and some 22,000 Muslims fled to adjoining British Indian territories [Chittagong]" (Karim 2016).

Shortly after Burma became independent in 1948, some Muslims carried out an armed rebellion, demanding an independent Muslim state within the Union of Burma. Though the rebellion was quashed in 1954, Muslim distrust of the Burmese administration remained, and a backlash ensued that even echoes today (see, for details, Ware and Laoutides 2018: 14). For example, "Muslims were removed and barred from civil posts, restrictions on movement were imposed, and property and land were confiscated" (see MSF Report 2002). Even so, the Rohingyas, as Muslims, were close to having their ethnicity and autonomy formally recognized in the 1950s under the democratic government of U Nu, but these plans were thwarted by the military coup of General Ne Win in 1962 (Uddin 2012).

After the military took over the state power, the plight of the Rohingya people started to deteriorate and was gradually pushed to the margin of the state. In 1978, a massive campaign took place against the Rohingya people by the Burmese military which triggered an influx of 250,000 Rohingyas to Bangladesh. Still the Rohingya people were enjoying a particular form of citizenship in the Arakan state of Burma until 1982. However, the Rohingya people became stateless soon after Myanmar in

1982 enacted its *Citizenship Law*, which conferred citizenship to 135 nationals excluding the Rohingyas. Since then many Rohingyas started migrating to Bangladesh, Thailand, Malaysia, and Middle Eastern countries to flee persecution (Hossain 2014[2010]) on the regular basis. In 2007, the Rohingyas drew global media attention, yet at minimal level, and attracted the concerns of rights organization as a "new boat people" (see Lewa 2008) because hundreds of Rohingyas died in the sea in their journey toward Thailand and Malaysia. But, in 2017, the Rohingya people heavily captured the attention of international community, leading global media outlets, and rights organizations due to the massive influx (more than 700,000) in Bangladesh. In fact, in the framework of modern nation state, the Rohingyas are nonexistent human beings as they are nowhere in the legal and structural framework of either Bangladesh or Myanmar (Uddin 2012, 2015). Therefore, the Rohingya people experience persecution, atrocities, and everyday forms of discrimination committed by the state despite their stateless people. In fact, the Rohingya people were denied all sorts of rights in Myanmar because "citizenship is considered as the rights of have rights" (see Arendt 1994; Kesby 2012).

The Rohingya people started migrating to the southeastern part of Bangladesh in the late 1970s, but big in number came in the early 1990s. The first influx took place in 1978 when about 200,000 fled to Bangladesh. "It is said that oppression, discrimination, violence and forced labour practices by the Myanmar authorities triggered an exodus of more than 250 thousand Rohingya Muslims to cross the border between 1991 and 1992. Since then the flow of this migration to the Bangladesh territory continued which contributed to shape a big figure living as refugees in this country" (Uddin 2010). Over the years, approximately 230,000 refugees have been reportedly repatriated to Myanmar under the supervision of the UNHCR. However, most of them along with new group of Rohingyas again returned to Bangladesh in many illegal ways and started living as unregistered Rohingyas in various localities of Teknaf and Ukhia. The number of such Rohingya returnees is estimated about 250,000. Besides, 125,000 Rohingyas came in 2012, and 85,000 crossed the border to Bangladesh in 2016. In a recent remark, the Minister of the Ministry of Expatriate Welfare informed that there are 250,000 Rohingyas who live in the Middle Eastern countries with Bangladeshi passport (Muntaha 2018). With the recent influx following August 25, 2017, it is estimated that more than 700,000 Rohingyas crossed the border. Bangladesh government has recently prepared a biometric database of around 1.3 million Rohingyas as part of the repatriation process, while still many have remained undocumented. Excluding expatriates, now approximately 1.3 million Rohingya people live in Bangladesh. They live in almost 30 temporarily built refugee camps in Ukhia and Teknaf of Cox's Bazar which is now considered as the biggest refugee camps in the world (World's Refugee Camp 2018).

In Myanmar, the Rohingya people are deprived of their social, economic, civil, political, and basic human rights because the state treats them as if they are lesser than human being what I call "subhuman" (Uddin 2019, forthcoming) due to their ethnic, religious, and racial difference. In Bangladesh, they are not well-received because Bangladesh is already an overpopulated country and southeastern part of

Bangladesh is resource-poor area which I have discussed earlier. Besides, Bangladesh is not one of the signatory states of *the UN Refugee Convention 1951* and hence does not feel obliged to host the Rohingya people as refugees. Besides, "the critical experience of dealing with Rohingyas who crossed the border in 1978, 1991/92, 2012, 2016 and 2017 have also discouraged Bangladesh to be cordial and sympathetic to them" (Uddin 2019, forthcoming). Given the scenario, the Rohingyas are in an acute vulnerable stage in both Bangladesh and Myanmar which has been created by Myanmar.

Evidence of Ethnic Cleansing

What Myanmar state force, Burmese ethnic extremists, and Buddhist fundamentalists are currently doing with the Rohingya people is called by the UN Human Rights Council as "a text book example of Ethnic Cleansing" (Safi 2017). In fact, the statistical figures are good enough to provide an adequate rationale that it is a clear ethnic cleansing. From August 25, 2017, more than 700,000 Rohingyas fled the Rakhine state (Safi 2018), more than 25,000 people were killed, and 19,000 women and girls were raped (The Daily Star 2018). Sixty-two percent of villages of Maungdaw were completely destroyed as the satellite images showed, and a total of 470 villages turned into ashes (The Independent 2017). Hundreds of thousands of Rohingya became wounded, and many more became paralyzed. Now, no more than 250,000 Rohingyas live in 3 townships (Maungdaw, Buthidaung, and Rathedaung) since the rest of the majority were "cleaned" from their settlement (see, for more details, HRW 2017). So, the fugues stated above clearly demonstrate that what the Myanmar security forces did in the Rakhine state is a clear ethnic cleansing.

In fact, the degree of atrocity was so intense that many internationally acclaimed scholars (e.g., Zarni and Cowley 2014; Ibrahim 2016; Green et al. 2015) and globally credible media outlets (e.g., *The New York Times* (Kristof 2018), *The Guardian* (Tisdall 2018), the BBC (2018), Al-Jazeera (2013), etc.) have termed it "genocide" (Uddin 2017). I would also like to use the term "genocide" instead of "ethnic cleansing" because what the Myanmar security forces did in 2017 is not just "cleaning" the Rohingya people from the Rakhine state but something far more than what could easily qualify as genocide in the framework of the United Nations Convention on the Prevention and Punishment of Genocide adopted in 1948 and the Rome Statues of the International Criminal Court (ICC) adopted in 1998 (see Uddin 2017). I have some firsthand evidences and eyewitnesses of such atrocities perpetrated by the Myanmar security forces, Burmese ethnic extremists, and Buddhist fundamentalists. I have recorded 500 narratives in descriptive form of newly arrived Rohingyas who have gone through an extreme level of atrocities, an acute form of brutalities, and an unexplainable torture following the massive campaign that started from August 25, 2018. I am giving three cases here which are strong enough to provide a feel about the ethnic cleansing in the Rakhine state of Myanmar.

Case 1: Fatema Begum (27)

I have lost my everything and have nothing to say. I got married when I was 17 years old. My husband was a businessman and used to sell household goods in Maungdaw Bazar. His earning was good enough to run our family of six members. I had three sons and one daughter. Of three, one was still at breast-feeding age. We had our own wood-made two-storied house in Koillarbah area of Northern Maungdaw. We were living with tension and constant insecurity because time and again some Rakhine youths and Burmese military used to visit our house under the pretext of searching illegal arms and Rohingya militants. Every time, we had to pay big amount of money to convince them. This was the way how we were living in Maungdaw. But this time Burmese military came in August 30, 2017, listened to none and nothing, and started ransacking the household goods and available essentials at home. They vandalised the entire house. They picked me up and taken to a bed room. My all children were crying. My husband was trying to snatched me away from them and he attempted couple of times. Suddenly one of the soldiers shot him on his head and he fell down on the ground and died on the spot. I was so shocked to see dying my husband in front of me. Then, four of them did gang-rape me in front of my children. I was severely bleeding and soon after I lost my sense. When my sense came back, I was lying down on the yard and saw my kids crying around me. I also saw that my house turned into ashes as they burnt the house and my husband was burnt inside the house. At night with many other Rohingyas, I with my four children also joined the march towards the border of Bangladesh. On the way, Borma military suddenly started random firing and many of our co-walkers were killed on the spot. I saw that my two sons also laying down on the street as bullets hit their body. The living ones started running and I also did so leave my two sons' dead bodies on the street. Finally, we could enable to cross the border and now in Bangladesh. I don't have any idea what I will do with my two children; where I will go; how I will survive; and where the destination of our lives is. I see dark in everywhere of my life. [Interviewed on September 24, 2017, at a Roadside temporary tent, Teknaf, Cox's Bazar, Bangladesh. I have used this case in elsewhere (see Uddin 2018), but I am using it here considering its intensity and high relevance.]

Case 2: Hasheuzzaman (41)

I used to work in the field all day long as a farmer. I was living in Tulatoli where mass killing took place in Maungdaw township with my wife, two children and parents. I had my own land for agriculture and used to rear domestic animal. I had my own house build on a sizable land. However, I was compelled to leave everything to flee a definite death. I had two options: either to living in Tulatoli for the sake of my huge property being ready to accept death any moment or to flee the definite death giving up all properties. I chose the second option. I saw military killing poor Rohingya people mercilessly in front of my eyes which compelled others to cross the border. Nobody could escape the military oppression. They came to my house, tortured me, and my parents. My wife was hiding, but they found her under a curt. Then they undressed her in front of us. I was kept on gun-point. My two children were holding me tightly and crying loudly. My parents couldn't endure it anymore and then went to refrain them, but one of the military soldiers shot my parents. Both my father and mother died in a minute. I became senseless watching this horrible scenario in front of my eye. My two children were crying. The military personnel gang-raped my wife in front of my children while I was senseless. I couldn't do anything. They looted my wife's ijjat *(honour) and killed my parents. As husband, it was horrible to see my wife being gang-raped but I couldn't do anything. We – my raped wife, my two children and I – spent the night and joined others towards Bangladesh border at dawn. It took 2 days to cross the border. On the way to cross the border, I saw hundreds of thousands of Rohingya people running. I saw many of them seriously wounded, raped; burnt on legs and hands; and terribly traumatized to see their near and dear ones being died in front of their eyes. Now I am in Kutupalong struggling to take care of my wife as she has become literally abnormal and hence my two children remain unattended. I don't know what to do, where to go and what my destination is.*

[The interview was conducted on October 10, 2017, in Teknaf.]

Case 3: Mohammad Mainuddin (46)

I was born in Keo Tan Kauk and raised there. Keo Tan Kauk was the place where Arakan Rohingya Salvation Army (ARSA0 attacked the Borma military camp on the 25th of August. Soon after the attack took place, Borma military surrounded the village and started firing guns and burning the houses. I was there at that time. Almost all houses in the village were burnt down, and almost all villagers were killed. Only few manage to escape and I was one of them. On the way to escape, the Borma military fired guns and the bullet hit me. I took shelter in a nearby village. One of my relations gave a bandage to my wounded leg. See my leg [showing his wounded place of leg and bandaged foot] and try to understand the brutality of Borma military. I was there for 2 days and left because military and Rakhine Buddhist young started ransacking the village to drive the villagers out of their homes. I saw hundreds of people ranging from children to aged ones running towards Bangladesh border. I also joined one of the groups. We were the first group of Rohingya who fled Borma and crossed the border to Bangladesh. I can't bear the pain anymore when I feel that all members of my family except myself are death now. My father and mother, my wife, my three daughters and two sons were died on the very 1st day of military attack. Many of them were wounded, but burnt alive as firing and burning were going together. Not only my family members, many villagers first received bullets, became wounded, and later brunt alive since nobody dared to flee as random firing was going on during the whole night. I with my wounded leg walked miles after miles to reach the Bangladesh border. I saw many babies were born on the roads as pregnant mothers were fleeing and many new born babies died thereafter. I saw many were maimed by land mines placed at the border by Borma military. I saw hundreds of death-bodies lying both sides of the road. I still stick to the horrible experience I have gone though. I can't remove the scene of brutality and atrocity from my eyes. I even can't sleep properly since I often go through some horrible nightmares as countless death-bodies, red flaming of fire, and the scared sounds of burning people always hunt me even while sleeping.

[Interview was taken on October 16, 2017, in Teknaf, Cox's Bazar.]

Conclusion

I could give an analysis separately based on the three cases, but I think these cases do not need any academic interpretation as they themselves are strong enough to provide a vivid scenario of why the UN called it the "textbook example of ethnic cleansing" (Uddin 2017). The three cases clearly demonstrate that what is happening in Rakhine state of Myanmar following August 25, 2017, is definitely an ethnic cleansing. What does ethnic cleansing mean? United Nations Office on Genocide Prevention and the Responsibility to Protect says, "A United Nations Commission of Experts mandated to look into violations of international humanitarian law committed in the territory of the former Yugoslavia defined ethnic cleansing in its interim report S/25274 as "... *rendering an area ethnically homogeneous by using force or intimidation to remove persons of given groups from the area.*" In its final report S/1994/674, the same Commission described ethnic cleansing as "... *a purposeful policy designed by one ethnic or religious group to remove by violent and terror-inspiring means the civilian population of another ethnic or religious group from certain geographic areas.*" The commission also suggests some features which qualify some form of atrocities as ethnic cleansing such as "murder, torture, arbitrary arrest and detention, extrajudicial executions, rape and sexual assaults, severe physical injury to civilians, confinement of civilian population in ghetto areas, forcible removal, displacement and deportation of civilian population, deliberate military attacks or threats of attacks on civilians and civilian areas, use of civilians as human shields, destruction of property, robbery of personal property, attacks on hospitals, medical personnel, and locations with the Red Cross/Red Crescent emblem, among others." If we deeply consider and analyze the case of Fatema Begum, Hasheuzzaman, and Mohammad Mainuddin which reflects a glimpse of hundreds of thousands of cases, we could easily say that what has happened in 2017 in Rakhine state of Myanmar with the Rohingyas people clearly justifies what the UN Human Rights Council said as "the text book of example of ethnic cleansing."

References

Ahmed I (2002–2003) State and stateless in South Asia: reaping benefits from a reconstructed discourse on state and nationality Theor Perspect 9 & 10

Ahmed I (ed) (2014 [2010]) The plight of the stateless Rohingyas. The University Press Limited, Dhaka

Akhanda M (2013) The history of Muslims in Arakan [in Bengali]. Bangladesh Co-operative Book-Society, Chittagong

Akhanda M (2018) The Rohingya problem and Bangladesh. Porilekh, Rajshahi

Alam AM (1999) A short historical background of Arakan. Arakan Historical Society, Chittagong. Available at: https://www.kaladanpress.org/images/document/2018/A%20Short%20Historical%20Background%20%20of%20Arakan.pdf. Accessed 02 Feb 2018

Al-Jazeera (2013) The hidden genocide. 16 Jan 2013. Available at: https://www.aljazeera.com/programmes/aljazeerainvestigates/2012/12/2012125122215836351.html. Accessed 28 Oct 2018

Amanullah (1997) The etymology of Arakan. ARAKAN 10(2):4–5

Arendt H (1994) The origins of totalitarianism. Harcourt Books, New York
Bahar A (2012) Racism to Rohingya in Burma. Source: http://www.kaladanpress.org/images/document/Racism-to-Rohingya-in-Burma.pdf. Accessed 04 Nov 2017
British Broadcasting Corporation (BBC) (2018) Myanmar Rohingya: UN says military leaders must face genocide charges. BBC Rep August 27, 2018. Available at: https://www.bbc.co.uk/news/world-asia-45318982. Accessed 28 Oct 2018
Buchanan F (1799) A comparative vocabulary of some of the languages spoken in the Burma empire. Asiat Res 5:219–240
Chan A (2005) The development of a Muslim enclave in Arakan (Rakhine) state of Burma (Myanmar). SOAS Bull Burma Res 3(2):396–420
Charney, Michael W (1999) Where Jambudipa and Islamdom converged: religious change and the emergence of Buddhist communalism in early modern Arakan (fifteenth to nineteenth centuries. A PhD dissertation, Department of History, University of Michigan
Chowdhury MA (2004) Bengal-Arakan relations. Firma KLM Private Limited, Kolkata
Cotterell A (2015) A history of South East Asia. Marshall Cavendish International (Asia) Private Limited, Singapore
Eaton R (1993) The rise of Islam and the Bengal frontier, 1204–1760. University of California Press, Berkeley
Elahi KM (1987) The Rohingya refugees in Bangladesh: historical perspectives and consequences. In: Rogge J (ed) Refugees: a third world dilemma. Rowman and Littlefield, New Jersey
Ezzati A a-F (2002) The spread of Islam: the contributing factors. Islamic College for Advanced Studies Press, London
Farzana KF (2015) Boundaries in shaping the Rohingya identity and the shifting context of borderland politics. Stud Ethn Natl 15(2):292–314
Farzana KF (2016) Memories of Burmese Rohingya refugees: contested identity and belonging. Palgrave Macmillan, New York
Farzana K Fahmida (2017) Memories of burmese rohingya refugees: Contested identities and belonging. Palgrave MacMillan, London
Forster R (2011) Magh marauders, Portuguese pirates, white elephants and Persian poets: Arakan and its bay-of-Bengal connectivities in the early modern era. Exp Dermatol 11(1):63–80
Gerhrz, Eva, and et al. 2018. INDIGENEITY ON THE MOVE: Varying Manifestations of a Contested Concept. Berghahn, Oxford & New York
Green P, Thomas MM, Venning A (2015) Count down annihilation: genocide in Myanmar. International State Crime Initiative, London
Gutman P (2001) Burma's lost kingdoms: Splendours of Arakan. Orchid Press, Bangkok
Hamilton W (1820) Geographical, statistical, and historical description of Hindostan and its adjacent countries. John Murray, London. Albemarle Street
Harvey GE (2000 [1925]) History of Burma: From the earliest time to the 10 march, the beginning of the English conquest. Asian Education Services, New Delhi
Hossain D (2014 [2010]) Tracing the plight of the Rohingyas. In: Ahmed I (ed) The plight of the stateless Rohingyas. The University Press Limited, Dhaka, pp 11–40
Human Rights Watch (HRW) (2017) Massacre by the river: Burmese army crimes against humanity in Tula Toli. December 19, 2017. Available at: https://www.hrw.org/report/2017/12/19/massacre-river/burmese-army-crimes-against-humanity-tula-toli. Accessed 28 Oct 2018
Ibrahim A (2016) The Rohingyas: Inside Myanmar's hidden genocide. Hurst & Company, London
Iqbal I (2017) Locating the Rohingya in time and space. In: In the shadow of violence (Dhaka Courier Weekend), October 13 Issue: 03–07
Karim A (2016 [1997]) The Rohingyas: a short account of their history and culture. Jatya Shahitya Prakash, Dhaka
Kesby A (2012) The rights to have rights: citizenships, humanity and international law. The Oxford University Press, Oxford
Kristof N (2018) I saw a genocide in slow motion. The New York Times, March 2, 2018. Available at: https://www.nytimes.com/2018/03/02/opinion/i-saw-a-genocide-in-slow-motion.html. Accessed 28 Oct 2018

Leiden JP (2018) Rohingya: The history of a Muslim identity in Myanmar. In: Ludden D et al (eds) The Oxford research encyclopedia of Asian history. The Oxford University Press, New York

Leider JP (2013) Rohingya: the name, the movement, the quest for identity. In: Myanmar EGRESS (ed) Nation building in Myanmar. Myanmar Peace Center, Myanmar, pp 204–255

Leider JP (2015) Competing identities and the hybridized history of the Rohingyas. In: Egreteau R, Robinne F (eds) Metamorphosis: studies in social and political change in Myanmar. NUS Press, Singapore, pp 151–178

Leitich K (2014) Decoding the past: the Rohingya origin enigma. Paper presented at the Third Annual Southeast Asian Studies Symposium, Keble College, University of Oxford, 22–23 Apr 2014

Lewa C (2008) Asia's new boat people. Available at: http://www.fmreview.org/sites/fmr/files/FMRdownloads/en/burma/lewa.pdf. Accessed 02 Jan 2018

Médecins Sans Frontiers Report (2002) 10 years for the Rohingya refugees in Bangladesh: past, present and future. Available at: http://www.rna-press.com/data/itemfiles/5ae98e43d068cb749b3060b002601b95.pdf. Accessed 28 Oct 2018

Médecins Sans Frontiers Report (2017)

Muntaha S (2018) Expatriate minister: 250,000 Rohingyas went abroad with Bangladeshi passports. Available at: https://www.dhakatribune.com/bangladesh/2018/04/28/expatriate-minister-250000-rohingyas-went-abroad-bangladeshi-passports/. Accessed 02 June 2018

Phayre AP (1883) History of Burma including Burma people, Pegu, Taungu, Tennaserim, and Arakan. Trubner & Co., London

Radio Free Asia (2017) Bengalis, not native to Myanmar. 12 Oct 2017. Available at: https://www.rfa.org/english/news/myanmar/bengalis-10122017191055.html. Accessed 02 Sept 2018

Rohingya not native, Myanmar army chief says. Al Jazeera, October 12, 2017. Available at: https://www.aljazeera.com/news/2017/10/rohingya-muslims-native-myanmar-army-chief-171012064646341.html. Accessed 12 Sept 2018

Safi M (2017) Myanmar treatment of Rohingya looks like 'textbook ethnic cleansing', says UN. The Guardian, September 11, 2017. Available at: https://www.theguardian.com/world/2017/sep/11/un-myanmars-treatment-of-rohingya-textbook-example-of-ethnic-cleansing. Accessed 28 Oct 2018

Safi M (2018) Lives will be lost': 700,000 Rohingya face cyclone season under tarpaulin. The Guardian, April 27, 2018. Available at: https://www.theguardian.com/world/2018/apr/27/rohingya-refugees-cyclone-monsoon-season-bangladesh-myanmar. Accessed 20 Oct 2018

Saw KM (2001) Islamization of Burma through Chittagonian Bengalis as Rohingya refugees. Available at: http://www.burmalibrary.org/docs21/Khin-Maung-Saw-NM-2011-09-Islamanisation_of_Burma_through_Chittagonian_Bengalis-en.pdf. Accessed 10 Nov 2017

Siddiquee M (2012) Who are Rohingyas and how? Origin and development of Rohingyas in Arakan. In: Uddin N (ed) To host or to hurt: counter narratives on the Rohingya refugee issues in Bangladesh. ICDR, Dhaka, pp 15–28

Singer N (2008) Vaishali and the Indianization of Arakan. A P H Publishing Corporation, New Delhi

Sussman RW (2014) The myth of race: the troubling persistence of an unscientific idea. The Harvard University Press, Cambridge, MA

Tarling N (2001) Southeast Asia: a modern history. The Oxford University Press, Australia

The Classical Journal (1811.) https://archive.org/details/in. ernet.dli.2015.20962. Accessed 7 Nov 2017

The Daily Independent (2017) 300 of 470 Rakhine villages completely destroyed. The Daily Independent, October 26, 2017. Available at: http://www.theindependentbd.com/post/120700. Accessed 28 Oct 2018

The Daily Star (2018) Killing of Rohingyas: death toll could be up to 25,000. The Daily Star, August 18, 2018. Available at: https://www.thedailystar.net/news/frontpage/killing-rohingyas-death-toll-could-be-over-10000-1622392. Accessed 28 Oct 2018

The United Nation (2018) The United Nations genocide prevention and the responsibility to protect. Definition of Ethnic Cleansing. Available at: http://www.un.org/en/genocideprevention/ethnic-cleansing.html. Accessed 25 Sept 2018

Tisdall S (2018) World's awkward silence over Rohingya genocide warnings. The Guardian, January 03, 2018. Available at: https://www.theguardian.com/world/2018/jan/03/worlds-awkward-silence-over-rohingya-genocide-warnings. Accessed 28 Oct 2018

Tonkin D (2014) The Rohingya identity: further thoughts. Network Myanmar. Available at: www.networkmyanmar.org/ESW/Files/Rohingya-Identity-II.pdf. Accessed 02 Nov 2018

Uddin N (2010) Treatment of unwelcome guests: A case of Rohingya refugee in Bangladesh. The paper presented at an international conference on Political Economy of South Asian Migrants organized by South Asian Regional Formation Research Society held on November 24–26, The University of Delhi, India

Uddin N (2012) Of hurting and hosting: crises in co-existence with Rohingya refugees in Bangladesh. In: Uddin N (ed) To host or to hurt: counter narratives on the Rohingya refugee issues in Bangladesh. ICDR, Dhaka, pp 83–98

Uddin N (2015) "State of Stateless People: The Plight of Rohingya Refugees in Bangladesh" in Rhoda Howard – Hassmann and Margaret Walton-Roberts eds. Human Rights to Citizens: A Slippery Concept. The University of Pennsylvania Press, USA, pp 62–77

Uddin N (2017) Not Rohingya, but Royanga: stateless people in the struggle for existence [in Bengali]. Murdhanno Prokashon, Dhaka

Uddin N (2018) Life in everyday death: A case of Rohingyas. In: Berkeley centre for global religion. Georgetown University, Washington, DC

Uddin N (2019, forthcoming) The Rohingyas: a case of "subhuman". Oxford University Press, Delhi

Vater JS (ed) (1816) Examples of German vernaculars: Dr. Seetzen's linguistic legacy and other linguistic research and collections, in particular on East India. Gerhard Fleischer, the Disciple, Leipzig

Ware A, Laoutides C (2018) Myanmar's 'Rohingya' conflict. Hurst & Company, London

World Health Organization (WHO) Report (2018) WHO appeals for international community support; warns of grave health risks to Rohingya refugees in rainy season. Published on March 29, 2018. Available at: https://reliefweb.int/report/bangladesh/who-appeals-international-community-support-warns-grave-health-risks-rohingya. Accessed 28 Oct 2018

World's largest refugee camps in (2018.) Available at https://www.raptim.org/largest-refugee-camps-in-2018/. Accessed 02 Oct 2018

Yunus M (1994) A history of Arakan: past & present. Magenta Colour, Chittagong

Zarni M, Cowley A (2014) Slow-burning genocide of Myanmar's Rohingyas. Pac Rim Law Policy J 23 (30):683–754

Displaced Minorities: The Wayuu and Miskito People

82

Christian Cwik

Contents

Introduction	1594
The Making of the Miskito and Wayuu People	1595
The Wayuu of the Guajira Peninsula	1596
The Miskito on the Mosquito Coast	1599
Displacement During the Long Twentieth Century	1603
Conclusion	1605
References	1606

Abstract

Among the many displaced indigenous minorities in Latin America and the Caribbean, the Wayuu of northern South America and the Miskito of eastern Central America took on a specific role. On the one hand, both ethnic groups are the result of displacement triggered by the Conquista and the transatlantic slave trade, and on the other hand both kept strong ties to non-Spanish European powers such as the English, the Dutch, and the French which gave them access to alternative markets. During the so-called independence period of the early nineteenth century, the territories of the Miskito and the Wayuu remained largely autonomous because of British protection. It was not until the mid of the nineteenth century that the young Latin American nation states succeeded in invading the area in their struggle for territorial integrity but failed because the British protected them against all these attempts. The situation changed when the USA came into dispute with the UK over steamship routes, coal storages, and the establishment of interoceanic connections, although both Nicaragua and Honduras and Colombia and Venezuela finally succeeded in incorporating the still unconquered areas into their state territory at the beginning of the twentieth

---

C. Cwik (✉)
Department of History, The University of the West Indies, St Augustine, Trinidad and Tobago
e-mail: christian.cwik@sta.uwi.edu; christian.cwik@uni-graz.at

© The Author(s), under exclusive license to Springer Nature Singapore Pte Ltd. 2019
S. Ratuva (ed.), *The Palgrave Handbook of Ethnicity*,
https://doi.org/10.1007/978-981-13-2898-5_117

century and even though the two now transnational ethnic groups were able to maintain autonomous structures. Since the 1960s civil and drug wars as well as guerrilla activity in Central America and in Colombia and Venezuela increased, which again led to mass murder and displacement of Wayuu and Miskito which persist in the case of Wayuu to this day.

Keywords

Genocide · Maroonage · Zambo · Proto-states · Imperialism · Autonomy · Displacement · Sandinism · Drug war

Introduction

In 1981 the so-called Contra War against the *Sandinistas* government in Nicaragua has reached the Miskito Coast on the Atlantic. Around the same time, the Civil War in Colombia hits the territory of the Wayuu on the Guajira Peninsula. One of the consequences of these brutal territorial penetrations by the several armed forces (military, paramilitary, police, mafia, and guerrilla) was displacement. Most of the Miskito people escaped to Honduras by crossing the Río Coco border to Honduras but remained in their traditional Miskito territory which extends to Cape Cameron. A small number of Miskito in the southern districts around the city of Bluefields escaped also to Costa Rica by crossing the Río San Juan, and some flew by boats via the Corn Islands to San Andres Island (Colombia). But also for the Wayuu, border crossing to Venezuela has been often the easiest option to escape because their ancestral territory extends far into neighboring Zulia. Another option has been the route to the Colombian interior through the Valle du Par and by boat to the Dutch island of Aruba.

But it was not only the wars that forced the groups to flee abroad but also the attempt of the central state to put an end to the uncontrollable activities of their indigenous people. Both the Miskito and the Wayuu were deeply involved in the smuggling trade and historically linked to the non-Spanish-speaking Caribbean. They used the Caribbean Sea as their trading area for short- and long-distance trade. Due to their trading activities, the two ethnic groups have been in contact with English (later British), Dutch French, and even Danish and Swedish colonies in the Caribbean for centuries. At the end of the nineteenth century, trade contacts with the USA became vital. All these economic relationships undermined the state monopoly on trade and the control of the state territory and borders. Particularly in the twentieth century, intense relations with the USA developed, often using conflicts between the central state and indigenous autonomous territories for their geopolitical interests. This is one of the reasons why the Miskito and the Wayuu remained active protagonists and many of them did not end up as defenseless victims despite persecution and displacement. Some of the Miskito refugees in Honduras joined, e.g., the so-called Contras, a CIA-backed army of Somoza loyal Ex-National Army officers and soldiers as well as mercenaries from all over and entered in their uniforms into the Nicaraguan territory to liberate it from the Sandinista government.

Their fight was mainly inspired as resistance against the establishment of a centralistic state run by the Sandinistas and not so much against the leftist ideology by itself. But also among the Wayuu refugees, we can find refugees especially those who became internally displaced persons (IDPs) in Colombia who joined one of the militarized groups (not the National Army) and became part of the Civil War.

If we trace the history of the two groups back to their beginnings, we find that displacement led to the formation of the two groups during the seventeenth and eighteenth centuries. Most of them were displaced persons of different indigenous cultures and African slaves from European haciendas, farms, estancias, ranchos, plantations, mines, ships, boats, and other places of work or war refugees from the many wars of the Conquista. The above means that neither the Miskito nor the Wayuu has existed before as independent ethnic groups. For the displaced remained only the last areas of retreat, the swampy areas of the rainforest of Central America's Atlantic Coast between *Cabo Cameron* and the Bay of Bluefields and the barren and desert of the Guajira Peninsula between the *Río Ranchería* and the Gulf of Venezuela. In addition to the common aspect of the extreme settlement areas, the Miskito and Wayuu shared the willingness to ally with British, Dutch, and French seafarers and colonists against the Spaniards, who began conquering unoccupied areas at the beginning of the seventeenth century.

The works of María Cristina Navarrete, Manuel Vicente Magallanes, Weildler Guerra Curvelo, Henri Candelier, Michel Perrin, José Polo Acuña, and Christian Cwik dealt with the history of the Guajiro Natives during the seventeenth and eighteenth centuries (Navarrete 2003; Magallanes 1975; Guerra Curvelo 1997, 2001; Candelier 1994; Perrin 1987; Polo Acuña 2000a, b, 2005; CWIK Christian 2014). Also I would like to mention the edition of documents of the Cabildo de Santa Marta between 1529 and 1640 by Antonino Vidal Ortega and Fernando Alvaro Baquero Montoya and for the history of the Wayuu during the nineteenth century again the work of José Polo Acuña (Polo Acuña 2011a, b) as well as Antonino Vidal Ortega and Baquero Montoya (2007). About the early history of the Miskitos, you find works written by Eugenia Ibarra Rojas, Karl Offen, Baron Pineda, Claudia García, Mary Helms, Michael Olien, Barbara Potthast Yuri Zapata Webb, and Christian Cwik (Ibarra Rojas 1999, 2002, 2008, 2011; Offen 2002; Pineda 2006; García 1996; Helms 1983; Olien 1983; Potthast-Jutkeit 1993; Zapata Webb 2006; CWIK Christian 2011–2012).

The Making of the Miskito and Wayuu People

Zambos are the result of the ethnic mixture between Africans and first natives. This is comparable with the genesis of the Mestizo. Where Zambo cultures emerged, large numbers of runaway slaves can be found. Runaway slaves or maroons escaped from their masters or rescued themselves from slave ships after rebellions or shipwrecks. To survive in the new and impassable surroundings, the maroons had to join Amerindian settlements (Thompson 2006). Within the settlements, their role differed from cases to case: they were enslaved, had to work as servants, intermingled with the indigenous groups, or even have been sold as slaves or into slavery. The first evidence about the existence of Zambos in maroon societies in the Americas can be found among the resistance communities of Chief Enriquillo in Santo Domingo (1519–1533), King Bayamo and President Filipinho in Panama (1532–1554), or King Miguel in Venezuela (1551–1554) (Lara 2006). But there were also white and even Asian people who have been displaced from colonial towns, fortresses, mines, plantations, farms, and ships.

Let us now take a closer look at the Wayuu on the Caribbean coast of Colombia and Venezuela and the Zambo-Miskito on the Caribbean coast of Honduras and Nicaragua – two examples of Africanized Amerindian societies in the Greater Caribbean. Both regions were never conquered by Spanish troops and therefore could develop independently. Around 1750, two centuries after the Spanish conquest of the Aztecs and Incas, independent native people still controlled over a half of Iberoamerica (Weber 2002). The development of the communities as refuge for outlawed people, mainly of African origin, influenced the native societies of the two said regions heavily. The Africanization of the natives throughout the centuries transformed the allochthon societies. The new allochthon societies were based mostly on African and Amerindian and just a little bit on European heritage.

The Wayuu of the Guajira Peninsula

In 1536 the first Europeans began to settle on the Guajira Peninsula. The hidalgo Antonio de Chávez founded the first European settlement of Nuestra Señora de las Nieves in the delta of the Ranchería River by order of the German-speaking conqueror Nicolas Federmann (Muñoz Luengo 1949; Polo Acuña 2000a). First pearl exploitation started across Cabo de la Vela by the Welser, a German company from the present-day Bavarian town of Augsburg in 1537. Pearl traders from the Venezuelan island of Cubagua founded de town of Cabo de la Vela in 1538. Two of the founders, Rodrigo de Gabraleón and Juan de la Barrera, started to organize the economy and policy of the town through the decree of 27th of March 1539 (Otte Enrique 1977). The pearl (and salt) exploitation of the southern Caribbean began around 1508 in the area between the present-day Venezuelan islands of Margarita, Cubagua, and Coche and the Araya Peninsula (Bernáldez 1869). In Enrique Otte's book *Las perlas del Caribe: Nueva Cádiz de Cubagua*, we can find some descriptions of the early enslavement of indigenous people and Africans as pearl divers on the island of Cubagua. After permanent attacks of Caribs from the Guianas and a heavy earthquake in 1539 which destroyed the center of Nueva Cádiz, the pearl traders and their slaves moved to Cabo de la Vela on the Guajira Peninsula.

Throughout the centuries, the different Amerindian groups of the South American coast resisted the Spanish conquerors. This was one of the reasons why the conquerors, after a period of thorough explorations of the sea- and landscapes, were only able to establish a few settlements (Turbaco 1509, Cumaná 1515, Santa Marta 1525, Coro 1526, Cartagena de Indias 1533 and Tolú 1534) before the foundation of Cabo de la Vela.

Among this generation of explorers, traders, and settlers were many of Portuguese origin with experiences in West Africa and the Afro-Atlantic islands. Some of them have been transculturated (The term "Transculturation" was introduced by the Cuban Anthropologist Fernando Ortiz (ORTIZ Fernando 1987, [1]1963).) and changed their appearance. They adopted African customs like skin scarification marks and tattoos, wore African dresses, and talked at least two African languages (Sweet 2003; Mark 2002; Brooks 2003). These Luso-Africans of European and African origin were called Lançados, Tangomaos, Pombeiros, Baquianos, or Imbangalas (Schorsch 2008; Queirós Mattoso 1982; Elbl 1986; Zeuske 2006). Many of them had a Jewish or a Muslim background. They negotiated with the most powerful African Kingdoms and intermarried with local African merchant families. Lançados developed important trading ports and villages on the Senegambian and Guinee river systems like Rufisque, Porto de Ale, Joala, Ziguinchor, Cacheu, Bolama, Porto da Cruz, Bissau, or even the famous port of Mina (Newitt 2005; Kagan and Morgan 2009). When they came to the Caribbean, they adapted quickly and negotiated with the American Native traders. In the case of the Guajira, they purchased "Amerindian slaves" from the different Carib-speaking traders for the pearl industries and silver and gold mining. The Colombian historian María Cristina Navarrete describes these slave raids in her article about rebellion and resistance of slaves between 1570 and 1615 (Navarrete 2003).

The history of the Guajira Peninsula remained throughout the sixteenth century a history of outlaw economies. The independence of the "Guajira societies" was based on different factors. The support by several native groups guaranteed the pearl elites (*Señores de Canoas*) of Cabo de la Vela their independence, and in reverse the allied indigenous groups preserved their own independence as well. Intermarriage strengthened the alliances between the two groups.

Besides the slave trade with natives, the demand for African salves increased during the 1550s. The import of thousands of African slaves began. Smugglers and interlopers from Africa and Europe guaranteed this supply. One of these smugglers was the English captain Sir John Hawkins from Plymouth. His father William Hawkins already founded around 1530 a family trading enterprise mainly based on slave trade between Europe, Africa, and Brazil. John Hawkins and his cousin Francis Drake continued this business. Piloted by Luso-African Atlantic Creoles (About the Portuguese Atlantic Creoles, who worked for John Hawkins Lançados as pilots see (Kelsey 2003).), Hawkins sold African slaves to the *Señores de Canoas* (a small group of about 15–30 men) in Cabo de la Vela and Río de la Hacha (present-day Riohacha) during the 1560s and 1570s. In 1568 Miguel de Castellanos had bought 144 African slaves from John Hawkins (Miranda Vázquez 1976). Among the chiefs of Cabo de la Vela, we find even an Africanized Baquiano (slave hunter) named Francisco de Castellanos as treasurer. Together with first natives of the region and several maroon groups, they controlled the illicit trade in indigenous and African slaves. The indigenous slaves were mostly captured in the Sierra Nevada mountains west of the Peninsula. The Guajira alliances sold the imported African slaves to the Neogrenadian Highlands via Valledupar or used them as slaves for their own pearl, lumber, divi-divi, and salt exploitation.

The end of the pearl exploitation in the 1580s led to a strong emigration from Cabo de la Vela to Río de la Hacha. However, most of the first natives and maroons stayed north and east of the Rancheria River where they controlled almost the entire Peninsula. After 1580, craftspeople and jewelers from different regions in the Caribbean reached the town of Río de la Hacha. María Eugenio Ángeles Martínez found out that a group of approximately 20 Señores de Canoas and 600 slaves of African ancestry were living in that town (Ángeles Martínez 1992). The Spanish colonial government in Maracaibo established a military post in Río de la Hacha and founded a council (cabildo) there. The colonial influence of Maracaibo and later Santa Marta on Río de la Hacha remained weak. On the contrary, the Señores de las Canoas used their intercultural relations with the first natives and maroons to dominate the town of Río de la Hacha, and they extended their influence on Maracaibo, Santa Marta, and even Cartagena de Indias (Navarrete 2003).

During the personal union between Spain and Portugal (1580–1640), the influence of Portuguese traders in the Americas grew fast. The establishment of an Inquisition Tribunal in Cartagena de Indias after 1610 was a reaction of the "old elites" against the economic activities of the Portuguese traders. From then on, all Portuguese were suspected as "Crypto Jews." Inquisition documents of 1627 tell us the story of two Portuguese traders who dominated the pearl trade between Cartagena and Río de la Hacha: Gramaxo was suspected to be a Secret Jew (Ventura 2001). At the end of the sixteenth century, the Gramaxo family established an Atlantic network of slave trade between Angola, the Cape Verdean islands, the rivers of Guinea, Brazil, and Lisbon (Vila Vilar 1977). Antonio Núñez Gramajo was one of the pioneers in the contraband in pearls, slaves, salt, and Brazil wood between Río de la Hacha and the nearby island of Curacao, where the Dutch founded a colony in 1634. After the conquest of the islands of Curacao, Aruba, and Bonaire between 1634 and 1636, the independent Guajira became an important point of commercial interest for the Dutch West Indian Company which established on the island of Curacao a center of slave trade in the mid-seventeenth century.

At the same time, the Guajira Peninsula was still an area which had never been controlled by the Spaniards. Different maroon groups of Africanized indigenous people dominated the area of the Central Guajira around Maicao and blocked the main connections between Santa Marta, Río de la Hacha, and Valledupar with Maracaibo (Vidal Ortega and Baquero Montoya 2007). The less Africanized Amerindian clans controlled the entire Upper Guajira. Dutch traders from Curacao and English traders from Jamaica intensified their business with the independent groups and supported their war against the Spaniards. In the national archive in Willemstad on the island of Curacao, several documents about Jewish and New Christians merchants are demonstrating the trade networks between Curacao and the Guajira Peninsula as well as the Mosquito Coast and the isthmus of Darién (Langebaeck 2006). All of them were independent territories under the control of indigenous and Zambos.

The WIC government sent its cultural brokers to the Guajira Peninsula to trade with the indigenous chiefs and maroon captains as well as with outlawed European merchants. The close relations to the Dutch increased the economic situation for the "outlaw societies" and the possibilities to expand the so-called contraband economy. The illegal trade in firearms was the most successful business, not only from an economic point of view but also considering the possibilities of self-defense against attacks of Spanish troops.

Since the beginning of the eighteenth century, Great Britain intensified its colonial interest in the Americas. One part of British policy was the support of independent first natives and maroons in their war against Spanish colonialism, like the Dutch did too. This selective armament of Indigenous and maroons of the Guajira Peninsula promoted the process of alliances between the different indigenous groups and maroons. This development culminated in the birth of a new ethnic group: the Wayuu. We do find the notion Wayuu for the first time around 1750 (CWIK Christian, Muth Verena, Polo Acuña José, and Zeuske Michael, 2009). Before that time, only the name "Guajiros" existed in colonial maps and documents. In 1727, more than 2000 Guajiros attacked the troops of the Viceroyalty of New Granada. Other attacks followed in 1741, 1757, 1761, and 1768 (Barrera, Internet source). On the 2nd of May 1769, the Wayuu set the Spanish town of El Rincon afire, burning down the church and two Spaniards who had taken refuge in it. Supported by the English and Dutch, the Wayuu defended their independence and regained their territory.

Wayuu are organized in clans following matrilineal structures. Some of the clans are more "indigenous" than other clans which are more "African" or even "Europeans." There are still distinct local and regional differences. Before slavery was abolished in the Dutch colonies in 1863, slaves escaped from Curacao, Bonaire, and Aruba to the South American coasts where these displaced individuals and groups joined the Wayuu. Despite the high percentage of intermingling with Afro-Caribbean and white European people, the Wayuu describe themselves as genuine first natives and as descendants of the Caribs. To this day most of Wayuu people deny any racial mixture with people of African descent.

The Miskito on the Mosquito Coast

Spanish colonialism failed completely on the Caribbean coast of Central America. At least until the end of the nineteenth century, not a single Spanish settlement could be established between Trujillo in present-day Honduras and the Chagres River in Panama. As part of the western Caribbean, the Caribbean coast of Central America is a region of intense Jamaican-British influence and a high degree of African-Amerindian mixture. Since the second half of the seventeenth century, these groups of Afro-Amerindian descent appear in different documents as "Zambos," "mosquitos," "moscos," "zambo-mosquitos," and "Zambos del Mosquito" (Rogers 2002). From an ethnohistorical point of view, Mary Wallace Helms had already discussed the question "Negro or Indian" in 1977 (Helms 1977; Ibarra Rojas 2007).

The name "Miskito" as notion for a tribe or a special indigenous group didn't exist until the beginning of the seventeenth century. Some scholars like Barbara Potthast, Germán Romero, and Karl H. Offen doubted that the name Miskito refers to a river named "Moschitos," "Moscomitos," or "Mesquitos" located in the south of the Cape Gracias a Dios. We can find this name in Spanish maps of the years 1536, 1562, 1587, and 1600 as well as in Dutch maps of 1595 and 1613 (Potthast 1988; Romero Vargas 1995; Offen 2007). According to English sources from the Colonial Office, the term Miskito derived from the weapon musket. Therefore they called the indigenous people around the Cape Gracias a Dios "muskeetos" or "Indiens de Moustique (PRO CO 124/1f. 2 (Kew/London).). Missionaries like Fray Pedro de la Concepción called the first natives, who traded in firearms and other weapons with the English, "Guaianes." In his dictionary "Español-Sumo, Sumo-Español," the linguist Götz von Houwald determined the same group as "Wayah" (Von Houwald 1980).

Miskito chiefs were able to communicate in English and traveled with English buccaneers as sailors to places all over the world. In 1633 or 1634, the Puritans of the island of Old Providence invited the successor of the Miskito chief to London, where he spent 3 years (Ibarra Rojas 2011). Almost the entire well known "piracy literature" concerning the Mosquito Coast contains similar information like the writings of Pedro de la Concepción. The "pirate" M.W. who traded with the Miskito around 1695–1705 Olien (1983) mentioned in his report "The Mosquito Indian and his Gold River" that the Miskito chief Oldman who governed probably the region of Cape Gracias a Dios between 1655 and 1686 was fluent in English language and traveled even until Jamaica (M.W. 1732). The indigenous groups of the "mosquitos," "Guaianes," and "wayah" (we are talking about one or probably more tribes as ancestors of the later Miskitos) as well as other first native cultures (Carey 2002; Ibarra Rojas 2011) like the Hicacas, Panamcas, Towacas, Cackeras, Ulvas, Jicaques, Payas, Sumos, Cucras, Caribes, and Ramas together populated the region between Cape Cameron, San Juan River, and the Segovia mountains. We can conclude that the population of this region was not homogenous.

Some Dutch merchants who traded with the indigenous people of the Mosquito Coast were of Sephardic Jewish origin. One example is the famous "buccaneer" (Knight 2000) Abraham Blauvelt (alias Bluefield) who visited the Mosquito Coast several times between 1625 and 1640. With the conquest of Curacao in 1634, the Dutch West Indian Company (DWIC) developed the island as home base for all their activities in the western and southern Caribbean. To smuggle African slaves to Trujillo, Campeche, Veracruz, or even Cuba, Dutch ships had to pass the Central American shores where they often shipwrecked because of the shallow waters.

Long before slaves from Dutch and English slave ships survived the shipwrecks of the seventeenth century, the Spanish Crown had already imported some thousands African slaves to the silver mining areas of Honduras as well as to the plains of the Pacific Nicaraguan coast between 1530 and 1600. African slave labor was important in the Honduran mountains since the beginning of colonial economy. Any form of slavery produced maroonage. Also in the mining areas of Honduras thus find references to maroon groups close to Trujillo around 1540. (Conversation with Dra. Rina Caceres, History Professor at the University of Cost Rica during her visit to Cartagena in May 2010.) To survive in the inhospitable areas of the Mosquito Coast, the black runaways needed the support of local native groups. One of the results was of course ethnic mixture. This new Zambo-Miskito population produced changes in the demographic, social, and political structure of the first native cultures and affected the economic relations between the different Amerindian groups. Some first natives did not allow the runaways to settle among them; they even killed or enslaved some of them. Enslaved Africans intermingled with indigenous people, but this happened not before the next generation because slavery was not inheritable.

The rise of the slave trade during the seventeenth century influenced the African population everywhere in the Americas. Small trading companies and new groups of colonizers of Spanish and non-Spanish origin increased the importation of African slaves to the western Caribbean like to the mostly uninhabited Bay and Corn islands as well the island of Old Providence. In 1633 the Puritan settlers of Old Providence (Providence) established commercial relations with the indigenous people in the surroundings of the Cape Gracias a Dios (Ordahl Kupperman 1993). With the beginning of the seventeenth century, the Spanish colonial government of Guatemala, which dominated the Pacific coast of Nicaragua, supported the development of a well-developed plantation system. For a better management of the slave importation to Nicaragua, the Spanish extended the port of Trujillo. Maroon groups, mostly from Dutch ships, populated the mountains of the Río Dulce and the neighboring islands of Guanaja, Roatan, Hog, and Utila (AGCA A1. 4060.31537 (1645)). Despite a permanent process of intermingling during the first two centuries of European invasion, the Miskito still believe in myths of shipwrecking slave ships.

The already mentioned English slave trader M.W. wrote in 1699 about a group of runaway slaves rescued from a slave ship from Guinea which shipwrecked in 1639 on the coast close to the Río Coco (M.W. 1732). M.W. dated a second shipwreck in 1649. Lic. Ambrosio Tomás Santaella Melgarejo, an officer of the Audiencia of Guatemala, described the shipwreck of a slave ship in 1652. It is possible that the owner of this ship was the Portuguese Jewish slave trader Lorenzo Gramajo from Curacao, a son of the mentioned Antonio Núñez Gramaxo (or Gramajo). Pedro de Rivera reported in 1742 that the ship shipwrecked on the Mosquito Coast in 1652 (CWIK Christian 2011–2012). According to the text of Robert Hodgson senior, at least two Dutch slave ships shipwrecked on the southern section of the Mosquito Coast before he became Superintendent between 1749 and 1759 (Hodgson 1779). Also Barbara Potthast mentioned a Dutch slave ship, wrecked in 1710 (Potthast 1988). Probably the most famous slave shipwrecking was the one of 1641. In this year English buccaneers took over a Portuguese slave ship and left the booty on the Mosquito Coast close to the banks of the Río San Juan (Potthast-Jutkeit 1993). The Nicaraguan bishop Garret y Arlovi described in 1711 the "famous ship wreck" of 1641 as the birth of the Zambo-Miskito culture. He refers to a black man named Juan Ramón who told him the story. Ramón reported that about one third of the slaves who survived the shipwreck escaped and founded their own "state" of palenques (runaway slave communities). Further he told him about the several armed conflicts between the Amerindian groups and the African maroons belonging to the "state." Bishop Garret y Arlovi described these Amerindian groups as "Caribs" (Peralta 1898). Finally the Africans defeated the indigenous tribes, and they escaped to the mountains of Segovia and Chontales. The Africans kidnapped Amerindian women, reproduced by intermarriage, and thus built the fundament for the Zambo-Miskito culture (Ibarra Rojas 2011).

Currently most of the Miskito of Nicaragua are regarding the shipwreck of 1641 as the birth of their nation. But not all Miskito are feeling like Zambo-Miskito due to their different decrees of intermingling with Africans as well as with white people. The Miskito who almost did not mix with the African maroons of the Coast were often called Tawira. Despite the physical differences, both groups shared a lot of similarities like famous Olaudah Equiano recorded already in 1773. Although the Miskito are practicing several African traditions (often without any knowledge that those traditions originally came from Africa), the Amerindian traditions predominate. The strongest feature of their shared identity until the present day is their language Miskito.

The degree of intermingling depended mainly on two factors: (1) the areas where, because of the shallow waters, most slave ships shipwrecked and (2) the intensity of Amerindian resistance against Africanization. We can establish the main areas of Zambo-Miskito population around Cape Gracias a Dios and Sandy Bay in the northern section and around the Pearl Lagoon in the southern section of the Mosquito Coast. According to the French buccaneer Raveneau de Lussan who visited the Mosquito Coast in 1688 the Zambo-Miskito settled largely in the valley of the Wanks River (modern Río Coco) (CWIK Christian 2011–2012). Also M.W. located their settlements on the banks of the mentioned river.

Due to the lack of census in the Mosquito Coast, we know neither how many Miskito lived there nor how big was the group of Zambo-Miskito. It is difficult to study the number of inhabitants of the regions outside of Spanish control like the Mosquito Coast, the Darién and the Talamanca mountains, the Petén, or the Guajira Peninsula. Even though it is difficult to study the number of inhabitants due to a lack of reliable data, it is not impossible (Muth 2012). Robert Hodgson who lived as Superintendent in Bluefields estimated in 1757 about 10–11,000 Miskito (Ibarra Rojas 2011). Exact data is only available for the British colony of Black River and its vicinity where around the year 1766, approximately 450 white men (mostly English settlers and soldiers), 4.400 African, and c. hundred native slaves as well as 10.000 Zambos and Miskito lived (Dawson 1983).

By the end of the seventeenth century, the leader of the Zambo-Miskito held titles like "General" and "Captain." A known Zambo-Captain was Captain Kit who lived in the delta of the Coco River, where he controlled the river navigation (M.W. 1732) Author Eugenia Ibarra Rojas created a map of the Miskito settlements at the Coco River based on the information of M.W. (Ibarra Rojas 2011). Under the rule of the mulatto King Jeremy I. between 1687 and c. 1720, the term "mulatto" was used by M.W.; the Miskito developed Sandy Bay as their capital and held the title of "King" (M.W. 1732); Olien 1983). Within the political union of all Miskito, the Tawira held the titles of "Governor" and "Admiral." During the eighteenth century, the Zambo-Miskito became more and more dominant. From the first decade until the official end of the Miskito kingdom in 1894, the function of the king was held by the Zambo-Miskito.

Displacement During the Long Twentieth Century

The quasi-independence of the Wayuu and Miskito opposed the still young republics in their efforts at territorial integrity. The governments of Nicaragua and Honduras as well as of Colombia and Venezuela failed in their individual attempts to bring these indigenous territories under state control, similar to the situation of the Spaniards before. During the transition from the nineteenth to the twentieth century, the USA and its companies (in the first place the United Fruit and the Standard Fruit Company) initially invaded the areas previously dominated by the British. In doing so, they helped the Latin American states in conquering territories. In the case of the Miskito Coast, these companies forced the immigration of English-speaking West Indians most of whom have been Afro-Jamaicans. The areas of Bluefields and Pearl Lagoon especially became populated by West Indians. This led to the displacement of the native population during the first two decades. Also in Honduras the two already mentioned big US corporations have imported English speaking West Indians but their plantations where not established on Miskito territory. In the case of Honduras, the Black Caribs better known as Garifuna who settled northwest of the port city of Trujillo were displaced. Between 1880 and 1920, hundreds of Garifunas from Honduras immigrated mostly to the area of Pearl Lagoon, south of Sandy Bay Sirpi.

Richard M. Juang and Noelle Morrissette are claiming that the first Garifunas under the leadership of Joseph Sambola had already come to Nicaragua's Caribbean coast in 1882 and probable founded the community of St. Vincent (Square Point). However, they mentioned no evidence for this thesis (Davidson 1980; Juang and Morrissette 2008). It is unclear whether this was a colonization project of a certain Joseph Sambola (the name refers to the denotation Zambo) or this group of Garifunas had escaped from Honduras because of internal wars. The main region for the immigrants was the Honduran coast east of Trujillo. The most important and largest Garifuna community of today is the town of Orinoco founded on the shores of the Pearl Lagoon in 1907. In an interview with Kensy Sambola in 2003 made by the author, Mrs. Sambola said that all Garifunas came to work for the Americans and were employed in cutting mahogany and working on sugar and banana plantations as well as saw mills. In contrast to the imported black West Indians, who became the majority population of the South of the Miskito Coast and became the "Black Creoles" of this coast, Garifunas and Miskitos had already lived in the immediate vicinity for centuries. A direct displacement by the Garifuna thus did not take place, because among other things immigration remained numerically low. Houses were typically of lumber and thatch, in the style of modem Miskito dwellings (Davidson 1980).

Immigration and the brutal method of territorial incorporation by the Nicaraguan military under the presidency of José Santos Zelaya finally led to the end of the autonomous kingdom in 1894. The last Miskito King Robert Henry Clarence abdicated in 1908 after the kingdom had been conquered bit by bit by 1894. The former Mosquito Coast was established as the Nicaraguan department of Zelaya and led to the displacement of many Miskito. In the first two decades after the abdication of King Robert Henry Clarence, Miskitos left the coastal areas and settled in the hinterland. The Jinotega Department in the north, where Miskitos had already settled before the mentioned displacement, became a refuge for many Miskitos from the coast. During the conflict in 1927–1933 between Augusto Sandino and the USA over the US occupation of Nicaragua, some Miskitos in the Jinotega region joined Sandino's liberation army. After Sandino's assassination in 1934, Miskitos became victims of Somoza's National Guard purges. The regime established a harsh type of administration on the Miskito Coast that concerned itself mainly with law and order. In order to exploit the gold, silver, and platinum mines of the region, the regime promoted the migration of the Mestizo population of the Pacific coast to the east. Between 1945 and 1975, over hundred thousand moved into the mining areas of the "Atlantic Coast" (Sollis 1989).

All these developments produced new displacement among the Miskitos and Sumos of the region. A new problem for the Miskito population arose in 1960 when the International Court of Justice ruled in favor of Honduras in a border dispute between Honduras and Nicaragua by awarding it a portion of Nicaraguan territory north of the River. The loss of traditional lands along the River Coco became a major issue for the Miskitos. Subsistence food production was negatively affected, and malnutrition and hunger became a major problem during the 1960s. The crises of this period led to the displacement of about 5000 Miskitos who were forced to relocate in Nicaragua and to take Nicaraguan citizenship (Sollis 1989). During the 1970s, the conflict between the Spanish-speaking migrants from the Pacific and the Miskito escalated and resulted in some deaths prior to 1979. This conflict continued after the triumph of the Sandinista revolution in 1979 but hardly had to do with the ideological orientation of the socialist revolution led by the FSLN.

Around the same time, as in Nicaragua, namely, in 1893, the government of Colombia conquered the Wayuu territory but has been less successful (Paz Reverol 2000), because of the decentralized political structure of the 14 clans (Aapushana, Epieyu, Iguana, Jayaliyuu, Jusayuu, Pausayuu, Sapuana, Tijuana, Uliana, Uliyuu, Uraliyuu, Ulewana, Walepushana, and Walapuana) and their semi-nomadism (in particular, during periods of drought, the Wayuu have to move their animals to areas where they can get water stored in wells.) Officially the Guajira became an intendancy in 1898 and a commissary in 1911. A survey made by Coronel Rafael E. Benítez in 1874 calculated 38.000 inhabitants (included only 10 clans) on the Guajira Peninsula (Benítez 1957). In addition to territorial control over the peninsula, the governments of Colombia and Venezuela promoted the takeover of the successful trading network of the Wayuu which they criminalized by calling it contraband trade. Simultaneously with the efforts of national governments, the Catholic Church sought to be at influence, in the "civilization process" of the Wayuu. In 1887 Capuchin friars under Reverend Brother José María de Valdeviejas returned, and in 1905, Pope Pius X created the Vicariate of La Guajira to "civilize" the Wayuu.

In 1935 the government founded a square circular around the population of Uribia, in the center of the indigenous territory, which allowed them to control the interior of the peninsula and nearby ports. The declared aim was an advance for the colonization of the north of the Guajira Peninsula, but finally they failed. Nevertheless, the settlement area of Wayuu was severely restricted due to these measures.

During the 1960s, the cultivation of marijuana in the neighboring Sierra Nevada increased, and the Guajira Peninsula became the most important transportation corridor for the illegal trade. Especially knowledge of the landscape terrestrial and maritime had been in demand by the drug mafia; hence some Wayuu became popular collaborators. This did not change after the drug mafia switched to cocaine production and trade in the 1970s. As a result, the Guajira Peninsula developed into a battlefield of the anti-drug war, and displacement was the consequence.

Despite displacement, and according to a 1997 census in Colombia, the Wayuu population numbered approximately 144,003 and represented 20% of Colombia's total Amerindian population and 48% of the population of the Department of La Guajira. This demonstrates their power of endurance. One of the reasons for this is the enormous maritime mobility of the Wayuu. Wayuu are using maritime routes to Jamaica, the Cayman Islands, San Andres, Providencia, Aruba, Curacao, and Bonaire, and we can trace their tracks even to the Dominican Republic. The migration is often temporarily limited and depends not only on currents and winds but also on their economic ties and sometimes even their family relation. When the civil wars in Colombia broke out in the 1960s, these destinations became a temporarily refuge for the Wayuu.

Conclusion

Miskito and Wayuu per se are the result of displacement due to the Spanish Conquista from the sixteenth to the nineteenth centuries and the subsequent war of the nation states for territorial control and unrestricted exploitation of natural resources. As enemies of the colonial Spanish Government and later the National Government, they became partners of the enemies of the Spanish Colonial powers, namely, the English, French, and Dutch. Another feature of both groups is the high degree of mingling with other people persecuted by wars, conflicts, and trafficking in human beings, many of whom were escaping African slaves. Through cooperation with the abovementioned European players, they were able to defend their territory until the twentieth century. However, the maritime orientation of both groups also made them useful partners, even for the hostile colonial power of Spain and its successor states. Their territories remained largely independent and remained autonomous regions even after the formal conquest in the twentieth century.

After very slow military progress, the national and regional governments tried to force aggressive settlement policies in the twentieth century which produced a high grade of displacement. With the help of missionaries, both Catholic (Wayuu) and Moravian (Miskito), they tried to break the defense of groups which were not willing to integrate into the system as citizens. But ultimately even this strategy did not lead to success. Both groups remained ultimately resistant and open to cooperation with the enemy regardless of whether they were rebels like Augusto Sandino or counter-revolutionaries such as the Contras or are guerrillas like the ELN or the Colombian drug mafia.

In the case of the Miskito, the Sandinista Government of Nicaragua has seen no other way out than to legalize the already existing autonomy and therefore founded in 1985/1986 two autonomous regions: the North Atlantic Autonomous Region (RAAN) today's North Caribbean Coast Autonomous Region (RACN) and Autonomous Region of the South Atlantic (RAAS) today's South Caribbean Coast Autonomous *Region* (RACS). Political autonomy such as the Miskitos have guaranteed whether by Venezuela nor Colombia, although autonomy is lived politically, legally and culturally due to their internal political organization.

References

Ángeles Martínez ME (1992) La esclavitud Indígena, impulsora de las pesquerías de perlas en Nuestra Señora de los Remedios. Actas del Congreso de Historia del Descubrimiento (1492–1556). III. Real Academia de la Historia/Confederación Española de Cajas de Ahorros, Madrid

Barrera E La rebelión Guajira de 1769. Algunas constantes de la Cultura Wayuu y razones de supervivencia. Edición en la biblioteca virtual del Banco de la República. http://www.banrepcultural.org/blaavirtual/revistas/credencial/junio1990/junio2.htm. 14 Sept 2018

Benítez RE (1957) Recuerdos de mis viajes por la Guajira y noticias recogidas de paso Maracaibo, Venezuela. Publicaciones de la Universidad del Zulia

Berlin I (1996) From Kreole to African: Atlantic creoles and the origins of African-American Society in Mainland North America. William Mary Q, third series, 53(2):251–288

Bernáldez A (1869) Historia de los Reyes Católicos. Capítulo I. Imprenta J. M. Geofrin, Seville

Brooks GE (2003) Euroafricans in Western Africa. Commerce, social status, gender and religion observance from the sixteenth to the eighteenth century. Ohio University Press, Ohio

Candelier H (1994) Riohacha y los indios guajiros. Ecoe Ediciones, Santafé de Bogotá

Carey M (2002) La influencia mayagna (sumo) en la historia de la costa Atlántica nicaragüense. Rev Hist 14:73–88

CWIK Christian (2011–2012) Africanidad con repugnancia: los zambos y el problema de la identidad en el Caribe centroamericano. In: Ariadna Tucma Revista Latinoamericana. Buenos Aires. www.ariadnatucma.com.ar

CWIK Christian (2014) Africanization of Amerindian tribes in the Greater Caribbean: case studies of the Wayuu and Miskito during the 17th and 18th centuries. In: Knight FW, Iyob R (eds) Dimensions of African and other diasporas. The University of the West Indies Press, Kingston, pp 83–104

Davidson WV (1980) The Garifuna of pearl lagoon: ethnohistory of an Afro-American enclave in Nicaragua. Ethnohistory 27(1):31–47

Dawson FG (1983) William Pitt's settlement at black river on the mosquito shore: a challenge to Spain in Central America, 1732–1787. HAHR 63(4)

de Peralta MM (1898) Costa Rica y Costa de Mosquitos. Imprenta General de Lahure, Paris

de Queirós Mattoso KM (1982) To be a slave in Brasil, 1550–1888. Rutgers University, New York

Elbl I (1986) The Portuguese trade with West Africa 1440–1521. University of Toronto Press, Toronto

García C (1996) The making of the Miskitu people of Nicaragua. The social construction of ethnic identity, Uppsala

García C (2002) Hibridación, interacción social y adaptación cultural en la Costa de Mosquitos, siglos XVII y XVIII. Anu Estud Am 59(2):441–462

Guerra Curvelo W (1997) La ranchería de perlas del Cabo de la Vela (1538–1550). Huellas 49–50:33–51

Guerra Curvelo W (2001) La disputa y la palabra. La Ley en la sociedad Wayuu. Ministe-rio de Cultura, Bogotá
Guerra Curvelo W (2003) La Guajira, Colombia. In: IM Editores, Bogota
Helms MW (1983) Miskito slaving and culture contact: ethnicity and opportunity in an expanding population. J Anthropol Res 39:179–197
Helms MW (1977) Negro or Indian: the changing identity of a frontier population. In: Old roots in new lands. Historical and anthropological perspectives on black experiences in the Americas. Greenwood Press, Westport Conn
Hodgson R (1779) The defense of Robert Hodgson. Esq, London
Ibarra Rojas E (2008) ¿Prisoneros de guerra o esclavos? Los Zambos y los mosquitos ante la práctica de la esclavitud en los siglos XVII y XVIII. In: Cáceres R, Lovejoy P (eds) Haiti-Revolución y emancipación. Editorial UCR, San José, pp 119–127
Ibarra Rojas E (2007) La complementariedad cultural en el surgimiento de los grupos zambos del Cabo Gracias a Dios, en la Mosquitia, durante los siglos XVII y XVIII. Rev Estud Soc 26:105–115
Ibarra Rojas E (2011) Del arco y la flecha a las armas de fuego. Los indios mosquitos y la historia centroamericana 1633–1786. Editorial UCR, San José
Israel JI (2002) Diasporas within a diaspora. Jews, crypto-Jews and the world maritime empires. Brill, Leiden
Juang RM, Morrissette N (2008) Africa and the Americas. Culture, politics, and history. A multidisciplinary encyclopedia, Vol. I. Abc-Clio, Santa Barbara
Kagan RL, Morgan PD (2009) Atlantic diasporas: jews, conversos and crypto-jews in the age of mercantilism, 1500–1800. John Hopkins University Press, Baltimore
Kelsey H (2003) Sir John Hawkins. Queen Elizabeth's slave trader. Yale University Press, New Haven
Knight, Franklin, Imperialism and slavery. Hilary McD Beckles/Verena Shepherd, Caribbean slavery in the Atlantic world. Marcus Wiener Publishers. Princeton 2000
Landers J (1999) Black Society in Spanish Florida. University of Illinois Press, Urbana
Langebaeck CH (2006) El diablo vestido de negro y los cunas del Darién en el siglo XVIII: Jacobo Walburger y su breve noticia de la Provincia del Darién, de la ley y costumbres de los Yndios, de la poca esperanza de plantar nuestra fe, y del número de sus naturales, 1748. Edicion Uniandes, Bogotá
Landers J (2010) Atlantic creoles in the age of revolutions. Harvard University Press, Harvard
Lara O (2006) Space and history in the Caribbean. Marcus Wiener Publishers, Princeton
Magallanes MV (1975) Historia política de Venezuela. Monte Ávila Ediciones, Caracas
Mark P (2002) "Portuguese" Style and Luso-African Identity: pre-colonial Senegambia, sixteenth-nineteenth centuries. Indiana University Press, Bloomington
M.W. (1732) The Mosquito Indian and his Golden River. In: A collection of voyages and travels, vol 6. Churchills, London
McNeill JR (2010) Mosquito empires. Ecology and war in the Greater Caribbean, 1620–1914. Cambridge University Press, New York
Miranda Vásquez T (1976) La gobernación de Santa Marta (1570–1670). Escuela de Estudios Hispanoamericanos, Sevilla
Muñoz Luengo M (1949) Noticias sobre la fundación de la Nuestra Señora de los Remedios de Cabo de la Vela. Rev Anu Estud Am IV:757–797
Muth V (2012) The Tule Proto-State between disappearance and historical reconstruction. Paper presented at the 44th conference of the Association of Caribbean Historians, Curacao (unpublished paper)
Navarrete MC (2003) La granjería de las perlas del Río de la Hacha. Historia Caribe 3(8):35–50
Newitt M (2005) A history of Portuguese overseas expansion 1400–1668. Routledge, London
Newson LA (1986) The cost of conquest. Indian decline in Honduras under Spanish rule. Westview Press, Boulder
Offen K (1999) The Miskitu kingdom: landscape and the emergence of a Miskitu ethnic identity, Northeastern Nicaragua and Honduras, 1600–1800. University of Texas, Austin

Offen K (2002) The Sambo and Tawira Miskitu: the colonial origins and geography of intra-miskitu differentiation in Eastern Nicaragua and Honduras. In: Ethnohistory, vol 49, 2: The Caribbean Basin. Duke University Press, Durham, pp 319–372

Offen KH (2007) Creating Mosquitia: mapping Amerindian spatial practices in Eastern Central America, 1629–1779. J Hist Geogr 33:254–282

Olien MD (1983) The Miskito kings and the line of succession. J Anthropol Res 39(2):198–241

Ordahl Kupperman K (1993) Providence Island (1630) -1641. The other Puritan Colony Cambridge University Press, Cambridge

Otte E (1977) Las perlas del Caribe: Nueva Cádiz de Cubagua. John Boulton Fundación, Caracas

Paz Reverol CL (2000) La sociedad wayuú ante las medidas del estado venezolano (1840–1850). Rev Cienc Soc VI(3):399–415

Perrin M (1987) The way of the dead Indians. Guajiro myths and symbols, vol 13. University of Texas Press, Austin

Pineda BL (2006) Shipwrecked identities: navigating race on Nicaragua's mosquito coast. Rutgers University Press, Chapel Hill

Polo Acuña J (2000a) En Defensa de la tierra: Colonización y conflicto en la Guajira. Siglo XVIII. Fondo Mixto para la promoción de las Artes y la cultura guajira, Riohacha

Polo Acuña J (2000b) Contrabando y pacificación indígena en una frontera del Caribe: La Guajira, 1750–1800. Agüaita 3:31–62

Polo Acuña J (2005) Etnicidad, Conflicto Social y Cultura Fronteriza en la Guajira. (1700–1850). Uniandes, Ceso, Ministerio de Cultura, Celikud, Bogotá

Polo Acuña J (2011a) Los indígenas de La Guajira y su articulación política al Estado colombiano (1830–1880). Hist Crít 44:80–103

Polo Acuña J (2011b) Territorios indígenas y estatales en la península de la Guajira (1830–1850). In: Polo Acuña J, Solano SP (eds) Historia Social del Caribe Colombiano. Territorios, indígenas, trabajadores, cultura, memoria e historia. La Carreta Editores, Cartagena de Indias, pp 45–74

Potthast B (1988) Die Mosquitoküste im Spannungsfeld Britischer und Spanischer Politik 1502–1821. Verlag Böhlau, Köln

Potthast-Jutkeit B (1993) Indians, blacks, and zambos on the mosquito coast, 17th and 18th centuries. América Negra 6:53–65

Restall M (2000) Black conquistadors: armed Africans in early Spanish America. Americas 57 (2):171–205

Rogers N (2002) Caribbean borderland: empire, ethnicity, and the exotic on the Mosquito Coast. Eighteen Cent Life, 26(3) 117–138

Romero Vargas G (1995) Las sociedades del Atlántico de Nicaragua en los siglos XVII y XVIII. Colección Cultural Banco Nicaragüense, Managua

Schorsch J (2008) Swimming the Christian Atlantic. Judeoconversos, Afroiberians and Amerindians in the seventeenth century. Brill, Leiden

Sollis P (1989) The Atlantic Coast of Nicaragua: development and autonomy. J Lat Am Stud 21 (3):481–520

Sorsby WS (1969) The British superintendency of the mosquito shore 1749–1787. Phd. Thesis. University College London

Sweet J (2003) Recreating Africa: culture, kinship, and religion in the African-Portuguese World, 1441–1770. University of North Carolina Press, Chapel Hill

Thompson AO (2006) Flight to freedom. African runaways and maroons in the Americas. University of the West Indian Press, Kingston

Thornton J (1992) Africa and the Africans in the formation of the Atlantic World, 1450–1680. Cambridge University Press, Cambridge, MA

Ventura María da Graça Mateus A, Os Gramaxo (2001) Un caso paradigmático de redes de influencia en Cartagena de Indias. Cad Estud Sefarditas 1:65–82

Vidal Ortega Antonino/Baquero Montoya Fernando Alvaro, De las Indias Remotas ... Cartas del Cabildo de Santa Marta 1529–1640. Ediciones Uninorte. Barranquilla 2007

Vila Vilar E (1977) Hispanoamérica y el comercio de esclavos. Estudios Hispanoamericanos de Sevilla, Sevilla
Von Houwald G (1980) Diccionario Español-Sumo, Sumo-Español. Ministerio de Educación, La Habana. Managua
Weber, David, Bourbons and Bárbaros. Center and periphery in the reshaping of Spanish Indian policy. Christine Daniels/Michael V. Kennedy. Negotiated empires: centers and peripheries in the Americas, 1500–1820. Routledge. New York 2002, 79–104
Zapata Webb YH (2006) Historiografía, Sociedad y Autonomía. Desde Tuluwalpa hasta las Regiones Autónomas de la Costa Caribe nicaragüense: Un pasado y un presente diferente. URRACAN, Managua
Zeuske M (2006) Sklaven und Sklaverei in den Welten des Atlantiks, 1400–1940. Umrisse, Anfänge, Akteure, Vergleichsfelder und Bibliografien. Band 1: Sklaverei und Postemanzipation. LIT Verlag, Münster/Hamburg/London

Ethnic Conflict and Genocide in Rwanda

83

Wendy Lambourne

Contents

Introduction	1612
The Ethnic Groups of Rwanda: Tutsi, Hutu, and Twa	1613
Mythmaking and Construction of Identities in Precolonial Rwanda	1615
European Colonization and the Entrenchment of Ethnic Identities	1618
Interethnic Conflict and Genocide	1621
Post-Genocide Rwanda and the Elimination of Ethnic Identity	1630
Conclusion	1637
Cross-References	1640
References	1640

Abstract

Identity and ethnicity have played a significant and contested role in the history of Rwanda, the genocide of 1994 and its aftermath. This chapter traces the origins of ethnicity as the most salient identity marker for Rwandans since colonization and independence. Starting with an overview of precolonial relations between the three identity groups provides a backdrop for understanding how ethnic identity was constructed by the colonial powers, reinforced by the postindependence governments and became a driver for violent conflict and ultimately genocide. Continuing this tradition of mythmaking and manipulation of identity for social and political purposes, the government of Rwanda post-genocide has sought to replace ethnic identity with a superordinate Rwandan national identity in order to maintain stability and promote unity and reconciliation. The chapter concludes by examining the contemporary challenges and implications of this approach to identity transformation for peace in Rwanda. Central to the analysis is the

---

W. Lambourne (✉)
Department of Peace and Conflict Studies, University of Sydney, Sydney, NSW, Australia
e-mail: wendy.lambourne@sydney.edu.au

recognition of how ethnicity has been constructed, reconstructed, and deconstructed for strategic and pragmatic purposes before, during, and after the genocide, rather than being seen as a primordial and definitive marker and determinant of social and political relations and violence in Rwanda. Nevertheless, ethnic identity, although recognized as a political and historical construct, is also seen as a potential powder keg because of its powerful mythological characteristics and capacity to engender deep affective responses based on collective memories of oppression and violence.

Keywords
Rwanda · Genocide · Ethnicity · Identity · Gacaca

Introduction

At the center of Rwandan history lies the controversial debate about the origins of the three ethnic groups that inhabit Rwanda: the Batwa, the Bahutu, and the Batutsi. All three speak the same Bantu language, Kinyarwanda, and have lived together on the same land for at least five centuries. Intermarriage between the two main groups, the Bahutu and Batutsi, has been common and the physical characteristics said to distinguish between them are not consistent nor always easily apparent, even to fellow Rwandans. It has also been claimed that Hutu and Tutsi share the same religious and cultural traditions, leading to arguments that they should not be regarded as separate ethnic groups at all. And yet, despite the lack of clarity and contested nature of the relationship historically, the distinction between Hutu and Tutsi became the source of one of the most significant genocides of the twentieth century.

An analysis of the ethnic nature of the conflict and the 1994 genocide against the Tutsi requires an understanding of Rwandan history, with all its apparent contradictions and complexities. Rwandan precolonial cultural tradition is oral, with history being created through stories passed on from one generation to the next. These stories are open to interpretation and alteration over time and to deliberate manipulation for political or other purposes. Furthermore, the strongly hierarchical nature of Rwandan society suggests that stories told by the more powerful would receive more credence. In addition to folktales and legends, Rwandan history was "supplemented by the memory of court historians whose task was to hand down to posterity the glorious traditions of the realm – not as history might have it but, rather, as royal ordinance prescribed" (Lemarchand 1970, p. 32).

In the absence of a reliable record of precolonial Rwandan history, the theories and observations of the European colonizers became the primary written source of historical analysis available to both Rwandans and the outside world. As will be discussed in this chapter, the historians and anthropologists who first studied Rwanda were influenced by the theoretical outlook of their time and the colonists were driven by motivations beyond the purely scientific. Subsequent studies have sought to produce more balanced and thoroughly researched accounts of precolonial and colonial Rwanda, which have contributed to a more nuanced understanding of the changing nature of the relationship between Hutu and Tutsi. Yet even so biases remain, and the reader is constantly reminded to be alert to how writers of Rwandan history can be influenced by sociocultural, psychological, and political factors and motivations often associated with seeking to defend and justify, as well as to explain, past actions or current policies and practice. Assuming that all writers will carry such biases can be misleading, but it does suggest the importance of considering the possibility of bias in reading any account of the Rwandan genocide and its aftermath. This chapter therefore draws on a range of authors, including Rwandan and European, representing Francophone and Anglophone, Hutu and Tutsi, and a range of disciplines including history, political science, psychology, sociology, and anthropology, in order to analyze the role of ethnicity in the genesis and conduct of the Rwandan genocide along with the implications and challenges for peacebuilding.

The first part comprises four sections exploring the issue of ethnicity in the context of precolonial, colonial, and postcolonial history and changing constructions of the identities of Hutu and Tutsi in Rwanda. This is followed by a discussion of the role of ethnicity in the conflict and genocide of 1994. The final section examines the consequences and contemporary implications in terms of ethnicity and identity deconstruction and reconstruction as part of building a new Rwanda based on national unity and reconciliation. Throughout the chapter, themes of complexity and contradictions are highlighted in order to build an understanding of Rwandan social and political dynamics that avoids perpetuating assumptions and stereotypes about ethnic primordialism, but at the same time underscores the ongoing potential for the use of such mythmaking and polarizing discourse to promulgate interethnic hatred and violence.

The Ethnic Groups of Rwanda: Tutsi, Hutu, and Twa

> What is a Tutsi? What is a Hutu? What is a Twa? A Tutsi is a person whose father is Tutsi. A Hutu is a person whose father is a Hutu. A Twa is a person whose father is a Twa. That is about the only point on which everyone agrees. If you go beyond this fact, you enter the debate which ended in genocide. (Sibomana 1999, p. 83)

Sibomana's attempt to depoliticize the distinction between Rwanda's three ethnic groups oversimplifies the "facts" and masks the realities of identity construction. It fails to take into account the precolonial fluidity of the identities of Hutu and Tutsi, the impact of intermarriages, and the consequent variability of physical attributes associated with each. As argued by the anthropologist historian, David Newbury (2009, p. 299), "social categorization judged by unilineal descent through the male line does not adequately account for biological reality."

The significance of physical differences between Hutu and Tutsi has been challenged by Rwandans themselves as well as by foreign commentators who refer to the many exceptions to the stereotypical picture of a Hutu as short and stocky and Tutsi as tall and thin (Sibomana 1999, p. 84). For example, a Rwandan was quoted by

Gourevitch (1998, p. 50) as saying: "We can't tell us apart. I was on a bus in the north once and because I was in the north, where they [Hutus] were, and because I ate corn, which they eat, they said, 'He's one of us'. But I'm a Tutsi from Butare in the south." On the basis of shared language and cultural practices, it has therefore been argued by some (such as the French social geographer Dominque Franche quoted in Sibomana 1999, p. 83) that the Batutsi, Bahutu, and Batwa should not be described as different ethnic groups, but rather as different social groups or classes within the same Rwandan ethnic identity.

However, the claim that historically all Rwandans practiced the same animist religion and cultural traditions is not universally accepted. Destexhe (1995, p. 36), for example, claims that: "It would be extremely difficult to find any kind of cultural or folkloric custom that was specifically Hutu or Tutsi." Yet others point out that the animist "kubandwa" possession cult is thought to have been of Hutu origin (Prunier 1995, p. 15), and that particular ceremonial dances are associated exclusively with the Tutsi group. Sibomana (1999, pp. 83–4) claims that Hutu and Tutsi children are told different stories in the evenings, and that a particular type of war poetry exists in Tutsi but not Hutu culture. Sibomana (1999, p. 84) also refers to differences in attitudes toward sexual modesty between the three Rwandan ethnic groups, and references to differences in eating habits have also been made.

The Twa (or Batwa in the plural) are a pygmoid people thought to come from the forests and to be the original inhabitants of what is today called Rwanda. They represent only about 1% of the Rwandan population and are generally regarded as inferior by Hutu and Tutsi alike (Destexhe 1995, p. 39). The European colonizers who arrived at the turn of the century observed that the Batwa lived either as hunter-gatherers in the forested areas or "served the high-ranking personalities or the King in a variety of menial tasks" (Prunier 1995, p. 5). According to Destexhe (1995, p. 39), the first European on Rwandan soil, Count von Goetzen, declared them to be "a caste of dwarfs." Like other marginalized minority groups throughout the world, the Batwa have continued to engage in a struggle for their rights and recognition in Rwandan society.

The Bahutu comprise some 85% of the population and at the time of European colonization were agriculturalists or peasants who cultivated the soil. European historians identified them as the first "tribe" to settle Rwanda, most probably coming from the south and west (Lemarchand 1970; Gourevitch 1998). The Bahutu were described by the colonizers as a Bantu people with typical negroid features and were regarded as superior to the Batwa but inferior to the Batutsi. Adolphus Frederick, Duke of Mecklenburg, wrote in 1910 that the Bahutu "are a medium-sized type of people whose ungainly figures betoken hard toil, and who patiently bow themselves in abject bondage to the later arrived yet ruling race, the Tutsi" (Lemarchand 1970, p. 19). In 1948, a Belgian doctor described the Hutu as "possessing all the characteristics of the negro: flat noses, thick lips, low foreheads, brachycephalic skulls. They are like children, shy and lazy and usually dirty" (quoted in Destexhe 1995, p. 39).

The remaining 14% of the population were the cattle-herding Batutsi. The Batutsi were described as much taller and thinner, with sharp, angular facial features and a somewhat regal appearance that led the European invaders to conclude that they were of a different and superior racial stock to the local Hutu peasants (Prunier 1995, p. 5).

Mecklenburg said of the Batutsi that "they possess that same graceful indolence in gait which is peculiar to Oriental peoples, and their bronze-brown skin reminds me of the inhabitants of the more hilly parts of northern Africa. Unmistakable evidence of a foreign strain are betrayed in their high foreheads, the curve of their nostrils, and the fine, oval shape of their faces" (Lemarchand 1970, p. 18). The same Belgian doctor referred to above wrote of the Batutsi in 1948 that they "are 1.09 metres tall. They are slim. They have straight noses, high foreheads, thin lips. The Hamites [or Tutsi] seem distant, reserved, polite and refined" (quoted in Destexhe 1995, p. 39).

These differences in physical appearance and occupational ties observed by the European colonizers led to theories about the distinct ethnic origins of the three groups, and the subsequent consolidation of differences to the extent that the Hutu, Tutsi, and Twa came eventually to consider themselves to be separate ethnic groups. There is evidence, however, that myths of Tutsi supremacy in the form of folktales and dynastic poems that set out the "fundamental and 'natural' differences among Tutsi, Hutu, and Twa" long predated the coming of the Europeans (Lemarchand 2009, pp. 52–3). One of these relates to *Ibimanuka* ("those who descended from heaven") and the mythical celestial origins of the Tutsi, while the other tells of how God determined who should rule over whom in the ancient kingdom of the Gatutsi, Gahutu, and Gatwa. Entrusted with a pot of milk each to watch over during the night, the greedy Gatwa drank the milk, the lazy Gahutu fell asleep and spilt the milk, and only the dependable Gatutsi stayed awake and kept guard over his milk until dawn (Lemarchand 2009, p. 53).

Whether or not these three groups can be substantiated biologically or anthropologically as separate ethnic categories, they are undoubtedly of political and sociological significance. Mamdani (2001) provides an account of how interpretations of the relationship between Hutu and Tutsi have since colonial times been framed in political terms. From his assessment of the anthropological and other evidence for the two main schools of thought concerning the origins of Hutu and Tutsi, Mamdani (2001, pp. 73–75) concludes that they are historical and political identities that have changed over time in relation to changes in power but are descended from one cultural identity (Banyarwanda). Newbury (2009, p. 302) goes further to argue that "while ethnicity serves as a powerful construct" in societies such as Rwanda, "regional diversities, ecological transformations, and political particularities are much more important than ethnic determinism in understanding the history." Fujii (2009, p. 56) concludes similarly that in the history of Rwanda, "politics and power trumped ethnic loyalties every time." In this chapter, I argue that it is the interplay between ethnicity and identity and politics and power that underpins the cycles of violent conflict and genocide experienced by Rwandans from precolonial times until today.

Mythmaking and Construction of Identities in Precolonial Rwanda

According to Lemarchand (1970, pp. 19–20), Rwandan society was highly centralized prior to colonization. However, while the south of the country was dominated by a single Tutsi monarchy (the "mwami," who was revered as a divinity, absolute, and infallible) (Gourevitch 1998, p. 49), the north was still ruled by several Hutu kings (Sibomana 1999, p. 81). The amalgamation of autonomous chieftaincies into a small nuclear kingdom centered around Kigali under the leadership of a royal clan (the Tutsi monarchy) probably took place in Rwanda during the fifteenth century (Lemarchand 1970, p. 19). This was followed by a period of expansion involving the gradual incorporation of outlying areas, with the last of the small Hutu kingdoms not being annexed until after colonization in the early 1920s (Lemarchand 1970, p. 21). The Tutsi dynasty had gradually defeated the Hutu kings and chiefs since the seventeenth century, but it was the European invaders, and especially the Christian missionaries, who reinforced the Tutsi lineage as the most important and formalized the centralization of political control under the Tutsi King, Mwami Yuhi Musingwa (Destexhe 1995, p. 40; Prunier 1995, p. 19; Sibomana 1999, pp. 81–2).

The Tutsi as a group most probably acquired economic and hence political power using the ownership of cattle as a lever (Lemarchand 1970, p. 19). The Tutsi possessed *ubuhake* – the right to own cattle – which was passed down from father to son (Destexhe 1995, p. 39). This ensured their socioeconomic and political domination over the Hutu who, like the Twa, were required to sell their labor and agricultural produce in return for protection from the chief (who was usually a Tutsi). The ownership of cattle thus formed the basis of a clientage system in which reciprocal bonds of loyalty were built up through the exchange of commodities and services between patron and client (Lemarchand 1970, p. 36). Tutsi would generally provide their Hutu clients with cow's milk and access to pasture land, as well as protection, in return for labor and agricultural produce. However, as Lemarchand (1970, p. 37) points out, the roles of patron and client were not mutually exclusive, and the client–patron relationships "formed a web of reciprocities embracing a wide segment of the population." The relationship between Tutsi and Hutu at this point could thus be seen as more symbiotic than exploitative.

Although the social and political structure of precolonial Rwanda has been described as feudal, this does not imply that the relationship between the aristocracy and peasants was fixed as in Europe in the twelfth century. As argued by Grimes (1975), Maquet's depiction of Tutsi as a class or caste ruling over Hutu was inconsistent with the indications that some Tutsi were "commoners" and some Hutu were chiefs. The ideology that Tutsis were "born to rule" should arguably be replaced by one that identifies Tutsi as "born fit for a special, ritual association with cattle, Hutu were born to be agriculturalists and Twa – hunters" (Grimes 1975, p. 55). The categories of Hutu and Tutsi were fluid: a Hutu could become a Tutsi by acquiring cattle or becoming a chief, and a Tutsi could become a Hutu by losing his cattle-owning status and turning to cultivation (Watson 1991, p. 3). However, as soon as he acquired cattle or became a chief of sufficient power, a Hutu was reclassified as a Tutsi – "they are absorbed into the upper caste. Their Hutu origins are 'forgotten'" (Lemarchand 1970, p. 39). Therefore, as argued by Lemarchand (1970, p. 39), the Hutu as a group "were inevitably destined to remain in an inferior position. A Tutsi could be both a client and a patron; but a Hutu could only be a client." As explained by Mamdani (2001, p. 75), "to be a Tutsi was thus to be in power, near power, or simply to be identified with power," while to be a Hutu was increasingly identified with being a subject.

The Tutsi were thus "not strictly a hereditary group but socially defined; for given the clientage system and intermarriage, Hutu could become Tutsi" (Grimes 1975, p. 66), based on what Fujii (2009, p. 115) classified as "status" or "hereditary" criteria. Intermarriages were possible, if not common, and the tracing of ethnic heritage could be arbitrary as Rwandans do not normally carry family names (Feil 1998, p. 34). Furthermore, many Tutsi were in a similar position economically to the Hutu, and often did not own cattle, but socially these "*petits* Tutsi" retained the privileges afforded to the rich Tutsi but not to the Hutu (Mamdani 2001, p. 74). According to Catharine Newbury (1988, p. 6), the strong identification as a socially oppressed group was not developed by the Hutu until the era of European colonialism that overwhelmingly favored the Tutsi group thereby transforming the structure of domination to one of blatant exploitation.

Vansina (2004) argues that the Hutu did begin to develop their identity as an oppressed group during the second half of the nineteenth century under the Tutsi clan dynasty, the Nyiginya kingdom, and that the first institutionalization of the distinction between Tutsi and Hutu that spread throughout Rwanda predated colonization. According to Vansina (2004, p. 136), the "absolute division between Hutu and Tutsi institutionalized by the daily practice of *uburetwa* rapidly displaced the older social class consciousness" as only farmers or Hutu (and not herders, the Tutsi) were obliged to perform the menial work associated with the new exploitative system of *uburetwa* introduced in 1870. The introduction of this new system continued the trend of increasing inequalities studied by Catharine Newbury (1988) in which the original reciprocal *umuheto* cattle clientship was replaced by the more unequal system of *ubuhake* which could involve families without cattle and thus expose them to "more arbitrary forms of exploitation" (Mamdani 2001, p. 65). *Uburetwa* as a completely nonreciprocal form of agricultural clientship was imposed on the newly landless Hutu farmers in the wake of the shift in land control from the lineages of land chiefs, many of whom were Hutu, to the king (Mamdani 2001, p. 66).

In order to justify and preserve this new social order that placed absolute authority in their hands, the Nyiginya clan promulgated an official account of Rwandan history that "claimed a primordial basis for Tutsi rule and superiority" (Fujii 2009, p. 57). Taylor (1999, p. 68) further points out how discrimination against the Twa was entrenched in the "local model of difference." As argued by Lemarchand (2009, pp. 52–4), precolonial Rwandan myths of origins were intended not only to make the past intelligible, but also legitimize the present for both Hutu and Tutsi and thus promote social cohesion while at the same time validating oppression. This Tutsi-centric version of history maintained that specialized roles for the Tutsi, Hutu, and Twa "emanated from each group's unique background" as pastoralists, cultivators, and forest dwellers, respectively, thus laying the foundation for the construction of ethnic identities by the European explorers and missionaries based on the Hamitic hypothesis of Tutsi superiority (Fujii 2009, p. 57). Lemarchand (2009, pp. 52–4) comments on the "uncanny fit" between European Hamitic theories and Rwandan myths of origins and how the "distortion of historical reality" through such myth-making was also used "to inspire division and to inflame ethnic passions" in a way that made atrocities against the demonized other possible.

Vansina's detailed account of the Nyiginya dynasties that dominated Rwanda in the eighteenth and nineteenth centuries reveals how the differing sociocultural and political experiences of Hutu and Tutsi grew during this period and ultimately led to violence between the two groups, including an armed anti-Tutsi insurrection that broke out in the northwest in 1897 and spread to a number of local areas. The armed revolt was eventually suppressed by the armies of the court in 1899, but not in all areas, and Vansina (2004, p. 138) concludes "not only that the population at this time was conscious of a great divide between Tutsi and Hutu, but also that the antagonism between these two social categories had already broken into the open." Nevertheless, Vansina (2004) and other historians maintain that the difference between Hutu and Tutsi was still more socioeconomic and political than it was ethnic, and it was only the promulgation of the Hamitic hypothesis and identity card system by the colonial powers that fixed and thus transformed the two social categories into ethnic groups.

The interethnic hatred and cycles of violence and revenge between the two groups that culminated in the genocide of 1994, did not begin until the end of the colonial era, but the seeds were sown in the "double-edged aspect of the clientage system" and the development of a superiority/inferiority relationship between Tutsi and Hutu (Lemarchand 1970, pp. 43–44). According to Kamukama (1993, p. 25), "the people of Rwanda were subjected to both monarchical and colonial exploitation and oppression" that fueled the Hutu revolution and subsequent cycles of violent conflict. Mamdani (2001, p. 74) also argues that the Hutu and Tutsi "emerged as state-enforced identities" derived from their history of state centralization and changes in clientship "that led to the social degradation of the Hutu." According to Lemarchand (1970, pp. 40–41), the clientage system not only created "a web of intercaste solidarities," it also created "the conditions of its rupture" by seeming to reinforce social and political inequalities between Hutu and Tutsi. Furthermore, he argues, "submissiveness and self-doubt remained the most enduring characteristics of Hutu behaviour" and resulted in pathological extremes of violence that could be "regarded as the blind reaction of a people traumatised by a deep and lasting sense of inferiority" (Lemarchand 1970, pp. 43–44). In his later work, Lemarchand (2009, pp. 49–68) went on to attribute the scale of depravity and bloodshed seen in 1994 to the power of divisive mythmaking that created not just "imagined communities" of Hutu, Tutsi, and Twa, but also "communities of fear and hatred" (p 57).

European Colonization and the Entrenchment of Ethnic Identities

Rwanda was colonized relatively late due in part to the inaccessibility of the region, and to the "ferocious exclusiveness" of the Rwandans that repelled even the slave traders (Gourevitch 1998, pp. 53–4). The first European explorers arrived in Central Africa in the mid-nineteenth century, and in 1885, a conference of major European powers designated the separate kingdoms of Rwanda and Burundi as provinces of German East Africa. The first European to enter Rwanda was a German count named von Gőtzen, who visited the royal court in 1894. The following year, the long-reigning Mwami Rwabugiri died and as Rwanda fell into political turmoil, the

Germans set up administrative offices and a system of indirect rule over the combined territory of Ruanda-Urundi. The feuding Tutsi clan leaders collaborated with the German colonizers in return for patronage and support for the system of political dominance over the Hutu majority. The German system of indirect rule "reinforced the absolutism of the monarchy, and hence the hegemony of the ruling caste" (Lemarchand 1970, p. 62).

Following the defeat of Germany in World War I the colony became a trustee territory of Belgium, administered under a League of Nations mandate, and after World War II as a United Nations Trust Territory. As in other parts of the world, Belgium followed the colonial strategy of "divide and rule," reinforcing the division between Tutsi and Hutu. Legitimacy was, however, favored over violence, whereby the Belgian administration operated through the Tutsi kings as the "prime legitimisers of Belgian colonial policies and practices" (Lemarchand 1970, p. 66). The colonial administration also continued the precolonial clientship systems of *ubuhake* – but as a more coercive arrangement – and *uburetwa*, as a requirement for "all Hutu men except for the small number who had salaried jobs" (Fujii 2009, p. 64). *Uburetwa* thus came to represent a system of Tutsi dominance that reinforced competition between the elites, and a means of colonial extraction from the poorest Hutu that reinforced a sense of discrimination against Hutu as a group (Fujii 2009, p. 64; Newbury 1988, p. 141).

The hypothesis was developed that the Tutsis were descended from nomadic pastoralists who had migrated from the north, most probably from southern Ethiopia, and conquered the indigenous Bantu societies in the fifteenth century. The British explorer J. H. Speke first suggested this theory in 1863 based on his observations of Rwandans from a vantage point in Tanzania (Destexhe 1995, p. 86). The physical features of the Tutsi suggested an ethnic link with the Galla or Oromo nomadic Cushitic tribes of southern Ethiopia (traditionally connected with the monarchic institution), along with extended racial links to peoples in the Middle East and Europe (Prunier 1995, p. 7). According to this "Hamitic hypothesis," the Tutsis were one of the African tribes descended from Noah's son, Ham, who along with his descendants was cursed after seeing his father naked, their color being a result of the curse (Destexhe 1995, pp. 37–8). The other "blacks" (including the Hutu of Rwanda), meanwhile, were classified according to their physical characteristics (such as skin color and skull shape) as different (and lesser) human beings not descended from Noah. This racist categorization of peoples based on "objective" criteria that was developed from social Darwinism during the early twentieth century was also used as an ideology to support the killing of Jews and other "lesser human beings" during the Nazi holocaust.

The Belgians thus regarded the Tutsi as superior and used the Hamitic hypothesis as justification for their discrimination in favor of the Tutsi minority. They ruled indirectly through the existing power structure of the Tutsi aristocracy and gave preferential treatment to the Tutsi in terms of education, employment, and political office. The lower level of school participation and university education enjoyed by the Hutu under colonial rule reinforced their lower socioeconomic standing in Rwandan society. The Belgians used the Tutsi as the administrators of their harsh policies and the Hutu became increasingly resentful – not of their colonial masters, but of the Tutsi monarchical system. The Tutsi, meanwhile, became more attached to the idea that they were the superior ethnic group and deserved to be in power.

The introduction of native tribunals by the Belgians in 1936 served to further entrench the power of the Tutsi elite as they used them to "legitimise abuses and wrong-doings" rather than to dispense justice (Lemarchand 1970, p. 76). The Belgian administrative reforms also resulted in the deposing of most of the remaining Hutu chiefs through a process of Tutsification, and the introduction of identity cards that had the effect of fixing the formerly fluid ethnic categories of Hutu and Tutsi. However, the allocation of identity cards by the Belgians was somewhat arbitrary, with those possessing at least ten head of cattle being considered Tutsi (Klinghoffer 1998, p. 6). The ethnic category of the whole family was determined by that of the father, and many Hutu chiefs were redefined as Tutsi in line with the Belgian preference for Tutsi rule.

The theory of Tutsi superiority was adopted by the church as it was consistent with its claim that all the peoples of the earth are descended from Noah, and the Roman Catholic Church was quite influential in the Belgian decision to give preference to the Tutsi (Destexhe 1995, pp. 38 & 40). The European missionaries of the Roman Catholic Church, known as the White Fathers, and those of the various Protestant churches – Anglican, Seventh Day Adventist, and Presbyterian – were instrumental in supporting the development and fixing of ethnic identities during the colonial period. According to Longman (2010, p. 58), the White Fathers pursued an alliance with the dominant political class in society as part of their mission, and as "they perceived political power in Rwanda in primarily ethnic terms" this led to "ignoring or downplaying important divisions of class, region, lineage, clan, and political faction." The missionaries "working together with the colonial administration ... helped to make this interpretation reality" by supporting the Tutsi power structure (Longman 2010, p. 58); imposing a racialization of the Tutsi/Hutu relationship both ideologically and institutionally (Mamdani 2001, p. 87); and providing data for the classification of Rwandans as Hutu, Tutsi, or Twa as part of the official census of 1933–1934 as a complement to physical measurements and the application of the "ten-cow rule" (in which those who owned ten or more cows were classified as Tutsi). So as a result of these measures, "by the end of the colonial period, the division among Hutu, Tutsi, and Twa had indeed become the predominant cleavage in Rwandan society" (Longman 2010, p. 58). And the church could claim to have significantly affected "how Rwandans perceived their own identities" (Longman 2010, p. 65); as Fujii (2009, p. 67) suggests, "many Rwandans had internalized the precepts of Tutsi superiority" by the time of the struggle for independence.

The anthropologist Jacques-Jean Maquet and other social scientists who studied Rwanda in the 1940s and 1950s were also responsible for reinforcing the early European theories that the ethnic and class stratification between Hutu and Tutsi was a fixed feature of traditional Rwandan society. To the colonizers, it seemed that the minority Tutsi pastoralists held political power and controlled the sources of wealth, and exploited their Hutu subjects (Newbury 1988, p. 3). However, the situation was much more complex than that: "ethnic identities were not primordial; they were contextually created, they altered over time, and they evolved differently in different places and contexts" (Newbury 2009, p. 297). According to Newbury (2009), the consolidation of identity into separate ethnic groups occurred as a result of the gradual encroachment of the state and the exercise of mutual agency in a complex process that saw the emergence of a "collective Hutu identity that transcended lineage and hill" (p 300). This broad social identity only became salient in a particular political context and "was based on concepts drawing on descent, occupation, class, and personal characteristics in various combinations" (p 301).

An important aspect of the growing resentment between the Hutu and Tutsi has been attributed to the lack of natural resources, high population density, and subsequent poverty and hardship that was not equally shared (Lemarchand 1970, p. 15; Uvin 1998). The Hutu revolution that secured Rwandan independence was largely driven by economic grievances and the struggle for access to the means of production (Newbury 1988, p. 213). For the majority of the population, ethnicity and class overlapped: "most of the people who were poor and exploited were categorized as Hutu" (Newbury 1988, p. 213). There were Hutu professionals who were better off, and not all Tutsi were rich and powerful. But by the end of colonial rule, a strong ethnic awareness had been developed (at least among the elite) and the Hutus as a group were generally regarded as inferior or subordinate.

Toward the end of colonial rule, it was the church, led by a new generation of socially progressive Flemish-speaking White Fathers, that began to educate the Hutus thereby producing the first generation of Hutu intellectuals (Fujii 2009, p. 66; Longman 2010). Under the influence of this "Christian socialism" now spreading throughout Europe, the Belgian Church in Rwanda began to support the Hutus in their quest for emancipation, and the Tutsi gradually lost their religious as well as political authority in Rwanda. Whether supporting the Tutsi or Hutu, the Catholic Church maintained its focus on ethnicity as a marker of social and political hierarchy, thereby playing its part in the fomenting of interethnic conflict in Rwanda and explaining how the church became so heavily implicated in the genocide itself (Longman 2010, p. 59).

The influence of the Roman Catholic Church in Rwanda gradually increased, while the role of the monarchy was diluted by the policies of the colonizers. After converting the Tutsi chiefs to Christianity, the missionaries used them to convert the Hutu masses. Rwanda thus experienced an unusually high conversion rate, with almost 65% of Rwandans having joined the Catholic Church by the end of the colonial era, and by the time of the genocide in 1994, the percentage of Christians in Rwanda had reportedly risen to 95%, with 85% belonging to the Catholic Church (Longman 2010).

Interethnic Conflict and Genocide

During the latter part of their rule, the Belgians responded to pressure from the United Nations and the Catholic Church, and began to open up the political and socioeconomic system to the majority Hutu. The Hutu ascendancy of the 1950s and

1960s was encouraged by the Belgians in a policy turnaround that saw the establishment of political parties and more democratic elections. Belgian policy now sought to bring an end to the feudal system of clientage, but the policies of democratization were, according to Lemarchand (1970, p. 79), "a classic example of 'too little and too late.'" The Belgians allowed Hutu riots against the authority of the Tutsi chiefs to escalate into full-scale civil war, and thousands of refugees began fleeing to neighboring countries (Uganda, Tanzania, Burundi, and former Zaire). The Hutu shed their loyalty for the Mwami in a political backlash against the monarchical system of exploitation that had been encouraged by the colonial powers, and Hutu extremists adopted the Hamitic hypothesis as justification for labelling the Tutsi as outsiders who should be expelled or killed. The Hutus attained political control within the colonial framework, and the Tutsi monarchy of four centuries came to an end.

The growing resentment and cycles of violence between Hutu and Tutsi could thus be blamed on the Belgian colonizers, both because of their policy of "divide and rule" and because of their switch in ethnic group loyalty that supported a reversal in power relations between the two groups. And yet, as argued by Sibomana (1999, p. 87), Hutu and Tutsi extremists were also both responsible for perpetuating the stereotypes and interethnic violence as part of their own ongoing power struggle:

> If power had not been given in its entirety to one group (the Tutsi) to the detriment of the other two groups (the Hutu and the Twa) and if, subsequently, it had not been taken away in its entirety from that group and handed over in its entirety to another group (the Hutu), we might have been able to avoid a genocide ... The Belgian settlers implanted racist stereotypes which we were not able to shake off. But the responsibility of these settlers should not obscure the responsibility of Hutu and Tutsi extremists who, one after the other and each in their own way, exploited these stereotypes which served the purposes of their struggle to conquer or to hold onto power.

The Hutu revolution in Rwanda was extremely violent and was driven as much (if not more) by the internal conflict between Hutu and Tutsi as by the conflict between colonial society and the colonizer (Lemarchand 1970, p. 81). Nationalism was more of a by-product rather than a cohesive force for independence from the colonial power. According to Lemarchand (1970, p. 95), the Hutu revolution was a "long and painful enterprise, which may not have succeeded without the auxiliary support extended by the Belgian administration to the insurgents." The Hutu were not, at that time, a united group, and could not all be classified as "peasant" due in part to their albeit limited upward social mobility. In fact, Lemarchand (1970, p. 95) argues that the revolution was led by the more elite Hutus of the northern region who remained a political force despite the superimposing of Tutsi rule.

Following the revolution and civil war during which an estimated 20,000 Tutsi were killed and approximately 200,000 Tutsi became refugees, Rwanda achieved its independence and became a republic under Hutu leadership on 1 July 1962. The first president was Gregoire Kayibanda, a Hutu from Gitarama in the south-central region of the country, who belonged to the Parmehutu party that became institutionalized in 1965 with the establishment of a one-party state. However, in July 1973, the defense minister, Major-General Juvenal Habyarimana, took power through the military and created a new one-party system with the formation of the Mouvement Révolutionnaire National pour le Développement (MRND) in 1975. Habyarimana came from Gisenyi prefecture in the northwest. Following his takeover, 40 southern politicians associated with the former regime were killed in jail (Klinghoffer 1998, p. 8). This shift in power to the Hutu of the north was to last until the civil war and genocide of 1994.

The Hutu governments of Kayibanda and Habyarimana maintained the ethnic identity system instituted by the Belgians and initiated a policy of discrimination against the minority Tutsi population in retaliation for the years of subjugation under Belgian/Tutsi rule. They scapegoated the Tutsi in order to deflect attention away from grievances of the Hutu masses who remained "desperately poor" and the educated revolutionaries "who had been promised much, but received little" (Fujii 2009, pp. 70–1). The Habyarimana government also introduced a quota system that discriminated against Hutus from the south as well as Tutsi: Hutus from the north received 60% of university places and civil service positions, while Tutsis were limited to 9% and were excluded from the military (Klinghoffer 1998, p. 8). A social hierarchy was formed, with Habyarimana and his wealthy Hutu business associates at the top of the pyramid, followed by the northern Hutu, southern Hutu, Tutsi, and Twa at the bottom. By 1994, the number of Rwandan Tutsi living outside the country had risen to almost 500,000. Only one of the eleven Rwandan regions or prefectures was headed by a Tutsi prefect, and none of the 143 local government areas was headed by a Tutsi bourgemaster (Klinghoffer 1998, p. 8). The Habyarimana regime, citing Rwanda's problem of chronic overpopulation, had refused to repatriate the refugees (Gourevitch 1998, p. 73).

During this period of discrimination, violence, and exile under Hutu rule, the ethnic identities of Hutu and Tutsi and the cycles of revenge became entrenched. A culture of impunity also became the norm, as the Rwandan government failed to bring to trial or prosecute anyone for the Tutsi massacres (Gourevitch 1998, p. 94) that were evidently a politically planned elite tactic for again "diverting attention away from the real crises that threatened various leaders' legitimacy and power" (Fujii 2009, p. 74). An emphasis on the underlying "tribal" nature of the killings was used by the government to satisfy any concerns expressed by the international community (Des Forges 1999, p. 91). But it was becoming clear that in Rwanda, "ethnicity was a strategy of politics, not its foundation" (Fujii 2009, p. 75).

Between 1973 and 1990, there was a period of relative calm within Rwanda, but political and ethnic tensions continued to rise as the Tutsis faced the limitations of institutionalized discrimination and social inequalities, and their fellow Tutsis remained in exile in neighboring countries. These tensions were exacerbated even further when, on 1 October 1990, the Rwandan Patriotic Front (RPF) launched its first offensive from Uganda. The Tutsi exiles and Hutu dissidents resident in Uganda had formed the RPF in 1988 with the aim of removing Habyarimana and allowing the return of Rwandan refugees (both Hutu and Tutsi) to their homeland. The RPF, while primarily Tutsi and originating in Uganda, was supported by Tutsi exiles in the former Zaire, Burundi, and Tanzania and was not calling for the reestablishment of the Tutsi monarchy (Klinghoffer 1998, p. 14). Led by Major-General Fred Rwigyema until his death in battle, and later by Major Paul Kagame, the RPF launched several attacks on Rwanda between 1990 and 1993 to which the Habyarimana government responded with periodic massacres of Tutsis in Rwanda.

At the same time as the RPF was exerting military pressure on the Habyarimana regime, the international community was pressuring the Rwandan government to introduce political reforms. In July 1990, Habyarimana announced that multiple political parties would be legalized and that a commission would be established to draft a new constitution. He also promised to remove ethnicity from identity cards. While the latter promise was never fulfilled, the new constitution was introduced in June 1991 and the first coalition government was formed in December. Among the new parties were the Mouvement Democratique Republican (MDR), the successor to Parmehutu, and the Hutu extremist Coalition pour la Défense de la République (CDR).

The Rwandan government was also engaged in negotiations with the RPF under the auspices of regional governments, primarily Tanzania. Known as the Arusha process, these negotiations resulted in two ceasefire and power-sharing agreements being signed in October 1992 and January 1993. However, the more extremist Hutu groups including the CDR were not represented at these negotiations. Under the agreements, the RPF and MRND would receive five out of 21 ministerial posts, while the MDR would receive three plus the post of Prime Minister. Several other parties were also to be included, but not the Hutu extremist CDR. The role of President was to be weakened, but Habyarimana was entitled to retain his position during a transitional period. The ceasefire agreements did not hold, however, while negotiations on military issues, refugees, and the proposed transitional government continued at Arusha (United Nations 1996; Jones 1999).

The civil war coincided with economic decline in Rwanda triggered by falling coffee prices and escalating population growth. Foreign aid donors imposed a structural adjustment program that included reducing the civil service, freezing salaries, lowering government spending, and increasing exports. These austerity measures, combined with the effects of the war and poor management practices, contributed to a declining standard of living. Famine in the southern regions exacerbated the hardships, and the levels of refugees and internally displaced people increased throughout Rwanda. These conditions made it more attractive for young Hutu men to join the army and militias, while creating an environment conducive to ethnic propaganda against the former elite Tutsi group (Uvin 1998). At the same time, the failure of the Rwandan government to resolve the refugee issue was a major impediment to ending the civil war (Kamukama 1993, p. 59).

Elite level Hutu extremism grew in opposition to the RPF military invasions and democratization and power-sharing proposals, while local level frustrations with the economic hardships also increased. The creation of Tutsi youth democratic and liberation movements, and fears regarding the decline of MRND political dominance, led to the formation of the MRND's *Interahamwe* militia, as well as the CDR's *Impuzamamugambi* militia. Propaganda against the "Hamitic invaders" became blatant, and the Hutu Ten Commandments were published in the Hutu paper *Kanguara*

('Wake Up!') in December 1990 calling for Hutu domination of political and economic positions, an exclusively Hutu army, and guidelines against mixed marriages and Hutu–Tutsi business partnerships. From as early as 1990, more than a dozen newspapers in Kinyarwanda and French that "systematically exploited ethnic hatred" had begun to appear (Human Rights Watch/Africa 1996, p. 16). The Belgians, meanwhile, had withdrawn their support from the Hutu government in 1990 and the vacuum was filled by the French who became identified with the Hutu majority and later implicated for failing to prevent the 1994 genocide, if not actively supporting it through the provision of weapons and other measures (Callamard 1999).

The Radio Télévision Libre des Mille Collines (RTLM), founded by relatives and associates of President Habyarimana in July 1993, reportedly to counter the influence of the RPF's Radio Muhabura, began broadcasting anti-Tutsi and anti-Arusha peace process messages that became increasingly inflammatory leading up to the genocide in April 1994. A speech given by Leon Mugesera, vice-president of MRND in Gisenye prefecture, on 22 November 1992 implied that "Tutsi should be killed and recommended that their bodies be thrown into the Nyabarongo River as a means of returning them to their supposed Ethiopian homeland" (Klinghoffer 1998, pp. 21–22). The Rwandan Minister of Justice, Stanislas Mbonampeka, issued an arrest warrant against Mugesera for inciting hatred, but instead of going to jail Mugesera received protection from the army and then emigrated to Canada, while Mbonampeka was dismissed from his post as Justice Minister (Gourevitch 1998, p. 97).

Approximately 6500 Rwandans were killed in the civil war. However, against all odds, by the end of July 1993, the country appeared to be relatively peaceful; an African peacekeeping mission was in place and the United Nations (UN) had dispatched an observer mission to the Ugandan border region where the RPF were concentrated. Habyarimana was never fully aligned with the Arusha process, but under pressure from the international community, the Arusha Peace Agreement was formally signed in August 1993.

According to the peace accord, the Rwandan Army (FAR) and the Rwandan Patriotic Army (the RPF military wing) were to be integrated on a 60:40 ratio basis, and an RPA battalion was to be stationed in Kigali to protect RPF members of the new transitional government. Again, ethnic identifications on documents were to be eliminated, but this was never implemented. The United Nations Assistance Mission for Rwanda (UNAMIR) was to manage the implementation of the peace agreement, but its establishment was delayed until October which belatedly paved the way for the RPF battalion to set up in Kigali by the end of December (United Nations 1996). The transitional government that was to have been installed by 10 September 1993 was also delayed by the late deployment of UNAMIR, and on 5 January 1994 Habyariamana declared himself the president of the nonexistent transitional government. The RPF objected to this breakdown in the Arusha peace agreement.

UNAMIR commander, Brigadier-General Dallaire, cabled the UN in New York on 11 January, warning about assassination plans aimed at preventing the transitional government from taking power; Interahamwe plans to kill Tutsi in Kigali; and a plot to kill Belgian peacekeepers in order to cause UNAMIR's withdrawal from Rwanda (Ronayne 2001, p. 155). The UN Peacekeeping Office denied Dallaire's request to seize weapons secreted for use by Hutu militia and instead advised him to share his information with the Habyarimana government and other Western diplomats (Dallaire 2003). Evidence of planning for the Rwandan genocide had been discovered by UN peacekeepers as early as December 1993 when they received an anonymous letter from Hutu army officers "warning of a plan for assassinations and massacres" (Ronayne 2001, p. 155). On 17 February, the UN Security Council reported on deteriorating security in Kigali and noncompliance with a weapons-free zone agreement. Other warning indications received and ignored by the UN included: information about illicit arms trading and weapons stockpiling; RTLM anti-Tutsi radio propaganda; past massacres and assassinations; and political maneuvering by extremists to undermine the peace process (Berry 2001; Dorn and Matloff 2000). Interahamwe violence around the country was increasing, and on 21 February an opposition Hutu, designated to be a minister in the transitional government, was assassinated.

On 6 April 1994, Habyarimana attended a meeting with regional leaders in Dar es Salaam, Tanzania, that appeared to augur well for the peace process. However, as the plane carrying Habyarimana and Burundian president, Cyprien Ntaryamira, approached Kigali airport on the evening of 6 April, it was struck by two missiles and crashed, killing all nine passengers and three French crewmen. Responsibility for the crash became a matter of some controversy, with blame being placed on Hutu extremists determined to stop the power-sharing agreement about to be implemented by Habyarimana, and competing claims that the RPA was responsible as part of an RPF plan to attack Kigali and take power in Rwanda. Either way, the impact on triggering the onset of the mass killings by Hutu extremists of Tutsis and moderate Hutus perceived as their political enemies is not in question.

During the night of the plane crash that killed president Habyarimana, hit squads killed twelve opposition political figures, including eleven Hutu and one Tutsi. During the following day, Prime Minister Agathe Uwilingiyimana, a moderate Hutu, was killed by members of the presidential guard who also killed the ten Belgian peacekeepers who were protecting her. These and other Hutu were killed on the basis of previously prepared death lists, but Tutsi were slaughtered without such selectivity (Klinghoffer 1998, p. 44). A curfew was imposed at 6 am on 7 April, and on 8 April telephone connections in Kigali were cut and the indiscriminate killing of Tutsi began (African Rights 1995). Hutu were killed because of their perceived political opposition, and thus southern Hutu were also indiscriminately targeted, at least at the beginning. The foreign community in Rwanda was evacuated, and the UNAMIR contingent was reduced after the loss of the Belgian peacekeepers.

The organizers of the genocide aimed to create an exaggerated fear in the Hutu masses in order to mobilize them to kill the Tutsis and their allies. Through a massive propaganda campaign, in which the Tutsi were described as "cockroaches" (*Inyenzi* in Kinyarwanda) to be stamped out, the Hutu population were instilled with the belief that invading Tutsi soldiers would mutilate, kill, or even eat them alive (Berry and Berry 1999, p. 3). Once the genocide began, Radio Rwanda joined RTLM in broadcasting extremist propaganda in Kinyarwanda, describing the Tutsi as "the enemy" and the RPF as "revengeful Ugandans" (Klinghoffer 1998, p. 45). Hutu were encouraged to "finish the 1959 revolution" and to "gather in the harvest," "get to work," and "clean around their houses," all euphemisms for murder and killing. They were urged to "do their duty" and to "fill up the half-empty graves with Tutsis" (Berry and Berry 1999, p. 116; Chalk 1999; Schabas 1999). In an ironic and deadly twist, the Hamitic hypothesis was used to justify the killing of Tutsis by referring to them as outsiders and invaders who should be thrown in the river and returned to Egypt from whence they came. In this way, the Hutu extremists continued to reproduce the colonial essentialization of ethnicity (Taylor 1999, p. 57).

Government ministers also played a role in inciting the genocide in speeches and at public meetings. For example, the interim president Sindikubwabo called for the "killing" of accomplices in his hometown of Butare (Klinghoffer 1998, p. 45). Rwanda's only Tutsi prefect, the prefect of Butare, was then replaced by a northern Hutu, and the militia and presidential guard were brought in to begin the killings in the area.

Militiamen and the presidential guard were the main perpetrators, but soldiers of the Rwandan army (FAR) also participated in the killing along with the militia and ordinary Rwandans (Klinghoffer 1998, p. 44). The Interahamwe were joined by the Impuzamugambi to create a militia force of approximately 30,000. These young militiamen ran riot, setting up their own roadblocks, murdering in return for payment in the form of alcohol from businessmen, and targeting wealthy Tutsi for their houses, cattle, and other possessions. Ordinary Hutu also killed for economic gain and the desire to take land and property from the Tutsi who were perceived to be wealthier than the majority of Hutu. They were frequently forced to kill or be killed themselves. According to Human Rights Watch, Africa (1996, p. 14), "many ordinary citizens acted from fear, both fear of the Tutsi whom they had been taught were coming to kill them, and fear of other Hutu who threatened reprisals on any who did not join in the carnage."

Whole Tutsi families were killed in their homes, sometimes being forced to kill fellow family members before being killed themselves. Tutsi women were often raped and mutilated prior to being killed. Testimonies from survivors confirmed that rape was extremely widespread (Human Rights Watch, Africa 1996). Hutu husbands were forced to kill their Tutsi wives or be killed themselves. Roadblocks were set up by armed militiamen who killed anyone with a Tutsi identity card, and sometimes even those who looked Tutsi or had no identity card (African Rights 1995). In this way, those who tried to escape being killed at home faced almost certain death on the road. Those who did manage to escape took refuge in churches and missions. These places had previously been considered safe havens, but this was not to be the case in Rwanda in 1994. Gourevitch (1998) claims that many priests participated in the killings or did not do anything to protect the people, although some Hutu priests did provide safe hiding places for Tutsi. According to Prunier (1995, p. 250), although ordinary Christians performed some "admirable acts of courage ... the church hierarchies were at best useless and at worst accomplices in the genocide." At the same time, many priests, nuns, and other religious officials were killed during the genocide (African Rights 1995).

Organized groups of armed militia came and massacred Tutsis taking refuge in public places, including churches, missions, the stadium in Kigali, hotels, hospitals, and the UNAMIR compound after the UN force had departed (African Rights 1995). Those who were not killed in the massacres lay still among the dead bodies until they were able to crawl out to the hills to hide (Des Forges 1999, p. 217). In many instances, the Tutsi formed organized groups of resistance, the most well-known being the case of Bisesero, "a mountainous ridge in Kibuye, where Tutsi stood off militia and military from April 8 until July 1" (Des Forges 1999, pp. 217–218).

Some Tutsis were unaccountably saved by former friends or colleagues or other officials at roadblocks, through bribery or other means (Staub and Pearlman 2001, pp. 201–2). For example, Ndamyumugabe (2000, pp. 83–5) recounts how he paid 1000 Frw to a militiaman with a machete and was allowed to go on his way down the road, and on another occasion was able to pass through a roadblock by acting confident and greeting them in a way that seemed to confuse them. Many Tutsi survived because they were protected by Hutu neighbors, but others were not so lucky if they were found by the militia. In one case, as related by Sibomana (1999, p. 104): a Hutu peasant managed to hide and feed a Tutsi family for several weeks, but when the militia came they ordered him to kill the family he had hidden or they would kill his wife and family. So, the man killed the family he had been hiding, but the militia still killed the man's family as punishment.

It has been argued that a Rwandan tendency to conformity and unquestioning obedience to authority, reinforced by both the German and Belgian colonial administrations, contributed to the effectiveness of the genocide (Prunier 1995, p. 245, Gourevitch 1998, p. 23). This enabling factor has been emphasized by some but downplayed by others. Sibomana (1999, p. 31), for example, suggested that the unbelievable "power of submission of Rwandan peasants" could be attributed to the fact that "the vast majority of the illiterate peasants who live in the countryside live under the moral guidance of chiefs." This view is supported by observations of the role of radio as a medium to spread messages of hatred and fear, and instructions to kill the Tutsis. According to Berry & Berry (1999, p. 116), the use of radio was significant "in preparing and orchestrating the genocide" among the masses of "illiterate peasants [who tend] to believe that anything said on the radio is the truth" (Berry and Berry 1999, p. 116). For example, a captured *Interahamwe* killer interviewed by Berkeley (1998, p. 26) said that he believed the army radio broadcasts that told him "you must kill or you will be killed" and that "the RPF was Tutsi and if it wins the war all the Hutus will be killed."

However, anthropological and other studies of the genocide which include interviews with those who participated in the killing have revealed that they did so for a multitude of reasons, often unconnected with the political propaganda inciting hatred and/or fear of the Tutsi invader (Fujii 2009). Researchers have found, for example, that Hutu in local communities were more likely to be responding to pressure and fears of reprisal from fellow Hutus and were unaware of the Hamitic hypothesis as justification for killing their neighbors (Straus 2006). Others such as Uvin (1998) have focused on the ongoing impact of economic and social inequalities exacerbated by the inadequacies of development aid policies that led so many ordinary local Hutus to participate in the violence. Smith (1998) attributes the intensity of the genocidal killing to a combination of such structural factors (poverty, class inequities, the coffee crisis and IMF pressure), fuelled by psychocultural factors including propaganda, sexual projectivity, aspects of traditional religion, and authoritarianism.

Fujii (2009) shows how such factors were distributed unevenly across the country, with Hutus in the north being driven more by fear associated with the civil war and advancing RPF based on lived local experience more than by propaganda (p 184). In other areas, fear was more strongly associated with local Hutus with power who responded violently to resistance or refusal to follow orders (p 184). As mentioned above, Tutsis were often hidden and saved by Hutus, so they needed to distinguish between Hutus they feared and those they could trust (p 184). Fujii (2009, pp. 185–6) therefore concludes from her ethnographic study that the genocide was driven more by local factors of power and influence than by fears and hatreds of the Tutsi as a group. Her research documents the role of local group dynamics in creating a performance of ethnic claims over who was to be killed and who was not, made possible by the flexibility of stereotypes to satisfy the needs and goals of local leaders, rather than being based on ethnicity as such (Fujii 2009, pp. 121–5). These group dynamics played a role in constructing a new social identity for those who participated in the killing, Fujii (2009, p. 186) argues, such that "performing violence reconstitutes the identities of the performers" and ethnicity becomes an outcome as well as a precondition for violence (p 188).

The ongoing civil war and culture of violence, along with the strong administrative authority and local group dynamics, thus enabled the violence to flourish with some semblance of legitimacy. Within 100 days, thousands of Tutsi women were raped and an estimated 1 million people were killed – that is, 10,000 people per day or approximately 400 per hour or one person every 10 s. While some massacres were achieved with the assistance of guns, most of the killing was done individually using machetes and clubs with nails. This rate of killing could only be achieved with the complicity of a large percentage of the general population. As in Nazi Germany, bystanders (including the international community) played a part in enabling the genocide to proceed so rapidly and successfully, with the United Nations reducing its peacekeeping force and failing to recognize the genocide for what it was or send in forces to protect civilians until it was too late.

After 3 months of intense violence, the RPF won a military victory and installed a new Tutsi-led government in July 1994. During their advance toward Kigali, the RPF were also guilty of killing civilians, including the massacre of Hutu civilians in Gitarama prefecture on 19 June and the assassination of the Catholic Archbishop of Kigali on 3 June (Klinghoffer 1998, p. 46; African Rights 1995). In May 1995, the largest documented RPF revenge killing took place at the overcrowded internally displaced persons (IDP) camp at Kibeho, with the slaughter of an estimated 2000–4000 Hutus including many *génocidaires* as well as innocent Hutus who were seeking refuge from the Tutsi army (Schofield 1996, p. 155; Gourevitch 1998, pp. 188–194). According to Lemarchand (n.d.), there is "little question that many such killings stemmed from a sense of uncontrolled rage by Tutsi troops, many of whom had lost members of their family during the genocide."

As the RPF advanced into Rwanda in response to the genocide and ceasefire breakdown, two million, mostly, Hutu refugees (including the genocide perpetrators) fled to the neighboring Congo (former Zaire) and Tanzania regions, creating a massive humanitarian emergency that finally attracted some assistance from the international community. Operation Support Hope was deployed by the US in July 1994 to provide food and medical services to the refugees suffering from hunger and disease. "Seemingly oblivious to the genocide that preceded and caused the refugee crisis, President Clinton called Goma [a town near the northwest border of Rwanda] 'the worst humanitarian crisis in a generation'" (Ronayne 2001, p. 183). This rapid and extensive humanitarian response saved lives, but at the same time it served to strengthen the domination of the refugee camps by the Hutu extremists. For example, it was reported that the *Interahamwe* in the camps regarded it as a "sort of ethnic public service" to impregnate as many women as possible in order to breed more Hutus (Gourevitch 1998, p. 269). The humanitarian agencies focused on feeding people and saving lives, rather than thinking about the political implications (Gourevitch 1998, p. 268). The possibility of disarming the militia was never really addressed (Prunier 1999, p. 299). As the Hutu extremists were able to survive and consolidate their power, the stage was set for the continuing violence and insecurity experienced in the northwest of Rwanda, and over the border in the DRC, in the period following the genocide (Destexhe 1995, p. 58; Ronayne 2001, p. 182).

Post-Genocide Rwanda and the Elimination of Ethnic Identity

Most of the 1994 Hutu refugees who stayed in Africa were repatriated and after 30 years of exile, more than 750,000 Tutsi refugees returned to their home country following the RPF victory, "nearly a one-to-one replacement of the dead" (Gourevitch 1998, p. 230). According to Gourevitch (1998, p. 232), in 1996 more than 70% of the population in the major towns of Kigali and Butare and in some rural areas of eastern Rwanda were said to be newcomers. The percentage of Tutsi in the urban areas had risen to 40%, with an estimated 90% of the residents of Kigali being Tutsi (Middleton 1997). As a result, many of those who stayed, both Hutu and Tutsi, felt displaced from their homes and expressed resentment of the newcomers taking the jobs and business opportunities:

> We survivors find it very difficult to integrate into the present society and – I hate to say it – into the government, too. They have their own style from outside, and they don't have much trust in us either. When they came they took the country as in a conquest. They thought it was theirs to look after. They said of us Tutsis who were here, 'The smart ones are dead and those who survived are traumatized.' ... 'If they killed everyone and you survived, maybe you collaborated.' (Tutsi survivor quoted in Gourevitch 1998, p. 233)

As described by Carr (1999, p. 220), one of the few foreign residents who returned to Rwanda after the genocide: "the once fertile potato fields of the Hutu are now pastures for the long-horned cattle of the Tutsi." According to Gourevitch (1998,

p. 234), there was also discontent within the Tutsi returnee population as they discovered the differences that had developed among them as a result of their long periods of exile in Uganda or Burundi, Zaire or Belgium, or elsewhere. English was added as a third official language in Rwanda, along with French and Kinyarwanda, reflecting the influx of returnees from English-speaking Uganda and Tanzania who now dominated the political elite.

In the aftermath of the 1994 genocide and civil war, the divisions of Hutu and Tutsi had thus been broken into an intricate array of further categories and subcategories of Rwandans, including Tutsi survivors and returnees; those who spoke English or French, and even some who no longer speak Kinyarwanda; old case (1959–1973) and new case (1990–1994) refugees; RPF, non-RPF, and anti-RPF Tutsis; current or former urban and rural Tutsis; Hutu survivors with good records and suspect Hutus; former militia extremists and refugees; Hutus who worked with the RPF, anti-Hutu Power and anti-RPF Hutus; Hutus from the north and Hutus from the south; rich and poor; and Catholics, Protestants, Muslims, and animists. There was a "significant cultural and attitudinal" distinction between "old case" Tutsi refugees who had returned from Zaire and Burundi (Francophones) and from Uganda and Tanzania (Anglophones) (Middleton 1997, p. 13). Overall, the Tutsi survivors felt marginalized by the returnees, and the Hutu felt the most marginalized as well as stigmatized by the label of being a *génocidaire*. The voices and experiences of the Twa, meanwhile, remained completely marginalized.

The new Rwandan government emphasized the significance of the genocide as the defining event for categorizing the Rwandan population into five categories: returnees, refugees, victims, survivors, and perpetrators (Mamdani 2001, p. 266). The official application of this system, that recognized only Tutsi as survivors of the genocide, greatly oversimplified the lived experience realities of the many Rwandans who now made up the population. By excluding Hutu from the category of survivor, the Rwandan government was implying that all Hutu were perpetrators, either as active participants or passive onlookers (Mamdani 2001, p. 267). Those with mixed parentage or other complex political identities, meanwhile, found themselves missing from the official narrative, and sometimes persecuted for their alleged association with the genocide perpetrators despite having seen their Tutsi relatives killed (Hintjens 2008). This categorization was therefore not helping to heal the ethnic divisions in Rwandan society, even though it was designed to support the elimination of ethnic identity as a defining feature of Rwandan social and political life.

The policy of the new Government of National Unity (GNU) has been one of inclusiveness, to the point where ethnic categories are no longer officially recognized. The crime of divisionism was added to the Rwandan penal code in order to enforce the government's determination that the terms Tutsi, Hutu, and Twa would no longer be used (Lemarchand 2008, p. 66). Rwandan identity has therefore been redefined and the old Hutu-Tutsi ideology associated with the colonial policy of divide-and-rule that "sowed the seeds of hate that culminated in genocide," has been rejected in favor of "building a shared sense of 'Rwandaness'" (Ndangiza 2006). As described by the public affairs officer of the RPA during a conference in Kigali in

January 1995, the goal was to dispel the distorted myth of Rwandan history brought by the colonizers and "to forge unity and to focus on the common values that we have shared for 500 years" (Berry and Berry 1999, pp. 58–64). Building on commonalities of history, language, geography, religion, and culture, the post-genocide government of President Paul Kagame has instituted policies and programs to eliminate ethnicity by promulgating a new myth, emphasizing the common ancestry of all Rwandans and promoting unity through national rather than ethnic solidarity.

After an initial focus on revenge and retributive justice for the crimes of the genocide (as further discussed below), the GNU recognized the need to focus on reconciliation as well as unity in order to build a sustainable future for the country. The National Unity and Reconciliation Commission (NURC) was subsequently created in March 1999, in line with the original terms of the Arusha Peace Agreement, with a mandate to "promote unity, reconciliation, and social cohesion among Rwandans and build a country in which everyone has equal rights and contributing to good governance." The NURC has focused on civic education including running the *Ingando* solidarity camps to educate students, returnees, ex-prisoners, and other community groups in the history of Rwanda and the lessons of unity and reconciliation (Mgbako 2005). According to the NURC (2009, p. 11), more than 90,000 Rwandans had participated in *Ingando* peace education camps in the first 15 years, resulting in an "increased trust and cooperation among the citizens" and more than 200 Student' Clubs of Unity and Reconciliation (SCUR) in universities and secondary schools which are "combating genocide ideology among youth." The NURC also conducts national summits, community consultations, training seminars, and research works, in addition to coordinating community-based programs with an emphasis on cultural renewal and celebration through social and cultural expressions of Rwandan identity such as drumming, dance, art, and theatre (NURC 2009).

The Rwandan "Law Relating to the Punishment of the Crime of Genocide Ideology" was passed in 2008 as an additional means of promoting unity and outlawing divisionism. While not specifically proscribing reference to ethnic identity, Nigel Eltringham (2011, p. 274) argues that research "demonstrates that Rwandans interpret these laws as mostly requiring public silence regarding ethnicity." Yet as Eltringham (2011) and a number of other scholars have observed, Rwandans still think and identify privately in ethnic terms, their memories of the past are constructed along ethnic lines (Lemarchand 2008), and ethnic cleavages continue to exist below the surface (Buckley-Zistel 2008). Eltringham (2011, pp. 277–8) found that the Rwandans he interviewed drew on ethnicity "to find guidance on who they should trust and with whom they should reconcile in the present," and he therefore concluded that "ethnicity has to be present as an index by which coexistence can be envisaged and evaluated." From a psychosocial perspective, in order to be transcended, ethnic memories and identities may need to be recognized and addressed in order to be transformed rather than suppressed.

The government-mandated public silence on ethnicity applies also to the expressions of ethnic memory, as pointed out by Lemarchand (2008, p. 72), except, paradoxically, in the official terminology introduced by the government in 2006 to refer to the genocide as the *jenoside yakorewe Abatutsi*, meaning "genocide against the Tutsi." The GNU has also required all Rwandans to participate in national commemoration activities each year to remember the genocide, which serves to further reinforce the focus on Tutsi as victims. Consequently, only Tutsi memory is being commemorated in post-genocide Rwanda, but Hutu and Twa have also been victimized and suffered from human rights violations and mass killings (Burnet 2009). As argued by Buckley-Zistel (2008, pp. 133–4), "different groups in Rwanda have different views on the past' and 'different attitude(s) to remembering." For Pottier (2002, p. 126), the distinction that only Tutsi can be victims of the genocide while Hutus are victims of politicide and massacres implies a moral hierarchy that reinforces ethnic divisions despite the official discourse of "we are all Rwandans." While the annual commemoration events seem to combine opportunities for mourning and honoring within a language of unity and reconciliation, by remembering only Tutsi victims of the genocide, it is not surprising that large sections of the Rwandan population have felt alienated from these commemoration events (Longman and Rutagengwa 2004). As Lemarchand (2008, p. 72) argues "the selectivity of public memories helps nurture ethnic enmities."

The Kigali Genocide Memorial located in Gisozi, and other national memorial sites throughout Rwanda, have similarly served to reinforce oppositional ethnic identities in Rwanda. All of these memorials remember the victims of the genocide against the Tutsi; there are no memorial sites which commemorate the victims of RPF massacres (Longman and Rutagengwa 2004, p. 167). The displays at Gisozi highlight the horrors of the genocide, and while stopping short of blaming one ethnic group for the killings, they implicitly focus on the Tutsi ethnic group as the victims. This emphasis is entirely appropriate, but may not be conducive to creating a single Rwandan identity while other memories of loss are excluded. The Murambi Genocide Memorial in southern Rwanda provides an example of how Rwandans are allowing some alternative memories to be included in the official discourse: Hutu are not only perpetrators, they are also "saviors." However, the acknowledgement of Hutu and Twa as victims and Tutsi as perpetrators could provide a more complete account of the past that acknowledges multiple memories and supports a more inclusive approach to national unity and reconciliation.

The Rwandan government has thus determined that how the country's history is understood and portrayed is a critical part of its policy to eradicate the divisions of the past and create a unified nation. The GNU's policies and programs have succeeded in transforming the devastated and divided nation into a politically stable country with a productive economy and a peace that has so far lasted 25 years. However, memory, linked with personal and national agendas about how history is perceived and communicated, can often become a controversial and contested terrain (Hamber et al. 2010, p. 398). The promotion of a nationally unified historical memory has been seen as exclusive, antagonistic, controversial, and contested, while at the same time repeating the historical pattern of "giving ideological legitimacy to the consolidation of Tutsi power" (Lemarchand 2008, p. 72). And state-mandated commemoration events and sites of memory which focus on remembering only Tutsi as victims have failed to acknowledge complexity and plural narratives, hence reinforcing divisions rather than promoting unity and reconciliation. By mandating the elimination of ethnic identity in public discourse while simultaneously denying and reinforcing shared memories associated with each ethnic group, the Rwandan government is creating the possibility that ethnicity maintains its latent power as a potential driver of identity-based violence.

The Rwandan government's policy of achieving justice for the victims of the genocide has also been seen as divisive as thousands of prisoners, mostly Hutus, were held in terrible jail conditions and faced unfair trials and possible execution. According to some estimates, up to 25% of those who were in jail were innocent. From the Rwandan government's perspective, the detention and trial of perpetrators of the genocide was an important step toward ending the culture of impunity prevailing in Rwanda. It passed the Organic Law No. 08/96 of 30 August 1996 which enabled the prosecution in domestic courts of those accused of perpetrating the genocide. The first 22 of those accused of genocide and sentenced to death by the Rwandan courts were executed by public firing squad in May 1998 (IRIN 27 September 2001). Tutsi genocide survivors and returnees interviewed in Kigali in July 1998 indicated that the executions had brought hope that the *génocidaires* would be punished if found guilty (Lambourne 2002). In addition, according to Reyntjens (1997), "many Hutus realise that the prosecution and conviction of those responsible for the 1994 genocide is the only way to rid themselves of collective guilt."

There were, however, huge logistical problems involved in the domestic prosecution of all those accused of committing crimes during the genocide. Rwanda's jails were overflowing with up to 130,000 detainees of whom about 2100 would have been subject to the death penalty if tried and found guilty (the Rwandan government later repealed the death penalty in line with international norms and standards). Some 95% of Rwanda's lawyers and judges were either killed or in exile or in prison, making it very difficult for the criminal justice system to cope. As of September 2001, more than 2500 of the accused had been tried and more than 300 sentenced to death in Rwanda. Still some 115,000 remained in overcrowded jail conditions throughout the country and it was estimated that it would take more than 100 years to try all those accused. In order to speed up trials and sentencing, as well as for revealing the truth about the genocide and fostering reconciliation, the Rwandan government decided to revive the traditional community justice system of *gacaca* in a modern form adapted to deal with the crimes of the genocide.

As with traditional gacaca, the modern form of gacaca also involved hearings held "on the grass" in local communities with the intention that all members of the community would be present and able to have their say without the intervention of legal representatives (Reyntjens and Vandeginste 2005). The judges – *Inyangamugayo* or people of integrity – were elected by the local community in a manner intended to reproduce the respect traditionally given to the elders. The equal participation of men and women was actively promoted, unlike the traditional gacaca which reinforced the social hierarchies of traditional Rwandan society by excluding women as well as young people from participating, except if they were directly involved in the dispute (Mattioli 2000–2001, p. 30). A Compensation Fund for Victims of the Genocide was established in 1999 to be used in conjunction with the gacaca as a vehicle for awarding damages to victims (Rambouts 2004).

As explained by Reyntjens and Vandeginste (2005, p. 119), traditional gacaca relied on a sense of community that engendered "common values, norms of reciprocity, mutual trust, and confidence." This social capital was destroyed by the genocide both geographically and psychologically (Uvin undated, p. 8). Returning refugees and released prisoners often did not return to the communities where they originally lived, while the "old case" refugees from 1959 returned having lived much or all of their lives outside Rwanda. This meant that the local community base for reintegration and reconciliation was not present in many communities, and especially in Kigali where the proportion of returnees was relatively high. The typical interdependence of rural communities was still evident, but rather than encouraging authentic reconciliation, gacaca seemed to be resulting in no reconciliation at worst or pragmatic reconciliation at best (Lambourne 2010). A psychological and social barrier to the success of gacaca was also created by the polarization of experiences during the genocide that correlated with ethnic identity. Feelings of anger, hurt, and fear resulting directly from the genocide could not be so easily eliminated (Lambourne 2010). For example, survivors living in Byumba said they were afraid because former *génocidaires* living in the community – including released prisoners – would still voice extremist ideas and insults, threatening the survivors that they would "finish the job" (Lambourne 2010).

A divisive factor inherent in the modern gacaca was that even though the gacaca courts operated under the Organic Law which covers crimes associated with the genocide and civil war (1990–1994), only Hutus (the perpetrators of the genocide) were able to be accused and tried in the gacaca courts. Those who lost loved ones in the civil war or massacres perpetrated by the RPF therefore could not seek justice through gacaca. The promotion of reconciliation and eradication of a culture of impunity were further limited by the temporal restrictions of the gacaca which made it impossible to address the accusations of human rights violations perpetrated by the RPA in neighboring DRC in 1996 (Pottier 2002). The resulting perception of victor's justice undermined the legitimacy of gacaca for the Hutu majority and the psychological openness toward reconciliation of those who were denied justice through the gacaca courts (Zorbas 2004).

The perception of victor's justice and the perpetuation of ethnic division were reinforced by the official designation that only Tutsis could be survivors in postgenocide Rwanda and only Hutus could be perpetrators. As discussed earlier and outlined by Burnet (2009, p. 89), while ethnic identities were removed from the official discourse, they were replaced by terms that were essentially synonymous with the two main ethnic groups and subject to differential treatment. The term survivor was used exclusively to describe Tutsi who survived the genocide, and only Tutsi survivors could claim financial support from the Fund for the Survivors of the Genocide (FARG). Hutu widows and others who lost family, Hutu women who were raped, or Hutu who were targeted but survived were not regarded as victims for the purposes of assistance or recognition of their losses or special needs arising from being a survivor (Tiemessen 2004). Conversely, as indicated above, only Hutu could be perpetrators, accused and tried in the gacaca courts. By denying the status of Hutus as victims or survivors, and Tutsi as perpetrators, what has been officially acknowledged and remembered is only part of the truth and works against the potential for reconciliation.

Jealousy and resentment of the other ethnic group based on perceived socioeconomic injustice because of the delays in implementing the victims' compensation fund, insufficient funding from FARG, and perceptions of limited assistance for those who were not identified as survivors or victims has also undermined the potential for reconciliation (Lambourne 2010). According to Mamdani (2001, p. 282), the continuing fusion of ethnic and political identity where the majority of Hutu population is politically and economically marginalized by the minority Tutsi-led government is not encouraging authentic reconciliation and may be creating a "simmering volcano" just waiting to erupt again (Mamdani 2001, p. 282). On the surface the language of unity – "we are all Rwandans" – seems neutral, but in practice it may be masking and perpetuating a deep ethnic cleavage (Mamdani 2001). Buckley-Zistel (2008, pp. 140–1) similarly reported on "deep fissures that continue to run through local communities."

Despite these criticisms and challenges, there is evidence to support President Kagame's conclusion at the gacaca closing ceremony in 2012 that gacaca had been successful in its mission to promote reconciliation amongst Rwandans. The NURC (2009) reported stories of survivors who had forgiven and reconciled with perpetrators as a result of gacaca, and where Hutu and Tutsi were living together and helping each other as friends and neighbors. These interethnic relationships were strengthening communities and building resilience through unity and reconciliation, according to the NURC (2009). Breed (2014, p. 98) reported that even though Rwandans acknowledged the risk of required performances of contrition as part of gacaca being insincere and undermining reconciliation, on the other hand the performance of reconciliation in itself, repeated at the weekly gacaca hearings, could contribute to healing communities (just as the performance of killing reinforced participation according to Fujii 2009). Clark (2010) concluded from his extensive field research that in some communities gacaca had promoted profound relationship transformation that contributed to reconciliation and social cohesion.

On the other hand, Clark (2010) reported that in some communities gacaca had stirred up tensions and resulted in retraumatization, while Purdekova (2015, p. 119) indicated there was evidence of an increase in distrust and suspicion resulting from participation in gacaca. The national service of Gacaca courts report (2012, p. 42) produced for the closing of gacaca acknowledged the factors contributing to a lack of social trust and the challenge of "strong trauma manifested during Gacaca court proceedings." The factors relating to gacaca that both undermined and indicated a lack of social trust included accusations of genocide crimes directed at the community-elected judges; violence perpetrated against genocide survivors, witnesses, and judges; lack of full truth being told by the accused; collusion of witnesses against survivors; and exclusion of RPF crimes from the process (National Service of Gacaca Courts 2012).

Thus, while annual commemoration events have reinforced a memory of one group (the Tutsi) being victimized by the other (the Hutu), the imprisonment of accused *génocidaires* and the conduct of *gacaca* community justice processes have seen one group (the Hutu) punished for crimes against the other (the Tutsi). What amounts to an official denial of ethnic difference has therefore been contradicted by a number of government policies in practice, including the application of a genocide framework for categorizing the population politically, the way the past is remembered, and how justice has been administered through *gacaca*, along with the lived reality of Hutu, Tutsi, and Twa in post-genocide Rwanda (Pottier 2002).

The stated aim of the government was to promote peaceful coexistence, but it seems that ethnic discrimination is still alive and well in practice, raising fears of a return to greater ethnic violence again in the future. The Tutsis took effective control and occupied most of the key positions in the country, adding to the alienation and resentment felt by the Hutu population (Prunier 1997). In the first 5 years of the Kagame government, a number of Hutu members of the government resigned and fled the country including one who was assassinated in Nairobi, while others remained but were progressively marginalized (Vandeginste 2001, p. 228). Some Tutsi members of the government also fled the country after criticizing government policy for failing to match its performance with its rhetoric in relation to inclusiveness and nondiscrimination. More specifically, the RPF-Tutsi in power were said to discriminate against other Tutsis because they did not fully trust them, wondering how they survived the genocide. As a result of the Hutu resignations, the Rwandan government became less representative of both ethnic groups, and the completion of the political transition process to a genuine power-sharing between Hutu and Tutsi, as mandated by the Arusha peace agreement, has remained an unfulfilled promise.

Conclusion

This chapter has shown how at each stage of Rwandan history, from precolonial to post-genocide, group identities have been constructed, reconstructed, and deconstructed for strategic and pragmatic purposes. Ethnic conflict and violence are therefore not seen as the inevitable outcome, but rather as a constituted result of the construction of identity around group differences equated with access to socioeconomic resources and political power. These politically constructed identities and their relationship to ethnicity thus need to be understood as historically situated as well as geographically located, before embarking on an analysis of their contemporary implications.

In the precolonial kingdoms of Rwanda, the two categories of Hutu and Tutsi were defined primarily in social and economic terms, without the immutable elements and distinctive characteristics normally associated with ethnic groups. A shared language and geography were offset against different occupational groupings and some differences in religious and cultural traditions. Cohabitation, intermarriage, and cultural exchange over centuries had created, what Mamdani (2001, p. 74) claims was, a single cultural community with Hutu and Tutsi constructed as political identities by the newly emerging state of Rwanda which brought together the scattered kingdoms and populations of Hutu and Tutsi across the country. There have always been poor, nonelite Tutsi, according to Mamdani (2001, p. 74), as well as Hutu chiefs and officials with social status, so even the precolonial groupings cannot be defined in purely socioeconomic terms. It was the social mobility and definition of Tutsi as a political construct associated with power which ensured that the groups did not take on the character of essentialist ethnic categories.

Toward the latter stages of the nineteenth century, however, the symbiotic relationship of the Tutsi herders and Hutu farmers began to take on a more exploitative form, as the Tutsi clan leaders took advantage of their more powerful position to extract menial labor from the less powerful Hutu farmers. The roots of interethnic conflict and violence were thus laid down during the precolonial era, and most especially during the Nyiginya kingdom when Hutus began to rise up against their Tutsi overlords. However, this conflict was not based on Hutus seeing themselves as an ethnic group nor on racial hatred toward the Tutsi as a group, according to Vansina (2004, pp. 138–9). But rather, it was the result of the Tutsi elite manufacturing discontent based on discrimination in order to consolidate their power, a precursor to the "divide and rule" policies later used by the colonial powers (Fujii 2009, p. 45).

The group identities of Hutu, Tutsi, and Twa were constructed as ethnic identities by the German and Belgian colonizers building on what they found and reinforcing the power and elite status of the Tutsi over the inferior Hutu and insignificant Twa. Racist ideologies from Europe were overlaid onto the existing precolonial power structure in Rwandan society, based on the Hamitic hypothesis and an identity card system that conclusively ended the fluidity of Hutu and Tutsi identity groups with eventual devastating consequences. The Tutsification of the customary system of rule and increasing discrimination against the Hutu as a group reinforced the relationship between power and ethnic identity, thus paving the way for the Hutu revolution against Tutsi rule associated with decolonization.

The independence struggle and postcolonial experiences of Rwandans reinforced the ethnic character of the two identity groups as they developed distinct historical memories of a common past as victims of discrimination and violence perpetrated by the "other" ethnic group, bolstered by a myth of common ancestry as Hutus and Tutsis respectively and a growing sense of solidarity within each group (Hutchinson and Smith 1996, p. 7). These factors of difference could thus be seen as outweighing the commonalities of language, geography, religion, and culture in reinforcing the ethnic character of the conflict that led to genocide. Further adding fuel to the interethnic fire were events in the region, including most particularly the assassination of the first Hutu president in neighboring Burundi in November 1993. However, it was the regional factors within Rwanda of political power struggles within the Tutsi elite prior to independence, and between the Hutu power factions post-independence, that were decisive in leading the country to pursue policies of ethnic discrimination and genocide.

The genocide itself was by definition an outpouring of violence and killing directed toward destroying the Tutsi ethnic group. However, as discussed, it was not that simple. The primary targets for assassination at the outset of the killing were those mostly Hutu seen as political enemies of the ruling Hutu clan from the northwestern region of Rwanda. Hutu were also killed during the genocide because they were identified as looking like or having some association with Tutsi, as a friend, relative, sympathizer, or protector – or simply being in the wrong place at the wrong time. Tutsi, by contrast, were often hidden or otherwise saved by Hutu, thus belying the essential ethnic character of the violence as being based on fear or hatred for the whole of the other group. Even at the height of the genocide, the identities of victims could thus be seen as social or political constructions rather than in purely ethnic or cultural terms.

Ambiguity and flexibility in relation to ethnic identity remained beneath the surface in postindependence Rwanda, as evidenced by Rwandans choosing to take "strategic action" to change their official ethnic identity by obtaining a new identity card (Fujii 2009, p. 115). The decision to change from Hutu to Tutsi, or Tutsi to Hutu, would be made for strategic reasons such as attaining privileges, avoiding discrimination, or escaping death. Keane (1995, p. 11), for example, claims that the leader of the *Interahamwe* militia, Robert Kajuga, was a Tutsi whose father had succeeded in changing the family's identity to Hutu. Fujii (2009, p. 118) argues that the choice made by many Rwandans to abandon their ethnic identity for strategic and pragmatic purposes indicates a lack of "deeply held, affective attachment" to ethnicity.

Despite this analysis of the essentially political and socioeconomic nature of the root causes of the genocide, the impact of this devastating experience on reinforcing ethnic identities needs to be understood with its deep and far-reaching psychological and sociocultural as well as political consequences. For the Hutu group now branded as perpetrators, and the Tutsi group as victims, intermarriage now became unthinkable, living together an incomprehensible and painful prospect, and in the words of one Tutsi survivor "the death penalty is not enough" to provide justice for what happened (Lambourne 2002). As Lemarchand (2009, p. 70) observes, "the horrors of genocide profoundly alter the image that one has of the other" that creates immense challenges for reconstruction and peacebuilding.

Following an initial period of revenge killings and retributive justice, the new Rwandan government embarked on a remarkable sociocultural and political journey: to eliminate Hutu and Tutsi identities and replace them with a new Rwandan national identity that would enable perpetrators, survivors, and returnees to live together in unity and reconciliation despite the newly laid down historical memories of interethnic violence, pain, and loss. This policy of national unity and reconciliation has been accompanied by aggressive programs of socioeconomic development designed to eliminate the root causes of interethnic violence and provide a stable and attractive environment for foreign investors. Only time will tell if these programs and policies of national development and community healing and reconciliation will be sufficient to quell the potential for future political or socioeconomic crises to again feed the seeds of discontent along ethnic lines in Rwanda.

Cross-References

▶ Historical Memory and Ethnic Myths
▶ The Threat of Genocide: Understanding and Preventing the "Crime of Crimes"

References

African Rights (1995) Rwanda: Death, Despair and Defiance, rev. edn. African Rights, London
Berkeley B (1998) Genocide, the Pursuit of Justice and the Future of Africa. *The Washington Post Magazine*, 11 October 1998, pp 10–29
Berry K (2001) Rwanda and the United Nations: A Case of Active Indifference. *IT Network* (International Network on Holocaust and Genocide & the *Newsletter* of the Australian Institute for Holocaust and Genocide Studies), 14(2–3): 10–20
Berry JA, Berry CP (eds) (1999) Genocide in Rwanda: A Collective Memory. Howard University Press, Washington, DC
Breed A (2014) Performing the Nation: Genocide, Justice, Reconciliation. Seagull Books, London
Buckley-Zistel S (2008) We are Pretending Peace: Local Memory and the Absence of Social Transformation and Reconciliation in Rwanda. In: Clark P, Kaufman ZD (eds) After Genocide: Transitional Justice, Post-Conflict Reconstruction and Reconciliation in Rwanda and Beyond. Hurst & Company, London, pp 125–143
Burnet JE (2009) Whose Genocide? Whose Truth? In: Hinton AL, O'Neill KL (eds) Genocide: Truth, Memory, and Representation. Duke University Press, Durham/London, pp 80–110
Callamard A (1999) French Policy in Rwanda. In: Adelman H, Suhrke A (eds) The Path of a Genocide: The Rwanda Crisis from Uganda to Zaire. Transaction Publishers, New Brunswick, NJ, pp 157–183
Carr RH with Halsey AH (1999) *Land of a Thousand Hills: My Life in Rwanda*. Viking Penguin, New York
Chalk F (1999) Hate Radio in Rwanda. In: Adelman H, Suhrke A (eds) The Path of a Genocide: The Rwanda Crisis from Uganda to Zaire. Transaction Publishers, New Brunswick, NJ, pp 93–107
Clark P (2010) The Gacaca Courts, Post-Genocide Justice and Reconciliation in Rwanda: Justice Without Lawyers. Cambridge University Press, Cambridge, UK
Dallaire R (2003) Shake Hands with the Devil: The Failure of Humanity in Rwanda. Random House, London
Des Forges A (1999) 'Leave None to Tell the Story': Genocide in Rwanda. Human Rights Watch, New York
Destexhe A (1995) Rwanda and Genocide in the Twentieth Century. Pluto Press, London
Dorn AW, Matloff J (2000) Preventing the Bloodbath: Could the UN Have Predicted and Prevented the Rwandan Genocide? Journal of Conflict Studies 20(1):9–52
Eltringham N (2011) The Past Is Elsewhere: The Paradoxes of Proscribing Ethnicity in Post-Genocide Rwanda. In: Straus S, Waldorf L (eds) Remaking Rwanda: State Building and Human Rights After Mass Violence. University of Wisconsin Press, Madison, Wisconsin, pp 266–282
Feil SR (1998) *Preventing Genocide: How the Early Use of Force Might Have Succeeded in Rwanda*. A Report to the Carnegie Commission on Preventing Deadly Conflict. Carnegie Corporation, New York
Fujii LA (2009) Killing Neighbors: Webs of Violence in Rwanda. Cornell University Press, Ithaca, NY
Gourevitch P (1998) We wish to inform you that tomorrow we will be killed with our families: Stories from Rwanda. Farrar, Strauss & Giroux, New York
Grimes S (1975) The Formation of Traditional States: An East African Case Study of the Role of Economy, Conquest and Trade. Master of Arts thesis, University of Sydney

Hamber B, Sevcenko L, Naidu E (2010) Utopian Dreams or Practical Possibilities? The Challenges of Evaluating the Impact of Memorialization in Societies in Transition. International Journal of Transitional Justice 4(3):397–420

Hintjens H (2008) Reconstructing Political Identities in Rwanda. In: Clark P, Kaufman ZD (eds) After Genocide: Transitional Justice, Post-Conflict Reconstruction and Reconciliation in Rwanda and Beyond. Hurst & Company, London, pp 77–99

Human Rights Watch/Africa (1996) Shattered Lives: Sexual Violence during the Rwandan Genocide and its Aftermath. Human Rights Watch, New York

Hutchinson J, Smith AD (1996) Ethnicity. Oxford University Press, Oxford

Jones BD (1999) The Arusha Peace Process. In: Adelman H, Suhrke A (eds) The Path of a Genocide: The Rwanda Crisis from Uganda to Zaire. Transaction Publishers, New Brunswick, NJ, pp 131–156

Kamukama D (1993) Rwanda Conflict: Its Roots and Regional Implications. Fountain Publishers, Kampala, Uganda

Keane F (1995) Season of Blood: A Rwandan Journey. Penguin, London

Klinghoffer AJ (1998) The International Dimension of Genocide in Rwanda. New York University Press, Washington Square, New York

Lambourne W (2002) *Justice and Reconciliation: Post-Conflict Peacebuilding in Cambodia and Rwanda*. PhD Thesis. University of Sydney

Lambourne W (2010) Transitional Justice After Mass Violence: Reconciling Retributive and Restorative Justice. In: Irving H, Mowbray J, Walton K (eds) Julius Stone: A Study in Influence. Federation Press, Sydney, pp 214–237

Lemarchand R (1970) Rwanda and Burundi. Pall Mall Press, London

Lemarchand R (2008) The Politics of Memory in Post-Genocide Rwanda. In: Clark P, Kaufman ZD (eds) After Genocide: Transitional Justice, Post-Conflict Reconstruction and Reconciliation in Rwanda and Beyond. Hurst & Company, London, pp 65–76

Lemarchand R (2009) The Dynamics of Violence in Central Africa. University of Pennsylvania Press, Philadelphia, Pennsylvania

Lemarchand R (n.d.) Genocide in Comparative Perspective: Rwanda, Cambodia and Bosnia', *Conflits Ethniques et Genocides*, http://www.iep.u-bordeaux.fr/iep/scolarite/lemarchand.htm (accessed 7 April 2000)

Longman T (2010) Christianity and Genocide in Rwanda. Cambridge University Press, New York

Longman T, Rutagengwa T (2004) Memory, identity, and community in Rwanda. In: Stover E, Weinstein HM (eds) My Neighbor, My Enemy: Justice and Community in the Aftermath of Mass Atrocity. Cambridge University Press, Cambridge, UK, pp 162–182

Mamdani M (2001) When Victims Become Killers: Colonialism, Nativism, and the Genocide in Rwanda. Princeton University Press, Princeton, NJ

Mattioli G (2000–2001) The Human Rights Debate about Non-Judicial Mechanisms of Accountability and Redress: The Case of the Proposed Gacaca Jurisdiction in Rwanda. European Master in Human Rights and Democratisation Thesis, Katholieke Universiteit Leuven

Mgbako C (2005) *Ingando* Solidarity Camps: Reconciliation and Political Indoctrination in Post-Genocide Rwanda. Harvard Human Rights Journal 18:201–224

Middleton J (1997) (ed) Encyclopedia of Africa South of the Sahara, Volume 4. Simon & Schuster Macmillan, New York

National Service of Gacaca Courts (2012) Summary of the Report Presented at the Closing of Gacaca Courts Activities, Kigali, Republic of Rwanda, June 2012

Ndamyumugabe P (2000) Rwanda: Beyond Wildest Imagination. Lesley Books, Berrien Springs, USA

Ndangiza F (2006) National Unity and Reconciliation Commission Report, Kigali

Newbury C (1988) The Cohesion of Oppression: Clientship and Ethnicity in Rwanda, 1860–1960. Columbia University Press, New York

Newbury D (2009) The Land beyond the Mists: Essays on Identity and Authority in Precolonial Congo and Rwanda. Ohio University Press, Athens, Ohio

Pottier J (2002) Re-Imagining Rwanda: Conflict, Survival and Disinformation in the Late Twentieth Century. Cambridge University Press, Cambridge, UK

Prunier G (1995) The Rwanda Crisis 1959-1994: History of a Genocide. Hurst & Company, London

Prunier G (1997) The Rwanda Crisis: History of a Genocide, 2nd edn. Columbia University Press New York

Prunier G (1999) Operation Turquoise: A Humanitarian Escape from a Political Dead End. In: Adelman H, Suhrke A (eds) The Path of a Genocide: The Rwanda Crisis from Uganda to Zaire. Transaction Publishers, New Brunswick, NJ, pp 281–305

Purdekova A (2015) Making Ubumwe: Power, State and Camps in Rwanda's Unity-Building Project. Berghahn Books, New York

Rambouts H (2004) Victim Organisations and the Politics of Reparation: a Case-Study on Rwanda. Intersentia, Antwerp/Oxford

Republic of Rwanda, National Unity and Reconciliation Commission (2009) *15 Years of Unity and Reconciliation Process in Rwanda: The Ground Covered To-Date*. Republic of Rwanda, Kigali, Rwanda

Reyntjens F (1997) Rwanda: 'The Planner of Apocalypse': The Case Against Bagosora. The Hague, 28 February 1997, reposted by Africa Policy Information Center, 7 March 1997

Reyntjens F, Vandeginste S (2005) Rwanda: An Atypical Transition. In: Skaar E, Gloppen S, Suhrke A (eds) Roads to Reconciliation. Lexington Books, Lanham, Maryland, pp 101–127

Ronayne P (2001) Never Again? The United States and Prevention and Punishment of Genocide since the Holocaust. Rowman & Littlefield, Lanham, Maryland

Schabas WA (1999) Hate Speech in Rwanda: The Road to Genocide. Paper presented to the international conference Hate, Genocide and Human Rights Fifty Years Later: What Have We Learned? What Must We Do?. McGill Law School, Montreal, Canada, 27 January 1999

Schofield J (1996) Silent Over Africa: Stories of War and Genocide. HarperCollins, New York

Sibomana A (1999) *Hope for Rwanda: Conversations with Laure Guilbert & Herve Deguine*, Translated and with a Postscript by Carina Tertsakian, Pluto Press, London

Smith DN (1998) The Psychocultural Roots of Genocide: Legitimacy and Crisis in Rwanda. Am Psychol 53(7)

Staub E, Pearlman LA (2001) Healing, Reconciliation, and Forgiving After Genocide and Other Collective Violence. In: Helmick RG, Petersen, RL (eds) Forgiveness and Reconciliation: Religion, Public Policy, and Conflict Transformation. Templeton Foundation Press, Radnor, PA, pp 195–217

Straus S (2006) The Order of Genocide: Race, Power, and War in Rwanda. Cornell University Press, Ithaca, NY

Taylor CT (1999) Sacrifice as Terror: The Rwandan Genocide of 1994. Berg, Oxford

Tiemessen AE (2004) After Arusha: Gacaca Justice in Post-Genocide Rwanda. African Studies Quarterly 8(1):57–76

United Nations (1996) *The United Nations and Rwanda 1993–1996*. Blue Book Series, Volume X. Department of Public Information, United Nations, New York

Uvin P (1998) Aiding Violence: The Development Enterprise in Rwanda. Kumarian Press, West Hartford, Connecticut

Uvin P (undated) The Introduction of a Modernized Gacaca for Judging Suspects of Participation in the Genocide and the Massacres of 1994 in Rwanda: A Discussion Paper. Prepared for the Belgian Secretary of State for Development Cooperation

Vandeginste S (2001) Rwanda: Dealing with Genocide and Crimes Against Humanity in the Context of Armed Conflict and Failed Political Transition. In: Biggar N (ed) Burying the Past: Making Peace and Doing Justice after Civil Conflict. Georgetown University Press, Washington, DC

Vansina J (2004) Antecedents to Modern Rwanda: The Nyiginya Kingdom. University of Wisconsin Press, Madison, Wisconsin

Watson C (1991) *Exile from Rwanda: Background to an Invasion*. Issue Paper. US Committee for Refugees, Washington, DC, February 1991

Zorbas E (2004) Reconciliation in Post-Genocide Rwanda. African Journal of Legal Studies 1(1)

Part IX

Ethnicity, Migration, and Labor

Part Introduction

This part casts new light on the emergence of ethnic alignments in the context of global labor migrations, colonialism, and refugee flows. The key concerns that underpin the research showcased here are ones canvassed in the classic ethnic studies works by anthropologists like Clyde Mitchell, A.L. ("Bill") Epstein, Fredrik Barth, and Abner Cohen. How can we best explain the creation of ethnic categorizations, boundaries, and identifications in particular circumstances? What is the relationship between ethnic configurations and labor migrancy, the introduction of capitalist systems of production, and state-building in colonial and postcolonial societies? The chapters that follow address these kinds of questions, raise others, and speak to powerful global histories of the plantation, imperial exploitation, and forced migration, as well as far more benign labor flows across international borders. And, at the vital center of these movements, we find ordinary people trying to shape their everyday lives as best they can in – sometimes dreadful – conditions that were not entirely of their own choosing.

The trans-Atlantic slave trade has rightly been the subject of an incisive and voluminous scholarship, but slavery also existed outside the Americas. In an exciting new work, Sadasivam Jaganada Reddi and Sheetal Sheena Sookrajowa survey the demography of the slave labor force on Mauritius, one of the Britain's most significant slave colonies, during the eighteenth and nineteenth centuries. Drawing on a range of source materials, they show that a shortage of women, inadequate food, poor health, natural disasters, and terrible social and economic conditions contributed to high mortality rates and a decline in the slave population across the French and British administrations. This pattern continued even after emancipation in 1839. The authors trace how the continuation of a slave workforce depended on the further importation of labor and demographic decline as a result of the legacies of the plantation economy also marked the post-Emancipation era. Brinsley Samaroo's chapter moves attention from the Indian Ocean world to its wider connections with the Atlantic and Pacific. He outlines the broader global history of slavery and indenture. The numbers are startling. He estimates that around 2.2 million men and women from China, India, Java, Madagascar, and Africa were contracted to work on tropical plantations around the world between 1837 and 1920. "Queen Sugar" and the pursuit of profit were central to this story and the human exploitation that it entailed. Like other contributors to this part, Samaroo speaks to on-going legacies: from music and dance to flora and fauna, and from syncretic forms of spirituality to foodways.

The theme of legacies in the context of colonial labor migration is further pursued in the context of Mauritius by Kathleen Harrington-Watt. She examines one aspect of the British indentured labor system on the island that followed the cessation of chattel slavery and led in this case to particular patterns of ethnicization. The emigration of Indian laborers under the contract system was a structured and selective process. These workers sailed from three principal ports – Calcutta, Madras, Bombay – and left particular villages in Eastern India, Bihar, Uttar Pradesh, the Madras Presidency, and Western India, with later flows from northern regions. Their arrival and settlement in large numbers had a major impact on local demography, economics, politics, and society, and the circumstances on the island led to the emergence of a particular ethnic configuration that differed from other plantation colonies like Trinidad and Guyana. A comparison here with Sherry-Anne Singh's chapter is instructive. She shifts our geographical focus to the Caribbean and to the experiences of the thousands of indentured laborers who made their way there from India between 1838 and 1920. As in the Mauritian case, this movement emanated from specific places and backgrounds with a predominance from the Bhojpuri belt. Singh teases out the roles played by caste, religion, and transposed traditions such as the *panchayat*, and documents contrasting outcomes in terms of ethnic formation across the region. Her work speaks to the "deep resonance" of these diasporic journeys and the need to attend to the varied shades and textures of ethnic organization over time and space.

The remaining chapters in this part bring us into the present day and contributors examine aspects of migrant labor mobility and refugee flows. Sheetal Sheena Sookrajowa and Antoine Pécoud set the scene for these case studies with their overview of the International Convention on the Protection of the Rights of All Migrant Workers and Members of their Families (ICMW) that was adopted by the United Nations in 1990 to protect the human rights of migrant workers and their families. Their research identifies a number of obstacles that stand in the way of ratification and effective implementation of the Convention globally. As a consequence, they suggest, the future of the ICMW is by no means certain. Yet its very existence highlights a crying need for "alternative political approaches to migration, grounded in multilateralism, cooperation, and human rights." In a different vein, Isabelle Bartkowiak-Théron and Nicole L. Asquith deal with vulnerability in relation to the "over-policing" of minorities globally. They identify comparable patterns of exclusion and domination in several contemporary contexts and see an antidote to current practices in the adoption of "critical diversity" by law enforcement agencies.

The protection of vulnerable people on the move is also the theme of the chapters that deal with refugees. Louise Humpage investigates the nature of refugee and settlement policies in New Zealand with a particular focus on the impact for the sector of its new labor-led government. Although there have been some very important shifts, she argues that political and economic considerations have dominated humanitarian motives in terms of refugee policy.In the immediate future, at least, New Zealand's response will be "driven by mixed agendas with discriminatory outcomes." Bruno Mendelski's study of the rhetoric employed by Hungarian Premier Victor Orban in the wake of Europe's recent refugee crisis suggests another outcome in a context where the immediacy of inflows and the need for action was substantially greater than in New Zealand. He argues that Orban constructed two "outsiders" who posed a twin threat to the nation's sovereignty and its sense of identity: a large wave of Muslim migrants and the stance of the EU's liberal-left elite. The immediate consequence has been the control and militarization of the Hungarian borders, a decisive move away from the integrationist dynamics of EU, and a more strident isolationist nationalist policy. The contrast with the incorporation of Muslims in Austria and Germany is striking. Although there have been well-documented tensions, Ryosuke Amiya-Nakada's chapter investigates differing institutional arrangements and historical legacies which have nonetheless pushed both nations toward convergence around shared ideals of "Liberal Multiculturalism."

The reception of Rohingya refugees in the aftermath of the recent Myanmar crisis is the subject of two chapters. In a provocative study, Sangit Kumar Ragi asks why there has been such polarization within India around the influx of these desperate Muslim newcomers. The answer, he suggests, can be found in the fears held by Hindus that their settlement would alter fragile "demographic equations" irrecoverably and threaten pluralistic and democratic values central to a predominantly Hindu India. His work further underlines the importance of context in shaping ethnoreligious alignments and the need to retain a sensitivity to the genuinely held concerns of host populations. This research is supplemented by Badrus Sholeh's chapter on Indonesia's policy toward Rohingya refugees in the Southeast Asian sea. He examines the nation-state's management of regional meetings, the question of regional agreements around the principle of noninterference, and government support for mediation in the Rakhine conflict and the democratization of Myanmar. As William Maley has observed, refugees are indeed "a symptom of a system of states that has failed properly to live up to its responsibilities" (2016, 12).

Two chapters deal with contrasting cases of modern labor mobility. Sam Scott notes that migration researchers have tended to ignore "ordinary" middle-class professional migrants, despite the fact that they are growing globally and now constitute a significant international flow. In a highly suggestive chapter, he identifies five key themes to guide future research: the relationship between migration, social mobility, place, and middle-class membership; the connections between age and decisions to move; the role played by lifestyle factors; the emergence of gendered household strategies; and social and cultural "emplacement" of middle-class migrants in everyday life. Remus Gabriel Anghel, Stefánia Toma, and László Fosztó, on the other hand, examine large-scale migratory flows of Romanian citizens across Europe. Theyemphasizea diversity of backgrounds and ethnoreligious identities among a migrant cohort that includes Roma, Romanian Germans, and Romanian

Hungarians. In an interesting move, they focus our attention on the role of informal networks that are based on ties of local identity, kinship, ethnicity, and religious belonging. Identity and ethnicity, they argue, are forms of social capital deployed by migrants during the migration process and their incorporation into host societies.

Lyndon Fraser

Policing Ethnic Minorities: Disentangling a Landscape of Conceptual and Practice Tensions

84

Isabelle Bartkowiak-Théron and Nicole L. Asquith

Contents

Introduction	1648
Definitions and Positioning	1648
Unraveling the Landscape	1650
Over-policing and Racial Profiling	1651
Institutional Racism	1656
Border Control: The Post 9/11 Context	1659
Community Policing and Procedural Policing: Do They Work?	1659
Training	1663
Recruitment and Retention of Ethnic Minorities into the Police Workforce	1663
Conclusion	1665
References	1666

Abstract

The policing of ethnic minorities has been a challenge for law enforcement agencies. After decades of research, inquiries into policing, policy-making, and attempts at changing practice, some progress has been made, but we are still far from an ideal picture of equity and procedural fairness. Conceptually, and in practice, issues of racial profiling, institutional racism, and over-policing still plague the everyday police business. The many innovative initiatives to increase trust and accountability, build confidence, and close gaps between ethnic minorities and police officers are commendable. However, they go but a small step into the right direction. Some further efforts are needed toward human rights policing and

I. Bartkowiak-Théron (✉)
Tasmanian Institute of Law Enforcement Studies, University of Tasmania, Hobart, TAS, Australia
e-mail: isabelle.bartkowiaktheron@utas.edu.au

N. L. Asquith
Western Sydney University, Kingswood, NSW, Australia
e-mail: n.asquith@westernsydney.edu.au

© The Author(s), under exclusive license to Springer Nature Singapore Pte Ltd. 2019
S. Ratuva (ed.), *The Palgrave Handbook of Ethnicity*,
https://doi.org/10.1007/978-981-13-2898-5_122

critical diversity in policy to make up for the enduring and entrenched tensions that are the legacy of past colonialist and, in some case, genocidal practices.

Keywords
Police · Policing · Ethnicity · Race · Racism · Minorities · Vulnerability

It must be recognised that racial discrimination, both direct and indirect, and harassment are endemic within our society, and the police service is no exception. (HMIC 1997, 2)

Introduction

Exploring the landscape of police interaction with ethnic minorities is like disentangling a complex web of issues where geopolitics meet issues of social identity, sociocultural understandings of difference, philosophical frameworks, and globalization. While newer generations of global citizens are more adroit at bringing these issues to the fore – largely by way of social media – the context of, and responses by, policing organizations appears, at first glance, to remain unchanged. The recent cases of Eric Gardner, Michael Brown, Dylan Voller, Julieka Dhu, or Laquan McDonald and the many others that have flooded the press and social media since 2010 have just replaced the imagery generated by the stories of Rodney King, Stephen Lawrence, Amadou Diallo, Abner Louima, TJ Hickey, or Patrick Dorismond in an earlier time.

The policing of minorities, especially visible ethnic minorities (i.e., individuals whose physical traits are different to the local majority and to the governing few), has been a subject of political, criminological, sociological, and cultural research for many years. Specifically, policing and criminological research has focused on the tense relationships between police and minorities and attempted to explain, occasionally help address, the abusive use of power by police and the "criminalization of race." Our discussion here is focused on the experiences of democratic policing services in the Global North. While some of our points reflect the situation in transitional societies, there is a dearth of research in this field in the Global South, where the ethnic minorities of the Global North are ethnic majorities. After positioning our approach, we consider various factors that have contributed to issues such as racial profiling and over-policing, institutional racism, border control, community policing, training, and the recruitment and retention of ethnic minority police officers. Each of these aspects of the relationship between policing and ethnic minority communities highlights that a single strategy will not answer problems that date back to colonization, slavery, and the formation of modern policing.

Definitions and Positioning

The expression "ethnic minorities" automatically evokes notions of race and physical difference (Carpenter and Ball 2012). Specifically, it suggests notions of race, skin color, and religion and is associated with issues of colonization, oppression, and, in some circumstances, the distressing histories of slavery and genocide (Holmes et al. 2015; Carpenter and Ball 2012). More recently, the larger and supposedly more politically correct notions of "culture" or "cultural or linguistic background" have been juxtaposed to issues of ethnicity, especially in countries where multiculturalist policies have attempted to write a better pathway for inclusive diversity and where images of "unity in diversity" have punctuated political discourses (Holmes et al. 2015, 91). In this chapter, "ethnic minorities" will be defined as communities who differ from the cultural norm; "racism" is defined as an "ideology based on the unfounded belief in the existence of different 'races' that involves locating social subgroups on a hierarchy" (Carpenter and Ball 2012; Holmes et al. 2015, 43).

The policing of minorities, ethnic or otherwise, has long been associated with the policing of migrants and, from a geopolitical point of view, the control of borders or colonies (de Koster and Reinke 2016). Embedded in maladroit and simplistic definitions of diversity, the policing of ethnicity is enshrined in discrimination and politics of exclusion which, despite attempts at remediating the situation, and due to a long-standing history of abuse and prejudice, have never been quite successful at fostering climates of inclusion and acceptance (Holmes et al. 2015).

Similarly, "policing" evokes images of brutal encounters with members of law enforcement organizations, often framed in paramilitary contexts. Images of shootings or vigorous management of urban protest fuel, rather justly, this imagery, and have stimulated a new debate about the relationships between what is seen as repressive law enforcement agencies and members of the community. Here, policing will be understood and defined as the broader range of services delivered by policing organizations, and not solely limited to "crime fighting," such as pure law enforcement, crime prevention, order maintenance, and peace-keeping. It will see policing as inclusive of the usually mundane activities performed by individual police officers (traffic or patrol duties, call and emergency response, or crowd control), as well as the more strategic operations conducted by officers, such as community liaison activities, problem-solving, and transnational or international cooperation. However, while policing is also defined as a range of services delivered by police organizations as well as other government, private, or third parties (such as private security, nongovernment specialist organizations, health agencies, etc.), we will limit our discussion to public police organizations and law enforcement personnel only (Fleming and Wakefield 2006).

Our discussion will be premised on the foundations of critical criminology discourse (Anthony and Cunneen 2008). As such, our argument will attempt to challenge some of the traditional understandings of policing and law enforcement, as much in concept as in practice, by putting them into perspective in the broader context of studies and scholarship in criminal justice, sociology, and criminology (Anthony and Cunneen 2008; White et al. 2017). This discussion will analyze the various dynamics at stake in the management of social difference, cultural diversity, and "othering," in societies where multiculturalist policies, since their inception in the 1960–1970s, should have solved a number of tensions between minorities and the law enforcement arm of governments (Cashmore 2002; Bartkowiak-Théron

2012b; Carpenter and Ball 2012). These policies, as part of a vision about the public good, were intended to act as governance mechanisms for ethnic diversity in constantly changing communities. They are based on four hypotheses: (1) multiculturalism is in the best interest of a nation; (2) multiculturalism can foster social, cultural, and economic benefits; (3) according to principles of social justice, society should become fairer because of multiculturalism; (4) social cohesion can only be achieved if governments overcome difference by embracing diversity (Bartkowiak-Théron 2012b; Holmes et al. 2015). These precepts however have a tendency to highlight difference and social fragmentation, as opposed to embracing them, and therefore divide more than they include (Body-Gendrot 1998; Bowling and Phillips 2003). Such policies are therefore confusing, in that they aim to challenge the social status quo, though never quite succeed in depolarizing debates.

Research has had a tendency to focus on some ethnic and cultural minorities more than others (e.g., African-Americans, indigenous populations, Hispanics or Asians; Zhao et al. 2015). However, it is agreed that police responses or interactions with ethnic minorities are as much a matter of personal attitudes and beliefs, as they are of operational practice and policy (White 2009). With "whiteness" (a "European-based system of justice": a scholarly, political, and judicial discourse often about or directed at ethnic minorities and imposed on these ethnic minorities) at the basis of most of the functioning of the criminal justice system, the "level-playing field" is rhetorical, privileges dominant classes, and disadvantages ethnic minorities (Cooper 2005; Holmes et al. 2015). However, it should be acknowledged that although racism seems to be rampant in policing organizations, most policing encounters happen without any problem, and while tensions may be felt by the individuals interacting with each other, exchanges are usually cordial, if not respectful (Fridell and Scott 2005). In saying that, the picture provided by the media, and several international inquiries into policing and law enforcement, have shown that prejudice and cynicism remain entrenched (Wieviorka 1999). Most of this polarization has to do with simplistic, mediatized images of moral panics (Goode and Ben-Yehudfa 2009; Wieviorka 1999) and urban "gangs," linked to the behavior of young African-American, Bangladeshi, Lebanese, Sudanese, or Vietnamese men (Jones and Newburn 2001; White 2004, 2009).

Unraveling the Landscape

Ethnic minority groups living (or arriving) in Australia, Canada, the USA, and most Western European countries have particularly problematic and poor relationships with police (Murphy and Cherney 2011; Zhao et al. 2015). These tensions have been long-standing and have created historically endemic strains on the ways these communities and law enforcement agencies approach and interact with each other (Jones and Newburn 2001). In fact, while police abuses of power usually evoke images of American police shooting members of indigenous or African-American communities, we can trace similar matters back to fifteenth-century Europe (in particular France's *ancien régime*). Long before the consolidation of policing as a profession, the movement of Roma or Gypsies challenged the early beginnings of the territorialization process (Holmes et al. 2015; de Koster and Reinke 2016). In those days, the management of poverty, begging, and vagrancy ranged from either brutal forms of eviction to the passive escorting of individuals to city gates. As a form of exclusion, such practices were used to translate policies aimed at consolidating borders or territories, and the privileges of ruling classes, from royalty to the lower *bourgeoisie*. As systematic ideas of racial stratification dominated colonization and understandings of social dominance (superiority) over inferior classes or races (Carpenter and Ball 2012), "domination by the 'superior race' was considered inevitable and desirable, because it was [mistakenly] thought to lead to human progress" (Holmes et al. 2015, 43).

With time, such practices extended to the mismanagement of the industrial revolution, colonization, and decolonization practices (Holmes et al. 2015; Body-Gendrot 1998). Some commentators have indicated that racist policing practices in European countries could be merely an extension of colonial policing, with media exacerbating the demonization of social groups and associating the myths of "folk devils" with that of the "enemy within" (Bowling and Phillips 2003; Cyr 2003; Body-Gendrot 1998; Wieviorka 1999). The withdrawal of large European empires (e.g., the departure of France from Algeria when the nation voted for its independence) created systems of disadvantage, and neither catered for the return or arrival of populations into metropolitan areas nor for the sociocultural dynamics created by workforce demands. The world wars exacerbated existing ethnic tensions, as well as the process of independence suffered by some Mediterranean countries, which remain the source of violent conflict between law enforcement and second- or third-generation minorities in Europe (de Koster and Reinke 2016; Body-Gendrot 1998, 2011; Wieviorka 1999; Bui-Trong 2000).

A focus on contemporary practices of police violence minimizes the historical legacy of colonization, which is replete with actual police massacres. Recently, criminology research has begun to map the links between colonial past and current practice (see, e.g., the work of the Université de Montréal in indigeneity and Michelle Alexander's (2010) critical work on the links between slavery and mass incarceration in the USA). Since the emergence of civil rights discourses, ethnic minority communities – particularly African-Americans in the USA, Caribbean migrants in the UK, and post-WWII migrants to Commonwealth countries such as Australia, South Africa, New Zealand, and Canada – have been represented "disproportionately among persons killed by police through the use of deadly force" (Goldkamp 1976, 169; Zhao et al. 2015). While, in this chapter, we focus on contemporary policing practices, we are cognizant that these do not exist in a vacuum; they are part of a longer history of territorialization, border control, and genocidal practices.

Over-policing and Racial Profiling

Over-policing is defined as "the imposition of police control on individual or community activities at a level unlikely to occur in the dominant society" (AJIC 1999). Over-policing is linked to two schools of thought. One largely deals with the fundamentally "racist machinery of policing" (Goldkamp 1976, 170; Holmes et al. 2015), while the other more fundamentally deals with a so-called *underclass* argument (Body-Gendrot 1998). Strongly associated with labeling theory, both schools of thought however stress the idea that law enforcement administration has encouraged policies and practices that focus on people at the margin, therefore feeding a self-fulfilling prophecy that minorities (of any kind) will systematically know or generate high-volume crimes, more altercations between communities and law enforcement personnel, and therefore more possible deaths by police. More arrests will therefore occur among these (usually lower socioeconomic) minorities and naturally attract further police attention. The fact that some marginalized social subgroups are more prone to being arrested, and that there are organizational and informal pressures that encourage this, is not new (Cain and Sadigh 1982). Research in those matters spans many decades, and the study of law enforcement activities shows an alienation of minority members in poor, ghettoized neighborhoods and peaks in reported incidents of police brutality or race-based policing (Zhao et al. 2015).

Stop-and-Search

I have long been concerned about the use of stop-and-search. Although it is undoubtedly an important police power, when misused it can be counter-productive. It can be an enormous waste of police time. When innocent people are stopped and searched for no good reason, it is hugely damaging to the relationship between the police and the public. In those circumstances it is an unacceptable affront to justice. Rt Hon Theresa May, Home Secretary, 2014 (Home Office 2014)

The Met must continue to ramp up its fight against violent crime ... This will include a significant increase in the use of targeted stop and search by the police across our city. When done badly, stop and search can cause community tensions. But when based on real intelligence, geographically focused and performed professionally, it is a vital tool for the police to keep our communities safe. Sadiq Khan, Mayor of London, 2018, in response to increases in reported knife crime (Crerar 2018)

Along with discretion, stop-and-search is probably the power most used by the police. Its practice is under strict scrutiny by governments as well as scholars, with regular inquiries as to its use, and questions as to the necessity to bolster its remit. It is now common knowledge that stop-and-search is linked to racism and that ethnic community members are overrepresented in stop-and-search statistics around the world, despite the fact that stop-and-search needs to occur under "reasonable grounds for suspicion" or "reasonable suspicion" (Murray 2018). However, while tacit knowledge, experience, and suspicion are a part of the police officer's decision to stop-and-search a person, research has shown that labeling and stereotypes, as well as "race-out-of-place," are central to making that decision (Quinton 2011).

(continued)

There are now several mechanisms and organizations in the UK specifically monitoring police use of stop-and-search. For example, the Northern Ireland Police Service now openly publishes statistics about stop-and-search and allows researchers as well as other community members to download full databases on Excel spreadsheets. Regrettably though, these databases provide select information, such as the gender of the person stopped-and-searched and the legislation under which the power was used. The ethnicity is not an information recorded in these databases. Similarly, the London Metropolitan Police publishes stop-and-search data regularly, via an online "dashboard," which helps track stop-and-search occurrences according to legislation, borough, etc. (Metropolitan Police 2018). Community-based agencies have also consolidated partnerships with various organizations to collect and record data on policing, with specific campaigns organized around stop-and-search (see, e. g., StopWatch: http://www.stop-watch.org/about-us/). Such community initiatives are informative, and in addition to focusing on creating new, visible, and accessible mechanisms for police accountability, they also help relay information reported by police organizations on their stop-and-search activities.

Overall, while data about stop-and-search seems to be at a record low in the UK, Home Office statistics covering 2016–2017 indicate that:

- black people are eight times more likely to be stopped than white people.
- black and minority ethnic groups are four times as likely to be stopped and searched.
- the proportional rise in searches of ethnic minorities contrasts with an actual 21% drop in stop-and-search overall in England and Wales since 2013.
- only 15–17% of these detentions led to an arrest.
- only 25% were conducted under justifiable cause.

Discussions about stop-and-search powers are not limited to the UK, although a large portion of the early literature has focused on that country as a response to the uncomfortable truths triggered by the Scarman and MacPherson reports (Bowling and Phillips 2007). In Australia, the Office of Police Integrity conducted a review of Victoria Police use of stop-and-search in 2012, further to new legislation passed in 2009, and especially with regard to the control of weapons. While the inquiry failed to reveal any misuse of power toward social subgroups, it found some entrenched failures in terms of accountability and data collection, concluding that Victoria Police did not meet legislative requirements in those areas. The inquiry failed to demonstrate an impact of stop-and-search onto crime reduction, especially violent crime or weapon-related crime. In acknowledging stop-and-search as an intrusive form of surveillance, the report ends in recommendations that the power be exercised in proportion to a perceived risk and informed by police intelligence

(*continued*)

> (the latter recommendation being echoed by the Mayor of London in the above quote). The report aligns with research suggesting that instead of focusing on "race," other attributes should be factored into the study of stop-and-search (Parliament of Victoria 2012).

Racial profiling consists of the use of generalizations and prejudicial inference based on not only race but also gender, language, ethnicity, culture, or age to guide police practice and decision-making, such as detention, arrest, searches, traffic stops, etc. (Fridell and Scott 2005; Delsol 2006). With some origins in the 1980s' war on drugs, racial profiling concerns itself with the idea that some individual attributes are indicators that a person is more likely to commit a crime or found guilty of an offense if confronted by law enforcement personnel. "Driving while black" (and all its declinations, such as "Flying While Arab") are derivatives of racial profiling practices (Zhao et al. 2015). Minimalist understandings of racial profiling concern an officer's decision to interact with a member of the community solely based on the observable attributes of this individual. Much criticism since the 2000s has been directed at debunking this minimalist definition, as an attempt to hide more pervasive discriminatory practices which included race as well as other individual attributes, such as age, clothing, or behavior or even occurrences of probable cause (Fridell and Scott 2005). While policing services are beginning to address this issue in more comprehensive and justified ways, and construct the practice in layers of observable factors (such as skin color, age, dress code, place and time of day), they continue to encroach into urban planning policies and over-police minorities in ghettoized, disadvantaged communities (Body-Gendrot 1998, 2011; Bui-Trong 2000). It is important to note that such issues as over-policing can sometimes be exacerbated by research innovations such as hot spot policing, which is sometimes guided in its geographical orientation on earlier generations of over-policing. Good research monitoring and methodological design is paramount to avoid such drawbacks in applied research and operational practice.

To continue our earlier point, research on policing conducted in the later part of the twentieth century – as part of the many inquiries into law enforcement and policing in Western countries, or following these – has actually found that police commonly use a wide range of labels, stereotypes, and descriptors outside race characteristics, to classify people according to various social attributes, from their age to their ethnic origin, housing status (even physical address), levels of education, state of health, etc. (Bowling and Phillips 2003; Bartkowiak-Théron and Asquith 2012). Among those, however, race (with determinants such as "Asian," "Black," "Indians," "Gypsies," "Lebanese," etc.) remains a prominent "marker," which is associated in policy and practice with dominant understandings of social conformism and law-abiding behavior, and is linked too often with gang, terrorist, and/or drug-dealing behavior. Entrenched racism continues to inform community attitudes such as "police have one trigger finger for whites and another for blacks" (Takagi, in Goldkamp 1976, 171). This nurtures tensions during encounters with members of ethnic minority communities. In a way, such stereotypes confirm Reiner's positioning of racist practices toward ethnic minorities as a form of "police property." According to such practices, the social majority consent to police dealing, as they see fit, with what is perceived as a socio-ethnic underclass (Reiner 2000; Sharp and Atherton 2007). Others have also labeled such practices and attitudes "functional racism," as part of broader injustices within police culture (Body-Gendrot 2011).

Police Shootings

"If you encounter these Negroes, shoot first and ask questions later." This quote, from the Christopher Commission, which investigated instances of police brutality by the Los Angeles Department in the context of the Rodney King Riots, highlights that some policing organizations have endorsed "shoot first, then ask question" policies (Cooper 2005).

Police shootings are vastly different between countries such as the UK and the USA. In Australia, for example, the Australian Institute of Criminology accounts 13 police shootings between 2013 and 2015. Numbers are significantly different in the USA, where the Washington Post (which started compiling a systematic database of police shootings since the 2015) shows 995 deaths by police shooting in 2015, 963 in 2016, 987 in 2017, and 707 as of 30 August 2018.

Statistics indicate significant overrepresentations of ethnic minority deaths, with race as a prominent factor in these police shootings.

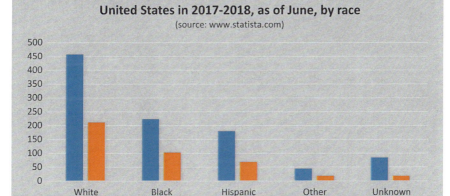

Number of people shot to death by the police in the United States in 2017-2018, as of June, by race (source: www.statista.com)

While the extent of the overrepresentation of black minorities in police shootings was questioned in earlier research, there is now overwhelming evidence that demonstrate an overrepresentation of ethnic minorities in statistics dealing with police use of force and use of deadly force (Zhao et al. 2015; Kearns 2017).

Institutional Racism

The idea that racism spans not only individual practice but every layer of the police organization has been widely discussed since the 1960s in America and specifically since the 1981 Scarman Report and the 1999 MacPherson Report in the UK (Jones and Newburn 2001). The Scarman Report was an inquiry ordered by the UK Home Secretary immediately after 3 days of urban unrest in Brixton in 1981. Tensions between black communities and the police had rapidly escalated into public disorder in the communities of Bristol, Brixton, Manchester, Liverpool, and Birmingham. The 1981 Brixton riots were triggered by the police saturation of the community, and the constant application of "stop-and-search" powers to no other probable cause than "looking suspicious." Fraught with methodological and theoretical positioning that only allowed identifying a limited number of police failures, the Scarman Report remains a touchstone in policing history. It started a process of denunciation of abusive practices by police. While not specifically mentioning institutional racism (racist practices which are endemic and normalized), it clearly criticized the "insufficient formal liaison between the black community and the police" (Jones and Newburn 2001), and paved the way for much "soul searching" (Bowling and Phillips 2003), and stronger, more provocative inquiries later (Cain and Sadigh 1982).

Scarman denounced the difficulties, social and economic, "which beset the ethnically diverse communities who live and work in inner cities," and urged the police to "fully recognise the problems of ethnic minorities" including recommendations to undertake "speedy and positive action to overcome them" (Williams 1982, 2; Scarman 1981). Scarman identified various problems in policing "a multi-racial community in a deprived inner city area where unemployment, especially among young black people, is high, and hopes low" (1981, 15), and the report found that while a strong racial element was at play during the riots, the media had played a part in escalating the situation. While Scarman found that "the police strategy and tactics in handling the disorders were to be commended and not criticised," the final part of his report suggests significant amendments to police organizational procedures and policies, including, but not limited to, better and more culturally friendly recruitment practice, community relations, training, supervision of officers, stop-and-search policies, and disciplinary action (the latter specifically focused on severe organizational responses to prejudicial police behavior) (Williams 1982; Bowling and Phillips 2003). He also pointed at a wide-ranging lack of public trust in the police, "unsafe statistical generalisations," and police abuse of power. The report finishes on a strong recommendation for the police to consider "more coherent and better directed [police] responses to the challenge of policing modern, multi-racial society" (Scarman 1981, s5.5).

The MacPherson Report was a later inquiry into the 1993 death and subsequent botched investigation of the murder of Stephen Lawrence in London (Rowe 2006; Bartkowiak-Théron and Asquith 2015), which acted as a "lightning rod" for a new consideration of police practice and policy in the UK (Bowling and Phillips 2003). The MacPherson Report, deemed a "bombshell on the British political and cultural landscape" (Younge 1999, 329), directly accused the police organization of institutional racism and specifically put blame on police organizations for an inability to provide a multicultural society with adequate and culturally appropriate problem-solving, service, and leadership. In shifting the focus from individual prejudice to institutional discrimination, the inquiry is a watershed in race relations, which made some damning points about the lack of ethnic representativity of the organization, disproportionate levels of discriminatory practices ("random" breath tests, stop-and-search, curfew or identity checks, etc.), racist violence, and harassment toward diverse community members (Younge 1999; Bowling and Phillips 2003).

To date, the Scarman and MacPherson reports remain landmarks in international policing and, just as the Royal Commission into Aboriginal Deaths in Custody in Australia, present race as a forefront issue in policing practice and policy (some say "canonical," presenting them like the "Pillars of Hercules in British race relations" – Cashmore 2002, 328). These inquiries are unprecedented in that they triggered annual (or less regular, albeit equally important) mandatory reporting mechanisms for law enforcement agencies as to the progress made on all or part of the recommendations aimed at improving more culture-friendly policies and operational frameworks. For example, recommendation 61 of the MacPherson Report insists that records be made of all "stop-and-searches" under any legislative provision. Initially discarded as "yet another piece of bureaucracy," these policing "progress statuses" are usually accompanied by academic commentaries, such as the one published in a special issue of *Policing: a Journal of Policy and Practice* in 2015 (see Bartkowiak-Théron and Asquith 2015).

The Australian Royal Commission into Aboriginal Deaths in Custody
The 1987 Royal Commission into Aboriginal Deaths in Custody (RCIADIC) was commissioned after 99 indigenous people died in custody between 1980 and 1989, of which 63 occurred within the first few hours of police custody (often by hanging). The inquiry revealed no instance of unlawful behavior on the part of the police. However, it severely criticized a lack of awareness, training, accountability, and reporting toward Aboriginal and Torres Strait Islander communities across all police jurisdictions and across all stages of the policing and justice process. Many of the 339 recommendations contained in the report are directly relevant to police. Such recommendations include:

- Improved standard of care in police cells
- Concerns around overrepresentation of indigenous people in public order offenses
- Better investigative practices in cases involving indigenous people or communities
- Lack of data about remand and police detainees

(continued)

- Institutional racism and violence by police
- Alternatives to detention for intoxication
- Arrest as a last resort for minor offenses
- Better recruitment, training, and placement of officers
- Attempts at recruiting indigenous police officers into police organizations

Further to the inquiry, the Indigenous Law Bulletin published progress reports for each Australian jurisdiction in 2001 (the first anniversary of the inquiry) and 2007. However, one of the main outcomes of the RCIADIC was the creation of the National Deaths in Custody Monitoring and Research Program at the Australian Institute of Criminology (AIC 2017), which monitored all deaths in custody (prison or police) over 20 years. The reports of the program are intended to guide criminal justice stakeholders in developing policy and practice initiatives to reduce deaths in police and prison custody.

The 2011 report found that the indigenous and nonindigenous rates of deaths in custody had decreased between 2001 and 2011, which was praised as significant progress. In 2011, death rates were lowest ever seen (0.16 per 100 and 0.22 per 100 for indigenous prisoners and nonindigenous prisoners, respectively), and the indigenous rate of death in prison was lower than the equivalent nonindigenous rate between 2003 and 2011. The report however stated that:

> While Indigenous prisoners continue to be statistically less likely to die in custody than non-Indigenous prisoners, there is a concerning trend emerging, as the actual number of Indigenous deaths in prison are rising again, with 14 in 2009–10 which is equal to the highest on record. More concerning still is that over the 20 years since the Royal Commission, the proportion of prisoners that are Indigenous has almost doubled from 14% in 1991 to 26% in 2011.

In 2018, the Australian Institute of Criminology further reported on deaths between 2013–2014 and 2014–2015 (Ticehurst et al. 2018). The report indicates that of the 34 deaths that occurred during that time, 6 (19%) were of indigenous. During the 26 years of the program monitoring, 782 deaths occurred in police custody and custody-related operations, 153 (20%) of which were indigenous. This is a significant overrepresentation given that the Aboriginal and Torres Strait Islander community is only 3.3% of the Australian population. In spite of the RCIADIC and the work done since the commission, overrepresentation of indigenous people in custody in Australia continues to be a significant problem. In the case of the Northern Territory in 2018, 100% of all young people in detention are Aboriginal or Torres Strait Islanders (Allam 2018).

Border Control: The Post 9/11 Context

Issues of territorialization are complex. They span the control of immigration with the physical control of borders by customs officers, or police officers seconded into the role, the enforcement of overstayed visas, and the control of asylum seekers (Murphy and Cherney 2011). Issues of terrorism have long been on the agenda of governments and their policing services, with most Global North countries reorienting much of their policing resources to manage a perceived uptick in terrorist activity since 2000. Yet, the disastrous events of 9/11 cast a new picture of the "enemy within," which labeled Muslims and Islam generally as sources of potential threats (Burnett 2012). Social tensions have escalated since, and racist attacks toward Muslim minorities have increased the regularity of police encounters with members of religious minorities. With antagonism encouraged by some hardened right wing political parties since the 1970s, and then with the Gulf War (Wieviorka 1999), police have had to readjust to new social dynamics, and to tensions amplified by riots in the 1980s, particularly in France and England (Williams 1982; Bui-Trong 2000). Crystallized by the images of the World Trade Center under attack, and the subsequent attacks in Bali, and on the London and Paris public transportation systems, "the enemy within" has become a component of many territory-focused enforcement initiatives, such as the "Plan Vigipirate," across the whole French territory.

As a result of political and social anxiety about terrorism, and its prominent position at the bureaucrats' agendas, much legislation and policy aimed at tackling terrorism or addressing radicalization have been enacted without regard to their potential effect on the policing of ethnic minorities (Pickering et al. 2007). In the UK, the Anti-Terrorism Act 2001 is "argued to be discriminatory against Muslim people in particular, and perceived to be eroding many basic rights on the grounds of national security" (Bowling and Phillips 2003, 22; Spalek and Imtoual 2007). While exodus and migration are typical traits of human nature (Egan-Vive and Fraser 2012), resettlement policies have accompanied colonization and civil war history. The acceleration of human movement due to world conflicts has made race and ethnicity a fundamental aspect of border control. Legislation and resettlement policies have been a feature of most dominant countries in the Global North and are a usual part of the law enforcement landscape in these countries. Yet, and while their arrival and settlement should be expected, refugees or migrants of different ethnic origins systematically face various levels of racial profiling and discrimination (Egan-Vive and Fraser 2012), resulting in overrepresentation in stop-and-search, traffic stops, and fine statistics (Holmes et al. 2015).

Community Policing and Procedural Policing: Do They Work?

A large portion of critical discussions about the policing of ethnic and cultural minorities focuses on mishaps in the field and entrenched racism in police organizations. These are artifacts of histories of tense relationships between community members and police officers. Literature also focuses on the various initiatives that have been created in order to build bridges between communities and government agencies, using social capital and local knowledge as pivotal aspects of positive interventionist frameworks such as community policing and procedural policing/ justice. Indeed, contrary to major social phantasmagoria, ethnic and religious community organizations more often than not promote forms of solidarity and engagement geared at citizenship and social harmony (Wieviorka 1999). It is therefore unsurprising to see the increased use of community-oriented policing initiatives to foster relationships with these communities, and for police to acquire a better understanding of the communities they serve and create real partnership-based problem-solving initiatives.

Community policing has been presented by many as a fundamental shift in paradigm from a traditional model of centralized, command-and-control policing. More of a feature of England, Canada, Australia, and US policing than it is in France, for example (Body-Gendrot 2011), community policing is defined as a proactive problem-solving approach used to address some inherent, sometimes chronic, threats to public safety. Aimed at building longer-lasting mutual respect between law enforcement and the public, community policing has been adopted, with varied terminology, as a foundational or strategic pillar for most democratic police organizations (Skogan 2006).

The topic of community policing needs to be approached cautiously and critically. While it is one of the primary strategies used to fix estranged relationships between police and communities, community policing has been widely documented, analyzed, and criticized for its many evaluation and measurement flaws. Its precept as well, while admirable, stands on shifting sands: the expression "community" has been pluralized, yet "communities" remain ill-defined, amorphous, and in a constant state of flux (Brogden and Nihar 2005; Bartkowiak-Théron and Corbo Crehan 2010). As a result, community policing initiatives have suffered from a lack of measurable indicators on which to judge efficacy of these approaches. Specifically, police organizations have struggled to increase trust in policing or crime reporting to the police. Additionally, as Fleming (2010) notes, community policing is not applied across all communities, and those who engage with community policing initiatives are probably those who need these the least (Fleming 2010). In a way, one could say that at a time when evidence-based policing is an ever-increasing paradigmatic framework on which some organizations focus their policies and practices, police organizations have a political and community obligation to account for the use of the softest, nonevidence-based approach for addressing one of the most intractable problems in policing. Furthermore, when embedded in the counter-terrorism framework, and despite calls to capitalize on existing social cohesion and capital, the "get tough" on the policing of terrorism weakens the community policing message conveyed to ethnic minorities and contributes to the precariousness of police-community relationships (Pickering et al. 2007). Engagement in such context, and despite efforts to make it look otherwise, functions according to binary conceptualizations of communities (us vs. them; legal vs. illegal), which hinders engagement and actual community participation and trust (Spalek and Imtoual 2007).

Scarman was one of the first officials to recommend the adoption of forms of community policing, specifically focused on consultation with communities, with accountability as a key aspect of those initiatives (Cain and Sadigh 1982; Jones and Newburn 2001; Skogan 2006). However, not all organizations have been successful at embedding community policing principles and practices in their everyday operational policies. Fundamentally based on the availability of budgetary resources, and the propensity of individual police officers to engage with communities and community members, community policing is often relegated to a philosophical backdrop, in favor of initiatives that generate more visible and faster results according to neoliberal budgetary frameworks (such as a drop in reported crime rates). Community policing has been applied to many types of communities, yet it has found more success in rural communities, where social networks are stronger and more developed (Kearns 2017). Race has been shown to significantly impact on police-community relationships, though, with "damaged relationships between police and minority communities," the ethnic composition of neighborhoods and the ethnic background and cultural beliefs of police officers cited as impeding community-policing initiatives (Kearns 2017, 1216; Zhao et al. 2015).

Police Liaison Schemes
Community liaison schemes are seen as crucial in the building of community relationships with police (AHRC 2010). These approaches have been established, particularly in the UK, Canada, the USA, Australia, and New Zealand, to "build positive, trusting and cohesive relationships with communities," promote information sharing and trust, capitalize on cultural differences, and improve relations between officers themselves (AHRC 2010, 1).

> At the heart of the liaison officer role is an effort to build a bridge between two groups whose relations, historically and contemporaneously, have often been fractious and marked by power imbalances and distrust. (Willis 2010, 43)

Often, these schemes are focused on specific subsections of the community, despite the fact that no ethnic or cultural community is a coherent, cohesive entity (Bowling and Phillips 2003; Carpenter and Ball 2012). Accordingly, some of these schemes focus on youth solely, or women, within these ethnic communities; others are applicable to only some sections of the national territory, such as remote and rural communities.

Some schemes have been particularly successful. A review of the "Community Partnership Project" (a project implemented under the Australian Human Rights Commission's Community Partnerships for Human Rights) by the Centre of Excellence in Policing and Security showed some local initiatives contributed to a better understanding of police officers and community members, although the positive impact of such initiatives is often thwarted

(*continued*)

by the constant rotation of police officers into different roles (AHRC 2010), or the appointment to these roles as secondary to officers' general duties.

By "extending the police family" through the pluralization of policing, recruitment of police auxiliaries, training and deployment of specialized officers, and the creation of corporate liaison roles dedicated to vulnerable populations, police liaison schemes have provided a way to symbolically advance a political intent to do things differently with diverse communities (Bartkowiak-Théron 2012a, b). However, we can only regret the fact that liaison schemes, due to their very wide nature, are never exactly comprehensive, and either target specific ethnicities or cultures (e.g., the Aboriginal Liaison Officer in New South Wales) or vaguely group different cultures under the same collective identification (e.g., ethnic liaison officers in Victoria or community liaison officers in Tasmania). These liaison roles fail to consider the layers of vulnerability often present in ethnic minority communities and do not adequately consider the ways in which intersections in vulnerability may change the nature of what is required from policing.

Procedural justice is defined as fairness in process and in the allocation of problem-solving processes, in order to guarantee just outcomes for all the parties involved. Recent research has focused on how procedural justice applies to the whole criminal justice system, in terms of relationships with disadvantaged communities, and particularly to the police, as the gatekeepers of that system (Tyler 2005; Bradford 2014). One of the strongest arguments made in favor of procedural justice in policing, particularly community policing, is that "given the history of police and ethnic group relations, enhancing legitimacy in the eyes of ethnic groups should be a priority for police agencies" (Murphy and Cherney 2011, 238). The research suggests that "if police adhere to principles of procedural justice in their dealings with ethnic minority group members, then they may be able to successfully engage these people and shape their willingness to cooperate with police in a range of matters" (Murphy and Cherney 2011; Tyler 2005).

It is natural, therefore, to see procedural justice research in policing flourish in the last 20 years. Although group and individual experiences of procedural justice are important in encouraging, building, or maintaining cooperative links with police (Bradford 2014), such research has concluded that "procedurally just encounters are not sufficient to alter general views of police and cooperation for ethnic minorities" (Murphy and Cherney 2011, 251). In light of the enduring tensions that have existed in the social control of multicultural communities, such findings are disappointing, but not overall surprising. Centuries of abuse, over-policing and sometimes genocide, cannot be overcome with process systems. In light of this, police organizations have since reverted back to more embedded forms of community engagement which not only aim at the resolution of social problems that have been identified by police but also defined and identified by communities themselves (VicPol 2013). Such joined-up approaches to social issues are a better, more significant step toward building more efficient and legitimized problem-solving and social capital building.

Training

Police training and education is the perennial "go-to" response in times of crisis. Escalating or ongoing tensions between police and vulnerable people are not an exception to this rule, and commentators are quick to insist on boosting cultural awareness components in police recruit training. According to this "go-to" answer, in order to make a police organization less racist and discriminatory, organizations need to not only "weed" racist and heavily biased applicants at recruitment but also need to make the organizations more culturally aware of difference (Stenning 2003; Zhao et al. 2015). While this is a laudable comment, much research has been conducted in this area since the 2000s, and evidence has shown that while education on ethnicity, culture, and critical diversity can bear some fruit, such training alone cannot change practice (Kearns 2017). It can even come with drawbacks that can aggravate tensions and stereotypes, as opposed to easing them (Stenning 2003), such as siloing police responses, generalizing about communities so much so that it becomes a caricature of what is needed, and creating a "competition of suffering" (Mason-Bish 2013) that is only remedied by dedicated modules in police training.

Cross-cultural training or cultural awareness training implies that the syllabus will focus on a number of attributes featured in ethnic minority communities. Various aspects of culture, religion, language, and relationships are expected to be featured in the curriculum. However, the multiplicity of such features makes the design of such curriculum a difficult task, and much of this curriculum has reverted to "areas of priorities" for law enforcement agencies, that is, cultural training specifically focused on those communities with which the police have experienced enduringly tense relationships and conflict. Training also focuses on communities' "deficits," as opposed to strengths, which has a tendency to aggravate stigma (or create new ones) as opposed to fostering new platforms for mutual comprehension (Victoria Police 2013). As such, curriculum has focused on ethnic minorities with a history of criminal or riotous behavior, indigenous communities, and migrant (often refugee) communities (Egan-Vive and Fraser 2012).

Recruitment and Retention of Ethnic Minorities into the Police Workforce

Most police organizations have been active in trying to address ethnic discord, urban disorder, and lack of community trust in law enforcement. As part of a professionalization and democratization process, a large part of their effort to address these tensions has been to increase the representation of ethnic groups in their organizations, often by establishing quotas and recruitment practices across all levels of their hierarchy (McLeod 2018). As indicated earlier, one of the major recommendations made in successive inquiries into policing has focused on the recruitment of ethnic minorities into the police workforce (Cain and Sadigh 1982; Cahsmore 2002; Bartkowiak-Théron 2012a, b; Shepherd 2014). This recommendation is based on the beliefs that (1) the police force must be representative of the communities they serve (including gender, McLeod 2018), (2) multiethnic organizations are likely to promote understanding and tolerance, and (3) a diverse workforce fosters climates of tolerance, legitimacy, and accountability in and outside the organization, in addition to economic benefits. Indeed, the idea of increasing the ethnic representation of the police force has been presented as a way to boost trust between minorities and police and contribute to ending negative encounters between police and members of these ethnic minorities (Rowe and Ross 2015). Police organizations have therefore implemented a number of laudable initiatives, and structured imaginative interventions, largely inspired from affirmative action principles, to redress discriminatory hiring policies (Jones and Newburn 2001; Stenning 2003; Fridell and Scott 2005; Shepherd 2014; McLeod 2018). These initiatives have however faced a number of barriers and obstacles that have now been widely documented in research literature (Cashmore 2002). Most of these obstacles have to do with the above three hypotheses, which have ill-posited the extent of existing tensions between police and minorities, and the exacerbating effect these positive discrimination policies would have on hiring practices.

In Australia and New Zealand, the Australasian Police Multicultural Advisory Bureau (APMAB) worked on assisting police services in establishing benchmarks for the management of cultural and linguistic diversity, with the particular aim to recruit and retain Culturally and Linguistically Diverse (CALD) police officers (APMAB 2006). Ending with 46 recommendations, most of which taken with serious consideration by policing leadership and management, the report concluded that most jurisdictions understood the challenges of recruiting and retaining a multicultural workforce and that cultural change had to be accompanied by stronger forms of engagement with ethnic minorities (Jones and Newburn 2001). Despite these initiatives, under-recruitment remains a problem, and police organizations are still struggling to meet the "unreachable" quotas initially thought out by policy-makers. In Canada, younger members of ethnic minorities did not respond enthusiastically to these recruitment campaigns, in large part because they could not see themselves being part of organizations that they have experienced as biased and racist (Stenning 2003). Research has indeed reported high levels of negative attitudes from young ethnic community members toward the police, not only because of the confrontational nature of interaction in the field (with white *and* black police officers, the latter "acting tough" to prove their worth) but also, at recruitment level, out of fear of subjection to sexist and racist practices within the force itself (Sharp and Atherton 2007). Focusing on the appointment of individual officers from ethnic minorities also fails to consider the ways in which the organization itself is antithetical to cultural diversity. For example, there are problems in recruiting ethnic minority communities when HR policies and practices are primarily aimed at ethnic (white) communities (such as the privileging of Christian public holidays, and little or no provision for religious practices such as those required by Muslim and Jewish officers).

However, recruitment and retention of an ethnically and culturally diverse force is a problem linked to the scarred history between police and minority communities, and "lofty goals have either not been achieved or are still being met" (Rowe and Ross 2015, 33). In 2012, the chief of the London Metropolitan Police admitted that he wished one in three police officers in London were of ethnic background, instead of one in ten (Anon 2012). This was reiterated by the then Home Secretary, Theresa May, in 2015, who "criticised the race record of the police in England and Wales, saying they are 'too white', with not one of the 43 forces looking like the communities they serve" (Dodd 2015). In 2016, the London Metropolitan Police appeared to have made some progress, with "3% of the Met's total police workforce [being] non-white," and "the number of black and minority ethnicity (BME) officers in the force rising from 3,163 in 2013 to 4,033 at the end of August" (Anon 2016). While laudable that the proportion of ethnic minority officers had increased, this, in no way, reflects the cultural diversity of London communities nor addresses the "pale, stale, and male" environment that these ethnic minority officers must negotiate once recruited.

Conclusion

One paradox to highlight is that while ethnic tensions, protest, and rioting were at the forefront of political and media commentary in the 1990s and 2000s – possibly exaggerated to renew police legitimacy (Bowling and Phillips 2003) – prominent members of these communities were advising peaceful resolution of conflict and demanding further police action to quench hostilities. It would not be fair to unpack a complex web of tension, brutality, and resentment without acknowledging the significant efforts that have been made to try and rectify the situation and bring forth more culturally appropriate forms of democratic policing. Nor is it fair to ignore the fact that many of the communities who rightly complain about biased practices of over-policing often seek solutions that increase the police contact with these same communities, albeit, positive rather than negative encounters.

Law and order is a catch phrase for most politicians and governments during elections. However, "strong on crime" stances, when turned into practice, have always been counterproductive in the context of addressing tensions between police and ethnic minorities. Attempts to remediate conflicts between police and minorities have been in response to highly mediated, often brutal incidents occurring in public spaces. As a result of such knee-jerk attempts at "crafting policy on-the-go," such policies have consistently come at a time where police organizations were "ill-equipped to meet the challenges of policing multicultural societies" (Stenning 2003, 17).

Today, much attention is being lent to "critical diversity" as a better framework to examine forms of inequality, oppression, and stratification within society (Herring and Henderson 2011). Critical diversity is inherently important to policing, in that it analyzes the mechanics of exclusion and discrimination and challenges white-based elite discourses revolving around "inclusive" diversity and color blindness (Herring and Henderson 2011). It embraces cultural difference within and between what has been erroneously perceived as cohesive social groups. While critical diversity decries the approach of existing multiculturalist policies, it still acknowledges the central precept that diversity is institutionally beneficial to societies and provides competitive advantages through social complexity (Bradford 2014; McLeod 2018).

Awareness of issues relevant to ethnicity and culture is pertinent and paramount to policing, especially in globalized, multicultural countries. As pointed out by Egan-Vive and Fraser (2012, 145): "the impact of well-informed police cannot be emphasised enough. Ignorance of the complex issues can have long-term implication for the life of [ethnic minority members] and for future interaction with the community." Nowadays, police organizations are moving toward a greater acknowledgment of diversity. Beyond ethnic or racial diversity, police organizations are increasingly focused on a variety of vulnerability attributes that can present alone or in layers, individually or institutionally instantiated, and can be enduring or sporadic (Asquith et al. 2017). Race and ethnicity are being "re-problematized" as part of a larger framing of diversity, which is not solely limited to visible racial markers. With identity politics at its zenith, issues of human rights and due process in policing are under acute scrutiny, and organizational response to police misconduct in cases involving ethnicity or vulnerability is almost immediate. This acknowledgment, however, comes with significant struggles toward embedding changes into policies and procedures. While much progress has been made, recent racial and discriminatory incidents in policing across the world indicate that there is still a long way to go.

References

Aboriginal Justice Implementation Commission (1999) Report of the Aboriginal Justice Inquiry of Manitoba. Retrieved at http://www.ajic.mb.ca/volume.html. Accessed 10 Sept 2018

Alexander M (2010) The new Jim Crow: mass incarceration in the age of color blindness. New Press, New York

Allam L (2018) All children in detention in the Northern Territory are Indigenous. The Guardian. https://www.theguardian.com/australia-news/2018/jun/25/all-children-in-detention-in-the-northern-territory-are-indigenous. Accessed 24 Sept 2018

Anon (2012) Met police chief: 1 in 3 officers should be from a minority. LBC. https://www.youtube.com/watch?v=LrCwq7tVUXk. Accessed 10 Sept 2018

Anon (2016) Met police 'more representative' of diverse London. BBC News. https://www.bbc.com/news/uk-england-london-37317671. Accessed 10 Sept 2018

Anthony T, Cunneen C (eds) (2008) The critical criminology companion. Hawkins Press, Annandale

Asquith NL, Bartkowiak-Théron I, Roberts K (eds) (2017) Policing encounters with vulnerability. Palgrave Macmillan, London

Australasian Police Multicultural Advisory Bureau (2006) Annual report. APMAB, Melbourne

Australian Human Rights Commission (2010) Building trust: working with Muslim communities in Australia: a review of the community policing partnership project. AHRC, Sydney

Australian Institute of Criminology (2017) National deaths in custody program. https://aic.gov.au/publications/mr/mr20/national-deaths-custody-program. Accessed 24 Sept 2018

Bartkowiak-Théron I (2012a) Regard Critique sur le Multiculturalisme Australien. Inf Soc 171:54–63

Bartkowiak-Théron I (2012b) Reaching out to vulnerable people: the work of police liaison officers. In: Bartkowiak-Théron I, Asquith NL (eds) Policing vulnerability. The Federation Press, Annandale, pp 84–100

Bartkowiak-Théron I, Asquith NL (2012) The extraordinary intricacies of policing vulnerability. Australas Polic 4(2):43–50

Bartkowiak-Théron I, Asquith NL (2015) Policing diversity and vulnerability in the post-Macpherson era: unintended consequences and missed opportunities. Policing 9(1):89–100

Bartkowiak-Théron I, Corbo Crehan A (2010) The changing nature of communities: implications for police and community policing. In: Putt J (ed) Community policing: current and future directions for Australia – research and public policy. Australian Institute of Criminology, Canberra

Body-Gendrot S (1998) Les villes face à l'insécurité: des ghettos américains aux banlieues françaises. Bayard, Paris

Body-Gendrot S (2011) Police marginality, racial logics and discrimination in the banlieues de France. In: Amar P (ed) New racial missions of policing. Routledge, London, pp 82–99

Bowling B, Phillips C (2003) Policing ethnic minorities. In: Newburn T (ed) Handbook of policing. Willian Publishing, Devon, pp 528–555

Bowling B, Phillips C (2007) Disproportionate and discriminatory: reviewing the evidence on police stop and search. Mod Law Rev 70(6):936–961

Bradford B (2014) Policing and social identity: procedural justice, inclusion and cooperation between police and public. Polic Soc 24(1):22–43

Brogden M, Nijhar P (2005) Community policing: national and international models and approaches. Willan Publishing, Portland

Bui-Trong L (2000) Violences urbaines: Des vérités qui dérangent. Bayard, Paris

Burnett J (2012) After Lawrence: racial violence and policing in the UK. Race Class 54(1):91–98

Cain M, Sadigh S (1982) Racism, the police, and community policing: a comment on the Scarman report. J Law Soc 9(1):87–102

Carpenter BJ, Ball M (2012) Justice in society. The Federation Press, Annandale, NSW

Cashmore E (2002) Behind the window dressing: ethnic minority police perspectives on cultural diversity. J Ethn Migr Stud 28(2):327–341

Cooper C (2005) An Afrocentric perspective on policing. In: Dunham RG, Alpert GP (eds) Critical issues in policing. Waveland Press, Long Grove, pp 325–349

Crerar P (2018) Sadiq Khan reveals police will 'significantly' increase stop and search to tackle soaring knife crime. Evening Standard. https://www.standard.co.uk/news/crime/sadiq-khan-reveals-police-will-significantly-increase-stop-and-search-to-tackle-knife-crime-a3736501.html. Accessed 24 Sept 2018

Cyr JL (2003) The folk devil reacts: gangs and moral panic. Crim Justice Rev 28(1):26–46

De Koster M, Reinke H (2016) Policing minorities. In: Knepper P, Johansen A (eds) The Oxford handbook of the history of crime and criminal justice. Oxford University Press, Oxford, pp 268–284

Delsol R (2006) Racial profiling. In: Fleming J, Wakefield A (eds) The Sage dictionary of policing. Sage, London, pp 263–266

Dodd V (2015) Theresa May: police forces are 'too white'. The Guardian. https://www.theguardian.com/uk-news/2015/oct/21/theresa-may-criticises-police-chief-bernard-hogan-howe-stop-search-race-record. Accessed 10 Sept 2018

Egan-Vive P, Fraser K (2012) Policing vulnerable offenders: police early encounters with refugees. In: Bartkowiak-Théron I, Asquith NL (eds) Policing vulnerability. The Federation Press, Annandale, pp 132–146

Fleming J (2010) Community policing: the Australian connection. In: Putt J (ed) Community policing: current and future directions for Australia – research and public policy. Australian Institute of Criminology, Canberra

Fleming J, Wakefield A (2006) Policing. In: Fleming J, Wakefield A (eds) The Sage dictionary of policing. Sage, London, pp 232–234

Fridell L, Scott M (2005) Law enforcement responses to racially biased policing and the perception of its practice. In: Dunham RG, Alpert GP (eds) Critical issues in policing. Waveland Press, Long Grove, pp 304–322

Goldkamp JS (1976) Minorities as victims of police shootings: interpretations of racial disproportionality and police use of deadly force. Justice Syst J 2(2):169–183

Goode E, Ben-Yehudfa N (2009) Moral panics: the social construction of deviance. Blackwell, London

Her Majesty's Inspectorate of Constabulary (1997) Winning the race: policing plural communities. HMIC thematic inspection report on police community and race relations. Home Office, London

Herring C, Henderson L (2011) From affirmative action to diversity: toward a critical diversity perspective. Crit Sociol 38(5):629–643

Holmes D, Hughes K, Julian R (2015) Australian sociology. Pearson, Melbourne

Home Office (2014) Stop and search: comprehensive package of reform for police stop and search powers. Theresa May Oral Statement to Parliament. 30 April 2014. https://www.gov.uk/government/speeches/stop-and-search-comprehensive-package-of-reform-for-police-stop-and-search-powers. Accessed 24 Sept 2018

Jones T, Newburn T (2001) Widening access: improving police relations with hard to reach groups. Police research series paper 138. Home Office, London

Kearns EM (2017) Why are some officers more supportive of community policing with minorities than others? Justice Q 34(7):1213–1245

Mason-Bish H (2013) Conceptual issues in the construction of disability hate crime. In: Roulstone A, Mason-Bish H (eds) Disability, hate crime and violence. Routledge, London, pp 11–24

McLeod A (2018) Diversity and inclusion in Australian policing: where are we at and where should we go? AIPM Public Saf Leadersh Res Focus 5(2):1–7

Metropolitan Police (2018) Stop and search dashboard. https://www.met.police.uk/sd/stats-and-data/met/stop-and-search-dashboard/. Accessed 24 Sept 2018

Murphy K, Cherney A (2011) Fostering cooperation with the police: how do ethnic minorities in Australia respond to procedural justice-based policing? Aust N Z J Criminol 44(2):235–257

Murray K (2018) The modern making of stop and search: the rise of preventative sensibilities in post-war Britain. Br J Criminol 58(3):588–605

Parliament of Victoria (2012) Review of Victoria Police use of 'stop and search' powers. https://www.parliament.vic.gov.au/file_uploads/VPARL2010-14No128_bJxK7r5D.pdf. Accessed 24 Sept 2018

Pickering S, Wright-Neville D, McCulloch J, Lentini P (2007) Counter-terrorism policing and culturally diverse communities. Australian Research Council Linkage final report. Monash University Publishing, Melbourne

Quinton P (2011) The formation of suspicions: police stop and search practices in England and Wales. Polic Soc 21(4):357–368

Reiner R (2000) The politics of the police. 3rd Edition. Oxford, Oxford University Press

Rowe M (2006) Institutional racism. In: Fleming J, Wakefield A (eds) The Sage dictionary of policing. Sage, London, pp 171–173

Rowe M, Ross JI (2015) Comparing the recruitment of ethnic and racial minorities in Police Departments in England and Wales with the USA. Policing 9(1):26–35

Scarman L (1981) The Scarman report. HMSO, London

Sharp D, Atherton S (2007) The experiences of policing in the community of young people from Black and other ethnic minority groups. Br J Criminol 47:746–763

Shepherd SM (2014) Why diversity many not mend adversity – an Australian commentary on multicultural affirmative action strategies in law enforcement. Curr Issues Crim Just 26(2):241–248

Skogan WG (2006) Police and community in Chicago. Oxford University Press, New York

Spalek B, Imtoual A (2007) Muslim communities and counter-terrorism responses: "hard" approaches to community engagement in the UK and Australia. J Muslim Minor Aff 27(2):185–202

Stenning PC (2003) Policing the cultural kaleidoscope: recent Canadian experience. Polic Soc 7:13–47

Ticehurst A, Napier S, Bricknell S (2018) National deaths in custody program: deaths in custody in Australia 2013–14 and 2014–15. Statistical reports no. 5. Australian Institute of Criminology, Canberra

Tyler TR (2005) Policing in Black and White: ethnic group differences in trust and confidence in the police. Police Q 8(3):322–342
Victoria Police (2013) Equality is not the same... Victoria Police response to community consultation and reviews on field contact policy and data collection and cross cultural training. VicPol, Melbourne
White R (2004) Police and community responses to youth gangs. Trends & issues in crime and criminal justice, 274. Australian Institute of Criminology, Canberra
White R (2009) Ethnic diversity and differential policing in Australia: the good, the bad and the ugly. Int Migr Integr 10:359–375
White RD, Haines F, Asquith NL (2017) Crime and criminology, 6th edn. Oxford University Press, Melbourne
Wieviorka M (1999) Violence en France. Seuil, Paris
Williams DGT (1982) The Brixton disorder. Camb Law J 41(1):1–6
Willis M (2010) Aboriginal Liaison Officers in community policing. In: Putt J (ed) Community policing: current and future directions for Australia – research and public policy. Australian Institute of Criminology, Canberra
Younge G (1999) The death of Stephen Lawrence: the MacPherson report. Polit Q 70:329–334
Zhao JS, Lai Y-L, Ren L, Lawton B (2015) The impact of race/ethnicity and quality-of-life policing on public attitudes toward racially biased policing and traffic stops. Crime Delinq 6(3):350–374

Romanian Identity and Immigration in Europe

85

Remus Gabriel Anghel, Stefánia Toma, and László Fosztó

Contents

Introduction	1672
Ethnic Migration from Romania	1674
Romanian Germans	1674
Romanian Hungarians	1676
The Labor Migration of Majority Romanians	1678
Migrating Minorities	1681
The Migration of the Roma	1682
Conclusions	1684
References	1686

Abstract

In the past 20 years, Romanian migration has grown from small numbers to one of the largest migratory flows in Europe. Much of the literature on this topic covers case studies of the labor migration of ethnic Romanians. In the past few years, there has also emerged a literature focusing on the migration of the Romanian Roma. As these two broad topics rarely meet, this chapter seeks to provide a more comprehensive view of Romanian migration, focusing on migrants' social identities and putting together studies on the migration of people with different ethnic backgrounds.

Romania is a rather diverse society, with significant ethnic and religious minorities; therefore, we took into account the diversity of ethno-religious identities rather than considering Romanian identity as a homogeneous category. In order to provide a comprehensive view of migration, the chapter distinguishes between *ethnic migration*, where migrants migrate to their kin states, *labor migration of the majority*, where migrants use their social capital in order

R. G. Anghel (✉) · S. Toma · L. Fosztó
The Romanian Institute for Research on National Minorities, Cluj Napoca, Romania
e-mail: remusgabriel@yahoo.com; tomastefania76@yahoo.com; Laszlo.foszto@gmail.com

© The Author(s), under exclusive license to Springer Nature Singapore Pte Ltd. 2019
S. Ratuva (ed.), *The Palgrave Handbook of Ethnicity*,
https://doi.org/10.1007/978-981-13-2898-5_124

to migrate, and *migration of minorities*, where migrants belonging to minorities use ties and networks in the same ethnic group. For the first case, the study analyzed the migration of Romanian Germans and Hungarians; for the second, that of ethnic Romanians; and for the third, the migration of Romanian Roma, a migratory flow that has attracted much attention in the past decade. Using this typology, the chapter not only provides a more comprehensive and accurate image of migration from Romania but also discusses how identity and ethnicity can be meaningful categories in migration studies.

Keywords
Romanian migration · Ethnicity · Religion · Ethnic migration · Labor migration

Introduction

In the past 20 years, Romanian citizens have become some of the most mobile Europeans, migrating in large numbers not only within the borders of the European Union but also beyond it. From the limited migration at the beginning of the 1990s immediately after state socialism collapsed, until recently, more than 3.5 million people have migrated to Europe permanently or temporarily. In the past decades, large Romanian communities emerged in many parts of Europe, especially in Italy, Germany, Spain, UK, and Hungary. Migration from Romania was very visible in the past, as it heated up the debates on immigration in many Western European countries. Migrants from Romania were often typified as poor immigrants, challenging public order and representing a burden on state budgets. However, in spite of the homogenizing tendencies of the debates, this large migration was highly diversified in terms of migrants' socioeconomic status, level of education, ethnicity, and religion.

This chapter provides an overview of the existing literature on Romanian migration, highlighting the diversity in the ethnic and religious identities of the migrants. Romania is a multiethnic and multireligious country with significant minorities and we show that especially ethnicity, but also religion, was important for how migration from Romania evolved. It uses the concept of identity to shed light on different social phenomena that influence the life of Romanian citizens and discusses the interrelatedness of identity and migration, inclusion and exclusion, ethnicization and the formation of networks.

It has often been observed that migrants from Romania rely more often on informal channels and networks than on formalized intermediary structures, employment agencies, or manpower companies. Kinship, local identity, ethnicity, and religious belonging shape how these informal networks develop (Sandu 2006) and how migration has developed as a massive social process encompassing large parts of the population in most parts of the country. Migrant social capital, social ties, and networks all play a role, both within the communities of origin and, depending on the context, in the countries of destination, in migrant adaptation and even long-term incorporation. Identity-based networks also stretch across the geographic distances and contribute to the development and maintenance of translocal/transnational connections between migrants and their stay-at-home relatives.

However, how identity (especially ethnicity) played out in this migratory process was not systematically addressed. Based on the existing literature, the chapter proposes a typology which distinguishes between different types of migration processes depending on the degree of institutionalization of ethnicity and related identities. (1) There are minority groups that have their kin states within Europe. These migrants are recognized by their kin states as co-ethnics; they are entitled to special rights – most importantly, privileged access into the country and citizenship. In this case, we speak of *ethnic migration* (Münz and Ohliger 2003), since ethnicity offers a privileged status for the migrants. For this case, the chapter considers the migration of Romanian Germans and Romanian Hungarians. Besides these two cases, ethnic migration from Romania was more diverse, as there were also Jewish people migrating to Israel, Croats migrating to Croatia, or Czechs migrating to the Czech Republic. (2) In the case of ethnic and religious minorities, community ties facilitate migration and incorporation into Western societies. These may involve members of new religions in Romania, such as Adventists or Baptists, as well as members of ethnic minorities such as the Roma, but also Hungarians (migrating to destinations other than Hungary) or Csángó. These are mostly groups which do not gain recognition in the form of preferential access to citizenship in their national kin state or do not have such a state. In these cases, ethnic and religious networks and ties can still provide resources for migration and we can speak of *the migration of minorities*. This chapter presents the case of the Romanian Roma, which is included here as a typical example. (3) Finally, labor migrants are those whose migration involves the use of migrant networks and social ties. Thus, identity and belonging also play a role in the case of the majority of Romanians. Numerous case studies have shown how Romanian identity, in this case kinship and local solidarity, friendship, and emerging ethnic Romanian communities in Western Europe shapes the migration process.

Accordingly, the analysis considers identity and ethnicity as a form of social capital and identification that migrants and would-be migrants use for migration and incorporation that can play an important role in processes of incorporation (see also Moroşanu and Fox 2013). Much of the literature on Romanian migration does not critically assess the role of ethnicity when comparing different forms and patterns of migration. In this way, this chapter intends to provide a more accurate image of Romanian migration, distinguishing it from accounts that pay little attention to ethnicity and religion. It thus portrays Romanian migration as highly diversified, comprising people of different ethnicities and religions who, due to their ethnic or religious affiliations, had different access to migration and employed different migration strategies. It finally considers the importance of addressing the politicization of Romanian migration. As studies have shown, depending on the context of the destination countries, Romanian identity in its different forms often becomes a stigma. While the chapter is mostly concerned with identity as a resource for migration and migrant incorporation, here it is also necessary to consider how belonging, and in particular external perception, can hinder social insertion at the destination. Studies of stalled social mobility or racialization of the migrants offer insights into these processes, as in the case of the Roma migrants.

Ethnic Migration from Romania

Ethnic migration from Romania started first after the First World War and became more intense in the wake of the Second World War. It is among the oldest types of international migration from Romania. Initially, ethnic migration involved Hungarians who migrated to Hungary after the First World War, ethnic Germans who were relocated to Germany during and after the Second World War, and Jews who migrated after the war towards Israel. The German and Jewish migrations especially continued during state socialism over more than 40 years. In the 1980s, Hungarians started to migrate to Hungary again. Causes of migration and migrants' incorporation took various forms, but in all these cases, officially recognized ethnicity offered migrants a privileged status. Due to the fact that Germans and Hungarians remained within the European context and represented a sizeable portion of the Romanian migration, in this section we focus mainly on the migration of these two large communities. Furthermore, the flows of ethnic migration, in particular the migration of Germans to Germany, played an important role in the emerging Romanian labor migration towards Western Europe. In the following sections, these cases are presented and discussed based on the existing literature.

Romanian Germans

The migration of Romania's Germans started during the Second World War with the relocation of Germans from the eastern territories of Romania to areas in Poland under German occupation. This was conducted by the Third Reich as an ethnic engineering policy meant to ensure that "assimilable Germans" would remain German. Later, towards the end of the Second World War and immediately afterwards, there was a movement of German refugees and war prisoners, mostly towards West Germany. As a consequence, of the 750,000 Germans who were living in Romania before the war, only about 350,000 remained in the country after the war. With the arrival of communism in Romania after 1948, international migration was severely restricted, including that of ethnic Germans. However, due to the previous migration to Germany, many families had relatives who had already migrated to Germany. During the first period of the Cold War, this migration was regulated by family reunions negotiated by the Red Cross and later by an intergovernmental agreement between Romania and Germany. Romanian Germans were supported by the German federal states for their migration. This ethnic migration policy was based on the fact that, after the Second World War, East European Germans encountered much discrimination, including mass deportation, and millions of individuals became refugees (Dietz 1999). *Aussiedler* – ethnic

Germans from Eastern Europe – were entitled to receive citizenship, state support and compensation when they arrived in Germany.

The Romanian-German agreement was signed in 1978 and concerned the family reunion of Romanian Germans, for whom the German state was willing to pay a ransom. Initially, this was about 5,000 DM/person. It was later raised by the Romanian authorities to 10,000 DM/person. In addition, there was a commonly agreed yearly allotment of about 10,000 people who could use this framework to migrate to West Germany. In principle, the program was designed to facilitate family reunions. In practice, German ethnicity was the basis of qualification within the agreement. However, the yearly allotment was insufficient for the large numbers of those wishing to migrate to Germany (Weber et al. 2003: 142). State pressure was strong during state socialism. Those wishing to migrate had to go through the administrative procedures of the Romanian state; they lost their jobs and had to sell their houses, often at ludicrously low prices. They faced pressure from the Securitate, the oppressive communist secret service, and the Romanian Militia (the police). Because of the limited number of available places for a large number of applicants, informal practices developed: potential applicants had to offer informal payments to state bureaucrats (often from the Securitate and Militia) in order to obtain legal migration approval from the Romanian authorities. However, not all were able to qualify for these legal procedures. Therefore, irregular exits from Romania developed, especially in the regions neighboring the Yugoslav border. Because borders were militarized, irregular crossings were risky, often including the risk of losing one's life.

The later period of Romanian communism was experienced by many people as a period of very severe food and goods deprivation. In the context of West Germany becoming Europe's wonderland and the most important migratory destination from Romania, a culture of migration oriented towards Germany developed in the communities of origin. Germans also faced an existential problem: the exodus of the entire ethnic community. Most members of the minority felt they had to migrate, since there was no possibility of maintaining the culture and life of the German communities. In order to prevent the exodus of priests, for instance, the German Protestant Church in Romania tried to convince the Protestant Church in Germany not to offer parishes to migrant priests from Romania (Wien 2018). However, such initiatives were in vain, and up to 1989 about 170,000 Germans migrated, amounting to about half of the Romanian German community.

Post-communist migration was sudden. After 1989, when state socialism collapsed, Germans migrated *en masse*, with entire communities vanishing in less than 2 years. Thus, in addition to those who migrated during communism, another 180,000 Germans and their family members migrated up to 1996 (Anghel 2013). The composition of migratory flows also changed. During communism, mainly unmixed families migrated. Afterwards, an increased number of mixed families and families where Romanians could claim German ancestry followed. This is because German families from Romania ceased to be homogeneous; in the last decades of communism, intermarriage was very frequent (Poledna 1998). Thus, the ethnic migration of ethnic Germans paved the way for the migration of

Romanian family members and later enhanced the migration of Romanians to Europe.

Romanian Germans' incorporation into Germany was very successful, at least in economic terms. The majority migrated towards the southern federal states of Bavaria and Baden-Württemberg (Münz and Ohliger 1997: 246–250). Migrants arriving there had first to go to reception camps for East-European Germans (*Aussiedler*). Administrative procedures changed for potential migrants. During communism, migrants had to apply and prove their ethnicity in Romania, but in 1990 exiting Romania was no longer controlled and migrants came to Germany directly. After reception in the camps and successful administrative registration, migrants could move out of the camps. They very quickly obtained German citizenship, financial support for integration and support for language schools and education. Before 1989, there was also compensation for those whose houses had been confiscated by the Romanian state (Groenendijk 1997). Labor-market incorporation was very good for these migrants. Their education and competencies were automatically recognized. Their German language proficiency was very good (Münz and Ohliger 1997), as most of them were German speakers. Thus, according to a study conducted among many *Aussiedler* groups from Romania, Poland, and Russia, Romanian *Aussiedler* performed very well in the labor market (Bauer and Zimmermann 1997).

In conclusion, ethnic Germans' migration was a politically motivated migration driven by Germany's migration policy towards East-European Germans (Weber et al. 2003). Ethnicity was the main selection criterion. However, migration by no means involved only ethnic Germans. In fact, many Romanians and Hungarians followed the same path, together with their German family members and friends. As Anghel (2013) shows, migration after 1989 was accompanied by the marriage migration of (mostly) Romanian women. If Romanian Germans planned no return, before 1989 they had usually encountered enormous difficulties in maintaining their ties to Romania, but after 1989 they could develop ties to Romania more easily. People who managed to retain properties in Romania were able to travel easily between Romania and Germany, and networks of temporary labor migration and businesses developed, stretching between the two countries (Anghel et al. 2016). Pensioners also spent much of their vacation time in their localities of origin. In many of these cases, ethnicity functioned as access to the right to migrate and obtain citizenship. Upon migration, the migrants' social capital encompassed non-ethnic Germans also, and migration diffused to other ethnic groups.

Romanian Hungarians

The ethnic migration of the Hungarians from Romania has some similarities with the case of the Germans, but it is also markedly different. Before 1918, Hungarians formed the politically dominant stratum in Transylvania, which was part of the Dual Monarchy of Austria-Hungary, although statistically, the Romanian population was dominant in the region. As a consequence of the Treaty of Trianon (1920),

Transylvania and Banat became part of Romania. About 1.6 million Hungarians became Romanian citizens. This period signaled the commencement of the systematic migration of Hungarians from Romania to mainland Hungary. While migrations continued at different paces and intensities during the various periods of the past century, the size of the Hungarian population decreased. However, it has been able to itself within Romania to this day, as the 2011 census recorded about 1.2 million ethnic Hungarians. The reasons for the sustained ethnic population, as well as for the ethnic migration of the Hungarians include internal factors, such as the historical political economy of the population and its identity formation, domestic policies of Romania towards minorities, and the external politics of the Hungarian state oriented towards Hungarians living abroad.

Immediately after the end of the First World War, a significant wave of refugees reached Hungary. Between 1918 and 1924, about 197,000 Hungarians left Greater Romania for Hungary, and a further 10,000 left in the period up to 1940 (Stark 2011). This migration was generated by pressures such as the restrictive policies of Romania, which introduced a compulsory oath of loyalty and Romanian language exams for public administration employees, as well as occurring for economic reasons. In the interwar period, the external politics of Hungary aimed to preserve the territorial distribution and residence of the Hungarians living in the successor states of the Monarchy, and there were sustained efforts to demand territorial revision. These contributed to the maintenance of the community within Romania. For a 4-year period (1940–1944) during the Second World War, the northern part of Transylvania became part of Hungary. Thousands of Hungarians from southern Transylvania, still part of Romania, fled to Northern Transylvania during this period. The Hungarian administration proceeded with the deportation of the Jewish population, most of whom were Hungarian speakers. By the end of the war, only 44,000 of the original 151,000 remained in Northern Transylvania (Stark 2011).

As stated previously, after the Second World War, international migration was limited by the Romanian communist authorities during the 1950s and 1960s. There was increased pressure to assimilate and relations with foreigners, including the Hungarians from Hungary, were under strict control. By the late 1980s, due to economic shortages and the declining possibilities for careers, many Hungarians planned emigration, although the socialist Hungary had no policies in place similar to those in Germany to welcome them. Those Hungarians who managed to flee were granted refugee status in Hungary (although Hungary did not sign the Geneva Convention until 1989). The numbers of these refugees reached a peak during the period between 1988 and 1990; totaling 47,954 persons, half of whom crossed the border illegally (Gödri 2004).

Romanian citizens could submit requests for residence permits and naturalization after 1990. Labor migration also became regularized between Romania and Hungary in the form of work permits issued for Romanian citizens. Hungarians from Romania continued to be the most significant immigrant group in Hungary. On the eve of Hungary joining the EU in 2004, about half of all immigrants were from Romania (and about an additional quarter from the former Yugoslavia and the

Ukraine), most of whom were ethnic Hungarians. The overwhelming majority of labor migrants were also from these same countries. The geographical proximity and the cultural and linguistic similarity facilitated the relatively smooth integration of these groups.

However, the immigration of Hungarians from Romania was not without adverse effects, as the level of xenophobia gradually increased and ethnic Hungarians from Romania were also targeted. As Fox shows (2007), Transylvanian Hungarians migrating to Hungary for work very often encountered negative stereotyping from the majority population. He concluded that a policy intended to produce national unity and solidarity produced ethnic disunity and economic exclusion among Transylvanian migrant workers in Hungary. In December 2001, Hungary gave special status to ethnic Hungarians living across the borders, to ease their access (Stewart 2003). Issues related to unwelcome labor migrants became topical during the 2002 election campaign; according to opposition leaders, the government wanted to "unleash millions of Romanian workers" to outcompete the Hungarian workers. In spite of the language and cultural closeness and the rights they had, towards 2007 Transylvanian Hungarians started to prefer new and richer labor markets in western and southern Europe and did not continue going to Hungary to the same extent as before.

Romania joined the EU in 2007 and a simplified procedure for obtaining Hungarian citizenship for ethnic Hungarians was introduced by the Hungarian government in 2010. As an outcome of this procedure for extraterritorial citizenship, increasing numbers of ethnic Hungarians from Romania acquired Hungarian citizenship, enabling them to access the labor market and social services within Hungary if they decided to migrate there. Even if they decided to stay in Romania, they could have political influence during the national elections, from without. This change brought the promise of full political membership and compensation for what they perceived as a century-long political marginality within their home country of Romania. However, the block vote of the new citizens also fueled controversies both in Hungary and to a lesser degree in Romania, during the recent parliamentary elections.

The Labor Migration of Majority Romanians

Migration of ethnic Romanians began to develop more substantially during the later period of communism. Like the migration of Germans and Hungarians, this was mostly a politically motivated migration. People could migrate while visiting foreign countries in professional exchanges, while visiting relatives or by leaving Romania irregularly. Legal migration was in principle possible for purposes of family reunion. The number of those migrating legally grew during the late years of communism, but the numbers were smaller than the numbers of ethnic Germans migrating legally (Horváth and Anghel 2009). After the collapse of state socialism, migration motivations were mostly economic. Labor migration from Romania, encompassing mostly ethnic Romanians but also members of other ethnic groups, evolved differently from the migration of ethnic migrants. Romanians' labor migration developed largely through the use of migrants' social capital, i.e., migrant networks and social ties (Sandu 2005). Over the years, the use of migrant networks and ties was employed differently in relation to migration and the labor opportunities Romanians had at different periods of time. Migration passed through several distinctive periods – first one of pioneers after the collapse of communism, followed by large-scale labor migration and later, one of diversified migration, especially after 2007 when Romania joined the EU (idem).

After 1989, the migration of majority Romanians was tied to that of Romania's ethnic minorities in its initial phases. Migration towards Germany of ethnic Germans was the first major migration from Romania. Germany was also the main European destination after 1990, as migrants from Romania went there during late communism and in the first years after 1989. Up to 1993, for instance, Romanians represented the largest group of asylum seekers (Anghel 2013). As Diminescu points out (Diminescu 2003), Germany was the "entry point" for Romanians going to Europe in the 1990s. As studies on the early migrations of Romanians unfolded, it was seen that Romanians used their ties to Romanian Germans in order to get to Germany and from there to different European countries (Bleahu 2004; Cingolani 2009; Elrick and Ciobanu 2009). In this period, when Romanians were pioneers of migration, migration was an innovative social practice, with pioneers looking for new destinations (idem). Romanian migrants were initially marginal migrants (Diminescu 2003; Marcu 2015). In a few years, Romanian migration grew, due to the development of migrant networks (Sandu 2006). Various studies (Şerban and Grigoraş 2000; Bleahu 2004; Sandu 2006; Elrick and Ciobanu 2009; Anghel 2013) show how these migrant networks were established, not only among kin members but also among friends and acquaintances from the same localities of origin. The study by Bleahu (2004) shows how a large network of migrants arrived in Spain. Using social capital, the pioneer migrant who initiated the network helped friends and relatives to migrate. In this case, he often helped friends first and relatives later. In a different study (Anghel 2013), networks developed between northern Romania and Milan, based almost exclusively on large kinship networks. Such case studies, concerning migrants from small Romanian localities, demonstrate social closure towards various other migrants, including Romanians. These studies and some others showed that social capital among co-ethnic Romanians was mobilized for migration, with extended migrant networks based on local trust and solidarity. Migrant networks provided funds for migration, knowledge of migratory strategies, and accommodation opportunities. They rapidly extended from one or two individuals to families and groups. Labor was also most often obtained via migrant networks. For migrants without social support, labor was obtained by relying on new acquaintances, usually made by Romanian co-ethnics, in risky and dynamic social environments in Western European cities (Perrotta 2011). As much of the labor was informal, newly arrived immigrants sought for jobs in the places where Romanians and other migrants were meeting. In places such as Madrid, Milan, or Rome, where there was a larger concentration of Romanian immigrants, Romanian migrants met in various open places in a search for jobs, accommodation, and new acquaintances. In many cases, Romanian entrepreneurs also relied on socializing with newly arrived Romanians to run their businesses and to obtain a certain social position (Anghel et al. 2016).

The development of this large migration was caused by the massive growth of labor demands in secondary labor markets in the countries of southern Europe (Italy, Spain, Portugal, and Greece) that became major attractors of international migration after 1990 (Anghel et al. 2016). In Romania, migration was driven by the massive collapse of the socialist economy, a process that left much of the population without jobs (Horváth and Anghel 2009). The level of employment fell dramatically. Between 1990 and 1999, 40% of jobs disappeared from the labor market. In industry, 48% of jobs disappeared (idem). Furthermore, in so-called mono-industrial cities and regions, the collapse of the former communist industry resulted in massive unemployment for the population. This large migration of Romanians took place between 2000 and 2008, when aggregate labor demand was very high in southern Europe.

Later, this labor migration, where migrants were needed in construction, care, or agriculture, decreased drastically when labor opportunities dropped in these countries, due to the economic crisis that struck southern Europe. After 2007, with the accession of Romania to the European Union, Romanian citizens became EU citizens; they had more rights than before and after a period of restrictions they were able to travel, reside, and work freely within the EU. The economic crisis resulted in another push for Romanian migrants, as it also hit the Romanian economy, putting pressure on salaries and labor opportunities. Institutionally mediated migration intensified over the years. Romanian state authorities enabled labor recruitment policies conducted by Spain and Germany, even from the early 2000s. However, the numbers of those recruited within these frameworks were small in comparison to the overall numbers of migrants (Horváth and Anghel 2009). As European citizens, Romanians could be employed formally through a variety of means, not only using state-mediated contracts but also through manpower companies operating both in Romania and abroad, through Romanian companies operating abroad or through direct employment in the labor market. Thus, as Romania became part of the EU, Romanians could easily find jobs in labor-intensive sectors, such as construction, care, butcheries, or agriculture.

Furthermore, Romanians started to migrate towards northern European countries, such as the Netherlands, Belgium, and the UK, and diversified their lines of business. Studies conducted in this period mention the ties used by migrants, rather than the extended networks used previously, together with flexible migratory projects (Meeus 2012). The concept of liquid migration (Engbersen and Erik 2013) may aptly describe migration in this period. Migratory practices were more temporary in nature and there was a less solid labor demand than there had been in southern Europe, where construction and care demanded very large numbers of workers. Furthermore, Romanians migrated towards the northern destinations not only from Romania but also from southern destinations such as Spain, using their ties to friends and relatives (Ciobanu 2015). Thus, migration after the economic crisis was more complex, as it involved many temporary practices, changes in migratory destinations, returns, and a wider diversity of migratory profiles. It also involved jobs mediated by both social networks and manpower companies and people using networks of co-ethnics or mixed networks. In addition, migration involved both temporary and long-term migration. For example, the migration of highly qualified Romanians followed a different path: migration was more selective and involved fewer social networks. Many Romanians migrated first as students and later prolonged their stay (Csedö 2008; Morosanu 2013). As European citizens, the migration of highly qualified workers was more flexible and less structured. One consistent migration was of medical doctors and nurses, whose recruitment was actively sought by Western European manpower companies and hospitals (Anghel et al. 2016).

Due to this migration, there emerged large communities of Romanian immigrants in Western European countries, with greater concentrations around cities such as Rome, Turin, Madrid, Barcelona, London, Nuremberg, and Stuttgart. In such places, Romanian ethnicity was mobilized by migrant organizations and Romanian Churches, especially the Orthodox Church. Although few studies have been undertaken on this important subject, the studies of Ciornei, Cingolani and Coşciug stress that religion had an important role, not only in the development of migration but also in integration and mobilization of migrants' social capital both at home and abroad (Coşciug forthcoming; Cingolani 2009; Ciornei 2012). Ethnic solidarity and new forms of ethnic connectedness appeared in larger urban areas, also manifesting via Internet sites, such as Facebook groups of Romanian migrants living in certain European cities, where those seeking information on jobs, accommodation, and various bureaucratic procedures could find support from more established Romanian migrants.

Ethnic mobilization may be of increased relevance in the context of the politicization of migration also. Romanian migrants were often the subject of heated anti-Romanian debates in major destination countries such as Spain, Italy, or the UK (McMahon 2015). They were often stereotyped as social security concerns or as poverty migrants. Although policy reactions to the arrival of Romanians have been analyzed in some studies, less research has been done on how Romanians reacted to these situations (idem). Their status had passed from one of irregular migrants to one of freely moving European citizens. However, a large majority of them performed lower-status jobs in construction, care, or agriculture. A topic also less covered by research is how Romanians experienced ethnicity. Studies conducted in the UK point towards two main strategies: playing "invisible" and focusing on personal worthiness and skills (Moroşanu and Fox 2013) or transferring the stigma to other migrants, most often Roma originating from Romania (idem). The second strategy, especially, that of racializing and stigmatizing the Roma, was not only adopted in emigration contexts: whenever public debates erupted in relation to Romanian migrants, the media in Romania emphasized this strong stereotyping of the Roma.

Migrating Minorities

The migration of Romania's ethnic and religious minorities also differed from that of ethnic and labor migrants. Ethnic migrants were, of course, members of minority groups. However, the defining feature of ethnic migrants is that *identity as status* (here *ethnicity*) provides the means to migrate. For migrating minorities, it is social capital, whether confined or not to members of the same ethnic or religious group, that drives migration. Romania has 18 recognized national minorities. As in the situation of the majority Romanians, members of these ethnic minorities were significantly involved in migration. This was the situation for Croats, Czechs, and Ukrainians. For this second category of migrating minorities, this study uses the case of the Romanian Roma. A similar framework could be used to understand the migration of members of different minority Churches and religious groups, especially the new religious denominations which developed in the country after 1989: Baptists, Jehovah's Witnesses, and Adventists. Despite the fact that ethnic identity differs from religious identity, some studies attest that migration propagated as a group strategy among members of the same religious community.

Ethnic and religious communities were the most mobile communities from Romania in the first years after 1989 when Romanians could exit the country without restrictions, but they started to face travel and migration restrictions from Western European countries. While there is substantive research on migration of ethnic minorities, there is less on Romania's minority religions. However, existing studies seem to suggest that religious social capital played a role in the migration of many Romanians. What makes the case particularly interesting is that members of these religious denominations could capitalize on their religious capital abroad, obtaining access to foreign countries, labor markets, and a community of co-believers they could rely on. The studies of Stan (cited in Anghel 2013) and Cingolani (2009), in three different villages in eastern Romania, show that members of religious minorities in Romania, i.e., Catholic and Pentecostal believers, migrated first to Western Europe. After their migration, their relatives migrated also, using kinship ties to neo-Protestant and Catholic Romanians. The study of Cingolani goes even further – he showed that multiethnic Romanian-Italian religious ties were used for labor-market incorporation. The Pentecostals' ties to the community of origin in Romania made them a transnationalized religious community, whereas the transnationalism of Orthodox Romanians was more individualized and less intense (Cingolani 2009). However, in spite of these results and the importance of the topic, little research is devoted to the migration of members of minority religious communities from Romania. However, based on these studies, the chapter hypothesizes that religious social capital played an important role in the migration of many Romanians and their labor-market incorporation abroad. More consistent literature exists, however, with respect to the migration of ethnic minorities, particularly the Roma, which has received much attention in the past 10 years. The following section details this migration, also paying attention to some effects of the migration of this discriminated-against group in the country of origin.

The Migration of the Roma

The first accounts of the mobility of the Roma from Romania in the early 1990s focus on the high number of asylum applications (Matras 2000), especially in Germany, France, and Ireland. In this period, accounts of ethnic conflicts and discrimination and persecution of the Roma in the home localities were common. After this period, however, the public discourse shifted toward a more stigmatizing presentation, often speaking about "waves of migrant Roma" or even an "exodus" or an "invasion." Such discourses were heightened prior to 2007, the moment when Romania joined the EU. The European Commission criticized Romania for not being able to regulate the policies for migration and free movement of its citizens and recommended that the Romanian authorities take more severe action to stop illegal migration. This was mirrored by public discourse; an analysis by an Agency for Press Monitoring (Ganea and Martin 2006) shows that the Roma minority was presented in a negative way and often associated with "criminality." A journal started a national campaign entitled "Gypsy instead of Roma" in which the authors argued that there is a need to dissociate the majority population from the Roma minority, who were said to "spread the negative image of Romanians in the world." The campaign was followed by heated disputes – even a legislative debate – regarding the proposal to change the ethnonym of the Roma. At the request of the Romanian Government, the Romanian Academy of Sciences issued an official statement recommending the use of the term "Gypsy" when speaking about the Roma minority of Romania (Fosztó 2018).

Press outlets, not only in Romania but also in Italy, published derogatory reports on the Romanian Roma (Italy being one of favorite destination countries for their migration in this period). Several studies concluded that after the EU enlargement, the number of negative depictions of Romanian migrants – Roma among them – had increased significantly. Surveys among Italian citizens showed that more than half of their respondents felt personally threatened by the presence of the Roma and Roma camps. The Roma represented the "number one enemy" for Spanish citizens also, Spain being the other favored destination country (López Catalán 2011). These situations, and especially the reaction of the French authorities to the presence of Romanian Roma (Nacu 2012), led to the launch of the EU Framework for National Roma Integration Strategies in 2011. However, many measures focused more on ways of excluding Romanian Roma from destination countries by preventing or restricting movement or by facilitating the expulsion of Roma migrants, framed by increasing anti-Gypsyism.

In this context, a growing number of empirical case studies emerged contributing to the deeper understanding of the migration of the Roma population from Romania. While the migration of Romanian citizens generally is characterized by more or less well-defined frameworks (Horváth and Anghel 2009), the case studies on the migration of the Romanian Roma provide us with an image of a more complex phenomenon, partially due to the diversity of the Roma groups (Tesăr 2015), while at the same time, it is not clearly independent of the migration of the majority population (Nacu 2011). Early field studies focused on the structural integration of Roma migrants, both in the country of origin and in the destination countries, highlighting that decisions and the potential to migrate are structured by available informal networks and resources (Pantea 2012, 2013). Pantea (idem) drew a distinction between communities rich in migration and those poor in migration. Migration was thus not a levelled, uniform process among the Roma from Romania; it varied widely between communities where migration is a more sustained process and those where migration is rare, with respect to the ways people were able to mobilize their social capital. Some case studies similarly showed that, in many cases, migration of the Roma was separated from that of Romanians or Hungarians (Anghel 2016; Toma et al. 2018). Networks and resources also play a role in their integration into the receiving society: as Nacu (2011) observed, many Romanian Roma migrants are concentrated in the suburbs of large cities, living in more or less temporary camps or in inadequate homes lacking basic and proper infrastructure (running water, electricity, heating, etc.), making it difficult for them to access basic social services.

During the past few years there have been increasing numbers of studies on the European policies for, and the local context of, Roma migration, with a particular focus on the destination countries. A large part of this scholarly literature highlights the limitations of European citizenship in effectively protecting the rights of the most vulnerable during their sojourns within the Union (van Baar et al. 2019) and demonstrates that their social mobility is stalled at the destination (Beluschi-Fabeni et al. 2018). In addition, their exclusion continues or even intensifies after they return home (Crețan and Powell 2018). A 4-year-long EU-funded research project (MigRom) empirically investigated the mobility of the Romanian Roma (Matras and Leggio 2018). Recent studies also focus on the ethnically mixed communities of origin within Romania (Anghel 2016; Toma et al. 2018). Social relations and local networks within these localities shape how migration patterns develop, the effect of social distance between the different segments of the local population (Toma and Fosztó 2018), the strategies of repositioning of the returnees and the diverging paths of local social development. On the other hand, for poor Roma, migration represented an opportunity for financial betterment and even a way of decreasing the sharp inequality that exists between the poor Roma, often living in segregated quarters, and the Romanian or Hungarian majority (Anghel 2016; Toma et al. 2018).

The issue of identity is ingrained in all these studies in intricate ways. In the ethnically mixed localities of origin, which are often residentially segregated, Roma identity is stigmatized. Mobility might offer escape from the local stigma, but racial stigma is also present in the context of destination countries. Nevertheless, migrants are able to navigate between different identity constructions, for example, the multiple geographical and social anchorages of the mobile Roma families, their Romanian national identity or the new residence in the destination country, even though that might be a shantytown. At the same time, returnees often reposition themselves upon return: some challenge the local categorizations and the hierarchy of identities at home, and spontaneous residential desegregation processes are underway as part of the migration-induced local development in places of origin.

Conclusions

Most studies on Romanian migration have focused either on the labor migration of ethnic Romanians or, in recent years, on the migration of Roma. Ethnicity as a relevant category for the structuration of Romanian migration was less frequently addressed in a comprehensive manner. Romania is a rather diverse society, with significant ethnic and religious minorities. Therefore, we considered the diversity of ethno-religious identities rather than considering Romanian identity as a homogeneous category. Identities, forming the basis for networks and solidarities which contribute to the emerging processes of migration in the communities of origin, can be important resources for migrants in the destination countries. If their identity is perceived as a stigma, it can hinder the incorporation or stall the social mobility of migrants in the context of their new home. Translocal and transnational ties stretch identities across state borders, channel remittances, and direct returns.

This chapter presented research focused on the Romanian Germans and the Romanian Hungarians as cases of so-called *ethnic migration*. In these cases, *ethnicity-as-status* is rather well institutionalized and serves as a basis for migration, entitlement to rights, and citizenship acquisition in the destination countries. Ethnic and linguistic similarity eases the process of inclusion in the labor market and society of the destination. Moreover, as the case of ethnic Germans exemplified, ethnic migration can also facilitate the large labor migration of the majority Romanians. State policies can make a crucial difference in the development of ethnic migration, as the contrasting cases of the Hungarians and Germans showed. Hungary's external policy towards the Hungarians abroad did not encourage immigration and naturalization over long periods, until recently when procedures for extraterritorial citizenship were introduced. In contrast, West Germany (and later Germany) held the door open for Germans from Eastern Europe, due to the country's political responsibility towards people who had to suffer after the Second World War because of their German ethnicity.

The case of *migration of ethnic minorities* is exemplified by the recent mobility of the Roma, which intensified over the last decade. In this case, ethnicity is not a basis for citizenship in the destination country. Rather the opposite: Roma identity is stigmatized very often at home and is also stigmatized abroad in the context of the destination country. Nevertheless, Roma migrants can take advantage of the resources available to them in the form of local social networks at home or abroad and the labor and financial resources available. The interplay between overcoming exclusion, returning, and repositioning in the local context offers a fertile ground for analysis of the role that identities play in the migration process.

The *migration of the majority* Romanians, both the Orthodox Christians and other religious groups, provides yet another angle from which to view migrants' social identity. Here, the chapter focused mostly on how migrants used their social networks and ties to migrate and adapt to the destination countries. Social networks based on kinship, friendship, and locality of origin supported the large migration of Romanians to Western Europe. As research developed and as the chapter discusses, it was shown that Romanians' social capital was employed differently at different periods of time: the periods with migration based on extended networks coincided with the contexts of strong pushing factors in Romania, which was experiencing crises and economic decay, and strong pulling factors abroad, especially the strong demand for laborers in southern Europe. As pushing factors became less intense and labor offers diversified into many more localities and countries of destination, extended networks were replaced by ties and, in some contexts, by institutions that mediated the migration of labor migrants. Furthermore, another relevant factor was the emergence of large Romanian communities abroad, providing support and assistance to newly arriving immigrants.

In conclusion, using this typology, the chapter gathered and compared cases that have generally been treated separately: the migration of ethnic Romanians and that of ethnic minorities from Romania. In so doing, it provided a broader and more comprehensive view of how one of the most important migratory flows in Europe emerged and developed, i.e., that of Romanian citizens. It also addresses how migrants fared at their destinations and the contexts they encountered, including politicization of migration and emerging anti-immigrant sentiments.

References

Anghel RG (2013) Romanians in Western Europe. Migration, status dilemmas and transnational connections. Lexington Books/Rowman and Littlefield, Lanham

Anghel RG (2016) Migration in differentiated localities: changing statuses and ethnic relations in a multi-ethnic locality in Transylvania, Romania. Popul Space Place 22:356–366. https://doi.org/10.1002/psp.1925

Anghel RG, Botezat A, Cosciug A, et al (2016) International migration, return migration, and their effects: a comprehensive review on the Romanian case. Bonn. http://migrationcenter.ro/wp/wp-content/uploads/2017/07/Anghel-Remus-et.-al.-2017.-International-Migration-Return-Migration.pdf

Bauer T, Zimmermann FK (1997) Network migration of ethnic Germans. Int Migr Rev 31:143–149

Beluschi-Fabeni G, Leggio DV, Matras Y (2018) A lost generation? Racialization and stalled social mobility in a group of Roma migrants in the UK. Migr Stud. https://doi.org/10.1093/migration/mny003

Bleahu A (2004) Romanian migration to Spain. Motivation, networks and strategies. New Patterns Labour Migr Cent East Eur 20–35

Cingolani P (2009) Romeni d'Italia. Migrazioni, Vita Quotidiana e Legami Transnazionali. Il Mulino, Bologna

Ciobanu RO (2015) Multiple migration flows of Romanians. Mobilities. https://doi.org/10.1080/17450101.2013.863498

Ciornei I (2012) The political incorporation of immigrant associations and religious organizations of the Romanian residents in Spain. Stud Sociol 57:51–76

Coșciug A (forthcoming) Religion, return migration and change in an emigration country. In: Anghel RG, Fauser M, Boccagni P (eds) Transnational return and social change. Social hierarchies, cultural capital and colelctive identities. Anthem Press: London

Crețan R, Powell R (2018) The power of group stigmatization: wealthy Roma, urban space and strategies of defence in post-socialist Romania. Int J Urban Reg Res 42:423–441. https://doi.org/10.1111/1468-2427.12626

Csedö K (2008) Routes leading to London: negotiating skills in the global city. London School of Economics

Dietz B (1999) Ethnic German immigration from Eastern Europe and the former Soviet Union to Germany: the effects of migrant networks. Discussion paper no. 68. IZA Discussion paper series. IZA, Bonn

Diminescu D (2003) Visible Mais peu Nombreux. Les Circulations Migratoires Roumaines. Éditions de la Maison de Science des L'Homme, Paris

Elrick T, Ciobanu O (2009) Migration networks and policy impacts: insights from Romanian-Spanish migrations. Glob Netw J Transnatl Aff 9:100–116(17)

Engbersen G, Erik S (2013) Liquid migration. Dynamic and fluid patterns of post-accession migration flows. In: Grabowska-Lusinska I, Kuvik A, Glorius B (eds) Mobility in transition. Migration patterns of EU enlargement. Amsterdam University Press, Amsterdam, pp 21–40

Fosztó L (2018) Encounters at the margins. Activism and research in Romani studies in post-socialist Romania. In: Beck S, Ivasiuc A (eds) Roma activism. Reimagining power and knowledge. Berghahn Books, Oxford/New York, pp 65–87

Fox J (2007) From national inclusion to economic exclusion: ethnic Hungarian labour migration to Hungary. Nations Natl 13:77–96

Ganea L, Martin R (2006) Minorități și discriminare în agenda presei. Agenția de Monitorizare a Presei, Bucharest

Gödri I (2004) A special case of international migration: ethnic Hungarians migrating from Transylvania to Hungary. In: Finnish yearbook of population research. Väestöliitto, The Family Federation of Finland, pp 45–72

Groenendijk K (1997) Regulating ethnic immigration: the case of the Aussiedler. New Community 23:461–482

Horváth I, Anghel RG (2009) Migration and its consequences for Romania. Südosteuropa Zeitschrift für Polit und Gesellschaft 57:386–403

López Catalán Ó (2011) Mobilitate forțată, poziții marginale și accesul la drepturile fundamentale. Migranții romi și politicile locale din Zona Metropolitană Barcelona. In: Toma S, Fosztó L (eds) Spectrum. Cercetări sociale despre romi. ISPMN /Kriterion, Cluj-Napoca, pp 231–266

Marcu S (2015) From the marginal immigrant to the mobile citizen: reconstruction of identity of Romanian migrants in Spain. Popul Space Place. https://doi.org/10.1002/psp.1845

Matras Y (2000) Romani migrations in the post-communist era: their historical and political significance. Camb Rev Int Aff 13:32–50. https://doi.org/10.1080/09557570008400297

Matras Y, Leggio DV (eds) (2018) Open borders, unlocked cultures Romanian Roma migrants in Western Europe. Routledge, London/New York

McMahon S (2015) Immigration and citizenship in an enlarged European Union : the political dynamics of intra-EU mobility. Palgrave Macmillan, Basingstoke

Meeus B (2012) How to "catch" floating populations? Research and the fixing of migration in space and time. Ethn Racial Stud 35:1775–1793. https://doi.org/10.1080/01419870.2012.659272

Morosanu L (2013) Between fragmented ties and "soul friendships": the cross-border social connections of young Romanians in London. J Ethn Migr Stud. https://doi.org/10.1080/1369183X.2013.733858

Moroşanu L, Fox JE (2013) "No smoke without fire": strategies of coping with stigmatised migrant identities. Ethnicities. https://doi.org/10.1177/1468796813483730

Münz R, Ohliger R (1997) Deutsche Minderheiten in Ostmittel – und Osteuropa, Aussiedler in Deutschland, Eine Analyse ethnisch privilegierter Migration. In: Kaelble H, Schriewer J (eds) Diskurse und Entwicklungspfade. Der Gesellschaftsvergleich in den Geschichts- und Sozialwissenschaften. Campus, Frankfurt am Main, pp 217–270

Münz R, Ohliger R (2003) Diasporas and ethnic migrants. Germany, Israel and post-soviet succesor states in comparative perspective. Frank Cass, London/Portland

Nacu A (2011) The politics of Roma migration: framing identity struggles among Romanian and bulgarian Roma in the Paris region. J Ethn Migr Stud. https://doi.org/10.1080/1369183X.2010.515134

Nacu A (2012) From silent marginality to spotlight scapegoating? A brief case study of France's policy towards the Roma. J Ethn Migr Stud. https://doi.org/10.1080/1369183X.2012.689192

Pantea MC (2012) From 'making a living' to 'getting ahead': Roma women's experiences of migration. J Ethn Migr Stud 38:1251–1268. https://doi.org/10.1080/1369183X.2012.689185

Pantea MC (2013) Social ties at work: Roma migrants and the community dynamics. Ethn Racial Stud. https://doi.org/10.1080/01419870.2012.664282

Perrotta D (2011) Rischio e disposizione predatoria. I rumeni irregolari in Italia tra il 2002 e il 2006. Mondi Migranti 67–84. https://doi.org/10.3280/MM2011-001004

Poledna RI (1998) Transformări Sociale la Sașii Ardeleni după 1945. Universitatea Babeș-Bolyai, Cluj Napoca

Sandu D (2005) Emerging transnational migration from Romanian villages. Curr Sociol 53. https://doi.org/10.1177/0011392105052715
Sandu D (2006) Locuirea temporară în străinătate. Migrația economică a românilor: 1990–2006. The Foundation for an Open Society, Bucharest
Şerban M, Grigoraş V (2000) Dogenii din Teleormani în Țară și în Străinătate. Sociol Românească 2:30–54
Stark T (2011) Population movements in the Carpathian Basin. In: Bárdi N, Fedinec C, Szarka L (eds) Minority Hungarian communities in the twentieth century. Atlantic Research and Publications, Distributed by Columbia University Press, Boulder/Budapest, pp 680–695
Stewart M (2003) The Hungarian status law: a new European form of transnational politics? Diaspora J Transnatl Stud 12:67–101. https://doi.org/10.1353/dsp.2011.0056
Tesăr C (2015) Begging: between charity and profession. Reflections on Romanian Roma's begging activities in Italy. In: Tauber E, Zinn D (eds) The public value of anthropology: engaging critical social issues through ethnography. Bozen-Bolzano University Press, Bozen-Bolzano, pp 83–111
Toma S, Fosztó L (2018) Roma within obstructing and transformative spaces: migration process and social distance in ethnically mixed localities in Romania. Intersect East Eur J Soc Polit 4:1–20
Toma S, Tesăr C, Fosztó L (2018) Romanian Roma at home: mobility patterns, migration experiences, networks, and remittances. In: Matras Y, Leggio DV (eds) Open borders, unlocked cultures : Romanian Roma migrants in Western Europe. Routledge, London/New York, pp 57–82
van Baar H, Ivasiuc A, Kreide R (2019) The European Roma and their securitization: contexts, junctures, challenges. In: van Baar H, Ivasiuc A, Kreide R (eds) The securitization of the Roma in Europe. Palgrave Macmillan, Cham, pp 1–25
Weber G, Nassehi A, Weber-Schlenter R, et al (2003) Emigration der Siebenbürgen Sachsen. Studien zu Ost-West Wanderungen im 20. Jahrhundert. Westdeutscher Verlag, Wiesbaden
Wien UA (2018) Biserica Evanghelică C.A. din România începând cu anul 1918. In: Trașcă O, Anghel RG (eds) Un Veac Frământat. Germanii din România după 1918. Institutului pentru Studierea Problemelor Minorităților Naționale, Cluj-Napoca, pp 199–254

Refugee Protection and Settlement Policy in New Zealand

86

Louise Humpage

Contents

Introduction	1690
Current and Proposed Refugee Protection Policy	1691
Quota Pathway	1691
Convention Pathway	1692
Family Reunification Pathway	1693
Emergency Protection Pathway	1695
Community Sponsorship Pathway	1695
Pacific Climate Change Pathway?	1696
Settlement Policy	1698
Initial Orientation and Settlement	1699
Housing	1700
Self-Sufficiency	1701
Education	1702
Health and Well-Being	1703
Participation	1704
Conclusion	1706
Cross-References	1707
References	1707

Abstract

New Zealand is a small country that often frames itself as making a big contribution regarding refugee protection and settlement. This chapter highlights where New Zealand is world leading but also where scholars believe it does not meet international obligations, with particular focus on how refugees selected via an annual quota are prioritized over other refugees when it comes to initial orientation and settlement, family reunification, and access to social services. This form of institutional discrimination is exemplified by the 2012

L. Humpage (✉)
Sociology, Faculty of Arts, University of Auckland, Auckland, New Zealand
e-mail: l.humpage@auckland.ac.nz

© The Author(s), under exclusive license to Springer Nature Singapore Pte Ltd. 2019
S. Ratuva (ed.), *The Palgrave Handbook of Ethnicity*,
https://doi.org/10.1007/978-981-13-2898-5_125

New Zealand Refugee Resettlement Strategy which focuses only on Quota refugees. A new coalition government formed in 2017 promised significant change in refugee policy, including an extension of the refugee quota, a new humanitarian visa for those displaced by climate change, and further investment in many under-resourced public services. But an overall context where economic and political factors shape policy as much as humanitarian needs remains the biggest obstacle to radically improving the lives of refugees settled in New Zealand.

Keywords

Refugee protection · Refugee settlement · Institutional discrimination · New Zealand · Policy

Introduction

The 1951 United Nations Convention Relating to the Status of Refugees defines a "refugee" as a person with a well-founded fear of persecution for reasons of race, religion, nationality, membership of a particular group or political opinion. As a signatory to the Refugee Convention and the related 1967 Protocol, New Zealand is one of the 196 countries who have committed to protecting refugees and asylum seekers and one of 35 countries with an annual settlement program (United Nations High Commissioner for Refugees – UNHCR 2017). Beaglehole (2009) notes that New Zealand's long history of accepting refugees since World War II is often framed as exceptionally humanitarian but has actually been driven by mixed intentions and, until the early 1980s, by a general reluctance to take refugees from non-European origins.

Today, New Zealand accepts refugees from a variety of ethnic and national backgrounds. Between July 2017 and May 2018, New Zealand welcomed 1020 refugees representing 23 different nationalities with Syria, Myanmar, Colombia, and Afghanistan being the most common (Immigration New Zealand – INZ 2018a). Moreover, in 2017, New Zealand elected a new government led by the Labour Party in coalition with the New Zealand First Party and supported in confidence and supply by the Green Party. The Labour and Green parties promised big changes in refugee protection and, to a lesser extent, settlement policy. This chapter argues that the Labour-led coalition government's reforms and modest funding increases are welcome but insufficient to overcome institutional discrimination resulting in assistance for newly resettled refugees being unevenly distributed, as well as significantly underfunded. Moreover, although New Zealand's policies are far less controversial than those espoused by Donald Trump in the United States of America or far-right groups in Europe, Beaglehole's (2009) argument that economic and political factors – not just humanitarian ones – play a part in the admission and the selection of refugees in New Zealand remains true in the twenty-first century.

Current and Proposed Refugee Protection Policy

The Immigration Act 2009 provides a process for New Zealand to meet its international obligations and support the settlement of refugees but Marlowe and Elliott (2014: 46) contend that: "Despite a nearly 70-year history of refugee resettlement, New Zealand does not have a formal refugee policy." As in many other policy areas, refugee protection has developed in a rather ad hoc manner over several decades, enabling world-leading humanitarianism to sit alongside what Mahoney et al. (2017) and the Human Rights Commission (HRC 2017) believe to be significant breaches of international obligations. This section highlights the four major pathways to protection available to refugee claimants, as well as a new community sponsorship pathway and proposals for a unique climate change humanitarian visa being considered by the new Labour-led government, because very different lived experiences result from these varied protection pathways.

Quota Pathway

Most refugees in New Zealand are selected overseas in UNHCR camps using Refugee Convention criteria and granted refugee status before arriving in New Zealand. They are known as "Quota refugees" because New Zealand committed to resettling a quota of up to 800 refugees annually in 1987; reduced to 750 in 1997, this refugee quota remained unchanged for three decades until a National Party-led government agreed to raise the quota to 1000 from July 2018 (Labour Party 2017). The new Labour-led government plans a further increase to 1500 per year by 2021 (Ministry of Business, Innovation and Employment – MBIE 2017). Although 1500 is somewhat less than the 4000 quota places promoted by the Green Party (2017a), the New Zealand First Party coalition partner indicated in September 2018 that it had not agreed to even this increase (see Bramwell 2018); it seems likely the historic rise in the quota will go ahead but this turn of events highlights the challenges of making policy in a Mixed Member Proportional representation environment where political compromise within coalition governments is commonplace.

The increased quota also represents only a fraction of the 68,000 immigrants arriving in 2018 (Statistics New Zealand 2018) and the total number resettled through the quota is extremely small compared to other countries (for example, Australia's quota is 20,000 people per year). This contributes to New Zealand ranking 90th in the world in per capita assistance to refugees (Amnesty International 2017). Although 1020 people were actually settled under the quota in 2017–2018, in some years it has not been fully subscribed: 527 were approved 2010–2011 and 679 accepted in 2011–2012 (Immigration New Zealand – INZ 2018b). Beaglehole (2009: 111) notes that, on occasion, New Zealand's small geographical size "has provided a convenient excuse for declining to accept a specific group of refugees, further groups or significant numbers of refugees."

The refugee quota program operates on a 3-year rolling program based on UNCHR recommendations regarding global resettlement priorities, but "political" factors can still determine government decisions regarding refugee protection. In 2010, Cabinet allocated 50% of the quota to the Asia-Pacific region and 50% to the Americas, Middle East, and Africa but chose not accept refugees coming from the latter two regions unless they already had family living in New Zealand; this criteria proved difficult to meet, meaning the quota for these areas was undersubscribed (Green Party 2017a; HRC 2017). Presumably refugees from such regions were assumed to be Muslim and potential "terrorists," highlighting how New Zealand governments are not immune to global shifts in political and public attitudes that view some refugees as more "deserving" than others. In contrast, in 2017–2018, the National-led government allocated the 100 places within the quota for large-scale refugee crisis situations to ethnic Rohingya and Syrians (MBIE 2017), two groups (currently) viewed as worthy of urgent humanitarian action. It is important to acknowledge, however, New Zealand's broader leadership in settling refugees rejected by other countries. Since 1959, the country has accepted refugee families with "handicapped" members, and it was also one of the few countries in the world to accept refugees with HIV/AIDS (Beaglehole 2009: 108). Today, the refugee quota reserves 75 places for "women at risk" and 75 places for "medical/disabled" applicants (MBIE 2017).

Convention Pathway

New Zealand receives approximately 300 applications each year from asylum seekers. Many arrive on valid visas, with nearly 50% living in the community for 1 year or more before making their claim, and only around 5% seek asylum upon arriving at a New Zealand airport, usually without documentation or travelling on a false passport (MBIE 2017). Research suggests this latter group receive poor treatment upon arrival (Bloom and Udahemuka 2014) and a small number will be detained in the Mangere Refugee Resettlement Centre or prison until identity/security issues are addressed (MBIE 2017). People claiming refugee status, however, are usually granted a visa to work, study, or live in the community, provided with free legal aid if required and will not be removed until their claim has been finally determined, which takes at least 3 months (HRC 2017).

Approximately one half of asylum seekers have their claims approved, either by the Refugee Status Branch of Immigration New Zealand (INZ) or, if unsuccessful there, the Immigration and Protection Tribunal. Successful asylum claimants are referred to as "Convention refugees" and can apply for permanent residence, but this is not granted automatically (MBIE 2017). Indeed, Bloom and Udahemuka's (2014: 79) research identifies the journey towards permanent residency as:

> ... laden with hurdles, from poor guidance, misinformation and/or mistreatment from airport officials and government agencies, to exploitation and corruption from community members. Participants faced prolonged periods of uncertainty resulting in anxiety, fear and low self-esteem, with severe health and well-being impacts.

In 2013, a National Party-led government introduced legislative amendments to deter large groups of asylum seekers arriving in New Zealand. Although no boat carrying asylum-seekers has ever made it to New Zealand's distant shores (Beaglehole 2009) and policies of deterrence have been unsuccessful in reducing asylum seeker numbers (Amnesty International 2014), this legislation states that any asylum seeker arriving in a group of more than 30 people (referred to as a "mass arrival") and successful in gaining refugee status, will have his or her situation redetermined after 3 years. Only if redetermination is successful can they then apply for permanent residence, with restricted family reunification provisions. Moreover, the legislation provides for the detention of a mass arrival of asylum seekers under a group warrant for up to 6 months, restricts access to judicial review proceedings, and allows claim processing to be suspended if reliable country information is unavailable or fluid (see Immigration Amendment Act 2013). Submissions on the proposed legislation highlight that many organizations and individuals across the refugee sector viewed such measures as breaching human rights obligations but, significantly, Bloom and Udahemuka (2014: 71–72) note:

> Immigration New Zealand policies are exempt from the Human Rights Act 1993, which means that the Human Rights Commission, which is the agency that receives discrimination (and other) complaints under the Human Rights Act 1993, cannot receive complaints of alleged discrimination in relation to immigration.

Family Reunification Pathway

Many people are sponsored by refugee family members under one of four family reunification immigration policies, a process of bringing separated families together that people from refugee backgrounds identify as a crucial determinant of positive settlement and mental health outcomes (ChangeMakers 2009; Choummanivong et al. 2014). Mahoney et al. (2017) note a number of areas where New Zealand policy on family reunification of refugees meets or exceeds New Zealand's international obligations but overall policy treats Quota refugees more favorably compared to other refugees.

In fact, the first of the four family unification policies – the Refugee Quota Family Reunification Category (RQFRC) – is directly linked to the quota program. Reunification of immediate family members of Quota refugees begins immediately upon arrival if they have already declared spouses, dependent unmarried children and parents of a young Quota refugee to INZ during the refugee's initial Refugee Quota Branch interview. The person being reunified does not need to pay an application or airfare fee and does not require standard immigration documentation because they are effectively included within the annual quota by their association with someone already approved as a Quota refugee (HRC 2017; Mahoney et al. 2017).

The main family reunification policy is the Refugee Family Support Category (RFSC), which allows both Quota and Convention refugees with New Zealand permanent residence to sponsor family members. The first tier of the RFSC system allows for up to 300 sponsored people (including their partners and dependent children) to settle in New Zealand each year. To be eligible, refugees must live alone in New Zealand or be the sole carer of dependent relatives and have no other family member eligible to apply for residency under any other New Zealand immigration category. Applications can be made at any time but are placed in a queue (INZ 2018c). Sponsorship can be achieved without independent referral from UNHCR and the individuals are not counted as part of the annual quota (MBIE 2017; Mahoney et al. 2017). However, sponsors must hold a residence class visa, meaning the partner/spouse of a Convention refugee is not eligible to be a Tier 1 sponsor if the couple separate (as is the case for Quota refugees) because that partner was granted residence on the basis of partnership with the person granted refugee status, not as a refugee. Reunification can be sought only for those whom New Zealand authorities have deemed to be the closest of relatives, not extended family. Although "New Zealand takes a fairly liberal approach to the definition of immediate family including spouses, partners, children up to the age of 24 and children adopted by custom" (Mahoney et al. 2017: 11), this policy causes much confusion and anguish for potential applicants (see Choummanivong et al. 2014). Mahoney et al. (2017) further argue that the narrow understanding of "family" could be considered discrimination under article 26 of the International Covenant on Civil and Political Rights on grounds of sociocultural beliefs, although not in domestic law.

Tier 2 registration is for applicants who already have family in New Zealand (including "extended" family) and their sponsors must have been New Zealand residents for at least 3 years (Immigration NZ 2018d). INZ only accepts Tier 2 applicants when the RFSC quota is not already filled by Tier 1 applicants, so families could not apply in the periods 2007–2011 and 2013–2017, and in other years, very limited numbers of Tier 2 applications were approved (INZ 2018b, e). Between 2007 and 2018, there were a total of 4320 applications for Tiers 1 and 2, accounting for 17,753 applicants of whom only 2452 (57%) were granted residence visas (INZ 2018e). Even successful Tier 1 and 2 applicants must pay for flights and all other costs, with sponsors required to ensure the provision of accommodation for the first 2 years. While various trusts fundraise to help cover such costs, this is a major stress for families and their supporters (ChangeMakers 2009). Moreover, those sponsored to New Zealand under the RQFRC or RFSC are not themselves eligible to apply for other family members to come to New Zealand because technically they have not been granted refugee status (HRC 2017; Mahoney et al. 2017; MBIE 2017). Given the constraints noted above, some refugees end up achieving family reunification via temporary or permanent residence visas through normal immigration channels. Classed as "migrants" not "refugees," they face additional requirements in order to obtain residency (Mahoney et al. 2017).

Finally, reunification can be achieved through a last resort "Special Directions" request to the Associate Minister of Immigration where strong humanitarian grounds exist. Until 2001, refugees were able to seek family reunification under a "humanitarian category" which allowed refugees with family members who did not meet the requirements for reunification under other categories to apply for residence. With the abolition of this category, refugee supporters suggest that cases of exceptional humanitarian concern brought to the attention of the Associate Minister of Immigration are almost always unsuccessful (ChangeMakers 2009; Mahoney et al. 2017).

It is therefore significant that the Labour Party and Green Party (2017) confidence and supply agreement agreed to review the family reunification system. The Green Party (2017b: 3) argues that the "The current visa application process for the reunification of refugee families is unfair and inhumane" and advocates for clearly published priorities and standards of acceptance, as well as an increase in the powers and funding of the Immigration and Protection Tribunal to allow for the consideration of more family reunification cases. At the time of writing, it remained to be seen whether the review achieved these aims; the New Zealand First Party campaigned on a policy of ensuring "immigration under 'family reunion' is strictly controlled" (see Weiner 2017: n.p), so political compromise may again be necessary.

Emergency Protection Pathway

Although not a process by which refugees can apply, refugees have also entered New Zealand in exceptional circumstances when requested by the UNHCR. In 1999, for instance, New Zealand accepted over 400 Kosovars for resettlement who had family in New Zealand, in response to the Kosovo humanitarian crisis. Again in 2001, New Zealand accepted 130 Afghan asylum seekers picked up by the freighter, MS Tampa, after their craft capsized in the Indian Ocean but was refused entry to Australian waters (Beaglehole 2009). Between 2015 and 2018, New Zealand also settled 600 refugees from Syria. These were in addition to the annual refugee quota but this is not always the case; in 2017, Prime Minister Jacinda Ardern (2017) indicated that New Zealand would be willing to accept refugees currently detained by Australia on Manus Island and Nauru as part of the quota. This offer was declined but it exemplifies how seemingly "humanitarian" gestures in times of emergency have attempted to avoid any overall increase in refugee numbers and the economic costs associated with their settlement. Neither the Labour nor the Green Party appears to support Amnesty International's (2014) call for a "Crisis Quota" that is separate from the annual quota so as to provide protection in unplanned circumstances at reduced notice.

Community Sponsorship Pathway

In June 2018, an additional 25 refugees were accepted into New Zealand under a pilot community sponsorship category initiated by the previous National-led Government. Although only a fraction of the additional 1000 community sponsorship refugees desired by the Green Party (2017a), this trial represents a significant shift in policy because it relies even more heavily than in the past on community organizations to provide sponsorship and the majority of settlement support. INZ conducts assessment and screening of all refugees in the new category because they must be mandated by the UNCHR as refugees and it funds a 2-week program at the Mangere Refugee Resettlement Centre. But community sponsors are responsible for: domestic travel to settlement locations; arrangement of privately funded accommodation, furniture, and household goods; community orientation and settlement assistance; and "meaningful and sustainable" employment or training that leads to employment (MBIE 2017). Minister of Immigration, Iain Lees-Galloway (2018a), described the pilot program as a grassroots approach that would encourage communities to get involved with supporting refugees in their resettlement. Four church-based organizations were chosen for the trial in Wellington, Timaru, Christchurch, and Nelson. The spread of community organizations outside of Auckland, New Zealand's largest city, and into regional areas aligns with the views of the New Zealand First coalition partner which believes that the intensification of immigrants generally in Auckland is not sustainable (Weiner 2017).

Other countries such as Canada, Australia, and the United Kingdom reportedly find the community sponsorship model a positive means for refugee settlement (MBIE 2017). It also seems likely that refugees taking this pathway will be able to access both the RQFRC and RFSC for family reunification. But applicants for this category in New Zealand must meet a higher bar than other refugees. Not only must they be UNHCR-mandated, meet security health and immigration risk assessments, and not be eligible to be sponsored for residence under any family category but also they must be aged between 18 and 45 years and have a minimum 3 years work experience or a tertiary qualification which took a minimum of 2 years to complete. The Minister of Immigration (Office of the Minister of Immigration – OMI 2017: 3) noted in a Cabinet paper that: "During consultation, there were concerns expressed about the inclusion of language, skill and age requirements due to the perception that these requirements are not consistent with the principles of the broader refugee and humanitarian programme." These concerns reportedly reduced the number of community sponsors wanting to be involved: "However, I consider that the potential benefits of improved settlement outcomes for sponsored refugees support the inclusion of language, skill and age requirements" (OMI 2017: 3). This desire to select refugees who it is hoped will find paid work quickly suggests economic factors outweigh humanitarian criteria (INZ 2018f); later discussion highlights that concern with paid work also dominates settlement policy, even under the new Labour-led government, suggesting this focus will not be addressed following an evaluation in December 2018 (OMI 2017). It is also unclear whether such refugees will have preferential access to family reunification since they are UNCHR-recognized but are not technically Quota refugees.

Pacific Climate Change Pathway?

The new government proposes a new humanitarian visa category for people displaced by climate change. Referring to saltwater intrusion in fresh water supplies, rising sea levels and extreme weather events affecting Pacific nations such as Samoa, Tonga, Niue, and the Cook Islands, Prime Minister Jacinda Ardern (2018: n.p) commented: "Collectively these islands represent a tiny portion of global emissions. They play almost no role in creating the crisis we now face, but they are already the first to face its devastating impacts." Because many people wish to stay living on their islands for as long as possible, New Zealand is helping to install renewable energy supplies, while maintaining a role in disaster relief and resilience building (Ardern 2018). But the climate change humanitarian visa acknowledges that remaining on some islands may be impossible in the long term. The visa is supported by the Green Party (2017a), which would trial the new category at 100 places per year, although refugees were not mentioned in discussion of climate change in its supply and confidence agreement with the Labour Party.

The government has also promised to establish a Ministerial Advisory Group to examine outstanding immigration issues within the Pacific (Immigration NZ 2017a). This is perhaps not surprising since:

> New Zealand has long-standing ties and a unique set of relationships with the Pacific Island nations including: the three realm countries of Niue, Tokelau and the Cook Islands; the Samoan Quota, the Pacific Access Quota, the Treaty of Friendship with Samoa, the Recognised Seasonal Employer Scheme, and its sizeable Pacific population who have made Aotearoa their permanent home. (Labour Party 2017: 5–6)

Alongside the review of family reunification, the government is thus reviewing the Pacific Access Quota to ensure both are accessible for Pacific people, working effectively and consistent with wider Pacific development commitments (Labour Party 2017).

Such discussions involve both INZ and the Ministry of Foreign Affairs and Trade (2018: 1) and it seems unlikely progress will be speedy given: "The complexity of the issues associated with Pacific climate change-induced displacement, resettlement and migration, and the significant implications for New Zealand and the Pacific region." Nonetheless, such a move aligns with the New York Declaration on Refugees and Migrants, adopted by all UN member states in 2016, which committed to specific (although unbinding) Global Compacts on refugees and on safe, orderly, and regular migration to provide a state-led global approach to "upholding human rights and wellbeing of migrants and their families" (MBIE 2018: 2). The first "Zero Draft" of the Migration Compact proposes to strengthen joint analysis to better map, predict, and understand migration relating to climate change and other environmental factors (MBIE 2018). In this context, the Labour-led government may be bold enough to establish the world's first climate change humanitarian visa. Although the government has been careful not to use the term "refugee" because persecution is not involved, this move could facilitate international discussion as to the appropriateness of broadening the Refugee Convention to include environmental causes for displacement.

In summary, this section has highlighted that current refugee protection policy offers a number of pathways to New Zealand. Quota refugees are clearly favored by family reunification processes, in that only they are practicably able to secure family unity without enduring the enormous cost and stress of other immigration processes, and it is unclear whether the new community sponsorship category or proposed climate change visa will change this focus. The next section highlights that Quota refugees can also access significantly higher levels of settlement support than other refugees, even though Article 31 of the Refugee Convention states that people should not be penalized based on their mode of arrival (Bloom and Udahemuka 2014). Although there is no evidence that Quota refugees are selected from one particular ethnic group, country, or region more than another, it is argued that this constitutes a form of systematic institutional discrimination because legally sanctioned organizational practices and procedures consciously favor one group over another based on their immigration pathway (see Fleras and Elliott 2017). This discrimination has yet to be addressed by the Labour-led government's proposed changes in a range of policy areas.

Settlement Policy

INZ is the lead government agency for the operational coordination of refugee-specific services and for undertaking longitudinal research on settlement outcomes with a particular emphasis on refugees. Since 2013, it has implemented the whole-of-government New Zealand Refugee Resettlement Strategy to provide greater cohesion to settlement policies which, as with refugee protection, have been developed over a number of years. Table 1 indicates the five goals guiding the establishment, development, and monitoring of all services funded by the government for refugee resettlement, which were developed in consultation with refugees and community groups. The refugee-focused strategy runs alongside the broader New Zealand Migrant Settlement and Integration Strategy 2014 (Altinkaya 2016) and regional settlement strategies for newcomers to New Zealand's larger cities (Mahoney et al. 2017).

Implementation of the Resettlement Strategy has thus far focused on providing greater information to Quota refugees before arrival, changes to their 6-week reception program, and the establishment of orientation and driver training programs in the community. English language service provision to refugees has also been mapped, while work is underway to improve language assistance services and refugee employment outcomes (MBIE 2017). Further priorities until 2020 include an evaluation of the reception and community orientation programs, changes to

Table 1 The five goals of the New Zealand Refugee Resettlement Strategy

Housing	Refugees live in safe, secure, healthy, and affordable homes, without needing government housing assistance
Self-sufficiency	All working-age refugees are in paid work or are supported by a family member in paid work
Education	English language skills help refugees participate in education and in daily life
Health and well-being	Refugees and their families enjoy healthy, safe, and independent lives
Participation	Refugees actively participate in New Zealand life and have a strong sense of belonging here

Source: INZ (2012)

evaluating refugees' settlement outcomes, and strengthening the delivery and coordination of health and disability services (INZ 2018g).

The remainder of this section highlights the rather narrow focus of Resettlement Strategy goals as well as constraints inhibiting their achievement. It is worth noting, however, two general problems with the Resettlement Strategy. First, although the original Cabinet documents mandated consideration that other categories of refugees be included in its focus, it still officially serves only Quota refugees. This is most obviously evident in the initial settlement and orientation period discussed below but arguably this favoritism continues to shape refugee experiences for years to come. The settlement needs of Convention refugees are currently being explored by INZ but it seems unlikely the Resettlement Strategy will ever encompass refugees arriving under all of the pathways identified earlier (MBIE 2017). Second, non-government organizations (NGOs) are the main provider of refugee-specific services in New Zealand (Marlowe and Humpage 2016; Mahoney et al. 2017). The committed individuals who run these organizations do a fantastic job but have long been constrained by underfunding and short-term contractual arrangements, forcing them to rely on volunteers and limiting their capacity for advocacy (McIntosh and Cockburn-Wootten 2018). Government tenders for refugee-focused services now require such organizations to link their services to the Resettlement Strategy's goals (Marlowe and Elliott 2014), thus further inhibiting their ability to service needs not prioritized in this document.

Initial Orientation and Settlement

Upon arriving in New Zealand, Quota refugees stay for 6 weeks, free of charge, in the Mangere Refugee Resettlement Centre to participate in a reception program that includes: general information about life in New Zealand; an English language assessment with follow-up language courses; medical screenings and mental health assessments; as well as free primary health, dental, and counselling care (INZ 2018h). The previous National-led government rebuilt the World War II-era Resettlement Centre buildings to address complaints about substandard conditions (MBIE 2017) and the Labour-led government's 2018 Budget provided further operating and capital investment funding to improve capacity and effectiveness (Lees-Galloway 2018b).

Upon leaving the Resettlement Centre, Quota refugees are settled in key sites where refugee-specific support is available: Auckland, Waikato, Manawatu, Wellington, Nelson, Canterbury (from 2019, after being on hold since the devastating earthquakes there in 2010–2011) and, more recently, Otago and Invercargill (Immigration NZ 2018b). The New Zealand Red Cross, an NGO, is contracted by MBIE to provide a settlement program to Quota refugees for up to 12 months via social workers, cultural workers, and trained community volunteers (HRC 2017; MBIE 2017). The use of trained volunteers to support families in the community is the strength of the program – providing a diverse range of community contacts for newcomer families that would be impossible to achieve through agency support alone (see Elliott and Yusuf 2014) – yet also results from the limited funding made available for refugee services. Other refugee organizations do important work but few have a national focus, meaning considerable diversity across regions. Overall, the contracting out of the provision of settlement services results in fragmentation of delivery, while access to such services is also heavily-dependent upon the population center where Quota refugees are settled (Mortensen et al. 2012).

Refugees using other pathways to protection receive no orientation but can choose to live anywhere in New Zealand except those arriving under the pilot community sponsorship category who, following a 2-week orientation at the Resettlement Centre, must settle in the sponsoring community (INZ 2017b). All non-Quota refugees can seek general information/advice from the Red Cross and access its employment program but cannot benefit from their case management services (HRC 2017). The remaining discussion further identifies that they are also excluded from many housing, employment, health, and educational opportunities afforded Quota refugees.

Housing

Since 2000, Quota refugees have been prioritized upon arrival for state-owned Housing New Zealand (HNZ) homes, where the maximum rent is set at 25% of weekly income. They are also eligible for a one-time reestablishment grant of $1200 if they apply within a year of arrival in New Zealand. Refugees arriving via other pathways must find their own housing in the private rental market (HRC 2017). RFSC and Community Sponsorship refugees have to rely on the persons sponsoring them to provide or help them find accommodation, with eligibility to apply for housing assistance dependent on eligibility to receive an income support benefit. The Auckland Refugee Council provides the country's only asylum seeker hostel but government funding stopped in 2013, so it now relies solely on donations and can provide accommodation to asylum seekers only for 3 months (HRC 2017). If New Zealand ever receives a "mass arrival," such asylum seekers will have to wait at least 3 years before they are able to gain permanent residence and thus access to full housing and other entitlements.

The Resettlement Strategy (INZ 2012: 7) identifies "reduced housing subsidy for refugees (after 2 years and 5 years in New Zealand)" as the desired integration outcome. This focus on reducing the cost to the state, rather than on positive outcomes for refugees, is troubling given affordable housing is in high demand, with housing shortages in some regions facilitating significant price increases. This makes housing subsidies necessary for many New Zealand households and increases to the Accommodation Supplement available to those in the private housing market in 2018 are unlikely to improve affordability in the long term (Robertson 2018). Moreover, adequacy of housing is not reflected in the Resettlement Strategy outcomes, despite this being a major concern in New Zealand where poor insulation means cold and damp houses are common. New government funding is targeted towards "greater resources to assist refugees to find affordable housing"

(Lees-Galloway 2018b: n.p), the Labour-led government is building more state housing and legislation now requires landlords to ensure homes are warm and dry. But in the context of what has been called a national "housing crisis" (Robertson 2018: 7), accommodation issues for refugees are unlikely to be resolved quickly.

Self-Sufficiency

This Resettlement Strategy goal focuses on ensuring all working-age refugees are in paid employment or supported by a family member in paid work. Refugees who are permanent residents/citizens have the same employment rights as other New Zealanders, while asylum seekers and Convention refugees must reapply for work visas until permanent residence is gained (HRC 2017). Although New Zealand has relatively low rates of unemployment, unemployment and underemployment are common among refugees (ChangeMakers 2012; O'Donovan and Sheikh 2014). Marlowe et al. (2014: 63) thus believe that "employment must not become the implicit principal measure that eclipses other important considerations for defining 'successful' settlement for refugee individuals, families or communities."

This comment was made at a time when a National-led government placed a strong, neoconservative focus on reducing welfare dependency which was arguably reflected in the Resettlement Strategy's emphasis on ensuring that refugees do not rely heavily on government income support (O'Donovan and Sheikh 2014). A focus on employment, however, remains strong under the new government and comments such as "limited English and a lack of formal qualifications still create barriers to employment for refugees" (INZ 2018g: 6) suggest that the problem is viewed as one of individual skills rather than shaped by broader structural factors. These include the dominance of poorly paid and insecure part-time or casual work versus full-time work (New Zealand Council of Trade Unions 2013) and discrimination by employers against foreign qualifications/experience, accents, names, or practices such as Muslim women wearing the hijab (HRC 2017; Ibrahim 2012). More specifically, asylum seekers find employers reluctant to employ them due to their short-term work visas (HRC 2017). Low English proficiency is, of course, an important factor inhibiting refugees gaining employment (see ChangeMakers 2012) but it is not the *only* factor.

At present, only refugees with permanent residence can access the free Red Cross refugee-specific Pathways to Employment program (HRC 2017). Free migrant-focused employment programs also run in larger cities by local councils and business groups, focusing on employment mentoring and matching (INZ 2018i). Although important, these programs are not available nationwide and are insufficient to meet demand and need. O'Donovan and Sheikh (2014) argue that a cross-political party commitment is needed to adequately fund the individualized, intensive programs that research suggests are most successful.

In the absence of paid work, many refugees who have permanent residency rely on conventional income support benefits as well as a range of additional benefits (such as the Accommodation Supplement, Child Care Subsidy or Disability

Allowance), while Convention refugees and successful RFSC applicants are entitled only to the emergency unemployment benefit and Temporary Additional Support (which must be reapplied for every 13 weeks) until they gain permanent residence (HRC 2017). In recent years, many forms of income support have become more discretionary and require benefit recipients to meet work, parenting, and other obligations to retain their income support payment. As a result, O'Donovan and Sheikh (2014) argue that more needs to be done to educate people from refugee backgrounds about these reforms in their own languages, otherwise refugees risk not meeting obligations and being financially sanctioned. While the Labour-led government is undertaking a review of the welfare system and has promised to remove inappropriate financial sanctions (Labour Party and Green Party 2017), refugees who rely on benefit payments will likely continue to struggle to meet work obligations and other requirements.

Education

As with employment, the Resettlement Strategy's focus on education focuses heavily on English language skills, rather than on education more widely, and again favors some refugee pathways over others. All children who have permanent residency or citizenship have a right to free compulsory education from ages 6–19. Child asylum claimants and children arriving under the RFSC can enroll in school, but while young RFSC refugees can access the same entitlements as children arriving under quota, additional support (including English as a second language) for child asylum seekers is assessed case by case (HRC 2017).

This is significant because the Ministry of Education (MoE 2018) provides funding for 5 years of English language support for each refugee background student (2 years of intensive support followed by 3 years of standard ESOL funding) if their assessment score is below a set threshold. MoE will further fund a range of other activities, such as homework and academic support programs; bilingual liaison support to link schools with refugee families; in-class bilingual support staff; and computers (with training) for refugee families. Such resources are coordinated by Regional Refugee Education Coordinators, who are employed in Auckland, Hamilton, Wellington, and Christchurch to help with student enrollment and adjustment into schools. Part of this role includes liaising with families and community groups to communicate about the education system, its expectations and identify particular children's needs, while a "Refugee Flexible Funding Pool" can be used by specific schools to address some of the broader issues preventing refugee background students from participating and achieving in mainstream school programs (MoE 2018).

Not all children from refugee backgrounds will attend a school with such support, so the Ministry of Education (2003) publishes *English for Speakers of Other Languages: Refugee Handbook for Schools* to assist schools in adapting to refugee learner needs. However, while the quality of compulsory education in New Zealand is highly regarded internationally, various studies indicate that limited access to information technology, English language ability, gender, geographic region, and level of disability may affect a refugee student's access to compulsory education, as does a school's response to bullying and discrimination (Ibrahim 2012). Additional funding for compulsory education in Budget 2018 does not specifically address these issues (Robertson 2018).

Regarding adult education, all permanent residents/citizens are eligible to apply for entry to tertiary education and benefit from government-subsidized tuition fees and access to the Student Loan scheme. Given many refugee families live on low incomes, permanent residents are likely also eligible for the means-tested Student Allowance, which covers basic living costs and does not need to be repaid. Convention refugees can access these forms of financial support once they have been given refugee protection status (HRC 2017). However, research suggests that people from refugee backgrounds are more likely to delay their entry into tertiary education because they cannot afford it. This may be related to a lack of awareness regarding the Student Loan Scheme and not having lived in New Zealand long enough to qualify for assistance; 6 months after arrival, only 28% of refugees were successful in obtaining a student loan; 2 years after arrival, that figure increased to 89% (Joe and Kindon 2011). The Labour-led government's commitment to 3 years of free postsecondary school education, initially beginning with 1 year free in 2018 (Robertson 2018), is therefore significant only if refugees know about and can take advantage of this policy.

There is no nationwide, free English language support for adults as in countries like Australia (Fozdar and Banki 2017), but adult refugees are eligible to work with a volunteer instructor through English Language Partners (Marlowe and Humpage 2016). Quota refugees may also be eligible for English language training provided through employment-focused schemes. Asylum seekers issued with a work visa while their refugee and protection claim is being processed may obtain permission to attend fee-paying ESOL classes in some regions and if they have been in New Zealand for fewer than 2 years but are not eligible for student loans or Student Allowance. Overall, non-Quota refugees have greater difficulties finding or doing study/training than Quota refugees, likely because they receive less information and support during initial settlement process (HRC 2017; Joe and Kindon 2011).

Health and Well-Being

New Zealand has a well-regarded public health system which all types of refugees can legally access, including subsidized primary health care and prescription medicines (both free for children under 14). Free basic dental care is available for children aged 18 but only emergency dental care is free for adults. Low income earners are also eligible for the Community Services Card, allowing access to certain healthcare services at reduced cost; the Labour-led government extended eligibility in 2018 (Robertson 2018) but low refugee take-up due to poor awareness limits the likely effect of this change (Mortensen et al. 2012). The Refugee Health Services program provides funding for some general practices to deliver primary health care services if they have a large enrolled refugee population. However, only Quota refugees definitely receive a free full health screening at MRRC; although this may also be free for asylum seekers, information about what services are accessible to other refugees is not well known (Mortensen et al. 2012; HRC 2017).

The Ministry of Health (Mortensen et al. 2012) publishes a handbook for professionals providing health services that describes common medical issues faced by refugees in New Zealand and suggests ways to provide culturally sensitive services for diverse refugee groups. There are also initiatives aiming to ensure refugee groups receive culturally appropriate healthcare, including cultural competency training, training programs for working with culturally and linguistically diverse populations, and additional funding for cross-cultural training. But because New Zealand has 20 District Health Boards responsible for health objectives, there can be considerable variance in terms of the services offered, the cost involved in using them and the length of waiting lists depending on where refugees live (Mortensen et al. 2012).

In particular, free refugee-specific mental health services are provided for Quota refugees and Convention refugees but only in Auckland and Wellington and even these run on extremely limited funding, with no government funding available for specialist mental health services for asylum seekers released into the community or children from refugee backgrounds (Amnesty International 2014; HRC 2017). These gaps are significant given research has identified mental health issues as an ongoing issue during resettlement, particularly for asylum seekers who not only must face uncertainty while waiting for their refugee status determination but also cannot access many of the same services as quota refugees (Bloom and Udahemuka 2014; Shrestha-Ranjit et al. 2017). It is unclear if significant investment in mental health, especially among young people, from 2018 will include refugee-specific programs (Robertson 2018).

A further barrier is limited access to professional interpreters and healthcare professionals trained to respect customary practices (Mortensen et al. 2012). Interpreting services are currently offered through Language Line which offers services through 44 languages and is funded by the Citizens Advice Bureau. However, nongovernment agencies and some government agencies are not eligible to use this service and need to employ bilingual workers, use community interpreters, or have access to specific funding for this service. A lack of national training, qualification or codes of practice for interpreters also means varying levels of access (particularly to those outside of main centers) and appropriateness for particular groups. Patients often end up using family members (even children) as interpreters to discuss health-related information (Mahoney et al. 2017). It is therefore significant that an improved language assistance program is one of the Resettlement Strategy's 2018–2020 priorities (INZ 2018g).

Participation

Just as with education and employment, the Resettlement Strategy goal for "participation" is framed only in terms of improving adult refugees' achievement of English language. This is troubling because it assumes that participation is not possible without English and thus excludes many refugees from ever feeling they can participate. However, there are no legal barriers to full civic participation for refugees who are permanent residents or citizens (Marlowe et al. 2014), particularly since even the former have the right to vote in New Zealand general elections.

Moreover, despite the limitations of the official participation goal, government has actually placed considerable focus on strengthening the refugee sector in recent years. Since 2006, INZ's Strengthening Refugee Voices (SRV) initiative in Auckland, Hamilton, Wellington, and Christchurch has provided modest funding to enable refugee groups to meet and discuss issues affecting their communities, hoping to shift power relationships between refugee groups and nongovernmental organizations. SRV also enables refugee community members to participate in setting the agenda for the National Refugee Resettlement Forum, an annual national consultation between government agencies and the NGO/refugee community sector. Since 2009, the National Refugee Network, composed of representatives from the regional SRV groupings, also provides a collective voice for refugees at a national level (Elliott and Yusuf 2014).

At a more general level, INZ developed the Welcoming Communities Standard for nine local government councils to pilot and use as a benchmark to mobilize and involve local residents to make New Zealand more welcoming for newcomers (defined as recent migrants, former refugees, and international students). This includes partnering with local indigenous peoples, businesses, community groups, other government agencies, and NGOs. Communities are supported to access other funds, make connections, and share best practice and lessons learned (INZ 2018j). This is important because:

> ... public receptivity to increased diversity as a result of changing immigration priorities has not been universally positive ... Refugee groups from countries such as Afghanistan, Burma, Iraq, Somalia, Bhutan, Iran and Ethiopia carry ethnic markers that distinguish them, physically (i.e. as 'non-white') as well as culturally, from most of the host society. Thus, for these and other groups, the potential remains for the persistence of social barriers to participation and belonging. (Marlowe et al. 2014: 64)

The HRC (2018) has embarked upon a nationwide campaign against racism using well-known celebrities, while organizations such as the Auckland Resettled Community Coalition (2018) focus more specifically on changing public perceptions towards refugees. Yet complaints to the HRC about racism are at an all-time *high*; that 16% of complaints in 2018 came from members of the ethnic majority suggests significant resistance to valuing diversity, with scholar Camille Nakhid (cited in Te 2018: n.p) commenting that, in terms of race relations, New Zealand had "not even gotten on the road much less started the journey."

In summary, this section has argued that the immigration pathway taken matters when it comes to refugee settlement in New Zealand, for different types of refugees receive varied rights and access to services. Although in some cases rights exist but refugees are not aware of them, it is telling that the Resettlement Strategy focuses only on Quota refugees. Given the limited support available to refugees who did not arrive under the Quota pathway, it is not surprising that research shows some extremely negative settlement outcomes for these groups (see Bloom and Udahemuka 2014; HRC 2017). This reinforces the argument that the day-to-day practices of organizations and institutions are having a harmful, if unintended, impact on non-Quota refugees in New Zealand (Fleras and Elliott 2017), as well as potentially reinforcing public perceptions that refugees are not "deserving" of more assistance.

Conclusion

New Zealand's refugee policies, which are ostensibly driven by humanitarian motives, are in fact constrained by economic and political considerations. These limit the government's commitment to ensuring all refugees are sufficiently protected and receive the same treatment once living in New Zealand, arguably constituting a form of institutional discrimination. There is little indication the Labour-led government elected in 2017 will radically change this situation. Although the new government is reviewing family reunification, the inclusion of Convention refugees in the Resettlement Strategy and two new refugee categories, there has yet been no commitment to treating all types of refugees equally regarding family reunification and settlement.

The current focus on Quota refugees is heavily shaped by the economic factors associated with offering all refugees the same access to services and rights such as family reunification. The extra funding provided by the new government since 2018 is unlikely to meet current needs, never mind this extra burden, since insufficient resourcing has historically been a significant issue for the refugee sector, and there is some evidence of underuse of existing rights and resources due to poor awareness. Indeed, despite INZ's efforts to promote collaboration, inconsistent and project-focused funding streams simply encourages organizations to *compete* with each other rather than share their knowledge and skills (McIntosh and Cockburn-Wootten 2018). Moreover, the Labour-led government has bound itself to Budget Responsibility Rules (Robertson 2018) that focus on producing a surplus and reducing government debt, making significant spending increases difficult.

Although the new government has not chosen to discourage certain groups of refugees for "political" reasons, nor has it reversed the decisions made by the previous administration regarding the "mass arrival" of asylum seekers and restrictions placed on African and Middle Eastern Quota refugees. Mahoney et al. (2017: 12) note that: "It is important to acknowledge that the differential treatment of varied types of refugees in New Zealand is not explicitly prohibited grounds for discrimination either under the Refugee Convention or New Zealand's Human Rights Act 1993." Yet they highlight a number of ways that New Zealand's position could be viewed as not meeting its international obligations. It remains to be seen whether the Labour-led government will prioritize humanitarian outcomes, as indicated at election time, or whether New Zealand policy will remain driven by mixed agendas with discriminatory outcomes. Given political and public concerns about the impact of diversity and the economic costs of settling refugees, along with the international implications of recognizing climate change as a cause for displacement for the first time, prioritizing humanitarian goals will take some bravery – but far less than refugees themselves have shown in establishing new lives in New Zealand.

Cross-References

▶ Immigration Policy and Left-Right Politics in Western Europe
▶ State Hegemony and Ethnicity: Fiji's Problematic Colonial Past
▶ The Significance of Ethno-politics in Modern States and Society

References

Altinkaya J (2016) New Zealand Migrant Settlement and Integration Strategy: a framework for collaborative action. In: Immigration New Zealand (ed) Settlement summit 2016 proceedings: collaborating for outcomes. Immigration New Zealand, Wellington, pp 5–9

Amnesty International (2014) Spotlight on the vulnerable. https://www.amnesty.org.nz/sites/default/files/Spotlight_on_The_Vulnerable.pdf. Accessed 31 Aug 2018

Amnesty International (2017) It's time for New Zealand to double the quota. https://www.amnesty.org.nz/sites/default/files/Double%20the%20quota%20fact%20sheet_0.pdf. Accessed 29 July 2018

Ardern J (2018) Climate change – challenges and opportunities – a Pacific perspective. https://www.beehive.govt.nz/speech/climate-change-challenges-and-opportunities-pacific-perspective. Accessed 29 July 2018

Auckland Resettled Community Coalition (2018) Projects. https://arcc.org.nz/projects/. Accessed 4 Sept 2018

Beaglehole A (2009) Looking back and glancing sideways: refugee policy and multicultural nation-building. In: Neumann K, Tavan G (eds) New Zealand does history matter? Making and debating citizenship, immigration and refugee policy in Australia and New Zealand. ANU E Press, Canberra, pp 105–124. https://www.oapen.org/search?identifier=459079. Accessed 3 Sept 2018

Bloom A, Udahemuka M (2014) "Going through the doors of pain": asylum seeker and Convention refugee experiences in Aotearoa New Zealand. Kōtuitui: NZ J Soc Sci 9(2):70–81

Bramwell C (2018) Labour and NZ First differ over refugee increase. Radio New Zealand. https://www.radionz.co.nz/news/political/365603/labour-and-nz-first-differ-over-refugee-increase. Accessed 31 Aug 2018

ChangeMakers (2009) Refugee family reunification in Wellington. Changemakers, Wellington

ChangeMakers (2012) People with refugee backgrounds can do the job. Refugee-background experiences of employment in Wellington. ChangeMakers, Wellington

Choummanivong C, Poole GE, Cooper A (2014) Refugee family reunification and mental health in resettlement. Kōtuitui: NZ J Soc Sci 9(2):89–100

Elliott S, Yusuf I (2014) "Yes we can; but together": social capital and refugee resettlement. Kōtuitui: NZ J Soc Sci 9(2):101–110

Fleras A, Elliott JL (2017) Unequal relations: an introduction to race and ethnic dynamics in Canada, 8th edn. Pearson Education Canada, Toronto

Fozdar F, Banki S (2017) Settling refugees in Australia: achievements and challenges. Int J Migr Bord Stud 3(1):43–66

Green Party (2017a) Welcoming more refugees: for a fairer society: Green Party election priority. https://www.greens.org.nz/sites/default/files/Green%20Party%20Refugee%20Full%20Policy%20Wording.pdf. Accessed 28 July 2018

Green Party (2017b) Immigration policy. https://www.greens.org.nz/sites/default/files/immigration_20170710_0.pdf. Accessed 28 July 2018

Human Rights Commission (2017) Discussion paper: treating asylum seekers with dignity and respect. Human Rights Commission, Wellington

Human Rights Commission (2018) Give nothing to racism. https://www.hrc.co.nz/news/give-nothing-racism/. Accessed 4 Sept 2018

Ibrahim H (2012) From warzone to godzone: towards a new model of communication and collaboration between schools and refugee families. Unpublished PhD thesis, University of Canterbury, Christchurch

Immigration Amendment Act (2013) http://www.legislation.govt.nz/act/public/2013/0039/latest/DLM4439209.html

Immigration New Zealand (2012) Refugee resettlement: New Zealand resettlement strategy. Ministry of Business Innovation and Employment, Wellington

Immigration New Zealand (2017a) Briefing: immigration policy priorities, and data and evidence. http://www.mbie.govt.nz/info-services/immigration/oia-responses/pacific-climate-migration/Immigration%20Policy%20priorities%20data%20and%20evidence.pdf. Accessed 30 Aug 2018

Immigration New Zealand (2017b) Invercargill chosen as new refugee settlement location. http://www.scoop.co.nz/stories/PO1705/S00015/invercargill-chosen-as-new-refugee-settlement-location.htm. Accessed 30 Aug 2018

Immigration New Zealand (2018a) Refugee and Protection Unit: Refugee Quota Branch (RQB) arrival statistics. https://www.immigration.govt.nz/documents/statistics/statistics-refugee-quota-arrivals. Accessed 30 Aug 2018

Immigration New Zealand (2018b) Refugee and Protection Unit: Refugee Quota Branch (RQB) resettlement statistics. https://www.immigration.govt.nz/documents/statistics/statistics-refugee-quota-settlement. Accessed 20 July 2018

Immigration New Zealand (2018c) Ballot system: B1 – Applicants decided by ballot. https://www.immigration.govt.nz/documents/statistics/statistics-applicants-decided-by-ballot. Accessed 20 July 2018

Immigration New Zealand (2018d) Refugee and Protection Unit: Refugee Status Branch (RSB) statistics. https://www.immigration.govt.nz/documents/statistics/statistics-refugee-and-protection-status-pack. Accessed 20 July 2018

Immigration New Zealand (2018e) Refugee and Protection Unit: Refugee Family Support Category (RFSC) statistics. https://www.immigration.govt.nz/documents/statistics/statistics-refugee-family-support-category-pack. Accessed 20 July 2018

Immigration New Zealand (2018f) Refugee and protection. https://www.immigration.govt.nz/about-us/what-we-do/our-strategies-and-projects/supporting-refugees-and-asylum-seekers/refugee-and-protection-unit. Accessed 20 July 2018

Immigration New Zealand (2018g) New Zealand refugee resettlement strategy: priorities to 2020. https://www.immigration.govt.nz/documents/refugees/settlement-strategy-priorities-2020.pdf. Accessed 20 July 2018

Immigration New Zealand (2018h) New Zealand Refugee Quota Programme. https://www.immigration.govt.nz/about-us/what-we-do/our-strategies-and-projects/supporting-refugees-and-asylum-seekers/refugee-and-protection-unit/new-zealand-refugee-quota-programme. Accessed 20 July 2018

Immigration New Zealand (2018i) Settlement services we support. https://www.immigration.govt.nz/about-us/what-we-do/our-strategies-and-projects/settlement-strategy/settlement-services-supported-by-immigration-new-zealand. Accessed 20 July 2018

Immigration New Zealand (2018j) What is Welcoming Communities? https://www.immigration.govt.nz/about-us/what-we-do/welcoming-communities/what-is-welcoming-communities. Accessed 20 July 2018

Joe A, Kindon S (2011) An equitable education: achieving equity status and measures to ensure equality for refugee-background tertiary students in Aotearoa New Zealand. ChangeMakers, Wellington

Labour Party (2017) New Zealand Labour Party manifesto 2017: immigration. https://d3n8a8pro7vhmx.cloudfront.net/nzlabour/pages/8193/attachments/original/1505192392/Immigration_Policy.pdf?1505192392. Accessed 31 Aug 2018

Labour Party and Green Party (2017) Confidence and supply agreement. https://www.greens.org.nz/sites/default/files/NZLP%20%26%20GP%20C%26S%20Agreement%20FINAL.PDF. Accessed 31 Aug 2018

Lees-Galloway I (2018a) Community organisations chosen to sponsor refugees in New Zealand. https://www.beehive.govt.nz/release/community-organisations-chosen-sponsor-refugees-new-zealand. Accessed 31 Aug 2018

Lees-Galloway I (2018b) New services to support refugees. https://www.beehive.govt.nz/release/new-services-support-refugees. Accessed 31 Aug 2018

Mahoney C, Marlowe J, Humpage L, Baird N (2017) Aspirational yet precarious: compliance of New Zealand refugee resettlement policy with international human rights obligations. Int J Migr Bord Stud 3(1):5–23

Marlowe J, Elliott S (2014) Global trends and refugee settlement in New Zealand. Kotuitui: NZ J Soc Sci Online 9(2):43–49

Marlowe J, Humpage L (2016) Policy responses to refugees in Aotearoa New Zealand: a rights-based analysis. In: Beddoe E, Maidment J (eds) New Zealand social policy for social work and human services: diverse perspectives. Canterbury University Press, Christchurch, pp 150–163

Marlowe J, Bartley A, Hibtit A (2014) The New Zealand refugee resettlement strategy: implications for identity, acculturation and civic participation. Kōtuitui: NZ J Soc Sci 9(2):60–69

McIntosh A, Cockburn-Wootten C (2018) Refugee-focused service providers: improving the welcome in New Zealand. Serv Ind J, online, 17 pages. https://doi.org/10.1080/02642069.2018.1472243

Ministry of Business, Innovation and Employment (2017) Briefing: increasing New Zealand's contribution to global humanitarian efforts – update and next steps for refugee policy. http://www.mbie.govt.nz/info-services/immigration/oia-responses/pacific-climate-migration/Updates%20and%20next%20steps%20for%20refugee%20policy.pdf. Accessed 28 July 2018

Ministry of Business, Innovation and Employment (2018) Briefing: global compact for migration: first round of negotiations. http://www.mbie.govt.nz/info-services/immigration/oia-responses/pacific-climate-migration/Global%20Compact%20for%20Migration%20-%20first%20round%20of%20negotiations.pdf. Accessed 28 July 2018

Ministry of Education (2003) English for speakers of other languages: refugee handbook for schools. Ministry of Education, Wellington

Ministry of Education (2018) Refugee background students. http://www.education.govt.nz/school/student-support/student-wellbeing/refugee-background-students/. Accessed 28 July 2018

Ministry of Foreign Affairs and Trade (2018) Cabinet paper progress update: a New Zealand response to Pacific climate migration. https://www.mbie.govt.nz/info-services/immigration/oia-responses/pacific-climate-migration/Pacific%20climate%20migration%20cabinet%20paper%20progress%20update.pdf. Accessed 28 July 2018

Mortensen A, Rainger W, Hughes S (2012) Refugee health care: a handbook for professionals. Ministry of Health, Wellington

New Zealand Council of Trade Unions (2013) Under pressure: a detailed report into insecure work in New Zealand. New Zealand Council of Trade Unions, Wellington

O'Donovan T, Sheikh M (2014) Welfare reforms and the refugee resettlement strategy: an opportunity to achieve meaningful employment outcomes for New Zealanders from refugee backgrounds? Kōtuitui: NZ J Soc Sci 9(2):82–88

Office of the Minister of Immigration (2017) Community Organisation Sponsorship Category. http://www.mbie.govt.nz/info-services/immigration/oia-responses/folder-community-organisation-refugee-sponsorship-category/cabinet-paper-community-organisation-refugee-sponsorship-category.pdf. Accessed 28 July 2018

Robertson G (2018) Budget speech 2018. https://treasury.govt.nz/sites/default/files/2018-05/b18-speech.pdf. Accessed 31 Aug 2018

Shrestha-Ranjit J, Patterson E, Manias E, Payne D, Koziol-McLain J (2017) Effectiveness of primary health care services in addressing mental health needs of minority refugee population in New Zealand. Issues Ment Health Nurs 38(4):290–300

Statistics New Zealand (2018) Annual net migration continues to fall slowly. https://www.stats.govt.nz/news/annual-net-migration-continues-to-fall-slowly. Accessed 31 Aug 2018

Te M (2018) Racism complaints to Human Rights Commission hit five year high. Stuff. https://www.stuff.co.nz/national/101587476/racism-complaints-to-human-rights-commission-hit-five-year-high. Accessed 31 Aug 2018

United Nations High Commissioner for Refugees (2017) Global trends: forced displacement in 2017. http://www.unhcr.org/5b27be547.pdf. Accessed 31 Aug 2018

Weiner (2017) Election 2017: party policies: immigration: refugees. https://www.interest.co.nz/news/87073/election-2017-party-policies-immigration-refugees. Accessed 31 Aug 2018

Indian Indentured Laborers in the Caribbean

87

Sherry-Ann Singh

Contents
Introduction	1712
On the Plantation	1713
Beyond the Estates	1719
Conclusion	1725
References	1726

Abstract
Between 1838 and 1920, more than half a million Indians (South Asians) migrated to the Caribbean as Indian indentured laborers. During the 82-year tenure of the system, Indians had an indelible impact on the Caribbean landscape, not just by fulfilling their ascribed economic role as the proverbial "saviors" of the sugar industry but also in terms of their social, cultural, and emotional presence. The system was terminated in 1920, which set the stage for a new dynamic for those Indians who had opted to make the Caribbean their home, especially since they were now unfettered by the rules, regulations, and restrictions of the system of Indian indenture. This chapter endeavors to trace the experiences of these indentured laborers as, at first, sources of labor on the various plantations and, as they left said plantations, as migrants embarking on the very complex journey of settlement in a foreign location, the Caribbean.

Keywords
Indian · Caribbean · Indenture · Labor

S.-A. Singh (✉)
The University of the West Indies, St. Augustine, Trinidad and Tobago
e-mail: Sherry-Ann.Singh@sta.uwi.edu

© The Author(s), under exclusive license to Springer Nature Singapore Pte Ltd. 2019
S. Ratuva (ed.), *The Palgrave Handbook of Ethnicity*,
https://doi.org/10.1007/978-981-13-2898-5_94

Introduction

Between 1838 and 1920, more than half a million Indians (South Asians) migrated to the Caribbean as Indian indentured laborers (Table 1).

Most of these indentured laborers were drawn from the agricultural and laboring classes of the Uttar Pradesh and Bihar regions of north India, with smaller numbers being recruited from Bengal and various regions of south India. This predominance of immigrants from the "Bhojpuri belt" (Western Bihar and Eastern Uttar Pradesh) inevitably generated Indian cultural, social, and religious transfigurations throughout the Caribbean that are predominantly rooted in the Bhojpuri traditions of Uttar Pradesh and Bihar (Vertovec 1992). Approximately 85% of the immigrants were Hindus and 14% Muslims (Vertovec 1992). The predominant age group of the immigrants was 20–30 years (Laurence 1994), and, while most came as unmarried men and women, some came as small family units (Tinker 1974). Initially, the journey from India to Trinidad took about 3 months but became shorter and less turbulent with the opening of the Suez Canal in 1869. For those Indians who had not truly understood the realities of their journey, the realization that they had left Indian soil was often quite traumatic, sometimes resulting in attempts at casting themselves overboard in a desperate effort to return to their homeland. Conditions onboard the ships were cramped and dismal. There were frequent outbreaks of cholera, typhoid, dysentery, and measles resulting in high mortality rates on some of the journeys, especially during the early years of the scheme (Tinker 1974; Table 2).

There were separate sleeping sections for single males, single females, and couples. Daily life on the ships was fairly routine. Indians were brought on deck on mornings and daily exercise/walk was encouraged. They were served meals twice daily which were prepared by Indian cooks. During turbulent weather no cooking was done, and instead, a dry meal comprising biscuits with sugar and tamarind or salt and raw onions was served (Tinker 1974). The immigrants were encouraged to engage in such harmless diversion such as music, song, dance, stick fighting, and

Table 1 Indian indentured laborers to the Caribbean

Locations	Period	No. of Indians
British Guiana	1838–1917	238,909
Trinidad	1845–1917	143,939
Guadeloupe	1854–1887	42,595
Jamaica	1845–1916	38,681
Surinam	1873–1918	34,024
Martinique	1848–1884	25,509
French Guiana	1853–1885	19,296
St. Lucia	1858–1895	4354
Grenada	1856–1885	3200
St. Vincent	1860–1880	2472
St. Kitts	1860–1861	337

Source: Verene Shepherd (2006)

Table 2 Mortality on ships to the Caribbean, 1856–1857

Ship	Passengers	Deaths
Wellesley	382	22
Bucephalus	380	45
Sir Robert Seppings	291	61
Roman Emperor	313	88
Adelaide	304	25
Sir George Seymour	354	36
Eveline	387	72
Maidstone	375	92
Merchantman	385	120
Granville	309	37
Burmah	326	49
Scindian	288	60

Source: Hugh Tinker (1974)

wrestling. Yet, depression, seasickness, and attempted suicide were constant features of the journey to the Caribbean.

Comparison between Indian indenture and African enslavement has generated the debate of whether or not Indian indenture was "a new system of slavery." The general consensus shared by the most proficient works on Indian indenture by Hugh Tinker (1974), K.O. Laurence (1994), Walton Look Lai (2004), Marina Carter (1995), and Brij V. Lal (2006) is that the former was not a system of slavery but, rather, was one that exhibited features of several systems of bonded labor and, by extension, varying shades of unfreedom. According to historian Bridget Brereton, Slavery and indenture "...were fundamentally different systems of labour control" (Brereton 1994). Another debate permeating discussions on Indian indenture surrounds the degree of voluntariness of Indian immigration under the system. A holistic consideration of this issue mandates taking into account all facets of the system of Indian indenture: recruitment practices, the contracts, the journey, conditions on the estates, legal sanctions, and the authenticity of the system. Questions surrounding the nature and workings of the system of Indian indenture are multifaceted and rather open-ended. A substantial degree of ambiguity has plagued the system, especially during its first three decades. These include the recruitment process in India; British role in the impoverishment of nineteenth-century India – a main push factor of Indian indenture; whether or not the Indians were truly and fully aware of the nature and details of the system; and their level of cognizance of the fact that they were leaving Indian soil.

On the Plantation

The first two decades of the system were very experimental in nature, with highly fluid regulations and conditions (Laurence 1994; Tinker 1974). There were, however, two central and enduring features of the system: immigrants were contracted with a single employer for long periods of time, and there were penal sanctions for breaches of the contract. From the Immigration Ordinance of 1854 until 1917, the system remained largely constant with a few discernible changes. However, there were a few features of the system that distinguished its operations on specific colonies. For example, in Trinidad, a land commutation scheme was implemented between 1869 and 1880 which granted Indians 10 and, later, 5 acres of land in lieu of their return passage (Brereton 1985). During the 1890s, a similar offer was made to Indians in Surinam (Hoefte 2006). On arrival in the various Caribbean colonies, the indentured immigrants spent a period of quarantine before being assigned to estates. In Trinidad, they were quarantined on Nelson Island. Immigrants were then assigned to the various estates for the contracted 3-year period; this was followed by a 2-year period which completed the "industrial residence" of 5 years. At the end of this 5-year period, the Indian immigrant was granted his Certificate of Industrial Residence, a type of "freedom paper" indicating that he/she was no longer indentured. However, in order to qualify for the free return passage back to India, the immigrant had to re-indenture himself for an additional 5 years but was then free to choose both employer and occupation. The only other option for returning to India without completing the 10 years of labor was at one's own expense.

For the indentured immigrants, life on the estates was fettered by the terms and conditions of the contract which they had signed, though most were illiterate in all of the three languages in which the contract was written. In essence, the Indians were not absolutely free. They could not demand higher wages, leave the estate without permission, live off the estates, or refuse the work assigned to them. The minimum wage stipulated in the contract was 25 cents per day or task for adult males and 16 cents for adult females. Although this amount could not be legally reduced, tasks were often increased (Brereton 1985). The contract stipulated a 45-hour workweek, but during crop time it was often six 9-hour days. There was no work on Sundays. Wages also varied according to the type of work, season, and the location (Tinker 1974; Laurence 1994). Withholding and cutting of wages were a persistent problem during the entire period of Indian indenture (Tinker 1974).

A rather irksome feature of the system for the indentured laborers was the fact that they were prosecuted as criminals for what were essentially civil offences: breach of contract and immigration laws (Brereton 1982). Indians leaving their respective estates had to carry a pass indicating that they had been granted permission to do so. Being found off the estate without this pass or "Ticket of Leave" led to many Indians being imprisoned for vagrancy or being found "at large" (Laurence 1994). For example, in Trinidad, 11,149 indentured Indians were prosecuted for absenteeism, desertion, vagrancy, or idleness between 1898 and 1905 (Kirpalani 1945). In British Guiana, between 1876 and 1910, 20,058 desertions were recorded (Seecharan 2006). Such "unlawful" absence from the estate could entail a maximum fine of $14.40 or 3 months in prison (Laurence 1994). By 1876, extension of indenture was the most common form of punishment for absenteeism, with fines and imprisonment being reserved for the more serious cases (Laurence 1994). Official investigations indicated that the common occurrence of both absenteeism and desertion was rooted in the issue of management on the estates, harsh treatment of the Indians, and unscrupulous employers conspiring for desertion by unfit or unwanted immigrant laborers (Tinker 1974). In attempting to deal with absenteeism and desertion, Indians who were no longer indentured were required to carry their Certificate of Industrial Residence at all times, to prove that they were not deserters and in seeking employment. Other offences carrying sentences included deliberate disobedience, threatening or verbally abusing the employer, and deception in performing work. The courts were heavily skewed against the Indians, who were often unfairly charged with excessive sentences (Brereton 1985). Very few Indians actually understood the immigration laws and regulations could defend themselves or pay for legal aid. By the 1870s, immigration laws were becoming increasingly arbitrary and confusing. Also, each revision of the law resulted in more stringent and comprehensive penalties.

While, in theory, there were a number of mechanisms put in place for the welfare and protection of the immigrants, these were more often than not very ineffectual. The Immigration Department led by the Protector of Emigrants/Agent General was established to secure the interests of the Indians through its regulations and regular estate inspections and even act as the last "court of appeal" (Tinker 1974). However, this office was very vulnerable to demands from the planters. The various authorities often failed in discharging their duties of protecting the immigrants, and inspection of the estates was too sparse. Not many immigrants lodged complaints because of an inherent fear of victimization and a general suspicion of the impartiality of the magistrate's court, which more often than not accepted the evidence of the estate authorities over that of the Indians. These, together with the pervasive influence of the planters, underlying administrative weaknesses, and general laxity in the operation of reformed laws, saw excessive exploitation being an integral facet of the system of Indian indenture (Laurence 1994). However, the ultimate sanction against the mistreatment of the Indians was the power of the Governor to remove laborers from an estate. Two such instances occurring in Trinidad were on the Patna Estate for unhealthy conditions and on the La Gloria Estate where the Indians were not being treated properly (Laurence 1994).

Throughout the period of Indian indenture in the Caribbean, living conditions on the estates were extremely unpleasant and many times subhuman. Indians were assigned barrack-type quarters, usually the same barracks used for the formerly enslaved Africans. Each room of the barrack building measured 10 ft^2 and 8–10 ft high. Since the partitions between rooms did not reach the roof, there was a total lack of privacy. Ventilation was inadequate. Each room housed either a married couple and their children or two to four single adults. Cooking was usually done outside, on the stairs (Brereton 1985).

Two constant problems on the estates were sanitation and the provision of drinking water. Even though some of the estates had sunk wells and water pumps, the facilities for storing rainwater on the estates were often deficient. Even when there was sufficient storage, the water was often polluted since both employer and the Indians were careless about maintaining its purity. The Indians themselves further aggravated the situation by drinking water from the ponds, streams, and canals. Throughout the nineteenth century, stagnant drains and the absence of latrines created serious sanitation problems on almost all of the estates. Indians had to use the fields, which resulted in malaria, dysentery, cholera, and such parasite-related diseases as hookworm, ground itch, and anemia being rampant on almost all of the estates (Brereton 1985). There were also occasional epidemics of yellow fever and smallpox. By law, each of the estates had a hospital for the Indian indentured laborers, which the District Medical Officers visited at set times. However, the condition of these hospitals ranged from good to appalling. In the worst cases, ill Indians continued staying in their barracks and were hurried to the hospital only when the doctor visited (Brereton 1985). So distasteful did the Indians find such dilapidated conditions that a law imposing jail sentences on those who ran away from the hospital was passed. Despite sustained attempts at improving the health of the immigrants, investigations revealed that, on average, an indentured laborer in Trinidad was ill for up to 4 weeks a year. In 1911, out of an indentured population of about 10,000, over 24,000 cases of illness were treated, the chief scourges being malaria and ancylostomiasis (Williams 1964). During the early decades of indentureship, the health conditions of the Indians in Surinam were extremely deplorable, leading to the temporary suspension of the system in 1875 (Hoefte 2006). High infant mortality rate was a grim reality throughout the entire period of Indian indenture (Laurence 1994). Due to the general lack of privacy in the living quarters, the disintegration of the extended family system, and the slackening of conjugal bonds, family life on the estates suffered enormously.

Throughout the entire period of Indian indenture, there was an acute imbalance in the ratio of male to female immigrants. From a total of 95,707 immigrants between 1874 and 1917, 65,084 were males, and 30,623 were females (Laurence 1994). There was an even more severe imbalance in the earlier decades; at its worst, the ratio stood at one female to five males. Recognizing the inherent problems of not addressing this issue, and under strong pressure from the Colonial Office, in 1868, the Secretary of State for India issued instructions that, heretofore, the proportion of 40 women to 100 men should be adhered to (Tinker 1974). This 2:5 ratio was obtained until the termination of the system of Indian indenture. The reasons for female immigration were manifold and located in the social and economic framework of nineteenth-century India. Many were women fleeing oppressive social situations including widowhood, dowry-related conflicts, domestic problems, and abusive husbands. Some came as wives of male immigrants, from pre-existing marital unions or unions that were established either in the holding depots or on the ships. A small number of women came as prostitutes or became prostitutes on the plantations. Underscoring all of the foregoing, however, were the economic push factors of destitution, extreme poverty, glut in the labor market, and starvation.

The paucity of Indian women had a profound impact on family life on the plantations, especially in Trinidad since most Indian men did not marry or cohabitate with African women (Wood 1986). In colonies such as British Guiana, Trinidad, and Jamaica, competition for Indian women resulted in an erosion of caste restrictions and generated grave tension which often erupted in violence against unfaithful women and, sometimes, the loss of lives. According to calculations done by Laurence, between 1872 and 1880, "...21 of the 22 Indian murders in Trinidad involved wives or reputed wives, while in British Guiana in the period 1873–1880 the number was 43 out of 71" (Laurence 1994). Traditional Indian male-female dynamics crumbled. The practice of dowry in the Hindu marriage ceremony where the bride's family gave gifts to the groom was reversed and replaced by the bride price where, now, the groom had to pay for his bride (Tinker 1974). Marriages were visibly unstable, and keeper unions were quite common with their stability largely contingent on the satisfaction of the female. Inter-caste marriages and Hindu-Muslim marriages were common on the estates.

A wide cross section of the Indian caste system manifested itself among the Hindu indentured laborers. These figures, however, carry with them a deep-seated ambiguity on the issue of authenticity of caste ascriptions by the indentured Indians. There are numerous accounts of individuals changing their castes upon arrival in the Caribbean or even at the depots in India (Laurence 1994). However, there was a rapid attenuation and reconfiguring of the Indian social system which could not reproduce itself under the Caribbean's quite variant social, political, economic, ethnic, and religious composition (Tinker 1974). Thus, rather than the system itself, some elements of caste ideology and practices survived on the estates in variously attenuated and diluted forms (Schwartz 1967). In fact, the process of caste disintegration and dilution began on the depots in India and on the ships where all the immigrants, regardless of caste, had to share common space and facilities (Tinker 1974). This process continued on the estates where shared living facilities and consequent indiscriminate contact among all the laborers further diluted many of the traditional taboos such as those associated with eating and touch. Almost all of the immigrants were ascribed the same social status. Occupation, instead of, as traditionally, being determined by caste, was now decided by the estate overseer. Yet, though small in number, high caste men – or those with claims to high caste – continued to exercise some level of influence among the Indians. Of these, the Brahmins (the priestly caste), due to their role in religious and ritual performance and preservation, would emerge at the fore of Hindu sociocultural and even sociopolitical life on the estates. Yet, even this dynamic was often interestingly conditioned by context. For example, in British Guiana, subversion was at work when the tiny Brahmin population (about 2%) found themselves having to minister to even the lowest castes in order to save their flock from Christian proselytizers (Seecharan 2006).

Castes	British Guiana (%)	Trinidad (%)
Brahmins and high castes	11.84	14.45
Agriculturists	31.38	30
Artisans	7.63	6.60
Low castes	33.84	34.87
Muslims	15.21	14.01
Christians	0.10	0.07

Source: K.O. Laurence (1994)

In general, life on the plantation, focused on the maximum extraction of labor, was not conducive to significant reconstruction of any aspect of religious, cultural, or family life. In addition to the highly labor-intensive days, there were rules and regulations that directly curtailed Indian religious and cultural practices. For example, Hindus were prohibited from beating drums at their wedding ceremonies which were traditionally held at nights since they disturbed the peace. Yet, despite the many hindrances, facets of Indian religion and culture were evident on almost all of the estates. By the 1860s, the earliest Hindu temples, very basic 2–3-ft-tall structures, began dotting the plantations; spaces were similarly claimed by the Muslims (Wood 1986). Simple domestic ceremonies such as the *puja* – with or without an animal sacrifice – and the Madrasi "firepass" ceremony were being conducted (Wood 1986). Recitation from the religious texts such as the *Ramayana* (Sankalia 1982) was common after a long day's work, providing the indentured laborers with the much needed respite from their otherwise wretched and harsh situation (Seecharan 1997). In Trinidad, communally observed festivals took birth on the plantations in the form of the *Muharram/Hosay* (Singh 1988) celebration and the *Ramlila* festival. Even in Grenada, where the Indian indentured laborers were an extremely small minority, Hosay was the only Indian festival that was openly observed during the period of indenture (Sookram 2006). The intense social, religious, and cultural diversity due to the wide sweep of immigration saw the process of cultural, religious, and social reconstruction being a highly creative one, marked by substantial levels of telescoping, adjustment, and substitution.

Life on the plantations rarely took into account the vicissitudes of Indian social life. Thus, Indian marriages were not recognized as legal unless registered with the District Immigration Agent, and the offspring of such unions were deemed illegitimate. Consequently, there were persistent complications over inheritance of property, and governors had to sometimes regrant lands to the children of Crown grantees who had not registered their marriages and had died intestate (Laurence 1994). This presents a very vivid example also of the clash of civilizations wherein, for the Indians, their religious ceremony was all the validation needed, while the Colonial authorities recognized just those unions that were officially registered; something that the Indians did not subscribe to. Additionally, Hindus were forced to bury their dead since permission was not granted for the traditional method of cremation.

Before the 1870s, hardly any effort was made to provide education for the children of the indentured laborers. Indians were also hesitant to send their children to the ward schools because of the linguistic, racial, and religious differences. In Trinidad, British Guiana, and Jamaica, a small number of estates and churches had established their own schools for the Indian children during the 1860s (Laurence 1994). It was, however, the persistent efforts of the Canadian Mission (C.M.), initiated in 1868 in Trinidad, in 1885 in British Guiana, and later on in Jamaica (Mansingh and Mansingh 1999), that saw a substantial rise in the formal education of Indian children in these three colonies. However, in Surinam, the education of Indian children was a (Dutch) government concern. In 1878, the compulsory education law was applied to Indian children, and in 1890, the first "coolie school" was opened (Hoefte 2006).

At the C.M. schools, teaching was initially done in English, but both standard Hindi and the vernacular were used "to explain the English." The emphasis was on reading, writing, and Bible knowledge (Morton 1916). The number of Indian children attending these C.M. schools slowly but steadily grew. However, because of the practice of child marriage and the primary roles of Indian women as wives and mothers, it proved extremely difficult to persuade the Indians to send their daughters to school. A noticeable number of the Indian males became teachers at the C.M. schools, and some became catechists and preachers. The C.M. schools were also providing Hindi interpreters for the government and clerks for offices (Morton 1916). Most of the Indians who had post primary education and subsequent employment via the Canadian Mission, however, fell prey to its underlying objective of conversion to Presbyterianism. It was grudgingly acknowledged by the Indians that, during the period of indenture, the only way out of the cane fields was through conversion. In Grenada, an official body responsible for the transformation of Indians into Christians, The Association for the Instruction of Indian Immigrants, was set up in 1864. Operating within an actively anglicizing and assimilative framework, this body was specifically aimed at coercing the Indians in Grenada "...to abandon their ancestral culture and embrace the cultural values perpetuated by the British" (Sookram 2006).

Beyond the Estates

During the 1880s, competition from beet sugar and the full implementation of the 1946 Sugar Duties Act saw depression looming over the British West Indian sugar industry. Planters quickly shifted the burden of the necessary economic adjustment on the Indian laborers, which generated strikes, disturbances, and other passive forms of resistance in many of the colonies. Most of these were due to the non-payment of wages, extending of tasks, and harsh and unfair treatment on the estates (Laurence 1994). In Trinidad, there were disturbances on the Cedar Hill Plantation and the Perseverance Estate. The situation, however, was most intense in British Guiana where, between 1976 and 1910, 20,058 cases were recorded (Seecharan 1997). By 1870, violence among indentured laborers on estates in British Guiana became widespread, giving birth to a "tradition of militancy" in that colony wherein Indian lives were lost and many more were injured (Seecharan 1997). Though substantially smaller in number, the Indians in Jamaica expressed their dissatisfaction with conditions on the estates in a similar manner. Between 1847 and 1921, 18 strikes were recorded on Jamaican estates, and production was further undermined by such more passive forms of resistance as desertion, feigning illness, committing suicide, and buying themselves out of contract (Shepherd 2006).

For Indians, estate life had become increasingly unbearable. This saw Indians exiting the estates in large numbers to become independent farmers, settle on, and cultivate lands granted to them through the land commutation scheme (in the case of Trinidad) or that they had purchased from the State. The Indians' deeply ingrained affinity for land, along with their total disenchantment with estate life, saw many of them becoming peasant proprietors at the end of their periods of indenture. Between 1870 and 1915, Indians in Trinidad had purchased about 102,000 acres of land

(Laurence 1994). In Jamaica, until 1906, Indians were offered either GBP12 or 4 ha of land in lieu of their return passage. However, similar to Trinidad, most of the lands granted were uncultivable, too mountainous, and arid and were eventually abandoned (Shepherd 2006). Plots of land were also offered to immigrants in Surinam during the 1890s.

By the 1890s villages of former indentured laborers were established in both British Guiana and Trinidad. As Indians moved off the estates, they embarked on the process of community reconstruction, facilitated by factors such as the acceptance of the colonies as their homelands by those immigrants who had stayed in the colonies, the evening of the male-female ratio and the age imbalance, and the noticeable increase in the birth rate of Indians. This would, in turn, generate a focus on and acceleration of social change and further integration into their respective larger societies.

Even before the system of Indian indenture was formally brought to an end in 1917, Indians had more than fulfilled their primary purpose of revival and expansion of the sugar industry and had converted Trinidad, British Guiana, and other colonies from societies of small farmers to large plantation societies (Brereton 1985). By 1915, 9202 Indian cane farmers were cultivating about 10,000 acres of sugar cane, about 24.3% of the total cane ground in the factories in Trinidad (Laurence 1994). The period between 1870 and 1920 has been classified as the "Golden Age" of the cocoa industry in Trinidad, and Indians played a significant role as laborers and contractors (Brereton 1985). Wet rice cultivation was introduced into Trinidad and British Guiana by Indians, along with its associated agricultural methods and technology (Seecharan 1997). By 1896, 6000 acres of lands owned by Indians in Trinidad were dedicated to wet rice cultivation, accounting for one-sixth of the local consumption (Niehoff and Niehoff 1960). By 1913, 13,714 ha of land in British Guiana were dedicated to wet rice cultivation by Indians, which also saw the expansion of the cattle-rearing industry (Seecharan 1997). By 1903, Indian smallholders in Surinam owned or leased 14,000 ha of land, dedicated to rice, vegetable, milk, meat, and fruit production (Hoefte 2006). In Jamaica, agriculture remained the main occupation of Indians, and a few Indians even became estate owners (Shepherd 2006). This prominent role of Indians in agriculture persisted in the Caribbean for decades.

From as early as the 1920s, notwithstanding the Indians' predominant engagement in agriculture and a variety of agriculture-related activities, Indian entrepreneurial endeavors were already being viewed as a viable alternative to agriculture. On the one level, there was a multitude of small-scale shopkeepers, hucksters, taxi drivers, proprietors, and transportation services. Nonagriculture-based caste-related skills brought by the Indian indentured laborers and passed on to their descendants added considerably to this level of Indian entrepreneurial effort (Brereton 1985). On the other level, a number of larger more established commercial businesses were already dotting the landscape of the major towns in Trinidad, British Guiana, and Surinam. Catering to the perceived needs and tastes of Indians, such larger establishments, often labelling themselves "General Provision Merchants" or "Importers of Indian Goods," procured from India dry goods, haberdashery, gold and silver jewelry, cotton and silk garments, brassware, furniture, household items, oriental curios, and Indian food staples such as rice, *dhall* (split peas), *ghee* (clarified butter), and a variety of whole spices. By the 1940s, Indians in Trinidad were also contributing significantly to the petroleum and energy sectors, either by leasing out the mineral rights of their land to oil developers or by working as professionals and technicians and often rising to the highest levels of management.

Indian organizational structure and function became increasingly active during the first half of the twentieth century. Even from the last decade of the nineteenth century, organizations such as the East Indian National Congress (EINC) or the East Indian National Association (EINA) in Trinidad were functioning as an organ and voice of the newly emergent Indian middle class (Malik 1971). A similar trend was visible in British Guiana with the formation of the British Guiana East Indian Association in 1916 and the Wesleyan East Indian Young Men's Society in 1919 (Mangru 1996). By the 1930s, Hindu organizations such as the Sanatan Dharma Board of Control and Sanatan Dharma Association were already serving as representatives of the Hindu population in Trinidad. Similar attitudes and trends would also be evident within the Muslim Indian community, with the Tackveeyatul Islamia Association (TIA), incorporated in 1931, and the Anjuman Sunnat-ul-Jamaat Association, incorporated in 1935 (Kassim 2002). The British Guiana Sanatan Dharma Maha Sabha incorporated in 1927 and the Sad'r Anjuman-E-Islam incorporated in 1937 functioned similarly for the Hindu and Muslim populations in British Guiana. However, in locations throughout the Caribbean with substantially smaller numbers of Indian immigrants, an Indian middle class was never consolidated during the period of indenture. In Grenada, for example, elements of an Indian middle class emerged much later on, "...at a time when the social system had already established the terms of their incorporation within the Grenadian mainstream: essentially, as persons devoid of Indian cultural supports" (Sookram 2006).

The increasing gravitation toward Western education provided Indians with another, though complicated, agent of mobility – that of conversion. Conversion has been a persistent concern among Indians in Trinidad and British Guiana since the advent of the Presbyterian Canadian Mission (C.M.) in 1868 (Seesaran 2002) and 1885, respectively. Under the shroud of education, the C.M. embarked on very vigorous attempts at communicating their "light and knowledge" to a "lamentably degenerate and base" group of people who retained but a "feeble sense of moral obligation" (Grant 1923). The techniques employed were formulated and administered in such an astute manner that it was both indiscernible by the members of the Hindu community and possibly misinterpreted by several scholars as a natural, practical dimension of the C.M.'s efforts at educating and "socializing" Indians in Trinidad and British Guiana.

Possibly the most skillful tactic was the incorporation of Indian forms of organization and worship into their efforts, thus packaging the fundamentally Christian values, beliefs, and principles in a veneer of Hinduism. Some of these techniques included the naming of Presbyterian churches, such as *Dharm ka Suraj* (the splendor of truth) and *Jagat ka Prakash* (light of the world), in Hindi so that they conveyed Christian messages in Hindi words (Samaroo 1975). In some cases, the meeting of the Presbyterian minister and elders rechristened "the panchayat" (Samaroo 1975). Hindi terminology was also extended to aspects of the Christian service. For example, Jesus Christ was renamed Yeshu Masih and hailed as *Ishwari-ji* (the lord), and the wearing of traditional Indian clothing to attend church services was encouraged (Seecharan 1997). Prayer meetings were renamed *Yeshu Katha* (literally, the story of Christ but also imbibing all of the religious connotations of a Hindu *katha* which, among Hindus, often refer to the reading of Hindu scriptures within the context of a puja). The consecrated bread distributed at Christian Communions was duly named j*ewan ki roti* (bread of life). Another method was the sale of Christian literature in Hindi. These included the Bible, *bhajans* (Hindu religious songs) with Christian messages, a critique of the *Valmiki Ramayana*, and Hindi editions of Church periodicals. Drawing on the deep-seated emotional bonds held by Indians in the Caribbean toward India, the C.M. also brought missionaries, pastors, and other helpers from India (Seecharan 1997).

Throughout the period of indenture, the predominance of such traditional social institutions as the *panchayat* (a group of five village elders responsible for resolving conflict), *bhaiyachaarya* (a cooperative brotherhood in building homes and cultivating crops), *kujat* (state of outcaste), and *praja* (traditional Indian patron-client relationship) and caste sentiments also tightened the sense of village (Klass 1961). Off the estates, this was enhanced by the de-emphasis of the individual in favor of the collective body, rooted in the secondary position of the individual to the family unit. The socioeconomic and emotional ties to ancestral lands and property and the persistence of traditional Indian structures and values surrounding Indian family life created a situation where male members of the family usually continued residing in their ancestral villages. This generated a high degree of consanguinity within villages which, in turn, prohibited marriages within villages. In addition, the kinship sentiment of the *jahaji bhai* relations (relationships established aboard the Indian immigrant ships and usually sustained during and after the indenture period) albeit fictive continued to exist among the descendants of the indentured immigrants, though in increasingly diluted degrees. Thus, along with the actual event of the wedding, affinal bonds generated by such unions greatly enhanced inter-village interaction and relations and the gradual crystallization of Indian group sentiments.

However, just one decade after the termination of Indian indenture, it was both imminent and evident that other elements were beginning to influence and, in some cases, even supersede the importance of traditional ideologies and institutions. Such factors included literacy, education, occupation, the acquisition of wealth, and in some cases power, which began to either work with or displace some of the traditional values and virtues as a formula for status, authority, and power (Haraksingh 1976). The decline of the traditional *panchayat* system provides a most potent example of this. Internally, being a member of the *panchayat* meant occupying the highest social position in the community; one accorded possibly the greatest degree of respect and authority. Judgments of the *panchayat* could have direct bearing on the status of both individuals and entire families in the village (Laurence 1994). The most outstanding evidence of this was the application of the state of *kujat* (outcaste) which involved the barring of the offender(s) from any kind of social interaction with fellow villagers; with the duration of the ban dependent on the gravity of the offence. Such offences included intra-village, inter-religious, or, worst of all, interracial marriages; and the time period could range from a few months to a few years, to life. Until the early 1920s, the composition of the *panchayat* was based on a flexible combination of caste, age, moral uprightness, scriptural and religious knowledge, and a sound sense of judgment. By the late 1930s, however, factors such as English education and economic status were added to, and sometimes even superseded, the more traditional determinants. In addition to the presence of wealthy non-Brahmins, the age restriction was being broken with the infiltration of some comparably younger members on the basis of their level of English education. However, the one enduring prerequisite for members was good character (Singh 2012). As with most tradition-based systems and institutions, the authority of the *panchayat* remained unquestioned as long as the traditional order which sanctioned its role remained intact and its rulings could be enforced.

The immediate post-indenture period saw several key developments that contributed to the restructuring of various aspects of Indian religious life, festivals, and observances. There was a steady rise in the quantum and scale of religious observances and celebrations performed at the community level (Haraksingh 1988). This was facilitated by a marked increase in the appearance of Hindu temples and Muslim mosques in almost every major area where Indians lived. Such activities organized by groups usually mirrored an awareness of the perceived need to revive, reform, and promote religion in a manner which would impart a greater degree of visibility and acceptability of both the religion and its adherents (Singh 2012). Temples and mosques also served as the preferred meeting places where issues pertaining to the Hindu and Muslim communities, many times in relation to their social mobility as a group, were discussed, debated, and sometimes resolved. Thus, they functioned as both the basis and markers of the increase in Indian socioreligious organizational development during this period.

In both practice and the ideal, the extended family structure prevailed among Indians during this period. This notion of "extended," however, should be tempered with the fact that it involved a number of compositional variations at the different stages of the cycle of the Indian family structure (Mandelbaum 1972). At strategic points, there would be the breaking away of a specific subgroup which would then proceed to form the nucleus (nuclear family) of another imminent extended system (Klass 1961). In a period where male siblings usually earned their livelihood by working on family-occupied (owned, rented, or leased) land, the common situation was one where the sub-unit would set up household either adjacent to or on the same property of the original unit or would even choose to stay at the same house while setting up separate kitchens. While factors such as Western education, non-agricultural occupations, and the geographical location of such occupations would influence the rate, extent, and nature of this breaking away, there would almost always be strong ideological and emotional ties with the original extended system (Klass 1961). However, the death of the patriarch inevitably led to the weakening of the ideal of fraternal relations and often set the stage for the materialization of formerly subtle, internal conflicts, often rooted in inheritance struggles. One fallout was the subdivision of landholdings and other property according to traditional prescriptions. This promoted greater autonomy for the resultant subdivisions, since the cohesive powers of neither parent figure nor common property were at work (Singh 2012).

Though monogamy was held as the ideal among Indians in the Caribbean by the twentieth century, there were digressions on the part of both men and women. These digressions, viewed against the ideal, impacted directly on the status of the individual within both the family and the larger community. The most glaring aspect of this was the discrepancy in attitude toward males and females. With a mixture of pious castigation, grudging admiration, and sometimes not so secret approval and understanding, the social standing of the adulterous male remained relatively intact. This was especially where it was suspected that the wife was barren. It may even be said that extramarital relationships were covertly expected of the more prominent men in the community. In the case of those whose status was based on ritual purity such as the Brahmins and the pundits, there was a more pronounced effect. This involved a combination of largely private ridicule, a decline in the individual's viability as a religious leader, and yet, paradoxically, the continued faithful following of his disciples. Women, on the other hand, still viewed as "the receptacles of the ancestral seed," the sustainers of the lineage, the foundation of family life and honor, and through whose fidelity male sexual prowess was measured were heavily reprimanded, ridiculed, beaten, and even ostracized by immediate family members and, often, the community as well (Kanhai 2008). The status of Indian women during the immediate post-indenture decades was highly conditioned by the desire to control female sexuality through early marriages, glorifying female reproductive powers, and preferring sons over daughters. The selective shaping of religious texts and doctrines aided this mood.

Tangible property, especially land, was almost never inherited by daughters on the same or comparable scale as sons, since it would in turn become the property of her husband. Daughters either received none or, sometimes, a very small plot of the ancestral land as "a gift." This notion of keeping the wealth/land in the family was also compounded by the attitude that women should be provided for by their husbands and not their parents (since upon marriage she became the "property" of her husband). The woman's "share of the wealth" was given as her dowry (which re-emerged during the post-indenture period) and other gifts upon her marriage. This usually included jewelry, money, cows, an occasional plot of land, and household appliances. Daughters received the majority of their father's wealth only if there were no sons in the family (Kanhai 2012). Even that too was sometimes deflected to other male members of the extended family, all to keep the land "in the family." However, it was quite common for the wealthier individuals to gift their daughters quite generously. Also, many widowed women were often given small plots of land by their relatives upon which they could construct homes. However, during this period, there were many cases of women, usually widows, or those separated from their husbands, purchasing or leasing property (land) on their own (Roopnarine 2007). It should be noted that the personal agency and highly prized position of Indian women during the indenture stymied attempts at absolute reproduction of patriarchal systems as they obtained in India. Within the essentially patriarchal values and ideology that permeated the Indian community until the 1960s, "women invariably negotiate[d] within their domestic spaces for changes which will improve the conditions of their lives and that of their families" (Mohammed 2002).

On 27 March 1917, the Viceroy of India terminated the shipping of Indian laborers overseas, setting the stage for the termination of the system of Indian indenture in 1920, when all of the indentured laborers in the various colonies would have ended their contracted periods of indentureship. Initial arguments against the system of Indian indenture were raised during the 1890s by Mahatma Gandhi during his prolonged stay in South Africa where, for 20 years, he fought against the atrocities of the system, as faced by Indian indentured laborers in South Africa. His arguments were later taken up and propelled into the forefront as one of many anti-colonial arguments of a rapidly increasing group of Indian nationalists who had been questioning colonial rule in India and who, by 1910, were advocating for self-rule in India. Highlighting the poor conditions, ill-treatment, punishment, and especially the abuse of Indian women, a massive campaign against the system of Indian indenture was initiated. Therein, numerous public meetings, the Indian press, resolutions, and petitions to both the Government of India and the British Imperial Government collectively saw the anti-indenture campaign reaching an all-India level. By 1915, the British Imperial Government could no longer ignore the growing threat of the campaign. Thus, in 1917, the shipping of Indian labor overseas was terminated.

Conclusion

When the system of Indian indenture was terminated by 1920, about 75% of the immigrants had chosen to make the Caribbean their permanent home (Laurence 1994). One hundred seventy-five years later, Indians have become an integral yet often distinct compositional element of the Caribbean landscape. The descendants of these indentured laborers now form an ethnic majority in Trinidad and Tobago, Guyana, and Surinam. Though substantially smaller, the Indian communities in Jamaica, Martinique, Guadeloupe, and St. Vincent are definitely visible, both demographically and culturally (Shepherd 1993; Singaravelou 1976). However, in such countries as Grenada, St. Lucia, St. Kitts, and Belize, the extremely small numbers together with variant factors have seen an almost total absorption of the Indian immigrant communities into their respective societies (Sookram 2009; Mahabir 2011). In most of the foregoing Caribbean locations, the decades following the termination of the system of Indian indenture generated a focus on and acceleration of social, economic, political, cultural, and religious transformation within and among the Indian communities in the Caribbean which would, ultimately, contribute to the process of identity formation, both within the various locations and as a larger Caribbean community. This would entail a dynamic interplay between "Indian" and "Caribbean," the traditional and the modern, the religious and the secular, retention and transformation, between being and belonging. Today, Indians in the Caribbean stand as an integral part of the Caribbean landscape. And, while such appellations as "Indo-Caribbean" and "Indians in the Caribbean" have been largely accepted by both Indians and the larger Caribbean community, they are a running reminder that, like all diaspora communities, the emergent identities of migrant communities would usually carry with them varying degrees and manifestations of hyphenation. Indeed, this in itself bears testimony of the intricacy and deep resonance of the physical, emotional, and psychological journey from India to the Caribbean.

References

Brereton B (1982) A history of modern Trinidad 1783–1962. Heinemann International, Kingston
Brereton B (1985) The experience of indentureship: 1845–1917. In: La Guerre J (ed) Calcutta to Caroni: the East Indians of Trinidad. Extra Mural Studies Unit, U.W.I, St. Augustine, pp 23–24
Brereton B (1994) The other crossing: Asian migrants in the Caribbean, a review essay. J Caribb Hist 28(1):99–122
Carter M (1995) Servants, sirdars and settlers:Indians in Mauritius, 1834–1874. Oxford University Press, London
Grant KJ (1923) My missionary memories. The Imperial Publishing Company, Halifax
Haraksingh K (1976) Aspects of the Indian experience in the Caribbean. In: La Guerre J (ed) Calcutta to Caroni: the east Indians of Trinidad. Extra Mural Studies Unit, U.W.I. St. Augustine, pp 155–169
Haraksingh K (1988) Structure, process and Indian culture in Trinidad. In: Immigrants & minorities. Frank Cass and Company Limited, London
Hoefte R (2006) Surinam. In: Lal BV (ed) The encyclopedia of the Indian diaspora. Editions Didier Millet, Singapore
Kanhai R (2008) Matikor: the politics of identity for Indo-Caribbean women. The University of the West Indies School of Continuing Studies, St. Augustine
Kanhai R (2012) Bindi: the multifaceted lives of indo-Caribbean women. University of the West Indies Press, Jamaica
Kassim H (2002) The transformation of Trinidad Islam: the works of Moulvi Ameer Ali and Moulvi Nasir Ahmad, 1935–1942. In: Paper presented at conference on religions of the new world. University of the West Indies, St. Augustine
Kirpalani MJ (1945) Indian centenary review. 100 years of progress 1845–1945. Indian Centenary Review Committee, Port-of-Spain
Klass M (1961) East Indians in Trinidad: a study of cultural persistence. Waveland Press, Illinois
Lal BV (ed) (2006) The encyclopedia of the Indian diaspora. Editions Didier Millet, Singapore
Laurence KO (1994) A question of labour: indentured immigration into Trinidad and British Guiana, 1875–1917. Ian Randle Publishers, Jamaica
Look Lai W (2004) Indentured labour, Caribbean sugar: Chinese and Indian migrants to the British West Indies, 1838–1918. John Hopkins University Press, Baltimore
Mahabir K (2011) The Indian diaspora in Belize, Guadeloupe and Suriname. In: Indian arrival day commemorative Magazine. Indo-Caribbean Cultural Centre, Trinidad
Malik Y (1971) East Indians in Trinidad: a study in minority politics. Oxford University Press, London
Mandelbaum DG (1972) Society in India: volume one. Continuity and change. University of California Press, Los Angeles
Mangru B (1996) A history of East Indian resistance on the Guyana Sugar Estates, 1869–1948. Edwin Mellen Press, New York

Mangru B (1999) Indians in Guyana: a concise history from their arrival to the present. Adams Press, New York

Mansingh A, Mansingh L (1999) Home away from home: 150 years of Indian presence in Jamaica, 1845–1995. Ian Randle Publishers, Jamaica

Mohammed P (2002) Gender negotiations among Indians in Trinidad, 1917–1947. Palgrave, New York

Morton S (1916) John Morton of Trinidad. Westminster Company, Toronto

Niehoff A, Niehoff J (1960) East Indians in the West Indies. Milwaukee Public Museums Publications in Anthropology, Milwaukee

Roopnarine L (2007) Indo-Caribbean indenture: resistance and accommodation, 1838–1920. University of the West Indies Press, Jamaica

Samaroo B (1975) Missionary methods and local responses: the Canadian Presbyterians and the East Indians in the Caribbean. In: Proceedings of conference on East Indians in the Caribbean: colonialism and the struggle for identity. University of the West Indies, St. Augustine

Sankalia HD (1982) The Ramayana in historical perspective. Macmillan India Limited, Delhi

Schwartz BM (ed) (1967) Caste in overseas Indian communities. Chandler Publishing Company, California

Seecharan C (1997) "Tiger in the stars" the anatomy of Indian achievement in British Guiana 1919–29. Macmillan Education Ltd., London

Seecharan C (2006) Guyana. In: Lal BV (ed) The encyclopedia of the Indian diaspora. Editions Didier Millet, Singapore

Seesaran R (2002) From caste to class: the social mobility of the Indo-Trinidadian community 1970–1917. Rosaac Publishing House, Trinidad

Shepherd V (1993) Transients to settlers: the experience of Indians in Jamaica 1845–1950. University of Warwick and Peepal Tree Books, England

Shepherd V (2006) Jamaica. In: Lal BV (ed) The encyclopedia of the Indian diaspora. Editions Didier Millet, Singapore

Singaravelou (1976) Indian religion in Guadeloupe, French West Indies. Caribbean Issues 11(3): 39–51

Singh K (1988) Bloodstained tombs: the Muharram massacre 1884. Macmillan Caribbean, London

Singh S (2012) The Ramayana tradition and socio-religious change in Trinidad, 1920–1990. Ian Randle Publishers, Jamaica

Sookram R (2006) Culture and identity of the Indian Community in Grenada, 1857–1960. Aust Hist Stud 7:42–44

Sookram R (2009) Challenges and achievements: the history of Indians in Grenada. VDM, Germany

Tinker H (1974) A new system of slavery: the export of Indian labour overseas, 1830–1920. Oxford University Press, London

Vertovec S (1992) Hindu Trinidad: religion, ethnicity and socio-economic change. Macmillan Education Ltd., London

Williams E (1964) History of the people of Trinidad and Tobago. Andre Deutsch, London

Wood D (1986) Trinidad in transition: the years after slavery. Oxford University Press, London

New Middle-Class Labor Migrants

88

Sam Scott

Contents

Introduction 1730
Spatial and Social Mobility 1733
Age and Migration 1738
Culture and Migration 1739
Household Migration 1741
Emplacing Middle-Class Migrants 1743
Conclusions 1744
Cross-References 1745
References 1745

Abstract

Migration researchers have tended to focus on social extremes: either highly skilled elites, on the one hand, or low-wage workers on the other. Less attention has been directed toward "ordinary" middle-class professional movers, and there have been no reviews of this literature to date. The chapter addresses this gap and identifies five important themes to guide future class-orientated migration research. First, the complex relationship between migration, social mobility, place, and middle-class membership is examined. Second, age is shown to be an important consideration in middle-class migration decision-making. Third, the cultural versus economic basis of the mobile middle-class is explored, and the role of lifestyle factors in shaping migration is critically examined. Fourth, middle-class migration decisions are connected to gendered household strategies, with the preponderance of dual-career couples now taking migration

S. Scott (✉)
University of Gloucestershire, Cheltenham, UK
e-mail: sscott@glos.ac.uk

© The Author(s), under exclusive license to Springer Nature Singapore Pte Ltd. 2019
S. Ratuva (ed.), *The Palgrave Handbook of Ethnicity*,
https://doi.org/10.1007/978-981-13-2898-5_95

decision-making well beyond the individual career path. Finally, the social and communal emplacement of middle-class migrants is considered as an important but neglected dimension of research. Overall, it is clear that the class-based analysis of migration is an important yet neglected field of study, and this is especially true for middle-class movers.

Keywords
Labor · Middle class · Middling · Migrant · Mobility · Transnational

Introduction

> Who cares about the middle classes? They are not, or at least do not at first glance appear to be, a 'social problem' (and) they do not appear to have spectacular amounts of power or influence. (Butler and Savage 1995: vii)

Traditionally, scholars have been attracted away from the mostly messy middle ground of class analysis toward the wealthy and powerful, on the one hand, and/or the poor and dispossessed on the other (Butler and Savage 1995). Migration, for instance, is commonly viewed at, and represented by, its socioeconomic poles. On the one extreme, the presence of a highly skilled professional elite has been researched (Beaverstock 2002) and the existence of a "transnational capitalist class" theorized (Sklair 2001). On the other extreme, there are low-wage (though not necessarily low-skilled) agricultural, manufacturing, and service workers who constitute a "secondary" labor force (Castles and Kosack 1973; Wills et al. 2010). The two extremes often exist side by side, most spectacularly within those world/global cities that are at the apex of the globalized economy. In fact, many have argued that these locations are where social polarization is most pronounced, with migration a key component part (Sassen 1991). However, it is clear – from students, to workers, to retirees – that middle-class migration is both highly significant and incredibly diverse. In short, migration scholars should care about the middle classes. To this end, the chapter that follows focuses in particular on middle-class labor migrants. The principal aim is to broaden the field of view with respect to migration studies away from the "elite" versus the "low-wage" extremes.

In an important contribution to the field of middle-class migration research, Conradson and Latham (2005a: 229) note:

> What is striking about many of the people involved...is their middling status position in their countries of origin. They are often, but not always, well educated. They may come from wealthy families, but more often than not they appear to be simply middle class. In terms of the societies they come from and those they are travelling to, they are very much of the middle. But the fact is that surprisingly little is known about these kinds of migrants.

In terms of benchmark national and international statistics, the data is patchy and/or dated. Recently, the US Bureau for Labor Statistics (2016) calculated that around one-third (32.2%) of foreign-born workers in the USA are employed within

Table 1 Proportion of foreign-born residents who are tertiary educated, by selected OECD country

Selected OECD country	Number native-born	Number foreign-born	% foreign-born	Number of foreign-born tertiary educated	% foreign-born tertiary educated
Australia	6,158,380	1,997,481	32.4	650,548	32.6
France	20,554,573	2,071,134	10.1	547,474	26.4
Germany	29,541,273	3,954,425	13.4	739,558	18.7
Italy	19,935,648	1,058,084	5.3	154,977	14.6
UK	24,247,796	2,327,938	9.6	965,470	41.5

Source: OECD.Stat/Demography and Population/Migration Statistics/Database on Immigrants in OECD Countries (DIOC)/Immigrants by Occupation. Available at: https://stats.oecd.org/Index.aspx?DataSetCode=DIOC_OCCUPATION
NB. The International Standard Classification of Education (ISCED; cf. UNESCO 1997) was used to classify educational level: primary level (ISCED 0/1/2); secondary level (ISCED 3/4); tertiary level 1 (ISCED 5A/5B); tertiary level 2 (ISCED 6). "Tertiary educated" thus corresponds to the ISCED 5/6 category. The Database on Immigrants in OECD Countries (DIOC) is mainly drawn from the 2000 round of censuses

"management, professional, and related occupations." International OECD figures, though dated, show a similar significance with respect to middle-class foreign workers. In the UK, for example, university graduates make up around four in ten (41.5%) foreign-born migrants, and around six in ten (59.8%) foreign-born migrants are employed within middle-class occupations. Corresponding figures for other selected OECD countries (Australia, France, Germany, Italy) are a little lower, though they still indicate significant middle-class migratory streams whether based on educational (see Table 1) or occupational (see Table 2) markers.

Thus, many international migrants are not part of a prestigious and privileged elite and are not able to move around freely and unconstrained by national bureaucracies. At the same time, they are also not dependent upon precarious low-wage work to survive. They do, put simply, occupy a "middling" status (Conradson and Latham 2005a). Arguably, the most studied group of international middle-class migrants are academics and researchers whose mobility is often understood as part of a broader process of transnational knowledge acquisition and exchange.

Exactly how middling migrants are constituted and who is represented by this category is a difficult question. Relatively few authors have attempted to delimit or define the middle-class as a migrant group (though see Scott 2006). More broadly, there is the thorny question of defining the middle class per se, irrespective of immigration. To this end, van Hear (2014) observes that, in migration studies, class has been underemployed by scholars (for exceptions, see Cederberg 2017; Wu and Liu 2014; Bonjour and Chauvin 2018; Rye 2019). It has been eclipsed by studies focused on gender, ethnicity, race, religion, generation, etc. This lack of coverage is worrying, though not entirely surprising. Class is a difficult, and highly politicized, concept to employ, and the "middle-class" category can be especially difficult to pin down. As Butler (1995: 26) laments: "Traditionally (academics) have found it much easier to examine the working-class or the 'ruling class' than the more messy and fragmented middle-class."

Table 2 Foreign-born residents by middle-class occupation, by selected OECD country

Selected OECD country	Number of foreign-born "legislators, senior officials, and managers"	% of foreign-born who are "legislators, senior officials, and managers"	Number foreign-born "professionals"	% Foreign-born who are "professionals"	Number of foreign-born "technicians and associate professionals"	% of foreign-born who are "technicians and associate professionals"	Number of foreign-born "clerks"	% of foreign-born who are "clerks"	% Foreign-born who are in a "middle-class" occupation
Australia	211,761	10.6%	396,268	19.8	232,663	11.6	238,743	12.0	54.0
France	184,181	8.9%	267,539	12.9	288,107	13.9	171,320	8.3	44.0
Germany	51,360	1.3%	350,672	8.9	523,030	13.2	284,638	7.2	30.6
Italy	95,031	10.0%	88,584	8.4	145,308	13.7	63,859	6.0	37.1
UK	379,885	16.3%	411,539	17.7	303,576	13.0	298,094	12.8	59.8

Source: OECD.Stat/Demography and Population/Migration Statistics/Database on Immigrants in OECD Countries (DIOC)/Immigrants by Occupation. Available at: https://stats.oecd.org/Index.aspx?DataSetCode=DIOC_OCCUPATION

NB. Occupations are recorded in the OECD DIOC database according to the International Standard Classification of Occupations (ISCO-88, cf. ILO 1990). There are 11 categories used in the OECD DIOC database: legislators, senior officials, and managers; professionals; technicians and associate professionals; clerks; service workers and shop and market sale workers; skilled agriculture and fisheries workers; craft and related trades workers; plant and machine operators and assemblers; elementary occupations; armed forces; unknown. The first four of these categories were used as surrogates for "middle-class" occupations. The Database on Immigrants in OECD Countries (DIOC) is mainly drawn from the 2000 round of censuses

Goldthorpe's (1982) concept of the "service class" is important here as it marks an attempt to distinguish between routine nonmanual white-collar workers (little different from manual workers) and the more powerful members of the (professional and managerial) middle class. The latter are distinguished by the trust that employers place in them and the associated roles they perform and responsibilities they hold within the contemporary workplace. The service class is characterized by relative stability and homogeneity. There is also, however, the work of Savage et al. (1992) which suggests that the middle class is changing and becoming increasingly fragmented and that the "service class" concept needs to be replaced by a more nuanced framework in order to capture the subtleties and fluidity of the new middle classes (see also Butler and Savage 1995).

Marxists perspectives would suggest, though, that capitalist societies will eventually tend toward polarization, with most people falling downward from the middle class into the proletariat, though a few will be co-opted upward into the capitalist class. This polarization thesis implies that the "middle class" is not in fact a stand-alone class category, but an extension (over a temporary time period) of a two-class system. Scholars argue over the degree to which contemporary society is polarizing, with some important contributions cautioning against the inevitability of an hourglass society (Hamnett 1994; Samers 2002). Correspondingly, the bifurcation of immigration flows is identified as a phenomenon by some, though many others continue to emphasize the importance of middle-class mobility. This is especially true in countries where a strong welfare state insulates citizens from the extremes of neoliberal capitalism. In the EU context, for example, Verweibe (2008: 1) observes that "recent European migration seems to be, above all, a middle-class phenomenon."

If there is debate within the developed world over the degree of social polarization and the loss of the middle class, there is relative agreement that globally the number of people identified as, or defined as, middle class is rising. Two countries feature prominently in this trend: China and India. Batnitzky et al. (2008: 54), for instance, state that since the mid-1980s, the middle class in India has more than tripled to an estimated 300 million, with some predictions suggesting that by 2040 half the country will be middle class. Similarly, Blau (2016) cites McKinsey research showing how there are now around 225 million middle-class households in China, up from just 5 million in 2000. Thus, the world is accommodating ever more middle-class citizens, and so one might expect this to feed through into studies of class and international migration.

Spatial and Social Mobility

One of the principal motives behind middle-class labor migration is to cement or increase one's socioeconomic status and/or income. There is an expectation among migrants that moving across international borders will lead to secure middle-class group membership, at very least, and possibly even to class advancement (either for migrants themselves or for subsequent generations). The relationship between spatial and social mobility, however, is complex, and there are instances where middle-class migrants experience, what they hope will only be a temporary, decline in their status and/or income. This is usually the result of not being able to transfer assets or "capital" (capital exists in three main forms according to Bourdieu (1984): economic (i.e., money and property); cultural (institutionalized via educational qualifications and often convertible into economic capital); and social (i.e., social connections, ties, and obligations)) across international borders. As Cederberg (2017: 149) observes: "It is well established that international migration involves not only geographical but also social mobility, as migrants achieve an improved socioeconomic position through increased economic opportunities, or experience downwards mobility as a result of not being able to transfer their economic, social or educational resources to the receiving country context."

In an extensive US study, Clark (2003: xiv) notes that "the allure of continuing upward social mobility often leads to migration" and goes on to find that there has been significant progress in this respect both in terms of a growing middle-class immigrant population and in terms of a "home-grown" second-generation immigrant middle class. Overall, Clark estimates there to be four million foreign-born and ethnic native-born middle-class household in the USA, making up 12.3% of all middle-class households (Clark 2003: 221). Thus, even if labor migrants do not move internationally as members of the middle class, their aim is often for themselves, or their children, to become middle class with international migration central to this aspiration.

There are certain occupations where international mobility has become highly prized and an expected part of any fast-track career. This is true, for example, among those in the highly paid financial service sector where certain world/global city destinations such as New York and London are essential locales to gain experience of and in (Beaverstock 2002). It is also true in academia where it is now the case that: "progression in science careers places a high premium on mobility" (Ackers and Gill 2008: 62). Essentially, then, certain professions now have career paths that extend beyond nation-state borders, and upward mobility can be facilitated by a willingness to acquire experience outside of one's home country.

For some, class status may no longer be defined exclusively within nation-state borders but may be transnational in constitution. Indeed, mobility itself is a key element of establishing and augmenting one's class position and brings with it various routes toward capital accumulation (see, e.g., Ong 1999). Cederberg (2017: 163), for instance, emphasizes "the importance of developing a transnational framework for understanding class processes." It may be, for example, that leading peripatetic lives with families often spread between nation-states is part of a class strategy. Or, it may be that moving according to an international career path, similarly, leads to capital accumulation. Either way, it is clear that class can no longer be understood purely within a nation-state framework and that transnational capital acquisition is a key element to understanding the contemporary relationship between spatial and social mobility (see also Rye 2019).

Ong (1999: 19), in a study of the transnational Chinese, observes figures such as "the multiple passport holder; the multicultural manager with 'flexible capital'; the 'astronaut' shuttling across borders on business; 'parachute kids' who can be dropped off in another country by parents on the trans-Pacific business commute; and so on." These examples of transnational flexibility have become something to strive for in certain social circles because of their role in underpinning social mobility. Perhaps most famously, there is the value now placed on Western education, in Asia in particular, as a grounding for subsequent professional employment and middle-class membership. This produces individuals "both technically adaptable to a variety of forms, functions, skills and situations and culturally adaptable to a variety of countries in Asia and the West" (Ong 1999: 170). Building on the work of Ong, Waters (2006) has shown how Western education enables the Hong Kong middle classes to accumulate valuable forms of "cultural capital." Overseas credentials then get converted into economic capital, particularly when graduates return to work in Hong Kong. In other words, transnational home and school environments create a distinct middle-class "habitus" that then enables a migrant to enter middle-class professional employment on leaving university. There is, then, a clear link between certain forms of childhood and early adult international education and subsequent middle-class labor migration, though this appears particularly prominent for Asian (especially Chinese) transnational families.

The notion that class is transnationally produced/reproduced, via capital acquisition away from one's home country, not only applies to those on the watershed between education and professional employment, it also applies to those forging international careers. Jöns (2011), for instance, talks about how international academics amass different forms of capital by virtue of their foreign sojourns, including prestige (symbolic capital); education and knowledge (embodied cultural capital); books and research infrastructure (objectified cultural capital); academic credentials and qualifications (institutionalized cultural capital); a network of relationships (social capital); and economic capital that is directly convertible into money. Similarly, in a recent study in Wroclaw, Jaskułowski (2017: 262) argues that experiences in the city among Indian middle-class migrants are used "for increasing social status and gaining new experiences that may be understood not only in terms of individualization processes but also in the context of building cultural capital." Or put another way, Indian migrants see their stay in Wroclaw in instrumental terms and as part of a longer-term goal of securing and perhaps even increasing their socioeconomic status. Wroclaw is not necessarily the final destination and is seen by many as an entry point on a longer journey of transnational middle-class production/reproduction.

In the literature on middle-class spatial and social mobility, it is clear that certain cities and regions occupy a particularly important place in terms of providing migrants with opportunities for advancement. The key concept in this respect is the "escalator" city/region. The origins of this can be traced back to the work of Watson (1964) and his concept of "social spiralism." Essentially, social spiralism is about achieving professional success, and the fact that this success may be blocked in certain places but available elsewhere. In other words, to get on professionally would-be and aspirant members of the middle class may have to move away from their place of origin. The "escalator" concept explicitly seeks to identify where "social spiralism" is occurring, and it is clear that world/global city destinations are key.

Most "escalator" research to date has been carried out on London and the surrounding southeast region (starting with Fielding 1992; Savage et al. 1992: Chap. 8). The area has been shown to facilitate a higher rate of upward social mobility than any other in the UK, especially among the young. Indicative of this, it has seen net in-migration of young adults, their promotion, and then net out-migration of older adults who are choosing to step off the escalator once their middle-class status is secured.

Clearly, the phenomenon of social spiralism and the escalator concept that emerged from this have the potential to apply globally: to a host of cities/regions and to international as well as internal middle-class labor migration. Looking beyond London and the southeast, for example, Fielding (2012: 107) has argued that a range of world/global cities: "act as 'engines' of promotion into middle and upper-class jobs." Similarly, Findlay et al. (2009: 876) stress that the escalator effect relates to international migrants too: "The increasingly global reach of major city regions such as London may well have enhanced the opportunities for upward mobility both for internal and international migrants with highly transferable and sought-after skills."

The link between spatial and social mobility is not always straightforward. It is not simply a case that getting the right education or moving to the right city/region will establish middle-class membership and possibly initiate upward mobility. The "transnational" and "cultural capital" explanations of middle-class family production/reproduction and the "social spiralist" and "escalator" effects are evident for some migrants but not for all. Moreover, and as noted above, migration may sometimes result in downward social mobility, with middle-class labor migrants prepared to work in low-wage jobs over the short to medium term in the hope of an eventual increase in socioeconomic status either for themselves or their children. This is particularly true, it seems, for those middle-class labor migrants moving from peripheral to core areas of the world economy.

Chiswick (1978) observed a temporary earnings dip for immigrants on entering the US labor market but also noted that over the long-term earnings drew level with and then eventually surpassed the native-born. This study is important because it demonstrates that migration may well lead to *both* downward and upward mobility depending upon the time period one examines. Ryan (2015), for example, has recently examined Polish workers in the UK, and her findings show that they may experience an initial de-skilling but that this is then followed by upward mobility. Such observations are important because a number of recent studies have observed what one might call "brain waste," i.e., university educated, middle-class migrants working in low-wage jobs, below the skill level to which they are qualified.

The "brain-waste" phenomenon appears to be most prominent where middle-class migrants cross a development gap and move from peripheral to core economies. Parreñas (2000), for example, has identified Filipino workers with tertiary qualifications employed in domestic care work and as nursing assistants, getting much lower rates of pay than their qualifications would imply. She uses the term "contradictory class mobility" to highlight the position of these largely skilled female migrants who raise their income via domestic work in Western countries but also experience downward social mobility by virtue of doing low-status work. Similarly, Kelly and Lusis (2006) have examined Filipino migrants in Canada and also note an overall pattern of de-skilling.

India has a growing middle-class, and Rutten and Verstappen (2014: 1217) note the plight of middling migrants from Gujarat to London who "dreamed of going to the West to earn money and improve their prospects at home but ended up in low-status, semi-skilled jobs to cover their expenses, living in small guesthouses crammed with newly arrived migrants." Others have observed a similar trend among the mobile Indian middle classes (Batnizky et al. 2008; Qureshi et al. 2013). Overall, then, it seems that there are considerable uncertainties with respect to the spatial mobility/social mobility relationship and that this translates into considerable ambivalence with regard to middle-class migrants' decisions to move abroad. Moreover, this is true mainly for those moving across a development divide. Thus, while international labor migration is now seen as an essential element in what is an increasingly transnational process of middle-class production/reproduction (see, e.g., Mapril 2014), there is great uncertainty as to whether the decision to migrate will pay off.

The task for scholars then, in light of the "brain-waste" phenomenon, is to identify reasons for middle-class migrants working at a level below that to which they are accustomed. Language skills are undoubtedly a key factor to explaining how well labor migrants do within the host country (Chiswick and Miller 2002). Nevertheless, lack of language skills does not mean inevitable brain waste. Chiswick and Taengnoi (2007), for instance, found that professional immigrants in the USA without English language skills were still able to enter certain occupations (such as computing and engineering), though others were less accessible. There also appear to be social and geographical nuances with respect to which middle-class migrants progress as expected and which are blocked from entering professional occupations. Haley and Taengnoi (2011), for example, found that professional migrants from the English-speaking developed world did better in the USA in terms of earnings. Underpinning this, they found that educational and professional experiences and qualifications from these countries were more transferable. Also in the USA, Mattoo et al. (2008) found that educated migrants from Latin American and Eastern European were more likely to end up in unskilled jobs than migrants from Asia and certain industrial countries. A key aspect of this, they observed, was the recognition of qualifications. Elsewhere, evidence from Canada points toward middle-class refugees struggling to gain suitable professional-level employment due to structural labor market barriers (Krahn et al. 2000).

Some middle-class migrants, however, appear willing to accept brain waste as a temporary step toward eventual upward social mobility. Based on research in Scotland, Piętka et al. (2013) observe how eastern European migrants often work below the level to which they are qualified but gain in terms of human capital: particularly language skills and self-confidence. Also in the UK, Batnitzky et al. (2008), in a study of Indian migrants in London, identify how certain forms of relatively low-status Western employment may be seen as "glamorous" (p51) back home. In addition, they argue that downward occupational mobility following migration is negotiated by migrants through conspicuous consumption patterns

(TVs, iPhones, etc.) and what might appear to be brain waste actually underpins middle-class status back in India. Migration, then, can be a transnational strategy tied to different class outcomes in the sending (positive) and receiving (negative) societies. Or, put another way, relatively routine low-wage service employment in core economies can underpin the production and reproduction of a middle-class identity in less economically developed home countries.

Waldinger and Lichter (2003: 9) usefully advance the idea of a "dual frame of reference" in relation to the acceptance, and even embrace, by migrants of apparently dead-end work. They argue that: "The stigmatized status of bottom-level work impinges differently on immigrants, who operate with a dual frame of reference, judging conditions 'here' by the standards 'back home'." Thus, if staying at home equates to class immobility, or even downward mobility, then it may well be worth moving abroad, even if there is brain waste. Middle-class migrants accept low-wage work because of the value of this work back home (e.g., via remittances) and/or because they see it as part of an international career path, a stepping-stone, that will eventually lead onto professional employment. In terms of the latter, Parutis (2014) identifies definite class advantage for eastern European migrants subject to brain waste in the UK. Provided they possess appropriate linguistic skills, migrants appear to progress from "any job" to a "better job" in search of an eventual "dream job." Thus, it is the stepping-stone role of certain jobs and migrants' short-stay horizons while in these jobs that can render brain-waste acceptable.

Finally, there are instances where middle-class migrants work for a long period of time below the skill level to which they are qualified but find this acceptable because of the hopes and class aspirations they have for their children. Lopez Rodriguez's (2010) research on Polish mothers, for example, suggests that children's opportunities are important motivations for migration. In a similar vein, Cederberg (2017) argues that: "The prospect of upwards mobility for migrants' children can help mitigate the experience of downwards mobility for the migrants themselves, confirming the importance of taking a family-wide and inter-generational perspective on social mobility" (p159).

Age and Migration

There is a very strong correlation between age and migration, as evidenced in the "model migration schedule" (Barcus and Halfacree 2017: 152). This shows how people in their late teens and twenties are highly mobile, more so than other age groups. These are ages when people often move to university and then for career forging and family forming reasons. Most obviously, and as we saw above, "escalator" cities/regions attract large numbers of young workers seeking to cement and augment their socioeconomic status. In many respects, then, migration both for education and work functions as a rite of passage into adulthood and can also function as a rite of passage into the middle classes.

For those who are part of the transnational elite, migration at a young age may go all the way back to prestigious international schooling. For many more members of the middle class, it is international experience while at university that helps to underpin subsequent mobility (see, e.g., Findlay et al. 2017). Those with international experience when in education may well be more likely to make a foreign move when working. Indeed, the normalization of the international through school and university, and the transnational employment trajectories that often develop from this, may actually underpin important forms of capital acquisition that are key to middle- and upper-class membership.

For young people outside of the transnational elite, and not on a highly skilled career path, international migration in early adulthood is well documented though it often relates to experience-seeking and self-development as much as economic opportunity. The lack of family ties and career commitment when young opens up possibilities for international experience. Work is important, but, crucially, it is used to pay for opportunities to experience other countries and cultures. Middle-class migration, then, needs to be understood as a phenomenon that involves individuals, especially when young, who might be termed "lifestyle" as much as labor migrants. Indeed, the period after education ends gives many young people, especially members of the middle classes, the chance to experience life abroad as a rite of passage into adulthood.

Clarke's (2005) study of working holiday makers in Australia and Conradson and Latham's (2005b) study of New Zealanders in London both capture this hybridized form of labor-lifestyle migration that has become reasonably common among the young middle class of the developed world (see also: Ryan and Mulholland 2014; Scott 2006; Wilson et al. 2009). For these individuals, labor market experiences may well be important, but immediate financial and career considerations are not always the main concern: with international cultural experience key. This experience may transfer into forms of capital that convey class distinction and advantage, but this is not usually a major strategic aim from the outset.

Conradson and Latham (2005b: 292) talk this type of mobility as a process of "societal individualization" which "places an enormous emphasis on the cultivation and nurture of the individual self" (see also Conradson and Latham 2005c). Some, however, have questioned how free migrants actually are in their aim of self-realization. Kennedy (2010: 480), for instance, argues that instrumental needs (i.e., a lack of opportunities at home versus employment available within the host country) are often dominant even among young skilled migrants who may appear at first glance to have a desire for adventure and cultural curiosity. Crucially, Kennedy does not dismiss cultural/lifestyle explanations for middle-class migration among the young, and he simply cautions against an overemphasis on this. The debate, then, is not about whether middle-class people work abroad when young, it is about how important employment and economic considerations are relative to cultural and lifestyle priorities.

Culture and Migration

The above leads us onto a broader discussion among scholars around what people look for in a place when they move there. Put simply, there is a debate about the primacy of economic opportunity (i.e., a job, a career path, a wider professional *milieu*, etc.) in locational decision-making versus the role of social and cultural factors in determining where members of the middle classes end up living. Some scholars argue that a city/region must have a particular economic prowess in order to draw in graduates and professionals from the outside. Others, however, maintain that the middle classes make locational decisions based often on who already lives in an area and/or on that area's cultural capital.

An economic versus sociocultural dichotomy is unhelpful, however, in explaining middle-class migration. In reality, both facets help us to understand why people choose particular places to live above others. The key point is that economic explanations may well have more or less power for some, while sociocultural explanations may well have more of less power for others. Hannerz (1996: 129–132), for example, in his analysis of the 'transnational city', identifies a group of "expressive specialists" alongside a "transnational managerial" category. His analysis underlines both the diversity of middle-class arrivals to the contemporary global city and also the fact that within this diversity, economic, social, cultural, and other factors are weighted differently by different groups and lifestyle types. The value of Hannerz's insight is that it teaches us, even for cities at the apex of the global economy, to look beyond the classic corporate career path mover to consider the full diversity of middle-class migration (see, e.g., Scott 2006).

Perhaps the most famous framework advocating for sociocultural factors to be considered in, and indeed central to, middle-class migration is that advanced by Richard Florida focusing on the mobility patterns of the "creative class" (Florida 2002, 2005; Mellander et al. 2013). The creative class are "people who are paid principally to do creative work for a living...the scientists, engineers, artists, musicians, designers and knowledge-based professionals" (Florida 2002, xiii). According to Florida, cities compete against each other, and one part of gaining competitive advantage rests in the people you are able to attract. Specifically, cities must try to attract the "creative class," and this is not just about having the requisite economic base. Instead, the creative class, especially immediately after graduating, are footloose and prefer certain types of places and spaces. Thus, if cities want to increase their competitiveness, they need to attract both firms and workers, and attraction is about more than just economics. To hackney a famous slogan: it's not just the economy, stupid.

Florida's arguments require one to believe that (1) there is a creative class; (2) the creative class is mobile; (3) the creative class are a key driver in economic development; (4) the creative class prefer certain types of place and thus concentrates within these; (5) the preferences of the creative class can be explained by "soft" factors (culture, leisure, environment, openness); and (6) overall cities/regions that are most successful will be endowed with the three Ts: technology, talent, and tolerance. Each of these assertions is open to contestation and indeed has been questioned in a sizeable sceptical literature.

While there is no space here to rehearse all the criticisms directed toward Florida's thesis, it is worth identifying key relevant critiques. Most notably, scholars point out that:

the idea that there are large numbers of 'footloose' creative individuals who are highly mobile and can chose freely between locations and who will be influenced by some vague notion of city attractiveness, rather than economic opportunity, seems barely credible. There might be some individuals for whom this condition is true but not so many that cities could use this as the basis of their economic development strategies. (Borén and Young 2013: 208)

Across a range of studies, there is considerable skepticism that place-based sociocultural factors can draw in the middle classes. As Storper and Scott (2009) argue, it is difficult to imagine how improving a city/region's attractiveness will draw in large numbers of people in the desired occupations in the absence of economic opportunities. Similarly, Murphy and Redmond (2009) found that members of the creative class were attracted to a city (Dublin) mainly on the basis of employment availability, family, and birthplace and that "soft" factors did not play an important role in decision-making. They concluded: "the validity of the creative class thesis for stimulating regional economic growth must be viewed with a high degree of caution" (p. 82). However, and to rebut these criticisms somewhat, one can surely accept that *both* economic and sociocultural factors might come into play in the locational decision-making of the middle classes and that they might come into play differently for different individuals.

Another criticism of Florida's work is that: "the migration dynamics of the creative class are little understood" (Borén and Young 2013: 196). This criticism is valid, in particular, with respect to international migration. There are very few examples of Florida's thesis being applied to the study of middle-class movers across international borders. A notable exception is Boyle's (2006) research on the Scottish creative class in Dublin. Boyle found that the city's sociocultural appeal was mainly for younger people before family formation but, even then, that the vast majority of Scottish expatriates moved to Dublin because of the city's career opportunities. Put another way, Florida's thesis did explain international migration of the Scottish middle classes to Dublin to a degree, but its role was at best a partial one.

Where does the above leave us, then, in understanding the migration patterns and preferences of the global middle classes? To be sure, Florida's "creative class" thesis is a convincing one. It has, though, been subject to a great deal of criticism. At worst, Florida leads us away from considering only a narrow group of international career path migrants to think about a more diverse mobile middle class. At best (and more controversially), Florida's thesis actually explains the geography of significant swathes of middle-class migration and helps us to understand why certain cities may attract significant numbers of international middle-class migrants.

Household Migration

Middle-class migration has, by some, been understood as a process involving largely male career path migrants making decisions to move that are often quite separate from the broader household unit. Kofman (2000, 2004) is critical of this narrow perspective and makes the case for a family-oriented and gendered migration framework looking beyond the individual economic motives of the male career path migrant. Similarly, Hardill (2002) is clear that middle-class membership is increasingly contingent upon dual careers and thus involves household level decision-making. Developing this point, Raghuram (2004), based on research with migrant doctors, argues that the nature of family migration and decision-making changes when migrants are skilled. In short, dual-career households are likely, and so choices over when and where to move can become very complex.

Overall, then, and especially within the past two decades, scholars have come to recognize that studies of middle-class mobility require gendered perspectives that acknowledge the role of women as workers, wives, and mothers in the migratory process. It is no longer sufficient to examine a single (usually male) career path and to use this as a basis for understanding migration. As Ackers and Gill (2008: 127) argue skilled migration is "simultaneously influenced by both family and employment considerations with the balance shifting over time."

This said, it is still commonplace to see the female career sacrificed when middle-class families move both internally and internationally (Boyle et al. 2001; Cooke 2007; Hardill 1998; Purkayastha 2005; Yeo and Khoo 1998). So, while our understanding of middle-class migration needs to be rooted within more complex and multilayered decision-making processes, there is still a need to examine and explain important gendered outcomes: most obviously, the continued phenomenon of the female "trailing spouse" and the associated career (and other) sacrifices that are made. Though the situation is changing, with up to one-third of tied professional movers now male (Clerge et al. 2017).

The above can have significant implications for how well women do in particular middle-class careers. To elucidate, certain professions expect internal, and in some cases international, mobility as part of career progression. Academia is a prime example. Several studies indicate, for instance, the necessity of geographic mobility for academic success; and this may account for why women appear more likely to drop out en route to top academic positions (Ackers and Gill 2008; Jöns 2011; Schaer et al. 2017). There is, then, an important gendered dimension infusing the relationship between social and spatial mobility, for some professions at least.

Alongside calls for gendered and familial perspectives on middle-class migration decision-making, scholars have also pointed out that some professional families engage in transnational patterns of behavior. Ong (1999), in a study of Chinese professional migrants, observed the phenomena of both "astronaut" parents shuttling across borders on business, and "parachute" children studying in foreign countries while their parents work (often transnationally). Often transnational family formation is both specific to certain nationalities and gendered. Commonly, for example, it has been observed among southeast Asian (especially Chinese and Taiwanese) professional whereby the man of the household works at distance from the rest of the family as the latter engage on a quest for an international (Western) education (Waters 2006). In such scenarios, the mother's professional life is often put on hold, and "the achievement of a mother lies in her children's education" (Chiang 2008: 516) which in turn is expected to convey class advantage. It is, therefore, education rather than employment that underpins the gendered transnational strategies of some middle-class professional families. Education explains why parents (usually the father) may work at a distance from the rest of their family and why the family may be spread transnationally across two or more nation-states.

Emplacing Middle-Class Migrants

In this final section, attention turns toward the ways in which middle-class migrants ground their life-worlds both within actual places and in terms of a more abstract sense of identity. The development of social networks, on the one hand, and a sense of place and belonging, on the other, is usually rooted both within and across nation-states. In the case of the latter, it is worth noting the "transnational turn" that took place within migration studies from the mid-1990s and the implications of this for the study of middle-class migrant communities (see, e.g., Beaverstock 2011; Colic-Peisker 2010; Conradson and Latham 2005b; Scott 2004). Notwithstanding this transnational turn, van Riemsdijk (2014) argues that the everyday experiences of ordinary skilled migrants have been neglected by researchers even though these experiences are extremely important in understanding processes of middle-class migrant integration.

One area where noteworthy insights have been made is in relation to the gendered nature of middle-class migration. There are, put simply, implications of the "trailing spouse" often being the female partner/wife. It seems that in-group communality is underpinned in many contexts by migrant women's ability to network (Ryan and Mulholland 2014; Willis and Yeoh 2002; Yeo and Khoo 1998). This is, in a sense, indicative of an adaptive strategy whereby middle-class migrant women often lose their productive/professional function and replace it by turning to the social and communal realm in order to ground their everyday life and identity. The presence of children and the use of specialist international schooling seem to further augment the importance of the social and communal realm in the life-worlds of the trailing spouse. This occurs through parents' "school-gate" networking and because the presence of specialist schooling can lead to middle-class residential clustering (White 1998).

This said, there are also ample studies demonstrating the in-group networking prowess of those migrants who are professionally employed (Beaverstock 2011; Cohen 1977; Colic-Peisker 2010; Conradson and Latham 2005b; Scott 2007). Further, in some contexts, this middle-class (often professional) networking involves certain types of "performance." Most notably, there are studies pointing to the importance of the club/society (Cohen 1977; Scott 2007) and studies pointing to role of alcohol, drinking, bars, nightclubs, and house parties in middle-class (Western) socio-communal behavior (Clarke 2005; Walsh 2007; Yeoh and Willis 2005).

Beyond actual in situ social networks, middle-class migrants have been shown to maintain transnational contacts and harbor transnational/multicultural identities (Colic-Peisker 2010; Ong 1999; Scott 2004). There is no simple process of integration happening, therefore, among middle-class migrants. Instead, foreign professionals often maintain in-group social and communal ties to different degrees depending upon the type of migrant they are (Scott 2006). Likewise, they attach to different places depending upon their own particular circumstances, their biography, and their future aspirations and expectations. Middle-class labor migrants, like all migrants, are engaged in a complex process of adaptation within the host country that places them both here and there in terms of their everyday life-worlds they inhabit.

Conclusions

This chapter has argued that it is important to consider migrants who are "in-between" the elite and the low-waged. These "middling" migrants are highly diverse and do not appear to constitute a stable or homogenous group. To this end, they have been referred to as "new middle-class labor migrants" to acknowledge their dynamism and complexity. Given the diversity, the chapter has sought to identify common themes emerging from a literature that has not been drawn together until now. Five core themes have emerged. The most significant concerns the link between spatial and social mobility and, specifically, the ways in which the middle class move in order to advance, or at least cement, their class position. The concept of the "escalator" city/region first advanced by Fielding is particularly important here. For some, however, the link between spatial and social mobility is one that stretches across generations: with migrants sometimes investing in their children and prepared, themselves, to accept "brain waste" and delayed gratification. Second, it is clear that some members of the middle class see international experience as a "rite of passage" into adulthood, and as part of this, cultural and lifestyle considerations are important in deciding to live and work abroad. The balance between culture and economics in explaining patterns of middle-class labor migration is developed further in the third theme of the chapter. Here, Florida's "creative class" thesis is significant in helping us to understand why certain places appeal more than others to graduates and professionals. Fourth, middle-class labor migration was connected to a household and gendered perspective to take us beyond a narrow notion of individual career path mobility. Finally, relatively little attention has been directed toward the everyday emplacement of middle-class migrants and their related socio-communal networks and cultural identities. The work that is available suggests that in-group communality is significant among middle-class migrants and that migrants' identities are complex and often transnational.

The above shows why one should not only care about the middle classes but care in particular about middle-class migration. The middle classes are growing globally, and middle-class labor mobility is a highly significant piece of the overall international migration jigsaw. Studying professionals on the move draws one into consider, inter alia, how class categories are defined; the relationship between spatial and social mobility; the role of age and life stage in mobility; the balance between culture and economics in migration decision-making the importance of the household and gender in the migration process; and the complexities of migrant integration and belonging. These are all issues that relate specifically to migration studies while, crucially, also drawing migration scholars into other areas of the social sciences. One may well be interested in middle-class labor migration per se, but this interest is one that inevitably connects to wider social issues, themes, and questions.

Cross-References

▶ Ethnicity and Class Nexus: A Philosophical Approach

References

Ackers L, Gill B (2008) Moving people and knowledge: scientific mobility in an enlarging European Union. Edward Elgar, Cheltenham
Barcus HR, Halfacree K (2017) An Introduction to population geographies: lives across space. Routledge, London
Batnitzky A, McDowell L, Dyer S (2008) A middle-class global mobility? The working lives of Indian men in a west London hotel. Glob Netw 8(1):51–70
Beaverstock JV (2002) Transnational elites in global cities: British expatriates in Singapore's financial district. Geoforum 33(4):52538
Beaverstock JV (2011) Servicing British expatriate 'talent' in Singapore: exploring ordinary transnationalism and the role of the 'expatriate' club. J Ethn Migr Stud 37:709–728
Blau R (2016) The new class war: special report. The Economist. July 9th 2016
Borén T, Young C (2013) The migration dynamics of the 'creative class': evidence from a study of artists in Stockholm, Sweden. Ann Assoc Am Geogr 103(1):195–210
Bonjour S, Chauvin S (2018) Social class, migration policy and migrant strategies: an introduction. Int Migr 56(4):5–18
Bourdieu P (1984) Distinction: a social critique of the judgement of taste. Harvard University Press, Cambridge, MA
Boyle M (2006) Culture in the rise of tiger economies: Scottish expatriates in Dublin and the 'creative class' thesis. Int J Urban Reg Res 30:403–426
Boyle P, Cooke TJ, Halfacree K, Smith D (2001) A cross-national comparison of the impact of family migration on women's employment status. Demography 38(2):201–213
Butler T (1995) The debate over the middle classes. In: Butler T, Savage M (eds) Social change and the middle classes. UCL Press, London, pp 26–36
Butler T, Savage M (eds) (1995) Social change and the middle classes. UCL Press, London
Castles S, Kosack G (1973) Immigrant workers and class structure in Western Europe. Oxford University Press, London
Cederberg M (2017) Social class and international migration: female migrants' narratives of social mobility and social status. Migr Stud 5(2):149–167
Chiang NLH (2008) 'Astronaut families': transnational lives of middle-class Taiwanese married women in Canada. Soc Cult Geogr 9(5):505–518
Chiswick BR (1978) The effect of Americanization on the earnings of foreign-born men. J Polit Econ 86(5):897–921
Chiswick BR, Miller PW (2002) Immigrant earnings: Language skills, linguistic concentrations and the business cycle. J Popul Econ 15(1):31–57
Chiswick BR, Taengnoi S (2007) Occupational choice of high skilled immigrants in the United States. Int Migr 45(5):3–34
Clark WA (2003) Immigrants and the American dream: remaking the middle class. Guilford Press, New York

Clarke N (2005) Detailing transnational lives of the middle: British working holiday makers in Australia. J Ethn Migr Stud 31(2):307–322

Clerge O, Sanchez-Soto G, Song J, Luke N (2017) 'I Would Really Like to Go Where You Go': rethinking migration decision-making among educated tied movers. Popul Space Place 23(2): e1990

Cohen E (1977) Expatriate communities. Curr Sociol 24:5–90

Colic-Peisker V (2010) Free floating in the cosmopolis? Exploring the identity–belonging of transnational knowledge workers. Glob Netw 10:467–488

Conradson D, Latham A (2005a) Transnational urbanism: attending to everyday practices and mobilities. J Ethn Migr Stud 31(2):227–233

Conradson D, Latham A (2005b) Friendship, networks and transnationality in a world city: antipodean transmigrants in London. J Ethn Migr Stud 31(2):287–305

Conradson D, Latham A (2005c) Escalator London? A case study of New Zealand tertiary educated migrants in a global city. J Contemp Eur Stud 13(2):159–172

Cooke FL (2007) Husband's career first: renegotiating career and family commitment among migrant Chinese academic couples. Work Employ Soc 21(1):4765

Fielding AJ (1992) Migration and social mobility: South East England as an escalator region. Reg Stud 26:1–15

Fielding AJ (2012) Migration in Britain: paradoxes of the present, prospects for the future. Edward Elgar Publishing, Cheltenham

Findlay A, Mason C, Houston D, McCollum D, Harrison R (2009) Escalators, elevators and travelators: the occupational mobility of migrants to south-east England. J Ethn Migr Stud 35:861–879

Findlay A, Prazeres L, McCollum D, Packwood H (2017) 'It was always the plan': international study as learning to migrate. Area 49(2):192–199

Florida R (2002) The rise of the creative class. Basic Books, New York

Florida R (2005) The flight of the creative class. Harper Business, New York

Goldthorpe J (1982) On the service class, its formation and future. In: Giddens A, MacKenzie G (eds) Classes and the division of labour. Cambridge University Press, Cambridge, UK

Haley MR, Taengnoi S (2011) The skill transferability of high-skilled US immigrants. Appl Econ Lett 18(7):633–636

Hamnett C (1994) Social polarisation in global cities: theory and evidence. Urban Stud 31(3):401–424

Hardill I (2002) Gender, migration and the dual career household. Routledge: London

Hannerz U (1996) Transnational connections: culture, people, places. Routledge, London

Hardill I (1998) Gender perspectives on British expatriate work. Geoforum 29(3):257–268

Jaskułowski K (2017) Indian middling migrants in Wrocław: a study of migration experiences and strategies. Asian Pac Migr J 26(2):262–273

Jöns H (2011) Transnational academic mobility and gender. Glob Soc Educ 9(2):183–209

Kelly P, Lusis T (2006) Migration and the transnational habitus: evidence from Canada and the Philippines. Environ Plan A 38:831–847

Kennedy P (2010) Mobility, flexible lifestyles and cosmopolitanism: EU postgraduates in Manchester. J Ethn Migr Stud 36(3):465–482

Kofman E (2000) The invisibility of skilled female migrants and gender relations in studies of skilled migration in Europe. Int J Popul Geogr 6:45–59

Kofman E (2004) Family-related migration: a critical review of European Studies. J Ethn Migr Stud 30(2):243–262

Krahn H, Derwing T, Mulder M, Wilkinson L (2000) Educated and underemployed: refugee integration into the Canadian labour market. J Int Migr Integr 1(1):59–84

Lopez Rodriguez M (2010) Migration and a quest for 'normalcy'. Polish migrant mothers and the capitalization of meritocratic opportunities in the UK. Soc Identities 16(3):339–358

Mapril J (2014) The dreams of middle class: consumption, life-course and migration between Bangladesh and Portugal. Mod Asian Stud 48(3):693–719

Mattoo A, Neagu IC, Özden Ç (2008) Brain waste? Educated immigrants in the US labor market. J Dev Econ 87(2):255–269

Mellander C, Florida R, Asheim B, Gertler M (2013) The creative class goes global. Routledge, New York

Murphy E, Redmond D (2009) The role of 'hard' and 'soft' factors for accommodating creative knowledge: insights from Dublin's 'creative class'. Ir Geogr 42(1):69–84

Ong A (1999) Flexible citizenship: the cultural logics of transnationality. Duke University Press, Durham

Parreñas R (2000) Migrant Filipina domestic workers and the international division of reproductive labour. Gend Soc 14(4):560–580

Parutis V (2014) Economic migrants or middling transnationals? East European migrants' experiences of work in the UK. Int Migr 52(1):36–55

Piętka E, Clark C, Canton N (2013) 'I Know That I Have a University Diploma and I'm Working As a Driver': explaining the EU post-enlargement movement of highly skilled polish migrant workers to glasgow, Scotland. In: Glorius B, Grabowska-Lusinska I, Kuvik A (eds) Mobility in transition: migrations patterns after EU enlargement. IMISCOE/Amsterdam University Press, Amsterdam, pp 133–154

Purkayastha B (2005) Skilled migration and cumulative disadvantage: the case of highly qualified Asian Indian immigrant women in the US. Geoforum 36:181–196

Qureshi KV, Varghese J, Osella F (2013) Indian Punjabi skilled migrants in Britain: of brain drain and under-employment. J Manag Dev 13(2):182–192

Raghuram P (2004) The difference that skills make: gender, family migration strategies and regulated labour markets. J Ethn Migr Stud 30(2):303–321

Rutten M, Verstappen S (2014) Middling migration: contradictory mobility experiences of Indian youth in London. J Ethn Migr Stud 40(8):1217–1235

Rye JF (2019) Transnational spaces of class: International migrants' multilocal, inconsistent and instable class positions. Curr Sociol 67(1):27–46

Ryan L (2015) Another year and another year: polish migrants in London extending the stay over time. Social Policy Research Centre, Middlesex University, London

Ryan L, Mulholland J (2014) 'Wives Are the Route to Social Life': an analysis of family life and networking amongst highly skilled migrants in London. Sociology 48(2):251–267

Samers M (2002) Immigration and the global city hypothesis: towards an alternative research agenda. Int J Urban Reg Res 26(2):389–402

Sassen S (1991) The global city. Princeton University Press, Princeton

Savage M, Barlow J, Dickens P, Fielding T (1992) Property, bureaucracy, culture. Routledge, London

Schaer M, Dahinden J, Toader A (2017) Transnational mobility among early-career academics: gendered aspects of negotiations and arrangements within heterosexual couples. J Ethn Migr Stud 43(8):1292–1307

Scott S (2004) Transnational exchanges amongst skilled British migrants in Paris. Popul Space Place 10(5):391–410

Scott S (2006) The social morphology of skilled migration: the case of the British middle class in Paris. J Ethn Migr Stud 32(7):1105–1129

Scott S (2007) The community morphology of skilled migration: the changing role of voluntary and community organisations (VCOs) in the grounding of British migrant identities in Paris (France). Geoforum 38(4):655–676

Sklair L (2001) The transnational capitalist class. Blackwell, Oxford

Storper M, Scott AJ (2009) Rethinking human capital, creativity and urban growth. J Econ Geogr 9:147–167

US Bureau for Labor Statistics (2016) Available at: https://www.bls.gov/news.release/forbrn.nr0.htm. Accessed 2 Feb 2018

van Hear N (2014) Reconsidering migration and class. Int Migr Rev 48:s1

van Riemsdijk M (2014) International migration and local emplacement: everyday place-making practices of skilled migrants in Oslo, Norway. Environ Plan A 46(4):963–979

Verwiebe R (2008) Migration to Germany: is a middle class emerging among intra-European migrants? Migr Lett 5(1):1–19

Waldinger R, Lichter MI (2003) How the other half works: immigration and the social organization of labor. University of California Press, Berkeley

Walsh K (2007) 'It got very debauched, very Dubai!' Heterosexual intimacy amongst single British expatriates. Soc Cult Geogr 8(4):507–533

Waters JL (2006) Geographies of cultural capital: education, international migration and family strategies between Hong Kong and Canada. Trans Inst Br Geogr 31(2):179–192

Watson W (1964) Social mobility and social class in industrial communities. In: Gluckman M (ed) Closed systems and open minds: the limits of naivety in social anthropology. Oliver and Boud, Edinburgh

White P (1998) The settlement patterns of developed world migrants in London. Urban Stud 35(10):1725–1744

Willis K, Yeoh B (2002) Gendering transnational communities: a comparison of Singaporean and British migrants in China. Geoforum 33(4):553–565

Wills J, Datta K, Evans Y, Herbert J, May J, McIlwaine C (2010) Global cities at work: new migrant divisions of labour. Pluto Press, London

Wilson J, Fisher D, Moore K (2009) Reverse diaspora and the evolution of a cultural tradition: the case of the New Zealand 'Overseas Experience'. Mobilities 4(1):159–175

Wu B, Liu H (2014) Bringing class back in: class consciousness and solidarity among Chinese migrant workers in Italy and the UK. Ethn Racial Stud 37(8):1391–1408

Yeoh BS, Khoo LM (1998) Home, work and community: skilled international migration and expatriate women in Singapore. Int Migr 36(2):159–186

Yeoh BS, Willis K (2005) Singaporean and British transmigrants in China and the cultural politics of 'contact zones'. J Ethn and Migr Stud 31(2):269–285

Slavery, Health, and Epidemics in Mauritius 1721–1860

89

Sadasivam Jaganada Reddi and Sheetal Sheena Sookrajowa

Contents

Introduction	1750
The Slave Labor Force in the Eighteenth Century	1751
British Period 1810–1870	1754
Ex-apprentices and the Epidemics of 1854, 1856, and 1867–1868	1760
Conclusion	1763
References	1764

Abstract

The decline of the slave population during French and British occupation from 1721 to 1870, the high mortality rate, and the impact of epidemics have been less thoroughly examined than other aspects of slavery. The standard work on slave demography remains Kuczynski's Demographic Survey of the British Empire published in 1949. A few detailed studies on some aspects of the slave population in recent years have helped to clarify certain issues, but most works on slavery remain general (Barker 1996; Teelock 1998; Valentine 2000). This chapter relies on existing studies to provide a survey of the slave population in Mauritius before and after abolition of slavery in 1835 and to look at the major factors that impacted on the slave demography, with a focus on health and epidemics.

Keywords

Slavery · Health · Epidemics · Population

S. J. Reddi
Réduit, Mauritius
e-mail: sada.reddi@yahoo.co.uk

S. S. Sookrajowa (✉)
Department of History and Political Science, Faculty of Social Sciences and Humanities, University of Mauritius, Réduit, Mauritius
e-mail: s.sookrajowa@uom.ac.mu; sheenasookrajowa@gmail.com

© The Author(s), under exclusive license to Springer Nature Singapore Pte Ltd. 2019
S. Ratuva (ed.), *The Palgrave Handbook of Ethnicity*,
https://doi.org/10.1007/978-981-13-2898-5_96

Introduction

Mauritius is a small island, 61 km long and 41 km wide, and is located in the Indian Ocean, 800 km, east of Madagascar. It had no indigenous population when the Dutch occupied the island in 1638. The Dutch occupied the island on two occasions, and when they finally left in 1710, the French colonized the island between 1721 and 1810. The British administered the island from1810 until independence in 1968. Both the Dutch and the French relied on a slave labor force during the period of colonization, and when the British occupied the island in 1810, there were about 67,000 slaves, 8,000 white and 7,000 colored. This made Mauritius one of the major slave colonies in the British Empire. The British abolished slavery in 1835, and slaves were set free in 1839 after a period of apprenticeship.

Several reasons can explain the lack of interest in the study of the slave population during the French and British occupation. Detailed investigation would have required a vast amount of research especially as the sources are dispersed in various archives. Available surveys and censuses during the early decades of the nineteenth century are marred by numerous inaccuracies, which have proved daunting for researchers. For example, the enumeration in the late eighteenth century and early nineteenth century were based on tax returns, and slave owners sought to minimize the number of slaves they owned to avoid paying taxes. In the British period, figures were compiled on different occasions. During the illegal slave trade, returns by slave owners were falsified to conceal the number of slaves obtained illegally. Even later, when the colonial government carried out surveys, there was resistance on the part of slave owners, and returns were defective and unreliable. After the termination of apprenticeship in 1839,the apprentices (ex-slaves) were labelled as ex-apprentices in the censuses but from 1861 the the ex-apprentices were merged with the white and the coloured in the category 'general population' so that it becomes difficult to identify the former slave population from the other social groups. Historians agreed that slave population figures are at best approximate except for the census of 1826 and that census too has its limitations but can nevertheless yield some insights about slave demography in this period (Barker 1996).

This paper is divided into three sections which cover three different and distinctive periods of the history of Mauritius, (i) the French period; (ii) the British period from 1810 which impacted on the slave population, first by illegal slave trading and second the development of a plantation economy based on sugar; and (iii) the post-emancipation period but also marked by the massive introduction of Indian indentured labor. Though they are distinctive periods in the country's history, there were a lot of continuities in the conditions and lives of slaves. It is against this broad background that the evolution of the slave population will be surveyed together with impact of the major epidemics on the slave and ex-apprentice population.

When surveying the slave demography in this period, health was just one of the factors which impacted on the population. Morbidity and mortality from epidemics were also linked to the general economic and social conditions of the population and their lack of resources. Inadequate sanitary measures and the failure of colonial administration to cope with ill-health and outbreak of epidemics played their part.

Epidemics had a major impact during the French and the British period – smallpox, cholera, and later malaria were responsible for excessive deaths among the population, particularly the slave population.

The Slave Labor Force in the Eighteenth Century

A starting point for studying the slave demography is the eighteenth century when Mauritius, formerly known as Isle de France, developed into a slave society during French colonization. Earlier, the Island had been occupied by the Dutch during two distinctive periods 1678–1694 and 1695–1710. During these years, the Dutch relied on the slave labor force to occupy the island, but the number of slaves never exceeded more than a hundred. The French occupied the island from 1721 to 1810, and slave labor was used by the French to develop the island.

In 1726 there were only 20 slaves in the island, and the figure rose to 638 in 1735. Under the governorship of Mahe de Labourdonnais, there was a rapid increase of slave population that reached 2,612 in 1740, and when Labourdonnais left the island in 1746, there was a slave labor force of 2,533. Between 1746 and 1767, slave population increased sixfold to reach 15,027. In the same period, the white population increased from 551 to 3,163 (North – Coombes 1978).

In 1777, the slave population reached 25,154 and 33,382 in 1787, and by 1807, its population had reached 63,367 slaves, 6,489 white and 5,912 free blacks or mixed black and white ancestry, and by 1810 it reached 68,177 (North – Coombes 1978; Noel 1991). The increase of free blacks was the result of both natural increase and those who had secured their emancipation (Nwulia 1981). These figures drawn by D'Unienville help to explain the trend in the slave population although he too conceded that the slave owners tended to conceal their wealth and evaded taxes and allocation of slaves for corvee (North – Coombes 1978; Table 1).

Slavery in Isle de France had its own characteristics. It was ethnically very diverse, and slaves were drawn mainly from Mozambique, Madagascar, and India. The increase of the population was due to importation and not to natural increase. Since the sources of slave labor were easily accessible given the relative proximity of either Madagascar or the east coast of Africa, slave owners had little interest in the natural reproduction of the labor force and preferred male slaves.

Table 1 Slave population in the eighteenth century

Year	White	Free blacks	Slaves	Ratio of freemen to slaves
1767	3,163	587	15,027	1:4
1777	3,434	1,173	25,154	1:5.5
1787	4,372	2,235	33,823	1:5.1
1797	6,237	3,703	49,080	1:4.9
1807	6,489	5,912	65,367	1:5.3

Source: North Coombes Problems in the Sugar Industry of Ile De France or Mauritius 1790–1842, p. 88

The island inhabitants relied on regular importation to replenish the slave labor force. Bernardin de St Pierre (2002) estimated that between 1768 and 1770, the 20,000 slaves had an annual decrease of 1/18 annually, a figure that North-Coombes (1978) considered probably to be inflated for that would have meant an annual rate of decrease of 55%. On the other hand, D'Unienville advances a figure of natural increase per annum based on a birth rate of 33.3% and a death rate of 30%. However, according to North-Coombes, in the manuscript version of D'Unienville, there was a natural decrease of 3%. In addition, a manumission rate 2.0% was assumed in the manuscript version, while in the published version, it was 0.8% (North – Coombes 1978). Analyzing these figures, North-Coombes concluded that there is a case for giving a greater role to slave importation, and the natural decrease was greater than the 3.3% assumed by D'Unienville (North – Coombes 1978).

Importation figures also vary with the sources. D'Unienville gives a figure of 61,400 for importation for the period 1769–1810 and 56,700 between 1773 and 1810. Toussaint's figure is 62,387 and Filliot's 105,000. From 1804 to 1806, the natural decrease of the slave population was 3.3% per annum compared to a rate of natural increase of 12% for the white population (North – Coombes 1978).

The shortage of women as well as other factors in the slave population inhibited population growth. The slave population in 1807 shows a ratio of 45 men for 19 women (Noël 1991). Government slaves showed the same imbalance in their sex ratio (Teelock 1998). Slave owners were not interested in developing family units among the slave labor force. Though there were some family units, families were easily broken by sale. Women showed low fertility because of the difficult working conditions, and these also deterred women slaves from having families. Marooning made it difficult for women to rear children for their maternal care made it difficult to leave their children behind when they marooned. Moreover, during the period they were marooning, children's cries would have made detection by maroon hunters easier. Since most women had been marooning at least one time or more, this would have been a major hindrance to their freedom. It was reported that women slaves also resorted to abortion to avoid their children living a miserable life under slavery (Arago cited in North – Coombes 1978). Freycinet (1996) also attributed it to promiscuity of the slave women. Dietary deficiencies militated against pregnancies and raised the high risks of mortality and miscarriage. Freycinet who visited the island in 1818 found while white women might have two children and women slaves might have three children and even five, they lived only a few weeks (Freycinet 1996).

Contemporary accounts of travelers though valuable are not easy to assess especially when the settlers hosted many of them. They are divided on the treatment of slaves. Milbert (1812) found slave conditions were reasonable, and the ship surgeon Avine saw that a few masters treated their slaves well, while de Bernardin de St Pierre (2002) was very critical of slavery, and the miserable life of the slaves was highlighted in his writings. Generally, the high incidence of mortality in the slave population was related to socioeconomic conditions that were very poor and harsh, and these made natural reproduction difficult. Economic and social conditions of the slaves varied from masters to masters, and slaves were employed in numerous occupations, domestics, field laborers, housemaids, artisans, and port workers. In the absence of labor-saving implements – carts and draught animals, slaves doing manual labor were excessively used with little concern for their health (North – Coombes 1978).

Slaves were generally poorly fed. The general population generally suffered from inadequate food according to the missionary Jean Pierre Teste. One can expect that the situation of the slaves would have been worst and it further aggravated during epidemics, cyclones, and wars. The ordinary white style of feeding was likened to a perpetual fast and worsened during hurricanes, epidemics, and lack of imported food during the war (North – Coombes 1978). One cannot deny that a few masters might have provided their slaves with adequate food but that would not be the case for the majority of slave owners. The ration of a slave was 2 lbs of maize or 5 lbs of manioc or 11/2 lbs of rice, supplemented by greens which they cultivated or fish (Noël 1991). Article 17 of the Code Noir of 1723 related to food and clothing was very vague (Wanquet 1979). An amendment of the law 1767, specifying the amount of food, suggests that previous food provision for slaves was not generally respected. Henceforth, those who were invalids or old abandoned by their masters were to be treated at the nearest hospital and be charged 4 to 6 sols a day. Later, in the 1820s, Charles Telfair refuted the criticism of the anti-slavery reporter on the quality of food on his estate at Bel-Ombre, but Barker concluded that the slaves enjoyed more than a tiny fraction.

In the eighteenth century, apart from sex disproportion of the slave population and low fertility, the excessive mortality among slaves is explained by the poor health, dietary deficiencies, and inadequate health facilities, dearth, hurricanes, and epidemics (North – Coombes 1978). Contemporary writers and travelers reported a wide variety of common diseases which afflicted the inhabitants such as chest pains, apoplexy, gout, scurvy, flux de sang, diarrhea, and intermittent and continuous fever. Urinary diseases, tetanus, small pox, and leprosy were also common ailments in the island among the white population (Freycinet 1996).

One can reasonably assume that slaves were most vulnerable to this disease environment as a result of grim economic and social conditions. Apart from diseases, nutrition must have been an important factor in the slave's health. It was reported that the constant use of manioc as a staple food created flux of blood or dysentery. Dependence of rice led to beriberi. In fact, epidemics of measles, dysentery, and beriberi were common among slaves. Bouron (cited in North Coombes 1978) added that abdominal diseases such as dysentery and associates were encountered frequently among slaves. He also reveals that scantily - clad slaves were prone to chest disease and that their weak constitution made treatment such as pneumonia difficult. Only in the large estates could some medical treatment be provided, and masters had to cope with the minor ailments. Later the law was updated in 1792, and the masters were charged 8 sols for every day a slave spent at the hospital in good health and 30 sols in case of medical treatment (Wanquet 1979).

In the eighteenth century, the population was afflicted by epidemics which resulted in sharp rises in mortality, particularly among the slave population. There were outbreaks in 1742, 1756, and 1758. There were cholera epidemics in 1775 and 1782. In 1756, half of the slave population was reckoned to have perished. In 1756, an outbreak killed half of the slaves belonging to the settlers and 1,800 slaves belonging to the company (Kuczynski 1949). In 1792, D'Unienville gives a figure of 4,000 persons who died in a population of 58,000 persons, excluding the garrison (Kuczynski 1949). One third of the black population and half of the white population died from the smallpox epidemic of 1792. Smallpox killed 8% of the population of Port Louis. It was reported that 556 of the 2,780 government slaves perished during the epidemic though they had better conditions of living compared to other slaves (Toussaint 1973). From 1793 to 1820, there was no serious outbreak of smallpox, and part of the explanation was the introduction of vaccine from India by Deglau in 1802 (North – Coombes 1978). In the eighteenth century, poor diet, constant whippings, diseases, the ravages of epidemics, a skewed sex ratio, and high mortality rate made life for the overwhelming majority of the slaves infinitely grueling, a situation which became even worse in the nineteenth century with development of the plantation economy.

British Period 1810–1870

When the British occupied Mauritius in 1810, slaves who had some hopes of emancipations were disappointed as the British administration issued proclamations to maintain slavery and the miserable socioeconomic conditions of the slave population during the French regime were perpetuated. In fact, the situation worsened. The abolition of the slave trade was not implemented in Mauritius until 1817, and illegal slave trade continued up to the 1830s. The transformation of the economy into a plantation economy based on sugar after 1825 intensified the misery of the slave population. The decrease in the slave population continued, and slave owners had recourse to importation to maintain and increase the level of their labor force. The decline of the slave labor force continued throughout the following decades up to the 1860s and possibly after. The termination of apprenticeship in 1839 registered a decline in their numbers. In 1856, it had fallen to 40,730, and in 1867 it was further reduced to 35,000. All the available figures, contemporary observations, censuses, as well as the judgment of historians point incontrovertibly to the decline of the slave and the ex-apprentice population during the period under study. This drastic reduction of population needs to be explained and placed in its historical context.

At the outset, it must be highlighted that the population figures for the slave population and the ex-apprentices for most of the period have been taken from various contemporary sources and were arrived through different computations so that there is very often wide variation in the numbers. The reasons are many: sometimes figures cover the island of Mauritius and its dependencies, and sometimes slaves for whom taxes are paid are listed excluding children under 6 years old, apart from underreporting to avoid paying taxes or simply inaccurate reporting or recording. According to the tax rolls in 1810, there were 60,000 slaves; a note from General Decaen to Governor Farquhar mentions 80,000, while returns from the collector of internal revenue give different figures from those tax rolls. Generally, figures for slaves population differed from those in the tax rolls (Nwulia 1981). The population figures were marred by inaccuracies, and it is difficult to be definitive about them for the period 1811–1834 (Kuczynski cited in Barker 1996). At best, the figures can only be approximate. Despite the rough estimates of the slave labor force and inaccuracies, they throw some light on the population dynamics – the direction in which the population numbers moved and its relationship to economic and social factors.

At time of British conquest, the continuation of the slave trade prevented the stabilization of the slave labor force and its natural reproduction because of the skewed sex ratio in favor of male slaves among the imports. Like in the French period, the labor force was only be replenished by importation so that an increase in the slave population was the result of importation. Historians have concluded that it is difficult to establish with any precision the number of slaves imported illegally and population figures vary from one source to another (Wanquet 1979).

In 1807, the population of Mauritius was constituted of approximately 65,637 slaves, 6,489 white and 5,912 colored (Barker 1996). Statistics of the slave population remains on a weak footing because slave owners would tend to conceal the identity of slaves introduced illegally (Valentine 2000). They might inflate the number to provide for the future acquisition of slaves from illegal importation or even transferred slaves from one estate to another at the time of enumeration (Reddi 1989). Farquhar estimated that the number of slaves imported from 1811 to 1821 was 30,000; other estimates suggest between 2,000 annually from 1793 to 1810 and 3,500 illegally introduced between 1811 and 1820 (Nwulia; Valentine 2000). The Commission of Inquiry on slave trade estimated in 1828 that of the 65,000 slaves in the island, 50,000 had been introduced illegally since 1814 which is considered high by several historians (Wanquet 1979; Teelock 1998). Carter and Gerbeau (1987 cited in Teelock 1998) advance a figure of 60,000, while Allen (2000) suggests an import figure of 52,550 to Mauritius and Seychelles between 1811and 1827. The debate on illegal importation rests on the numbers imported with estimates varying from the conservative figure of 30,000 to much higher figures.

Closer analysis of the slave demography by Barker, Coombes, and Valentine gives credence to higher figures for illegal importation. Barker's analysis of the adult population in 1826 gives a figure of 66.8% for foreign-born slaves compared with 33.2% for creole slaves (Barker 1996). North-Coombes figure in 1826–1827 for male adult population aged 17–60 is 35.1% foreign-born and 11.3% local-born slaves (North-Coombes 1978). Valentine's population pyramid in a data set of 26,672 slaves for 1835 slave population finds that slaves of foreign origins constituted 40.2% foreign born and 59.8% creoles. Moreover, she finds that there was an increase in the male population between ages 25 and 59 and a similar but smaller increase in the same age group for female slaves. Valentine's life table of the slaves in 1835 confirms that while the sex ratio in the data set is 123 for the slave population, the sex ratio of creole slaves was 91 compared with 198 for imported slaves. All these suggest a very high mortality and low life expectancy with a sharp decline in population numbers after the age of 40 (Valentine 2000). Though Barker finds an increase in the slave population by 14,126 between 1807 and 1817, there was a decline of 17% in the slave population due to cholera in 1819. However, Pitot advances a slave mortality of 20,000 during the epidemic which implies a 33% reduction in the slave population (Reddi 1989).

During the period of amelioration, later censuses and returns on the slave labor force failed to improve the accuracy of the population figures. Slave owners opposed registration of the slave population, and returns were falsified in various ways. As a result, in 1826 the slave population was variously estimated as 69,076, 62,634, and 69,201 (Barker 1996). Barker prefers to rely on the figure of 68,201 as it is based on the 1826 slave registers to Kuczynski's (1949) figure of 69,264 which may have included slaves from other islands, dependencies of Mauritius. Based on the figure of 69,076 of 1826 which is generally considered the most reliable, the slave population declined to 64,331 in 1834 and 61,045 in 1835, though these figures too are derived from the 1826 census (Blue Book 1826 B6; Blue Book 1834; Blue Book 1835).

In explaining the decline of the slave workforce, D'Unienville finds that the death rate of the slave population exceeded birth rate and a yearly decrease of 5% would have led to the extinction of the slave population in 20 years, a conclusion which is contested by North-Coombes (1978). North-Coombes (1978) points out that the decline of importation following the abolition of the slave trade changed the demographic profile of the slave population. The slaves who died in old age were no longer offset by fresh importation and that the absolute decrease which had started in 1826 was at an end in 1846. Since the slaves introduced illegally were overwhelmingly male, an improvement in the male-female ratio of the slave population over time would have ensured natural reproduction. But with an increasing proportion of creole slaves born in the colony rising from 26.6 of the total to 50.2 in the period 1826–1827, while in 1827 male slaves still outnumbered female by 1.6 to 1 compared to 2.1 in 1809, the balance between the sexes would have taken much longer time in Mauritius as a result of the slave trade. On the other hand, low fertility or infant mortality in the slave population retarded population growth. Women appeared to have few children and fewer survived to adulthood. Even a possible rise in the number of children in 1835 did not mean a rise in total fertility rate and that the slave population had become self-reproducing (Valentine 2000). Further the cholera epidemic of 1824–1825 might also have increased mortality among children. Overall, the slave pyramid of the slave population in 1835 reflected a high mortality rate and short life expectancy as well as the harshness of the slave regime (Valentine 2000).

The increased harshness of the slave regime resulted largely from the expansion of the sugar industry after 1825. Changes in the plantation economy had profound effects on the slave population (Teelock 1998). The expansion of cane cultivation resulted in general shortage of labour on sugar estsates. Planters hired personal and urban slaves or transferred labor from small and declining estates for sugar cultivation and production. The expansion of sugarcane cultivation increased the labor and the hardships of slaves; personal slaves faced several unstable situations as they were hired to work on different estates in different work situations resulting in increased alienation. Moreover, decline in food production resulting from the shift to sugarcane affected the diet of the labor force and its health. Slaves relied more and more on rice compared with the variety of food which they had in the past. Consumption of rice resulted in beriberi epidemics. In these difficult circumstances, there was a high incidence of morbidity and mortality.

Poor working conditions and harsh punishment in addition to change in diet also contributed to deteriorating health conditions. In the early years of the British occupation, Dr. Burke's report on the health of the slaves shows that health conditions were very bad (Teelock 1998). Housing conditions were dismal, and women slaves were deprived of any health facilities during pregnancy or for childcare. Later the Commission of Inquiry in the 1820s reported the same conditions prevailed on the sugar estates where severe labor and insufficient food resulted in the excess of deaths over births (Teelock 1998). Planters extracted the maximum labor from slave, men, women, and children since they regarded child-rearing and pregnancy as a loss of labor to the estates. Such an attitude meant that the planters gave scant regard to the health conditions of the slaves; they were made to work even when they feel sick or suffered from a particular disability. Complaints lodged at the protector's office reveal that with only a few exceptions, most sugar estates did not have proper hospital or medical personnel to treat the sick.

Amelioration policy inaugurated in 1825 was intended to improve the general conditions of the slave labor force. During that period measures to provide for the sick were resented by the proprietors. The old and the aged and those with incurable sickness were sent to government hospitals and even encouraged them to maroon so that they would be of little expense to the planters in terms of food and shelter. Amelioration measures were resisted by the planters, and their impact on the well-being of slaves was marginal. Barker (1996) concluded that masters were making physical labor difficult and the extreme measures contribute to the morbidity and mortality of the slave population.

The period of apprenticeship certainly brought some changes in the life of the apprentices who were able to purchase their freedom, but for the majority, apprenticeship equaled slavery. Conditions of living and work did not improve during apprenticeship, and the planters sought to extract the maximum labor from their apprentices especially that apprenticeship was viewed by the British government as a way to compensate the slave owners for the loss of slave labor as a result of abolition, while the other half was paid by the British government as compensation. In Mauritius, slave owners obtained 2 million pounds out of the 20 million pounds paid to all slave owners in the Caribbean and Mauritius. Even after abolition, the planters intended to secure the labor of the ex-apprentices through an ordinance in 1835, a piece of legislation that was very oppressive and was already in force for 1 year before it was disallowed. The ordinance of 1835 made provision for those apprentices unable to work or find work punishable by 3 years of imprisonment. Children 8 years old were to be employed. The thirst for freedom made the apprentices work much harder to secure their release from apprenticeship, and the fact that the planters raised the prices of apprentices meant they had to work much more and do overtime to secure their purchase. Apart from the law, a number of measures were passed to prevent apprentices from purchasing their freedom or even developing means of autonomous existence (Reddi 1989).

After 1835, the colonial state and the slave owners implemented a number of measures to the detriment of the apprentices. The imperial government did not consider that the ex-apprentices needed protection or had cause to complain from competition from Indian laborers on the ground that they had withdrawn their labor from the sugar estates (Deerpalsingh and Carter 2015). All these measures were unfavorable to the apprentices, and these meant apprenticeship could prove worse than slavery itself (Kloosterboer). The indifference of the colonial authorities continued after the termination of apprenticeship.

During the apprenticeship period 1835–1839, there was an absolute decline in the slave population. In 1835, two figures on the apprentice population are provided, 61,045 and 62,022 (Kuczynski 1949; Nwulia 1981). The second figure is higher because it may include 1,009 who were under 6 and not subject legally to apprenticeship. The number of effective apprentices was 51,929, excluding 9,084 of the aged and the infirm (Nwulia 1981). We still do not know if the above figures include those who went maroons. The number who went marooning in the years 1835, 1836, and 1837 averaged 7.7% (Allen 1999). The ex-slave population declined further between 1835 and 1851, with a slight increase in 1846 when the ex-apprentices numbered 49,365 compared to figure of 48,060 in 1835 (Census 1851).

There were also other factors to explain the decrease between 1835 and 1846. Ex-apprentices were confronted with varying conditions. Those who had obtained their freedom during apprenticeship no longer registered themselves as apprentices. For example, in the district of Grand Port, about 9,000 slaves had already secured their freedom before apprenticeship came to an end, and they would have merged in the category general population. Fluctuation in the population of ex-apprentices in the different districts was related to internal migration. Their numbers increased in the districts of Flacq, Grand Port, Black River, and Moka but decreased in the district of Riviere du Rempart (Census of Mauritius 1851). Many of the ex-apprentices relocated themselves in some districts and established themselves as small cultivators and took employment outside the sugar estates.

After the termination of apprenticeship in 1839 and 1840, conditions of the ex-apprentices seemed to have improved generally, as they had been released from the rigor of plantation life with the introduction of Indian indentured labor. Ex-apprentices lived in relative freedom; wages were high for skilled workers on the sugar estates. Others could live and gain their living outside the sugar estates where there was a general shortage of labor. Even those who worked on the estates welcomed the presence of Indian laborers as they helped to lessen the workload of the ex-apprentices. In a period of general labor shortage, the ex-apprentice slaves could also enjoy a stronger bargaining power. All these positive changes had beneficial effects on the health of the slaves and must have contributed to a lower mortality and morbidity among many in the ex-slave population. This was reflected possibly in the relatively small decrease in the mortality rate. Mortality between 1835 and 1846 averaged 3.2% annually and between 1846 and 1851 to 0.4% annually. Death rate continued to exceed birth rate although its average death rate between 1835 and 1846 had fallen to 1.3 between 1846 and 1851. This slight improvement in the conditions of the ex-apprentices could also be explained by the fact that the ex-apprentices had moved away to "the wooded and the less cultivated districts where they could purchase land at cheaper rates or occupy land without purchase. Many apprentices established small independent farms where they did not come under the pressure of the sugar economy. Many ex-apprentices settled outside the sugar estates and even in Port Louis so that they could find alternative jobs to laboring on the sugar estates" (Report from the Acting General Sanitary Inspector of the epidemic Fever of 1866–1867). One additional factor that can explain the direction toward demographic stability was that there was no major epidemic during that period.

The general improvement of the ex-apprentice population is borne out by several reports from contemporary observers. Governor Gomm remarked that mortality among the ex-apprentices was not excessive. Mortality averaged 3% throughout the 10 years following emancipation. However, the old and the infirm would not have necessarily improved the economic situation or even their health. A slight improvement in the sex ratio also raised the prospect of a balanced population. It is impossible to know whether these comments applied to those ex-apprentices who had purchased their freedom or those still under the apprenticeship system though we have shown earlier that those working during the apprenticeship system faced difficult conditions. Those who had purchased their freedom would have improved their conditions outside the apprenticeship system but not necessarily inside the system.

By 1840, most of the apprentices left the sugar estates. They could be divided into three classes – those who purchased small plots of land, on which they erected their dwellings and lived with their families, and a second group hired plots of ground at low rents and grew vegetables, manioc, sweet potatoes, or Indian corn. A small number worked on sugar estates as sugar makers and carters during the crop season and received high wages; others did some hawking and petty trafficking. A third group were masons and various tradesmen who hired their services regularly on the sugar estates or are in the employment of master tradesmen, and some are domestic servants (Stipendiary Magistrate to Colonial Secretary 19 December 1845 MA SD 28). At the time of the termination of apprenticeship, some 3,000 ex-apprentices worked on the sugar estates, but by 1845 the number had increased to 6,000 out of 52,000 workers in agriculture (Report of Rawson Committee 19 February 1845). The division of labor during slavery and apprenticeship was maintained during the indentured period. In 1846 ex-apprentices had varied occupations. There were 8,409 in commerce and trade, 4,826 in agriculture and laborers outside agriculture, 148 in government civil service, 796 in naval establishments, 4705 domestic servants, and 2,388 independent workers (Census of Mauritius 1851). These different categories of employment included clerks, watchmen, stone and tombstone cutter, porter and messengers, seamstresses, carpenter and joiner, mason and bricklayers, fishermen, and boatmen (Census of Mauritius 1851; North – Coombes 1978).

The post-emancipation period, despite several positive changes for many ex-apprentices, brought its own lot of setbacks. The colonial state discharged itself of its responsibility for ex-apprentices who refused to integrate the plantation labor and disqualified them from protection of the colonial government. Access to medical and other facilities was limited. In the 1820s vaccination has been compulsory, and with the relative disappearance of epidemics, the population paid little attention to vaccination apart from the fact that there was reluctance among ex-apprentices to be vaccinated. The relocation of many ex-apprentices population in remote areas meant they had to fare for themselves in case of epidemics. The presence of Indian

Table 2 Ex-apprentice population 1846–1851

Year	Male	Female	Total
1846	28,142	21,223	49,365
1847	28,101	21,397	49,498
1848	28,234	21,727	49,961
1849	28,031	21,836	44,867
1850	27,757	22,012	49,769
1851	26,653	21,677	48,330

Source: Kuczynski (1949), Part 4, "Mauritius and Seychelles," p. 777

Table 3 Population of Mauritius in 1846 and 1851

Type	Year 1846	Year 1851
General population	52,852	54,497
Ex-apprentices	49,365	48,330
Indians	56,245	77,996
Total	180,823	158,462

Source: Census 1851, Appendix No 4

laborers and old immigrants intensified competition in the labor market, and most of the ex-apprentices in all walks of life were reduced to a precarious existence. In spite of prosperity of the island in the 1850s, it is uncertain whether these conditions had any significant impact on their lives. The census of 1851 reported a decline in the ex-apprentice population of 2% or 0.4% per annum from 1846 to 1851. This decrease contrasts with a 3% increase in the general population though some women may have merged in the general population by marriage (Tables 2 and 3).

Ex-apprentices and the Epidemics of 1854, 1856, and 1867–1868

The three major epidemics of cholera in 1854 and 1856 and malaria in 1865–1868 occurred against a background of poor economic and social conditions which affected the lives of the population in several ways (Kuczynski 1949). A major role played by these epidemics was to aggravate mortalities and delay the demographic recovery of the ex-slave population. In the ordinary period of mortality, deaths among ex-apprentices were significantly higher compared with other social groups (Table 4).

For the year 1851, mortality figures show that ex-apprentices had a death rate of 52% compared with 26% for the general population (Kuczynski 1949). It is reasonable to assume that the death rate for the ex-apprentices remained consistently higher throughout the 1850s with excess mortality during the epidemic years. Although reports on epidemics did not specifically report on mortality of ex-apprentices, scattered references in reports and newspapers make occasional references to the fate of ex-apprentices thus confirming the mortality trend in the lower classes (Table 5).

Table 4 Mortality among the population

Years	Ex-apprentices	General population
1853	2,142	1,616
1854	4,200	1,700
1855	509	303
1856	2000	1,000

Source: Commercial Gazette 30 December 1854

Table 5 Mean rate mortality of the population

Year	Mean
1850	31.46
1851	26.50
1852	28.07
1853	29.66
1854	84.61
1855	33.01
1856	50.56

Source: Mauritius Almanac 1901

In 1851 ex-apprentices had 2,535 deaths compared with 1,401 among the rest of the general population (Kuczynski 1949). In 1853 there were 2,142 deaths among apprentices compared with 1,616 among the rest of the general population. Within the general population, the ex-apprentices constituted an important segment, and mortality was determined by the class structure. Compared with either the white or the colored elite, the ex-apprentice, the casual worker, and the manual worker living in crowded urban conditions suffered most compared with the better-off. In 1854, during the cholera epidemic, the total number of deaths for the whole island for the period of 25 May to 14 September was 8,496. In Port Louis, from 25 May 1854 to 1 August 1854, the number of deaths was 3,492. A detailed breakdown of the figure shows that between 25 May and 31 August 1854, of 7,650 deaths reported, there were about 3,832 deaths among ex-apprentices and 1,538 among the general population and 2,280 among Indians (Kuczynski 1949) (Table 6).

During the 1854 epidemic, cholera deaths in Port Louis were higher than in other districts. Port Louis had a population of 49,631 or 49,909, and cholera caused approximately 3,492 deaths in Port Louis. The victims of cholera among the ex-apprentices were 1854 and for Indians 543 and the general population 995. The figures for the district of Pamplemousses were 1385 and 718 the district of Flacq (Hoolass 1998). The mortality figures indicate that within the general population, it was the ex-apprentices who suffered the most and the rest of the general population was the least affected. In all districts, except Riviere du Rempart, ex-apprentices had the highest number of deaths. During the cholera epidemic of 1856, there were 3,532 deaths, 2,000 deaths among the ex-apprentices and much less than 1,000 among the rest of the general population. Altogether, there were 6,200 deaths among the ex-apprentices for cholera, and if deaths from smallpox are added, in the period of 1854–1856, there were

Table 6 Deaths from cholera (25 May 1854–31 August 1854)

General population	Ex-apprentices	Indians	Total
1,538	3,832	2,280	7,650

Source: Report on Cholera 1854, 1856

7,000 deaths. According to Governor Higginson, the number of apprentices declined from 48,366 in 1852 to 40,730 in 1856, and out of a decrease of 16% and 14.5%, 7,000 deaths were attributable to epidemic diseases (Kuczynski 1949).

Though from 1861 census does not distinguish between ex-apprentices and the category general population, occasional references and analysis of the ex-apprentice population occurred in Kuczynski's work drawn from contemporary sources. According to Kuczynski, between 1859 and 1866, there were 17,518 deaths among the ex-apprentices compared with 15,586 among the rest of the population. By 1866 he reckoned that in a population of 130,000 of the general population, there were about 35,000 who were apprentices to the utmost. In 1867 there were 9801 deaths among the ex-apprentices compared with 7223 among the rest of the general population though registration was apparently incomplete (Kuczynski 1949). An indication of the high mortality in Port Louis is evident in the rise of a death rate for fever and typhus per 1000 from 207.3 in 1866 to 840.8 in 1867. The deaths from fever amounted to 31,920 against 8544 from other causes giving a total mortality of 40,464 in a population of 360,378 on the 1 January 1867 (Report from the Acting General Sanitary Inspector of the epidemic Fever of 1866–1867) (Table 7).

Even before the outbreak of the malaria epidemic in 1867, the greater part of the ex-apprentice population faced dire economic and social conditions. The Acting General Sanitary Inspector in his report on the malaria epidemic of 1867 described the life of the ex-apprentices as one reduced to pauperism, "In the best of times since the emancipation, numbers of these people must have suffered great distress when the chief of the family was ill or out of work What then must have been their condition when provisions rose to a famine price." In the 1860s, the ex-apprentices were satisfied "with a bowl of rice, and 'bredes', a piece of salt fish or boiled salt beef or pork" (Report from the Acting General Sanitary Inspector of the epidemic Fever of 1866–1867). Moreover the high prices of rice in 1865 were beyond the reach of many. Destitution and misery were widespread, and "even families previously in easy circumstances experienced the sad effects of want and high prices." The distress was both in town and in the rural districts where the financial difficulties of the sugar industry has swelled the number of unemployed who flocked to town and increased the crowded conditions. According to Dr. Fitz Patrick, the ex-apprentices were living in idleness, and "these people accustomed to be taken care by others, had no notion of whatever of providing for the future; to earn enough for their daily wants was all they aimed at and were always in a state of pauperism." He concluded his report by blaming society for its indifference to ex-apprentices and indentured labor for, "neither of them has the community given any attention until some doleful mortality devours them, and nothing remained to be done but to find places to inter them." (Report from the Acting General Sanitary Inspector of the epidemic Fever of 1866–1867).

Table 7 Mortality in Mauritius in 1867

General population	7,223
Ex-apprentices	9,801
Indian immigrants	24,177
Total	41,201

Source: Kuczynski (1949), Part 4, Mauritius and Seychelles

Apart from the economic and social conditions of the poorer classes, the indifference of the colonial government and the plantocracy was reflected in the absence of health facilities. For example, there were hospitals and dispensaries on the sugar estates for Indian immigrants; for those not employed on the estates among whom were the old Indian immigrants and the ex-apprentices, there was practically no access to health services. It was found that there is a low death rate of malarious fever in the district prisons where the inmates were provided "good lodging, clothing, bedding, wholesome and sufficient food with medicines and medical care...sadly contrasted with the state of the bulk of the poor living in the neighborhood who did no themselves possess, who could not go to the appointed places to find, and to whom it was not possible during the height of the epidemics, to extend any of those benefits to a degree at all commensurate with their great need" (Report from the Acting General Sanitary Inspector of the epidemic Fever of 1866–1867). The same diagnostic of lack of food, medicine, and medical attention explains the thousands of deaths in 1867 as has been the case of previous epidemics of cholera that was the conclusion of the Report of the Fever Commission. For example, death rate on sugar estate was 6.1 per 100 compared with Indians not on sugar estate which was to be 12.9. There was a general lack of health infrastructure for the poor both in Port Louis and in the country districts. Though in Port Louis the Local Board of Health opened 11 hospitals and provided food medicine and clothing to the poor while the General Board of Health also opened dispensaries and provisional hospitals, "the inefficiency of these measures...disclosed in a pointed manner how backwards Mauritius remains as far as the great questions of public health are concerned" (Report from the Acting General Sanitary Inspector of the epidemic Fever of 1866–1867). In spite the opening of dispensaries to care for the sick, there was no medicine available. The high price of quinine made it inaccessible to the majority of the population and even those who could afford. There was a shortage of quinine in the island, and quinine had to be obtained from other countries such as reunion and South Africa. Among the poor, it was both the old Indian immigrants and the ex-apprentices who suffered the most.

Conclusion

An average death rate of 38 and a birth rate of 30 for the population of Mauritius between 1831 and 1870 means a natural decrease of the population in that period (Mauritius Alamanach 1900; Kuczynski 1949). On the other hand, the death rate of the ex-apprentice population always remained higher than the rest of the population.

With epidemics taking a dreadful toll on the population, it was always the ex-apprentices who fared the worst. This grim reality is mirrored in the slow natural growth of the population in general, and until the 1870 the ex-slave population was in continuous decline. Economic and social conditions of the apprentices and crowding in the urban area of Port Louis are important factors in the decline of the apprentices, but lack of sanitary practices and rudimentary health services were as important as was government and planters' attitude and policy after emancipation. While the economic and social conditions were never favorable for the growth of the slave and the ex-slave population except for a very brief period after emancipation in 1839, epidemic mortalities were not isolated events but cumulative effects of economic and social conditions before and after the development of a plantation economy. The structure of the slave population and the labor force remained dependent on regular and continued importation of labor as a result of colonial and planter's policy. This contributed significantly toward the demographic decline of the slave population during slavery and the post-emancipation period.

References

Allen RB (1999) Slaves, freedmen, & indentured laborers in colonial Mauritius. Cambridge University Press, Cambridge, UK

Allen RB (2000) The traffic of several nations – the Mauritius slave trade. In: Teelock, Alpers (eds) History, memory and identity. University of Mauritius 2000, Mauritius

Barker AJ (1996) Slavery and anti-slavery in Mauritius, 1810–33 – the conflict between economic expansion and humanitarian reform under British rule. Palgrave Macmillan, Basingstoke

Blue Book of the colony of Mauritius and its dependencies 1826 B6

Blue Book of the colony of Mauritius and its dependencies 1834

Blue Book of the colony of Mauritius and its dependencies 1835

Bernardin de Saint-Pierre B (2002) Journey to Mauritius (trans: Wilson J). Oxford

Census of Mauritius (1851) Report of the Commisioner appointed to take census of the Island of Mauritius and its dependencies, November 1851 JR Wilson & Co.1853

Deerpalsingh S, Carter M (eds) (2015) Stanley to Gomm. 22 January 1842. Select documents on Indian immigration Mauritius 1836–1926, vol 1. Mahatma Gandhi Institute, Mauritius, p 70

Freycinet RMP (1996) Rose des vents: journal de madame rose de saulces: voyage de l'Uranie autour du monde, (1817–1820). Collection Mascarin, Ste. Clotilde

Hoolass DCV (1998) Epidemiology and the lower classes: a case study of the Cholera Epidemic of 1854 in Mauritius. University of Mauritius, Reduit

Kuczynski RR (1949) Demographic survey of the British empire, vol 2. Oxford University Press, London

Milbert JG (1812) Voyage Pittoresque à l'Ile Maurice, au Cap de Bonne Espérance et à l'Ile de Teneriffe. A. Nepveu, Paris

Noel K (1991) L'esclavage à l'ile de France. Editions Two Cities, Paris

North- Coombes (1978) Labour problems in the sugar industry of Ile De France or Mauritius 1790–1842 (unpublished M.A dissertation Cape Town, 1978). p 88

Nwulia M (1981) The history of slavery in Mauritius and the Seychelles, 1810–1875. Rutherford Fairleigh Dickinson University Press, D. E., London/Toronto

Reddi S (1989) Aspects of slavery during the British administration. In: Bisoondoyal, Servansingh (eds) Slavery in the south West Indian Ocean. Mahatma Gandhi Institute, Mauritius, pp 106–123

Report from the Acting General Sanitary Inspector of the epidemic Fever of 1866–1867. Mauritius October 1868. p 20

Teelock V (1998) Bitter sugar: sugar and slavery in 19th century Mauritius. Mahatma Gandhi Institute, Moka

The Mauritius Alamanach (1900), The Mauritius Stationery and Printing Co. Ltd, 1900.

Toussaint, A (1973) Port Louis, a tropical city (trans. by W.E.F. Ward [R]). London : Allen and Unwin

Valentine B (2000) The dark soul of the people. Slaves in Mauritius, Computer file S0102. Rhodes University, Grahamstown, Pretoria: South African Data Archive, National Research Foundation 2001

Wanquet C (1979) Histoire d'une révolution. La Réunion (1789–1803). Annales historiques de la Révolution française. pp 495–506

The Legacy of Indentured Labor

Kathleen Harrington-Watt

Contents

Introduction	1768
Setting the Stage of the British Indentured Labor System	1768
Mauritius, Indentured Labor, and Indo-Mauritians	1771
Mauritius and the Indentured Labor System	1772
Ethnicity and Diversity	1778
Indentured Labor and Ethnic Boundaries	1781
The Categorization of Race and Ethnicity	1782
Mass Migration of Indian Laborers	1782
The Indentured Laborer Category	1783
Land Ownership	1784
The Reinvigoration of Endogamy	1784
Language, Religion, and Identity	1786
Independence and Indo-Mauritian Political Power	1787
Ancestral Heritage and Cultural Capital	1789
Conclusion	1791
Cross-References	1792
References	1792

Abstract

This chapter will present and discuss the system of indentured labor established by the British Empire during the nineteenth and early twentieth centuries as a new form of labor acquisition for the colonies. The indentured labor system was created in response to the British Abolition of Slavery Act of 1833. This chapter will outline the nature of the indentured labor system, why it was started, and how it functioned. It will then examine how such a migrant labor system impacted upon both the migrants and receiving colonies, paying particular attention to the notion of ethnicity and the development of multiethnic communities. Mauritius is

K. Harrington-Watt (✉)
Anthropology, Canterbury University, Christchurch, New Zealand
e-mail: kharringtonwatt@gmail.com

© The Author(s), under exclusive license to Springer Nature Singapore Pte Ltd. 2019
S. Ratuva (ed.), *The Palgrave Handbook of Ethnicity*,
https://doi.org/10.1007/978-981-13-2898-5_100

one such host society that dramatically changed due to the impact of indentured labor migrants arriving on its shores; it will therefore serve as a useful case study to examine the significant role indentured labor has played in the formation of Mauritian society today.

Keywords
Indentured labor · Indo-Mauritian · Plural society · Multiethnic · Ethnicity and diversity · Indian ancestry · Labor migration

Introduction

Like all events in history, it is important to understand the many contexts that exist in a particular time and place. The indentured labor system began in the British colonies during the early nineteenth century and was seemingly a well-controlled and highly structured model of labor acquisition and supply. It involved specific laws, work contracts, and administrative processes that were applied to each host nation; however, each colony developed differently as new ethnic groups and communities arrived, settled, and grew over time. One could premise that all migrations of people adapt to their environment accordingly. However, in this chapter, I argue that the British indentured labor system of the nineteenth century impacted greatly on the future ethnic makeup of indentured labor host societies. These impacts, what I term the "legacies of indenture," were the consequences of the various arrangements that were imposed or developed by the indentured labor system itself. With that said, because each host society has its own historical and cultural context, each site of indentured labor has developed its own flavor of nationhood and complex of ethnic identities. What is important to highlight is that the indentured labor process meant that there were large numbers of migrants dislocated from their homeland and adapting to their new circumstances. This chapter takes a cultural historical view of the legacies of indentured labor on the receiving societies. It will begin by setting the stage of indentured labor, explaining what it was and why it was established. Following this, it will look more specifically at the indentured labor system as it was applied in Mauritius and make links to specific indentured labor circumstances that influenced the makeup of ethnicity in Mauritius today (Fig. 1).

Setting the Stage of the British Indentured Labor System

Indentured labor was a form of labor recruitment for the plantation colonies of the British Empire. Indentured labor is labor based upon a voluntary work contract. This form of labor provision could be described as a global phenomenon of the last 200 years. The origins of a systemized form of indentured labor began as a consequence of the British Abolition of Slavery Act in 1833, where slavery, after

Fig. 1 Images of indentured laborers taken as ID photographs in Mauritius from 1865 to 1910. Photographs with permission from Mauritian National Archives and Mahatma Gandhi Institute, Moka Mauritius

much debate and criticism in the British parliament, was determined an immoral process of obtaining labor for the colonies. Royal assent was granted in the British Parliament on August 28, 1833, and the abolition of slavery took effect on August 1, 1834. This meant that hundreds of thousands of British slaves who had been kidnapped and made to work in the colonies were to be freed from bondage.

The British colonies who had relied on slavery to provide a workforce for their plantation economies had already experienced an influx of migrating populations. There were previous free settlers, traders, and laborers who had travelled to the colonies to establish new homes, businesses, and work opportunities, respectively. These migrants brought with them their own language, culture, and traditions. There were also those that arrived as slaves who came with their own language, culture, social systems, and traditions but were forced to live and work in a setting that attempted to forcibly stamp out all notions of their original culture, religion, and identity. It is essential that we understand that the foundations of indentured labor began in response to the cessation of slavery.

The transition of slavery and its abolition differed for each British colony according to its own colonial and/or indigenous history. The general impact of abolition meant that with the emancipation of slaves, the plantation owners had a problem obtaining enough labor to keep productivity and export markets profitable. The indentured labor system was proposed as a way to alleviate this crisis and was titled "the great labor experiment" (Carter 1996:19).

A voluntary contracted labor agreement was the foundation of the indentured labor process and was perceived as a new and improved method of acquiring labor. Indentured labor was deemed significantly different to slavery, because the system was voluntary and the labor contract specified wages, work and living conditions, and arrangements for transportation to and from the country of employment. This system aimed to encourage the mass migration of people from their homelands to outreaching colonies that were desperate to fill labor shortages (Fig. 3).

This new system of labor recruitment provided opportunities for laborers and the peasant classes in other countries to obtain much needed work. Many of these recruits had been displaced off their land, due to floods and famine, or from the impacts of capitalism that had effected massive economic changes in the colonies. Consequently, there was a ready-made population in countries such as India, China, and Africa, with masses of people needing work to support their families and villages. Like slavery, the indentured labor system saw, yet again, the large-scale movement of people from one country to another.

Alongside this large-scale movement of people, the laborers brought with them their language, social customs, religion, and cultural practices. The sheer number of laborers migrating from specific regions to the colonies meant they could continue to associate with others from their place of origin with similar cultural backgrounds. Unlike the circumstances of slavery, the employers were invested in trying to keep the laborers in their employ and paid greater attention to the significance of the laborer's individual, family, social, religious, and cultural needs. There have been numerous debates surrounding the differences and similarities of slavery and indentured labor, and for the purposes of this chapter, it is unnecessary to discuss this well-covered topic here, though it is important to appreciate, as does Brij Lal (1998), that both slavery and indentured labor systems were ultimately exploitative. What was significantly different between these two labor systems was that the indentured laborer had a greater freedom to transfer and adapt their social and cultural traditions to their new homes, something tragically absent for those subjected to slavery. While this chapter begins to discuss the legacy of indentured labor and ethnicity, it is important to keep in sight the background of slavery of which indentured labor emerged. At the core of this new labor system, while perhaps not intended in the minds of the colonial administrators who were more concerned with productivity and global trade, was the notion of ethnicity.

Colonies such as Mauritius, La Reunion, Fiji, Trinidad Tobago, Suriname, Guyana, Jamaica, and South Africa relied on this new form of labor supply. To obtain labor for the colonies, a new system regulating methods of recruitment, wages, and living conditions was required. At the heart of this new labor system was a complex administrative recording system (Addison and Hazareesingh 1984; Richard Allen 1999; Clare Anderson 2009; Satyendra Peerthum 2012). Consequently, the indentured labor system resulted in large numbers of people shifting from their place of origin to new locations, places with distinctly different geographies and ethnic populations. Ad Knotter (2015) refers to organized labor systems as "intervening institutions" where laborers were recruited from countries with large groups of people seeking employment and opportunity. The sheer number of laborers migrating to the colonies, over the span of approximately 80 years, meant that this system of labor migration had a significant impact on the communities in which they arrived, worked, and, for many, chose to permanently reside. As such, the indentured labor system directly and indirectly influenced how these varied cultural groups negotiated their place in their host settings and how these sites of cross-cultural migration have developed over time (Fig. 4).

One of the largest recruitment sites for indentured labor during the nineteenth and early twentieth century was India. It is no surprise that India became such a proficient provider of labor. At the time the official British indentured labor system began, in 1842, India was already an established British colony and had undergone major changes to land tax and land ownership laws imposed by the colonial administration. These changes impacted heavily upon the agricultural sector, particularly small landowners and farmers who could no longer afford to remain on their ancestral land. Consequently, there was a large and growing peasant class looking for employment, who were shifting towards populated centers hoping for new opportunities. As such we can see that the consequence of the British Land Tenure and Tax laws provided, somewhat surreptitiously, a desperate and available labor workforce.

The British colonial system of indentured labor and its relationship with India serves as a good example of shifting labor populations. The significance of the British colonial indentured labor enterprise on the history of South Asian global migration and ethnic group formation in indentured labor colonies should not be underestimated. Around the globe, we find South Asian-based communities/diasporas that were formed during the nineteenth century as a consequence of the extensive movement of laborers from India to many British colonies around the globe. As a result, these Indian-based communities have grown and developed their own understanding of their ethnic identity often holding onto their Indian ancestral origins. Indentured labor has had an important demographic, economic, cultural, and social impact on these colonial host societies. While indentured labor had its own social, cultural, and economic consequences in the countries of labor recruitment and employment, these consequences remain relevant to our understanding of migration and notions of ethnicity and identity today. To understand more fully the legacy of indentured labor on ethnicity, it is useful to focus on a particular site of indentured labor. This chapter will focus on the Island of Mauritius as a way of explaining how the system of indentured labor influenced the particular characteristics of ethnicity in Mauritius today.

Mauritius, Indentured Labor, and Indo-Mauritians

Krish Seetah (2016:265) states that, *"New plural societies, characterized by cultural hybridity, were created around the world as a consequence of labor diasporas in the late historic period."* Mauritius was one of these plural societies created as a consequence of the British Empire's indentured labor system. Mauritius is a small island situated in the middle of the Indian Ocean, often referred to as "Little India" as coined by Patrick Eisenlohr (2006), referencing its strong links to India as a nation today. Mauritius is located approximately 800 km east of Madagascar. It was uninhabited until seafarers attempted to settle on the island in the late 1500s. Since then, it has been under colonial control by Dutch, French, and the British Empire over the last 300 years. Mauritius has no original indigenous population and today consists of multiethnic communities that all originated as migrants from Europe, China, India, and Africa. Today, it has a population of 1.4 million and has been an independent republic since 1968.

Mauritius was the first site of the formalized indentured labor system. It also received the largest number of indentured laborers over a period of 68 years, from 1842 to 1910, approximately 453,000 people (Vijayalakshmi Teelock 2009). While the indentured laborers came predominantly from India, there were also smaller numbers of contracted laborers from China, Malaysia, and East Africa. For the purposes of exploring the legacy of indentured labor, this chapter will focus on the migration of indentured laborers from India, justified by the significantly large number of Mauritian indentured laborer's of Indian origin. Similar legacies of the indentured labor system in Mauritius can also be found in other countries whose Indian communities originally stemmed from the migration of indentured laborers from India. It is also important to stress that these other indentured labor colonies have their own local histories and influences that created their own national character and configurations of ethnic diversity. In other words, while the British system of indentured labor was very much mirrored in each receiving British colony, the particular dynamics of geography and other resident indigenous and ethnic communities means that each location has negotiated its own unique multiethnic character (Fig. 5).

To understand the unique cultural and social milieu of Mauritius and the legacies of the indentured labor system, we need to contextualize the history of Mauritius and how the implementation of an indentured labor system has influenced its ethnic and cultural makeup. To do this, this chapter discusses several topics that piece together the complex legacies of indentured labor in Mauritius. We start with a brief summary of the history of Mauritius before the arrival of the indentured laborers. We then consider the need for indentured labor in Mauritius and examine how the indentured laborers negotiated their new lives in Mauritius. The second half of this chapter will focus on the various forces operating during the indentured labor period in Mauritius, from both inside and outside the indentured labor community influencing the formation of distinct ethnically bounded communities.

Mauritius and the Indentured Labor System

The previous colonial rulers of Mauritius, in particular the French, played a significant role in the development of Mauritian society. Even though the British annexed Mauritius from the French in 1810, after defeating the French in the naval Napoleonic wars, they negotiated lenient terms for the population already living in Mauritius. The existing population were allowed to keep possession of their property and their way of life, including language, laws, religion, and customs (Addison and Hazareesingh 1984; Teelock 2009). Therefore, the influence of French culture in

Mauritius has persisted over time. Other migrant groups arrived in Mauritius during and after the French period, namely slaves from Africa who arrived during both periods of French and British colonial rule as well as British migrants and civil servants who came to Mauritius after the British took control of the colony. There were also Indian migrants who had arrived in Mauritius as either indentured laborers on private contracts or as free settlers or traders. A limited number of Chinese migrants also came as laborers or traders. The population of Mauritius is now made up of these main migrant groups (Fig. 6).

During the nineteenth century, sugarcane agriculture was labor intensive, requiring individuals to plant, water, harvest, and transport the sugar crop to the nearest sugar mill for processing. Prior to 1833, when the British Slavery Abolition Act came into force, the sugar plantation labor supply was obtained through the importation of slaves from nearby Madagascar and the East Coast of Africa (Teelock 2009). With specific reference to Mauritius, the enforcement of the Slavery Abolition Act happened in 1835 – a year later than other parts of the British colonial empire, due to the strong resistance from Mauritian planters (Addison and Hazareesingh 1984: 48). Prior to the abolition of slavery in Mauritius, planters had already foreseen the labor shortage and an apprenticeship system was established. The apprenticeship system, under the guise of retraining and educating ex-slaves, forced them to continue as paid laborers under a labor contract period for 6 years (Allen 1999: 55–56). In practice, this system forced ex-slaves to keep working on the sugar plantations, where they were paid a minimal sum and were restricted by laws that governed marriage, meetings, land ownership, vagrancy, and corporal punishment. Consequently, the apprentice was neither slave nor free. The Abolition of Slavery Act of 1833, and its potential impact on laborers on the sugar plantation in Mauritius, was thwarted by the apprenticeship system. Consequently, ex-slaves would choose either *maroonage* and run away from their place of work, or *manumission* and work out the remainder of their contracted period (Richard B. Allen 2002). As a consequence, by the time the apprenticeship system ceased in 1839, the general reaction of ex-slaves was to leave the vicinity of the sugar plantations altogether, distancing themselves from the tyranny of the plantation, and moving to more urban center's or unpopulated regions on the island where they could established their own communities (Mishra 2009).

One significant difference between the system of slavery and indentured labor was their administration. The indentured labor system involved the documentation of each individual's journey, from their point of recruitment overseas to their contracted employment on the sugar estate, to their death or departure from Mauritius. The British colonial administration recorded each laborer's name, father's name, age, village of origin, region, religion, caste, ship, date of arrival, place of contract, and physical features. This detailed documentation can be read in two ways: one as a criticism of the methods used by the colonizers to control and monitor their subjects; and two, as often presented in Mauritius today, a redeeming feature of the British colonial governing system, enabling histories to be traced and the laborer's points of origin and identities to be retrieved.

In Mauritius, the lack of detailed documentation for slaves continues to impact their descendants and their ability to make links with their ancestral history. In contrast, many descendants of the indentured laborers have a gamut of information available to research their ancestral and familial heritage. With this said, the level of documentation recorded under the indentured labor system was unlikely to have been done for the future good of the laborers and their descendants. Instead, it mirrored the documentation systems already in use by the British administration in other colonies. These systems were used to record and control the colonial population, as with the colonial recording systems used in India. The fact that the descendants of the indentured laborers have such a wealth of historical information about their ancestors today is by coincidence rather than design. Yet has had a great deal of influence on their perceptions of ethnicity and identity.

Emigration of the Indian laborers was carried out under a government-regulated recruitment strategy from three principal ports – Calcutta, Madras, and Bombay. The Indian emigrants who went to distant plantation settlements under the contract system came from diverse regions, including the tribal regions of Eastern India, Bihar, the North West Provinces (present Uttar Pradesh), the Madras Presidency, and Western India. In the later period, many laborers from the northern regions, such as Western parts of the United Provinces and present day Haryana, also emigrated. The main regions of labor supply were the tribal regions of Chota Nagpur in Eastern India, Saran, Chapra, Shahabad, Champaran, Gaya, and Patna in Bihar; Banaras, Ghazipur, Azamgarh, Gorakhpur, Basti, Bahraich, and Jaunpur in the United Provinces; Chingalpet, Tanjore, Tiruchirappalli, South and North Arcot, Salem, Coimbatore, and Vizagapatam in Southern India; and Ratnagiri in Western India, as shown on the following map (Mishra 2009) (Fig. 2).

The relative proximity of Mauritius to India, already a British colony, along with the abundant supply of potential laborers from the growing unemployed and landless classes, made the ports of Calcutta, Madras, and Bombay ideal recruitment and transportation centers for indentured labor. The regions around these ports were primarily agricultural, and the laborers from these areas were deemed to be knowledgeable about farming, as well as fit and strong. Regional events, such as floods, famine, and political unrest, and unemployment resulted in willing participants for the recruitment process. There have been several critiques of the "willingness" of laborers, in particular the inaccurate/false promises of recruiters and the exploitative operations of the indentured labor system. Frequently, the living, work, and pay conditions that actualized once the laborer was stationed in Mauritius did not meet the expectations of the laborers themselves (Teelock 2009; Hugh Tinker 1974; Allen 1999; Carter 1992, 1995, 1996).

Another fundamental difference between the indentured labor system and slavery was the temporality of the indenture contract. For instance, the Mauritian Ordinance of 1849 determined a 3-year contract, and a following ordinance in 1862 reauthorized the period to a 5-year contract (Allen 1999:60). Slavery, on the other hand, was indefinite. The indentured labor system followed a pathway from recruitment to the completion of the labor contract. This pathway became more regulated as

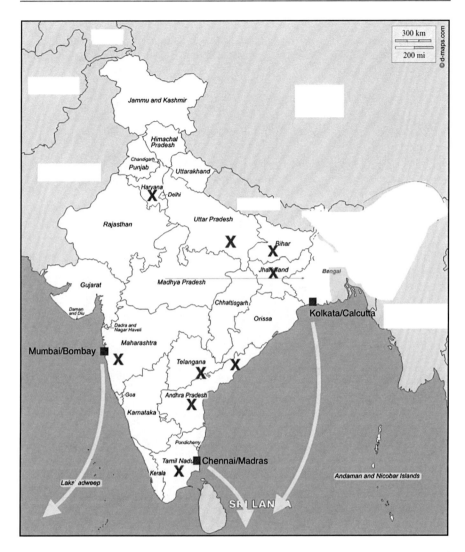

Fig. 2 Map showing the general regions of indentured laborers origins and the three main ports of Madras, Bombay, and Calcutta – used for ship transportation to Mauritius. Large crosses mark the general regions of Indian indentured labor origins

time passed. The following diagram depicts the indentured labor system as it was employed in Mauritius and other colonies (Table 1).

The pathway began with the ever increasing demand for sugar in England, as G.L. Beer (cited in Sidney Mintz 1985:39) stated in 1948: "From the middle of the eighteenth century these islands seem never to have been able to produce much more sugar than was needed for consumption in the mother country." When a planter

Fig. 3 Identification photographs of indentured laborers in Mauritius, from the indentured labor colonial ledger. Identification names and numbers removed as according to publication policy of the Mahatma Gandhi Institute Indentured Labor Archive, Moka Mauritius

(the owner of a sugar plantation) required new labor for his estate, they would make a request to the colonial government of Mauritius for new labor recruits. These requests were then transferred to India and other areas where recruitment agents were stationed. The recruitment agents sought out potential laborers and organized the signing of contracts and the placement of prospective laborers into immigration depots at the nearest port. From here, they awaited transportation to Mauritius by ship. On the signing of their contracts and registering as an indentured laborer, the immigrants' details were entered into administrative records and ledgers and became part of the detailed British colonial record. These records followed the immigrants' embarkation on the ship, their journey and arrival at their destination, their stay at the Immigration Depot in Port Louis, and their dispatch to specified plantations for their contracted period of labor. All these steps and movements were recorded at certain processing stages. One particular stage that is highly relevant to the topic of ethnicity was the immigrant ticket system.

The immigrant pass or "ticket," system identified the laborer as an indentured immigrant and therefore subject to specific rules. These rules governed the living and working arrangements of the indentured laborers while resident on the island. The immigrant ticket became an essential document in the laborers day-to-day lives. Containing identifying details such as name, immigration number, date of arrival, name of sugar estate, and from 1865 the ticket included an identification photograph.

The immigrant pass system played an active and vigorous role in the lives of the indentured laborers. In fact, as noted by Peerthum and Peerthum (2014), the ticket system and the high level of vagrancy due to lost or misplaced tickets were at the core of both the colonial government's attempt to control the laborers and the laborers attempt to resist the regulatory systems imposed on them. It could also be argued that the immigrant ticket system was one of the tangible differences between the systems of slavery and indenture, as it served to classify and identify the laborer with a direct link to their work contract and the terms of the contract agreement. While acting as a controlling and monitoring device, it also ambiguously provided

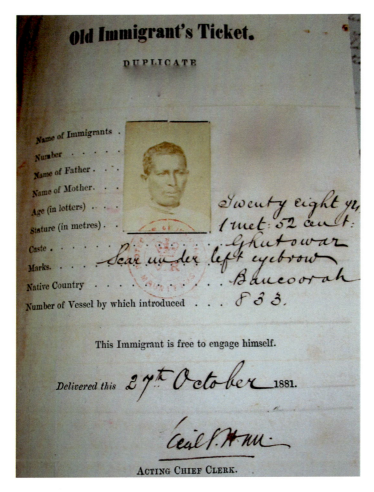

Fig. 4 Example of Old Immigrant Ticket, given to indentured laborer once they had completed their work contract. Original document as found in colonial ledgers, Mauritian National Archives

the laborer with a form of verification and legitimacy of movement around the island, keeping the laborer from being labelled and charged as a vagrant. The pass system also served to identify the laborer as a particular kind of immigrant, one from another country, encouraging the identification of a very specific migrant group. The regulatory indentured labor immigrant ticket system and the lengths the colonial government and planters went to keep the required level of laborers available for work emphasizes just how high the economic stakes of the sugar industry were.

In Mauritius, the recruitment of indentured laborers ended in 1910. The Indian indentured labor population was expanding rapidly. The laborers had already formed community groups associated with language, religious practices, and points of origin in the labor camps. A large percentage of laborers had chosen to remain in Mauritius and settle. Some laborers had taken the opportunity to become landowners often in

Fig. 5 Muslim prayer shrine, Creve Couer Mauritius. Surrounded by newly planted sugar crop. Authors photo, 2014

the same area in which they had worked on the sugar plantation, keeping them close to their established social networks. Identifying temples began to dot the land as well as mosques and churches. The growing Indo-Mauritian community had a clear idea of their ancestral heritage, and began to perceive each other and their ancestors as having a significant historical Mauritian story, one of struggle and survival. The growing population of the descendants of the indentured laborers has, in turn, impacted greatly on the demography and cultural landscape of Mauritius, today contributing to what Rosabell Boswell (2006:196–197) describes as, "... the island's rich tapestry of cultures" or what Erikson (1998: ix) refers to as, a "laboratory of diversity' that can 'profoundly' deepen our understanding of ethnic processes."

Ethnicity and Diversity

Ethnicity: "The systematic and enduring social reproduction of basic classificatory differences between categories of people who perceive each other as being culturally discrete" (Erikson 1993:3).

Mauritius is frequently described as a country made up of multiple ethnic groups and is often referred to metaphorically as a "rainbow nation." In fact, Megan Vaughan (2006) describes Mauritius as, "... the most ethnically diverse country on Earth." The following discussion attempts to explain this ethnic diversity in

Fig. 6 Kalimai shrine found amidst sugar plantations, Flaq Mauritius. Author Photo, 2014. (Performing rituals at the *Kalimai* shrine is still strong today, especially in rural Mauritius and especially among women who perform rituals asking for the protection of the goddess Kali and making offerings to appease her. The shrines are used by different people for different rituals that vary based primarily on gender and caste, and although Sanantanist Hindi-speaking Hindus are the primary practitioners, Mauritians from a variety of backgrounds make offerings and prayers at the Kalimai shrines, recognizing the powers of the goddess (Mauritian Hinduism, The Pluralism Project, 2018)

relation to the impacts of indentured labor on the sociocultural makeup of Mauritius. Today, the people of Indian descent (predominantly descendants of the indentured laborers) are called Indo-Mauritians and identify religiously as either Hindu or Muslim, with the exception of a small number of Indian Catholics who came as indentured laborers from India (Marcel Chowriamah 2010). The people of African descent are called Afro-Mauritians, or Creole, and Europeans are predominantly distinguished as Franco-Mauritians; both these communities associate largely with the Catholic Church. The minority group of Sino-Mauritians, those of Chinese origin, follow Buddhism or Christianity. According to the 2011 census conducted by Statistics Mauritius, Hinduism is the dominant religion with followers making up 48.5% of the population, followed by Christianity (32.7%), Islam (17.3%), and Buddhism (0.4%) (Mauritian Government 2011).

The Indo-Mauritian diaspora contains further complicated religious and cultural differentiations, based on religion and Indian regional languages. The Hindu community in Mauritius includes subgroups, these groups are defined

Table 1 Indentured labor system pathway

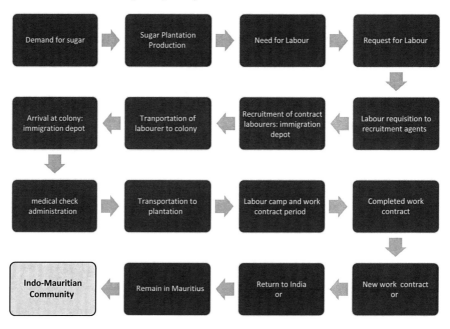

by corresponding languages and religious groups, such as Hindi, Tamil, Telugu, and Marathi. It is the religious and cultural identities that distinguish these Hindu groups, whereas religion remains a unifying signifier for the Muslim Indo-Mauritian community (Selvam 2003).

These diverse communities determine the cultural and religious makeup of Mauritius and while there is crossover for business, trade, employment, education, and national events, they remain markedly separate in social, cultural, and religious contexts. Multiple readings and research would suggest that in social, religious, and kinship matters, these different groups function exclusively. Metaphorically, the edges of each color of the rainbow are clearly bounded rather than blended.

Erikson (2001) refers to ethnicity as a social relationship that is negotiated between people, where ethnic identity is constructed by forces within and outside the group. There is a complex of pressures and ideologies that influence how the concept of an ethnic group forms, develops, and continues to change over time. These include laws, economic resources, language, marriage rules, cultural practices, religious practices, associations with place of origin, food, and dress. The development of ethnic identities and categories in Mauritius is no exception, and the indentured labor system and its legacies have played an important role in the construction of existing community ethnic boundaries. Tijo Salverda (2015:546) comments that, "Most Mauritians see themselves through a mental framework of ethnic belonging and accept ethnicity as a dominant organizing principle of social life."

The descendants of the indentured laborers are very much entrenched in the organizing principle of ethnicity. The Indian indentured laborers came from highly structured social systems in India. At the time of the indentured labor system, India was predominantly ruled by the British colonial government, functioning as a colonial hierarchical system. The social structure of the Hindu caste system was also a highly structured and hierarchical system. At the time of indenture, the caste system functioned as the dominant social system in India. At the top of this system is the Brahmin, the temple priests who are believed to be the link between the people and gods. Next is the Kshatriya, the rulers and warriors, and after them comes the Vaishya, the merchants and farmers. Beneath them are the Shudras, the unskilled labor classes, and at the bottom of (or below) this group are the untouchables. Lying at the heart of the caste system are Hindu concepts of purity and pollution, where the higher the caste category, the more pure, and the lower the caste category, the more polluted. While this is an extremely simplistic description of a very complex social structure, what is important to recognize in the indentured labor context is that the majority of indentured laborers were Hindu and were familiar with living inside defined social categories where caste laws influenced and governed all areas of social life, such as: (a) the importance of endogamy (marrying within one's own community), (b) the maintenance of religious rituals and practices, (c) the significance of ancestral genealogy and family origins, (d) the importance of language and culture, (e) the significance of rules around food preparation and consumption, and many more...

The notion of caste was weakened during the process of the indentured labor system and some would argue that it actually dissipated during this time, where the recruitment and transportation circumstances of the laborers meant a mixing of all recruits at the immigration depots, on the ships, and in the labor camps regardless of an individual's caste. It was difficult for labor migrants to maintain traditions and intentions of purity and religious ritual in such settings. However, even though the laborers found it difficult to maintain caste and religious purity, the idea of a bounded community remained a familiar concept, and as Hollup (1994) argues, the notion of caste became again more relevant in Mauritius post-independence especially within the Indo-Mauritian political domain.

Indentured Labor and Ethnic Boundaries

The following section considers the impacts of the indentured labor system on the formation of distinct ethnic boundaries in Mauritius. If we unpack the indentured labor system as it existed in Mauritius, we find certain features that have helped shape the formation of an ethnic group identity. These features are listed below and will be discussed in detail.

(1) The categorization of race and ethnicity
(2) Mass migration of Indian laborers
(3) The indentured laborer category

(4) Land ownership
(5) The reinvigoration of endogamy
(6) Language, religion, and identity
(7) Independence and Indo-Mauritian political power
(8) Ancestral heritage and cultural capital

The Categorization of Race and Ethnicity

Before Mauritius became a British colony in 1810, the British empire had already been actively categorizing people into specific racial and ethnic groupings through scientific and anthropological investigations, determining categories of racial types through physical, cultural and behavioral differences. These investigations treated communities of race in a similar way to other colonial scientific investigations such as the study of exotic (foreign) flora, fauna, and geography. "Foreign" subjects were subjected to being measured, photographed, and observed. These investigations sought to clearly define a hierarchy of race and distance the colonial empire from "other" races. The colonial administrators in the colonies sought to make clear distinctions between the multiethnic communities they found themselves governing in the colonies.

The categorization of people during the colonial period helped to structure what we can still see today as official categories of race and ethnicity. The census was one such tool that ordered and classified the various populations in the colonies. In Mauritius, beginning as early as 1830, the census referred to three categories: European, Free Black, and Slave. With private Indian indentured labor contracts beginning in 1834, by 1837 the census included European/Free Black, Apprentice, and Indian categories. The Mauritian census has continued to change and adjust to population and political shifts, such as the further distinction between Hindu and Muslim Indians, Chinese, and a broadening General Population category. Today, as with other postindependence colonies, the use of an ethnic question in the census was removed to help symbolically "forge a common nationalism" and replaced today by a question of language (A. J. Christopher 2005).

Mass Migration of Indian Laborers

Yancey et al. (1976) describe ethnicity as a phenomenon rather than a category; it is something that develops and changes as groups and individuals change over time. For post-migrant communities, to identify as a particular ethnicity, the members of this migrant network must expand, form, and maintain ties with, what Grieco (1998: 705) describes as, other "co-ethnics". The large numbers of indentured laborers to Mauritius during the nineteenth century meant that their community in Mauritius was already buoyed by large numbers of Indian laborers who were working and living together. These social networks were strengthened by a variety of ties between other indentured laborers. The decision to distribute the newly arrived laborers to the same plantations as other family members or with those from the same village or region encouraged the association of laborers with family ties and similar connections through language, religious practices, and familiar cultural expressions. This intention, though there were many exceptions to this rule, was an attempt by the colonial administration to ensure the labor population remained in Mauritius by encouraging connections with other co-ethnics with similar Indian regional identities. The laborers were therefore able to find support and maintain ties with their Indian origins and what could be described as a continued sense of "Indianness."

Initially, the indentured labor recruits were predominantly male. In 1839, the ratio of male to female was 56:1. This gender disparity became a concern for the colonial authorities in Mauritius, who saw a close link between the shortage of women and the lack of moral restraint in the indentured labor camps resulting in difficulties maintaining law and order in the colony. As a strategy to correct this imbalance and stabilize the indentured labor population, the authorities introduced new recruitment laws, beginning in 1857, that specified that at least 35% of immigrants arriving in Mauritius had to be women. This was increased to 40% in 1858 and 50% from 1859 to 1865 (Allen 1999:162). Not all women who came to Mauritius were contracted as laborers, some came as wives and daughters, or free migrants. While not contracted laborers, they still performed important roles on the sugar estates. They planted and looked after the labor camp gardens, managed livestock, and were often employed as staff on the sugar estate. The increase in women arriving in Mauritius impacted on the social dynamics of the camps, increasing the practice of religious rituals and marriage. The birth of children in the labor camps encouraged the development of *baitkas,* (a social meeting place to pray, perform religious rituals and instruction) and a greater desire to settle in Mauritius permanently. By the 1880s, fewer old immigrants returned to India at the cessation of their work contract. In 1880, the island became home to more than 113,000 Indo-Mauritians who had been born in Mauritius and who accounted for 45% of the Islands Indian residents (Allen 1999: 162).

The Indentured Laborer Category

With specific regard to the indentured labor system in Mauritius and ethnic categories, the indentured labor system classified the Indian migrants as a specific kind of migrant in Mauritius. They were governed by different laws regarding work contracts, living conditions, wages, food, and the ability to move around the island. These laws enforced identification processes, criminal convictions, marriage, private trade, and so on. From the moment they arrived in Mauritius, they were numbered, distributed, and monitored as a distinct group. Their records contained specific details that documented their name, origins, tribe, village, religion, caste, physical markings, and photographic identification. They were effectively branded by their status as an "indenture immigrant" and while restrictive in practice, unintentionally over time, allowed for the continued connection between the indentured laborer, their place of origin and ancestral heritage. Today, the indentured labor category is perceived as one of ancestral pride and honor, what Eisenlohr (2006:100) refers to as an ideology of "ancestral culture." This has encouraged the forming of strong ties between the Indo-Mauritian groups and their Indian origins, and invigorated an ancestral collective memory of struggle, survival, and achievement, helping to legitimize the rise of Indo-Mauritian political power in contemporary Mauritius (Eisenlohr 2006).

Land Ownership

During the mid-nineteenth century in Mauritius, the Indian indentured labor population grew and continued to grow within the labor camps of the sugar estates, as well as in nearby villages where the old laborers would set up homes, and shops. By the 1880s, there were two changes to the plantation economy in Mauritius that created a dramatic shift in the indentured labor landscape greatly influencing the social and political makeup of Mauritius. Firstly, in the late nineteenth century, the sugar industry became more centralized, where the size of sugar mills expanded but decreased in number due to greater efficiency. Secondly, as a result of a drop in the global market for sugar, many small plantation owners lost their business and larger sugar estates sold off parcels of land to survive the slump (Teelock 2009). As a consequence, the indentured laborer was given the opportunity to buy land, called *the grand morcellement*. Most of the newly available land was purchased by Indian families and laborers. This developed into a growing Indo-Mauritian land owning class. By 1935, 39% of sugar cane plantations were owned by Indo-Mauritians (Eisenlohr 2006; Teelock 2009). As a consequence of land acquisition, there was a movement away from the sugar estates and Indian village communities developed around the rural areas of Mauritius.

The Reinvigoration of Endogamy

One of the most powerful ties in post-migrant communities is the practice of *endogamy* (marrying only within one's own community) serving to reinforce a form of social closure and establishing a clear boundary marked by a commitment to a particular ethnic identity. Ari Nave (2000:348) suggests that, " ... an adequate understanding of ethnic group boundaries requires knowledge of the proximate mechanisms driving endogamy and cultural reproduction."

The majority of Indian indentured laborers practiced endogamy in their Indian homelands, both Hindu and Muslim laborers. Just as with the practice of the caste system, endogamy was difficult to maintain at the time of the indentured labor scheme. Initially, the low levels of female laborers and the mixing of laborers from varied regions made following an endogamous system difficult. As we have already discussed, initially the indentured labor recruits were predominantly male, in 1839, the ratio of male to female was 56:1. Consequently, during the period of indenture, mixed marriages were common. By 1891, the colonial administration in Mauritius produced guidelines on how to collect data on the children of intermarriages, where the child was assigned the ethnic identity of the father, no matter their appearance or cultural identification. The increase in women arriving in Mauritius impacted on the social milieu of the camps, with an increase in the practice of religious ritual and endogamous marriages.

As the population of Indian indentured laborers grew, the traditional practice of endogamy was reinvigorated. Mauritians in general have a clear preference for marrying someone of the same ethnic group. Franco-Mauritians' also have a preference for marrying "white" conforming to the endogamous marriage patterns of all Mauritian communities (Nave 2000: 548). We understand these preferences to be based upon a preference to marry someone with shared social norms and values. Research done on interethnic marriage by Nave (2000) found that ethnic groups in Mauritius maintained distinct boundaries through dress, religious beliefs and cultural practices, and the practice of endogamy.

Mauritius is commonly described as a plural society: a "fruit salad" of multiculturalism. The discourse about unity in diversity is strong in Mauritius. It has been widely assumed by researchers that in plural societies, rates of interethnic (involving people of different ethnicities) marriage is a common indicator of the level of social integration between groups. However, in Mauritius, we find that interethnic marriages are uncommon, and that intra-ethnic (involving people of same ethnicity) marriages are the predominant organizing principle of marriage. Endogamy and intra-ethnic marriage is important for the continuation of ethnic culture, whereas interethnic marriages reduce the possibilities of passing on ancestral cultural practices and beliefs to the next generation. This is particularly true in Mauritius where heritage and cultural diversity are celebrated and endorsed as National ideologies, where ethnicity and the practice of endogamy is socially accepted (Ng Tseung-Wong and Verkuyten, 2015: 690).

There are of course exceptions to the rule where intermarriage occurs, and in the Indo-Mauritian context, where endogamy is well entrenched. The practice of interethnic marriage is often socially challenging for those families involved (Erikson 1997 cited: Hans Vermeulen and Cora Govers ed. 1997). This is particularly so with marriages between Muslim and Hindu couples, due to strict religious doctrines and tensions between these two groups. Ng Tseung-Wong and Verkuyten (2015) found Mauritius exemplifies a country that is multicultural at the national and public level but is ethnically bounded at the family and cultural community level. They use a descriptive phrase from their research on intermarriage in Mauritius in their title which references directly the common attitude towards endogamy, "I'd rather we be neighbors than lovers": the two-sidedness of multiculturalism (Ng Tseung-Wong and Verkuyten 2015:690). The common Mauritian discourse rejects "mixed" marriages and is found among all communities. This discourse is encouraged by the significance of ethnic affiliation in Mauritian society, and as Erikson (2012) notes, there is little appeal to having a hybrid identity. So, with the practice of endogamy prevalent in Mauritius, we see how cultural ethnicity can remain a powerful invigorator of social boundaries and ethnic identities within essentially plural societies.

Language, Religion, and Identity

The circumstances of language in Mauritius reflect a similar dichotomy to both nationalism and pluralism. Language in Mauritius can symbolize both unity and disunity. At the time of the 2000 National Census, the languages spoken, in order of prevalence and followed by the number of speakers, were: Creole (806,152); Bhojpuri (142,387); French (39,953); Hindi (7250); Tamil (3623); Telugu (3623); Marathi (1888); Urdu (1189); and Chinese/Hakka (1606). Today, Creole remains the vernacular language of Mauritius, cutting across group boundaries and identities (Tiroumalechetty 2014:17–18). There are many languages spoken in Mauritius and many people speak three or more of them. Language in Mauritius is heavily caught up in debates around communalism and ethnic division in Mauritius. The ideology of a united and inclusive multicultural nation is undermined by post-colonial policies that foster ancestral culture and heritage (Eisenlohr 2006: 264). In recent times, there have been attempts to standardize and institutionalize Mauritian Creole, where it is described as the only cultural feature that transcends all ethnic boundaries in Mauritius. Yet, there has been strong opposition within the dominant Hindu community, who take issue with favoring a national Creole language for fear that the Creole community will claim Creole as their own distinct language base as the national language (Eisenlohr 2006). Consequently, the "ancestral cultural" ideology is gaining a stronger foothold in Mauritius as more and more Indo-Mauritians choose to promote their own ancestral language. The growth in speaking, writing, and publishing of Indian ancestral languages in Mauritius continues to demark ethnic subgroups.

Religion also plays a deciding role in the ethnic divisions of Mauritius. There are three broad religious groupings in Mauritius: Catholic, Hindu, and Islam. As Selvam (2003:28) comments, in the case of Mauritius, " ... in addition to factors such as language and place of origin, religion and places of worship play a significant cementing role in the formation and existence of ethnic groups and maintenance of an ethnic consciousness." With respect to the indentured labor migrants, religion and identity have gone hand in hand. As previously explained, the indentured laborers were able to continue their religious rituals and practices, albeit in adapted forms and settings that accommodated their new circumstances on the sugar plantations and in the villages of Mauritius.

Today, it is still possible to find clear links between the indentured laborers, the sugar plantation, and traditional religious practices, such as small shrines or temples found among the sugar plantation fields. During the indenture period, the sugar plantation owners realized that religious practice was essential to the well-being of the laborers and therefore allowed for the construction of religious prayer structures in the labor camp. For the Indian indentured laborers, the faithful performance of religious tradition and ritual was directly related to their sense of survival in what was initially experienced as a hostile and laborious circumstance. As is believed in the performance of rituals such as *Shivratri* and *Kavadee* today, if these rituals were not performed or done properly, a great misfortune would befall the laborer, their family, village, and community (Tiroumalechetty 2014:67).

Tiroumalechetty (2014:67) suggests as an example that religious rituals for Tamil indentured laborers, "... provided the emotional support and strength to face the miseries and injustices of the time and, secondly, it became a binding force grouping the Tamils together under common beliefs, customs and traditions." The sugar plantations today exemplify how laborer religious practices and rituals continue to signify religious affiliations and traditions by the Indo-Mauritian community. Although there are different religious subgroups within the broader Hindu community, there also exists an overall Hindu unity that functions as a powerful tool for mainatining political influence in Mauritius. So much so, that the advancement of Hinduism in Mauritius is perceived as a threat to the well-being of other ethnic communities (Clare Sisisky 2016). Leo Couacaud (2013) agrees that religion has become the most significant indicator of ethnic differentiation in Mauritius, especially in view of the extent to which religion has been instrumental in constructing group identity and belonging, particularly for Indo-Mauritian ethnic groups.

Independence and Indo-Mauritian Political Power

Throughout the twentieth century and more recently the start of the twenty-first century, we can still see the impacts of indentured labor on ethnicity being played out in the social and political realms of Mauritius. In the words of Patrick Eisenlohr (2011:262), "...peaceful coexistence through the acceptance and promotion of ethnic and religious pluralism is considered "a supreme common good" in Mauritius. Mauritius is described as a plural society, a medley of people who mix, but do not combine. Each distinct group represents different sections of Mauritian society where they live side by side, but separate, yet governed within the same political system (Mehta 1995). Mehta defines Mauritian society as one based on a cultural pluralist model. Ethnicity has a significant influence on Mauritius society, where it continues to divide communities into multiethnic, heterogenous groups. Consequently, each group has its own dynamics of population size, majority or minority groupings, history, and socioeconomic conditions. As such, some groups have greater representation and political force than others.

Throughout the twentieth century, the descendants of the indentured laborers grew in numbers becoming the largest population group in Mauritius, of which Indo-Mauritians were the largest group of indentured laborers. The next largest ethnic category is what the census defines as "the general population" made up of European white settlers, African Creoles, and mixed Creoles, making up 25% of the population. Within this group, and who represent only 1% of the population, are the Franco-Mauritians, who hold the greatest economic power (Mehta 1995). Although the Franco-Mauritians have the greatest economic power in Mauritius, as the dominant land and international business owners, it is the Indo-Mauritian ethnic community that holds the greatest political power. Unlike other British indentured labor colonies, the indentured labor descendant population of Mauritius has managed to forge their way into a dominant political position.

There are a variety of complex factors that have supported this development, and for the purposes of this chapter, we will focus on factors that are directly linked to the history of indentured labor. As previously mentioned, the fast expanding demographics of the post-indentured labor population has played a large role in Indo-Mauritians having a powerful stake hold in the government of Mauritius. The postindependence electoral voting process has favored rural constituencies which have been dominated by Hindu Mauritian communities. Historically, over the last century, there has been strong protest and debate around the exploitation and subjugation of indentured laborers, which led to the implementation of progressive laws that protected their rights.

While the Hindu Indo-Mauritian community was improving its social and economic position in Mauritius, there were also growing tensions between the ethnic communities, concerned with their growing political dominance over minority groups. By the 1960s leading up to the independence of Mauritius from British colonial rule in 1968, there was a growing fear among non-Indian communities that their political and social position would be overshadowed by a dominant Indo-Mauritian Hindu community. This tension saw a large number of Mauritians migrate outside of Mauritius, in particular, members of Catholic Creole communities. To help balance the fears of minority groups being swamped by a Hindu-based government, the Best Loser System (BLS) was introduced as part of the new postindependence electoral system. The aim was to guarantee political representation of "all" communities, especially minority groups. The implementation of the BLS system incorporated ethnic distinctions into the constitution, namely, Hindus, Muslims, Sino-Mauritians, and General Population (Salverda 2015:540).

Again we see the use of ethnic categories to identify the separate communities of Mauritius. As Boswell (2006) suggests, instrumentalization of ethnicity is hard to undo. In plural societies, behind the outward appearance of interethnic compromise, there exists competition between the various ethnic groups who are all attempting to improve their social, economic, and political position. As such, competition and tensions occur between groups, where each aim to have their own priorities and needs met. This is also true for Mauritius.

With the growing indentured labor descendant population and greater political representation, there came a growing interest in the promotion of Indian regional languages, traditions, and cultural events. With an emerging Indo-Mauritian middle class, the community became more confident in the development of family businesses, accessing comprehensive education and the strengthening of intra-ethnic ties through kinship, marriage, business, and caste networks (Salverda 2015: 549).

Hollup noted in 1994 that since post-independence, there has been a revival of caste consciousness in political contexts. Generally speaking, mentioning the caste system in Mauritius is politically incorrect, where the question of a caste structure in the Indo-Mauritian community is highly controversial (Claveyrolas 2016). For some Mauritians, it exists, and for others, it does not. Whether caste is relevant or not relevant in Mauritius today is a complex topic that cannot be addressed sufficiently here; however, what is apparent in Mauritius is the notion of "backing" that can be described as a derivative of the caste system. Rosabell Boswell (2006:155) claims that "backing" is widely used in Mauritius. This practice results in the preferential employment of European and Indo-Mauritian descendants in the private sector and civil service, respectively. Today, jobs and promotions within government and business sectors are still commonly influenced by an employee's ethnic network (Bunwaree 2002). These links may exist through family and kinship networks, caste or religious group membership. The existence of "backing" serves to create further tensions between the different ethnic communities in Mauritius, where some groups appear to have greater access to resources and opportunities than others (Lyn M Hempel 2009).

Even though there exist marked differentiations between each ethnic community in Mauritius, Mauritians manage to unconsciously and routinely navigate these differences at a national level, where there does exist a sense of social cohesion. This is exemplified by the creole term *"Lakorite,"* a word that does not have a direct equivalence (or roots) in the English or French language but means a common nationhood (Salverda 2015). Erikson (1998) has commented on the positive atmosphere of interethnic compromise and cooperation in Mauritius; however, Boswell (2005: 201) also suggests that this sense of social cohesion is a veneer, covering over the real competition and struggles that exist between groups for hegemony (leadership) and control. One such example of this is the underlying negative discourse associated with the descendants of slaves, identified as belonging to the Creole community, where they are perceived by other Mauritian ethnic groups to be of mixed heritage and therefore a hybrid group, with no clear ethnicity. This becomes particularly difficult for the Creole community when the majority of Mauritians emphasize ethnicity and ancestral origins as highly significant in Mauritian society. Consequently, today there is a great push towards connecting the descendants of Afro-Mauritians and Slaves with their African origins (Boswell 2005). This is a way for the Creole community to strengthen their political position in Mauritius, as a bounded community determined by a similar heritage and particular cultural traits. As Boswell (2005:212) observed, "…knowing one's origins and celebrating it … was becoming more important because it had become the only thing that tells others who one is and establishes belonging." Hence, there is a focus on researching Afro-Mauritian history in Mauritius, including research of archaeological sites and a growing interest in promoting music, dance, and language that can be linked to their African heritage.

Ancestral Heritage and Cultural Capital

The shifting status of the indentured laborers as colonial subjects (objects of labor) to the transformation over time of the status of their descendants is astounding given their subservient beginnings. The transformative narrative of the Indo-Mauritian community is central to their sense of identity and belonging. For the descendants of the indentured laborers today, the valorization of ancestors has become a form of "cultural memorialization" through a repetitive narrative (Hirsch 1997:4). In Hirsch's words: "this involves an activity occurring in the present in which the past is continuously modified and re-described, even as it continues to shape the future." Ancestral heritage and memorialization could also be described as a form of cultural capital: an asset that can be institutionalized, objectified, or embodied, that helps promote social mobility, that is different to financial capital (David Throsby 1999). The narrative of the indentured laborers as brave, strong, and tenacious helps to further substantiate the Indo-Mauritian's social status and negates any old narratives of the indentured laborers as slaves, victims, as downtrodden, sick, or weak. This narrative is reinforced by the descendants' continual reference to their indentured labor ancestors with pride, honor, and gratitude.

Ancestor worship takes on a very powerful role in reaffirming family and descendant community histories and is inherently involved in Indo-Mauritian religious practices and rituals. Because the Indo-Mauritian community dominates national and political arenas, indentured labor heritage sites, objects, and cultural traditions have become important cultural capital in Mauritius. These findings resonate with those of Eisenlohr (2006:100), where he claims that the improved social and political status of the Indo-Mauritian community is explained by their adherence to ancestral traditions, "Hindus in Mauritius have in the end been redeemed by their steadfast attachment to ancestral traditions and values, which are responsible for their economic success and climb upward from a previously inferior position in the political system." According to Eisenlohr (2006), because all communities in Mauritius have origins from "elsewhere," the cultivation of ancestral traditions and historical narratives help to cement the successes of the postcolonial experience.

Hinduism, while remarkably old, complex, and diverse, has always incorporated ideas of ancestral worship and ancestral rites (Sayers 2015). These ideas and practices most certainly travelled with the indentured laborers from India and were cultured and nurtured amidst the new environment of the indentured labor camps. While these traditions and religious practices have adapted over time, having a more Mauritian flavor, they have nevertheless remained a stable indicator of Indo-Mauritian identity and culture. The practice of Indo-Mauritian religious pilgrimages, such as *Shivratri* and *Kavadee*, and the ancestor ritual of *Gran Dimoun* are good examples of just how important ancestral and religious traditions are in contemporary Mauritius today.

Gran Dimoun is a family ritual usually conducted in the home on the 1st January each year. It is specifically practiced to honor family ancestors. *Thaipoosam Cavadee* is a yearly celebration performed in devotion of Lord Murugan. On this day the Tamil people show deep thanks and appreciation for having a prosperous year and ask for the deity's blessing. It involves, purity rituals and fasting as well as physical sacrifice, such as body piercing, walking on nailed shoes, carrying the heavy wooden *cavadee* (mountain) etc. It is considered so significant it has been given public holiday status. The Mauritian *Maha Shivaratri* festival is the largest Hindu pilgrimage outside of India. Thousands of devotees walk from all corners of the island to Ganga Talao the sacred lake in the centre of the island also called Grand Bassin, where the great night of Lord Shiva is celebrated. The festival exemplifies the Hindu tradition of pilgrimage, an imperative aspect of Hindu religion that connects the human world with the sacred. (cited from *The Pluralism Project* Harvard University http://pluralism.org/). In the Indo-Mauritian context, these are not only religious performances but also collective re-enactments and commemorations of the past sufferings of the immigrant ancestors (Eisenlohr 2004:93). There are many examples of religious performances enacted in Mauritius depending on the particular religious community (Telugu, Tamil, Marathi, etc.) and their calendar of religious festivals and auspicious days. The social lives of Indo-Mauritians are centered around these religious events and auspicious occasions. As such, we also find the celebration of festivals and ethnic group identity celebrated and supported at the Government level, where public holidays include specific days for each ethnic community in Mauritius.

As previously discussed, language has also played an important role in defining ethnic boundaries in Mauritius and also performs as an important form of cultural capital. Patrick Eisenlohr (2006:173) discusses the attachment and reinvigoration of ancestral languages in Mauritius performing in similar ways to religious traditions. He notes how traditional ancestral languages have grown as a political focus in Mauritius since post-independence. Today, the teaching of regional Indian languages in respect to ancestral tradition also continues the "valorization" of their ancestral heritage and helps to ensure the continuity of their Indian origins and culture. In turn, the practice of ancestral language keeps the Indo-Mauritian community tightly bound.

Conclusion

The indentured labor system, by its reliance on migrant labor and its innate categorizing structure, encouraged the development of a plural society; a society with strong ethnic affiliations that differentiate each group from another. While the influx of indentured laborers does not explain fully the development of a multiethnic society in Mauritius, as there were already clear divisions between the Franco-Mauritians, slaves, and others before the arrival of the indentured laborers, it has, however, fostered clear divisions between the indentured labor migrants, their employers, and other Mauritian communities. The indentured laborers were perceived as distinctly different to any other group. They were allowed to speak their own language, practice religious rituals and cultural traditions, remain endogamous, eat and dress according to their own customs, build temples and shrines, own parcels of land, and eventually become business owners. These opportunities all began within the auspices of the indentured labor system, a system that strongly signified difference and bounded this particular group through specific laws and administrative processes. It is no surprise that as the indentured laborers completed their work contracts and chose to remain in Mauritius, they had already established strong social networks and belonged to clearly marked ethnic communities. The sheer number of indentured laborers that arrived and remained in Mauritius had a pronounced impact on the demographics of Mauritius and altered the social, economic, and political constitution of the island. At a broader social level, this has resulted in an imbalance of ethnic group population numbers, political representation, and access to resources and equal opportunities. While there does exist a perception of social cohesion at the national level, the significance of ethnicity and group identity remains a dominant force. The growing interest in ethnic group identity, history, and ancestral heritage would suggest that the cultural plurality of Mauritius is likely to continue with further cultural and ethnic distinctions and boundaries being further defined and encouraged.

Cross-References

▶ Diaspora as Transnational Actors: Globalization and the Role of Ethnic Memory
▶ Global Capitalism and Cheap Labor: The Case of Indenture
▶ Indian Indentured Laborers in the Caribbean
▶ New Middle-Class Labor Migrants
▶ Religion and Political Mobilization
▶ State Hegemony and Ethnicity: Fiji's Problematic Colonial Past
▶ The Significance of Ethno-politics in Modern States and Society

References

Addison J, Hazareesingh K (1984) A new history of Mauritius. Editions de l'Ocean Indien, Stanley
Allen RB (1999) Slaves, Freedmen, and indentured laborers in colonial Mauritius. Cambridge University Press, Cambridge
Allen RB (2002) Maroonage and its legacy in Mauritius and in the colonial plantation world. Outre-Mers. Revue d'histoire 336(/337):131–152
Anderson C (2009) Convicts and coolies: rethinking indentured labour in the nineteenth century. Slavery Abolition 30(1):93–109
Boswell R (2005) Unravelling Le malaise creole: hybridity and marginalisation in Mauritius. Identities 12(2):195–122
Boswell R (2006) Le malaise creole: ethnic identity in Mauritius. Berghahn, New York, Oxford
Bunwaree S (2002) Economics, conflicts and interculturality in a small island state: the case of Mauritius. Polis 9(1):1–19
Carter M (1992) The family under indenture: a mauritian case study. J Mauritian Stud 4(1):1–21
Carter M (1995) Servants, sirdars and settlers, Indians in Mauritius 1834/1874. Oxford University Press, Delhi
Carter M (1996) Voices from Indenture: experiences of Indian migrants in the British Empire. Leicester University Press, London
Chowriamah M (2010) Preserving a multidimensional heritage in a plural society. J Mauritian Stud 5(Special Edition):91–101
Christopher AJ (2005) Race and the census in the commonwealth. Population, Space and Place. 11:103–118
Claveyrolas M (2016) The land of the Vaish? Caste Structure and Ideology in Mauritius. South Asian Multidisciplinary Academic Journal (online) (Free-Standing Articles)
Couacaud L (2013) Recognising Mauritius's unique heritage: the relevance of estate temples and shrines. Angage: Post Independence Mauritius 3:135–155
Eisenlohr P (2004) Temporalities of community: ancestral language, pilgrimage, and diasporic belonging in Mauritius. J Linguist Anthropol 14(1):81–98
Eisenlohr P (2006) Little India. Diaspora, time, and ethnolinguistic belonging in Hindu Mauritius, 1st edn. Los Angeles. University Of California Press, London

Eisenlohr P (2011) Religious media, devotional Islam, and the morality of ethnic pluralism in Mauritius. World Dev 39(2):261–269
Erikson TH (1993) Us and them in modern societies: ethnicity and nationalism in Mauritius Trinidad and beyond. Scandinavian University Press, Oslo
Erikson TH (1997) Tensions between the ethnic and the post-ethnic. In: Vermeulen H, Govers C (eds) The politics of ethnic consciousness. Macmillan, London
Erikson TH (1998) Common denominators: ethnicity, nation building and compromise in Mauritius. Berg, Oxford
Erikson (2001) Small places large issues: an introduction to social and cultural anthropology. London, Virginia: Pluto Press
Erikson TH (2012) Ethnicity and nationalism: anthropological perspectives (anthropology, culture and society), 3rd edn. Pluto Press, London/New York
Grieco EM (1998) The effects of migration on the establishment of networks: caste disintegration and reformation among the Indians of Fiji. Int Migr Rev 32(3):704–736
Hempel LM (2009) Power, wealth and common identity: access to resources and ethnic identification in a plural society. Ethn Racial Stud 32(3):460–489
Hirsch M (1997) Family frames: photography narrative and postmemory. Harvard University Press, Cambridge/London
Hollup O (1994) The disintegration of caste and changing concepts of Indian ethnic identity in Mauritius. Ethnology 33(4(Autumn)):297–316
Knotter A (2015) Migration and ethnicity in coalfield history: global perspectives. IRSH 60(Special Issue):13–39
Lal B (1998) Understanding the Indian indenture experience. South Asia J South Asian Stud 21(s1):215–237
Mauritian Government (2011) National Census. Statistics, ed, vol 2. Mauritian Government, Mauritius
Mehta SR (1995) Power dynamics of Indian immigrants in Mauritius: a study in ethnic relations. Ind Anthropol 25(1):1–11
Mintz SW (1985) Sweetness and power: the place of sugar in modern history. Penguin Books, New York
Mishra AK (2009) Indian indentured Labourers in Mauritius: reassessing the 'new system of slavery' vs free labour debate. Stud Hist 25(2):229–251
Nave A (2000) Marriage and the maintenance of ethnic group boundaries: the case of Mauritius. Ethn Racial Stud 23(2):329–352
Ng Tseung-Wong C, Verkuyten M (2015) Multiculturalism, Mauritian style: cultural diversity, belonging, and a secular state. Am Behav Sci 59(6):679–701
Peerthum S (2012) A cheap reservoir of mankind for labour: the genesis of the indentured labour system in Mauritius,1826–1843. Angage: explorations into the history. Soc Cult Indentured Immigrants Descendents Mauritius 1:155–178
Peerthum S, Peerthum S (2014) Incorrigible, defiant and determined: vagrants, vagrancy, worker resistance and the function of the Bagne prison during the late 1820's and 1830's. In: Hassankhan M, Lal B, Munro D (eds) Resistance and Indian indenture experience: comparative perspectives. Ajay Kumar Jain for Manohar Publishers, New Delhi
Salverda T (2015) (Dis)unity in diversity: how common beliefs about ethnicity benefit the white Mauritian elite. J Mod Afr Stud 54(4):533–555
Sayers M (2015) The Śrāddha: the development of ancestor worship in classical Hinduism. Religion Compass 9(6):182–197
Seetah K (2016) Contextualizing complex social contact: Mauritius, a microcosm of global diaspora. Camb Archaeol J 26/2:265–283
Selvam S (2003) Religion and ethnicity in the Indian diaspora: Murugan worship among Tamil-Hindus in Mauritius. J Mauritian Stud 2(1):1–29
Sisisky C (2016) Mauritian Hinduisms and post-colonial religious pluralism in Mauritius. Committee on the study of religion, Harvard University, http://www.pluralism.org/affiliates/sisisky/index.php
Teelock V (2009) Mauritian history: from its beginnings to modern times. Mahatma Gandhi Institute, Moka, Republic of Mauritius

The Pluralism Project (2018) Harvard University. http://pluralism.org/
Throsby D (1999) Cultural capital. Journal of Cultural Economy 23:/1 Barc Conf Plenary Papers 23(1):3–12
Tinker H (1974) A new system of slavery: the export of Indian labour overseas, 1830–1920. Oxford University Press, London/New York
Tiroumalechetty P (2014) Tamil cultural identity in Mauritius: a sociolinguistic perspective. Printed and self published in Mauritius
Vaughan M (2006) Creating the Creole Island: slavery in eighteenth-century Mauritius. Itinerario 30(1):109–111
Yancey IL, Ericksen EP, Juliana RN (1976) Emergent ethnicity: a review and reformulation. Am Sociol Rev, 41:391–403

Global Capitalism and Cheap Labor: The Case of Indenture

91

Brinsley Samaroo

Contents

Introduction	1796
Creation of the Plantation System	1797
Transition to Indentureship	1798
Indian Indentureship	1801
Indentured Women	1804
The Movement Toward Abolition	1805
The Legacy of Indentureship	1807
Descendants of the Immigrants	1809
Conclusion	1810
References	1811

Abstract

The system of indentureship, utilizing mainly Chinese and Indian labor in the post-slavery period, was a continuation of the capitalist desire of sourcing cheap labor under the aegis of the plantation system. That system, originating in Brazil from the sixteenth century, provided a model which was effectively used by the other Western European countries to create a plantation society. This was a rigidly stratified polity using race as a major determinant of one's place in the pyramid. The model was transferred from Portuguese Brazil under the auspices of Dutch entrepreneurs, to the Caribbean colonies transforming them from poverty into prosperity. Its success in the Caribbean led to its transference to the Indian Ocean by the same European powers which had established parallel patterns of trading in the East, complementing their Western, Atlantic enterprises. In this continuance of labor exploitation, China and India were major sources of "coolie" labor under less brutal conditions than in slavery. For both peoples, however, this bondage was not the end of their world. Most of them survived using new opportunities

B. Samaroo (✉)
History Department, University of the West Indies, St. Augustine, Trinidad and Tobago
e-mail: bsamaroo40@gmail.com

© The Author(s), under exclusive license to Springer Nature Singapore Pte Ltd. 2019
S. Ratuva (ed.), *The Palgrave Handbook of Ethnicity*,
https://doi.org/10.1007/978-981-13-2898-5_102

provided by new situations, discarding some of the old traditions selectively. Both Chinese and Indians came from ancient societies guided by beliefs and traditions sanctified by time. As they adapted to their adopted societies, they used their ancestral moorings as enablers in new homelands in the Atlantic and Pacific worlds. Through the complex interaction of sugar, slavery-bonded labor, and European capitalism, the international economy was transformed leading to the industrialized world of the nineteenth and twentieth centuries.

Keywords
Plantation system · Cuban Chinese · Guandong · Calcutta · Girmitya (agreement signer) · Arkatia (recruiting agent) · Jahaji bandal (ship's belongings) · Gender imbalance

Introduction

> To what purpose do you bring me frankincense from Sheba and the sweet smelling cane from a far country? Your offerings are not acceptable nor are your sacrifices pleasing to me (Jeremiah 6:20)

During the period 1837–1920, just over 2.2 million Chinese, Indians, Javanese, Malagasy, and free Africans were indentured on tropical plantations worldwide. This activity occurred as European mercantilists continued the process of industrializing human energy in the pursuit of profit which had been an ongoing activity during the previous two centuries of African enslavement. From the start of the nineteenth century, the movement toward abolition gained increased momentum with the British ban on slave-trading in 1807 and their prohibition of slavery between 1834 and 1838. Mauritius ended its slave trade in 1839 and the French colonies in 1848 followed by the Dutch in 1863, Cuba in 1886, and Puerto Rico in 1873. At the center of this long story of slavery and indentureship was the sugarcane, the boon and the bane of the modern world.

This narrative of the interlocking roles of sugar, slavery, and indentureship has been the focus of many studies, some of which have been described by contemporary analysts as *Sweet Malefactor: the story of sugar* (Aykroyd 1967), *Fruits of Empire* (Walvin 1997), *Bitter Sugar* (Teelock 1998), *Sweetening bitter sugar* (Seecharan 2005), and *Sugar in the blood* (Stuart 2012).

From its Asiatic roots, the plant was transferred to the Iberian peninsula by the Arabs from the time of their invasion in 711 to the end of the fifteenth century when Christopher Columbus introduced sugarcane to the Caribbean. Most of the canes cultivated by Spain and Portugal was done on the offshore islands such as Madeira, the Canaries, and Cape Verde where the labor was provided by African slaves fetched from Northwest Africa. The Spaniards were the first to introduce the plant to the Caribbean when Columbus brought the first set to Hispaniola in 1493 on his second voyage to the New World. In 1506 a second consignment was brought by the Spaniard Avignon. But this early introduction of sugar to the Northern Caribbean did not mean its diffusion to the rest of the islands. Spain was far more interested in precious metals and pearls than in agriculture. Hence sugar cultivation was secondary to the search for metallic wealth. Even so there was a significant sugar industry in Cuba and Hispaniola. At the same time the Spaniards prohibited the export of both plants and technology to their possessions in the Southern Caribbean. Here the challenge of the interlopers (British, French, and Dutch) posed a serious threat. In fact as Spain concentrated on Mexico and Peru, its Caribbean possessions from Jamaica to the Guianas were increasingly being conquered by these interlopers.

Creation of the Plantation System

With the Spanish embargo on the export of sugar technology, the task of introducing the product to the British and French islands was undertaken by the Dutch whose traders considered this transference as essential to their roles as international carriers in the Atlantic world and in the Indian Ocean and as sugar refiners in Europe. The Dutch occupation of Pernambuco in Northern Brazil from 1621 to 1651 was an integral part of this process. The Portuguese had introduced sugar cultivation to their Brazilian colony from 1520 under the donatario system which became the foundation for the evolution of the plantation model. This system was largely responsible for the prosperity of Brazil for the next two centuries providing the wherewithal for the penetration of the sertao (interior). Like the Spaniards, the Portuguese were reluctant to pass secrets to their northern neighbors in the Caribbean. Such secrets remained as secrets until the Dutch gained temporary ascendancy in Brazil for just over three decades from 1621. During this period the Dutch invited British and French investors to Brazil. These persons were pleased to observe a ready-made system which effectively utilized slave labor, creating a stratified society for the profitable production of sugar and its by-products (Davis 1973, p. 173). Dutch investors also moved to the Caribbean.

The plantation system established a clearly defined class system based on ethnic origins where one's "caste" position determined one's occupation and place in a well-defined pyramid. This enabled a large cohort of plantation owners to live in Europe, while the local "compradore" class made up of Europeans and European creoles managed the plantations as attorneys, accountants, commercial agents, and overseers. Over time, mixed-race (colored) functionaries ascended into the compradore class. Beneath these upper echelons, there was the mass of Africans, themselves classified as soldiers, policemen, drivers of gangs, house slaves, and field slaves. The plantation system was devised to allow one crop to one region as this suited the metropolitan interests. In this way sugar was allotted to Mauritius, Natal, Fiji, and the Caribbean, cotton and tobacco to the North American colonies, and rice and textiles to India. In this regulated crop system, other necessities were imported from those colonies whose assignment was different and from metropolitan producers and colonists who were socialized into the acquisition of foreign tastes. The plantation system dissuaded slaves or indentured servants from developing independent livelihoods so as to increase dependence on a centralized center. In this way, rice production was discouraged in the swamplands of British Guiana or Suriname whose post-indentureship development became heavily based on rice production.

Similarly Fijians and Mauritians were not encouraged to exploit the abundant fisheries which existed in the Indian Ocean. Seafoods had to be imported. In the Caribbean the workers were fed on a diet of Canadian cod, New Brunswick sardines and herrings, and "Irish" potatoes. Native root crops such as cassava, yams, or arrowroot were hardly welcome. Another essential element of the plantation system was the constant presence of a wide range of Protestant and Roman Catholic missionaries who were willing upholders of the model, using the Bible to justify servitude while denigrating native ontologies, African or Asian ways of seeing. In Mauritius, Catholic schools dominated, acting as socializing agents, in other words, bringing the population into a Catholic culture (Teelock 2009, p. 281).

Because of their crucial role in transferring an immediately applicable model for the establishment of the plantation, loans for the purchase of machinery, markets for the raw sugar (to be refined in Dutch factories), and a ready supply of slaves, the Dutch have been called the foster parents of the Sugar Revolution which was started in the Caribbean in the mid-seventeenth century. In this way, Jamaica, Barbados, St. Kitts, Martinique, and Guadeloupe became immediate beneficiaries of Dutch enterprise as sugar cultivation created a new canescape. Under the aegis of this system, a large number of unprofitable crops (indigo, cotton, tobacco, cocoa, and coffee) were replaced by a single crop, namely, sugar. Similarly a large number of smallholdings gave way to a small number of large holdings (Davis 1973, p. 184). As the industry developed, centralization of factories became increasingly important as in the case of Cuba and Fiji. When Fiji was ceded to Britain in 1874, its first governor Sir Arthur Gordon, fresh from Trinidad and Mauritius, introduced the plantation model using Indian indentured laborers of whom 60,063 arrived between 1879 and 1916 (Lal 2006, p. 370).

It must be remembered, too, that Dutch enterprise was not restricted to the Atlantic world; the Dutch were global traders. During the seventeenth century, the Dutch East India Company was selling Indian and South Asian slaves to the Cape Colony and to factories in Indonesia and Sumatra. French traders, too, were offering services to the Caribbean while selling Indian slaves to Mauritius and Reunion (Allen 2016, p. 41). Through these global networks, the plantation model was internationalized and was boosted by two other considerations. One was the availability of African slaves initially and Asian indentured workers subsequently. To the plantation owners, Asia, like Africa, had an unlimited supply of unemployed men eager to go abroad. The second consideration was the high price for sugar in the European market. During the eighteenth century, alternative sea routes were developed between colonizers and the colonized, and this facilitated easier trading. It became safer to travel from a colony to a metropole than it was to travel among the Fijian islands or among the French colonies in the Caribbean. In the case of Fiji, the new colonizer was Australia whose Colonial Sugar Refining Company controlled its sugar industry.

Transition to Indentureship

The system of indentureship which flourished during the nineteenth century was a revival of an earlier indentureship which was practiced in North America from the mid-seventeenth century to the late eighteenth. Between 1660 and 1775, some

400,000 British indentured servants had been transported to the North American colonies, many to work as field laborers but not on the plantation model (Allen 2016, p. 39). Most had to work for up to 3 years after which they would be given freedom and allotments. The treatment of these indentured servants was far better than the later Asiatic indentured servants. In the immediate post-slavery era, an effort was made to revive this system through the importation of European "engagés" from Iberia, France, Malta, Ireland, and Germany. These European settlers, it was believed, would assist in maintaining an ethnic balance and provide an example of diligence to the former enslaved people. However, this experiment failed since the Europeans could not adapt to sugar cultivation in the tropical heat. Unsuccessful efforts were also made in the Caribbean to recruit free Africans from the Chesapeake Bay area of Eastern USA after the Anglo-American War of 1812 as well as former soldiers after the end of the Napoleonic Wars of 1815. It was after the failure of these experiments that Asia became the major source of labor for the Indian Ocean and the Atlantic colonies.

In the continuing search for suitable replacements, it was China, not India, which was the first target. As early as 1760, Chinese were being brought to Mauritius when, in that year, 300 Chinese laborers were brought and in 1829 another 200 were imported. However, these efforts collapsed like the simultaneous experiments in the Atlantic world (Teelock 2009, p. 320).

After that time, hundreds of Chinese came to Mauritius, but these came as traders between China and Mauritius. This trading contact increased after the British liberalized Chinese immigration in 1877. The first Chinese to arrive in the Caribbean came to Trinidad in 1806, but these did not come from China. The 200 Chinese were an assortment of Chinese who were based in Calcutta together with others who had been recruited in Penang (modern Malaysia). This experiment failed, to be restarted later on. From 1847 to 1887, around 165,000 Chinese were brought to the Caribbean (Table 1).

In the midst of this largely unregulated traffic, British and French officials sought to regularize the trade through negotiation with the Chinese government. At the Kung Convention in 1866, the parties agreed to terms based on the Indian indentured model. From this time the trade in Chinese bodies was expected to increase, but then the West Indian planters subverted this plan by purchasing their "coolies" from India

Table 1 Chinese immigrants to the Caribbean, 1806–1924

Colony	Years	Indentured	Non-indentured
Cuba	1847–1874	126,000	
	1901–1924		17,000
French West Indies	1853–1887	2,129	
Suriname	1853–1874	2,839	
British Guiana	1853–1879	13,539	
Trinidad	1806–1866	2,984	
Jamaica	1854–1884	1,196	
British Honduras	1865	474	
Antigua	1882	128	

which incurred less costs than from Guandong or Macao (Looklai 1993, p. 48). By 1872 the Europeans were able to wring more consciousness from a weak Manchu government, but by this time the plantocracy had switched to the Indian sources. As a result a small number came to the non-Hispanic Caribbean: 2,645 to Suriname, about 2,984 to Trinidad, and 1,196 to Jamaica. British Guiana received 13,359 and Cuba 126,000. Compare this with 239,000 Indians who went to British Guiana, 147,000 to Trinidad, and just over 68,000 who went to Martinique and Guadeloupe. From the late nineteenth century, there was an exodus of Chinese from British Guiana to Trinidad and the other British Caribbean colonies because of the unfair advantages given to the Portuguese who had also come as indentured laborers. The Portuguese had shorter terms of indentureship and were afforded special facilities for trading because they were European. In the process the Chinese who were also traders had to find other havens.

The Chinese indentured experience in Cuba deserves our special attention since it was the harshest of all. Indentureship from India was better organized with tighter state controls. In the Chinese case, such controls were absent as European traders and Chinese officials conspired to extract as many Chinese as possible from a politically unstable kingdom. The voyage from China was itself most hazardous. The trip to the Caribbean took an average of 125 days compared to those from India which averaged 90 days. Out of 142,000 who left for Cuba between 1847 and 1874, as many as 16,000 died during the crossing in "rebellions, assassinations of crews, reprisals against captains, suicides and death by thirst" (Helly 1993, p. 21). The eminent Chinese historian Lyn Pann has correctly observed that "It was a very unlucky Chinese who found himself transported to Cuba" (Pan 1966, p. 67). It is no accident that the Chinese "coolie" trade has given us the word "Shanghaied" and was generally referred to as the "pig trade."

In the free-for-all situation in Cuba, Chinese were indentured for unusually long periods (8–10 years in the first instance), and their subsequent freedom was blocked by the Madrid government. From 1860 those whose indentures had expired had to leave the island at their own expense or re-indenture themselves. For many who sought to claim their freedom and leave, employers regularly withheld their certificates of completion, forced them in re-indentureship, or detained them in depots (Cuba Commission 1876, pp. 77, 81).

A major disincentive to Chinese settlement in Cuba was the marked absence of women among the immigrants. From 1852 importers of Chinese labor into Cuba had agreed to ensure that at least one-fifth of each consignment were to be women. The record, however, points to the blatant disregard of this convention. Chinese migration to Latin America and the Caribbean was overwhelmingly bachelor migration. Out of 126,000 Chinese who went to Cuba between 1847 and 1874, there were about 62 women. By the 1860s when free Chinese were opting to start families in Cuba, there were 1.6 Chinese women for every thousand men (Northrup 1995, p. 75). This gender disparity created problems for the Chinese in the Caribbean and in Mauritius since there was competition between Chinese and Africans for available women. The importation of Chinese was also seen as a means of depressing wages, causing further conflict. Despite these hindrances the Chinese contribution to Caribbean development was considerable. In Cuba they facilitated industrialization of the sugar industry. Denise Helly, an authority on the Chinese in Cuba found that:

> The adaptation of the Cantonese to industrial labour was so rapid that not a single informant to the 1874 investigation mentioned the technical difficulty in carrying out the tasks in the sugar mills. (Helly 1993, p. 22)

In the Atlantic and Indian Ocean colonies to which there was Chinese migration, the Chinese filled a variety of roles: domestics, charcoal burners, laundry men, and vegetable farmers. In all of these places of migration, they played a major role in promoting retail trading in far-off rural communities to which the European merchants would not go. Generally, the Chinese tried to escape the rigors of plantation life as quickly as possible, after buying out the remaining years of servitude and assisting others to do so. The Chinese saw the neglected rural communities as their niche markets, so they went and set up shops in nooks and crannies, often taking local women as partners. The "Chinese shop" became the community center where groceries, alcohol, bread, and pudding were readily available. In this way they formed an integral part of the plantation network by supplying local workers with daily necessities prior to field labor. From the early twentieth century, they migrated from rural to urban locations, setting up larger enterprises and availing better opportunities for their children.

Indian Indentureship

The island of Mauritius deep in the Indian Ocean became the initial testing ground for the "great experiment" of the production of sugar by free labor (Carter 2006, p. 267). As we have seen, the British and French used the Indian model as the basis for their negotiations with the Chinese authorities, hoping to avoid the abuses of the Cuban situation. In this way Chinese indentureship in the non-Hispanic Caribbean was far less abusive than in Spanish Cuba. Being close to India, Mauritius had a long and intimate relationship with India. From the time of its possession by France in 1721, who named it "Ile de France," the island saw a constant influx of Indian slaves, artisans, and soldiers through the activities of the French East India Company. After all, the French held a strong base at Pondicherry on India's southeastern coast. At the beginning of the nineteenth century, just before British conquest in 1810, there were about 6,000 Indian slaves on the island together with many other free Indians, some of whom were themselves owners of slaves. The prohibitive cost of bringing skilled workers from Europe enabled Indian jewellers, shopkeepers, seamen, and sailors to be recruited on contract from 1729. Mauritius was also an exile station for Indian convicts.

British conquest in 1810 signalled a boost in sugar production as a viable alternative in the same way that the Sugar Revolution had earlier changed the Caribbean economy. The technology had been developed for the Caribbean, the price of sugar in Europe was attractive, and there were willing Mauritian and British investors. The presence of a previously settled Indian community, derived from sugar-producing areas of Northern India, was a favorable factor. To top it all, the British government granted tariff equality with British West Indian sugar, for entering the British market in 1821. Between 1834 and 1838, a total of 25,468 Indians were contracted in India for labor in Mauritius. By 1917 when the Indian government ended the further recruitment of Indians, no less than 450,000 girmityas (agreement signers) had arrived in Mauritius. By this time too, 152,189 had gone to Natal, 60,695 to Fiji, and 4,579 to Reunion. The Indian Ocean contingent was certainly larger than the Atlantic.

The administrative model developed in Mauritius became the basis for the opening up of further indentureship, first to British Guiana in 1838, to the wider Caribbean in 1845, to Natal in 1860, and to Fiji in 1879. The same model was used by the Dutch in respect of Suriname and by the French in Reunion, Martinique, and Guadeloupe. As the system matured, there were stops and starts as the administrators sought to correct abuses pointed out by ship captains, doctors, the Anti-Slavery Society, and anti-indenture groups in India.

The initial period of indentureship did not go well. In Mauritius and in British Guiana, accommodation and health facilities were poor, contracts were not clear, and the gender disparity was atrocious. When the Calcutta agents of Sir John Gladstone (the initiator of Indo-Caribbean indentureship) asked the noble lord about the proportion of women to be sent to British Guiana, they were given the Mauritian formula. This was one woman for every ten men "for cooking and washing" (Bahadur 2014, p. 79). In 1839 the trade was stopped as reforms were pondered. In 1842, under pressure of continuing demand from the plantocracy in the Atlantic and Indian ocean colonies, the British government allowed the resumption under new government controls. Among the reorganized plans, immigration depots were set up in Calcutta, Madras, and Bombay with staff appointed to oversee the recruitment, accommodation, and dispatch of the girmityas from India. To remedy the gender imbalance, bounties were offered to migrating families, and immigration depots were also established in the receiving colonies to be presided over by a protector of immigrants. This officer replaced the stipendiary magistrate in the former slave colonies, who had been appointed to oversee the proper treatment of the former enslaved. The protector of immigrants, like the stipendiary magistrate, was drawn from the European ruling class. Most of these "protectors" showed little sympathy for the girmityas; there were few exceptions. In India contractors called "arkatias" or "maistries" were appointed to recruit potential agreement signers. Many of these arkatias used trickery to entice their targets. For example, they told rosy tales about a place called Chinidad (land of sugar) instead of Trinidad; Mauritius was Mirch Desh (country of peppers), and Suriname was Sri Ram (God's abode). In the colonies "sirdars" (labor supervisors) were hired as intermediaries between the planters and the workers. In the colonial setting, these sirdars emerged as local overlords. Many of them opened shops near the estates and pressured their workers to patronize those places where credit could be obtained during the slack season. The one item which was abundant and cheap was rum, a product of slave and indentured labor and the bane of family life in the Atlantic and Indian Ocean plantations. This of course provided an attractive base for North American and European temperance groups which, like the Anti-Slavery Society, was constantly seeking for new things to abolish. None of these groups attacked the plantation system, the root of the evil.

As part of the reorganization of the system, immigration agents were appointed at the ports of embarkation. In Calcutta there were two such agents located at Garden Reach on the Hooghly River, a regular point of departure. One agent was recruited for British Guiana and Natal; the other handled Fiji, Mauritius, and the Caribbean. The Bombay depot scoured the Western Ghats for the plantation colonies, and the French depot was located at Pondicherry, recruiting for the French Caribbean and Reunion. In 1882 the British closed this French station. As the nineteenth century progressed, there were frequent changes and amendments as the system matured. As Brij Lal has asserted "the patterns varied but the process remained the same" (Lal 2012, p. 44). For most of the period of indentureship, the girmitya was indentured for 5 years, on an estate to which he was allocated by the colonial administration. He then had to spend another 5 years either as a re-indentured or free person. It was only after this period of "industrial residence" that he and family were entitled to a return passage.

While the majority of the immigrants worked on sugar estates, some were indentured to other occupations such as clearing forests, cocoa, and coconut plantations and rearing animals in a system in which animal power was used up to the twentieth century. A good example of the diverse ways in which Indian indentured labor was spread out can be found in Natal. In addition to their use in sugar areas on the coast, Natal employed them as farm laborers and domestics. Some were indentured in coal mines and in the tea industry which was dependent on Indian women. After indentureship this industry collapsed (Beall 1990, p. 96). A working day consisted of 9 h except on Sundays and public holidays. Adult men, that is, those above 15, were paid a shilling a day, and women, children, and "weakly men" earned 9 pennies, three quarters of a shilling. The workers received rations for the first 6 months, rent-free dwellings in logies or barracks which offered little privacy, and free medical care. A strict legal regimen operated in which desertion and vagrancy were considered criminal offences and, in the absence of trade unions, the workers had to depend on the protector of immigrants.

Despite the efforts of the British government to keep the system under control, the planters in the colonies were constantly seeking loopholes to reduce their costs of maintaining the system. They had to pay two-thirds the cost, the other one-third coming from the tax-paying public. As aforementioned, the Indian and his family were entitled to a return fare after 10 years. Colonial administrators did their best to discourage repatriation by offering concessions. In 1869 Indians were offered 10 acres if they abandoned their right of return. In 1872 this offer was modified when the time expired Indian was offered 10 acres or an alternative of 5 pounds and 5 acres. In 1881 the offer was reduced to 5 pounds, and in 1889 the incentive of land or money was withdrawn. Five years later when it was clear that most of the Indians were opting to remain, the incentive was further reduced. The men had to contribute

Table 2 Indentured Indians to the Caribbean, 1838–1917

Territory	Number of immigrants
British Guiana	238,909
Trinidad	147,000
Guadeloupe	42,326
Jamaica	37,027
Suriname	34,404
Martinique	25,404
French Guiana	8,500
Grenada	3,200
Belize	3,000
St. Vincent	2,472
St. Kitts	337
St. Croix	300

25% and the women 16 2/3%. In 1898 these rates were doubled (Laurence 2011, p. 42). On average about 75% of the Indians remained in the colonies (Table 2).

Indentured Women

As we have already noted, there was a marked paucity of Chinese women in Cuba. In the case of the Southern Caribbean, the situation was better since there were Christian missionaries in South China who were actively promoting family migration. Because of this, 16.6% of Chinese who went to British Guiana were women, and 14.7% of those who went to Suriname were women. In the Indian case the disparity was lower but still inadequate for the formation of stable family life. Indian men were unwilling to cohabit with non-Indians because of their religious belief so there was intense competition for the available women. Despite repeated efforts of the Indian government to recruit women, the proportion of women rarely topped 33% until the 1890s from which time there was a gradual increase. From that time until 1917 the proportion rose to around 45%. As more and more women arrived, they joined the labor force, many as field laborers doing weeding, planting vegetables among the cane rows, carrying manure, and being paniharis (water carriers). They worked alongside the men, but at lower wages and at the end of the field day, they went home to cooking, house cleaning, and looking after children. Prior to the colonial experience, they were often victims of abuse on the ships by sailors, topazes (cleaners), and other shipmates. On the estates they were abused by sirdars, white overseers, and other persons in authority. Because of Christian prejudice, Hindu and Muslim marriages were not recognized during indentureship, so that widows could not claim their husbands' inheritance. Many a widow had to vacate the family home as the state seized and sold their properties. Of course those who had converted to Christianity did not suffer such indignity, and their children were not registered as "illegitimate" with all disadvantages inherent in that designation.

Table 3 Indentured Indians to the Indian and Pacific Ocean, 1834–1917

Colony	Year	Number
Mauritius	1834–1917	453,000
South Africa (Natal)	1860–1911	152,189
Reunion	1860–1882	4,579
Fiji	1879–1916	60,695

Despite these odds, both Indian and Chinese women were able to creatively adapt to the new Atlantic and Pacific worlds into which they were transported. Their scarcity gave them the opportunity to choose partners, unlike the practice in their ancestral places. The Indian custom of dowry (bride price) was now irrelevant. Women could now embark on professions outside of their castes and class. Those who had dared to cross the dark waters were a cut above their peers and were the driving force behind reconstitution of their culture through maintenance of the ancestral identity in formative societies such as Mauritius, Natal, Reunion, or Suriname. They were the ones who insisted on the maintenance of the *rites de passage* for their children. On these occasions the leading singers were the women who preserved the chants and melodies transported from India. This practice continues today in the diasporic homelands. That process of personality change had in fact started in Asia, at the "coolie depots" in Guandong or Calcutta. In these collecting centers, people of all castes, regions, and religions were bundled together for long periods as they awaited the next ship. That mixing continued on the ships which did the long crossings across many seas. Misery acquainted strange bedfellows, and among the Indians a camaraderie developed, a brotherhood of the boat (jahagi bhai/bahin) which bonded the shipmates permanently. In the colonies these jahagis sought continuous contact and gave needy assistance in times of celebrations and of troubles on the plantation. Many mixed marriages took place at the depots, on board ship, and on the sugar estates. The colonial Indian after indentureship was no longer the same Indian who had earlier crossed the kala pani (dark waters). The experience abroad changed the Indian personality so much that most of those who were repatriated sought re-indentureship. Many were rejected by kith and kin because they had lost caste by crossing the dark waters. In India they were called "tapuha" island people who drank alcohol, felt superior to their Indian brother, dressed differently, and greeted with a handshake rather than the graceful clasped hands ("namaste"). Many of these returnees were fleeced by relatives and holy men and formed a colony in Metiabruz on the Hooghly River eagerly hoping to be re-indentured abroad. This colony was the source for many of these who were re-indentured. After 1917 this was impossible (Table 3).

The Movement Toward Abolition

In March of 1917, the Indian Legislative Council resolved to end the further recruitment of Indians for indentured service abroad. This decision came at the end of a long campaign waged on many fronts, to end the system. There was considerable agitation in the colonies themselves particularly in Natal, Mauritius, and Fiji. When the benefits came, the Caribbean Indians also gained their freedom although their participation was minimal. Among the immediate causes, the demands of the First World War (1914–1918) figured prominently. Indian men were required for the theaters of war, agricultural workers were needed in India to provide food for the British army and fodder for the horses, and the threat of German submarines made oceanic movement hazardous. This was particularly noticeable for the Atlantic passage. In addition, tea planters in Assam and jute producers in Bengal renewed their clamor for more and more cheap labor. Why should Indians be exported when they were needed at home? In India itself, the major pressure group in the struggle for independence, the Indian National Congress (INC), made this issue a major item in their nationalist struggle. At the rural level in India, a folk tradition had developed highlighting the evils of indentureship. A typical song was as follows:

> The arkatia came with promise and lies Oh! The suffering and the pain of the journey
> Few were there who did not cry
> Many preferred to die
> We were told that were going to a land with so much gold
> Now that we are here Oh! Our bodies are melting like gold. (Mahase 2007, p. 159)

Pamphlets were printed and distributed widely in the villages warning people about arkatias:

> Don't get enmeshed in their meshes, you will repent
> They take you overseas!
> To Jamaica, Fiji, Damra, Mauritions
> British Guiana Trinidad and Honduras. (Mahase 2007, p. 162)

The Anti-Slavery and Aborigines Protection Society took up the issue in Britain, adding to the other pressures from all around. As the agitation picked up during the First World War, the Colonial Office became increasingly worried that the agitation might reach the Caribbean. One intelligence report indicated that some Indians had been visiting the Caribbean gathering information which could be made public (Mahase 2007, p 241). Such information, circulated during wartime, could be useful propaganda for Germany. It was now necessary to keep the Caribbean outside of the international campaign. The abolition of the system in Natal in 1911 came about largely as a result of the leadership of Gandhi. This set the stage for further abolition. By 1917 the system had become very unpopular. The British Guiana Immigration Agent in Calcutta advised the Colonial Office in early 1917 that emigration had "not a single friend in India outside of the walls of the Emigration Agencies." The European resident was either lukewarm or opposed to the system, and the general public had accepted the views of Andrews, Gandhi, and other campaigners. There were also caste objections to overseas travel (Mahase 2007, p. 237). In 1917 all further recruitment was stopped, and in 1920 the system was abolished.

The Legacy of Indentureship

As we have seen, Chinese indentureship in Cuba contributed significantly to the further development of the profitable plantation system, started earlier under slavery. Chinese food became part of the Cuban diet, and Little Havana remains as a haven of Chinese activity to this day. The Lion Dance became part of the Cuban Carnival, and many Chinese fought in the 10 Years War (1868–1878) which was the first part of the Cuban Revolutionary struggle against Spain. In the British, French, and Dutch Caribbean, the Chinese opened up the rural interior areas through their vegetable gardens but more significantly through the provision of goods and services where most of the laboring population resided. Because of their thrift and industry, they established themselves in these rural communities and later moved to the urban centers as merchants whose children became part of the professional elite. The Chinese were not religious in the Indian sense but followed the principles of Confucianism and Taoism which stressed ancestor worship, filial piety, the importance of the clan and the family, and the benefits of hard work, courage, and fearlessness.

In the case of the Indians, there was a similar development of the sugar industry on the plantation model. The investors here were European and North American, and in the case of Fiji, the overlords were Australian. All of these formed part of a global cartel which wielded enormous power in parliaments and elite societies such as the West India Committee in London. European warships were always close at hand to quell workers' uprisings and to appoint a Commission of Inquiry as a sop to the dead or injured. Such Commission reports invariably placed the blame on "troublemakers" and "ring leaders" or "Communists" after the First World War. At the ground level, the indentured workers brought prosperity to the plantation owners. In Fiji sugar replaced cotton as a viable alternative, and in Mauritius forest lands were converted into prosperous sugar estates. In the Caribbean, Indians were used to open up swamps and jungles in newly conquered colonies such as British Guiana (1810) and Trinidad (1803). These two colonies prospered, while their neighbors declined during the second half of the nineteenth century.

Indian survival and productivity in the colonies of the Old and New World can be ascribed to spiritual values which informed their physical activity. Their major religions, Hinduism and Islam, were in fact their culture. Coming from an agrarian society, this culture was based on gleanings from the natural environment which have been sacralized. The earth is Mother Earth (Dharti Mata), and the cow is Mother Cow (Gai Mata). The natural environment is therefore more than a physical space. It is, rather, a collection of sacred objects to be worshipped or to be used in worship.

The majority of the agreement signers had advanced notice that they were going to do agricultural work. Those who were not informed through official channels received information from returnees from the colonies. To encourage them into colonial agricultural production, the British allowed the Indians to carry on board a cloth handbag called the jahaji bandal (ship's belongings) in which they were allowed to carry a few items. The Muslims stored a copy of the Holy Qu'ran, and the Hindus stored a text such as the Ramayana which is a tale of exile and return of the deity Lord Rama. These texts served as their sources of spiritual sustenance in far-off lands – such as Suriname, Natal, and Fiji. Equally important was the wide array of seeds and cuttings, fruits, and herbs which changed the geography of all the new destinations. These items of flora can be found as readily in the markets of Patna in India, Starbroek in Guyana, or Port Louis in Mauritius.

The list of items of flora which were fitted into this *jahaji bandal* is long and impressive. Among these were mango (aam), guavas (amrudh), pomegranate (anar), string bean (bodi), Indian drumstick (saijan/moringa), pumpkins (khora, khadu), loofa (jinghi), marijuana, datura, rice (chawal), sapodilla (chicu), betel nut (supari), turmeric (haldi), bitter gourd (caraillee), ginger (adhrak), curry plant (karapillay), cinnamon (dalchini), mustard (sarson), black pepper (kali mirch), onion (pyaj), cumin (geera), fennel (sauf), fenugreek (maithi), long gourd (lowki), and cloves (laung), as well as the seeds of the ashoka, bael, neem, and lotus (kumud). In the *jahaji bandal*, they brought a whole range of spinach (bhaji) seeds as well as the full panoply of Indian lentils (dhal). Some of the seeds brought, like guava and citrus, had been brought to the region before the arrival of the Indians, but India now supplied new varieties which improved the native stock.

In other trading arrangements, Indian plants were introduced. For example, the jackfruit (*A. integrifolia*), known as "cowa." Black pepper (*Piper nigrum*) was brought from Travancore and Malabar in South India. In 1806, two nutmeg plants were brought from India to Trinidad, and those were sent to St. Vincent where they were successfully cultivated. In 1820, mature plants were sent back to Trinidad where they were soon cultivated commercially in the valleys of the Northern Range. At this time also Grenada received its nutmeg seeds from which a major industry – still in profitable existence today – was started. Similarly, through inter-botanical garden transfers, the hibiscus (*Hibiscus tiliaceus*) was brought to the colonies, becoming as prolific as the mango, a constant sight in all countries, used for daily worship, as a toothbrush, as a fodder for animals, and for the creation of pretty hedges and flower gardens. In addition, cocoa producers found, in the Poovan banana plants, imported from Mysore, an ideal shade for their young plants, as well as a delicious fruit which sold well in the market place.

The introduction of animals for the promotion of the sugar industry is perhaps as important as the flora just described. Colonial plantation owners were very concerned about snake and rat infestation of their fields. In this regard, the Indian mongoose was brought to Jamaica in 1860, Barbados in 1870, and St Lucia in 1885. From these islands, the animal was exported to sugar estates as far north as Cuba and Puerto Rico. Eventually these rodents became pests, particularly to poultry farmers who have had to take all kinds of precautionary measures to control their flock. Another useful animal brought to the colonies was the goat. Hundreds of goats were introduced as leftovers from the indenture ships. Goats and sheep were taken on board to supplement the shipboard meals for the lascars (Indian seamen) and for nonvegetarian immigrants. Some of these animals reached the colonies and were distributed among the estates, where their hardiness ensured their reproduction in the new place. As British breeders realized the potential of these ruminants for meat, milk, and hide production, they were crossed with other varieties sent to the colonies. Another animal brought on the indenture ships was the Indian zebu cattle whose huge humps store water for use when normal sources are unavailable. These strong animals were used as replacements for estate mules which often foundered in the heavy clay soils of the plantations. During the second half of the nineteenth century, they were extensively used in the British, Dutch, and French colonies, not only for haulage but also for meat, leather, and milk.

Over time, however, poor husbandry on the estates led to a high incidence of tuberculosis causing considerable loss among the herds. A search was then made for an alternative animal which was hardier than the cattle. This search again led to India where the water buffalo (*Bos bubalis*) had been in use since around 3000 BC. In addition to being a good haulage animal, the "bhaisa" was an excellent milk producer and, at the beginning of the twentieth century, India was an exporter of over five million hides annually. The animal's thick skin kept mites away, and they were rarely troubled by flies and screwworms, which normally wrought havoc among cattle. From 1905, water buffaloes were imported by colonial planters and, by the time of the First World War, they were being widely used on the estates. Such importation continued until 1949, by which time at least eight breeds had arrived in the colonies. Among these were the Murrah, Surti, Jaffarbadi, Mehsana, Nagpuri, Nelli, Ravi, and Bhadawaria. Over the decades these breeds were intermixed as they became popular, not only on the sugar plantations but also in the rice fields. In Trinidad, as in Venezuela, Jamaica, Colombia, and Guyana, it was found that the buffaloes thrived in grass that was high in fiber and that they were well adapted to the hot humid tropical conditions. In addition, they were much easier to break in than zebu cattle. A study published by researchers at the University of the West Indies in 2017 reported that water buffalo meat is more tender than beef from Brahma cattle of the same age, gender, and diet. The study also indicated that water buffalo milk is higher in fat than cow's milk and has been used locally to make cottage cheese (paneer), yogurt (dahi), ghee, and sweets (barfi).

The grand finale of the faunal development was the creation of a new animal through a project of genetic selection and crossbreeding undertaken by scientists at the University of the West Indies. Led by veterinarian Dr. Steve Bennett, the team was able to produce an animal which combined the best qualities of the Indian breeds, producing an animal that gave meat, milk, leather, and haulage qualities, so that the benefits could be widespread. The new animal was called the buffalypso which was a combination of *buffalo* and *calypso*, which is Trinidad's most popular musical genre. By 1967, production of the buffalypso was in full swing as these animals were exported to Argentina, Costa Rica, Miami, Brazil, Mexico, and Columbia where buffalypso milk was used in the making of soft cheeses, ice cream and mozzarella, queso blanco, and queso de mano. The water buffalo and its successor, the buffalypso, remain one of India's prize contributions to the tropical world.

Descendants of the Immigrants

In addition to their impact on the physical environment, indentured workers were able to rise above their assigned plantation roles to become leaders in many spheres of colonial life. A sampling will be given here. Dai Ailian (1916–2006) was the granddaughter of Ah Sek (Little Pebble) who was indentured in the canefields of central Trinidad. After his bondage, Ah Sek established a shop at a major junction which today continues to bear his name. His son Dai Yao continued the business and was able to send his daughter Dai Ailian to the capital city where she started her career as a ballet dancer in the English mode. In 1931 her mother took her to London where she perfected her art which she took back to Hong Kong. In China she revived Chinese ethnic dances, and in 1954 she was appointed principal of the Beijing Dance School where she produced signature works. During the Cultural Revolution, she was sidelined, but after Mao's death in 1976 she was reinstated, becoming Director of the Chinese National Ballet. In this capacity she popularized Chinese dance worldwide (Glasstone 2007). In a similar manner, Arthur Raymond Chung (1918–2000) arose from a rural Chinese settlement in Guyana to become an Appeal Court judge and the first President of Guyana when it became a Republic in 1970. Similarly Sir Solomon Hochoy (1905–1983) son of Chinese laborers transported first to Jamaica and later to Trinidad worked his way up in the Civil Service, becoming Trinidad's first Governor-General at that nation's Independence in 1962. There were Chinese from the colonies who travelled to China to liberate the mother land from European and Japanese occupation. Diasporic Indians also returned to join India's freedom struggle. To them Mahatma Gandhi was a major inspiration in their colonial battles. In Mauritius Sir Seewoosagur Ramgoolam, son of Indian immigrant from Bihar, India, became the first prime minister of that island upon its Independence in 1968, holding that office until his death in 1985. In a nation of considerable diversity, he was able to forge unity and to create a viable, prosperous nation. This of course was in marked contrast to the career of Dr. Cheddi Jagan who initiated the anti-colonial struggle during the Second World War. Sadly for Jagan his ascendancy during the Cold War was the cause of his exclusion from office and his imprisonment. His Marxism was like a red rag to the British and the Americans who effectively curbed his bids for high office. In 1992, with the Communist threat lessened, he returned to high office as President of Guyana, holding that office until his death in 1997.

Conclusion

The system of indentureship was a major movement in world history. It saw the transference of millions of laboring folk, mainly from India and China to the Atlantic and Pacific regions in a complex network of arrangements. The system was supervised from European capitals to which the profits of this lucrative trade gravitated, affording European capitalist development. The fortunes of this enterprise hardly reached the major producers of the wealth, namely, the enslaved African or the indentured Asian. These lives were influenced by factors over which they had no control. When, for example, bounty-fed beet sugar arose as a serious competitor to cane sugar, plantations in all the colonies went into decline during the late nineteenth century. As the sugar colonies picked up during the early twentieth century, the First World War interrupted the transfer of sugar and its derivatives because of the hazards of shipping on open seas. In these fluctuations, it was the working class which suffered, at the base of the plantation pyramid. To their credit, the working class creatively survived these traumas. They had come from civilizations of ancient vintage, bringing with them a penchant for hard work, persistence in the face of adversity, close family bonding, and a deep spiritual attachment to the land as the major sustainer of life. They introduced new schools of Islam as well as Hindu philosophy and practice. As these ancestral beliefs interacted with Christianity, new syncretic forms evolved, adding to the cultural diversity of the receiving colonies. Oriental forms of music, dance, culinary practice, different forms of dress and of ways of seeing now added to the evolution of cosmopolitan societies. In this way the immigrants disproved the prediction of the English poet Laureate Rudyard Kipling that East is East and West is West and ne'er the twain shall meet. Perhaps a more appropriate conclusion can be that of Williams Shakespeare who wisely wrote that "Sweet are the uses of adversity, which like the toad, though ugly and venomous, wears yet a precious jewel on its head."

References

Allen R (2016) New perspectives on the origins of the new system of slavery. In: Hassan-Khan et al (eds) The legacy of Indian indenture. Manohar, Delhi
Aykroyd WR (1967) Sweet malefactor: sugar, slavery and human society. Heinemann Press, London
Bahadur G (2014) Coolie woman. University of Chicago Press, Chicago
Beall J (1990) Women under indenture in Natal. In: Bhana S (ed) Essays on indentured Indians in Natal. Peepal Tree Press, Leeds
Carter M (2006) Mauritius. In: Lal BV (ed) Encyclopedia of the Indian diaspora. University of Hawaii Press, Honolulu
Cuba Commission (1876) Chinese emigration: report of the commission sent by China to ascertain the condition of Chinese Coolies in Cuba. Imperial Maritime Customs Press, Shanghai
Davis R (1973) The rise of the Atlantic economies. Cornell University Press, New York
Glasstone R (2007) The story of Dai Ailian. Dance books, London
Helly D (1993) Introduction to the Cuba Commission Report (1876). In: A hidden history of the Chinese Cuba. Johns Hopkins University Press, Baltimore
Lal BV (ed) (2006) Encyclopedia of the Indian diaspora. University of Hawaii Press, Honolulu
Lal BV (2012) The odyssey of indenture. Australian National University, Canberra
Laurence KO (2011) The importation of labour and the contract system. In: Laurence KO (ed) General history of the Caribbean, vol IV. UNESCO Publishing, Paris
Looklai W (1993) Indentured labour, Caribbean sugar. John Hopkins University Press, Baltimore
Mahase R (2007) Indian indentured labour in Trinidad. PhD thesis. University of the West Indies, Trinidad
Northrup D (1995) Indentured labour in the age of imperialism. Cambridge University Press, Cambridge
Pan L (1966) Sons of the yellow emperor: the story of the Chinese overseas. Mandarin paperback, London
Seecharan C (2005) Sweetening bitter sugar. Ian Randle, Jamaica
Stuart A (2012) Sugar in the blood. Portobello Books, London
Teelock V (1998) Bitter sugar: sugar and slavery in 19th century Mauritius. Mahatma Gandhi Instituted, Moka
Teelock V (2009) Mauritian history. Mahatma Gandhi Institute, Moka
Tinker H (1974) A new system of slavery. Oxford University Press, London
Walvin J (1997) Fruits of empire: exotic produce and British trade. New York University Press, New York

United Nations Migrant Workers Convention

92

Sheetal Sheena Sookrajowa and Antoine Pécoud

Contents

Introduction	1814
Historical Background	1815
Content	1816
Obstacles to the ICMW	1818
Legal Barriers	1818
Economic Obstacles	1819
Political Obstacles	1820
Lack of Awareness	1821
Public Attitudes	1821
National Sovereignty	1822
Limitations of the ICMW	1822
Conclusion	1824
References	1825

Abstract

The International Convention on the Protection of the Rights of All Migrant Workers and Members of their Families (ICMW) is a comprehensive international human rights mechanism adopted by the United Nations in 1990 with the purpose of protecting the migrant workers and members of their families. However, as compared to other international human rights treaties, the ICMW has been less recognized by States. Till date there are only 54 States which have ratified the Convention, 13 signatories, and 131 No action. The aims of this

---

S. S. Sookrajowa (✉)
Department of History and Political Science, Faculty of Social Sciences and Humanities, University of Mauritius, Réduit, Mauritius
e-mail: s.sookrajowa@uom.ac.mu; sheenasookrajowa@gmail.com

A. Pécoud
University of Paris 13, Paris, France
e-mail: antoine.pecoud@univ-paris13.fr

© The Author(s), under exclusive license to Springer Nature Singapore Pte Ltd. 2019
S. Ratuva (ed.), *The Palgrave Handbook of Ethnicity*,
https://doi.org/10.1007/978-981-13-2898-5_142

chapter are therefore to provide a general assessment of the Convention and to identify the major obstacles that explain the low level of ratification. The obstacles include political will, legal barriers, economic obstacles, political obstacles, lack of awareness, public attitudes, and national sovereignty. This chapter also sheds light on the limitations of the ICMW in States which have ratified it, namely, Guatemala, Ecuador, Mexico, and Sri Lanka. Overall, the findings reveal that though these States have ratified the ICMW, they do not fully conform to its obligations as there are still legal discrepancies, lack of awareness, corruption, and poor governance. However, the ICMW remains an important and highly relevant international human rights framework to govern the transnational mobility of people.

Keywords
United Nations · International human rights law · Migrant workers · Migration governance

Introduction

Since the early 1990s, the world has experienced an ongoing "migration crisis", as the mobility of people – in relation to major geopolitical turbulences such as the war in the Balkans, the collapse and instability in countries of the former Soviet Union, the fall of the apartheid system in South Africa, conflicts in Africa and the Middle East, or the Arab uprisings – has been apprehended as a destabilizing process for States and societies. This has cast doubts on States' capacity to govern migration while also fueling anti-immigrants' feelings among host populations and exclusionary policies. Foreigners and people of foreign origin face a wide range of difficulties, such as discrimination, unemployment or deplorable living and working conditions (Weiner 1995; Castles, de Haas and Miller 2013). According to the International Organization for Migration (2017), the number of international migrants worldwide was approximately 244 million in 2015, a rise from the year 2000 estimates of 155 million people.

Adopted by the United Nations (UN) General Assembly in 1990, the International Convention on the Protection of the Rights of All Migrant Workers and Members of their Families (ICMW) is a major human rights treaty that addresses some of the most pressing issues in the "age of migration" (Castles et al. 2013). As one of the nine core international human rights instruments adopted between 1965 and 2006 (Office of the High Commissioner for Human Rights (OHCHR) 2018), the ICMW is designed to uphold the rights of migrant workers, whether in a regular or irregular situation. It details the way fundamental human rights – such as civil, political, economic, social, cultural rights or access to courts, and tribunals – apply to migrants and members of their families (de Guchteneire and Pécoud 2009; Pécoud 2009).

However, the ICMW is among the most forgotten treaties in international human rights law (Batistella 2009; Pécoud 2017). It suffers from a low number of State Parties, as only 54 States have ratified it, 13 have signed it, and 131 have taken no action (OHCHR 2018). According to Taran (2009), such under-ratification is an expression of the conflict between globalization and the necessary mobility of labor across borders on the one hand and the need for protection and for a right-based approach toward the governance of migration on the other. Ruhs (2012) argues that this low ratification record shows that most governments do not consider the rights of migrants as "real" human rights that should be guaranteed by international law.

Yet, despite the diverse setbacks pertaining to its ratification, the ICMW is perhaps more significant today than it ever was, as more and more people are on the move. With an increasing number of migrants worldwide and the relative rise of human rights violations toward migrants, the ICMW represents a potentially relevant strategy to safeguard the human rights of migrants (Desmond 2017). In this context, this chapter aims at providing a general assessment of the ICMW, identifying the major obstacles that prevent its ratification, and highlighting the diverse limitations toward its full implementation.

Historical Background

After World War I, at the time of the 1919 Treaty of Versailles, States founded the League of Nations, with the purpose of stabilizing the relationships between countries and to prevent another devastating war. The International Labour Organization (ILO) was created on the same occasion, as a "specialized agency" whose mandate was to enhance the conditions of workers worldwide; States thus recognized that peace required not only diplomatic efforts between States but also decent living and working conditions for their populations (Hasenau 1991; Batistella 2009). Importantly, this included the protection of migrant workers, and the preamble of the draft constitution of the ILO thus mentioned "the protection of the interests of workers when employed in countries other than their own." The ILO regularly reaffirmed this principle, notably in the 1944 Philadelphia Declaration and the 1998 Declaration on Fundamental Principles and Rights at Work. It also adopted two international conventions on migrant workers' rights: the Migration for Employment Convention (Revised) in 1949 (ILO Convention 97) and the Migrant Workers (Supplementary Provisions) Convention in 1975 (ILO Convention 143) (ILO 2009). These treaties have however had "mixed success" with regard to ratification (Pécoud 2017, p. 25).

The human rights of migrant workers have also been a matter of concern for the UN, at least since a 1972 session of the Economic and Social Council (ECOSOC) during which the unlawful trafficking of African workers was reported and discussed. On 17 December 1979, the UN General Assembly adopted a resolution entitled "Measures to Improve the Situation and Ensure the Human Rights and Dignity of All Migratory Workers," and a working group was set up to prepare the ICMW (Rao Penna 1993, p. 180). The working group was composed of UN member states and other institutions, like the UN Commission on Human Rights; the UN Commission for Social Development; the ILO; the UN Educational, Scientific, and Cultural Organization (UNESCO); and the World Health Organization (WHO) which also took part in the drafting of the Convention (Edelenbos 2005). The drafting process took around 9 years, from 1980 to 1989; the working group finalized the draft in June 1990, and the ICMW was approved by the UN General Assembly on 18 December 1990. In 2003, 13 years after adoption, the ICMW entered into force after obtaining the 20 ratifications needed (de Guchteneire and Pécoud 2009). Confronted to a slow and uncertain process of ratification, a number of international organizations (IOs) and non-governmental organizations (NGOs) launched a Global Campaign for Ratification of the Convention in 1998, both at local and international levels, which contributed to subsequently raise the number of ratifications (Edelenbos 2005).

Content

The ICMW is designed to ensure that migrant workers benefit from the protection afforded by human rights, including civil, political, economic, social, and cultural rights. In so doing, the ICMW hinges mainly on already-existing international human rights treaties, whose application to migrant workers had not been explicitly delineated. It does also provide a number of new rights targeting migrant workers, such as the right to transfer remittances or to have access to information on the migration process (Pécoud 2017).

The ICMW (1990) is a long document, composed of 9 parts and 23 articles. Part I presents its scope and definition. Part II provides a general statement with regard to "non-discrimination with respect to rights" stipulating that State Parties should conform to the Convention by respecting the rights of all migrant workers and members of their families irrespective of the "sex, race, colour, language, religion or conviction, political or other opinion, national, ethnic or social origin, nationality, age, economic position, property, marital status, birth or other status."

Part III (Articles 8–35) focuses on the "Human Rights of All Migrant Workers and Members of their Families." This therefore also pertains to migrants in an irregular situation (Article 35). The rights include the right to leave any State, including their State of origin (Article 8); the right to life (Article 9); the right not to be exposed to torture or to cruel, inhuman or degrading treatment or punishment and not to be held in slavery or servitude or carry out forced or compulsory labour (Article 10 and 11); the right to freedom of thought, conscience and religion (Article 12); the right to hold opinions without interference and the right to freedom of expression (Article 13); the right not to be exposed to arbitrary or unlawful interference (Article 14); the right not to be indiscriminately deprived of property (Article 15); the right to liberty and security (Article 16); the right to be treated with humanity, particularly for migrants who are deprived of their liberty (Article 17); the right to equality with nationals of the receiving State before courts and tribunals (Article 18); the right not to be "held guilty of any criminal offence on account of any act or omission that did not constitute a criminal offence under national or international law at the time when the criminal offence was committed" (Article 19); the right not to be "imprisoned merely on the ground of failure to fulfil a contractual obligation" (Article 20); not to destroy any identity documents such as passport of a migrant worker (Article 21); not to be exposed to measures of collective expulsion (Article 22); the right "to have recourse to the protection and assistance of the consular or diplomatic authorities of their State of origin...whenever the rights recognized in the present Convention are impaired" (Article 23); the right to recognition everywhere as a person before the law (Article 24); the right to join in trade union (Article 26); the right to social security (Article 27); the right to medical care (Article 28); the right to a name, birth registration, nationality (Article 29); the right to education of each child of migrant worker (Article 30); the right to have their culture respected (Article 31); the right for migrants to transfer their earnings upon termination of their stay and return to their country (Article 32); and the right to be informed (Article 33).

Part IV (Articles 36–56) lists the "Other Rights of Migrant Workers and Members of their Families who are Documented or in a Regular Situation." Apart from the rights that are listed in Part III, Part IV extends more rights to migrant workers in a regular situation. These rights include the right to be fully informed by the State of origin or the State of employment on the conditions of employment and possibilities for temporary absences (Article 37 and 38); "the right to liberty of movement in the territory of the State of employment and freedom to choose their residence there" (Article 39); "the right to form associations and trade unions in the State of employment" (Article 40); the right to participate in elections in their State of origin (Article 41); the right to have equal treatment as nationals of the State of employment in terms of education, training, housing, social and health services and participation in cultural life (Article 43 and 45); the right to the unity of migrants' families (Article 44); and the right to transfer earnings (Article 47 and 48).

Part V (Articles 57–63) addresses the rights of specific groups of migrant workers, such as frontier workers, seasonal workers, itinerant workers, project-tied workers, and self-employed workers. Part VI refers to the "Promotion of sound, equitable, humane and lawful conditions in connection with international migration of workers and members of their families," requiring the development of appropriate policies and measures with regard to such type of migration (Article 65–71). Article 68 of the Convention also calls for the prevention and eradication of "illegal or clandestine movements and employment of migrant workers in an irregular situation." Part VII refers to the application of the Convention. Part IX relates to the final provisions.

A key feature of the ICMW is that it incorporates a comprehensive range of human rights for undocumented migrant workers and members of their families, a category of people that had never been explicitly addressed by international human rights law. The ICMW extends beyond labor rights only (which are mentioned in ILO conventions) and includes civil/political, economic, social, and cultural rights (Böhning 1988). The inclusion of migrants in an undocumented situation has been a particularly controversial issue since adoption of the ICMW, as the extent of State's responsibility to protect such migrants is the object of much political debates (Bosniak 1991).

Georgopoulou et al. (2017) argue that, even if the ICMW replicates to some extent with other international human rights treaties, it is important because it is the only treaty that jointly considers three groups of rights: "entry and stay rights, health and social security rights, and access to justice." The ICMW is thus distinct as it establishes a comprehensive standard on a particular group of people that has not been addressed specifically elsewhere. In the same vein, Grange (2017) recalls that the ICMW explicitly mentions the situation of migrant workers who are placed in detention and lists their rights in this respect (such as the right to receive visits by members of their families), whereas this issue is not even stipulated in other human rights treaties like the International Covenant on Civil and Political Rights (ICCPR).

Obstacles to the ICMW

State Parties to the ICMW come mainly from the Global South and are on the sending side of the migration process. For example, States that played a key role in drafting and advocating the ICMW include Mexico, Morocco, or the Philippines. By contrast, developed states – understood as those that compose the majority of States at the Organisation for Economic Cooperation and Development (OECD) – have displayed a very strong reluctance to ratify the ICMW, with the consequence that States in which important migrant populations live and work are also those that do not implement the provisions contained in the Convention. This situation is at odds with the long-standing commitment of liberal democratic States to human rights and with their traditional role as "champions" of human rights (Vucetic 2007). The fact that no European Union (EU) State has ratified the ICMW is particularly bewildering in this respect. This raises the issue of what obstacles prevent greater acceptance of the ICMW.

According to Patrick Taran (2009), who was the Coordinator of the Global Campaign for ratification from 1998 to 2002, the lack of political will is the prime hurdle to ratify the ILO and UN conventions on the rights of migrant workers. For example, in Asia, in Western countries, and in South Africa, France, or Mauritius, the lack of political will is the major cause for non-ratification (Piper 2009; Grange and d'Auchamp 2009; Crush et al. 2009; Oger 2009; Sookrajowa and Joson 2018). For de Guchteneire and Pécoud (2009), governments that display a political will to ratify the ICMW do so despite possible financial, legal, and administrative obstacles. In sum, there is evidence that governments worldwide do not see migrant workers' rights as a political priority, which is a clear obstacle to the ICMW.

Legal Barriers

In certain countries, domestic laws are deeply incompatible with the provisions of the ICMW: in such cases, ratification faces clear legal obstacles as States would need to substantially modify their legislation (de Guchteneire and Pécoud 2009). Yet, Nafziger and Bartel (1991) note that the provisions of the ICMW intersect with, and resemble very much to, the provisions of other human rights treaties such as the Universal Declaration of Human Rights (UDHR); the International Covenant on

Economic, Social, and Cultural Rights (ICESCR); the International Covenant on Civil and Political Rights (ICCPR); the International Convention on the Elimination of All Forms of Racial Discrimination (ICEAFRD); the Convention on the Elimination of All Forms of Discrimination Against Women (CEAFDAW); the Convention on the Rights of the Child (CRC); and the European Social Charter (ESC). This means that legal obstacles to the ICMW are likely to take place within a broader context of reluctance toward human rights. As far as migrant workers are concerned, the most evident example in this respect is the situation in the Gulf States, where important numbers of migrant workers are active and where governments display negative attitudes toward international human rights law in general (Piper 2009).

By contrast, in OECD countries with a strong ratification record of other human treaties, the legal provisions of the ICMW tend to correspond to existing legislation (Pécoud 2017). For example, Oger (2009) notes that in France, the ratification of the ICMW would be legally congruent with "minor reservations." Touzenis (2009) also argues that the provisions of the ICMW generally conform with Italy's domestic legislations. In a similar vein, Vanheule et al. (2005) sustain that Belgian national law is largely compatible with the Convention and that ratification by the Belgian government would rather be a matter of "high legal symbolic value" than of actual legal change.

There are nevertheless situations in which, even in Western *état de droit*, the ICMW would require important changes in domestic legislation. In Canada, Piché et al. (2009) show that, in the event of ratification, the government would have to reconsider its legal and institutional structure pertaining to the employment of low-skilled foreign workers. Likewise, in Japan, government officials noted that the ICMW contravenes with the domestic laws and the constitution, which hence explain the unwillingness of the government to ratify the Convention (Piper 2009). Similarly, in the United States of America (USA), there would be significant legal implications if the ICMW was to be ratified: even if migrant workers and members of their families are already protected under national laws and the USA Constitution, discrepancies have been noted with regard to undocumented migrants and the right of migrant workers to assume public jobs, social benefits, immigration law, and civil rights (Helton 1991).

Economic Obstacles

Given the economic implications of labor migration, ratification of the ICMW is also a matter of a cost-benefit analysis. Reliance upon migrant labor is often associated with the low wages paid to foreign workers: by increasing their labor protection, the ICMW may therefore have an economic impact, which may fuel States' reluctance toward this treaty. Touzenis and Sironi (2013) show that the ratification and the implementation of the ICMW involve financial and administrative costs, such as "law enforcement, for pursuit of due process and justice, for training of authorities and for public education." Likewise, in Mauritius, as the country is already undergoing economic adversities such as unemployment and has an aging population, the former Minister of Labor affirmed that the main reason for not ratifying the Convention was due to the financial costs that the country would have to bear in terms of social welfare (Sookrajowa and

Joson 2018). This should be nuanced, however, as other studies show that the input of migrant workers through their employment and tax payment in countries of employment exceeds their costs in terms of welfare benefits (Touzenis and Sironi 2013). For example, in Mauritius, migrant workers take up jobs that locals are unwilling to do and contribute to the Mauritian export economy (Sookrajowa and Joson 2018). Rights may also enhance the productivity of workers and hence increase their economic contribution to the economy of receiving countries.

It remains however that the ICMW is at odds with the neoliberal logic according to which, particularly in Western advanced economies, migration has become a source of cheap, flexible, and often semi-legal labor. This takes place in a context that sees States combatting irregular migration while at the same time tolerating such abuses in the name of competitiveness and under employers' pressure. By contrast, the ICMW presupposes that receiving States are willing to intervene to protect labor rights. Finally, it is to be noted that the economic consequences of ratification impact differently sending and receiving countries, as destination countries tend to bear most of the costs of affording rights while origin countries have much less obligations under the ICMW (Ruhs 2012).

Political Obstacles

The unwillingness to ratify the ICMW can be understood as merely a political or electoral obstacle: given that migrants are not citizens, they cannot vote, and governments are therefore unlikely to take measures to improve their situation. Beyond this observation, migrants' rights have important implications in terms of citizenship: traditionally, access to rights has been closely associated with citizenship or at least with a strong membership in the political community. By granting rights to all foreigners, even those in an undocumented situation, the ICMW challenges the privileges of citizenship and blurs the boundaries between insiders and outsiders. While this is deeply logical from a human rights standpoint, it is a challenge for States that echoes Hannah Arendt's classical observations on the "right to have rights" and the difficulty of conciliating the sovereign logic of the State with the universality of human rights.

This is all the more the case because the ICMW calls for a kind of political recognition of migrant workers. According to Article 42:

> (1) States Parties shall consider the establishment of procedures or institutions through which account may be taken, both in States of origin and in States of employment, of special needs, aspirations and obligations of migrant workers and members of their families and shall envisage, as appropriate, the possibility for migrant workers and members of their families to have their freely chosen representatives in those institutions. (2) States of employment shall facilitate, in accordance with their national legislation, the consultation or participation of migrant workers and members of their families in decisions concerning the life and administration of local communities. (3) Migrant workers may enjoy political rights in the State of employment if that State, in the exercise of its sovereignty, grants them such rights.

Such provisions provide migrant workers with a political status that constitutes a challenge for many receiving societies, especially those that do not recognize themselves as countries of immigration or that have racial or ethnic understandings of membership. In countries such as Malaysia or Singapore, characterized by their multiethnic nature, migration policy also serves to preserve a specific ethnic/religious equilibrium, which is why only highly skilled migrants or those who are married to a citizen are granted permanent residence status (Piper 2009). Likewise, in Mauritius, ratification of the ICMW is practically impossible at this stage due to the multiethnic composition of the country and its constitutional arrangement: since the Constitution of Mauritius already classifies the population into communities, ratification of the ICMW would disturb the demographic structure and also require a constitutional review; politicians in Mauritius have thus been very prudent in preserving the ethnic balance (Sookrajowa and Joson 2018).

Lack of Awareness

Along with the obstacles mentioned above, research on the ICMW has evidenced the low awareness that surrounds this treaty (de Guchteneire and Pécoud 2009). Despite initiatives by certain IOs and a handful of NGOs, there have not been continued efforts to raise the consciousness and ratification of the Convention. Although the International Organization for Migration has a newly established department on international migration law to provide training to its member states, it does not have a full human rights mandate and lacks the capacity and legitimacy to uphold and regulate international legal standards (Pécoud 2018; Taran 2009). For example, in South Africa, France, and Germany, the lack of awareness and understanding of the ICMW is the highest current problem to ratification. The ICMW is known to very few activists, academics, and policymakers, to the extent that Convention is in practice "unknown" (Crush et al. 2009; Oger 2009; Hillman and Von Koppenfels 2009). In Italy, Touzenis (2009) shows that low awareness has led to the absence of the ICMW from the political agenda and to a total lack of funding to foster acceptance of this treaty.

Public Attitudes

Taran (2009) classifies "discrimination and xenophobic hostility" toward migrants as a severe obstacle to the global governance of migration. Usually, when there are hostile attitudes such as "racist attitudes or discriminatory behaviors" by nationals toward migrant workers in destination countries, governments are reluctant to provide more rights to migrant workers as this would constitute a political risk (de Guchteneire and Pécoud 2009). In South Africa, as noted by Crush et al. (2009), the perceptions toward migrant workers are increasingly pessimistic and xenophobic, and any policy for the protection of migrants' rights is therefore likely to be unwelcome. Similar problems exist in Europe (Beutin et al. 2006). In Italy, it was reported that in 2004, 72% of the population display negative attitudes toward migrants by stating that "the economic situation in Italy means that we cannot take any more migrants" (Touzenis 2009). For de Guchteneire and Pécoud (2009), racism, xenophobia, and discrimination reflect the uncertain socioeconomic situation such as "unemployment, labour market deregulation, decreasing resources for social security and welfare programmes, political populism…globalisation and terrorism." Whitaker and Giersch (2015, p. 1536) studied attitudes toward immigration in Africa and conclude that in countries which are more democratic; possess leading party systems; are ethnically diverse; and have greater economic development, and when the study is carried out just prior and after election, "oppositions to immigration" are higher and more probable. Tunon and Baruah (2012) maintain that public attitudes are important to be considered while designing policies for migrant workers as attitudes add to situation where there is already unequal treatment of migrant workers.

National Sovereignty

Ratification of the Convention is often associated with "a loss of national sovereignty" (de Guchteneire and Pécoud 2009). However, the ICMW does not restrict the State's sovereignty: Article 79 mentions that "Nothing in the present Convention shall affect the right of each State Party to establish the criteria governing admission of migrant workers and members of their families. Concerning other matters related to their legal situation and treatment as migrant workers and members of their families, States Parties shall be subject to the limitations set forth in the present Convention." Oger (2009) thus sustains that even under ratification "sovereignty is maintained, as states retain monopoly on access to their territory and their labour market." Yet, in South Africa, for example, the question of "political sovereignty" was raised as policymakers feared that the Convention would prevent the state from designing its own policies with regard to the admission of migrants (Crush et al. 2009). Moreover, once human rights treaties are in force, State Parties have to submit periodic reports on their practices and compliance with treaties and may be blamed for human rights violations. States may then be unwilling to ratify international treaties due to the "sovereignty cost" (Wotipka and Tsutsui 2008).

Limitations of the ICMW

The non-ratification of the Convention by EU countries, by traditional countries of immigration such as the USA, Canada, or Australia, as well as by major receiving States in the Global South such as South Africa, is a major and obvious limitation to the ICMW, as it is at odds with the universal nature of human rights as envisaged in the UN Charter and the UDHR. Yet, even in countries in which the Convention has been ratified, there are a number of implementation problems. This section examines the situation in four countries for which in-depth analysis is available.

Ecuador ratified the ICMW in 2002 and has since then promoted the rights of migrants in its 2008 Constitution; yet, major legal inconsistencies have been noted in terms of the implementation of the Convention: the country's 1971 migration law is still effective and determines whom to admit in the country on the basis of potential migrants' contribution to the development of the country. In 2007 and 2010, the Committee on Migrant Workers (CMW), the UN body in charge of monitoring the Convention, has addressed the disparities between Ecuador domestic legislations and the ICMW and concluded that "selectivity, control, security and sovereignty, rather than human rights" are still regulating migration policies in Ecuador. Furthermore, it has also been noted that the ICMW is barely mentioned when debating migration law and policy and is rarely taken into account when it comes to ascertaining the responsibilities of Ecuadoran authorities to protect the rights of migrants in the country. Hence, the "lack of reference suggests a lack of awareness of the ICMW in Ecuador, maybe as a consequence of the proliferation of human rights treaties ratified by Ecuador and the lack of dissemination of such treaties" (Salazar 2017, p. 201).

Another Latin American country, Guatemala, ratified the ICMW in 2003. However, it has been noted that although the government has devised new policies to conform to the provisions of the Convention to protect certain rights of migrants, the ICMW has not been fully applied by the government in general, and the developments have been rather sluggish. Initiatives concern "the detention and expulsion of migrants, regularisation of the irregular migrant population, human trafficking," but are not really in conformity with the Convention. There remain legal differences as Guatemala has not amended its migration law to be in line with the ICMW (Caron et al. 2017). It has, for instance, been observed that Guatemala organizes collective expulsion of migrants, which is incompatible with the ICMW and infringes international norms, and that there are violations of migrants' rights to legal defense. Caron et al. (2017, p. 213) thus assert that "international conventions like the ICMW can in the end become a dead letter if signatories fail to tailor the country's legislation to meet their obligations, and if they lack the will to propose, pass and implement favourable policies for its implementation. Without these measures to ensure internal compliance, the ICMW and other human rights conventions become an empty promise."

The first country to sign the ICMW, in 1991, was Mexico. Although there are progresses in the legal and policy domains, Mexico does not conform to all the obligations of the Convention. The main obstacles to fully abide by the standards of the ICMW are "corruption and impunity endemic" due to the ineffective rule of law in the country and its geographical location as a transit country for Central American irregular migrants and asylum seekers to the USA. Moreover, there is a lack of information that hampers migrants' access to rights, in a context in which transit migration comes along with a serious humanitarian crisis, particularly for women who suffer from oppressive situations. Also, Mexico does not follow the Convention as it does not safeguard child migrants, who are regularly kept in detention centers because of human and financial constraints. According to Prieto and Kuhner (2017, p. 235), there have been significant initiatives to standardize Mexico's domestic legislations with the Convention, and new laws have been developed with regard to "the protection of refugees and asylum seekers; to prevent, punish and eradicate trafficking in persons; to promote assistance for victims of crime and human rights violations; and to guarantee access for women to a life free from violence." The Mexican labor legislation needs to be reinforced to provide more protection to women.

In Asia, Sri Lanka ratified the Convention in 1996 but also faces serious problems in implementing it. Although Sri Lanka has established a comprehensive migration administration system over the past years, it has not yet made significant efforts to bring its domestic legislations in line with the ICMW. For example, the Constitution of Sri Lanka emphasizes the granting of certain rights to citizens only, such as the "protection against discrimination and the right of peaceful assembly, freedom of association, freedom to form and join a trade union, freedom to engage in any lawful occupation, or profession, and freedom of movement" (Wickramasekara 2017, p. 256). The country also has also to cope with a difficult local context, marked by the predominance of low-skilled migration to the Gulf region and the major role by private brokers in governing these flows (Wickramasekara 2017).

In terms of the monitoring of the ICMW, Grange (2017) identifies two final challenges. Firstly, State parties do not always submit their reports to the Committee on Migrant Workers (CMW), which makes it difficult to evaluate compliance with the Convention. Second, the members of the CMW are appointed by State parties and usually occupy positions that are very much associated to their countries' government, rather than serving "in their individual capacity" as stipulated in the Convention. Grant and Lyon (2017) further note that, as all UN human rights treaty bodies have included the rights of migrants in their mandates, there are issues of "overlapping jurisdictions," which creates the possibility of different understandings and interpretations of international human rights law, as well as the risk of treaty bodies acting separately while dealing with the rights of migrants. Grant and Lyon also note that the CMW is not usually mentioned by treaty bodies while referring to issues related to the rights of migrants.

Conclusion

By recognizing the vulnerability of migrant workers and their families, and by encompassing a broad range of rights and situations, the ICMW is an all-inclusive international human rights mechanism that encompasses civil, political, social, economic rights for both regular and irregular migrants. Yet, there are major obstacles toward its ratification. These include political will, legal barriers, economic obstacles, political obstacles, lack of awareness, public attitudes, and national sovereignty.

In December 2018, the international community adopted the Global Compact for Safe, Orderly and Regular Migration, a non-binding soft law instrument that is expected to help States address the challenges of migration in a concerted and human rights-friendly manner. To a large extent, the Compact was born out of the migration crisis in the Euro-Mediterranean region. This document hardly mentions the ICMW and does not call for its ratification: while prepared under the auspices of the UN, the Compact neglects one of the key tools developed by the UN to foster respect for migrants' rights. This is in line with ongoing discussions, at the international level, that aim at better "managing" migration and in which international human rights law is given secondary importance to the benefit of managerial and socioeconomic objectives (centered on development, border management, interstate cooperation, etc.)

This state of affair inspires mixed feelings. On the one hand, the Compact makes clear that migration is high on the political agenda, that it raises serious human rights concerns, and that it deserves a multilateral approach in which States and international organizations get involved in the search for global solutions – precisely the premises upon which the ICMW was designed in the first place. On the other hand, current efforts largely ignore the Convention: they seem to take for granted that the ICMW is unpopular among States and rejected by the governments of Western receiving countries; they favor soft law normative instruments to the detriment of international human rights law. This is yet another obstacle to the ICMW, which is not even supported by the very organization that created it.

The future of the ICMW is therefore highly uncertain. Its very existence, however, testifies to the need of alternative political approaches to migration, grounded in multilateralism, cooperation, and human rights. This is far from a new idea, as it was already expressed by the ILO a century ago, in 1919. Yet, today more than ever, the failure of State policies leads to major political and humanitarian crises – and this calls for alternatives in which, on the long run, the ICMW may prove useful.

References

Batistella G (2009) Migration and human rights: the uneasy but essential relationship. Cholewinski R, de Guchteneire, P, Pécoud, A, Migration and Human Rights: the United Nations Convention on Migrant Workers' Rights. Cambridge University Press, New York, 47–69

Beutin R, Canoy M, Horvath A, Huber A, Lerais F, Smith P, Sochacki M (2006) Migration and public perception. Bureau of European Policy Advisers (BEPA). European Commission, Brussels

Böhning WR (1988) The Protection of Migrant Workers and International Labour Standards. International Migration 26(2):133–146. https://doi.org/10.1111/j.1468-2435.1988.tb00618.x

Bosniak LS (1991) Human rights, state sovereignty and the protection of undocumented migrants under the international migrant workers convention. Int Migr Rev 25(4):737–770. Retrieved from: http://www.jstor.org/stable/2546843

Caron C, Griesbach K, Roldan U, Sandoval R (2017) Guatemala's implementation of the ICRMW: emerging efforts. In: Desmond A (ed) Shining new light on the UN Migrant Workers Convention. Pretoria University Law Press, Pretoria, pp 204–228

Castles S, de Haas H, Miller MJ (2013) The age of migration. International population movements in the modern world. Macmillan Press Ltd., London

Crush J, Williams V, Nicholson P (2009) Migrants' rights after apartheid: South African responses to the ICRMW. In: Cholewinski R, de Guchteneire P, Pécoud A (eds) Migration and Human Rights: the United Nations Convention on Migrant Workers' Rights. Cambridge University Press, New York, pp 247–277 de Guchteneire P, Pécoud A (2009) Introduction: the UN Convention on Migrant Workers' Rights. In: Cholewinski R, de Guchteneire P, Pécoud A (eds) Migration and Human Rights: the United Nations Convention on Migrant Workers' Rights. Cambridge University Press, New York, pp 1–44

Desmond A (2017) Introduction: the continuing relevance of the UN ICRMW. In: Desmond A (ed) Shining new light on the UN Migrant Workers Convention. Pretoria University Law Press, Pretoria, pp 1–22

Edelenbos C (2005) The international convention on the protection of the rights of all migrant workers and members of their families. Refug Surv Q 24(4):93–98. https://doi.org/10.1093/rsq/hdi088

Georgopoulou A, Schrempf TA, Venturi D (2017) Putting things into perspective: the added value of the ICRMW's substantive provisions. In: Desmond A (ed) Shining new light on the UN Migrant Workers Convention. Pretoria University Law Press, Pretoria, pp 129–150

Grange M (2017) The migrant workers convention: a legal tool to safeguard migrants against arbitrary detention. In: Desmond A (ed) Shining new light on the UN Migrant Workers Convention. Pretoria University Law Press, Pretoria, pp 72–100

Grange M, D'Auchamp M (2009) Role of civil society in campaigning for and using the ICRMW. Cholewinski R, de Guchteneire, P, Pécoud, A, Migration and Human Rights: the United Nations Convention on Migrant Workers' Rights. Cambridge University Press, New York, 70–99

Grant S, Lyon B (2017) Indirect success? The impact and use of the ICRMW in other UN Fora. In: Desmond A (ed) Shining new light on the UN Migrant Workers Convention. Pretoria University Law Press, Pretoria, pp 101–128

Hasenau M (1991) Part I: The genesis of the convention: ILO standards on migrant workers: The fundamentals of the UN Convention and their Genesis. International Migration Review 25(4):687–697. https://doi.org/10.1177/019791839102500402

Helton AC (1991) The new convention from the perspective of a country of employment: the U.S. case. Int Migr Rev 25(4):848–858. Retrieved from: http://www.jstor.org/stable/2546848

Hillman F, Koppenfels AKV (2009) Migration and human rights in Germany. Cholewinski R, de Guchteneire, P, Pécoud, A, Migration and Human Rights: the United Nations Convention on Migrant Workers' Rights. Cambridge University Press, New York, 322–342

International Convention on the Protection of the Rights of All Migrant Workers and Members of Their Families (1990) Adopted by General Assembly resolution 45/158 of 18 Dec 1990

International Labour Organization (2009) Protecting the rights of migrant workers: A shared responsibility. International Labour Office, Geneva

IOM (2017) Migration and migrants: a global overview. In: IOM (ed) World Migration Report 2018. IOM, Geneva

Nafziger JAR, Bartel BC (1991) The Migrant Workers Convention: its place in human rights law. Int Migr Rev 25(4):771–799. Retrieved from http://www.jstor.org/stable/2546844

Oger H (2009) The French political refusal on Europe's behalf. Cholewinski R, de Guchteneire, P, Pécoud, A, Migration and Human Rights: the United Nations Convention on Migrant Workers' Rights. Cambridge University Press, New York, pp 295–321

Pécoud A (2009) The UN Convention on Migrant Workers' Rights and international migration management. Glob Soc 23(3):333–350. https://doi.org/10.1080/13600820902958741

Pécoud A (2017) The politics of the UN Migrant Workers Convention. In: Desmond A (ed) Shining new light on the UN Migrant Workers Convention. Pretoria University Law Press, South Africa, pp 24–44

Pécoud A (2018) What do we know about the International Organization for Migration? J Ethn Migr Stud 44(10):1621–1638

Piché V, Depatie-Pelletier E, Epale D (2009) Obstacles to ratification of the ICRMW in Canada. In: Cholewinski R, de Guchteneire P, Pécoud A (eds) Migration and Human Rights: the United Nations Convention on Migrant Workers' Rights. Cambridge University Press, New York, pp 150–168

Piper N (2009) Obstacles to, and opportunities for, ratification of the ICRMW in Asia. In: Cholewinski R, de Guchteneire P, Pécoud A (eds) Migration and Human Rights: the United

Nations Convention on Migrant Workers' Rights. Cambridge University Press, New York, pp 171–192

Prieto GD, Kuhner G (2017) Mexico and the ICRMW: protecting women migrant workers. In: Desmond A (ed) Shining new light on the UN Migrant Workers Convention. Pretoria University Law Press, Pretoria, pp 229–248

Rao Penna L (1993) Some salient human rights in the UN Convention on Migrant Workers. Asian Pac Migr J 2(2):179–197. Retrieved from http://www.smc.org.ph/administrator/uploads/apmj_pdf/APMJ1993N2ART4.pdf

Ruhs M (2012) The human rights of migrant workers: why do so few countries care? Am Behav Sci 56(9):1277–1293. https://doi.org/10.1177/0002764212443815

Salazar D (2017) Universal citizens globally, foreign migrants domestically: disparities in the protection of the rights of migrant workers by Ecuador. In: Desmond A (ed) Shining new light on the UN Migrant Workers Convention. Pretoria University Law Press, Pretoria, pp 176–203

Sookrajowa SS, Joson MBC (2018) An analysis of the challenges and implications of the UN migrant workers convention: the case of Mauritius. Migration and Development 7(2):262–281. https://doi.org/10.1080/21632324.2017.1419544

Taran PA (2009) The need for a rights-based approach to migration in the age of globalization. In: Cholewinski R, de Guchteneire P, Pécoud A (eds) Migration and Human Rights: the United Nations Convention on Migrant Workers' Rights. Cambridge University Press, New York, pp 150–168

Touzenis K (2009) Migration and human rights in Italy: prospects for the ICRMW. In: Cholewinski R, de Guchteneire P, Pécoud A (eds) Migration and Human Rights: the United Nations Convention on Migrant Workers' Rights. Cambridge University Press, New York, pp 343–359

Touzenis K, Sironi A (2013) Current challenges in the implementation of the UN International Convention on the Protection of the Rights of all migrant workers and members of their families. Directorate-General for External Policies of the Union, European Parliament, Brussels

Tunon M, Baruah N (2012) Public attitudes towards migrant workers in Asia. Migr Dev 1(1):149–162. https://doi.org/10.1080/21632324.2012.718524

Office of the High Commissioner for Human Rights (2018) International convention on the protection of the rights of all migrant workers and members of their families. Accessed: https://www.ohchr.org/en/professionalinterest/pages/cmw.aspx

Vanheule D, Foblets MC, Loones S, Bouckaert S (2005) The significance of the UN migrant workers' convention of 18 December 1990 in the event of ratification by Belgium. Eur J Migr Law 6:285–321. Retrieved from http://dlx.booksc.org/42400000/libgen.scimag4243800042438999.zip/browse/10.1163/1571816044088818.pdf

Vucetic S (2007) Democracies and international human rights: why is there no place for migrant workers? Int J Hum Rights 11(4):403–428. https://doi.org/10.1080/13642980701659930

Weiner M (1995) The global migration crisis. The challenge to states and to human rights. Harper Collins, New York

Wickramasekara P (2017) The ICRMW and Sri Lanka. In: Desmond A (ed) Shining new light on the UN migrant workers convention. Pretoria University Law Press, South Africa, pp 249–276

Whitaker BE, Giersh J (2015) Political competition and attitudes towards immigration in Africa. Journal of Ethnic and Migration Studies 41(10):1536–1557. https://doi.org/10.1080/1369183X.2014.996534

Wotipka CM, Tsutsui K (2008) Global human rights and state sovereignty: State ratification of international human rights treaties, 1965–2001. Sociological Forum 23(4):724–754. https://doi.org/10.1111/j.1573-7861.2008.00092.x

The Rhetoric of Hungarian Premier Victor Orban: Inside X Outside in the Context of Immigration Crisis

Bruno Mendelski

Contents

Introduction	1830
Method and Theoretical Structure: Post-structuralist Discourse Analysis	1831
Challenging the EU and Pushing Away the *Other* Foreigner: Orban's Politics to Immigration	1834
Analysis of Orban's Speeches	1836
Speech of September 04, 2015	1836
Speech of September 05, 2015	1838
Speech of October 22, 2015	1840
Speech of November 04, 2015	1842
Speech of November 16, 2015	1843
Speech of December 19, 2015	1845
Orban's Discursive Framework on the Immigration Crisis	1846
Conclusions	1848
Cross-References	1849
Annex I	1849
Amendment of the Asylum Government Decree (in effect from 1 April 2016)	1849
Amendment of the Asylum Act (in effect from 1 June 2016)	1849
References	1850

An earlier version of this paper was presented at the International Political Science Association (IPSA) World Congress, Brisbane, Australia, July 21 - 25, 2018.

B. Mendelski (✉)
Institute of International Relations (IREL), University of Brasilia, Brasilia, Brazil

International Relations at Department of Economics, University of Santa Cruz do Sul, Santa Cruz do Sul, Viamão, Brazil
e-mail: brunomendelskidesouza@gmail.com

© The Author(s), under exclusive license to Springer Nature Singapore Pte Ltd. 2019
S. Ratuva (ed.), *The Palgrave Handbook of Ethnicity*,
https://doi.org/10.1007/978-981-13-2898-5_155

Abstract

This chapter analyzes the impact of the rhetoric of Hungarian premier Viktor Orban on the current wave of refugees in Hungary. Based on the theoretical assumptions of Post-structuralism in International Relations, it examined six Orban discourses in the year 2015 (the apex of the immigration crisis). Methodologically, it relies on Hansen (Security as practice: discourse analysis and the Bosnian War. Routledge, Londres, 2006) model of Discourse Analysis to investigate the process of linking and differentiation that opens space for ethnic or racist discrimination against individuals. It argues that the Hungarian premier presents the issue within a binary framework, with an *inside* × *outside* logic. Thus, Orban constructs the Hungarian *inside* as opposed to a pair of *outsiders*: the immigrants (primordial *outsider*) and the EU left-liberal elite (secondary *outsider*). To the first is given a threatening Muslim identity, while to the second it's given a religionless, borderless, and nationless identity. Both outsiders are counterpoints with the Hungarian Christian-peaceful identity. The hypothesis of this chapter is that Orban's *inside* × *outside* rhetoric reasserts the importance of the Nation State, updating to the Post-structuralist challenges of the 1990s. The common point between these periods lies in the efforts of political leaders to present themselves as protectors of the *inside* in the face of (*outside*) threats, thus legitimizing xenophobic policies towards the foreigner "other." The new element in this discussion is the affirmation of sovereignty through the questioning of the supranational power of the EU.

Keywords

Hungarian identity · European immigration crisis · Xenophobia · Post structuralism in IR · Critical discourse analysis

Introduction

Contemporary discussions over state identity and **xenophobia** are particularly relevant in Europe, where migration has become a major issue of interest especially since the beginning of the refugee crisis in 2015. Hungary was one of the countries that most received this population. For that reason, this chapter analyzes the impact of the Hungarian premier Viktor Orban's rhetoric on the current wave of refugees in Hungary.

Based on the theoretical assumptions of Post-structuralism in International Relations, it examined six Orban discourses of the year 2015 (at the peak of the immigration crisis). It relies methodologically on Hansen (2006) model of Discourse Analysis to investigate the process of linking and differentiation that opens space for ethnic or racist discrimination against individuals.

It argues that the Hungarian premier presents the issue within a binary framework, with an ***inside*** × ***outside*** logic. Thus, Orban constructs the Hungarian *inside* as opposed to a pair of *outsiders*: the immigrants (primordial *outsider*) and the EU left-liberal elite (secondary *outsider*). To the first is given a threatening Muslim identity, while the second is given a religionless, borderless, and nationless identity. These two outsiders are counterpoints with the Hungarian Christian-peaceful identity. The immigrant is the primordial *outsider* because it represents the immediate and concrete danger to the loss of Hungarian sovereignty. The EU left-liberal elite are the secondary *outsider* for providing the theoretical-institutional framework that reduces the sovereign power of Hungary and consequently favors the entry of the immigrants. Besides representing distinctive ideologies, Orban in his speeches presents several times the left and the liberal doctrines as part of the same group. These ideologies have the same objectives in Orban's view: eliminate the borders, destruction of the nation state, ended with the sovereignty and marginalize Christian identity and values.

In this context, borders guarantee the separation between the internal and the external, justifying measures of exception to the foreigners and the non-adoption of some EU procedures. The hypothesis of this chapter is that the nationalist rhetoric based on the dichotomy *inside* × *outside* reasserts the importance of the Nation State, updating to the Post-structuralist challenges of the 1990s.

The common point between these periods lies in the efforts of political leaders to present themselves as protectors of the *inside* in the face of (*outside*) threats, thus legitimizing xenophobic policies towards the foreigner "other." Several Hungarian laws provide evidence to support this argument, particularly those related to the following areas: cuts in social subsidies to asylum seekers (2016), automatic detention of migrants seeking asylum (2017), and the construction of fences and the militarization of the Hungarian borders (2015–2017).

The new element in this discussion is the affirmation of **sovereignty** by questioning the supranational power of the European Union. Such position can be clearly seen in the non-adoption of the Budapest quota system proposed by the European bloc. Biased national consultations about the issue also act as domestic legitimating mechanisms. The EU placed as an outsider not only reinforces Post-structuralist observations about State's necessity on affirm its identity but also rises more uncertainty about the future of the organization.

Method and Theoretical Structure: Post-structuralist Discourse Analysis

The post-structuralist approach, through a careful analysis of language, aims to deconstruct the dominant discourses and the power relations contained in them (Derian 1989). It also defends that reality alone does not exist, but only representations of that, which achieve meaning from language (Shapiro 1989). Then the dominant groups, which seek to construct and universalize their worldviews, construct these representations discursively through the establishment of antagonistic identities.

In this process of constructing identities, it is essential to point out that language is both social and political configuring itself as an inherent and dynamic system of signs that generates meaning through the simultaneous construction of identity and difference (Hansen 2006). Language is social when it allows the socialization of individuals through their creation of terms and meanings; it is political because it is a place where particular subjectivities and identities are produced and reproduced, while others are simultaneously excluded (Hansen 2006). The joint analysis of the social and political spheres in the study of language is crucial, since at the individual level personal beliefs, rather than perennial and natural ones, are textualized from a historical production of an epistemological code, which is deeply involved with other historical developments (Shapiro 1989).

Furthermore, Hansen (2006) suggests thinking identities within a dynamic process where subjects and objects are continually reaffirmed, negotiated, and redone. Campbell (1992), in turn, proposes an understanding of the state as dependent on a constant affirmation of its identity, which occurs through the demarcation of its "other" opponent. This "other" is constructed linguistically as one that is beyond state borders. Therefore, borders are the mechanism that allows and potentiates the demarcation of the "inside" and "outside," "self" and "other," "citizen" and "foreign" (Campbell 1992).

Working on a similar line to Campbell (1992), Walker (1993) uses these dichotomous tools to problematize the concept of state sovereignty. The author (1993) affirms that sovereignty is a trait of modern political thought, since it represents the evolution of medieval political organization: it institutionalizes the separation of two political spheres, the national and the international, the inside and the outside, and thus creates the conditions for the state to exist. This state identity dichotomous logic also permits the state to present itself as the defender of the people against the different "other" foreigners.

According to Campbell (1992), the demarcation of **borders** between territories allows the constant creation of the "self" national as opposed to the "other" foreign. These constructions tend to emerge in security discourses that are "traditionally constituted through a national self against one or more threatening others, whose identities are radically different from the self" (Hansen 2006: 6). Thus, the construction of difference, the exclusion of the different and its conversion to "otherness" are fundamental for the affirmation of the "self" and as a legitimation for the state's existence itself (Resende 2009).

Therefore, security is an ontological necessity of the **state**: its identity requires the constant construction of external threats. Danger and insecurity constitute the state, and not only constitute their potential destroyers: the state only knows itself through their juxtaposition against the threatening other (Campbell 1992). To Walker (2006) the delimitation of the internal and the external by the borders is related to almost all the difficult issues of our time: distinctions/discriminations, inclusions/exclusions, beginnings/ends, etc.

In methodological scope, Hansen (2006) proposes a useful model to understand the relations among identities in the discourses. Her framework provides theoretical concepts and methodological tools to investigate how identities establish acts as legitimation of foreign policy actions. Initially one should identify those terms that indicate a clear construction of the other or of the self. These features are contained within the same identity, as indicated in the two pentagons of the figure below.

This identities must be deconstructed in relation to the other, so that what may appear to be a "positive" construction of the self. Building a relationship of hierarchy and position between other and self (Hansen 2006). The author (2006: 38) exemplifies its model through the identity relationship between the Balkans and Europe (Fig. 1).

Hansen model helps in the process of deconstructing discourses in order to indicate their dichotomous contents. Besides, the above figure evidence two fundamental points of post-structuralist thought. First, it reaffirms the view of identities as constituted in opposition to the differences. Second, it highlights the role of language as a central constructor of meanings in reality. Its only through the language construction that "things" – objects, subjects, states, living beings, and material structures – are given meaning and endowed with a particular identity (Hansen 2006: 18). Shapiro (1981: 218) adds that language is the field of social and political practice, and hence there is no objective or "true meaning" beyond the linguistic representation to which one can refer.

Hence, the **identities** pointed by the discourse are fundamental for the establishment of roles and duties, since language constructs reality and the things need an

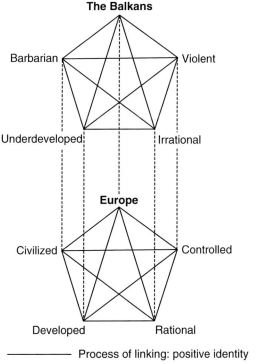

Fig. 1 Hansen model of linking and differentiating identities

identity to create its own meaning. Accordingly to Hansen (2006: 19) "identities are thus articulated as the reason why policies should be enacted, but they are also (re) produced through these very policy discourses: they are simultaneously (discursive) foundation and product." Thus, the goal of post-structuralist discourse analysis is to hold that foreign policy discourses always involve a construction of responsibility, even if only implicitly applicable toward a national citizenry (Hansen 2006).

In relation to the discursive corpus analyzed in the chapter, some considerations are necessary. Orban's speeches are available fully in English on the Hungarian government official website. Furthermore, the choice of the year 2015 for the analysis of the speeches is due to two reasons: this year marks the beginning of immigration crises and the start of Orban's **anti-immigration policies**. Once exposed the theoretical-methodological structure of the chapter, one can proceed to investigate Viktor Orban's rhetoric and politics about immigration in 2015.

Challenging the EU and Pushing Away the *Other* Foreigner: Orban's Politics to Immigration

Since the beginning of the immigration crisis in 2015, Orban's government seeks to politicize it. Ruling party since 2010, the Hungarian Civic Alliance, Fidesz (right wing), took the opportunity of the 2015 migration/refugee crisis to create new enemies aiming to mobilize popular support due its low levels of popularity (Vidra 2017). The spectacularization of politics marks its **populist** rhetoric with constant need of creating opposition between "us" and "them" by the government (Szalai and Göbl 2015; Vidra 2017). Then, Orban represents the immigrant crisis as a battle between the Muslim immigrants *outsiders* supported by EU left-liberal elite against the Hungarian Christians *insiders*.

Biased national consultations complement this process. With them Fidesz has achieved the population's support for its anti-immigration measures and noncompliance with EU policies. Orban's government implements three major national consultations on immigration: national consultation (April 2015), quota referendum (October 2016), and national consultation (March 2017).

In the first case, the government launched a questionnaire poll on "immigration and terrorism" complemented by a billboard campaign. Accordingly to the European Parliament (2015 online), the survey was highly misleading, biased, and unbalanced, establishing a biased and direct link between migratory phenomena and security threats. Likewise, the government increases xenophobia through manipulative propaganda campaign, with aggressive billboards urging refugees to respect the country's laws, customs, and not to take away Hungarians jobs (Juhász et al. 2015: 6; Sereghy 2016: 230).

The second consultative measure was directed to oppose **EU** refugee quotas. Before the October 2016 quota referendum, Orban's government started an intensive campaign calling for the rejection of the quota system. Large billboards featured with controversial messages such as "Did you know? The Paris terrorist attacks were carried out by immigrants" or "Did you know? Since the start of the immigration crisis, sexual harassment of women has increased in Europe?" (Sereghy 2017: 264). Accordingly to Freedom House (2017: 15), the government disseminated xenophobic propaganda connecting asylum seekers and immigrants to acts of crime and **terrorism**.

The third national consultation titled "Let's Stop Brussels" *Állítsuk meg Brüsszelt* was again a biased and misleading questionnaire regarding EU politics. On the subject of immigration, the second of the six questions were: "In recent times, terror attack after terror attack has taken place in Europe. Despite this fact, Brussels wants to force Hungary to allow illegal **immigrants** into the country. What do you think Hungary should do? (a) For the sake of the safety of Hungarians these people should be placed under supervision while the authorities decide their fate. (b) Allow the illegal immigrants to move freely in Hungary" (The Budapest Beacon 2017 online).

For Sereghy (2018: 312), the 2017 national consultation "was a repeated attempt to gain popular legitimation to act against European Union policies and domestic civil society supporting refugees." The European Commission (2017b online) points out that several of the claims and allegations made in the consultation are factually incorrect or highly misleading. All these **national consultations** received the support of the overwhelming majority of the Hungarian population, allowing that Orban's government executes a hard-line immigration policy (Hungarian Government 2015g, 2017; Human Right Watch 2017).

Hence, the Hungarian government starts the alteration of its asylum system in August 2015. The adoption of an Amendment to the Asylum, denied the asylum procedure to asylum-seekers who first pass through a list of countries the Hungarian authorities have deemed "safe," including Serbia and Macedonia (Amnesty International 2016). The measure was criticized for hampering access to Hungary for the asylum seekers access to Hungary. Therefore, the European Commission open an infringement procedure against Hungary in the end of 2015 (European Commission – Press release 2015 online).

In addition, in July 2015, the government began to construct the first fence along the 175-km border between Hungary and Serbia. Since Croatia directed the migrants toward the Hungarian border, Budapest has started to build the second fence along the 348-km border between Hungary and Croatia (RT 2017). The new barriers proved to be efficient in reducing the flow of immigrants: the number of successful attempts to illegally border crossing fell from 391,000 in 2015 to 18,236 in 2016, and then to only 1,184 in 2017 (RT 2017). Complementarily, the government promoted the border's militarization, employing "coercive weapons,' and restricting civil liberties of the immigrants (Freedom House 2016: 15).

The construction of the border fences has three important consequences. First, it became the symbol of the Hungarian position against the supranational quotas policy proposed by the EU (Vidra 2017). Second, these barriers represent a clear deny of the refugee's human rights, people who are in a great vulnerable situation (Krekó and Rakt 2015). Third, the construction of fences portrays a desperate attempt by a state to secure control of its primary function: the decision about who enters and leaves. By losing the border control, the state identity is in a great crisis, since it can no more offer security to its citizens in the face of a world of danger (Campbell 1992).

Moreover, in 2016, Orban's government approved two draconian legislative amendments: Amendment of the Asylum Government Decree and Amendment of the Asylum Act (the full contend of this and the earlier amendments are available in the Annex I of this chapter). The first is on effect since April 1, 2016, and the second since June 1, 2016. As results of this new legislation, refugees are now obliged to move out from the reception center where they are accommodated, already a month after the grant of their status, and will not receive any targeted support for their integration, such as financial benefits, housing allowance, language course, etc. (The Hungarian Helsinki Committee 2016: 1). In practice, these provisions may immediately force the refugees to homelessness and destitution, constituting as a serious violation of refugee's human rights (The Hungarian Helsinki Committee 2016: 1; Amnesty International 2016).

In March 2017, the Hungarian government passed a law, which prescribes police to pushback unlawfully staying migrants who wish to seek **asylum** in Hungary across the border fence, without any legal procedure to challenge this measure. Furthermore, now all asylum-seekers must submit their application in the transit zones at the border, where they will be detained in border camps made of containers for the entire asylum procedure without no legal basis or judicial remedies (The Hungarian Helsinki Committee 2017: 1; Amnesty International 2017: 1). This law has been widely criticized by organizations such as Amnesty International and the Hungarian Helsinki Committee (Heinrich Böll Stiftung 2017). The law changing also led European Commission to open another infringement procedure against Hungary in May 2017 (European Commission – Press release 2017).

After pointing out the main anti-immigration politics of the Orban's government, one can now investigate its binary and alarming rhetoric, fundamental to build the legitimize for this measures.

Analysis of Orban's Speeches

Speech of September 04, 2015

The first Orban's speech analyzed is an interview with journalist Éva Kocsis for the "programme 180 min" of the Hungarian *Kossuth* radio station. In this discourse, there is a common strategy in Orban's speech on immigration: the represent of it as a threat to the Hungarians. This alarmist tone serves Orban's purpose of constructing an environment of danger, thus justifying and legitimating not only his government but also the Hungarian state itself.

> **The truth is that Europe is being threatened by massive immigration on an unprecedented scale.** (...) Today we are talking about hundreds of thousands, **but next year we will be talking about millions, and that will never end** [our griffins].

In this way, the immigrant as a threat provides the demand for the state to carry out its primary function: the promotion of the **security** of its citizens (Walker 1993).

The dramatic sense employed by Orban continues in the following section, where it is exposed the impossibility of coexistence between the Hungarian "us" and the "other" immigrant.

> **And one morning we can wake up and realize that we are the minority on our own continent.**
> (...) I personally believe in a Europe, I would like to live in a Europe, and I would like my children to live in a Europe and a Hungary that is the **continuation of an age-old tradition maintained by our parents, our grandparents and our Great-grandmothers.**
> This can change: **they can occupy Hungary, something unprecedented in our history – or they can introduce communism** [our griffins].

Expressions like "one morning we can wake up and realize that we are the minority on our own continent" evidence the continuous process of constructing Hungarian state identity. Campbell (1992) adds that the threats constitute the state: it only knows who it is by confronting the threatening 'other." The author goes even further by stating that "states are never finished as entities; the tension between the demands of identity and the practices that constitute it can never be fully resolved because the performative nature of identity can never be fully revealed" (Campbell 1992: 11).

In addition, its important deconstruct Orban's rhetoric about the **Hungarian identity**. The premier represents the Hungarian people as a homogeneous unity, but as attests Hall, "the identities connect itself with the use of the resources of history, language and culture" (2012: 108, free translation). The author (2012) adds that identities are never unified, but multiply constructed across discourses, practices, and positions that may intersect or be antagonistic. This view highlights the idealized representation of Hungarian identity in Orban's speech. Hansen (2006) adds that the national security discourses draw its powerful political identity at the same time as it masks its specificity and its history. Thereby, the political leader constructs the security of his national community as an objective and dehistoricized demand.

The danger exacerbation in the last passage (although close to fantasy) has the important aspect of generating a fear in the Hungarian population, thus guaranteeing greater legitimacy for the use of authoritarian measures for the matter of immigration. Accordingly, to Shapiro (1989: 20) as "we live in a world in which danger is institutionalized, persons interested in relating their fears to situations of danger have become consumers of representations from institutions that have the legitimacy to produce interpretations of danger." Hansen (2006) complements arguing that security discourses have a double dynamic: they give legitimate power to the actors who execute these policies, but they also construct these agents with a particular responsibility to do so.

Still, in this discourse, the state sovereignty acts as the legitimation for the *inside* × *outside*. This recourse will be recurrent in the Orban's strategic on the demarcation of Hungarian identity versus its primordial (Muslims immigrants) and secondary *outsider* (**left-liberal EU elite**). Here, the premier makes it clear his wish for the maintenance of the national Christian Hungarian identity to the detriment of a 'supposed" increase in the Muslim population in his country:

> I believe we must **respect the decisions of countries that have already decided that they want to live with large Muslim communities:** the decisions of countries like France or Germany [our griffins].
> We cannot criticize them – this was their decision. But we also have the right to decide whether we want to follow their example or not. I, for example – and this is my personal opinion – would advise the Hungarian people not to follow this example.

The right of states to be sovereign in their domestic decisions protects Orban's prejudiced rhetoric against Muslim immigrants. Thus, the argument that states are sovereign to decide their internal affairs, in fact, supported the construction of a boundary between "us" **Christian** and "they" Muslims, revealing the impossibility of coexistence between the "self-internal" with the "external other." Connolly (2002) points out that the state is the privileged place for the production of otherness since its interior represents a clearer line between internal and external. The Islamophobia is an important element in Orban's Muslim otherness.

Historical elements of Hungarian identity supported the construct of this border. Accordingly, to Vidra (2017: 13), the Hungarian national identity has the strong element of protecting Christian Europe against the invasion of Muslims. Equally, the elements of Hungary's Ottoman occupation (1541–1699) are still present in the country's collective memory (Sereghy 2017: 261). The minuscule **Muslim** community in Hungary and the widespread ignorance about **Islam** among the population also contributes to anti-Muslim narratives enjoy the unconditional support of an overwhelming portion of Hungarians (Sereghy 2016: 235; Sereghy 2017: 258).

Speech of September 05, 2015

This discourse was address by Orban at the 14th Kötcse civil picnic (annual gathering of Fidesz and Fidesz-tied circles). In the passage below, one can observe the use of a recurring strategy in Orban's rhetoric: the attempt to criminalize immigration through his representation as a threat to Hungary.

> **Now we are inundated with countless immigrants: there is an invasion, they break down fences,** and it is clear to us all that they are not seeking refuge, and are not running for their lives [our griffins].

Recalling post-structuralist notes, the passage above indicates an Orban effort to represent immigration as a threat to Hungarians, according to the use of the terms "flood," "numerous immigrants," and "invasion." In this sense, it is salutary to consider that this description (immigration as dangerous to Budapest) consists of only one of several realities about this conjuncture (Shapiro 1989). Likewise, according to Campbell (1992), the sense of danger is not given an objective, but rather associated with the interpretation of who does it.

The construction of this danger's scenario caused by immigrants, in turn, allows a stronger and more incisive action from the state in order to protect citizens from this external threat. This logic of defining the foreign "other" as a threat contributes to the state asserting its identity and its functionality. Thereby, "the state grounds its legitimacy by offering the promise of security to its citizens who, it says, would otherwise face manifold dangers" (Campbell 1992: 56). Moreover, danger scenarios favor the existence of a greater state action, strengthening the power of the groups who control it, being of their interest the representation of these realities. Therefore, Shapiro (1989) states that it is appropriate to conceive of security discourse as a type of discourse that represents structures of authority and control.

As can be seen below, the Orban's binary framework follows the logic of the "clash of civilization," with its idealized and prejudiced view of national identities. Since the other is portrayed as different and threatening, this construction acquires a schmittian view of the state, favors the **nationalism,** and encourages xenophobic feelings and actions.

> (…) Hungary – and now I do not want to speak for other countries, but I would like to think that most of Europe think as we do – **must protect its ethnic and cultural composition**.
> (…) Allow me to mention a conversation I had with a talented, experienced, but not very hopeful European politician, who was no longer in frontline politics, and who asked me to explain what I meant when **I said that we do not want a significant Muslim community in Hungary**.
> (…) **Why can we not talk about the right of every state and every nation to decide on whom they want to live on their territory?**
> In Europe, many countries have decided on this – for example the French or the British, or the Germans with regard to the Turks. I think they had the right to make this decision (…). **And we can say that we like Hungary just as it is. It is colorful and diverse enough.**
> **I am convinced that Hungary has the right – and every nation has the right – to say that it does not want its country to change.** (…) **But we should not argue about whether a community has the right to decide if it wants to change its ethnic and cultural composition in an artificial way and at an accelerated pace**. And if Hungarians say that they do not want this, no one can force them to do so [our griffins].

The sovereignty concept is a key element in this Orban discourse. For Walker (1993), the sovereignty relates with the primordial existence of the state itself, by demarcating the boundary between **internal** and **external**. According to the author (1993), the *outside* (in this case, the Muslim immigrants) is not only the strange, foreign, and threatening; it is responsible for asserting the identity of the *inside*. At the same time, the basilar principle of international relations, the sovereign relationship between states, acts as a legitimizing element for Orban exclusionary view of the "other" Muslim immigrant. When the premier states that the decision of the countries should be respected in determining who has the right to live within its borders, he is only reaffirming the principle of borders and state sovereignty, which, together with its identity, are the pillars of its existence (Campbell 1992). This point also indicates the actuality of the post-structuralist critique on the nation-state's exclusionary character.

If in the part analyzed above, Orban focuses on the external enemy, in the following part he focuses on the internal enemy. Primordial to this is the establishment of the identities. The Hungarian Christian identity is established for operate as distinct to the Muslims refugees (primordial *outsider*), and to the left-liberal thought of the EU (secondary *outsider*), as the fragment above shows.

> A liberal person who does something in order to present themselves in a good light knows full well that they are in fact a hypocrite. Please don't misunderstand me – I'm not talking now about the grand old liberals like Lajos Kossuth, Deák or Graf Lambsdorff; **but we have always thought of the modern left-liberal school of thought** – alongside which we live and which is dominant – as hypocrisy organized into a system at the individual level and at state level [our griffins].

Orban continues and articulates his language in order to represent discursively the current theme of asylum and mass migration as liberalism's crisis. Conveniently, Orban ignores the causes of the phenomenon and the role of the states in the issue, constructing a view of **reality**, which suits his interests of weakening the supranational power of EU.

> (…) Earlier we have talked about identity crises among ourselves: The Christian identity crisis, or the national identity crisis. But now, Ladies and Gentlemen, **we are witnessing the liberal identity crisis**. Viewed from the right perspective, **the whole issue of asylum and mass migration, the whole problem of economic migration is nothing more than the identity crisis of liberalism.**
>
> (…) **Of course The Good Lord will help the person who fights for good causes,** because in such times it turns out, for example, that the Hungarian constitution – adopted at a time when an immigration crisis was still nowhere to be seen – **is superbly suited to strengthening this Christian and national identity in the eyes of all and in opposition to the ruling liberal identities in Europe today** [our griffins].

In addition, he openly opposes The Hungarian Christian identity to liberal identity, his secondary *outside*. Vidra (2017) argues that traditional Hungarian narrative against Islam is different from general Western European countries, which endorsement liberal values. Specifically, "Hungarian anti-Muslimism explicitly refutes liberal values as they are considered as not being part of the Hungarian 'nationalist semantics of self'" (Vidra 2017: 13). As Campbell (1992) remembers, the states are never ready as entities: the tension between the demands for identity and the practices that constitute it can never be fully resolved. Therefore, the premier seizes the opportunity of the **refugee crisis**, to associate its negatives aspects to the liberal identity, confronting it with the good national-Christian identity.

Speech of October 22, 2015

Speaking at The European People's Party Congress in Madrid, **Orban** again frames his immigration discourse towards his primordial and secondary *outsiders*. About the first, he initially represents the issue as an emergency question.

I would like to congratulate Partido Popular and the Spanish Prime Minister, Mariano Rajoy for the outstanding performance of their government. Today I would like to speak about the migration crisis. This issue will determine the future of our political family. **We are in a deep trouble. The migration crisis is able to destabilize governments, countries and the whole European continent** (...).

The danger we have been facing demands open and honest speech. First of all, dear Friends, **what we have been facing is not a refugee crisis. This is a migratory movement composed of economic migrants, refugees and also foreign fighters. This is an uncontrolled and unregulated process**.

I would like to remind you that free choice of a host country is not included in the international law. I also want to underline that there is an unlimited source of supply for people, after Syria, Iraq, Pakistan, Afghanistan, Africa is now also on the move. **The dimension and the volume of the danger is well above our expectations** [our griffins].

Catastrophic terms signalized the urgency of the issue: "the migration crisis is able to destabilize governments, countries and the whole European continent," "this is an uncontrolled and unregulated process" and "the dimension and the volume of the danger is well above our expectations." However, as remember Campbell (1992: 1) "danger is not an objective condition. It (sic) is not a thing which exists independently of those to whom it may become a threat." Thus, this feeling of danger allows that Hungarian state rebuild its identity as a different for this *outsider*, through its borders (Walker 1993). Furthermore, these *outsiders* are not just refugees: they are also *economic migrants* and *foreign fighters*. Orban, through this reading of reality, stresses the seriousness of the issue and better justifies his role of protector of Hungarian borders.

After, Orban seeks to define the European left as its secondary *outsider*. He establishes its main characteristics and strategically opposes it with his understanding of the true European identity. The left is religionless, borderless, and nationless, while the European tradition is based in family, **nation**, subsidiarity, and responsibility. According to Connolly (2002: 64), "an identity is established in relation to a series of differences that have become socially recognized. These differences are essential to its being." Thereby, this confrontation of identity reinforces the post-structuralist view that language is social and political, which constantly generate meaning through a simultaneous construction of identity and difference (Hansen 2006: 15).

We cannot hide the fact that **the European left has a clear agenda. They are supportive of migration.** They actually import future leftist voters to Europe hiding behind humanism. It is an old trick but I do not understand why we have to accept it. They consider registration and protection of borders bureaucratic, nationalist and against human rights. **They have a dream about the politically constructed world society without religious traditions, without borders, without nations. They attack core values of our European identity: family, nation, subsidiarity, and responsibility.**

We are the European People's Party – *Partie Populaire, Volkspartei, Partido Popular*, Party of the People – our responsibility is towards the people. Listen to the people. Let's be determined, let's defend Europe. **Do not let the leftist mess up and reconstruct Europe**! And do not let them oust the soul of Europe! **Do not let liberals and socialists take away Europe from the people!** [our griffins].

The last fragment of this speech assumes a classically dichotomous tone, pointing again the two secondary *outsider*s: the liberals and the socialists. This binary logic demonstrates a political relationship to the differences, which the "self" it seeks to fix (Connolly 2002). Vidra (2017: 13) states that Orban, besides the "Muslim other" created in the horizontal dimension, makes a further opposition in the vertical dimension between us (Hungarians) and them (EU, Western Europeans).

Speech of November 04, 2015

In his speech in the Opening of the World Science Forum (Budapest), Orban again represents the current wave of immigration to **Europe** as a dangerous and threatening. The pejorative terminology used to describe the immigrants ("mass immigrants," "avalanche of people," and "invaders") contributing to the insertion of the theme from a security perspective.

> We are living in interesting – indeed, crazy – times. **Europe is under pressure from mass migration on a colossal scale**.
> (...) **We must confront a flood of people pouring out** of the countries of the Middle East, and meanwhile, the depth of Africa has been set in motion
> (...) **This is an uncontrolled and unregulated process**, and – now that I am speaking before the scientific community – **the most precise definition of this is "invasion"**. (...) **Our continent** is yet to appreciate the gravity of the problem: **there is a challenge to its very culture, the way of life and pattern of existence up to now**. (...) It is as if we did not yet want to see that the **Western world** is facing an unprecedented challenge which could crush and bury under itself the form of existence we have known up to now. The stakes are therefore enormous. At the same time, what is happening, what will happen and what we allow to happen to have significance far beyond the **borders of Europe or Western civilization** [our griffins].

The presentation of the theme framed by the dichotomous relationship between *inside* × *outside* allows the criminalization of immigration. The foreign identity is represented as "a challenge to our own culture, the way of life and pattern of existence so far." As post-structuralist thought advocates, the modern state constantly needs to define the **boundaries** between the internal and the external, and traditionally it does so by constructing its identity in opposition to the identity of some foreign people or group (Waever 2002). Moreover, according to Connolly (2002), state identity operates as a pressure to allow the fullness of self-identity by marginalizing, degrading or excluding the differences on which it depends to self-specify. Thus again, the identity of the "other" immigrant not only poses a threat to national identity but also the possibility of its own existence (Campbell 1992).

The use of the dichotomous terms "Western world" and "borders of Europe or Western civilization," indicate the traditional border-building strategy between internal and external (Shapiro 1989; Campbell 1992). Said (1995) draws attention to the European tradition of constructing Christian identity in opposition to Islam, through binary terms such as "we" x "them," "West" x "East," "Christian" x "Muslims." It is important to emphasize that the terms Muslim or Islamic are implied in the excerpt above, although are not expressly mentioned. Identity is a relational concept: It exists through something that it is not (Hansen 2006).

Speech of November 16, 2015

Orban in this discourse at the Hungarian Parliament systematize the immigration issue at a three-point threat. First, he associates the mass immigration to terrorism rise. Talking in the wake of the deadly Paris terrorist attacks of November 13, 2015, Orban undertakes an inconsistent and prejudiced connection between terrorism and **mass immigration**.

> (...) Beyond the financial and economic realities, mass migration presents three serious risks, each of which is on its own sufficient reason to hold back the flood of people. Firstly, on Friday night **we witnessed the fact that mass migration represents an exponentially increasing terror threat** – indeed today we are not even talking about the threat of terror, but the fact and reality of terror [our griffins].

Posteriorly, he relates the current immigrant crises to the rise of crime, and as a threat to the culture, the European-Hungarian way of life. Thus, the *outsider* refugee represents the classical elements of the *threatening other*, which endangers the *national inside*.

> Secondly, **mass migration increases the risk of crime**. It is not PC, not politically correct, to talk about this –indeed in the Western world, this fact is publicly denied – but it is a fact for all that. **In those places in Europe with high numbers of immigrants, crime has increased significantly and public security has deteriorated. There is more theft, robbery, physical assault, grievous bodily harm, rape, and murder.** Whether we talk about them or not, these facts are still facts.
> Thirdly, **mass resettlement of people arriving from other continents and cultures represents a threat to our culture, way of life, customs and traditions**. Now those who have lived in the delusion of multi-culturalism – and who have sought to force this delusion on us – can see where all this is leading [our griffins].

Likewise, since the concept of identity is relational, the Hungarian state can reconstruct its identity in opposition to the foreign other (Hansen 2006). Orban presents the Hungarian identity as peaceful, orderly, and Christian, juxtaposing it to the terrorist, criminal, and Muslim identity of the refugees. As pointed out by Hall (2012), identities emerge within the context of power relations, thus being more a product of the marking of difference and exclusion, than a sign of an identical unity.

Orban's effort to challenge EU power focuses on building these identities. Also, he connects the national *inside* and the refugee's *outsider* with EU supranational power.

> In the light of what has happened, we must also speak about the issue of **compulsory resettlement quotas**. It is still the case that, **from somewhere outside Hungary, people want to tell us Hungarians who we should live alongside. This is what the quotas are about**.
>
> I propose to the Honourable House that we continue **to reject the quotas and continue to insist that we ourselves should decide whom we want to let in and whom we want to live together with**. Mandatory resettlement quotas are quite simply not Europe: they are a complete contradiction of the spirit of Europe [our griffins].

Initially, the denomination of European Union as an *outside* is symptomatic with Orban's dichotomous rhetorical strategic. This binary separation between the state (*inside*) and the European Union (*outside*) is fundamental to reaffirm the national identity of Hungarian state (Walker 1993). Further, the **Hungarian state** is ontologically challenged by EU's supranational power and by the *other* Muslims refugees. The loss of Hungarian sovereignty for EU means that the state cannot exercise its basic function: the control of its borders. The second part of the fragment illustrates this point.

Nevertheless, it is necessary to construct the *others* refugees as a threat to the state, to ensure its *outside* condition and the state power:

> In the light of the terrorist attacks, Brussels can no longer question Member States' right to defend themselves, **given that mandatory resettlement quotas are dangerous because they would spread terrorism across Europe** [our griffins].

The refugee's association with terrorism is the central element in this narrative. Likewise, Shapiro (1989: 13–14) remembers "representations are not descriptions of a world of facticity, but are ways of making facticity." Thereby, Orban will benefit domestically and externally on this negative representation of refugee's. Domestically, it will support his anti-immigration policies. Externally, it will act as legitimizer of his EU's challenging posture.

Orban exposes his ideas on how EU should be managing the refugee crisis at the end of this speech.

> I suggest that we return from the realm of ideologies to common sense, and reconsider our European policy on the basis of four self-evident commandments.
>
> First of all, **we must protect the external borders of the European Union**, because security begins with the protection of the borders. Secondly, **we must protect our culture, because Europe's essence lies in its spiritual and cultural identity**. Thirdly, we must protect our economic interests, because we Europeans must remain at the center of the world economy. And fourthly, **we must give the people the right to have a say in European decisions, because the European Union must be based on democratic foundations** [our griffins].

The last sentence deserves a special attention. There, Orban attacks the representative character of EU in favor of his nationalist approach. His national consultations are the mechanism for legitimizing his challenging stance to the EU.

The 2015 consultation pointed out that 80% of Hungarians think that the Brussels' policy on immigration and terrorism has failed (Hungarian Government 2017). The EU's migrant quotas were rejected for 98% of respondents in the 2016 quota referendum (Sereghy 2017). Although the low turnout (44%) making the referendum invalid, the government declared the results as "politically valid" and regarded it as a political mandate to "defend the country against the compulsory quota" (Sereghy 2017: 261).

Moreover, in the March 2017 national consultation, 90% of respondents supported the tightening of measures on immigration (Hungarian Government 2017). Orban's defiant posture to the EU and his anti-immigration policies strengthened with the Hungarian overwhelming majority supports.

Speech of December 19, 2015

This discourse is constituted of an Orbán's interview given to the Czech daily newspaper *Lidové Noviny*. There, Orban reaffirms his nationalism and confronts it is with the European liberal thought.

> We have the suspicion that there is also a secret – or not openly acknowledged – importation of voters into Europe. The third problem is **the idea that the nation is seen as a source of danger**. They do not see the nation as an integral, indispensable, positive element in the evolution of European society, but as something which bears threats, because it is the hotbed of nationalism. **These groups have done everything within their power to eliminate nations**.
>
> And the followers of these **internationalist traditions** – which are now emerging in the guise of **supranationalism** – take the view that the ethnic foundations of European nations must be shaken since if we replace the population, the problem of the nation will change. So in my view, the current situation has developed for several different reasons, and in this situation, the number of power groups which support immigration and regard it as a positive phenomenon is larger than expected [our griffins].

The Hungarian leader openly accuses this political view of trying to destruct the nation states. His mentions to *supranationalism* is a clear critique to EU policy in regard to the refugee crisis, which Orban sees a threat to the supposed **Hungarian homogeneity**. Orban creates new identities for the EU elite in order to strengthen his disapprobation to them:

> **Europe is dealing with questions which are not insignificant – fine, gracious things: human rights, progress, same-sex marriage, tolerance and issues of a similar nature. At the same time, Europe is not dealing with the roots from which these important issues stem: Europe is disregarding its Christian traditions or traditions associated with nations**. Europe has forgotten who or what it actually is, and what the truly important things are [our griffins].

Subtly and ironically, he exposes liberal characters that can be easily opposed with conservative's ideas. Therefore, again, the premier points out two different identities: the liberal with its defenses of human rights, progress, same-sex marriage, and tolerance versus conservative's Christian and nationalist traditions. As stated by Connolly (2002: 64), "identity requires a difference in order to be, and it converts difference into otherness in order to secure its own self-certainty."

Moving forward, Orban intensifies its efforts to de-legitimize the **liberalism** by indirectly associating it with Bolshevism and National Socialism:

> Europe is an extremely fertile continent intellectually. It always has been: it has been the source of a wide range of ideas, economic, political and social teachings. Of course, amidst such an array of fertile thoughts, not only useful ones tend to emerge, but also dangerous ones. **There have been instances in Europe when this intellectual fertility brought dangerous and destructive theories to the surface, and there have been times when the people of Europe were not strong enough to control the destructive ideas which seized the continent**.
> I think this is how **Bolshevism** – which is a Marxist ideology with roots in Germany – spread in a Europe which lacked the strength to protect itself. **National Socialism** also grew from the same European soil. **The idea of a Europe without nations, the idea of a United States of Europe, the gradual weakening of nations, is also an insane and dangerous idea** [our griffins].

As state by Laclau (1990), the constitution of a social identity is always an act of power, since it can only affirm itself from the repression of what threatens it. Thus, the representation of a progressive liberal Europe as a dangerous idea like the Bolshevism and the National Socialism, as bizarre as it may seem, aims to link the negative feelings of these two historical experiences into European liberal.

With this rhetoric, Orban intends to domestically present himself as the "protector of the Hungarian nation" and, at the regional level, as the "defender of European nations" against immigrants and against the bureaucracy in **Brussels** (Juhász et al. 2015: 6).

Orban's Discursive Framework on the Immigration Crisis

After analyzing Orban's discourses, one can systematize its fundamental axes. Based on Hansen (2006) processes of linking and differentiation, and Walker (1993) conception of *inside* × *outside*, the chapter present the Orban's discursive framework on the immigration crisis. The premier minister constructs the Hungarian national identity in opposition to two different *outsiders*: the primordial (immigrants) and secondary (EU liberal-left elite). As shown below in Fig. 2.

These two *outsiders* are central to Orban's efforts to reconstruct the Hungarian national identity and legitimize his power. As stated by Campbell (1992), the state's construction of "its" national identity is only possible through a simultaneous delineation of something which is different. At this point, Derrida's (1978) ideas are precious: language is a system of differential signs, and meaning, established not by the essence of a thing itself but through a series of juxtapositions, where one element is valued over its opposite. Thus, the positive *inside* depends on the negative *outsider* to operate: "peaceful" x "terrorist," "sovereign" x "multiculturalist."

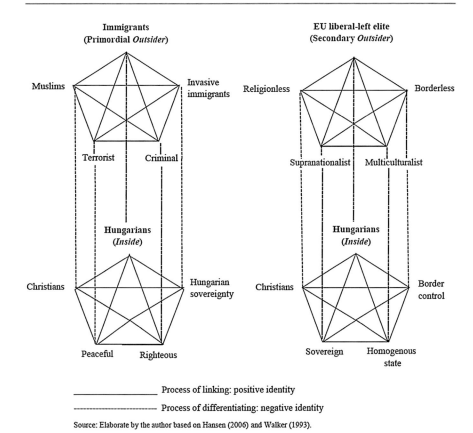

Fig. 2 Orban's discursive framework on the immigration crisis

Nevertheless, the Hungarian case presents the specificity of constructing two simultaneous *outsiders* that expose a double capacity for differentiating Hungarian national identity. This double construct of difference occurs due to the emergence of a new outsider who challenges state sovereignty: the EU. In the context of intensification of European integration, the EU shares space with the traditional "**other**" **foreign** and threatening. The pro-immigration politics of EU's liberal-left elite make it the secondary *outside*. In Orban's vision, the EU permissiveness to the dangerous Muslims immigrants (primordial *outsider*) is also a danger coming from "outside."

In his discursive framework, Orban places the Christian character of Hungarian identity, both in opposition to the immigrants' Muslim aspect and to the EU's secular-liberal element. This is the central aspect of his argument. Orban likewise combines the threat posed by the two *outsiders* in reinforcing the sovereign concept. Thereby, the sovereign guarantees the isolation of immigrants, and at the same time, moves away from EU supranational impulses. Additionally, the sovereign allows the Hungarian leader to keep his rhetoric of clash of civilizations, complemented by his critics of **multiculturalism**.

In this sense, Orban's nationalist rhetoric distances the Hungarian *inside* by correlating its primordial and **secondary** *outsiders* with each other. Accordingly, to Sereghy (2018: 311), Orban's discourse is building upon a Migration-Islamization-Terrorism nexus supported by anti-Christian, liberal `elite which is seeking to undermine European nation states and the continent's Christian identity through mass illegal immigration and consequent Islamization.

Conclusions

The chapter pointed out that Orban's binary and alarming rhetoric in the wake of refugee's crises were organized through the construction of two *outsiders*. The Muslims immigrants (primordial *outsider*) represent the classical threat to the homogeneous national identity sentiment. Orban portrays the immigrants especially as Muslims, terrorists, and criminals, ignoring the wide range of immigrants, juxtaposing them with the Christian, good, and pacific Hungarians.

The mass immigration and the possibility of the Hungarian state lose the border's control put it in crisis, reaching the immigrants as the main *outsider*. The control and militarization of the Hungarian borders are examples of the Hungarian state's effort in not lose its ontological function: the power to determine and construct the foreigner.

Together with the **primordial** *outsider*, Orban constructs the EU's liberal-left elite as his second *outsider*. The supranational character of EU means a new challenge for nation-state's sovereignty, driven by the current refugee crisis. Thus, the Hungarian national-state was doubly confronted by the traditional foreign other and for EU's liberal institutionality.

Thereby, Orban astutely associates these two *outsiders*, reinforcing the Hungarian state identity. The Christian characteristic of Hungarian identity is represented as opposed to Islam (immigrants) and to religionless (EU). In addition, the EU liberal features (supranationalism and multiculturalism) are represented as dangerous for facilitating the entry of Muslim *outsiders*. This construction strengthens the basic principle of the state, challenged by the two *outsiders*: the sovereignty.

The reification of the border notion captained through the sovereign concept is the operative mechanism of these antagonist identities. The sovereign exercise allows the Hungarian state to construct a border to separate the *inside* to immigrant and EU *outsiders*. For the first, the border is physical and discouraging; to the second is affirmative and symbolic.

In addition, the establish these different identities was fundamental to build legitimize for Hungarian anti-immigration and xenophobic measures, as well as in the confrontational position with the EU. Moreover, the national consultations provided internal legitimation for these two measures. Furthermore, the open condemnation of migration and the challenge of **EU supranational power**, supported by the construction of these identities, represent the weakening of the European liberal doctrine of **human rights**. By ignoring the EU principles and regulations, Hungarian moves away from the integrationist dynamics of EU and deepens its isolationist nationalist policy.

Cross-References

▶ Ethno-cultural Symbolism and Group Identity
▶ Religion and Political Mobilization
▶ The Significance of Ethno-politics in Modern States and Society

Annex I

Amendment of the Asylum Government Decree (in effect from 1 April 2016)

Termination of monthly cash allowance of free use for asylum-seekers (monthly HUF 7125 / EUR 24);
Termination of school-enrolment benefit previously provided to child asylum-seekers (Hungarian Helsinki Committee 2016: 1).

Amendment of the Asylum Act (in effect from 1 June 2016)

Terminating the integration support scheme for recognized refugees and beneficiaries of subsidiary protection introduced in 2013, without replacing it with any alternative measure;
Introducing the mandatory and automatic revision of refugee status at minimum 3-year intervals following recognition or if an extradition request was issued (previously refugee status was not limited in time, yet it could be withdrawn any time);
Reducing the mandatory periodic review of the subsidiary protection status from 5- to 3-year intervals following recognition;
Reducing the maximum period of stay in open reception centers following the recognition of refugee status or subsidiary protection from 60 days to 30 days;
Decreasing the automatic eligibility period for basic health care services from 1 year to 6 months following the recognition of refugee status or subsidiary protection (Hungarian Helsinki Committee 2016: 1).

References

Amnesty International (2016) Hungary: Appalling treatment of asylum-seekers a deliberate populist ploy. September 27, 2016. https://www.amnesty.org/en/latest/news/2016/09/hungary-appalling-treatment-of-asylum-seekers-a-deliberate-populist-ploy/. Accessed 18 June 2017

Amnesty International (2017) Hungary: container camp bill is flagrant violation of international law. March 7, 2017. https://www.amnesty.org/en/latest/news/2017/03/hungary-container-camp-bill-is-flagrant-violation-of-international-law/. Accessed 18 June 2017

Campbell D (1992) Writing security: United States foreign policy and the politics of identity. University of Minnesota Press, Minneapolis

Connolly W (2002) Identity difference: democratic negotiations of political paradox. University of Minnesota Press, Minneapolis

Der Derian J (1989) The boundaries of knowledge and power in international relations. In: Der Derian J, Shapiro M (eds) International/intertextual relations: postmodern readings in world politics. Lexington Books, Lexington, pp 3–10

Derrida J (1978) Writing and difference. Routledge and Kegan Paul, London

European Commission (2015) European Commission – Press release: Commission opens infringement procedure against Hungary concerning its asylum law. http://europa.eu/rapid/press-release_IP-15-6228_en.htm. Accessed 18 June 2017

European Commission (2017a) European Commission – Press release migration: Commission steps up infringement against Hungary concerning its asylum law. http://europa.eu/rapid/press-release_IP-17-5023_en.htm. Accessed 18 Jan 2018

European Commission (2017b) "Stop Brussels": European Commission responds to Hungarian national consultation. https://ec.europa.eu/commission/publications/stop-brussels-european-commission-responds-hungarian-national-consultation_en. Accessed 18 Jan 2018

European Parliament. Online. European Parliament resolution of 10 June 2015 on the situation in Hungary (2015/2700(RSP)). http://www.europarl.europa.eu/sides/getDoc.do?pubRef=-//EP//TEXT%20TA%20P8-TA-2015-0227%200%20DOC%20XML%20V0//EN. Accessed 18 Jan 2018

Freedom House (2016) Freedom in the World 2016: Hungary Profile. https://freedomhouse.org/report/freedom-world/2016/hungary. Accessed 20 Jan 2018

Freedom House (2017) Freedom in the World 2017: Hungary Profile. https://freedomhouse.org/report/freedom-world/2017/hungary. Accessed 18 Jan 2018

Hall S (2012) Quem Precisa da Identidade? In: Silva T (ed) Identidade e Diferença: a Perspectiva dos Estudos Culturais. Vozes, Petrópolis, pp 103–133

Hansen L (2006) Security as practice: discourse analysis and the Bosnian War. Routledge, Londres

Heinrich Böll Stiftung (2017) Serious human rights violations in the Hungarian asylum system. https://www.boell.de/en/2017/05/10/serious-human-rights-violations-hungarian-asylum-system. Accessed 13 Mar 2018

Human Right Watch (2017) Hungary: Draft law tramples asylum seekers' rights. March 2017. https://www.hrw.org/news/2017/03/07/hungary-draft-law-tramples-asylum-seekers-rights. Accessed 24 Apr 2017

Hungarian Government (2015a) Viktor Orbán's interview given to the Czech daily newspaper Lidové Noviny. December 19, 2015. http://www.kormany.hu/en/the-prime-minister/the-prime-minister-s-speeches/prime-minister-viktor-orban-s-interview-given-to-the-czech-daily-newspaper-lidove-noviny. Accessed 15 Jan 2017

Hungarian Government (2015b) Viktor Orban's speech address in the Hungarian Parliament, Budapest. November 16, 2015 http://www.kormany.hu/en/the-prime-minister/the-prime-minister-s-speeches/prime-minister-viktor-orban-s-address-in-parliament-before-the-start-of-daily-business. Accessed 25 Nov 2016

Hungarian Government (2015c) Viktor Orban's speech address in the opening of the world science forum, in Budapest. November 04, 2015 http://www.kormany.hu/en/the-prime-minister/the-prime-minister-s-speeches/viktor-orban-s-speech-at-the-opening-of-the-world-science-forum. Accessed 26 Nov 2016

Hungarian Government (2015d) Viktor Orban's speech address in the The European People's Party Congress in Madrid. October 22, 2015. http://www.kormany.hu/en/the-prime-minister/the-prime-minister-s-speeches/speech-of-viktor-orban-at-the-epp-congress20151024. Accessed 26 Nov 2016

Hungarian Government (2015e) Viktor Orban's speech address in the 14th Kötcse civil picnic. September 05, 2015. http://www.kormany.hu/en/the-prime-minister/the-prime-minister-s-speeches/viktor-orban-s-speech-at-the-14th-kotcse-civil-picnic. Accessed 25 Nov 2016

Hungarian Government (2015f) Viktor Orban's interview with journalist Éva Kocsis for the "programme 180 minutes" of the Kossuth radio station. September 04, 2015. http://www.kormany.hu/en/the-prime-minister/the-prime-minister-s-speeches/if-we-do-not-protect-our-borders-tens-of-millions-of-migrants-will-come. Accessed 25 Nov 2016

Hungarian Government (2015g) Prime Minister Viktor Orbán's presentation at the 26th Bálványos Summer Open University and Student Camp. July 27. http://www.kormany.hu/en/the-prime-minister/the-prime-minister-sspeeches/prime-minister-viktor-orban-s-presentation-at-the-26th-balvanyos-summer-open-university-and-studentcamp.

Hungarian Government (2017) Prime Minister Viktor Orbán's address in Parliament before the start of daily business. http://abouthungary.hu/speeches-and-remarks/prime-minister-viktor-orbans-address-in-parliament-before-the-startof-daily-business/.

Hungarian Helsinki Committee (2016) Hungary: recent legal amendments further destroy access to protection. April–June 2016. https://www.helsinki.hu/wp-content/uploads/HHC-Hungary-asylum-legal-amendments-Apr-June-2016.pdf. Accessed 05 Jan 2018

Hungarian Helsinki Committee (2017) Hungary: law on automatic detention of all asylum seekers in border transit zones enters into force, despite breaching human rights and EU law. http://www.helsinki.hu/wp-content/uploads/HHC-Info-Update-rule39.pdf. Accessed 05 Jan 2018

Juhász A, Hunyadi B, Zgut E (eds) (2015) Focus on Hungary: refugees, asylum and migration. Political Research & Consulting Institute, Prague. https://www.boell.de/sites/default/files/2015-focus-on-hungary_refugees_asylum_migration.pdf. Accessed 18 Nov 2016

Krekó P, Rakt E (2015) Foreword. In: Political Research & Consulting Institute, Juhász A, Hunyadi B, Zgut E (eds) Focus on Hungary: refugees, asylum and migration, vol 5. Heinrich-Böll-Stiftung, Prague

Laclau E (1990) New reflections on the revolution of our time. Verso, London

Resende É (2009) Americanidade, Puritanismo e Política Externa: a (re)produção da ideologia puritana e a construção da identidade nacional nas práticas discursivas da política externa norte-americana. 334p. PhD Thesis (Postgraduate Program in Political Science – Master's and Doctorate) – University of São Paulo

RT (2017) Hungary credits razor-wire border fence for almost 100 percent drop in illegal migration. 18 Sep 2017. https://www.rt.com/news/403738-hungary-border-fence-migrants/. Accessed 05 Jan 2018

Said E (1995) Orientalismo: a Invenção do Oriente pelo Ocidente. Companhia das Letras, São Paulo

Sereghy Z (2016) Islamophobia in Hungary: national report. In: Bayrakli E, Hafez F (eds) European Islamophobia Report 2015. SETA – Foundation for Political, Economic and Social Research, pp 223–238

Sereghy Z (2017) Islamophobia in Hungary: national report. In: Bayrakli E, Hafez F (eds) European Islamophobia Report 2016. SETA – Foundation for Political, Economic and Social Research, pp 255–276

Sereghy Z (2018) Islamophobia in Hungary: national report. In: Bayrakli E, Hafez F (eds) European Islamophobia Report 2017. SETA – Foundation for Political, Economic and Social Research, pp 305–324

Shapiro M (1981) Language and political understanding: the politics of discursive practices. Yale University Press, New Haven

Shapiro M (1989) Textualizing global politics. In: Der Derian J, Shapiro M (eds) International/intertextual relations: postmodern readings in world politics. Lexington Books, Lexington, pp 11–22

Szalai A, Gőbl G (2015) Securitizing migration in contemporary Hungary. Working paper. Center for EU Enlargement Studies, Central European University, Budapest

The Budapest Beacon (April 3, 2017) "Let's stop brussels!": Here is the new National Consultation. https://budapestbeacon.com/lets-stop-brussels-new-national-consultation/. Accessed 14 June 2017

Vidra Z (2017) Counter-Islamophobia Kit. 'Workstream 1: dominant Islamophobic Narratives Hungary'. Working Paper – CERS, University of Leeds. https://cps.ceu.edu/sites/cps.ceu.edu/files/attachment/publication/2923/cps-working-paper-countering-islamophobia-dominant-islamophobic-narratives-hungary-2017_0.pdf. Accessed 13 June 2017

Walker R (1993) Inside/Outside: international relations as political theory. Cambridge University Press, Cambridge

Walker R (2006) The double outside of the modern international. Ephemera: Theory and Politics in Organization 6(1):56–69. http://www.ephemerajournal.org/sites/default/files/6-1walker.pdf. Accessed 13 June 2017

Waever O (2002) Identity, communities and foreign policy: discourse analysis as foreign policy theory. In: Hansen L, Waever O (eds) European integration and national identity: the challenge of the Nordic States. Routledge, London/New York, pp 20–49

Suggested Readings

Eran S (2019) The ethnic construction of terrorism. In: Naidu V (ed) Racial prejudice and stereotypes. Palgrave Macmillan, London

Fraser L (2019) Immigration, Borders, and refugees. In: Fraser L (ed) Ethnicity, immigration, and labor. Palgrave Macmillan, London

Ramesh S (2019) State hegemony and ethnicity. In: Rudolph J (ed) The state, society, and ethnopolitics. Palgrave Macmillan, London

Villegas P, Villegas F (2019) Migrant illegalization and impact on minorities. In: Anae MS (ed) Globalization and diaspora. Palgrave Macmillan, London

Different Legacies, Common Pressures, and Converging Institutions: The Politics of Muslim Integration in Austria and Germany

94

Ryosuke Amiya-Nakada

Contents

Introduction	1854
Germany and Austria: Commonalities and Differences	1854
Focus of the Chapter	1855
Nationality and Citizenship Provision: Is *Jus Sanguinis* a Cultural "Type?"	1856
Germany as a Nation-State	1856
Acceptance of Foreign Workers in West Germany	1857
Policy Change Under the Red-Green Coalition	1858
Austria from the Empire to the Republic	1860
State and Religious Education in Austria and Germany	1862
Legacy of the Habsburg Empire in Austria	1862
Approval of the Islamic Faith Community: Successful Integration?	1864
Islamic Religious Education in Austria	1866
Challenges to the Austrian Official Recognition Regime: Transparency and Plurality	1868
Muslims and the State in Germany: Toward "Austrification?"	1870
Conclusion: Historical Diversity Facing Common Challenges	1873
Cross-References	1874
References	1875

Abstract

Austria and Germany have shared similar nationality rules and political landscape with strong Christian Democratic parties. This would lead readers to expect similar, non-multicultural policies toward Muslim inhabitants. However, Austria has long maintained an official Muslim recognition regime, while there had been no such recognition in Germany throughout the twentieth century. How do we explain such divergence?

This chapter has two main aims. First, it investigates why Austria and Germany had different institutional arrangements incorporating Muslim

R. Amiya-Nakada (✉)
Tsuda University, Kodaira, Japan
e-mail: r.amiya-nakada@nifty.com

© The Author(s), under exclusive license to Springer Nature Singapore Pte Ltd. 2019
S. Ratuva (ed.), *The Palgrave Handbook of Ethnicity*,
https://doi.org/10.1007/978-981-13-2898-5_156

inhabitants. Based on historical analysis, this chapter elucidates different contexts which surrounded respective institutional formation. This divergence is explained by different historical legacies, especially an experience of multinational empire, in the case of Austria, and an imperial nation state, as for Germany.

Recently, both regimes have shown signs of institutional changes. In Austria, traditional a-liberal incorporation regime has been criticized for its disregard for transparency and non-democratic procedures within organizations, which eventually led to the change of laws. In Germany, increasing number of Muslim inhabitants led to recognition of dual citizenship and the steps towards official recognition of Islamic religious education has been taken. The second aim of the chapter is to show the way established institutions are put under the common pressure and how they are converging.

Through these two case studies, it is shown that history matters, but common pressure pushes different incorporation regimes toward convergence in the direction of Liberal Multiculturalism.

Keywords

Austria · Germany · Multiculturalism · Religious governance · Religious education

Introduction

Germany and Austria: Commonalities and Differences

Germany and Austria are often categorized under common headings in many respects. It goes without saying that they share languages and many cultural elements. In terms of citizenship, they have long maintained the *jus sanguinis* (literally law of blood, meaning inheritance of citizenship from parents) principle and have been reluctant to grant nationality to immigrants. Regarding the relationship between the states and religious groups, they have not adopted a strict political separation model (like the French one) and have given a privileged position to some religious organizations.

This chapter is an attempt to analyze the relationships between the states and Muslims in these two countries. Although there are many analyses on the German case, especially in the form of contrasting the case against the French, the Austrian case is poorly covered in relevant literature. However, Austria is an interesting research subject, and various insights can be gained from its comparison to Germany in the form of a most similar case design.

For example, while liberal multiculturalism has been widely discussed, Austria is more a case of non-liberal multiculturalism. It is interesting to note that the relationship between Muslims and the state is more problematic in more liberal Germany; Austria has not experienced an intense debate over scarves like France and Germany, and culturalism vs. leading culture was inconspicuous until the end of the twentieth century, even though the Muslim proportion of the population is high. From this contrast, we will see the complex relationship between liberalism and multiculturalism.

Behind such differences between Austria and Germany lies the legacy of the empire. Many of the problems of multiculturalism are problematic in the context of the nation-state model, but to what extent and in which way was each European country a nation-state? Which conception of the nation did the governance system of each country rely on? This chapter tries to provide new viewpoints to through case studies.

Focus of the Chapter

In analyzing multiculturalism, many approaches have relied on the citizenship model (Brubaker 1992) (for literature review, see Rosenberger and Sauer 2008). This overlaps with the older typology of nation (Kohn 1944) and interprets citizenship rules as embodying the principle constituting a political community. Although they are useful as a heuristic, they also have some drawbacks. One is that they are static. They cannot explain the historical changes in each country regarding the provisions of granting citizenship. The other is that there is not necessarily a correlation between policies on citizenship and other policies, such as education and welfare.

The state–church relationship is another factor. This is linked to criticism that the citizenship model cannot handle the problem of the collective rights of cultural minorities well (Koopmans et al. 2005, 8). However, even in France, which is a typical example of the separation-type, we find attempts to incorporate Muslim delegates into policy processes in recent years (Laurence 2009). If the state–church relations are regarded as a fixed "type," criticism against staticity is applicable, as well as the citizenship model. In addition, the strength of right-wing populism (Dolezal et al. 2010) and the tradition of anti-discrimination policy, etc., are used as explanatory factors in comparative research.

Although this chapter does not deny the explanatory power of these approaches, we focus on the empire as a historical factor in addition to the citizenship model and national church relations. This point was also taken up in two noteworthy recent studies. (These studies have been built on recent developments in the historical study on various empires. For historiography, see Dickinson (2008) and Leonhard and Hirschhausen (2009).) Howard (2009) tried to avoid categorization and staticization by building a citizenship policy index (CPI), paying attention to the acquisition of citizenship, mainly nationality granting. The factors that create the difference in CPI are the presence or absence of large colonies (this determines the size of human diversity) and the presence or absence of early democratization (the degree of tolerance for diversity is determined) in particular. Janoski (2010) tried to explain the magnitude of the naturalization rate as the dependent variable using the differences in the stages of colonial construction. In comparison with Howard (2009), it is characterized by a more fine-grained classification of the relationship between colony and home country. This chapter shares the perspective of these studies but emphasizes the domestic religious governance (Koenig 2007) and the differences in empire experience that bring about the difference between Austria and Germany.

In section "Nationality and Citizenship Provision: Is *Jus Sanguinis* a Cultural "Type"?," we will first discuss nationality provisions to confirm that there is no significant difference between the two countries; however, it should also be noted that the German provision has been influenced by short-term policy needs and that the citizenship model is relative and contingent. In section "State and Religious Education in Austria and Germany," we analyze religious education in public schools show that the difference here between the two is large (despite the similarity of the citizenship model) and that legacy of the Empire has been influential in the case of Austria. However, recent trends indicate a convergence of the two countries, and, in that sense, the "type" of each country is relative, as in the previous section.

Nationality and Citizenship Provision: Is *Jus Sanguinis* a Cultural "Type?"

Germany as a Nation-State

In 1913, the Nationality Act was enacted in the Second Empire Germany. The Second Empire was the first nation-state established in Germany. The nationality law was enacted about 40 years after the Unification. This law has drawn researchers' attention as a prime example of the ethnic and cultural understanding of nationality and citizenship in Germany. This principle is put in contrast to the civic nationality model based on birthplace (*jus soli*) (Brubaker 1992).

In both models, the nation-state attempts to unify and homogenize the people living within it, as well as to unify and consolidate the inside of the border with respect to institutions of governance (the "modern state" in a narrow sense). The French model also has the logic of inclusion and exclusion. While the residents who conform to the ideals of France regardless of their origins are said to be granted citizenship, those judged not to conform are excluded. That point becomes clear when a school excludes French-citizen students who wear religious symbols of Islam. Nevertheless, ethnic citizenship principles have been linked to the Nazi's "blood and soil" slogan, which has been linked to backwardness and nondemocracy. Regarding West Germany after World War II, the existence of this citizenship principle was regarded as a major factor in the exclusion of foreigners.

The German Special Path (*Sonderweg*) thesis emphasizes the difference in the nature of modernization between Germany and Western Europe in the same way. The thesis has insists that the establishment of the second imperial rule, or the "inner empire construction" in 1878 at the latest, was crucial in deciding the German special path. On the basis of this understanding, we would expect that the citizenship principle was consolidated at this stage.

Actual historical sequence does not match this expectation (Fahrmeir 1997). Citizenship provisions after 1815 were based on settlement sites, and the regulators were each *Land*. This basic structure did not change even after the unification process throughout the 1848 Revolution. It was maintained even after the German Unification in 1871. It was the 1913 Nationality Law that changed it to the *jus sanguinis*. In other words, linking nationality provisions and regime-level characteristics, such as the nature of nationalism, is over-reading (Gosewinkel 2008).

The 1913 Law should be put into context. Fahrmeir (1997) noted that blood-powered principles are a product of Europe's imperialist atmosphere before the First World War, not a traditional characteristic of the German nationality law. Specifically, it is a product of two wide-spread European trends: the restriction of immigration from Eastern Europe and the expansion of the military power base by intensifying the draft. One motivation for the enactment of the 1913 Law was to prevent the inflow of Jews from Eastern Europe by the Land administration, which was tolerant of granting nationality. The other was to keep the loyalty of the Germans migrating to the United States and South America.

It is noteworthy that the 1913 Nationality Law and *imperialism* in the usual sense are related, but this imperialism is different from the empire experience this chapter emphasizes. Janoski (2010, 135) pointed out that Germany did not have a colony long enough to exceed the simple military occupation stage and had only about 100 black Africans on the German mainland. In other words, unlike Britain and France, Germany entered World War I without becoming a large colonial empire, which facilitated the fiction of the German nation. With a large colony, maintaining the difference between the mainland inhabitants and the colonial residents at the level of nationality and citizenship is increasingly difficult, as human interaction intensifies in terms of political and economic rationale. Even if they had had a *jus sanguinis* regulation, they would have had to somehow revise it. In contrast, Germany was able to maintain the character of a purer nation-state because it failed to become a colonial empire. (Ther (2001) pointed out similarities in the German and the Russian cases and contrasted them with the Habsburg case.)

Acceptance of Foreign Workers in West Germany

After the Second World War, the principle of *jus sanguinis* was maintained in West Germany, which can be also explained by a specific circumstance. The division of Germany attributed an important political meaning to the citizenship provision. While East Germany stressed discontinuity with the pre-war Germany, West Germany regarded itself as a legitimate heir to the pre-war German state, which represented the German nation. Consequently, West Germany assumed a position of successor to wartime obligations and reparations and inherited various treaties. Moreover, insisting on existence as the only German state, the West German government refused to recognize East Germany and later insisted on the so-called Hallstein doctrine, which stipulated that it would not have formal diplomatic relations with countries that established formal relationships with East Germany.

In relation to this claim, it was necessary to maintain the *jus sanguinis* nationality law. This made it possible for Germany to automatically acquire West German nationality for the Germans based on the border in 1937 and their descendants.

This also allowed for granting nationality to Russian and German residents who lived in former Eastern European countries, but it directly facilitated the inflow of residents from East Germany.

Furthermore, this provision was also related to the Eastern border problem. West Germany considered the 1937 border a legitimate boundary and had not approved the Polish reign west of the Oder-Neisse Line. To claim this point, it was necessary to regard descendants of the Germans of 1937 as (potential) nationals.

Nonetheless, it was the influx of workers from outside that supported the economic growth of West Germany. Initially, the influx from East Germany became the foundation of growth, but as it became impossible with the construction of the Berlin Wall in August 1961, the West German government decided to establish a planned import of foreign workers based on bilateral treaties. They responded to the labor shortage by promoting the introduction of an immigrant labor force. Within this framework, Turkey has supplied the largest share of the immigrant labor. Based on the turbulence of the economy after the oil shock and the increase in unemployment, the planned solicitation of workers was stopped after 1973, and the influx of foreigners temporarily declined. However, many foreign workers had not returned home after a certain period of labor, and, due to the births of their family members and the second generation, they continued to live in West Germany. After the temporary decline, the total number of foreigners increased.

The increase in foreigners was a big challenge for understanding West German citizenship based on the *jus sanguinis* nationality provisions. In particular, the second generation of foreign workers was born and raised in Germany, spoke German, worked in Germany and, even if there was a symbolic bond with their nationality country, their real lives were based in the West German society. The fact that they were virtually placed in the position of second-class citizens was a big problem and has attracted attention since the 1980s.

In this context, the Muslim problems came to be treated as Turkish-minority issues rather than religion issues. Therefore, related problems were also treated in the context of the integration of foreigners. The next section gives an overview of the change in this problem.

Policy Change Under the Red-Green Coalition

The Red-Green coalition government under Gerhard Schröder, who was elected in September 1998 as a chancellor, began reform of the nationality law, and the draft was presented in December. This draft added "birth in Germany" to the conditions for nationality acquisition, suggesting a withdrawal from *jus sanguinis*.

The opposition parties, the Christian Democrats and the Free Democrats, made an active attack. With a view to the Hessian state parliamentary election, which was Schroeder's first state legislature election, the Christian Democrats initiated a signature campaign, which was quite unusual for the rather conservative party, and succeeded. Contrary to expectations, the Christian Democrats became the first party and took power. This defeat had direct federal political repercussions. As the

Upper House of Germany consists of the state governments, the new Red-Green federal government lost the majority in the Upper House and was forced to cooperate with the opposition just 4 months after the establishment of the federal government.

The Red-Green Coalition's legislative initiative now depended on the government of Rheinland-Palatinate, a coalition government of the Social Democratic Party and the Liberal Democrats. The Red-Green accepted the revision proposal of the Free Democrats. As for the dual-nationality provision, they had to endure setbacks. With this revision, it became necessary for immigrants to select one nationality at the age of 18. However, the introduction of birthplace principle remained. When one parent had stayed legally for more than 8 years or had acquired permission to stay indefinitely 3 years prior, their child was supposed to acquire German nationality from the time of birth.

As mentioned above, the Red-Green Coalition government implemented reforms to introduce the principle of birthplace into the nationality regulations, but the real impact was diluted by the prohibition of dual nationality. Also, as seen in the success of the campaign at the Hessian State Council, the national statue based on the traditional nation-state model was still strong.

However, after this, the discourse on immigration in Germany changed gradually but dramatically. The cause for the change in the trend was economic necessity. Although structural unemployment continued, the shortage of professional workers, such as in the IT sector, was being emphasized. In February 2000, Prime Minister Schröder unveiled the plan to introduce a green card system targeting specialized workers. Naturally, the Christian Democratic Party opposed this proposal, but the industry expressed its support. In the middle of the controversy, the North-Rhine-Westphalia election was held in March 2000. The top candidate of the Christian Democratic Party criticized this proposal and used the slogan *Kinder statt Inder* (Children instead of the Indians). Although he seemed to intend to promote education, he was forced to withdraw the statement due to criticism that the slogan was racist. The election campaign had been in close battle, but the Christian Democratic Party could not take the position of the first party and allowed the state Red-Green regime to continue. The nationality appeal had failed as an election strategy.

In addition, the Schröder government established the Immigration Law Investigation Committee in July 2000. He took advantage of a disagreement within the Christian People's Party to avoid the reoccurrence of the Hessian State Parliamentary election. He appointed liberal Rita Süssmuth of the Christian Democratic Party, who was a senior politician with the experiences of the Lower House Chair, to chair the committee in order to give it a bipartisan flavor. To counter and to collect media attention, the leader of the Lower House Parliamentary group of the Christian Democrats, Friedrich Merz, stated in October 2000 that the German leading culture (*Leitkultur*) was necessary for the social integration of immigrants. After the internal dispute among the Christian Democrats, this phrase was not taken as the official strategy. Through these two episodes, it was clear that the trend was changing and that simple non-recognition of the immigrants would not work any longer.

This was a major change from the era of the Kohl government (1982–1998), when the position of "Germany-is-not-an-immigrant-state" was staunchly maintained. Now, the problem had changed from the acceptability of immigrants to the extent to which they accepted immigrants and how they should respond in policy terms.

In July 2001, the Süssmuth Committee issued a report. Immigrants were regarded as an essential element of economic growth, and a comprehensive policy framework that governed immigrants was presented. In November, the Cabinet passed immigration bills, which passed through Congress in March 2002 with the welcome of business circles, labor unions, churches, and NGOs. But the problem was the Upper House, the *Bundesrat*. For the passage of the bills, it was necessary to gain the assent of the state government with Christian Democratic participation. The negotiations between the federal government and the opposition state government were unfruitful. In the voting at the Upper House in March 2002, the Social Democratic representatives of the Brandenburg government, consisting of the Social Democratic Party and the Christian Democratic Party, voted for the bill without obtaining the consent of the Christian Democrats. The Social Democratic chairman declared that it approved this, but the constitutionality of the decision was questioned immediately, and the problem was postponed until after the election of the Lower House in September.

The Red-Green coalition narrowly won the election, but in December 2002, the Federal Constitutional Court invalidated the voting in the Bundesrat. The resubmitted government draft was rejected in June 2003, and, after the long-term negotiations in the Upper House, the new immigration law was passed in June 2004. It was a major revision. The point system, which had been the main feature since the Süssmuth report, had been eliminated.

As is shown above, under the Schröder government, important changes were made to the organizing principle of the German state. There is no doubt that historical inertia to path-dependence was in force, as is evident in the Nationality Law and Immigration Law compromise forced on the government proposals. However, the actual multiculturalization in daily lives and the economic demands from the business community acted as fundamental drivers to push the change. This example shows that it is inappropriate to view the principle of citizenship solely as a historical or cultural legacy or as a predefined regime. After the formal revision in principles, the German discourse on immigrants and nationality changed even further. In the 2008 Hessen State Parliamentary election, the Christian Democratic premier tried to situate crimes committed by the foreigners as the central issue of the electoral campaign to repeat the success in 1999, but it failed this time.

Austria from the Empire to the Republic

The first citizenship provision in Austria was stipulated in the 1811 Civil Code (hereinafter Stern and Valchars 2013). It was decided that acquisition of Austrian citizenship would be based on *jus sanguinis*. Other acquisition conditions included public office, business, and continuing residence for 10 years and so on. As in Germany, nationality was conferred on a bottom-up basis in the late nineteenth century. That is, nationality was added to the residential citizenship in municipal units (*Heimatrecht*, literally "the hometown right") introduced in 1859.

While the Habsburg Monarchy experienced defeat against Prussia in the fight over the shape of the German nation-state in 1867 and the so-called double monarchy was broken up in 1918 due to the World War I, the Republic of Austria inherited many legal provisions from the Empire. Despite major political changes, there was no fundamental change in nationality provisions. Significant reduction of the territory should have required decisions on the belonging of many residents, but in principle, nationality was given to those who had resident citizenship in the territory of the Republic of Austria. However, as many of the Jews did not have resident citizenship, problems arose. In 1920, the citizenship decision came under the competence of the Federation, but the citizenship law of 1925 stipulated that attribution of nationality to the province citizen (*Land*) and acquisition of resident citizenship was essentially still premised. In addition, acquisition of a professorial position at an Austrian university and marriage with an Austrian male were automatic nationality acquisition requirements.

However, there were differences from Germany at this stage in the provisions concerning post-World War I settlement. It is well known that minorities' protection provisions were paired with the self-determination principle in the construction of the post-World War I order. From a functional point of view, they were necessary compensation measures when constructing nation-states in the Central and Eastern Europe region where ethnic groups co-inhabited. In reality, however, it was the reduction of German and Hungarian territory and the emergence of massive German and Hungarian ethnic minorities in the new countries that spurred new legal provisions. For this reason, the new independent countries, such as Czechoslovakia and Poland, were required to protect ethnic minorities modeled on the so-called Polish Minority Treaty, but this provision was not included in the Versailles Convention against Germany (Mazower 2004). Regarding Austria, Section V of the Saint-Germain Treaty was the "Protection of Minorities," and the minority protection provision of the Convention was regarded as the National Basic Law. This can be seen as the empire's legacy, which makes a marked contrast with Germany.

Austria was annexed by Germany in 1938, and the German 1913 Nationality Law was also applied to Austria. When Austria was rebuilt in 1945, as in many other areas, the former Austrian law was resurrected. As for the nationality regulation, in principle, it was treated as if the 1925 law continued even after 1938, and Austrian nationality was granted to those who and been given nationality before the Annexation and to those who should automatically acquire nationality under the 1925 Law. However, those who had acquired the nationality of another country in the past 7 years were excluded.

Although there have been changes in naturalization requirements, etc., the outline of Austrian nationality law has not changed. Since 1985, the naturalization requirements have been tightened, and the naturalization rate has been low.

The comparison of these two cases shows that common cultural and linguistic traditions did not automatically determine nationality provisions. Rather, they were influenced by contingent contextual factors. Among them, "empire-ness" (or "nation-state-ness") has been a key factor. Does this difference have policy implications? We examine this point in the next section, taking the Austrian case as a prime example.

State and Religious Education in Austria and Germany

Legacy of the Habsburg Empire in Austria

According to the 2001 census, there were approximately 340,000 Muslims in Austria, or about 4% of the total population. This is a fairly small proportion compared to Catholics, who accounted for about three quarters, and the non-religious population of 12%. However, it was the fourth largest group, almost equivalent to the Protestants. Among Muslims, 125,000 inhabitants have Turkish citizenship and 96,600 Bosnian. There were 96,000 Muslims with Austrian citizenship. In addition, compared to the 15 former EU countries before the expansion to the East, Austria was the third largest after France (about 8%) and the Netherlands about (4.5%). According to the aggregate figure based on the resident register as of 2009, the number further increased to more than 510,000, or 6.2% of the total population. Among the increase of 170,000 people, inflows accounted for about 70,000 people, and the remaining 100,000 people were born to Muslims who resided in Austria (Janda and Vogel 2010, 6–8). Many were Sunnis, but 5–15% were Shias, and an estimated 20–30% were Alevi. The proportion of the Alevi has been high, as many of the labor migrants from Turkey in the 1960s and 1970s were from rural areas of Central and Eastern Anatolia, where the proportion of Alevi is high (Schmidinger 2007, 242–244).

The Habsburg Empire in the second half of the long nineteenth century was a multi-ethnic empire that remained in the sea of emerging nation-states. Moreover, they had to face the various problems of modernization without abandoning the characteristic of multiethnic empire. From this situation, unique ideas and systems concerning the relationships of diverse ethnic groups and religious groups were created. Among the former are the well-known concepts of socialists such as Otto Bauer and Karl Renner (cf. Ra'anan et al. 1991; Nimmi 1999, 2005). They conceived a dual system consisting of a regionally based Federal solution for political problems and a personalized solution based on attribution to ethnic groups regarding cultural issues. The latter type of idea has influenced the inclusion of Muslim organizations, which is the subject of this chapter.

Islam was recognized as a religion by the Imperial Government in 1874. In 1781, a tolerance decree had already been promulgated, and the religious homogenization of the Catholic was over. This 1874 "Approval Law" officially recognized the Jewish, the Orthodox Church, Protestants and Muslims and allowed them the freedom to gather and practice religion. Potz (2010, 14–15), who is in charge of Religious Law at the University of Vienna, commented on the characteristics of this approval of multiple religions as follows: "Individual rights have not played any role for a long time. The individual is subsumed in a religion as a sub-society with compulsory affiliation." As a result, "it was better for the members of certain religious minorities than in Western Europe."

As the Habsburg Empire occupied Bosnia and Herzegovina in 1878, the incorporation of Islam proceeded. In response to the request of the Muslim leader in the area, the Habsburg government appointed a public religious leader (*mufti*) and founded a council of four Islamic representatives with the intent to weaken the religious tie with the Ottoman Empire (Schwarz n.d.; Hunt 2002; Bair 2002, 15–16). In 1878, the first prayer place was built in Vienna, for Muslims belonging to the military (Abdel-Fattah 2004). The Bosnians, known as the emperor's imperial guards and as elite troops, wore Islamic traditional hats (*Fezzes*), which provided an image of the "good Muslim" (Sticker 2008, 42–45; Kurier-Serie 2005, 4).

In 1908, the area was consolidated as the imperial territory. The Basic Law was promulgated in 1910, and it was officially approved to apply Islamic law between Muslims on family, marriage, and inheritance matters. However, these regulations were limited to Bosnia and Herzegovina. Therefore, to guarantee the rights of Muslims outside, the government presented the bill to the House of Lords of the Empire in 1909 (Bair 2002). The government intended to recognize Muslims as religious organizations throughout the Imperial territory. Although Islam did not fulfill the requirements for religious organizations by the Approval Law, it was deemed necessary to approve the Hanafi faction who occupied a majority in Bosnia and Herzegovina under special law. Although the bill was initially dismissed, it was approved in July 1912 (Reichsgesetzblatt, No. 159/1912).

This Islam Law (*Islamgesetz*) was unique among European countries and clearly shows the imperial nature of Austria-Hungary, in the sense that it was a political order that encompassed heterogeneous ethnic, cultural and political entities. The Habsburg dynasty, which was defeated in the German nation-state construction, had to redefine itself as a multi-ethnic empire.

This granted the Muslim sectarian community the status of "public institution," equivalent to Catholics, etc. Now the Hanafi faction became "*privilegierte öffentliche Korporation*" (Bair 2002, 27ff.). Specifically, in addition to being able to construct praying places, burial ceremonies and religious gatherings were to be excluded from application of general assembly laws. Furthermore, this approval resulted in the right of religious education at school. According to Article 17 of the Basic Law, religious organizations were responsible for providing religious education, conducting direct supervision. The point is that the law was to approve and integrate Muslim people as a group.

Such a position was passed down even after the disintegration of the empire and the establishment of the Republic of Austria. This provision was also being carried over after World War II. (As of the end of 2016, 27 churches or religious communities and 8 registered faith communities were officially recognized, www.bka.gv.at/religiose-bekenntnisgemeinschaften; www.bka.gv.at/kirchen-und-religionsgemeinschaften).

Approval of the Islamic Faith Community: Successful Integration?

Other organizations aimed for official recognition as Muslim organizations after the Islam Law in 1912, but many were short-lived and not certified. (For historical overview until the establishment of the IGGiÖ is based on Hunt (2002), Potz (2005) and Bair (2002).) After the First World War, Bosnia became part of Yugoslavia, and only a few Muslims remained in Austria.

However, due to the influx of immigrants, the Muslim population has increased since the 1960s. According to the 1961 census, only about 4500 Muslim residents with Jugoslav citizenship and 200 with Turkish citizenships resided there. These had increased to 93,000 and 16,000 people, respectively, in 1971 and grew further to 126,000 and 60,000 in 1981 (Kraler and Sohler 2005, 8). Along with this, in 1962, the Bosnian intellectuals group established the Muslim Social Working Group to provide social services to Muslims in cooperation with the United Nations High Commissioner for Refugees based in Vienna. As the population of Muslims increased, they also played a role as the center of diverse groups.

The Muslim Social Working Group filed for the establishment of a Muslim sectarian community in 1971. The subsequent process was complicated, but with the support of the Bishop of Vienna and Prime Minister Bruno Kreisky, who was intending friendship with the Middle Eastern countries, the Austrian Islamic Belief Community (IGGiÖ: *Islamische Glaubens-gemeinschaft in Österreich*) was founded in 1979. This consisted of the Vienna-Muslim religious community, which was based on the Muslim Social Working Group, as well as three organizations representing Muslims in other areas. In 1988, according to the Federal Constitutional Court ruling, the limitation to the Hanafi faction, which was in accordance with the 1912 law, was deleted, and the position was changed to the representatives of all Muslims under the leadership of the faction.

Due to the existence of this legal status, some of the problems seen in other European countries have been avoided in Austria (Strobl 2007, 534–535). For example, since religious education is conducted under public supervision, there is no problem of the "Quran schools," religious schools outside public supervision, like in Germany or Switzerland. As for the headscarf problem, the situation is different from that of France and Germany (Abid 2006; Strobl 2007). In 1995, the chairman of the IGGiÖ instructed teachers of Islamic religious education that female students must wear hijabs during class. However, confronting criticism from various sides, he withdrew it, and the wearing of hijab became optional after that.

The status of Muslims in Austria was constitutionally protected as an approved public association. As a result, Prime Minister Wolfgang Schüssel was reported to have said that the headscarf problem did not exist in Austria (*der Standatd*, 26 Feb 2007, https://derstandard.at/1976191/Gesetze-in-Europa-das-islamische-Kopftuch), when the German Constitutional Court issued a judgment that admits headscarf regulation on The Education minister also repeated that there was no intention to ban. In 2004, students wearing scarves became a problem at the public school of Linz, but the Ministry of Education confirmed the acceptance of wearing them under the ministerial ordinance again. In addition, the hospital of Vienna approved the wearing of scarves by Muslim women on duty, and turbans were allowed for Sikh city bus drivers, regardless of the hat-wearing rules (Abid 2006).

In the spring of 2005, then Interior Minister Liese Prokop mentioned banning the wearing of head scarves for public school teachers. However, 2 days later, a meeting with the IGGiÖ was set up, and a joint statement was announced. There, it was confirmed that freedom of religion was a constitutional right together with the right of religious practice and that it was not subject to any discussion, including wearing hijabs. The meeting also confirmed that violence against women and forced marriage were problems of tradition rather than of Islam as a religion. Further, the Interior minister clarified that she had never intended the hijab prohibition (*Gemeinsame Pressemitteilung der Bundesinen ministerin Liese Prokop und der Islamischen Glaubensgemeinschaft in Österreich*, 10 Mar 2005; Abid 2006).

Islamic method of slaughtering, which is in conflict with animal protection regulations in some countries and restricted, had been regulated by the government until 1988, but it was later certified by the Federal Constitutional Court ruling (Montadel n.d.). In the ruling, the Constitutional Court stated that the provisions of Article 63 (2) of the Treaty of Saint-Germain stipulated the scope of religious regulation by laws narrower than those of Article 15 of the National Basic Act (1867) and Article 9 of the European Convention on Human Rights. Further, only those laws which have essential meanings for human symbiosis in the state could be incorporated as "public order" and that animal protection was not such "public order" (VfGH Erkenntnis vom 17 Dec 1998, B3028/97).

Such lines are also based on political motivation. In Vienna in particular, there are many Muslim residents with immigrant backgrounds. In the 2001 Vienna City Council election, the Social Democratic Party candidate Omar Al-Rawi won 2558 votes and achieved third place in the Social Democratic Party list. Following this, the People's Party, the Liberal Party and the Green Party also held Muslim candidates (Montadel n.d.). In addition, in the national Parliamentary elections of 2008, the Social Democratic Party also created pamphlets in Turkish and Serbian-Croatian (Mourão Permoser and Rosenberger 2010, 1473). The Communist Party began hosting the party of Ramadan (*iftbar*) in Vienna in 2002, and in 2003, the People's Party followed suit (Abdel-Fattah 2004). In May 2003, the mayor of Vienna hosted an official banquet at City Hall, and in 2004, President Franz Fischer invited Muslim representatives to the Hofburg Palace and held a banquet. From 2006, National Assembly Chairman Andreas Khol also followed this (Eurofound 2010, 22).

As a result, the relationship between Muslims and the majority society in Austria has been relatively stable and less conflicting.

According to a survey on discrimination experiences conducted by the EU's Basic Rights Agency, Austrian Turks have the second lowest percentage of discrimination in the past year, as low as 9%, with an average of 3.2 times on average (FRA 2009). They have the lowest experiences of being called to by the police, and they are third lowest in feeling investigated at border checkpoints due to ethnicity, following Bulgaria and Slovenia. Meanwhile, knowledge on laws and bodies that prohibit discrimination is lower than average and contrasts with Nordic countries and France. In addition, in a 2008 survey of immigrants, more than 80% of respondents of Turkish and Bosnia–Herzekovina origins responded that they are completely or partly integrated (Ulram 2009, 21). According to a study (Dolezal et al. 2010) comparing the state of discussions on Muslims with Germany and Switzerland, there were more pragmatic discussion frames in the Austrian debate than in the other two countries. It pointed out that Muslims' own remarks were often taken up by civil society actors.

Nonetheless, Austria was not exceptionally open or tolerant. According to a survey conducted in 2005 by the Federal Ministry of Interior, while 23% had positive evaluations for Muslims, 40% had negative responses, and 37% had neutral responses (Rohe 2006, 26). However, only 14% answered that they had personally had a bad experience. Among the majority residents, although the evaluation was divided, 43% were positive as to whether integration was functioning well, while 54% held a negative opinion (Ulram 2009, 66). In addition, 51% responded that there were many foreigners who were not prepared for integration, and 22% said that most foreigners were not prepared for integration (Ulram 2009, 67). From the side of the minorities, half of the respondents who answered that they were "completely integrated" admitted that there was exclusionism (Ulram 2009, 32).

In fact, there were concrete cases of conflict. In Terfus, a city with a population of 15,000 people in the Tyrol Province, when a minaret construction plan became clear, a civil opposition movement was developed. The reason was traffic congestion and noise. Although the town did not object to the construction of the prayer place and was only concerned about the sound of Azan, it was reported that a dislike for the existence of Muslims being visible was the reason for objection (Sticker 2008, 78–80). In the end, a minaret was built, but lighting-up and Azan were forbidden.

In addition, in May 2006, referencing the results of the abovementioned survey, Minister Prokop said that 45% of Muslims did not have intentions to integrate. However, the author of the report refuted that there was no will of integration, saying that Muslims and the majority had distant attitudes and that they had reported vague anxiety. Some even questioned the quality of the survey, showing the counter-evidence that 80% were positive in integrating among the second generation (*der Standatd*, 28 Mai 2006, https://derstandard.at/2460907/Uni-Wien-Studien-zu-zweiter-Generation-80-Prozent-integrationsbereit).

Although it became politically controversial in this context, the overall description of the relationship in the report, "peaceful but distanced parallel existence (*Nebeneinander*)" (Rohe 2006, 44) had certain relevance. In the next section, as an example of such coexistence, we take the case of religious education in public schools.

Islamic Religious Education in Austria

Religious education is one of the most important of the specific rights obtained by becoming an authorized sectarian community (Potz 2005). Religious education is conducted in public schools in Austria. The government prepares only institutional and organizational aspects, such as facilities and salary provision, and the content of the education is determined by each sectarian organization. Specifically, each sectarian organization is responsible for preparing guidelines and teaching materials and the approval of faculty members, and no teaching materials have been censored.

According to a 2003 survey (Khorchide 2009), 31,890 children in 1716 primary schools and 4400 students in 191 secondary schools in Austria receive Islamic religious education. This is estimated to be about half of the Muslim pupils and students. Although religious education is supposed to be compulsory, it is possible not to take classes by notification.

Faculty who implemented religious education was initially introduced from overseas by the IGGiÖ. Regarding educational content, traditional doctrinal education was central, rather than being adapted to the relationship between students and their life world (Mohr 2002). However, similar tendencies were strong in Catholic and Protestant education. The IGGiÖ's emphasis was on providing infrastructure to support life as a Muslim, and each individual was supposed to be integrated into Austrian society through participation in the Islamic community. In the survey of Muslims (Ulram 2009, 52), only 30% answered that they were not satisfied with religious education, but just 35% answered with high appreciation.

There was an attempt to train the teachers in Austria. In 1998, the Academy of Islamic Religious Education was founded. This Academy was supposed to train religious teachers in primary education through an eight-semester program (the second semester being preparatory education in German and Arabic) (Öffentliche Sicherheit 3–4/2006, 24–25). In addition, in the winter semester of 2006, an Islamic religious education master's program for acquiring secondary-education teaching qualifications was established at the Department of Education at the University of Vienna (Islamische Religionspädagogik, https://slw.univie.ac.at/studieren/masterstudien/islamische-religionspaedagogik-master/). In this program, the graduates of the abovementioned Academy of Islamic Religious Education as well as related bachelor's degree holders were admitted. Over the course of 2 years, Islam-related subjects such as "Koran, the prophet's thought and action" and "Education of faith and Islam of daily life," as well as religious studies in general and subjects and methods of social pedagogy studies, were supposed to be taken.

In the 2009 winter semester, as a pilot project under the financial aid of the city of Vienna, a recurrent Imam curriculum entitled "Muslim in Europe" was also established at the university (Muslime in Europa, https://www.postgraduatecenter.at/weiterbildungsprogramme/internationales-wirtschaft/muslime-in-europa/). The purpose of this course was to give Imams a better understanding of Austrian political and legal realities, thereby preparing them to tackle the challenges in Austria. In addition to the pedagogy-related subjects, students were obliged to take courses such as "Law, Politics, Education in Austria" and "Islam in Europe" (*oe24*, 16 Nov 2009, https://www.oe24.at/oesterreich/politik/Uni-Wien-startet-Weiterbildung-fuer-Imame/678387). In the first year, 81 people applied for the 30 available spots, he said. Among them, women were included, and the professor in charge said that the emergence of female imam was also a matter of time (*der Standatd*, 15 Oct 2009, https://derstandard.at/1254311287171/Uni-Lehrgang-Imame-lernen-oesterreichische-Werte).

Challenges to the Austrian Official Recognition Regime: Transparency and Plurality

Among the problems surrounding Muslims in Austria, the most noteworthy point was the question of the nature of the Islamic representative organization.

The problem is that institutionalized incorporation of a specific group can be inconsistent with the diversity of real foreign nationals. In this respect, there was a tension with the largest population group, the Turks. Regarding Turkish residents, there were several organizations reflecting conflicts in their home country. One of them was the Turkish-Islamic Union for Cultural and Social Cooperation in Austria (ATiB), the overseas representative of the Turkish Ministry of Agriculture. The ATiB represents about 50 independent religious associations, more than half of which are civil servants of the Turkish Government Deputy Administrative Office engaged in duties. Since 1991, nearly 30 Imams have been working in Austria in 4 years change (Kroissenbrunner 2003, 195). The ATiB was appealing for improving its position in the IGGiÖ, but since the IGGiÖ Supreme Council limited representatives from individual ethnic groups to a maximum of four (one third), there was a conflict.

There was also a conflict over religious education. Under the bilateral agreement between Austria and Turkey, faculty members dispatched from the Turkish government were to be approved by the IGGiÖ. Although their academic backgrounds were high, they could not speak German fluently enough, which caused problems in classes that included many non-Turkish children. Therefore, the IGGiÖ intended to give priority to those who completed the Academy of Islamic Religious Education. From the viewpoint of the ATiB, this meant that only the ability to speak German was an asset, and only teachers with educations equivalent to theological education held in Turkey were recognized.

Meanwhile, the Islamic Federation, established in 1988, opposed the ATiB in Turkish domestic politics. The Islamic Federation was an affiliate organization of the Islamic Welfare Party. The Federation represented 26 mosques and ran a private Islamic high school in Vienna. In addition, youth organizations and women's organizations were also being constructed (Kroissenbrunner 2003).

From the beginning, a problem of internal governance has been present, as the IGGiÖ was originally created from top down and internal decision-making procedures has been untransparent. One manifestation of this is criticism of the conservative nature of the IGGiÖ. In 2006, a popular newspaper reported that Admen-Ibrahim, the Imam of Vienna's Alshula Mosque, had praised Hamas and Hezbollah and criticized Arab leaders who did not support the Lebanese uprising. In the following year, a lecturer of the University of Vienna, Thomas Schmidinger, made a critical comment about the IGGiÖ in a reputable paper. He alleged that Adnan-Ibrahim's relationship with the Muslim Brotherhood was an open secret and that the IGGiÖ leadership, including Anas Schakfeh and Al-Rawi, was very close to Adnan-Ibrahim. He stated that the followers of the Muslim Brotherhood got the leadership of the c and monopolized the voice of Islam in Austria (*Die Presse*, 9 Jan 2007, https://homepage.univie.ac.at/thomas.schmidinger/php/texte/pol_islam_debatte_scheich_adnan_ibrahim.pdf).

Apart from personal relationships, questions have been raised about the transparency of organizational management of the IGGiÖ. Although the IGGiÖ's key position was supposed to be elected, its effectiveness has been questioned (Schmidinger 2007, 249–250). In response to this, strict criticism has been also voiced among Muslims, for example from the Islamic Information and Document Center. Although the statute of the IGGiÖ was revised in 2008, there were calls for democratization of the organization on the grounds that the protection of minorities such as Shiites and Alevis was unsatisfactory.

With this background, the Alevi applied for official recognition as their own sectarian community in March 2009. The Ministry of Education, Culture and Arts of Jurisdiction, under the request of the IGGiÖ, dismissed this application in August. In response, the Vienna-Alevi cultural federation lodged a constitutional objection to the Constitutional Court. Prior to this application, many new religions had already begun to seek official status in recent years. Indeed, the Jehovah's Witnesses won approval as a sectarian community after a successful lawsuit at the European Court of Human Rights. The Alevi faction's application was based on this precedent. Authorities argued that under the Islamic law after the 1988 revision, approval of Islamic organizations other than the IGGiÖ was not expected.

The Constitutional Court found that the 1987 ruling deemed forcing Muslims to organize into a single sectarian community unconstitutional, but that it should not be interpreted as denying the existence of other Muslim communities. Following this ruling, the Austrian-Islamic-Alevi faith community (*Islamische Alevitische Glaubensgemeinschaft in Österreich*) was approved as a registered faith community in December 2010 (Erkentniss vom 1 Dec 2010, B 1214–09/35). In addition, an application for status as a religious community was also allowed in May 2013 (BGBl. II Nr. 133/2013, 22 May 2013). Following this development, the Austrian-Islamic-Schiiti community (*Islamische-Schiitische Glaubensgemeinschaft in Österreich*) and the Paleo-Alevi faith community have been approved as faith communities (GZ BMUKK-12.056/0005-KA/2012; Bescheid vom 23 Aug 2013, GZ BMUKK-12.056/0006-KA/2012).

Here, we can observe a unique dynamic of the Austrian religious governance. A faction of Islam has acquired the status of accredited religions along with Catholicism, Protestantism, Greek Orthodoxy and Judaism. This system has not caused problems as long as the organizational scope of the subject of Muslims was self-evident.

Lacking in democratic selection and transparency, the past IGGiÖ leadership had still given due consideration to the Austrian established political parties and relationships with Austrian democracy. In the Graz City Council election in January 2008, the top candidate of the populist Free Democratic Party developed a campaign to criticize "excessive foreignization" and "Islamization" (Mourão Permoser and Rosenberger 2010, 1470–1471). In response to this, the IGGiÖ tried to calm the problem and persuaded the mosques not to make counter-mobilization. Further, the government began to consult the IGGiÖ as a symbolic policy partner of immigration problems, as seen in participation in the Integrated Forum in January 2008 (Mourão Permoser and Rosenberger 2010).

As the pressure of diversification and liberalization grew, however, the criteria for official recognition were disputed, which eventually has led to pluralization of the Muslim representatives. The election of the IGGiÖ chairman took place in 2010, and the Turks successfully occupied many delegates due to the mobilization by the Turkish organizations such as the ATiB. The new chairman was Fuat Sanac, a Turk. His succession itself was not surprising, as it has been expected since Schakfeh announced his intention to retire. But it is also a revelation of the competitive dynamics intensified by the democratization of the IGGiÖ. Having worked in Germany as a full-time employee of Millî Görüş, a large Turkish Islamist organization known for its critical stance against Western Values, Sanac, made remarks appreciating Millî Görüş even before his inauguration, which caused concern. The new leadership had stronger democratic legitimacy, but there was a possibility that relations with government and political parties may become difficult. This was also a problem of Islamization caused by democratization, which was also related to the position of the Welfare Party in mainland Turkey.

In 2015, a new Islam Law was enacted to fully revise the 1912 Law. The law aimed to further strengthen the Austrian Muslim by prohibiting continuous funding from abroad and training religious education leaders in Austria.

In this way, the religious governance of Austria has been relatively stable, but there is constant fluctuation in the structure of the representative organizations of Muslims that support it. Let's move on to a case in Germany that historically does not have a Muslim representative.

Muslims and the State in Germany: Toward "Austrification?"

At the end of 2015, about 4.5 million Muslims lived in Germany, around 5.5% of the population, of which it was estimated that the Turks account for about half (Stichs 2016). The proportion was lower than in 2008 when they exceeded two-thirds. However, the number of residents from the Middle East, including Syria, has increased by about 500,000 in the 5 years since 2011. In the 2008 survey, the Sunnis were nearly three quarters, 13% were Alevi, and 7% were Shias (Haug et al. 2009, 97).

As already mentioned, most Muslim residents in Germany had been foreigners, and no integration policy had been adopted for a long time. However, following the change of the trend triggered by the formation of the Red-Green Coalition government, integration policies towards Muslims began to take shape in Germany as well.

In 2005, the Merkel Grand Coalition government, consisting of the Christian Democrats and the Social Democrats, replaced the Red-Green Coalition. From the party-political composition of the government, it might be possible to expect policy reversal from the former government, but there was no retrogression. Rather, the continuity came to the fore, such as with the "Integration Summit" inviting Muslim delegates under aegis of the Interior Minister Wolfgang Schäuble of the Christian Democratic Party. The summit (the German Islamic Council) was held on September 27, 2006 for the first time, and a total of four meetings were held by 2009. In 2009, the Grand Coalition was replaced by the Conservative-Liberal Coalition from the

Christian Democrats and the Free Democrats. Schäuble was succeeded by Demezier. But the conference was held once a year.

One of the background factors of policy continuity was the heightened attention to educational problems. According to the results of the 2000 PISA survey reported at the end of 2001, Germany ranked low in every subject (20th in mathematics, 21st in reading comprehension and 20th in natural science among 32 countries). Although the ranking improved in the next 2003 survey, it was evident that pupils and students with immigration background had problems. Furthermore, in 2006, it was reported that the class collapse occurred in a district of Berlin (Ito 2008).

President Christian Wulff, who took office in 2010, delivered a speech entitled "Addressing Diversity and Promoting Unity" in his first address on the day of German Unification, in which he stated that "Christianity undoubtedly belongs to Germany. There is no doubt that Judaism belongs to Germany. This is our Judaeo-Christian history, but Islam also belongs to Germany in the meantime" (Vielfalt schätzen – Zusammenhalt fördern, http://www.bundespraesident.de/SharedDocs/Reden/DE/Christian-Wulff/Reden/2010/10/20101003_Rede_Anlage.pdf). Although there was controversy over this remark, there was enormous symbolic significance that the president formally recognized Islam on the very day commemorating German Unification.

So, what is the relationship between the state and Islam in this changing trend towards integration? There are important issues, such as learning German, acquiring social value in Germany and so on (Ito 2008). Here, we focus on the relationship between religion and education, which shows clear difference from the Austrian case. Let's look at the headscarf problem as an example.

In the beginning, when headscarves began to be problematized in France, there was no similar case in Germany; there was no concept of *Laïcité* in Germany, which prohibits bringing religion into public spaces (Tezuka 2008, 2009). In 1998, however, problems arose in Germany as to whether a teacher of public schools in Baden-Württemberg could wear scarves: students' religious freedom might be transgressed due to the teacher's power in the classroom. As the state did not hire this teacher, she sued the state government in an administrative trial. In 2003, the Federal Constitutional Court determined the disposition was unconstitutional. At the same time, however, the prospective legislative measures prohibiting headscarves were allowed as long as neutrality was maintained.

Because issues concerning education and religion fall within the authority of the state, the scarf problem has seen very different treatments in each state (Henkes and Kneip 2010). Among the 16 states, state law does not exist in the 5 states of former East Germany. Among the 11 states of former West Germany, provisions allowing Christian symbols while prohibiting Islamic ones were established in the 6 states where the Christian Democrats led the government. State law was also established by the two Social Democrat-led government, namely Bremen (coalition with the Christian Democratic Party) and Berlin (coalition with the Left Party), but both laws banned religious symbols in general. Furthermore, there were no laws in Schleswig-Holstein, Rheinland-Palatinate and Hamburg.

However, the state laws enacted with the Christian Democratic push led to an unexpected result. In the relevant lawsuits, most judgments found that a full ban on religious symbols, including Christian monk's clothes, was the Constitution-conforming interpretation of the laws, as the Federal Constitutional Court had requested neutrality. For this reason, the Interior Minister de Maizière said, "The more you try to drive away the symbols of other religions from public life, the greater the risk that attacks on Christian symbols in public daily life will be effective" (*FAZ. net*, 7 Mar 2010, http://www.faz.net/aktuell/politik/inland/im-interview-thomas-de-maiziere-in-der-koalition-wird-zu-viel-herumgequatscht-1638637.html).

As a result, the circumstances surrounding religious education have also changed, and the voice of Muslim religious education was raised by the Christian Democrats and the Free Democrats. For example, President Wullf was known to advocate official recognition of Islam by a sort of Concordat in 2007, when he was the Lower Saxony State Prime Minister (*Die Welt*, 26 Jun2007, https://www.welt.de/politik/article976070/Wulff-hofft-auf-Staatsvertrag-mit-Muslimen.html). In Hessen, the Liberal Democrat Phil Hearn aimed for the introduction of Islam education by 2013 (*FAZ.net*, 31 Jul 2009, http://www.faz.net/aktuell/rhein-main/hessen/islam unterricht-hahn-schmueckt-sich-mit-der-integration-1577450.html; 17 Aug 2010, http://www.faz.net/aktuell/rhein-main/hessen/schwierige-traegersuche-hahn-unterri cht-fuer-muslime-spaetestens-in-drei-jahren-11025432.html). Throughout 2012, the conflict between the Free Democratic Party and the Christian Democratic Union continued, but at the end of the year, they decided to introduce it in the fall of 2013 (*FAZ.net*, 18 Dec 2012, http://www.faz.net/aktuell/rhein-main/schulpolitik-weg-frei-fuer-islamischen-religionsunterricht-11997308.html). As is already the case in the Netherlands, the conservative Christian Democrats may become an ally to Islamic religious education in order to resist the secularization of education.

In this regard, too, the organization of the Muslims was problematic. As in the Austrian case, religious organizations in Germany also occupied a special status of "public corporation." As religious matters are under the authority of the state, the recognized denominations differed according to the state, but they were almost restricted to Christianity and Judaism. From the German side, the lack of church-like organizations by Muslims had been often regarded as a cause of difficulty in incorporating them into the existing legal frameworks.

Although the Integration Summit mentioned above did not result in concrete policies, it is noteworthy that the coordinating organization of Muslims was built in the process. During the 2007 summit, the German Muslim Coordination Council (KRM) was established by the four Muslim organizations. Participating were the German-Muslim Central Assembly (*Zentralrat*), the Turkish-Islamic Union for Religious Affairs (DitiB), the Islamic Council of Islam (*Isramrat*), and the Federation of Islamic Cultural Centres. Based on this, the German-Muslim Coordination Council sought to implement religious education similar to that of Catholicism. North Rhine-Westphalia State issued a joint statement with these four organizations in February 2011 to clarify the schedule of introducing Islamic religious education (*Gemeinsame Erklärung des Koordinationsrats der Muslime und der Ministerin für Schule und Weiterbildung des Landes Nordrhein -Westfalen über den Weg zu einem bekenntnisorientierten Islamunterticht*, 22 Feb 2011, https://www.gruene-hessen.de/landtag/files/2011/02/Gemeinsame-Erklaerung.pdf).

There is no room to discuss the concrete effect of Islamic religious education, but as it is a policy within the framework of integration, it should be noted that there was a change in the discourse from the past. In some provinces, some classes similar to Islamic religious education had already been implemented as pilot projects. In North Rhine-Westphalia, the subject "Religion knowledge" (*Religionskunde*) had been established, and in Bayern, this had been implemented within the framework of supplementary education for foreigners. These two are religious education for foreigners and a part of education by mother tongue. It is evident here that German policy concerning Islam had been a kind of foreign policy. The content of the education implemented in Germany had put emphasis on the world-wide Muslim community and was not based on the idea of "Islam in Germany."

The current policy direction is contrary. Education for Muslims in German society should be taught in German. For this purpose, the Academic Council (*Wissenschaftsrat*) recommended the establishment of religious teachers and Islamic research centers for the development of Imams at a couple of universities in 2010 (Empfehlungen zur Weiterentwicklung von Theologien und religionsbezogenen Wissenschaften an deutschen Hochschulen, 29 Jan 2010, https://www.bmbf.de/files/WissenschaftsratEmpfehlung2010.pdf). In the past, some pilot-projects were set up in several universities, such as Erlangen, Osnabrück, in cooperation with trials of religious education as mentioned above. Based on these experiences, the program of Islamic Studies was set up in Tübingen, Münster/Osnabruck in October 2010 and received a four-million-euro startup subsidy from the federal budget (*FAZ, net*, 14 Oct 2010, http://www.faz.net/aktuell/politik/inland/hochschulen-tuebingen-und-muenster-osnabrueck-wollen-islamstudiengaenge-einfuehren-1575039.html). It was also approved for Frankfurt/Giessen and Erlangen/Nürmberg in February 2011 (Budesministerium für Bildung und Forschung, "Zeitgemäße Integrationspolitik: Islamische Theologie an deutschen Hochschulen," 30 Oct 2012, http://www.bmbf.de/de/15619.php).

Conclusion: Historical Diversity Facing Common Challenges

Let's compare the cases in Germany and Austria reviewed above and examine the meaning. First, the primary factor that brought about the difference between the two countries was the difference in historical circumstances. There can be various factors, but this chapter emphasizes the contrast between the "nation-state" and "empire" in particular. Whereas Germany aimed at the "empire" in the sense that it expands its version on the basis of the nation-state, the Habsburg monarchy, as a multi-national empire, had to include heterogeneous communities. As a result, while the German Nationality Act in 1913 was enacted to strengthen the homogeneity of citizens, the Habsburg Islam Law in 1912 institutionalized religious diversity. (In a similar vein, Gosewinkel (2008) argued that integration of the British Empire has been based on the feudal *jus sanguinis* principle and loyalty to the Crown.)

Second, the circumstances after the World War II consolidated these differences. In Austria, not only were the Habsburg legal provisions inherited, but also the former Yugoslavian source of labor migrants, among whom the Bosnian Muslims were included. The problem of their integration was incorporated into existing church–state relations. In Germany, foreign workers are Turkish, and the image of "Muslim" is almost restricted to the Turks. For this reason, West Germany had not admitted for a long time that it was an immigrant country, and the integration of Muslims has long been a problem of foreigners.

Third, the differences in institutionalized relationships between Islam and the state also affect the direction of Muslim organizations. In Austria, there is a representative organization of Muslims, emphasizing the identity of Muslims in Austria. In Germany, however, the focus had been on the aspect of cultural and religious intergenerational transfer. The aspect of German Muslims was only recently taken up through the integration summit.

Despite these historically conditioned divergences, we can also see the similarities or converging trends. In Germany, creating Muslim representative organizations had been an important issue. Austria had been referred to as a model, and the division of German Muslim organizations, or the differences in treatment by state, were regarded as problems. In June 2013, the Hesse state government finally approved the Ahmadi faction, seemingly because the faction is reform-oriented, and the organization is Christian type (*Die Welt*, 13 Juni 2013, https://www.welt.de/politik/deutschland/article117076904/Der-Islam-gehoert-nun-offiziell-zu-Deutschland.html). Further, at the end of 2012, the Hamburg city-state government signed an agreement with three Islamic groups and the Alevi faction, and in January 2013, Bremen had signed a similar agreement. In Austria, however, the monopoly of representation by the IGGiÖ has been problematized in recent years. In both cases, the balance between collective group rights and internal diversity within a religion is becoming a problem.

In addition, there is a common trend to invest in teacher training and expansion of higher education for that purpose. Here you can see the intention to promote the European value order and the adaptive Muslims symbolized by the word *Euro-Islam*. However, there is still tension between the networks of Muslims with transnational extensions and the fact that they are part of public education in Germany/Austria.

Group-based religious governance is an important issue in considering multiculturalism in Europe, specifically the relationship between the state and Muslims (cf. Bader 2007). This chapter emphasized the contrast between Austria and Germany and insists that such a framework depends on concrete historical conditions.

Cross-References

▶ Immigration Policy and Left-Right Politics in Western Europe
▶ Multiculturalism and Citizenship in the Netherlands

References

Abdel-Fattah B (2004) Muslims in Austria: the early recognition of religious rights. http://www.siyassa.org.eg/esiyassa/ahram/2004/4/1/FILE4.htm. Accessed 5 Aug 2008

Abid LJ (2006) Muslims in Austria: integration through participation in Austrian society. J Muslim Minor Aff 26:263–278. https://doi.org/10.1080/13602000600937770

Bader V (2007) Secularism or democracy? Associational governance of religious diversity. Amsterdam University Press, Amsterdam

Bair J (2002) Das Islamgesetz. Springer, Vienna/New York

Brubaker R (1992) Citizenship and nationhood in France and Germany. Harvard University Press, Cambridge, MA

Dickinson ER (2008) The German Empire: an empire? Hist Work J 66:129–162. https://doi.org/10.1093/hwj/dbn028

Dolezal M, Helbling M, Hutter S (2010) Debating Islam in Austria, Germany and Switzerland: ethnic citizenship, church–state relations and right-wing populism. West Eur Polit 33:171–190. https://doi.org/10.1080/01402380903538773

Eurofound (2010) Intercultural policies and intergroup relations. Case study: Vienna, Austria. European Foundation for the Improvement of Living and Working Conditions, Dublin

Fahrmeir AK (1997) Nineteenth-century German citizenships: a reconsideration. Hist J 40:721–752

FRA (European Union Agency for Fundamental Rights) (2009) EU-MIDIS. Data in focus report 2: Muslims. https://fra.europa.eu/sites/default/files/fra_uploads/448-EU-MIDIS_MUSLIMS_EN.pdf. Accessed 15 Sept 2018

Gosewinkel D (2008) The dominance of nationality? Nation and citizenship from the late nineteenth century onwards: a comparative European perspective. Ger Hist 26:92–108. https://doi.org/10.1093/gerhis/ghm005

Haug S, Müssig S, Stichs A (2009) Muslimisches Leben in Deutschland. Bundesamt für Migration und Flüchtlinge, Berlin

Henkes C, Kneip S (2010) Von offener Neutralität zu (unintendierten) Laizismus: Das Kopftuch zwischen demokratischen Mehrheitswillen und rechtsstaatlichen Schranken. Leviathan 38:589–616

Howard MM (2009) The politics of citizenship in Europe. Cambridge University Press, Cambridge

Hunt R (2002) Islam in Austria. Muslim World 92:115–128

Ito N (2008) Doitsu ni okeru togo seisaku (Integration policy in Germany). Yoroppa Kenkyu (Eur Stud) 7:181–190

Janda A, Vogel M (eds) (2010) Islam in Österreich. Österreichischer Integrationsfonds, Vienna

Janoski T (2010) The ironies of citizenship: naturalization and integration in industrialized countries. Cambridge University Press, Cambridge

Khorchide M (2009) Der islamische Religionsunterricht zwischen Integration und Parallelgesellschaft. VS Verlag, Wiesbaden

Koenig M (2007) Europeanising the governance of religious diversity. An institutionalist account of Muslim struggles for public recognition. J Ethn Migr Stud 33:911–932. https://doi.org/10.1080/13691830701432756

Kohn H (1944) The idea of nationalism: a study in its origins and background. Macmillan, New York

Koopmans R, Statham P, Giugni M, Passy F (2005) Contested citizenship: immigration and cultural diversity in Europe. University of Minnesota Press, Minneapolis

Kraler A, Sohler K (2005) Active civic participation of immigrants in Austria. Country Report prepared for the European research project POLITIS. www.politis-europe.uni-oldenburg.de/download/Austria.pdf. Accessed 15 Sept 2018

Kroissenbrunner S (2003) Islam and Muslim immigrants in Austria: socio-political networks and Muslim leadership of Turkish immigrants. Immigr Minor 22:188–207. https://doi.org/10.1080/0261928042000244826

Kurier-Serie (2005) Eine Kurier-Serie zum Thema Islam in Österreich (1–5 August 2005). http://www2.mcdaniel.edu/german/islamindach/islkamindach_PDF/Islam%20in%20%D6sterreich%20-%20Kurier%20August%202005.pdf. Accessed 15 Sept 2018

Laurence J (2009) The corporatist antecedent of contemporary state-Islam relations. Eur Polit Sci 8:301–315. https://doi.org/10.1057/eps.2009.15

Leonhard J, Hirschhausen U (eds) (2009) Empires und Nationalstaaten im 19. Jahrhundert. Vandenhoeck und Ruprecht, Göttingen

Mazower M (2004) The strange triumph of human rights, 1933–1950. Hist J 47(2):379–398. https://doi.org/10.1017/S0018246X04003723

Mohr IC (2002) Islamic instruction in Germany and Austria: a comparison of principles derived from religious thought. Cahiers d'Etudes sur la Mediterranee Orientale et le monde Turco-Iranien (CEMOTI) 33:149–166

Montadel D (n.d.) Islam in Austria. http://www.euro-islam.info/country-profiles/austria/. Accessed 25 Apr 2011

Mourão Permoser J, Rosenberger SK (2010) Religious organisations as political actors in the context of migration: Islam and Orthodoxy in Austria. J Ethn Migr Stud 36:1463–1481. https://doi.org/10.1080/1369183X.2010.500819

Nimmi E (1999) Nationalist multiculturalism in late imperial Austria as a critique of contemporary liberalism: the case of Bauer and Renner. J Polit Ideol 4:289–314. https://doi.org/10.1080/13569319908420800

Nimmi E (ed) (2005) National cultural autonomy and its contemporary critics. Routledge, London

Potz R (2005) Islamischer Religionsunterricht in Österreich und Deutschland. http://www.abif.at/deutsch/download/Files/31_Islamischer_Religionsunterricht-SummaryNeu.pdf. Accessed 11 Aug 2011

Potz R (2010) State and religion in Austria. In: Potz R, Kroissenbrunner S, Hafner A (eds) State, law and religion in pluralistic societies – Austrian and Indonesian perspectives. V&R Unipress, Göttingen, pp 13–20

Ra'anan U et al (eds) (1991) State and nation in multi-ethnic societies: the breakup of multinational states. Manchester University Press, Manchester

Rohe M (2006) Perspektiven und Herausforderungen in der Integration muslimischer MitburgerInnen in Österreich. Bundesministerium für Innen, Berlin

Rosenberger S, Sauer B (2008) Islam im öffentlichen Raum. Debatten und Regulationen in Europa. Eine Einführung. Österr Z Polit 37:387–399

Schmidinger T (2007) Islam in Österreich – zwischen Repräsentation und Integration. In: Khol A et al (eds) Österreichisches Jahrbuch für Politik 2007. Böhlau, Vienna, pp 235–256

Schwarz K (n.d.) Staat und Kirche im Donau- und Karpatenraum in historischer Perspektive. http://kgdk.org.txt/Schwarz%20-%20Staat%20und%20Kirche%20im%20DK.htm. Accessed 12 Feb 2008

Stern J, Valchars G (2013) EUDO citizenship observatory. Country report: Austria. Robert Schuman Centre for Advanced Studies. http://eudo-citizenship.eu/admin/?p=file&appl=countryProfiles&f=2013-28-Austria.pdf. Accessed 15 Sept 2018

Stichs A (2016) Wie viele Muslime leben in Deutschland? Eine Hochrechnung über die Anzahl der Muslime in Deutschland zum Stand 31. Dezember 2015. Im Auftrag der Deutschen Islam Konferenz. Bundesamt für Migration und Flüchtlinge. https://www.bamf.de/SharedDocs/Anlagen/DE/Publikationen/WorkingPapers/wp71-zahl-muslime-deutschland.pdf. Accessed 15 Sept 2018

Sticker M (2008) Sondermodell Österreich? Die Islamische Glaubensgemeinschaft in Österreich (IGGiÖ). Drava, Klagenfurt

Strobl A (2007) Der österreichische Islam: Entwicklung, Tendenzen und Möglichkeiten. SWS-Rundsch 45:520–543

Tezuka K (2008) Isuramu jyosei kyoshi to sukafu kinshi (Muslim female teacher and the ban on headscarves) Mie daigaku kyoiku gakubu kenkyu kiyo. Bull Fac Educ 59:113–131

Tezuka K (2009) Isuramu no sukafu kimchi mondai (the ban on Islamic headscarves issues). Mie daigaku kyoiku gakubu kenkyu kiyo. Bull Fac Educ 60:117–133

Ther P (2001) Imperial instead of national history: positioning modern German history on the map of European empires. In: Miller A, Rieber AJ (eds) Imperial rule. Central European University Press, Budapest, pp 47–65

Ulram PA (2009) Integration in Österreich: Einstellungen, Orientierungen, und Erfahrungen von MigrantInnen und Angehörigen der Mehrheitsbevölkerung. GfK-Austria, Vienna

Intended Illegal Infiltration or Compelled Migration: Debates on Settlements of Rohingya Muslims in India

95

Sangit Kumar Ragi

Contents

Introduction	1878
Conclusions	1887
References	1888

Abstract

Settlement of Rohingya migrants in some parts of India has triggered schism and polarization in the Indian politics. While most of the political parties opposed to the BJP and Muslim social and cultural organizations supported the settlement of the migrants and asked the government to consider their case from humanitarian perspectives, the BJP party and other rightwing social and cultural organizations called upon the people to stage protests against it. The government at the center also opposed their settlements and publicly declared to identify and send them back to their country. From places of settlements to religion of the migrants became the subjects of debate. This chapter critically examines why the settlements of Rohingya migrants evoked so much protests and noise at national level? Secondly, were the locations of settlements a well-considered choice of the migrants or they were taken to these destinations by people this side of the border? These questions became pertinent because instead of settling in the North East provinces of India they traveled deep far into the Indian territory, comprising extreme North in Kashmir to Southern city of Hyderabad. It analyzes why Hindus were so much agitated on the issue and what it meant for the Muslims who came forward to support the settlements of Rohingyas in India.

S. K. Ragi (✉)
Department of Political Science, Social Science Building, North Campus, University of Delhi, Delhi, India
e-mail: sangit_ragi@yahoo.co.in

© The Author(s), under exclusive license to Springer Nature Singapore Pte Ltd. 2019
S. Ratuva (ed.), *The Palgrave Handbook of Ethnicity*,
https://doi.org/10.1007/978-981-13-2898-5_159

Keywords

Rohingya migrants · People Democratic Party · Jammu and Kashmir · National Conference

Introduction

Migration and settlements of Rohingya Muslims in India dominated the national debates for weeks in India in the month of January 2018 and continued to capture headlines with intermittence. Though the issue had been compounding for few years, it captured the national attention only after two of the Rohingya migrants filed a case in the Supreme Court against the government proclamations to deport them. It further got momentum when the nation came to know that the state of Jammu and Kashmir government had allowed the settlement of 5700 Rohingyas in Jammu and Ladakh regions. The people in Jammu, particularly Hindus, opposed such settlements, whereas the valley-centric parties like the National Conference and People Democratic Party supported this. The valley-centric parties like the PDP and the National Conference used humanitarian arguments to support their decisions. Others in the valley also joined the chorus. On the other hand, Hindus in Jammu did not like it. They resented and organized protests against the settlement of Rohingyas in the state. The resentment was because the same sets of people who were instrumental in exodus of Pandits from Kashmir valley, and did not work for their rehabilitation, were talking about now settlements of people coming from across the border.

Following this, Rohingya settlements triggered a national debate which involved not only the political parties but also academia, media, human rights activists, and other social organizations in the country. A high degree of ethnic and ideological polarization across academia, intellectuals, and political class was seen across the country. The non-BJP political formations competed against each other in support of Rohingyas' settlements. From Samajwadi Party and Bahujan Samaj Party in Uttar Pradesh to left parties, All India Trinamool Congress (AITMC) and the Indian National Congress (INC) came in defense of Rohingyas' settlements in India. All India Trinamool Congress, a major regional and ruling party in Bengal, openly contested the central government. A member of the legislative assembly of Bengal from TMC said that sheltering Rohingyas was not illegal. Mamata Banerjee also had twitted in support of giving shelter to these migrants and opposed central government decision to deport them. She in her tweet said that she supported the appeal of the UN which said that they should be treated as persecuted humans. She further said that all comers are not terrorists (The Hindustan Times 2018). The CPI (M) not just asked the government not to deport the migrants but also take up their cause with the United Nations Human Rights Commission (UNHRC) and other international forums besides taking up the matter in bilateral talks between the two governments at the highest level (Donot Deport Them 2017). In other words, CPM wanted that the Government of India should take the initiative and use its offices to influence Myanmar government in support of Rohingyas. The Congress party accepted that the matter is very serious, but it did not come out with a clear stand on the issue. The party asked the government to take all the parties into confidence while formulating a policy and response to Rohingyas' settlements (The Hindu 2017). But soon what it did clearly exposed the party taking a stand in favor of migrants. The party allowed its Delhi unit to make demonstration on roads in support of Rohingyas (Times Now 2017). The party also invoked humanitarian issue and argued that the Rohingyas are victims of the state repression in Burma and the Indian government should not do something like forceful deportation as that will hurt the image of the government.

The extreme response, however, came from the Muslim organizations in particular. All India Majlis-e-Ittehadul Muslimeen (AIMIM) president Asaduddin Owaisi held that "if refugees from Tibet and Sri Lanka can stay in India, why not the Rohingya Muslims from Myanmar." (The Hindu 2017) It was on expected lines. The thrust of the argument was that if Hindus persecuted elsewhere can come and settle here why not Muslims? Owaisi wanted to convey that the government policy toward the migrants is selective and discriminatory and so is the response of the majority community as there is no national outrage against the non-Muslim migrants and their settlements. In fact, Muslims in general and their organizations expressed solidarity with the migrants. They held demonstrations and submitted their memorandum to the government to take care of the interests of Rohingyas at different levels and do not deport them forcibly. At Aurangabad, in Maharashtra, they held a rally and submitted memorandum to the district magistrate. It was represented by 21 organizations, mainly the Muslims except for the Samajwadi Party (The organizations included: Numainda Council, JamiaIslamiaKashifulUloom, Jama Masjid, Jamiat Ulema-e-Hind, Maharashtra Muslim Awami Committee, All India Imams Council, Khidmat-e-Hujjaj, MdQaisar Iqbal Siddiqui, Raza Academy, MIM, Samajwadi Party, Ameer MarkazUloom e Sharia, Muslim Personal Law Board, Al-Hira Educational & Welfare Society, JamiatUlemaMarathwada, Majlis-Ul-Ulema, Happy To Help Foundation, Late Farhan Education & Welfare Society, Anjuman-e-KhademulMasoomin, Muslim Youth Forum Marathwada, K K Group and Azad Yuva Brigade were among the organisations that participated in the rally.). Though the settlements of Rohingyas extended to states like Delhi and Rajasthan as well, Jammu and Hyderabad settlements became the major contesting points.

Right-wing social and cultural organizations, and parties like BJP and its allies, openly opposed it. Rashtriya Swayamsevak Sangh (RSS) held that both Rohingyas and Bangladeshis are not the refugees. They are the foreigners who have illegally sneaked into India, and therefore they should be deported. The Prant Karyavah (executive head of a province) of the state Purushottam Dadhichi held that they are security threat to both the center and the state, and therefore they should not be allowed to settle (The Indian Express 2018b). Vishwa Hindu Parishad (VHP), a Hindu organization having pan-India impacts too, made demands from the government to immediately deport the migrants. It passed the resolution against the migrants and appealed to the people to boycott them socially and economically (The Indian Express 2018a). These pressures worked as the government filed affidavit in the Supreme Court against the migrants' settlements. The party criticized the Congress and the other opposition for their stands on the issue which it depicted were driven by political considerations at best. Needless to say, the case of the two Rohingyas who had filed the case in the Supreme Court requesting the court to direct the government to stop their deportation created a national furor in which there was an explicit polarization of stands across political and ethnic lines.

As discussed, it is not only the political parties but media also carried the debates where a sharp ideological and perceptional positioning was visible. There were channels which went into to suggest that their investigation showed no links between the Rohingya migrants and the terror groups or terrorist activities. For instance, NDTV did a story which showed that only 0.25% of Rohingyas had FIR (First Information Report) against them in the state of J&K. Out of the 15 FIRs, most of them were related to minor crimes like thefts, violation of VISA rules, etc. The nature of crimes committed by them proved that they were not involved in terror activities (Rohingyas 2017). No proof of links between them and the Pakistani terrorists and Rakhine Rohingya Liberation Army was established. Quoting Inspector General of Police, Dr. S D Singh of Jammu region the report concluded that the migrants' settlers individually or in group were not involved in organized or any serious crimes (Ibid.). Obviously, the report dented the narrative of the government which claimed that Rohingyas had terror links and they are threat to the national security.

On the other hand, Zee group and News 18 group, The Republic and channels like Times Now anchored the debates against Rohingyas. The Republic debates titled like, Will pro-Rohingya Brigade Explain? Rohingya Terror Exposed, and so on. All these channels focused on three things: first how Rohingyas are involved in Hindu killings in Burma; second, how they are linked with the terrorists groups; and third, why PDP and NC do not show similar concerns toward the Hindu migrants from Kashmir and why there is secular silence against the human rights violation in Muslim countries. For the first time, Indian media got so polarized on such subjects where vertical division was clearly visible which explained their ideological positioning on such subjects.

Why has there been so much polarization on Rohingya Muslims in the country? After all there has been influx of Buddhist Chakmas and Hindus from Bangladesh. Similarly, there has been migration of population from Sri Lanka, and they have been allowed to settle in India. There have been also Afghani settlements which are primarily Muslims, and yet the government or the civil society has not made too much noise of it then why only against Rohingyas? Is it because Rohingyas are primarily Muslims by religion? In what sense of terms settlements of Rohingyas are threat to the national security? Why did Rohingya migrants who came from Burma cover such a long distance from the Far East to travel to the extreme North in Kashmir and in Hyderabad in the South? Why did they not sneak into the North-East states of India which are racially and geographically close to them? Is there any pattern of settlements? Further, is this only coincident or their selection of destinations for settlements are part of well-thought-of plan and agencies behind it? Were their migrations to Hyderabad and Jammu done because they found it safer compared to the other states because they happened to be the Muslim-dominated places? Is there an agency which is working for their settlements in such areas in order to increase the numerical dominance of followers of Islam to alter the religious demography of the places? Further that how has the rise of violent form of global Islam increasingly shaped the mind of the common people toward the Muslims in general? These are the questions which become important to understand the Rohingya issues in India.

Rohingya Muslims are the people settled in the Rakhine state of Burma. They stay in Burma, but as per the new constitution, they are not the citizens of the state. Burmese government has snatched away the citizenship rights that they used to enjoy. Muslim constitutes nearly 8% of the total population. They are widely dispersed across the country because they are of different origins. There are Muslims from China, Malaya, India, Sri Lanka, and so on. While the Chinese and Malayan Muslims are white in complexion, the Muslims migrated from India and Sri Lanka are black in color. Further, while the Chinese Muslims are located in different parts of Northern Burma, the Muslims of Malaya origin and Indian Muslims are mostly settled in far south-east of the country, Rangoon, and its near vicinity, respectively. However, the majority of Muslims nearly 1.1 million are settled in the north-west state of Rakhine. This part of Burma once was called Arakan areas, and it borders with Bangladesh.

Burma is a Buddhist-dominated country. Buddhist population is roughly around 45 million. Muslims concentration is very high only in the Arakan or Rakhine region. There are contested accounts of History. The Muslim intellectuals and historians argue that the Muslims in Rakhine state were the original inhabitants since the eighth century in Burma. They came into contact with the Arab traders and converted themselves to Islam. (Al-Mehmood 2016) They also hold that Arakan was an independent Kingdom which became part of Burma only in the eighteenth century when the Burman king Bodapaya conquered it in 1784 and annexed the territory. Burmese nationalists, however, hold that the Arakan was part of Burma since the time immemorial. Further, Burma remained under the British occupation from 1824 when it was made to be the part of British India till it was given independence in 1948.

As the Arakan or Rakhine province was Muslim dominated, it wanted to be part of Pakistan. Buddhist nationalists confronted this, and this became a bone of contention between the two communities in subsequent years. They harbored apprehensions against them which continued even after independence. When the new government after independence came into power, it used ruthless power to suppress the possible Muslim revolts. The tension started brewing up, and in 1950 an armed insurgency was started by a section of the Muslim community named Mujahideen. However, it failed to make much impact. But this made the majority community to understand that the Muslim's loyalty is not toward Burma. It made a permanent mark of mistrust between the two communities.

In 1962, when *General Ne Win* came to power, the government took strong measures toward the extremists. The government came out with national registration cards to its citizens, and Rohingyas were given identity cards which treated them as foreigners. It needs to be placed here for clear understanding that even in the Citizenship Act of 1948, Rohingyas were not included in the ethnic groups which were to be given citizenship. However, they did not feel so much hardship initially. The Burmese government also held that the Muslims settled in Arakan areas are the ones who were brought by the British from Bangladesh, and therefore they are illegal migrants. Advancing this argument in 1982, a new citizenship law was introduced which declared them noncitizens and thereby snatched away all the citizenry rights from them. A three level citizenship law was enacted in which Rohingyas were not recognized as one of the indigenous ethnic groups of the country. They were now supposed to provide proofs that their families lived before 1948, and they are able to speak one of the national languages. It was difficult for them as they lacked the documents of stay before 1948. As a result they overnight became foreigners. They not only were now denied the right to vote in the system but their other activities were also restricted, including some movements. They could not enter now certain professions like law and medicine and were not allowed to run their own business. They were not natural but naturalized people of Burma. It needs to be understood that the rights of citizens are not withdrawn from all the Muslims but only those who the government found after screening as foreigners settled from Bangladesh. As the crackdown on outsiders had started already in 1978, over 250,000 Rohingyas left their homes and migrated to Bangladesh who returned after UN arranged a settlement formula between Bangladesh and Myanmar.

Decades of isolation and alienation has allowed the radicalization of Muslims in the Arakan region, especially after the appearance of Wahhabi Islam on the global map (Wahavi Islam divides the world into Darul Harab and Darul Islam. Darul harb is the land which is governed by Non-Muslims whereas Darul Islam is the land which is governed by the followers of Islam. It propagates that the territory of Darul Harab must be converted into the land of Islam and all means are acceptable to it.). In 2016, Arakan Rohingya Salvation Army (ARSA) came to fore with attacks on three police posts which resulted into killing of nine police officers (BBC Asia News 2017). The army retaliated with disproportionate force resulting into killing of over 400 Rohingya Muslims. The army claimed that it killed only the ultras, whereas the Rohingyas and human rights organizations indicated that the majority of the people who were killed were the innocent civilians (Ibid BBC Asia News.). While the army and the government establishment claim that the Arakan Rohingya Salvation Army (ARSA) is primarily a terrorist group, the group justifies its organization and such actions on the ground that the government is involved in genocide of Muslims, and therefore they are left with no option but to take arms in the hands. While the Rohingya ultras justify their action on the ground that the state has been coercing them and they are being denied even the basic human rights, the state justifies its actions on the ground that they are the ultras and therefore cannot be treated with soft hands.

While there is one narrative that the ARSA has a no link with international Jihadi groups and its activities are limited to resistance to state atrocities against the Rohingyas, recent revelations have debunked this premise. The October 9, 2016, attacks by Rohingyas have revealed that the assailants had link with people in

Pakistan and Saudi Arabia where they were trained and exposed to handling weapons (https://in.reuters.com/article/us-myanmar-rohingya/myanmars-rohingya-insurgency-has-links-to-saudi-pakistan-report-idINKBN1450Y7). It was found that the Rohingyas who were involved in attacks were trained by Afghans in the Rakhine state for almost 2 years. The Brussels-based International Crisis Group revealed that Rohingyas have also fought for Jihads in other parts of the world (http://www.dw.com/en/is-saudi-wahhabism-fueling-rohingya-muslim-insurgency/a-36791809). There are also reports that they receive funds from some of the gulf countries for Jihads. The matter of fact is that the whole scenario in the Rakhine province worsened with taring of the Muslims in Guerilla warfare and formation of Harakah al-Yaqin by Atah Ullah Khan (ISI 2017). This organization further has links with other terrorist organizations in the name of Islam. Atah Ullah Khan was instrumental in issuance of Fatwa to the Rohingya Muslims to support extremist activities of Harakah al-Yaqin. This extremist organization used sophisticated weapons to attack the armed forces of Myanmar. This resulted into retaliatory violence by the armed forces in which even the common Muslims suffered heavily.

Further, in the Muslim-dominated Rakhine state, if military and Buddhists have come out openly against the Muslims, the latter also has targeted the Hindu and Buddhist populations (https://www.washingtonpost.com/world/asia_pacific/we-are-going-to-kill-you-villagers-in-burma-recount-violence-by-rohingya-muslim-militants/2017/11/14/409ff59b-849d-4459-bdc7-d1ea2b5ff9a6_story.html?utm_term=.d7527703e6d9). The report of Annie Goven filed in the Washington Post on 15 November 2017 reveals that Hindus and Buddhists also have their own terror stories to share with. There are several internally displaced people settled currently in the Western Burma who hold that they would never like to go back to their homes. They fear that Rohingyas will slit their throat and kill the entire family. Hindus also became targets of the Rohingya Muslims. On 27 September 2017, the Government of Myanmar found out mass graves of 45 dead bodies of Hindus near Fakira Bazar (Hasnat 2017). It claimed that ARSA had come to the Hindu village, gathered up around 100 of them, chased them to their fields, and finally killed them with knives (Tun 2017). One can understand the violence between the local Buddhists and the state on the one hand and Rohingya Muslims on the other, but why the Hindus were killed is still an idiom to be resolved. Is it not because the Rohingyas are also intolerant to other faiths? Even the Christians living in Burma acknowledge that it is the terror activities of the Rohingya Muslims that the state has resorted to repressive attitude (https://learningenglish.voanews.com/a/rohingya-immigrants/4065689.html). The stories of Hindus being killed by the Rohingya Muslims also infuriated Hindus in India.

Needless to say, in the last three decades, over 1.1 million Rohingyas have left the country. The major destinations have been Bangladesh, Malaysia, and India. Since the border of Bangladesh meets the Arakan region, the major exodus has been to Bangladesh. According to one estimate, nearly 890,000 Rohingyas have fled to Bangladesh followed by 350,000 in Pakistan, 200,000 in Saudi Arabia, 150,000 in Malaysia, and 40,000 in India. The matter of fact is that now Bangladesh, and even Malaysia, Pakistan, and Saudi Arabia have refused to welcome Rohingya migrants. Bangladesh thinks that it cannot bear further the burden of population coming from Myanmar (Ashrq Al-Awsat 2017). This applies to other Muslim countries as well. This gives ammunition to the right-wing organizations in India to argue that when the Muslim countries are not ready to accommodate their coreligionists, why should India give them the shelter? There is a substance in this argument. Is pan-Islamism mere rhetoric for political consolidation? These questions become valid in context of idea of Muslim brotherhood dominating the Islamic ideology at moment.

The Malaysian government made several statements against the government of Myanmar, but it was not ready to accommodate the refugees. So is with other Muslim countries. For example, Turkey government issued strong statements in support of Rohingyas, but they are not ready to give space for settlement of these stateless people. Gulf countries are the richest countries in the Muslim world. They are ready to extend financial help, but they are not ready to accommodate them on their soil. It is not only in case of Burma. What happened in case of Syrian refugees are for all to see. It is finally Germany and the European countries which gave them refugee status. No Muslim country came forward to give land for their settlement and grant citizenship. The 2014 Report of Amnesty International is really shocking. The report noted that none of the countries of the Gulf Cooperation Council which included rich gulf countries accommodated even a single Syrian refugee (Dehlvi 2017a).

The religion for which they aspire to die did not come for their rescue. The argument can be made that why the people from far distant land like Myanmar should be accommodated in their countries, but the fact is that after the start of Syrian crisis, there has been mass migration of population from Syria, but there has been no helping hand from the Arab world. The Gulf Cooperation Council which comprises of several Islamic countries like Saudi Arabia, Oman, Qatar, Kuwait, Bahrain, UAE, etc. did not extend the hands of support (Dehlvi 2017b). United Nations has termed it as the biggest humanitarian crisis, but no affirmative action has come up from the world communities. While the Muslim nations such as Malaysia, Bangladesh, Indonesia, and Pakistan tried to convey their anguish over the on-going ethnic violence against the Rohingya Muslims, the Western countries remained rather reluctant. When the secretary of the USA visited Myanmar, he termed the violence against the Rohingyas as "ethnic cleansing" and indicated of applying sanctions against Burma, but they did not take any substantial stand (Reuters 2017). This was again used by the right-wing organizations and the government to argue against Rohingyas.

Further, the conditions of the non-Muslims in the Muslim countries also allowed the non-Muslims in the country to display a sense of apathy to the Rohingya cause. This was raised not only by the Hindus but also the Muslims in the country. Sultan Shahin, the founder and editor of the New Age Muslim, while participating in a news channel debate argued that why do Indian Muslim leaders and Ulemas remain silent spectators when the human rights of non-Hindus are violated in Muslim-dominated countries like Bangladesh, Pakistan, Indonesia, Malaysia, etc.? Why do Muslims of the world do not speak against the human rights violations in Islamic countries?

Do the human rights belong only to the Muslims and not to the other religious communities? This question became pertinent in light of exodus of Hindus from Pakistan and Bangladesh (The New Age 2017).

In the recent past, there have been several stories of torture and abduction of Hindu women in Pakistan which created national outrage. Unfortunately, the Muslims organizations and leaders never hit the streets for the Hindus. That is why when Muslim organizations invoked cultural, civilizational, and humanitarian arguments to defend settlements of Rohingyas in the country, there were few takers. The cultural and civilization logic emanated from the great saying that this country celebrates the ethos of *Atithi Devo Bhavah* (Guests are God). And therefore, if India denies the shelter to the persecuted communities, it would be going against its own ethos which the right-wing organizations and nationalists always boast off. The President of All India Ulema and Mashaikh Board, Syed Mohammad Ashraf Kichhouchhwi, and Syed Salman Chisti of Ajmer Dargah Sharif used this argument and demanded that the government of India must give shelter to the Rohingya Muslims (The Indian Express 2017a). But such appeals to the government did not go well with the masses. The reaction went worse when the Chief Minister of the state of J&K Mahbooba Mufti Sayed made a statement that Rohingyas are not found in terror activities, and the central government should be generous to their settlement. She said so on the floor of the legislative assembly (The Indian Express 2017b). She accepted that some madrasas are associated with Rohingyas in the valley. Hindus took serious objection to her statements as this amounted to her duplicity on the settlement as she has been opposed to any outsider to settle in the state. But the government of India rejected all such appeals and filed its reply with the Supreme Court in which it categorically stated that Rohingyas are threat to the national security (The affidavit said "...this obligation is binding only in respect which are party to the convention. Since India is not party to the said convention, or the said protocol the obligations contained therein are not applicable to India."). When Rajnath Singh, the central home minister, visited the state, he told in a press conference clearly that Rohingyas are threat to the national security (The Kashmir Horizons 2017). And further that they will be deported soon to the land from where they came in (Masih 2017). The government reiterated its stand that Rohingyas are involved in terror activities, and they have overseas links with the terrorists groups, and therefore they cannot be allowed to settle in India. Surprisingly, while the religious organizations belonging to the Muslim community supported Rohingyas on humanitarian ground, the Grand Mufti of Syria, Sheikh Ahmad Badreddin Hassoun, supported India's stand. In an interview to Indian News Channel WION, he endorsed India's stand and said that there was propaganda against the Myanmar government (http://www.middleeasteye.net/news/syrias-grand-mufti-concurs-india-rohingya-muslims-are-security-threat-1087331340).

Interestingly, the political parties in valley who do not welcome back Kashmiri Pandits in the valley came out enthusiastically to advance the humanitarian logic to support the stay of Rohingyas in Jammu region. This, however, infuriated the Hindus of the region who saw in it a deliberate design to alter the numerical strength of Hindus. And, therefore, Hindus of the Jammu region vehemently criticized the state government decision to give shelter to these refugees. The question was not inappropriate as the political parties like PDP and National Conference otherwise are very sensitive on Article 35 A (Article 35 A is an article which was inserted into the Indian constitution not through constitutional amendments under Article 368 but through presidential order. It pertains to the right given to the legislature of the state of Jammu and Kashmir to decide the permanent citizen of the state.) and don't want it to be disturbed in order to perpetuate the numerical preponderance of Muslims in the valley, but they had no problems if Rohingya Muslims come from Burma and settle there in Jammu region. The coverage of the distance by the migrants from Burma to remote Jammu also raised questions. Why the migrants did not settle in the other states close to Burmese border. It is interesting that the Rohingyas settled in the state are not in the valley but in Jammu and Ladakh regions.

Hindu organizations have protested against such settlements because they fear that settlements of the Muslims would alter the demographic equations in the future, and that would have far-reaching political and cultural consequences for the Hindus. Their understanding of Islam emanates from the experience they had in the Kashmir valley where Hindus who had been there for thousands of years were forced to leave their homes and properties. For them, humanitarian call had no meaning, and therefore they wanted nothing less than eviction and deportation of Rohingyas. They fear that the refugee of today will turn out to be the mercenary of Islam tomorrow bringing turmoil for the other religionists. The massive level of radicalization of the Muslim youths across the world and rise of the cult of violent form of Islam has gone into forming this psyche among other religionists in general and Hindus in particular.

The way the global Islam has accelerated radicalization, the idea has gained ground that there is something inherent within Islam which makes it fanatic and radical and unfit therefore for a society which believes in coexistence. A numerically dominant Muslim community does not give the same cultural and civil rights to other religious and cultural communities, and therefore rising numerical strength of Islam is a threat to the pluralistic and democratic predominantly Hindu India. Already there have been chains of protests and movements by these organizations against the Bangladeshi Muslims who have got settled in different parts of India and have changed the religious and cultural geography of many states like Assam, West Bengal, Bihar, Tripura, Uttar Pradesh, and even Delhi (Both the BJP and RSS have passed resolutions several times in the past against the migrants from Bangladesh into India. And supported the demand of identifying and deportation of the migrants. But unfortunately, nothing substantial have been done to this effect despite government at the centre.).

Human rights organizations, both national and international, have come out to openly support the cause of Rohingyas. Their main arguments are that India has a long-standing tradition of giving shelters to the persecuted communities in order to save their lives. If the Rohingyas are sent back, they too will be persecuted by the hostile state apparatus in Burma. The National Human Rights Commission chaired by the former Chief Justice of the Supreme Court of India justified their stay on the ground of long tradition of giving such refuse as well as on the grounds of extended and enlarged explanations of fundamental rights by the Supreme Court that even the noncitizens have the right to life. It observed that even though the country has not signed the Convention on Refugee of 1951 and the Protocol of 1967 on the same as yet, it has been signatory to many such conventions which seek to protect the human rights. It held that the country had so far stricken a balance between the human and humanitarian cause on the one hand and security and national interests on the other (The Times of India 2017). The Supreme Court of India led by the Chief Justice of India while hearing the petition of the two migrants, namely, Mohammad Salimullah and Mohammad Shaqir, observed that it was a huge humanitarian crisis, and the court would not ignore the humanitarian aspects in dealing with the matter, though in its same breath it held that it will balance the interests of the national security, economic interest, labor interests, and demographic considerations (NDTV 2017). Government, on the other hand, does not seem to be in mood to paying heed to the Supreme Court. The ISI angle of training the Rohingya Muslims has given food for thought to the government to investigate into larger design of Pakistan to alter the demographic characters of Jammu and other parts of the state where they have settled in. Many jurists have also objected to the intervention of the Supreme Court on the issue. They argue that Supreme Court does not have jurisdiction in this matter. The security of the state is basically the responsibility of the executive. It is the executive which examines and evaluates the magnitude of the security threat to the country immediate as well as prospective. And therefore the court has no business to enter into the domain of the executive.

Conclusions

Migration of population with strong ethnic orientation has larger impacts in the society in which they come and settle in. In the initial years, they don't assert their cultural and political identity and just wish to be part of the society. This is the time when they need the cooperation of the sheltering state. But with the growth of population, they not only demand more share in the cultural and political space but that becomes the issue of contestations with the indigenous communities. Down the generations they start asserting themselves for the same. India is witness to over 300 Million Bangladeshi Muslims who have altered the political and cultural geography of states like Assam, Tripura, West Bengal, Bihar, and many other states of India. Bangladeshi settlers in Assam and Bengal today have started influencing the politics and culture of the areas they have settled in. In the state of West Bengal, they pushed out the Hindus from the border areas to settle in the cities selling their lands and properties. Now no party, except for the right-wing political and social organizations, has courage to demand their repatriation to Bangladesh. In Bengal, they have gone so offensive that with their support the Muslim communities have started coercing the Hindus in many villages where they are in dominating positions. In last few years, Bengal witnessed several one-sided communal riots in which the Muslim masses aggressively attacked the Hindu processions and forced the government to issue directives to restrict their religious processions and rituals in public space. Migrants thus are not the individuals but the part of political and cultural communities which they come from. They begin with individual rights and then go for equal rights in cultural and political space. Thus, with advance of time, they throw larger challenges to the hosting countries, and therefore there has been opposition to their settlements. This becomes all the more relevant and complex in case of India which witnessed partition in the name of religion in 1947 and continues to face Islamic extremism in many parts of the country. Opposition to the Rohingyas by the right-wing political and cultural organizations is driven by such thinking which has gathered popular strength in recent years.

References

Al-Mehmood SZ (2016) Timeline: a short history of Myanmar's Rohingya minority. The Wall Street Journal

Bangladesh refuses to accept more Rohingyas refugees. Ashrq Al-Awsat, 29 August 2017. Accessed 23 Mar 2017

Business standard, Rohingyas are refugees. Donot Deport Them, 7 September 2017. Accessed 1 July 2018

Dehlvi GulamRasool (2017a) The war within Islam: why are the Islamic countries not coming forward to take Rohingyas? The New Age Islam.com

Dehlvi GhulamRasool (2017b) Why aren't Muslim countries absorbing the Rohingyas. Asia Times

Hasnat MA (2017) Who really attacked the Rohingyas Hindus in Rakhine? Dhaka Tribune

http://www.dw.com/en/is-saudi-wahhabism-fueling-rohingya-muslim-insurgency/a-36791809. Accessed 21 Mar 2018

http://www.middleeasteye.net/news/syrias-grand-mufti-concurs-india-rohingya-muslims-are-security-threat-1087331340. Accessed 1 July 2018

https://in.reuters.com/article/us-myanmar-rohingya/myanmars-rohingya-insurgency-has-links-to-saudi-pakistan-report-idINKBN1450Y7. Accessed 21 Mar 2018

https://www.washingtonpost.com/world/asia_pacific/we-are-going-to-kill-you-villagers-in-burma-recount-violence-by-rohingya-muslim-militants/2017/11/14/409ff59b-849d-4459-bdc7-d1ea2b5ff9a6_story.html?utm_term=.d7527703e6d9. Accessed 21 Mar 2018

ISI Behind Rohingya Crisis (September 9, 2017) S Balakrishnan, PGURUS. https://www.pgurus.com/isi-behind-rohingya-crisis/. Accessed 12 Sept 2018

Masih N (2017) Look at us as humans and not as Muslims. The Hindustan Times

Mehbooba silence on Rohingyas crisis. The Kashmir Horizons, 15 September 2017

NDTV, 13 Oct 2017. Accessed 01 July 2018

Quoted in Dehlvi, GulamRasool The war within Islam: why are the Islamic countries not coming forward to take Rohingyas? The New Age Islam.com, 10 September 2017

Reuters, 22 November 2017. https://www.reuters.com/article/us-myanmar-rohingya-usa/u-s-calls-myanmar-moves-against-rohingya-ethnic-cleansing-idUSKBN1DM1N3. Accessed 23 June 2018

Rohingya Muslims issue: Delhite out on streets, Congress leads the march. Times Now, 13 September 2017

Rohingyas a Terror threat: NDTV finds little evidence of government claims, 16 September 2017. Accessed 1 July 2018

Rohingyas are external, internal security threat: VHP. https://indianexpress.com/article/india/rohingya-are-internal-external-security-threat-vhp-resolution-5233309/. The Indian Express. Accessed 1 July 2018a

Tensions follow Rohingyas refugees to United States. https://learningenglish.voanews.com/a/rohingya-immigrants/4065689.html. Accessed 26 Mar 2018

The Dewan of Ajmer Sharif Dargah, one of the most noted Muslim shrines in India depicted the attack on Rohingyas as an act of cowardice. The Indian Express, 18 September 2017a, New Delhi

The Hindu, 15 September 2017

The Hindustan Times, E Paper updated on 17 March 2018, Rohingya refugee find safe heaven near Kolkata

The Indian Express, New Delhi, 20 January 2017b. In a written reply to the BJP MLA, Sat Pal Sharma she said that 5700 Rohingyas are reported to have been staying in the state

The Indian Express, Delhi. https://indianexpress.com/article/india/rohingyas-a-security-threat-deport-them-rss-5101212/. Accessed 1 July 2018b

The Times of India, New Delhi, 2017

Tun SZ (2017) Slaughtered Hindus a testament to brutality of Mynmar conflict. Reutors

What sparked latest violence in Rakhine? BBC Asia News, 19 September 2017. https://www.bbc.com/news/world-asia-41082689. Accessed 1 July 2018

Indonesia and ASEAN Responses on Rohingya Refugees

96

Badrus Sholeh

Contents

Introduction	1892
Theoretical Framework	1893
Indonesian Policy	1895
Bali Process and Indonesian Leadership	1897
ASEAN Response	1900
Second Track Diplomacy	1902
Challenge	1904
Conclusion	1904
References	1905

Abstract

Rohingya refugees crisis have challenged ASEAN and regional institutions. Asian institution-building remains state-centric, especially covering the issues of human rights (Acharya, Int Stud Rev 13:12–17, 2011). In addition, humanitarian intervention meets the gap of noninterference ASEAN Way. The principle of noninterference leads to states ignoring human rights violations. More than 1.2 million Rohingya refugees live in the border of Bangladesh and Myanmar and around a hundred thousands stay at temporary shelters with a very limited facility in Indonesia, Malaysia, and Thailand. This needs urgent strategic national, regional, and international policy involving bilateral and multistate role in overcoming the crisis. This chapter examines the Indonesian foreign policy on the issue of Rohingya refugees and how the Indonesian government led the regional initiatives in overcoming the problem. This chapter is based on in-depth interviews to Rohingya refugees, governments, and policy makers in Southeast Asia

---

B. Sholeh (✉)
Department of International Relations, Faculty of Social and Political Sciences, Syarif Hidayatullah State Islamic University, Jakarta, Indonesia
e-mail: badrus.sholeh@uinjkt.ac.id

© The Author(s), under exclusive license to Springer Nature Singapore Pte Ltd. 2019
S. Ratuva (ed.), *The Palgrave Handbook of Ethnicity*,
https://doi.org/10.1007/978-981-13-2898-5_170

and on analyzing documents related to the issue from 2016 to 2018. It argued the ASEAN way and international pressures toward ASEAN, and Myanmar will strengthen the policy to reduce the tension of the conflict and stabilize regional security sue to the refugees.

Keywords
Indonesia · ASEAN · Rohingya Refugees

Introduction

Hundreds of thousands of Rohingya people have fled to Asian countries since 2012. From January 2014 to May 2015, 88,000 Rohingya and Bangladesh refugees took boats across the Bay of Bengal transiting Thailand to reach Malaysia and Indonesia (Ha and Htut 2016; Tan 2016). The International Organization for Migration described the condition of the refugees in Andaman Sea as "maritime ping-pong with human life." Malaysia and Thailand government ordered their maritime forces to push back the boats toward international water (Beech 2015). They survived in Andaman Sea with lack of food and water. Some of them got stranded near Aceh beach in May 2015 and were rescued by Acehnese fishermen although Indonesian authority initially followed the policy of Thailand and Malaysia to refuse the refugee boats. Indonesian government later changed the policy welcoming the refugees. The 2015 Rohingya refugee issues tested the commitment of ASEAN on how non-interference policy deals with human rights (Tan 2016; Ullah 2016). Rohingya's stateless status and existence of human rights violations against them can be a strong reason for the threat of regional and international security which urgently needs humanitarian intervention (Ullah 2016).

In April 2016, Acehnese fishermen rescued two boats carrying 84 Rohingya refugees. According to the law of the sea and Indonesia's Presidential Regulation no. 125 of 2016 Concerning the Handling of Foreign Refugees, they were allowed to disembark in Indonesia (Suryono 2018). Under the regulation, Indonesian authority and people are encouraged to help, rescue, and accommodate Rohingya refugees. Indonesia coordinated with international organizations in handling the refugees. Article 2 number 1 of the regulation stated that "the handling of refugees is carried out pursuant to cooperation between the central government with the United Nations through the United Nations High Commissioner for Refugees in Indonesia and/or international organizations" (Minister of Law and Human Rights 2016). UNHCR argued that the regulation "helped mitigate that risk, as demonstrated by the lives saved by the Indonesian government's support of the rescue, disembarkation and reception of these two recent groups" (Suryono 2018). The crisis in Rakhine State became worse after 2016. The Myanmar military (known as the Tatmadaw) began clearance operations in the aftermath of a small-scale attack to military forces by the Arakan Rohingya Salvation Army (ARSA) in October 2016 and August 2017 forced more than 700,000 Rohingya women, men, and children fled their homes in Rakhine State to Cox's Bazar, Bangladesh (Alam 2018). There are about 921,000 Rohingya refugees (215,796 families) in Cox's

Bazar by October 2018 with a high risk of health, security, and natural disaster (WHO 2018). Densely packed refugees in Cox's Bazar camp are at risk of diseases, community tensions, fires, domestic and sexual violence, and natural disaster like flooding and eroding (Human Rights Watch 2018).

This article examines the Indonesian foreign policy on the Rohingya refugees and how Indonesia led the effort to overcoming the challenges of the issue by managing regional meetings since the early period of Rohingya refugee influx in Southeast Asian sea. It is based on qualitative research method: observation and in-depth interviews. I conducted fieldworks in Indonesia and Thailand, interviewing refugees, government officers, civil society organizations, and scholars from 2016 to 2018. It argues Indonesia have to work more progressively along with regional states and persuading Myanmar to comprehensively solve the problem of Rohingya Muslims, not only providing supports for refugees but helping Myanmar to mediate ethno-religious conflict in Rakhine State province. UNHCR stated that Indonesia hosted some 13,840 refugees from about 49 countries as of December 2017, with half coming from Afghanistan (UNHCR 2018). In regional context, the article argues ASEAN way's approach, and international strategic pressures toward ASEAN and Myanmar will help to overcome ethno-religious conflicts in Rakhine State. In addition, the humanitarian intervention in this context will not cross over ASEAN non-interference policy. The intervention is how regional and international state and civil society have to mediate the conflicts of Rohingya in Rakhine State and comprehensively managing Rohingya refugees involving all countries.

Theoretical Framework

The theories of regionalism and humanitarian intervention will cover the discussion of the issue. The Rohingya refugees' case tested the regionalism of ASEAN as a unity of Southeast Asian states. ASEAN's regional institution emerged from the period of *konfrontasi* to the community-building initiatives strengthened ASEAN integration. The active global initiatives demonstrated "institutional adaptation, the construction of shared norms, and a common identity, mediated through, and, manifested in, an ASEAN way," the idea supported by liberal institutionalist and constructivist (Jones and Jenne 2016). Acharya said the integration deepened by an active engagement among track two parties such as academics, think tanks, and scholars in the region (Acharya 2011). Dealing with human rights issues, however, ASEAN community engagement is still struggling due to state-centric policy approach. Acharya argued "transnational social movements which usually champion human rights or social issues are yet to feature prominently in Asian institution-building, which remain state-centric and strongly wedded to national sovereignty" (Acharya 2011, 15). Instability in ASEAN states in the 1990s such as conflicts in Cambodia, Thailand, and Indonesia and in the 2000s when Myanmar failed to respond the rise of human rights violations against Rohingya challenged ASEAN as a solid security community (Ba 2014).

The second theory of humanitarian intervention responding the issue of Rohingya refugee in Southeast Asia will fill the gap of non-interference ASEAN way. Humanitarian intervention will be a strategic reason for regional and international institutions to support the crisis of Rohingya. Rohingya people are "susceptible to rape, torture, summary killings, confiscation and destruction of their homes and property, physical abuse, religious persecution, and forced and unpaid labor" (Ullah 2011), which forced them to search temporary safe shelters in the border of Bangladesh and paid smugglers to join the boats to get a protection in Indonesia, Thailand, and Malaysia. The ASEAN Charter respects member states' national sovereignty; however, it is argued that "non-interference without any doubt leads to states ignoring human rights violations at the domestic level in other member state territories, and this is particularly the case with the Rohingya in Myanmar" (Kaewjullakarn 2015, 8).

Argument of ASEAN's accessibility to protect human rights violations against its people is the establishment of AICHR (the ASEAN Intergovernmental Commission on Human Rights). The AICHR is a judicial mechanism founded under Article 14 of the ASEAN Charter to promote human rights with a decision-making based on consensus and consultation. Therefore, the way of AICHR assisted Myanmar in solving the problem of Rohingya is by having institutional discussion and informal consultation. The AICHR has a limit by the ASEAN way to respect national sovereignty of member states. Indonesian civil society groups established Indonesian Humanitarian Alliance for Myanmar, which is expected to reduce the tension in Rakhine State. However, Myanmar restricted them operating freely to deliver humanitarian aids in 2017 in Rakhine State. Humanitarian intervention, therefore, will be blocked by two aspects: non-interference principle of ASEAN and strong reason for Myanmar to protect its national sovereignty. China supported the argument of Myanmar on sovereignty right reason responding the statement of UNSC on human rights violation against Rohingya (UN 2018; Robert 2009).

Rohingya refugees should get international interests from causes to effects of the refugee influx. Causes came from the ethno-religious conflicts between Rohingya Muslims and Rakhine Buddhists. It affected to the rise of Rohingya people leaving their home. Rakhine Buddhists killed Rohingya Muslims and burned their houses. Many Rohingya overseas still plan to return to their home. The conflicts need mediation from third parties from state and civil society groups. It includes aid organizations and donors which can help on post-conflict rehabilitation and reconstruction. Myanmar kept the issue of Rohingya becoming home affairs and successfully forced ASEAN and international states not to interfere the conflicts.

ASEAN has to remind Myanmar on how ASEAN, Japan, and China helped Myanmar during the period of international pressures due to military authoritarianism and human rights violation of Myanmar government. The conflicts between Rohingya Muslims and Rakhine Buddhists need international mediation in order to prevent further political violence discriminating against Rohingya Muslims. The conflicts attracted the interests of terrorist groups which stated that they will fight against Myanmar government to protect Rohingya Muslims. This will increase regional security threats.

Karl DeRouen, Jr., argued that:

> According to the U.S. Institute of Peace, external partners can provide resources, insurance, expertise, and experience supporting peace agreement implementation. Third parties, such as allies or neighboring states, can assist in ensuring that promises are kept, timetables respected, and matching commitments fulfilled...A network of donors, including governments, aid organizations, and reconstruction agencies, can help pay for implementation, such as reconstruction bills. (DeRouen 2015, 164)

The Ministry of Foreign Affairs of the Republic of Indonesia is committed in managing Rohingya refugee crisis in Southeast Asia. Indonesia accommodated more than 10,000 Rohingya refugees in Aceh and joined regional ministerial meetings with Thailand, Malaysia, and Myanmar to overcome the problem of Rohingya refugees in the region. ASEAN summits also raised Rohingya refugee crisis issues as part of regional agenda to cope with. However, ASEAN and its state members prevent to interfere Myanmar as part of regional norm and value agreement on non-interference policy of ASEAN. Some scholars consider this issue challenged ASEAN due to human rights violations against Rohingya Muslims in Rakhine State.

There are three levels of Indonesia actively supporting Rohingya refugees. Firstly, in regional level, Indonesia supports regional dialogues and facilitates meetings discussing Rohingya issues. The Ministry of Foreign Affairs took an active role. It includes bilateral and multilateral meetings among ASEAN states and states outside Southeast Asia, such as Bali Process. Secondly, Indonesia coordinates among ministries of Indonesian government to manage Rohingya refugees. They are the Ministry of Foreign Affairs; Ministry of Social; Coordinating Ministry for Political, Legal and Security Affairs; and government in provincial and district levels, especially in Aceh. Lastly, Indonesian people and civil society groups are actively support Rohingya as Muslim solidarity.

After the outbreak of Rohingya in 2012, and their arrivals in neighboring countries especially Malaysia and Indonesia, Vice President Jusuf Kalla said that Indonesia will help Rohingya refugees. However, Indonesia cannot work alone. Indonesia needs a regional consensus among states in ASEAN. Numerous meetings have been made in Bali, Jakarta, Kuala Lumpur, Bangkok, Tokyo, and other cities in the Asia Pacific discussing the challenge of Rohingya refugees and asylum seekers. Vice President Jusuf Kalla argued conflicts in ASEAN state members will influence other regions, and it becomes responsibility of all states. Vice President Kalla said "these humanitarian measures were important to prevent the spread of radicalism in ASEAN. The rise of Islamic State in the Middle East was due to the radicalization of people from failed states in their region" (Channelnewsasia 2015).

Indonesian Policy

Indonesian civil society criticized the statement of General Moeldoko, Commander in Chief of the Indonesian Military (TNI), who said Indonesian military will prevent any refugees to enter Indonesian territory. It was on 8 May 2015, 418 Bangladeshi and 230 Rohingya refugees, including 55 children and 62 women, got stranded in the Strait of Malacca about 20 miles from Pusong beach, East Aceh district. Two days later, 587 Rohingya refugees got stranded in the water of North Aceh district and were rescued by Acehnese fishermen after finding the vessels of the refugees sinking. On 10 May 2015, Moeldoko stated: "They will not be allowed to enter Indonesian region. If they do, they may create social problems. If they have no water or food, we will help because it will then be a humanitarian problem. However, if they enter our region, it will be the TNI's duty to safeguard the country's territory" (Supriyadi 2015). Beka Ulung Hapsara at the Wahid Institute argued Indonesia is a great power in ASEAN and therefore Indonesian government has to lead humanitarian assistance to Rohingya refugees (Kuwado 2015). The Ministry of Foreign Affairs attempted to clarify General Moeldoko's statement. Ministry of Foreign Affairs spokesperson, Arrmanatha Nasir, said: "the Indonesian authorities were not allowed to seize or drive away foreign vessels transporting undocumented migrants in the strait because of the implementation of a peaceful sailing principle" (*The Jakarta Post* 2015). A month after this controversial statement, President Joko Widodo replaced the position of General Moeldoko by Army chief of staff General Gatot Nurmantyo on 9 June 2015.

Nahdlatul Ulama and Muhammadiyah have urged the Indonesian government to proactively helped Rohingya Muslim refugees. They said that "the Indonesian government should engage or pressure the Myanmar government in order to ensure the Rohingya's rights. Yet to date, most of the support shown towards the Rohingya by governments and organizations has been limited to rhetoric" (Singh 2014, 13). President Joko Widodo's foreign policy is strongly influenced by national interests and domestic politic factors. It is reflected to how Minister of Foreign Affairs, Retno Marsudi, responded to Rohingya refugee issues in national and regional level.

Indonesian Ministry of Foreign Affairs responded the Rohingya refugee very carefully to prevent pulling factors for other refugees toward Indonesian territory. Minister of Foreign Affairs Retno Marsudi argued Indonesian government has to measure precisely how to accommodate Rohingya refugees under international humanitarian law. Furthermore, after active participation of Acehnese fishermen helping the Rohingya boat people, and the critique from media, Indonesian government seriously helps the community. Critique also came from international community. Zeid Ra'ad al-Hussein, the United Nations' human rights chief, criticized Indonesia, Malaysia, and Thailand "for turning away the vessels while the European Union has urged Myanmar to end the persecution of its Rohingya minority" (Xiong 2015).

After gaining the pressures, ministers of foreign affairs of Indonesia, Malaysia, and Thailand conducted an emergency meeting on 20 May 2015 in Kuala Lumpur discussing the Rohingya crisis. It was contrary to the previous position of the navies of those governments which pushed refugees' boats away from their shores in what international human rights and aid groups characterized as "a dangerous game of human ping-pong" (Cochrane 2015). In the meeting, Indonesia and Malaysia agreed to offer shelter to 7,000 refugees and migrants temporarily. They said in a joint statement in Kuala Lumpur on 20 May 2015 that "they would offer resettlement and repatriation, a process that would be done in a year by the support of the international community" (*The Guardian*, 20 May 2015).

Indonesian government has to manage the Rohingya asylum seekers by domestic and regional approaches. In the domestic policy, Indonesian government protects the Rohingya asylum seekers fulfilling international standard of how international state have to take care of them. In regional level, Indonesia has to deal with ASEAN, especially Malaysia, Thailand, and Myanmar, on how regional organization have to protect refugees. It tested Indonesian leadership in the region. Minister of Foreign Affairs Retno Marsudi stated that Indonesian government is committed to take care of Rohingya boat people for some period and to respect regional agreement in Southeast Asia. Minister Marsudi said: "we only provided humanitarian assistance. However, we do not want to send out a message that Indonesia has created a pull effect as it could attract refugees to come here" (Fardah 2015).

Indonesian foreign policy on Rohingya asylum seekers considered weightily on the stability of domestic politics and the responses of human rights organization, as well as political leaders. It considers *kedaulatan* (sovereignty) and *kemandirian* (autonomy), popularly called *diplomasi membumi* (diplomacy brought down to earth) (Connelly 2015). Therefore, Acehnese fishermen's actions to help Rohingya boat people stranded in the sea changed government policy to accept them, although government stated that the shelters for Rohingya and other refugees are provided temporarily until the Third World countries agree to accept them permanently (Fardah 2015).

State and civil society organizations of Indonesia have visited Myanmar negotiating with government of Myanmar to protect Rohingya and overcome conflicts between Muslim (Rohingya) and Buddhist (Rakhine). President Susilo Bambang Yudhoyono stated that he did a constructive "intervention" on the issue of Rohingya. In April 2013, President Yudhoyono visited Myanmar and talked to President Thein Sein. President Yudhoyono said: "I asked (him) to fairly overcoming conflict which affected to Rohingya ethnic group. It includes rehabilitation and humanitarian approach after the conflict, I suggested Myanmar to work with UN and OIC" (Yudhoyono 2014, 712).

Bali Process and Indonesian Leadership

Amitav Acharya argued that Indonesia, the largest country in Southeast Asia, has moved toward regional and global leadership role. Therefore, the way of managing Rohingya refugees tested Indonesian regional influence on democracy, security and stability. It includes to ensure the commitment of regional states on human rights and democracy in the ASEAN Charter, the ASEAN Political-Security Community, and its drive for the ASEAN Intergovernmental Commission on Human Rights (AICHR), the construction of the Bali Democracy Forum (BDF), and Indonesia's voting in the UN Third Committee (Humanitarian, Social, Cultural Committee that deals with human rights and humanitarian issues) on Syria, Myanmar, North Korea, and Iran (Acharya 2014).

Indonesia's foreign policy on dealing with Rohingya asylum seekers is also affected by the demands of domestic politics that as the largest Muslim country Indonesia has to accept Rohingya asylum seekers. Foreign policy on Rohingya refugees is in line with Indonesian people expression. The decision-making of foreign policy is currently more dispersed, "there is a more diverse constituency for foreign policy, a sense of public ownership and participation in the policy making, even in post-makers during the dissemination phase to earn the support of public, to get feedback, sell the policy. So, overall the system is much more inclusive" (Acharya 2014, 13).

The problem in regional level is uneasy communication among states in ASEAN. Myanmar refused to join the meeting initiated by Indonesia and Malaysia. It is contrary to the spirit of democracy in Myanmar (Singh 2014). In addition, democratic process in Myanmar is criticized by some scholars for not regarding Rohingya people refuged to other states including Indonesia as a human rights violation. Not only Burmese State disregarded Rohingya's citizenship state, but also Buddhist monk and community refused the existence of Rohingya in Rakhine province. Buddhist monks did rally pressuring government to force Rohingya get out of the state.

More than 723,000 Rohingya seek refuge in Bangladesh after the violence broke out in Rakhine State on 25 August 2017. The vast majority arriving Bangladesh are women, children and elderly people. More than 40 percent children are under age 12. Bangladesh government managed a strict policy against Rohingya refugees and considers more on bilateral relations between Bangladesh and Myanmar. Bangladesh government claimed that Rohingya refugee had created criminal problems in Bangladesh (Datta 2015). It also affected bilateral relations between Bangladesh and Myanmar (Pamini 2011).

Indonesia took a strategic leadership in the Bali Process and Bali Democracy Forum discussing the issue of Rohingya and making a regional agreement in managing Rohingya refugees in Southeast Asia. The meetings confirmed that refugee and asylum seekers become the common interests for more countries, how they have to cope with the problem with responsibility of all countries. The challenge is Third World countries are still reluctant to open their immigration policy. Some countries in Europe, Asia, Australia, and the USA tend to close for more immigrants. On the other hand, leaders of other countries declared to welcome refugees. Canadian Prime Minister is very popular government leader who welcome Syrian refugees to be Canadian citizens.

Further regional mechanism is conducted through the Bali Process. The dynamics of refugees are responded by regional states to making a constructive regional forum called the Bali Process. It is stated the Bali Process on People Smuggling, Trafficking in Persons, and Related Transnational Crime (Bali Process), including refugees and asylum seekers, is "a voluntary and non-binding process with 48 members including the United Nations High Commissioner for Refugees (UNHCR), United Nations Office on Drugs and Crime (UNODC) and the International Organization for Migration (IOM)" ("The Bali Process").

Regional states and international organizations involved in the Bali Process managed under the Regional Support Office (RSO) facilitated the operationalization of the Regional Cooperation Framework (RCF) to decrease irregular migration and refugees in the Asia Pacific region. RSO operated under direction of the Co-Chairs of the Bali Process (Indonesia and Australia) and in consultation with UNHCR and IOM.

Bali Process was established by Indonesia and Australia in 2002. It provided a meeting forum for transit, destination, and source countries. Hassan Wirajuda, Indonesia's former minister of foreign affairs and one of the founders of the Bali Process, called for its co-chairs to step up or step aside, as a comparison between 2013 and 2016 of the Bali Process and its regional influence. In August 2013, about 50 member countries joined the Bali Process on People Smuggling, Trafficking in Persons, and Related Transnational Crime, and forced migration movement was acknowledged as a global challenge and threats. The number of displaced persons according to UNHCR by 2013 was 51.2 million. It grew 20% by 60 million in March 2016 (McLeod 2016).

Speaking ahead of a regional forum on people smuggling, Indonesian Foreign Minister Retno Marsudi said:

> We already hosted more than 13,000 refugees and asylum seekers that have been years in Indonesia waiting to be resettle. In May 2015, we received almost 2000 coming from Bangladesh and Myanmar. Of course, there is hope for Indonesia not only to Australia but to every country to be more receptive to these migrants who have been waiting for resettlement. (Topsfield 2016)

Indonesia expected the role of Third World countries, especially from industrial countries to host and finance the refugees more openly. The burden of influx of refugees due to war and conflict is higher, and it needs to share the burden.

The Royal Thai government also confirms the importance of burden sharing on refugee crisis. Burden sharing can be a regional cooperation between state and civil society as well. Saw Khu, senior researcher of International Rescue Committee (IRC), claimed that the issue of Rohingya refugees and asylum seekers is transnational and it becomes the matters of international community. Khu said that all countries and civil society have to cope with the Rohingya refugee comprehensively by having regional meetings involving state and civil society (Khu 2016), using Karl DeRouen, Jr.'s argument on how Third World countries and foreign aid can be effective groups persuading Myanmar in giving international supports to end the conflict in Rakhine province between Rohingya Muslims and Rakhine Buddhists. However, Myanmar government refused any international intervention and pressures toward conflicts in Rakhine State. In addition, ASEAN carefully deals with the problem of Rohingya refugees leaving their home due to the conflict.

International NGOs, aid, and human rights groups criticized the finding of graveyards of Rohingya and human rights abuse and smuggling against Rohingya refugees in the border between Southern Thailand and Malaysia. Thailand joined ministerial meetings with Indonesia and Malaysia and expected to share the burden of refugee crisis, especially after 10,000 Rohingya stranded in Andaman Sea affected territorial security in Thailand, Malaysia, and Indonesia (Idiris 2015). In the ministerial meetings of ASEAN, Thailand government proposed an open border for members of ASEAN for refugees. However, ASEAN members disagreed to the proposal. Currently, refugees challenge regional political and security community among ASEAN members and the Asia Pacific region. People seek refuge due to wars in the Middle East and because religious prosecution in South Asia and Southeast

Asia is rising. On the other hand, the policy of resettlement, repatriation, and reintegration cannot fill the gap. The process of refugee and the acceptance of resettlement of refugees to Third World countries are very slow. Many refugees in Thailand still wait for more than 5 years to resettle to Third World countries. Thailand provided more Rohingya refugees than Indonesia due to availability of land routes toward Malaysia.

ASEAN Response

The Rohingya refugees crisis issues have impacted the Southeast Asian security since 2012. It highlighted ASEAN's lack of a legal framework to deal with refugees issues. Among ten ASEAN nations, only the Philippines and Cambodia are parties to the 1951 Convention Relating to the Status of Refugees and its 1967 Protocol. ASEAN does not have an institutional mechanism dealing with Rohingya and other refugees in the region (Shivakoti 2017). This is the challenge for ASEAN member states.

Some ASEAN sates concerned the refugee crisis and responded by having some regional meetings and summits between 2012 and 2016 which discussed the issues of refugees and cope with the crisis. However, the numbers of meetings did not move ASEAN efficiently to overcome the Rohingya refugees. It was an effect of regional norms and consensus constructed among ASEAN leaders, called non-interference policy. Indonesia is among few countries in Asia approaching Myanmar to transform from authoritarian to democratic country before ASEAN gave authority for Myanmar to chair ASEAN. In 2014, Myanmar hosted ASEAN Summit, and international community expected Myanmar government provide enough space to talk on the issue of Rakhine conflict and Rohingya problem. Myanmar kept the issue as internal affairs, and it was not allowed to any ASEAN Summit participants to discuss the issue.

Indonesian government became more active after getting public pressures following the upsurge of violence against Rohingya Muslims in Rakhine State in May–June 2012. Jusuf Kalla, the Chairman of Indonesia's Red Cross, visited Rohingya refugee camps in Myanmar in August 2012. President Susilo Bambang Yudhoyono appointed Jusuf Kalla as the special envoy on the Rohingya issue. President Yudhoyono said: "Mr. Kalla, with his extensive experience, can become our special envoy, so that Indonesia's solidarity and attention on the humanitarian issue of the Rohingya is accurate, does not give rise to misunderstanding for Myanmar but also helps our Rohingya brothers and sisters" (Singh 2014, 14).

The 24th ASEAN Summit in Nay Pyi Taw on May 2014 did not raise the issue of Rohingya refugee. U Aung Htoo, Deputy Director General of the Ministry of Foreign Affairs of Myanmar, said the issue of Rohingya was not raised during the foreign ministers' meeting due to ASEAN's charter calls for non-interference policy on internal affairs of member states. Vo Xuan Vinh said: "ASEAN will be put in the dilemma since Myanmar government has been unwilling to discuss the issue of the Rohingya people at ASEAN meetings after it took over the chair. In retrospect, ASEAN Foreign Minister released a statement in August 2012 on the recent developments in the Rakhine State" (Vinh 2014: 30). It becomes a great challenge for ASEAN to reconsider international norms of human rights violations, especially ASEAN itself established human rights commission in regional level. Matthew Smith, Executive Director at the Thailand-based Fortify Rights, claimed: "ASEAN countries have never taken an active stance on regional human rights abuses and that needs to change if the region is going to grow in economic and political influence" (Mclaughlin and Shin 2014).

Decha Tangseefa, Professor of Political Sciences of Thammasat University, said: "it is the notion of non-interference, until later we have the notion of constructive engagement, and then flexible engagement" (Tangseefa 2016). Non-interference policy of ASEAN affected how the meetings and summits became ineffective, especially to push Myanmar on human rights violation. Prof. Tangseefa added that "ASEAN is state based organization. You have to respect d'etat of the state, the reason of the state, which is what territory integrity" (Tangseefa 2016).

In 2015, the official meetings of foreign ministers of Indonesia, Thailand, and Malaysia resulted in an agreement which is to accommodate them before being transferred in a Third World country. This meeting is crucial to address Rohingya refugees at sea. This also became a regional solidarity among ASEAN states and community to reduce the burdens of refugee crisis. They agreed for burden sharing and burden responsibility for all ASEAN state members. They realized non-interference consensus of ASEAN affected the fact that ASEAN have no rights to pressure and persuade Myanmar. It is fully the home affairs of Myanmar. ASEAN only provide humanitarian assistantship to all Rohingya refugees and give them temporary shelters for certain period before transferring them to third parties (*Masyarakat ASEAN* 2015).

In the ASEAN ministerial meetings in Kuala Lumpur on "Transnational Crime Concerning Irregular Movement of Persons in Southeast Asia," 2 July 2015, the establishment of the task force and the trust fund was formulated. This meeting talked about the conduct of polemic Rohingya refugees and legal immigrant. The ministerial meeting in Kuala Lumpur delivered some endorsements to save as many as 4,800 Rohingyas who became human trafficking victims (Dompet Dhuafa 2015). They were stranded in several Southeast Asian countries, such as Indonesia, Thailand, and Malaysia. Malaysia accommodated 134,175 asylum seekers and refugees with Rohingyas majority as of March 2017 (Ahmad et al. 2017, 67).

ASEAN needs a more progressive regional policy toward refugees for regional development, security, and stability. On 6 September 2016 at the 11th East Asian Summit, Chairman of the Summit declared:

> We called on the Governments of all countries involved source, transit and destination to provide responses in the spirit of cooperation and collective efforts acting with humanity, compassion and in accordance with international law, and to the extent permitted by domestic law, to refugees and migrants. In this regard, we welcomed the adoption of the East Asia Summit Declaration on Strengthening Responses to Migrants in Crisis and Trafficking in Persons. ("Chairman's Statement" 2016)

The statement however did not respond specifically to Rohingya crisis. The government of Malaysia requested the Organization of Islamic Cooperation to hold an emergency ministerial meeting in Kuala Lumpur in January 2017 discussing the situation of Rohingya crisis. Malaysia called ASEAN to investigate atrocities committed against Rohingya Muslims and to coordinate humanitarian aid. Malaysia also requested Myanmar to have a regional informal meeting with ASEAN foreign ministers in Yangon in December 2016 responding international pressures (Shivakoti 2017). Aung San Suu Kyi during the meeting stated that Myanmar agreed to provide regular information to ASEAN members and worked with them in coordinating humanitarian aids. The Government of Myanmar allowed some media to visit Maungdaw, one of the important sites of conflicts. Suu Kyi also founded an Advisory Commission on Rakhine State chaired by Kofi Annan on 5 September 2016 (Shivakoti 2017).

The Advisory Commission investigated security sector in Rakhine State, one of urgent issues related to the crisis. The commission reported two points: Firstly, potential violent confrontations between Muslims and Buddhists communities occurred from 2012 clash. Secondly, anti-government sentiments attracted the rise of paramilitary groups, such as the Arakan Rohingya Salvation Army (ARSA) and the Arakan Army (AA) to challenge Myanmar's security. However, the commission founded that there is "alleged human rights violations carried out by the security forces have further strained relations between the authorities and the Muslim community, especially in the north," following the extensive military and police operations responding the attack on the Border Guard Police (BGP) in October 2016 (Commission 2017, 53).

Other than the factors of conflicts and wars, migration of people in Southeast Asian countries is pulled by other factors, economic growth and industrialization in the 1980s and 1990s. Professor Tangseefa stated: "Thailand is one among five tigers, Thailand, Taiwan, South Korea, Malaysia and Indonesia. They were called NIC, New Industry Countries. So in the 1990s, Thailand economy became progressive. For a lot of reason, that economic vibrant, how a lot of illegal (and legal) migrant workers from Burma" (Tangseefa 2016). The rise of migration, refugees, and trafficking pulled by new industry policy of Thailand is not prepared by national regulation on refugees. Civil society organizations responded to filling the gap by strengthening their participation to advocacy on refugees, trafficking, and migrant workers.

Second Track Diplomacy

Popular supports for Rohingya refugees come from second track diplomacy. Civil society organizations actively manage to overcoming refugees. In Indonesia, civil society groups criticized government not to accommodate refugees well. Indonesian Foreign Minister Retno Marsudi argues Indonesia is not a signatory state on the 1951 UN Convention which affected to passively respond to refugees. Foreign Minister Retno said Rohingya refugees are responsibility of international organizations like UNHCR and IOM. This argument raised critiques from Muslim community and civil society organizations who constantly accommodated and supported Rohingya refugees in Aceh and other cities of Indonesia.

Civil society groups managed second track diplomacy on overcoming Rohingya refugees. It covered national and regional levels. Indonesian government coordinated with civil society in Aceh in managing the camps of Rohingya. Indonesian government tried to avoid breaking the international laws to give more spaces and burdens for civil society. Government facilitated supports under some ministries like Ministry of Social, which provided humanitarian programs coordinating with local government and civil society in Aceh. Nahdlatul Ulama and Muhammadiyah, two largest Muslim organizations with each member 60 million and 40 million, respectively, managed programs for Rohingya Muslims. They provided food, clothes, and other trainings.

Indonesian Muslim coalition also managed an important support to Myanmar. The Indonesian Humanitarian Alliance for Myanmar called the AKIM, Indonesian abbreviation of Aliansi Kemanusiaan Indonesia untuk Myanmar, was initiated by Indonesian Muslim civil society groups in early 2017. As of September 2017, 25 groups already supported the organization (Fauzia 2017).

Foreign Minister Retno Marsudi invited representatives of 11 Indonesian Muslim humanitarian groups to discuss a partnership between state and civil society to support aids to Rakhine State on 5 January 2017. Among the organizations are Muhammadiyah Aid (Muhammadiyah's humanitarian affiliate); Climate Change and Disaster Management Institution of Nahdlatul Ulama (LPBI-NU); Dompet Dhuafa; DPU Daarut Tauhiid; Rumah Zakat; LAZIS Wahdah; PKPU; Forum Zakat, BAZNAS, LAZ Al-Irsyad al-Islamiyah, and Pusat Zakat Umum; and LAZNAS LMI. The meeting resulted in the foundation of Indonesia Humanitarian Alliance for Myanmar (AKIM). AKIM developed a $2 million humanitarian program called Humanitarian Assistance for Sustainable Community, focusing on developing schools, hospitals, and markets in Rakhine State, especially in Rathedaung, Sittwe, and Maungdaw (IPAC 2018).

In regional level, INGOs and NGOs actively work to support Rohingya and other refugees. Indonesia and Thailand are transit countries for Rohingya refugees. Thailand suffered more as Rohingya refugees use land routes toward destination country, Malaysia through Thailand. Noor Muhammad, coordinator of Rohingya refugees in Thailand, argued Rohingya people were treated very badly by Thai government. Police and immigration arrested Rohingya people, and some of them were just sold to smugglers. Muhammad claimed Thai government just attempted to get rid of Rohingya refugees. He concerned how detention centers are under international standard and some of refugees died due to the condition of detention centers (Muhammad 2016). Muhammad expected majority Muslim country of Indonesia to support Rohingya refugees and to lead ASEAN to persuade Myanmar government to provide security assistantship to Rohingya in Rakhine State.

International critical responses on human rights violations in Rakhine State gained negative signals from Rakhine activists, especially who advocated the movements against Rohingya Muslims. Burke argued: "International isolation and the lack of rule-based domestic institutions meant that Rakhine activists were cynical of the notion that any institution acts according to principles of neutral humanitarianism" (Burke 2016, 273–274). This is a consequence of international pressures and critiques to Myanmar government which allowed Buddhist militant movements to act violently against Rohingya Muslims. It is therefore the pressures using international aid and donors may be ineffective.

Challenge

The crisis of Rakhine State continued with some challenges. Firstly, domestic politics of Myanmar keep the crisis hard to resolve. The politics of identity affected to interfaith and inter-ethnic relations. They used to have a harmonious relation. However, relations worsen after the conflicts. Initiatives of Indonesian civil society groups attempt to mediate them to reflect current problem and how they could fix it through peaceful dialogue.

Secondly, in regional level power relations did not move the conflict into significant permanent peace. ASEAN's non-interference policy is challenged by human rights groups to consider a certain standard for regional organization dealing with human rights violations. The Rohingya human rights coalition claimed ASEAN way of non-interference policy as "a silence in crime." The reason is that member states of ASEAN tend to keep silent and avoid critical discussion in regional forums.

Thirdly, the fact-finding of UNSC took an international pressure to Myanmar and it was responded negatively by the government of Myanmar, China, and their allies. The ideas to bring the case to International Criminal Court (ICC) have double impacts. The process in national and bilateral peace initiatives will be affected.

Conclusion

Liberal institutionalists and constructivists argued ASEAN's transformation from the period of Cold War to the development of community integrated the regional institution resilient from global pressure (Acharya 2011). It includes the instability of the region in the 1990s in Cambodia and Indonesia and 2000s in Myanmar due to ethnic conflicts, internal wars, and human rights issues. Adaptability and accessibility of ASEAN on legal protection is challenged by rise of Rohingya refugees in Bangladesh, Indonesia, Thailand, and Malaysia.

The Indonesian foreign policy on Rohingya refugee referred to regional and international norms and values, especially respected the non-interference consensus of ASEAN. However, Indonesian government actively initiated meetings among states and established regional forum in dealing with refugees and asylum seekers including the problem of Rohingya refugees. Indonesian government is expected to take a stronger role in pushing Myanmar government on seriously solving the conflict between Rohingya Muslims and Rakhine Buddhists which is accused to discriminate against Rohingya Muslims. Minister of Foreign Affairs Retno Marsudi believed democratization of Myanmar will transform the country to handle the conflict more peacefully.

Former Minister of Foreign Affairs of the Republic of Indonesia, Hassan Wirajuda, initiated the Bali Process, co-founder with Australia in 2002. It became an active forum in Asia Pacific region discussing the challenge of refugees and asylum seekers in 2013 and 2016. The forum gave Indonesia leading country managing the problem of refugees. Indonesia also worked with Malaysia, Thailand, and Myanmar in dealing with Rohingya refugees responding the influx of Rohingya and Bangladeshi refugees in May 2015.

The Royal Thai government expected burden sharing on overcoming the Rohingya refugees with all states in Southeast Asia. Indonesian government urged Third World countries like Australia and other industrial countries to open their doors for refugees.

The challenge for refugees come from global politics. Anti-migrant views of governments and political parties in the West are rising. Some European countries managed a more stern policy against refugees. The Australian government in the latest decade tended to close their door for refugees, although it agreed to sign a coalition agreement to receive 1,000 number of Syrian refugees. Indonesian government expected Australia to open more for Rohingya and Bangladeshi refugees and change "return the boat" policy toward refugees.

References

Acharya A (2011) Engagement or entrapment? Scholarship and policymaking on Asian regionalism. Int Stud Rev 13:12–17

Acharya A (2014) Indonesia matters Asia's emerging democratic power. World Scientific, London

Advisory Commission on Rakhine State (2017) Towards a peaceful, fair and prosperous future for the people of Rakhine final report of the advisory commission on Rakhine State. Retrieved from http://www.rakhinecommission.org/app/uploads/2017/08/FinalReport_Eng.pdf

Ahmad AA, Rahman AZ, Mohamed AMH (2017) The role of non signatory state to the 1951 refugee convention: the Malaysian experience. Pertanika Journal of Social Sciences and Humanities 25(October):61–72

Alam M (2018) Country in focus enduring entanglement the multi-sectoral impact of the Rohingya crisis on neighboring Bangladesh. Georgetown J Int Aff *XIX*:20–26. Retrieved from http://search.ebscohost.com/login.aspx?direct=true&db=buh&AN=57958743&site=ehost-live&scope=site

Ba A (2014) Institutional divergence and convergence in the Asia- Pacific? ASEAN in practice and in theory. *Cambridge Review of International Affairs* 27(2):295–318

Beech H (2015) The nowhere people. TIME, June

Burke A (2016) New political space, old tensions: history, identity and violence in Rackhine state, Myanmar. Contemp Southeast Asia 38(2):258–283

Cohrane J (2015) Indonesia and Malaysia agree to care for stranded migrants. The New York Times, 20 May

Cornelly AL (2015) Sovereignty and the sea: president Joko Widodo's foreign policy challenges. Contemp Southeast Asia 37(1):1–28

Channelnewsasia (2015) Indonesia urges nations to help solve refugee problem in Southeast Asia. Retrieved October 15, 2018, from http://www.channelnewsasia.com/news/asiapacific/indonesia-urges-nations/1862844.html

Datta SK (2015) Rohingya's problem in Bangladesh. Himal Cent Asian Stud 19(½)

DeRouen KJ (2015) An introduction to civil wars. CQ Press, Los Angeles

Dompet Dhuafa (2015) Di Aceh, Dompet Dhuafa Kembali Gulirkan Bantuan bagi Pengungsi Rohingya. May

Galache CS (2015) Hearrowing voyage for Rohingya Muslims. *The Christian Century*, 132(13), June 24

Fardah (2015) Rohingya asylum seekers treated with compassion in Aceh. AntaraNews

Fauzia A (2017) Islamic philanthropy in Indonesia: modernization, Islamization, and social justice. Austrian J South-East Asian Stud 10(2):223–237. https://doi.org/10.14764/10.ASEAS-2017.2-6

Ha HT, Htut Y (2016) Rakhine crisis challenges ASEAN' s non-interference principle (70):1–8

Human Rights Watch (2018). "Bangladesh is not my country" the plight of Rohingya refugees from Myanmar. Retrieved from https://www.hrw.org/sites/default/files/report_pdf/bangladesh0818_web2.pdf

Hunt for undocumented foreign vessels intensifies (2015) The Jakarta post. Retrieved from http://www.worldaffairsjournal.org/content/indonesian-government-continues-hunt-undocumented-foreign-vessels

IPAC (2018) Indonesia and the rohingya crisis 29(46)

Jones DM, Jenne N (2016) Weak states' regionalism: ASEAN and the limits of security cooperation in Pacific Asia. 16(July 2015):209–240. https://doi.org/10.1093/irap/lcv015

Kaewjullakarn S (2015) What legal measures should ASEAN apply to help the Rohingya? *South East Asia Journal of Contemporary Business, Economics, and Law* 6 (4):6–14

Khu S (2016) Personal interview in Bangkok, 21 July. Saw Khu is senior researcher at International Rescue Committee (IRC) of Thailand

Kuwado FJ (2015) Panglima TNI Diingatkan untuk Tak Beri Pernyataan Kontroversial soal Rohingya. Kompas.Com. Retrieved from https://nasional.kompas.com/read/2015/05/21/12292781/Panglima.TNI.Diingatkan.untuk.Tak.Beri.Pernyataan.Kontroversial.soal.Rohingya

McLaughlin T, Shin A (2014) Graft scandal sinks without trace.*Myanmar Times*, 9 June

McLeod T (2016) A new hope for Myanmar's Rohingya migrants? Southeast Asia Globe, 9 May

Minister of Law and Human Rights. Regulation of the president of the Republic of Indonesia number 125 year 2016 concerning the handling of foreign refugees (2016)

Muhammad N (2016) Personal interviews in Bangkok, 21 July. Noor Muhammad is a coordinator of Rohingya refugees and migrant worker based in Bangkok

Parnini SN (2013) The crisis of the Rohingya as a Muslim minority in Myanmar and bilateral relations with Bangladesh. J Muslim Minor Aff 33(2)

Robert WR (2009) Principal-agent problems in humanitarian intervention: moral hazards, adverse selection, and the commitment dilemma. International Studies Quarterly 53:871–884

Shivakoti R (2017) ASEAN's role in the Rohingya refugee crisis. Forced Migr Rev (56):75–77

Singh B (2014) ASEAN, Myanmar and the Rohingya issue. Himal Cent Asian Stud 18(1/2)

Supriyadi E (2015) Will not allow refugees to land in Indonesian territory: TNI. *AntaraLampung.Com*. Retrieved from http://lampung.antaranews.com/berita/281607/will-not-allow-refugees-to-land-on-indonesian-territory-tni

Suryono M (2018) Indonesian fishermen rescue Rohingya. Retrieved from http://www.unhcr.org/news/latest/2018/5/5b0e962c4/indonesian-fishermen-rescue-rohingya.html

Tan NF (2016) The status of asylum seekers and refugees in Indonesia. Int J Refug Law 28(3):365–383. https://doi.org/10.1093/ijrl/eew045

Tangseefa D (2016) Personal interviews in Bangkok, 20 July. Decha Tangseefa is Professor in Political science at Tammasat University Bangkok

Topsfield J (2016) Indonesian foreign minister hopes countries will assist to resettle refugees. *Sydney Morning Herald*, 19 May

Ullah AA (2011) Rohingya refugees to Bangladesh: historical exclusions and contemporary marginalization. J Immigr Refug Stud 9(2):139–161

Ullah AKMA (2016) Rohingya crisis in Myanmar: seeking justice for the "Stateless." https://doi.org/10.1177/1043986216660811

UN (2018) Head of human rights fact-finding mission on Myanmar urges security council to ensure accountability for serious violations against Rohingya. Retrieved January 27, 2019, from https://www.un.org/press/en/2018/sc13552.doc.htm

UNHCR (2018) UNHCR in Indonesia. Retrieved 26 Jan 2018, from https://www.unhcr.org/id/en/unhcr-in-indonesia

Vinh VX (2014) ASEAN's approach to Myanmar. Himal Cent Asian Stud 18(1–2)

WHO (2018) Emergency type: Rohingya refugee crisis. Bangladesh

Xiong DHG (2015) Rohingya refugee crisis: testing Malaysia's ASEAN chairmanship. RSIS Commentary 128(128)

Yudhoyono SB (2014) Selalu Ada Pilihan untuk Pencinta Demokrasi dan para Pemimpin Indonesia Mendatang. Kompas, Jakarta

Part X

Cultural Celebration and Resistance

Part Introduction

As cultures interact and change in complex ways, communities also response in multiple fashions, depending on particular circumstances at the time and interests of groups concerned or powerful elements within those groups. People may mobilize to resist external cultural domination in a variety of ways or even celebrate either diversity or one's own identity as a way of affirming one's place in the modern world.

In many societies, celebration of identity takes place simultaneously with cultural resistance. Sereana Naepi and Sam Manuela examine how Pacific cultures and people are framed in the media and how the constructed public stereotypes can be countered through cultural resistance. Two ways in which many Pacific peoples celebrate and reproduce their identities are through kava ceremonies and associated cultural and cosmological discourses as Apo Aporosa examines and through cultural preservation by museums as Tarisi Vunidilo observes.

Artistic expressions are also significant in expressing and reproducing identity. This is the theme of the chapter by Murtala Murtala, Alfira O'Sullivan, and Paul Mason as they weave together the relationship between artistic expressions and ethnocultural identity by using the case study of Acehnese body percussions in Indonesia. The use of films as an artistic form of cultural expression, celebration, and resistance in politically repressive environments can be powerful and transformative. This is the case in South Africa where ethnic films were used to critique apartheid while at the same time celebrate black culture, as Gaioonisa Paleker and Bart Barendregt discuss in their chapter.

Celebration of multiculturalism is seen as a counterforce to racial demarcation and anti-immigrant policies. Many modern states are framing their national identity around multiculturalism and common citizenship, a theme which Igor Boog discusses in the case of the Netherlands.

Steven Ratuva

Rewriting the World: Pacific People, Media, and Cultural Resistance

97

Sereana Naepi and Sam Manuela

Contents

Introduction	1910
Identity Development and the Media	1911
Consuming the Pacific	1913
Dusky Maidens	1913
Noble Savages	1915
Consuming Our Ancestors	1918
Populating the Pacific	1920
Conclusion	1921
Cross-References	1921
References	1921

Abstract

This chapter explores how media is used both to create and resist hegemonic constructions of identity. Using Pacific peoples as an example, this chapter explores how media continues to portray colonial understandings of Pacific peoples and how Pacific peoples rewrite these hegemonic understandings using the same media that constructs them. This chapter considers various forms of media including poetry, film, blogs, online newspapers, and social media and how each is utilized to resist mainstream understandings of the Pacific.

Keywords

Pacific · Media · Identity · Resistance

S. Naepi (✉)
Thompson Rivers University, Kamloops, Canada
e-mail: sepatterson@tru.ca

S. Manuela
University of Auckland, Auckland, New Zealand
e-mail: s.manuela@auckland.ac.nz

© The Author(s), under exclusive license to Springer Nature Singapore Pte Ltd. 2019
S. Ratuva (ed.), *The Palgrave Handbook of Ethnicity*,
https://doi.org/10.1007/978-981-13-2898-5_132

Introduction

Media as a communication tool has the power to both resist and create hegemonic narratives about who people are. Media is used to tell stories about individuals and communities; these stories are then consumed and can be used to define an individual or community of people. When a single story is told of people over and over again, that story becomes them (Adichie 2009); it therefore becomes imperative that these stories are resisted through retelling or rewriting. Currently rewriting the world is seen as a social justice moment. When we write from the perspective of those unable to pass in the world, we diversify the narrative of this world (Ahmed 2012, 2017; Naepi 2018); we begin to tell multiple stories of the same people and communities, thereby resisting the hegemonic ideology. This resistance is necessary as those with more political power have used their power to not only oppress others but to also rewrite "the other." Pacific peoples experienced a rewriting of their ontological and epistemological understandings of this world as part of the colonial project (Hau'ofa 1994; Jolly 2007). The colonial project defined Pacific peoples in relation to Europeans and found Pacific peoples as lacking in some way (Jolly 2007). From the very moment of European encounter, Pacific peoples have had to work to define themselves on their own terms as colonial powers used, and others continue to use media to define the Pacific and Pacific peoples with single stories.

Media provides gateways for the construction and deconstruction of hegemonic ideologies. A simple exercise to show the hegemonic construction of Pacific peoples is to read the front page of a newspaper in Aotearoa New Zealand. The single story that is told of Pacific peoples on the front page of the newspaper is that we play sport, we provide entertainment (consumption of Pacific peoples), we are underachievers in education, or the Pacific is a tourist destination. However, it is possible to resist these hegemonic constructions, and hegemony is not permanent. When hegemonic ideas are resisted and challenged, we create space for the hegemonic idea to be shifted or moved toward a more nuanced understanding of what it means to be Pacific. We begin to create a diverse narrative of being Pacific with multiple stories. This chapter records current hegemonic ideologies of "being Pacific" and how these are currently challenged through the use of alternative media sources.

Pacific peoples in this chapter refer to both Pacific people located within the Pacific region and Pacific people who have migrated outside of the Pacific region. The Pacific region refers to Samoa, American Samoa, Tonga, Cook Islands, Niue, Tokelau, Fiji, Rotuma, Solomon Islands, Vanuatu, New Caledonia, Papua New Guinea, Kiribati, Tuvalu, Palau, Marshall Islands, Federated States of Micronesia, Wallis and Futuna, Hawaii, French Polynesia, and Rapanui. As such the identities of Pacific peoples are complex, multifaceted, and dynamic. There is no agreed-upon definition of what it means to be a Pacific person, as Pacific identities can be as diverse as the nations that fill the Pacific Ocean and as dynamic as the currents that flow within it. While it is important to recognize the uniqueness each nation brings to the Pacific, there are common threads of connection that speak toward a broader collective identity. These include an emphasis on family, spirituality, and views of the self as an integral part of a wider collective. In essence, the Pacific self is relational and defined in terms of relationships with people and places.

This chapter will map how media has played a role in the "writing" of Pacific ethnicities and how Pacific peoples have used media to resist hegemonic portrayals of Pacific peoples. First this chapter will explore the role of media in the development of identity with a specific focus on Pacific identity formation. Second, we will examine how Pacific people have been established as a people whose bodies and ancestral heritage can be consumed through the use of the dusky maiden, noble savage, and Disney's *Moana* (2017). Third we will consider how mainstream media has constructed the Pacific as an empty space for Western audiences to escape to. Throughout this chapter we will explore how Pacific peoples use media to resist hegemonic ideologies of Pacific people in an effort to establish and reinforce a Pacific identity that affirms Pacific peoples view of themselves. It is only possible to tell this story of media misrepresentation and re-storying because of Pacific people's own use of media to resist hegemonic constructions of the Pacific, and we wish to acknowledge the Pacific people who record our stories in order to ensure the world can see us.

Identity Development and the Media

Lived experiences of identity formation for Pacific peoples have been likened to that of a journey with many ups and downs, and the formation and development of what it means to be a Pacific person develops through a series of challenges to the self, when the self becomes distinct in varying social spaces, when physical differences belie cultural differences, and when challenges from the biased assumptions of non-Pacific others force one to define their self in relation to others both Pacific and non-Pacific. Before exploring the role of media in the formation of Pacific identities, a theoretical discussion of Pacific identities that has informed contemporary, colonial, and indigenous views of Pacific identity development is necessary. This will serve a basis on which to discuss the way media can influence Pacific identity development.

Drawing on psychology, ethnic identity has been understood from a developmental framework. Early theories on identity development have drawn on Erikson's (1968) model of ego identity development, which posits that questions about who one is become more salient during adolescence. Identity development would occur over time as one observed and reflected on their own values, interests, and identifications, eventually reaching an *achieved identity status* which is based on a unified understanding of oneself. Marcia (1980) extended upon this and posed identity formation via a process of exploring identity issues and committing to an identity, both of which when considered together suggest four identity statuses. Phinney and Ong (2007) articulate these statuses in relation to ethnic identity where one could (a) not have a clear concept of their ethnic identity (*ethnic identity diffusion*), which could lead to (b) a commitment to an ethnic identity without having explored its content or meaning (*ethnic identity foreclosure*), or (c) engaging in a period of exploration of what it means to be a member of their ethnic group (*moratorium*), finally leading to (d) having a clear idea of what their ethnicity means to them and being committed to that ethnicity (*ethnic identity achievement*).

While ethnic identity development offers explanations of how one can come to understand their ethnic self, it does little to explain what ethnic identity consists of and the meanings it has for individuals. Ethnic identity has been understood from a social identity theory framework (Tajfel and Turner 1986) which posits that ethnic identity can be derived from one's self-perceived membership with a group, together with emotional significance attached to that group. Extending upon social identities, Phinney and Ong (2007) proposed ethnic identity as a construct consisting of self-identification with an ethnic group, a sense of belonging to that ethnic group, positive/negative attitudes toward the group, and involvement in practices associated with an ethnic group. Essential to Phinney's conceptualization of ethnic identities is how it is marked by its multidimensional and dynamic nature as indicated by discourses relating to ethnic identity development.

Psychological research on ethnic identity highlights two broad perspectives – one relating to the content of ethnic identity and the other on its development. Yip (2014) suggests these two perspectives have grown in parallel with each other. Within this broad narrative, some Pacific theorists have attempted to define what it means to be a Pacific person and how one comes to developing that self-consciousness. Anae (1998) examines identity through her personal journey in her study of Samoan identity. Her research draws parallels with Phinney and Ong's (2007) articulation of ethnic identity development but furthers this perspective by offering how ethnic identity is developed in contexts that provide content for what it means to be Samoan. For instance, Anae discusses interactions with family, church members, and non-Pacific people that challenged an individual's sense of self. Some of these challenges included the role of language as a marker of identity, discrimination in increasingly diverse contexts, and changing social networks. From Anae's perspective, a secure identity is one in which the sense of self as Samoan is persistent and in which one has found a resolution between internal and external conflicts of what it means to be Samoan. In a similar vein, Tiatita's (1998) early work positions Pacific peoples at the interface between two cultural worlds, where their involvement in one could be seen as denial of the other. Mila-Schaaf (2010) provides a description of polycultural capital for Pacific peoples in which experiences in diverse social settings are marked by feelings of inclusion, exclusion, similarities, and differences and provide an accumulation of cultural resources that allows people to engage with identities in relation to the contexts they are in. For instance, Pacific peoples would behave and react in particular ways to counter negative social narratives they perceived were being expressed by their non-Pacific peers. With a focus on the contents of Pacific identities, Manuela and Sibley (2013, 2015) put emphasis on family, relationships with society, a sense of belonging, positive attitudes toward Pacific others, the embeddedness of religiosity and spirituality, and engagement with one's culture. In relation to this, Pacific ethnic identity development is seen as influenced by relationships in various levels of New Zealand society. These perspectives of Pacific ethnic identities also speak of sociohistorical contexts, experiences of discrimination, responses to stereotypes, celebrations of self, and affirmations of the self with similar others.

When viewed against this backdrop of ethnic Pacific identity development, the role of media in identity formation becomes quite complex. In this sense, media can serve a dual role. In one sense, media can be a broad social influence from which one can gain information about what it means to be Pacific as one explores one's Pacific identity. In addition, the media's representation of Pacific peoples also creates, constructs, and defines the content of Pacific ethnic and cultural identities. However, the content of these ethnic meanings differs as a function of who produces Pacific media representations: Pacific or non-Pacific. As will be shown in this chapter, non-Pacific people often produce media narratives and imageries that reinforce Pacific peoples as consumable objects, whereas Pacific peoples tend to produce media imageries that tell complex stories of who we are and what can be used to reinforce strong positive Pacific identities.

Consuming the Pacific

The Pacific is often framed as a place and people to be consumed by the western gaze and western experience (Naepi 2016, 2018). This is evident in centuries old depictions of Pacific people as dusky maidens and noble savages right through to this contemporary moment in the Disney movie Moana where Pacific ancestors are depicted in multi-million-dollar films in order to advance profits by corporations.

Dusky Maidens

The dusky maiden refers to a centuries old practice of "sexualizing and eroticizing the Polynesian female form through titillating visual representations of bare-breasted, nubile Polynesian wāhine (women), which functioned as soft porn for art connoisseurs" (Tamaira 2010, p,1). More recently the dusky maiden has developed to be a "simultaneous portrayal of Polynesian women as sexually receptive as well as distant and dangerous (as signified by the tattoos inscribed on their bodies), served to intensify rather than curb their exotic and erotic appeal in the Western imagination" (Tamaira 2010, p. 11). This problematic positioning of Pacific women continues. In a contemporary example, Netflix's popular series, The Crown, Prince Philip is seduced by Pacific women while on tour. In the scene, Pacific women are dancing and beckoning to him over a fire, and he is then led away by a dancer with a knowing smile. The dusky maiden trope is designed to remove agency and power from Pacific women by presenting them as vulnerable maidens for men's consumption as opposed to the genealogical descendants of powerful goddesses (Tamaira 2010). Naepi (2018) argued that this portrayal of Pacific women as consumable objects can be counteracted by building a more complex understanding of Pacific women, one that is built from Pacific people's own understandings of the world.

This movement toward developing a more nuanced understanding of Pacific women is not only important for how the rest of the world sees Pacific people but also for providing alternatives that allow Pacific peoples to resist internalizing these problematic images (Jolly 2007). Poetry is one media device that is being used by Pacific women to dispel the myth of the dusky maiden. Pacific female poets such as Konai Thaman, Karlo Mila, Tusiata Avia, Courtney Sina Meredith, Teresia Teaiwa, and Katerina Teaiwa continue to share poetry that calls into question the hegemonic understanding of Pacific women as dusky maidens. Some Pacific women poets such as Selina Tusitala Marsh's *Statued (stat you?) Traditions* (1997) directly refer and critique the dusky maiden trope so that it becomes possible to reimagine Pacific women from a place of strength. Karlo Mila's poetry (below) speaks to Pasifika (people of Pacific ancestry in Aotearoa New Zealand) efforts to relocate themselves within the ancient beat of Pacific women, to find the grace and ease of movement that their grandmothers had. This poem of loss and reconnection is an important insight into how Pacific women experience the world outside of the hegemonic understanding of Pacific women. Pacific dance is not something that is done to allure (white) men away from their faithful wives and into the arms of a Pacific maiden (the narrative in *The Crown*). Pacific dance is something that reconnects us with our ancestors. Poetry is a form of media that gives Pacific women the opportunity to rewrite the world from Pacific perspectives disrupting and resisting the dangerous dusky maiden trope.

> On joining Pasifika
> When I first met you
> we were learning to siva
> wearing lavalava tied in awkward knots
> our work clothes carefully folded away
> both of us
> learning a new dance
> both of us
> finding a different way to move
> through life
> We have hustled and bustled
> and power-walked well
> somehow
> sacrificing the grace
> and ease of movement
> our grandmothers held in their hands
> When we met
> both of us
> were trying to remember
> that earlier beat
> Both of us trying to reclaim
> a new dance from old memories
> both us standing shyly
> in the back-row
> trying to siva in our sports socks
> both of us searching for a rhythm
> we'd never quite
> been able to find
> within ourselves
> All of us trying to find time
> to ta'olunga

to meke
to tamule
to siva
into our truest selves.
(Mila 2005)

If we consider these two depictions of Pacific women next to each other, it is possible to see how different media sources can reinforce Pacific identities. Pacific produced media creates media that resists hegemonic ideologies of Pacific women and instead ensures that all the complexities of being Pacific are explored.

Noble Savages

Pacific masculinities have been constructed through the lens of "the other." The construction of Pacific masculinities can be tied back to the "world historical processes of colonialism, Christian conversion, market penetration and urbanisation" (Biersack 2016, p.198). Of particular importance in the construction of Pacific masculinities is the noble savage trope. The noble savage construction can be tied back to European desire to experience a "state of nature" that can be found within the South Pacific. It is a complex idea which both celebrates Pacific peoples in a state of nature (Campbell 1980) and suggests that when Pacific people engage in civilization, they become ignoble as they are tainted by the modern world usually due to their "simple" nature (Taylor 2008). While Campbell (1980) noted that it is the tourism industry keeping the idea of the noble savage alive, it is possible to see the same narratives within mainstream media today. The narrative of the noble savage which began during early colonization of the Pacific continues to impact on how Pacific men are portrayed today. The concept of the noble savage and Pacific masculinities can be seen within sports.

Pacific influence in sports is growing. Prominent Pacific names can be found in NFL with the likes of Troy Polamalu, sports entertainment with Dwayne "The Rock" Johnson, and in both Rugby Union and Rugby League codes internationally, particularly New Zealand and Australia. Perhaps rearticulating the noble savage trope in a contemporary age, Pacific men are seen to be displaying their raw and "savage" prowess on the sporting field. The increasing representation of Pacific men in rugby and league focus on the "natural athlete" stereotype and the "white flight" narrative (Cleaver and Napier 2018) – a movement of white players away from rugby because of the size and physicality of Pacific players. This positions white athletes as victims of the supposed natural athleticism of Pacific athletes, thus requiring the regulation of Pacific athletes in media narratives. The stereotype of the naturally gifted Pacific athletes is often paired with language that emphasizes their physicality and simultaneously downplaying their intelligence. Commentary on white athletes highlights their intellect, decisiveness, and leadership prowess, while Pacific athletes are generally spoken about in terms of their strength, power, and speed (Stevenson 2015). This is a common trope of athletes of color relative to their white counterparts (Gane-McCalla 2009; Eastman and

Billings 2001). Similarly, decisions of Samoan rugby player, rugby league player, and boxer, Sonny Bill Williams, were met with derision by media outlets, where he was simultaneously praised for his physical prowess but chided about his personal agency (Meagher 2017). The same media regularly reinforces the idea that Pacific nations could not possibly participate in rugby tournaments most recently citing that Pacific men would not return from high-paying European teams to play for their own national teams (Napier 2018). In this narrative, Pacific players who are noble in the game of rugby (as the media acknowledges their natural ability) are seen as unable to resist the corruption of the civilized dollar; their natural athleticism has become a source of greed in the face of capitalism. The media also points to governance issues using the "corruption" of one Pacific nation as an excuse to exclude all Pacific nations, suggesting that Pacific peoples are not capable of managing themselves.

In spite of the mainstream media's belief that the "noble savage" will be corrupted by the dollar, it has been proven otherwise. In the lead up to the 2017 Rugby League World Cup, Taumalolo announced that he would be representing Tonga's national team, Mate Ma'a Tonga. In New Zealand, the media were swift to characterize him as traitorous, having turned his back on New Zealand despite Taumalolo doing what the media now argues Pacific people will not do, which is give up a more lucrative contract to represent their home countries. Perhaps even more disheartening was how the mainstream media portrayed Taumalolo. The interplay between ethnic and national identities for Pacific peoples in the context of sport-related media places Pacific identities between competing patriotic loyalties, where they can be either New Zealand or Pacific, but not both. It is from this that competing narratives were developed – one by mainstream media that positioned Taumalolo as the anti-villain – one who displays heroic attributes in their quest for a goal but with questionable means on how to get there. According to media portrayals, it was admirable for Taumalolo to want to represent Tonga, but a slap in the face to New Zealand for doing so and perhaps an unwise decision for his future possibilities of national representation. This highlights an expectation by New Zealand media to see Pacific athletes as New Zealanders and New Zealanders only. It creates a sense that identity for Pacific peoples means surrendering their sense of Pacific-ness to the New Zealand national identity. However, their Pacific-ness is not viewed in terms of their culture, identities, and relationships with others but in terms of an essentialist physicality – the noble savage's place is on the sports field. There are of course examples of Pacific athletes that have challenged this idea, showing how one can be both Pacific and New Zealander, such as Tana Umaga leading the All Blacks in haka, a role usually reserved for the indigenous Maori or tagata whenua (Teaiwa and Mallon 2005). When Pacific athletes exhibit any sense of personal agency, this runs counter to the narrative New Zealand media has produced, and the response is one of questioning loyalty to a New Zealand national identity – the "noble savage" has become morally corrupt. It is then when their Pacific cultural and ethnic identity becomes a centrally defining aspect of the narrative but in a way that is disruptive to NZ's sporting goals.

Furthermore, Taumalolo was not the only target of negative media portrayals, but so too were Tongan fans. Media representations of Tongan rugby league fans presented an unruly, violent crowd, situating their place in South Auckland suburbs and highlighting the number of arrests made (South Auckland population has a high proportion of Pacific peoples and is stereotyped as a high-crime area). This presented three stories that all relate to Pacific identities as presented in media: one playing stereotypes of the Pacific criminal (McCann 2017) one in which Pacific success is tainted with problematic and antisocial behavior ("Tongan supporters well behaved despite 21 fans arrested" 2017). In instances where mainstream media outlets centered the Pacific voice, this was also shaped by dominant narratives. Centering of Pacific voices was a response to negative reactions by Pacific peoples of the unfair portrayals of Pacific players and fans who did not view themselves as the problematic images the media produced but as passionate and proud fans (New Zealand Herald 2017). While this could be seen as an attempt to challenge their own narratives, in essence it relied on them to provide a platform for the Pacific voice.

New Zealand media's portrayal of the noble Pacific athlete and its construction of their identity presents a misunderstanding of what and how Pacific identities inform sporting endeavors and thus how they could be presented in media. Pacific productions and accounts of Mate Ma'a Tonga's 2017 Rugby League World Cup campaign painted an image in which ethnic and cultural values were fully embedded in the teams approach to the tournament. Coconet TV's summary of the 2017 Rugby League World Cup highlighted that these culture and ethnic behaviors were written as part of the normative behavior:

> The Tongan team played their cards well in this tournament. They came in quietly and got down to the job of training and getting the basics right. Catch the ball and finish the sets. Off the field, they went to church, sang songs, ate well, and kept a humble camp. When tensions amongst Tongan and Samoan fans looked to spill over, they were on your facebook page telling their fans to calm down and increase the peace. The fans loved them, and they in turn played for their fans. All up, they had the perfect build up to this tournament and the results of good on field and off field training, became apparent on game days, where they muscled and then moonwalked themselves to the semi finals. (Kosokoso 2017)

In one paragraph, this excerpt highlights how a normative positioning of Pacific cultural values provides the construction of the Pacific athlete as a whole person – cultural, spiritual, professional, successful, and with a focus on relationships. This piece also referred to the problematic white gaze upon Mate Ma'a Tonga, acknowledging the problematic portrayal of Taumalolo's agency, but not making the traitor narrative central, instead turning the narrative back on to mainstream media. "This is in no small part to the "defectors" (Taumalolo and co) who made themselves available to Mate Ma'a Tonga, earning the evil eyes of David Kidwell and the Kiwi team" (Kosokoso, ibid). This act of resistance both challenged the white narrative and asserted the Pacific narrative as one of equal and positive competition.

Consuming Our Ancestors

Disney's Moana is a contemporary example of how Pacific peoples and their cultures are understood to be something that can be consumed. Disney a multi-billion-dollar media giant profited off the depiction of Pacific ancestral imageries. Disney utilized ancestral stories of Māui to create a Disney princess story that centered on a Pacific girl's journey across the Pacific with the demigod Māui to save her people. Disney profited immensely from this retelling of Pacific navigational stories and its inclusion of Māui as a sidekick. Disney's Moana was the second-highest Thanksgiving debut in America (after Frozen) making 81.1 million over the Thanksgiving holiday (Reuters 2016). Disney alludes to the significance of Māui in his song *You're Welcome*:

> Hey, what has two thumbs and pulled up the sky
> When you were waddling yay high? This guy
> When the nights got cold, who you stole you fire from down below?
> You're looking at him, yo!
> Oh, also I lassoed the sun, you're welcome
> To stretch your days and bring you fun
> Also, I harnessed the breeze, you're welcome
> To fill your sails and shake your trees…
> …Well, come to think of it,
> Kid, honestly, I can go on and on
> I can explain every natural phenomenon
> The tide, the grass, the ground
> Oh, that was just Māui messing around
> I killed an eel, I buried its guts
> Sprouted a tree now you've got coconuts.

Māui's exploits throughout the Pacific were designed to upset the universe the Gods had created to benefit themselves and instead shift the universe to benefit all of humankind (Luomala 1986). The inclusion of these deeds in Māui's song shows that Disney is aware and understands the significance of Māui to Pacific peoples.

In order to understand the significance of Disney choosing to represent and profit off Māui on film, it is important to understand who Māui is to Pacific people. Māui is a Pacific ancestor who has been characterized as a trickster or demigod. Māui is found throughout the Pacific (Luomala 1986; Howe 2006). Tonga has three Māui, the youngest of which is Māui Kisikisi, son of Māui 'Atalanga, son of Māui Motu'a (old Māui) (Mila 2016). In Samoa Māui is Ti'iti'i son of Talaga and brings fire from the underworld (Mila 2016). These may sound myth-like to people today, but they refer to stories of a Pacific ancestor. Mila (2016) outlines that many people consider that the hook Māui uses in so many stories to fish up islands refers to a set of constellations that were used to navigate to islands. Mila explains that:

> All over Oceania we have named stars, cities, giant stone sculptures, landmarks, beaches, and islands after him. Our stories about Māui helped us make sense for centuries of morals, mortality, land, death, power, fire, mana, authority – and who and what you can be in this

world, regardless of birth. He has featured in story, symbol and song. He is both demigod and ancestor. (Mila 2016, n.p)

However, this inclusion of Pacific ancestral tales within a Disney film was not without some controversy. The problem was how Disney portrayed Māui; he went from a powerful ancestor to a:

> pot-bellied, barrel-chested man-baby, with eyes too close together, pupils perfectly aligned with his widespread nostrils in nice savage symmetry......an oafish, neckless wonder with large lips and an ooga-booga mask-like mouth. Our great hero has more in common with the cartoon fare of the hunchback of Notre Dame, more affinity with the Beast than any Beauty. (Mila 2016, n.p)

Mila (2016) outlines how despite Disney's protests that they were representing Pacific people on film, at the end of the day, they had created a Pacific male archetype that Pacific people did not identify with. Diaz slammed *Moana* as:

> Disney's 21st century imagineering of primitivist desire for noble savagery, now dressed up in a story of a would-be anti-heroine; a brave and amazing navigatress/princess (lets call her Moana 1) in synergistic touch with the power of nature, in particular with the ocean (Moana 2), in the company of a buffoonish, but ultimately lovable caricature (Disney Maui) of an actual pan-Polynesian demigod and revered ancestor (Maui the Real)......The sad fact is, Disney is a capitalist culture-vulture that cannibalizes and then spits (or shits) out other people's cultural traditions and birthrights, a domain into which it has no real business sticking its nose, especially in such seemingly sensitive, but actually crassly commercialized ways. (2016, n.p)

Disney's portrayal of Māui and the Pacific is problematic because of the audience reach they have (Teaiwa 2016), they are able to create a hegemonic understanding of the Pacific and Pacific peoples. In spite of this, Pacific peoples were able to use online media outlets to protest this depiction of Pacific peoples and their ancestors (as shown above). It is clear that people are engaged in these alternative readings of Moana beyond a high-grossing film for Disney as shown in the YouTube video *Beyond Disney's Moana: In the Spirit of Maui* which has over 7000 views (Iron Lion 2016).

However, not all Pacific peoples used online media to resist Disney's representation of Pacific peoples in Moana. Thompsen (2016) argued that Moana could be good for Pacific peoples. Thompsen's central argument was that Moana was a story of female empowerment that provides a counternarrative to the patriarchy which was installed during colonization. Thompsen notes that:

> I feel comfortable riding Moana's wave, because she makes space for us Pacific Islanders in global discussions. As adults, academics, activists, parents, aunts, uncles – we have the job now to reshape those spaces into something future Pacific generations will feel capable of claiming as their own. (2016, n.p)

Thompsen's view seems to be reinforced within the comment sections of his online piece in e-tangata (a Sunday online magazine for Māori and Pacific peoples) where Pacific people from around the globe share that they too felt that Moana gave them at least one character in mainstream media that they could identify with.

The online debate of *Moana* among the Pacific community shows how media can be used to inspire complex discussions on identity and how we understand ourselves. The media gives us a platform to consider how we wish to be understood by the outside world and to also resist or agree with the depictions of our own people. This shows that not all hegemonic understandings of Pacific people can be considered just good or bad but that we should have a more nuanced discussion about what makes a depiction "good" or "bad" and if we see ourselves within this construction.

Populating the Pacific

The Pacific is often used as both a physical place for filming and as a plot device in film and television. Fiji serves as an example of how Hollywood both uses and frames the Pacific. Many movies have been shot in Fiji from *Mr. Robinson Crusoe* (1932), a film about a man living on an abandoned island; numerous reincarnations of *The Blue Lagoon* (1979, 1992), a film about castaways lost in the Pacific; to *Castaway* (2000), a film about a single castaway lost in the Pacific. What these films have in common is that Fiji provides the backdrop of uninhabited islands for Westerners to be lost in. This is taken even further in television where *Survivor* has filmed multiple seasons (four seasons) with plans to make Fiji its permanent filming home (Ross 2017). *Survivor* is a reality TV show predicated on the idea that American must survive being "abandoned" on uninhabited islands. In The Truman Show (1998), Truman famously talks about escaping from his manufactured life by fleeing to Fiji; in one particular scene when he is asked where Fiji is, he replies "FIJI, You can't get any further away before you start coming back." Fiji is understood to be a remote location where he can escape his life. This referencing of Fiji as a distant and remote place to escape trouble is common in Hollywood films and television.

In comparison feature films created by Pacific people show the Pacific as not only inhabited but also as a place from which life's lessons can be learned. *Three Wise Cousins* (2016) written, produced, and directed by Samoan filmmaker Stallone Vaiaoga-Ioasa tells the story of a New Zealand-raised Pacific male returning to Samoa to learn how to become a "real islander" in order to win a girl's heart. The theme is about the main character who learns from his cousins about the importance of putting family first while also tackling the difficult and complex issue of being Pacific when raised elsewhere. *Three Wise Cousins* is one of the few feature films created by Pacific people about Pacific people, and Vaiaoga-Ioasa said the best thing for him apart from the box office results was "the real impact is just the feedback that it's cool to be an Islander" (Tapaleao 2016). This reflection shows the impact of creating Pacific films that reflect the Pacific, not as "islands in the far sea" (Hau'ofa 1994) but as islands with people, traditions, and knowledge.

Conclusion

Although this chapter has outlined very specific examples of Pacific peoples responding to negative portrayals of Pacific peoples, it is important to note that there is a significant amount of media out there that is by Pacific for Pacific and that honors the diversity within the Pacific. These include *Truths She Wrote* (a blog about successful Pacific women), *The Coconet* (a website that uses multimedia to connect Pacific peoples to their heritage through language, history, stories, etc.), and *Fresh* (a television show dedicated to Pacific-oriented pop culture). The media is a powerful tool for defining people, but as Pacific peoples in New Zealand have experienced, the media is also powerful as a tool to resist these definitions.

Cross-References

▶ Faamatai: A Globalized Pacific Identity
▶ Kava and Ethno-cultural Identity in Oceania
▶ Media and Stereotypes
▶ Nuclear Testing and Racism in the Pacific Islands
▶ Race and Racism: Some Salient Issues
▶ Racism and Stereotypes

References

Adichie C (2009) The danger of a single story. Retrieved from: https://www.ted.com/talks/chimamanda_adichie_the_danger_of_a_single_story?language=en
Ahmed S (2012) On being included: racism and diversity in institutional life. Duke University Press, Durham
Ahmed S (2017) Living a feminist life. Duke University Press, Durham
Anae M (1998) Fofoa-i-vao-'ese: the identity journeys of NZ-born Samoans (Unpublished doctoral dissertation). University of Auckland, Auckland, New Zealand
Biersack A (2016) Introduction: emergent masculinities in the Pacific. Asia Pac J Anthropol 3–4:197–212
Campbell I (1980) Savages noble and ignoble: the preconceptions of early European voyagers in Polynesia. Pac Stud 4(1):45–59
Cleaver D, Napier L (2018) Special report: white flight – a detailed look at race and Auckland rugby. The New Zealand Herald. April 14
Diaz V (2016) Disney craps cute grass skirt. The Hawaiian Independent. September 29
Eastman S, Billings A (2001) Biased voices of sports: racial and gender stereotyping in college basketball announcing. Howard J Commun 12:183–201. https://doi.org/10.1080/106461701753287714
Erikson E (1968) Identity: youth and crisis. Norton, New York
Gane-McCalla C (2009) Athletic blacks vs smart whites: why sports stereotypes are wrong. Huffington Post. May 20
Hau'ofa E (1994) Our sea of islands. In: Waddell E, Naidu V, Hau'ofa E (eds) A New Oceania: rediscovering our sea of islands. School of Social and Economic Development, University of the South Pacific, Suva, pp 126–139
Howe KR (ed.) (2006) Vaka moana: voyages of the ancestors: the discovery and settlement of the Pacific. David Bateman

Iron Lion (2016) Beyond Disney's Moana: in the spirit of Maui. https://www.youtube.com/watch?v=OdsRO4i7pFM
Jolly M (2007) Imagining Oceania: indigenous and foreign representations of a sea of islands. Contemp Pac 19:508–545
Kosokoso JS (2017) Referee parts the Red Sea – a summary of the rugby league world cup for our Pacific Island teams. Retrieved from: http://www.thecoconet.tv/coco-talanoa/sports/referee-parts-the-red-sea-a-summary-of-the/
Luomala K (1986) Voices on the wind: Polynesian myths and chants. Honolulu, Bishop Museum Press
Manuela S, Sibley CG (2013) The Pacific Identity and Wellbeing Scale (PIWBS): a culturally-appropriate self-report measure for Pacific peoples in New Zealand. Soc Indic Res 112:83–103. https://doi.org/10.1007/s11205-012-0041-9
Manuela S, Sibley CG (2015) The Pacific Identity and Wellbeing Scale-Revised (PIWBS-R). Cult Divers Ethn Minor Psychol 21:146–155. https://doi.org/10.1037/a0037536
Marcia J (1980) Identity in adolescence. In: Handbook of adolescent psychology. Wiley, New York, pp 159–187
McCann M (2017) Tongan rugby league fans cause problems in Otahuhu. Newshub. November 11
Meagher G (2017) Sonny Bill Williams bears brunt of criticism after All Blacks defeat. The Guardian. July 2
Mila K (2005) Dream fish floating. Huia Publishers
Mila K (2016) Why Disney's Maui is so wrong. E-Tangata
Mila-Schaaf K (2010) Polycultural capital and the Pasifika second generation: Negotiating identities in diasporic places. (Doctoral dissertation). Massey University, Albany
Naepi S (2016) Indigenous feminisms: A South Pacific perspective, Canadian Graduate J Social Justice 1:1–10
Naepi S (2018) Beyond the Dusky Maiden: Pasifika women's experiences working in higher education (Doctoral dissertation). University of British Columbia, Vancouver
Napier L (2018) Rugby: the key factors stopping a Pacific Island Super Rugby franchise. The New Zealand Herald. September 16
New Zealand Herald (2017) League: Taumalolo turns his back on kiwis, opts to represent tonga at world cup. New Zealand Herald. 4 October
Phinney JS, Ong AD (2007) Conceptualization and measurement of ethnic identity: current status and future directions. J Couns Psychol 54:271–281. https://doi.org/10.1037/0022-0167.54.3.271
Reuters (2016) 'Moana' rules the thanks giving box office as 'The Rules Don't Apply' bombs. Fortune. November 28
Ross D (2017) Jeff Probst wants survivor to stay in Fiji permanently. Entertainment Weekly. September 12
Rudin S (Producer), Weir P (Director) (1998) Truman Show [Motion Picture]. Paramount, United States of America
Stevenson S (2015) Racial stereotyping is alive and well in the language of NZ sport. The New Zealand Herald. July 29
Tajfel H, Turner J (1986) The social identity theory of intergroup behaviour. In: Austin W, Worchel S (eds) Psychology of intergroup relations. Nelson-Hall, Chicago, pp 7–24
Tamaira AM (2010) From Full Dusk to Full Tusk: Reimagining the "Dusky Maiden" through the Visual Arts. The Contemporary Pacific 22(1):1–35
Tapaleao V (2016) Low-key movie three wise cousins a $1m Pacific hit. The New Zealand Herald. 07 March
Taylor JP (2008) Changing Pacific masculinities: the 'problem'of men. Aust J Anthropol 19(2):125–135
Teaiwa T (2016) I once was seduced by Disney but no more. E-Tangata. October 08
Teaiwa T, Mallon S (2005) Ambivalent kinships? Pacific people in New Zealand. In: Liu J, McCreanor T, McIntosh T, Teaiwa T (eds) New Zealand identities: departures and destinations. Victoria University Press, Wellington, pp 207–229
Thompsen P (2016) Why Moana could actually be good for us. E-Tangata. December 10
Yip T (2014) Ethnic identity in everyday life: the influence of identity development status. Child Dev 85:205–219. https://doi.org/10.1111/cdev.12107

Kava and Ethno-cultural Identity in Oceania 98

S. Apo Aporosa

Contents

Introduction	1924
Origination of Kava in Oceania	1924
Kava Preparation, Effect, and Oceanic Identity	1925
Yaqona (Kava) and National Ethno-cultural Identity in Fiji	1926
Yaqona (Kava) and Other Symbols of Collectivism	1929
Fijian-ness, Yaqona, and Government	1930
What Do Fijians Say About Yaqona	1931
Yaqona and Ethno-cultural Identity in Diaspora	1931
Critics of "Yaqona as a Symbol of Cultural Identity"	1931
Fundamental Questions as to the Role of Yaqona	1933
Conclusion	1934
Cross-References	1934
References	1934

Abstract

Garibaldi and Turner (Ecol Soc 9:1, 5, 2004) explain the role that particular plants play in facilitating the shared ancestry, practices, and social experience of an ethnicity. This can include spiritual connections, cultural expression and practice, ceremony, exchange, linguistic reflection, socialization, and medicinal and/or dietary systems. They term these plants "cultural keystone species" and icons of identity, plants that if removed would cause some disruptions to the cultural practices and identity of an ethnic group. Undoubtedly, kava (*Piper methysticum*) is the cultural keystone species for many Oceanic and Pacific peoples, a "differentiating element of common culture" (Zagefka, Ethnicity, concepts of. In: Smith AD, Hou X, Stone J, Dennis R, Rizova P (eds) The Wiley Blackwell

---

S. A. Aporosa (✉)
Te Huataki Waiora: Faculty of Health, Sport and Human Performance, University of Waikato, Hamilton, Waikato, New Zealand
e-mail: apo.aporosa@waikato.ac.nz

© The Author(s), under exclusive license to Springer Nature Singapore Pte Ltd. 2019
S. Ratuva (ed.), *The Palgrave Handbook of Ethnicity*,
https://doi.org/10.1007/978-981-13-2898-5_134

encyclopedia of race, ethnicity, and nationalism. West Wiley, Sussex, pp 761–763, 2016) informing their ethno-cultural identity. That influence is also extending to new non-Pacific Island user groups who have embraced elements of kava ethno-cultural identity in what has been termed diasporic identity formation in reverse. This chapter will discuss kava with specific reference to ethnic positionality in Fiji while recognizing the tensions from inside and outside the region that support and threaten the continuance of the kava drinking tradition.

Keywords
Identity · Kava · Yaqona · Fiji · Oceanic Pacific cultural identifiers · Evangelical

Introduction

Garibaldi and Turner (2004, p. 1, 5) explain the role that particular plants play in facilitating the shared ancestry, practices, and social experience of an ethnicity. This can include spiritual connections, cultural expression and practice, ceremony, exchange, linguistic reflection, socialization, and medicinal and/or dietary systems. They term these plants "cultural keystone species" and icons of identity, plants that if removed would cause some disruptions to the cultural practices and identity of an ethnic group. Undoubtedly, *kava* (*Piper methysticum*) is the cultural keystone species for many Oceanic and Pacific peoples, a "differentiating element of common culture" (Zagefka 2016, p. 761) informing their ethno-cultural identity. That influence is also extending to new non-Pacific Island user groups who have embraced elements of *kava* ethno-cultural identity in what has been termed *diasporic identity formation in reverse*. This chapter will discuss *kava* with specific reference to ethnic positionality in Fiji while recognizing the tensions from inside and outside the region that support and threaten the continuance of the *kava* drinking tradition.

Origination of Kava in Oceania

The *kava* plant, of the genus *Piper methysticum*, is found across much of tropical Oceania. Growing several meters tall and with six to eight thick noded stems and heart-shaped leaves extending from a central basal stump, *kava*'s importance is reflected in the traditional narratives of Pacific Oceanic people groups from Papua New Guinea in the west to Hawaii in the east (Lebot et al. 1992, p. 121). Lindstrom (2004) explains that although there is some variation in these narratives, they contain a common theme of regeneration and fertility empowered by local ancestral spirits and gods, with these recited "to legitimate contemporary behavioural patterns and understandings" (p. 12).

Botanical, linguistic, and genetic evidence suggests that the *kava* plant was originally found by the Austronesian Lapita culture in northern Vanuatu around 3000 years ago (Lebot et al. 1992). That "finding" has led to other narratives. For instance, this tropical shrub is asexual – without seeds and requiring manual propagation – which has led to its status becoming a "plant of the gods," believed to have been nurtured by the gods until the arrival of those first Austronesians in Vanuatu. This link with the gods is argued to imbue *kava* with *mana* (or spiritual power) (Aporosa 2014). *Mana* is also believed to give *kava* its medicinal efficacy, which includes mild anesthetic, analgesic, and anti-inflammatory properties and antifungal, amebicidal, anticonvulsant, antimicrobial, anticancer, and anxiolytic activity (Lebot and Cabalion 1988; Lim 2016).

Vanuatuan anthropologist Kirk Huffman (2012), reflecting on the spread of *kava* from Vanuatu, has observed: "Well cut and wrapped fresh kava branches can be planted after sea voyages of up to two weeks... Thus, we can attribute the entire distribution of drinkable kava across the Pacific to the earlier maritime explorers of the region, long before the late arrival of European explorers" (p. 25). In their Eastern Polynesian anthropologically focused text, Kirch and Green (2001) agree with Huffman's thesis: "we can be certain it [*kava*] was introduced from the West. Most probably, this occurred with or just after the initial Lapita settlement of Fiji-Tonga-Samoa region" (p. 256). It is speculated that early trading by Lapita peoples also introduced *kava* to areas west of Vanuatu, including selected regions of Papua New Guinea (Lebot et al. 1992).

Although trade is cited as a significant reason for *kava*'s distribution across the Pacific, Lebot et al. (1992) also cite the role of "traditional exchange ... [which] links people with their gods and ancestral spirits" (p. 120). That union between *kava* and traditional spiritualism and mana suggests that early traders, who frequently negotiated dangerous stretches of open water, would have carried *kava* with them for protection while also having an item of spiritual significance on hand to offer to, and acknowledge, those they met en route and to forge trading alliances (Lebot et al. 1992, p. 142). That connection with gods and ancestral spirits is believed to have been enhanced through the consumption of *kava* beverage (Lebot et al. 1992).

Kava Preparation, Effect, and Oceanic Identity

Kava is made by steeping the crushed green or dried roots of the *kava* plant in water to make a slightly peppery earthy flavored drink (Fig. 1). In Vanuatu and the kava using regions to the west, *kava* is mixed with less water and therefore is stronger in concentration than typically prepared in Fiji and the islands to the east (Aporosa 2014). Active properties within *kava*, called kavalactones, dull receptors in the central nervous system leading to a slight numbing and slowing in the response time in the muscles, limbs, and brain creating a relaxed, peaceful, lethargic feeling (Aporosa 2011, 2017). This does not lead to marked euphoria or hallucination, as *kava* "intoxication" includes a clear mindedness, which facilitates quality conversation and decision-making (Aporosa and Tomlinson 2014).

Lebot et al. (1992) report that *kava* "plays a unique role in the social life of many Pacific societies... [as part of] asserting their cultural identity" (p. 198). Pacific and Social Science researchers have reported widely on the link between identity and

Fig. 1 Contemporary kava mixing using cloth 'mixing bag'. (Source: Payson 2008, p. 122)

kava use across Oceania (Aporosa 2014, pp. 35–44). This includes selected areas of Papua New Guinea, notably in the Middle Fly District, where the Gogodala people continue to use *kava* today (Crawford 1981) together with the islanders of Pohnpei in the Federated States of Micronesia. Balick and Lee (2009) report that both the plant and the drink made from it play a critical role in "defining Pohnpeian cultural identity" (p. 165).

Kava in Vanuatu is described as important to outworking *kastom*, being a "symbol of national identity" (Young 1995, p. 61). Finau et al. (2002) also highlight *kava* use in Tonga through which "Tongan's have maintained their cultural identity" (p. 59). Fehoko (2014) adds that *kava* consumption venues act as sites of cultural continuance in which values, language, traditions, and beliefs are "reinforced... thus reaffirming their Tongan identity" (p. 91; also see Matthias 2014). In Samoa, *kava* is considered "an important cultural symbol and a traditional sign of hospitality" (Minahan 2012, p. 279). Tengan (2008) tells an alternate story, an account of the impact of missionization, colonization, and cultural loss in Hawaii. This has now being addressed through a reengagement with *kava* as part of reestablishing traditional knowledge and enhancing identity. Anthropologist Dr. Nancy Pollock (1995) summarizes the importance of *kava* to ethno-cultural identity across Oceania: "In Tonga, Samoa, Futuna, Fiji and Pohnpei kava usage persists as an 'external symbol' of both current and past ideologies" (p. 2). Pollock's reference to Fiji provides the focal point for this chapter, the cultural keystone role that *yaqona* (*kava*) plays in Fijian ethnicity and identity both in Fiji and the Fijian diasporic communities.

Yaqona (Kava) and National Ethno-cultural Identity in Fiji

Yaqona (more commonly known as *kava*), when coupled with its associated rituals and practices, is commonly recognized as a potent symbol of Fijian ethno-cultural identity (Aporosa 2008). Fijians colloquially refer to *kava* as *grog* (Geraghty 1996), although when spoken of in more formal discussion, both *yaqona* and particularly *wainivanua* (or "water of the *vanua*") are used. To explain this connection, and particularly the linguistic significance of the word *wainivanua* in more detail, Ravuvu (1983) states:

> Vanua literally means land, but also refers to the social and cultural aspects of the physical environment identified with a social group. On the social plane it includes people and how they are socially structured and relate to one another. On the cultural plane it embodies the values, beliefs and the common ways of doing things. (p. 76)

Therefore, when combining understandings of *vanua* with the word *wainivanua*, this "infers an ingestible representation of the land, people and culture ... which is deeply rooted in their sense of identity and customary practices" (Aporosa 2014, p. 68). Once prepared, *yaqona* (the descriptor that will predominantly be used in this chapter when referring to *kava* in Fiji) becomes a sacred and living entity that both embodies *mana* and has the ability to enhance a person's *mana* (Turner 1986; Tomlinson 2004).

In most villages across Fiji, when the working day ends, men, and occasionally women, sit cross-legged at the *tanoa* (*yaqona* bowl) to discuss the day and plans for the next, along with the latest news or gossip (Aporosa 2008). *Yaqona*'s expression of Fijian-ness, and as an embedded symbol of ethno-cultural identity, has led to icons such as the *tanoa* and the preparation and/or serving of *yaqona* frequently being drawn on as a symbol of Fiji (Fig. 2). For instance, the *tanoa* is depicted on the Fijian one-cent piece

Fig. 2 Postcard: Fijian serving yaqona. (Unknown producer)

(Fig. 3) and also comprises the logo and trophy for the annual *Ratu Sukuna Bowl* and interservices (police vs. army) rugby competition (Fig. 4) (Dean and Ritova 1988).

According to Ratuva (2007, pp. 92–99) and Vakabua (2007, p. 103), the drinking of *yaqona* demonstrates, externalizes, and personifies "Fijian-ness" and the Fijian way. Such notions are demonstrated through the union of the *tanoa* with *Ratu Sir Lalabalavu Sukuna* (1888–1958), a Fijian chief, decorated soldier (French Foreign Legion), statesman, and Oxford University scholar who many argue personifies the "ideal Fijian" (Scarr 1980; Lal 1985). By uniting one of Fiji's most revered leaders with the *tanoa* – and vicariously *wainivanua* carried in the *tanoa* – to represent the logo and trophy for the annual *Ratu Sukuna Bowl* interservices rugby competition (see Fig. 4), this provides a potent metaphoric symbol of "Fijian-ness" and authority, reinforced through inferred power associated with Fiji's military and police who compete for the *Ratu Sukuna Bowl*. More overt references can be seen within Tourism Fiji advertising and on postcards and prepaid telecards (see Figs. 5, 6, and 7).

Fig. 3 Fijian one-cent piece. (Source: Government of Fiji 2006)

Fig. 4 Polo shirt logo: Ratu Sukuna Bowl. (Source: Republic of Fiji Military Forces 2009)

Fig. 5 Postcard: iTaukei serving yaqona. (Source: Siers, J., c1979, author of Fiji in color)

Fig. 6 Postcard: tanoa (yaqona bowl) and images of sale, export, and research. (Source: University of the South Pacific, undated)

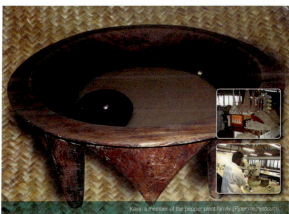

Yaqona (Kava) and Other Symbols of Collectivism

Symbols and icons are an important part of defining collectivist identities (Linnekin 1990). Hamrin-Dahl (2013) goes further, suggesting that collectivism through Pacific Islanders' use of traditional objects, icons, and practices in the postcolonial

Fig. 7 Telecard: Fijian mixing yaqona. (Source: Fiji Posts and Telecommunications Limited 1994)

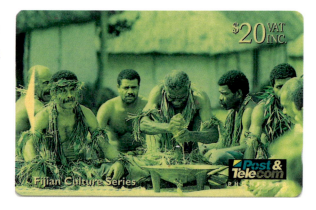

Fig. 8 Official seal of Western Samoa

period affirms a construct of identity in contrast with the European "other." She states that in contemporary Hawaii and Samoa, the *kava* bowl has now been adopted as a "national symbol" of postcolonial identity and sovereignty (ibid., 2013, p. 32). In addition to a *kava* bowl, the official Seal of American Samoa (Fig. 8) includes a *fue* (fly switch), another object of traditional significance to a number of Oceanic Pacific ethnicities. Other Pacific icons include the *taro* plant, coconut palm, *frangipani* flower, and *kava*.

Fijian-ness, Yaqona, and Government

The Fijian Government also acknowledges the importance of *yaqona* to ethno-cultural identity, supported by the *Institute of iTaukei Language and Culture (IiTL&C)* who are tasked with "preserving iTaukei [indigenous Fijian] identity" (Ministry of Information, 2010, p. 1). In an article discussing the work of the *Institute*, a large photograph of two Fijian's dressed in traditional costume mixing *yaqona* is included, clearly linking the practice with the stated objective of preserving cultural identity. Drawing on a number of scholars, former *IiTL&C* researcher Sekove Degei (2007) remarked: "To the Fijians, yaqona is a link to the past, a tradition so inextricably woven into the fabric of culture, that life and social processes would be unimaginable without it. Although the use of kava is common among other people groups in the South Pacific, for the Fijian, yaqona is clearly linked to concepts of identity" (p. 3).

What Do Fijians Say About Yaqona

In 2014, Fijian school teachers were interviewed about their *yaqona* use and questioned as to whether restrictions on nightly *yaqona* use were necessary to limit *kava* hangover aimed at improving teaching ability (Aporosa 2014). A school principal objected strongly to the idea of *yaqona* prohibition stating: "No one can stop us from drinking *yaqona*. People might try to stop us but they can't because it is part of our culture" (p. 153). A teacher agreed, arguing that *"Yaqona* is the cornerstone of our culture" (p. 151). Yet another teacher responded, "People can encourage us to stop [drinking *yaqona*], but this is about our culture, *itovo* [custom, manner], the *vanua*" (p. 159), inferring *yaqona*'s significance to cultural practice and as an ingestible representation of the land, people and culture.

Yaqona and Ethno-cultural Identity in Diaspora

As Fijians and other Oceanic *kava* using peoples have migrated, they have taken their *yaqona/kava* drinking practices with them. That use of *yaqona/kava* in diaspora acts as a "visible means of affirming and demonstrating their Pasifika-ness," playing a key role in maintaining connectedness to one and the other in both their new and old "homelands" and to assert their ethno-cultural identity (Aporosa 2015, p. 62). Some of that diasporic *kava* use has also influenced the opening of contemporary *kava* outlets modeled on café's and alcohol-styled bars to cater for non-Pacific *kava* users (Wolinski 2018). However, of greater interest is a growing cohort of non-Pacific *kava* users who are joining Pacific diasporic *kava* using groups and embracing aspects of Oceanic ethno-cultural *kava* identity and practice. This has been termed *diasporic identity formation in reverse* and is interpreted by Pacific peoples as affirming the significance of their "cultural keystone specie" and icon of identity which further entrenches ethno-cultural *kava*-related identity (Aporosa 2015).

Critics of "Yaqona as a Symbol of Cultural Identity"

Overwhelmingly the literature and ethnographic evidence presented points to *yaqona/kava* as a significant ethno-cultural identifier in Pacific Oceania and particularly Fiji. Although there is a sector within Fiji who criticizes the overuse of *yaqona*, asserting that this negatively impacts on productivity (Baba 1996; Kava 2002; Singh 2007; Rawalai 2014; for counterargument, see Kumar and Aporosa 2018), this has not lead to a rejection of this cultural keystone species and its related practices in any significant manner. However, more recently Fiji has seen a small but increasing number argue that *yaqona* is not part of their identity or ethno-cultural expression. Most of these critics tend to belong to evangelical Christian denominations such as the *All Nations*, *New Methodist*, and *Assemblies of God* Churches (Aporosa 2014, pp. 154–157). Countering this message are the older denominations such as the *Wesleyan* and *Catholic* Churches who mostly continue to support *yaqona* use and practice. Ryle (2010) points out: "Pacific theologians have even related the kava ceremony to the Christian Eucharist,... [paralleling this with] themes of self-sacrifice, leadership and service" (p. 20). The Samoan Catholic Church, for instance, identifies "Jesus Christ as a Heavenly Kava Root at Bethlehem" (Taofinu'u 1973, p. 2).

Samoan Wesleyan Methodists believe that *kava* has a redemptive significance in the same manner as the Blood of Christ (Fa'asi'i 1993, p. 62). In the case of Fiji, Toren (1988, p. 709) also sees a likeness between images of Christ's *Last Supper* with the *yaqona* circle. She advances that Leonardo da Vinci's tapestry of *The Last Supper* "evokes the image of a group of clan chiefs [drinking *yaqona*] with the paramount chief [Jesus] at their centre." The tapestry image and symbolism, Toren argues, is "a material manifestation of 'the Fijian way'" (p. 696), thereby epitomizing "Fijian-ness" (see also Ryle 2010, pp. 23–5).

What then has influenced Fijians from the newer Pentecostal Christian denominations to deny the link between *yaqona* and their identity? This appears to have its roots in the pre-colonial use of *yaqona* as a conduit for communication between traditional priests and their ancestral gods (Turner 1986; Lebot et al. 1997; Linnekin 1997). *New Methodist* Church co-founder Reverend Atu Vulaono has declared that *yaqona* "is a hold-over from pre-Christian religion and not from God" (Titus 2009; also see Vulaono 2001). He has stipulated that *yaqona* is the "drink of Satan," used to disrupt Fijian lifeways (Fiji Times 2008a, p. 2, b, p. 2). The idea that *kava* is the "drink of Satan" has become one of Vulaono's signature messages (FBC 2017) and has been adopted by other Pentecostal Churches aimed at eliminating the consumption of *yaqona* in Fiji (Aporosa 2014).

While some view the criticism of *yaqona* by Pentecostal Christians as an opportunity for lighthearted joking, what has been more revealing are comments that Vulaono has rejected his culture. In the minds of many, Vulaono has forfeited his identity and cultural standing, not because he has ceased *yaqona* consumption but because he believes *yaqona* is the drink of and instrument of Satan (Aporosa 2014, p. 153). This connection to the devil is considered a threat to what *yaqona* symbolizes, an ingestible manifestation of the *vanua* and an icon that demonstrates Fijian-ness and therefore Fijian identity.

The Biblical reference often cited by Pentecostal preachers to support their anti-*yaqona* message is "Therefore, if anyone is in Christ, he is a new creation; the old has gone, the new has come!" (NIV 2011: 2 Corinthians 5:17). With many of the practices associated with *yaqona* having their foundations in the precontact pre-

Christian era, neo-Christian denominations frequently categorize *yaqona* as belonging to "the old." Additionally *the old* can also include selected *meke* (traditional dance) and the use of *tabua* (whale's teeth) and *yaqona* as part of marriage negotiation (Ravuvu 1983, p. 46). In contrast, "the new" is deemed to be an abandonment of "the old" traditional ways, with members of these new Pentecostal denominations encouraged to embrace alternative forms of cultural expression such as the giving of boxes of soap instead of *tabua* and the consumption of orange juice as a replacement for *yaqona*, in marriage negotiations.

Fundamental Questions as to the Role of Yaqona

For many, *yaqona*'s link to *mana* and the *vanua* prevents it from being substituted with other offerings, items some argue represent "plastic protocols." This is particularly the case in solemn ceremonies such as the ethno-culturally based restorative justice process of *matanigasau* (Ratuva 2002; Cretton 2005). In these apology ceremonies, parties meet, present, and mix *yaqona* and discuss the issues that led to conflict or relational breakdown and seek resolution. As *yaqona* is seen as an ingestible manifestation of the *vanua*, the apology ceremonies, with its sharing of *yaqona*, symbolically demonstrates the reuniting of the *vanua*, a process that many argue would lack efficacy with orange juice – or the Pentecostal substitute that has no connection to the *vanua*. This not only has the potential for the loss of traditional knowledge and cultural identity but also has the likelihood to disrupt sociocultural harmony.

Twenty-five years ago, the UNESCO reported that "the loss of culture," or cultural identity, is at "the heart of our... social problems" (Teasdale and Teasdale 1992a, p. 1). This they argued was not limited to indigenous cultures but also the "dominant societies of the west, who have moved so far along the road of capitalism, with its emphasis on competition, the consumption of goods and services, and the exploitation of the world's non-renewable resources, that they too are losing their deepest roots" which in turn has seriously impacted sociocultural stability. The UNESCO report concluded that "Culturally appropriate teaching and learning is integral" to sociocultural stability, a process and goal that is reliant upon depth of ethno-cultural identity (Teasdale and Teasdale 1992b, p. 70). Thaman (1992) concurs, arguing that a lack of understanding of one's personal culture is a factor in the breakdown of sociocultural values (see also Rao and Walton 2004).

Regardless that a strong divide exists between Fijians who argue that *yaqona* does and does not comprise or reflect their identity, Dalton et al. (2001) initiate valuable commentary which brings clarity to this implied impasse. They draw on Community Psychology's Ecological Levels (also known as systems theory) and state that "Individuals, societies, and the layers of relationships between them are interdependent" (p. 13). Newman and Newman (2011) add:

> Systems theories take the position that the whole is more than the sum of its parts... Any system – whether it is a cell, an organ, an individual, a family, or a corporation – is composed of interdependent elements that share some common goals, interrelated functions,

boundaries, and an identity. The system cannot be wholly understood by identifying each of its component parts. The process and relationships of those parts make for a larger, coherent entity. The language system for example, is more than the capacity to make vocal utterances, use grammar, and acquire vocabulary. It is the coordination of these elements in a useful way in a context of shared meaning. Similarly, a family system is more than the sum of the characteristics and components of the individual members. (p. 50)

As Newman and Newman (2011) note, system theory includes identity. Therefore the identity of the majority "cannot be ... [altered or subverted, by the personal opinions of] its component parts." It is the majority that dictate the "context of shared meaning" or, in the case of this chapter, ethno-cultural identity. As such, assertions that "*yaqona* is not part of some Fijians' identity," whether imagined or hoped for, do not alter *yaqona*'s fundamental link with ethno-cultural identity for the majority of Fijians, a union also found throughout other Oceanic Pacific *kava* using societies in both original and diasporic locations.

Conclusion

This chapter has examined *yaqona/kava* as an ingestible representation, manifestation, and embedded symbol of ethno-cultural identity in Oceania and in particular Fiji. This chapter has demonstrated that *yaqona/kava* not only plays a critical role in Fijian ethno-cultural identity but has also been adopted by selected non-Pacific peoples to enhance their own notions of self. However, this in turn has raised questions as to why some believe this iconic symbol and ritual drink does not comprise their identity in the same way. Reasons argued against *yaqona* include impacts to productivity and anti-*yaqona* rhetoric stemming from inside Fiji from the newer neo-Christian fundamentalist Churches with their foundations outside of the country. This tension however is not considered sufficient to limit *yaqona/kava* in Fiji or Oceania in general, owing to the depth of observance and practice. In summing up, while some may dispute and wish to undermine the significance of *yaqona/kava* as the dominant symbol of ethno-cultural identity – such as asserting that "yaqona is not part of my identity" – this simply reflects a minority opinion.

Cross-References

- ▶ Ethno-cultural Symbolism and Group Identity
- ▶ Faamatai: A Globalized Pacific Identity
- ▶ Museums and Identity: Celebrating Diversity in an Ethnically Diverse World

References

Aporosa S (2008) Yaqona and education in Fiji: a clash of cultures? VDM Verlag, Germany
Aporosa S (2011) Is kava alcohol?: the myths and the facts. J Commun Health Clin Med Pac 17(1):157–164

Aporosa S (2014) Yaqona (kava) and education in Fiji: investigating 'cultural complexities' from a post-development perspective. Massey University, Directorate Pasifika@Massey, Albany

Aporosa S (2015) The new kava user: diasporic identity formation in reverse. N Z Sociol 30(4):58–77

Aporosa S (2017) Understanding cognitive functions related to driving following kava (*Piper methysticum*) use at traditional consumption volumes. J Psychopharmacol 31(8):A84

Aporosa S, Tomlinson M (2014) Kava hangover and gold-standard science. Anthropologica (J Can Anthropol Soc) 56(1):163–175

Baba P (1996) Yaqona: it is getting the nation doped? Weekend: Fiji Times Mag. 6 April, 2

Balick M, Lee R (2009) The sacred root: Sakau en Pohnpei. In: Balick M (ed) Ethnobotany of Pohnpei: plants, people, and island culture. University of Hawai'i Press in association with The New York Botanical Garden, Honolulu, pp 165–203

Crawford AL (1981) Aida: life and ceremony of the Gogodala. National Cultural Council & Robert Brown & Associates, Bathurst

Cretton V (2005) Traditional Fijian apology as a political strategy. Oceania 75(4):403–417

Dalton J, Elias MJ, Wandersman A (2001) Community psychology: linking individuals and communities. Wadsworth, Belmont

Dean E, Ritova S (1988) Rabuka: no other way. Doubleday, Sydney

Degei S (2007) The challenge to Fijian Methodism: the vanua, identity, ethnicity and change, (unpublished Master's thesis), Anthropology Program, The University of Waikato

Fa'asi'i U (1993) Gospel and culture in the ava ceremony. J Theol sIIn10:61–63

FBC: Fiji Broadcasting Commission (2017) Cucurui (S01E01): Yaqona – Pastor Atunaisa Vulaono. April 2. Retrieved from https://www.youtube.com/watch?v=WY8XE4W7doo

Fehoko E (2014) Pukepuka fonua: an exploratory study on the faikava as an identity marker for New Zealand-born Tongan males in Auckland, New Zealand. (unpublished Master's thesis), Auckland University of Technology

Fiji Times (2008a) Kava is evil, says minister, Fiji Times 24 August, 2

Fiji Times (2008b) New Methodist warns on kava, Fiji Times 22 August, 2

Finau S, Stanhope J, Prior I (2002) Kava, alcohol and tobacco consumption among Tongans with urbanization. Pac Health Dialog 2:59–68

Garibaldi A, Turner N (2004) Cultural keystone species: implications for ecological conservation and restoration. Ecol Soc 9(3):1–19

Geraghty P (1996) "When I was a lad...": thoughts on our national drink. Fiji Post: 16. April 28

Hamrin-Dahl T (2013) The kava bowl wonders: can the fetish be named? Etnografiska, Germany

Huffman K (2012) Kava: a Pacific Elixir. MUSE (J Sydney Univ Mus) 1:24–25

Kava R (2002) The adverse effects of kava. Pac Health Dialog 2:293–296

Kirch PV, Green RC (2001) Hawaiki: ancestral Polynesia. Cambridge University Press, Cambridge, UK

Kumar A, Aporosa S (2018) Anti-kava campaign: give up for a month and feel the difference. Radio Tarana (via Stuff.co.nz), Sept. 14. Retrieved from https://www.stuff.co.nz/tarana/107029166/antikava-campaign-give-up-for-a-month-and-feel-the-difference

Lal B (1985) Review of Fiji: the three-legged stool. Selected writings of Ratu Sir Lala Sukuna. Aust Hist Stud 21(84):433–466

Lebot V, Cabalion P (1988) Kavas of Vanuatu: cultivars of *Piper methysticum* frost (vol. technical paper no.195). South Pacific Commission, Noumea

Lebot V, Merlin M, Lindstrom L (1992) Kava: the Pacific drug. Psychoactive Plants of the World Series. Yale University Press, New Haven

Lebot V, Merlin M, Lindstrom L (1997) Kava, the Pacific elixir: The definitive guide to its ethnobotany, history and chemistry. Vermont, Healing Arts Press

Lim TK (2016) Edible medicinal and non-medicinal plants: volume 11, modified stems, roots, bulbs. Springer, New York

Lindstrom L (2004) History, folklore, traditional and current uses of kava. In: Singh YN (ed) Kava: from ethnology to pharmacology (medicinal and aromatic plants – industrial profiles volume 37). CRC Press, Boca Raton, pp 10–28

Linnekin J (1990) The politics of culture in the Pacific. In: Linnekin J, Poyer L (eds) Cultural identity and ethnicity in the Pacific. University of Hawaii Press, Honolulu, pp 149–174

Linnekin J (1997) The ideological world remade. In: Denoon D, Meleisea M, Firth R, Linnekin J, Nero K (eds) The Cambridge history of the Pacific islanders. Cambridge University Press, Cambridge, UK, pp 397–438

Matthias J (2014) AUT study: kava keeps young Tongans out of trouble, The New Zealand Herald. Online at: http://www.nzherald.co.nz/education/news/article.cfm?c_id=35&objectid=113671 62

Minahan JB (2012) Ethnic groups of South Asia and the Pacific: an encyclopedia. ABC-CLIO, California

Ministry of Information, National Archives and Library Services (2010) Going back to our roots: IILC to preserve iTaukei identity. New Dawn: Gov Fiji 2(5):1

Newman B, Newman P (2011) Development through life: a psychosocial approach (11th ed). Wadsworth/Cengage Learning, California

NIV – New International Version (2011) The Bible: 2 Corinthians. Online at: http://www.biblica.com/en-us/bible/online-bible/?translation=niv&book=2+corinthians&chapter=5

Payson R (2008) The culture of kava: a visual journey of rituals and ceremonies among rural Fijians. (unpublished Master's of Social Science thesis). Brooks Institute of Photography

Pollock N (1995) Introduction: the power of kava. In: Pollock N (ed) The power of kava, vol 18. Australian National University, Canberra, pp 1–19

Rao V, Walton M (2004) Culture and public action: relationality, equality of agency, and development. In: Rao V, Walton M (eds) Culture and public action. Stanford Social Sciences, Stanford, pp 3–36

Ratuva S (2002) Re-inventing the cultural wheel: re-conceptualizing restorative justice and peace building in ethnically divided Fiji. In: Dinnen S, Jowett A, Newton T (eds) A kind of mending: restorative justice in the Pacific Islands. Pandanus, Canberra, pp 149–163

Ratuva S (2007) Na kilaka a vaka-Viti ni veikabula: indigenous knowledge and the Fijian cosmos: implications for bio-prospecting. In: Mead A, Ratuva S (eds) Pacific genes and life patents: pacific indigenous experiences and analysis of the commodification and ownership of life. Call of the Earth Llamado de la Tierra and the United Nations University of Advanced Studies, Wellington, pp 90–101

Ravuvu A (1983) Vaka i Taukei: the Fijian way of life. University of the South Pacific, Suva

Rawalai L (2014) 'Kavaholics' told to drink in moderation. Fiji Times. Online at: http://www.fijitimes.com/story.aspx?id=278962. Accessed 1 Sept 2014

Ryle J (2010) My god, my land: interwoven paths of Christianity and tradition in Fiji. Ashgate, Surrey

Scarr D (1980) Ratu Sukuna: soldier, statesman, man of two worlds. Macmillan Education, London

Singh M (2007) The good and bad of kava, Fiji Sunday Times, 2 September, 7

Taofinu'u P (1973) O le 'ava o se peloferaga: the kava ceremony as a prophecy. Roman Catholic Church, Apia

Teasdale J, Teasdale B (1992a) Introduction. In: Teasdale K, Teasdale B (eds) Voices in a seashell: education, culture and identity. Institute of Pacific Studies, University of the South Pacific and United Nations Educational, Scientific and Cultural Organisation, Suva, pp 1–5

Teasdale J, Teasdale B (1992b) Culture and the context of schooling. In: Teasdale K, Teasdale B (eds) Voices in a seashell: education, culture and identity. Institute of Pacific Studies, University of the South Pacific and United Nations Educational, Scientific and Cultural Organisation, Suva, pp 54–70

Tengan TPK (2008) Native men remade: gender and nation in contemporary Hawai'i. Duke University Press, North Carolina

Thaman K (1992) Cultural learning and development through cultural literacy. In: Teasdale K, Teasdale B (eds) Voices in a seashell: education, culture and identity. Institute of Pacific Studies, University of the South Pacific and United Nations Educational, Scientific and Cultural Organisation, Suva, pp 24–36

Titus P (2009) Fijian Methodist Church challenges military government, Touchstone: monthly newspaper of The Methodist Church of New Zealand. August, 1,8

Tomlinson M (2004) Perpetual lament: kava-drinking, Christianity and sensations of historical decline in Fiji. J R Anthropol Inst 10:653–673

Toren C (1988) Making the present, revealing the past: the mutability and continuity of tradition as process. Man 23(4):696–717

Turner J (1986) The water of life: kava ritual and the logic of sacrifice. Ethnology 25(3):203–214

Vakabua J (2007) A Fijian's perspective on the uses and ownership of intellectual property. In: Mead A, Ratuva S (eds) Pacific genes and life patents: pacific indigenous experiences and analysis of the commodification and ownership of life. Call of the Earth Llamado de la Tierra and the United Nations University of Advanced Studies, Wellington, pp 102–109

Vulaono A (2001) Revelation on kava/snake, Online at http://www.visionprovider.net/prophecies/yaqona-prophecy.html. Accessed 20 Aug 2010

Wolinski C (2018) This ancient South Pacific sipper is officially trending. VinePair (online), March 21. Retrieved from https://vinepair.com/articles/what-kava-kava-drink/

Young M (1995) Kava and Christianity in Central Vanuatu (with an appendix on the ethnography of kava drinking in Nikaura, Epi). In: Pollock N (ed) The power of kava, vol 18. Australian National University, Canberra, pp 61–96

Zagefka H (2016) Ethnicity, concepts of. In: Smith AD, Hou X, Stone J, Dennis R, Rizova P (eds) The Wiley Blackwell encyclopaedia of race, ethnicity, and nationalism. Wiley, West Sussex, pp 761–763

Museums and Identity: Celebrating Diversity in an Ethnically Diverse World

99

Tarisi Vunidilo

Contents

Introduction	1940
Understanding Museums	1941
Modern Museums	1944
Ethnicity and Museums	1945
Museums and Ethnic Memories	1947
Museums and Social Connections	1947
Museum and Cultural Appreciation	1948
Museum and Cultural Wealth	1948
Museum and Cultural Tourism	1949
Museum Technology and Education	1949
Museum and Celebration of Identity	1949
Concluding Remarks	1952
References	1954

Abstract

Issues of national identity are the subject of much discussion and debate, particularly in the fields of social and cultural studies. Museums lie at the center of these debates – their collections, and the presentation and interpretation of these collections, being inextricably linked to national identity. This chapter reviews these current debates within the social and cultural spheres, and locates museums within them. Its purpose is to develop a deeper understanding of the ways in which museums negotiate and construct meanings of national identity.

Over the past few decades, relationships between museums and ethnic societies, including indigenous people have changed dramatically for the better. Communities have demanded a bigger voice in how their cultural heritage, in both tangible and intangible forms, is curated and represented in museums. These

T. Vunidilo (✉)
Department of Anthropology, University of Hawaii-Hilo, Hilo, HI, USA
e-mail: tarisiv@hawaii.edu

© The Author(s), under exclusive license to Springer Nature Singapore Pte Ltd. 2019
S. Ratuva (ed.), *The Palgrave Handbook of Ethnicity*,
https://doi.org/10.1007/978-981-13-2898-5_135

changes have led to increased collaborations between museums and source communities. Such collaborative work, among other things, has revealed diversity in the way people experience and understand their cultural heritage. Changing relationships have also given rise to new museum ethics that recognizes this diversity and reflects greater respect for people's cultural and human rights.

Museums as educational and cultural institutions started as places of learning for learned people. This changed over time as the role of museums increasingly focused on community groups showcasing *ethnic identity* of people. With history as the main focus of such institutions, museums were seen as *institutions that celebrated ethnic identity* of its visitors and stakeholders.

Keywords
Museums · Ethnic identity · Tangible heritage · Intangible heritage · Source communities

Abbreviations
ICOM	International Council of Museums
MAA	Museum of Archaeology and Anthropology
MOA	Museum of Anthropology
NMAI	National Museum of the American Indian
PCAP	Pacific Collections Access Project
PIMA	Pacific Islands Museums Association

Introduction

Museums are important institutions in any society. They are repositories for knowledge and objects of value in many nations. Some view museums as a place for finding solace, healing, cultural reflection, and inspiration. Others compare museums to schools and view them as educational institutions where one can learn about their past, culture, and tradition. Some view museums as keepers of the past, since museums manage artifacts that previously were used by a group of people, many of whom have passed on. They believe that their elders have left behind a legacy for the new generation to carry on the culture and tradition of a people. Even though museums may be compared with other institutions, such as schools, it has been argued that museums can provide services to the community that other institutions cannot (Karp 1992, p. 5).

In recent times, culturally specific museums have been developed because the point of view reflected by traditional museums was perceived as excluding the experiences of certain cultural and ethnic groups. Mainstream museums were also perceived as places where objects associated with the histories of these groups were not being collected, and where the broad or specific stories of these groups were not being told though exhibits. Some key questions that remain to be asked are: Are these specialty museums no longer necessary today, as some have contended? Are they just jostling for political influence or expressing outdated identity politics?

Such questions do not reflect how much influence these museums have had on the museum world in recent decades.

All museums around the world today strive to be relevant to their communities, to be places of community, and to be organizations where scholarship and inspiration take place. Culturally specific museums set the example in how to achieve these goals. In fact, they have shown how programs that serve the community can be placed at the center of the museum model – so much so that many museums today, including natural history museums, have developed successful public programs that highlight a particular cultural group in the community.

In bad economic times, most museums are vulnerable. Culturally specific museums can weather this challenge if they remain relevant to their communities and reflect broader themes of universal human experience, provided they have prudent leadership. As long as these institutions think carefully about their mission, they will continue to play a vital part in expressing the ultimate museum experience. In a society that values diverse viewpoints, they can make an especially important contribution.

Some case studies that I will be discussing will feature situations in Africa, Canada, France, Singapore, England, and the United States where museums have become significant mediums for ethnic identity in a diverse world. It is imperative that we learn from these examples that showcase the diversity of their collections and connect with the diverse ethnic communities that they serve. Ethnic identity is all the more important today as it provides a safe space for migrants, refugees, and tourists, who are looking for a place of belonging.

Understanding Museums

According to the Oxford English Dictionary (2015), "a museum is a building where objects of historical, scientific, artistic or cultural interest are stored and exhibited" (Oxford Dictionary Online 2015). The International Council of Museums (ICOM) defines the museum as "a non-profit, permanent institution in the service of society and its development, open to the public, which acquired, conserves, researches, communicates and exhibits the *tangible and intangible heritage* of humanity and its environment for the purposes of education, study and enjoyment" (ICOM website 2015). Tangible heritage are physical manifestations of culture that a person can touch and feel. Intangible, on the other hand, are invisible to the naked eye, however can be heard, sung, spoken, and felt through emotions. Museums are places where objects are meant to invoke associations to trigger memories and to generate questions (Healey 1994, p. 34). Some view museums as keepers of the past.

Musaeum was traditionally defined as the place where muses dwell (Findlen 2000, p. 164). Whitlin (1949, p. 1) believed the word "museum" to have originated in ancient Greece. The Museum of Alexandria is believed to be the world's first museum (Genoway and Andrei 2008, p. 13). It was built in the third century BCE by Ptolemy Soter (Butler 2007, p. 17). Prior to the building of this museum, temples were built and dedicated to the nine goddesses and used by *muses* or learned men and women that studied the ancient Greek philosophies. Later museums have become known as the houses of knowledge (Findlen 2000, p. 164). Greek author Timon of Phlius wrote about the muses:

> [I]n the populous land of Egypt, they breed a race of bookish scribblers who spend their whole lives pecking away in the cages of the Muses (Findlen 2000, p. 164).

The main features of museums in ancient times involved worship of gods and goddesses and the temple was viewed as the place of worship and a knowledge bank. As museums became known as houses of knowledge, the reputation of learned men and women soared and the muses, as they were known then, were on an equal level to philosophers. Access to these places was only for the elite. As time passed, the collections varied and included collections of astronomical and surgical instruments, and hides of rare animals which led to the development of the zoology field of study. Alcohol was manufactured and used to preserve animals. Some collectors began developing records and lists, which were exchanged among collectors. As travel became popular among the nobles, they also wanted to develop their own collections that reflected their interests and knowledge of the world. Overall, most of these muses and collectors were interested in the formation of the human race and classes of humankind. The classification of people had begun, in particular, in the categorizing of those who are powerful over those who are not. There was also a quest for knowledge and the studies of the animal kingdom, of minerals, and of astronomy added value to their search for knowledge. The result of such quests was the formation of museums in many parts of the ancient world.

The museum was also connected to the Great Library of Alexandria. This museum began the process of collecting astronomical and surgical instruments, as well as elephant tusks and hides of rare animals (Whitlin 1949, p. 1). According to Genoway and Andrei (2008), collections that began in the museum in Alexandria were scientific collections. As time went by, other types of artifacts were collected and added to the existing ones. Elements of sacred temples and of an educational institution seem to have been combined in the Greek schools of Philosophy. These museums became the source of inspiration for the development of museums in the beginning of the Renaissance (Lee 1997).

Strabo, the Greek geographer and historian of *Amaseia*, mentioned that the museum was part of the royal palace. There was also a large house where learned men (mostly philosophers) would gather with their leader, a priest, who was also in charge of the museum. Such priests were appointed by the King and later, priests' appointments were made by Caesar (Genoway and Andrei 2008, p. 15). Philosophers utilized museum spaces as their place of intellectual research and debate. As a result, the study of philosophy was regarded as a service to the Muses (Whitlin 1949, p. 1). The significance placed on Alexandria as the birthplace of museums has made the British Museum and the Louvre, among others, feel that they all share the same ancestry, and therefore they are referred to as the latter day Alexandrian mouseion (Butler 2007, p. 18).

Ernst (2000, p. 18) mentioned that the *musaeum* was an epistemological structure that encompassed a variety of ideas, images, and institutions. He further added that the museum was a text, occupying a position in the field somewhere between *bibliotheca*, *thesaurus*, *studio*, *galleria*, and *theatrum*. The muses focused a lot of their time and energy on developing new philosophies that related to life in the ancient world. In contrast, the role of postmodern museums is to teach museum users how to cope with information in museums. Museums became known as the inventory of the world (ibid).

There are many types of museums. Art museums offer a visual experience to their viewers, while museums of cultural and natural history produce exhibitions with more narrative content. In terms of museum classification in the United States, there are six types of museums and they are: museums of art, historical museums, anthropological museums, natural history museums, technological museums, and commercial museums (Conn 2010, p. 8). Museums are not free from political implications, as communities will always attempt to have a say on how the museum is run and what exhibitions they show (Karp 1992, p. 2).

Museums help people understand the world by using objects and ideas to interpret the past and present and to explore the future (Museum Australia Constitution 2002). According to Parman (2006), museums are themselves a part of history; they are living institutions that must continually cope with the present and imagine how to prepare for the future. Museums become the link between the past and the present. Key museum activities are collecting, preserving, studying, interpreting, and exhibiting (Karp 1992, p. 3).

From an indigenous perspective, museums are western institutions. The word "museum" has classical origins. In its Greek form, *mouseion*, it meant "seat of the muses" and designated a philosophical institution or a place of contemplation (Lewis 2012). Museums in the third century were only for the elite, where one could only visit the museum based on their status and educational background. Through time, museums began to open their doors to other members of society. The word "museum" was revived in fifteenth-century Europe to describe the collection of Lorenzo de' Medici in Florence, but the term conveyed the concept of comprehensiveness rather than denoting a building. This was in the 1700s where, for instance, in Europe, learned societies were establishing themselves in regional towns rather than in major cities where the elite were based. Museums were moving away from having private collections to developing exhibitions for the public to view. The first public museum was at the University of Oxford, which opened its doors to the public to visit and view its collection (ibid).

In the 1950s, left wing writers on museums took a critical approach and supported the idea that museums could be perceived as instruments of the elite that are used to assert class-based claims to interpret and control high culture (Karp 1992, p. 9). Through time and with new forms of museum studies and new ways of collecting, a move toward the new museum was developed. There has been international research and debate around the roles of museums, collections, and repatriation that is critical to this research (Nafziger and Nicgoski 2009; Rukundwa and van Aarde 2007).

The role and status of museums are often taken for granted; however, at the same time, museums were seen to be dominant features of our cultural landscape as they frame our most basic assumptions about the past and about ourselves (Marstine 2008, p. 1). In comparison with other heritage-led institutions such as libraries and archives, museums are versatile (Bouqet 2012, p. 3). They are versatile because museums are able to be adaptable to political and cultural changes in society and declare themselves as active players in the construction of meaning. Art historians such as McClellan (1999) support this by saying that museums have great flexibility and have been metamorphosing continually since their founding (Marstine 2008, p. 22). The new museum theory identifies four archetypes of museums: shrine, market-driven industry, colonizing space, and post-museum (Marstine 2008, p. x).

Museums were also viewed as a place where artifacts were rescued in times of distress. For example, in the case of the British Museum, it has in its possession artifacts taken from its former colonies under the guise of being rescued during turbulent political turmoil. For instance, the Elgin Marbles that originally belonged to Greece have now become part of the British heritage. Britain inherited democracy from ancient Athens, and universalization of the democratic ideals was then used as basis for colonization and domination of colonized people (Marstine 2008, p. 2).

Education was a fundamental factor influencing the way museums were built and what audiences could partake in the delivery of exhibitions. Elitism was another factor, where only individuals of high rank were privileged to view exhibitions and take part in the research and what took place behind the scenes. Between 1825 and 1925, there was a rapid increase in the number of museums in the United States (Genoways and Andrei 2008, p. 9). Marstine (2008, p. 3) said that museums have grown exponentially in number, size, and variety, and more people go to museums than ever before.

Modern Museums

Today, museums vary in their origin, discipline, scale, governance, structure, collections, sources of funding, endowment, staffing, facilities, and community setting (Weil 2002, p. 5). There are many types of museums. Some are privately owned, while others are publicly funded. There are also science museums, while others are based on art, ethnology, and history (Genoways and Andrei 2008, p. 10). The origin of museums goes back to the ancient times, where artifacts were kept for educational and religious purposes.

Museums in modern times are increasing in numbers and they vary in size, types, and narratives (Macdonald 1996, p. 1). In the twenty-first century, the term "museum" and its meaning has been debated. One such debate is questioning whether the focus of museums is collections or people. Modern museums are more inclined to satisfy the need of visitors, all the more so if they have to pay to enter and to ensure that programs and activities in the museum satisfy the needs of these museum visitors. Another debate is whether funding is paramount in order to provide a service, compared to the past where the learning from the objects was the priority. Museums, then, should be accessible places for encounters for everyone (Butler 2015). The narrow meaning is of a particular building or institution, but now museums are looked upon as a "potent social metaphor and as a means whereby societies represent their relationship to their own history and to that of other cultures" (ibid). Museums today are more than just buildings; however, Dana (in Genoways and Andrei 2008, p. 137) is critical of new museums which are so focused on their sheer size and architecture that they remain isolated from their communities.

Museums today are frequently seen on the news and also in the ever-expanding literature on museology. As mentioned earlier – that the number of museums has increased in an unprecedented rate – museums are also diversifying in form and content. Some museums are tackling controversial subjects, for example, the Holocaust Memorial Museum in Washington DC; the Museum of Famine, Ireland, and exhibitions on colonialism, warfare, gender, and on sexuality (Macdonald 1996, p. 1). They have also opened themselves up to diverse communities and exhibiting collections that would not have been thought of before, for instance, the Canadian *Fluffs and Feathers* exhibition (ibid).

Overall, the past is always the concern of museums (Lumley 1988). In the 1900s, technological advancement has greatly influenced museum experiences and programs that are offered to museum visitors. More emphasis is given to sound, electronic buttons, and experiential exhibitions that enable visitors to be physically engaged in activities. Macdonald (1996, p. 2) noted that museums are using new media and new techniques of creativity. Some museum critics compare these museums to theme parks, deviating from how traditional museums should be. In New Zealand, one example is the newly built five-storey Museum of New Zealand Te Papa Tongarewa, located in Wellington. It has a lot of interactive machines for its visitors and its galleries are in no way close to its predecessor, the Museum of New Zealand (previously located on Buckle Street), which had a much more traditional feel (ibid).

Museums today are also used to celebrate political events that celebrate certain cultures. For instance, the Holocaust Museum in Germany is a museum dedicated to the effects of the two World Wars that devastated the Jewish population under the leadership of Adolf Hitler. History, in this case, is used as a political resource whereby national identities are constructed and forms of power and privilege are justified and celebrated (Lumley, p. 1988). In the United Kingdom, the development of heritage museums has increased over the years. Even though the British Museum was founded in 1753 and is one of the oldest and greatest public-funded museums, it is one of the museums that have contributed to the development of new museums around the United Kingdom. Many smaller museums pay tribute to the British Museum for setting standards and leading the way in the field of museology. Over the years, museum developments are proceeding at different rates, bringing with them the demand for professionalism and training (Wilson 2002, p. 2).

Ethnicity and Museums

Ethnic identity can best be understood through an examination of its linguist origins. The term ethnic has Latin and Greek origins – *ethnicus* and *ethnikas* both meaning nation. It has been used historically to refer to people as heathens. Ethos, in Greek, means custom, disposition, or trait (Trimble and Dickson 2005). Ethnicas and ethos taken together therefore can mean a band of people (nation) living together who share and acknowledge common customs (Isajiw 1974). The second part of identity has Latin origins and is derived from the word identitas; the word is formed from the word *idem*, meaning same. This means that the term is used to express the notion of sameness, likeness, and oneness. More precisely, identity means "the sameness of a person or thing at all times in all circumstances; the condition or fact that a person or thing is itself and not something else" (Simpson and Weiner 1989, p. 620). Combining the definitions and interpretations of identity and ethnicity, it can be concluded that they mean, or at minimum imply, the sameness of a band or nation of people who share common customs, traditions, historical experiences, and, in some cases, geographical residence. At one level of the interpretation, the combined definition is sufficient to capture the manner in which the identity is generally conceptualized and used to understand enthno-cultural influences. At another level, identity is almost the same as ethnicity, prompting sociologists like Herbert Gans (2003) to suggest that identity is no longer a useful term. Additionally, due to the increasing popularity, identity has become a cliché and therefore more and more difficult to understand (Gleason 1996).

Definitions of ethnic identity vary according to the underlying theory embraced by researchers' and scholars' intent on resolving its conceptual meanings. The fact that there is no widely agreed upon definition of ethnic identity is indicative of the confusion surrounding the topic. Typically, ethnic identity is an affiliative construct, where an individual is viewed by themselves and by others as belonging to a particular ethnic or cultural group (Bentley 1987). An individual can choose to associate with a group especially if other choices are available (i.e., the person is of mixed ethnic or racial heritage). Affiliation can be influenced by racial, natal, symbolic, and cultural factors (Cheung 1993). Racial factors involve the use of physiognomic and physical characteristics; natal factors refer to "homeland" (ancestral home) or origins of individuals, their parents, and kin; and symbolic factors include those factors that typify or exemplify an ethnic group (e.g., holidays, foods, clothing, artifacts, etc.). Symbolic ethnic identity usually implies that individuals construct their identity; however, to some extent, the cultural elements of the ethnic or racial group have a modest influence on their behavior (Nafziger 1993).

One identifies with a particular ethnic group and continues to have a sense of belonging which involves one's perceptions, way of thinking, feelings, and behavior. Individuals then are labeled through classifying and naming of people. Once this notion of "self-concept" is solidified through socialization, one tends to look at material things to identify their origin and for people around them. Our relationships with people and things was part of life therefore societies create "material culture" that are tangible evidence of one's connection to their land and communities.

The relationship between ethnicity and museums is relatively complex and can be outlined in six ways. (1) Firstly, they build and invokes memories and strengthen love for the motherland of its citizens; (2) secondly, it enriches and renews the sense of national union and unity; (3) thirdly, they make people appreciate and enhance their cultural appreciation from a culture that has been inherited from their ancestors; (4) fourthly, museums introduces culture, natural wealth, and others to its people;

(5) fifthly, museums become key players in the tourism industry of a nation; and (6) lastly, museums help contribute actively to government's technological and annual development plans. I will discuss these six areas below:

Museums and Ethnic Memories

It is best to reflect on human memories, and how we, as individuals or as a social group, tribe, or society, attempt to keep our memory and history alive for the sake of our future generations. This is something that can be done in the confines of our homes (through our family heirlooms, photo albums, etc.) or done publicly, through physical spaces and proper buildings that one must enter to view displays that evoke memories and allow the viewer to learn about their history (Crane 2000, p. 1). Memory is not a passive process as it evokes emotions and desires, either positive or negative, and is also driven by a desire to remember or forget. One way of solidifying memories is through creation of forms of representation, in objects that we touch and see (ibid). Museums then have become storehouses, a repository of memory, and the location of the collections that form the basis of cultural or national identity (Crane 2000, p. 4). Ernst (2000, p. 17) supports this position, that "all museums are storehouses or containers of cultural heritage. They all participate in a universal adherence to preservation of memories." Museums have become places where memories are forged in physical form to prevent the natural erosion of memory, both personal and collective (Crane 2000, p. 9).

Museums and Social Connections

Some museums have developed an arrangement called "shared ownership" between artifacts and source communities. For example, at the Waikato Museum of Art and History in New Zealand, they developed a unique museum program known as "Cultural Days." A brain-child of the then Museum Director, Ms. Kate Vusoniwailala, such days were meant to showcase museum objects and cultures of ethnic communities that live in Hamilton City and represented in the Waikato District. Museum curators and education officers worked collaboratively with selected community members to deliver enriching exhibition openings and cultural programs that made ethnic community members "feel at home." In 2008, the museum won a national award with recognition by the Human Rights Commission New Zealand Diversity Action Program Award.

The museum was recognized based on how they promote cultural diversity including the award-winning exhibition "Rare View," which focused on Hamilton's Somali community; Keeping Faith, a major community exhibition on different religions in the Waikato; Qui Tutto Bene, which featured Italian New Zealanders; and Te Atairangikaahu, the Soaring Hawk of the Dawn, which showcased official photographs of the Maori Queen's tangi (funeral) as well as a standing exhibition on Tainui.

Museum and Cultural Appreciation

Museums have a long history that responds to the human natures of collecting and keeping memories alive. Before the modern era, some individuals spent their time and resources collecting artifacts of interest. Through time, some interested individuals have worked in groups to achieve their goal of collecting. Museums have now become institutions that preserve and interpret artifacts that are important to a group of people or for the human race. Museums started collecting in ancient and medieval times and continue to do so today. In medieval times, storehouses, royal treasure troves, and curiosity cabinets began the process of museum development (Simpson 1997). The Enlightenment and Romantic thinkers added historical values to economic, scientific, and aesthetic values of objects, and this prompted the construction of museums for the preservation of the past. In modern times, historical museums and heritage museums have expanded tremendously and scholars are now focused on the way the past has been interpreted for the present and for national audiences (Crane 2000, p. 4). Museums, then, have become more than cultural institutions and showplaces of objects. They have become sites of interaction between personal and collective identities and between memories and history (Crane 2000, p. 12). Hagen (born in 1876), who was a Professor of Entomology at the Museum of Comparative Zoology at Harvard University (1867–1893), noted that temples were used in the past to house artifacts that were collected from travels around the world. For example, Alexander the Great gave the horns of the Scythic bulls, which were exceedingly rare, to the temple of Delphi. Similarly, the horn of the steer from Macedonia was presented by King Philip to the temple of Hercules (Genoways and Andrei 2008, p. 40). Over time, these temples became repositories of such artifacts; however, the methods of how items were kept and their associated maintenance have been a subject of interest. Many artifacts, most of them from the natural sciences, were lost and destroyed. Preservation, as a result, through time became apparently important, and scientists began to develop ways of ensuring that they last long and can be enjoyed over many years (ibid).

Museum and Cultural Wealth

Museums though (to some researchers) have plundered to create their collections from a Eurocentric perspective. Marstine (2006, p. 14) highlighted that many claims to have had a benevolent motivation, which was to salvage objects that could not be protected by the source communities. The focus of such collecting was more for the wealth and status of the collector, the museum, and the state. It is thus important to identify the key motivating factor for collecting in the first place. In the case of New Zealand, the Auckland Museum has shifted this thinking from the collector to the source community. It has embarked on a 3-year project called the Pacific Collections Access project (PCAP). The museum has shifted its focus to the community as the source of "cultural wealth" that will enhance its current collection and relevant information. For the last 2 years, the museum has successfully collaborated with "Indigenous knowledge holders" from the Cook Islands, French Polynesia, Fiji, Hawaii, and Kiribati.

Museum and Cultural Tourism

Recent research has classified museums within the same groupings of theme parks and entertainment centers. Such museums have moved away from their traditional form to a more inclusive, modern way of enticing their visitors who are viewed as customers as they are required to pay for many services within the museum. Some museums employ full-time grant-writers to request funding from philanthropists and businesses to continue to meet the economic demands of their museum. With high turnover of exhibitions and museum programs, associated costs have pushed museums to make money, some through paid exhibitions, cafeterias, museum shops, and other paid events. Museums within this category are managed like a business and funders expect profits to be made at the end of every year. Cultural and ethnic artifacts become commodities to generate profit. Marstine (2006, p. 11) highlights how museums today have become part of a market-driven industry. Most museums need funding to operate and the work of museum directors, trustees, development officers, and even curators involves financial decision-making. As a result, many museums have become more open to economic realities and have adopted business models to generate adequate revenues (Marstine 2006, p. 12).

Museum Technology and Education

Another debate regarding collections is whether museums need a collection to make it a museum. It is indeed true that collections make a museum; however, with new technologies being used in museums today, some are challenging the notion that museums still need museum objects to qualify as a museum. Conn (2010) challenged the known museum reality that collections created museums. In this book, Conn demonstrated that museums are no longer seen as houses of objects but seen as places of knowledge, a place of reflection between culture and politics. Objects, according to Conn, have begun to lose their centrality within the museum. Education officers are hired within the museum to create experiences within the museum. Films and moving images have taken over the focus on objects (ibid).

Museum and Celebration of Identity

Museums were originally sites of mass-control, wherein the dominant group collects, organizes, and displays the culture of the minority. However, today they became the venues for the minority groups' identity formation and function as contact zones for both groups. Museums and arts are presenting identity to unite rather than divide. Curators and practitioners of the arts share a renewed focus on how culture and heritage shape who we are. In the United States, for example, a vibrant mix of the arts, natural history, and history museums contribute to the increasing numbers of ethnic museums around the country. In the last 40 years, there has been an increase in culture-specific museums such as the Museum of the American Indian in Washington DC, Arab American National Museum in Michigan, Japanese American National Museum in Los Angeles, and the Contemporary Jewish Museum in San Francisco.

In the case of Fiji, the Fiji Museum provides a common space for exhibiting diverse cultural artifacts representing indigenous Fijians (iTaukei), Indo-Fijians, European, Chinese, and Pacific Islanders. Given the history of Fiji's ethnic strife, the Fiji Museum through its exhibitions and programs has provided a common space for interethnic representation. For the last 2 years, the Fiji Museum has seen an increase in the number of visitors, most of whom were local. The bimonthly Fiji Museum open day, is an opportunity to showcase cultural symbolisms and celebrate cultural diversity. The themes in the past included the culture and experiences of the Girmitiyas (Indians that came to Fiji since 1879 to work on sugarcane plantations), as well as iTaukei culture and other cultures.

Another museum dedicated to cultural diversity is the Asian Civilizations Museum, the only museum in Singapore dedicated to exhibiting artifacts and collections representing different regions of Asia including China, Southeast Asia, South Asia, and West Asia/Islamic. The museum, located on the bank of the Singapore River, is where you can learn about Asia's history and cultures. With Singapore's multicultural history, this museum in particular showcases the migrations and conquests of leaders and kings thousands of years ago. The museum is also relevant to present generation where its rotating contemporary exhibitions meet the needs of its visitors. The Museum organizes monthly events targeting families to visit the museum and participate in its programs that showcases Asian culture through music, dance, drama, and artistic expressions. Highlight events include the Asian Culture and Music Series that focuses on the celebration of Indonesian culture under the Children's Season for this year. Children of Indonesian descent, now living in Singapore, can get the chance of reconnecting with their history and culture through public performances such as outdoor events hosted by the Asian Civilization Museum.

The Apartheid Museum in South Africa opened in 2001 and is acknowledged as the preeminent museum in the world dealing with twentieth-century South Africa, at the heart of which is the apartheid story. The museum is the first of its kind, illustrates the rise and fall of apartheid. An architectural consortium, comprising several leading architectural firms, conceptualized the design of the building on a seven-hectare stand. The museum is a superb example of design, space, and landscape, offering the international community a unique South African experience (Apartheid Museum 2018). The exhibits have been assembled and organized by a multi-disciplinary team of curators, filmmakers, historians, and designers. They include provocative film footage, photographs, text panels, and artifacts, illustrating the events and human stories that are part of the epic apartheid saga. A series of 22 individual exhibition areas take the visitor through a dramatic emotional journey that tells a story of a state-sanctioned system based on racial discrimination and the struggle of the majority to overthrow this tyranny. The museum is a beacon of hope showing the world how South Africa is coming to terms with its oppressive past and working toward a future that all South Africans can call their own. It is also a place of healing for many families.

In the United States, the Skirball is the oldest Jewish museum in the country, established in Cincinnati in 1913 and then transferred to Los Angeles in 1972. One of the key features of such museums is that they are created by immigrant or minority groups to trace their history, demonstrate their sufferings, and celebrate their triumphs, ending with an assertive embrace of their identities. This has been the traditional narrative shaping recent museums devoted to such groups as American Indians, Japanese-Americans, and African-Americans. The Smithsonian Museum followed the same path when it built 11 museums and galleries on the National Mall and 6 other museums. It has the African American Museum, African Art Museum, American Art Museum, and the American Indian Museum.

The National Museum of the American Indian (NMAI) looks after one of the world's most expansive collections of native objects, photographs, and media, covering the entire Western Hemisphere from the Arctic Circle to Tierra del Fuego. The museum's sweeping curvilinear architecture, its indigenous landscaping, and its exhibitions, all designed in collaboration with tribes and communities, combine to give visitors from around the world the sense and spirit of Native America. Architecture in this case becomes a prominent language of showcasing the ethnic identity of the indigenous American Indians. Education is the best tool to inform individuals or groups of people on the history of your host nation. One way the NMAI have done this is through the usual museum exhibitions and community programs. Another way they have done so is through digital media and online teaching. The content of the lessons is from the indigenous community members' perspectives and aims at informing students and teachers alike on an important and difficult part of US history.

Vancouver's Museum of Anthropology (MOA) was founded in 1949 in the basement of the Main Library at the University of British Columbia. Today, Canada's largest teaching museum is located in a spectacular building overlooking mountains and sea – its collections, exhibitions, and programs are renowned for giving access and insight into the cultures of indigenous peoples around the world. The Pacific collection component was collected between 1895 and 1923. Frank Burnett, a Canadian writer and traveler of Scottish descent, was the founding collector, and his deep interest in the Pacific brought over 200 Fijian artifacts to MOA. He not only collected artifacts from the Pacific, but also from indigenous communities within Canada, including two most important Musqueam house posts, which were acquired and donated by the UBC class of 1927 (Shelton 2007). Indigenous house posts at the MOA reconnect indigenous visitors and tourists alike, to celebrate their heritage through public art such as carvings.

From the Pacific to Asia, from Africa to the Americas, the permanent collection area presents 3.500 works geographically without partitions. The juxtaposition of these works encourages original dialog between the cultures of four continents. The museum holds ten or temporary exhibits per year, which are characterized by the diversity of approaches and fields of exploration. Designed by French or foreign figures from various backgrounds, the exhibits present works from the museum's collections, as well as prestigious loans from international institutions and private collections. Three hundred thousand works from Africa, Asia, Oceania, and the Americas make up the collection which the museum aims to conserve, document, and enrich. The collection housed by the muse du quai Branly-Jacques Chirac is extremely diverse, both in terms of its regions (Africa, Asia Oceania, and Americas) and its contents (photographs, textiles, sculptures, masks, etc.). The collection is the result of a history which extends from the Neolithic age via the kings of France to the explorers and great ethnologists of the twentieth century.

Apart from source communities visiting the Quai Branly Museum, the museum also invites performing artists, who are represented by the vast collections to be part of its program, showcasing their talents but also sharing their culture in a live setting. This is an Australian Aboriginal group from Australia "Crossing Roper Bar" performing in the museum space on November 10, 2012.

The Museum of Archaeology and Anthropology (MAA) is one of the nine museums at the University of Cambridge. The University's collections are a world-class resource for researchers, students, and members of the public. Cambridge has the country's highest concentration of internationally important collections outside of London (MAA website 2018). The MAA at the University of Cambridge holds world-class collections of art and artifacts from many parts of Oceania, Africa, Asia, and the Americas. These ethnographic objects include masks, canoes, and sculptures, some collected during the voyages of Captain Cook to the Pacific, others assembled by Cambridge fieldworkers from the late nineteenth century onwards. The museum also displays archaeological discoveries, ranging from the very earliest hominid tools excavated by Louis Leakey from Olduvai Gorge in eastern Africa, through to early South American textiles, to Roman and Anglo-Saxon finds from various parts of Britain (Elliott and Thomas 2011). The founding collection at the MAA was from Fiji.

Concluding Remarks

There are so many benefits of the roles museums in supporting positive ethnic identity of individuals in communities. This chapter has enabled us to define museums from ancient times to today. Changes are inevitable, and definitely, roles of museums have changed over time and types of museums have increased as well. Museums have to remain relevant to its stakeholders and visitors. One common denominator that remained unchanged is the role of collections and artifacts. These are definitely the physical manifestations of the cultures that they represent. These are the cultural markers and ethnic identifiers of people from around the world. Such objects have become embodiments of unity and empowerment for those that needs emotional strengthening and ethnic affirmations.

From this chapter, we can identify six key areas that highlights the role of museums and their role in ethnic identity: (1) firstly, they build and strengthen love for the motherland of its citizens; (2) secondly, it enriches and renews the sense of national union and unity; (3) thirdly, they make people appreciate and enhance their cultural appreciation from a culture that has been inherited from their ancestors; (4) fourthly, museums introduces culture, natural wealth, and others to its people; (5) fifthly, museums become key players in the tourism industry of a nation; and (6) lastly, museums help contribute actively to any the government's annual development plans.

Museums indeed have the ability to celebrate diversity. Museum collections and exhibitions bridge connections to a universal community. Museums that focus on identity need to include not only diversity and individuality, but universal connections. The challenge for museums is not to see one way or the other, but both at the same time. While nineteenth- and early twentieth-century public museums have been implicated in many nation–state's inculcating agenda, debate exists as to whether contemporary museum persists in such a role. Using the case studies from Canada, England, France, Singapore, South Africa, and the United States, this chapter argues that museums continue to be instrumental in the evolution of national identities. While much has been written on the roles of museums in curatorial content and program delivery, others have been largely writing on museum's architectural or design elements. The MOA Museum in Canada and the National Museum of American Indian possess architectural designs that signify indigenous knowledge and architecture. This chapter draws on a historical framework to examine the Museum's approach to the representation of Australian history. In doing so, it highlights the role of the nation–state and cultural institutions in the construction of national identities, which is particularly relevant in the wake of studies demonstrating visitors' trust in museums as objective institutions.

In order to explore the extent to which museums can go beyond expressing and influencing people's individual and communal identities, this chapter has demonstrated that ethnic identities can be celebrated in heritage locations such as museums. Many museums in metropolitan areas comprise of international quality collections of art, history, and natural history. Many cities also suffer from some of the worst levels of health, poverty, and educational attainment; however, within the context of these contrasts and of the interaction of diverse local, class, and religious identities, the museum service has tried to achieve its various objectives which is to make "high culture" widely accessible, providing a recreational and educational facility for local people, expressing civic pride, and promoting cultural tourism. This chapter has proven both the impact of these factors on selected case-study museums and their attempts to influence the identities of their visitors and to contribute to the creation of a more just society.

References

Apartheid Museum (2018) History and background. Downloaded from https://www.apartheidmuseum.org/about-museum-0
Bentley GC (1987) Ethnicity and practice. J Comp Stud Soc Hist 29(1):24–55
Bouqet M (2012) Museums: a visual anthropology. Berg, New York
Butler T (2007) Memoryscape: How audio walks can deepen our sense of place by integrating art, oral history and cultural geography. Geography Compass 1(3):360–372
Butler T (2015) The future museum project: what will museums be like in the future? Downloaded from http://www.museum-id.com/idea-detail.asp?id=283
Cheung YW (1993) Approaches to ethnicity: Clearing roadblocks in the study of ethnicity and substance use. International Journal of the Addictions 28(12):1209–1226
Conn S (2010) Do museums still need objects? University of Pennsylvania Press, Philadelphia
Crane S (2000) Museums and memory. Stanford University Press, Stanford
Elliott M, Thomas N (2011) Gifts and discoveries: The Museum of Archaeology and Anthropology. London: Scala
Ernst W (2000) Archi(ve) textures of museology. In: Crane S (ed) Museums and memory. Stanford University Press, Stanford, pp 17–34
Findlen P (2000) The modern muses: renaissance collecting and the cult of remembrance. In: Crane S (ed) Museums and memory. Stanford University Press, Stanford
Gans H (2003) Democracy and The News; Oxford: Oxford University Press
Genoways H, Andrei M (2008) Museum studies: an anthology. In: Elliott M, Thomas N (eds) Gifts and discoveries: the Museum of Archaeology & Anthropology, Cambridge (2011). Cambridge University Museum of Archaeology and Anthropology, London
Gleason P (1996) Identifying identity: a semantic history. In: Sollars W (ed) Theories of ethnicity: a classical reader. New York University Press, New York, pp 460–487
Healy C (1994) Histories and collecting: museums, objects and memories. In: Darian-Smith K, Hamilton P (eds) Memory and history in twentieth-century Australia. Oxford University Press, Melbourne, pp 33–51
ICOM (2015) Museum. Retrieved from http://icom.museum/the-vision/museum-definition
Isajiw W (1974) Definition of ethnicity. Ethnicity 1 & 2:111–124
Karp I (1992) Museums and communities: the politics of public culture, Woodrow Wilson International Center for Scholars. Smithsonian Institution Press, Washington, DC
Lee PY (1997) The Musaeum of Alexandria and the Formation of the Muséum in Eighteenth-century France. The Art Bulletin 79(3):385–412
Lewis R (2012) Hamlet, metaphor, and memory. Studies in Philology 109(5):609–641
Lumley R (Ed) (1988) The museum time-machine: Putting culture on display. London: Routledge
MAA website (2018) History and background of the Museum of Anthropology and Archaeology, Cambridge
Macdonald S (Ed.) (1998) The politics of display: Museums, science, culture. Psychology Press
Macdonald S, Fyfe G (Eds.) (1996) Theorizing Museums. Sociological Review Monographs. Oxford: Blackwell
Marstine J (2006) New museum theory and practice: an introduction. Blackwell, Malden
Marstine J (Ed.) (2008) New museum theory and practice: an introduction. John Wiley & Sons
McClellan A (1999) Inventing the Louvre: Art, politics, and the origins of the modern museum in eighteenth-century Paris. Univ of California Press
Museum Australia Constitution (2002) Museums Australia Incorporated-Constitution Rules, Registered NO: A 2359
Nafziger JAR, Nicgorski AM (eds) (2009) Cultural heritage issues: the legacy of conquest, colonization, and commerce [electronic resource]. Martinus Nijhoff Publishers, Leiden
Nafziger JA, Paterson RK, Renteln AD (2010) Cultural law: international, comparative, and indigenous. Cambridge University Press
Oxford Dictionary Online (2015)

Parman A (2006) The Museum's Community Role. Culture Work 10(1):305–408

Rukundwa LS, van Aarde AG (2007) The formation of postcolonial theory. HTS Teologiese Stud/Theol Stud 63(3):1171–1194

Shelton A (2007) Questioning locality: the UBC Museum of Anthropology and its hinterlands. Etnográfica. Revista do Centro em Rede de Investigação em Antropologia 11(2):387–406

Simpson MG (ed) (1997) Museums and repatriation: an account of contested items in museum collections in the UK, with comparative material from other. Museums Association, London

Simpson JA, Weiner ES (1989) The Oxford English dictionary, vol VII, 2nd edn. Clarendon Press, Oxford

Trimble JE (2000) Social psychological perspectives on changing self-identification among American Indians and Alaska Natives. In: Dana RH (ed) Handbook of cross-cultural and multicultural personality assessment. Lawrence Erlbaum Associates, Mahwah, pp 197–222

Trimble JE, Dickson R (2005) Ethnic identity. In: Fisher CB, M R (eds) Encyclopedia of applied developmental science, vol I. Sage, Thousand Oaks, pp 415–420

Weil S (2002) Making museums matter. Washington: Smithsonian Institution Press

Whitlin AS (1949) The museum: its history and its task in education. Routledge and Kegan Paul, London. https://www.smithsonianmag.com/smithsonian-institution/how-museums-arts-are-presenting-identity-so-it-unites-not-divides-180951560/#r8zfSK4IiYqoBJp0.99

Wilson DM (2002) The British Museum: A History. British Museum Press

Artistic Expressions and Ethno-cultural Identity: A Case Study of Acehnese Body Percussion in Indonesia

100

Murtala Murtala, Alfira O'Sullivan, and Paul H. Mason

Contents

Introduction	1958
Branding Culture	1959
Participating in the Dance	1962
Three Acehnese Dances	1963
Ratéb Meusekat	1964
Likok Pulo	1967
Saman	1969
Transformation and Change	1973
Conclusion	1975
Cross-References	1975
References	1975

Abstract

As the processes of globalization bring diverse ethnic groups from within and across national borders into contact, translocal communities of practice increasingly sustain previously localized visual and performance arts. How do connections between artistic expression and ethno-cultural identity become constructed and contested in this context? In this chapter, we consider Acehnese body percussion as a case study to examine artistic expression and ethno-cultural identity. The centrifugal forces of globalization have brought Acehnese body percussion into contact with new student populations and put this genre on display for naïve audiences in foreign performance spaces. Acehnese artist-

---

M. Murtala · A. O'Sullivan
Suara Indonesia Dance Troupe, Sydney, NSW, Australia

P. H. Mason (✉)
School of Social Sciences, Monash University, Clayton, VIC, Australia

Department of Anthropology, Macquarie University, North Ryde, NSW, Australia
e-mail: paul.mason@monash.edu

© The Author(s), under exclusive license to Springer Nature Singapore Pte Ltd. 2019
S. Ratuva (ed.), *The Palgrave Handbook of Ethnicity*,
https://doi.org/10.1007/978-981-13-2898-5_136

teachers have mobilized their art to capitalize upon these shifts but simultaneously found themselves needing to develop effective responses to resist cultural appropriation and assert their authority over this unique genre of body percussion. While it can be argued that no performance genre is truly fixed, stable, and bounded, the desire to maintain a coherent association to ethno-cultural identity impacts on the aesthetic features of an art as well as the politicized discourses surrounding integrity, authenticity, and creativity. Acehnese body percussion is a particularly compelling case example to consider given Aceh's 30-year conflict with the central Indonesian government as well as the political turn of events following the tragic tsunami on December 26, 2004. The maintenance of some semblance of purity in a performance genre is important to those who trade in the export of their culturally orchestrated skills, but even more important to a people whose sense of collective identity has been bolstered by external threats.

Keywords

Aceh · Body percussion · Globalization · Ethno-cultural identity · Artistic expression · Creativity · Performance art

Introduction

The opening ceremony to the 2018 Asian Games in Indonesia featured 1600 Jakartan high school students performing seated body percussion in striking unison. Highly coordinated patterns of movement rippled across 18 rows of dancers for over 4 min. Dynamic costume changes added to the visual splendor. Samples of traditional tunes backed by electronic music energized both dancers and crowd.

Choreographed by Indonesian singer and dancer, Denny Malik, the performance wowed audience members. The unity displayed in this performance genre has often been put on stage at national and international events to demonstrate the diverse cultures of Indonesia in harmony with one another. These artistic expressions of Indonesian identity, however, disguise the unsavory historical circumstances and political agendas impacting upon subnational, ethno-cultural identity across the archipelago. Denny Malik, for example, is not Acehnese. Moreover, the foundational work of Acehnese choreographers in teaching seated body-percussion to school students in Jakarta went unmentioned in media reporting about the opening ceremony.

The movement sequences of this crowd-pleasing dance performance had first been taught to Jakartan high school students by Acehnese choreographers who had descended upon their nation's capital to escape civil conflict and seek better employment. They taught a collection of coastal Acehnese dances known by diverse names, but which came to be branded as "Saman" in Jakarta. While Saman became the umbrella term for all Acehnese dance, it is actually the name of a men's dance from the Gayo people in the mountainous area of the Aceh highlands. Originally used to spread Islam in Aceh, the sitting body-percussion dances have become popular as secular performance and entertainment all over Indonesia, especially Jakarta, and overseas. Stripped of their histories and significance, symbols can become depoliticized markers of a hybrid identity (Lo 2000: 168). Long-standing historical tensions between Aceh and the central Indonesian government, however, have not left national representations of Acehnese body percussion uncontested. Ethno-cultural identity is strongly asserted by Acehnese artists who teach and perform unique and impressive genres of body percussion.

In this chapter, we examine the seated body-percussion dances of Aceh and how artistic expressions of ethno-cultural identity come to be constructed, experienced, mobilized, transmitted, appropriated, contested, misconstrued, and politicized. Saman, put forward by the Indonesian Government for listing on UNESCO's World Heritage List, was eventually inscribed in 2011 on the List of Intangible Cultural Heritage in Need of Urgent Safeguarding. This political act raised the profile of Acehnese dance nationally and internationally, but also misrepresented the diversity of coastal and highland Acehnese dance and heritage. Furthermore, subsuming Acehnese dance into a larger nationalistic project brushed aside historical political tensions between the Acehnese people and the Indonesian government. The history of the dances, their names, philosophy, and meaning have all been disrupted as a consequence of increasing the number of stakeholders involved in these shifting discourses.

Branding Culture

In the words of Jonathan Haynes, "Names conceal as well as reveal" (2007: 106). For example, the title of "Bollywood" covers up the production of Indian films in languages other than Hindi such as Tamil, Bengali, and Punjabi (ibid.). Similarly, the name "Nollywood" covers up the diversity of film productions in Nigeria (ibid.). With regard to Saman, Indonesian authority figures have sought to promote the ideology of "unity in diversity" and have grouped together the multitude of sitting dances from around Aceh under one title. "Saman" has become a metonym for multiple different sitting dances found throughout Aceh that have come to be recognized abroad as Indonesian.

Acehnese dance first started to appear in Jakarta in the 1960s when President Sukarno was still in power. During this time, nationalist symbols were established by taking local culture from various provinces to represent a "National culture" for the nation in order to forge a collective Indonesian identity (Hughes-Freeland 2008: 55–56). The Indonesian government in Jakarta requested the Acehnese government provide dance troupes to perform Acehnese dances at official events and for visiting overseas officials who stayed at the Presidential Istana (palace). Other dance troupes from different provinces were also asked to perform. At this point in time, Acehnese dances in Jakarta were not taught yet in schools and very rarely performed by non-Acehnese people.

When Suharto's regime began in 1966, dance troupes from Aceh –troupes who had previously visited Jakarta to perform Acehnese dances at official State events– commenced performances at nonofficial events where they were more accessible to the Indonesian public. In 1974, the Acehnese government brought the Saman Gayo arts team to Jakarta for the opening of Taman Mini Indah Park Indonesia. Tari Saman was simultaneously broadcast on TVRI, the Indonesian national TV station. The Tari Saman group from the Gayo highlands were subsequently asked to come back to Jakarta to perform at various official events. The 1974 performance, broadcast nationally, prompted the Indonesian public outside Aceh to consider all Acehnese sitting dances under the label of "Saman."

During 1970–1975, after the official opening of Taman Mini Indonesia Indah, Acehnese dance was still only practiced within the sphere of the Acehnese community. These communities then started to teach *sanggar* (dance troupes) around Jakarta. According to Marzuki, one of the first teachers of Acehnese dance in Jakarta, training and practice of Acehnese dances was initiated during this time by the Taman Iskandar Muda Acehnese community group as well as pockets of the Acehnese community in Jakarta. By the 1980s, there were a number of Acehnese dance groups around, and Taman Mini also started their own *sanggar*. Non-Acehnese people also started to participate in training in both sitting and standing Acehnese body percussion dances.

Indonesia's national motto was "Unity in Diversity" as proclaimed at the time of independence. As part of a nation and character building policy, arts education and activities were implemented into national pedagogical programs. In Jakarta during the 1990s, the Ford Foundation supported an Arts Appreciation Program, which introduced dances into schools in order to teach traditional forms of dance from different regions of Indonesia. Acehnese sitting dances were the most popular and easiest to learn. Schools started to have dance competitions instead of basketball or football teams. Having a winning Acehnese dance group became the pride of a school and community. Regional artistic representations that conformed to the nation building project were co-opted for the aims of the policy and offered a positive feedback for certain local arts. The nation building policy to promote *puncak daerah* (local peaks of cultural excellence) favored some performance genres over others. Versions of Acehnese sitting dance were taught at high schools, undergraduate courses at Indonesian Arts Institutes, and extracurricular programs in various sanggar. Through this association, Saman became recognized by a national pedagogy and integrated into national events. The integration of *Saman* into the opening ceremony of the 2018 Asian games is an example of, to borrow the words of Hughes-Freeland, how "dance becomes both implicated in, and is also constitutive of, the embodied and imagined community of the nation state" (2008: 17).

Civil conflict was occurring in Aceh at the same time that Acehnese dances were becoming popular in Jakarta. Indeed, the spread of Acehnese dance around the country was catalyzed by civil war and conflict. In the history of Aceh, its people, and cultures have always been a distinctive group, not only were they linguistically and socially different, the Acehnese considered themselves an independent polity (Reid 2004: 303). Aceh's efforts against the Dutch saw them active in the Indonesian struggle for independence. However, the relationship between Aceh and the central government has always been complex and broken promises by the central government caused two rebellions to ignite against them. The first time was in 1953; the Darul Islam rebellion which was lead by Daud Bereueh declared Aceh as part of the

Negeri Islam Indonesia (Sulaiman 2006: 130) and for Aceh to become autonomous within a Federal Islamic Indonesian State (Reid 2004: 302).

The second rebellion had most effect on the spread of Acehnese sitting dances outside Aceh. Hasan di Tiro proclaimed Aceh's independence from Indonesia on the December 4, 1976 (Sulaiman 2006: 135). The exploitation of Aceh's natural resources, their separate identity as a people, as well as the second rebellion being an extension of the continuity of Daud Beureuh's rebellion in the 1950s, were factors that are believed to have contributed to the second rebellion and conflict in Aceh (Reid 2006: 13). Edward Aspinall argues that a separate Acehnese identity, detached from Indonesia, was assisted by the long-standing abuses by the Indonesian military during the Darul Islam rebellion (2006: 149–176). Di Tiro in his speeches also claimed that the subversion of Aceh's history is to blame for the lack of Aceh's own national identity (Sulaiman 2006: 135). The conflict between the Acehnese Freedom movement (*Gerakan Aceh Merdeka*) otherwise known as GAM and the Indonesian government's military forces began in 1976 and lasted almost 30 years. In the early stages, many leaders of the separatist movement were killed, imprisoned, or exiled (Robinson 1998: 127–157), including Hasan di Tiro who fled to Sweden and led GAM in exile.

During the DOM (Daerah Operasi Militar) or Military Operations Zone in Aceh (1990–1998) (Aspinall 2009: 88), Jakarta not only sent dance troupes to Aceh but also performed Acehnese arts within Indonesia as well as abroad. Some Acehnese artists feel that this was one of the cultural maneuvers of Indonesia to outdo and outsmart Aceh on a cultural level, by claiming Acehnese dances as "Indonesian" which endorsed the situation of control over the province.

During the conflict in Aceh, the military imposed curfews (Kartomi 2006: 88), so that many activities and events held at night, such as performances and parties, came to an end. This included the practice and performance of traditional Acehnese art forms (traditional dances were practiced at night, starting from *Isya* night time prayers until *Fajr* or *Subuh* dawn prayers). The only groups that were able to continue performing were subsidized *sanggar* in government-sanctioned performances. Conflict came to an end on the August 15, 2005, after the devastating tsunami of 2004, and a Memorandum of Understanding was signed in Helsinki Finland between the Republic of Indonesia and GAM. Aceh was given the name Nanggroe Aceh Darussalam, with special autonomy status, and the freedom to choose and run its own government (Reid 2006: 317). Both GAM and the central government realized that a ceasefire was necessary for Aceh, in particular Banda Aceh, if the region was to recover.

During conflict in Aceh, it was difficult for dancers or trainers to get work, or perform, and hence many artists moved to the capital city and other cities in Indonesia to continue their art, especially Jakarta. Artists, such as Yusri Saleh and Mohammed Taufik, made decisions concerning their artistic careers and chose to move to Jakarta to develop their talents and art in the capital city where they were able to express their "Aceh-ness" by performing and practicing sitting dances through teaching at schools and various *sanggar*.

The move from rural Aceh to urban Jakarta led Acehnese teachers to make aesthetic changes to the dances in order to adapt them to local context. The most prominent change was that Acehnese body percussion went from being a private practice (such as Acehnese sitting dances in the mosques and private spaces of Aceh) into an organized cultural expression on stage (such as Acehnese sitting dances performed at festivals in Jakarta). This shift away from private spaces opened Acehnese body percussion out to public audiences. When a cultural practice shifts from private to public viewing, it "moves from mere self-representation to 'representation for someone'" (Lewis 1992: 3). As a consequence, visual aesthetics became a valued feature of Acehnese body percussion performances in Indonesia. Sitting dances in Jakarta became restructured to create a more visually intricate and aesthetically attractive performance genre, yet simplified in terms of the significance and devotional elements intended as supplications to God.

Driven by economic concerns, teachers marketed their product in a manner that maintained the interest of their clientele, which for the most part was Junior and Senior High schools. After all, subsistence comes before existential concerns. While non-Acehnese Indonesians may have attributed the name Saman as a collective umbrella term for Acehnese sitting dances, many Acehnese artists propagated the trend, even though they were aware of Saman's specificity. Just as the term "Nollywood" is simple to recall and implies a space alongside the of Hollywood and Bollywood in the international film industry (Haynes 2007), so too did the term "Saman" serve instrumental purposes in marketing and popularizing Acehnese dance, securing paid employment for Acehnese choreographers, and maintaining a steady flow of student clientele.

In what might be considered an effort to reclaim or reassert their authority over these ethno-cultural, artistic expressions, Acehnese artists popularizing seated body percussion in Jakarta have created a new term to categorize these dances, "Ratoh Jaroe" as the distinctive Jakartan style of Acehnese sitting dance. These dances use songs from a collection of coastal Acehnese dances including Likok Pulo, Rateb Meusekat, Ratoh Bantai, and Ratoh Duek. Teachers like Yusri Saleh and Mohammad Taufik claim that these dances are urban as they have changed in style, movement, vocals, and the *rapai* drum musical accompaniment. Discriminating, labeling, and categorizing markers of difference is a political act, one that defines and asserts boundaries between groups and reinforces in-group/out-group dynamics (Mason 2013). That the label "Ratoh Jaroe" has been respected by Indonesian journalists reporting on the opening ceremony to the 2018 Asian games might be taken as a good sign, but only time will tell if these labels will loop back and accentuate the differences between rural and urban forms of Acehnese dance and eventually perhaps even serve to crystallize the aesthetic markers of difference between these two forms.

Participating in the Dance

Collective participation in Acehnese sitting dances allows people to recognize themselves as, to repurpose the words of Michael Jackson, "members of a community, of a common body" (Jackson 1983: 338). The sense of solidarity is strong. Performing seated body-percussion in unison with others fills dancers with a strong feeling of belonging within a group and through shared action allows the group to feel like a community. Not only is the sense of togetherness strong and deeply experienced, this sensation can be achieved relatively quickly. Large groups in rank and file can learn these dances reasonably easily, because choreographed, multimodal, and self-referencing methods of teaching (see Mason 2017) allow rapid transmission of the genre. Becoming unanchored from its original social setting allowed Acehnese body percussion to become an autonomous performance genre, which allowed it to become contested as either an artistic expression of ethno-cultural or national identity.

During seated body-percussion performances, dancers sit close to one another, shoulder-to-shoulder, and knee-to-knee. Dancers form one or more lines and articulate movements together as a group. They rely on each other to coordinate carefully choreographed complex sequences. Each individual dancer has a responsibility to the next dancer sitting in the row to ensure the pace and rhythms are in time, even when rhythms are intertwined between the dancers, to create a sense of unification performing as one body as opposed to individual dancers with different roles. Margaret Kartomi refers to artists who primarily perform as dancers but use their body as the instrument to create rhythms and vocals while performing body movements as "dancer-musicians" (2004: 1). This self-accompanied dimension (see Mason 2014) of body percussion demands concentration and physical investment on behalf of the performers and provides them a strong sense of ownership over the performance.

Elite performers undertake intense training in order to perfect the technicalities of intricate sequences of movement. Movements might be synchronized in unison or in harmony, i.e., all members of a performance group will perform the same movements at the same time, or two or three complementary choreographies will be split across every second or third dancer in a row. Movements must be perfected and memorized. Teachers might use slightly divergent methods of teaching and emphasize different performative aesthetics. Teachers may also sculpt student interpretations by sharing knowledge, philosophy, and anecdotes about dance. To better understand the specifics of Acehnese body percussion, we will describe three Acehnese sitting dances in the next section.

Three Acehnese Dances

In this section, we discuss the history development and performance styles of three genres of Acehnese sitting dances: Ratéb Meusekat, Likok Pulo, and Saman. We explore the important differences in movement, song, and history in Ratéb Meusekat, Likok Pulo, and Saman. Ratéb Meusekat is a women's sitting dance from the West and Southern regions of Aceh. Likok Pulo is originally a men's dance from the Pulo Aceh community. Saman is a men's dance from the Gayo people in the mountainous area in the Aceh highlands. Likok Pulo and Ratéb Meusekat have songs that tell stories, which show Shia' influenced rituals still in practice. These three sitting dance genres all involve rhythms being made by beating on the chest, thighs, and floor, clapping, clicking of the fingers, and singing simultaneously. The characteristics of the body percussion seen in these dances and the accompanying songs about Hasan and Husain also point to a strong Shia' influence. Hitting and beating of oneself is reminiscent of the Shia' practice of self-flagellation during the day of Ashura (Mason 2016), which is believed by many in Aceh to be the origin of how the body percussion that is prevalent in Acehnese sitting dances started. Various movements and lyrics of the Acehnese sitting dance songs are full of the symbols of the Battle of Karbala: in Acehnese, "tumbok tumbok droe" meaning to beat oneself as a reflection of the mourning for Husain. The strong relationship to the history of Shia' in Aceh, especially in the distinctive percussive beating on the body, make the seated body-percussion a unique artistic expression of ethno-cultural identity.

With the advent of Islam in Indonesia in the thirteenth century, the Islamic Shia' tradition entered together with Sufism (Barorah 1976: 6) via India and Persia. The Shia' influence can be seen through local rituals and practices still prevalent in some provinces in Sumatra. There are many genres of dance, music, and arts that are influenced by Sufi expressions of Shia' traditions throughout Indonesia; the Tabuik festival of the Minangkabau people of West Sumatra and the Tabot festival of Bengkulu (Mason 2016). The Shia' influenced rituals shows the prevalence of cultural exchanges that occurred between locals, Arab travellers, traders, Sepoy Indians and Europeans. Interestingly, many Shia' practices still exist even though Indonesian Muslims are predominantly Sunni (Kartomi 1986: 141).

Ratéb Meusekat

Ratéb Meusekat dances were developed in Meudang Ara Rumoh Baro in South West Aceh. Ratéb comes from Arabic. Its etymology is from the word "ratib," meaning "to stand firm." In practical terms, ratéb appears as a form of worship based upon a number of particular prayer readings, which are performed as a religious exercise together making secular rhythms accompanied by singing (Hurgronje 1895: 159). The solo singer and the group take turns in singing sacred songs while performing body percussion kneeling, like the creed, the names of God, or praises to God and his messenger. The positioning of the hands varies from the chest and in front of the shoulder as well as hands being put out straight in front with palms facing to the audience. The hands also beat the thighs and floor and there is clapping, and also clicking of the fingers. Identical patterns are made in the air with hands and neck and heads going the same way or opposite to the next person. There may be pairs of odd-numbered performers creating one pattern, for instance, with their torso bent forward closer to the ground, and the even-paired numbers are sitting up (Kartomi 2004: 38). These movements are continuous for one song and then change when the next song starts.

The origins of the dance, as well as the name has a number of different sources; one theory, is that its name derived from "Maskawahi" – the name of a philosopher from Iraq, the Islamic Scholar (Ulema) Ibnu Maskawahi. Though this is believed by some to be legend, Maskawahi met Acehnese pilgram Teuku Muhammad Taib in

Bagdad in the seventeenth century (Kartomi 2006: 97–98) taught religion and arts in the form of what was believed to be the beginnings of Ratéb Meusekat, which he then brought back these teachings to the kingdom of Kuta Bate, in the southern district of Blang Pidie (present day region of the Aceh Barat Daya) where he became the religious leader of a school, teaching female students from all ages from surrounding villages in Rumoh Baro, later changing its name to Desa Medang.

The word "meusekat" may come from seukat which in Arabic means "to pray" or the word sakat meaning "quiet." According to Snouk Hurgronje, ratébi syèhs coerced their dancers to over stress the words of the ratéb poems which carried the creed and names of God, because deliberate mistakes were considered by many people to be unforgivable (khafir) (Hurgronje 1906: 60). In some cases, the words of the creed, the names of God, or alternative words like Hu, which mean "He the Lord," and many others, have been replaced with sounds that hold no meaning; so it is difficult to know or remember the original sources.

The spread of Ratéb Meusekat throughout West Aceh is believed to have been led by the daughter of Teungku Abdurrahim (aka Habib Seunagan) who came from Nagan Raya and taught the movements, while its poems or ratéb were created by Teungku Chik in Kala: an ulema (Islamic clerical scholar) in Seunangan. The content and unique characteristics of his poems consisted of adoration and praise to God and adoration of the Prophet Muhammad.

At first, Ratéb Meusekat was practiced in the pesantren, Islamic boarding schools, as an extra activity for students or santri (religious scholars) after learning and preaching (pengajian) or a religious lesson at night was over, as a form or entertainment in the space and grounds of the pesantren. However, after the santri completed their education from the boarding school, they also taught and spread this art in the heart of the community as dakwah, or a tool to promote Islam.

Originally, this dance was specifically performed and watched only by groups of women, but in its present development, this dance may be viewed by groups of men also. These dancers used traditional Acehnese clothing; cloth (selendang) that is crossed over the chest, with the ends tucked into a gold belt, over a long-sleeved blouse. The blouse is either white, silver, red, yellow or gold, and black, which are colors that are associated with the cardinal directional concepts of space which encompass Animist-Hindu-Buddhist associations, with certain colors also being influenced by Perso-Arabic arts like green (Kartomi 2004: 9). The dancers cover their heads with a head scarf called a jilbab with pants and a colorful songket, which is a woven Acehnese cloth type skirt over the pants. Today, the range in colors varies from pink, green, purple, blue, red to mention a few. The dance is performed by 9–15 female dancers and 2 singers, called aneuk syahè in Acehnese, who sit to the right of the dancers. The syèh who sits in the middle of the dancers and an apet syèh next to or two to three dancers down the line. Over time, the dance became more broadly imitated and became a regular activity for many people.

Kartomi notes Ratéb Meusekat was on the verge of extinction in the 1960s as men started to be prohibited to watch it because of traditional custom (adat). Even though women still performed it (as documented by Hasanuddin Daud) in 1961 in Betung village (Kartomi 2006: 98), it wasn't until 1972 that Ratéb Mesuekat had a revival.

This was due to a female choreographer Ibu Cut Asiah who went to Betung village to study Ratéb Meusekat from elderly women and brought it back to Melaboh to create new choreography and revived this art form. In the 1970s, the Ministry of Education and Culture had asked the people of Blang Pidie to identify local artistic genres and Ratéb Meusekat was not included initially perhaps because of adat (traditional custom) restricting men to not be exposed to it anymore, so the Ministry were ignorant of its existence at the time. According to Kartomi, the revival was so successful that later male dancers also appropriated this art form and performed it for national events, election campaigns, or tours (Kartomi 2006: 98).

Ratéb Meusekat is promoted on major religious days like Id al-Fithr (after the fasting month of Ramadhan) and Id al-Adha (remembrance of the sacrifice of Ibrahim) (Kartomi 2006: 98) and important national days, wedding celebrations, and other occasions as a form of entertainment that carries the values of religion within it.

Song Content in Ratéb Meusekat.

I will translate two songs from Ratéb Meusekat to show (1) advice for the community and (2) Shia' influence in the content of the following songs.

(1) Nyawong geu tanyoe didalam badan
/The soul inside our body/
Barang pinjaman siat tuhan bri
/is just an object lent to us from God/
Oh troh bak wate kagecok pulang
/when its time it will be returned/
Nyawong lam badan tuhan pe ce bre
/the soul that God will split away from our body/
Beingat-ingat wahe e tuboh
/remember, remember your body/
oh leh pajan troh nyawong geuhila
/one day your soul could be taken from you/
oh aleh uroe-oh aleh malam
/it could be day, it could be night/
nyawong lam badan tuhan pecebre
/the soul that God will split away from your body/
(2) Lon Bu lon Burak meunari-Burak menari/
(I'm offering a song about) a dancing flying horse, a dancing flying horse/
Lon a lon ateuh rueng gunong-ateuh rung gunong/
/On top of the back of the mountains, on top of the back of the mountains/
Lon bak lon bak cabeung bungong-bak cabeng bungong/
(I'm offering a song about) a flower sprig, a flower sprig
Lon a lon aneuk leue ku a-aneuk leue' kua/
(I'm offering a song about) a baby nightingale, a baby nightingale/

These songs are evident of the religious purposes of the dance. The first song warns the community about the concept of soul in Acehnese "nyawong," and that it can easily be taken back from God any time of day or night. The second song is symbolic of the Burak bird-like chariot of angels believed to have picked up the remains of Hasan and Husain and bring them to heaven. This shows the Shia' influence brought to Sumatra from earlier Sepoy Indians (Kartomi 1986: 145). At the beginning and end of the dance, there is always a Muslim greeting for the audience, Salam mualaikum: "Peace upon you."

Likok Pulo

Likok means "body movement" and even though it can describe body movement in many forms of sitting dances, it is the Likok Pulo genre of sitting dances form Aceh that has adopted the term "likok" in the title of this particular art form. It is believed that this was not the original name of this dance and that it came about when it was performed outside of the village where it originated. In this dance, movements are made in harmony with the rhythms of the songs and rapa'i percussion instrument. Because it exists in Pulau Aceh, this art form is called Likok Pulo Aceh, abbreviated and known more widely as Likok Pulo. It originates and has its roots in Ule Paya village on Pulau Beras. This island is one of a cluster of islands located in the area of Aceh Besar or the Greater Aceh Regency, Aceh Islands Municipality. The capital city of this area is Lampuyang. This art form appears to be the only one of its kind from this cluster of islands (Hasanuddin 1995: 5). Likok Pulo is believed to be created by Sheikh Amat Badron, an Ulema (Islamic clerical scholar) from the Middle East who was adrift at sea and cast ashore on Beras Island (Ibid.: 6). The time of his arrival is unknown. This Ulema settled on Pulau Beras and taught the religion of Islam. At the time Sheikh Amat Badron arrived, the people there already followed Islam. However, in general, they were still heavily influenced by their earlier pre-Islamic animistic or Hindu-Buddhist cultural mores (Ibid.: 6).

To deepen their awareness of the religion, Sheikh Amat Badron used alternative forms of art which could be enjoyed by the community and became a medium for the study of Islam. Songs were gradually inserted into these rapa'i performances and rapa'i procession songs, which were remembrance chants to God (zikir) or stories of the Prophet Mohammad. Gradually, rapa'i practices and performances were moved into the Meunasah (small religious schools often attached to the mosque) and after practices the men would pray together (Ibid.: 6). Activities like this invited the attention of the wider community, a process through which Sheikh Amat Badron added members until it was made into a regular religious practice. It was an activity that was performed additional to religious prayer, seen as an "extra" activity to do for practicing Muslims. This new art form attracted many people, which saw rapa'i players and groups developing with new movements in neighboring villages. Consequently, new syèh leading new dance groups also appeared (Ibid.: 7).

Likok Pulo is performed by men in a seated row (all these movements are performed while sitting on the heels) with accompanying rhythmic music created by two rapa'i drums. The rapa'i players traditionally were positioned sitting behind the dancers on the left hand side. However, since Likok Pulo has moved to the arena of entertainment, the accompanying rapa'i players sit to the left hand side of the dancers in a row so they can see the dancers. The vocals are started by a syèh, who is seated in the middle of the other dancers. The other dancers then join in the singing, the rapa'i player also sings the panton (verse) similar to the role of the aneuk syahè in Ratéb Meusekat. It is believed that traditionally the role of the syèh functioned as a leader who gave reproof and advice for the community and messages, which would be reiterated by the aneuk syahè playing the rapa'i (Hasanuddin 1995: 12).

Rhythms are made by clapping, beating of the chest, ground, and thighs, and clapping an odd-numbered partner, while the even-numbered partners are doing the same but in a bent torso position while the odd-numbered partners are sitting upright on their heels. Observing this male sitting dance, it is considered more masculine than the Ratéb Meusekat, not just because it is performed by males but also because the head movements are far more exaggerated than that of the female dances. There are 12–16 dancers sitting in a row with the aneuk syahè who sit behind.

Likok Pulo encompasses roles that are all needed to make the dance complete, these are the dancers, the songs that are sung by the syèh and the rapa'i drummers. The syèh sits in the middle of the dancers and gives the queue to start or end a movement. Traditionally, he was responsible for the successful result or failure of the performance.

There are two types of Likok Pulo forms of performance: tunang which are competitions between groups or the usual noncompetitive performance consisting of one group performing Likok Pulo. Tunang (which literally means betrothal) is believed to be a form of performance passed down by tradition because most of the groups from surrounding villages were able to perform Likok Pulo. Hence, this art form often became a competition between one group and another and could include as many as four competing groups at a time (Hasanuddin 1995: 15). This tunang was enacted among the coastal Acehnese community. A tunang is usually carried over a whole night. It would begin after the 'Issa night prayer and finished on observing the Subuh (predawn) prayer. The tunang was set-up on a spacious open field. The spectators were segregated by gender. Usually, the women sat behind the hosts, while the men sat next to the opponents. In the tunang, the selection of the winner was decided by a team which includes the previous winners among the Likok Pulo syèhs and well-known members of the community (Ibid.: 15).

Competition is staged by seating participants in straight lines, with the first group facing their opponents. The host group begins to perform their movements, making movements with the rhythms of prepared songs, while a group of opponents try to mirror their movements. If they are successful in copying these movements, points can be obtained by that group and vice-versa. After three or four movements are presented by the host group, the other group can have their turn to show what they can do. If there are four groups competing at the same time, they would take it turns to compete, the two groups not competing would sit as the audience while they wait their turn (Ibid.: 15).

Currently, Likok Pulo competitions outside this Acehnese art practice are performed by just one group as entertainment at events like weddings, festivals, organization events, parties, and religious and national holidays, in a similar manner to Ratéb Meusekat. In addition, Likok Pulo has become considered an indispensable component of formal occasions like official welcoming ceremonies and national reception nights. At occasions like this, the positions of dancers are arranged as appropriate for the occasion; so too the timing of the performance, the chosen dances, and the melodies that are presented to the audience.

The following is an example of a song that is an example of the commemoration of Hasan and Husain reflecting Shia' influence:

Dengo lon kisah Hasan ngon Husen
/Listen to my story (about) Hasan and Husain/
Yang puteh licen aso sirugaaaa
(who are) as white as the heavens/
Hasan ngon husen cuco dinabiii
/Hasan and Husain, the grandchildren of The Prophet/
Aneuk tuan siti, Fatima Dora
/The children of Fatima Dora/

Originally, the costumes which were worn by the Likok Pulo dancers were very simple, that is, they just wore ordinary tops and pants and everyday sarongs. As it developed, the Likok Pulo costume became more attractive for competitions: using long-sleeved shirts with embroidered gold patterns, long black pants with embroidery around the ankles, woven Acehnese sarongs (songket) with a belt and head cloth. The colors of the tops would alternate between the odd- and even-numbered dancers, so alternating two colors only. Today Likok Pulo dancers wear different colours, often encompassing more than one colour in the tops. This dance is now also performed by female dancers.

The two different coloured costumes adorned by every odd-numbered dancer is shown here, the two different colours worn here help emphasise the patterns, created with the torso bent down and upright- the 'cyclic spatial formation' concept of central-point in a circle (Kartomi 2004: 27).

The dancers set about creating 'waves' with their arms and torso, formations aimed at resembling the ocean. This is another example of 'cyclic spatial formation' (Kartomi 2004: 27) as the dancers move down toward the ground, then sit on their heels with their toes facing the floor, then they go up on high knees. We can also see the Sufi influence in that the dancers portraying the natural environment and the ocean, perhaps here, symbolising God as the ocean, an entity that is always there and never gone (Al-Attas 1963: 25–26).

Saman

"Saman" is believed to have originated from Sheikh Saman, an Ulema who spread Islam in the Gayo region, using native folkloric games (Pok-ane) as a method for spreading and planting its teachings (Kesuma 1992: 5).

The Saman dance, or what is also known informally as the 'thousand hands' dance, is a traditional highly-esteemed art of the Gayo and the Lokop region (Eastern Aceh), Blang Kejeren (in Gayo Lues Regency), and parts of Central Aceh. The poetic language used is a mixture of Gayonese and Arabic. It conveys dakwah messages, romantic poems, poems that ridicule, and advice for the community. There are two types of Saman that can be found in two areas, Gayo and Lokop. Saman Gayo was developed in Southeast Aceh, Gayo Lues, Bener Meriah, and

Central Aceh. Saman Lokop was developed in the Eastern Aceh Regency. The difference between the two can only be known by their dialects and the traditional style and colors of the Gayo kerrawang costume, the special costume for Saman which is worn by men who perform this art form. When Saman entered into the arena of national and international entertainment, the dance started to be called Saman Gayo, perhaps to reiterate the origins of Saman.

Saman is usually performed to celebrate important customary events and also performed on major religious and national days. Apart from that, this dance appears at formal events like the visit of a well-known personality or the opening of a festival, or to rejoice the end of a rice harvest (Kesuma 1992: 9). The most fundamental aim of the Saman performance is to strengthen the feeling of solidarity (Serinen) between one dancer to the next in the Saman group and also between one Saman group and the other in competition style (jalu) (Kesuma 1992: 19).

This dance has very dynamic, mystical, powerful movement and involves cooperation between dancers who are solid and able to produce very fast movements that demand a lot of energy. The basic element of such movement is body percussion, which is brought about by hand movements that slap the thighs and chest, and vocals sung by individuals or groups that are able to create a sacred and mystical atmosphere. The force behind the beauty of Saman combines elements of literature through the song, elegant art through the costumes and precision of movements through the body percussion, all accomplished without variations in formations like other developments of sittings dances. Saman is performed in one line and has not changed. Traditionally, Saman had become a part of life that could not be separated from the community; young men known to not yet feel "fulfilled" if they could not perform Saman. Elements of mysticism were known to be adopted by the religious people of Gayo within its own culture.

Technically, Saman is difficult to learn because of the complex movements, the language, as well as the costumes used in practice, restricting the dance's development. This dance is still studied and performed by the Gayo people, whether it is by those of the Gayo Lues in the highlands, (the Lokop areas in Eastern Aceh), Blangkejeren (Southeast Aceh), parts of Central Aceh, university students, or Gayo communities outside these areas, like Banda Aceh, Jakarta, or Yogyakarta. However, in Banda Aceh, there are a number of sanggars run by university students that have begun to compete with the Saman dance, such as: IAIN Ar-raniry and Unsyiah Law Faculty against MAN II (Madrasah Aliyah Negeri) (religious high schools) in Banda Aceh. The Governor's Sanggar Cut Nyak Dhien Meuligo has also been teaching and performing Saman as well. The teaching of Saman outside these Gayo communities only began around 5 years ago in Banda Aceh.

Saman is highly spectacular because of its dramatic movements, supported by very unique vocals addressing the audience. The Saman performance is split into four segments and is known to generate a response from the audience at each pause. Traditionally, Saman had to be performed as a *jalu* (competition) between two or more groups from the different villages which carried-over a day and night; even on occasion over a number of days and nights known as roa lao-roa ingi (Kesuma 1992: 16). The selection of the winner was decided by a jury that was made up of well-known people from the local community who understood the meanings embedded in the movements, authentic local customs, as well as religion. The different Saman groups were performed by a total of 15–25 male dancers.

In Saman, the performance is lead by a pengangkat (Ibid.: 10) who is placed in the middle of the dancers (similar to the position of the syèh in Ratéb Meusekat and Likok Pulo). He determines the dance movements, the volume of the reverberating pitch, the songs or syair, and those that rebute the enemy opponent if played in the jalu form. The pengangkat is assisted by two pengapit (like assistants) (Ibid.: 10) which are to his left and right, whose job it is to help the pengangkat with the dance moves or singing. There are two dancers who sit farthest to the left and right called the penupang or also called penamat kerpe jejerun (holders of the jejerun (a type of grass found in Gayo) grass who take on the role of the dancers to maintain the whole dance position so that it is perfectly straight and tight. Furthermore, other dancers called penyepit represent the dancers that support the dance or dance moves, as directed by the pengangkat.

Pesalaman (greetings) is made up of a rengum (Ibid.: 14–15) or group murmur to begin. The sounds of the initial murmur are not clear. However, essentially they are praises and magnifications of Allah. After regum immediately enters the salam, with the traditional Islamic greeting of "Assalamualaikum" (Peace upon you) to the audience, proper honor to the specific sides, and a request for permission to play Saman as expected courtesy and etiquette (Ibid.: 14–15).

Ulu Ni Lagu is the movement that follows the greeting (Ibid.:14–15). It marks the first main movement after "Assalamualaikum." In this section, the movements are variations between hand movements, clapping the chest, and moving the body and head, but are still in a slow tempo, during which the pengangkat sings a vocal solo. At this moment, the movements enter fast tempo, where the pengangkat with a high-pitched voice (called seek) gives the order to his fellow dancers in the row that they will soon enter the fast paced movements. Lagu-lagu are the movements in Saman. This section shows the richness of the moves of Saman. It represents the pinnacle of the Saman (Ibid.: 14) dance moves. Dancers move fast, being interspersed together with vocals, called redet. After the climax of the fast movement follows the slowing down of the movement and a return to the initial recitation of poems from the pengangkat.

After the climax of fast movements, the pace slows down and the dancers are given an opportunity to catch breath. This transition is called "to ease," or Uak Ni Kemuh (Kesuma 1992:14). When the condition of the dancers has returned to normal, the pengangkat will give commands for other movements. When the fast movements peak and reach a climax, the vocals stop and only the movements are seen and the percussive beats on the body and hands are heard.

The last part of the dance, Anak Lagu Penutup, involves simple movements. The dominant aspects are the poems, the parting words, pardons to the audience, and other particular aspects. In the tunggal Saman genre, there may be time constraints, and it can be adapted so that it is possible a few parts can be cut-out (Kesuma 1992: 16). Saman is not accompanied by any musical instruments; music is created by dancers by clapping hands, slapping of the chest and slapping on the lower thighs (before the knees), alternating raising of hands above the shoulders. Apart from rengum, songs that are used for the Saman dance aren't rigid; how the song or rhythm change depends on the location, time, and situation of the performance (ibid.: 15).

The styles of costume and accessories worn by the Saman dancers have identifiable colors and motifs making them special and specific to Gayo. The clothes worn by Saman dancers are believed to be clearly distinctive between Saman and other Acehnese sitting dances. Bulang teleng or bulang kerawang is a head-wrap decoration using tajuk kepies – a type of aromatic leaf (Ibid.: 58). Because this plant is now rare, it has been replaced with the pandan leaf. Special tops fitted to the body are worn called baju pokok, also known as baju kantong (Kesuma 1992: 60). The colors worn by Saman dancers from Gayo are yellow or gold, red, green, white embroidered onto black cloth. This is another example of colors associated with the cardinal directional concepts of space which encompass Animist-Hindu-Buddhist associations.

The dancers also wear long pants called suel naru which are made of black cloth and have ruje rino patterns and also encompass kerawang patterns specific to Gayo. For the sarong worn just over the pants, the material is called upuh pawak also pawak kerawang, this is the sarong worn from the waist to the knees. The dancers wear ikotni rongok or rongok which is a yellow handkerchief tied around the neck. It is folded in a triangle shape and also one is tied around the right wrist with its point of the triangle towards the fingers (Kesuma 1992: 60–61).

The lyrics in Saman are in the Gayo language. The following is an extract from the many songs in the dance. The time of the song is unknown; however, the song was likely made after Saman's popularity exceeded to national and international level, so as to let people know where Saman came from. Again, it shows the pride of the Gayo culture and Saman being part of it:

Tari Saman menurut sejarah
/The Saman dance according to history/
sara tukang tetah alim ulama
/was introduced by an ulema/
gerale Syeh Saman ari tanoh Mekah
/his name was Syeh Saman from Mecca/
Sire tuker rempah ngemang agama
/trading spices as he spread religion/
Sawah ku Gayo Islam berkembang
/when he got to Gayo, Islam flourished/
Ku sibebujang tengah berlagu
/to the young people who are singing/
Engone betepok bertebah runcang
/you can see by the beat on your chest/
I one i timang redet urum baju
/there the rules of song and clothes (costume) are made/
Ayone agama kutari Saman
/entered (also) religion into the Saman dance/
Gerak ite tahan kati semperne
/we have perfected the dance until its perfect/
Pok pok ane gerale pemulon
/the first naming of the dance started as "Pok ambe-ambe"/
Renye itukeren kerna wae gure

/after it was changed to something more beautiful/
Gerakni Saman menganung arti
/The movements of Saman full of meaning/
Katas kutuyuh kuen kukiri
/up to down, right to left/
Tebah kudede tepok jejari
/beating the chest, clicking of the fingers/
Sifet pahlawan membela diri
/characteristics of heroic defence/

Transformation and Change

Tracing the development of these art forms outside Aceh, it becomes clear that they have been modified and transformed to different degrees. Saman was performed at Pekan Kebudayaan Aceh ke II (the Second Acehnese Cultural Expo in 1972) and the formal opening of Taman Mini Indah Indonesia Theme Park in 1974. Saman became one of the art forms that frequently represented Aceh: raising it to a national level, as well as gaining international acclaim. In the 1980s, almost all the villages in the Blangkejeren district had a Saman group. This fostered a sense of pride in the community, especially when the group was able to perform in different areas and even overseas (for example, at the Kias festival in America 1990 and 1991). Saman, as an Acehnese sitting dance, was elevated and performed at the national and international levels, and its name became famous across the general population of Indonesia; to the extent that every sitting dance from Aceh is always called "Saman" now, even though occasionally these performances are not in fact Saman dances from Gayo.

There have been some changes, in that apart from the jalu form, Saman is now performed in a "tunggal" (literally meaning solo – not solo dancer, but just meaning without opponents). For the wider non-Gayo community, this dance performance is more popular, because it is often promoted outside its original region, such as promoted in the capital Jakarta. Saman is used as an entertaining dance form, used to celebrate grand occasions. This form of performance is used to fill-out various programs, performed for 8 or 10 min with a total of 10–12 dancers. Despite these modifications, Saman remains well known by the Gayo people and coastal Acehnese, because it's original form has been preserved. The dance is still performed by groups of men and is not performed by women.

In contrast, the performance and gender of dancers in the two other forms discussed here has changed more dramatically. In the beginning, Likok Pulo was performed by groups of 12–16 men. In its development outside Pulau Aceh, however, there were changes in the position of performers and men were replaced with women. This transformation then became one of the factors that caused Likok Pulo to develop rapidly outside Pulau Aceh, and now these performances are danced by women. Ratéb Meusekat was revived by Ibu Cut Asiah who went to Betung to learn Ratéb Meusekat (Kartomi 2004). Today, there are more women who perform Acehnese sitting dances not only in Indonesia but overseas. We agree with Kartomi

(2004) who finds that women have been the key to the revival, preservation, and spread of sitting dancers even if the teachers have often been men.

At first, a Likok Pulo performance which was performed by women was given the name "Likok Inong" (Inong meaning female or woman in Acehnese), but this name was lost and is not recognized anymore. Nowadays, there are often Likok Pulo competitions between young people in different villages. The Likok Pulo dance has developed further and now includes women whose movements vary slightly to that of the men's. Likok Pulo is relatively easy to learn because its movements are not fixed compositions and can be developed in different directions, though artists who are interested in preserving its original form are worried for the loss of its distinctive features and characteristics. At one point during the early development of this dance, it almost became classified as an extinct art form which had only occurred after planting or harvesting rice fields. In the 1980s, this dance saw a resurgence, however, and was also performed at the national level.

After these events, Likok Pulo became a source of pride to the Pulau Beras community, because it had raised the profile of the Island. Many sanggars taught this dance – primarily sanggars outside of Pulau Aceh, like in Banda Aceh, North Aceh, and even sanggars in Jakarta too – which were maintained by Acehnese dancers or choreographers.

Thus, the shape of Likok Pulo started to shift and develop, and its quality was raised by new arrangements and improvements on movement, tempo, rhythm, dynamics, poetic elements, and also performance costumes. However, in Pulau Aceh itself, Likok Pulo did not develop and experienced a decline at most of the sanggars that had once taught this dance, sanggars outside of Pulau Aceh were being invited more frequently to represent the dance.

In Aceh, Rateb Meusekat is still performed by girls in schools and *sanggar* with little change to its traditional form in song and movement. In Jakarta, students and dancers have adopted the gendered characteristic of Rateb Meusekat (a dance only performed by women) but have combined dances from both boys coastal and girls coastal dances. It has become popular to use the term, "Ratoh Jaroe" referring to Jakarta style sitting dances as seen at the opening of the Asian Games. Acehnese teachers such as Yuri Saleh and Mohammad Taufik have also come to realize that it is their style of urbanized sitting dances that have become popular and for too long the name Saman has been accredited in both media and among communities, most probably leading to its world heritage listing by UNESCO.

One difference between the Ratéb Meusekat and Likok Pulo is that the Likok Pulo performance is accompanied by rapa'i as opposed to Ratéb Meusekat, which does not use music accompaniment. Saman is also not accompanied by the rapa'i and only uses the hitting of the body and hands to create rhythms. Another difference with the Saman is that in the Saman dance performance they use the Gayo language but the Ratéb Meusekat and Likok Pulo dance songs are sung in Acehnese.

Moreover, Saman does not possess a musical instrument accompaniment, and the songs in the Saman are sung by one of the dancers who also joins the dancing (pengangkat-as mentioned above in the analysis of Saman). He becomes singer and dancer at the same time. On the other hand, in the Ratéb Meusekat the aneuk syahè, or singer does not follow the dancer, the aneuk syahè is only for singing the songs and carries the verse (pantun). In Jakarta, sitting dancers were made famous by Marzuki Hasan. Commonly known as Pak Uki, he is the one who popularized its movements within Jakarta and overseas. And nowadays, teachers like Yusri Saleh and Mohammad are also responsible for the widespread popularity of these dancers especially among junior and senior students in schools.

Conclusion

Hughes-Freeland observes that "dance became a legitimate object of study when globally it was being removed from its socially embedded conditions of practice" (2008: 12). In the context of globalization, artistic expression has to be understood within permeable and shifting locales. Acehnese artist-teachers in Jakarta have demonstrated unique perspectives and responses to the processes of globalization. They are aware that they may not be able to wholly control what happens to their art once it has been passed on, and they attempt to deliberately manipulate and sustain the social worlds that lend prestige to their art. In negotiating the transmission of an embodied art form, artists sometimes struggle to maintain authority and to control the shape and form of the art they teach. From person to person, and school to school, embodied art forms can be represented differently according to the skills of individuals, the influences of key practitioners, and the tendencies of a group. A constant interplay exists between the changes in individual representations and socially shared representations. In the "lived and representational" (Hughes-Freeland 2008: 22) world of translocal embodied arts, if ethno-cultural identity and artistic expressions are to be understood, then observations of the interaction between artist-teachers and performer-students should be captured and contextualized in the social environments where training takes place, within the demands of the cultural locale, and the framing of the historical moment.

Cross-References

▶ Ethno-cultural Symbolism and Group Identity

References

Al-Attas SN (1963) Some aspects of Sufism as understood and practised among the Malays. Malaya Publishing House, Singapore

Aspinall E (2006) Violence and identity formation in aceh under Indonesian rule. In: Reid A (ed) Verandah of violence: the background to the aceh problem. Singapore University Press, Singapore, pp 149–176

Aspinall E (2009) Islam and Nation: separatist rebellion in aceh. Stanford University Press, Stanford

Barorah B (1976) Shia elements in Malay literature. In: Kartodirdjo S (ed) *Profiles of Malay culture; historiography, religion and politics* organisatie: ministry of education culture, Indonesia. Directorate General of Culture, Yogyakarta

Hasanuddin D, (1995). Diskripsi Tari Likok Pulo, Bidang Kesenian Kanwil Department Pendidikan dan Budaya Propinsi Daerah Istimewa Aceh. Banda Aceh

Haynes J (2007) 'Nollywood': what's in a name? Film Int 5(4):106–108

Hughes-Freeland F (2008) Embodied communities: dance traditions and change in Java. Berghahn Books, Oxford/New York

Hurgronje CS (1895) The acehnese, vol. I (translated by O'Sullivan A. W. S.). E. J. Brill, Leiden/London

Hurgronje CS (1906) The acehnese, vol. II (translated by A.W.S. O'Sulliva). late E.J. Brill, Leyden

Jackson M (1983) Knowledge of the body. Man 2:327–345

Kartomi MJ (1986) Tabut – a Shi'a Ritual transplanted from India to Sumatra. In: Chandler DP, Ricklefs MC (eds) Nineteenth and twentieth century Indonesia; essays in Honour of Professor J.D. Legge. Centre of Southeast Asian Studies, Monash University, Melbourne, pp 141–162

Kartomi MJ (2004) Some implications of local concepts of space in the dance, music, and visual arts of aceh. Yearb Tradit Music 36:1–49

Kartomi MJ (2006) Aceh's body percussion: from ritual devotionals to global Niveu. Musiké: Int J Ethnomusicological Stud 1(1):85–108

Kesuma A (1992) *Diskripsi tari Saman*. Propinsi Daerah Istimewa Aceh Proyek Pembinaan Kesenian. Kantor Wilayah Departemen Pendidikan dan Kebudayaan Provinsi daerah Istimewa Aceh.

Lewis JL (1992) Ring of liberation: a deceptive discourse in Brazilian Capoeira. University of Chicago Press, Chicago

Lo J (2000) Beyond happy hybridity: performing Asian-Australian identities. In: Ang I, Chalmers S, Law L, Thomas M (eds) Alter/Asians: Asian-Australian identities in art, media and popular culture. Pluto Press, Annandale, pp 152–168

Mason PH (2013) Intracultural and intercultural dynamics of Capoeira training in Brazil. Global Ethnographic 1:1–8

Mason PH (2014) Tapping the plate or hitting the bottle: sound and movement in self accompanied and musician accompanied dance. Ethnomusicol Forum 23(2):208–228

Mason PH (2016) Fight-dancing and the Festival: Tabuik in Pariaman, Indonesia, and Iemanjá in Salvador da Bahia, Brazil. Martial Arts Stud J (2):71–90. https://doi.org/10.18573/j.2016.10065

Mason PH (2017) Combat-dancing, cultural transmission and choreomusicology: the globalization of embodied repertoires of sound and movement. In: Lesaffre M, Maes P-J, Leman M (eds) The Routledge companion to embodied music interaction. Routledge, New York, pp 223–231

Reid A (2004) War, peace and the burden of history in Aceh. Asian Ethnicity 5(3):301–314

Reid A (2006) Introduction: Verandah of violence: the background to the aceh problem. Singapore University Press, Singapore

Robinson G (1998) Rawan is as Rawan does: the origins of disorder in new order aceh. Indonesia 66:127–157

Sulaiman MI (2006) From autonomy to periphery: a critical evaluation of the acehnese nationalist movement. In: Reid A (ed) Verandah of violence. Singapore University Press, Singapore, pp 121–148

Ethnic Film in South Africa: History, Meaning, and Change

101

Gairoonisa Paleker

Contents

Introduction	1978
South African "National" and "Ethnic" Cinemas: Historical Overview	1979
The New "Ethnic Film"	1987
Conclusion	1990
Cross-References	1992
References	1992

Abstract

This chapter provides a discussion of ethnic films in South Africa by tracing the historical development of "national" and "ethnic" cinema in the context of apartheid where creative and financial control of filmmaking was controlled by the state and white individuals who acted as surrogates of the state. The chapter interrogates the extent to which the "ethnic film" category can be applied to film productions that represented an inauthentic African worldview, culture, and tradition. It further argues that the categories of national and ethnic have shifted since the democratic elections of 1994 and in the post-1994, context and sectors of the Afrikaans-language film industry have now moved to the margins in what can be described as an "inward migration." In the process, these films have become decentered and detached from the "national" industry and are now the new "ethnic" cinema in South Africa.

Keywords

South Africa · Afrikaans films · Black film industry · Cultural nationalism

---

G. Paleker (✉)
Department of Historical and Heritage Studies, University of Pretoria, Pretoria, South Africa
e-mail: nisa.paleker@up.ac.za

© The Author(s), under exclusive license to Springer Nature Singapore Pte Ltd. 2019
S. Ratuva (ed.), *The Palgrave Handbook of Ethnicity*,
https://doi.org/10.1007/978-981-13-2898-5_138

Introduction

Implicit in any discussion of "ethnic" cinema is the binary between a "national" and "ethnic" (other) cinema. In two of the globally dominant commercial film industries, Hollywood and Bollywood, "national" cinema can best be described as White Anglo-Saxon Protestant (WASP) and Hindu nationalist, respectively. Films produced outside the dominant industry, especially from different regions, linguistic, and cultural groups, are juxtaposed as ethnic/regional cinemas. In the South African context, ethnic and national cinemas have been historically contingent categories as defined firstly by apartheid and secondly by the end of political apartheid post-1994. Since 1994 both categories of national and ethnic cinema have been upended to the extent that the core of both has shifted as political power and a concomitant dislocation of political power has shifted.

Gary Keller's review essay of a series of books on ethnic cinema published in the early 1990s summarizes the shift in scholarship on ethnic cinema (Keller 1995). Keller describes this shift as a move away from considerations of representations of ethnic groups to considerations of control of production and finance. The "image of" approach in film scholarship, particularly focused on Hollywood cinema, tended to focus on what Stuart Hall has described as "positions of enunciation" where ethnic minority groups as subjects of films were spoken on behalf of, rather than speaking on their own behalf (Hall 1989). These "image of" approaches looked at "dominant regimes of representation" (Hall 1989:71) and the ways in which ethnic minority groups were positioned, framed, and bespoken.

The shift in the early 1990s took a more nuanced approach that distinguished between two categories of ethnic cinema: ethnic cinema produced within the commercial industry and independently produced ethnic cinema. The latter category considers ethnic participation beyond acting and technical support and looks instead at control of finance and production. From this vantage point, analyses of technique, themes, and genres acquire new meanings consonant with a shift in the position of enunciation. On the basis of these shifts in scholarly approaches to ethnic cinema, the term ethnic cinema itself is in transition.

Discussions and definitions of ethnic cinema are shaped by larger debates on ethnicity which, in turn, are shaped by resurgent and, frequently, aggressive identity politics as evident in locales as diverse as Johannesburg, Paris, and Poland, to name a few. Recent affirmations of ethnic identities allude to essentialist definitions, ignoring the hybrid, shifting, and dynamic nature of ethnicities. In the South African context, the ethnic binary that takes center stage in national debates is between whiteness and blackness where each is conceived as homogenous states of being. This binary excludes black people who fall within the apartheid racial categories of Colored and Indian. The exclusionary nature of black and white identity politics in South Africa has led to frequent eruptions of what could be called "Colored anger" – as opposed to "Black anger." At the core of this anger is a sense of "agrievedness" that the Coloured community is marginalized and denied access to resources and state services in the post-1994 dispensation. The discourse of the rainbow nation which flowed from the first democratic elections in 1994 and the witness-bearing of the South African Truth and Reconciliation Commission (TRC) has thus all but unraveled in the fabric of contemporary South African society.

More importantly though, shifts in meanings of ethnic cinema in the South African context are contingent on politics and power in a much more direct way than through identity politics. In the recent past, as part of the rainbow nation discourse, the narrowly conceived national cinema of the apartheid years has been displaced by an emerging inclusive definition of national cinema. Accompanying this shift has been a withdrawal of elements of Afrikaans cinema to the margins of a national cinema which could be argued to constitute the new "ethnic cinema" of South Africa. Most typically, this involved Afrikaans cinema produced as part of an entrenched Afrikaner nationalism vying for political and cultural space in a dramatically reorganized polity and society. These shifts in conceptualizing South African cinema and ethnic cinema have been largely due to the changed political order heralded by the democratic, inclusive elections of 1994 which for the first time opened up opportunities for black creative, financial, and production control in a manner inconceivable in the apartheid past.

South African "National" and "Ethnic" Cinemas: Historical Overview

Any attempt to understand the historical and contemporary composition and content of the South African film industry needs to pay attention to the role of the state. Furthermore, contemporary South African film has been distinctly shaped by a historical context characterized by racism, oppression, denial, and violence; cinematic language, techniques, narratives, and themes are only now beginning to emerge from the shadow of apartheid.

The shadow of apartheid also effectively insulated the South African film industry, both "national" and "ethnic," from the world in terms of audiences as well as growth and development in tune with global cinematic trends. More pertinently, South African film was isolated from the continent. Cinema in South Africa, due in large part to the ideological motivations behind films produced in the country, had historically been viewed with suspicion by the rest of the continent. Key historic moments which witnessed continent-wide meetings, resolutions, and agreements are characterized by the exclusion of a South African presence. The Algiers Charter on African Cinema (1972), the Niamey Manifesto of African Filmmakers (1982), and the Final Communiqué of the First Frontline Film Festival and Workshop (Harare 1990) have been some historical attempts by African filmmakers to crystallize and formulate continental resolutions and declarations with regard to film. South Africa was not represented in any of these gatherings except for the presence of ANC delegates at the Harare festival (Bakari and Cham 1992). African filmmakers have however tried to make provision for individual South African filmmakers not ideologically aligned to the apartheid state. The Pan African Federation of Filmmakers (FEPACI) whose membership consisted of different African national film bodies rather than individual filmmakers made an exception for individuals from an "occupied country such as South Africa or from a colonised country such as Mozambique" (Diawara 1992:40).

State intervention in South African film remains firmly entrenched, though revitalized and reconceptualized since 1994. The early development of cinema in South Africa is inextricably linked to the "building of white identity" within a national paradigm especially from 1910 onward when South Africa attained Union status (Maingard 2007:4). The articulation of a national identity and what constituted nationhood, through the medium of film, was later closely linked to Afrikaner nationalist aspirations which received state support from 1948 onward when the National Party came into power. The first formal route of state intervention was by means of a state subsidy introduced in 1956 by the apartheid National Party (NP) government (Tomaselli 1989; Paleker 2010). The general election of 1953 resulted in a far more decisive victory for the NP than was the case in the 1948 elections. This assured the NP government a greater degree of political confidence than it previously had to entrench and more confidently enact policies that were consonant with Afrikaner ideologies of racial differences, the place of Afrikaners and Afrikaner culture vis a vis both English and black South Africans. As Beinart (2001) comments, the dominant preoccupation of the nationalists in these early years of rule was more on the formulation and clarification of ethnic Afrikaner nationhood and identity. State intervention in film production at this point should be understood from twin perspectives: firstly, the specter of foreign domination and, secondly, the need to clarify and consolidate ethnic Afrikaner nationhood and power. Implicit in both imperatives was a full recognition of the potential of film as a propaganda and pedagogic tool.

The foreign domination (British and US productions) of the local film industry served not only to marginalize local producers, but importantly also it led to an increased diminishing of government's role in the production industry due to the increasing use of foreign co-production that accompanied this new phase of the local industry. The Motion Picture Producers Association which was established in 1956, exclusively white but comprising both English- and Afrikaans-speaking filmmakers, was a direct outcome of the apartheid government's desire to negotiate with industry. Jamie Uys, Afrikaner filmmaker, was its first chairperson and was to play a crucial role in subsequent years not only in the film industry generally but more specifically as "advisor" and unofficial ideologue of the National Party government (Tomaselli 1989: 32).

The state subsidy was paid on the basis of box office receipts. A number of conditions were attached to the subsidy at this point of its existence. Firstly, subsidy could only be claimed for 35 mm films. Secondly, this subsidy would be in the form of a refund of the entertainment tax paid for exhibition, and the amount to be refunded would not exceed £10,000 or 50% of the total production costs which could include the costs of printing six copies of the film. Thirdly, only South African films were eligible for funding. South African for the government meant that 75% of salaries and wages had to be paid to South African citizens and the production company as well as all partners had to be registered as South African companies for tax purposes. Fourthly, the condition was that payments would only be made on a half-yearly basis and claims had to be submitted by the end of June and December of each year. Fifthly, films had to be registered with the Department of Trade and Industry immediately after release. Applications for the registration of a film had to be accompanied by audited statements where the auditor had to certify that three-quarters of salaries had indeed been paid to South African citizens (see Tomaselli 1989; Paleker 2010). These application documents also needed to include an audited statement of the entertainment tax paid along with copies of daily returns from the exhibitors.

Due to the failure of film producers to notify the Department timeously of the amounts they would be claiming, a further set of conditions were applied from the 1960s onward. These included firstly the submission from producers of a report indicating their plans for the coming 6 months. This report had to indicate the names of films to be produced, estimated costs, and expected date of release. Secondly, producers also had to indicate the total amounts to be claimed at the end of each financial year.

In the late 1960s, the percentage of subsidy paid for ethnic Afrikaans-language films was increased from 44% to 55%, and in order for a film to qualify for this increased subsidy, 90% of the dialogue had to be in Afrikaans. This increase was an attempt to boost the production of Afrikaans-language films which were believed to be disadvantaged in terms of subsidy payments. But more importantly according to Nationalist MPs like J.A. van Tonder, the Afrikaans language, especially in bilingual films, was depicted as "being subservient to English, as being the language of ridiculous 'backvelders' (or country bumpkins). Such films earn a great deal more in state subsidies, while purely unilingual Afrikaans films, with a cultural value... will receive little or no subsidy..." (Tomaselli 1989: 34). This attempt to encourage the Afrikaans industry coincided with the South African National Life Insurance Company (SANLAM) takeover of 20th Century Fox's South African interests (for an in-depth study of Afrikaner capital, see, e.g., Dan O'Meara, *Volkskapitalsime* 1983). This meant an effective dominance of the production, distribution, and exhibition industries by Afrikaner capital. The next amendment to the subsidy was introduced in 1973 where the formula for subsidy payments was changed to read net box office earnings instead of gross box office earnings.

The films that were produced as part of this subsidy ranged in genre from action, romance, and drama to explicitly ideological films that furthered Afrikaner nationalist interests. One of the most popular genres within the Afrikaans-language industry was the filmic adaption of what is known as the *plaasroman* or farm novel. Land in general and the farm in particular occupied preeminent place in this genre as the origin of the *volk* or Afrikaner folk. The farm (land) was the space that was conquered by Afrikaner pioneers who went on to tame, civilize, and make it productive. It is the idyllic home and legacy where right of tenure is considered inalienable (van Coller and van Jaarsveld 2018). Contestations around land are currently a national debate with the ANC recently approving land expropriation without compensation, though government still has to adopt this as policy. Land therefore continues to be a central issue in political, economic, and cultural life, and particular discourses around land have filtered through to recent Afrikaans-language films such as *Treurgrond* (lit. mourning ground 2015).

The historical commitment of the apartheid government to developing a national film industry, within the ideological framing of the South African nation as exclusively white, was informed in no small measure by the anti-apartheid struggle. For example, in the aftermath of the Sharpeville massacre on 21 March 1960, there was a flurry of communication between various Native Affairs Commissioners. In the massacre, 69 people were killed, and many more wounded when police opened fire on the crowd participating in the anti-pass campaign organized by the Pan Africanist Congress (PAC). This was followed by the declaration of a state of emergency and the banning of the ANC and PAC. A further and immediate consequence of Sharpeville was international censure and disinvestment (Beinart 2001: 166–167). The necessity for a national film industry which could be used not only to mitigate the immediate backlash of Sharpeville but also to create positive propaganda, especially among Africans, was a pressing need. In view of this, considerable attention was given to attempts to "fight subversive propaganda with positive propaganda" as directed by the Chief Bantu Affairs Commissioner to all Commissioners in the Transkei Territories, dated March 1963 (Pretoria Archives, KAB1/BUT 88). This sentiment was accompanied by further suggestions to all Commissioners for the Transkei Territories to actively engage with local African leaders. The Commissioners were to hold regular meetings with "tribal authorities" as well as to "buttress the prestige of local leaders" and to give prominence to historical heroes and make "full use of Bantu superstition." Film was identified as an important component of these propaganda efforts.

In 1972 a state subsidy known as the B-Scheme was introduced by the apartheid state for the production of films in ethnic African languages. White entrepreneurs who were not filmmakers were at the forefront of successfully lobbying the apartheid government for the introduction of this second subsidy. This was a separate subsidy to the one that was introduced in 1956 and which was reformulated and amended at various times throughout the years with increasing amounts of money being set aside annually for the production of films. This general subsidy was predominantly for the production of "white" films in either English or Afrikaans though there were films such as *Dingaka* (1964) which were produced as part of this subsidy. With the majority of state funds being diverted to the production of English- and Afrikaans-language films, the production of African-language films was severely neglected and hence the introduction of a separate subsidy.

The B-Scheme film subsidy, from its inception, paid a maximum of R45 000, increased to R77 000 in 1977 and R80 000 in 1981 (Tomaselli 1989: 40). Comparatively, in 1981 a white film could earn up to R1.2 million in subsidy funding. The only criteria, as stated previously, for the state subsidy was firstly 75% of the actors had to be African and, secondly, three-quarters of the dialogue had to be in an African language. The state did not vet any scripts, and the final arbiter was the Censor Board. The subsidy was paid out on the basis of number of tickets sold. This meant that indirectly, the subsidy was controlled by the exhibitor and producers were assured of immediate income which could be considerable in cases of low-budget productions. The 1977 amendment as mentioned earlier included not only the increase in subsidy funding but importantly also films that were rented to mine compounds were now eligible for subsidy funding, and the period during which a film could qualify for subsidy had been reduced from 4 to 3 years from the date of first release (*SA Film Weekly*, 1977: 1).

Both the A- and B-Scheme subsidies were amended in 1977 as a result of a Commission of Inquiry instituted to investigate both subsidies. With regard to the "Bantu Film Industry" as reported in the *SA Film Weekly*, "the Board deems the existence of an independent Bantu film industry justified and in fact necessary, and concludes that this industry requires greater financial and technical assistance than is extended to it at present" (*SA Film Weekly* 1977: 2).

The differential subsidy paid for "white" as opposed to "black films" was in keeping with the political and concomitant economic ideology of "separate development." According to this, the apartheid government saw no need to expend vast resources on Africans who were not South African "citizens." This kind of expenditure needed to come from each of the ethnic homelands to which Africans belonged. The Bantu Investment Corporation (BIC) as a possible funding agency for "black" films became one possible avenue of funding African-language films.

The BIC was established in 1959 as part of the broader plan of "separate development" which in economic terms partly meant not only the decentralization of labor-intensive industry to the border areas of the homelands but also the financing of entrepreneurs within the homelands itself. Through financial assistance to approved individuals, the BIC aimed to promote not only the economic development (strictly along apartheid policies) of the homelands but also to stimulate a "Bantu film industry of their own" (Tomaselli 1989: 59). The BIC, according to the report in the *SA Film Weekly*, provided a sum of R500 000 toward the establishment of a Filmbank which was set up to finance film production. By 1977 eight films had been produced and five cinemas built in "Bantu" areas through funding from the Filmbank (*SA Film Weekly* 1977: 2).

The Promotion of Bantu Self-Government Act of 1959 established a total of ten "Bantu Homelands" along ethnic lines. Of these Transkei was the first to receive self-government with the 1963 Transkei Constitution Act which created a legislative assembly. Transkei became "independent" in 1976. Anticipating black political dissent and protest, the homelands were projected to absorb narrowly defined ethnic nationalism rather than a broader South African nationalism. Beinart argues that "A central tenet of apartheid was to divert the ambitions of the African educated classes from major cities so that they would help guide the journey towards separate development" (Beinart 1994: 208). Within the framework of ethnic Bantustan ideology, Africans in "white" South Africa were aliens whose proper place was within the geopolitical boundaries of the various reserve areas that were now being prepared for "statehood" under South African tutelage. Given this, any form of discrimination could rightly be argued to be on the basis of nationality rather than race, color, or ethnicity. Furthermore, as regards film, each Bantustan could theoretically develop its own "national" industry, thus obviating the necessity to incorporate "black" films into a "white" national industry.

Two interrelated consequences of separate development and ethnic Bantustan ideology were firstly the entrenchment of ethnic identities and divisions which would find violent expression in the early 1990s in KwaZulu/Natal. This is perhaps most obvious in the case of KwaZulu and Zulu nationalism as typified by the Inkatha Freedom Party. Mangosuthu Buthelezi, as leader of the KwaZulu homeland and Inkatha, refused independence, arguing instead an ideology not remarkably different to that of the National Party. Aiming for "reform" of apartheid from within, Buthelezi supported development along ethnic and regional decentralization. This in turn would earn him support not only from the South African government but also, importantly, from capitalists as well as foreign governments (see, e.g., Lowe 1991).

Secondly, separate development created ethnically based "systems of support, patronage, resource distribution and means of coercion and control" (Lowe 1991: 195). The creation of a class of petty bourgeoisie, the co-optation of local chiefs, and class of homelands bureaucrats furthered the aim of separate development. The nationalist government gave active support to the creation of an African homeland middle class through loans and grants to help establish capitalists and traders. This was given further impetus by the departure of white traders with established businesses in the homeland areas.

The threat of cultural hybridity and racial miscegenation was a preeminent preoccupation within this framework of separate development. The Bantustans were conceived not only as separate political and national entities but, importantly, also as separate cultural entities. This total separation meant not only separation from white (Afrikaner) South Africa and culture but also complete separation between various African ethnic groups. Nixon argues that apartheid in one sense was akin to cultural stasis because apartheid ideological conception of African ethnic culture and identity did not allow for dynamic change, interchange, and exchange but instead sought to fossilize this within the different boundaries of the homelands, and numerous devices were employed to ensure this fossilization (Nixon 1994: 5).

Many of the white filmmakers working in the "black" film industry assumed surrogate roles for the apartheid state in that many B-Scheme films either implicitly or explicitly supported this ideology of separate development. The "black film industry" was made up of white men, most of whom came from non-film backgrounds. The "chairperson" of this loosely organized industry was in construction blasting, and while working on special effects for two Afrikaner filmmakers, he saw African migrant workers watching imported films while tuned in to what was then known as Radio Bantu, a collection of radio stations broadcasting in some of the major indigenous African languages. Tonie van der Merwe saw this as an entrepreneurial opportunity and together with several others successfully lobbied the apartheid government for a separate subsidy for films in indigenous African languages. The state did not set any specific criteria apart from those of language and cast mentioned earlier. With the subsidy paid on the basis of box office returns, the films that were produced as part of this subsidy were largely profit driven. In the absence of formal theatres for African audiences in urban centers, the thousands of films that were produced as part of this subsidy were screened on the mobile circuit, which was essentially a panel van with a projector that toured the rural areas and homeland towns screening in makeshift theatres which were mainly school, church, and community halls. This created multiple opportunities for fraud; audience numbers were inflated for purposes of claiming maximum subsidy, and one film with several titles in some of the indigenous languages could be submitted multiple times for subsidy claims.

This fraudulent practice was not the only problem. Part of the problem according to van der Merwe was that the "black film industry" became too big.

> When I had a meeting once a month with the government because I'm the chairman (of the Association for Black Film Producers), they say, hey you guys are making too many movies, there's no money in this industry, you have to calm down you have to cut down and I go back to my people and I say listen, they say you must make less movies there's not enough budget money and I have to set an example and make less. I make probably the least movies of everybody. And they didn't even worry about it they just went on and produced like a factory. And the government officials were corrupt. They took bribes, they took presents, they took money and those people, a few companies involved, their claims went through like... record time they got their checks, in record time and obviously the signs was there.... (Personal interview, see Paleker 2010)

The signs van der Merwe speaks of were obvious both in terms of the corruption involved and also in terms of the quality of films produced. As Tomaselli argues, the subsidy system by its very nature did not support film as art. This was especially true for the B-Scheme films where, as van der Merwe points out, people were churning out movies at a rate of 12 per month.

> .. we wanted to create a certain, a bit of standards because some people really made total rubbish. They took the film, load a camera magazine and it runs for 11 minutes and they shoot a scene for 11 minutes long and then they change the magazine and they shoot it like a show on a stage, that kind of movies which was very bad, I think for the industry.... Unfortunately, some producers... the quality did increase and improve with the higher subsidy, but most of them kept to this really bad movies to make maximum profit. If they made 10 or 12 movies a month, that's not uncommon. I think most of those returns was 'jipoed' (creatively manipulated) like that, so it was purely, purely... nothing to do about the art, or the film industry, it was purely about financial gain. We said let's submit a script, look at the script first before you pass it. Some people didn't even shoot with a script. The script was on a cigarette box, then they shoot like that. (Personal interview)

A major player in the "black" film industry was Heyns Films which was identified as a front company for the Department of Information in the revelations which emerged around the Information Scandal in 1978–1979. From the mid-1970s, the Department of Information under the leadership of Minister Connie Mulder and Secretary Eschel Rhoodie instituted a number of secret projects broadly aimed at combating the "world-wide psychological and propaganda onslaught against South Africa" (Rees and Day 1980: 190). The mass media was a vital part of their strategy which included bankrolling election campaigns in the United States and United Kingdom. Film did not escape these enterprising men, and monies were set aside to, firstly, build cinemas for African audiences and, secondly, produce films for Africans. The plan was not only to control the types of films that were distributed and exhibited to black people but also administer the production of films.

The Department of Information argued that African people were major consumers of foreign films and their exposure to American cinema was creating a strong sense of identification with Hollywood heroes. The Department actively sought to counteract this Americanizing influence through the creation of local superheroes such as *Joe Bullet* (1974), who would be portrayed against their "ethnic background." This would improve not only the quality of films for Africans but simultaneously support the government ideology of separate ethnic development (Tomaselli 1989; Paleker 2011a). Film was seen as an ideal medium through which African cultural identity could be fostered. "... the rationalisation was that black films were essentially there to give people a cultural identity and to take their attention off other things" (Interview with filmmaker David Bensusan, Paleker 2011); the other things being the political situation in the country. This limitation to culture and tradition was strictly adhered to by most white filmmakers and even by black directors such as Simon Sabela who argued for portraying "actual life" in order to educate and inform people about those things that need to be "preserved – the traditions that are beautiful" (Deane 1978: 162). Admittedly, Sabela had no creative control over the content of the films which he directed or in which he acted, other than ensuring a degree of cultural authenticity. Sabela was one of the very few Africans directing films, for Heyns Films, as part of the B-Scheme subsidy. As an African though, he could not directly access the subsidy and worked for Heyns Films. Apart from directing, he also starred in many of the films such as *uDeliwe (Deliwe* 1974), *iKati Elimnyama (The Black Cat* 1975), and *The Advocate* (1978).

The films that were produced as part of this "black industry" were largely of the *skiet, skop en donner* (shoot, kick, and beat up) genre, drama, romance, and suspense centered on white conceptions of African traditions, spirituality, and witchcraft. Apart from a handful of films that attempted to subvert and offer oppositional readings of apartheid policies (*My Country My Hat* 1983 and *Mapantsula* 1989 among others), most B-films propagated various apartheid policies in theme and narrative. These, however, were also historically contingent and shifting as apartheid reinvented itself. In the 1970s, for example, a prominent theme was the "return to the homeland." Within these films, the hero (and a limited number of heroines) was afforded the opportunity to come to "white" South Africa, but to ensure success, they had to return to their ethnic homelands. A variation on this was the "crime doesn't pay" morality film in which the city in urban South Africa is represented as a corrupting influence on African people whose self-actualization could best be achieved only in their ethnic homelands. As apartheid readjusted itself to increasing African urbanization in the 1980s, so too did many B-films which now represented African success in urban, "white" South Africa. (For analyses of many of these films, see Paleker 2011a, 2011b.)

Ethnic African cinema under apartheid rule in South Africa was conceived within the ideological, political, economic, and racist imperatives of the apartheid state. Black African people had limited opportunities to creatively control the stories that were told on their behalf. African traditions, symbols, culture, and values were appropriated and reflected back to African audiences through the prism of apartheid ideologies. In view of this, the African "ethnic cinema" that was created was constructed rather differently to what this means in ethnicity scholarship.

The New "Ethnic Film"

Since 1994 and the coming to power of a majority black government under the rule of the ANC, state intervention and support continues, albeit differently formulated and more broadly inclusive. One of the first tasks undertaken by the newly established Ministry of Arts, Culture, Science and Technology in 1995 (since then two separate departments for Arts and Culture and Science and Technology have been created) was to undertake an extensive audit of the state of the South African film industry, with a view to restructuring it entirely.

The new ANC government under the auspices of this new Ministry first commissioned a substantial report on the state of the industry before introducing new mechanisms of state support for the industry. The Film Development Strategy which was compiled and published in 1996 made provision for the establishment of the National Film and Video Foundation. The NFVF was established by an act of parliament, namely, the National Film and Video Foundation Act of 1997 (Botha 2003: 182). The NFVF functions as an agency of the Department of Arts and Culture and is the primary state funding mechanism for the South African film industry. The Foundation's mission and vision is to "work with all stakeholders to support the development and promotion of the South Africa film industry and hopes to create an industry that represents our nation's aspirations and celebrates our diversity through the values of creativity, freedom of expression, entrepreneurship, equitable redress, and collaboration" (www.nfvf.org.za).

The Foundation is thus the official "face" of the South African film industry post-1994. The Foundation, along with industry, represents the South African film industry at international events and festivals. It assists emerging and established filmmakers with financing (limited as it is), sourcing additional funds and with co-financing agreements. In the latter regard, the NFVF has established co-financing agreements with, among others, the United Kingdom, France, Canada, Australia, Ireland, and Germany. Co-financing agreements are of two types; one type is exclusively financial with creative control residing with either signatory to the agreement, and the other type of agreement is based on shared financing and creative control. Other state agencies and departments that fund film include the Department of Trade and Industry and the Industrial Development Corporation. The South African Revenue Service (SARS) also offers tax incentives on income derived from film for both local and co-financed productions.

Despite this, the South African state is by no means the biggest funder of film. Private industry and capital are significant investors in the film industry. Afrikaner capital continues to be a significant role-player in funding. One of these is Naspers, a multinational entertainment and communications company, founded in 1915 as Nasionale Pers (National Press). It is the biggest media conglomerate in South Africa and has enjoyed a mutually beneficial relationship with the former apartheid government. Its subsidiaries M-Net and kykNET, pay-to-view channels, are significant funders of local productions. kykNET (kyk is Afrikaans for watch/view) has emerged as one of the biggest funders of recent Afrikaans-language films such as

Treurgrond (2015), *Modder en Bloed* (*Blood and Glory* 2016), *Vaselinetjie* (2017), and *Stroomop* (Upstream 2018).

Furthermore, kykNET is the biggest funder, along with Afrikaner cultural organization ATKV (Afrikaans Language and Culture Association), of the Afrikaans-language film festival, Silwerskermfees (lit. Silver Screen Festival), which was first hosted in 2010. The festival is a showcase for short films funded by kykNET. The festival screens both English and Afrikaans films, features, shorts, and documentaries, but it remains foremost a platform for showcasing emerging young filmmakers producing Afrikaans-language films (www.kyknet.dstv.com). Endeavors such as these by kykNET can be read against the backdrop of ethnic angst about the erosion of Afrikaner culture and language, as well as against dwindling audience numbers for Afrikaans films.

A 2015 study of ticket purchasing behavior among young Afrikaner audiences (Jordaan et al. 2015) provides useful information as a point of departure for further studies. The study, conducted among young Afrikaner respondents based at an Afrikaans-language university (North West University in Potchefstroom) and Afrikaans school-goers, found that young Afrikaner women were the largest demographic sector attending cinema screenings of Afrikaans films. Among these respondents, the most popular genres were romantic comedies, romance dramas, and action films. The study found that the factors impacting young Afrikaner filmgoers' viewing choices could be ranked from the most important to the least important, these being "proudly Afrikaans', quality facilities, marketing, production credentials and quality film" (Jordan et al. 2015: 198). The findings and recommendations offered by this study suggest a real concern for cultivating a future generation of Afrikaans-language film audience. Recommendations made by these authors range from cinemas offering targeted loyalty incentives to Afrikaans audiences to marketing efforts concentrating on communicating "a message that emphasizes the fact that these films are written by Afrikaans speaking people, tell Afrikaans stories that relate to Afrikaans culture and ultimately contribute to and support the Afrikaans film industry" (Jordaan et al. 2015: 201). What is evident from this is the historical continuity in the deployment of film for propagating Afrikaner cultural nationalism and an ethnic Afrikaner identity. From the 1930s to the present, Afrikaans-language film has served very specific political, cultural, and national interests and not merely or only through the use of the Afrikaans language.

More recent Afrikaans-language films have reprised a number of favorite tropes of historical Afrikaner nationalist cinema; English-Afrikaner tensions, the significance of farm and platteland (rural countryside) to Afrikaner identity, the pioneering and survival instinct of the Afrikaner, and the centrality of faith to Afrikaner identity are among the most important tropes that have been reclaimed by Afrikaans films. *Modder en Bloed* (Else 2016) is a period drama set in the midst of the South African War of 1899–1902 and represents the Boer-Brit struggle. This struggle is represented at the macro and micro level. At the macro level is the war, with a group of Afrikaner prisoners of war held on the island of St. Helena. At the micro level is a battle of wits and wills between the Afrikaner prisoners and their British warders which takes the form of a rugby match between the two groups. A historical irony is the manner in which the sport of rugby, globalized through British imperialism, has evolved into a central signifier of Afrikaner masculinity and Afrikaner leisure time. This film is similar to the 2001 Bollywood historical sports-drama, *Lagaan*, in which cricket features as the marker of honor, survival, and self-hood.

Films such as *Treurgrond* (Roodt 2015), *Platteland* (*Countryside*, Else 2011), and *Pretville* (*Funville*, Korsten 2012) all have as central themes the idea of space and home as significant to Afrikaner identity. Broodryk's (2016) analysis of these films suggests that these films represent Afrikaner nostalgia (for the "good old days" when Afrikaners were firmly rooted in space and time as in *Platteland*), Afrikaner triumphalism (despite political displacement the Afrikaner survival instinct is so strong that Afrikaners can pioneer new places of belonging whether it is in Canada or Australia as in *Pretville*), and Afrikaner victimhood as expressed in *Treurgrond*. The latter film has generated significant controversy not only due to the presence of Steve Hofmeyr (an Afrikaner entertainer and self-identified volk activist) as the protagonist but also in part for entrenching the discourse of "white (Boer) genocide" (Broodryk 2016: 70). The film deals with two contentious issues, namely, land (appropriation) and farm murders; the latter issue has led to the emergence of the white genocide discourse propagated by Afrikaner civil rights organization AfriForum and others.

Films such as *Faan se Trein* (*Faan's Train* 2014), *Saak van Geloof* (*A Case of Faith* 2011), *Roepman* (*Stargazer* 2011), and *Suiderkruis* (*Southern Cross* 2015) cover a range of genres but have as a central theme the importance of Christian belief and faith in the daily life of the Afrikaner (Joynt and Broodryk 2018). In these films, the church and faith are central to Afrikaner survival, redemption, and self-actualization. The idea of redemption through church and faith is important for another reason, as a counter and spiritual palliative for the guilt felt by many Afrikaners (and English speakers) for either direct participation and/or complicity in the atrocities of apartheid, despite the rejection of this guilt by some very conservative Afrikaners. Dan Roodt, the Director of PRAAG (Pro-Afrikaans Action Group), rejects the idea of Afrikaner guilt and would have Afrikaners forget the painstaking excavations and exculpations of the Truth and Reconciliation Commission as outright propaganda that distorted pre-1994 history. For Roodt, forgetting is the necessary precursor to reclaim history unblemished by the TRC revelations (Broodryk 2016: 65). Films such as *Platteland* serve this purpose well in the recreation of 1950s platteland South Africa with an insular Afrikaner community seemingly isolated from the turmoil of the 1950s with forced removals, population registrations, and civil disobedience campaigns. Likewise, films such as *Treurgrond* propagate the idea that without political interference, black and white lived, and can continue to live, in communal harmony on the farm and platteland.

Considering what have been identified as central "markers of Afrikaner identity: 'the presence of the Afrikaans language; the desire and love for land (as epitomised in the farm); a pervasive sense (and accompanying narrative) of survival; a strong sense of family; a sense of political conservatism; and a dominant religious position occupied by Christianity, especially in its Calvinist form" (Combrink in Broodryk 2016: 64), these films represent virtually all of these to varying degrees. And by virtue of the presence of these thematic and narrative elements, these films have been central to entrenching a very specific form of Afrikaner identity and cultural nationalism.

These films can also be read as representing what van der Westhuizen calls an "inward migration," a "wielding of ethnicity (Afrikanerhood) to withdraw from shared national spaces" (van der Westhuizen 2016: 2). In the absence (loss) of the white (Afrikaner) nation-state, alternative spaces (territorial – albeit much reduced such as Orania and Kleinfontein which are exclusive Afrikaner settlements – cultural and celluloid spaces) have become new ethnic sites of enunciation. The aim of this inward migration is community and cultural preservation in service of carving out autonomy in a changed political landscape. This inward migration is by no means shared by all Afrikaners. In fact the majority of Afrikaners have failed to take up the offer to move to the Afrikaans-only settlements at Orania and Kleinfontein, many opting instead to remain in suburbs that are becoming increasing multicultural, if not integrated.

As with the broader community, the Afrikaans-language film industry is likewise bifurcated with many filmmakers self-consciously situating themselves as part of the larger national industry with others choosing to remain within a distinctly "ethnic" industry. One of the ways in which Afrikaners have tried to step outside a cultural nationalist enclave is through strategic "alliances," in film, with especially the Colored Afrikaans-speaking community. These "alliances" translate as narratives that create shared celluloid spaces for Afrikaner and Colored. Films such as *Vaselinetjie* (2017) draw on the historically undeniable reality of miscegenation, much in the tenor of earlier films such as *Fiela se Kind* (*Fiela's Child* 1988). Vaselinetjie, the nickname of the protagonist, is a white girl raised by her Coloured grandparents until she is placed in a white orphanage due to cruel teasing from the Coloured children in the village where she grew up. The film is an adaptation of a novel of the same name, and it deals with issues such as belonging and identity in a society in which identity touchstones have been dislocated. More importantly, as with *Fiela's Child*, the film conveys the idea of a shared heritage between Afrikaner and Coloured, with heritage conceived very narrowly and predominantly in terms of the Afrikaans language.

Conclusion

Ethnic cinema in South Africa, as ethnic cinema more globally, is in a state of flux. In the South Africa context, the meaning, composition, and structure of ethnic cinema have changed dramatically in the last 100 years or so. Since the period of Union in 1910 and into the 1950s when under apartheid rule, a "national" cinema was supported by the National Party government through the establishment of a state subsidy until the early 1990s; ethnic cinema was conceived as a parallel industry to the "national" white industry. This parallel industry was also created by means of a state subsidy introduced in 1972 for the production of films in indigenous African languages. This ethnic, parallel cinema was primarily a white entrepreneurial enterprise in which African cultural symbols, traditions, and values were appropriated by white men and reflected back to African audiences.

The "black film industry" that developed as a result of the B-Scheme subsidy cannot be considered indigenously African in character despite the presence of many Africans working within it, primarily as actors but some also as technical crew members and even a few as directors. This is mainly due to the fact that African people had little power to control production or exhibition of these films. At best, this "black film industry" was a group of white men exploiting an untapped market of African audiences, though there were some exceptions to this also. The "black film industry" was not, however, the outcome of a deliberate intention on the part of the apartheid state to develop a parallel industry but rather the unintended outcome of the B-Scheme. This did not mean that the apartheid state did not see the propaganda and pedagogic value of this industry, but as it has become historically evident, it exploited this opportunity to maximize political profit through various forms of intervention. This self-conscious identity of a black film industry then originated organically from among some of the white people who were involved in producing, distributing, and exhibiting films for African audiences.

Since 1994 the South African film industry has been radically restructured to open up creative and financial opportunities for black people. In keeping with its political objective of fostering a broadly inclusive South African nation-state, the ANC government established state mechanisms to fund, support, and nurture a "national" film industry that reflects the multicultural and multiracial composition of South African society. These mechanisms include a National Film and Video Foundation which is an agency of the national Department of Arts and Culture, the Department of Trade and Industry, the Industrial Development Corporation, and the South African Revenue Services.

But state funding is one component and still minor (given the developmental priorities of the SA state) compared to private capital investment in the film industry. In this regard, Afrikaner private capital continues to play a significant role with Naspers, through its subsidiaries M-Net and kykNET, providing significant funding to established and emerging filmmakers. kykNET in particular is at the forefront of growing and nurturing the Afrikaans-language film industry. It does this through direct financing as well as sponsoring the Silwerskermfees to showcase Afrikaans-language films.

In post-1994 South Africa, the binary of "national" and "ethnic" cinemas has shifted significantly with sectors of the Afrikaans-language industry now occupying the marginal "ethnic" space previously occupied by films for African audiences. This shift has been less the result of a "push" and more a conscious withdrawal or "inward migration" by sectors of Afrikaner society. The film productions emerging from this new ethnic cinema display many of the tropes and discourses of earlier Afrikaner nationalist cinema which supports the idea of Afrikaner aspirations channelled into cultural rather than political nationalism.

Cross-References

▶ Ethno-cultural Symbolism and Group Identity
▶ Historical Memory and Ethnic Myths
▶ State Hegemony and Ethnicity: Fiji's Problematic Colonial Past

References

Bakari I, Cham M (eds) (1992) African experiences of cinema. British Film Institute, London
Beinart W (1994, 2001) Twentieth Century South Africa. Oxford University Press, Oxford
Botha M (2003) Current film policy in South Africa: the establishment of the National Film and Video Foundation of South Africa and its role in the development of a post-apartheid film industry. Communicato 29(1&2):182–198
Broodryk C (2016) Ons sal antwoord op jou roepstem: Steve Hofmeyr and Afrikaner identity in post-apartheid Afrikaans cinema. Communicare 35(1):59–76
Deane DS (1978) Black south Africans: a who's who, 57 profiles of Natal's leading blacks. Oxford University Press, Cape Town
Diawara M (1992) African cinema: politics and culture. Indiana University Press, Bloomington
Hall S (1989) Cultural identity and cinematic representation. Framework: The Journal of Cinema 36:68–81
Jordaan J-M, Botha K, Viviers P-A (2015) Analyzing the ticket purchasing behaviour of younger Afrikaans cinema attendees. South Afr Theatr J 28(2):180–208
Joynt S, Brookryk C (2018) Screening the church: a case study of clergy representation in contemporary Afrikaans cinema. HTS Theol Stud 74:1–8. ISSN: (Online) 2072-8050
Keller Gary D (1995) The Boom in Ethnic Cinema and the Breakthrough in its Analysis. Bilingual Review 20(1):77–89
Lowe C (1991) Buthelezi, Inkatha and the problem of ethnic nationalism in South Africa. In: Brown J et al (eds) History from South Africa: alternative visions and practices. Temple University Press, Philadelphia
Maingard J (2007) South African national cinema. Routledge, London
Nixon R (1994) Homelands, harlem and hollywood: South African culture and the world beyond. Routledge, New York
O'Meara D (1983) Volkskapitalisme: class, capital and ideology in the development of Afrikaner nationalism 1934–1948. Ravan Press, Johannesburg
Paleker G (2010) The B-scheme subsidy and the black film industry in apartheid South Africa, 1972–1990. J Afr Cult Stud 22(1):91–104
Paleker G (2011a) Ethnic films for ethnic homelands: black film and separate development in apartheid South Africa, 1972–1979. South Afr Hist J 63:127–147
Paleker G (2011b) On the town and underworld in South Africa: representations of urban Africans in 'black films'. Afr Hist Rev 43:37–54
Rees M, Day C (1980) Muldergate. Macmillan Press, Johannesburg
Tomaselli K (1989) The cinema of apartheid: race and class in south African films. Routeledge, London
van Coller HP, van Jaarsveld A (2018) The indigenous Afrikaans film: representation as a nationalistic endeavour. Literator: J Lit Crit, Comp Linguistic Lit Stud 39:1–13. ISSN: (Online) 2219–8237
van der Westhuizen C (2016) Afrikaners in post-apartheid South Africa: inward migration and enclave nationalism. HTS: Theol Stud 72:1–9

Multiculturalism and Citizenship in the Netherlands

102

Igor Boog

Contents

Introduction: Multiculturalism and Multicultural Citizenship	1994
Perspectives on National Belonging	1996
National Belonging in the Netherlands: Policies and Debates	1998
Perspectives on Social Equality	2001
Social Equality in the Netherlands: Policies and Debates	2004
Perspectives on Cultural Distinctiveness	2005
Cultural Distinctiveness in the Netherlands: Policies and Debates	2007
Conclusion	2009
Cross-References	2011
References	2011

Abstract

In this chapter, it is argued that to understand the current debates about cultural diversity in the Netherlands, several historical developments have to be taken into account. One development is the contradictory conception of the nation-state, which includes inclusive as well as exclusive criteria for national belonging. Another development is the changing pattern of migration, resulting in an increase of cultural diversity in Dutch society. Finally, the debates take place in the context of the human rights revolution since World War II, in which historical hierarchies are being challenged by emphasizing social equality on various grounds, including ethnic background, gender, and sexual orientation. Part of this human rights revolution is the ideology of multiculturalism, which generally stresses liberal values including social cohesion and national belonging, and social equality of all groups in society. The most defining aspect of multiculturalism is the recognition of cultural or religious distinctiveness of ethnic and

I. Boog (✉)
Institute of Cultural Anthropology and Development Sociology, Leiden University, Leiden, The Netherlands
e-mail: i.boog@fsw.leidenuniv.nl

© The Author(s), under exclusive license to Springer Nature Singapore Pte Ltd. 2019
S. Ratuva (ed.), *The Palgrave Handbook of Ethnicity*,
https://doi.org/10.1007/978-981-13-2898-5_139

cultural groups in society, which is considered to be essential to achieve social cohesion and social equality. In the 1990s and 2000s, this recognition was increasingly criticized in the Netherlands, with mostly right-wing politicians considering certain norms and values of immigrants, especially Muslims, to be incompatible with the norms and values of Dutch natives. In the 2000s, Dutch parliament debated several proposals to prohibit certain cultural or religious expressions of Muslims in the Netherlands, despite the Dutch interpretation of freedom of religion. Currently, this culturalization of citizenship is still evident, mostly from views and statements of right-wing populist and ultra-orthodox Christian politicians.

Keywords
Citizenship · Multicultural citizenship · Multiculturalism · National belonging · Social equality

Introduction: Multiculturalism and Multicultural Citizenship

Diversity in society has become an almost inescapable topic in public, political, and scientific debates in the Netherlands and other Western European countries. These debates often concern cultural and ethnic diversity resulting from immigration since World War II. A central topic in these debates is the cultural distinctiveness of immigrants: whether certain practices, norms, and values of immigrants are compatible with the norms and values of the immigrant receiving societies, a question that in the last three decades has been increasingly asked about Muslim immigrants.

An example is the debate about whether Muslim immigrants should be allowed to wear a headscarf in school or at work. Another example is the discussion whether multiple citizenship and transnational ties of immigrants undermine their loyalty to the nation-state. In more general terms, the relevance of cultural boundaries of national belonging is increasingly being discussed. Scholars in the Netherlands refer to this process as a culturalization of citizenship, "in which emotions, feelings, norms and values, symbols and traditions (including religion) come to play a pivotal role in defining what can be expected of a Dutch citizen" (Duyvendak 2011: 81).

These debates are accompanied by changing discussions, attitudes, policies, and regulations regarding social equality. Since the 1960s, the Netherlands and many other countries developed a wide range of equality policies and antidiscrimination legislation, following United Nations conventions such as the International Convention on the Elimination of All Forms of Racial Discrimination (ICERD) which came into force in 1969. Scientific studies and political debates increasingly paid attention to the questions of how to prevent discrimination of and achieve social equality for citizens with various group characteristics, including those with a migrant background.

A key concept in the contemporary debates about cultural and ethnic diversity is "multiculturalism." This concept, in use since the 1960s (Kymlicka 2012: 5), refers to specific responses – policies or ideologies – to diversity in society. While there are many different interpretations of this concept, there are three aspects or values that are considered fundamental by most proponents of multiculturalism. These aspects include national belonging (or social cohesion), social equality, and the *recognition* of cultural distinctiveness. The importance attached to specifically these values indicates that most proponents of multiculturalism advocate a specific *liberal* form of multiculturalism (Kymlicka 2012, 2014; Modood 2010).

These three aspects are closely related to fundamental debates on citizenship and are therefore by some authors referred to as dimensions of "multicultural citizenship" (Boog 2014; Modood 2010). The first aspect is the importance that is attached to social cohesion and national belonging in society. The question here is whether citizens of various ethnic and cultural backgrounds are recognized as full members of the national group. In diversity debates, it is questioned, for example, whether "integration" of immigrant citizens is possible while simultaneously respecting (elements of) their cultural or religious distinctiveness. This relates to a fundamental issue in debates on citizenship, as the concept of citizenship in modern nation-states always "entails a tension between inclusion and exclusion" of individuals (Bloemraad et al. 2008: 155).

The second aspect of multiculturalism is the importance attached to non-discrimination principles that concern social equality of the various groups in society, not only on grounds of race or ethnic background but also on grounds such as gender and sexual orientation. This, of course, relates to the fact that legal citizenship in Western countries entails the right to equality, which is expressed in regulations and policies regarding equal treatment and nondiscrimination.

These first two aspects are closely related to the third and most defining aspect of multiculturalism, which is the recognition of cultural distinctiveness of the various groups in society. Proponents of multiculturalism argue that this recognition of cultural distinctions, but also of other distinctions such as gender and sexual orientation, is essential to achieve social cohesion and equality (Parekh 2000). An important reason for this recognition is, according to these authors, that the state and other institutions may strive for "neutrality" and being "difference-blind" but are always susceptible to an explicit or implicit bias towards the majority group.

These aspects and their interrelationships are discussed in more depth in the next sections. The primary focus in this chapter is on the multiculturalism debates in the Netherlands. Before the discussions of these debates below, analytical perspectives will be provided on the concepts used. This chapter is largely based on research carried out in the period 2010–2014, and on courses on "race" and diversity taught between 2015 and 2018 at Leiden University. For a more extensive discussion of the issues covered in this chapter, see Boog (2014).

It is important to note that various terms are and have been used in the Netherlands to describe immigrants and Dutch citizens of various origins. In this chapter, the terms "native Dutch" and "immigrants" or "immigrants and their descendants" will be used. Of course, in practice, many so-called "native Dutch" are also descendants of immigrants. In this chapter, however, following similar definitions in use by Statistics Netherlands (CBS) and in the policies and debates that will be discussed, the term native is taken to mean that both parents are born in the Netherlands, while the term immigrant indicates that at least one parent was born outside the Netherlands.

Perspectives on National Belonging

Individuals who possess the legal status of a nation-state's citizenship legally belong to this nation-state's national group. However, citizens of this nation-state can still disagree about who of their fellow citizens *fully* belongs to their national group, disagreements that potentially have negative effects on social cohesion. An example is the use of the term "foreigners" to describe immigrants and their descendants, even those who have full legal citizenship. Furthermore, in the Netherlands and other Western European countries, discussions about national identity that have flared up since the 2000s show that some citizens are of the opinion that fellow citizens who have a certain immigrant background cannot be fully part of their national group. An example is the use of arguments in which it is claimed that a certain national identity is essentially "Judeo-Christian," a claim that excludes Muslim citizens from being accepted as a full member of the national group.

Importantly, these views on national belonging are also expressed in terms of citizen rights. As will become clear in the next sections, citizens can disagree in their views on to what extent certain citizen rights, such as freedom of religion, should be upheld equally for both "natives" and naturalized immigrants and their descendants.

These disagreements about who fully belongs to the national group illustrate that views on belonging are socially constructed and therefore dynamic. In other words, to understand the issues of national belonging and social cohesion as an aspect of responses to immigration and the resulting cultural diversity in a nation-state, the nation itself should be studied as a social construct. (On social construction, see, for example, Brubaker 2004; Vera 2006.)

Categories such as the nation, ethnicity and race are social constructs that are being reproduced (and thus also changed) by individuals in daily life (Brubaker 2004; Anderson 1991). Research has shown that individuals and groups categorize themselves and others as part of such categories, a process that is often referred to as social categorization (Tajfel 1981). The daily reproduction of these categories or groups includes the maintenance of group boundaries (Barth 1969) and negotiations about the importance of these boundaries, or criteria, for belonging to a certain group.

These social categorizations do not just provide labels for groups. They also have cultural and emotional dimensions, often called stereotypes: expectations and perceptions regarding the norms and behavior of individuals who are categorized as member of a certain group. Research has shown that individuals tend to favor their own group over other groups, and that they tend to overestimate both the differences between groups and the homogeneity of groups they do not belong to as well (Brubaker 2004).

Importantly, the process of categorization is an intervention; it has effects on people's lives. These interventions can be useful; categories are essential tools to bring order in social life. But it is also clear that categorization and stereotyping can have unwanted effects, such as discrimination (discussed in the next section), identity conflicts, and a lower sense of belonging (Huynh et al. 2011). More generally, categories can serve, and are constructed, to justify and maintain social hierarchies. History provides an abundance of examples, such as denying women voting rights and the use of racial categories to justify colonialism.

Categories have a history of (social) construction, as they are socially being reproduced and changed. Understanding the history of a category is important when analyzing its contemporary uses. Thus, aspects of contemporary Western European discussions and policies regarding multiculturalism and national belonging can be traced back to the "contradictory 19th-century conception of the modern nation-state" (Stolcke 1995: 12). Two criteria for national belonging were, and still are, influential in this conception. One stressing the free choice of individuals to live together as citizens in a nation-state, and the other stressing the importance of all citizens sharing a common ethnic or cultural heritage. The first criterion is inclusive, while the second is an example of an exclusive boundary as it does deny full membership of citizens with a different ethnic or cultural background. In studies of nationalism, a similar distinction is often made between inclusive "civic nationalism" and exclusive "ethnic nationalism" (see Bakke 2000 for a discussion).

Several scholars have analyzed the connection between ethnic nationalism and racism, both constructing exclusive boundaries by invoking ideas about common ethnic or racial origins and heritage (Balibar and Wallerstein 1991; Lentin 2004). These ideas about ethnic and racial origins of the nation, a clear example of which is twentieth century Nazism, were influential in the nineteenth century formation of modern nation-states and can be traced back to imperialist colonialism (Arendt 1951; Foucault 1980).

While ideas about race and social equality have changed considerably since World War II, the idea that a nation is defined by a common cultural heritage of its citizens – an exclusive boundary – is very much alive in contemporary debates about multiculturalism and national belonging in Western Europe. Culture, norms, and values of immigrants and their descendants are considered by some to be incompatible with those of the immigrant receiving societies. The above mentioned claim about the "Judeo-Christian" essence of (Western European) national identities is a clear example. The contemporary use of such ideas to exclude citizens with a (certain) migration background from being accepted as full members the national group has been compared to the nineteenth century mix of ethnic nationalism and racism. While some authors argue that the contemporary rhetoric of exclusion is to an important extent different from "traditional racism" (e.g., Stolcke 1995), others stress the similarities and the continuity of racism and argue that the category "culture" is replacing the category "race" in reifications of differences between human groups (e.g., Lentin 2000, also see Visweswaran 1998).

The contemporary emphasis on the cultural distinctiveness of immigrants in Western Europe is reflected in debates about the integration of immigrants and their descendants. The concept of integration essentially refers to the process of change elicited by migration to a different society. This process consists of various aspects, including changes in immigrants' educational status and their position in the labor market, and more complex issues such as immigrants' social relationships with "natives," discrimination, and real or perceived differences between their norms and values and those of "natives" (Erdal and Oeppen 2013). Governments in Western Europe have developed integration policies, for example, to further equal treatment and equal opportunities for immigrants and their descendants (Penninx 2005). However, in recent years, integration policies in several European countries have been amended to also include knowledge of norms and values of the receiving society.

The cultural distinctiveness of immigrants has also been linked to their loyalty to the nation-state. Some authors argue that immigrants' transnational ties and multiple citizenship can lead to multiple loyalties immigrants might have to their ethnic groups and countries of origin, and that such loyalties can undermine or conflict with their loyalty to the nation-state (e.g., Huntington 2004). However, as other authors point out, every citizen has multiple loyalties (for example to their multinational employer, their family) which can potentially conflict with his or her loyalty to the nation-state. As Baron (2009: 1040) suggests, this clash of loyalties does not differ from "the usual conflict of commitments that characterize politics." Importantly, when the accusation of conflicting loyalties is exclusively directed at immigrants, it creates an exclusive boundary, denying that immigrants can be full members of the national group.

National Belonging in the Netherlands: Policies and Debates

As mentioned in the section "Introduction," contemporary discussions about multiculturalism started after World War II. This is certainly the case in the Netherlands. While the Netherlands has always been an immigration country, relatively few immigrants settled in the Netherlands between 1850 and 1940. Their number and ethnic and cultural diversity increased again after 1945, as a result of decolonization, the recruitment of labor migrants and their subsequent family reunification in the 1970s and 1980s, and, mostly since the 1980s, asylum migration (Lucassen and Lucassen 2011).

The percentage of "individuals with a migration background," a term used by Statistics Netherlands (CBS) to designate individuals of whom at least one parent has been born outside the Netherlands, increased from 9% of the Dutch population in 1972 to 22.6% in 2017. This percentage includes "individuals with a non-Western migration background" (12.7% of the Dutch population in 2017): those of whom at least one parent was born in Turkey or on the continents of Africa, South America, or Asia (excluding Japan and former colony Indonesia) (CBS Statline). Part of these non-Western immigrants are Muslims, mainly originating from Turkey and Morocco, who constituted around 5% of the Dutch population in 2015 ("De religieuze kaart van Nederland, 2010–2015," CBS 2016).

Since the 1980s, the debates about immigrants and cultural diversity in the Netherlands have become increasingly politicized. In this period, both the national and local governments have developed policies designed to integrate immigrants and their descendants, policies that address national belonging, multiple citizenship, social equality, and cultural distinctiveness. Key developments and changes in these debates and policies will be discussed below (national belonging and multiple citizenship) and in the following sections (social equality and cultural distinctiveness).

Before 1980, the Dutch government did not see the need to develop structural policies for immigrant integration. Immigrants from former Dutch colonies were seen as repatriates, and the presence of individuals who since the 1950s came to the Netherlands as labor immigrants – guest workers as they were called then – was seen as temporary. This changed in the 1970s, when it became clear that many labor immigrants wanted to remain in the Netherlands. The national government developed its first integration policy, known as the Ethnic Minorities Policy. The goals of this policy were not limited to equality and participation of immigrants but also included sociocultural emancipation which was considered necessary for the improvement of their socioeconomic position and which could prevent identity conflicts (Penninx 2005). In the late 1980s and the 1990s, this policy was increasingly criticized for including the goal of sociocultural emancipation, and critics called for the focus to be limited to the socioeconomic position of immigrants and their descendants. Consequently, in 1994, the government presented a new national integration policy with "civic integration" as the main goal. It stressed the obligation of all citizens, including immigrants, to learn the Dutch language and acquire basic knowledge of Dutch society.

The debates and political discourse changed again around the year 2000. Several authors and politicians claimed that the integration of immigrants had failed. More specifically, they argued that the social cohesion of Dutch society was being threatened because certain norms and values of immigrants and their descendants, especially those of Muslims, are not compatible with those of the "native" Dutch. After the year 2000, these ideas were combined in a political discourse by right-wing populist politician Pim Fortuyn, and important parts of this discourse were appropriated by other political parties (Penninx 2005; Prins 2004). The culturalization of citizenship became mainstream, a process, already referred to in the introduction of this chapter, "in which emotions, feelings, norms and values, symbols and traditions (including religion) come to play a pivotal role in defining what can be expected of a Dutch citizen" (Duyvendak 2011: 81). In other words, exclusive boundaries for national belonging were once again stressed, by emphasizing the idea that the Dutch nation is defined by a common cultural heritage.

In the policy document that outlined the once again revised national integration policy in 2003, the government problematized the social and cultural distance between Dutch natives and immigrants and their descendants. The government stressed the importance of not just learning the Dutch language but "basic Dutch norms" as well (Tweede Kamer 2003–2004, Brief Integratiebeleid Nieuwe Stijl, 29,203, nr. 1). Furthermore, to strengthen social cohesion, several politicians thought it necessary to focus on Dutch national identity. Especially politicians on the right of the political spectrum argued that Dutch norms and values had to be protected by recognizing that there is one fundamental Dutch national identity, which is, according to some of those politicians, essentially based on Christian, Jewish, or humanist values. In this context, a national canon of Dutch history was compiled, which became part of school curricula in 2010. The use of this canon has been criticized, however, because it limits the debate on interpretations of Dutch history. Although the authors of the canon have stressed that national identity is a dynamic social construction (WRR 2007), it "just gives one story about what the Netherlands is" (Kremer 2013: 10).

In the same period, the use of the term *allochthon* was debated, a term used to describe Dutch citizens of whom at least one parent was born outside the Netherlands. This term means "other" or "not from here," and in 2004, several members of Parliament argued that the term was increasingly used to suggest that those who are designated as such do not fully belong in Dutch society. Since then, several municipalities and Statistics Netherlands (CBS) have decided to stop using the term. However, some politicians on the right of the political spectrum proposed instead to extend the definition and the use of the term. They argued that immigrants' grandchildren, of whom both parents are born in the Netherlands, should also be designated as *allochthon*, thereby trying to make the criteria for national belonging more exclusive.

The culturalization of Dutch citizenship is also evident from debates on the issue of multiple citizenship. While settled immigrants were provided with easier access to Dutch citizenship in the 1980s and the requirement that applicants for Dutch citizenship renounce their original citizenship was abolished in 1991, Dutch citizenship laws became more restrictive after 1997. Politicians on the right of the political spectrum then doubted the commitment to the Netherlands of immigrants who retained their original citizenship. Once again, immigrants who applied for naturalization officially had to renounce their original citizenship, unless this was impossible, for example, when their countries of origin did not allow such renunciation. In the 2000s, Dutch politicians who opposed multiple citizenship considered it to be a possible symptom of failed integration, which could undermine an immigrants' loyalty to the nation-state. Interestingly, these debates were mainly focused on Muslim immigrants who held multiple citizenship, indicating that their ethnic, cultural, or religious backgrounds were also assumed to undermine their loyalty to the nation-state (De Hart 2005). Currently (as of 2018), the Dutch government still requires applicants for citizenship to renounce their original citizenship, despite studies by government advisory bodies that denied clear relationships between multiple citizenship on the one hand and integration and loyalty to the nation-state on the other (WRR 2007; ACVZ 2008).

Finally, scholars have shown that the discussions about radicalization and terrorism in the last few decades can contribute to negative views of Muslims and a culturalization of citizenship in general. Such discussions have led to a "popular assumption that Islam is to 'blame' for the violence of individuals" and to a binary view of Muslims being either radical or moderate (Brown 2018). This binary view is an example of a singular and therefore misleading view of identity, which can lead to further polarization (Sen 2006).

In recent years, the Dutch governments have in their policy documents on integration mostly focused on "civic integration." The latest policy document published in 2018, for example, mostly stresses the importance of learning the Dutch language and participation on the labor market. However, the culturalization of citizenship is still evident from political and public debates. Politicians representing the PVV (the right-wing populist Party for Freedom), led by parliamentarian Geert Wilders, claim that Islam is a threat to Dutch society, and the SGP (ultra-orthodox Protestant Reformed Political Party) wants to limit manifestations of "cultures and religions that do not belong in Dutch society" (SGP Electoral program of 2012). Furthermore, various statements by Thierry Baudet, leader of the FvD (the right-wing populist Forum for Democracy), suggest that he has an exclusive, ethnic nationalist conception of Dutch national belonging. In an interview in 2015, for example, he said that he wanted Europe to remain "predominantly white and culturally as it is" (Radio AmsterdamFM, September 17, 2015), and in an election meeting on March 8, 2017, he claimed that "our elite is busy diluting [Dutch society] homeopathically" by allowing immigrants and refugees to settle in the Dutch nation-state.

As mentioned above, the culturalization of citizenship is not just evident from such claims by right-wing populist or ultra-orthodox politicians. Since the early 2000s, politicians representing other parties have appropriated parts of the culturalization discourse. Stef Blok, as Minister of Foreign Affairs, claimed in the summer of 2018 that he didn't know of any peaceful multiethnic, multicultural society. To some, this came as a surprise, as Blok, member of the VVD (the right-wing liberal People's Party for Freedom and Democracy), currently the largest party in Dutch parliament and part of the government coalition, chaired a parliamentary research committee that in 2004 concluded that the process of integration of "many immigrants has been fully or at least partially successful" (Blok Commission 2004: 105).

Perspectives on Social Equality

After World War II, and partly in reaction to it, attitudes regarding social equality changed, as part of what has been described as a human rights revolution (Kymlicka 2012). UNESCO started initiatives aiming at condemning racism by educating people about scientific insights concerning "race." In 1965, the United Nations adopted the International Convention on the Elimination of All Forms of Racial Discrimination (ICERD). After the ICERD came into force in 1969, many countries, including the Netherlands, developed a wide range of equality policies and anti-discrimination legislation. The concept of "race" was increasingly seen as a social construction rather than as a biological reality. This was reflected in equality policies and legislation, in which the race concept is generally used as a legal term that refers to distinctions made in social life on the basis of *perceived* group characteristics, including skin color and ethnic background.

The debates about multiculturalism that started in the 1960s can also be seen as part of this human rights revolution. Proponents of (liberal) multiculturalism stress the importance of social equality of the various groups in society, not only on grounds of race or ethnic background but also on grounds such as gender and sexual orientation (Kymlicka 2012; Modood 2010). The connection between the issues of national belonging and social equality is clear; discrimination of citizens on the basis of their race, ethnicity, gender, or other for citizenship irrelevant group characteristics implies that these individuals are not being accepted as full citizens or equal members of the national group.

To understand the debates about equality policies, it is important to distinguish between two types of equality: formal equality and substantive equality of opportunity. Formal equality refers to the ideal that all persons should be treated equally in equal circumstances, a principle that is laid down in the law of many countries. In the Netherlands, for example, Article 1 of the Constitution stipulates that "All persons in the Netherlands shall be treated equally in equal circumstances. Discrimination on the grounds of religion, belief, political opinion, race, or sex, or on any ground whatsoever shall not be permitted." However, the act of equal treatment does not guarantee equality of opportunity, as the latter also requires equal starting conditions. Unequal starting conditions can be the result of historical processes of discrimination, resulting in disadvantages for certain groups. They can also be the result of processes that are still current, such as the recruiting of new employees through informal social networks to which certain groups do not have equal access – a practice known as nepotism. The concept of equality that includes measures to overcome such limitations and to level the playing field is known as substantive equality of opportunity. These measures are referred to as positive action or affirmative action, and more recently, "diversity policies" (cf. Ahmed 2007).

In Western European countries, including the Netherlands, various policies and regulations have been developed to achieve both formal equality and substantive equality of opportunity for all citizens. Specific attention has been and still is paid to disadvantaged groups, including women and migrants with diverse ethnic and cultural backgrounds. These efforts include policies designed to assist immigrant integration, positive action, diversity policies, and measures and regulations to combat and prevent prejudice and discrimination.

Discrimination is the most widely discussed obstacle to social equality. It refers to behavior, actions, policies, or structures which in a specific context might result in a relative disadvantage for members of groups whose group characteristics are irrelevant in that context. As such, discrimination, in a legal sense, can be defined as a prohibited form of unequal treatment. Despite the above mentioned human rights revolution after World War II, empirical studies indicate that discrimination is still prevalent and persistent, even in countries where there is strong support for the principle of formal equality (Bobo and Fox 2003; Pager and Shepherd 2008; Havinga 2002; Andriessen et al. 2012).

Several sets of scientific theories address this persistence. (For a more extensive discussion of some of these theories, see Bobo and Fox 2003.) One set of theories is based on research which indicates that discriminatory behavior is not confined to individuals who have an explicit ideology that can be used to justify inequality or discrimination, such as racism or sexism. Unequal treatment is a consequence of social categorization and accompanying stereotypes and prejudice. As described in the previous section, individuals tend to overestimate the differences between social categories and underestimate the differences between individuals within their own social category. This leads to bias which implies, "reacting to a person on the basis of perceived membership in a single human category, ignoring other category memberships and other personal attributes" and can be described as, "a narrow, potentially erroneous reaction, compared with individuated impressions formed from personal details" (Fiske 2002: 123). Biases underlie stereotypes, prejudice, ethnocentrism, discrimination, and unequal treatment in general.

Another set of theories explains discrimination as a consequence of conflicting group interests, where bias originates when people perceive a threat to their own group. This threat can emerge when in the perception of "natives" their jobs are being taken by immigrants, or that traditional values are threatened (Fiske 2002: 127). Moreover, dominant groups among whose members these biases originate, "develop and propagate ideologies that maintain and even legitimize their higher social status" (Bobo and Fox 2003: 323), such as racism and sexism.

Bobo and Fox (2003) also discuss how members of majority groups can oppose equality policies on grounds of fairness or individualism, and not because of racist or sexist ideas. Some people, for example, oppose positive action because they think it implies reverse discrimination or because they think the government should not interfere in issues of inequality and discrimination.

The persistence of discrimination can also be explained by the accumulation of its effects (Pager and Shepherd 2008: 199) and the fact that it is maintained by feedback effects between social domains (Reskin 2012: 31). A disadvantage in one domain, for example, the level of prosperity of the neighborhood one lives in, can lead to relative disadvantages in other domains, such as education, which in its turn leads to a lower level of income. Moreover, relatively high unemployment rates in a specific group can lead to the negative stereotype that its members are unwilling to work. Discrimination then occurs when, on the basis of this stereotype, employers refrain from employing members of this group. This implies a self-fulfilling prophecy and an accumulation of disadvantage. Such self-fulfilling prophesies show that inequality itself can cause and maintain discrimination and consequently, inequality.

Another reason for the limited effectiveness of the equal treatment principle is that it does not directly address the problem of unequal opportunities. Because of this, in various countries, measures for positive action (or affirmative action, as similar measures are called in the United States) have been introduced. These measures include outreach efforts, for example, by advertising a vacancy in such a way that it reaches all groups in society, instead of exclusively using informal networks to recruit employees. Other such measures are used to give preference to a member of a disadvantaged group in application procedures, usually under the condition that his or her qualifications are at least equal to those of other qualified candidates. In recent years, similar policies aimed at leveling the playing field and creating equal opportunities (in equal circumstances) are often referred to as "diversity policies" (Ahmed 2007).

Social Equality in the Netherlands: Policies and Debates

Considering the extent of the Dutch equality policies and regulations, the Netherlands has been called "Europe's champion of anti-discrimination policy" (Joppke 2007: 260). And indeed, the Netherlands has developed a wide range of such policies, with the backing of wide political support across the political spectrum (Blok Commission 2004).

Following the Dutch acceptance of the International Convention on the Elimination of All Forms of Racial Discrimination (ICERD, see above), in 1971, the Dutch Penal Code was adapted to include specific provisions against racial discrimination. In 1983, Article 1 of the Dutch Constitution was adapted to include the prohibition of discrimination. This chapter was elaborated in more detail in the Equal Treatment Act (ETA) of 1994, by which various forms of discrimination in various social domains were prohibited. The regulations that have been developed did not only concern social equality of ethnic and cultural minorities but also social equality on grounds such as gender, sexual orientation, age, and disability.

Apart from the development of legislation, since the 1980s, equality policies have been developed by the national and local governments and by various organizations as well. As mentioned in the previous section, one of the goals of the national integration policy in the 1980s was social equality, and discrimination was considered to be a main obstacle to integration. To prevent (by creating awareness) and combat discrimination, codes of conduct in organizations have been established in various sectors, and the national government adopted a law in 2010 that requires all municipalities to provide their residents with access to a local office that is able to handle complaints of discrimination.

In addition, the Dutch government, municipalities, and organizations have implemented a limited range of measures for positive action. Between 1994 and 2003, for example, organizations were obliged to publicly monitor the representation of ethnic minorities among their employees. However, one of the most widely discussed of these measures is preferential treatment, which is legally allowed for women, ethnic minorities, and the disabled. This means that preference can be given to an applicant (for example, for a job or a promotion) who belongs to one of these groups but only when it is clear that this group is in a disadvantaged position in the specific application procedure and only when the applicants' qualifications are at least equal to those of other qualified candidates. These measures for positive action have been and still are controversial. Many employers doubt the beneficial effects and considered preferential treatment to be unfair. Members of ethnic minority groups fear the risk of stigmatization; they did not want to be known as the employee who got the job because of his or her ethnic background (Glastra et al. 1998; Schaafsma 2006). Since the early 2000s, no nationwide measures for positive action have been implemented. However, some organizations have developed the so-called "diversity policies" with the same goals: actively promoting the representation of various groups in organizations, to further the ideal of social equality (cf. Ahmed 2007).

Despite this development of legislation and policies, the problem of inequality is persistent. While statistics show that immigrants and their descendants are making clear progress in education and on the labor market, their unemployment rate remains disproportionally high. Research indicates that this is at least partly caused by discrimination (Andriessen et al. 2012). Apart from the explanations for the persistence of discrimination discussed in the first part of this section, research in the Netherlands has shown that the effectiveness of the existing antidiscrimination legislation is limited (Havinga 2002). One reason is that the enforcement of this legislation depends principally on individuals who feel discriminated against to take action. However, victims of discrimination are sometimes reluctant to step forward for fear of escalation or retaliation (cf. Sechrist et al. 2004). Research also shows that some individuals do not recognize or do not want to admit that they are being discriminated against (Andriessen et al. 2007; Crosby et al. 2003), or, instead of lodging a complaint, they adapt their behavior to avoid further discrimination (Andriessen et al. 2007).

The difficulty in overcoming inequality and discrimination is just one of the indications that the integration of immigrants and their descendants is a process that takes time. The fact that integration is a process was clearly recognized by the already mentioned research committee established by the Dutch parliament to investigate the effects of the national integration policies in the beginning of the 2000s. In its findings, published in 2004, the socioeconomic progress of immigrants and their descendants was recognized, and it was concluded that the integration of "many immigrants has been fully or at least partially successful" (Blok Commission 2004: 105). However, those politicians who claimed that integration had failed (see above), criticized the commission for not paying enough attention to the alleged problematic norms and values of (specifically Muslim) immigrants (Duyvendak and Scholten 2012).

The mainstreaming of the culturalization of citizenship around the year 2000 appears not to have had much direct effect on the wide political support for antidiscrimination efforts. Only a few right-wing populist politicians, including Fortuyn and Wilders, have called for the abolition of Article 1 of the Constitution, essentially because they claimed that they were prevented from criticizing Islam by the principle of equal treatment (as reported in the Dutch daily "De Volkskrant" on February 9, 2002, and March 21, 2006). On the other hand, proponents of multiculturalism would argue that the culturalization of citizenship can hinder social equality, for example, by causing bias and discrimination (see above). In the next section, the culturalization of citizenship will be discussed in more detail.

Perspectives on Cultural Distinctiveness

The contemporary debates about multiculturalism that started in the 1960s are grounded in the above described human rights revolution after World War II (Kymlicka 2012). The most defining aspect of contemporary multiculturalism is the recognition of (cultural) distinctiveness of the various groups in society. Without this recognition, proponents of multiculturalism argue, it is not possible to achieve social cohesion and social equality for all groups in society (Parekh 2000). A Muslim citizen, for example, might not be accepted as a full member of the national group when it is claimed that the national group is defined by a "Judeo-Christian" heritage. Furthermore, when a citizen is denied employment because she is wearing an Islamic headscarf, a cultural and religious distinction, this can amount to discrimination. In short, while organizations and institutions, including the state, may strive for neutrality and being "difference-blind," they are always susceptible to an explicit or implicit bias towards the majority group. Opponents of multiculturalism, however, argue that the recognition of cultural distinctiveness can hinder immigrants' integration or warn that a formal recognition is incompatible with the neutrality of the state.

Contemporary debates on cultural distinctiveness, in the Netherlands but also in other Western European countries, primarily concern religious practices, norms, and values of Muslim immigrants and their descendants (Maliepaard and Phalet 2012). Therefore, the discussion of the regulations, debates, and views on this subject in Dutch society will focus on the perceived incompatibility between Dutch norms and values and the norms and values embraced by Muslim immigrants.

The most discussed argument against multiculturalism is that the recognition of cultural (or religious) distinctiveness hinders immigrant integration. Opponents of multiculturalism claim that this recognition does not incentivize immigrants and their descendants to learn the language of the host country or to develop interethnic contacts (e.g., Koopmans et al. 2005), that it prevents them from developing a sense of national belonging (e.g., Barry 2002) or that it can undermine their loyalty to the nation-state (see above). Furthermore, multiculturalism is seen as incompatible with the ideal of social equality, as it can lead to the preservation of certain immigrants' norms and values which encourage the unequal treatment of women or individuals who do not identify as heterosexual. More generally, it is argued that recognition of cultural distinctiveness can lead to an emphasis of differences and even to a reification of cultural or religious groups, which can result in segregation, conflicts, and discrimination (e.g., Barry 2002).

However, other authors have pointed out that it is often unclear how these opponents define "multiculturalism" (Kymlicka 2012, 2014; Pakulski and Markowski 2014). In the Netherlands, for example, opponents have criticized policies which they label "multicultural," even though these policies clearly did not fit the qualification (Duyvendak and Scholten 2012). The criticism of opponents often appears to be directed at a caricaturish model of multiculturalism (Kymlicka 2012) which does not imply the *recognition* of cultural distinctiveness but rather the *preservation* of cultural identities. Most multicultural policies can, however, be characterized as *liberal*, implying *recognition* of cultural distinctiveness (Kymlicka 2014). Where an emphasis on the *preservation* of cultural identities can understandably lead to concerns about essentializing identities, obstacles to integration, and a process of segregation (for a discussion, see Kymlicka 2014), the *recognition* of cultural distinctiveness does not preclude cultural change or the adherence to legal principles of equal treatment and is necessary to achieve social cohesion and citizen equality, as the examples in the beginning of this section illustrate. In the overview of the political debates in the Netherlands below, the meaning and possible implementation of the *recognition* of cultural or religious distinctiveness will be discussed in more detail.

Debates about multiculturalism do not only suffer unclear definitions or the use of caricaturish models. They are also mostly theoretical and hypothetical. So far, there seems to be no strong empirical evidence for the hypothesis that multicultural policies hinder the process of social and political inclusion and political engagement of immigrants (Wright and Bloemraad 2012). This is not surprising, as the process of immigrant integration is influenced by a wide range of factors, government policies being just one element among many. This situation complicates empirical comparisons between the effects of policies which are multicultural and policies which are not.

Cultural Distinctiveness in the Netherlands: Policies and Debates

As mentioned, the debates on multiculturalism in the Netherlands have in the last decades increasingly concentrated on cultural and religious practices of Muslim immigrants and their descendants. Proponents of multiculturalism argue for a combination of social equality and recognition of cultural and religious distinctiveness, while opponents of multiculturalism often argue for prohibiting certain religious practices or manifestations.

These debates take place in a legal context: both freedom of religion and freedom of education are enshrined in the Dutch Constitution. Where freedom of religion implies the legal protection of the observance of religious practices and expressions of religious convictions, the Dutch principle of freedom of education guarantees denominational schools the same funding conditions, rights, and duties as public secular schools. The latter freedom is an example of the Dutch system of neutrality of the state in religious affairs, or, in other words, church-state relations. In this system, anyone is allowed to express his or her religious identity in the public sphere, and every citizen enjoys equal rights to obtain state support for religious and cultural activities (Shadid and Van Koningsveld 1995). Therefore, it can be argued that the Dutch state neutrality implies formal recognition of religious and cultural distinctiveness.

As discussed in the above section about national belonging, the cultural or religious distinctiveness of immigrants and their descendants was not seen as an obstacle to integration in the first national integration policies the Dutch government devised in the 1980s. Rather, sociocultural emancipation was considered to have positive effects on the integration process. Much later, in the debates about the perceived failure of multiculturalism that started in the 1990s, it has been claimed that the integration policies of the 1980s had failed because these policies emphasized the importance of the *preservation* of the cultural identities of immigrants, resulting in segregation and unsurmountable differences between groups with conflicting norms and values. However, this criticism is not correct. The national integration policies in the 1980s were based on the assumption that the *recognition* of cultural identities is necessary to achieve social cohesion and social equality (cf. Duyvendak and Scholten 2012; Vink 2007). Moreover, these integration policies were implemented in a context of Dutch pillarization, a development between the 1900s and 1970s in which secular and religious groups established their own institutions, including political parties and schools, with the support of the national government (Duyvendak and Scholten 2011).

Thus, a process started in which existing rights, such as the freedom of religion and freedom of education, were extended to religious and cultural immigrant groups. Where, for example, Dutch Christians had the right to build churches and Christian schools with government support, Dutch Muslims obtained equal rights to build mosques and Muslim schools. In collective labor agreements, provisions were included to give Muslim employees the right to ask and receive for paid leave to observe the two main Islamic holidays, similar to long standing provisions regarding Christian holidays (Shadid and Van Koningsveld 2008). This focus on sociocultural emancipation was increasingly criticized during the 1990s, and the Dutch government shifted the focus to "civic integration" in the new integration policy of 1994. The debates continued, however, with opponents of the recognition of cultural and religious distinctiveness of immigrants arguing that this recognition would hinder the integration process.

The political debates entered a new phase around the year 2000, as described above. Opponents of the recognition of cultural distinctiveness argued that immigrant integration and multiculturalism had failed and claimed that the norms and values of the Dutch "natives" are incompatible with norms and values of immigrants and their descendants, especially those of Muslims. These arguments became part of a political discourse that was appropriated by several politicians and political parties across the political spectrum. Members of parliament frequently debated religious practices, norms, and values of Muslim immigrants and their descendants, including the Islamic headscarf, ritual slaughter, and the refusal of some Muslims to shake hands with individuals of another gender. Some parliamentarians, for example, argued that the principle of state neutrality implies that public officials in certain functions should not display their religious affiliation (Lettinga and Saharso 2012). Still, the majority of parliament members were of the opinion that a prohibition of wearing an Islamic headscarf by employees and pupils in public schools was not warranted by the principle of state neutrality. However, this discussion did lead in 2007 to the prohibition of displaying religious, political, or other affiliations for police officers. The latter prohibition has in recent years once again become subject of discussion, in the context of policies that have been implemented to increase diversity in the police force.

The debates did not only concern interpretations of state neutrality but also the norm of gender equality. The Islamic headscarf was increasingly being discussed in terms of Islamic norms and values and whether these conflict with the emancipation of women. Those who considered the headscarf as a symbol of unequal treatment of women often assume that Muslim women do not have a free choice in whether or not to wear it and therefore argued that it should be banned. Others, however, argued that emancipation is the way to gender equality and not a ban on religious dress (Lettinga and Saharso 2012).

The political debates in the Netherlands about the cultural and religious distinctiveness of Muslim immigrants and their descendants appear to have peaked in the years 2004–2006. Since then, this issue is barely mentioned in the Dutch governments' policy documents on immigrant integration. In its policy document on integration published in 2011, the government stressed that the right of freedom of religion also applies for Muslim citizens, and, as mentioned, the most recent integration policy document, published in 2018, mostly focuses on civic integration and participation in society. (For a more extensive analysis of Dutch political and public views on the issue of religious distinctiveness, see Boog 2014.)

This does not mean, however, that there is consensus about the issue. As of 2018, some politicians continue arguing that cultural or religious manifestations and expressions of Muslim citizens do not belong in Dutch society. Most of these politicians represent one of two political parties: the PVV (right-wing populist Party for Freedom) led by parliamentarian Geert Wilders and the SGP (ultra-orthodox Protestant Reformed Political Party). Currently (as of 2018), these parties have respectively 20 and 3 seats in the Dutch parliament, out of 150 total seats. The PVV claims that Islam is a threat to Dutch society and calls for the ban of various religious expressions, including the Quran and the building of mosques (PVV, electoral program of 2012). The SGP also wants to ban the construction of mosques and wants to limit "cultures and religions that do not belong in Dutch society" (SGP, electoral program of 2012). These proposals are clearly incompatible with the rights of freedom of religion, but also with the non-discrimination principles in the Dutch law, as these parties do not propose similar bans on expressions of other religions.

While the FvD (Forum for Democracy, two seats in Dutch parliament), the other right-wing populist party in Dutch Parliament, appears to respect these rights, it does argue that the norms and values of Muslim immigrants and their descendants conflict with core values in the Dutch society, as is evident from the official views published on the FvD-website. Moreover, as discussed in the section on national belonging, statements by FvD-leader Baudet suggest that he has an exclusive, ethnic nationalist conception of Dutch national belonging.

Conclusion

In this chapter, it is argued that to understand the current debates about cultural and ethnic diversity in the Netherlands (and other Western European countries), several historical developments have to be taken into account. One relevant development is that of the conception of the nation-state in Western Europe since the nineteenth century. This conception is contradictory as it includes inclusive – civic – as well as exclusive – ethnic or cultural – criteria for national belonging (Stolcke 1995). Another development is the changing pattern of migration since World War II. While The Netherlands has always been an immigration country, relatively few immigrants settled in the Netherlands between 1850 and 1940. Their number and ethnic and cultural diversity grew again after 1945, increasing diversity in Dutch society. And importantly, the diversity debates take place in the context of a developing human rights revolution that started after World War II (Kymlicka 2012). In this revolution, historical hierarchies are being challenged by ideologies of social equality and nondiscrimination, and policies and regulations have been and still are being developed to achieve social equality on grounds such as gender, ethnic background, and sexual orientation.

A central topic in contemporary diversity debates is the cultural and religious distinctiveness of immigrants and their descendants; whether certain practices, norms and values of immigrants are compatible with the norms and values of the immigrant receiving societies, a question that in the last three decades has been increasingly asked about Muslim immigrants. In other words, the relevance of cultural – more exclusive – boundaries of national belonging is increasingly being discussed. Scholars in the Netherlands refer to this process as a culturalization of citizenship, "in which emotions, feelings, norms and values, symbols and traditions (including religion) come to play a pivotal role in defining what can be expected of a Dutch citizen" (Duyvendak 2011: 81).

A key concept in these debates is multiculturalism, a concept that refers to specific responses to diversity in society that are grounded in the aforementioned human rights revolution. While many interpretations of this concept are in use, most proponents agree on three fundamental values or aspects that emphasize the liberal character of multiculturalism: national belonging or social cohesion, social equality, and the *recognition* of cultural or religious distinctiveness. These values are closely related to fundamental debates on citizenship, as they refer to citizen rights such as the right of equal treatment and the right of freedom of religion, and also to the issue of the tension between inclusion and exclusion that the concept of citizenship entails (cf. Bloemraad et al. 2008).

In the Netherlands, the first national policies for the integration of immigrants and their descendants were developed and implemented in the 1980s. The goals of these policies included participation in society and social equality. The policy goal of social equality for immigrants and their descendants was and is part of a larger development of policies and regulations to achieve social equality on grounds that include ethnic background, gender, sexual orientation, age, and disability. To this end, the Dutch Constitution was amended, provisions have been included in penal and civil law, and various policy measures have been implemented, including codes of conduct in organizations and a nationwide system of offices that can handle discrimination complaints.

Apart from social equality, the Dutch integration policies of the 1980s were also meant to achieve sociocultural emancipation of the culturally diverse groups of immigrants and their descendants. This was considered necessary to achieve social cohesion and social equality. Thus, existing rights, such as the freedom of religion and freedom of education, were extended to religious and cultural immigrant groups. Where, for example, Dutch Christians had the right to build churches and Christian schools with government support, Dutch Muslims obtained equal rights to build mosques and Muslim schools. Furthermore, given the legal nondiscrimination principles and the Dutch interpretation of freedom of religion, it was clear that the unequal treatment of, for example, an employee because she is wearing an Islamic headscarf, would in most cases amount to discrimination.

However, the political debates about the sociocultural emancipation of immigrants and their descendants, and especially of Muslims, became heavily politicized in the 1990s and 2000s. Despite the fact that the process of socioeconomic integration of immigrants and their descendants was successfully progressing (as statistics clearly showed), politicians on the right of the political spectrum claimed that integration was failing. Their argument was that the goals of social equality and social cohesion were threatened by the cultural and religious distinctiveness of immigrants. More specifically, they argued that certain norms and values of Muslim citizens were incompatible with those in Dutch society. Right-wing populist politician Pim Fortuyn combined these ideas in a political discourse, parts of which were appropriated by other political parties in the 2000s.

Religious practices, norms, and values of Muslim immigrants and descendants were frequently debated in Dutch parliament. While the antidiscrimination efforts continued to enjoy wide political support, parliamentarians did debate possibilities to prohibit certain Islamic practices, including the wearing of the headscarf. Some politicians, mostly on the right of the political spectrum, considered the Islamic headscarf to be a symbol of unequal treatment of women and therefore argued that it should be prohibited. Others argued, however, that emancipation, and not a ban on religious dress, is the way to gender equality. Moreover, a prohibition of religious expressions such as the Islamic headscarf would in many cases violate the Dutch interpretation of freedom of religion.

These discussions appeared to have peaked in the years 2004 and 2006. Recently (as of 2018), the Dutch government mostly focuses on civic integration of immigrants and their descendants: participation in society and learning the Dutch language. However, the culturalization of citizenship is still evident from public debates and from the views and statements of various politicians. The right-wing populist PVV and the ultra-orthodox SGP still want to ban Islamic expressions and manifestations from Dutch society, and statements by FvD-leader Thierry Baudet suggest clearly that he has an exclusive, ethnic nationalist conception of Dutch national belonging.

Cross-References

▶ Immigration Policy and Left-Right Politics in Western Europe
▶ Race and Racism: Some Salient Issues

References

ACVZ (2008) Nederlanderschap in een onbegrensde wereld. English edition: Dutch nationality in a world without frontiers. ACVZ, Den Haag

Ahmed S (2007) The language of diversity. Ethn Racial Stud 30(2):235–256
Anderson BR (1991) Imagined communities: reflections on the origin and spread of nationalism, revised and extended edn. Verso, London
Andriessen I, Dagevos J, Nievers E, Boog I (2007) Discriminatiemonitor niet-westerse allochtonen op de arbeidsmarkt 2007. Sociaal en Cultureel Planbureau/Art.1, Den Haag/Rotterdam
Andriessen I, Nievers E, Dagevos J (2012) Op achterstand. Discriminatie van niet-westerse migranten op de arbeidsmarkt. Sociaal en Cultureel Planbureau, Den Haag
Arendt H (1973 [1951]) The origins of totalitarianism. Harcourt Brace Jovanovic, New York
Bakke E (2000) How voluntary is national identity? Revised version of a conference paper presented at the 8th national political science conference, Tromsø
Balibar E, Wallerstein I (1991) Race, nation, class: ambiguous identities. Verso, London
Baron IZ (2009) The problem of dual loyalty. Can J Polit Sci 42(4):1025–1044
Barry B (2002) Culture and equality: an egalitarian critique of multiculturalism. Harvard University Press, Cambridge, MA
Barth F (1969) Introduction. In: Barth F (ed) Ethnic groups and boundaries: the social organization of culture difference. Universitetsforlaget, Oslo
Bloemraad I, Korteweg A, Yurdakul G (2008) Citizenship and immigration: multiculturalism, assimilation and challenges to the nation-state. Annu Rev Sociol 34:153–179
Blok Commission (2004) Bruggen bouwen. Eindrapport van de Tijdelijke Parlementaire Onderzoekscommissie Integratiebeleid. SDU, Den Haag
Bobo LD, Fox C (2003) Race, racism, and discrimination: bridging problems, methods and theory in social psychological research. Soc Psychol Q 66(4):319–332
Boog I (2014) Multiculturalism and multicultural citizenship: public views on national belonging, equality and cultural distinctiveness in the Netherlands. PhD dissertation, Leiden University, Leiden
Brown K (2018) Introduction: radicalisation and securitisation of Muslims in Europe. J Muslims Eur 7(2):139–145
Brubaker R (2004) Ethnicity as cognition. Theory Soc 33(1):31–64
Crosby FJ, Iyer A, Clayton S, Downing R (2003) Affirmative action: psychological data and the policy debates. Am Psychol 58(2):93–115
De Hart B (2005) Het probleem van dubbele nationaliteit. Politieke en mediadebatten na de moord op Theo van Gogh. Migrantenstudies 21(4):224–238
Duyvendak JW (2011) Feeling at home in the nation. Understanding Dutch nostalgia. In: Harbers H (ed) Strangeness and familiarity. Global unity and diversity in human rights and democracy. Proceedings international conference Groningen, The Netherlands, FORUM/University of Groningen, Utrecht, 21–22 October 2010
Duyvendak JW, Scholten P (2011) Beyond the Dutch "multicultural model". The coproduction of integration policy frames in the Netherlands. Int Migr Integr 12(3):331–348
Duyvendak JW, Scholten P (2012) Deconstructing the Dutch multicultural model: a frame perspective on Dutch immigrant integration policymaking. Comp Eur Polit 10(3):266–282
Erdal MB, Oeppen C (2013) Migrant balancing acts: understanding the interactions between integration and transnationalism. J Ethn Migr Stud 39(6):867–884
Fiske ST (2002) What we know about bias and intergroup conflict. The problem of the century. Curr Dir Psychol Sci 11(4):123–128
Foucault M (1980) The history of sexuality, vol 1. Vintage, New York
Glastra F, Schedler P, Kats E (1998) Employment equity policies in Canada and the Netherlands: enhancing minority employment between public controversy and market initiative. Policy Polit 26(2):163–176
Havinga T (2002) The effects and limits of anti-discrimination law in the Netherlands. Int J Sociol Law 30(1):75–90
Huntington SP (2004) Who are we? The challenges to America's national identity. Simon & Schuster, New York
Huynh Q, Devos T, Smalarz L (2011) Perpetual foreigner in one's own land: potential implications for identity and psychological adjustment. J Soc Clin Psychol 30(2):133–162

Joppke C (2007) Transformations of immigrant integration: civic integration and antidiscrimination in the Netherlands, France, and Germany. World Polit 59(2):243–273

Koopmans R, Statham P, Giugni M, Passy F (2005) Contested citizenship: immigration and cultural diversity in Europe. University of Minnesota Press, Minneapolis

Kremer M (2013) The Netherlands. From national identity to plural identifications. Migration Policy Institute, Washington, DC

Kymlicka W (2012) Multiculturalism. Success, failure, and the future. Migration Policy Institute, Washington, DC

Kymlicka W (2014) The essentialist critique of multiculturalism: theories, policies, ethos. EUI working paper RSCAS 2014/59, European University Institute, Fiesole

Lentin A (2000) 'Race', racism and anti-racism: challenging contemporary classifications. Soc Identities 6(1):91–106

Lentin A (2004) Racial states, anti-racist responses. Picking holes in 'culture' and 'human rights'. Eur J Soc Theory 7(4):427–443

Lettinga D, Saharso S (2012) The political debates on the veil in France and the Netherlands: reflecting national integration models? Comp Eur Polit 10(3):319–336

Lucassen L, Lucassen J (2011) Winnaars en verliezers. Een nuchtere balans van vijfhonderd jaar immigratie. Bert Bakker, Amsterdam

Maliepaard M, Phalet K (2012) Social integration and religious identity expression among Dutch Muslims: the role of minority and majority group contact. Soc Psychol Q 75(2):131–149

Modood T (2010) Multicultural citizenship and Muslim identity politics. Interventions 12(2):157–170

Pager D, Shepherd H (2008) The sociology of discrimination: racial discrimination in employment, housing, credit, and consumer markets. Annu Rev Sociol 34:181–209

Pakulski J, Markowski S (2014) Globalisation, immigration and multiculturalism – the European and Australian experiences. J Sociol 50(1):3–9

Parekh B (2000) Rethinking multiculturalism. Cultural diversity and political theory. Harvard University Press, Cambridge, MA

Penninx R (2005) Bridges between research and policy? The case of post-war immigration and integration policies in the Netherlands. Int J Multicul Soc 7(1):33–48

Prins B (2004) Voorbij de onschuld. Het debat over de multiculturele samenleving. Herziene versie. Van Gennep, Amsterdam

Reskin B (2012) The race discrimination system. Annu Rev Sociol 38:17–35

Schaafsma J (2006) Ethnic diversity at work. Diversity attitudes and experiences in Dutch organisations. Aksant, Amsterdam

Sechrist GB, Swim JK, Stangor C (2004) When do the stigmatized make attributions to discrimination occurring to the self and others? The roles of self-presentation and need for control. J Pers Soc Psychol 87(1):111–122

Sen A (2006) Identity and violence: the illusion of destiny. Issues of our time. W.W. Norton & Co, New York

Shadid WA, Van Koningsveld PS (1995) De mythe van het islamitische gevaar. Hindernissen bij integratie. Kok Pharos, Kampen

Shadid WA, Van Koningsveld PS (2008) Islam in Nederland en België. Peeters, Leuven

Stolcke V (1995) Talking culture: new boundaries, new rhetorics of exclusion in Europe. Curr Anthropol 36(1):1–24

Tajfel H (1981) Human groups and social categories. Cambridge University Press, Cambridge

Vera H (2006) Rebuilding a classic: the social construction of reality at 50. Cult Sociol 10(1):3–20

Vink M (2007) Dutch multiculturalism: beyond the pillarization myth. Polit Stud Rev 5(3):337–350

Visweswaran K (1998) Race and the culture of anthropology. Am Anthropol 100(1):70–83

Wright M, Bloemraad E (2012) Is there a trade-off between multiculturalism and socio-political integration? Policy regimes and immigrant incorporation in comparative perspective. Perspect Polit 10(1):77–95

WRR (2007) Identificatie met Nederland. Amsterdam University Press, Amsterdam

Correction to: Diaspora and Ethnic Contestation in Guyana

Ralph Premdas and Bishnu Ragoonath

Correction to: Chapter 69 in: S. Ratuva (ed.), *The Palgrave Handbook of Ethnicity*, https://doi.org/10.1007/978-981-13-2898-5_45

The co-author name has been inadvertently retained as "Ragoonat" and the same has been updated now as "Ragoonath" in the chapter.

The updated online version of this chapter can be found at
https://doi.org/10.1007/978-981-13-2898-5_45

© The Author(s), under exclusive license to Springer Nature Singapore Pte Ltd. 2020
S. Ratuva (ed.), *The Palgrave Handbook of Ethnicity*,
https://doi.org/10.1007/978-981-13-2898-5_171

Index

A
Abangan, 795, 802
Abkhazia, 154
Aboriginal authors, *see* Indigenous scholars
Aboriginality
　complexity of, 1000
　concepts of, 995
　definition of, 996
　and ethnicity, 997
　as fluid concept, 997–998
　idea of, 994
　political movement, 1005
Aboriginal land title, 726
Abuse of human rights, 852
Academic dis-identification, 1412
Accommodation, 113
Accommodative constitutional designs, 112
Acculturation, 844, 1192, 1193, 1197
Aceh, 968
　highlands, 1958
Acehnese choreographers, 1958
Acehnese Freedom movement, 1961
Adat, 794, 1453, 1454, 1456, 1458–1461
Adventures of a Child of War, 420
Affective tie, 1225
Affirmative action, 21–23
　Ali baba practice, 1510
　benefits, 1509
　black community, 1508
　culture and value, 1502
　demand, 1504
　discrimination, 1503, 1506
　education, 1507
　eligibility in US, 1510
　equality and justice, 1502
　group eligibility, 1508
　identity symbols, 1505
　incidence, 1503
　individualism and merit, 1505
　inequality, 1503
　injustice, 1503
　institutional reform, 1504
　laws/legislation, 1505
　legal instruments, 1510
　minorities, 1506
　polity participation, 1507
　preferences, 1502
　procedural rectification, 1507
　redistribution, 1502
　riots, 1504
　societies, 1507
　South Africa, 1509
　success and failure, 1505
　symbolic goods, 1508
　zero-sum contest, 1504
Africans, 660, 663, 665
　organic exporting, 1429
Afrikaans films, 1981, 1988
Afrikaner audiences, 1988
Afrikaner cultural nationalism, 1988
Afro-Amerindian, 1599
Afro-Mauritians, 1789
Aganuu, 1239
Agency, 1225
Age of migration, 1814
Agricultural production, 1016
Ahle Sunnah wal Jamaah, 830
Ahmadi/Qadiani, 833, 834
Ahmadiyah, 830
Aiga (family), 1225
Alataw Pass, 1025
Alawite community, 134
Aliansi Kemanusiaan Indonesia untuk Myanmar (AKIM), 1902, 1903
Alii (sacred chief) titles, 1237
Ali, Moulvi Ameer, 830, 833
Ali, Muhammad, 828
Aliran, 795

Alliance Party, 259
Allochthon, 2000
All India Majlis-e-Ittehadul Muslimeen (AIMIM), 1879
Al Murabitoun Battalion, 762
Al Shabab, 760
Ambon, 1452, 1457
Amelioration policy, 1757
American Civil Rights Movement, 393
American Civil War, 393
Amerindian Land Commission, 1354
Anachronistic equality, 943–944
Anak Lagu Penutup, 1971
Ancestor worship, 1790
Ancestral culture, 1784
ANC government, 1991
Ancien régime, 1650
Animist-Hindu-Buddhist associations, 1965
Anjuman Sunnatul Jamaat Association (ASJA), 842
Ankle bracelets and electronic monitoring, 1345
Ansar al-Din, 765
Ansar al-Din Front, 762
Ansari, Maulana, 831
Anthropology, 1447, 1449, 1450, 1461
Anti-capitalism, 1035
Anti-Fur policy, 663
Anti-immigration policies, 1834
Antipodes, 1271
Anti-racist struggles, 392–393
Anti-Semitism, 389, 393
Anti-Tamil pogrom, 640
Aotearoa/New Zealand, 870, 877, 1266–1280, 1283, 1285, 1366
Apartheid, 79–83, 86–89
Apartheid Museum, 1950
Apartheid state, 464
    African identity, 474–475
    Afrikaner identity, 470–474
    colonial era, 464–466
    coloured identity, 475–476
    Indian identity, 476–477
    mining and criminalisation of race, 467–468
    non-racialism, 478–480
Apprenticeship system, 1773
Arab(s), 660, 663–666
Arab-African dichotomy, 660, 661
Arab-Fur war, 663
Arab-Islamic project, 658
Arab Spring, 132, 133, 135, 139, 140
Arab world, 132, 133, 135, 140
Arakan/Rakhine region, 1578, 1881–1882

Arakan Rohingya Salvation Army (ARSA), 1882–1883
Argentina, 851, 858
Aristotle, 68
Arkatia (recruiting agent), 1802, 1806
Armenian genocide, 1548
Art museums, 1943
Aruba, 1605
Aryans, 485
ASEAN
    charter, 1894, 1897
    and Myanmar, 1893
    regionalism, 1893
    response, 1900–1902
    summits, 1895
    way, 1892, 1893
ASEAN Intergovernmental Commission on Human Rights (AICHR), 1893, 1897, 1898
Asian Americans, 1484
    academic success, 1484
    admissions discrimination charges, 1485–1488
    discrimination complaints, admissions, 1493
    Harris' framework, 1493
    Harvard's holistic approach, 1491
    race conscious admissions, 1486–1487
Asian Casino Economy, 1319–1321
Asian Civilizations Museum, 1950
Asian Development Bank (ADB), 1228
Asia, political subjectivity and LGBTIQ rights in, *see* Lesbian, gay, bisexual, transgender, intersex and queer (LGBTIQ)
Aspinall, Edward, 1961
Assam
    Bodo community, 1530
    community's political representation, 1529–1530
    elections and voting, 1528
    Garo community, 1530
    grievance redressal, 1531–1533
Assimilation, 17–18, 844
Assimilationist perspective, 1168
Assimilationist policies, 1172
Association of Southeast Asian Nations (ASEAN), 1314
Ästerxan (Astrakhan) Khanate, 320
Asylum, 1836
Asylum seekers, 1692
Atarashii Rekishi o Tsukurukai, 1477
Atithi Devo Bhavh, 1885

Atoalii, 1239
Atomic Energy Commission (AEC), 886, 894
Atrocities, 387, 1587
Audiences, 399, 400, 403, 405–406, 408–410
Audit model, 1437, 1438
Aussiedler, 1674
Australia, 887, 888, 891, 895, 1085, 1086
Austria, 350, 352
    challenges to official recognition regime, 1868–1870
    and Germany, 1854–1855
    Islamic faith community, 1864
    legacy of Habsburg empire in, 1862–1863
    Republic of, 1860–1862
Authoritarian rule, 1357
Authority, 66, 68, 70, 71, 73
Authority-focused demands, 159
Autonomy, 284, 285, 287–289, 291, 294–297, 852, 858, 860, 863, 968, 1606

B

Baitkas, 1783
Bali Democracy Forum (BDF), 1897
Bali process and Indonesian leadership, 1897–1900
Bangladesh, 55, 1576
Bangladesh-China-India-Myanmar and the China-Pakistan Economic Corridors, 1025
Bantu Investment Corporation (BIC), 1983
Bantustan, 469, 473, 479, 1984
Barefoot in Fire: A World War II Childhood, 420
Barthes, Roland, 66
Basilone, John, 1213
Batırşa, 321
Battle of Karbala, 1964
Batu, 318
Bau, 248, 250, 253, 261
Beche-de-mer, 248
Beijing University, 1020
Belief in a common descent, 43
Belmokhtar, Mokhtar, 758
Belonging, 80–82, 89, 1252, 1255
Belt and Road, 1012
Berk, F., 65
Bersiap, 793–794
Best Loser System (BLS), 1788
Bhojpuri belt, 1712
Biculturalism
    inequalities and neoliberalism, 874–875
    in social policy, 878–880

Big Man politics, 275
Big-tent' policy, 668
Big Three, 1488, 1490
Bikini Atoll, 886, 887, 891, 899
Bipolar partisan order, 813
Black community, 1508
Black consciousness, 479
Black film industry, 1984, 1985, 1991
Blackness, 1978
Black Panther party, 1216
Black people in Europe, 524–527
    ethinc differences, 517–522
    languages, 519
    racial similarities, 522–524
    religion and faith communities, 520
Black peril, 433–436
Bluefields, 1594
Body snatchers, 1048–1056
Bokayo, 422
Boko Haram, 767
Bolivia, 851, 856, 857, 859, 861
Bonjol, Tuanku Imam, 792
Bonnett, J., 68
Borders, 1248, 1254
    enforcement, 1343
    internal, 1255
Border Security and Immigration Enforcement Improvements Executive Order, 1340
Bosnia, 1546
Bosnia-Herzegovina
    ethnicized history of, 597–601
    ethnic nationalism, affect and descent into war, 545–549
    fragmented political elites of, 605–609
    power-sharing institutions, 601–605
    non-war in, 549–552
Bosnian political system, 604
Bosnian public discourse, 550
Bosnian War, 540, 549, 553
Bradford, 448, 449, 452
Brain-waste, 1736
Branding culture, 1959–1962
Bravo operation, 886, 899
Bravo test, 886, 888, 892, 895, 896, 899
Brazil, 853, 859
Britannia, 1277, 1278
British, 1581
    colonial rule, 658
    indirect rule, 254
British Abolition of Slavery Act in 1833, 1768
British East India Company, 1273, 1276
British Indentured Labor system, 1768–1771
British Land Tenure and Tax laws, 1771

British National Party (BNP), 449
British nuclear testing, 896
British Rāj, 1295
Brixton, 1656
Brussels, 1846
B-Scheme film subsidy, 1982
Buchanan, 1581
Budi Utomo, 793
Building trust, 1570
Burma, 1576
Burnham, Forbes, 1354, 1357
Burnley, 448, 449, 451
Burns, Creighton, 260

C
Cabo de la Vela, 1596, 1598
Cakobau, Ratu Seru, 248
Cakobau government, 248
Calcutta, 1799, 1802, 1803, 1805, 1806
Calder, Alexander, 792, 805
Caliphate State, 768
Calvi, G., 69
Campanilismo, 1204, 1206–1208, 1212
Candidate-centric elections, 743
Capital accumulation, 1224
Capital acquisition, 1735
Capital investment, 1012
Capitalism, 1035, 1041, 1044, 1052, 1053, 1055, 1056, 1058, 1059, 1228, 1770
Caribbean
    estates, 1719–1725
    plantation, 1713–1719
    Indian indentured labourers in, 1711–1726
Carr, E.H., 67, 68, 70
Casino, 1314–1328
Caste laws, 1781
Catholics, 1779
Cayman Islands, 1605
Census, 1267, 1272, 1283–1306
    2010 census, 1015
Center-periphery dynamics, 657–659
Central African Republic, 625
Central Americans, 1336
Central Asia, 1021
Centralized planning policy, 1562
Chain immigration, 1176
Chain migration, 1206
Chen Quanguo, 1017
Chiefly system, 249
Chiefs, 248, 258, 260, 262
Children's literature, 417, 418, 421, 424, 425

Chile, 851, 852, 856, 858, 861
China and the Indo-China Peninsula, 1024
China-Central Asia, 1024
China-Europe trains, 1025
China-Mongolia-Russia, 1024
China Railway Construction Heavy Industry company, 1025
China's ethnic policy, 307
China's land bridge to Asia, 1024
China's State Grid Corporation, 1021
China's territorial integrity, 1026
Chinese, 1335
    colonialism, 1019
    emigration, four patterns of, 1168
    employees, 1326
    Exclusion Act, 1173
    immigrants, 1354
    indentureship, 1801
    migrants, 1773
Chinese Communist Party (CCP), 295, 1013
Chinese Islamic Association, 289
Chinese language Internet, 1019
Chinese Nationalism, 1018, 1019
Chineseness, 1170
    historical identity of, 1177
    loss of, 1178
    in multicultural societies, 1179
Chinese People's Political Consultative Conference (CPPCC), 98
Chongqing, 1023
Christian, 1838
Christianity, 1228, 1452, 1454, 1458
Christian missionaries, 251
Christmas (Kiritimati) Island, 887, 892, 898, 900, 901
Ciarrocchi, Giuseppe, 1215
Citizenship, 79, 80, 89, 1249, 1252, 1254, 1678, 1995
    Amendment Act of 2005, 238
    Chinese, 1171
    Indonesian, 1171
Citizenship policy index (CPI), 1855
Civic identity, 150
Civic nationalism, 9
Civic nationhood, 121
Civic virtue, 277
Civil conflict, 1960
Civil Rights Act, 391
Civil war, 134, 140, 142–144, 657–659, 663–666, 671
    in Colombia, 1594
Clash of civilizations, 174
Classification, 78, 79, 83, 86–89

Class struggle, 1058
Climate change humanitarian visa, 1691, 1697
Clinton, Bill, 1218
Coalition-building, 736, 737, 739
Coal pollution, 1022
Coal production and power generation, 1021
Coal reserves, 1021
Coal to gas and gasoline, 1022
Co-ethnics, 1681, 1782
Cohen classification, 1151–1154, 1161
Cold War, 1541
Collective action, 172
Collective approach, 1375
Collective identity, 1158, 1450, 1460
Collective memory, 1151, 1152, 1161
    comfort women, 1157
    Halbwachs, Maurice, 1156
    needs, 1157
    public and social commemoration, 1157
    social identity, 1158–1159
Collectivism, 1929
Colonial administration, 1773
Colonial discourse, 1131, 1132, 1134, 1136, 1139, 1140
Colonialism, 80, 86, 200, 202, 385, 387, 389, 393, 464, 916, 920, 921, 1228, 1354
Colonial period, 994, 998, 1004, 1006
Colonial powers, 133, 1452, 1453
Colonial Secretary Office, 255
Colonisation, 431, 1648
Color-blindness, 111
Colourblind ideology
    challenge, 500
    diversity and, 501
    white supremacy, 507
Columbus Day, 1213
Combat stereotypes, 410, 411
Comedy, 484, 496
Comfort women, 1155, 1157, 1159
2012 Commission's draft constitution, 120
Committee on Migrant Workers (CMW), 1824
Commodification of culture, 51–54
Common nationhood, 1789
Common roll, 258
Communal boundaries, 8
Communal conflict, 657, 665, 666, 668, 677
    active, 678
    boundaries and local authority, 686–687
    cattle raids, 683–685
    in Darfur, 661–663
    devolution, 689–691
    electoral politics, 680–683
    natural resources, 685–686

Communal elections, 1355
Communalism, 6
Communal violence, 1452–1454
Communication, 42, 44, 45
Communism, 1035, 1036, 1046, 1055, 1056, 1058
    transition from, 322–327
Community, 80–82
    cohesion, 448, 457–460
    participation, 1373
    peace building, 1454, 1459
    policing, 1660
    sponsorship category, 1695
Community-based conflict resolution service, 588
Comparative advantage, 1231, 1234, 1242, 1243
Competition of suffering, 1663
Competitive edge, 1242
Complex inequalities, 1314–1318
Comprehensive Peace Agreement (CPA), 658, 667–669
Compulsory education, 1702
Conard, Robert, 892, 893
Concertación, 852, 856, 857
Concertación de Partidos por la Democracia, 852
Conflict, 596, 600, 609
    analysis model, 624
    complexity, 671
    interlinkages, 657
    management, 617, 688, 968, 969, 971
    in Northern Ireland (*see* Northern Ireland)
    resolution, 617, 624, 811, 1570
    transformation, 617
Conflict-ridden Mindanao, 981–987
Congolese migrant
    education and understanding of manhood, 1123–1124
    Manhood and migration, 1125
    work and manhood, 1124
Congress of Peoples (COP), 815
Consociational, 332
    arrangement, 602
    democracy, 162, 626
Consociationalism, 14
Constitution, 736
    1966 Constitution, 260
    1970 Constitution, 116
    1990 Constitution, 116
    1997 Constitution, 117
    2013 Constitution, 110
    democracy, 110

Constitution (*cont.*)
　engineering, 160
　making, 110
　reform, 110, 119
Constitutional Review Committee (CRC), 117
Consultas, 857, 860
Consultations, 852, 855, 857, 858, 861, 1661
Contemporary conflicts, 614
Contestation, 804
Contra War, 1594
Convention on Refugee of 1951, 1887
Cook, James, 1270, 1273, 1276
Cook Islands, 223, 235, 237
　Cook Islands Party, 231
　geography, 228–229
　history, 231–234
　politics, 230–231
　population, 230
Coolies, 1175
Cooperative republic, 1356
Co-optations, 277
Copenhagen Criteria, 369
Corruption, 1243
Cosmopolitanism, 213–214, 372, 377
Cosmopolitan workplace, 1315, 1317
Counterinsurgency, 659, 665
Counter-stereotyping, 407, 410
Coup, 118
Coup attempt, 670
Cox's Bazar, 1892
Creative
　class, 1740
　nationalism, 277
Creepiness, 1052, 1053
Creolization, 832
Crime, 400–403, 406
Crime of crimes, 1539–1551
Criminal, 400, 401
Criminalization
　definition, 1337
　post-civil rights, 1337
　pre-civil rights, 1337
　of race, 1648
Crimmigration
　after 9/11, 1339
　definition, 1337, 1338
Crisis equilibrium, 1558, 1560
Critical discourse analysis, 1830
Critical Race Theory (CRT), 492
Cronyism, 799, 800
Cross-cutting cleavages, 598
Cross-ethnic alliances, 741
Cross-ethnic coalitions, 736, 737, 741, 742, 752

Crypto Jews, 1598
Cubagua, 1596
Cuban Chinese, 1801, 1807
Cukong, 800
Cultural awareness, 1663
Cultural capital, 1790
Cultural conservatism, 1181
Cultural days, 1947
Cultural distinctiveness, 2006
　in Netherlands, 2007–2009
　perspectives on, 2005–2007
Cultural hegemony, 786
Cultural hybridization, 39
Cultural identity, 597, 887, 890, 891, 897, 902
Culturalization, 1994
Cultural keystone species, 1924
Cultural law, 70
Cultural markers, 54
Cultural memory, 1197
Cultural nationalism, 333, 1473
　Afrikaner, 1988
　Afrikaner identity and, 1990
Cultural pluralist model, 1787
Cultural regulation, 72
Cultural Revolution, 1810
Cultural socialization and ethnic consciousness
　development, 57–59
　neoliberal globalization, 51–54
　social media, 59–61
　tourism, 54–57
Cultural symbols, 36, 39, 45
Cultural traits, 1314
Cultural turn, 1447
Cultural wounding, 716
　and ethnicity, 718–720
　healing, 727–730
　violence and ethnic conflict, 720–722
　Yanyuwa families, land rights, 722–727
Culture, 82, 83, 86, 89, 1082, 1084, 1086, 1087,
　　1089, 1091–1093, 1096, 1097,
　　1447–1454, 1456, 1457, 1459–1461
　of migration, 1675
Curacao, 1599, 1600
Customary law, 1451, 1452, 1459

D

Daesh and Salafist discourse, 757, 759–761,
　765, 768
Darfur, 657
　communal conflicts in, 661–663
　communal conflicts to civil war and ethnic
　　cleansing, 663–666
　land and identity in, 660

Darfur Peace Agreement (DPA), 665, 671
Darién, 1602
Darul Islam, 802
Database expansion, 1344
Dayton Peace Agreement, 601
De Horatiis, Joseph, 1215
Deadly force, 1655
Decentralization, 805, 1455
　despotism, 274, 277
Decision making, 1376
Decolonial turn, 862, 863
Decolonization, 259, 484
Deep ethnic division, 811, 814, 815
De-ethnicization, 20–22, 119
　of politics, 114
Deliberative democratic political theory, 1431
Democracy
　building activities, 163
　consolidation, 110
　and representation, 1518–1521
Democratic Labor Party (DLP), 813
Democratic Republic of Congo (DRC), 614, 616, 619–622
Democratic Unionist Party (DUP), 338–343
Democratization, 1663
Demography, 1266, 1267, 1284, 1301, 1302, 1306
Demonisation, 1651
Deng Xiaoping government, 1012
Department of Justice (DOJ), 1342
Depoliticisation, 1083
　of Tibetan ethnicity, 307–309
Deportability
　concepts of, 1251
　of migrants, 1248
　threat, 1257
Deportation, 1251
　continuum, 1346
　regime, 1346
Deservingness, 1258, 1260
Deterritorialization, 1169
　imagined communities, 1153
Development, 853
　projects, 858, 861
Dewan Dakwah Islamiyah Indonesia, 804
Diachronic discourse analysis, 544
Dialect groups, 1170
Dialectical materialism, 1038
Diaspora groups, 1079–1085, 1186–1188, 1191, 1194, 1196–1199, 1242
　assimilationism, 1153
　Cohen classification, 1151, 1152, 1154
　collective memory, 1151
　comfort women, 1155
　deterritorialization, 1153
　ethnic identity, 1153
　ethnonationalistic group, 1155
　imagined community, 1152
　Indian diaspora, 1161–1164
　role of ethnic memory (see Ethnic memory)
　Safran classification, 1151, 1152, 1154
　transnationalism, 1154, 1155
　Yaqona and ethno-cultural identity in, 1931
Diet, 1192, 1193, 1199
Diligent, 1314
Diouf, S., 827
Direct air links between Xinjiang and Western European cities, 1025
Discourses, 543, 544
Discrimination, 942, 949, 956, 958, 1694, 1701, 2002
　assimilation, 800
　laws, 79, 82
Disidentification, 1416–1418
Disintegration of national economy, 1561
Disproportionate force, 1013
Dissident sub-nationalism, 274
Distribution sits, 1507
Distributive justice, 213, 214, 216
District Peace Committees, 688
Diversity, 1649
　ideology, 502, 506
Divide and rule, 115
Divided societies, 110, 112, 118
Divided state, 811, 815
Divisive racial campaign, 821
Domestic labour, 69
Domestic laws, 1818
Domestic print and on-line media sources, 1027
Double-consciousness, 1053
Driving while black, 1654
Drug war, 1605
Dual frame of reference, 1738
Dual identity, 45, 1198
Dusky maiden, 1913
Dutch East India Company, 799
Dutch East Indies, 793
Dutch Ethical Policy, 793
Dwifungsi, 797

E

Earliest arrival, 1267, 1269, 1270
Eastern Fiji, 248
Economic and Social Council (ECOSOC), 1815

Economy, 1243
  cost, 1695
  factors, 1706
  obstacles, 1819
  power, 1787
  reforms, 1560
Education, 83, 84, 87, 443, 484, 486, 491, 931, 932, 934, 938, 939, 941–946, 951, 953, 954, 957, 958, 1256, 1417, 1418, 1702
  and housing projects, 1014
  and institutions, 1017
  stereotypes, 491–493
Effective tie, 1234
Eisenbud, Meril, 886
Election-related communal violence, 680–683
Elections, 1527
Electoral features, 736, 737
Electoral system, 1229
Eligibility rules, 1510
Elites, 275, 276, 657, 658, 668, 669, 671
  bargains, 278
  factions, 278
  institutions, 1488, 1492–1495
Elitism, 590
El Socorro Islamia School, 841
Embedded achievement, 1420
Employment, 1701
  opportunities, 1029
Empowerment, 1228, 1371
Enemy aliens, 1214
Enemy within, 1659
Enforcement party, 1559
English language support, 1702, 1703
Entrepreneurial choices, 61
Environmental pollution, 1029
Epeli Hau'ofa, 890
Episodes and pockets' of social unrest, 1012
Epistemic exploitation, 501
  definition, 501
  philosophical context of, 502
Epistemological decolonization, 862
Epistemological violence, 716
Epton, Bernard, 1216
Equality, 931, 938–941, 1503
  of opportunity, 2002
Equal treatment, 2002
Equiano, Olaudah, 1602
Escalator, 1735
Essentialist, 35, 38, 39
  construction of identity, 272
Eternal City, 73, 74
Ethicized voter preferences, 817

Ethnic, 31, 33–35, 38–43, 45
  Afrikaans-language films, 1981
  Afrikaner nationhood, 1980
  Bantustan ideology, 1983
  bipolarity, 1361
  blindness, 111, 112, 121–123
  characteristics, 44
  consciousness (see Cultural socialization and ethnic consciousness)
  defensiveness, 1210
  discontent, 1017
  distinctions, 799
  diversity, 124
  divisions, 615
  elites, 268
  entrepreneurs, 275, 276
  equity, 810
  exclusion, 811
  extremists, 1585
  group identity, 1781
  groups, 80, 86, 87, 277, 737, 1014
  identity, 67, 70, 266, 274, 627, 696, 711, 792, 1020, 1153, 1155, 1163, 1768, 1945–1947, 1951
  identity-based politics, 266
  intra-elite competition, 277
  issues, 1016
  labour market, 1317
  markers, 1705
  migrants, 1316–1318
  militias, 564, 571
  minorities, 1019, 1648
  minority language, 409
  minority prisoners, 1027
  mobilisation, 274, 563, 565, 568, 571
  murder, 516
  nationalism, 112, 276, 545–549, 1997
  partisan politics, 824
  partisan preference, 814, 821
  plurality, in Indonesia (see Indonesia)
  politic(s), 278
  political mobilisation, 276
  political violence, 276, 278
  relation, 448, 458
  stereotypes, 17
  tensions, 798, 1014
  unrest, 1013, 1016
  violence, 541, 543–545
Ethnic media, 406–410
  cinema, 1990
  cultures, 30, 31
  identity, 32, 34, 41, 44
  imageology, 42

Ethnic community, 376
    language, 43
    markers, 41, 43
    pluralism, 33
    violence, 1884
Ethnically-blind' constitution, 110, 114
Ethnically-diverse students, 1409–1412, 1415–1418
Ethnically divided societies, 112
Ethnically bi-polar state, 810
Ethnical nationalism, multiethnic communities, 783–787
Ethnic-class-territorial politics, 154
Ethnic cleansing, 665, 1585, 1884
    evidence of, 1585
Ethnic Community/State Respondents, 1535
Ethnic conflicts, 112, 180, 560, 563, 571, 811, 824, 1446, 1450
    characteristics, 623
    and cultural wounding, 720–722
    internally displaced peoples, 621
    and peace building, 624–627
Ethnicity, 31–40, 44, 268, 275, 276, 384, 386, 390, 391, 909, 922, 1225, 1267, 1269, 1283–1293, 1296, 1297, 1299, 1302, 1304, 1305, 1316, 1447–1448, 1459, 1461, 1543, 1548, 1613, 1621, 1632, 1649, 1666, 1672–1674, 1676, 1684
    affirmative action, 21–23
    and assimilation, 17–18
    and civil wars, 618–624
    and communal boundaries, 6
    and conflict, 195–197
    definition, 615
    globalization and, 777, 781–782
    and intersectionality, 20–21
    and LGBTIQ (*see* Lesbian, gay, bisexual, transgender, intersex and queer (LGBTIQ))
    and nationalism, 7–9, 193–195
    and race, 9–10
    soft skills, 1321–1325
    and specialism, 774
    theoretical engagement, 1315
    and the state, 12–14
    transactional, 11
Ethnicity and class, 1034–1044
    Badiouian procedure, 1056–1059
    psychoanalytic and philosophical contribution, 1044–1048
Ethnicized intra-elite competition, 277
Ethnic memory, 1161, 1163
    collective memory (*see* Collective memory)
    social networks, 1159–1161
Ethnic migration, 1673
    Romanian Germans, 1674–1676
    Romanian Hungarians, 1676–1678
Ethnic politics, 273, 677, 690
    and global justice theory (*see* Global justice)
Ethnic Power Relations (EPR) dataset, 1523, 1525
Ethnization, 31
Ethnoburb, 1174
Ethnocentrism, 490, 780
    definition, 779
    dispersion in world, 780–781
    ethnics and, 781
Ethno-class conflict, 152
Ethno-communal conflict, in South Sudan, *see* South Sudan
Ethnocratic state, 274
Ethno-cultural community, 1503
Ethno-cultural division, 1511
Ethno-cultural identities, 794
Ethno-cultural symbolism and group identity
    belief in a common descent, 43
    communication, 44
    cultural hybridization, 39
    dual identity, 45
    ethnic imageology, 42
    ethnos/ethnicity, 32, 35
    general, 37
    global era, 33
    group boundaries, 41
    identity markers, 39
    language, 43
    mobility, migration and refugees, 30
    modern and global inventions, 32
    multiple identities, 33
    national culture, 31
    neo-Marxist "ethnos theory", 33
    particular, 37
    political and economic factors, 32
    "primordialist" position, 35
    quality of ethnic groups, 33
    religion, 44
    "self-other" distinctions, 37
    situational ethnicity, 34
    traditional attachments, 36
    universal cultural features, 37
Ethnographic data, 1234
Ethnographic research, 1447, 1452
Ethno-nationalism, 7, 1013, 1020
Ethnonym, 42, 43
Ethnos, 32–35, 39
Ethno-symbolism, 37–39, 44
Euphoria of nationalism, 1569

Eurasian economic corridors, 1024
Europe, 248, 250, 255, 257, 259, 261, 369–370, 1842
　citizens, 1681
　ethnic differences in black populations, 517–522
　historical background of black people in, 524–527
　immigration crisis, 1834, 1846–1848
　imperialism and colonialism, 389
　model of organic certification, 1437
　peasantry/serfs, 388
　racial similarities in black populations, 522–524
　settlers, 252
European Union, 371
Evangelical Christian denominations, 1932
Exclusionary nationalism, 150
Exclusionary practices, 805
Exclusive economic zone (EEZ), 228
Exit costs, 1558
Exodus, 1683
Exploitative operations, 1774
Export agriculture, 1430
Exteriority, 1050
External intimacy (extimacy), 1048, 1051, 1059
Extra-constitutional politics, 162
ExxonMobil, 1360, 1361

F

Faalavelave, 1236
Faamatai, 1224, 1228, 1229, 1241
Faasinonomaga, 1243
Facebook monitoring, 1344
Faifeau (Church ministers), 1237
Failed state, 133
Faizrakhmanists (Fäyzraxmançılar), 326
False consciousness, 276, 277
Family reunification, 1693
Family systems, 829
Fantasy, 66, 1035, 1044–1050, 1053, 1059
Far right, 348–356, 358
Federal constitution, 1561
Federation Party, 259
Feminist, 69
　scholars, 1316
Fiji, 110
　politics, 117
　pre-Cession Fiji, 249–253
　as republic, 116
　tri-ethnic discourse, 253–261
　Yaqona (kava) and national ethno-cultural identity in, 1926–1930

Fijian, 898, 900
Fijian Affairs Board, 257
Filipinos, 417
　employees, 1318
Film, 399, 400, 403, 404
First contact, 1271, 1273, 1306
First-past-the-post electoral system, 816, 824
Folk dancing, 1193
Food and supply committees, 588
Forced migration, 1116
Foreign terrorists, 1028
Foreshore and Seabed Act, 876
Foresti, Felice, 1208
Forgiveness, 71, 72
Formal and informal religious institutions, 179
Formal education, 840
Formal rules, 1556
Franco-Mauritians, 1785
Fraser, Nancy, 211, 214, 217
Fraud and abuse, 1566
Free association, 224, 234, 236, 239
Freedman's perspectives, 776
Freedom of religion, 2007
French bourgeoisie, 70
French culture, 1772
French India spiepr132Company, 1273
French model, 1856
French nuclear testing, 897
French Polynesia, 888, 890, 897, 898, 902
Freud, S., 66, 67, 71, 74
Frozen conflict, 154
Fur, 660, 663

G

Gacaca, 1451, 1634–1636
Gagnon, Alan-G., 317
Gandong, 1456, 1458
Garang, John, 666–669
Gardening, 1192
Garibaldi, Giuseppe, 1205
Garifunas, 1603
Gas exploitation, 1022
Gas reserves, 1021
Gawaian Bodkin-Andrews, 1385–1386
Ğayaz İsxaqıy (Iskhaki), 321
Gayo language, 1972
Gayo people, 1958
Gaza Strip and the West Bank, 581
Gender, 1253
Gender disparity, 1783
Gendered migration, 1741
Gender imbalance, 1802
General Ne Win, 1881

Generic humanity, 1036, 1046, 1056–1058
Genericity, 1035, 1048, 1051, 1057
Genghis Khan, 318
Genocide, 72, 1585, 1649
    causes of, 1547–1549
    characteristics of, 1541–1546
    debate, 1542, 1549
    distinctiveness of, 1549–1550
    efforts and failures to prevent or halt, 1540–1541
    and interethnicconflict, 1621–1630
    Justice, 1632, 1634
    post-genocide Rwanda, 1630–1637
    Rwanda, 1613–1615
    ten stages, 1548
Genocide Convention, 1540–1544, 1546, 1550
Geo-economic realities, 1026
Geographic origin, 1189
Gerakan Aceh Merdeka (GAM), 968
Germany, 205
    and Austria, 1854–1855
    foreign workers in, 1857–1858
    Muslims in, 1870–1873
    Red-Green coalition, 1858–1860
Ghair Mukallid, 830, 834
Ghana, 1433, 1434
Ghetto Act, 79
Girard, R., 66
Girmityas (agreement signers), 1269, 1802, 1803
Global capitalism and cheap labour, 1796–1797
    immigrants, descendants of, 1809–1810
    indentured women, 1804–1805
    legacy of indentureship, 1807–1809
    movement towards abolition, 1805–1806
    plantation system, 1797–1798
    Indian indentureship, 1801–1804
    transition to indentureship, 1798–1801
Global economy, 1225
Global Financial Crisis, 1028
Globalization phenomenon, 30–32, 34, 44–46, 210–212, 774, 1154, 1225
    from below, 1228
    characteristics, 776
    definition, 775
    ethnicity, 777
    ethnocentrism, 779
Global justice, 211–212, 215–218
    cosmopolitanism, 213–214
    definition, 210
    distributive justice, 213
    emergence of, 210
    internationalism, 214–215

Global North, 1648
Global South, 1648
Godelier, M., 69
Golden Horde, 318–320
Golkar, 797, 798
Goode, W. Wilson, 1216
Good Friday (Belfast) Agreement, 332
Good Night, Lala, 421
Gorbachev, Mikhail, 321
Gordon, Arthur, 248
Government collection of information, 1018
Government 'regulation' of religion, 1027
Government sponsored force, 1014
The Grand Morcellement, 1784
Grass-roots discontent, 1028
Great Lakes, 621
Great Leap Forward (GLF), 287
Great Proletarian Cultural Revolution (GPCR), 288
Great Western Development campaign, 1023
Greek(s), 1186, 1188–1190, 1194, 1196, 1199
    culture, 1188, 1193, 1195, 1196, 1198
    language, 1187, 1190, 1191, 1193, 1195, 1198, 1199
Greek identity, in Australia, 1198
    acculturation, 1192
    Australian Greek community, change in, 1193–1195
    cultural community, 1191
    cultural memory, 1197
    diet, 1192
    folk dancing, 1193
    gardening, 1192
    geographic origin, 1189
    Greek settlement, 1189
    history of Greek diaspora, 1186–1188
    language, 1189–1191
Greekness, 1188, 1193, 1195–1199
Greek Orthodox Church, 1190, 1194, 1195, 1199
Group Areas Act (GAA), 82, 83, 85, 86, 88
Group boundaries, 41
Group eligibility, 1508
Group identities, and ethno-cultural symbolism, see Ethno-cultural symbolism and group identity
Guajira peninsula, 1595, 1597
Guandong, 1800, 1805
Guard committees, 588
Guatemala, 855, 858, 860
Guilt, 72, 74
Guinea, 1601
Gujarat, 1295

Gujarati, 1266
Ghulam Ahmad, Mirza, 833
Guyana, 1359, 1360
    decolonization and ethnic mass politics, 1354–1356
    economy, 1360
    ethnic distribution, of Guyanese population, 1352
    multi-ethnic state, 1352–1354
    seizure of power and ethnic domination, PNC, 1356–1359
Gwadar Port, 1025
"G" word, 1540
Gypsies, 1650

H

Haji Ruknudeen, 829, 830, 834
Halbwachs, Maurice, 1156
Hamitic hypothesis, 1622
Han, 284–288, 290–294, 296
    and Hui immigrants, 1013
    minority relations, 1019
    paternalism, 1014
Hanifa, Imam Abu, 830
Hard power, 1014
Hardworking, 1314, 1317
Harff, B., 1548
Haruku Island, 1457
Hatuhaha, 1457–1459
Hau'ofa, 890
Hawaiian sovereignty
    Ea and other pre-Western understanding, 951–954
    in federal courts, 930–933
    federal recognition, 934, 944–947
    Native Hawaiian narratives, 948–951
    pre-loaded narratives, 939–944
    race and colorblindness, 934
    restorative and remedial self-determination, 936–937
    UN Declaration on the Rights of Indigenous Peoples 2007, 954–959
    validation, need for, 937–939
Hawkins, John, 1597
Health care, 1256
Health disparities, 1369, 1376
Health equity, 1368, 1369, 1376, 1377
Health promotion, 1374
Health service provision, 1372
Hegel, G.W.F., 71
Hegemonic ethnic enterprises, 272
He Korowai Oranga (HKO), 1370
Herder-farmer, 661

Heritage, 1190, 1192–1195, 1199
Heterogeneity, 804
Hezbollah, 136, 139
Hill Tribes, 252
Himpunan Mahasiswa, 804
Hindu, 1779
Hinduism, 838, 1790
Hindu-Muslim, 840
Hiroshima, 1545
Historical memory, 66, 68, 70, 72, 74, 426
Historical trauma, 1389
History, 66, 74, 1266–1269, 1271, 1272, 1279, 1280, 1282, 1283, 1286, 1299, 1301, 1306, 1447, 1455, 1458
History textbooks of Japan, see Japanese history texbooks
Hokkien, 1169
Holocaust, 71, 72, 1549
Home, 720
Homophobia, 1082
Homosexuality, 1078, 1087, 1088, 1090, 1092–1098
Honduras, 1599
"Hosay" festival, 832
Hosay Riots, 832
Hostility, 489, 490
Hot-spot policing, 1654
Household migration, 1741–1743
Housing, 1700
Houthis, 136
Htoo, U Aung, 1900
Hu Angang, 1020
Hua, C., 69
Huaqiao, 1178
Huayi, 1178
Human capital, 1564
Humanitarian, 1690, 1695
    colonialism, 253, 256
    colonial policy, 259
Human radiation experiments, 892, 894, 902
Human rights, 94, 99, 100, 102, 370, 1026, 1588
    Chinese tradition, 103
    Euro-American tradition, 104
    European tradition, 102, 103
    of migrant workers, 1815
    organizations, 1886–1887
    violations, 852
Humour, 484, 495–496
Hungarian state, 1844
    homogeneity, 1845
    identity, 1837
Hybrid ethnocide, 317

Hybrid identity, 1198
Hybrid system, 161
Hypervisibility, 490

I
Iberoamerica, 1596
ICMW, 1814–1821
    limitations of, 1822–1824
Idel-Ural state, 322
Identification, 267
    card system, 1018
Identitarianism, 1034, 1035
Identity, 31–33, 36, 40, 43, 908–910, 912, 914, 915, 920–922, 1178, 1224, 1373, 1447, 1448, 1450–1454, 1457, 1461, 1621, 1631–1637
    of Aboriginal people, 994
    from adversity, 1005–1006
    collective, 1910
    concepts, 995–996
    conflict, 132, 133, 135, 137, 140–144
    cultural, 1003
    development and media, 1911–1913
    development of, 1911
    dual, 45
    ethnic, 31, 32, 34, 37, 41–43
    Greek identity, in Australia (*see* Greek identity, in Australia)
    Indian identity, in South Africa (*see* Indian identity, in South Africa)
    indigenous, 996–997
    kava and ethno-cultural, 1924–1934
    markers, 39
    multiple, 33
    national, 38, 43–45
    and nation state, 1003–1005
    in Northern Ireland (*see* Northern Ireland)
    politics, 801
    religious, 44
    rivalry, 810
    symbols, 1505
    threat, 494
    tribal, 995
Ideological films, 1981
Ideology, 1052, 1054
Ijtihad, 836
Ikatan Cendekiawan Muslim Indonesia, 804
Imagination, 277
Imagined community, 7
Imagined decolonization, 803
Imagined transnational communities, 1152
Immigrant ticket system, 1776

Immigration, 1217, 1998
    industrial complex, 1346
    reform, 1173
Imperialism, 389, 430
Indentured labor, 78, 79, 89, 255, 1353, 1712, 1714, 1768
    ancestral heritage and cultural capital, 1789–1791
    British, 1768–1771
    categorization of race and ethnicity, 1782
    ethnic boundaries, 1781–1791
    indentured laborer category, 1783
    independence and Indo-Mauritian political power, 1787–1789
    land ownership, 1784
    language, religion and identity, 1786
    mass migration of Indian laborers, 1782–1783
    Mauritius, 1772–1778
    recruitment sites, 1771
    reinvigoration of endogamy, 1784–1785
Indentureship, 1796
    indentured women, 1804–1805
    legacy of, 1807–1809
    Indian indentureship, 1801–1804
    transition to, 1798–1801
Independence, 110
India, 1771
Indian(s), 255, 262
    ancestry, 1786
    diaspora, 1266–1268, 1285, 1286, 1300, 1303
    electoral democracy and representation, 1521–1522
    immigration, 1353
    indentured labourers in Caribbean, 1711–1726
    indentureship, 1801–1804
    militancy, 258
    presence, 1267–1280, 1283, 1287, 1288, 1290, 1295, 1301, 1306
    settlement, 1266, 1267, 1280–1283, 1299, 1301, 1306
Indian identity, in South Africa
    community and belonging, 80–82
    fixed identity, 86–87
    Ghetto Act, 79
    isolation and exclusiveness, 82–86
Indian National Congress (INC), 1806
Indigeneity, 53, 943, 944
    concepts of, 1002
    vs. ethnicity, 997

Indigenist research
  indigenous people voice, 1387
  indigenous standpoint theories, 1386, 1387
  non-indigenous standpoints, 1387
Indigenous activists, 856, 862
Indigenous Australians, 720–722, 1386, 1388
Indigenous belief systems, 801
Indigenous communities, 53
Indigenous ethno-methodology
  indigenist research principals, 1391–1392
  procedure, 1392
  qualitative research (*see* Qualitative yarning method)
  quantitative research method, 1397–1401
Indigenous organizations, 858, 860, 861
Indigenous peoples, 1387, 1388, 1402
Indigenous resources, 248
Indigenous rights, 872, 877, 879
Indigenous scholars, 863
  Gawaian Bodkin-Andrews, 1385–1386
  Shannon Foster, 1386
  Treena Clark, 1386
Indigenous state-nations, 1172
Indirect rule, 114
Individual identity, 1505
Individualisation, 61
Indo-Caribbean dishes, 837
Indo-Mauritians, 1779
  diaspora, 1779
  Mauritius, indentured labor and, 1771–1772
  Muslim, 1780
  political power, 1787–1789
  religious practices, 1790
Indonesia, 792, 968, 1447, 1452, 1454, 1455, 1458, 1460
  Bersiap, 793–794
  ironies of, 1070
  Islam and nation-building, 801–804
  Orde Baru, rise of, 795–798
  Pancasila, 794–795
  political identity, 792
  post-independence, 799
  pre-independence, 798
  repressive developmentalism, 799
  and sexuality, 1066–1067
Indonesian leadership, 1897–1900
Indo-Trinidadians, 826
Inequality, 1013, 1503, 1684
Informal rules, 1557
Information committees, 588
Information Scandal, 1985
Infrastructure construction, 1017
Injustice, 1503

Inner Mongolia, 696, 698, 701, 703, 705
Institutional discrimination, 87, 1698
Institutional protection for whites, 1488–1490
Institutional racism, 392, 486–488
Institutional stagnation, 1557–1560
Institutional weaknesses, 1569
Instrumental/situational/mobilizationist, 36
Instrumentalised ethnicity, 266, 268, 273
Instrumentalists, 7
Instrumentalization, 1451, 1454, 1457
Instrumentalized ethnicity, 278
Intangible heritage, 1941
Integration, 113, 114, 1997
Integrationist constitutional frameworks, 112
Integrative models of conflict management, 603
Intent to destroy, 1543
Inter-ethnic conflict, 278
Inter-ethnic violence, 266
Inter-generational challenges, 1237
Intergenerational loyalty, 1194
Intergroup attitudes, 405–406
Interiority, 1050
Intermarriage, 1785
Internal control system (ICS), 1438
Internal enforcement, 1343–1344
Internalised racism, 1081
Internally displaced peoples, 621
Internally Displaced Persons (IDP's), 1595
Internal wars, 135
International community, 1570
International community intervention, 625
International Criminal Court (ICC), 1544
International criticism, 1026
International human rights law, 1814, 1817, 1819, 1824, 1825
International interventions, 1447
Internationalism, 214–215, 371, 374
International Labor Organization passed Convention 169 (ILO 169), 852, 854, 857, 858, 1815
International migration, 1226
International Monetary Fund (IMF), 851, 1228
International Romani Union (IRU), 374
Interpreters, 1704
Intersectionality, 1038
Intervening institutions, 1770
Interventions, 1541, 1549
Intifada, 586–587
Intra-communal dynamics, 261
Intra-elite cleavages, 276

Intra-state conflicts, 616
Investment, 1013
Inward migration, 1990
Iran, 136
Iraq, 132, 197, 198, 1561
    collective action, 1566–1567
    exit-enter costs, 1567–1568
    path dependence, 1562–1564
    The Neighbors' effect, 1564–1566
Irish Language Act, 339, 340, 344
Irish nationalism, 332, 334, 336, 340
Irish Republican Army (IRA), 156, 332, 335–337
ISIS, 838
Islam, 175, 1452, 1454, 1458, 1838
    and sexuality, 1067–1068
Islamic Party of North America, 828
Islamic religious belief and practice, 1016
Islamic Resource Society (IRS), 828
Islamic State, 757, 1895
Islamic State organisation (DAESH), 136
Islamic Trust, 843
Islamist Resistance Movement (Hamas), 585
Israel, 189, 191, 192
Italian(s), 1334, 1335
Italian Americans, 1205, 1210–1215, 1217, 1218
Italian identity
    Columbus Day, 1213
    enemy aliens, 1214
    ethnic defensiveness, 1210
    Italianness, 1210–1212
    Little Italies, 1212, 1213
    mafia, 1209
    Mussolini's government, 1212
    Order Sons of Italy in America, 1213
    post-ethnic identity, 1217–1218
    Quota Acts, 1210
    whiteness, 1215, 1216
    World War II, 1212–1215
Italianness, 1210–1212
Italo-Ethiopian war, 1211, 1212
Ivan IV (the Terrible), 320

J
Jadidism, 321
Jagan, Cheddi, 1354, 1358
Jahaji bandal (ship's belongings), 1807, 1808
Jakarta Charter, 801
Jakartan style, 1962
Jakeway, Dereck, 258
Jamaat-al-Muslimeen, 828

Jamaica, 1605
Jammu and Kashmir
    community's political representation, 1528
    elections and voting, 1527–1528
    grievance redressal, 1530
Janjaweed, 664–666
Jankélévitch, V., 71, 74
Japan, 189, 205, 416, 425
Japanese, 1335
    representation, 417, 418, 424, 425
Japanese Emperor, 416
Japanese history textbooks
    continental migration, 1471
    culture and minzoku, 1466
    emotive language, 1466
    Jōmon era, 1468
    migrants of the Yayoi era, 1467
    Ministry of Education, 1468
    race and culture, 1473
Jaspers, K., 72
Java, 792, 795, 800, 802
Jean François Marie de Surville, 1270, 1273
Jehadi groups, 1883
Jetnil-Kijiner, Kathy, 902
Jewish Problem, 1488
Jews, 485, 1334
Juba, 659, 668–670
Jus sanguinis, 1857–1858
Justice and Equality Movement (JEM), 664, 665

K
Kalimantan, 792, 800, 802, 805
Kalla, Jusuf, 1895, 1900
Kamanchi, 1579
Kandyan Sinhalese, 636
Kanem-Bornu, 757
Kanuri, 763
Kariu, 1458, 1459, 1461
Kartosuwiryo, S.M., 802
Kashgar, 1023, 1025
Kasimov Khanate, 320
Katuulo cooperatives' capacity, 1439–1440
Kavalactones, 1925
Kava, *see* Yaqona
Kazak, 1015, 1024
Kazan Khanate, 319, 320
Kazan Tatars, 319
Kebatinan, 801
Kenya, 676
    communal conflict (*see* Communal conflict)
    political developments, 677
    waves of violence, 676

Kenya, ethnicity and politics in
  atavistic /residual cultural ghost thesis, 268–269
  class struggle, 275–277
  colonial state power, 270
  imagined community, 277–278
  nationalistic response, 274–275
  social resistance, 270–274
  theoretical approaches, 267–268
Kiir, Salva, 667–670
King Jeremy I, 1602
Kiribati, 887, 890, 891, 897, 898
Klan, K.K., 151
Kleptocratic, 804
Know India Programme (KIP), 1162
Knowledge, 193, 199
Kojève, A., 70, 71
Komando Jihad, 803
Komik, 418, 421
Komite Indonesia Untuk Solidaritas dengan Dunia Islam, 804
Kongsi, 1170
Kubuna, 249
Kurdistan Regional Authorities, 138
Kurdistan Region of Iraq (KRI), 1561
  collective action, 1566–1567
  exit-enter costs, 1567–1568
  path dependence, 1562–1564
  The Neighbors' effects, 1564–1566
Kurds, 134

L
Labour
  camps, 1784
  migration, 1771, 1781
Labourers, in Caribbean, 1711–1726
Labour-lifestyle migration, 1739
Labour Party, 454
Lagden Commission, 469
Lake Chad, 768
Lançados, 1597
Land, 248, 249, 251, 252, 254, 257, 259, 262, 436–438
  alienation, 254
  conflict, 686
Land and Titles Court, 1231
Language, 33–36, 38, 40–45, 472, 1186, 1187, 1189–1199
Lascars, 1273–1282, 1285, 1286
Law, 1095–1098
Lawrence, S., 1656
Leadership, 1370
Lebanon, 132
Left-liberal EU elite, 1837
Left-right, 348, 350–354, 356, 358
Legacy of indentured labor, 1771
Legal barriers, 1818–1819
Legal instruments, 1510
Legal narratives, 930, 938
Legal status transitions, 1251
Legitimacy, 1662
Lemkin, Raphael, 1540
Lenin, 68, 70
Lesbian, gay, bisexual, transgender, intersex and queer (LGBTIQ), 1078
  Asian migration, 1086–1087
  Australian perspectives, 1085–1086
  in China, 1094–1095
  in India, 1088–1093
  in Indonesia, 1098
  in Japan, 1096
  in Korea, 1096
  in Malaysia, 1097
  MCMF, 1080, 1084, 1085
  in Nepal, 1094
  in Pakistan and Bangladesh, 1094
  race-based marginalisation and exclusion in, 1079
  in Singapore, 1097
  in Taiwan, 1095
  technological, economic, social and political changes, 1080
  in Thailand, 1096–1097
  in Vietnam, 1097
Levi-Strauss, C., 72
Lhasa, 1013
Liberalism, 1846
Liberal peace, 1449
Liberation Tigers of Tamil Eelam (LTTE), 635, 649, 650
Libya, 132
Lijst Pim Fortuyn (LPF), 348
Likok Pulo, 1967–1970, 1974
Lima malosi and loto alofa, 1234
Lindsay, John, 1216
Linnaeus, Carl, 385
Liquid migration, 1680
Little Italies, 1207, 1211–1213, 1217, 1218
Living dead, 1056, 1059
Liwayway, 418
Local agency, 1446, 1460
Local government officials, 1022
Local moral order, 271
Local ownership, 1449

Local peacebuilding, 1447
Local powerbrokers, 798
Local turn, 1449–1452
London Missionary Society (LMS), 232
Low country' Sinhalese, 636
Low-grade warfare, 154
Lumads, 970, 987

M
Macau, 1314, 1316, 1318–1320, 1322, 1325–1327
   casino resorts research, 1318
   local workers, 1318
Machar, Riek, 667
Macina Battalions, 763
Macina Liberation Front, 767
Mackerras, Colin, 1015
MacPherson Report, 1656
Macphersons, 1231
Maddock, Kenneth, 258
Mafia, 1209
Magazines, 403, 404, 407
Majelis Ulama Indonesia, 804
Majority black government, 1987
Malaysian employee, 1318
Malcolm X, 828
Maluku, 1447, 1450–1461
Mamalu, 1238
Mamdani, Mahmood, 798
Managerial school, 1559
Managing manhood, 1112
Mandal Commission, 1525
Mandela, Nelson, 393
Manhood
   country of origin, 1124–1125
   education and understanding, 1123–1124
   and migration, Congolese migrant in Durban, 1125
   and work, Congolese migrant in South Africa, 1124
Manumission, 1773
Māori, 870, 879, 1266, 1269, 1366–1370
   communities, 871
   definition, 868
   and Pacific students, 1412
   renaissance, 872–874
   Waitangi Tribunal, 875–877
Māori Language Act, 877, 878
Mapuche, 852, 856, 857, 862
Mara, Kamisese, 258
Maracaibo, 1598

Maralinga, 888, 896
Marginalisation, 1372
Marion du Fresne, 1275
Marketplace of religion, 171
Ma Rong, 308, 1020
Maroonage, 1600, 1773
Marriot/Mayhew, 841
Marsden project survey, 1227, 1231
Marshall Islands, 886–888, 890, 894, 896–898, 902
Marsudi, Retno, 1896, 1898
Marxist approach, 103
Masjumi, 801
Masked Battalion, 762
Mass immigration, 1843
Matai, 1224
Matai palota, 1229
Matanitu, 249
Mato oput, 1451
Mau Mau rebellion, 273
Mauriora, 1373
Mauritian Ordinance of 1849, 1774
Mauritius 1721-1860
   British period 1810-1870, 1754–1760
   ethnicity and diversity, 1778–1781
   ex-apprentices and the epidemics, 1760–1763
   and Indentured labor, 1772–1778
   Indo-Mauritians and indentured labor, 1771–1772
   slave labour force, 1751–1754
   slavery, health and epidemics in, 1750–1764
Mayroz, E., 1547
Media, 484, 490, 494, 495, 1249
   as gateways, 1910
   identity development and, 1911–1913
   stereotypes and, 493–495
   uses, 1910
Media and stereotypes
   effects, 405–406
   ethnic, 406–410
   news media, 400–403
   popular, 403–405
Medical committees, 588
Medical services, 1017
Meiteization, 912, 920
Memorialization, 1633
Mental health, 1704
Merchants' committees, 588
Merit principle, 1506
Mesuji, 802
Metaphoric return, 1226
Meta-Samoa, 1242

Metropoles, 1228
Mexicans, 1336
Mexico, 853, 855, 857
Microstates, 224–228, 238, 241
Middle-class labour migrants
   age and migration, 1738–1739
   culture and migration, 1739–1741
   household migration, 1741–1743
   spatial and social mobility, 1733–1738
   transnational turn, 1743
Middle East, 774, 783–785, 787, 1026
Middling migrants, 1731
Migrants, 1582
   human rights of, 1815
   networks, 1679
   workers, 1317
Migration, 30, 34, 36, 41–45, 911, 912, 916, 920, 921, 1112, 1186, 1188, 1191, 1197, 1224, 1268–1271, 1279, 1295, 1302
   among men, 1119–1120
   around the world, 1115–1116
   compact, 1697
   consequences of, 1114–1115
   crisis, 1814
   and economy, 1116–1117
   and gender, 1117–1119
   manhood and masculinity, 1120–1122
   need for, 1113–1114
   qualitative approach, 1122–1123
Milad-un-nabi, 831
Miles, R., 487
Militancy, 1036, 1040, 1056, 1057
Military, 1583
Military coup, 116
Military occupations, 188
   colonialism and ethnicity, 197–198
   foreign, 188–193
Miller, David, 215
Mindanao, 968, 987
Mindanao peace process, 987–988
Ministry of Overseas Indian Affairs, 1162
Minority(ies), 18
   identities, 1019
   nationality, 1015
   preferences, 1017
   splitism, 1019
Mintimer Shaymiev, 324
MINZU, 696, 698, 703
   distribution of, 699
   identification, 712
   Mongol from 1949 to 1979, 704–709
   as social transformation, 707
MINZUism, 697

Misrepresentation, 304, 307
Missionaries, 1228
Mitigation of national sovereignty, 784
Mobile Caliphate state, 764
Mobility, 30, 31, 33, 34, 38, 39, 41, 43, 45, 1225, 1226
Model migration schedule, 1738
Model minority, 1174
Modernization and development, 1012
Modernization globalization, 922
Modern protected states, 224–227, 241
Moeldoko, 1895
Moluccan conflict, 1447, 1457, 1458
Mongolian, 1015
   elites before 1949, 696, 699–704
Monogamy, 1724
Monotaga, 1236
Monstrosity, 1059
Monstrous 'living dead', 1048
Moral economy, 270, 271, 277
Moral ethnicity, 267, 268, 271, 277
Moral panic emergence, 449
Moral panics, 1340
Moretti, F., 70
Moro Islamic Liberation Front (MILF), 968
Moruroa, 897, 899, 900
Moruroa Atoll, 902
Moruroa e Tatou, 897
Moses, D., 1542
Mouloud, 831
Movement for Social Justice (MSJ), 815
Mufti, 833
Mughal, 1580
Muhammadiyah, 796, 801, 803, 804, 1895, 1902, 1903
Muharram massacre, 832
Mujahids, 1881
Multicultural, 855, 857, 861, 862
   citizenship, 1995
   coalition, 811
Multicultural and multi-faith (MCMF), 1080, 1084–1086, 1099
Multiculturalism, 45, 348, 352, 353, 356, 358, 854, 855, 857, 859, 860, 1175, 1178, 1194, 1650, 1847, 1854, 1855, 1994, 2006
Multi-ethnic communities, 1772, 1782, 1787
Multi-partyism, 276
Multiple citizenship, 1998
Multiple identities, 33
Musa Bigiyev, 321
Muscovy, 319–320

Museum
- and celebration of identity, 1949–1952
- and cultural appreciation, 1948
- and cultural tourism, 1949
- and cultural wealth, 1948
- definition, 1941
- and ethnic identity, 1945–1947
- and ethnic memories, 1947
- features of, 1942
- modern, 1944–1945
- origins, 1943
- role and status of, 1943
- and social connection, 1947
- technology and education, 1949
- types of, 1943

Museum of Archaeology and Anthropology (MAA), 1952
Muslim, 1016, 1579, 1779, 1838
Muslim Ban, 1341
Muslim Brotherhood (MB), 585
The Muslim Standard, 843
Mussolini, Benito
- anti-fascists, 1211
- anti-semitic provisions, 1212
- colonial military campaign, 1212

Myanmar, 1576
Myth, 66, 67, 69, 74
Myth of nationhood, 794, 803
Myth of return, 1225

N

Nadi, 260
Nagas identity and nationalism
- Baluch and Pakhtoon movements, 908
- British colonialism, 921
- ceremonies, 911
- Christian missionaries, 913, 916
- cultural identities, 910
- identity formation, 908
- southerners' (Rongmeis) settlement, 911
- women and the subordinate ethnicities, 909
- Zeliangrong movement, 920

Nahdlatul Ulama, 796, 801
Nahkid, 1225
Nakama, 420
Nakba, 580
Nanay Coring, 422
Narcissus, 67
Narrative, 66, 67, 70, 72
Naspers, 1987
Natal Indian Congress (NIC), 80, 81

Nation, 150
National, 31, 32, 35, 38, 40, 43–45
National belonging, 1996
- in Netherlands, 1998–2001

National Congress Party (NCP), 658
National consciousness and civic education, 1026
National consultations, 1835
National delimitation, 161
National Film and Video Foundation, 1987
National Human Rights Commission, 1886
National identity, 132
National identity formation, 804
National interests, 1016
National Islamic Front (NIF), 658
Nationalism, 190, 193, 195, 372, 375–377, 470, 792–794, 799, 1839
- Afrikaner, 471, 478
- black, 479

Nationalist ideology, 9
Nationalist leaders, 792, 793, 798, 804
National Italian American Foundation, 1218
Nationality, 94–100, 102, 104, 105
- definition, 94–96

National Joint Action Committee (NJAC), 815, 822
National minorities, 1015
National minority blind, 1020
National Museum of the American Indian (NMAI), 1951
National Party (NP), 78, 79, 606, 1980
National People's Congress (NPC), 98, 289, 290
National sovereignty, 1822
National unity, 1013
National Unity and Reconciliation Commission, 1632
Nation branding, 57
Nation building policy, 1960
Nation-state, 133, 134, 141, 996, 1003, 1005, 1996
Nation-state of Samoa, 1224
Native Hawaiians, 929–937
Native Land Husbandry Act (LHA), 438
Native Land Ordinance, 248
Na tribe, 69
Natsir, 801, 802
Natural dispositions, 1314
Nayacakalou, Rusiate, 257
Nazi, 71, 72
Negara integralistik, 795
Negara Islam Indonesia, 802, 803
Negrophiliacs, 1055

Neighbour, 1045, 1047, 1059
Neighbouring relations, 600
Neo-fascist, 448
Neoliberal capitalism, 1056, 1059
Neoliberal development, 859
Neoliberal globalisation, 51–54
Neoliberalism and indigenous rights, in Latin America
  post-neoliberal and/or post-multicultural moment, 858–863
  social suffering and early resistance, 850–854
Neoliberal multicultural, 856, 859, 860
Neoliberal multiculturalism, 855, 861
Netherlands, 348, 350, 352
Neutrality of the state, 2007
New Economic Policy, 1172
New Order (Orde Baru), 795–798
News media, 398, 400–403, 406
New York Declaration on Refugees and Migrants, 1697
New Zealand, 1266–1272, 1274, 1277, 1279, 1281–1306, 1366, 1367
  health policy, 1369–1370
New Zealand Citizenship Act of 1977, 238
New Zealand Refugee Resettlement Strategy, 1698
Ngā manukura, 1370, 1371
Nihon bunkaron, *see* Nihonjin-ron
Nihonjin-ron
  ethnocentrism and racism, 1471
  hard, 1469, 1473, 1476–1478
  Jiyūsha and Ikuhōsha, 1469
  mixture of hard and soft, 1466
  soft, 1471, 1476
Nihonron, *see* Nihonjin-ron
Nihon shakairon, *see* Nihonjin-ron
Nikulin, D., 73
9/11 attacks, 448
Niue, 223
  geography, 229–230
  history, 235
  politics, 231
  population, 230
Nomadic Gypsies, 366
Nonconceptual, 1042
Nonconcurrent electoral cycles, 749
Non-discrimination
  anachronistic equality, 943–944
  real-time equality, 941
Non-national block, 607
Non-negotiable principles, 119
Normativity, 1035, 1037, 1038

Normikhla, 1578
North American Free Trade Agreement (NAFTA), 853
Northern Cyprus Turkish Republic, 154
Northern Ireland, 332
  cultural nationalism, emergence of, 333
  IRA, 335
  Irish Protestantism, 334
  Northern Catholics, 335
  political culture in, 334
  politics of identity, 336–339
  sectarianism, 340–343
  Unionism, 334
Northern Ireland Life and Times Survey (NILT), 341
Nuclear Free and Independent Pacific movement (NFIP), 889, 895
Nuclear racism, 887
Nuer, 666–670
Nuremberg trials, 1541
NZ-born, 1231

O
Obeah, 837
O' Brien, George, 256
Occupation, 188, 193, 197, 198, 200
  termination strategies, 201–205
Occupied Palestinian territories, 581
Oceania
  kava and ethno-cultural identity in, 1924–1934
  origination of kava in, 1924–1925
Office diplomacy, 163
Office of Civil Rights of the Department of Education (OCR), 1485
Ohrni, 835
Oil and gas extraction, 1021
Oil pollution, 1022
Oil reserves, 1021
Oldham, 448–450
Old Providence, 1600, 1601
O le ala i le pule o le tautua, 1224, 1234
Ontologicallly, 1036
Opportunity gap, 492, 493
Opposition, 1229
Oppression, 1648
Orang Tionghoa-Indonesia, 799, 800
Orban, 1840
Order of the Orange, 156
Order Sons of Italy in America, 1208, 1211–1213, 1217

Organic agriculture
    expansion, 1429
    export-led certified, 1429
    governance, 1432–1433
    group certification and democracy legitimacy, 1437–1440
    standard setting and deliberative capacity, 1435–1437
    in Uganda and Ghana, 1433–1435
Organisation for Economic Co-operation and Development (OECD), 1818
Organisation for National Reconstruction (ONR), 814
Organisation of the Great Sahara, 762
Orientalism, 1131, 1132
Orisha, 837
Oslo Peace Agreement, 590
Othered, 800
Othering, 333, 334, 340, 343, 344, 1649
Outbound power transmission, 1021
Outer Mongolia, 701
Outputs, 158
Over-policing, 1651–1655
Overseas-born, 1236

P

Pacific Collections Access project (PCAP), 1948
Pacific islanders, 886–888, 890, 891, 893, 900
Pacific masculinities, 1915
Pacific media, 407, 408
Pacific nations, 1696
Pacific people
    ancestors, 1918–1920
    character, 1910
    inhabiting, 1920
    in media, 1910
Pākehā, 868, 870, 873, 879, 1266, 1269, 1306
Pakistani community, 457
Palenques, 1601
Palestine, 191
Palestine Liberation Organisation (PLO), 581
Palestinian civil society
    civil society and national initiatives, 587–588
    committees of, 589–590
    conflictual relations, 583
    Islamist framewok, 585–586
    occupation, 581–586
    political framework and institutional growth, 582–583
    prior to 1948, 579–581
    social organisations, 584–585

Panafrican Federation of Filmmakers (FEPACI), 1979
Pancasila, 794–795, 796, 801–803
Papua, 792, 800
Parmusi, 803
Partai Komunis Indonesia (PKI), 795, 801
Participation, 1704
Partnership failure, 1556
Party of Political Progress Groups (POPPG), 813
Party systems, 349–353, 356, 358, 606
Pasifika, 1268
Pastoralist, 660, 661, 668
Pastoralist conflict, 683, 688
Patel, A.D., 258
Paternalism, 99
Paternalistic tax policy, 255
Patronage, 277
    networks, 275
    opportunities, 278
Patron-client relationships, 274
Peace and conflict studies, 1449, 1461
Peacebuilding, 1447, 1448, 1450, 1452, 1457, 1459, 1461
    aims, 617
    and ethnic conflicts, 624–627
Peace industry, 1446, 1449
Peacekeeping operations (PKOs), 625
Peace process, 338, 339, 344
Peace research, 1449
Pela, 1455–1457, 1459, 1460
Pellico, Silvio, 1205
Pemerintah Revolusioner Republik Indonesia, 802
Pendatang, 800
Pengangkat, 1971
People's Progressive Party (PPP), 1354, 1359
People's Daily website, 1027
People's Liberation Army (PLA), 286
People's National Congress (PNC), 1355–1359
Peoples National Movement (PNM), 810, 813, 823
People's Partnership (PP), 815, 817, 820, 822
People's Republic of China (PRC), 284
    autonomy, 294–296
    diversity in, 284–286
    ethnic relations, 296–298
    Maoist era, 286–288
    reform era, 288–294
Peranakans, 1169
Perasaan senasib sepenanggungan, 793
Performance burden, 1413–1416
Perpetual foreigners, 88

Persistent Samoan identity, 1229
Perso-Arabic arts, 1965
Personal model of exchange, 1558
Pesalaman, 1971
Petén, 1602
PetroChina, 1021
Petroleum reserves, 1021
Peusijuek, 1451
Philippines, 416, 418, 420, 424, 426, 968, 987
Philosophy, 1034–1037, 1040, 1041, 1046
Pioneer, 1236
Pipelines, 1021
Pirate, 1600
Pisicano, Paul, 1213–1215
Place, 719
    destruction and designification, 722
Plantation system, 1797–1798, 1803, 1807
Plan vigipirate, 1659
Plural societies, 1771, 1785, 1787, 1788
Plurinationality, 861
Plurinational state, 855, 856, 859–861
Pogge, Thomas, 214
Polarization, 1733
Polarized pattern of voting, 815, 822
Police
    custody, 1657
    liaison schemes, 1661–1662
    property, 1655
    shootings, 1655
    stop-and-search, 1652
    training and education, 1663
    violence practices, 1651
    workforce, 1663–1665
Police checkpoints, 1018
Policing, 454, 1649
    community, 1660
    over-policing, 1651–1655
    procedural, 1662
Polish minority treaty, 1861
Political economy of violence, 278
Political factors, 1690, 1692
Political geography, 775
Political identity, 792
Political legitimacy, 368, 370–374
Politically-motivated migration, 1676
Political mobilisation, 171, 266
Political obstacles, 1820
Political party, 744
Political representation of ethnic groups (PREGs), 1524
Political stability, 110
Political tribalism, 267, 268, 276

Political truth, 1035, 1036, 1057
Political violence, 278, 279
Politics, 268, 274, 276, 1083
    Australian, 1086
    LGBTIQ identity, in Asia (*see* Lesbian, gay, bisexual, transgender, intersex and queer (LGBTIQ))
Polynesian labor trade, 389
Pondicherry, 1273
Popular culture, 490, 494, 496
Popular education committees, 588
Popular media, 403–405, 417
Popular Mobilisation Forces, 138
Population Registration Act (PRA), 83, 88
Positive action, 2003
Postcolonial critique, 200
Post-colonial discourse, 7
Postcolonial identity, 804
Postcolonial insights
    into occupations, 198–201
Postcolonial mind, 193
Post-colonial situations, 994
Postcolonial societies, 197
Postcolonialstate, 798
Postcolonial theories, 198
Post-conflict Aceh, 970–981
Post-conflict institution-building, 160
Post-ethnic identity, 1217–1218
Post-Helsinki Aceh, 975–981
Post-ideological, 1041, 1052, 1054
Post-independence history, 110
Post-modern approach, 7
Post-multicultural, 860
    moment, 858
    question, 859
Post-neoliberal moment, 858
Post-neoliberal multiculturalism, 861
Post-structuralism in international relations, 1830
Postwar nationalist discourses, 550
Pouvanaa a Oopa, 888
Power resources, 271
Power sharing, 332, 626, 627, 689, 736
Power vertical, 325, 327
Practice turn, 1448
Prasad, Ayodhya, 258
Pravasi Bharatiya Divas, 1162
Praxis, 1054, 1057
PRC, *see* People's Republic of China (PRC)
Precarious immigration status, 1250, 1258
pre-Cession Fiji, 249–253
Pre-electoral coalition making, 739

Preferential development programmes, 1014
Preferential policies, 94, 96, 99, 105
Preferential treatment, 2004
Preferential voting, 118
Prejudice, 486, 487, 489, 490, 496
Presidential candidates, 737
Presidential elections, 736, 737–742
Presidential terms limits, 747
Pribumi, 799, 800, 1172
Primitive natives, 892
"Primitive" peoples, 891, 892
Primitivism, 891
Primordialism, 268
Primordialist, 4, 35
Primordial public, 274
Primordial realm, 274
Priority Enforcement Program (PEP), 1341, 1343
Procedural justice, 1662
Procedural rectification, 1507
Professionalisation, 1663
Professional politicians, 608
Pro-government militias (PGMs), 561–563
    defector, 565–566
    effects on conflict dynamics, 568–572
    rival, 566–568
Project 4.1, 892, 893
Project Sunshine, 894
Promotion of Bantu Self-Government Act, 1983
Propaganda, 1991
Prophet Muhammad cartoons, 496
Proportional representation, 824
Proportional representation (PR) systems, 159
Protected groups, 1543
Protestant, 826
Proto-affirmative action, 1504
Protocol of 1967, 1887
Proto-state, 798
Protracted conflicts, 154
Proxies, 798, 800
Prunier, G., 1551
Psychoanalysis, 70, 1035, 1044–1048, 1059
Public attitudes, 1821
Public Order Act, 455
Pule, 1224
Pulo Aceh community, 1963
Punjab, 1295
Punjabi, 1266
Putin, V., 325
Putra daerah, 800
Pygmalion, 65, 66

Q

Qaddafi, 135
Qadiani, 834
al-Qaeda, 136, 757–762, 765–769
Qasida, 831
Qing dynasty, 100
Qualitative yarning method, 1393
    experience, 1397
    no racism, 1396
    physical racism, 1396
    racism as erasure, 1395–1396
    racism on the outside, 1394
    racist slurs, 1394
    stereotyping subleties, 1395
    teacher racism, 1396–1397
Quantitative research method, 1397–1399
    aboriginal students, 1400
    inferential analyses, 1399–1400
Queer, 1079, 1084, 1086, 1088, 1089
    activism and scholarship, 1091
    identity, 1089
    in India, 1089, 1091
Quota(s), 1663
Quota Acts, 1210, 1217

R

Race, 80, 82–89, 484–491, 493, 1648, 2001
    denial of, 1388–1389
    group, 83, 84, 86, 87
    illusion of, 1387
    thinking, 89
Race and ethnicity
    empire, discourse of, 1132–1134
    intergenerational conflict, sexuality and migrant families, 1139–1143
    young people and sexualised media, 1134–1139
Race and racism
    anti-Semitism, 389
    cognitive and behavioral dimensions, 391
    English language, 390
    and ethnic group, 385
    'old' and 'new' racism, 391–392
    Polynesian labor trade, 389
    race relations and anti-racist struggles, 392–393
    racial and ethnic stereotypes and prejudices, 390
    racial discrimination, 391
    racialization, 385–388

Racial and ethnic minorities, media representation, *see* Media and stereotypes
Racial capitalism, 1253
Racial centrality, 491
Racial community, 84, 85
Racial discrimination, 516–517, 1391
Racial equality, 393, 1508
Racialization, 78, 484, 485, 487, 489, 490, 493, 496, 1332
  immigrants, 1332
  migrant, 1252
Racial justice
  issues, 506
  racism and, 501
  21st century problem, 502
Racial politics, 1354
Racial prejudice, 15
Racial profiling, 1654
Racial unrest, 1216
Racism, 14–17, 484–489, 490, 492, 496, 1079, 1081–1083, 1085, 1099, 1370, 1372, 1384, 1409–1412, 1705, 1997
  aboriginal and Torres Strait Islander adults, 1390
  and black peril, 433–436
  definition, 430
  denial of, 1388–1389
  descriptive statics, 1399
  as erasure, 1395–1396
  experience, 1397
  historical trauma, 1389
  illusion of, 1388
  impact, 1390
  indigenist research, 1386–1387
  labour regime, 439–441
  multi-levelled in nature, 1389
  physical, 1396
  positioning, 1385–1386
  quantitative measures, 1398
  scientific, 431–432
  teacher, 1396–1397
  white, 436–438
Racist
  slurs, 1394
  truth, 496
Radicalism, 792
Radical religious ideology, 175
Radioactive contamination, 886
Radio Bantu, 1984
Rail and road networks, 1017
Rainbow nation, 1979

Raja, 1455–1456, 1459, 1460
Rakhine Buddhist, 1587
Rakhine State, 1892–1894, 1899–1903
Ramadan, 1016
Rancière, J., 67
Ratéb Meusekat, 1964–1966, 1974
Ratoh Jaroe, 1962
Rawls, John, 213, 214
Real, 1045
Reality, 1840
Real-time equality, 941
Rebellion, 792, 802, 805, 969
Rebel-rebel conflicts, 657
Recognition, 854, 862
Reconciliation, 1448, 1451, 1454, 1456, 1458, 1460, 1613, 1632–1636, 1639
Recruitment strategy, 1774
Red-Green coalition, 1858–1860
Red Guards, 288
Redistribution, 853, 855, 856, 860, 862
Re-education, 1024
  camps, 1027
Reeves, E., 1550
Referendum for independence, 1568
Reform and modernisation, 1012
Reformasi, 804
Refugees, 30, 31, 43, 137, 142, 1576, 1583–1585, 1690
  crisis, 1840
  protection, 1690
  quota, 1691
Regime change, 160
Regional autonomy, 626
Regional conflict system, 620
Regional counter-terrorism law, 1018
Regional government, 1017
Regions of labor supply, 1774
Registration card, 1014
Reintegration of society, 1447, 1454
Religion, 34–36, 38–41, 43–45, 176–178, 585, 1447, 1448, 1452–1454, 1457, 1459, 1461, 1648, 1672, 1681
Religious conversion, 920
Religious education, 1863, 1864
  in Austria, 1866–1867
  Islamic, 1872
Religious framing, 174
Religious governance, 1856, 1870
  Austria, 1869
Religious institutions, 178–179
Religious minorities, 141
Reluctant matai, 1235
Remittances, 1224

Rent-seeking, 278
  rebellions, 668, 670
Repatriation, 1458, 1460, 1461, 1584
Repeat visits, 1224
Representation, 217
  situational analysis, 1522–1534
Repressive developmentalism, 799
Resilience, 317
Resistance, 200, 201, 203, 205, 1910, 1917
Resource curse, 1361
Resource exploitation, 1014
Resource reserves, 1016
Responsibility to Protect (R2P), 1541
Reverend John Morton, 829
Reverse discrimination, 1506
Reverse racism, 391
Revival of local traditions, 1451
Rhodes, C., 431, 441
Rhodesia, 432
  political marginalisation, 443–444
  racism (*see* Racism)
  white racism and alienation and racialisation of land, 436–438
Riots, 448
  2001 riots, 448, 449, 454, 457, 458, 460
Risorgimento, 1204
  identity of, 1205–1206
Rituals, 173, 1447, 1449, 1451, 1459, 1460
Rival discourses, 551
Rizzo Frank, 1216–1217
Roatan, 1601
Rodney, Walter, 1357
Rohang, 1578
Rohingya, 1576–1583
Rohingya muslims
  Arakan/Rakhine region, 1881–1882
  Arakan Rohingya Salvation Army, 1882–1883
  Asaddudin Owaisi, 1879
  channels, 1880
  ethinic violence, 1884
  human rights organisations, 1886–1887
  in Jammu region, 1885
  major destinations, 1883
  polarisation, 1880–1881
  2014 Report of Amnesty International, 1884
  threat to national security, 1885
  Trinmool Congress, 1878
Rohingya refugees
  in Andaman sea, 1892
  ASEAN commitment, 1892
  ASEAN response, 1900–1902
  Bali process, 1898
  challenge, 1903–1904
  and Indonesian government, 1891
  Indonesian policy, 1895–1897
  second track diplomacy, 1902–1903
  theories of regionalism and humanitarian intervention, 1893–1895
Roma, 366–369, 1650
  minority, 1683
Roman Catholic, 826
Romanian migration, 1674
  Germans, 1674–1676
  Hungarians, 1676–1678
  labor migration, 1678–1681
Romani identity, 367
Romaphobia, 368
Rooinga, 1582
Rorlich, Azade-Ayşe, 317
Royal Commission into Aboriginal Deaths in Custody, 1657
Ruijin ethos, 104
Rummel, R., 1545
Runit Island, 902
Russia *vs.* Tatarstan treaty, 327
Rwanda
  colonisation, 1618–1621
  ethnic groups of, 1613–1615
  genocide, 1613–1615, 1630
  post-genocide, 1630–1637
  precolonial, 1615–1618

S

Saddam Hussein, 137
Safran classification, 1153, 1154
Sahel, African, 623, 756–759, 764, 766, 769, 770
Salafi, 836
Salamasina, 1238
Salim, Agoes, 801
Saman, 1958, 1970
Samoan culture, 1224
Samoan language, 1237
Samoan observe, 1241
Samoan transnationalism, 1228
Samoa's comparative advantage, 1231, 1242
San Andres Island, 1594
Sanctuary cities, 1341
Sandalwood trade, 250
San Diego, 1238
Santa Marta, 1595
Santri, 795, 802
Sa'o (paramount chiefs), 1241
Sarekat Islam, 803
Savage, Charles, 251

Scandella, Giuseppe, 1210
Scapegoats, 800
Scarman Report, 1656
Schabas, W., 1542
Scheffer, D., 1550
Schröder government, 1859
Scientific racism, 431–432
Second-order ethnic minorities, 969
Second-order minorities, 969
   in conflict-ridden Mindanao, 981–987
   Mindanao peace process and, 987–988
   in post-conflict Aceh, 970–981
   post-helsinki Aceh and, 975–981
The Secret, 418
Secret societies, 1170
Sectarian, 333, 335–336, 339–341, 344
Sectarianism, 137–139, 335, 340–343
Secularization theory, 171–174
Secure Communities (S-Comm), 1341
Security forces, 687
Security vacuum, 680
Sedentary, 660
Seemab, Nazeer Ahmad, 830
Segregated sport, 84, 85
Segregation, 459, 468, 469, 478, 1047
Self-determination, 150, 153, 945, 946, 949, 951, 955–961
Self-government, 254
Self-identify, 267
"Self-other" distinctions, 37
Self-representation, 407–410
Semi-exclusiveness of religious community, 599
Separatism, 792, 1026–1028
Separatist/Islamist ideas, 1018
Sepoys, 1276–1278
Seram, 1456, 1457
Serb nationalist discourse, 540
Service class, 1733
Settlement policy, 1690
Settler
   colonialism, 869–872
   Rhodesia, 431–432
   societies, surviving exclusion in, 1173
Sexuality, 1132–1134, 1135, 1138–1143
   in ancient times, 1064–1066
   Indonesia and, 1066–1067
   Islam and, 1067–1068
Sexual racism, 1081
Shannon Foster, 1386
Shared citizenship, 224, 227, 235–240
Sharpeville massacre, 479, 1982
Sheikh Amat Badron, 1967

Shia, 134
   influence on, 1964
Shi'ite, 832
Shirk, 835
Siddiqi, Maulana, 831
Simab, Moulvi Nazeer Ahmad, 835, 836
Singapore, 1314, 1316, 1318–1327
   casino resorts research, 1318
   local workers, 1318
Sinn Féin, 338–340, 342, 343
Sinophone studies, 1180
Situational definition of ethnicity, 596
Situational ethnicity, 34
Slave demography, 1751, 1755
Slave labour force, 1751–1754
Slavery, 484–486, 494, 1354, 1649
Small arms and light weapons (SALW), 683
Small states, 222, 224, 225, 227, 233
Smith, R., 1545
Smithsonian Museum, 1951
Soccer, 1193
Social capital, 1226, 1672, 1679, 1682
Social categorization, 1996
Social closure, 1679
Social cohesion, 1789
Social construction, 267
   of ethnicity, 274
Social constructionist, 7
Social control, 488–490, 497
Social Democratic and Labour Party (SDLP), 338
Social engineering, 1450, 1451, 1459, 1460
Social equality, 2001
   in Netherlands, 2004–2005
   perspectives on, 2001–2003
Social field, 1225
Social identity, 409, 1648
Social identity theory (SIT), 490, 491
Social imaginaries, 792, 804
Social imagination, 277
Social infrastructure and services, 1014
Social media, 59–61
Social mobility, 1733–1738
Social networks, 1743
Social reform committees, 588
Social relations
   restoration of, 1447, 1450, 1454
Social stability, 1013
Social suffering, 852, 854, 857, 858, 863
Social ties, 1679
Societal individualisation, 1739
Societal pluralism, 134
Society, 1078–1081, 1084, 1085

Socio-structural factors, 1375
Soft power, 1014
Somoza, 1594
Source communities, 1948
South Africa, 1979
    cinema in, 1979
    film industry, 1979
    Indian identity in (*see* Indian identity, in South Africa)
South Asian, 448–452, 454, 459, 460
    based communities/diasporas, 1771
Southeast Asia, 1319
    after WWII, 1178
    Chinese communities in, 1169
    decolonisation and Chinese in, 1171–1172
    diasporic population in, 1168
    immigrants from, 1181
    maritime trade and Chinese in, 1169–1171
    postcolonial politics in, 1178
South Ossetia, 154
South Sudan, 623, 656
    CPA, 669
    Dinka-Nuer war, 670
    interim period, 667–669
    SPLM/A, 666, 667
    SPLM/A-IO, 669, 670
Sovereign Christian states, 123
Sovereignty, 222, 223, 225–227, 232, 234, 237, 1248, 1368, 1831
    See also Hawaiian sovereignty
Special intent, 1544
Spiralism, 1735
Splitism, 1026–1028
Splitting, 1044
SPLM/A-In Opposition (SPLM/A-IO), 669, 670
Sri Lanka
    ethnicization and ethic war colonial impact, 636–640
    ethnic riot, 640–643
    ethnic violence of July 1983, 648–649
    historical emergence of ethnic identities, 635
    post war violence, 650–651
    violence in Puttalam, 643–646
    violence of 1981, 646–648
Stalin, 1015
State and minority nationalities, in China
    Chinese nationalities policy, 96–99
    Hui nationality, 94
    human rights, 102–105
    preferential policy, 94, 96, 99, 105
    terrorism/separatism, 100–102

State subsidy, 1980
Stereotypes, 83, 87, 484–486, 488, 489–491
    consciousness, 491
    and education, 491–493
    and humour/satire, 495–496
    and media, 493–495
    subleties, 1395
Stereotype threat, 1408
    in Aotearoa New Zealand context, 1412–1413
    combating, 1418–1421
    disidentification, 1416–1418
    impacts of, 1413–1421
    performance burden, 1413–1416
    racism and ethnicity, 1409–1412
Stop-and-search, 1652
Strategic alterity, 1317, 1326
Strategic ethnic divides, 799
Strike forces, 587
Structural adjustment reforms, 851, 852
Students for Fair Admissions (SFFA), 1486, 1491
Subaltern, 203
    co-ethnics, 275
Subconscious bias, 14–17
Subidentities, 133
Subjectivization, 1037, 1043, 1047, 1050, 1054, 1055
Subordinate groups, 276
Substantive rectification, 1507
Sudan, 132, 656
    center-periphery dynamics and civil wars in, 657–659
    Darfur (*see* Darfur)
Sudan Liberation Movement/Army (SLM/A), 664, 665
Sudan People's Liberation Movement/Army (SPLM/A), 658, 659, 663, 666–668
Suel naru, 1972
Sufism, 833, 1964
Sugar
    industry, 256
    plantation, 1353, 1776
Sugar cane, 258, 1773
Suharto, 794–800, 803–805
Sukarno, 792–795, 799–804
Sukuna, Ratu, 257
Sulawesi, 792, 800, 802, 805
Sumatra, 792, 800, 802
Sunni, 137, 828
Sustainable peace, 1447
Suu Kyi, Aung San, 1902

Syed Abdul Aziz, 829
Symbols, 1447, 1450, 1451, 1455, 1458, 1460, 1461
   ethnicity, 1217
   goods, 1508
   production, 1042, 1043, 1059
   universes, 1168
Symbolism, 12
Syncretisms, 837
Syria, 132
Systemic inequities, 1371

T
Tabligh/ Dar ul Uloom, 838
Tabot festival of Bengkulu, 1964
Tabuik festival, 1964
Taiwanese, 1179
Taiwanese nationalism, 1181
Takveeatul Islamic Association (TIA), 841, 842
Talamanca mountains, 1602
Tangata whenua, 868, 1268
Tang Dynasty, 95
Tangible heritage, 1941
Tangomaos, 1597
Tanjung Priok massacre, 803
Tarim Oilfield, 1021
Tari Saman group, 1960
Tasman, Abel, 1273
Tatar, 316, 318
Tatar Declaration of Sovereignty, 324
Tatar language, 316
   classes ban, 327
Tatar Public Center (TOTs), 323
Tatarstan, 325
Tatarstan Airlines Boeing 737-500 crash, 327
Tatar Yoke myth, 318
Tauiwi, 1272, 1306
Tautala faasamoa, 1237
Tautua, 1224, 1227, 1236
Tazeem, 831
Teacher racism, 1396–1397
Teaiwa, T., 891
Technology, 1012
Television shows, 403, 406, 407
Te mana whakahaere, 1371
Temporary Protected Status (TPS), 1342
Tentara Islam Indonesia, 802
Tentara Nasional Indonesia, 797
Te Oranga, 1375
Te Pae Mahutonga, 1368
Te reo Māori, 871
Territorialisation, 1651
Terrorism, 94, 99–102, 327, 1026–1028, 1835

Terrorist incidents, 325
Terrorist jihadist organisations, 138
Tertiary education, 1703
Te Tiriti o Waitangi, 869–870, 1367
Theology, 175–176
Theories of ethnos and ethnicity, 38
Third-party peacekeeping operations, 163
30th September Movement, 795
Thurn, Everard im, 256
Tiananmen incident, 1012
Tibet, 1013
   de-politicisation, 307–309
   non-separatism self-representation, 309–310
Tibetans, 284, 285, 287, 292–296, 1015
Tibetan Autonomous Region (TAR), 286, 293
Tibetan Lamaism, 702
Tibetan uprising, 1013
Timbuktu, 767
Tino rangatiratanga, 874
Tjokroaminoto, H.O.S., 803
Tobago Organisation of Peoples (TOP), 815
Toiora, 1374
Tongans, 249
Torres Strait Islander, aboriginal and
   adults, 1390
   children, 1390
   voices, 1391
   youth, 1390
Tourism, 54–57, 1243
Tradition, 1447, 1451, 1452, 1454–1459
Traditional alliances, 1454, 1456
Traditional attachments, 36
Traditional justice, 1449–1452, 1455
Traditional justice mechanisms (TJM), 1450, 1451, 1459, 1460
Traditional leaders, 1450, 1452, 1454, 1455
Traditional Unionist Voice (TUV), 340
Traditional village union, 1457
Training schools, 1018
Trans-and international activism, 852
Trans-Asia Railway, 1024
Trans-border ethnic groups, 616
Transformation, 1229, 1237
Transformational approach, 1376
Transition to democracy, 119
Transmigration policies, 800
Transnational contacts, 1743
Transnational framework, 1224
Transnational imagination, 1152
Transnationalism, 372–374, 1153, 1155, 1169, 1180, 1225
Transnationalized religious community, 1682

Transnational matai, 1224
Transnational network, 1179–1180
Transnational reincorporation, 1224, 1243
Transnistria, 154
Transport and communication networks, 1024
Trauma, 66, 67, 71, 72, 74
Treaty of Waitangi, 869–870, 880, 1271, 1301
Treena Clark, 1386
Tribalism, 267, 269
Tribal Trust Lands (TTLs), 438
Trinidad and Tobago (TT), 810, 811
    Crown Colony governance, 813
    economy, 812
    election results, 821–822
    2010 elections, 815–817
    ethnic groups, 811
    ethnic types, 817
    non-ethnic types, 817
    population, 813
    UDeCOTT, 816, 818, 819
Trinidad Muslim League (TML), 834, 842
Trinmool Congress (TMC), 1878
Trobriand Islands, 70
Trump, D., 384
Truth claims, 496
Tuaregs, 758
Tui Viti, 252
Tulafale (orator chief), 1237
Tunggal Saman genre, 1971
Turaga ni koros, 257
Turkey, 137
Turkic peoples, 1016
Turkish-Islamic Union for Cultural and Social Cooperation in Austria, 1868
Twice-migrants, 1163, 1164
Two-ness, 1053

U
Uganda, 1433–1435
Ulama, Nahdlatul, 1896, 1902, 1903
Ulster Defence Association (UDA), 332
Ulster Unionist Party (UUP), 339, 340
Ulster Volunteer Force (UVF), 332
Ulu Ni Lagu, 1971
Uncanny, 1048–1051, 1053, 1055
Unconscious cognitions, 490
UN Declaration on the Rights of Indigenous Peoples 2007, 954–959
Underclass, 1652
Underground fires in coalfields, 1022
Underperformance, 1416
UNESCO, 485

UNESCO Declaration on Race and Racial Prejudice, 385
UNHCR, 1892, 1898
Unionism, 332, 334, 339, 340, 342, 343
United Democratic Front (UDF), 480
United Fruit and the Standard Fruit Company, 1603
United Kingdom, 332, 333, 341
United National Congress (UNC), 810, 812, 815, 817, 819, 821, 823
United Nations (UN), 374, 1588
United Nations Committee on the Elimination of Racial Discrimination, 1027
United Nations High Commissioner for Refugees, 1690
United Nations' sources, 1027
United States Citizenship and Immigration Services (USCIS) website, 1342
Unity in diversity, 1649
Universal cultural features, 37
Universal suffrage, 1229
University entrance examination (EGE), 327
Uppsala Conflict Data Program (UCDP), 661
Upuh pawak, 1972
Urumqi Airport, 1017
Urumqi riots, 1013
US nuclear test, 886, 902
Uyghurs, 284, 285, 287, 292–296, 1015
    activists resident overseas, 1027
    architectural inheritance, 1024
    labour force, 1016
    nationalism, 1014
    resentment, 1021
    residents, 1013
    unrest, 1013

V
Valle du Par, 1594
Values, 1187, 1194, 1196, 1198
Vancouver's Museum of Anthropology (MOA), 1951
Van Mook, H., 793
Victimhood politics, 1567
Video games, 400, 403, 404
Vietnam War refugees, 1176
Village council (fono), 1238
Villages, 1236
Violence, 277, 278, 615, 1057
    capacity, 278
    ethnic lines, 1518
    and intimidation, 1030
Violent non-state actors, 142

Visman Commission, 793
Visual representation, 402
Voice, 1705
Volga Bulgar state/Volga Bulgaria, 318, 319
Volga Tatars, ethnogenesis of, 319
Voluntary contracted labor, 1770
Volunteers, 1699
Voting, 1527
Vulnerability, 1662

W

Wahhab, Muhammad Ibn Abdul, 835
Wahabbism, 835
Wahavi Islam, 1882
Waiora, 1374
Waitangi Tribunal, 874–877, 879
Wallace, G., 1216
War preparation, 1563
Washington, Harold, 1216
Water shortages, 1022
Wayuu, 1599
Weibo, 1019
Weiner, A., 70
Welfare system, 1702
Western Europe, 348
    expert survey data and analyses, 352
    far right, 349–352
    immigrants and immigration policy, theoretical implications for, 356–357
    immigration, multiculturalism, and traditional left-right, 352–356
Western metropoles, 1243
Western press, 1022, 1027
Westphalian regime, 1156
Whānau Ora, 1375
White fragility/guilt, 506, 509, 510
White genocide, 1989
Whiteness, 489, 1214, 1215, 1978
White privilege, 1488–1490
White racism, 436–438
White Anglo-Saxon Protestants, 1488
White Settler Societies, 1173

Wog, 1198
Women as matai, 1238
Women's Committees, 587
Wong, Gilbert, 1232
Work, 1257
World Bank, 851, 857, 1228
World Uighur Congress, 1028
World War I, 1205, 1207, 1210
World War II, 1205, 1212–1215, 1218

X

Xenophobia, 88, 1830, 1834
Xi Jinping, 1012
Xinjiang, 1013
Xinjiang Uyghur Autonomous Region, 1013
Xinjiang–Western Europe rail connections, 1024

Y

Yaqona, 1926–1934
    role of, 1933–1934
    as symbol of cultural identity, 1931
Yasin Abu Bakr, 828
Yellow peril, 1174
Yeltsin, 321
Yemen, 132
Young, Iris Marion, 216
Yudhoyono, Susilo Bambang, 1897, 1900
Yugoslavia, 602

Z

Zambos, 1595, 1598
Zapatista, 853
Zapatista National Liberation Army (EZLN), 853
Zero-sum contest, 1504
Zero-sum games, 746
Zionism, 578, 580, 590
Žižek, 68, 70, 74
Zuid Afrikaanse Republiek (ZAR), 471